W9-APK-149

Selected Highlights

Chapter	You Make the Call	Current Happenings	Using the Information	Did You Know?
<14>	• Engineer • Farmer • Teacher	• Declining dividends • Reporting income • Stock options	• Earnings per share • Dividend yield • Price-earnings	• Buybacks explode • Earnings expectations • Fortunes in options
<15>	• Bond rater • Retailer • Bond investor	• Return of junk bonds • Convertible bonds • Amortization software	• Bond vs stock financing • Collateral agreements • Analyzing pledged assets	• Muni bonds • Bond quotes • Rating bonds
<16>	• Money manager • Home builder • Retailer	• Classifying investments • International investments • Reporting investments	• Interpreting investments • Foreign exchange rates • Return on total assets	• Trading secrets • Mob on Wall Street • Tinseltown securities
<17>	• Reporter • Community activist	• Measuring cash flows • Classifying cash flows • Reporting cash flows	• Cash vs net income • Analyzing sources & uses • Cash flow on total assets	• Cash valuation • E-cash • Free cash flow
<18>	• Banker • Auditor	• Data from the Web • Building blocks of analysis • Reporting analysis results	• Horizontal analysis • Vertical analysis • Ratio analysis	• Chips and brokers • Ticker prices • Bears and bulls
<19>	• Budget officer • Purchases manager • Salesperson	• Customer orientation • Global economy • Manuf. mgmt. principles	• Classifying costs • Quality management • Contribution margin	• Airline quality • Banished to overhead • Continuous improvement
<20>	• Mgmt. consultant • Sales director • Systems consultant	• Manufacturing activities • Job order manufacturing • Job order documents	• Applying overhead • Analyzing cost flows • Multiple overhead rates	• Build-to-order PCs • Job order colleges • Software modules
<21>	• Budget officer • Process manager • General manager	• Customer-interaction software • Flexibility & standardization • Process cost summary	• Analyzing process cost • Cost per equivalent unit • Spoiled units	• Training programs • Service companies • Teamwork
<22>	• Operations manager • Officer • Center manager	• Responsibility accounting • Activity-based costing • Contribution reporting	• Assigning overhead • Allocating joint costs • Analyzing centers	• Overhead kills • Healthcare costing • Nonfinancial measures
<23>	• Trainee • Operations manager • Marketing manager	• Cost-volume-profit analysis • Cost behavior • Multiproduct analysis	• Estimating costs • Break-even • Operating leverage	• Compaq's break-even • Price-cutting • Graphical analysis
<24>	• Environmental manager • Budget staffer • Sales manager	• Administering budgets • Master budgeting • Linking budgets	• Expense planning • Managing cash • Zero-based budgeting	• Budget calendar • Budgeting acquisitions • Activity/Process budgeting
<25>	• Human Resource Mgr. • Sales manager • Internal auditor	• Standard costing • Management by exception • Performance reports	• Cost variances • Flexible budgeting • Sales variances	• Setting standard costs • Strategic partnerships • Benchmarking
<26>	• Systems manager • Production manager • Investment manager	• Using payback • Analyzing rate of return • Net present value	• Capital budgeting • Relevant costs • Break-even time	• The winner is ... • Deciding new products • 'Make or Buy' services

Volume 1   Chapters 1-12

Fundamental Accounting Principles

Fifteenth Edition

Volume 1 Chapters 1-12

Fundamental Accounting Principles

Fifteenth Edition

Kermit D. Larson
University of Texas at Austin

John J. Wild
University of Wisconsin at Madison

Barbara Chiappetta
Nassau Community College

Boston   Burr Ridge, IL   Dubuque, IA   Madison, WI
New York San Francisco   St. Louis
Bangkok   Bogotá   Caracas   Lisbon   London   Madrid   Mexico City
Milan   New Delhi   Seoul   Singapore   Sydney   Taipei   Toronto

▶ To the Instructor

Changes in accounting education have led to the most significant revision in the history of **Fundamental Accounting Principles**. The call for change in introductory accounting is upon us, and we responded. This fifteenth edition gives you more flexibility and options for innovation than preceding editions. At the same time, it maintains the rich content that has made it a market-leading textbook in accounting principles. See the Preface and its "To the Instructor" comments to learn more about this new and exciting edition and all its supporting materials. We know you will enjoy teaching from this new edition.

▶ To the Student

Accounting is one of the most valuable subjects you will study. Understanding accounting—the language of business—is essential for business success. **Fundamental Accounting Principles** gives you this understanding. Its content, features, and insights make learning accounting exciting and relevant. Please see the preface's "To the Student" comments to learn more about this book and how it can help you achieve success. Described in the preface are many student supplements that will help you succeed. We are confident you will find this book relevant and fun.

To my wife **Nancy**.

To my wife **Gail** and children, **Kimberly, Jonathan, Stephanie,** and **Trevor**.

To my husband **Bob**, my sons **Michael** and **David**, and my **mother**.

Irwin/McGraw-Hill

A Division of The McGraw·Hill Companies

FUNDAMENTAL ACCOUNTING PRINCIPLES

Copyright © 1999 by The McGraw-Hill Companies, Inc. All rights reserved. Previous editions © 1955, 1959, 1963, 1966, 1969, 1972, 1975, 1978, 1981, 1984, 1987, 1990, 1993, and 1996, by Richard D. Irwin, a Times Mirror Higher Education Group, Inc., company. Printed in the United States of America. Except as permitted under the United States Copyright Act of 1976, no part of this publication may be reproduced or distributed in any form or by any means, or stored in a data base or retrieval system, without the prior written permission of the publisher.

This book is printed on acid-free paper.

International   2 3 4 5 6 7 8 9 0 VNH/VNH 9 3 2 1 0 9
Domestic   3 4 5 6 7 8 9 0 VNH/VNH 9 3 2 1 0 9

ISBN 0-256-25534-2
ISBN 0-07-366125-2
ISBN 0-07-366126-0
ISBN 0-07-366127-9
ISBN 0-07-365857-X
ISBN 0-07-365858-8
ISBN 0-07-030722-9
ISBN 0-07-030723-7
ISBN 0-07-366315-8

Vice president and editorial director: *Michael W. Junior*
Publisher: *Jeffrey J. Shelstad*
Developmental editor: *Tracey Klein Douglas/Jackie Scruggs/Burrston House*
Senior marketing manager: *Rhonda Seelinger*
Senior project manager: *Denise Santor-Mitzit*
Production supervisor: *Lori Koetters*
Interior Designer: *Ellen Pentengell*
Cover Design: *Z Graphics*
Cover photos: *Front image: © Tony Stone Images, Chris Specdic;*
                          Back image: Tony Stone Images, David Madison
Senior photo research coordinator: *Keri Johnson*
Supplement coordinator: *Rose Hepburn*
Compositor: *York Graphic Services, Inc.*
Typeface: *10.5/12 Times Roman*
Printer: *Von Hoffmann Press, Inc.*

INTERNATIONAL EDITION
Copyright © 1999. Exclusive rights by The McGraw-Hill Companies, Inc., for manufacture and export. This book cannot be re-exported from the country to which it is consigned by McGraw-Hill. The International Edition is not available in North America.

When ordering the title, use ISBN 0-07-115818-9

http://www.mhhe.com

About the Authors

A progressive new authoring team further establishes F.A.P.'s market leadership . . .

Kermit D. Larson

Kermit D. Larson is the Arthur Andersen & Co. Alumni Professor of Accounting Emeritus at the University of Texas at Austin. He served as chairman of the University of Texas, Department of Accounting and was visiting associate professor at Tulane University. His scholarly articles have been published in a variety of journals, including *The Accounting Review, Journal of Accountancy,* and *Abacus.* He is the author of several books, including *Financial Accounting* and *Fundamentals of Financial and Managerial Accounting,* both published by Irwin/McGraw-Hill.

Professor Larson is a member of the American Accounting Association, the Texas Society of CPAs, and the American Institute of CPAs. His positions with the AAA have included vice president, southwest regional vice president, and chairperson of several committees, including the Committee of Concepts and Standards. He was a member of the committee that planned the first AAA doctoral consortium and served as its director.

Professor Larson served as president of the Richard D. Irwin Foundation. He also served on the Accounting Accreditation Committee and on the Accounting Standards Committee of the AACSB. He was a member of the Constitutional Drafting Committee of the Federation of Schools of Accountancy and a member of the Commission on Professional Accounting Education. He has been an expert witness on cases involving mergers, antitrust litigation, consolidation criteria, franchise taxes, and expropriation of assets by foreign governments. Professor Larson served on the Board of Directors and Executive Committee of Tekcon, Inc., and on the National Accountants Advisory Board of Safe-Guard Business Systems. In his leisure time, he enjoys skiing and is an avid sailor and golfer.

John J. Wild

John J. Wild is a professor of business and the Vilas Research Scholar at the University of Wisconsin at Madison. He has previously held appointments at Michigan State University and the University of Manchester in England. He received his BBA, MS, and PhD from the University of Wisconsin.

Professor Wild teaches courses at both the undergraduate and graduate levels. He has received the Mable W. Chipman Excellence-in-Teaching Award and the departmental Excellence-in-Teaching Award at the University of Wisconsin. He also received the Beta Alpha Psi and Roland F. Salmonson Excellence-in-Teaching Award from Michigan State University. Professor Wild is a past KPMG Peat Marwick National Fellow and is a recipient of fellowships from the American Accounting Association and the Ernst and Young Foundation.

Professor Wild is an active member of the American Accounting Association and its sections. He has served on several committees of these organizations, including the Outstanding Accounting Educator Award, National Program Advisory, Publications, and Research Committees. Professor Wild is author of *Financial Statement Analysis* published by Irwin/McGraw-Hill. His research appears in *The Accounting Review, Journal of Accounting Research, Journal of Accounting and Economics, Contemporary Accounting Research, Journal of Accounting, Auditing and Finance, Journal of Accounting and Public Policy,* and other business periodicals. He is associate editor of *Contemporary Accounting Research* and has served on several editorial boards including *The Accounting Review, Accounting and Business Research,* and the *Journal of Accounting and Public Policy.*

Professor Wild, his wife, and four children enjoy travel, music, sports, and community activities.

Barbara Chiappetta

Barbara Chiappetta received her BBA in Accountancy and MS in Education from Hofstra University and is a tenured full professor at Nassau Community College. For the past 17 years, she has been an active executive board member of the Teachers of Accounting at Two-Year Colleges (TACTYC), serving 10 years as vice president and currently as president since the fall of 1993. As an active member of the American Accounting Association, she has served on the Northeast Regional Steering Committee, chaired the Curriculum Revision Committee of the Two-Year Section, and participated in numerous national committees.

In April 1998, Professor Chiappetta was inducted into the American Accounting Association Hall of Fame for the Northeast Region. She received the Nassau Community College dean of instruction's Faculty Distinguished Achievement Award in the spring of 1995. Professor Chiappetta was honored with the State University of New York Chancellor's Award for Teaching Excellence in 1997. As a confirmed believer in the benefits of the active learning pedagogy, Professor Chiappetta has authored *Student Learning Tools,* an active learning workbook for a first-year accounting course, published by McGraw-Hill.

In her leisure time, Professor Chiappetta enjoys tennis and participates on a U.S.T.A. team. She also enjoys the challenge of bridge. Her husband, Robert, is an entrepreneur in the leisure sport industry. She has two sons — Michael, a lawyer, currently manages David's rock band, Blindman's Sun.

v

About the Contributors

An expert set of contributors complements the authors' rich experiences and success . . .

Jo Lynne Koehn

Jo Lynne Koehn received her PhD and Master's of Accountancy from the University of Wisconsin at Madison and is an associate professor at Central Missouri State University. Her scholarly articles have been published in a variety of journals including *The CPA Journal, Accounting Enquiries,* and *The MSCPA casebook.* Professor Koehn is a member of the American Accounting Association and the American Institute of CPAs. She also holds a Certified Financial Planning license and is active in developing a financial planning curriculum at Central Missouri State University. In the spring of 1997, she received the Faculty Excellence in Teaching Award from the Harmon College of Business Administration's Advisory Board. In her leisure time, Professor Koehn indulges her passion for golf and participates in the Executive Women's Golf Association of Kansas City. Professor Koehn also enjoys reading, traveling, and visiting bookstores.

Suresh Kalagnanam

Suresh Kalagnanam is an associate professor of accounting at the University of Saskatchewan in Canada. He received his B.Eng. from the University of Madras, MBA from Gujarat University (both in India), MBA and MSc in Accounting from the University of Saskatchewan, and PhD from the University of Wisconsin—Madison. His scholarly articles have been published in *Accounting, Organizations and Society, The Journal of Cost Management,* and *Management Accounting.* He has also written a teaching case which has been published by the Institute of Management Accountants. Dr. Kalagnanam is a member of the American Accounting Association, American Society for Quality, Canadian Academic Accounting Association, and the Institute of Management Accountants and an associate member of the Society of Management Accountants of Saskatchewan. Dr. Kalagnanam has two children, Pallavi and Siddharth. His wife, Viji, is a homemaker and a part-time university student.

Thomas L. Zeller

Thomas L. Zeller is associate professor of accountancy and university scholar/teacher in the Department of Accounting at Loyola University, Chicago. He received his Doctor of Philosophy from Kent State University in 1991. He has published numerous articles addressing managerial accounting, financial statement analysis and health care financial measurement issues. His research has appeared in several journals, including *Business Horizons, Healthcare Financial Management, Journal of Accounting and Public Policy, Business and Economic Review,* and *Journal of Applied Business Research.* Dr. Zeller is a member of the American Accounting Association and American Institute of Certified Public Accountants.

Carol Yacht

Carol Yacht received her MA in business and Economic Education from California State University, Los Angeles and BS in Business Education from the University of New Mexico. She is the author of Irwin/McGraw-Hill's *Computer Accounting with Peachtree for Microsoft Windows* books, and is a recognized expert in payroll accounting and reporting. She has worked as an educational consultant for IBM Corporation, an accounting instructor at Yavapai College, and a business education department chair at Beverly Hills High School in California. She chairs the Distance Learning Committee of the Computer Education Task Force, National Business Education Association. Professor Yacht's son, Matthew, is completing his accounting degree at Northern Arizona University. Her husband, Brice Wood, is an artist and part owner of a fine arts gallery. She is active in community activities and chairs the Planning and Zoning Commission of her town.

Preface

Let's Talk

Through extensive market-based surveys, focus groups, reviews, and personal correspondence with instructors and students, we discovered several interests and needs in accounting education today. In a nutshell, these desires can be grouped into eight pedagogical areas: (1) motivation, (2) organization, (3) preparation, analysis, and use; (4) ethics, (5) technology, (6) real world; (7) active learning, and (8) flexibility. Our main goal in this edition of Fundamental Accounting Principles (F.A.P.) is to address these needs and create the most contemporary, exciting, relevant, and flexible principles book in the market. A quick summary of these areas follows.

Motivation. Motivation drives learning. From the chapter's opening article and its focus on young entrepreneurs to the decision-making prompted by You Make the Call, **F.A.P.** motivates readers. It brings accounting and business to life and demonstrates that this material can make a difference in your life.

Organization. Organization serves the learning process, and **F.A.P.**'s outstanding organization aids that process. From "Chapter Linkages" and learning objectives organized by the *CAP Model*™ to its chapter outline and Flashbacks, **F.A.P.** is the leader in lending readers a helping hand in learning about accounting and business.

Preparation, Analysis, and Use. Accounting involves preparing, analyzing, and using information. **F.A.P.** balances each of these important roles in explaining and illustrating topics. From the unique Using the Information section to the creative Hitting the Road projects, **F.A.P.** shows all aspects of accounting.

Ethics. Ethics is fundamental to accounting. **F.A.P.** highlights the roles of ethics and social responsibility in modern businesses. From the Judgment and Ethics decision-making feature to its Ethics Challenge assignments, **F.A.P.** alerts readers to relevant and important ethical concerns.

Technology. Technology continues to change business and accounting, creating new and exciting accounting opportunities. **F.A.P.** is the leader in applying and showing technology in accounting. From the innovative Taking It to the Net projects to its Web-based assignments, **F.A.P.** pushes the accounting frontiers.

Real World. Accounting is important to the information age. From features and assignments that highlight companies like NIKE, Reebok, and America Online to the Teamwork in Action and Communication in Practice activities, **F.A.P.** shows accounting in a modern, global context. It also engages both accountants and nonaccountants. From the exciting Did You Know? features to its *Business Week* Activities, **F.A.P.** shows accounting is relevant to everyone.

Active Learning. Active learning implies active inquiry and interaction. **F.A.P.**'s instructor's edition (F.A.S.T.) gives new annotated links to pedagogical materials for those interested in applying active learning activities. **F.A.P.** is the undisputed leader in offering a strong pedagogical support package for active learning. Also, the *MHLA* service is a new, special addition to our support package.

Flexibility. Accounting involves conceptual, analytical, and procedural aspects. **F.A.P.** offers a new CAP Model to help choose the preferred teaching or learning approach. The CAP Model establishes color-coded learning objectives as either Conceptual, Analytical, or Procedural, and assigns them to chapter content, assignments, and test items. This gives maximum flexibility and choice in teaching and learning structure.

This is just a sneak preview of **F.A.P.**'s new and exciting features. From communication, interpersonal, and critical thinking skills to the development of ethical and global awareness, **F.A.P.** is the leader. We invite you to take a complete look at these and other special features in the remainder of this preface to see why **F.A.P.** is the *first choice* in accounting principles books.

Motivation

Motivation is a main goal of **F.A.P.** We know information retention is selective—if it doesn't apply to the lives of readers, they typically aren't motivated to learn. **F.A.P.** explains and illustrates how accounting applies to the reader. Here is a sampling of materials that motivate the reader.

The **Chapter Opening Article** sets the stage and shows how the chapter's contents are relevant to the reader. Articles often focus on young entrepreneurs in business who benefit from preparing, analyzing, and using accounting information. These articles bring the material to life in concrete terms.

Tax Cop

DETROIT, MI—Carmen Benish and her two comrades jump out of their battered Zhiguli and walk briskly to the door of a bicycle sales and services shop in the Moscow suburb of Podolsk. Ducking under bicycle frames hanging from the ceiling, they approach a salesclerk and flash their badges. A few days earlier, an undercover colleague made a purchase that wasn't reported. Benish, Mikail Nikolas, and Val Yaroslav are investigating whether the business is underreporting sales to avoid paying

You Make the Call features develop critical thinking and decision-making skills by requiring decisions using accounting information. Each chapter contains two to four of these features. They are purposely chosen to reflect different kinds of users. Examples are investors, consultants, programmers, financial planners, engineers, appraisers, and political and community activists. Guidance answers are provided.

Entrepreneur
You are the owner of a small retail store. You are considering allowing customers to purchase merchandise using credit cards. Until now, your store only accepted cash and checks. What form of analysis do you use to make this decision?

You Make the Call

Company Excerpts call attention to well-known organizations to illustrate accounting topics. These excerpts are often accompanied by a photo drawing attention to the nature of the business and its relevance to readers.

Sales are generally recorded by the Corporation when products are shipped to independent dealers.

General Motors

Financial Statements of familiar companies are used to acquaint readers with the format, content, and use of accounting information. The financial statements for NIKE, Reebok, and America Online are reproduced in the book and referenced often.

NIKE, INC. CONSOLIDATED STATEMENT OF INCOME

(in thousands, except per share data)

YEAR ENDED MAY 31,	1997	1996	1995
Revenues	$9,186,539	$6,470,625	$4,760,834
Costs and expenses:			
Costs of sales	5,502,993	3,906,746	2,865,280
Selling and administrative	2,303,704	1,588,612	1,209,760
Interest expense (Notes 4 and 5)	52,343	39,498	24,208
Other income/expense, net (Notes 1, 9 and 10)	32,277	36,679	11,722

Organization

Organization is crucial to effective learning. If it isn't well-organized or linked with previous knowledge, learning is less effective. **F.A.P.** helps readers organize and link accounting concepts, procedures, and analyses. A **Preview** kicks off each chapter. It introduces the importance and relevance of the materials. It also links these materials to the opening article to further motivate the reader. Here are some additional materials to enhance learning effectiveness.

A Look Back

Chapter 1 began by considering the role of accounting in the information age. We described accounting for different organizations and identified users and uses of accounting. We saw that ethics and social responsibility are crucial to accounting.

A Look Ahead

Chapter 3 explains the recording of transactions. We introduce the double-entry accounting system and show how T-accounts are helpful in analyzing transactions. Journals and trial balances are also identified and explained.

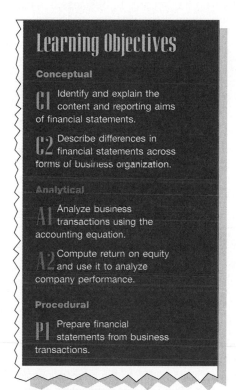

Learning Objectives

Conceptual

C1 Identify and explain the content and reporting aims of financial statements.

C2 Describe differences in financial statements across forms of business organization.

Analytical

A1 Analyze business transactions using the accounting equation.

A2 Compute return on equity and use it to analyze company performance.

Procedural

P1 Prepare financial statements from business transactions.

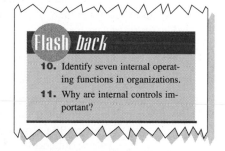

Flash back

10. Identify seven internal operating functions in organizations.
11. Why are internal controls important?

Chapter linkages launch a chapter and establish bridges between prior, current, and upcoming chapters. Linkages greatly assist readers in effectively learning the materials and help them link concepts across topics.

Learning Objectives are shown at the beginning of the chapter to help focus and organize the materials. Each objective is repeated in the chapter at the point it is described and illustrated. Self-contained summaries for learning objectives are provided at the end of the chapter.

A series of **Flashbacks** in the chapter reinforce the immediately preceding materials. Flashbacks allow the reader to momentarily stop and reflect on the topics described. They give immediate feedback on the reader's comprehension before going on to new topics. Answers are provided.

A color-coded **Chapter Outline** is provided for the chapter. This gives a mental and visual framework to help readers learn the material.

Chapter Outline

▶ **Communicating with Financial Statements**
 ■ Previewing Financial Statements
 ■ Financial Statements and Forms of Organization

▶ **Transactions and the Accounting Equation**
 ■ Transaction Analysis—Part I
 ■ Transaction Analysis—Part II
 ■ Summary of Transactions

Preparation, Analysis, and Use

Accounting is a service focused on preparing, analyzing, and using information. **F.A.P.** presents a balanced approach to these three crucial aspects of accounting. The preparation aspect of **F.A.P.** is well established and highly regarded. A new and progressive emphasis on analysis and use continues to put **F.A.P.** on the frontier of practice. Here's a sampling of new or revised textual materials on analysis and use:

The **Accounting Equation** (Assets = Liabilities + Equity) is used as a tool to evaluate each journal entry. The accounting equation is especially useful in learning and understanding the impacts of business transactions and events on financial statements. **F.A.P.** is a pioneer in showing this additional analysis tool.

Aug. 31	Cash	6,300		Assets	= Liabilities	+ Equity
	Sales		6,000	+6,300	+300	+6,000
	Sales Taxes Payable ($6,000 × 0.05)		300			
	To record cash sales and 5% sales tax.					

The **Using the Information** section wraps up each chapter and emphasizes critical-thinking and decision-making skills. Each section introduces one or more tools of analysis. It applies these tools to actual companies and interprets the results. The section often focuses on use of ratio analyses to study and compare the performance and financial condition of competitors.

Return on Investment   USING THE INFORMATION

We introduced return on investment in assessing return and risk earlier in the chapter. Return on investment is also useful in evaluating management, analyzing and forecasting profits, and planning future activities. **Dell Computer** has its marketing department compute return on investment for *every* mailing. "We spent 15 months educating people about return on invested capital," says Dell's Chief Financial Offi-

A4 Compute and interpret return on investment.

Hitting the Road is a unique addition to the chapter's assignment material. This activity requires readers to work outside the book and often requires application of interpersonal and communication skills. Tasks range from visits to local merchandisers and Social Security headquarters to conducting phone interviews and Web searches. These activities help readers understand and appreciate the relevance of accounting.

Hitting the Road

C2

Select a company in your community that you can visit in person or interview on the telephone. Call ahead to the company to arrange a time when you can interview an employee (often an accountant) who helps prepare the annual financial statements for the company. During the interview inquire about the following aspects of the company's accounting cycle:

A **Business Week Activity** requires the reader to apply the chapter's material to read and interpret a *Business Week* article. It also aids in developing reading comprehension skills and gives exposure to business happenings. Students can purchase **F.A.P.** with a special *Business Week* subscription package.

Read the article "Michael Dell: Whirlwind on the Web" in the April 7, 1997, issue of *Business Week*. Answer the following questions:
1. How many days of sales does Dell have in inventory?
2. How does Dell's days of sales in inventory compare with one of its chief competitors?

Business Week Activity

A3

Ethics

Ethics is the most fundamental accounting principle. Without ethics, information and accounting cease to be useful. **F.A.P.** is the leader in bringing ethics into accounting and demonstrating its importance. From the first chapter's opening article to the ethics codes at the end of the book, **F.A.P.** sets the standard in emphasizing ethical behavior and its consequences. Here's a sampling of how we sensitize readers to ethical concerns and decision making:

The **Judgment and Ethics** feature requires readers to make accounting and business decisions with ethical consequences. It uses role-playing to show the interaction of judgment and ethics, the need for ethical awareness, and the impact of ethics. Guidance answers are provided.

Judgment and Ethics

Certified Public Accountant
You are a CPA consulting with a client. This client's business has grown to the point where its accounting system must be updated to handle both the volume of transactions and management's needs for information. Your client requests your advice in purchasing new software for its accounting system. You have been offered a 10% commission by a software company for each purchase of its system by one of your clients. Do you think your evaluation of software is affected by this commission arrangement? Do you think this commission arrangement is appropriate? Do you tell your client about the commission arrangement before making a recommendation?

A new **Ethics Challenge** is provided in the *Beyond the Numbers* section. It confronts ethical concerns based on material from the chapter. Many of these challenges involve actions where the ethical path is blurred.

Ethics Challenge

P2

Randy Meyer is the chief executive officer of a medium-size company in Wichita, Kansas. Several years ago Randy persuaded the board of directors of his company to base a percent of his compensation on the net income the company earns each year. Each December, Randy estimates year-end financial figures in anticipation of the bonus he will receive. If the bonus is not as high as he would like he offers several accounting recommendations to his controller for year-end adjustments. One of his favorite recommendations is for the controller to reduce the estimate of doubtful accounts. Randy has used this

Social Responsibility is a major emphasis of progressive organizations. **F.A.P.** is unique in introducing this important topic in Chapter 1. We describe social responsibility and accounting's role in both reporting on and assessing its impact. **F.A.P.** also introduces social audits and reports on social responsibility.

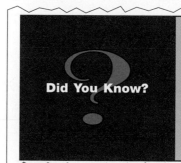

Did You Know?

In Pursuit of Profit
How far can companies go in pursuing profits? **Converse** proposed to name a new footwear product Run N' Gun. This sparked debate on ethics, social responsibility, and profits. Converse says Run N' Gun is a basketball and football team. Critics claim it invites youth violence and links with the gun culture. To the credit of Converse, it changed the name from Run N' Gun to Run N' Slam prior to its sale to consumers.

Technology

Technology and innovation can be exciting and fun. **F.A.P.** makes the transition to new technologies easy. It is the leader in demonstrating the relevance of technology and showing readers how to use it. Here's a sampling of items pushing the technology frontier:

F.A.P.'s **Home Page,** www.mhhe.com/business/accounting/fap, is the starting point for accessing accounting and business resources on the Web. The book's Web site harnesses technological resources to provide the most up-to-date and powerful Web services available.

PeachTree

A **Student Software CD** provides several technology-assisted educational activities. These include (1) *Essentials*—reviewing the entire accounting cycle, (2) *PeachTree Templates*—uses leading software for accounting support, (3) *Tutorial*—interactive review of topics, and (4) *GLAS* and (5) *SPATS*—instructional software to solve problems.

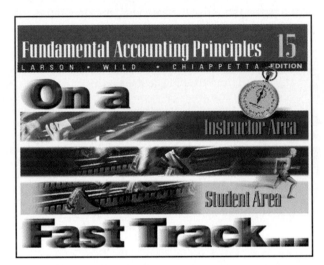

Taking It to the Net requires accessing a Web site and obtaining information relevant to the chapter. It aims to make readers comfortable with Web technology, familiar with information available, and aware of the power of Web technology.

| Taking It to the Net
C1, A2 | Access the **Cannondale** promotional Web site at http://www.cannondale.com. Visit several hotlinks on the site to get a feel for the company's products.
1. What is the primary product that Cannondale sells?
2. Review the Cannondale 10K—this is the annual financial data required by the SEC. You can access this from the SEC's Edgar system (see this book's Web page). (Hint: Edgar Web site lists numerous |

PowerPoint® Presentations and Supplements augment each chapter with colorful graphics, interesting charts, innovative presentations, and interactive activities. The PowerPoint® materials are flexible and can be customized for any use.

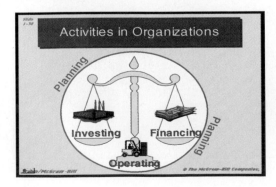

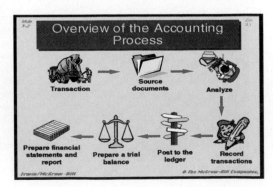

Real World

Showing readers that accounting matters is part of an effective learning package. **F.A.P.** is the leader in real world instructional materials. It offers unique assignments challenging the reader to apply knowledge learned in practical and diverse ways. These challenges include analytical problems, research requirements, comparative analysis, teamwork assignments, and communication exercises. They also allow greater emphasis on conceptual, analytical, communication, and interpersonal skills. Here's a sampling of these materials:

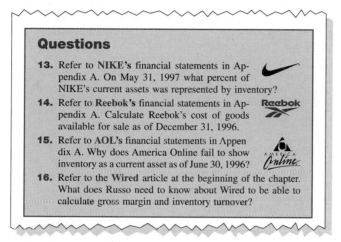

Questions

13. Refer to **NIKE's** financial statements in Appendix A. On May 31, 1997 what percent of NIKE's current assets was represented by inventory?

14. Refer to **Reebok's** financial statements in Appendix A. Calculate Reebok's cost of goods available for sale as of December 31, 1996.

15. Refer to **AOL's** financial statements in Appendix A. Why does America Online fail to show inventory as a current asset as of June 30, 1996?

16. Refer to the **Wired** article at the beginning of the chapter. What does Russo need to know about Wired to be able to calculate gross margin and inventory turnover?

Reporting in Action requires analysis and use of NIKE's annual report information. The unique *Swoosh Ahead* feature allows use of the most current information in the marketplace.

Reporting in Action
A1, A3, A4

NIKE designs, produces, markets, and sells sports footwear and apparel. Key financial figures for NIKE's fiscal year ended May 31, 1997 are:

Key figure	In millions
Financing (liabilities + equity)	$5,361
Profit	796
Sales	9,187

Required

1. What is the total amount of assets invested in NIKE?

2. What is NIKE's return on investment? NIKE's assets at May 31, 1996 equal $3,952 (in millions).

3. How much are total expenses for NIKE?

Analysis component:

4. Does NIKE's return on investment seem satisfactory if competitors average a 5% return?

Swoosh Ahead

5. Obtain NIKE's most recent annual report. You can also access NIKE's annual report at its Web site **(www.nike.com)** or at the SEC's Web site **(www.sec.gov)**. Compute NIKE's return on investment using this updated annual report information you obtain. Compare the May 31, 1997, fiscal year-end return on investment to any subsequent years' returns you are able to compute.

Comparative Analysis compares the performance and financial condition of NIKE and Reebok using the accounting knowledge obtained from the chapter. These activities help develop analytical skills.

Both **NIKE** and **Reebok** design, produce, market, and sell sports footwear and apparel. Key comparative figures ($ millions) for these two organizations follow:

Comparative Analysis A2

Key figures*	NIKE	Reebok
Total liabilities	$2,205	$1,405
Total equity	$3,156	$ 381

* NIKE figures are from its annual report for the fiscal year ended May 31,1997. Reebok figures are from its annual report for the fiscal year ended December 31, 1996.

Comprehensive and Serial Problems are included in several chapters and focus on multiple learning objectives from multiple chapters. They help integrate and summarize key principles.

Comprehensive Problem
Alpine Company
PeachTree
G S

Assume it is Monday, May 1, the first business day of the month, and you have just been hired as the accountant for Alpine Corporation, which operates with monthly accounting periods. All of the company's accounting work has been completed through the end of April and its ledgers show April 30 balances. During your first month on the job, you record the following transactions:

May 1 Issued Check No. 3410 to S&M Management Co. in payment of the May rent, $3,710. (Use two lines to record the transaction. Charge 80% of the rent to Rent Expense—Selling Space and the balance to Rent Expense—Office Space.)

2 Sold merchandise on credit to Essex Company, Invoice No. 8785, $6,100. (The terms of all credit sales are 2/10, n/30.)

2 Issued a $175 credit memorandum to Nabors, Inc., for defective merchandise sold on April 28 and returned for credit. The total selling price (gross) was $4,725.

Problems often cover multiple learning objectives and usually require preparing, analyzing, and using information. They are paired with **Alternate Problems** (at the end of the book) for further review of the same topics. Problems are supported with software and other technology options. Many include an **Analytical Component** focusing on financial statement consequences and interpretations.

Problem 7-3ᴬ
Income comparisons and cost flows—periodic
A1, P4

Green Jeans, Inc., sold 5,500 units of its product at $45 per unit during 1999, and incurred operating expenses of $6 per unit in selling the units. It began the year with 600 units and made successive purchases of the product as follows:

January 1 (beginning inventory) . . .	600 units @ $18 per unit
Purchases:	
February 20	1,500 units @ $19 per unit
May 16	700 units @ $20 per unit
October 3	400 units @ $21 per unit
December 11	3,300 units @ $22 per unit
	6,500 units

Check Figure Net income (LIFO), $69,020

Required

Preparation Component

1. Prepare a comparative income statement for the company, showing in adjacent columns the net incomes earned from the sale of the product, assuming the company uses a periodic inventory system and prices its ending inventory on the basis of: (*a*) FIFO, (*b*) LIFO, and (*c*) weighted average. Assume an income tax rate of 30%.

A **Demonstration Problem** is at the end of the chapter. It illustrates important topics and shows how to apply concepts in preparing, analyzing, and using information. A problem-solving strategy helps guide the reader.

Demonstration Problem

On July 14, 1999, Tulsa Company paid $600,000 to acquire a fully equipped factory. The purchase involved the following assets (we include additional facts related to each):

Asset	Appraised Value	Estimated Salvage Value	Estimated Useful Life	Depreciation Method
Land	$160,000			Not depreciated
Land improvements ...	80,000	$ -0-	10 years	Straight line
Building	320,000	100,000	10 years	Double-declining balance
Machinery	240,000	20,000	10,000 units	Units of production*
Total	$800,000			

*The machinery is used to produce 700 units in 1999 and 1,800 units in 2000.

Required

1. Allocate the total $600,000 cost among the separate assets.

Infographics and Artwork aid in visual learning of key accounting and business topics. Photos, color, highlighting, and authentic documents all help with visual learning.

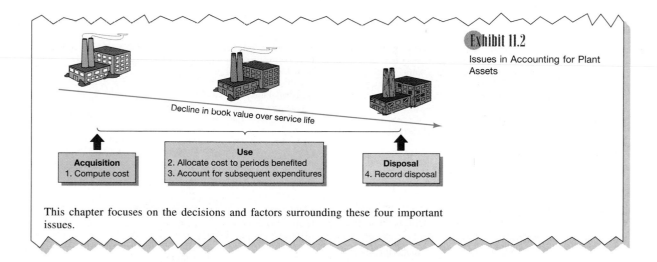

Exhibit 11.2

Issues in Accounting for Plant Assets

Decline in book value over service life

Acquisition	Use	Disposal
1. Compute cost	2. Allocate cost to periods benefited 3. Account for subsequent expenditures	4. Record disposal

This chapter focuses on the decisions and factors surrounding these four important issues.

Active Learning

Active learning requires effective assignments. **F.A.P.** is the student-proven and instructor-tested leader in assignment materials. Proven and thoughtful assignments not only facilitate but motivate effective and active learning. Many assignments include writing components. Here's a sampling of relevant assignment materials:

Teamwork in Action assignments require preparing, analyzing, and using information in teams. They can be completed in or outside of class. These active learning activities reinforce understanding of key topics and develop interpersonal skills.

A team will be called upon to personify the operation of a voucher system. Yet all teams must prepare for the potential to be selected by doing the following:

1. Each team is to identify the documents in a voucher system. The team leader will play the voucher, and each team member is to assume "the role" of one or more documents.

2. To prepare for your individual role you are to:
   a. Find an illustration for the document within the chapter.
   b. Write down your documents function, where you originate, and how you flow through the voucher system.

3. Rehearse the role playing of operating the system. You may use text illustrations as props, and for visual effect you may wear a nametag identifying the part you play.

Teamwork in Action
P2

Communicating in Practice exercises aim at applying accounting knowledge to develop written and verbal communication skills.

The class is divided into teams. Teams are to select an industry, and each team member is to select a different company in that industry. Each team member is to acquire the annual report of the company selected. Annual reports can be obtained in many ways including accessing this book's Web page or through the SEC's EDGAR database [www.sec.gov]. Use the annual report to compute total asset turnover. Communicate with teammates via a meeting, e-mail, or telephone to discuss the meaning of this ratio, how different companies compare to each other, and the industry norm. The team must prepare a single memo reporting the ratios for each company and identify the conclusions reached during the team's discussion. The memo is to be duplicated and distributed to the instructor and all classmates.

Communicating in Practice
A2

Student Learning Tools (SLT) is a pedagogical support package aimed at helping in the teaching and learning process geared to active learning. The instructor's F.A.S.T. Edition offers links to SLT and its related Instructor's Manual (IM) when appropriate.

Fast Hint   Active Learning: *SLT* provides Activity 29 for introducing plant asset disposals in an active learning environment (see pp. 132–136 in *SLT* and notes in *IM*).

Flexibility

Learning and instructing requires flexibility. **F.A.P.** offers flexibility in meeting the unique demands of individual students and teachers. From the conventional classroom to the active learning environment, **F.A.P.**'s new edition and its pedagogical package give more flexibility and options for innovation in learning and instruction. It does this while maintaining the rich content that has made it the market-leading book in accounting principles. Here's a sampling of relevant assignment materials:

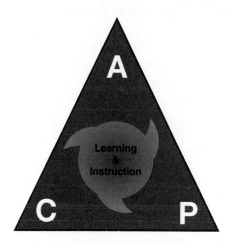

CAP Model

The new **CAP Model,** as already discussed, allows courses to be specially designed to meet instructional and learning needs—whether they be conceptual, analytical, procedural, or some combination of the three. The CAP Model recognizes the strength of each approach. Its identification of learning objectives, textual material, assignments, and test material by **C, A,** or **P** provides the flexibility to readily adapt **F.A.P.** to the preferred instructional and learning emphasis. It also allows the instructor to vary the emphasis by topic.

Packaging Options

Unique **packaging options** support **F.A.P.**'s flexibility. Nobody matches Irwin/Mc-Graw-Hill when it comes to packaging options for accounting principles. Drawing on user feedback, we offer several new options with this edition:

- Hardcover splits—with a special introductory price and exciting packages. This new option is a hit with both instructors and students.
- *Business Week* Editions—The new *Business Week* Edition gives students a 16-week subscription for under $10! *Business Week* excerpts in the book further peak students interest in both accounting and business.
- F.A.S.T. Edition splits—with a two-volume Instructor's Edition to "lighten the load". The F.A.S.T. annotations have been revised by Barbara Chiappetta and offer added value.

Innovations and Enhancements

In preparing this edition, we asked questions of instructors and students. We asked what topics to add, delete, or change in emphasis. We asked what pedagogical aids would help in teaching and learning. We wanted to know what innovations and enhancements would help them and maintain **F.A.P.** leadership in accounting principles. From these questions came several requests. We listened, and this edition is the result. We've already described major content and pedagogical changes. This section identifies many other chapter-by-chapter innovations and enhancements:

Chapter 1

- New focus on the information age and the relevance of accounting.
- Early introduction to income, revenues, and expenses using Nike.
- New discussion of return and risk as part of all business decisions.
- New introduction to the Web with reference to **F.A.P.**'s homepage.
- New description of business activities: financing, investing, and operating.
- New and unique presentation of ethics and social responsibility.

Chapter 2

- *FASTForward,* an athletic service company, introduced as the new focus company for Chapters 2–5.
- New company transactions to add realism and interest.
- Revised discussion and presentation of accounting principles.
- Added analysis of each transaction using the accounting equation.
- New presentation and integration of cash flow statement with other financial statements.
- New description of reporting differences between proprietorships, partnerships, and corporations.

Chapter 3

- Revised presentation of transactions and source documents.
- New exhibits on the accounting equation and double-entry accounting.
- New exhibits and discussion linking transactions to financial statements, including the statement of cash flows.
- Revised discussion and exhibits for recording transactions.
- Expanded discussion of debt ratio with new comparative analyses.

Chapter 4

- New discussion of the accounting period and the motivation for adjusting accounts.
- New framework for preparing and analyzing adjustments.
- Several new exhibits and graphics illustrating adjusting accounts.

- New presentation linking adjustments to financial statements.
- Several new features highlighting current happenings in revenue recognition and the role of technology.
- Revised discussion of profit margin using Ben & Jerry's along with comparative analyses.

Chapter 5

- Revised presentation and new exhibits for the closing process.
- New contemporary presentation of the work sheet using Excel. [*A traditional acetate overlay presentation is available in full color teaching transparencies. PowerPoint slides mimic the overlay.*]
- Revised presentation and discussion of the statement of cash flows as an integral part of the full set of financial statements.
- New exhibits presenting the accounting cycle.
- New presentation of the classified balance sheet.
- Revised current ratio discussion using Harley-Davidson and industry analyses.

Chapter 6

- New discussion comparing a service company and a merchandiser.
- New presentation of the operating cycle of a merchandiser with credit or cash sales.
- New design of source documents including an invoice and debit and credit memoranda.
- Revised presentation of merchandising sales and purchases using the perpetual inventory system.
- Revised discussion on the transfer of ownership for inventory.
- New discussion and presentation of merchandising cost flows across periods.
- New comparison of cash and accrual measures of sales and costs.
- Revised acid-test ratio and gross margin discussion using J.C. Penney and industry analyses.
- New appendix on accounting for merchandising sales and purchases under both the periodic and perpetual inventory systems.

Chapter 7

- Revised presentation of assigning costs to inventory using the perpetual inventory system.
- Revised discussion of inventoriable items and costs.
- New explanation of both financial and tax reporting for inventory.
- New exhibits illustrating statement effects of inventory errors.
- Revised presentation of alternative inventory valuation methods.
- New appendix presentation assigning costs to inventory using the periodic inventory system.
- Expanded merchandise turnover and days' sales in inventory ratio discussion using Toys 'R' Us and industry analyses.

Chapter 8

- New section on fundamental system principles.
- Contemporary and streamlined presentation on components of accounting systems.
- Revised discussion of hardware and software for systems.
- Contemporary presentation of Special Journals.
- Revised discussion of technology-based accounting systems.
- Revised layout for Special Journals reflecting current practice.
- New discussion of *enterprise-application software*, including SAP and Oracle.
- New analysis of business segments using a contribution matrix and Woolworth's data.

Chapter 9

- New sections on the purpose of internal control and its limitations.
- Revised discussion on the principles of internal control.
- New feature boxes involving current technological developments.
- Revised discussion on control of cash.
- New presentation and exhibits on the voucher system of control.
- New depictions of important source documents.
- New presentation on using banking activities as controls, including the bank reconciliation.
- Revised discussion of days' sales uncollected using comparative analyses of Hasbro and Mattel.

Chapter 10

- New organization focuses on receivables first and short-term investments second.
- Revised discussion of credit sales, including use of credit cards.
- New presentation on accounting for accounts receivables.

- New ordering of (simpler) write-off method before (more complex) allowance method.
- New presentation and exhibits for estimating bad debts.
- Revised presentation and exhibits for notes receivable.
- Streamlined accounting for investments including unrealized gains and losses.
- Revised discussion of accounts receivable turnover using comparative analyses of Dell and Compaq.

Chapter 11

- New introduction and motivation on accounting for plant assets.
- New discussion to describe and illustrate depreciation.
- Streamlined MACRS depreciation for tax reporting.
- Revised presentation and exhibits for disposals of plant assets.
- New discussion on natural resources and intangible assets.
- New discussion on the cash flow impacts of long-term assets.
- Revised total asset turnover illustration using Coors and Anheuser-Busch.

Chapter 12

- New introduction on accounting for liabilities.
- Revised presentation of known (determinable) liabilities.
- New exhibits and discussion on promissory notes.
- Revised presentation and exhibits for payroll-related liabilities.
- Revised discussion of accounting for long-term liabilities.
- Transfer of present value discussion of liabilities to Chapter 15.
- New appendix on **Payroll Accounting and Reports**.
- New exhibits, including form 941, W-2, payroll register, check, and withholding table.
- Use of **PeachTree**® to generate payroll-related reports.
- Revised presentation of times interest earned with application to Best Buy.

Chapter 13

- Reorganized chapter with partnerships first and corporations second.
- New discussion of LPs, LLPs, S Corporations, and LLCs.
- New discussion of partnerships, including financial statements, admission/withdrawal, and liquidation.
- New exhibits include the Boston Celtics' partnership report.
- Revised corporation coverage to focus on its characteristics and both common and preferred stock.
- New summary exhibit highlighting differences across alternative forms of organization.
- New exhibits including Green Bay Packer stock certificate.
- Streamlined coverage of stock subscriptions.

- Transfer of cash dividends discussion to Chapter 14.
- Revised book value per share discussion with references to Anheuser-Busch and Ride (snowboard manufacturer).

Chapter 14

- Reorganization into four main sections: dividends; treasury stock; reporting income; and retained earnings.
- New dividend presentation with new exhibits and infographics.
- Revised and streamlined discussion on treasury stock.
- Streamlined presentation on reporting income information.
- Revised earnings per share discussion to reflect new standard.
- New section on accounting for stock options.
- Revised presentation of reporting retained earnings.
- New presentation of dividend yield and price-earnings ratios using The GAP, Microsoft, Chevron, and Philip Morris.

Chapter 15

- New introduction to bond (long-term debt) financing.
- Revised bond presentation with new exhibits and infographics.
- New layout for effective interest amortization tables.
- Revised presentation of accounting for bond retirements.
- Revised presentation for notes payable.
- New explanation of present value concepts.
- New discussion on computing present values using interest tables.
- New discussion of collateral agreements for bonds and notes.
- Revised presentation of pledged assets to secured liabilities with reference to Chock Full O'Nuts.

Chapter 16

- Streamlined coverage of investments and international accounting.
- Reorganized into 3 sections: classification of investments; long-term investments in securities; and international investments.
- New exhibits and infographics on accounting for securities.
- Revised presentation of accounting for international investments.
- New presentation on the components of return on total assets with application to Reebok and Nike.

Chapter 17

- New presentation on the motivation for cash flow reporting.
- New exhibits on the format of the statement of cash flows.
- Revised discussion on cash flows from operating activities—both direct and indirect methods.

- New flexible presentation allows coverage of either or both direct or indirect methods.
- New exhibits summarize adjustments for both the direct and indirect methods.
- Revised discussion of cash flows from investing activities.
- Revised discussion of cash flows from financing activities.
- Revised presentation of analysis of cash sources and uses.
- New presentation of cash flow on total assets ratio with references to Nike, PepsiCo, Wal-Mart, and Wendy's.

Chapter 18

- New discussion on the basics of financial statement analysis.
- New explanation of the building blocks of analysis.
- Revised discussion on analysis tools and standards for comparisons.
- Revised presentation of horizontal and vertical analysis.
- New application of financial statement analysis to Nike.
- New comparative analysis of Nike and Reebok along with other competitors (Converse, LA Gear, Stride Rite).
- Revised graphical analysis using pie charts and bar graphs.
- Revised summary exhibit of financial statement analysis ratios.
- New section on analysis reporting.

Chapter 19

- New introduction to managerial accounting.
- New section and exhibit on the purpose of managerial accounting.
- Revised presentation of reporting manufacturing activities.
- New section on cost accounting concepts emphasizing cost identification and classification.
- New discussion of manufacturing management principles.
- New introduction to important managerial topics including prime, conversion, product, and period costs.
- New infographics augment many new and revised topics.
- Transfer of discussion of a manufacturing statement and a general accounting system to Chapter 20.
- New presentation on unit contribution margin with illustrations using a bike manufacturer.

Chapter 20

- New focus on manufacturing and job order cost accounting.
- Revised presentation of manufacturing activities and reporting.
- Revised discussion of the job order cost accounting system.
- Streamlined discussion of underapplied and overapplied overhead.
- New presentation on multiple overhead allocation rates.

- Revised discussion of general accounting system (periodic) in a new appendix.

Chapter 21
- Revised introduction with discussion of motivation for a process manufacturing system.
- New exhibit and discussion comparing job order and process manufacturing systems.
- New exhibit to explain process manufacturing operations.
- Revised discussion of computing and using equivalent units.
- New discussion on the physical flow of units and preparation of a cost reconciliation.
- New presentation on spoilage in process costing and its effects on costs per equivalent unit.

Chapter 22
- New section and exhibits on two-stage cost allocation.
- New presentation and exhibits for activity-based costing.
- Transfer of activity-based costing upfront to link with Chapter 21.
- Revised discussion of decision making relevance of cost allocation and performance measurement.
- Revised discussion of departmental expense allocation.
- New exhibit and presentation of joint costs.
- New presentation of return on assets by investment centers.
- Transfer of discussion of "eliminating an unprofitable department" to Chapter 26.

Chapter 23
- Revised discussion on describing and identifying cost behavior.
- Revised presentation and comparison of the high-low, scatter diagram, and regression methods.
- Revised presentation on applying cost-volume-profit analysis.
- New presentation of operating leverage and its role in determining income.

Chapter 24
- New presentation of the budget calendar.
- New exhibit showing the master budget sequence.
- Expanded discussion and new exhibits of production and manufacturing budgets.
- Revised discussion motivated by new material on planning objectives.
- New presentation on zero-based budgeting.

Chapter 25
- New discussion and exhibit on the process of budgetary control.
- Revised emphasis on a decision making role for budgets and standard costs.
- New presentation of standard costs and the standard cost card.
- Revised organization of variance analysis.
- New presentation of and visual orientation to variance analysis.
- New separate analysis of variable and fixed overhead variances.
- New presentation on sales variances with illustrations.

Chapter 26
- Revised presentation of capital budgeting.
- New exhibits illustrating capital budgeting and its computations.
- New presentation of the internal rate of return for capital budgeting.
- New section comparing methods of analyzing investments using capital budgeting.
- New section on managerial decision making, information, and relevant costs.
- Revised presentation of short-term managerial decision tools.
- New section on qualitative factors in managerial decisions.
- New presentation of break-even time with illustrations.

Supplements

Instructor

Fully Annotated Support for Teaching Edition
Marginal annotations labeled **Fast Hints** have been revised and expanded. These annotations include: *Points* of interest or emphasis; *Discussion* suggestions; *Terminology,* offering alternate terminology; *Application,* referencing end-of-chapter quick studies and exercises; *Tools,* referencing instructional visuals found in the Instructor's Resource Manual; *Critical Thinking* questions; *Active Learning,* referencing class activities and team presentation assignments; and *Hint,* offering teaching suggestions.

Instructor's Resource Manual
By Barbara Chiappetta, Nassau Community College, and Jeannie Folk, College of DuPage. This manual contains materials for managing an active learning environment and provides new instructional visuals. Each chapter provides a Lecture Outline, a chart linking Learning Objectives to end-of-chapter material, a list of relevant active learning activities, transparency masters, and digital files on disk. For instructors' convenience, student copies of these visuals are provided in the *study guide.* If students do not acquire the study guide, adopters are permitted to duplicate these visuals for distribution.

Solutions Manual
The manuals, prepared by John J. Wild, along with Suresh Kalagnanam, Jo Lynne Koehn, and Thomas Zeller, contain

solutions for all assignment materials. An electronic version and transparencies in large, boldface type are also available.

Test Bank

Prepared by Jane G. Wiese of Valencia Community College and Robert Landry of Massassoit Community College. The Test Bank contains a wide variety of questions, including true-false, multiple-choice, matching, short essay, quantitative problems, and completion problems of varying levels of difficulty. All Test Bank materials are grouped according to learning objective. A computerized version is also available in Macintosh and Windows.

Ready Shows, Ready Slides, Ready Notes

These teaching enhancement packages were prepared by Jon A. Booker, Charles W. Caldwell, Susan C. Galbreath, Richard S. Rand, all of Tennessee Technological University.
Ready Shows. This is a package of multimedia lecture enhancement aids that uses PowerPoint® software to illustrate chapter concepts. It includes a viewer so that they can be shown with or without Microsoft PowerPoint® software.
Ready Slides. These selected four-color teaching transparencies are derived from the Ready Shows presentation screens. The package also includes a booklet of black and white transparency masters.

Instructor's Manual for Student Learning Tools.

This manual illustrates how to approach a traditional accounting principles curriculum and meet the objective set forth by the AECC. The approach employs a concept and user focus and aims at developing intellectual, communication, and interpersonal skills. Active learning strategies and structures, group formation, and assessment techniques are discussed. Transparency masters for instructional visuals to facilitate mini-lectures are also provided.

Presentation CD-ROM

This integrated CD-ROM allows you to maneuver from PowerPoint® slides to solutions to test bank questions and much more. Now the disk supplements that come with the text are packaged in one convenient CD-ROM.

Distance Learning

McGraw-Hill Learning Architecture

This Web-based learning environment distributes product course materials for viewing on any PC compatible or Macintosh computer. This on-line learning center is packed with dynamically generated pages of text, graphics, PowerPoint® slides, exercises, and more. Customization possibilities are easily implemented.

LeCroy Center (Dallas Community College District) Telecourse

An exciting new Telecourse is being developed in partnership with the LeCroy Center, the world leader in Telecourse education. Approximately 13 hours of new videos will be developed for **F.A.P.,** as well as a student Telecourse Guide and

additional Web support. Consult your Irwin/McGraw-Hill representative for more details.

Videos

Lecture Enhancement Video Series. These short, action-oriented videos provide the impetus for lively classroom discussion. There are separate *Financial Accounting* and *Managerial Accounting* libraries.

Student Software CD

Achievement Tests

Student

Working Papers

These new volumes are prepared by John J. Wild to match end-of-chapter assignment material. They include papers that can be used to solve all quick studies, exercises, serial problems, comprehensive problems, and Beyond the Numbers activities. Each chapter contains one set of papers that can be used for either the problems or the alternate problems.

Study Guide

By Barbara Chiappetta, Nassau Community College, and Jeannie Folk, College of DuPage. For each chapter and appendix, these guides review the learning objectives and the summaries, outline the chapter, and provide a variety of practice problems and solutions. Several chapters also contain visuals to illustrate key chapter concepts.

Student Learning Tools

Written by Barbara Chiappetta, this supplement contains material for creating an active learning environment in the classroom. Class activities, writing assignments, and team presentation assignments are provided; suggestions for their implementation and evaluation are provided in the accompanying instructor's manual. Accounting working papers are also provided for duplication.

Ready Notes

These note-taking tools contain printouts of the text-specific Ready Shows (PowerPoint®) presentation screens.

Software CD-ROM

Five pieces of software on one CD-ROM enable students to practice accounting applications such as journal entries and spreadsheets as well as take a self-test on text vocabulary, procedures, and concepts.
GLAS (General Ledger Applications Software) by Jack E. Terry, ComSource Associates, Inc.
SPATS (Spreadsheet Applications Template Software) by Jack E. Terry, ComSource Associates, Inc.
Peachtree Problems by Jack E. Terry, ComSource Associates, Inc.

Tutorial Software by Leland Mansuetti and Keith Weid-kamp, Sierra College

Essentials of Financial Accounting: A Multimedia Approach

Manual Practice Sets
FastMart, Inc.
Republic Lighting Company
Republic Lighting Company, Extended Version
Cogg Hill Camping Equipment
Freewheel Corporation, Inc.
KJC Manufacturing Company, Inc.

Computerized Practice Sets

From Leland Mansuetti and Keith Weidkamp, both of Sierra College
Business Simulations for Microsoft® Windows®
Granite Bay Jet Ski, Level 1
Granite Bay Jet Ski, Level 2
Wheels Exquisite, Inc., Level 1
Practice Set for Microsoft® Windows® by Donald V. Saftner, University of Toledo *and* Rosalind Cranor, Virginia Polytechnic Institute and State University.

Acknowledgments

We are thankful for the encouragement, suggestions, and counsel provided by the many instructors, professionals, and students in preparing the 15th edition. This new edition reflects the pedagogical needs and innovative ideas of both instructors and students of accounting principles. It has been a team effort and we recognize the contributions of many individuals. We especially thank and recognize those individuals who provided valuable comments and suggestions to further improve this edition, including:

Patricia Ayres	*Arapahoe Community College*	Frank Korman	*Dallas Community College District*
Russell Baker	*Florida Metropolitan University*	Charles Lacey	*Henry Ford Community College*
Bill Barribeau	*Fox Valley Technical College*	John Lacey	*Montgomery County Community College*
Abdul Baten	*Northern Virginia Community College—Manassas*	Bruce Leauby	*La Salle University*
Irene Bembenista	*Davenport College*	Tuan Luong	*Northern Virginia Community College—*
Judy Benish	*Fox Valley Technical College*		*Woodbridge*
James Beisel	*Longview Community College*	Florence McGovern	*Bergen County College*
Stuart Brown	*Bristol Community College*	Rosalie Morgan	*Delaware County Community College*
Ed Browning	*Northwest Missouri State University*	Ali Naggar	*West Chester University*
Jo Ann Buchmann	*Rockland Community College*	Don Noseworthy	*Hesser College*
Don Bush	*Regis University*	Lynn Pape	*Northern Virginia Community College*
Howard Clampman	*Bronx Community College*	Sam Pedregon	*Pueblo Community College*
Ronald Clute	*Metropolitan State College of Denver*	Clarence Perkins	*Bronx Community College*
Robert Coburn	*Franklin Pierce College*	Ann Price	*Shepherd College*
Kenneth Coffey	*Johnson County Community College*	Tac Ryu	*Metropolitan State College*
Jim Crowther	*Kirkwood Community College*	Mary Scott	*Northwest Missouri State University*
Lyle Dehning	*Metropolitan State College of Denver*	Carl Smith	*West Chester University*
Paul Donohue	*Delaware County Community College*	Dennis Smith	*Consumnes River College*
Thomas Edmonds	*Regis University*	Thomas Szczurek	*Delaware County Community College*
Brad Farr	*Arapahoe Community College*	Jim Thomas	*Consumnes River College*
Thomas Franco	*Wayne County Community College*	Tom Thompson	*Madison Area Technical College*
Linda Frye	*Northwest Missouri State University*	Marilyn Uecker	*Fox Valley Technical College*
John Gorham	*Bronx Community College*	Martin E. Ward	*DeVry Institute of Technology*
Jerry C.Y. Han	*SUNY—Buffalo*	Henry Weiman	*Bronx Community College*
David Hancock	*Northwest Missouri State University*	Kenneth L. Wild	*University of London*
Sara Harris	*Arapahoe Community College*	Rahnl Wood	*Northwest Missouri State University*
Ken Kettelhohn	*Milwaukee Area Technical College*	Orville Wright	*Morgan State University*
Shirley Kleiner	*Johnson County Community College*	Mike Zematis	*Davenport College*
Judy Korb	*Johnson County Community College*		

We also wish to thank our accuracy checkers, Barbara Schnathorst of The Write Solution Inc. and Marilyn Sagrillo of the University of Wisconsin—Green Bay, and also our supplement proofreader, Kalista A. Johnston of Nash KalistaAnn Graphics Inc.

Kermit D. Larson
John J. Wild
Barbara Chiappetta

Contents in Brief

ontents

CHAPTER 1

Accounting in the Information Age

Chapter Outline

► **Living in the Information Age**
 ▪ Power of Accounting
 ▪ Business and Investment
 ▪ Focus of Accounting
 ▪ Accounting and Technology
 ▪ Setting Accounting Rules

► **Forms of Organization**
 ▪ Business Organization
 ▪ Nonbusiness Organization

► **Activities in Organizations**
 ▪ Planning
 ▪ Financing
 ▪ Investing
 ▪ Operating

► **Users of Accounting Information**
 ▪ External Information Users
 ▪ Internal Information Users

► **Ethics and Social Responsibility**
 ▪ Understanding Ethics
 ▪ Social Responsibility

► **Opportunities in Practice**
 ▪ Financial Accounting
 ▪ Managerial Accounting
 ▪ Tax Accounting
 ▪ Accounting Specialization
 ▪ Accounting-Related Opportunities

► **Using the Information—Return on Investment**

Winning at Giving

PITTSBURGH, PA—Just a few years ago, Stephanie Williams was working as a salesclerk, but spent much of her time dreaming about getting a degree and a better job. In September of that year, her dreams came true. She quit her job and returned to college. Yet no one would have predicted that Williams, now 25, would soon be living the American Dream.

Williams signed up for her first accounting course with no idea of what to expect. "I took accounting because people I trusted said it would be useful," says Williams. "What I got in return was a career, lots of friends, and a partner!" Her accounting course included a community service requirement. Students had to pair up and help less advantaged individuals.

My partner, Brett Fulwood, and I volunteered our services to a senior citizens community." Williams and Fulwood never looked back. On their first visit, Williams says they helped more than a dozen seniors, fielding questions on reading bank statements, interpreting pension checks, and analyzing financial reports of companies in which a few had invested their modest savings. "It was great," says Williams. "I saw the relevance of accounting and I was able to give something to others."

In the weeks that followed, Williams and Fulwood answered several follow-up questions. "We even got a call from a woman's nephew in Harrisburg asking if we could help with recordkeeping in the family trucking business," says Williams. "He offered to pay us a decent fee if we'd do it," added Fulwood. "That's when we knew we were onto something."

Today, Williams and Fulwood are running their own business, **W&F Financial Services.** "We still visit with seniors on the second Saturday of every month with free financial advice," says Williams. "It's the most rewarding work I do."

CHAPTER PREVIEW

Accounting in the information age is about people like Stephanie Williams and Brett Fulwood. Today's world is one of information—its preparation, communication, analysis, and use. Accounting is at the heart of the information age. Knowledge of accounting gives us opportunities and the insight to benefit from them. By studying this course and this book, you will learn about many concepts, procedures, and analyses that are useful in our everyday lives. This knowledge reduces our reliance on hunches, guesses, and intuition and, in turn, improves decision making.

In this chapter we describe accounting in the information age, the users and uses of accounting information, the forms and activities of organizations, and the importance of ethics and social responsibility. We also explain several important accounting concepts, procedures, and analyses. This chapter provides a foundation for those who have little or no understanding of business. Chapter 2 will build on this foundation when we consider transactions and financial statements.

Living in the Information Age

We live in the **information age**—a time of communication, data, news, facts, access, and commentary. The information age encourages timeliness, independence, and freedom of expression. Access to and understanding of information affect how we live, whom we associate with, and the opportunities we have. We use information to pick and choose among products and services like cars, bikes, clothes, computers, hotels, and restaurants. We pay people to analyze information for us. Examples are product rankings (*Consumer Reports*), medicinal advice (*American Medical Association*), and credit rating (*Standard & Poor's*).

Communication with and access to data are a major part of the information age and make up much of the *information superhighway*. The information superhighway has redefined communication, especially business communication. Global computer networks and telecommunications equipment allow us access to all types of business information. As it did for Stephanie Williams and Brett Fulwood (mentioned in the opening article), information provides us with powerful tools and opportunities. To take advantage of these, we need knowledge of the information system.

An information system is the collecting, processing, and reporting of information to decision makers. Knowing the information system means personal opportunities and real increases in pay. Two-year degree graduates with this knowledge can make upwards of 20 to 30 percent more than high school graduates, and bachelor degree graduates can make at least 55 percent more than high school graduates.[1] This added pay is due to an ability to understand and process information. Understanding and processing information is the core of accounting.

To get the most from our education and opportunities in life, we must know accounting. Your instructor will provide you with many assignments from this book and related materials to help you master accounting. We also encourage you to join us on the information superhighway to explore the opportunities awaiting you. For your help, we devote an entire Web site solely for your use and enjoyment with this book. You can access this site at **[www.mhhe.com/business/accounting/fap]**. The time and effort you spend in this course will repay you many times over.

Power of Accounting

C1 Explain the aim and power of accounting in the information age

One of the most important roles of the information superhighway is the reporting of business activities. Providing information about what businesses own, what they owe, and how they perform is the aim of accounting. **Accounting** is an information and mea-

[1] "The Sheepskin Paradox," *Business Week*, October 6, 1997, p. 30.

surement system that identifies, records, and communicates relevant, reliable, and comparable information about an organization's economic activities. It helps people make better decisions, including assessing opportunities, products, investments, and social and community responsibilities. Opportunities abound and accounting opens our eyes to new and exciting possibilities.

Completing this course will help you apply information in a way you can use in your everyday life. The use of information is not limited to accountants or even to people in business. Often the greatest benefits from understanding accounting come to those outside of accounting and business. We can use accounting to get a loan for a house or to start a business. We can use accounting to make better investment decisions. We are able to use accounting knowledge wherever we go and in whatever career we choose.

The World Wide Web is a part of our lives. This book is supported by a Web site to help in your studies.

Business and Investment

A **business** is one or more individuals selling products or services for profit. Products such as athletic apparel (**NIKE, Reebok, Converse**), computers (**Packard-Bell, Hewlett-Packard, Apple**) and clothing (**Levis, REI, GAP**) are part of our lives. Services like information communication (**America Online, CompuServe, Microsoft**), dining (**McDonald's, Burger King, Wendy's**), and car rental (**Hertz, Budget, Alamo**) make our lives easier. A business can be as small as an in-home child care service or as massive as **Wal-Mart.** Nearly 1 million new businesses are started in the United States each year, no different than **W&S Financial Services** in the opening article. Most of these are started by people who want freedom from ordinary jobs, a new challenge in life, or the advantage of extra money.

A1 Describe profit and its two major components.

Business Profit

A common feature of all businesses is the desire for profit. **Profit,** also called **net income** or **earnings,** is the amount a business earns after subtracting all expenses related to its sales. **Sales,** also called **revenues,** are the amounts earned from selling products and services. **Expenses** are the costs incurred with sales. For **W&F Financial Services,** profit is the amount earned from consulting with clients less expenses such as travel, meals, advertising, and promotion. Not all businesses make profits. A **loss** arises when expenses are more than sales. Many new businesses incur losses in their first several months or years of business. Yet no business can continually experience losses and stay in business.

Let's look at **NIKE**'s profit breakdown in Exhibit 1.1. If we pay $100 for a pair of **NIKE** athletic footwear, $8.66 is profit to **NIKE.** The rest goes to cover expenses such as materials and labor ($53.51) and advertising ($10.65). **NIKE** also pays $5.43 per pair in total taxes. One question confronting our society today is what is the "right" amount of profit. Should business pay more for charitable giving or community services? Are taxes too high or too low? For us to even begin to consider important questions like these we must understand accounting.

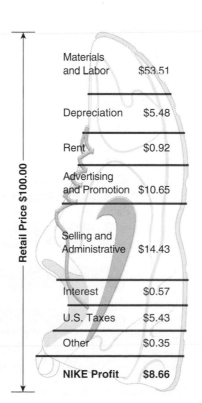

Retail Price $100.00	
Materials and Labor	$53.51
Depreciation	$5.48
Rent	$0.92
Advertising and Promotion	$10.65
Selling and Administrative	$14.43
Interest	$0.57
U.S. Taxes	$5.43
Other	$0.35
NIKE Profit	**$8.66**

Exhibit 1.1

Where Our Money Goes When Buying a Pair of NIKEs

Return and Risk

Profit is often linked to **return.** The term *return* derives from the idea of getting something back from an investment, or return on investment. **Return on investment** is often stated in ratio form as profit divided by amount invested. For example, banks or savings and loans often report our return from a savings account in the form of an interest rate of return on investment. For example, we might have a 4% savings account or invest our college money in an 8% money market fund.

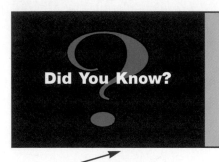

Did You Know?

Oprah Winfrey	27%
Steven Spielberg	19
Tiger Woods	15
Michael Jordan	14
Tom Cruise	8
Rosie O'Donnell	5
Jerry Seinfeld	4
Madonna	2

Celebrity Investment

How do fame and fortune translate into return and risk? A poll asked people which celebrity is the best investment. Similar to business investments, people named relatively young performers with years of earning power ahead. Oprah came out on top with high return and low risk. Source: *Business Week,* Dec. 7, 1998 and March 24, 1997.

Did You Know is a feature that extends throughout the book. This feature highlights important and interesting cases from practice.

A2 Explain the relation between return and risk.

We can invest our money in many ways. If we invest it in a savings account or in U.S. government treasury bills, we get a return of around 3% to 7%. We could also invest in a company's stock, or even start our own business like Williams and Fulwood. How do we decide among these investment options? Our answer rests on the trade-off between return and risk.

Risk is the amount of uncertainty about the return we expect to earn. All business decisions involve risk. But some decisions involve more risk than others. The lower the risk of an investment, the lower is our expected return. The reason why savings accounts pay such a low return is the low risk of our not being repaid with interest. The government guarantees most savings accounts from default. Also, U.S. government bonds pay a low return because of the low risk of the U.S. government's defaulting on its payments. But if we buy a share of **NIKE** or any other company, there is no guarantee of any return. There is even the risk of loss.

The bar graph in Exhibit 1.2 shows returns for bonds with different risks. **Bonds** are written promises by organizations to repay amounts loaned with interest. U.S. treasury bonds provide us a low expected return of 6.49%, but they also offer low risk since they are backed by the U.S. government. High-risk corporate bonds offer a much larger expected return (8.52%) but with much greater risk.

The trade-off between return and risk is a normal part of business. Higher risk implies higher, but more risky, expected returns. To help us make better business decisions,

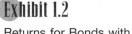
Exhibit 1.2

Returns for Bonds with Different Risks

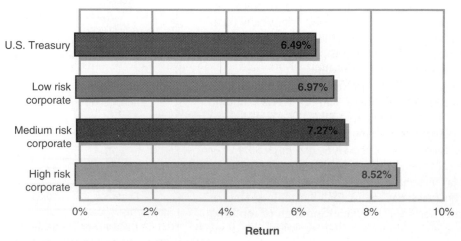

Source: *The Wall Street Journal,* August 4, 1997.

we use accounting information in measuring both return and risk. We decide on our desired level of return and risk and use accounting information to help achieve it.

Answer—p. 27

Programmer

You are considering two job offers. Both require your computer programming skills. One is with a new start-up Internet provider at an annual salary of $31,000; the other is with an established medical supply company for $25,500 a year. Which offer do you accept? *[Note: Guidance answers to "You Make the Call" are at the end of chapter.]*

You Make the Call

"You Make the Call" are role-playing exercises extending throughout the book. These exercises stress the relevance of accounting for people in and outside of business.

Accounting Information

Factors of production are the means businesses use to make profit. *Land, labor,* and *plant and equipment* are the traditional factors of production. Today's information age suggests we add accounting information to these traditional factors of production. Accounting information gives us knowledge to make better decisions, and good decision making is key to business success.

If we analyze recent business performance, we see it is not the traditional factors driving success. For example, we see **GTE** with its factors of production worth well over $40 billion reporting a recent loss of more than $2 billion. We see **Kmart,** which employs more than 250,000 employees, reporting a recent loss of $571 million. Other giants like **IBM, Woolworth,** and **Tandy** struggle to consistently yield a 5% or 10% return on investment. Yet smaller companies like **GAP, NIKE,** and **Mattel** consistently yield a 15% or greater return on investment. The common denominator in the success stories is relevant and reliable information.

Focus of Accounting

We need to guard against a narrow view of accounting. Accounting affects many parts of our lives and is crucial to modern society. Our most obvious contact with accounting is through credit approvals, checking accounts, tax forms, and payroll. Yet these experiences are limited and tend to focus on the recordkeeping parts of accounting. **Recordkeeping** or **bookkeeping,** is the recording of financial transactions and events, either manually or electronically. While recordkeeping is essential to data reliability in our information age, accounting is this and much more.

The primary objective of accounting is to provide useful information for decision making as shown in Exhibit 1.3. Accounting activities include identifying, measuring, recording, reporting, and analyzing economic events and transactions. They also involve interpreting information and designing information systems to provide useful reports that monitor and control an organization's activities. Whatever our career path, accounting is part of it. We benefit by understanding how accounting information is prepared and used. To gain this understanding, we need to know certain recordkeeping skills. This book provides opportunities for you to learn these skills. This knowledge helps us read and interpret financial data. Our opportunities are greater if we understand accounting and are able to use information effectively.

Identifying and measuring

Recording

Reporting and analyzing

Exhibit 1.3

Accounting Activities

Accounting and Technology

Technology is a key part of our modern society and business practices. It also plays a major role in accounting. Computing technology reduces the time, effort, and cost of recordkeeping while improving clerical accuracy. While some smaller organizations continue to perform various accounting tasks manually, they are still impacted by information technology.

As technology has changed the way we store, process, and summarize large masses of data, accounting has been freed to expand its field. Major consulting, planning, and other financial services are quickly becoming part of accounting. Now more than ever we need people who can quickly sort through masses of data, interpret their meaning, identify key factors, and analyze their implications.

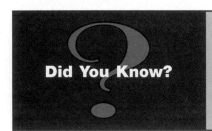

Did You Know?

Accounting Web

Technology is changing the face of business and accounting. Many organizations maintain their own Web pages that include substantial accounting information. You might want to visit **NIKE**'s **(www.nike.com)** or **Reebok**'s **(www.reebok.com)** Web site to see for yourself. You can also search the SEC's on-line database called **EDGAR** **(www.sec.gov)**. EDGAR has accounting information for thousands of companies.

Setting Accounting Rules

There are rules for reporting on an organization's performance and current condition. These rules increase the usefulness of reports, including their reliability and comparability. The rules that make up acceptable accounting practices are determined by many individuals and groups and are referred to as **generally accepted accounting principles,** or **GAAP.** Since accounting is a service activity, these rules reflect our society's needs and not those of accountants or any other single constituency. This is reinforced by the federal government, which regulates organizations that sell shares of ownership to the public. The **Securities and Exchange Commission (SEC)** is charged by Congress with the authority to set reporting rules for these organizations. For the most part, the SEC passes authority to set accounting rules to professionals in practice.

The **Financial Accounting Standards Board (FASB)** is currently responsible for setting accounting rules. The FASB is an independent group of seven full-time members with a large staff. It has issued six statements of accounting concepts to help guide accounting standard setting. Many interested groups and individuals involve themselves in setting accounting rules and lobby the FASB in their self-interests. They include unions, investors, government agencies, lenders, politicians, and other business and nonbusiness organizations. Individuals and leaders in these organizations must understand accounting information and any proposed rules to chart and defend a position in their best interests. The **American Institute of Certified Public Accountants (AICPA),** the largest and most influential national professional organization of certified public accountants, is especially active in the process of setting accounting rules.

Flashbacks *give you a chance to stop and reflect on key points in the book. Guidance answers to Flashbacks are given at the end of the chapter.*

Flash *back*

1. What is the aim of accounting?
2. Describe profit, sales, and expenses.
3. Explain the trade-off between return and risk.
4. What is the relation between accounting and recordkeeping?
5. Who sets accounting rules?

Answers—p. 27

Exhibit 1.4

Forms of Organizations

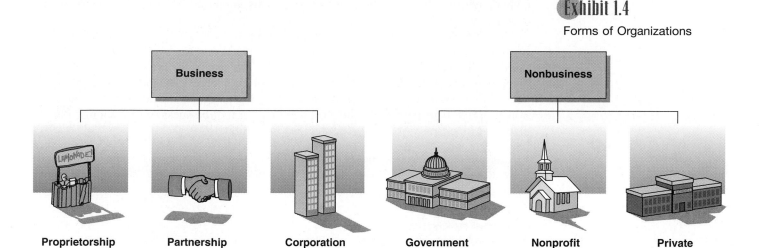

Organizations can be classified as either business or nonbusiness as shown in Exhibit 1.4. Typically, businesses are organized for profit, while nonbusinesses serve us in ways not always measured by profit.

Most organizations engage in economic activities. These can include the usual business activities of purchasing materials and labor and of selling products and services. They can also involve nonbusiness activities like collecting money through taxes, dues, contributions, investments, or borrowings. A common feature in all these organizations is the power and use of accounting.

Forms of Organization

C2 Identify forms of organization and their characteristics.

Business Organization

A business is organized and operated to make a profit. Because of this, a business is often called a *profit-oriented organization.* A principle that must be followed in accounting for organizations is the **business entity principle.** This principle means every organization is accounted for separately from its owner's personal activities. It also means that a set of accounting records and reports refer only to the transactions and events of that one organization. We will discuss this and other important accounting principles in the next chapter.

Businesses take one of three legal forms: a *sole proprietorship*, a *partnership,* or a *corporation.* Exhibit 1.5 gives us the proportion and revenues from these different organization forms.

Exhibit 1.5

Different Business Organizations and Their Revenues

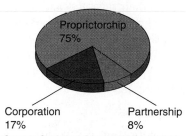

Forms of businesses

Proprietorship 75%

Corporation 17%

Partnership 8%

Source: *Statistical Abstract of the United States,* U.S. Bureau of the Census

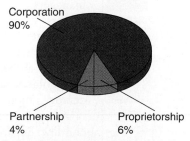

Revenues of businesses

Corporation 90%

Partnership 4%

Proprietorship 6%

Source: *Statistical Abstract of the United States,* U.S. Bureau of the Census

Sole Proprietorship

A **sole proprietorship,** or **single proprietorship,** is a business owned by one person. No special legal requirements must be met to start a sole proprietorship. While it is a separate entity for accounting purposes, it is *not* a separate legal entity from its owner. This means, for example, a court can order an owner to sell personal belongings to pay a proprietorship's debt. An owner is even responsible for debts that exceed an owner's net investment in the proprietorship. This *unlimited liability* of a proprietorship is sometimes a disadvantage.

Tax authorities do not separate a proprietorship from its owner. This means the profits of a proprietorship are not subject to a business income tax, but must be reported and taxed on the owner's personal income tax return. The rate of tax on a proprietorship's income depends on the level of total income from all sources that the owner had for the year. Small retail stores and service businesses often are organized as proprietorships. Sole proprietorships are by far the most common form of business organization in our society and its characteristics are summarized in Exhibit 1.6.

Exhibit 1.6

Characteristics of Business Organizations

	Proprietorship	Partnership	Corporation
Business entity	yes	yes	yes
Legal entity	no	no	yes
Limited liability	no	no	yes
Unlimited life	no	no	yes
Business taxed	no	no	yes
One owner allowed	yes	no	yes

Partnership

A **partnership** is a business owned by two or more people, called *partners*. Like a proprietorship, no special legal requirements must be met in starting a partnership. All that is required is an agreement between partners to run a business together. The agreement can be either oral or written and usually indicates how profits and losses are shared. A written agreement is preferred as it can help partners avoid or resolve disputes. A partnership, like a proprietorship, is *not* legally separate from its owners. This means that each partner's share of profits is reported and taxed on that partner's tax return. It also means *unlimited liability* for its partners.

There are two types of partnerships that limit liability. A *limited partnership* includes a general partner(s) with unlimited liability and a limited partner(s) with liability restricted to the amount invested. A *limited liability partnership* restricts partners' liabilities to their own acts and the acts of individuals under their control. This protects an innocent partner from the negligence of another partner. Yet all partners remain responsible for partnership debts. There are about one-tenth as many partnerships as proprietorships. **NIKE** began as a partnership and was originally called **Blue Ribbon Sports.** The partners, Philip Knight and Bill Bowerman, each contributed $500 and shipped shoes out of Knight's basement.

Corporation

A **corporation** is a business legally separate from its owners. This means a corporation is responsible for its own acts and its own debts. It can enter into its own contracts, and

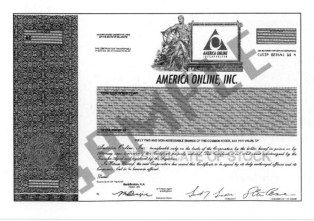

it can buy, own, and sell property. It can also sue and be sued. Separate legal status means a corporation can conduct business with the rights, duties, and responsibilities of a person. A corporation acts through its managers, who are its legal agents. Separate legal status also means its owners, who are called *shareholders,* are not personally liable for corporate acts and debts. Shareholders are legally distinct from the business and their loss is limited to their net investment in shares purchased. This limited liability is a key to why corporations can raise resources from shareholders who are not active in managing the business. It also encourages more risky investment with higher expected returns.

A corporation is legally chartered (*incorporated*) under state or federal law. Separate legal status results in a corporation having unlimited life. Ownership, or *equity*, of all corporations is divided into units called **shares** or **stock.** Owners of shares are called **shareholders** or **stock-**

holders. A shareholder can sell or transfer shares to another person without affecting the operations of a corporation. When a corporation issues only one class of stock, we call it **common stock,** or *capital stock.*

A corporation is subject to *double taxation.* This means a corporation is taxed on its net income. Any distribution of corporate earnings to its owners is also taxed as part of their personal income. An exception to this is an S corporation. An *S corporation* is a corporation with certain characteristics that give it special tax status.[2] This special tax status removes its double taxation. Instead, shareholders of S corporations report their share of corporate income or loss as part of their personal income.[3]

Exhibit 1.7

Partial List of Nonbusinesses

Nonbusiness Organization

Nonbusiness organizations plan and operate for goals other than profit. These goals often are met by government or nonprofit organizations and include security, health, education, transportation, judicial, and religious services and cultural and social activities. Examples are public schools meeting the needs of citizens and community care groups meeting the needs of the poor.

Nonbusiness organizations lack an identifiable owner. Still the demand for accounting information in nonbusiness organizations is high because they are accountable to their sponsors. Governments need to report receipts and expenditures of tax money, and colleges need to explain tuition increases. These organizations are accountable to taxpayers, donors, lenders, legislators, regulators, or other constituents. Accounting for these organizations is usually a *fund-based* system, but the basic principles are similar to accounting for business organizations.

Exhibit 1.7 lists a wide range of nonbusiness organizations affected by the power of accounting. This list is but a sampling of the roughly one-third of U.S. economic activity done by nonbusiness organizations. Some of these organizations, such as hospitals, are often run as private, nonprofit, or government operations. In all of these organizations, accounting captures key information about their activities.

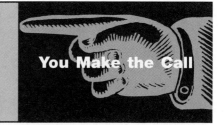

Entrepreneur
You and a friend develop a new design for mountain bikes that improves speed and performance by 25% to 40%. You plan to form a small business to manufacture and market these bikes. You and your friend want to minimize taxes, but your prime concern is potential lawsuits from individuals who will "push the limit" on these bikes and be injured. What form of organization do you set up?

You Make the Call

Answer—p. 27

---

[2] The required characteristics are listed in the *Internal Revenue Code.* These characteristics include: no more than 75 shareholders (not counting spouses), only one class of stock, and all shareholders are U.S. citizens or residents.

[3] A *limited liability company* (or LLC) is a new alternative form of business organization. It offers the limited liability of a corporation and the tax treatment of a partnership (or proprietorship).

Activities in Organizations

C3 Identify and describe the three major activities in organizations.

Organizations carry out their activities in many different ways. These differences extend to their products, services, goals, organization form, management style, worker compensation, and community giving. Yet the major activities of organizations are similar. We discuss the three major types of business activities: financing, investing, and operating. Each of these activities requires planning.

Planning

All organizations begin with planning. **Planning** involves defining the ideas, goals, and actions of an organization. Strategies and tactics need to be laid out. Employees must be informed and motivated. Managers must be credible and display leadership and vision. All of these tasks are part of planning and are the duty of *executive management*. Executive management sets the organization's strategic goals and policies that are captured in an *organization plan*. The owner or owners take on this duty in most organizations. Responsibility for this duty often carries with it the title of president, chief executive officer, or chairman of the board of directors. In nonprofit organizations the title for top managers is often executive director.

Planning assists an organization in focusing its efforts and identifying opportunities. External users benefit from knowledge of an organization's plans. They look for clues on tactics, market demands, competitors, promotion, pricing, innovations, and projections. Much of this information, both for internal and external users, is provided in accounting reports. **NIKE** (and most other public corporations) uses the Management Discussion and Analysis section in its annual report for this purpose:

> the Company is positioning itself to continue to expand markets and gain market share on a worldwide basis . . . The Company intends to continue to invest in growth opportunities and worldwide marketing and advertising in order to ensure the successful sell-through of the high level of orders.

It is important to remember that planning involves change and reaction to it. It is not cast in stone. This adds *risk* to both the development and analysis of an organization's plans. Accounting information can reduce this risk through more informed and better decision making. Both internal and external accounting reports affect the plans, decisions, and actions of management.

Financing

An organization requires financing to begin and operate according to its plans. **Financing activities** are the means organizations use to pay for resources like land, buildings, and machines to carry out plans. Organizations are careful in acquiring and managing financing activities because of their potential to determine success or failure.

There are two main sources of financing: owner and nonowner. *Owner financing* refers to resources contributed by the owner and any profits that the owner chooses to leave in the organization. *Nonowner* (or *creditor*) *financing* refers to resources contributed by creditors (lenders) that are called liabilities. Creditors can include banks, savings and loans, and other financial institutions. *Financial management* is the task of planning how to obtain these resources and to set the right mix between the amounts of owner and creditor financing. Government organizations can also acquire resources with taxes and fees, and nonprofit organizations can acquire resources from contributions by donors. **NIKE**'s total 1997 financing equaled $5,361 (in millions). It comprised $3,156 in owner financing and $2,205 in creditor financing.

Investing

Investing activities are the acquiring and disposing of resources (assets) that an organization uses to sell its products or services. These assets are funded by an organization's financing. **Assets** are economic resources that are expected to produce future benefits. They include land, buildings, equipment, inventories, supplies, cash, and all investments needed for operating an organization. **NIKE**'s 1997 assets totaled $5,361 (in millions). Organizations differ on the amount and makeup of their assets. Some organizations require land and factories to operate. Others might only need an office. Determining the amount and type of assets for organizations to operate is called *asset management.*

It is important to see that an organization's investing and financing totals are *always* equal. Invested amounts are referred to as *assets,* and financing is made up of creditor and owner financing. Creditors and owners hold claims, or rights, in assets. Creditors' claims are called **liabilities** and the owner's claim is called **owner's equity** (or simply *equity*). This equality can be written as:

$$\text{Assets} = \text{Liabilities} + \text{Equity}$$

This equality is called the **accounting equation. NIKE**'s 1997 assets of $5,361 equal the total of its liabilities of $2,205 plus its owner's equity of $3,156 (in millions):

$$\text{Assets} = \text{Liabilities} + \text{Equity}$$
$$\$5,361 = \$2,205 + \$3,156$$

The accounting equation works for all organizations at all times. It is an important part of accounting. We will return to and use the accounting equation in our analysis of transactions in the next several chapters.

> **A3** Explain and interpret the accounting equation.

Operating

An organization's main purpose is operating activities. **Operating activities** are the carrying out of an organization's plans and involve using assets to research, develop, purchase, produce, distribute, and market products and services. They include management activities like worker supervision and compliance with laws. Operating activities aim at selling the organization's products and services. Sales and revenues are the inflow of assets from selling products and services. Costs and expenses are the outflow of assets necessary to support operating activities. Examples of costs and expenses are salaries, rent, electricity, and supplies. *Strategic management* is the process of determining the right mix of operating activities for the type of organization, its plans, and its market. How well the organization carries out its operating activities determines its success and return.

Exhibit 1.8 summarizes these activities. Planning is part of every activity and is the common link between activities. Planning gives the activities meaning and focus. Investing (assets) and financing (liabilities and equity) are set opposite each other to stress their balance. Operating activities are shown below investing and financing activities. This is to emphasize that operating activities are the result of investing and financing. Financing, investing, and operating activities and the planning involved in all three are constantly changing to reflect the actions of an organization.

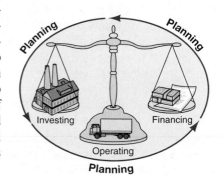

Exhibit 1.8

Activities in Organizations

6. What are the three common forms of business organizations?

7. Can you identify examples of nonbusiness organizations?

8. What are the three major activities in organizations?

Answers—p. 28

Users of Accounting Information

C4 Identify users and uses of accounting.

Organizations set up accounting information systems to help them and others make better decisions. Every organization uses some type of information system to report on its activities. The accounting information system is a service activity as shown in Exhibit 1.9. It serves the information needs of many kinds of users (or stakeholders) including managers, lenders, suppliers, customers, directors, auditors, employees, and current and potential investors. Knowledge of accounting improves their decisions.

External Information Users

External users of accounting information are *not* directly involved in running the organization. They include shareholders, lenders, directors, customers, suppliers, regulators, lawyers, brokers, and the press. Yet these users are affected by, and sometimes affect, the organization. External users rely on accounting information to make better decisions in pursuing their goals. For example, lenders are less likely to make bad loans or shareholders bad investments when they know current and past profits of a business.

Financial accounting is the area of accounting aimed at serving external users. Its primary objective is to provide external reports called financial statements to help users analyze an organization's activities. External users have limited access to an organization's valuable information. Their own success depends on getting external reports that are reliable, relevant, and comparable. Some governmental and regulatory agencies have the power to get reports in specific forms. But most external users must rely on *general-purpose financial statements*. The term *general-purpose* refers to the broad range of purposes for which external users rely on these statements. Generally accepted accounting principles are important in increasing the usefulness of financial statements to users. We discuss these principles along with financial statements in the next chapter.

Each external user has special information needs depending on the kinds of decisions one must make. These decisions involve getting answers to key questions, answers that are often available in accounting reports. This section describes several external users and questions they confront. Your accounting course will provide you many insights into where answers can be found.

Exhibit 1.9

Users of Accounting Information

Internal users	**External users**

Internal users		**External users**	
• Managers	• Sales managers	• Lenders	• Labor unions
• Officers	• Budget officers	• Shareholders	• External auditors
• Internal auditors	• Controller	• Government	• Customers

Lenders (Creditors)

Lenders loan money or other resources to an organization. Lenders include banks, savings and loans, co-ops, and mortgage and finance companies. Lenders look for information to help them assess whether an organization is likely to repay its loan with interest. External reports help them answer questions about organizations such as:

- Has it promptly paid past loans?
- Can it repay current loans?
- What are its current risks?
- What is its profit outlook?

The questions can change between short- and long-term lending decisions. The more long-term a loan, the more a lender's questions look like those of an owner.

Shareholders (Owners)

Shareholders have legal control over part or all of a corporation. They are the owners of corporations and in many cases are not part of management. Owners are exposed to the greatest return and risk. Risk is high because there is no promise of either repayment or a return on investment. They can lose their entire investment. Yet owners have a claim on assets after a business pays its debts. Many businesses do not give all or most of their profits back to owners but invest them in more assets to enable the company to grow. External reports aim to help answer shareholder (owner) questions such as:

- What is the income for current and past periods?
- Are assets adequate to meet business plans?
- Do expenses fit the level and type of sales?
- Are customers' bills paid promptly?
- Do loans seem large or unusual?

Corporations typically have a board of directors. *Directors* are elected representatives of shareholders and are charged to oversee their interests in an organization. Because directors are responsible to shareholders, their questions are similar. **NIKE**'s 1997 board of directors had 13 members.

External Auditors

External (or *independent*) auditors examine and provide an opinion on whether financial statements are prepared according to generally accepted accounting principles. External reports of competing organizations are used by auditors to help assess the reasonableness of a client's reports. **NIKE**'s independent auditor is **Price Waterhouse LLP.**

Employees

Employees, or their union representatives, have a special interest in an organization. They are interested in judging the fairness of their wages and in assessing future job prospects. External reports provide information useful in addressing these needs. External reports are also used in bargaining for better wages when an organization is successful.

Regulators

Regulators often have legal authority or significant influence over the activities of organizations. The Internal Revenue Service and other tax authorities require organizations to use various reports in computing taxes. These taxes include income, unemployment, sales, and social security. Tax reports usually require special forms and supporting records. Government and nongovernment agencies also use financial reports. Examples include utility boards that use accounting information to set utility rates and securities regulators that require special filings for businesses with publicly traded securities.

Other Important External Users

Accounting serves the needs of many other important external users. Voters, legislators, and elected officials use accounting information to monitor and evaluate a government's receipts and expenses. Contributors to nonprofit organizations use accounting information to evaluate the use and impact of their donations. Suppliers use accounting information to judge the soundness of a business before making sales on credit. Customers use external reports to assess the staying power of potential suppliers and the extent of products returned.

Internal Information Users

Internal users of accounting information are those individuals directly involved in managing and operating an organization. They include managers, officers, and other important internal decision makers. Internal users make the strategic and operating decisions for an organization. The internal role of accounting is to provide information to help improve the efficiency or effectiveness of an organization in delivering products or services. In this way, accounting helps businesses reach their goals.

Managerial accounting is the area of accounting aimed at serving the decision-making needs of internal users. Managerial accounting provides internal reports to help internal users improve an organization's activities. Internal reports are not subject to the same rules as external reports. This is because decisions of internal users are not constrained by the need to keep certain information private from external users because of competitive concerns. Internal users often have access to a lot of private and valuable information. Costs in preparing internal reports are usually the only constraint on internal reporting. Internal reports aim to answer questions like:

- What are manufacturing costs per product?
- What is the most profitable mix of services?
- What level of sales is necessary to break even?
- Which service activities are most profitable?
- What costs vary with sales?

Information to help answer these questions is very important for success. This book provides many tools to help in this task.

The responsibilities and duties of internal users extend to every function of an organization. There are at least seven functions common to most organizations. Accounting is essential to the smooth operation of each of these functions. The internal operating functions are shown in Exhibit 1.10 and include: research and development, purchasing, human resources, production, distribution, marketing, and servicing. The larger the business, the more likely these operating functions are separate units in the business. Each unit often has its own internal user (manager) who is responsible for decisions. Depending on the type of business, not all of these operating functions are necessary. For example, publishing companies usually don't require separate research and development units, and banks don't require production units. Less frequently used functions are often combined. We briefly describe the information needs of these internal users for each operating function:

- **Research and development** Research and development is aimed at creating or improving a company's products or services. Managers need information about current and projected costs and potential sales to decide on research and development projects.
- **Purchasing** Purchasing involves acquiring and managing materials needed for operations. Managers need to know what, when, and how much to purchase.
- **Human resources** Human resource management aims to locate, screen, hire, train, compensate, promote, and counsel employees. Managers need information about current and potential employees, payroll costs, employee benefits, and other performance and compensation data.

- **Production** Production is the mix of the factors of production to produce products and services. Good production methods depend on information to monitor costs and ensure quality.
- **Distribution** Distribution involves timely and accurate delivery of products and services. Relevant information is often key to quality distribution including its cost.
- **Marketing** Marketing is the promotion and advertising of products and services. Marketing managers use accounting reports about sales and costs to effectively target consumers and set pricing. Marketing also uses accounting to monitor consumer needs, tastes, and price concerns.
- **Servicing** Servicing customers after selling products or services is often key to success and includes training, assistance, installation, warranties, and maintenance. Information is needed on both the costs and benefits of servicing.

Exhibit 1.10
Internal Operating Functions

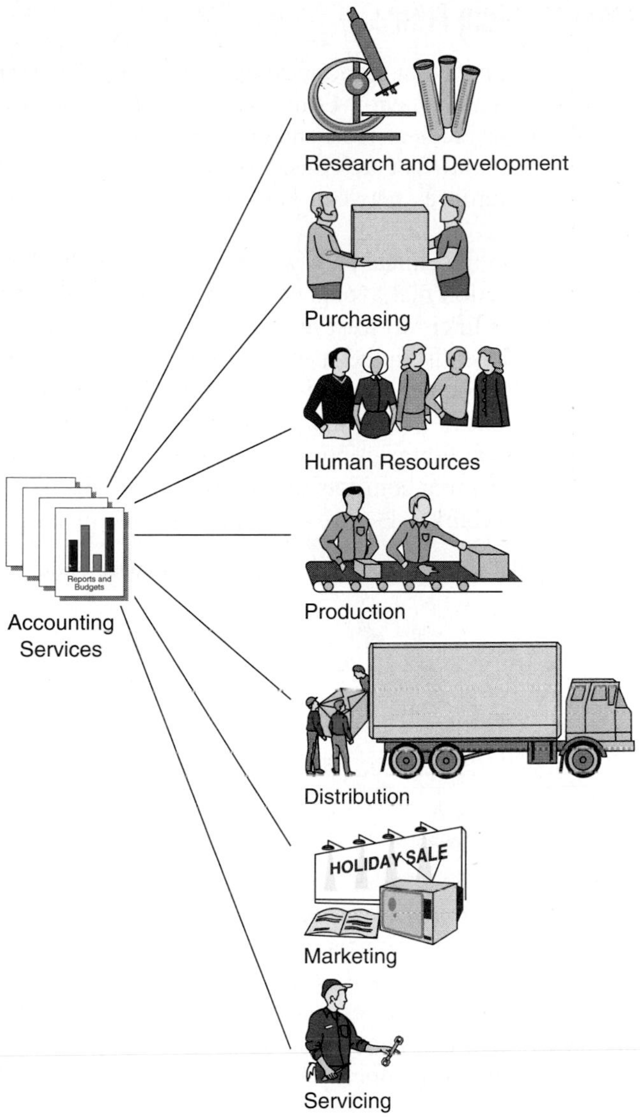

Research and Development

Purchasing

Human Resources

Production

Distribution

Marketing

Servicing

Accounting Services

Both internal and external users rely on internal controls to monitor these operating functions. **Internal controls** are procedures set up to protect assets, ensure reliable accounting reports, promote efficiency, and encourage adherence to company policies.

Ethics and Social Responsibility

Ethics and ethical behavior are important. We are reminded of this when we run across disappointing stories in the media or witness wrongful actions by individuals such as cheating, harassment, misconduct, and bribery. Such cases make it more difficult for people to trust one another. If trust is missing, our lives are more difficult, inefficient, and unpleasant.

This section explains the meaning of ethics and describes how ethics affect organizations. We take up ethics early in our study because of their importance to organizations, accounting, and everyday living. The goal of accounting is to provide useful information for decision making. For information to be useful, it must be trusted. This demands ethics in accounting. This section also discusses social responsibility for organizations.

C5 Explain why ethics and social responsibility are crucial to accounting.

Understanding Ethics

Ethics are beliefs that separate right from wrong. They are known as accepted standards of good and bad behavior. Ethics and laws often coincide, with the result that many unethical actions (such as theft and physical violence) are also illegal. Yet other actions are not against the law but are considered unethical, such as not helping people in need. Because of differences between laws and ethics, we cannot look to laws to keep people ethical.

Identifying the ethical path is sometimes difficult. The preferred ethical path is to take a course of action that avoids casting doubt on one's decision. For example, accounting users are less likely to trust an auditor's report on the fairness of accounting if the auditor's pay depends on the success of the reporting organization. To avoid questions and concerns of this type, ethics rules are often set. Auditors are indeed banned from any direct investment in their client, regardless of amount.[4] Auditors also cannot accept pay that depends on figures reported in a client's accounting reports.[5] These ethics rules are aimed at preventing conflicts of interest or even the appearance that an auditor is not independent. Exhibit 1.11 gives us guidelines for making ethical decisions.

Exhibit 1.11

Guidelines for Ethical Decision Making

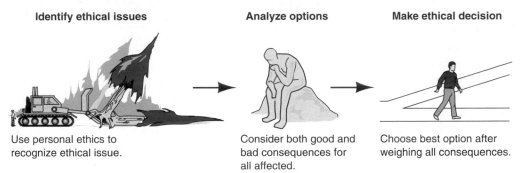

Identify ethical issues	Analyze options	Make ethical decision
Use personal ethics to recognize ethical issue.	Consider both good and bad consequences for all affected.	Choose best option after weighing all consequences.

Throughout our lives we will continue to face decisions with ethical aspects. These arise in our school, our workplace, and our personal relationships. A commitment to ethical behavior requires us to think carefully before we act, to be certain we are making ethical choices. Our success in making these choices affects how we feel about ourselves and how others feel about us. Ethics are not a personal matter. Our combined individual choices affect the quality of our community and the experiences of all of us.

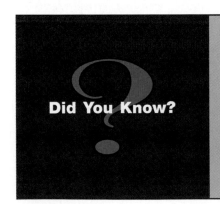

Did You Know?

In Pursuit of Profit

How far can companies go in pursuing profits? **Converse** proposed to name a new footwear product Run N' Gun. This sparked debate on ethics, social responsibility, and profits. Converse says Run N' Gun is a basketball and football term. Critics claim it invites youth violence and links with the gun culture. To the credit of Converse, it changed the name from Run N' Gun to Run N' Slam prior to its sale to consumers.

Organizational Ethics

Organizational ethics are likely learned through example and leadership. Companies like **McDonald's, Marriott, Ben & Jerry's Homemade Ice Cream,** and **IBM** work hard

---

[4] *AICPA Code of Professional Conduct,* Rule 101.

[5] *AICPA Code of Professional Conduct,* Rule 301.

at instilling ethics in employees. Yet we still hear people express concern about what they see as low ethics in organizations. A survey of more than 1,100 executives, educators, and legislators showed that 94% of the participants agreed with the comment that "the business community is troubled by ethical problems."[6] Yet this survey revealed that the vast majority of participants believe high ethical standards are followed by organizations that are successful over the long run. This finding confirms an old saying: *Good ethics is good business.* Ethical practices build trust, which promotes loyalty and long-term relationships with customers, suppliers, and employees. Because of this and the public interest in ethics, many organizations have their own codes of ethics. These codes set standards for internal activities and for relationships with customers, suppliers, regulators, the public, and even competitors.

Accounting Ethics

Ethics are crucial in accounting. Providers of accounting information often face ethical choices as they prepare financial reports. Their choices can affect both the use and receipt of money, including taxes owed and money shared with owners. It can affect the price a buyer pays and the wages paid to workers. It can even affect the success of products, services, and divisions. Misleading information can lead to a wrongful closing of a division where workers, customers, and suppliers are seriously harmed.

Because of the importance of accounting ethics, codes of ethics are set up and enforced. These codes include those of the American Institute of Certified Public Accountants and the Institute of Management Accountants. These codes are presented at the end of the book and can help us when confronting ethical dilemmas. For example, organizations often pay managers bonuses based on the amount of income reported. Managers can benefit from using accounting in ways to increase their pay. These choices can reduce the money available for employee wages, training programs, community giving, and other supported programs such as the **United Way.**

Ethics codes can also help in dealing with confidential information. For example, auditors have access to confidential salaries and an organization's strategies. Organizations can be harmed if auditors pass this information to others. To prevent this, auditors' ethics codes require them to keep information confidential.[7] Internal accountants are also not to use confidential information for personal gain.[8] These examples show the practical value of ethical codes. They provide guidance in knowing what action to take.

Social Responsibility

Social responsibility is a concern for the impact of our actions on society as a whole. Organizations, too, are increasingly concerned with their social responsibility. **Reebok** proclaims in its annual report:

> We have a deep-felt commitment to operate in a socially responsible way and we stand for human rights throughout the world.

Our society is increasing the pressure on organizations to give something back. Socially conscious employees, customers, investors, and others see to it that organizations back

---

[6] Touche Ross & Co., *Ethics in American Business* (New York, 1988), pp. 1–2.

[7] *AICPA Code of Professional Conduct,* Rule 301.

[8] *Institute of Management Accountants Standards of Ethical Conduct.*

up rhetoric with actions. There are several ways that organizations give something back. This section describes some of these programs and discusses social auditing as a means to monitor social responsibility.

Social Programs

An organization's social responsibility extends in many directions. It can include donations to nonprofit organizations such as hospitals, colleges, community programs, and law enforcement. It can also include programs to reduce pollution, increase product safety, improve worker conditions, support continuing education, and better use our natural resources. Yet most organizations are more likely to invest in their own social programs. For example, **NIKE** invests in its *P.L.A.Y.* (*Participate in the Lives of America's Youth*) program. It is aimed at activism, especially providing opportunities and facilities for kids to pursue fitness and fun. **Xerox** offers its workers up to a one-year leave to work for a nonprofit organization. During their leave, workers receive full salary and benefits and return to their same positions when the leave is finished. Many other organizations offer similar social programs. We are aware of well over 1,000 businesses that offer social programs to their employees to pursue community service activities. **Boeing**'s corporate citizenship is described in its annual report as follows:

> Company and employee contributions totaled nearly $60 million to support a full spectrum of community programs in the areas of education, health and human services, civic participation, and the arts. Boeing employees and retirees also volunteered more than one million hours of their own time to serve their communities.

A more detailed social responsibility report is that of **AT&T** shown in Exhibit 1.12. These programs are not limited to large companies. For example, many independently owned movie theaters and leisure sports businesses offer discounts to students and senior citizens. Still others help sponsor events such as the Special Olympics and summer reading programs with the local library.

Support for all of these types of social programs by organizations is not universal. Some argue that organizations are not unbiased in supporting social programs. There is a concern that an organization's interests might be quite different from its workers', customers', or the public's. It is sometimes argued that an organization should increase pay to its workers so that they can contribute to their own community concerns. While there will be continuing debate and disagreement with the charitable giving of organizations, the new era of social responsibility is here to stay.

Exhibit 1.12

AT&T's "Social Responsibility" Report

Commitment to Making a Difference

- The AT&T CARES program is granting 130,400 AT&T people a paid workday by the end of 1997 in which they may perform community service work. Our efforts can generate more than 1 million hours of volunteer local service. To date, some 10,000 employees have participated in projects that include planting trees, cleaning playgrounds and helping build houses.

- The AT&T Foundation donated $49 million in 1996 through our Matching Gift Program, the United Way and local contributions.

- Last year, 8.7 percent of AT&T's total purchases came from minority- and women-owned businesses (MWBE). We received the Distinguished Corporate Award from the U.S. Department of Commerce and U.S. Small Business Administration, while the Asian Entrepreneurs organization awarded AT&T its Corporate Advocate Award.

Returns on Social Responsibility
Virtue isn't always its own reward. Compare the **S&P 500,** which includes companies selling weapons, alcohol, and tobacco, with the **Domini Social Index** which covers 400 companies that don't, and have good records of social responsibility. Notice that returns for companies with socially responsible behavior are at least as large if not higher than those of the S&P 500.
Source: *Business Week,* May 26, 1997.

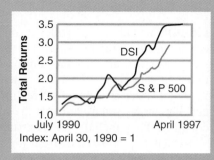

Index: April 30, 1990 = 1

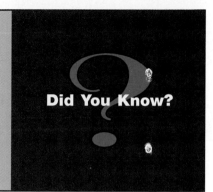

Social Auditing

How do we measure and evaluate an organization's activities aimed at social responsibility? **Chiquita** declares in its annual report:

> The **Chiquita Environmental Charter** is to protect the rainforest; to maintain clean water; to minimize the use of agrichemicals; to reduce, re-use and recycle waste; to support environmental education; and to ensure our workforce is well-trained and works safely.

While it is difficult to compute a net social contribution measure for declarations like these, we can use social auditing to help us out. A **social audit** is an analysis of an organization's success in carrying out programs that are socially responsible and responsive. There are different approaches in practice. But organizations that report these activities usually stick with disclosing *positive* actions (contributions, pollution reduction, minority business).

Flash back

9. Who are the internal and external users of accounting information?
10. Identify seven internal operating functions in organizations.
11. Why are internal controls important?
12. What are the guidelines in helping us make ethical decisions?
13. Why are ethics and social responsibility valuable to organizations?
14. Why are ethics crucial to accounting?

Answers—p. 28

Accounting information affects many aspects of our lives. The organizations we work for, the work we do, and the lives we live are impacted by accounting. When we earn money, pay taxes, invest savings, budget earnings, and plan for the future, we are influenced by accounting. Accounting helps us better perform and compete in society. To help us understand the opportunities for us in accounting, this section discusses four areas: financial, managerial, taxation, and accounting related. These areas differ by the kinds of information provided to and demanded by decision makers. Exhibit 1.13 lists selected opportunities for each of these areas. We also discuss unique aspects of these areas in business and nonbusiness organizations. These activities demand the work of millions of individuals employed in accounting or accounting-related areas.

Opportunities in Practice

C6 Identify opportunities in accounting and related fields.

Financial Accounting

Financial accounting provides information to decision makers not involved in the daily operations of an organization. These decision makers include customers, suppliers, planners, investors, and lenders. Information is normally reported through general-purpose financial statements. Financial statements describe the condition of an organization and its major transactions and events for a period of time. The process of preparing financial statements often demands the input of many individuals within and outside of accounting. They include lawyers, statisticians, doctors, artists, and photographers.

Exhibit 1.13 shows a demand for auditing in financial accounting. Many financial statements are issued with an *audit report* from a public accountant. An **audit** is a check of an organization's accounting systems and records using various tests. It increases the credibility of financial statements. Banks usually require audits of financial statements when companies apply for large loans. Also, federal and state laws require companies to have audits before their securities (stocks and bonds) are sold to the public. An auditor's objective is to decide whether the statements reflect the company's financial position and operating results using generally accepted accounting principles. When an audit is complete, an auditor writes a report expressing a professional *opinion* about whether the financial statements are fairly presented. It is an opinion because an auditor uses samples to examine the statements and does not verify every transaction and event. The auditor's reports accompanying the statements of **NIKE, Reebok,** and **America Online** are shown in Appendix A near the end of this book.

Government organizations such as the SEC are involved with regulating financial accounting practices and information issued to the public. SEC employees review companies' financial reports to be sure they comply with securities regulations. Employees who work for other regulatory agencies such as the Federal Trade Commission often review reports filed by businesses subject to the agencies' authority. They also help organizations understand and comply with regulations. Some government employees investigate and pursue violations of laws. Employees of the SEC investigate crimes related to securities, and others investigate financial frauds and white-collar crimes in their duties as agents of the Federal Bureau of Investigation (FBI). The FBI is a major employer of accounting-related professionals.

Managerial Accounting

Managerial accounting provides information to an organization's decision makers, or internal users. Managerial accounting reports often include much of the information in financial accounting. But managerial accounting reports also include information not reported outside the company. These reports generally fall within one of five major areas.

Exhibit 1.13

Opportunities in Practice

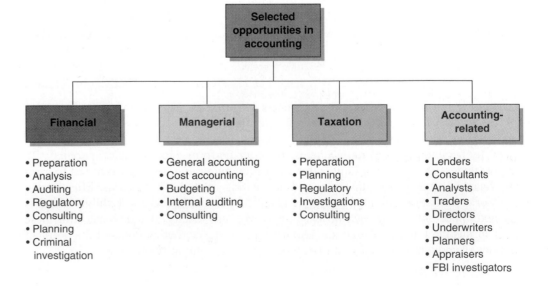

General Accounting

General accounting is the recording of transactions, the processing of data, and the preparing of reports for internal use. General accounting also includes preparing financial statements that companies issue to external users. An organization's own employees usually design the necessary information system, often with help from outsiders. The general accounting area is supervised by a chief accounting officer called the **controller.** This title reflects the fact that accounting information is used to control an organization's activities.

Cost Accounting

To plan and control operations, managers need information about the nature of costs incurred. **Cost accounting** is a process of accumulating the information managers need about costs. It helps managers identify, measure, and control costs. For example, **America Online** uses cost accounting in disclosing in its annual report that:

> The increase in cost of revenues was primarily attributable to an increase in data communication costs, customer support costs and royalties paid to information and service providers.

Cost accounting involves accounting for the costs of products, services, and other activities. Cost accounting information is especially useful for evaluating a manager's performance.

Budgeting

The process of developing formal plans for an organization's future activities is called **budgeting.** One goal of budgeting is to give individual managers an understanding of how their activities affect the entire organization. After the budget is adopted, it provides a basis for evaluating actual performance.

Internal Auditing

Organizations often employ individuals in **internal auditing** to add credibility to reports produced and used within the organization. **Reebok** includes a Report of Management in its annual report that states:

> The Company maintains an internal auditing program that monitors and assesses the effectiveness of the internal control system and recommends possible improvements thereto.

The value of internal auditors often goes beyond an examination of recordkeeping. Internal auditors assess whether managers are following established operating procedures and evaluate the efficiency of operating procedures.

Management Consulting

Individuals with knowledge of accounting are in demand by organizations that desire **management consulting** (or advisory) services. They include organizations like **Andersen Consulting, McKinsey,** and **Standard & Poor's.** Independent auditors gain a deep understanding of a client's accounting and operating procedures when they conduct their tests. As a result, auditors are in an excellent position to offer suggestions for improving an organization's activities. Most clients expect these suggestions as a useful by-product of an audit. Consultants with accounting knowledge often help organizations design and install new accounting and control systems, develop budgeting procedures, and set up employee benefit plans.

Tax Accounting

Taxes raised by federal, state, and local governments are usually based on income earned by taxpayers. These taxpayers include both individuals and organizations. The amount of taxes is computed on what the law defines as income. **Tax accounting** practitioners help taxpayers comply with the law by preparing their tax returns. **H&R Block** is one of the largest of such organizations. It claims that:

> **H&R Block** now processes the taxes for one out of every seven Americans who file returns.

Another tax accounting activity is planning future transactions to minimize taxes. Large organizations usually have employees who are responsible for tax returns and tax planning. But they often consult with other tax accounting experts when needing tax advice. Small organizations especially rely on these experts for much of their tax accounting. Nonbusinesses are major employers of tax services, especially the Internal Revenue Service **(IRS)**. The IRS is responsible for collecting federal taxes and enforcing tax law. IRS employees review tax returns filed by taxpayers. IRS employees also offer assistance to taxpayers, help write regulations, and investigate possible violations of tax law.

Accounting Specialization

The majority of accounting professionals work in **private** businesses as seen in Exhibit 1.14. A large business can employ 100 or more accounting professionals, but most have less. Another large number of accounting professionals are employed as **public accountants** whose services are available to the public. Many in public accounting are self-employed, while others work for public accounting firms that have a few or even several thousand employees. Another large number of accounting professionals work in nonbusiness organizations, with many of these in federal, state, or local government. *Government accountants* perform accounting services for government units, including business regulation and investigation of law violations. Many other accounting specialists are employed in education. Since accounting is a crucial service activity in modern society, there is a demand for educators who can teach accounting to a wide range of users.

Accounting specialists are highly regarded and require special abilities, including integrity and fairness. The professional standing of an accounting specialist often is denoted by a certificate. Certified Public Accountants **(CPAs)** are licensed in every state in the United States, the District of Columbia, Guam, Puerto Rico, and the Virgin Islands. The licensing process helps ensure a high standard of professional service. Individuals can legally identify themselves as CPAs only if they hold the license. To become licensed, an individual must meet education and experience requirements, pass the CPA examination, and exhibit ethical character. Most states require a college degree with the equivalent of a major in accounting. Some states allow persons to substitute experience for part of the education requirements. The CPA examination covers topics in financial and managerial accounting, taxation, auditing, and business law.

Many accounting specialists hold certificates in addition to or instead of the CPA license. Two of the most common are the Certificate in Management Accounting **(CMA)** and the Certified Internal Auditor **(CIA).** Holders of these certificates must meet ex-

Exhibit 1.14

Accounting Jobs by Area

Accounting Jobs by Area

Private accounting 60%
Public accounting 25%
Government accounting 12%
Accounting education 3%

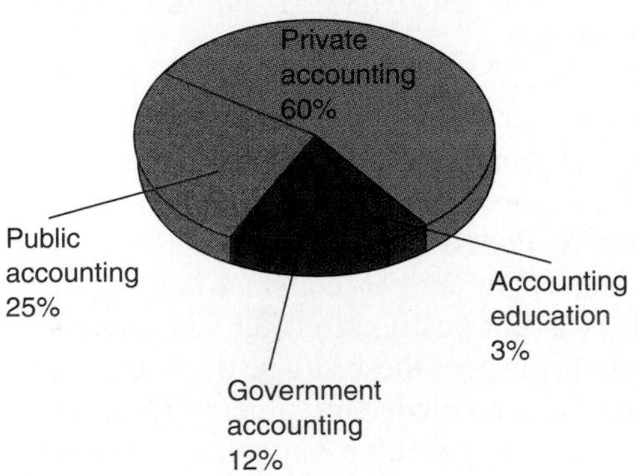

Source: Institute of Management Accountants

amination, education, and experience requirements similar to those of a CPA. The CMA is awarded by the Institute of Management Accountants and the CIA is granted by the Institute of Internal Auditors. Another prestigious certificate is the Chartered Financial Analyst **(CFA)**. It is awarded by the Association for Investment Management and Research (AIMR), an international nonprofit organization of investment practitioners and educators.

Accounting-Related Opportunities

Accounting-related opportunities are great. Accounting is the common language of financial communications. It spans professions, continents, and economies. Exhibit 1.13 lists several accounting-related opportunities including lenders, consultants, managers, and planners. Less traditional ones include community activist, political consultant, reporter, salesperson, union official, entrepreneur, programmer, engineer, and mechanic. All of these professions are made easier with a working knowledge of accounting. This course provides that knowledge.

Return on Investment

We introduced return on investment in assessing return and risk earlier in the chapter. Return on investment is also useful in evaluating management, analyzing and forecasting profits, and planning future activities. **Dell Computer** has its marketing department compute return on investment for *every* mailing. "We spent 15 months educating people about return on invested capital," says Dell's Chief Financial Officer T.J. Meredith.[9] This section describes return on investment and how it can help us with these tasks.

Return on investment (ROI), also commonly called *return on assets (ROA),* measures performance independent of its financing sources. It is viewed as an indicator of operating efficiency. We compute **return on investment** as shown in Exhibit 1.15.

A4 Compute and interpret return on investment.

$$\text{Return on investment} = \frac{\text{Net income}}{\text{Average total assets}}$$

Exhibit 1.15

Return on Investment

Net income is the profit earned over a specified time period. Average total assets is usually computed by adding the beginning and ending amounts of total assets for that same period and dividing by two. For illustrative purposes, let's consider **Reebok.** Reebok reports net income of $138.95 in 1996 (in millions). At the beginning of 1996, Reebok's total assets are $1,651.619 and at the end of 1996 they total $1,786.184 (in millions). Reebok's return on investment for 1996 is:

$$\text{Return on investment} = \frac{\$138.95}{(\$1,651.619 + \$1,786.184)/2} = 8.08\%$$

Is an 8.08% return on investment good or bad for **Reebok?** To help answer this question and others like it, we can compare **Reebok's** return on investment with its prior performance, the returns of similar companies (such as **NIKE, Converse,** and **L.A.Gear**), and returns from alternative investments. Reebok's return on investment for each of the prior six years is reported in the second column

---

[9] Gary McWilliams, "Michael Dell: Whirlwind on the Web," *Business Week,* April 7, 1997.

Exhibit 1.16

Reebok, NIKE, and Industry
Returns

Year	Reebok's Return on Investment	NIKE's Return on Investment	Industry Return on Investment
1996	8.1%	15.6%	2%
1995	10.0	14.5	4
1994	16.7	13.1	9
1993	16.3	18.0	7
1992	8.3	18.4	6
1991	16.7	20.5	7

of Exhibit 1.16. Reebok's return on investment for this period ranges from 16.7% in 1991 to 8.1% in 1996. This pattern suggests a recent decline in Reebok's efficiency in using its assets. We can also compare **Reebok** to a similar company such as **NIKE,** whose return on investment is shown in the third column of Exhibit 1.16. In five of six years, **NIKE's** return exceeds **Reebok's** and its average return is higher for this period. We can also compare Reebok's return to the normal return for manufacturers of athletic footwear. Industry averages are available from services like **Dun & Bradstreet's** (D&B) *Industry Norms and Key Ratios* and **Robert Morris Associates'** (RMA) *Annual Statement Studies.* Ratios computed from a select group of similar manufacturers are shown in the fourth column.[10] When compared to their competitors both **Reebok** and **NIKE** perform well.

Exhibit 1.17

Return on Investment for Other
Companies

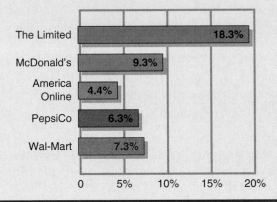

Another useful analysis is to compare returns to alternative investments. Exhibit 1.17 shows recent returns for five familiar companies. **The Limited** and **McDonald's** performed better than Reebok, while **AOL, PepsiCo,** and **Wal-Mart** did not. Using this information, Reebok's performance is probably "good." While not equal to NIKE, it is similar to the norm as judged by the returns of competitors both in and outside its business.

Summary

C1 Explain the aim and power of accounting in the information age. Accounting is an information and measurement system that aims to identify, record, and communicate relevant, reliable, and comparable information about economic activities. It helps us better assess opportunities, products, investments, and social and community responsibilities. The power of accounting is in opening our eyes to new and exciting opportunities. The greatest benefits from understanding accounting often come to those outside of accounting.

C2 Identify forms of organization and their characteristics. Organizations can be classified as either businesses or nonbusinesses. Businesses are organized for profit, while nonbusinesses serve us in ways not always measured by profit. Busi-

nesses take one of three forms: sole proprietorship, partnership, or corporation. These forms of organization have characteristics that hold important implications for legal liability, taxation, continuity, number of owners, and legal status.

C3 Identify and describe the three major activities in organizations. Organizations carry out three major activities: financing, investing, and operating. These activities are tied together by an organization's plans, including its ideas, goals, and strategies. Financing is the means used to pay for resources like land, buildings, and machines. Investing refers to the buying and selling of resources used in selling products and services. Operating activities are those necessary for carrying out the organization's plans.

---

[10] The industry ratio is the median value computed from 11 competitors including Fila, Converse, L. A. Gear, and Stride Rite, among others.

C4 **Identify users and uses of accounting.** There are both internal and external users of accounting. Some users and uses of accounting include: (a) managers in controlling, monitoring, and planning; (b) lenders for measuring the risk and return of loans; (c) shareholders for assessing the return and risk in acquiring shares; (d) directors for overseeing management; and (e) employees for judging employment opportunities. Other users are auditors, consultants, officers, regulators, analysts, unions, suppliers, and appraisers.

C5 **Explain why ethics and social responsibility are crucial to accounting.** The goal of accounting is to provide useful information for decision making. For information to be useful it must be trusted. This demands ethics and socially responsible behavior in accounting.

C6 **Identify opportunities in accounting and related fields.** Opportunities in accounting include traditional ones such as financial, managerial, and tax accounting. They also include accounting-related fields such as lending, consulting, managing, and planning. Nontraditional opportunities with accounting knowledge include careers as a community activist, political consultant, reporter, salesperson, union official, entrepreneur, programmer, and engineer.

A1 **Describe profit and its two major components.** Profit is the amount a business earns after subtracting all expenses necessary for its sales (Sales − Expenses = Profit). Sales are the amounts earned from selling products and services. Expenses are the costs incurred with sales. A loss arises when expenses are more than sales.

A2 **Explain the relation between return and risk.** Return refers to profit, and risk is the uncertainty about the return we hope to make. All business decisions involve risk. The lower the risk of an investment, the lower is its expected return. Higher expected return offsets higher risk. Higher risk means higher, but more risky, expected return.

A3 **Explain and interpret the accounting equation.** Investing activities are funded by an organization's financing activities. An organization cannot have more or less assets than its financing and, similarly, it cannot have more or less nonowner (liabilities) and owner (equity) financing than its total assets. This basic relation gives us the accounting equation: Assets = Liabilities + Owner's equity.

A4 **Compute and interpret return on investment.** Return on investment is commonly computed as profit, also called net income or earnings, divided by amount invested. For example, if we have an average balance in our savings account of $100 and it earns interest of $5 for the year, then our return on investment is $5/$100, or 5%. Return on investment is also called return on assets, where the amount invested is measured by the average assets for the period.

Guidance Answers to **"You Make the Call"**

Programmer

As the computer programmer, you are confronting a trade-off between return (salary) and risk (dependable employment). The new start-up company has an uncertain future and is willing to increase your pay to balance the added risk you have in working for them (this company could fail). The established medical supply company pays less, but you are assured of employment. If you or others are totally dependent on your income, the risk of the start-up company might be too high. Yet if you and others do not depend on your salary, the increased pay might be worth the risk.

Entrepreneur

You should probably form your business as a corporation if potential lawsuits are of prime concern. The corporate form of organization protects your personal property from lawsuits directed at the business and would place only the corporation's resources at risk. A downside of the corporate form is double taxation—the corporation must pay taxes on earnings and you must pay taxes on any money distributed to you from the business (even though the corporation already paid taxes on this money). You should also examine the ethical and socially responsible aspects of starting a business where you anticipate injuries to others.

Guidance Answers to Flash backs

1. Accounting is an information and measurement system that identifies, records, and communicates relevant information to people that helps them make better decisions. It helps people in business identify and react to investment opportunities. It also helps us better assess opportunities, products, investments, and social and community responsibilities.

2. Profit is the money a business earns after paying for all expenses necessary for its sales. Sales, also called revenues, are the amounts earned from selling products and services. Expenses are the costs incurred with sales.

3. The trade-off between return and risk is a normal part of business. The lower the risk of an investment, the lower is our expected return. Similarly, higher expected return offsets higher risk. Remember that *actual* return usually differs from *expected* return. Higher risk implies higher, but more risky, expected returns.

4. Recordkeeping is the recording of financial transactions and events, either manually or electronically. While recordkeeping is essential to data reliability, accounting is this and much more. Accounting includes identifying, measuring, recording, reporting, and analyzing economic events and transactions. It involves interpreting information and designing information systems to provide useful reports that monitor and control an organization's activities.

5. Accounting rules are determined by many individuals and groups. Since accounting is a service activity, these rules reflect our society's needs and not those of accountants or any other single constituency. Major participants in setting rules include the Securities and Exchange Commission (SEC), the Financial Accounting Standards Board (FASB), and the American Institute of Certified Public Accountants (AICPA).

6. The three common forms of business organizations are sole proprietorships, partnerships, and corporations.

7. Nonbusiness organizations often include airports, libraries, national defense, museums, churches, cities, police, mail, colleges, bus lines, utilities, highways, fraternities, shelters, parks, hospitals, and schools.

8. Organizations pursue financing, investing, and operating activities. These three major activities all require planning.

9. External users of accounting information are not directly involved in running the organization and include lenders, shareholders, directors, customers, suppliers, regulators, lawyers, brokers, and the press. Internal users of accounting information are those individuals directly involved in managing and operating an organization. They include managers, officers, and other important internal decision makers involved with the strategic and operating decisions.

10. The internal operating functions are: research and development, purchasing, human resources, production, distribution, marketing, and servicing.

11. Internal controls are procedures set up to protect assets, ensure reliable accounting reports, promote efficiency, and encourage adherence to company policies. Internal controls are crucial if accounting reports are to provide relevant and reliable information.

12. Ethical guidelines are threefold: (1) identify ethical issues using personal ethics; (2) analyze options considering both good and bad consequences for all individuals affected; and (3) make ethical decisions choosing the best option after weighing all consequences.

13. Ethics and social responsibility are important for us because without them our lives are more difficult, inefficient, and unpleasant. They are equally important to organizations for these same reasons. In addition, they often translate into higher profits and a better working environment.

14. Accounting aims to provide useful information for decision making. For information to be useful it must be trusted. Trust of information demands ethics in accounting.

Glossary

Accounting an information and measurement system that identifies, records, and communicates relevant information about a company's economic activities to people to help them make better decisions. (p. 4).

Accounting equation the equality where Assets = Liabilities + Owner's Equity. (p. 13).

American Institute of Certified Public Accountants (AICPA) the largest and most influential national professional organization of certified public accountants. (p. 8).

Assets economic resources that are expected to produce future benefits. (p. 13).

Audit a check of an organization's accounting systems and records using various tests. (p. 22).

Bonds written promises by organizations to repay amounts loaned with interest. (p. 6).

Bookkeeping the part of accounting that involves recording economic transactions and events, either electronically or manually (also known as *recordkeeping*). (p. 7).

Budgeting the process of developing formal plans for future activities, often serving as a basis for evaluating actual performance. (p. 23).

Business one or more individuals selling products or services for profit. (p. 5).

Business entity principle every business is accounted for separately from its owner's personal activities. (p. 9).

CFA Chartered Financial Analyst; a certification from the Association for Investment Management and Research that an individual is professionally competent in the area of investments. (p. 25).

CIA Certified Internal Auditor; a certification from the Institute of Internal Auditors that an individual is professionally competent in internal auditing. (p. 24).

CMA Certificate in Management Accounting; a certification from the Institute of Management Accountants that an individual is professionally competent in managerial accounting. (p. 24).

Common stock the name for a corporation's stock when only one class of stock is issued (also called *capital stock*). (p. 11).

Controller the chief accounting officer of an organization. (p. 23).

Corporation a business that is a separate legal entity under state or federal laws with owners that are called shareholders or stockholders. (p. 10).

Cost accounting a managerial accounting activity designed to help managers identify, measure, and control operating costs. (p. 23).

CPA Certified Public Accountant; an accountant who has met examination, education, and experience requirements; CPAs are licensed by state boards to practice in public accounting. (p. 24).

Earnings the amount a business earns after subtracting all expenses necessary for its sales (also called *net income* or *profit*). (p. 5).

Ethics codes of conduct by which actions are judged as right or wrong, fair or unfair, honest or dishonest. (p. 18).

Expenses the costs incurred to earn sales. (p. 5).

External users persons using accounting information who are not directly involved in the running of the organization; examples include shareholders, customers, regulators, and suppliers. (p. 14).

Factors of production the means businesses use to make profit; land, labor, and plant and equipment are the traditional factors of production. (p. 7).

Financial accounting the area of accounting aimed at serving external users. (p. 14).

Financial Accounting Standards Board (FASB) an independent group of seven full-time members who are currently responsible for setting accounting rules. (p. 8).

Financing activities the means organizations use to pay for resources like land, building, and machines. (p. 12).

General accounting the task of recording transactions, processing data, and preparing reports for managers; includes preparing financial statements for disclosure to external users. (p. 23).

Generally accepted accounting principles (GAAP) the rules that indicate acceptable accounting practice. (p. 8).

Information age a time period that emphasizes communication, data, news, facts, access, and commentary. (p. 4).

Internal auditing activity conducted by employees within organizations to assess whether managers are following established operating procedures and to evaluate the efficiency of operating procedures. (p. 23).

Internal controls procedures set up to protect assets, ensure reliable accounting reports, promote efficiency, and encourage adherence to company policies. (p. 17).

Internal users persons using accounting information who are directly involved in managing and operating an organization; examples include managers and officers. (p. 16).

Investing activities the buying and selling of resources that an organization uses to sell its products or services. (p. 13.)

IRS Internal Revenue Service; the federal agency that has the duty of collecting federal taxes and otherwise enforcing tax laws. (p. 24).

Liabilities creditors' claims on an organization's assets. (p. 13).

Loss arises when expenses are more than sales, or revenues. (p. 5).

Management consulting activity in which suggestions are offered for improving a company's procedures; the suggestions may concern new accounting and internal control systems, new computer systems, budgeting, and employee benefit plans (also called *advisory services*). (p. 23).

Managerial accounting the area of accounting aimed at serving the decision-making needs of internal users (also called *management accounting*). (p. 16).

Net income the amount a business earns after subtracting all expenses necessary for its sales (also called *profits* or *earnings*). (p. 5).

Operating activities the use of assets to carry out an organization's plans in the areas of research, development, purchasing, production, distribution, and marketing. (p. 13).

Owner's equity the owner's claim on an organization's assets. (p. 13).

Partnership a business that is owned by two or more people that is not organized as a corporation. (p. 10).

Planning the term for defining the ideas, goals, and actions of an organization. (p. 12).

Private accountants accountants who work for a single employer other than the government. (p. 24).

Profit the amount a business earns after subtracting all expenses necessary for its sales (also called *net income* or *earnings*). (p. 5).

Public accountants accountants who provide their services to many different clients. (p. 24).

Recordkeeping the recording of financial transactions and events, either manually or electronically (also known as *bookkeeping*). (p. 7).

Return derives from the idea of getting something back from an investment in a business. (p. 6).

Return on investment a financial ratio serving as an indicator of operating efficiency; net income divided by average total assets. (p. 6, 25).

Revenues the amounts earned from selling products or services (also called *sales*). (p. 5).

Risk the amount of uncertainty about the return to be earned. (p. 6).

Sales the amounts earned from selling products or services (also called *revenues*). (p. 5).

Securities and Exchange Commission (SEC) the federal agency charged by Congress to set reporting rules for organizations that sell ownership shares to the public. (p. 8).

Shareholders the owners of a corporation (also called *stockholders*). (p. 10).

Shares equity of a corporation divided into units (also called *stock*). (p. 10).

Single proprietorship a business owned by one individual that is not organized as a corporation (also called *sole proprietorship*). (p. 9).

Social audit an analysis of an organization's success in carrying out programs that are socially responsible and responsive. (p. 21).

Social responsibility involves considering and being accountable for the impact actions might have on society. (p. 19).

Sole proprietorship a business owned by one person that is not organized as a corporation (also called *single proprietorship*). (p. 9).

Stock equity of a corporation divided into units (also called *shares*). (p. 10).

Stockholders the owners of a corporation (also called *shareholders*). (p. 10).

Tax accounting the field of accounting that includes preparing tax returns and planning future transactions to minimize the amount of tax; involves private, public, and government accountants. (p. 24).

Questions

1. Identify four external users and their uses of accounting information.

2. Identify three types of organizations that can be formed as either profit-oriented businesses, government units, or non-profit establishments.

3. What type of accounting information might be useful to those who carry out the marketing activities of a business?

4. Explain return and risk. Discuss the trade-off between return and risk.

5. What is the purpose of accounting in society?

6. Describe the internal role of accounting for organizations.

7. Explain business profit and its computation.

8. What are at least three questions business owners might answer by looking at accounting information?

9. Technology is increasingly used to process accounting data. Why then should we study accounting?

10. Define and explain return on investment (assets).

11. Why do organizations license and monitor accounting and accounting-related professionals?

12. What is the relation between accounting and the information superhighway?

13. Identify three types of services typically offered by accounting professionals.

14. Describe three forms of business organizations and their characteristics.

15. An organization's chief accounting officer is often called the controller. Why?

16. Identify at least four managerial accounting tasks performed by both private and government accountants.

17. Describe three important activities in organizations.

18. Identify at least two management advisory services offered by public accounting professionals.

19. Explain why investing (assets) and financing (liabilities and equity) totals are always equal.

20. List at least three examples of the types of tasks performed by government accounting professionals.

21. Identify three businesses that offer services and three businesses that offer products.

22. What work do tax accounting professionals perform in addition to preparing tax returns?

23. Why is accounting described as a service activity?

24. What is a social responsibility report?

25. What ethical issues might accounting professionals face in dealing with confidential information?

26. Identify the chief financial officer for **NIKE** from its financial statements in Appendix A. How many directors does **NIKE** have?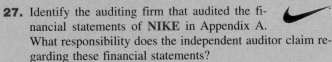

27. Identify the auditing firm that audited the financial statements of **NIKE** in Appendix A. What responsibility does the independent auditor claim regarding these financial statements?

28. The chapter's opening article discussed **W&F Financial Services.** This business is organized as a partnership. Identify important characteristics of partnerships and their implications.

Quick Study exercises give readers a brief test of key elements in every chapter.

Quick Study

QS 1-1
Identifying transactions and events

Accounting provides information about an organization's economic transactions and events. Identify examples of economic transactions and events.

QS 1-2
Identifying planning activities

Identify three responsibilities in the overall *executive management* (planning) activity of organizations.

QS 1-3
Explaining internal control

An important responsibility of many accounting professionals is to design and implement internal control procedures for organizations. Explain the purpose of internal control procedures.

QS 1-4
Accounting opportunities

Identify at least three main areas of work for accounting professionals. For each accounting area identify at least three accounting-related opportunities in practice.

Accounting professionals must sometimes choose between two or more acceptable methods of accounting for certain transactions and events. Explain why these situations can involve difficult matters of ethical concern.

QS 1-5
Identifying ethical concerns

C5

Use **America Online's** 1996 annual report printed in Appendix A near the end of the book to answer the following:

a. Identify the dollar amounts of America Online's 1996 (1) assets, (2) liabilities, and (3) equity.

b. Using America Online's amounts from (a), verify that: Assets = Liabilities + Equity.

QS 1-6
Identifying and computing assets, liabilities, and equity

A3

Presented below are descriptions of several different business organizations. Determine whether the situation described refers to a sole proprietorship, partnership, or corporation.

a. Ownership of Cola Company is divided into 1,000 shares of stock.

b. TexTech is owned by Kimberly Fisher, who is personally liable for the debts of the business.

c. Jerry Forrentes and Susan Montgomery own Financial Services, a financial services provider. Neither Forrentes nor Montgomery has personal responsibility for the debts of Financial Services.

d. Nancy Kerr and Frank Levens own Runners, a courier service. Both Kerr and Levens are personally liable for the debts of the business.

e. MRC Consulting Services does not have separate legal existence apart from the one person who owns it.

f. Biotech Enterprises has one owner and does not pay taxes.

g. Tennessee Technologies has two owners and pays its own taxes.

Exercises

Exercise 1-1
Distinguishing business organizations

C2

Select the internal operating function from the two choices provided that is most likely to regularly use the information described. While the information is likely used in both functions, it is most relevant to one.

a. Which internal operating function is most likely to use payroll information: marketing or human resources?

b. Which internal operating function is most likely to use sales report information: marketing or research and development?

c. Which internal operating function is most likely to use cash flow information: finance or human resources?

d. Which internal operating function is most likely to use financial statement, budget, and performance report information: research and development or executive management?

e. Which internal operating function is most likely to use product quality information: finance or production?

Exercise 1-2
Determining internal operating functions

C4

Identify at least three external users of accounting information and indicate some questions they might seek to answer through their use of accounting information.

Exercise 1-3
Identifying accounting users and uses

C4

Many accounting professionals work in one of the following three areas:

A. Financial accounting   **B.** Managerial accounting   **C.** Tax accounting

Identify the area of accounting that is most involved in each of the following responsibilities:

_____ **1.** Auditing financial statements.   _____ **5.** Reviewing reports for SEC compliance.

_____ **2.** Planning transactions to minimize taxes.   _____ **6.** Budgeting.

_____ **3.** Cost accounting.   _____ **7.** Internal auditing.

_____ **4.** Preparing financial statements.   _____ **8.** Investigating violations of tax laws.

Exercise 1-4
Describing accounting responsibilities

C6

Exercise 1-5
Identifying ethical
concerns

C5

Assume the following role and describe a situation where ethical considerations play an important part in guiding your action:
a. You are a student in an accounting principles course.
b. You are a manager with responsibility for several employees.
c. You are an accounting professional preparing tax returns for clients.
d. You are an accounting professional with audit clients that are competitors in business.

Exercise 1-6
Learning the language of
business

C1–C6

Indicate which term best fits each of the following descriptions:
A. Audit   C. Cost accounting   E. Ethics   G. Budgeting
B. Controller   D. GAAP   F. General accounting   H. Tax accounting

_____ 1. An accounting area that includes planning future transactions to minimize taxes paid.
_____ 2. A managerial accounting process designed to help managers identify, measure, and control operating costs.
_____ 3. Principles that determine whether an action is right or wrong.
_____ 4. An examination of an organization's accounting system and records that adds credibility to financial statements.
_____ 5. The task of recording transactions, processing recorded data, and preparing reports and financial statements.
_____ 6. The chief accounting officer of an organization.

Exercise 1-7
Learning the language of
business

A1, A2, C4, C6

Indicate which term best fits each of the following descriptions:
A. Government accountants   C. IRS   E. CIA   G. Risk   I. AICPA
B. Internal auditing   D. SEC   F. Profit H. Public accountants   J. CMA

_____ 1. Responsibility of an organization's employees that involves examining the organization's recordkeeping processes, assessing whether managers are following established operating procedures, and appraising the efficiency of operating procedures.
_____ 2. Amount of uncertainty associated with an expected return.
_____ 3. Money a business earns after paying all expenses associated with its sales.
_____ 4. Federal agency responsible for collecting federal taxes and enforcing tax law.
_____ 5. Accounting professionals who provide services to many different clients.
_____ 6. Accounting professionals employed by federal, state, or local branches of government.

Exercise 1-8
Using the accounting
equation

A3

Answer the following questions. (*Hint*: Use the accounting equation.)
a. Doug Stockton's medical supplies business has assets equal to $123,000 and liabilities equal to $53,000 at the end of the year. What is the total of the owner's equity for Stockton's business at the end of the year?
b. At the beginning of the year, ParFour Company's assets are $200,000, and its owner's equity is $150,000. During the year, assets increase $70,000 and liabilities increase $30,000. What is the owner's equity at the end of the year?
c. At the beginning of the year, Navy Company's liabilities equal $60,000. During the year assets increase by $80,000 and at year-end they equal $180,000. Liabilities decrease $10,000 during the year. What are the beginning and ending amounts of owner's equity?

Exercise 1-9
Calculating return on
investment

A4

Java Jimmies reports net income of $20,000 for 1999. At the beginning of 1999, Java Jimmies had $100,000 in assets. By the end of 1999 assets had grown to $140,000. What is Java Jimmies' return on investment?

Exercise 1-10
Using the accounting
equation

A3

Determine the amount missing from each accounting equation below.

	Assets	=	Liabilities	+	Equity
a.	?	=	$30,000	+	$65,000
b.	$89,000	=	22,000	+	?
c.	132,000	=	?	+	20,000

Bell Systems manufactures, markets, and sells cellular telephones. The average amount invested, or average total assets, in Bell Systems is $250,000. In its most recent year, Bell earned a profit of $55,000 on sales of $455,000.

Required

1. What is Bell Systems' return on investment?
2. Does return on investment seem satisfactory for Bell Systems when its competitors average a 12% return on investment?
3. What are total expenses for Bell Systems in its most recent year?
4. What is the average total amount of financing (liabilities plus equity) for Bell Systems?

Problems

Problem 1-1
Determining profits, sales, costs, and returns
A1, A3, A4

Coke Company and Sprite Company both produce and market beverages and are direct competitors. Key financial figures (in $ millions) for these businesses over the past four years are:

Key figures	Coke Company	Sprite Company
Sales	$400	$250
Profit	$50	$37.5
Average invested (assets)	$625	$312.5

Problem 1-2
Computing and interpreting return on investment
A4

Required

1. Compute return on investment for (*a*) Coke Company and (*b*) Sprite Company.
2. Which company is more successful in sales to consumers?
3. Which company is more successful in earning profits from its amount invested?

Analysis component:

4. Write a brief memo explaining which company you would invest your money in and why.

All business decisions involve risk and return.

Required

Identify the risk and return in the following activities:
1. Investing $1,000 in a 4% saving account.
2. Placing a $1,000 bet on your favorite sports team.
3. Investing $10,000 in America Online stock.
4. Taking a $10,000 college loan to study accounting.

Problem 1-3
Identifying risk and return
A2

Write a description of an organization's three major activities.

Problem 1-4
Describing organizational activities
C3

A new startup company often engages in the following transactions during its first year of operations. Classify these transactions within one of the three major categories of an organization's business activities.

A. Financing   **B.** Investing   **C.** Operating
_____ 1. Leaving profits in the business.   _____ 5. Purchasing equipment.
_____ 2. Obtaining necessary licenses.   _____ 6. Distributing products.
_____ 3. Purchasing land.   _____ 7. Conducting an advertising campaign.
_____ 4. Obtaining credit at bank.

Problem 1-5
Describing organizational activities.
C3

BEYOND THE NUMBERS

Reporting in Action
A1, A3, A4

NIKE designs, produces, markets, and sells sports footwear and apparel. Key financial figures for NIKE's fiscal year ended May 31, 1997 are:

Key figure	In millions
Financing (liabilities + equity)	$5,361
Profit	796
Sales	9,187

Required

1. What is the total amount of assets invested in NIKE?
2. What is NIKE's return on investment? NIKE's assets at May 31, 1996 equal $3,952 (in millions).
3. How much are total expenses for NIKE?

Analysis component:

4. Does NIKE's return on investment seem satisfactory if competitors average a 5% return?

Swoosh Ahead

5. Obtain NIKE's most recent annual report. You can also access NIKE's annual report at its Web site (**www.nike.com**) or at the SEC's Web site (**www.sec.gov**). Compute NIKE's return on investment using this updated annual report information you obtain. Compare the May 31, 1997, fiscal year-end return on investment to any subsequent years' returns you are able to compute.

Comparative Analysis
A1, A3, A4

Both NIKE and Reebok design, produce, market, and sell sports footwear and apparel. Key comparative figures ($ millions) for these two organizations follow:

Key figure*	NIKE	Reebok
Financing (liabilities + equity)	$5,361	$1,786
Profit	796	139
Sales	9,187	3,483

*NIKE figures are from its annual report for fiscal year-end May 31, 1997.
  Reebok figures are from its annual report for fiscal year-end December 31, 1996.

Required

1. What is the total amount of assets invested in (a) NIKE and (b) Reebok?
2. What is the return on investment for (a) NIKE and (b) Reebok? NIKE's beginning assets equal $3,952 (in millions) and Reebok's beginning assets equal $1,652 (in millions).
3. How much are expenses for (a) NIKE and (b) Reebok?

Analysis components:

4. Is return on investment satisfactory for (a) NIKE and (b) Reebok [competitors average a 5% return]?
5. What can you conclude about NIKE and Reebok from these computations?

Ethics Challenge
C5

Rupert Jones works in a public accounting firm and hopes to eventually be a partner. The management of ShadowTech Company invites Jones to prepare a bid to audit ShadowTech's financial statements. In discussing the audit's fee, ShadowTech's management suggests a fee range where the fee amount depends on the reported profit of ShadowTech. The higher its profit, the higher the audit fee paid to Jones' firm.

Required

1. Identify the parties potentially affected by this situation.
2. What are the ethical factors in this situation?
3. Would you recommend that Jones accept this audit fee arrangement? Why or why not?
4. Describe some ethical considerations guiding your recommendation.

Refer to this chapter's opening article about **W&F Financial Services.** Before establishing the business, Williams and Fulwood met with a loan officer of a Pittsburgh bank to discuss a loan.

Required

1. Prepare a brief report outlining the information you would request from Williams and Fulwood if you were the loan officer.
2. Indicate whether the information you request, and your loan decision, are affected by the form of business organization for **W&F Financial Services.**

**Communicating in Practice
A2, C2**

There is extensive accounting and business information available on the Internet. This includes the SEC's on-line database referred to as EDGAR (**www.sec.gov**) and numerous other Web sites offering access to financial statement information or related data. Examples are the AICPA (**www.aicpa.org**), the IRS (**www.irs.ustreas.gov**), and the AAA (**AAA-edu.org**). You can access the Web site devoted to this book (**www.mhhe.com/business/accounting/fap**) for updated links to several of these databases in case Web addresses change.

Required

Access at least one of the Web sites, selected by either you or your instructor, and answer the following:

1. Write a brief report describing the types of relevant information available at this Web site.
2. How would you rate the importance of the information available at this Web site for accounting and business?

**Taking It to the Net
C1, C4**

Effectively implementing a team approach in both business and education requires scheduling team meetings and maintaining ongoing communication between team members. Cooperation and support are key elements in effective teams. As part of a team, you have the right to receive assistance from your teammates when you need or request it, and you have the responsibility to provide it when possible. This activity is designed to open channels of communication to provide ongoing opportunities to fulfill team rights and responsibilities.

Required:

1. Open a team discussion and determine a regular time and place where your team will meet between each scheduled class meeting.
2. Develop a list of telephone numbers and/or e-mail addresses of your teammates.
3. Notify your instructor, via a memo or e-mail message, as to when and where your team will hold regularly scheduled meetings.

**Teamwork in Action
C1**

You are to interview a local business owner. (This can be a friend or relative.) Opening lines of communication with members of the business community can provide personal benefits of business networking. If you do not know the owner, you should call ahead to introduce yourself and explain your position as a student and your assignment requirements. You should request an appointment for a face-to-face or phone discussion to discuss the form of organization and operations of the business. Be prepared to make a good impression.

Required:

1. Identify and describe the primary operating activity and the form of organization for this business.
2. Determine and explain why the owner(s) chose this particular form of organization.
3. Identify any special advantages and/or disadvantages the owner(s) experiences in operating with this form of business organization.

**Hitting the Road
C2**

Business Week publishes a ranking of the top 1,000 companies based on several performance measures. This issue is called the **BUSINESS WEEK 1000.** Obtain the March 25, 1996 (or more recent) publication of this issue (**Business Week** also maintains a web site with access to its articles at **www.businessweek.com/**).

Required

1. What are the top 10 performing companies on the basis of sales?
2. What are the top 10 performing companies on the basis of profits?
3. What are the top 10 performing companies on the basis of assets?

***Business Week*
Activity
C1**

2
CHAPTER

Financial Statements and Accounting Transactions

Chapter Outline

Shoes on Trial

LOS ANGELES—Tucked along an oceanside street, **FastForward** could be another trendy sports shop. But its small back lot, where Chuck Taylor runs up grassy mounds, through sand pits, and in mud, makes clear this is something far different. These obstacles are product research tools.

FastForward consults on athletic footwear. In just one year, Chuck Taylor has become a consultant sought after by sports clubs, schools, and athletes. In the first six months of 1998, his company's profits are rising at a 35% rate.

FastForward's story is the envy of every entrepreneur. Taylor, 29, loved sports—but he hated his shoes. He never seemed to have the right shoes for the right conditions. Independent tests of shoe performance were either nonexistent or outdated.

So in September 1997, Taylor had an idea. He went out and purchased 21 pairs of the best basketball shoes on the market. He ran the shoes through a battery of tests under many different court conditions. His results were striking. Many lower priced, lesser known shoes performed on par or better than many big ticket, big name shoes. He carried his findings to athletic teams and athletes, and got a welcome reception and payment for his services.

In November 1997, Taylor quit his job to devote full time to his new business. "I instantly needed accounting skills to keep track of receipts, bills, everything," says Taylor. "When I later applied for a loan, the bank couldn't believe my poor accounting records. But what'd you expect from a sports junkie!"

Taylor eventually cleaned up his accounting and got the loan. To boost growth, **FastForward** is now moving into the testing of soccer, track, and football shoes. "We are meeting a market need and making people happy," added Taylor. And you can count Taylor as one of the happy.

CHAPTER PREVIEW

Financial statements report on the financial performance and condition of an organization. They are one of the most important products of accounting, and are useful to both internal and external decision makers. Chuck Taylor of **Fast-Forward** recognized the importance of accounting reports in running his own business and in applying for a loan. Financial statements are the way business people communicate. Knowledge of their preparation, organization, and analysis is important.

In this chapter, we describe the kind of information captured and revealed in financial statements. We also discuss the principles and assumptions guiding their preparation. This discussion includes the organizations that regulate and influence accounting. An important goal of this chapter is to illustrate how transactions are reflected in financial statements and how they impact our analysis. This helps us see the immediate usefulness of financial statements. Special attention is devoted to a discussion of **FastForward,** whose first month's transactions are the focus of our analysis.

Communicating with Financial Statements

C1 Identify and explain the content and reporting aims of financial statements.

In Chapter 1 we discussed how accounting provides information to help people make better decisions. These decision makers include investors, lenders, managers, suppliers, and customers. Many organizations report their accounting information to internal and external users in the form of financial statements. These statements are useful in revealing an organization's financial health and performance in a summarized and easy to read format. They give an overall view of an organization's financing, investing, and operating activities. They also are the primary means of financial communication.

Previewing Financial Statements

There are four major financial statements: income statement, balance sheet, statement of changes in owner's equity, and statement of cash flows. We begin our study of these statements with a brief description of these statements. We cover all four statements in detail by the end of this chapter. How these statements are linked in time is illustrated in Exhibit 2.1.

A balance sheet reports on an organization's financial position at a *point in time*. The income statement, statement of changes in owner's equity, and statement of cash flows

Exhibit 2.1

Links between Financial Statements

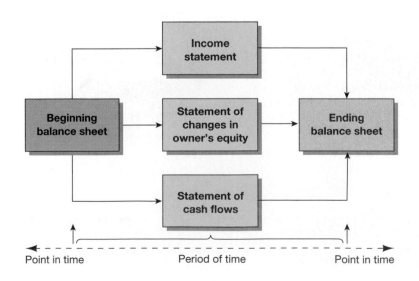

report on performance over a *period of time*. The three statements in the middle column of Exhibit 2.1 link balance sheets from the beginning to the end of a reporting period. They explain how the financial position of an organization changes from one point to another.[1]

Selection of a reporting period is up to preparers and users (including regulatory agencies). A one-year, or annual, reporting period is common, as are semiannual, quarterly, and monthly periods. The one-year reporting period is also known as the *accounting,* or *fiscal, year*. Businesses whose accounting year begins on January 1 and ends on December 31 are known as *calendar year* companies. But many companies choose a fiscal year ending on a date other than December 31. **NIKE** is a *noncalendar year* company as reflected in the headings of its May 31 year-end financial statements shown in Appendix A. Some companies choose a fiscal year-end when sales and inventory are low. For example, the **GAP's** 1997 fiscal year-end is February 1, after the holiday season.

Income Statement

An **income statement** reports revenues earned and expenses incurred by a business over a period of time. Expenses are subtracted from revenues on the income statement to show whether the business earned a net income. A **net income** means revenues exceed expenses. A **net loss,** or simply *loss,* means expenses exceed revenues.

The income statement for FastForward's first month of operations is shown in Exhibit 2.2 (FastForward is a sole proprietorship). An income statement does not simply report net income or net loss. It lists the types and amounts of both revenues and expenses. This is crucial information for users as it helps in understanding and predicting company performance. For example, **Walt Disney** classifies its revenues and expenses in three categories: theme parks, filmed entertainment, and consumer products. Also **McDonald's** separates its revenues into two groups: company-operated restaurants and franchised and affiliated restaurants. This information is more useful for making decisions than simply an income or loss number.

FASTFORWARD Income Statement For Month Ended December 31, 1997		
Revenues:		
Consulting revenue	$3,800	
Rental revenue	300	
Total revenues		$4,100
Expenses:		
Rent expense	$1,000	
Salaries expense	700	
Total expenses		1,700
Net income		$2,400

Exhibit 2.2

Income Statement

Revenues

Revenues are inflows of assets in exchange for products and services provided to customers as part of a company's primary operations.[2] Assets include cash, land, equipment, and buildings. The income statement in Exhibit 2.2 shows that FastForward earned total revenues of $4,100 during December from consulting services and rental revenue.

---

[1] Some view Exhibit 2.1 like a motion picture where points in time are freeze frames and periods of time are the actions occurring between freeze frames.

[2] Financial Accounting Standards Board, *Statement of Financial Accounting Concepts No. 6,* "Elements of Financial Statements" (Norwalk, CT, 1985), par. 78.

Expenses

Expenses are outflows or the using up of assets from providing products and services to customers.[3] The income statement in Exhibit 2.2 shows FastForward used up some of its assets in paying for rented store space. The $1,000 expense for store space is reported in the income statement as rent expense. FastForward also paid for an employee's wages at a cost of $700. This is reported on the income statement as salaries expense. The income statement heading identifies the company, the type of statement, and the time period covered. Knowledge of the time period is important in judging whether a company's performance is satisfactory. In assessing whether FastForward's $2,400 net income is satisfactory, we must remember it earned this amount during a one-month period.

Answer—p. 63

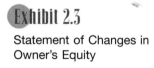

Chef
You are working as a chef at a restaurant and feel your wages are too low. You decide to ask the owner for a raise. How can you use the income statement of the restaurant to help in your request?

Statement of Changes in Owner's Equity

The **statement of changes in owner's equity** reports on changes in equity over the reporting period. This statement starts with beginning equity and adjusts it for events that (1) increase it—investments by the owner and net income, and (2) decrease it—net loss and owner withdrawals.

The statement of changes in owner's equity for FastForward's first month of operations is shown in Exhibit 2.3. This statement describes events that changed owner's equity during the month. It shows $30,000 of equity created by Taylor's initial investment. It also shows $2,400 of net income earned during the month, and Taylor's $600 withdrawal. FastForward's equity balance at the end of the month is $31,800.[4]

Exhibit 2.3

Statement of Changes in Owner's Equity

FASTFORWARD Statement of Changes in Owner's Equity For Month Ended December 31, 1997		
C.Taylor, capital, December 1, 1997		$ 0
Add: Investment by owner	$30,000	
Net income	2,400	32,400
Total		$32,400
Less: Withdrawal by owner		(600)
C.Taylor, capital, December 31, 1997		$31,800

Balance Sheet

The **balance sheet** reports the financial position of a company at a point in time, usually at the end of a month or year. Because of its emphasis on financial position it is also called the **statement of financial position.** The balance sheet describes financial

---

[3] Ibid., par. 80.

[4] The beginning capital balance in the statement of changes in owner's equity is rarely zero. An exception is for the first period of a company's operations. Since FastForward began operations in December 1997, its beginning capital balance for the month of December is zero. But the beginning capital balance in January 1998 for FastForward will be $31,800 (this is December's ending balance).

FASTFORWARD Balance Sheet December 31, 1997			
Assets		**Liabilities**	
Cash	$ 8,400	Accounts payable	$ 1,100
Supplies	3,600	Note payable	5,100
Equipment	26,000	Total liabilities	$ 6,200
		Owner's Equity	
		C. Taylor, capital	31,800
Total assets	$38,000	Total liabilities and owner's equity	$38,000

Exhibit 2.4

Balance Sheet

position by listing the types and dollar amounts of assets, liabilities, and equity. Exhibit 2.4 shows the balance sheet for FastForward as of December 31, 1997. The balance sheet heading lists the company, the statement, and the specific date on which assets, liabilities, and equity are identified and measured. The amounts in the balance sheet are measured as of the close of business on that specific date.

The balance sheet for FastForward shows it owns three different assets at the close of business on December 31, 1997. The assets are cash, supplies, and equipment. The total dollar amount for these assets is $38,000. The balance sheet also shows total liabilities of $6,200. Owner's equity is $31,800. Equity is the difference between assets and liabilities. The total amounts on each side of the balance sheet are equal (assets = liabilities + equity). This equality is why the statement is named a *balance sheet*. This name also reflects the reporting of asset, liability, and equity *balances* in the statement.

Assets

Assets are resources owned or controlled by a company. A common characteristic of assets is their ability to provide future benefits to the company.[5] Assets are of many types. A familiar asset is cash. Another is accounts receivable. An **account receivable** is an asset created by selling products or services on credit. It reflects amounts owed to a company by its credit customers. These customers and other individuals and organizations who owe a company are called its **debtors.** Other common assets include merchandise held for sale, supplies, equipment, buildings, and land. Assets also can be intangible rights such as those granted by a patent or copyright.

Personal Assets

Assets of U.S. households have more than tripled in the past 15 years. They now exceed $20 trillion. But as Wall Street has soared and inflation has cooled, the asset mix has changed. Where we once saw savings and money market accounts, we now see stocks, mutual funds, and pension assets.

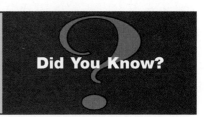

Did You Know?

---

[5] Financial Accounting Standards Board, *Statement of Financial Accounting Concepts No. 6,* "Elements of Financial Statements" (Norwalk, CT, 1985), par. 25.

Liabilities

Liabilities are obligations of a business. They are claims of others against the assets of the business. A common characteristic of liabilities is their potential for reducing future assets or requiring future services or products.[6] Liabilities take many forms. Familiar liabilities are accounts payable and notes payable. An **account payable** is a liability created by buying products or services on credit. It reflects amounts owed to others. A **note payable** is a liability expressed by a written promise to make a future payment at a specific time. Other familiar liabilities are salaries and wages owed to employees and interest payable.

Individuals and organizations who own the right to receive payments from a business are called its **creditors.** Creditors own the right to be paid by a business. One entity's payable is another entity's receivable. If a business fails to pay its obligations, the law gives creditors a right to force the sale of business assets to obtain the money to meet creditors' claims. When assets are sold under these conditions, creditors are paid first, but only up to the amount of their claims. Any remaining money, the residual, goes to the owner of the business. Creditors often use a balance sheet to help decide whether to loan money to a business. They compare the amounts of liabilities and assets. A loan is less risky if liabilities are small in comparison to assets. This is because there are more resources than claims on resources. A loan is more risky if liabilities are large compared to assets.

Equity

Equity is the owner's claim on the assets of a business. It is the *residual interest* in the assets of a business after deducting liabilities.[7] Equity also is called **net assets.** Since FastForward is a sole proprietorship, the equity heading of its balance sheet in Exhibit 2.4 is *owner's equity*. If it was organized as a corporation, its owner would be a shareholder and equity would be called *shareholders', or stockholders', equity.*

Owner's equity is increased by owner investments and by revenues. It is decreased by owner withdrawals and by expenses. Exhibit 2.5 shows these important relations. Owner investments are assets put into the business by the owner. Owner withdrawals are assets taken from the business by the owner. These changes in owner's equity are reported in the statement of changes in owner's equity and give us the ending balance of owner's equity. This ending balance is also reported in the balance sheet.

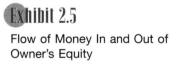

Exhibit 2.5

Flow of Money In and Out of Owner's Equity

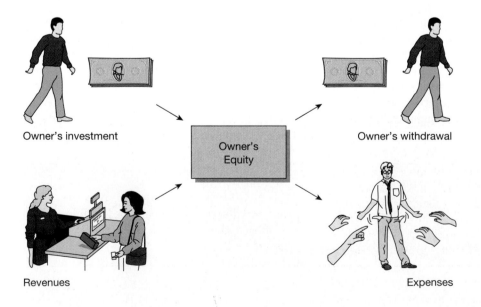

Owner's investment

Owner's Equity

Owner's withdrawal

Revenues

Expenses

---

[6] Ibid., par. 35.

[7] Ibid., par. 49.

FASTFORWARD
Statement of Cash Flows
For Month Ended December 31, 1997

Cash flows from operating activities:

Cash received from clients	$4,100	
Cash paid for supplies	(2,500)	
Cash paid for rent	(1,000)	
Cash paid to employee	(700)	
Net cash used by operating activities		$ (100)

Cash flows from investing activities:

Purchase of equipment	$(20,000)	
Net cash used by investing activities		(20,000)

Cash flows from financing activities:

Investment by owner	$ 30,000	
Partial repayment of note	(900)	
Withdrawal by owner	(600)	
Net cash provided by financing activities		28,500
Net increase in cash		$ 8,400
Cash balance, December 1, 1997		0
Cash balance, December 31, 1997		$ 8,400

Exhibit 2.6
Statement of Cash Flows

FASTForward

Statement of Cash Flows

The **statement of cash flows** describes the sources (inflows) and uses (outflows) of cash for a reporting period. It also reports the amount of cash at both the beginning and end of a period. The statement of cash flows is organized by a company's major activities: operating, investing, and financing. Since a company must carefully manage cash if it is to survive and prosper, cash flow information is important.

FastForward's statement of cash flows for December is shown in Exhibit 2.6. The first section shows cash outflows from operating activities equal to $100. This is the result of $4,100 of cash received from customers less $4,200 paid for supplies, rent, and salaries. The second section reports on investing activities and shows a $20,000 cash outflow for buying equipment. The third section reports a $28,500 cash inflow from financing activities. FastForward's financing activities included an owner investment, a loan repayment, and an owner withdrawal.

Financial Statements and Forms of Organization

Chapter 1 described three different forms of business organization: proprietorships, partnerships, and corporations. While there are many differences between these forms of business organization, financial statements for these organizations are very similar.

Probably the most important difference in financial statements is in the equity section of the balance sheet. A proprietorship's balance sheet lists the equity balance beside the owner's name as in Exhibit 2.4. A partnership's balance sheet uses the same approach, unless there are too many owners for their names to fit in the available space. For example, if Chuck Taylor is part of an equal partnership with his sister Jane, then the equity section of the balance sheet would look like the one in Exhibit 2.7.

C2 Describe differences in financial statements across forms of business organization.

FASTFORWARD
Partial Balance Sheet
December 31, 1997

Partners' Equity

Chuck Taylor, capital	$15,900
Jane Taylor, capital	15,900
Total partners' equity	$31,800

Exhibit 2.7
Equity Section of a Partnership Balance Sheet

FASTForward

Exhibit 2.8

Equity Section of a Corporation Balance Sheet

FASTFORWARD Partial Balance Sheet December 31, 1997	
Shareholders' Equity	
Contributed capital:	
Common stock	$30,000
Retained earnings	1,800
Total shareholders' equity . . .	$31,800

A corporation's balance sheet does not list the names of its shareholders. Instead, equity is divided into **contributed capital** (also called **paid-in capital**) and **retained earnings.** Contributed capital reflects shareholders' investments. Retained earnings are the corporation's profits that have not been distributed to shareholders. For example, assume Chuck Taylor had set up FastForward as a corporation in which he was the sole shareholder. If he is issued common stock for his $30,000 investment, then the equity section of the balance sheet would look like the one in Exhibit 2.8.

Retained earnings is a corporation's accumulated net income (loss) for all prior periods' operations that has not been distributed to shareholders. FastForward has earned $2,400, of which $600 was distributed to Taylor as a dividend, leaving $1,800 in retained earnings.

When an owner of a proprietorship or a partnership takes cash or other assets from a company, the distributions are called **withdrawals.** When owners of a corporation receive cash or other assets from a company, the distributions are called **dividends.** Withdrawals and dividends are not reported as part of the income statement because they are *not* expenses incurred to generate revenues. Also, when the owner of a proprietorship is its manager, no salary expense is reported on the income statement for these services. The same is true for a partnership. But since a corporation is a separate legal entity, salaries paid to its managers are always reported as expenses on its income statement. This different treatment of owners' salaries requires special consideration when analyzing an income statement. We explain one special adjustment near the end of this chapter.

The emphasis in the early chapters of this book is on sole proprietorships. This allows us to focus on important measurement and reporting issues in accounting without getting caught up in the complexities of organizational form. We do discuss forms of organization and provide examples when appropriate. Chapters 13 and 14 return to this topic and provide details about the financial statements of partnerships and corporations.

Flash *back*

1. What are the four major financial statements?

2. Describe revenues and expenses.

3. Explain assets, liabilities, and equity.

4. What are three differences in financial statements for different forms of organizations?

Answers—p. 63

Generally Accepted Accounting Principles

We explained in Chapter 1 how financial accounting practice is governed by rules called *generally accepted accounting principles,* or *GAAP.* For us to use and interpret financial statements effectively, we need an understanding of these principles. A primary purpose of GAAP is to make information in financial statements relevant, reliable, and comparable. Relevant information affects the decisions of its users. Information must be reliable so decision makers can depend on it. Information is comparable for different companies if the companies use similar practices. GAAP impose limits on the range of accounting practices companies can use. We describe in this section the current process for setting GAAP and many of the most important accounting principles.

Financial Reporting Environment

Generally accepted accounting principles are developed in response to the needs of users. While accounting professionals prepare financial statements, independent auditors (CPAs) often examine them and prepare an audit report to give users more assurance in the statements' reliability. Statements along with an audit report then are distributed to users.

Exhibit 2.9 shows how accounting principles, auditing standards, and various parties interact in the financial reporting environment. Accounting principles are applied in preparing financial statements. Preparers use preferred procedures in accounting for business transactions and events. Audits are performed in accordance with **generally accepted auditing standards (GAAS),** which are the accepted rules for conducting audits of financial statements. Both accounting and auditing help assure users that financial statements include relevant, reliable, and comparable information. An audit does not ensure success, and does not reduce the risk that a company's products and services will be unsuccessful or that adverse factors will cause it to fail. Instead, it tells us the statements are prepared using accepted accounting principles. **Ernst and Young** says in its audit report of **Harley-Davidson:**

> In our opinion, the consolidated financial statements . . . present fairly, in all material respects . . . in conformity with generally accepted accounting principles.

C3 Explain the financial reporting environment.

Setting Accounting Principles

Accounting principles were historically developed through common usage. A principle was acceptable if it was permitted by most professionals. This history is reflected in the phrase *generally accepted.* As business transactions became more complex, users were less satisfied with the lack of more concrete guidance. Many of these users desired more

Exhibit 2.9

Financial Reporting Environment

FASB

GAAP

Preparers

Financial statements

Auditors

Audit report

Decision makers

ASB

GAAS

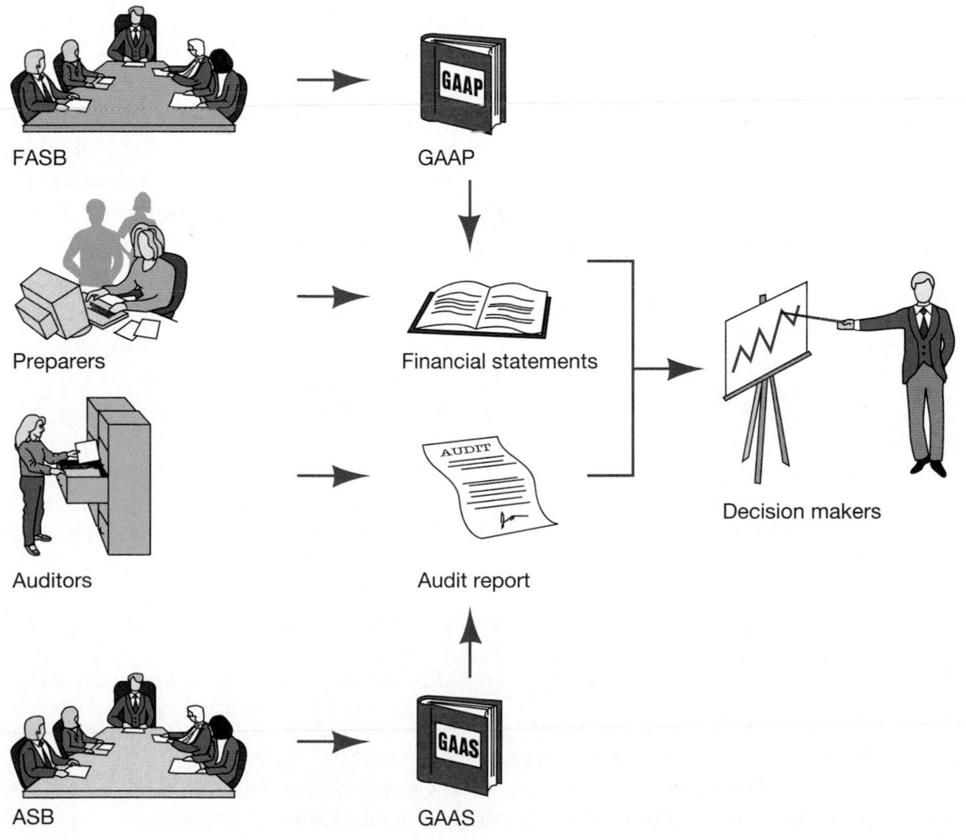

C4 Identify those responsible for setting accounting and auditing principles.

uniformity in practice. Authority for developing accepted principles was eventually assigned to a select group of professionals in the field. These committees or boards have authority to establish GAAP. The authority of these groups has increased over time.

We show two organizations in Exhibit 2.9 that are the primary authoritative sources of GAAP and GAAS. The Financial Accounting Standards Board (FASB) is the primary authoritative source of GAAP. It is a nonprofit organization with a large research staff to help identify accounting problems and solutions. The Board seeks advice from all users and often holds public hearings for this purpose. Its goal is to improve financial reporting and balance the interests of all users. The FASB communicates its decisions in various publications. Most notable are **Statements of Financial Accounting Standards (SFAS).** These statements set generally accepted accounting principles in the United States and often affect international practices.[8]

The FASB draws its authority from two major sources. The first is the Securities and Exchange Commission (SEC). Congress created the SEC to regulate securities markets, including the flow of information from companies to the public. The SEC designates the FASB as its primary authority for setting GAAP. It can overrule the FASB but rarely does so. The second source of authority is state boards that license CPAs. Independent auditors assure us that financial statements comply with FASB rules. State ethics codes require CPAs that audit reports to disclose any areas where statements fail to comply. If CPAs fail to report noncompliance, they can lose their licenses to practice. The AICPA's Code of Professional Conduct includes a similar provision. A member of the AICPA can be expelled from the institute for not objecting to financial statements that fail to comply with FASB rules.[9]

Authority for generally accepted auditing standards (GAAS) belongs to the **Auditing Standards Board (ASB).** The ASB is a special committee of the AICPA with unpaid volunteer members. The SEC is an important source of the ASB's authority.[10]

International Accounting Principles

In today's global economy, people in different countries increasingly do business with each other. It is common for companies in the United States to sell products and services around the world. We see examples of companies in countries such as Russia selling their shares to American and Japanese investors and borrowing from lenders in places such as Saudi Arabia and Germany. **Marriott** is a United States company providing lodging and contract services. While many of **Marriott's** operations are in the United States, it recently opened or scheduled to open businesses in Aruba, the Bahamas, Egypt, Lebanon, Puerto Rico, Costa Rica, Ecuador, Germany, Guatemala, Indonesia, Malaysia, Mexico, and Thailand. Also, **NIKE** says the following about its global operations:

> All NIKE regions outside the U.S. experienced revenue increases greater than 30%. Europe increased 33%, Asia Pacific, 41%, and the Americas, 35%. The most significant increases were in Japan, Italy, United Kingdom, Korea, and Canada.

Despite our growing global economy, countries continue to maintain their unique set of acceptable accounting practices. Consider a Singapore company selling stock to foreign investors. Should it prepare financial statements that comply with Singapore ac-

---

[8] Predecessors to the FASB were the Accounting Principles Board (APB) and the Committee on Accounting Procedure (CAP).

[9] Many other professional organizations support the FASB, including the American Accounting Association (AAA), Financial Executives Institute (FEI), Institute of Management Accountants (IMA), Association for Investment Management and Research (AIMR), and Securities Industry Association (SIA). They increase the Board's credibility by participating in its process for setting GAAP.

[10] Working alongside the FASB is the Governmental Accounting Standards Board (GASB), which identifies special accounting principles to be applied in preparing financial statements for state and local governments.

counting standards or with the standards of the United States, Japan, Saudi Arabia, or Germany? Should it prepare five different sets of reports to gain access to financial markets in all five countries? This is a difficult and pressing problem.

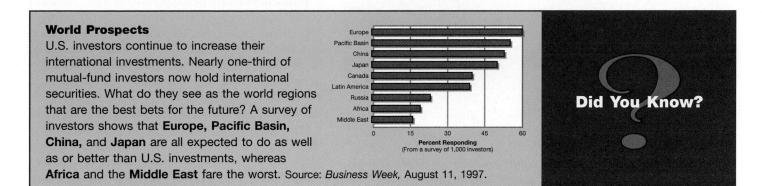

World Prospects

U.S. investors continue to increase their international investments. Nearly one-third of mutual-fund investors now hold international securities. What do they see as the world regions that are the best bets for the future? A survey of investors shows that **Europe, Pacific Basin, China,** and **Japan** are all expected to do as well as or better than U.S. investments, whereas **Africa** and the **Middle East** fare the worst. Source: *Business Week,* August 11, 1997.

Did You Know?

One response has been to create an **International Accounting Standards Committee (IASC).** The IASC issues *International Accounting Standards* that identify preferred accounting practices and encourages their worldwide acceptance. By narrowing the range of alternative practices, the IASC hopes to create more harmony among accounting practices of different countries. If standards are harmonized, a single set of financial statements can be used by one company in all financial markets. Many countries' standard setters support the IASC. Both the FASB and the SEC provide support and technical assistance. Yet the IASC does not have authority to impose its standards on companies. While interest is growing in moving United States GAAP toward the IASC's preferred practices, authority to make such changes rests with the FASB and the SEC.

Flash back

5. What organization sets GAAP? From where does it draw authority?

6. What is GAAS? What organization sets GAAS?

7. How are U.S. companies with international operations affected by international accounting standards?

Answers—p. 63

Principles of Accounting

Accounting principles are both general and specific. General principles are the basic assumptions, concepts, and guidelines for preparing financial statements. Specific principles are detailed rules used in reporting business transactions and events. General principles stem from long-used accounting practices. Specific principles arise more often from the rulings of authoritative groups.

We need an understanding of both general and specific principles to effectively use accounting information. Because general principles are especially crucial in using accounting information, we emphasize them in the early chapters of this book. The general principles described in this chapter include: business entity, objectivity, cost, going-concern, monetary unit, and revenue recognition. General principles described in later chapters (with their relevant chapter in parentheses) include: time period (4), matching (4), materiality (9), full-disclosure (9), consistency (10), and conservatism (10).[11] The specific principles are especially important for understanding individual items in financial statements and are portrayed as the building blocks for the *House of GAAP* in

C5 Identify, explain, and apply accounting principles.

---

[11] General principles are also commonly called *concepts, theories, assumptions,* or *postulates.*

Exhibit 2.10

Building Blocks for the House
of GAAP

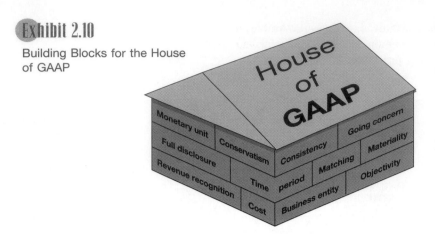

Exhibit 2.10. They are described throughout the
book as we come to them.

Business Entity Principle

The **business entity principle** means that a business
is accounted for separately from its owner or owners. It also means we account separately for each
business that is controlled by the same owner. The
reason for this principle is that separate information
about each business is relevant to the decisions of
its users.

We use FastForward to illustrate the importance of
the business entity principle. Suppose Chuck Taylor,
the owner, wants to know how well the business is
doing. For financial statements to address his need, FastForward's transactions must be
separate from Taylor's personal transactions. For example, Taylor's personal expenses (such
as entertainment and clothes) must not be subtracted from FastForward's revenues on its
income statement because they are not incurred as part of FastForward's business. A company's statements must not reflect its owner's *personal* transactions, assets, and liabilities.
It also must not reflect the transactions, assets, and liabilities of *another business.* For reports and decision making to be effective, businesses must follow the entity principle.

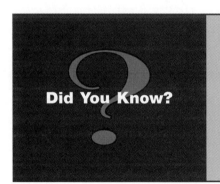

Did You Know?

Penthouse Suspicions
Abuse of the business entity principle brought
down executives at **Allegheny International.**
Allegheny's executives turned in expenses not
part of business activities. The worst? More
than $1 million was spent to renovate and pay
for a lavish penthouse for the CEO's son.
Source: Securities and Exchange Commission, AAER
No. 151.

Objectivity Principle

The **objectivity principle** means that financial statement information is supported by independent, unbiased evidence. It involves more than one person's opinion. Information
is not reliable if it is based only on what a preparer thinks might be true. A preparer can
be too optimistic or pessimistic. An unethical preparer might even try to mislead users
by intentionally misrepresenting the truth. The objectivity principle is intended to make
financial statements useful by ensuring they report reliable and verifiable information.

Cost Principle

The **cost principle** means financial statements are based on actual costs incurred in business transactions. **Business transactions** are exchanges of economic consideration between
two parties. Sales and purchases are examples of business transactions. Economic consideration can include products, services, money, and rights to collect money. Cost is measured
on a cash or equal-to-cash basis. This means if cash is given for an asset or service, its cost
is measured as the amount of cash paid. If something besides cash is exchanged (such as a
car traded for a truck), cost is measured as the cash equal of what is given up or received.[12]

The cost principle is accepted by users because of its emphasis on reliability and relevance. Cost is the amount given up to purchase an asset or service. It approximates market

---

[12] FASB, *Accounting Standards—Current Text* (Norwalk, CT, 1995), sec. N35.105. First published as *APB Opinion No. 29,* par. 18.

value of an asset or service when it is acquired. Most users consider cost information as relevant to their decisions. The cost principle is also consistent with *objectivity* in that information based on cost is considered objective. For example, reporting purchases of assets and services at cost is more objective than reporting a manager's estimate of their value.

To illustrate this principle, suppose FastForward pays $5,000 for equipment. The cost principle tells us to record this purchase at $5,000. It would make no difference if Chuck Taylor thinks this equipment is really worth $7,000. The cost principle requires that this purchase be recorded at a cost of $5,000.

Going-Concern Principle

The **going-concern principle,** also called the *continuing-concern principle,* means financial statements reflect an assumption that the business will continue operating instead of being closed or sold. This means a balance sheet does not report liquidation values of assets held for long-term use. Instead, these assets are reported at cost. Since costs change, a balance sheet seldom reflects a company's exact worth. If a company is to be bought or sold, buyers and sellers should obtain additional information from other sources.[13] Neither the going-concern principle nor the cost principle is appropriate if a company is expected to fail or be liquidated. Instead, market values are most relevant.

Monetary Unit Principle

The **monetary unit principle** means we can express transactions and events in monetary, or money, units. Money is the common denominator in business. Expressing transactions and events in money helps us use financial statements for communication in business. Examples of monetary units are the dollar in the United States, Canada, Australia, and Singapore, pound sterling in the United Kingdom, and peso in Mexico, the Philippines, and Chile. An *exchange rate* expresses the value of one currency relative to another. Exchange rates change frequently and are tied to many economic and political factors. The chart below is a partial listing of exchange rates in terms of U.S. dollars:

Country	U.S. $ equivalent†	Country	U.S. $ equivalent†
Canada (dollar)	0.70	United Kingdom (pound)	1.67
Taiwan (dollar)	0.03	Mexico (peso)	0.12
Germany (mark)	0.54	Philippines (peso)	0.03

†Rates as of April 2, 1998.

The monetary unit used by an organization usually depends on the country where it operates. But we are seeing more companies expressing financial statements in more than one monetary unit. For example, an excerpt in Exhibit 2.11 from **Nintendo's** financial statements shows results reported in *both* yen and dollars.

NINTENDO'S FINANCIAL HIGHLIGHTS Years Ended March 31, 1997 and 1996				
	Yen (¥) in Millions		U.S. ($000s) Dollars	
	1997	1996	1997	1996
Total revenues	¥462,922	¥400,707	$3,733,249	$3,231,512
Net income	65,481	59,870	528,077	482,828
Total assets	735,620	649,840	5,932,422	5,240,650
Total equity	563,718	512,524	4,546,120	4,133,260

Exhibit 2.11

Nintendo's Financial Highlights in Both Dollars and Yen

---

[13] In *SFAS 107,* the FASB requires supplemental disclosures (in notes to financial statements) of the current market values of many assets and liabilities.

Accounting generally assumes a *stable* monetary unit. This means we expect the value of a currency to not change. The more changes in the monetary unit, the more difficult it is for us to use and interpret financial statements, especially across time.

Flash *back*

8. Why is the business entity principle important?

9. How are the objectivity and cost principles related?

Answers—p. 63

Transactions and the Accounting Equation

A1 Analyze business transactions using the accounting equation.

Exhibit 2.12

Accounting Equation

We know financial statements reflect the business activities of a company. We also know many of these activities, such as purchases and sales, involve business transactions. To understand information in financial statements, we need to know how an accounting system captures relevant data about transactions, classifies and records data, and reports data in financial statements. This section starts us on an important path that continues through Chapter 5.

The basic tool of modern accounting systems is the **accounting equation** as shown in Exhibit 2.12.

$$\text{Assets} = \text{Liabilities} + \text{Owner's equity}$$

The accounting equation is also called the **balance sheet equation** because of its link to the balance sheet. Like any mathematical equation, the accounting equation can be modified by rearranging terms. Moving liabilities to the left side of the equality, for example, gives us an equation for owner's equity in terms of assets and liabilities:

$$\text{Assets} - \text{Liabilities} = \text{Owner's equity}$$

We next show how to use the accounting equation to keep track of changes in a company's assets, liabilities, and owner's equity in a way that provides us useful information.

Transaction Analysis—Part I

A business transaction is an exchange of economic consideration between two parties. Examples of economic consideration include products, services, money, and rights to collect money. Because two parties are exchanging assets and liabilities, a transaction affects the components of the accounting equation. It is important to remember that each transaction leaves the equation in balance. Assets *always* equal the sum of liabilities and equity. We show how this equality is preserved by looking at the transactions of Fast-Forward in its first month of operations.

Transaction 1: Investment by Owner

On December 1, 1997, Chuck Taylor formed an athletic shoe consulting business. He set it up as a proprietorship. Taylor is the manager of the business as well as its owner. The marketing plan for the business is to focus primarily on consulting with schools, sports clubs, athletes, and others who place orders of athletic shoes with manufacturers. Taylor invests $30,000 cash in the new company and deposits it in a bank account opened under the name of **FastForward.** After this transaction, the cash (an asset) and the owner's equity (called *C. Taylor, Capital*) each equal $30,000. The effect of this transaction on the accounting equation is:

	Assets	=	Liabilities	+	Owner's Equity
	Cash	=			C.Taylor, Capital
(1)	+$30,000	=			+$30,000 Investment

The accounting equation is in balance. It reveals that FastForward has one asset, cash, equal to $30,000. It also reveals no liabilities and an owner's equity of $30,000. The source of increase in equity is also identified as an investment to distinguish it from revenues.

Transaction 2: Purchase Supplies for Cash

FastForward uses $2,500 of its cash to buy supplies of brand name athletic shoes for testing. This transaction is an exchange of cash, an asset, for another kind of asset, supplies. The transaction produces no expense because no value is lost. It merely changes the form of assets from cash to supplies. The decrease in cash is exactly equal to the increase in supplies. The equation remains in balance.

	Assets		=	Liabilities	+	Owner's Equity
	Cash	+ Supplies	=			C.Taylor, Capital
Old Bal.	$30,000		=			$30,000
(2)	−2,500	+2,500				
New Bal.	$27,500	+ $2,500	=			$30,000
		$30,000			$30,000	

Transaction 3: Purchase Equipment for Cash

FastForward spends $20,000 to acquire equipment for testing athletic shoes. Like transaction 2, transaction 3 is an exchange of one asset, cash, for another asset, equipment. It is not an expense because no value is lost. This purchase changes the makeup of assets but does not change the asset total. The equation remains in balance.

	Assets				=	Liabilities	+	Owner's Equity
	Cash	+	Supplies	+ Equipment	=			C.Taylor, Capital
Old Bal.	$27,500	+	$2,500		=			$30,000
(3)	−20,000			+20,000				
New Bal.	$7,500	+	$2,500	+ $20,000	=			$30,000
			$30,000				$30,000	

Transaction 4: Purchase Equipment and Supplies on Credit

Taylor decides he needs more testing equipment and supplies of brand name athletic shoes. These purchases total $7,100. But as we see from the accounting equation in transaction 3, FastForward has only $7,500 in cash. Concerned that these purchases would use nearly all of FastForward's cash, Taylor arranges to purchase them on credit from CalTech Supply Company. This means FastForward acquires these items in exchange for a promise to pay for them later. Supplies of athletic shoes cost $1,100, the new testing equipment cost $6,000, and the total liability to CalTech Supply is $7,100. The effects of this purchase on the accounting equation are:

	Assets					=	Liabilities			+	Owner's Equity
	Cash	+	Supplies	+	Equipment	=	Accounts Payable	+	Note Payable	+	C.Taylor, Capital
Old Bal.	$7,500	+	$2,500	+	$20,000	=					$30,000
(4)		+	1,100	+	6,000		+$1,100	+	$6,000		
New Bal.	$7,500	+	$3,600	+	$26,000	=	$1,100	+	$6,000	+	$30,000
			$37,100					$37,100			

This purchase increases assets by $7,100 while liabilities (called *accounts payable* and *note payable*) increase by the same amount. Both of these payables are promises by Taylor to repay its debt, but the note payable reflects a more formal, written agreement. A note payable is often necessary when the repayment period is longer than a month or two. We discuss these liabilities in detail in later chapters.

Transaction 5: Services Rendered for Cash

A main objective of a business is to increase its owner's wealth. This goal is met when a business produces *net income.* Net income is reflected in the accounting equation as an increase in owner's equity. FastForward earns revenues by consulting with clients about test results on athletic shoes. FastForward earns a net income only if its revenues are greater than the expenses incurred in earning them.

We see how the accounting equation is affected by earning consulting revenues in transaction 5. FastForward provides consulting services to a Los Angeles athletic club on December 10 and immediately collects $2,200 cash. The accounting equation shows an increase in cash by $2,200 and in owner's equity by $2,200. This increase in equity is identified in the far right column as a revenue because it is earned by providing services. These explanations are useful in later preparing and interpreting a statement of changes in owner's equity and an income statement.

	Assets			=	**Liabilities**			+	**Owner's Equity**	
	Cash	+ **Supplies**	+ **Equipment**	=	**Accounts Payable**	+ **Note Payable**		+	**C.Taylor, Capital**	
Old Bal.	$7,500	+ $3,600	+ $26,000	=	$1,100	+ $6,000		+	$30,000	
(5)	+ 2,200							+	2,200	Consulting Revenue
New Bal.	$9,700	+ $3,600	+ $26,000	=	$1,100	+ $6,000		+	$32,200	
		$39,300					$39,300			

Transactions 6 and 7: Payment of Expenses in Cash

FastForward pays $1,000 rent on December 10 to the landlord of the building where its store is located. Paying this amount allows FastForward to occupy the space for the entire month of December. The effects of this event on the accounting equation are shown below as transaction 6. On December 12, FastForward pays the $700 salary of the company's only employee. This event is reflected in the accounting equation as transaction 7.

	Assets			=	**Liabilities**			+	**Owner's Equity**	
	Cash	+ **Supplies**	+ **Equipment**	=	**Accounts Payable**	+ **Note Payable**		+	**C.Taylor, Capital**	
Old Bal.	$9,700	+ $3,600	+ $26,000	=	$1,100	+ $6,000		+	$32,200	Rent Expense
(6)	−1,000								− 1,000	
Bal.	$8,700	+ $3,600	+ $26,000	=	$1,100	+ $6,000		+	$31,200	Salary Expense
(7)	− 700								− 700	
New Bal.	$8,000	+ $3,600	+ $26,000	=	$1,100	+ $6,000		+	$30,500	
		$37,600					$37,600			

Both transactions 6 and 7 are expenses for FastForward. They use up cash for the purpose of providing services to clients. Unlike the asset purchases in transactions 2 and 3, the cash payments in transactions 6 and 7 acquire services. The benefits of these services do *not* last beyond the end of this month. The accounting equation shows both transactions reduce cash and Taylor's equity. The accounting equation remains in balance after each event. The far right column identifies these decreases as expenses.

Summary of Part I Transactions

FastForward has net income when its revenues exceed its expenses. Net income increases owner's equity. If expenses exceed revenues, a net loss occurs and equity is decreased. Net income or loss is not affected by transactions between a business and its owner. This means Taylor's initial investment of $30,000 is not income to FastForward, even though it increased equity.

To stress that revenues and expenses yield changes in equity, we add revenues directly to owner's equity and subtract expenses directly from owner's equity in this chapter. In practice and in later chapters, information about revenues and expenses is compiled separately. These amounts are later added to or subtracted from owner's equity at the end of the period. We describe this process in Chapters 3–5. Because of the importance of properly recognizing revenues for a business, we interrupt our analysis of FastForward's transactions to describe the revenue recognition principle.

 **back**

10. How can a transaction not affect liability and equity accounts?

11. Describe a transaction increasing owner's equity and one decreasing it.

Answers—pp. 63, 64

Revenue Recognition Principle

Preparers need guidance in deciding when to recognize revenue. *Recognize* means to record a transaction or event for the purpose of reporting its effects in financial statements. If revenue is recognized too early, the income statement reports net income sooner than it should and the business looks more profitable than it is. If revenue is recognized late, the earlier income statement shows lower amounts of revenue and net income than it should and the business looks less profitable than it is. In both cases, the income statement does not provide decision makers with the most useful information about company success.

The **revenue recognition principle** provides guidance on when revenue should be recognized on the income statement. Recognition is also sometimes called *realization*. The recognition principle includes three important guidelines:

1. *Revenue is recognized when earned.* Preparing to provide services, finding customers, and promoting sales all contribute to earning revenue. Yet the revenue earned at any point in this process usually cannot be determined reliably until the process is complete, that is, when the business acquires the right to collect the selling price. This means revenue is usually not recognized on the income statement until the earnings process is complete. The earnings process is normally complete when services are rendered or the seller transfers ownership of products sold to the buyer. To illustrate, suppose a customer pays in advance of taking delivery of a product or service. Because the earnings process is not complete, the seller must not recognize revenue. The seller must complete the earnings process before recognizing revenue.[14] This practice is called *sales basis of revenue recognition*.

2. *Assets received from selling products and services do not have to be in cash.* A common noncash asset acquired by the seller in a revenue transaction is a customer's promise to pay at a future date. The seller views the customer's promise as an account receivable. These transactions are called *credit sales* and are often convenient for customers in purchasing products or services and paying for them later.

---

[14] FASB, *Accounting Standards—Current Text* (Norwalk, CT, 1995), sec. R75.101. First published as *APB Opinion No. 10,* par. 12.

FastForward did this in transaction 4 when it bought supplies and equipment on credit. If objective evidence shows that a seller has earned the right to collect from a customer, this seller should recognize an account receivable as an asset and record revenue earned. When cash is collected later, no additional revenue is recognized. Collecting the cash simply changes the makeup of assets from a receivable to cash.

3. *Revenue recognized is measured by cash received plus the cash equivalent (market) value of other assets received.* This means, for example, if a transaction creates an account receivable, the seller recognizes revenue equal to the value of the receivable, which usually is the amount of cash expected to be collected.

Notes to financial statements should include an explanation of the revenue recognition method used by a company. **General Motors,** for instance, reports in its annual report that:

> Sales are generally recorded by the Corporation when products are shipped to independent dealers.

Transaction Analysis—Part II

We return to the transactions of FastForward to show how revenue recognition works in practice.

Transaction 8: Services and Rental Rendered for Credit

FastForward provides consulting services of $1,600 and rental of test facilities for $300 to a small college sports team. The rental involves allowing selected team members to try recommended shoes at FastForward's testing grounds. The sports team is billed for $1,900. This transaction results in a new asset, account receivable from a client. The $1,900 increase in assets produces an equal increase in owner's equity. The increase in equity is identified as two revenue components in the far right column of the accounting equation:

	Assets				= Liabilities		+ Owner's Equity	
	Cash	+ Accounts Receivable	+ Supplies	+ Equipment	= Accounts Payable	+ Note Payable	+ C.Taylor, Capital	
Old Bal.	$8,000 +		+ $3,600	+ $26,000	= $1,100	+ $6,000	+ $30,500	
(8)		+ 1,900					+ 1,600	Consulting Revenue
							+ 300	Rental Revenue
New Bal.	$8,000 +	$1,900	+ $3,600	+ $26,000	= $1,100	+ $6,000	+ $32,400	
		$39,500				$39,500		

Transaction 9: Receipt of Cash on Account

An amount of $1,900 is received from the client 10 days after being billed for consulting services in transaction 8. Transaction 9 does not change the amount of assets and does not affect liabilities or equity. It converts the receivable to cash. It does not create new revenue. Revenue was recognized when FastForward rendered the services, not when the cash is now collected. This emphasis on the earnings process instead of cash flows is a goal of the revenue recognition principle and yields useful information to users. The new balances are:

	Assets				= Liabilities		Owner's Equity
	Cash	+ Accounts Receivable	+ Supplies	+ Equipment	= Accounts Payable	+ Note Payable	+ C.Taylor, Capital
Old. Bal.	$8,000	+ $1,900	+ $3,600	+ $26,000	= $1,100	+ $6,000	+ $32,400
(9)	+ 1,900	−1,900					
New. Bal.	$9,900	+ $ 0	+ $3,600	+ $26,000	= $1,100	+ $6,000	+ $32,400
		$39,500				$39,500	

Transaction 10: Payment on Note Payable

FastForward pays $900 to CalTech Supply on December 24. The $900 payment is for the earlier $6,000 purchase of testing equipment from CalTech, leaving $5,100 unpaid. The $1,100 amount due CalTech for supplies remains unpaid. The accounting equation shows this transaction decreases FastForward's cash by $900 and decreases its liability to CalTech Supply by the same amount. As a result, owner's equity does not change. This event does not create an expense even though cash flows out of FastForward.

	Assets				= Liabilities		Owner's Equity
	Cash	+ Accounts Receivable	+ Supplies	+ Equipment	= Accounts Payable	+ Note Payable	+ C.Taylor, Capital
Old Bal.	$9,900	+ $ 0	+ $3,600	+ $26,000	= $1,100	+ $6,000	+ $32,400
(10)	− 900					− 900	
New Bal.	$9,000	+ $ 0	+ $3,600	+ $26,000	= $1,100	+ $5,100	+ $32,400
		$38,600				$38,600	

Transaction 11: Withdrawal of Cash by Owner

Taylor withdraws $600 in cash from FastForward for personal living expenses. A proprietorship's distribution of cash, or other assets, to its owner is called a *withdrawal.* This decrease in owner's equity is not an expense. Withdrawals are not expenses because they are not part of the company's earnings process. Since withdrawals are not expenses, they are not used in calculating net income.

	Assets				= Liabilities		+ Owner's Equity
	Cash	+ Accounts Receivable	+ Supplies	+ Equipment	= Accounts Payable	+ Note Payable	+ C.Taylor, Capital
Old Bal.	$9,000	+ $ 0	+ $3,600	+ $26,000	= $1,100	+ $5,100	+ $32,400
(11)	− 600						− 600 Withdrawal
New Bal.	$8,400	+ $ 0	+ $3,600	+ $26,000	= $1,100	+ $5,100	+ $31,800
		$38,000				$38,000	

Summary of Transactions

FastForward engaged in transactions with five major entities: the owner, suppliers, an employee, customers, and the landlord. We identify the specific transactions by number with the specific entity in Exhibit 2.13.

We also summarize in Exhibit 2.14 the effects of all eleven transactions of FastForward using the accounting equation. Three points should be noted. First, the accounting equation remains in balance after each transaction. Second, transactions can be analyzed

Exhibit 2.13

FastForward's Transactions
Grouped by Entities

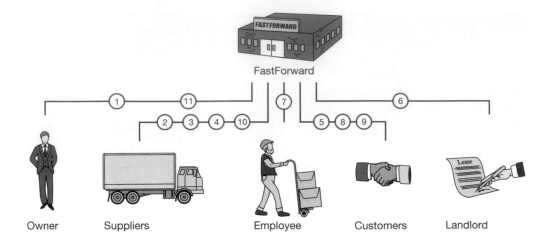

by their effects on components of the accounting equation. For example, total assets and
equity increased by equal amounts in transactions 1, 5, and 8. In transactions 2, 3, and
9, one asset increased while another decreased by equal amounts. For transaction 4, we
see equal increases in assets and liabilities. Both assets and equity decrease by equal
amounts in transactions 6, 7, and 11. In transaction 10, we see equal decreases in an asset and a liability. Third, the equality of effects in the accounting equation is crucial to
the double-entry accounting system. We discuss this system in the next chapter.

Exhibit 2.14

Summary of transactions using
the Accounting Equation

		Assets			= Liabilities		+ Owner's Equity	
	Cash	+ Accounts Receivable	+ Supplies	+ Equipment	= Accounts Payable	+ Note Payable	+ C.Taylor, Capital	
(1)	$30,000						$30,000	Investment
(2)	− 2,500		+$2,500					
Bal.	$27,500		$2,500				$30,000	
(3)	−20,000			+$20,000				
Bal.	$ 7,500		$2,500	$20,000			$30,000	
(4)			+1,100	+ 6,000	+$1,100	+ $6,000		
Bal.	$ 7,500		$3,600	$26,000	$1,100	$6,000	$30,000	
(5)	+ 2,200						+$2,200	Consulting Revenue
Bal.	$ 9,700		$3,600	$26,000	$1,100	$6,000	$32,200	
(6)	− 1,000						− 1,000	Rent Expense
Bal.	$ 8,700		$3,600	$26,000	$1,100	$6,000	$31,200	
(7)	− 700						− 700	Salary Expense
Bal.	$ 8,000		$3,600	$26,000	$1,100	$6,000	$30,500	
(8)		+$1,900					+ 1,600	Consulting Revenue
							+ 300	Rental Revenue
Bal.	$ 8,000	$1,900	$3,600	$26,000	$1,100	$6,000	$32,400	
(9)	+ 1,900	−1,900						
Bal.	$ 9,900	$ 0	$3,600	$26,000	$1,100	$6,000	$32,400	
(10)	− 900					− 900		
Bal.	$ 9,000	$ 0	$3,600	$26,000	$1,100	$5,100	$32,400	
(11)	− 600						− 600	Withdrawal
Bal.	$ 8,400	+$ 0	+$3,600	+ $26,000	= $1,100	+ $5,100	+ $31,800	

Flash *back*

12. Why is the revenue recognition principle important?

13. Identify a transaction decreasing both assets and liabilities.

14. When is the accounting equation in balance and what does it mean?

Answers—p. 64

We described financial statements at the beginning of this chapter. These statements are required under GAAP. In this section we show how financial statements are prepared from business transactions. Recall that the four major financial statements and their purposes are:

1. *Income statement* describes a company's revenues and expenses along with the resulting net income or loss over a period of time. It helps explain how owner's equity changes during a period due to earnings activities.

2. *Statement of changes in owner's equity* explains changes in equity due to items such as net income and an owner's investments and withdrawals over a period of time.

3. *Statement of cash flows* identifies cash inflows (receipts) and outflows (payments) over a period of time. It explains how the cash balance on the balance sheet changed from the beginning to the end of a period.

4. *Balance sheet* describes a company's financial position (assets, liabilities, and equity) at a point in time.

We now show how to prepare these financial statements using the transactions of Fast-Forward.

Financial Statements

P1 Prepare financial statements from business transactions.

Income Statement

FastForward's income statement is shown at the top of Exhibit 2.17. It is prepared from the December transactions of Fast-Forward. These transactions and information about revenues and expenses are conveniently taken from the owner's equity column of Exhibit 2.14.

Revenues of $4,100 are reported first on the income statement. They include consulting revenues of $3,800 resulting from transactions 5 and 8, and rental revenue of $300 from transaction 8. Pie charts shown in Exhibits 2.15 and 2.16 are often helpful in analyzing the makeup of revenues and expenses. If FastForward earned other kinds of revenues, they would be shown separately to help users better understand the company's activities.

Expenses follow revenues. We can list expenses in different ways. For convenience in this chapter, we list larger amounts first. Rent and salary expenses are from transactions 6 and 7. Expenses help users interpret events of the time period. Net income is reported at the bottom and is the amount earned during December. Owner's investments and withdrawals are *not* part of measuring income.

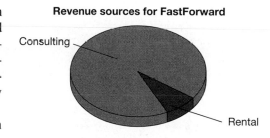

Revenue sources for FastForward

Exhibit 2.15

Pie Chart Analysis of Revenues

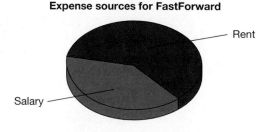

Expense sources for FastForward

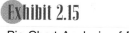

Exhibit 2.16

Pie Chart Analysis of Expenses

Exhibit 2.17

Financial Statements and Their Links

FASTFORWARD
Income Statement
For Month Ended December 31, 1997

Revenues:		
Consulting revenue	$3,800	
Rental revenue	300	
Total revenues		$4,100
Expenses:		
Rent expense	1,000	
Salaries expense	700	
Total expenses		1,700
Net income		$2,400

FASTFORWARD
Statement of Changes in Owner's Equity
For Month Ended December 31, 1997

C.Taylor, capital, December 1, 1997		$ 0
Plus: Investment by owner	$30,000	
Net income	2,400	32,400
Total		$32,400
Less: Withdrawal by owner		(600)
C.Taylor, capital, December 31, 1997		$31,800

FASTFORWARD
Balance Sheet
December 31, 1997

Assets		Liabilities	
Cash	$ 8,400	Accounts payable	$ 1,100
Supplies	3,600	Note payable	5,100
Equipment	26,000	Total liabilities	$ 6,200
		Owner's Equity	
		C.Taylor, capital	31,800
		Total liabilities and	
Total assets	$38,000	owner's equity	$38,000

FASTFORWARD
Statement of Cash Flows
For Month Ended December 31, 1997

Cash flows from operating activities:		
Cash received from clients	$ 4,100	
Cash paid for supplies	(2,500)	
Cash paid for rent	(1,000)	
Cash paid to employee	(700)	
Net cash used by operating activities		$ (100)
Cash flows from investing activities:		
Purchase of equipment	(20,000)	
Net cash used by investing activities		(20,000)
Cash flows from financing activities:		
Investment by owner	30,000	
Partial repayment of note	(900)	
Withdrawal by owner	(600)	
Net cash provided by financing activities		28,500
Net increase in cash		$ 8,400
Cash balance, December 1, 1997		0
Cash balance, December 31, 1997		$ 8,400

Statement of Changes in Owner's Equity

The statement of changes in owner's equity reports information about changes in equity over the reporting period. This statement shows beginning equity, events that increase it (investments by owner and net income), and events that decrease it (withdrawals and net loss). Ending owner's equity is computed from this statement and is carried over and reported on the balance sheet.

The second report in Exhibit 2.17 is the statement of changes in owner's equity for FastForward. Its heading lists the month of December 1997 because this statement describes events that happened during that month. The beginning balance of equity is measured as of the start of business on December 1. It is zero only because FastForward did not exist before then. An existing business reports the beginning balance as of the end of the prior reporting period (such as November 30). FastForward's statement shows $30,000 of equity is created by Taylor's initial investment. It also shows the $2,400 of net income earned during the month. This item links the income statement to the statement of changes in owner's equity. The statement also reports Taylor's $600 withdrawal and FastForward's $31,800 equity balance at the end of the month.

Balance Sheet

FastForward's balance sheet is the third report listed in Exhibit 2.17. Its heading tells us the statement refers to FastForward's financial condition at the close of business on December 31, 1997.

The left side of the balance sheet lists FastForward's assets: cash, supplies, and equipment. The right side of the balance sheet shows FastForward owes $6,200 to creditors. This is made up of $1,100 for accounts payable and $5,100 for a note payable. If any other liabilities had existed (such as a bank loan) they would be listed here. The equity section shows an ending balance of $31,800. Note the link between the ending balance from the statement of changes in owner's equity and the equity balance here.

Supplier

You open your own wholesale business selling home entertainment equipment to small retail outlets. You quickly find that most of your potential customers demand to buy on credit. How can you use the balance sheet in deciding which customers you extend credit to?

You Make the Call

Answer—p. 63

Statement of Cash Flows

The final report in Exhibit 2.17 is FastForward's statement of cash flows. This statement describes where Fast-Forward's cash came from and where it went during December. It also shows the amount of cash at the beginning of the period and the amount left at the end. This information is important for users because a company must

carefully manage cash if it is to survive and grow. **Delta Air Lines** reported net losses of more than $1.3 billion for the three-year period ending June 30, 1994. But Delta avoided bankruptcy by carefully managing its cash by delaying spending, increasing borrowings, and issuing stock. Delta earned a profit of $408 million in 1995 and $156 million in 1996.

Cash Flows from Operating Activities

The first section of the statement of cash flows reports cash flows from *operating activities*. The $4,100 of cash received from customers equals total revenue on the income statement only because FastForward collected all of its revenues in cash. If some credit sales are not collected, or if credit sales from a prior period are collected this period, the amount of cash received from customers will not equal the revenues reported on the income statement for this period.

This section also lists cash paid for supplies, rent, and salaries. These cash flows are from transactions 2, 6, and 7. We put these amounts in parentheses to indicate they are subtracted. Amounts for rent and salaries equal the expenses on FastForward's income statement because it paid expenses in cash. The payment for supplies is an operating activity because they are expected to be used up in short-term operations.

Cash used by operating activities for December is $100. If cash received exceeded cash paid for operating activities, we would call it "cash from operating activities." Decision makers are especially interested in the operating section of the statement of cash flows. This information allows users to answer questions such as how much of operating income is in the form of cash.

Cash Flows from Investing Activities

The second section of the statement of cash flows describes *investing activities*. Investing activities involve the buying and selling of assets such as land and equipment that are held for long-term use in the business. FastForward's only investing activity is the $20,000 purchase of equipment in transaction 3.

Decision makers are interested in this section of the statement because it describes how a company is preparing for its future. If it is spending cash on productive assets, it should be able to grow. But a user is also concerned that a company does not overly spend on productive assets and face a cash shortage. If a company is selling its productive assets, it is downsizing its operations.

Cash Flows from Financing Activities

The third section of this statement shows cash flows related to *financing activities*. Financing activities include borrowing and repaying cash from lenders, and cash investments or withdrawals by the owner. The statement of cash flows in Exhibit 2.17 shows FastForward received $30,000 from Chuck Taylor's initial investment in transaction 1. If the business had borrowed cash, that amount would appear here as an increase in cash. The financing section also shows $900 paid for the note to CalTech Supply from transaction 10 and the $600 owner withdrawal in transaction 11. The total effect of financing activities was a $28,500 net inflow of cash. The financing section shows us why FastForward did not run out of cash even though it spent $20,000 on assets and used $100 in its operating activities. Namely, it used the owner's investment and a note from a supplier. Decision makers are interested in the financing section because excessive borrowing can burden a company and reduce its potential for growth.

The final part of the statement of cash flows is the net increase or decrease in cash. It shows FastForward increased its cash balance by $8,400 in December. Because it started with no cash, the ending balance is also $8,400. This ending amount is the link from the statement of cash flows to the balance sheet. We give a more detailed explanation of the statement of cash flows in Chapter 17.

Flash back

15. Explain the link between an income statement and the statement of changes in owner's equity.

16. Describe the link between a balance sheet and the statement of changes in owner's equity.

17. Discuss the three major sections of the statement of cash flows.

Answers—p. 64

USING THE INFORMATION   Return on Equity

A2 Compute return on equity and use it to analyze company performance.

An important reason for recording and reporting information about assets, liabilities, equity, and income is to help an owner judge the company's success compared to other business or personal opportunities. One measure of success is the **return on eq-**

uity ratio. This ratio is computed by taking net income for a period and dividing it by average owner's equity as shown in Exhibit 2.18.

$$\text{Return on equity} = \frac{\text{Net income}}{\text{Average owner's equity}}$$

Exhibit 2.18

Return on Equity

Chuck Taylor's return on equity is computed as:

$$\text{Return on equity} = \frac{\$2,400}{[\$30,000 + \$31,800] \div 2} = 7.8\%$$

This shows Taylor earned a return on equity of 7.8% for the month of December.[15]

Taylor's return for December is very high compared to most investments, especially for the first month of operations. But we must remember that net income for a proprietorship does not include an expense for the effort exerted by the owner in managing its operations. To take this into consideration, we compute a **modified return on equity** for proprietorships and partnerships. This modified return on equity reduces net income by the value of the owner's efforts and is computed as shown in Exhibit 2.19.

$$\text{Modified return on equity} = \frac{\text{Net income} - \text{Value of owner's efforts}}{\text{Average owner's equity}}$$

Exhibit 2.19

Modified Return on Equity

Other employment opportunities suggest that Taylor's efforts are valued at $1,800 per month. Taylor's modified return on equity is then computed as:

$$\text{Modified return on equity} = \frac{\$2,400 - \$1,800}{[\$30,000 + \$31,800] \div 2} = 1.9\%$$

This modified return for Taylor of 1.9% per month is quite different from the 7.8% above.

Taylor compares this return with other opportunities to determine whether it is adequate. Examples of other opportunities are savings accounts, government bonds, and company stock. Because 1.9% per month is more than 20% per year,[16] it is likely Taylor will continue to operate FastForward. For further comparison, we graph in Exhibit 2.20 the return on equity for seven different industries. FastForward's return exceeds each of these.

Three additional points need mention. First, an evaluation of returns should also recognize risk. Risk can differ considerably across investment alternatives. Second, income can vary from month to month. Income variation is related to risk. Third, because of company, business, and economic fluctuations, a better measure of return is obtained by computing it over a longer period such as one year.

---

[15] A simple average equals the sum of beginning and ending equity balances divided by two, or [$30,000 + $31,800] ÷ 2. Since this is the company's first month of operations, we use the owner's initial investment as its beginning balance.

[16] The annual rate is approximated by taking the 1.9% monthly rate and multiplying by the 12 months in a year, or 22.8%.

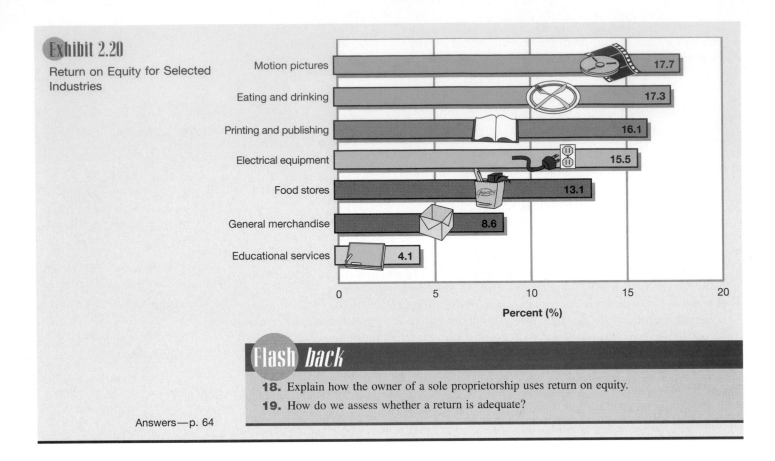

Exhibit 2.20

Return on Equity for Selected Industries

Flash back

18. Explain how the owner of a sole proprietorship uses return on equity.

19. How do we assess whether a return is adequate?

Answers—p. 64

Summary

C1 Identify and explain the content and reporting aims of financial statements. The major financial statements are: income statement, balance sheet, statement of changes in owner's equity, and statement of cash flows. An income statement shows a company's profitability including revenues, expenses, and net income (loss). A balance sheet reports on a company's financial position including assets, liabilities, and owner's equity. A statement of changes in owner's equity explains how owner's equity changes from the beginning to the end of a period, and the statement of cash flows identifies all cash inflows and outflows for the period.

C2 Describe differences in financial statements across forms of business organization. One important difference is in the equity section of the balance sheet. Proprietorship and partnership balance sheets list the equity balance beside the owner's name. Names of a corporation's shareholders are not listed in a balance sheet. Another difference is with the term used to describe distributions by a business to its owners. When an owner of a proprietorship or a partnership takes cash or other assets from a company, the distributions are called *withdrawals*. When owners of a corporation receive cash or other assets from a company, the distributions are called *dividends*. Recording payments to managers when managers are also owners is another difference. When the owner of a proprietorship or partnership is its manager, no salary expense is reported. But since a corporation is a separate legal entity, salaries paid to its managers are always reported as expenses on its income statement.

C3 Explain the financial reporting environment. Accounting professionals prepare financial statements, independent auditors often examine them and prepare an audit report, and users rely on them for making important decisions. Preparers use GAAP to decide what procedures are most appropriate for accounting for business transactions and events, and for proper reporting of statements. GAAS guide auditors in deciding on the audit procedures useful in determining whether financial statements comply with GAAP. Applying both GAAP and GAAS helps ensure that financial statements include relevant, reliable, and comparable information for users.

C4 Identify those responsible for setting accounting and auditing principles. The FASB is the primary authoritative source of GAAP. The FASB draws its authority from two major sources: the SEC and state boards that license CPAs. Authority for GAAS belongs to the ASB. The SEC is an important source of the ASB's authority.

C5 Identify, explain, and apply accounting principles. Accounting principles aid in producing relevant, reliable, and comparable information. The general principles described in this chapter include: business entity, objectivity, cost, going-concern, monetary unit, and revenue recognition. We will discuss others in later chapters. The business entity principle means that a business is accounted for separately from its owner. The objectivity principle means information is supported by independent, objective evidence. The cost principle means financial statements are based on actual costs incurred in business transactions. The monetary unit principle assumes transactions and events can be captured in money terms and that the monetary unit is stable over time. The going-concern principle means financial statements reflect an assumption that the business will continue to operate. The revenue recognition principle means revenue is recognized when earned, that assets received from selling products and services do not have to be in cash, and that revenue recognized is measured by cash received plus the cash equivalent (market) value of other assets received.

A1 **Analyze business transactions using the accounting equation.** A transaction is an exchange of economic consideration between two parties. Examples of economic considerations include products, services, money, and rights to collect money. Because two different parties exchange assets and liabilities, transactions affect the components of the accounting equation. The accounting equation is: Assets = Liabilities + Owner's equity. Business transactions always have at least two effects on the components of the accounting equation. The equation is always in balance when business transactions are properly recorded.

A2 **Compute return on equity and use it to analyze company performance.** Return on equity is computed as net income divided by average owner's equity. A modified return on equity for proprietorships and partnerships, that values the owner's efforts, is often useful and is computed as net income less the value of the owner's efforts and this quantity divided by average owner's equity. Return should be compared with other investment alternatives and opportunities to determine whether it is adequate. We should remember that net income can fluctuate and is a source of risk.

P1 **Prepare financial statements from business transactions.** Business transactions can be summarized using the accounting equation. Once transaction data are organized by the accounting equation we can readily prepare financial statements. The balance sheet uses the ending balances in the accounting equation at a point in time. The statement of changes in owner's equity and the income statement use data from the owner's equity account for the period. The statement of cash flows uses the numbers in the cash account for the period.

Guidance Answers to **You Make the Call**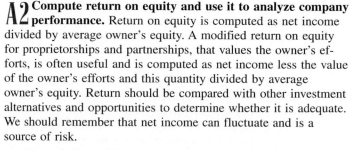

Chef

A chef's efforts are often reflected in the income statement. This statement reports information on the revenues and expenses associated with operating activities. If operating activities are successful and you can point to specific contributions such as increased sales or reduced expenses, then you are much more likely to be successful in getting a wage increase.

Supplier

We can use the accounting equation to help us identify risky customers to whom we would not want to extend credit. The accounting equation is: Assets = Liabilities + Owner's equity. A balance sheet provides us with amounts for each of these key components. The lower owner's equity is, the less likely you should be to extend credit. A low owner's equity means there is little value in the business that does not already have claims on it from other creditors.

Guidance Answers to Flash backs

1. The four major financial statements are: income statement, balance sheet, statement of changes in owner's equity, and statement of cash flows.

2. Revenues are inflows of assets in exchange for products or services provided to customers as part of the primary operations of a business. Expenses are outflows or the using up of assets that result from providing products or services to customers.

3. Assets are the resources owned by a business. Liabilities are the obligations of a business, representing the claims of others against the assets of a business. Equity is the owner's claim on the assets of the business after deducting liabilities.

4. Three differences are: (*a*) A proprietorship's balance sheet lists the equity balance beside the owner's name. Partnerships use the same approach, unless there are too many owners for listing purposes. Names of a corporation's owners, or shareholders, are not listed in the balance sheet. (*b*) Distributions of cash or other assets to owners of a proprietorship or partnership are called withdrawals. Distributions of cash or other assets to owners of a corporation are called dividends. (*c*) When the owner of a single proprietorship is also its manager, no salary expense is reported on the income statement. The same is true for a partnership. But salaries paid to a corporation's managers are always reported as expenses on its income statement.

5. The FASB sets GAAP. Its most notable decisions are reported in *Statements of Financial Accounting Standards*. The FASB draws authority from two main sources: the SEC and state boards that license CPAs.

6. GAAS refer to generally accepted auditing standards and are the guidelines for performing audits of financial statements. GAAS are set by the Auditing Standards Board (ASB).

7. U.S. companies with international operations are not directly affected by international accounting standards. International standards are put forth as preferred accounting practices. However, there is growing pressure by stock exchanges and other parties to narrow differences in worldwide accounting practices. International accounting standards are playing an important role in that process.

8. Users desire information about the performance of a specific entity. If information is mixed between two or more entities, its usefulness decreases. It is important for the usefulness of accounting that the business entity principle be followed.

9. The objectivity principle means that financial statement information is supported by independent, unbiased evidence. The cost principle means financial statements are based on actual costs incurred in business transactions. The objectivity and cost principles are related in that most users consider information based on cost as objective. Information prepared using both principles is considered highly reliable and often relevant.

10. A transaction that changes the makeup of assets would not affect any liability and equity accounts. Both transactions 2 and 3 offer examples. Each involves exchanging one asset for another asset.

11. Earning revenue by performing services for a customer, such as in transaction 5, increases the owner's equity (and assets). Incurring expenses while servicing clients, such as in transactions 6 and 7, decreases the owner's equity (and assets). Other examples include owner investments that increase equity, and owner withdrawals that decrease equity.

12. The revenue recognition principle gives preparers guidelines on when to recognize (record) revenue. This is important since if revenue is recognized too early, the income statement reports net income sooner than it should and the business looks more profitable than it is. If revenue is recognized too late, the income statement shows lower amounts of revenue and net income than it should and the business looks less profitable than it is. In both cases the income statement is less useful to users.

13. Payment of a liability with an asset reduces both asset and liability totals. An example is transaction 10 where a note payable is reduced by paying cash.

14. The accounting equation is: Assets = Liabilities + Owner's equity. This equation is always in balance, both before and after every transaction. *Balance* refers to the equality in this equation and it is always maintained.

15. An income statement presents a company's revenues and expenses along with the resulting net income or loss. A statement of changes in owner's equity shows changes in equity, including net income. Also, both statements report transactions occurring over a period of time.

16. A balance sheet describes a company's financial position (assets, liabilities, and equity) at a point in time. The owner's equity account in the balance sheet is obtained from the statement of changes in owner's equity.

17. The statement of cash flows reports cash inflows and outflows in three sections: operating, investing, and financing activities. Cash flows from operating activities include revenues and expenses from the primary business the company is engaged in. Cash flows from investing activities involve transactions from the buying and selling of assets. Cash flows from financing activities include borrowing cash or other assets from lenders and the investments or withdrawals of the owner. The net figure in the statement of cash flows is the increase or decrease in cash for the business over the period. This net figure links the statement of cash flows to the balance sheet.

18. An owner of a proprietorship uses return on equity to measure the success of the business. This return is compared to alternative investment opportunities an owner could engage in. If the owner also works in the business, a modified return on equity is appropriate. This modified return subtracts the value of the owner's effort from net income in the numerator of the return on equity formula.

19. The return should be compared with other investment alternatives to determine whether it is adequate. Investment alternatives include savings accounts, government bonds, stocks, and other business ventures. These alternatives should be compared on the basis of both return and risk.

Demonstration Problem

After several months of planning, Barbara Schmidt started a haircutting business called The Cutlery. The following events occurred during its first month:

a. On August 1, Schmidt put $3,000 cash into a checking account in the name of The Cutlery. She also invested $15,000 of equipment that she already owned.

b. On August 2, she paid $600 cash for furniture for the shop.

c. On August 3, she paid $500 cash to rent space in a strip mall for August.

d. On August 4, she purchased some new equipment for the shop that she bought on credit for $1,200. This amount is to be repaid in three equal payments at the end of August, September, and October.

e. On August 5, The Cutlery opened for business. Receipts from services provided for cash in the first week and a half of business (ended August 15) were $825.

f. On August 15, Schmidt provided haircutting services on account for $100.

g. On August 17, Schmidt received a $100 check for services previously rendered on account.

h. On August 17, Schmidt paid $125 to an assistant for working during the grand opening.

i. Cash receipts from services provided during the second half of August were $930.

j. On August 31, Schmidt paid an installment on the account payable.

k. On August 31, she withdrew $900 cash for her personal use.

Required

1. Arrange the following asset, liability, and owner's equity titles in a table similar to the one in Exhibit 2.14: Cash, Accounts Receivable, Furniture, Store Equipment, Accounts Payable, and Barbara Schmidt, Capital. Show the effects of each transaction on the equation. Explain each of the changes in owner's equity.

2. Prepare an income statement for August.

3. Prepare a statement of changes in owner's equity for August.

4. Prepare a balance sheet as of August 31.

5. Prepare a statement of cash flows for August.

6. Determine the return on equity ratio for August.

7. Determine the modified return on equity ratio for August, assuming that Schmidt's management efforts were worth $1,000.

Planning the Solution

- Set up a table with the appropriate columns, including a final column for describing the events that affect owner's equity.
- Analyze each transaction and show its effects as increases or decreases in the appropriate columns. Be sure the accounting equation remains in balance after each transaction.
- To prepare the income statement, find the revenues and expenses in the last column. List those items on the statement, calculate the difference, and label the result as *net income* or *net loss.*
- Use the information in the Explanation of Change column to prepare the statement of changes in owner's equity.
- Use the information in the last row of the table to prepare the balance sheet.
- To prepare the statement of cash flows, include all events listed in the Cash column of the table. Classify each cash flow as operating, investing, or financing. Follow the example in Exhibit 2.17.
- Calculate the return on equity by dividing net income by the average equity. Calculate the modified return by subtracting the $1,000 value of Schmidt's efforts from the net income, and then dividing the difference by the average equity.

Solution to Demonstration Problem

1.

	Cash	+	Accounts Receivable	+	Furni-ture	+	Store Equip-ment	=	Accounts Payable	+	Barbara Schmidt, Capital	Explanation of Change
			Assets					=	**Liabilities +**		**Owner's Equity**	
a.	$3,000						$15,000				$18,000	Investment
b.	− 600				+$600							
Bal.	$2,400				$600		$15,000				$18,000	
c.	− 500										− 500	Rent Expense
Bal.	$1,900				$600		$15,000				$17,500	
d.							I 1,200		+$1,200			
Bal.	$1,900				$600		$16,200		$1,200		$17,500	
e.	+ 825										+ 825	Haircutting Services Revenue
Bal.	$2,725				$600		$16,200		$1,200		$18,325	
f.			+$100								+ 100	Haircutting Services Revenue
Bal.	$2,725		$100		$600		$16,200		$1,200		$18,425	
g.	+ 100		− 100									
Bal.	$2,825		$ 0		$600		$16,200		$1,200		$18,425	
h.	− 125										− 125	Salaries Expense
Bal.	$2,700		$ 0		$600		$16,200		$1,200		$18,300	
i.	+ 930										+ 930	Haircutting Services Revenue
Bal.	$3,630				$600		$16,200		$1,200		$19,230	
j.	− 400								− 400			
Bal.	$3,230				$600		$16,200		$800		$19,230	
k.	− 900										− 900	Withdrawal
Bal.	$2,330 +				$600 +		$16,200 =		$800 +		$18,330	

2.

THE CUTLERY Income Statement For Month Ended August 31		
Revenues:		
Haircutting services revenue		$1,855
Operating expenses:		
Rent expense	$500	
Salaries expense	125	
Total operating expenses		625
Net income		$1,230

3.

THE CUTLERY Statement of Changes in Owner's Equity For Month Ended August 31		
Barbara Schmidt, capital, August 1		$ 0
Plus: Investments by owner	$18,000	
Net income	1,230	19,230
Total		$19,230
Less withdrawals by owner		(900)
Barbara Schmidt, capital, August 31		$18,330

4.

THE CUTLERY Balance Sheet August 31			
Assets		**Liabilities**	
Cash	$ 2,330	Accounts payable	$ 800
Furniture	600	**Owner's Equity**	
Store equipment	16,200	Barbara Schmidt, capital	18,330
		Total liabilities and	
Total assets	$19,130	owner's equity	$19,130

5.

THE CUTLERY Statement of Cash Flows For Month Ended August 31		
Cash flows from operating activities:		
Cash received from customers	$1,855	
Cash paid for rent	(500)	
Cash paid for wages	(125)	
Net cash provided by operating activities		$1,230
Cash flows from investing activities:		
Cash paid for furniture		(600)
Cash flows from financing activities:		
Cash received from owner	$3,000	
Cash paid to owner	(900)	
Repayment of debt	(400)	
Net cash provided by financing activities		1,700
Net increase in cash		$2,330
Cash balance, August 1		0
Cash balance, August 31		$2,330

6.

$$\text{Return on equity} = \frac{\text{Net income}}{\text{Average owner's equity}} = \frac{\$1,230}{\$18,165} = \mathbf{6.77\%}$$

Average owner's equity is ($18,000 + $18,330)/2 = $18,165

7.

$$\text{Modified return on equity} = \frac{\text{Net income} - \text{Owner's efforts}}{\text{Average owner's equity}} = \frac{\$230}{\$18,165} = \mathbf{1.27\%}$$

Glossary

Accounting equation a description of the relation between a company's assets, liabilities, and equity; expressed as Assets = Liabilities + Owner's equity; also called the *balance sheet equation*. (p. 50).

Account payable a liability created by buying goods or services on credit. (p. 42).

Account receivable an asset created by selling products or services on credit. (p. 41).

Assets resources owned or controlled by the business; more precisely, resources with an ability to provide future benefits to the business. (p. 41).

Auditing Standards Board (ASB) the authoritative committee of the AICPA that identifies generally accepted auditing standards. (p. 46).

Balance sheet a financial statement providing information that helps users understand a company's financial status; lists the types

and dollar amounts of assets, liabilities, and equity as of a specific date; also called the *statement of financial position*. (p. 40).

Balance sheet equation another name for the accounting equation. (p. 50).

Business entity principle the principle that requires every business to be accounted for separately from its owner or owners; based on the goal of providing relevant information about each business separately to users. (p. 48).

Business transaction an economic event that changes the financial position of an organization; often takes the form of an exchange of economic consideration (such as goods, services, money, or rights to collect money) between two parties. (p. 48).

Continuing-concern principle another name for the *going-concern principle*. (p. 48).

Contributed capital the category of equity created by shareholders' investments; also called *paid-in capital*. (p. 44).

Cost principle the accounting principle that requires financial statement information to be based on actual costs incurred in business transactions; it requires assets and services to be recorded initially at the cash or cash equivalent amount given in exchange. (p. 48).

Creditors individuals or organizations entitled to receive payments from a company. (p. 42).

Debtors individuals or organizations that owe money to a business. (p. 41).

Dividends distributions of assets by a corporation to its owners. (p. 44).

Equity owner's claim on the assets of a business; more precisely, the residual interest in the assets of an entity that remains after deducting its liabilities; also called *net assets*. (p. 42).

Expenses outflows or the using up of assets as a result of the primary operations of a business. (p. 40).

Financial statements the most important products of accounting; include the balance sheet, income statement, statement of changes in owner's equity, and the statement of cash flows. (p. 38).

Generally accepted auditing standards (GAAS) rules adopted by the accounting profession as guides for conducting audits of financial statements. (p. 45).

Going-concern principle rule that requires financial statements to reflect the assumption that the business will continue operating, unless evidence shows it will not continue; also called *continuing-concern principle*. (p. 49).

Income statement a financial statement in which expenses are subtracted from revenues to show whether the business earned a profit; it lists the types and amounts of revenues earned and expenses incurred by a business over a period of time; also called *profit and loss statement*. (p. 39).

International Accounting Standards Committee (IASC) a committee that attempts to create more harmony among the accounting practices of different countries by identifying preferred practices and encouraging their worldwide acceptance. (p. 47).

Liabilities debts owed by a business or organization; claims by others that will reduce the future assets of a business or require services or products. (p. 42).

Modified return on equity the ratio of net income minus the value of owner's effort to average owner's equity. (p. 61).

Monetary unit principle the expression of transactions and events in money units; examples include units such as the dollar, peso, and pound sterling. (p. 49).

Net assets another name for equity. (p. 42).

Net income the excess of revenues over expenses for a period. (p. 39).

Net loss the excess of expenses over revenues for a period. (p. 39).

Note payable a liability expressed by a written promise to make a future payment at a specific time. (p. 42).

Objectivity principle accounting guideline that requires financial statement information to be supported by independent, unbiased evidence rather than someone's opinion; objectivity adds to the reliability, verifiability, and usefulness of information. (p. 48).

Paid-in capital another name for contributed capital. (p. 44).

Retained earnings shareholders' equity that results from a corporation's profits that have not been distributed to shareholders. (p. 44).

Return on equity ratio of net income to average stockholders' equity; used to judge a business's success compared to other activities or investments. (p. 60).

Revenue recognition principle provides guidance on when revenue should be reflected on the income statement; the rule includes three guidelines: (1) revenue must be recognized at the time it is earned; (2) the inflow of assets associated with revenue may be in a form other than cash; and (3) the amount of revenue is measured as the cash plus the cash equivalent value of any noncash assets received from customers in exchange for goods or services. (p. 53).

Revenues inflows of assets received in exchange for goods or services provided to customers as part of the major or primary operations of the business. (p. 39).

Statement of cash flows a financial statement that describes where a company's cash came from (receipts) and where it went during a period (payments); cash flows are arranged by an organization's activities: operating, investing, and financing. (p. 43).

Statement of changes in owner's equity reports the changes in equity over the reporting period; beginning equity is adjusted for increases (owner investment and net income) and for decreases (owner withdrawals and net loss). (p. 40).

Statement of financial position another name for the balance sheet. (p. 40).

Statements of Financial Accounting Standards (SFAS) the publications of the FASB that establish generally accepted accounting principles in the United States. (p. 46).

Withdrawal a payment of cash or other assets from a proprietorship or partnership to its owner or owners. (p. 44).

Questions

1. What information is reported in an income statement?
2. What do accountants mean by the term *revenue?*
3. Why does the user of an income statement need to know the time period that it covers?
4. What information is reported in a balance sheet?
5. Define *(a)* assets, *(b)* liabilities, *(c)* equity, and *(d)* net assets.
6. Identify two categories of accounting principles.
7. What FASB pronouncements identify generally accepted accounting principles?

8. What does the objectivity principle require for information reported in financial statements? Why?

9. A business shows office stationery on the balance sheet at its $430 cost, although it cannot be sold for more than $10 as scrap paper. Which accounting principle justifies this treatment?

10. Why is the revenue recognition principle needed? What does it require?

11. What events or transactions change owner's equity?

12. Identify the four main financial statements that a business reports to its owners and other users.

13. What should a company's return on equity ratio be compared with to determine whether the owner has made a good investment?

14. Find the financial statements of **NIKE,** in Appendix A. To what level of significance are the dollar amounts rounded? What time period does the income statement cover?

15. Review the balance sheet of **Reebok** in Appendix A. What is the amount of total assets reported at December 31, 1996? Prove the accounting equation for Reebok for December 31, 1996.

16. Find **America Online's** income statement in Appendix A. How is the name of this statement different from FastForward's income statement? How does AOL's 1996 net income compare to the previous year's?

17. Review **FastForward's** financial statements presented in the chapter for the month ended December 31, 1997. Review the balance sheet and determine the business form Chuck Taylor has chosen to organize his business. How much cash did FastForward generate from the total of its operating, investing, and financing activities in December 1997?

In solving the assignment materials in this and later chapters, assume no income taxes unless they are specifically mentioned.

Identify the financial statement on which each of the following items appears:

a. Office supplies

b. Service fees earned

c. Cash received from customers

d. Owner, withdrawals

e. Office equipment

f. Accounts payable

g. Repayment of bank loan

h. Utilities expense

Quick Study

QS 2-1
Identifying financial statement items   C1

Identify which general accounting principle is best described by each of the following practices:

a. Tracy Regis owns Second Time Around Clothing and also owns Antique Accents, both of which are sole proprietorships. In preparing financial statements for Antique Accents, Regis should be sure that the expense transactions of Second Time Around are excluded from the statements.

b. In December, 2000, Classic Coverings received a customer's order to install carpet and tile in a new house that would not be ready for completion until March 2001. Classic Coverings should record the revenue for the order in March 2001, not in December 2000.

c. If $30,000 cash is paid to buy land, the land should be reported on the purchaser's balance sheet at $30,000.

QS 2-2
Identifying accounting principles

C5

Determine the missing amount for each of the following equations:

	Assets	=	Liabilities	+	Equity
a.	$ 75,000	=	$ 40,500	+	?
b.	$300,000	=	?	+	85,500
c.	?	=	$187,500	+	$95,400

QS 2-3
Applying the accounting equation

A1

Use the accounting equation to determine the:

a. Owner's equity in a business that has $374,700 of assets and $252,450 of liabilities.

b. Liabilities of a business having $150,900 of assets and $126,000 of owner's equity.

c. Assets of a business having $37,650 of liabilities and $112,500 of owner's equity.

QS 2-4
Applying the accounting equation A1

QS 2-5
Computing return on equity

A2

In a recent year's financial statements, **Boeing Company,** which is the largest aerospace company in the United States, reported the following:

Sales and other operating revenues	$21,924 million
Net income	856 million
Total assets	21,463 million
Total beginning-of-year equity	8,983 million
Total end-of-year equity	9,700 million

Calculate Boeing's return on equity.

Exercises

Exercise 2-1
Effects of transactions on accounting equation

A1

The table below shows the effects of five transactions *a* through *e* on the assets, liabilities, and equity of Pace Design. Write short descriptions of the probable nature of each transaction.

	Assets				= Liabilities + Owner's Equity	
	Cash +	Accounts + Receivable	Office + Supplies	Land	= Accounts + Payable	C. Pace Capital
	$7,500		$2,500	$14,500		$24,500
a.	−3,000			+3,000		
	$4,500		$2,500	$17,500		$24,500
b.			+ 400		+$400	
	$4,500		$2,900	$17,500	$400	$24,500
c.		+$1,050				+ 1,050
	$4,500	$1,050	$2,900	$17,500	$400	$25,550
d.	− 400				−400	
	$4,100	$1,050	$2,900	$17,500	$ 0	$25,550
e.	+1,050	−1,050				
	$5,150 +	$ 0 +	$2,900 +	$17,500 =	$ 0 +	$25,550

Exercise 2-2
Analysis using the accounting equation

A1

Carter Stark began a new consulting firm on January 3. The accounting equation showed the following balances after each of the company's first five transactions. Analyze the equations and describe each of the five transactions with their amounts.

		Assets			= Liabilities + Owner's Equity	
Trans-action	Cash +	Accounts Receivable +	Office Supplies +	Office Furniture =	Accounts Payable +	C. Stark, Capital
a.	$30,000	$ 0	$ 0	$ 0	$ 0	$30,000
b.	29,000	0	1,750	0	750	30,000
c.	21,000	0	1,750	8,000	750	30,000
d.	21,000	2,000	1,750	8,000	750	32,000
e.	20,500	2,000	1,750	8,000	750	31,500

Exercise 2-3
Computing net income

C1, C5

A business had the following amounts of assets and liabilities at the beginning and end of a recent year:

	Assets	Liabilities
Beginning of the year	$ 75,000	$30,000
End of the year	120,000	46,000

Determine the net income earned or net loss incurred by the business during the year under each of the following unrelated assumptions:

a. Owner made no additional investments in the business and withdrew no assets during the year.

b. Owner made no additional investments in the business during the year but withdrew $1,750 per month to pay personal living expenses.

c. Owner withdrew no assets during the year but invested an additional $32,500 cash.

d. Owner withdrew $1,750 per month to pay personal living expenses and invested an additional $25,000 cash in the business.

Linda Champion began a professional practice on May 1 and plans to prepare financial statements at the end of each month. During May, Champion completed these transactions:

a. Invested $50,000 cash along with equipment that had a $10,000 fair market value.

b. Paid $1,600 rent for office space for the month.

c. Purchased $12,000 of additional equipment on credit.

d. Completed work for a client and immediately collected the $2,000 cash earned.

e. Completed work for a client and sent a bill for $7,000 to be paid within 30 days.

f. Purchased $8,000 of additional equipment for cash.

g. Paid an assistant $2,400 as wages for the month.

h. Collected $5,000 of the amount owed by the client described in transaction *e*.

i. Paid for the equipment purchased in transaction *c*.

j. Withdrew $500 for personal use.

Required

Create a table like the one in Exhibit 2.14, using the following headings for columns: Cash; Accounts Receivable; Equipment; Accounts Payable; and L. Champion, Capital. Then, use additions and subtractions to show the effects of the transactions on the elements of the accounting equation. Show new totals after each transaction. Determine the modified return on Champion's initial investment, assuming that her management efforts during the month have a value of $3,000.

Exercise 2-4
Effects of transactions on accounting equation and computing return on equity

A1, A2

Check Figure Net income, $5,000

Seven pairs of changes in items of the accounting equation are described below in *a* through *g*. Provide an example of a transaction that creates the described effects.

a. Decreases a liability and increases a liability.

b. Increases an asset and decreases an asset.

c. Decreases an asset and decreases equity.

d. Increases a liability and decreases equity.

e. Increases an asset and increases a liability.

f. Increases an asset and increases equity.

g. Decreases an asset and decreases a liability.

Exercise 2-5
Effects of transactions on the accounting equation

A1

On November 1, Joseph Grayson organized a new consulting firm called The Grayson Group. On November 30, the company's records showed the following items. Use this information to prepare a November income statement for the business.

Exercise 2-6
Income statement

C1, P1

Cash	$12,000	Owner's withdrawals	$ 3,360
Accounts receivable	15,000	Consulting fees earned	15,000
Office supplies	2,250	Rent expense	2,550
Automobiles	36,000	Salaries expense	6,000
Office equipment	28,000	Telephone expense	660
Accounts payable	7,500	Miscellaneous expenses	680
Owner's investments	84,000		

Check Figure Net income, $5,110

Use the facts in Exercise 2-6 to prepare a November statement of changes in owner's equity for The Grayson Group.

Exercise 2-7
Statement of changes in owner's equity

C1, P1

Exercise 2-8
Balance
sheet C1, P1

Use the facts in Exercise 2-6 to prepare a November 30 balance sheet for The Grayson Group.

Exercise 2-9
Reporting financial
statement items
C1, P1

Match each of the numbered items below with the financial statement or statements on which it should be reported. Indicate your answer by writing the letter or letters for the correct statement in the blank space next to each item.

A. Income statement   **C.** Balance sheet
B. Statement of changes in owner's equity   **D.** Statement of cash flow

_____ **1.** Cash received from customers   _____ **5.** Accounts payable
_____ **2.** Office supplies   _____ **6.** Investments of cash by owner
_____ **3.** Rent expense incurred and paid in cash _____ **7.** Accounts receivable
_____ **4.** Consulting fees earned and received in cash _____ **8.** Cash withdrawals by owner

Exercise 2-10
Statement of changes in
owner's equity
C1, P1

Compute the amount of the missing item in each of the following separate cases a through d:

	a	b	c	d
Owner's equity, January 1	$ 0	$ 0	$ 0	$ 0
Owner's investments during the year	120,000	?	63,000	75,000
Owner's withdrawals during the year	?	(54,000)	(30,000)	(31,500)
Net income (loss) for the year	31,500	81,000	(9,000)	?
Owner's equity, December 31	102,000	99,000	?	85,500

Exercise 2-11
Accounting principles
C5, C3

Match each of the numbered descriptions below with the principle it best illustrates. Indicate your answer by writing the letter for the correct principle in the blank space next to each description.

A. General principle   **E.** Specific principle
B. Cost principle   **F.** Objectivity principle
C. Business entity principle **G.** Going-concern principle
D. Revenue recognition principle

_____ **1.** Requires every business to be accounted for separately from its owner or owners.

_____ **2.** Requires financial statement information to be supported by evidence other than someone's opinion or belief.

_____ **3.** Usually created by a pronouncement from an authoritative body.

_____ **4.** Requires financial statement information to be based on costs incurred in transactions

_____ **5.** Derived from long-used and accepted accounting practices.

_____ **6.** Requires financial statements to reflect the assumption that the business will continue operating.

_____ **7.** Requires revenue to be recorded only when the earnings process is complete.

Exercise 2-12
Return on equity
A2

Use information for each of the following separate cases a through d to calculate the company's return on equity and its modified return on equity:

	a	b	c	d
Average equity	$50,000	$800,000	$300,000	$572,800
Net income	10,800	216,000	91,500	177,930
Value of owner's efforts	4,400	100,000	66,000	150,000

Indicate the section in which each of the following cash flows would appear on the statement of cash flows.

A. Cash flow from operating activity   **C.** Cash flow from financing activity
B. Cash flow from investing activity

_____ **1.** Cash paid to suppliers   _____ **5.** Cash paid for rent
_____ **2.** Withdrawal by owner   _____ **6.** Investment by owner
_____ **3.** Cash paid to employee   _____ **7.** Repayment of note
_____ **4.** Purchase of equipment   _____ **8.** Cash received from customers

Exercise 2-13
Statement of cash flows

C1

George Hemphill started a new business called Hemphill Enterprises and completed the following transactions during its first month of operations:

a. Hemphill invested $60,000 cash along with office equipment valued at $30,000 in the business.
b. Paid $300,000 for a building to be used as an office. Paid $50,000 in cash and signed a note payable promising to pay the balance over several years.
c. Purchased $4,000 of office supplies for cash.
d. Purchased $36,000 of office equipment on credit.
e. Performed services and billed the client $4,000 to be received at a later date.
f. Paid a local newspaper $1,000 for an advertisement of the new business.
g. Performed services for a client and collected $18,000 cash.
h. Made a $2,000 payment on the equipment purchased in transaction d.
i. Received $3,000 from the client described in transaction e.
j. Paid $2,500 cash for the office secretary's wages.
k. Withdrew $1,800 cash from the company bank account to pay personal living expenses.

Required

Preparation Component

1. Create a table like the one in Exhibit 2.14, using the following headings for the columns: Cash; Accounts Receivable; Office Supplies; Office Equipment; Building; Accounts Payable; Notes Payable; and George Hemphill, Capital. Leave space for an explanation column to the right of the Capital column. Identify revenues and expenses by name in the explanation column.
2. Use additions and subtractions to show the transactions' effects on the elements of the accounting equation. Show new totals after each transaction. Indicate next to each change in the owner's equity whether it was caused by an investment, a revenue, an expense, or a withdrawal.
3. Once you have completed the table, determine the company's net income.

Analysis Component

4. Determine the return on Hemphill's average owner's equity. Also, assume Hemphill could have earned $6,000 for the period from another job and determine the modified return on equity for the period. State whether you think the business is a good use of Hemphill's money if an alternative investment would have returned 9% for the same period.

Problems
Problem 2-1
Analyzing effects of transactions and computing return on equity

C5, A1, A2

Check Figure Net income, $18,500

Kelly Young started a new business called Resource Consulting Co. and began operations on April 1. Young completed the following transactions during the month:

Apr. 1   Invested $60,000 cash in the business.
1   Rented a furnished office and paid $3,200 cash for April's rent.
3   Purchased office supplies for $1,680 cash.
5   Paid $800 cash for the month's cleaning services.
8   Provided consulting services for a client and immediately collected $4,600 cash.
12   Provided consulting services for a client on credit, $3,000.
15   Paid $850 cash for an assistant's salary for the first half of the month.
20   Received payment in full for the services provided on April 12.
22   Provided consulting services on credit, $2,800.
23   Purchased additional office supplies on credit, $1,000.

Problem 2-2
Preparing a balance sheet, an income statement, and a statement of changes in owner's equity

C1, A1, P1

28   Received full payment for the services provided on April 22.
29   Paid for the office supplies purchased on April 23.
30   Purchased advertising for $60 in the local paper. The payment is due May 1.
30   Paid $200 cash for the month's telephone bill.
30   Paid $480 cash for the month's utilities.
30   Paid $850 cash for an assistant's salary for the second half of the month.
30   Purchased insurance protection for the next 12 months (beginning May 1) by paying a $3,000 premium. Because none of this insurance protection had been used up, it was considered to be an asset called Prepaid Insurance.
30   Withdrew $1,200 cash from the business for personal use.

Required

1. Arrange the following asset, liability, and owner's equity titles in a table like Exhibit 2.14: Cash; Accounts Receivable; Prepaid Insurance; Office Supplies; Accounts Payable; and Kelly Young, Capital. Include an Explanation column for changes in owner's equity. Identify revenues and expenses by name in the explanation column.

2. Show effects of the transactions on the elements of the equation by recording increases and decreases in the appropriate columns. Do not determine new totals for the items of the equation after each transaction. Next to each change in owner's equity, state whether it was caused by an investment, a revenue, an expense, or a withdrawal. Determine the final total for each item and verify that the equation is in balance.

3. Prepare an income statement for April, a statement of changes in owner's equity for April, and an April 30 balance sheet.

Check Figure Ending owner's equity, $62,760

Problem 2-3
Computing net income, preparing a balance sheet, and calculating return on equity

CI, A2, PI

The accounting records of Goodall Delivery Services show the following assets and liabilities as of the end of 1999 and 2000:

	December 31	
	1999	2000
Cash	$ 52,500	$ 18,750
Accounts receivable	28,500	22,350
Office supplies	4,500	3,300
Trucks	54,000	54,000
Office equipment	138,000	147,000
Building		180,000
Land		45,000
Accounts payable	7,500	37,500
Notes payable		105,000

Late in December 2000 (just before the amounts in the second column were calculated), Travis Goodall, the owner, purchased a small office building and moved the business from rented quarters to the new building. The building and the land it occupies cost $225,000. The business paid $120,000 in cash and a note payable was signed for the balance. Goodall had to invest $35,000 cash in the business to enable it to pay the $120,000. The business earned a satisfactory net income during 2000, which enabled Goodall to withdraw $3,000 per month from the business for personal expenses.

Required

1. Prepare balance sheets for the business as of the end of 1999 and the end of 2000. (Remember that owner's equity equals the difference between assets and liabilities.)

2. By comparing owner's equity amounts from the balance sheets and using the additional information presented in this problem, prepare a calculation to show how much net income was earned by the business during 2000.

Check Figure Modified return on equity, 6.3%

3. Calculate the 2000 return on equity for the business. Also, calculate the modified return on equity assuming that Goodall's efforts were worth $40,000 for the year.

Stan Frey started a new business and completed these transactions during November:

Nov. 1 Stan Frey transferred $56,000 out of a personal savings account to a checking account in the name of Frey Electrical Co.

1 Rented office space and paid cash for the month's rent of $800.

3 Purchased electrical equipment from an electrician who was going out of business for $14,000 by paying $3,200 in cash and agreeing to pay the balance in six months.

5 Purchased office supplies by paying $900 cash.

6 Completed electrical work and immediately collected $1,000 for doing the work.

8 Purchased $3,800 of office equipment on credit.

15 Completed electrical work on credit in the amount of $4,000.

18 Purchased $500 of office supplies on credit.

20 Paid for the office equipment purchased on November 8.

24 Billed a client $600 for electrical work completed; the balance is due in 30 days.

28 Received $4,000 for the work completed on November 15.

30 Paid the assistant's salary of $1,200.

30 Paid the monthly utility bills of $440.

30 Withdrew $700 from the business for personal use.

Required

Preparation Component

1. Arrange the following asset, liability, and owner's equity titles in a table like Exhibit 2.14: Cash; Accounts Receivable; Office Supplies; Office Equipment; Electrical Equipment; Accounts Payable; and Stan Frey, Capital. Leave space for an explanation column to the right of Stan Frey, Capital. Identify revenues and expenses by name in the explanation column.

2. Use additions and subtractions to show the effects of each transaction on the items in the equation. Show new totals after each transaction. Next to each change in owner's equity, state whether the change was caused by an investment, a revenue, an expense, or a withdrawal.

3. Use the increases and decreases in the last column of the table from part 2 to prepare an income statement and a statement of changes in owner's equity for the month. Also prepare a balance sheet as of the end of the month.

4. Calculate the return on average owner's equity for the month.

Analysis Component

5. Assume the investment transaction on November 1 was $40,000 instead of $56,000 and that Frey obtained the $16,000 difference by borrowing it from a bank. Explain the effect of this change on total assets, total liabilities, owner's equity, and return on equity.

The following financial statement information is known about five unrelated companies:

	Company A	Company B	Company C	Company D	Company E
December 31, 1999:					
Assets	$45,000	$35,000	$29,000	$80,000	$123,000
Liabilities	23,500	22,500	14,000	38,000	?
December 31, 2000:					
Assets	48,000	41,000	?	125,000	112,500
Liabilities	?	27,500	19,000	64,000	75,000
During 2000:					
Owner investments	5,000	1,500	7,750	?	4,500
Net income	7,500	?	9,000	12,000	18,000
Owner withdrawals	2,500	3,000	3,875	0	9,000

Problem 2-4
Analyzing transactions, preparing financial statements, and calculating return on equity

C1, A1, A2, P1

Check Figure Ending owner's equity, $58,460

Problem 2-5
Calculating missing information using accounting knowledge

C1, A1

Required

1. Answer the following questions about Company A:
   a. What was the owner's equity on December 31, 1999?
   b. What was the owner's equity on December 31, 2000?
   c. What was the amount of liabilities owed on December 31, 2000?
2. Answer the following questions about Company B:
   a. What was the owner's equity on December 31, 1999?
   b. What was the owner's equity on December 31, 2000?
   c. What was the net income for 2000?
3. Calculate the amount of assets owned by Company C on December 31, 2000.
4. Calculate the amount of owner investments in Company D made during 2000.
5. Calculate the amount of liabilities owed by Company E on December 31, 1999.

Check Figure Co. C, Dec. 31, 2000, assets, $46,875

Problem 2-6
Identifying effects of transactions on financial statements

C1, A1

Identify how each of the following transactions affects the company's financial statements. For the balance sheet, identify how each transaction affects total assets, total liabilities, and owner's equity. For the income statement, identify how each transaction affects net income. For the statement of cash flows, identify how each transaction affects cash flows from operating activities, cash flows from financing activities, and cash flows from investing activities. If there is an increase, place a "+" in the column or columns. If there is a decrease, place a "−" in the column or columns. If there is both an increase and a decrease, place a "+/−" in the column or columns. The line for the first transaction is completed as an example.

		Balance Sheet			Income Statement	Statement of Cash Flows		
	Transaction	Total Assets	Total Liab.	Owner's Equity	Net Income	Operating	Financing	Investing
1	Owner invests cash	+		+			+	
2	Perform services for cash							
3	Purchase services on credit							
4	Pay wages with cash							
5	Owner withdraws cash							
6	Borrow cash with note payable							
7	Perform services on credit							
8	Buy office equipment for cash							
9	Collect cash on receivable from (7)							
10	Buy asset with note payable							

A new business, Do You Copy, has the following beginning cash balance and cash flows for the month of December:

Cash balance, December 1	$ 0
Withdrawals by owner	500
Cash received from customers ..	4,000
Repayment of debt	1,000
Cash paid for store supplies	2,600
Purchase of equipment	21,000
Cash paid for rent	2,000
Cash paid to employee	800
Investment by owner	32,000

Required

Prepare a statement of cash flows for Do You Copy for the month of December.

Problem 2-7
Preparing a statement of cash flows

C1, P1

Check Figure Cash bal., Dec. 31, $8,100

BEYOND THE NUMBERS

NIKE designs, produces, markets, and sells sports footwear and apparel. The financial statements and other information from NIKE's May 31, 1997, annual report are included in Appendix A at the end of the book. Use information from that report to answer the following questions:

1. Examine NIKE's consolidated balance sheet. To what level are the dollar amounts rounded?
2. What is the closing date of NIKE's most recent annual reporting period?
3. What amount of net income did NIKE earn for the fiscal year ended May 31, 1997?
4. How much cash (and equivalents) did NIKE hold at fiscal year-end May 31, 1997?
5. What was the net amount of cash provided by the company's operating activities during fiscal year ended May 31, 1997?
6. Did the company's investing activities for fiscal year ended May 31, 1997, create a net cash inflow or outflow? What was the amount of the net flow?
7. Compare fiscal year-end 1997's results to 1996's results to determine whether the company's total revenues increased or decreased. What was the amount of the increase or decrease?
8. What was the change in the company's net income between fiscal year-end 1997 and 1996?
9. What amount was reported as total assets at fiscal year-end 1997?
10. Calculate the return on equity that NIKE achieved for the fiscal year ended May 31, 1997.

Swoosh Ahead

11. Obtain access to NIKE's annual report for fiscal years ending after May 31, 1997. You can gain access to NIKE's annual report at its web site [www.nike.com] or through the SEC's EDGAR database [www.sec.gov]. Recompute NIKE's return on equity with the updated annual report information you obtain. Compare the May 31, 1997, fiscal year-end return on investment to any subsequent year's return you are able to calculate. Also compare how NIKE's total assets, total revenues, and net income have changed since May 31, 1997.

Reporting in Action

C1, A2

Comparative Analysis

A2

Reebok

Both **NIKE** and **Reebok** design, produce, market, and sell sports footwear and apparel. Key comparative figures ($ millions) for these two organizations follow:

Key figures	NIKE	Reebok
Beginning equity	$2431.4	$895.3
Ending equity	$3155.8	$381.2
Net income	$ 795.8	$139.0

Required

1. What is the return on equity for (a) NIKE and (b) Reebok?
2. Is return on equity satisfactory for (a) NIKE and (b) Reebok if competitors average a 26% return?
3. Would it be appropriate to calculate the modified return on equity for Reebok and Nike?
4. What can you conclude about NIKE and Reebok from these computations?

Ethics Challenge

C5

BJ Crist is a new entry-level accountant for a mail order company that specializes in supplying skateboards and accessories for the sport. At the end of the fiscal period, BJ is advised by a supervisor to include as revenue for the period any orders that have been charged by phone but not yet fulfilled by shipping the product. BJ is also advised to include as revenue any orders received by mail with checks enclosed that are also pending fulfillment.

Required

1. Identify relevant accounting principles that BJ should be aware of in view of the supervisor's instructions.
2. What are the ethical factors in this situation?
3. Would you recommend that Crist follow the supervisor's directions?
4. What alternatives might be available to Crist other than following the supervisor's directions?

Communicating in Practice

Understanding and using financial information is important in a wide range of careers. You are to obtain a copy of the article, "Why Neil Simon Decided to Turn His Back on Broadway" by Donald G. McNeil, Jr., *The New York Times,* November 21, 1994, pp. C9 and C13. After reading the article, prepare a brief written report that includes responses to the following questions.

1. How does this article illustrate the importance for Neil Simon, a playwright, of understanding financial statements?
2. Summarize and explain the financial considerations that brought Neil Simon and his producer to the conclusion it was a financially wise decision to produce off-Broadway. Do you agree with their conclusion? Why or why not?
3. Using the figures in the article, at what point does the decision to produce off-Broadway prove less profitable than the alternative one? Explain.

Taking It to the Net

C1, C5

Access the **Reebok** Web site (**http://www.Reebok.com**). After you arrive at Reebok's home page, click on the *company* hotlink. This link should take you to http://www.Reebok.com/company/company.html. Now click on *REEBOK CHARTER*.

Required

1. What does Reebok identify as its greatest asset in the Charter?
2. Using your knowledge of accounting principles write a brief memo listing reasons why Reebok has not included this "greatest asset" on its balance sheet.

This activity is aimed at generating a team discussion of business transactions. Understanding transactions provides the necessary background for dealing with more complex transactions later in the book.

Required

1. Each team member should write down as many different transactions they can think of that fall into one of the following categories:
   a. Transactions affecting assets.
   b. Transactions affecting liabilities.
   c. Transactions affecting owner's equity but not affecting revenues and expenses.
   d. Transactions affecting revenues and/or expenses.
2. Team members should exchange lists and write down the analysis of each transaction on the list received.
3. Each team member is to report the analysis in part 2 to other team members. If all members of the team agree with the analysis presented, they should proceed to other transactions and team members' reports. If there is disagreement, team members should discuss differences and consult the book in reaching a decision. If the discussion does not result in agreement, team members should consult the instructor.

Teamwork in Action
C5, A1

Use the **Edgar database [http://www.sec.gov]** and obtain the toll-free 800 number of a company that you are interested in learning more about. Once you have obtained the 800 number call the company and ask to speak to the Investor Relations department. Request a copy of that company's most recent annual report from the Investor Relations phone representative. You should receive the requested report within 1-3 weeks. Once you have received your report consult it throughout the term to see the principles you are learning in the classroom applied in practice.

Hitting the Road
C1

Business Week periodically publishes a ranking of the top 1,000 businesses in the world based on market performance. This issue contains charts labeled BUSINESS WEEK GLOBAL 1000. Obtain the most recent publication of this issue.

Business Week Activity
A2

Required

1. Is the company that is ranked number 1 in the world a United States company?
2. Of the top 10 global businesses, how many are United States companies?
3. What is the return on equity for the number 1 company in the world?
4. What is the industry of the number 1 company in the world?

Analyzing and Recording Transactions

A Look Back

We explained the value of accounting in the information age. We showed how financial statements, prepared according to accounting principles, communicate useful information. We also analyzed and prepared financial statements from transactions.

A Look at This Chapter

This chapter focuses on the accounting process. We describe transactions and source documents as inputs for analysis. We explain analysis and recording of transactions for preparing financial statements. T-accounts, postings, ledgers, and trial balances are shown as useful tools in carrying out these important steps.

A Look Ahead

Chapter 4 extends our focus on processing information. We explain the importance of adjusting accounts and procedures in preparing financial statements.

Chapter Outline

Spinning an Accounting Web

HOUSTON—Maria Sanchez's second year on the job was nearly her last. She was working as a staff accountant for a small medical center where she was assigned to payroll and accounts receivable. In late December of her second year, she was instructed to add 1% to all employees' end-of-year paychecks as a bonus. Instead, she keyed an extra zero and gave everyone a 10% bonus. "The controller was furious," says Sanchez. "To top it off, the employees were so grateful that the controller and board couldn't do anything but keep quiet, accept the error, and congratulate everyone."

Today, Sanchez accepts blame for the error. But it wasn't always that way. "I still partly blame our accounting technology. It was awful," says Sanchez. It was this experience that led Sanchez to add technology skills to her accounting background. While taking evening classes in computing, Sanchez became convinced that accounting packages could be more user friendly. She also foresaw the power of the Web.

Sanchez, 29, is now the owner of **RecordLink,** an accounting software firm that provides recordkeeping services for small businesses. It is unique in that it relies on the Web. This means there is no need for software purchases or special computing hardware requirements for small business. Clients link into her Web servers for their computing needs.

The convenience of clients having access to their accounting information anytime, anywhere, is attracting new clients. "We offer 24-hour accounting and computing advice, and we are expanding our software options to include strategic planning, budget analyses, and other sophisticated programs that few small businesses can individually afford." RecordLink spreads these costs over all its clients.

Sanchez sees recordkeeping services for small business as a lucrative and underserved market. She plans to expand her business to Dallas and San Antonio by year-end. So far, her creativity has been a hit with clients. Last year, RecordLink's revenues went over $850,000. Adds Sanchez, "Not bad for a high-tech recordkeeper!"

Learning Objectives

Conceptual

C1 Explain the steps in processing transactions.

C2 Describe source documents and their purpose.

C3 Describe an account and its use in recording information about transactions.

C4 Describe a ledger and a chart of accounts.

C5 Define debits and credits and explain their role in double-entry accounting.

Analytical

A1 Analyze the impact of transactions on accounts and financial statements.

A2 Compute the debt ratio and describe its use in analyzing company performance.

Procedural

P1 Record transactions in a journal and post entries to a ledger.

P2 Prepare and explain the use of a trial balance.

CHAPTER PREVIEW

The accounting process is crucial to producing useful financial information. We explained in Chapter 2 how the accounting equation (Assets = Liabilities + Equity) helps us understand and analyze transactions and events. In this chapter we describe how transactions are processed and how their effects are recorded in accounts. All accounting systems use procedures similar to those described here. These procedures are important steps leading to financial statements. Maria Sanchez of **RecordLink** uses a Web-based system, but the accounting procedures are essentially identical for manual systems.

We begin by describing how source documents provide crucial information about transactions. We then describe accounts and explain their purpose. Debits and credits are introduced and identified as valuable tools in helping us understand and process transactions. This background then enables us to describe the process of recording events in a journal and posting them to a ledger. We return to transactions of **FastForward,** first introduced in Chapter 2, to illustrate many of these procedures. We conclude the chapter by describing how to use a company's debt ratio to assess its risk.

Transactions and Documents

 **C1** Explain the steps in processing transactions.

We explained in Chapter 1 how accounting provides information to help people make better decisions. This information is the result of an accounting process that captures business transactions and events, analyzes and records their effects, and summarizes and prepares information in reports and financial statements. These reports and statements are used for making investing, lending, and other important decisions. We illustrate the steps in the accounting process in Exhibit 3.1.

Transactions and events are the starting points in the accounting process. Relying on source documents, we analyze transactions and events using the accounting equation to understand how they affect organization performance and financial position. These effects are recorded in accounting records, informally referred to as the *accounting books,* or simply the *books.* Additional processing steps such as posting and preparing a trial balance help us summarize and classify the effects of transactions and events. A final step in the accounting process is to provide information in useful reports or financial statements to decision makers. We begin our overview of the accounting process with a discussion of transactions and events.

Transactions and Events

Business activities can be described in terms of transactions and events. We know from Chapter 2 that business transactions are exchanges of economic consideration between two parties. We also know that the accounting equation is affected by transactions and events.

Exhibit 3.1

Accounting Process

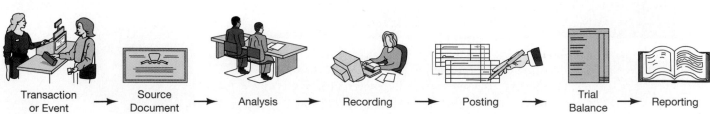

Transaction or Event → Source Document → Analysis → Recording → Posting → Trial Balance → Reporting

Transactions and events are the starting point in the accounting process. **External transactions** are exchanges between an organization and another person or organization. External transactions yield changes in the accounting equation. **Internal transactions** are exchanges within an organization. Internal transactions can also affect the accounting equation. One example is a company using equipment in its operating activities. As the equipment is used, its costs are reported as expenses.

Events are happenings that both affect an organization's financial position and can be reliably measured. These include financial events such as changes in the market value of certain assets and liabilities, and natural events such as floods and fires that destroy assets and create losses. The analysis and recording of events are explained in the next chapter.

Source Documents

Organizations use various documents when doing business. **Source documents,** or *business papers,* identify and describe transactions and events entering the accounting process. They are the sources of accounting information and can be in either hard copy or electronic form. Examples are sales tickets, checks, purchase orders, charges to customers, bills from suppliers, employee earnings records, and bank statements.

When we buy an item on credit, the store usually prepares at least two copies of a sales invoice. One copy is given to you. Another is sent to the store's accounting department and gives rise to an entry in the information system to record a sale. This copy is often sent electronically. Also, for both cash and credit sales, the item is usually rung up on a register that records and stores the amount of each sale. Many registers record this information for each sale on a tape or electronic file locked inside the register. Total sales for a day or for any time period can be obtained immediately from these registers. This record is used as a source document for recording sales in the accounting records.

The accounting procedures when buying an item are part of an information system designed to ensure the accounting records include all transactions. They also help prevent mistakes and theft. To encourage employees to follow procedures such as these, stores often give discounts or free goods if a customer is not provided a receipt. This is part of internal control procedures.

C2 Describe source documents and their purpose.

Cashier

You are a cashier at a cash-and-carry retail store. When hired, the manager explained to you the policy of immediately ringing up each sale. Recently, lunch hour traffic has increased dramatically and the assistant manager asks you to avoid delays by taking customers' cash and making change without ringing up sales. The assistant manager says she will add up cash and ring up sales equal to the cash amount after lunch. She says that in this way the register will always be accurate when the manager arrives at three o'clock. What do you do?

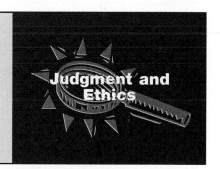

Answer—p. 109

Both buyers and sellers use sales invoices as source documents. Sellers use them for recording sales and for control purposes. Buyers use them for recording purchases and for monitoring purchasing activity. In both cases, a copy of the invoice is a source document.

Source documents, especially if obtained from outside the organization, provide objective evidence about both transactions and events, and their amounts. As we explained in the prior chapter, objective evidence is important because it makes information more reliable and useful.

There are still many accounting systems that require manual (pencil and paper) recording and processing of transaction data. These are mostly limited to small businesses. In today's information age, computers assist us in recording and processing data. Yet computers are only part of the process, and modern technology still demands human insight and understanding of transactions. In our discussion of the steps making up the accounting process, we use a manual system for presentation. The fundamental concepts of the manual system are identical to those of a computerized information system.

Flash *back*

1. Describe external and internal transactions.
2. Identify examples of accounting source documents.
3. Explain the importance of source documents.

Answers—p. 109

Accounts and Double-Entry Accounting

This section explains an *account* and its importance to accounting and business. We also describe several crucial elements that support an accounting system. These include ledgers, T-accounts, debits and credits, and double-entry accounting.

The Account

C3 Describe an account and its use in recording information about transactions.

An **account** is a detailed record of increases and decreases in a specific asset, liability, equity, revenue, or expense. Information is taken from accounts, analyzed, summarized, and presented in reports and financial statements useful for decision makers. A separate account is maintained for items of importance to information users. This means that separate accounts are kept for each important asset, liability, and equity item. It also means separate accounts are kept for important revenue and expense items. Important changes in owner's withdrawals and contributions are also captured in separate accounts.[1]

A **ledger** is a record containing all accounts used by a business. This is often in electronic form and is what we mean when we refer to the *books*. While most companies' ledgers contain similar accounts, there are often several accounts that are unique to a company because of its individual type of operations. Accounts are arranged into three general categories using the accounting equation as shown in Exhibit 3.2.

Exhibit 3.2

Accounting Equation

These accounts directly affect the preparation of financial reports and statements. The remainder of this section introduces accounts that are common to most organizations.

Asset Accounts

Assets are resources controlled by an organization that carry current and future benefits. Most accounting systems include separate accounts for the assets described here.

Cash

Increases and decreases in the amount of cash are recorded in a *Cash* account. A cash account includes money and any medium of exchange that a bank accepts for deposit. Examples are coins, currency, checks, money orders, and checking account balances.

Accounts Receivable

Products and services are often sold to customers in return for promises to pay in the future. These transactions are called *credit sales* or *sales on account*. The promises from buyers are called *accounts receivable* to sellers. Accounts receivable are increased by new credit sales and are decreased by customer payments. A company needs to know

---

[1] As an example of an account, see Exhibit 3.5 showing the Cash account for **FastForward.**

the amount currently due from each customer to send bills. A separate record for each customer's purchases and payments is necessary for this purpose. We describe the system for maintaining these records in Chapters 6 and 7. For now, we use the simpler practice of recording all increases and decreases in receivables in a single account called Accounts Receivable. The importance of accounts receivable, like many other accounts, depends on the nature of a company's operations as shown in this excerpt from practice:

ShowBiz Pizza Time's accounts receivable amount to less than 2% of its assets. In comparison, **NIKE**'s accounts receivable amount to more than 30% of its assets.

Notes Receivable

A **note receivable,** or **promissory note,** is a written promise to pay a definite sum of money on a specified future date(s). A company holding a promissory note signed by another party has an asset. This asset is recorded in a Notes Receivable account.

Prepaid Expenses

Prepaid Expenses is an asset account containing payments made for assets that are not used until later. As these assets are used up, the costs of these used assets become expenses. Common examples of prepaid expenses include office supplies, store supplies, prepaid insurance, prepaid rent, and advance payments for legal and accounting services. An asset's cost can be initially recorded as an expense *if* it is used up before the end of the period when statements are prepared. If an asset will not be used before the end of the reporting period, then its cost is recorded in an asset account. Prepaid expenses that are more crucial to the business are often accounted for in separate assets accounts. We describe three of the more common accounts: insurance, office supplies, and store supplies.

Prepaid Insurance

Insurance contracts provide us with protection against losses caused by fire, theft, accidents, and other events. An insurance policy often requires the fee, called a *premium,* to be paid in advance. Protection can be purchased for almost any time period, including month, year, or even several years. When an insurance premium is paid in advance, the cost is typically recorded in an asset account called *Prepaid Insurance.* Over time the expiring portion of the insurance cost is removed from this asset account and reported in expenses on the income statement. The unexpired portion remains in Prepaid Insurance and is reported on the balance sheet as an asset.

Office Supplies

All companies use office supplies such as stationery, paper, and pens. These supplies are assets until they are used. When they are used up, their cost is reported as an expense. The cost of unused supplies is an asset and is recorded in an Office Supplies account.

Store Supplies

Many stores keep supplies for wrapping and packaging purchases for customers. These include plastic and paper bags, gift boxes, cartons, and ribbons. The cost of these unused supplies is recorded in a Store Supplies account. Supplies are reported as expenses as they are used.

Equipment

Most organizations own computers, printers, desks, chairs, and other office equipment. Costs incurred to buy this equipment are recorded in an *Office Equipment* account. The costs of assets used in a store such as counters, showcases, and cash registers are recorded in a *Store Equipment* account.

Building

A building owned by an organization can provide space for a store, an office, a warehouse, or a factory. Buildings are assets because they provide benefits. Their costs are recorded in a Buildings account. When several buildings are owned, separate accounts are sometimes used for each of them.

Land

A Land account records the cost of land owned by a business. The cost of land is separated from the cost of buildings located on the land to provide more useful information in financial statements.

Liability Accounts

Liabilities are obligations to transfer assets or provide services to other entities. An organization often has several different liabilities, each represented by a separate account. The more common liability accounts are described here.

Accounts Payable

Purchases of merchandise, supplies, equipment, or services made by an oral or implied promise to pay later produce liabilities called *payables.* Accounting systems keep separate records about purchases from and payments to each creditor. We describe these individual records in Chapters 6 and 7. For now, we use the simpler practice of recording all increases and decreases in payables in a single account, Accounts Payable.

Notes Payable

When an organization formally recognizes a promise to pay by signing a *promissory note,* the resulting liability is a *note payable.* Its recording in either a Short-Term Notes Payable account or a Long-Term Notes Payable account depends on when it must be repaid. We explain details of account classification in Chapter 5.

Unearned Revenues

Chapter 2 explained that the *revenue recognition principle* requires revenues be reported on the income statement when earned. This principle means we must be careful with transactions where customers pay in advance for products or services. Because cash from these transactions is received before revenues are earned, the seller considers them **un-**  **earned revenues.** Unearned revenue is a liability that is satisfied by delivering products or services in the future. Examples of unearned revenue include magazine subscriptions collected in advance by a publisher, sales of gift certificates by stores, and rent collected in advance by a landlord. **Reader's Digest** reported unearned revenues of $408 million as of December 31, 1997.

When cash is received in advance for products and services, the seller records it in a liability account such as Unearned Subscriptions, Unearned Rent, or Unearned Professional Fees. When products and services are delivered, the now earned portion of the unearned revenues is transferred to revenue accounts such as Subscription Fees, Rent Earned, or Professional Fees.[2]

---

[2] There are variations in account titles in practice. As one example, Subscription Fees is sometimes called Subscription Fees Revenue, Subscription Fees Earned, or Earned Subscription Fees. As another example, Rent Earned is sometimes called Rent Revenue, Rental Revenue, or Earned Rent Revenue. We must use our good judgment when reading financial statements since titles can differ even within the same industry. For example, product sales are called revenues at **NIKE** and **K. Swiss,** but net sales at **Reebok** and **Converse.** The term *revenues* or *fees* is more commonly used with service businesses, and *net sales* or *sales* with product businesses.

Accrued Liabilities

Common accrued liabilities include wages payable, taxes payable, and interest payable. Each of these is often recorded in a separate liability account. If they are not large in amount, one or more of them may be added and reported as a single amount on the balance sheet.

> The liabilities section of **Harley-Davidson's** balance sheet at the end of 1997 included accrued liabilities of more than $160 million.

Equity Accounts

We described in the prior chapter the four types of transactions that affect owner's equity. They are (1) investments by the owner, (2) withdrawals by the owner, (3) revenues, and (4) expenses. We entered all equity transactions in a single column under the owner's name in Chapter 2. When we later prepared the income statement and the statement of changes in owner's equity, we reviewed the items in that column to classify them in financial statements.

A preferred approach is to use four separate accounts. They are: owner's capital, owner's withdrawals, revenues, and expenses. We show this visually in Exhibit 3.3 by expanding the accounting equation.

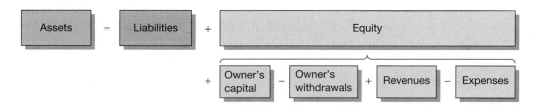

Exhibit 3.3
Expanded Accounting Equation

Information in these separate accounts is readily used to prepare financial statements without further analysis. We describe these four accounts below.

Owner's Capital

When a person invests in a proprietorship, the invested amount is recorded in an account identified by the owner's name and the title Capital. An account called *Chuck Taylor, Capital,* can be used to record Taylor's original investment in FastForward. Any further investments by the owner also are recorded in the owner's capital account.

Owner's Withdrawals

Owner's equity increases when a business earns income. The owner can leave this equity intact or can withdraw assets from the business. When the owner withdraws assets, perhaps to cover personal living expenses, the withdrawal decreases both the company's assets and owner's equity.

It is common for owners of proprietorships to withdraw regular weekly or monthly amounts of cash. We know that owners of proprietorships cannot receive salaries because they are not legally separate from their companies. Also, they cannot enter into salary (or any other) contracts with themselves. These withdrawals are neither income to the owners nor expenses of the business. They are simply the opposite of investments by owners.

Most accounting systems use an account with the name of the owner and the word *withdrawals* in recording withdrawals by the owner. An account called *Chuck Taylor, Withdrawals,* is used to record Taylor's withdrawals from FastForward. The owner's withdrawals account also is sometimes called the owner's *personal* account or *drawing* account.

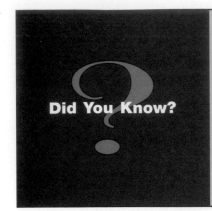

Revenues and Expenses

Decision makers often want information about revenues earned and expenses incurred for a period. Businesses use a variety of revenue and expense accounts to report this information on income statements. Different companies have different kinds of revenue and expense accounts reflecting their own important activities. Examples of revenue accounts are Sales, Commissions Earned, Professional Fees Earned, Rent Earned, and Interest Earned. Examples of expense accounts are Advertising Expense, Store Supplies Expense, Office Salaries Expense, Office Supplies Expense, Rent Expense, Utilities Expense, and Insurance Expense.

We can get an idea of the variety of revenues and expenses by looking at the *chart of accounts* near the end of this book. It lists accounts needed to solve some of the exercises and problems in the book.[3]

Ledger and Chart of Accounts

C4 Describe a ledger and a chart of accounts.

The actual recording of accounts can differ depending on the system. Computerized systems store accounts in files on electronic storage devices. Clients of **RecordLink,** as explained in the opening article, store their accounts on-line at another location. Manual systems often record accounts on separate pages in a special booklet. The collection of all accounts for an information system is called a ledger. If accounts are in files on a hard disk, those files are the ledger. If the accounts are pages in a booklet, then the booklet is the ledger. A ledger simply refers to the group of accounts.

A company's size and diversity of operations affect the number of accounts needed in its accounting system. A small company may get by with as few as 20 or 30 accounts, while a large company may need several thousand. The **chart of accounts** is a list of all accounts used by a company. The chart includes an identification number assigned to each account. Companies assign account identification numbers in an orderly manner. A small business might use the following numbering system for its accounts:

101–199	Asset accounts
201–299	Liability accounts
301–399	Owner's equity accounts
401–499	Revenue accounts
501–699	Expense accounts

[3] Different companies sometimes use different account titles than those in this book's chart of accounts. For example, a company might use Interest Revenue instead of Interest Earned, or Rental Expense instead of Rent Expense. It is only important that an account title describe the item it represents.

While this particular system provides for 99 asset accounts, a company may not use all of them. These numbers also provide a three-digit code that is useful in recordkeeping. In this case the first digit assigned to asset accounts is a 1, while the first digit assigned to liability accounts is a 2, and so on. The second and third digits also relate to the accounts' categories. A partial chart of accounts is shown below for FastForward.

Account Number	Account Name	Account Number	Account Name
101	Cash	301	C. Taylor, Capital
106	Accounts receivable	302	C. Taylor, Withdrawals
128	Prepaid insurance	403	Consulting revenue
125	Supplies	406	Rental revenue
167	Equipment	641	Rent expense
201	Accounts payable	622	Salaries expense
236	Unearned consulting revenue	690	Utilities expense
240	Note payable			

Ledger Bytes

What does technology mean for accounting information processing? **Sears Roebuck** provides an answer. For its annual financial plan, Sears at one time used a 100-square-foot flow chart with more than 300 steps. Using computing technology, this plan is now 25 steps on *one* 8½-by-11-inch sheet of paper! Technology also allows Sears' analysts to view and analyze budgets and financial plans on their PCs. Sears says it has slashed $100 million in costs. [Source: *Business Week*, October 28, 1996.]

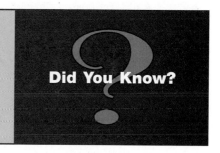

Did You Know?

T-Account

A **T-account** is a helpful tool in showing the effects of transactions and events on individual accounts. The T-account gets its name from its shape. Its shape looks like the letter "T" and is shown in Exhibit 3.4.

Account Title	
(Left side)	(Right side)
Debit	*Credit*

Exhibit 3.4

The T-Account

The format of a T-account includes (1) the account title on top, (2) a left, or debit, side, and (3) a right, or credit, side. A T-account provides one side for recording increases in the item and the other side for decreases. As we will discuss later, whether increases are recorded on the right or the left side depends on the type of account. The T-account for FastForward's Cash account after recording the transactions in Chapter 2 is shown in Exhibit 3.5.

Cash			
Investment by owner	30,000	Purchase of supplies	2,500
Consulting services revenue earned	2,200	Purchase of equipment	20,000
Collection of account receivable	1,900	Payment of rent	1,000
		Payment of salary	700
		Payment of note payable	900
		Withdrawal by owner	600

Exhibit 3.5

Cash T-Account for FastForward

Balance of an Account

An **account balance** is the difference between the increases and decreases recorded in an account. For example, the balance of a liability account is the amount owed on the date the balance is computed.

Putting increases on one side of an account and decreases on the other helps in computing an account's balance. To determine the balance, we start with the beginning balance and then (1) compute the total increases shown on one side, (2) compute the total decreases shown on the other side, and (3) subtract the sum of the decreases from the sum of the increases. The total increases in FastForward's Cash account are $34,100, the total decreases are $25,700, and the account balance is $8,400. The T-account in Exhibit 3.6 shows how we calculate the $8,400 balance.

Exhibit 3.6

Computing the Balance of a T-Account

Cash			
Investment by owner	30,000	Purchase of supplies	2,500
Consulting services revenue earned	2,200	Purchase of equipment	20,000
Collection of account receivable	1,900	Payment of rent	1,000
		Payment of salary	700
		Payment of note payable	900
		Withdrawal by owner	600
Total increases	**34,100**	Total decreases	**25,700**
Less decreases	**−25,700**		
Balance	8,400		

Debits and Credits

C5 Define debits and credits and explain their role in double-entry accounting.

The left side of a T-account is called the **debit** side, often abbreviated *Dr (or Db)*. The right side is called the **credit** side, abbreviated *Cr*.[4] To enter amounts on the left side of an account is to *debit* the account. To enter amounts on the right side is to *credit* the account. The difference between total debits and total credits for an account is the account balance. When the sum of debits exceeds the sum of credits, the account has a *debit balance*. It has a *credit balance* when the sum of credits exceeds the sum of debits. When the sum of debits equals the sum of credits, the account has a *zero balance*.

We must guard against the error of thinking that the terms *debit* and *credit* mean increase or decrease. Whether a debit is an increase or decrease depends on the account. Similarly, whether a credit is an increase or decrease depends on the account. But in every account, a debit and a credit have opposite effects. In an account where a debit is an increase, the credit is a decrease. And, in an account where a debit is a decrease, the credit is an increase. Identifying the account is the key to understanding the effects of debits and credits.

We must remember in working with T-accounts that a debit means an entry on the left side and a credit means an entry on the right side. To emphasize this, Exhibit 3.7 shows how Taylor's initial investment in FastForward is recorded in the Cash and Capital T-accounts:

Exhibit 3.7

Debits and Credits in T-Accounts

Cash			C.Taylor, Capital		
Investment	30,000			Investment	30,000

The cash increase is recorded on the *left side* of the Cash account with a $30,000 debit entry. The corresponding increase in owner's equity is recorded on the *right side* of the

---

[4] These abbreviations are remnants of 18th-century English recordkeeping practices where the terms *debitor* and *creditor* were used instead of *debit* and *credit*. The abbreviations use the first and last letters of these terms, just as we still do for Saint (St.) and Doctor (Dr.).

capital account with a $30,000 credit entry. This dual method of recording transactions on both the left and right sides is an essential feature of *double-entry accounting*, the topic of the next section.

4. Classify each of the following accounts as either an asset, liability, or equity: (a) Prepaid Rent, (b) Unearned Fees, (c) Building, (d) Retained Earnings, (e) Wages Payable, and (f) Office Supplies.

5. What is an account? What is a ledger?

6. What determines the number and types of accounts used by a company?

7. Does debit always mean increase and credit always mean decrease?

Answers—p. 109

Double-Entry Accounting

Double-entry accounting means every transaction affects and is recorded in at least two accounts. This means the *total amount debited must equal the total amount credited* for each transaction. Since each transaction is recorded with total debits equal to total credits, the sum of the debits for all entries must equal the sum of the credits for all entries. The sum of debit account balances in the ledger must equal the sum of credit account balances. The only reason the sum of debit balances would not equal the sum of credit balances is that an error has occurred. Double-entry accounting helps prevent errors by assuring that debits and credits for each transaction are equal.

The system for recording debits and credits follows from the accounting equation in Exhibit 3.8. Assets are on the left side of this equation. Liabilities and equity are on the right side. Two points are important here. First, like any mathematical relation, increases or decreases on one side have equal effects on the other side. For example, the net increase in assets must be accompanied by an identical net increase in the liabilities and equity side. Recall that some transactions only affect one side of the equation. This means that two or more accounts on one side are affected, but their net effect on this one side is zero. Second, we treat the left side as the *normal balance* side for assets, and the right side as the *normal balance* for liabilities and equity. This matches their layout in the accounting equation.

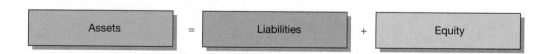

Exhibit 3.8
Accounting Equation

The normal debit balances of asset accounts and the normal credit balances of liability and equity accounts again follow from the accounting equation. This means that increases in asset accounts are recorded with debits, while increases in liability and equity accounts are recorded with credits. These important relations are captured in Exhibit 3.9.

Exhibit 3.9
Debit and Credit Effects for Accounts

Three important rules for recording transactions in a double-entry accounting system follow from the diagram in Exhibit 3.9:

1. Increases in assets are debits to asset accounts. Decreases in assets are credits to asset accounts.
2. Increases in liabilities are credits to liability accounts. Decreases in liabilities are debits to liability accounts.
3. Increases in owner's equity are credits to owner's equity accounts. Decreases in owner's equity are debits to owner's equity accounts.

We explained in Chapter 2 how owner's equity increases from owner's investments and revenues. We also described how owner's equity decreases from expenses and withdrawals. These important owner's equity relations are conveyed by expanding the accounting equation as shown in Exhibit 3.10.

Exhibit 3.10

Components of the Accounting Equation

Exhibit 3.11

Debit and Credit Effects for Component Accounts

We can extend Exhibit 3.10 to include debits and credits in double-entry form as shown in Exhibit 3.11.

Increases in capital or revenues increase owner's equity, while increases in withdrawals or expenses *decrease* owner's equity. These relations are reflected in the following important rules:

1. Investments are credited to owner's capital because they increase equity.
2. Withdrawals are debited to owner's withdrawals because they decrease equity.
3. Revenues are credited to revenue accounts because they increase equity.
4. Expenses are debited to expense accounts because they decrease equity.

Our understanding of these diagrams and rules is crucial to analyzing and recording transactions. It also helps us prepare and analyze financial statements.[5]

Marketing Manager
You are a company's marketing manager and you want to know your company's revenues for the current period. Financial statements are not yet available. Where do you direct your search for this information? Would the general journal or the ledger be more useful to you in getting revenue figures?

[Answer—p. 109]

[5] We can use good judgment to our advantage in applying double-entry accounting. For example, revenues and expenses normally (but not always) accumulate in business. This means they increase and rarely decrease during an accounting period. Accordingly, we should be alert to decreases in these accounts (such as debit revenues or credit expenses) to be certain this is our intent.

We return to the activities of **FastForward** to show how debit and credit rules and double-entry accounting are useful in analyzing and processing transactions. We analyze FastForward's transactions in two steps. Step one analyzes a transaction and its source document(s). Step two applies double-entry accounting to identify the impact of a transaction on account balances. We include in step two an analysis of statement links to identify the financial statements impacted by a transaction. Exhibit 3.13 shown later in this chapter summarizes these links. Three additional steps are necessary to fully process transactions. We identify and describe these three additional steps after we complete steps one and two.

We should study each transaction thoroughly before proceeding to the next transaction. The first 11 transactions are familiar to us from Chapter 2. We expand our analysis of these transactions and consider five other transactions (numbered 12 through 16) of FastForward that were omitted from Chapter 2.

Analyzing Transactions

A1 Analyze the impact of transactions on accounts and financial statements.

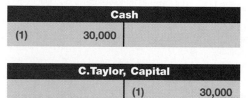

1. Investment by Owner

Cash	
(1) 30,000	

C. Taylor, Capital	
	(1) 30,000

Transaction. Chuck Taylor invests $30,000 in FastForward on December 1.
Analysis. Assets increase. Owner's equity increases.
Double-entry. Debit the Cash asset account for $30,000. Credit Taylor's Capital account in owner's equity for $30,000.
Statements affected.[6] BS, SCF, and SCOE

2. Purchase Supplies for Cash

Supplies	
(2) 2,500	

Cash	
(1) 30,000	(2) 2,500

Transaction. FastForward pays $2,500 cash for supplies.
Analysis. Assets increase. Assets decrease. This changes the composition of assets but does not change the total amount of assets.
Double-entry. Debit the Supplies asset account for $2,500. Credit the Cash asset account for $2,500.
Statements affected. BS and SCF

3. Purchase Equipment for Cash

Equipment	
(3) 20,000	

Cash	
(1) 30,000	(2) 2,500
	(3) 20,000

Transaction. FastForward pays $20,000 cash for equipment.
Analysis. Assets increase. Assets decrease. This changes the composition of assets but does not change the total amount of assets.
Double-entry. Debit the Equipment asset account for $20,000. Credit the Cash asset account for $20,000.
Statements affected. BS and SCF

4. Purchase Equipment and Supplies on Credit

Supplies	
(2) 2,500	
(4) 1,100	

Equipment	
(3) 20,000	
(4) 6,000	

Accounts Payable	
	(4) 1,100

Note Payable	
	(4) 6,000

Transaction. FastForward purchases $1,100 of supplies and $6,000 of equipment on credit. FastForward signs a promissory note for the $6,000 of equipment.
Analysis. Assets increase. Liabilities increase.
Double-entry. Debit two asset accounts: Supplies for $1,100 and Equipment for $6,000. Credit two liability accounts: Accounts Payable for $1,100 and Note Payable for $6,000.
Statements affected. BS

---

[6] We use abbreviations for the statements: Income Statement (IS); Balance Sheet (BS); Statement of Cash Flows (SCF); and Statement of Changes in Owner's Equity (SCOE).

5. Provide Services for Cash

Cash

(1)	30,000	(2)	2,500
(5)	2,200	(3)	20,000

Consulting Revenue

		(5)	2,200

Transaction. FastForward provides consulting services to a customer and immediately collects $2,200 cash.
Analysis. Assets increase. Owner's equity increases from revenue.
Double-entry. Debit the Cash asset account for $2,200. Credit the Consulting Revenue account for $2,200 (this increases owner's equity).
Statements affected. BS, IS, SCF, and SCOE

6. Payment of Expense in Cash

Rent Expense

(6)	1,000		

Cash

(1)	30,000	(2)	2,500
(5)	2,200	(3)	20,000
		(6)	1,000

Transaction. FastForward pays $1,000 cash for December rent.
Analysis. Assets decrease. Owner's equity decreases from expense.
Double-entry. Debit the Rent Expense account for $1,000 (this decreases owner's equity). Credit the Cash asset account for $1,000.
Statements affected. BS, IS, SCF, and SCOE

7. Payment of Expense in Cash

Salaries Expense

(7)	700		

Cash

(1)	30,000	(2)	2,500
(5)	2,200	(3)	20,000
		(6)	1,000
		(7)	700

Transaction. FastForward pays $700 cash for employee's salary for the pay period ending on December 12.
Analysis. Assets decrease. Owner's equity decreases from expense.
Double-entry. Debit the Salaries Expense account for $700 (this decreases owner's equity). Credit the Cash asset account for $700.
Statements affected. BS, IS, SCF, and SCOE

8. Provide Consulting and Rental Services on Credit

Accounts Receivable

(8)	1,900		

Consulting Revenue

		(5)	2,200
		(8)	1,600

Rental Revenue

		(8)	300

Transaction. FastForward provides consulting services of $1,600 and rents test facilities for $300 to a customer (both services are part of FastForward's normal operations). The customer is billed $1,900 for the services and FastForward expects to collect this money in the near future.
Analysis. Assets increase. Owner's equity increases from revenue.
Double-entry. Debit the Accounts Receivable asset account for $1,900. Credit two revenue accounts: Consulting Revenue for $1,600 (this increases owner's equity) and Rental Revenue for $300 (this increases owner's equity).
Statements affected. BS, IS, and SCOE

9. Receipt of Cash on Account

Cash

(1)	30,000	(2)	2,500
(5)	2,200	(3)	20,000
(9)	1,900	(6)	1,000
		(7)	700

Accounts Receivable

(8)	1,900	(9)	1,900

Transaction. An amount of $1,900 is received from the client in transaction 8 on the 10th day after being billed for the services and facilities provided.
Analysis. Assets increase. Assets decrease. This changes the composition of assets but does not change the total amount of assets.
Double-entry. Debit the Cash asset account for $1,900. Credit Accounts Receivable asset account for $1,900.
Statements affected. BS and SCF

10. Partial Payment of Note Payable

Note Payable			
(10)	900	(4)	6,000

Cash			
(1)	30,000	(2)	2,500
(5)	2,200	(3)	20,000
(9)	1,900	(6)	1,000
		(7)	700
		(10)	900

Transaction. FastForward pays CalTech Supply $900 cash toward the note payable of $6,000 owed from the purchase of equipment in transaction 4.

Analysis. Assets decrease. Liabilities decrease.

Double-entry. Debit the Note Payable liability account for $900. Credit the Cash asset account for $900.

Statements affected. BS and SCF

11. Withdrawal of Cash by Owner

C.Taylor, Withdrawals			
(11)	600		

Cash			
(1)	30,000	(2)	2,500
(5)	2,200	(3)	20,000
(9)	1,900	(6)	1,000
		(7)	700
		(10)	900
		(11)	600

Transaction. Chuck Taylor withdraws $600 from FastForward for personal living expenses.

Analysis. Assets decrease. Owner's equity decreases.

Double-entry. Debit the owner's equity withdrawal account for $600. Credit the Cash asset account for $600.

Statements affected. BS, SCF, and SCOE

12. Receipt of Cash for Future Services

Cash			
(1)	30,000	(2)	2,500
(5)	2,200	(3)	20,000
(9)	1,900	(6)	1,000
(12)	3,000	(7)	700
		(10)	900
		(11)	600

Unearned Consulting Revenue			
		(12)	3,000

Transaction. FastForward enters into (signs) a contract with a customer to provide future consulting. FastForward receives $3,000 cash in advance of providing these consulting services.

Analysis. Assets increase. Liabilities increase. Accepting $3,000 cash obligates FastForward to perform future services and is a liability. No revenue is earned until services are provided.

Double-entry. Debit the Cash asset account for $3,000. Credit an Unearned Consulting Revenue liability account for $3,000.

Statements affected. BS and SCF

13. Pay Cash for Future Insurance Coverage

Prepaid Insurance			
(13)	2,400		

Cash			
(1)	30,000	(2)	2,500
(5)	2,200	(3)	20,000
(9)	1,900	(6)	1,000
(12)	3,000	(7)	700
		(10)	900
		(11)	600
		(13)	2,400

Transaction. FastForward pays $2,400 cash (premium) for a two-year insurance policy. Coverage begins on December 1.

Analysis. Assets increase. Assets decrease. This changes the composition of assets from cash to a "right" to insurance coverage. This does not change the total amount of assets. Expense is incurred as insurance coverage expires.

Double-entry. Debit the Prepaid Insurance asset account for $2,400. Credit the Cash asset account for $2,400.

Statements affected. BS and SCF

14. Purchase Supplies for Cash

Supplies	
(2)	2,500	
(4)	1,100	
(14)	120	

Cash			
(1)	30,000	(2)	2,500
(5)	2,200	(3)	20,000
(9)	1,900	(6)	1,000
(12)	3,000	(7)	700
		(10)	900
		(11)	600
		(13)	2,400
		(14)	120

Transaction. FastForward pays $120 cash for supplies.
Analysis. Assets increase. Assets decrease. This changes the composition of assets.
Double-entry. Debit the Supplies asset account for $120. Credit the Cash asset account for $120.
Statements affected. BS and SCF

15. Payment of Expense in Cash

Utilities Expense	
(15)	230	

Cash			
(1)	30,000	(2)	2,500
(5)	2,200	(3)	20,000
(9)	1,900	(6)	1,000
(12)	3,000	(7)	700
		(10)	900
		(11)	600
		(13)	2,400
		(14)	120
		(15)	230

Transaction. FastForward pays $230 cash for December utilities.
Analysis. Assets decrease. Owner's equity decreases from expense.
Double-entry. Debit the Utilities Expense account for $230 (this decreases owner's equity). Credit the Cash asset account for $230.
Statements affected. BS, IS, SCF, and SCOE

16. Payment of Expense in Cash

Salaries Expense	
(7)	700	
(16)	700	

Cash			
(1)	30,000	(2)	2,500
(5)	2,200	(3)	20,000
(9)	1,900	(6)	1,000
(12)	3,000	(7)	700
		(10)	900
		(11)	600
		(13)	2,400
		(14)	120
		(15)	230
		(16)	700

Transaction. FastForward pays $700 cash for employee's salary for the two-week pay period ending on December 26.
Analysis. Assets decrease. Owner's equity decreases from expense.
Double-entry. Debit the Salaries Expense account for $700 (this decreases owner's equity). Credit the Cash asset account for $700.
Statements affected. BS, IS, SCE, and SCOE

Accounting Equation Analysis

Exhibit 3.12 shows the accounts of FastForward after all 16 transactions are recorded and the balances computed. The accounts are grouped into three major columns.

These columns represent the terms in the accounting equation: assets, liabilities, and equity.

Exhibit 3.12 highlights several important points. First, as with each transaction, the totals for the three columns must obey the accounting equation: Assets = Liabilities + Equity. Specifically, assets equal $40,070 ($7,950 + $0 + $2,400 + $3,720 + $26,000); liabilities are $9,200 ($1,100 + $3,000 + $5,100); and equity is $30,870 ($30,000 − $600 + $3,800 + $300 − $1,000 − $1,400 − $230). These numbers obey the accounting equation: $40,070 = $9,200 + $30,870. Second, the withdrawals, revenue, and expense accounts reflect the events that change owner's equity. Their ending balances make up the statement of changes in owner's equity. Third, the revenue and expense account balances are summarized and reported in the income statement. Fourth, components of the cash account make up the elements reported in the statement of cash flows.

Exhibit 3.12

Ledger for FastForward

Assets			=	Liabilities			+	Owner's Equity		
Cash				**Accounts Payable**				**C. Taylor, Capital**		
(1)	30,000	(2)	2,500			(4)	1,100		(1)	30,000
(5)	2,200	(3)	20,000							
(9)	1,900	(6)	1,000	**Unearned Consulting Revenue**				**C. Taylor, Withdrawals**		
(12)	3,000	(7)	700			(12)	3,000	(11)	600	
		(10)	900							
		(11)	600					**Consulting Revenue**		
		(13)	2,400	**Note Payable**					(5)	2,200
		(14)	120	(10)	900	(4)	6,000		(8)	1,600
		(15)	230			Balance	5,100		Bal.	3,800
		(16)	700							
Total	37,100	Total	29,150					**Rental Revenue**		
	−29,150								(8)	300
Balance	7,950									
								Rent Expense		
Accounts Receivable								(6)	1,000	
(8)	1,900	(9)	1,900							
Balance	0							**Salaries Expense**		
								(7)	700	
Prepaid Insurance								(16)	700	
(13)	2,400							Balance	1,400	
Supplies								**Utilities Expense**		
(2)	2,500							(15)	230	
(4)	1,100									
(14)	120									
Balance	3,720									
Equipment										
(3)	20,000									
(4)	6,000									
Balance	26,000									

Accounts in this white area reflect increases and decreases in owner's equity. Their balances are reported on the income statement or the statement of changes in owner's equity.

$40,070	=	**$9,200**	+	**$30,870**

Financial Statement Links

Exhibit 3.13 extends the analysis and summarizes how transactions and their related accounts impact financial statements. Some transactions such as purchasing supplies on credit (no. 4) impact only one statement. Others such as receiving cash for services performed (no. 5) impacts all of the statements. We should review this exhibit and understand how transactions link to financial statements. We return to explain the details of these links in Chapter 5, including the adjusting and closing processes required.

Flash *back*

8. What kinds of transactions increase owner's equity? What kinds decrease owner's equity?

9. Why are most accounting systems called *double-entry?*

10. Double-entry accounting requires:

   a. All transactions that create debits to asset accounts must create credits to liability or owner's equity accounts.

   b. A transaction with a debit to a liability account must create a credit to an asset account.

   c. Every transaction to be recorded with total debits must equal total credits.

Answers—p. 109

		Balance Sheet (BS)								
Transactions		**Assets**				=	**Liabilities**		+	**Equity**
No.	Description	Cash +	Accts. Rec. +	Prepd. Insur. +	Supp. +	Equip. =	Accts. Pay. +	Unearned Rev. +	Note Pay. +	Taylor Capital
1	Owner investment	30,000				=			+	30,000
2	Purch. supp.	(2,500)			2,500	=			+	
3	Purch. equip.	(20,000)				20,000 =			+	
4	Credit purch.				1,100	6,000 =	1,100		6,000 +	
5	Services for cash	2,200				=			+	2,200
6	Rent exp.	(1,000)				=			+	(1,000)
7	Salary exp.	(700)				=			+	(700)
8	Services for credit		1,900			=			+	1,600 300
9	Cash rec'd. on Acct. Rec.	1,900	(1,900)			=			+	
10	Payment of Note Pay	(900)				=			(900) +	
11	Owner Withdrawals	(600)				=			+	(600)
12	Cash for future service	3,000				=		3,000	+	
13	Payment of future insur.	(2,400)		2,400		=			+	
14	Purch. supp.	(120)			120	=			+	
15	Util exp.	(230)				=			+	(230)
16	Salary exp.	(700)				=			+	(700)
	Total	7,950	0	2,400	3,720	26,000 =	1,100	3,000	5,100 +	30,870

We used double-entry accounting in the prior section to show how transactions affect accounts. This process of analyzing transactions and recording their effects directly in accounts is useful in understanding the accounting system. Yet accounting systems rarely record transactions directly in accounts. This is to avoid the potential for error and the difficulty in tracking mistakes.

Instead, the accounting process includes a *third step* where we record transactions in a journal before recording them in accounts. A **journal** gives us a complete record of each transaction in one place. It also links directly the debits and credits for each transaction. The process of recording transactions in a journal is called **journalizing.**

Step four of the accounting process is to transfer (or **post**) entries from the journal to the ledger. This step occurs only after debits and credits for each transaction are entered into a journal. This process leaves a helpful trail in checking for accuracy. It also helps us avoid errors. The process of transferring journal entry information to the ledger is called **posting.** This section describes both journalizing and posting of transactions. *Step five,* preparing a trial balance, is explained in the next section. Each of these steps in processing transactions is depicted in Exhibit 3.14.

Recording and Posting Transactions

P1 Record transactions in a journal and post entries to a ledger.

Income Statement (IS)			Statement of Cash Flows (SCF)				Transactions	
Rev. − Exp. = Net Inc.			Oper. + Cash Flow	Inv. + Cash Flow	Fin. + Cash Flow	= Net Cash Flow	No.	Description
−	=				30,000	= 30,000	1	Owner investment
−	=		(2,500)			= (2,500)	2	Purch. supp.
−	=			(20,000)		= (20,000)	3	Purch. equip.
−	=					=	4	Credit purch.
2,200 −	= 2,200		2,200			= 2,200	5	Services for cash
− 1,000	= (1,000)		(1,000)			= (1,000)	6	Rent exp.
− 700	= (700)		(700)			= (700)	7	Salary exp.
1,600 −	= 1600						8	Services for credit
300 −	= 300							
−	=		1,900			= 1,900	9	Cash rec'd. on Acct. Rec.
−	=				(900)	= (900)	10	Payment of Note Pay
−	=				(600)	= (600)	11	Owner Withdrawals
−	=		3,000			= 3,000	12	Cash for future service
−	=		(2,400)			= (2,400)	13	Payment of future insur.
−	=		(120)			= (120)	14	Purch. supp.
− 230	= (230)		(230)			= (230)	15	Util exp.
− 700	= (700)		(700)			= (700)	16	Salary exp.
4,100 − 2,630	= 1,470		(550) +	(20,000) +	28,500	= 7950		Total

Exhibit 3.13

Financial Statement Links to Transactions

Exhibit 3.14

Steps in Processing
Transactions

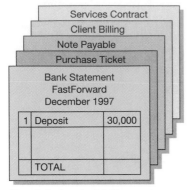

Step 1: Analyze transactions and source documents.

Step 2: Apply double-entry accounting.

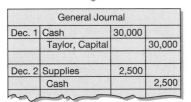

General Journal		
Dec. 1	Cash	30,000	
	Taylor, Capital		30,000
Dec. 2	Supplies	2,500	
	Cash		2,500

Step 3: Record journal entry.

Step 4: Post entry to ledger.

FastForward Trial Balance		
December 31, 1997		
	Debit	Credit
Cash	$7,950	
Accounts Receivable	0	
Prepaid Insurance	$2,400	

Step 5: Prepare trial balance.

The Journal Entry

The **general journal** shows the debits and credits of transactions and it can be used to record any transaction. A general journal entry includes the following information about each transaction:

1. Date of transaction.
2. Titles of affected accounts.
3. Dollar amount of each debit and credit.
4. Explanation of transaction.

Exhibit 3.15 shows how the first four transactions of FastForward are recorded in a general journal. A journal is often referred to as the *book of original entry*. The accounting process is similar for manual and computerized systems. Many computer programs even copy the look of a paper journal.

The fourth entry in Exhibit 3.15 uses four accounts. There are debits to the two assets purchased—supplies and equipment. There are also credits to the two sources of payment—accounts payable and note payable. A transaction affecting three or more accounts is called a **compound journal entry.**

Journalizing Transactions

There are standard procedures for recording entries in a general journal. We can identify nine steps in journalizing. It is helpful to review the entries in Exhibit 3.15 when studying these steps.

1. Enter the year on the first line at the top of the first column.
2. Enter the month in column one on the first line of the journal entry. Later entries for the same month and year on the same page of the journal do not require reentering the same month and year.
3. Enter the day of the transaction in column two on the first line of each entry.
4. Enter titles of accounts debited. Account titles are taken from the chart of accounts and are aligned with the left margin of the "Account Titles and Explanation" column.
5. Enter debit amounts in the "Debit" column on the same line as the accounts debited.
6. Enter titles of accounts credited. Account titles are taken from the chart of accounts and are indented from the left margin of the "Account Titles and Explanation" column to distinguish them from debited accounts.
7. Enter credit amounts in the "Credit" column on the same line as the accounts credited.
8. Enter a brief explanation of the transaction on the line below the entry (it is often a reference to a source document). This explanation is indented about half as far as the credited account titles to avoid confusing an explanation with accounts. We italicize explanations.
9. Skip a line between each journal entry for clarity.

A complete journal entry gives a useful description of a transaction and its effects.

The **posting reference (PR) column** is left blank when a transaction is initially recorded. Individual account numbers are later entered into the PR column when entries are posted to the ledger.

Computerized Journals

Journals in computerized and manual systems serve the same purposes. Computerized journals are often designed to look like a manual journal page as in Exhibit 3.15. Maria Sanchez of **RecordLink** in the opening article designed her Web-based system to look exactly like the paper-based system. Computerized systems typically include error-check-

Exhibit 3.15

Partial General Journal for FastForward

General Journal				Page 1
Date	**Account Titles and Explanation**	**PR**	**Debit**	**Credit**
1997 Dec. 1	Cash		30,000	
	C.Taylor, Capital			30,000
	Investment by owner.			
2	Supplies		2,500	
	Cash			2,500
	Purchased store supplies for cash.			
3	Equipment		20,000	
	Cash			20,000
	Purchased copy equipment for cash.			
6	Supplies		1,100	
	Equipment		6,000	
	Accounts Payable			1,100
	Note Payable			6,000
	Purchased supplies and equipment on credit.			

ing routines that ensure debits equal credits for each entry. Shortcuts often allow record-keepers to enter account numbers instead of names, and to enter account names and numbers with pull-down menus.

Balance Column Account

T-accounts are simple and direct means to show how the accounting process works. They allow us to omit less relevant details and concentrate on main ideas. Accounting systems in practice need more structure and use **balance column accounts.** Exhibit 3.16 is an example.

Exhibit 3.16

Cash Account in Balance Column Format

Cash					Account No. 101
Date		**Explanation**	**PR**	**Debit**	**Credit**	**Balance**
1997	1		G1	30,000		30,000
	2		G1		2,500	27,500
	3		G1		20,000	7,500
	10		G1	2,200		9,700

    The balance column account format is similar to a T-account in having columns for debits and credits. It is different in having a transaction's date and explanation. It also has a third column with the balance of the account after each entry is posted. This means the amount on the last line in this column is the account's current balance. For example, FastForward's Cash account in Exhibit 3.16 is debited on December 1 for the $30,000 investment by Taylor. The account then shows a $30,000 debit balance. The account is credited on December 2 for $2,500, and its new $27,500 balance is shown in the third column. On December 3, it is credited again, this time for $20,000, and its balance is reduced to $7,500. The Cash account is debited for $2,200 on December 10, and its balance increases to $9,700.

When a balance column account is used, the heading of the Balance column does not show whether it is a debit or credit balance. This omission is no problem because every account has a *normal balance*. The normal balance of each account (asset, liability, equity, revenue, or expense) refers to the left or right (debit or credit) side where increases are recorded. The earlier diagrams in this chapter highlight this. Exhibit 3.17 shows normal balances for accounts to emphasize their importance.

Exhibit 3.17

Normal Balances for Accounts

Assets		=	Liabilities		+	Owner's Capital		−	Owner's Withdrawals		+	Revenues		−	Expenses	
Dr. for increases	Cr. for decreases		Dr. for decreases	Cr. for increases		Dr. for decreases	Cr. for increases		Dr. for increases	Cr. for decreases		Dr. for decreases	Cr. for increases		Dr. for increases	Cr. for decreases
+	−		−	+		−	+		+	−		−	+		+	−
Normal				**Normal**			**Normal**		**Normal**				**Normal**		**Normal**	

Abnormal Balance

Unusual events can sometimes temporarily give an abnormal balance for an account. An *abnormal balance* refers to a balance on the side where decreases are recorded. For example, a customer might mistakenly overpay a bill. This gives that customer's account receivable an abnormal (credit) balance. An abnormal balance is often identified by circling it or by entering it in red or some other unusual color. Computerized systems often provide a code beside a balance such as *dr.* or *cr.* to identify its balance.

Zero Balance

A zero balance for an account is usually shown by writing zeros or a dash in the Balance column. This practice avoids confusion between a zero balance and one omitted in error.

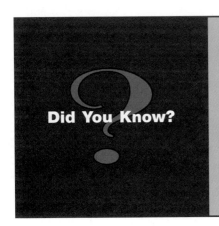

Did You Know?

STAR CFOs: The Next Generation
What are likely duties for the next generation of accounting professionals? A recent article on chief financial officers (CFOs) gives us a peek. CFOs were once perceived as: bean counters; nonplayers in corporate strategy; narrowly focused; and preoccupied with costs. CFOs are now major players in: long-term planning; revenue strategies; using technology; and interpreting accounting information. This suggests the next generation of accounting professionals will require more analytical and conceptual skills. [Source: *Business Week,* October 28, 1996.]

Posting Journal Entries

Exhibit 3.14 shows that journal entries are posted to ledger accounts. To ensure that the ledger is up to date, entries are posted as soon as possible. This might be daily, weekly, or when time permits. All entries must be posted to the ledger by the end of a reporting period. This is necessary so account balances are current when financial statements are prepared. It is why the ledger is referred to as the *book of final entry.*

When entries are posted to the ledger, the debits in journal entries are copied into ledger accounts as debits, and credits are copied into ledger accounts as credits. Exhibit 3.18 shows six steps of manual systems to post each debit and credit from a journal entry.

The usual process is to post in order debits and then credits. The steps in posting are:

1. Identify the ledger account that was debited in the journal entry.
2. Enter the date of the journal entry in this ledger account.
3. Enter the source of the debit in the PR column of the ledger, both the journal and page. The letter *G* shows it came from the general journal.[7]

---

[7] Other journals are identified by their own letters. We discuss other journals later in the book.

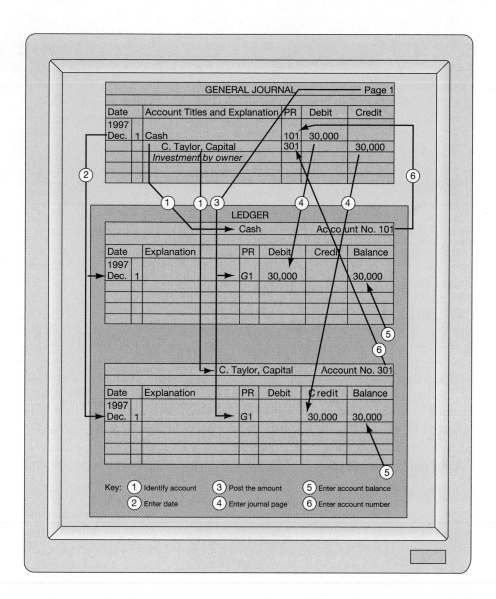

Exhibit 3.18

Posting an entry to the ledger

4. Enter the amount debited from the journal entry into the Debit column of the ledger account.

5. Compute and enter the account's new balance in the Balance column.

6. Enter the ledger account number in the PR column of the journal entry.

7. Repeat the six steps for credit amounts and Credit columns.

Step 6 in the posting process for both debit and credit amounts of an entry inserts the account number in the journal's PR column. This creates a link between the ledger and the journal entry. This link is a useful cross-reference for tracing an amount from one record to another. It also readily shows the stage of completion in the posting process. This permits one to easily start and stop the posting process.

Posting in Computerized Systems

Computerized systems require no added effort to post journal entries to the ledger. These systems automatically transfer debit and credit entries from the journal to the ledger. Journal entries are posted directly to ledger accounts. Many systems, including those of **RecordLink,** have programs testing the reasonableness of a journal entry and the account balance when recorded. For example, the payroll program might alert a preparer to hourly rates exceeding $500.

Flash back

11. When Maria Sanchez set up RecordLink, she invested $15,000 cash and equipment with a market value of $23,000. RecordLink also took responsibility for an $18,000 note payable issued to finance the purchase of equipment. Prepare the journal entry to record Sanchez's investment.

12. Explain what a compound journal entry is.

13. Why are posting reference numbers entered in the journal when entries are posted to accounts?

Answers—p. 109

Trial Balance

P2 Prepare and explain the use of a trial balance.

Double-entry accounting records every transaction with equal debits and credits. We know an error exists if the sum of debit entries in the ledger does not equal the sum of credit entries. The sum of debit account balances must equal the sum of credit account balances.

Step five of the accounting process shown in Exhibit 3.14 is to use a trial balance to check on whether debit and credit account balances are equal. A **trial balance** is a list of accounts and their balances at a point in time. Account balances are reported in the debit or credit column of a trial balance. Exhibit 3.19 shows the trial balance for Fast-Forward after the 16 entries described earlier in the chapter are posted to the ledger.

Another use of the trial balance is as an internal report for preparing financial statements. Preparing statements is easier when we can take account balances from a trial balance instead of searching the ledger. We explain this process in Chapter 4.

Preparing a Trial Balance

Preparing a trial balance involves five steps:

Exhibit 3.19

Trial Balance

FASTFORWARD Trial Balance December 31, 1997		
	Debit	**Credit**
Cash	$ 7,950	
Prepaid insurance	2,400	
Supplies	3,720	
Equipment	26,000	
Accounts payable		$ 1,100
Unearned consulting revenue		3,000
Note payable		5,100
C. Taylor, Capital		30,000
C. Taylor, Withdrawals	600	
Consulting revenue		3,800
Rental revenue		300
Rent expense	1,000	
Salaries expense	1,400	
Utilities expense	230	
Total	$43,300	$43,300

1. Identify each account balance from the ledger.

2. List each account and its balance. Debit balances are entered in the Debit column and credit balances in the Credit column.[8]

3. Compute the total of debit balances.

4. Compute the total of credit balances.

5. Verify total debit balances equal total credit balances.

The total debit balances equal the total credit balances for the trial balance in Exhibit 3.19. If these two totals were not equal, we would know that one or more errors exist. Equality of these two totals does not guarantee no errors were made.

---

[8] If an account has a zero balance, it can be listed in the trial balance with a zero in the column for its normal balance.

Using a Trial Balance

We know one or more errors exist when a trial balance does not balance (when its columns are not equal). When one or more errors exist they often arise from one of the following steps in the accounting process: (1) preparing journal entries, (2) posting entries to the ledger, (3) computing account balances, (4) copying account balances to the trial balance, or (5) totaling the trial balance columns.

When a trial balance does balance, the accounts are likely free of the kinds of errors that create unequal debits and credits. Yet errors may still exist. One example is when a debit or credit of a correct amount is made to a wrong account. This can occur when either journalizing or posting. The error would produce incorrect balances in two accounts but the trial balance would balance. Another error is to record equal debits and credits of an incorrect amount. This error produces incorrect balances in two accounts but again the debits and credits are equal. We give these examples to show that when a trial balance does balance, it does not prove all journal entries are recorded and posted correctly.

Searching for Errors

At least one error exists if the trial balance does not balance. The error (or errors) must be found and corrected before preparing financial statements. Searching for the error is more efficient if we check the journalizing, posting, and trial balance preparation process in *reverse order.* Otherwise we would need to look at every transaction until the error is found.

Several steps are involved. Step one is to verify that the trial balance columns are correctly added. If step one fails to find the error, then step two is to verify that account balances are accurately copied from the ledger. Our third step in identifying the error is to see if a debit or credit balance is mistakenly listed in the trial balance as a credit or debit. A clue to this kind of error is when the difference between total debits and total credits in the trial balance equals twice the amount of the incorrect account balance.

If the error is still undiscovered, our fourth step is to recompute each account balance. Our fifth step if the error remains is to verify that each journal entry is properly posted to ledger accounts. Our sixth step is to verify that the original journal entry has equal debits and credits.

One frequent error is called a *transposition.* This error occurs when two digits are switched, or transposed, within a number. If transposition is the only error, then it yields a difference between two trial balance columns that is evenly divisible by nine. For example, assume a $691 debit in a journal entry is incorrectly posted to the ledger as $619. Total credits in the trial balance are then larger than total debits by $72 ($691 − $619). The $72 error is *evenly* divisible by 9 ($72/9 = 8). The first digit of the quotient (in our example it is 8) equals the difference between the digits of the two transposed numbers (i.e., between the 9 and the 1). The number of digits in the quotient also tells the location of the transposition. Because the quotient in our example had only one digit (8), it tells us the transposition is in the first digit of the transposed numbers, starting from the right.[9]

Correcting Errors

If errors are discovered in either the journal or the ledger, they must be corrected. Our approach to correcting errors depends on the kind of error and when it is discovered.

If an error in a journal entry is discovered before the error is posted, it can be corrected in a manual system by drawing a line through the incorrect information. The cor-

[9] Consider another example where a transposition error involves posting $961 instead of the correct $691. The difference in these numbers is $270, and its quotient is $30 ($270/9). Because the quotient has two digits, it tells us to check the second digits from the right for a transposition of two numbers that have a difference of 3.

rect information is written above it to create a record of change for the auditor. Many computerized systems allow the operator to replace the incorrect information directly. If a correct amount in the journal is posted incorrectly to the ledger, we can correct it the same way.

Another case occurs when an error in a journal entry is not discovered until after it is posted. We usually do not strike through both erroneous entries in the journal and ledger. Instead, the usual practice is to correct the error in the original journal entry by creating *another* journal entry. This *correcting entry* removes the amount from the wrong account and records it to the correct account. As an example, suppose we recorded a purchase of office supplies in the journal with an incorrect debit to Office Equipment:

Assets = Liabilities + Equity
+1,600
−1,600

Oct. 14	Office Equipment	1,600	
	Cash		1,600
	To record the purchase of office supplies.		

We then post this entry to the ledger. The Office Supplies ledger account balance is understated by $1,600 and the Office Equipment ledger account balance is overstated by the same amount. When we discover the error three days later, the following correcting entry is made:

Assets = Liabilities + Equity
+1,600
−1,600

Oct. 17	Office Supplies	1,600	
	Office Equipment		1,600
	To correct the entry of October 14 that incorrectly debited Office Equipment instead of Office Supplies.		

The credit in the correcting entry removes the error from the first entry. The debit correctly records the supplies. The explanation reports exactly what happened.

Computerized systems often use similar correcting entries. The exact procedure depends on the system used and management policy. Yet nearly all systems include controls to show when and where a correction is made.

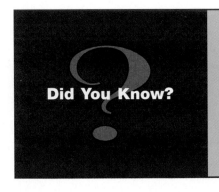

Did You Know?

Window on Accounting
Manual and computerized accounting systems mirror each other. Computerized systems often take on many routine tasks in accounting. They also give regular updating (batch time) or continuous (real time) processing of information. Many programs point out errors like unequal debits and credits or the transposing of numbers. They usually look like the paper-based ledger and general journal. Computerized systems have freed accounting professionals to spend more time and effort on analyzing and interpreting information for users. [Source: *Business Week*, September 16, 1996.]

Formatting Conventions

Dollar signs are not used in journals and ledgers. They do appear in financial statements and other reports, including trial balances. This book follows the usual practice of putting a dollar sign beside the first amount in each column of numbers and the first amount appearing after a ruled line indicating that an addition or subtraction has been performed. The financial statements in Exhibit 2.17 demonstrate how dollar signs are used in this book. Different companies use various conventions for dollar signs. For example, dollar signs are usually printed beside only the first and last numbers in columns of the financial statements for **NIKE.**

When amounts are entered manually in a journal, ledger, or trial balance, commas are not needed to indicate thousands, millions, and so forth. However, commas are used in financial statements and other reports. It is common for companies to round amounts to the nearest dollar, and even to a higher level for certain accounts. **NIKE** is typical of many companies in that it rounds its financial statement amounts to the nearest thousand dollars. But it continues to report its income per share amount in dollars with cents. NIKE's decision is usually linked with the perceived importance of rounding for users' decisions.

Flash back

14. Explain a chart of accounts.

15. When are dollar signs typically used in accounting reports?

16. If a $4,000 debit to Equipment in a journal entry is incorrectly posted to the ledger as a $4,000 credit, and the ledger account has a resulting debit balance of $20,000, what is the effect of this error on the trial balance column totals?

Answers—p. 110

Debt Ratio

USING THE INFORMATION

Accounting records are designed to provide useful information to users of financial statements. One important objective for many users is gathering information to help them assess a company's risk of failing to pay its debts when they are due. This section describes the debt ratio and how it can help in this task.

Most companies finance a portion of their assets with liabilities and the remaining portion with equity. A company that finances a relatively large portion of its assets with liabilities is said to have a high degree of *financial leverage*. While we will discuss more about financial leverage in Chapter 14, we should understand that higher financial leverage involves greater risk. This is because liabilities must be repaid and often require regular interest payments. The risk is that a company may not be able to meet required payments. This risk is higher if a company has more liabilities (more highly leveraged).

One way to assess the risk associated with a company's use of liabilities is to compute and analyze the debt ratio. The **debt ratio** describes the relation between a company's liabilities and its assets, and is defined in Exhibit 3.20.

A2 Compute the debt ratio and describe its use in analyzing company performance.

$$\text{Debt ratio} = \frac{\text{Total liabilities}}{\text{Total assets}}$$

Exhibit 3.20

Debt Ratio

To see how we apply the debt ratio, let's look at **Stride Rite**'s liabilities and assets (in millions) for 1992–1996. Stride Rite is the maker of Keds, Pro-Keds, and other footwear. Using these data, we compute in Exhibit 3.21 the debt ratio for Stride Rite at the end of each year.

	1996	1995	1994	1993	1992
a. Total liabilities	$103	$99	$104	$110	$112
b. Total assets	$364	$367	$397	$412	$384
c. **Debt ratio**	.283	.270	.262	.267	.292
d. Industry debt ratio*	.64	.47	.52	.50	.47

Exhibit 3.21

Computation and Analysis of Debt Ratio

* Industry debt ratio is the median value from ten of Stride Rite's competitors including NIKE, Reebok, Fila, Converse, L. A. Gear, and others.

Evaluating a company's debt ratio depends on several factors such as the nature of its operations, its ability to generate cash flows, its industry, and economic conditions. It is not possible to say that a specific debt ratio is good or bad for all companies. As we already discussed, we need to compare performance over time and across companies both in and outside of the industry.

We note that **Stride Rite's** debt ratio is stable over recent years, ranging from a low of .262 to a high of .292. This is low for most companies as evidenced by comparisons with industry figures. It is also unusual for a company like Stride Rite to carry no long-term debt as pointed out in its 1996 annual report:

> ... the Company had no long-term debt as the final payment on the Company's Senior Notes will be made during 1997.

This analysis implies a low risk from financial leverage for Stride Rite. There are other risk factors we need to examine and we will do this in later chapters.

Investor

You are considering buying stock in **Converse.** As part of your analysis, you compute the debt ratio of Converse for 1994, 1995, and 1996: 0.80, 1.10, and 1.17, respectively.* Based on these debt ratios, is Converse a low risk investment? Has the risk of buying Converse stock increased or decreased from 1994 to 1996?

*Converse's equity balances are negative in 1995 and 1996 because of losses.

Answer—p. 109

Summary

C1 Explain the steps in processing transactions. The accounting process captures business transactions and events, analyzes and records their effects, and summarizes and prepares information useful in making decisions. Transactions and events are the starting points in the accounting process. Source documents help in analyzing them. The effects of transactions and events are recorded in the accounting books. Postings and the trial balance help summarize and classify these effects. The final step is providing this information in useful reports or financial statements to decision makers.

C2 Describe source documents and their purpose. Source documents are business papers that identify and describe transactions and events. Examples are sales tickets, checks, purchase orders, bills, and bank statements. Source documents help ensure accounting records reflect all transactions. They also help prevent mistakes and theft, and are important to internal control. Source documents provide objective evidence making information more reliable and useful.

C3 Describe an account and its use in recording information about transactions. An account is a detailed record of increases and decreases in a specific asset, liability, equity, revenue, or expense item. Information is taken from accounts, analyzed, summarized, and presented in reports and financial statements for use by decision makers.

C4 Describe a ledger and a chart of accounts. A ledger is a record containing all accounts used by a company. This is what is referred to as the *books*. The chart of accounts is a listing of all accounts and usually includes an identification number assigned to each account.

C5 Define debits and credits and explain their role in double-entry accounting. Debit refers to left, and credit refers to right. Debits increase assets, withdrawals, and expenses, while credits decrease them. Credits increase liabilities, capital, and revenues, while debits decrease them. Double-entry accounting means every transaction affects at least two accounts and has at least one debit and one credit. The total amount debited must equal the total amount credited for each transaction. The system for recording debits and credits follows from the accounting equation. The left side of a T-account is the normal balance for assets, and the right side is the normal balance for liabilities and equity.

A1 Analyze the impact of transactions on accounts and financial statements. We analyze transactions using concepts of double-entry accounting. This analysis is performed by determining a transaction's effects on accounts. These effects are recorded in journals and posted to ledgers.

A2 Compute the debt ratio and describe its use in analyzing company performance. A company's debt ratio is computed as total liabilities divided by total assets. It tells us how much of the assets are financed by creditor (nonowner or liability) financing. The higher this ratio, the more risk a company faces in using liabilities to finance assets. This is because liabilities must be repaid.

P1 **Record transactions in a journal and post entries to a ledger.** We record transactions in a journal to give a record of their effects. Each entry in a journal is posted to the accounts in the ledger. This provides information in accounts that is used to produce financial statements. Balance column ledger accounts are widely used and include columns for debits, credits, and the account balance after each entry.

P2 **Prepare and explain the use of a trial balance.** A trial balance is a list of accounts in the ledger showing their debit and credit balances in separate columns. The trial balance is a convenient summary of the ledger's contents and is useful in preparing financial statements. It reveals errors of the kind that produce unequal debit and credit account balances.

Guidance Answer to **Judgment and Ethics**

Cashier

There are advantages to the process proposed by the assistant manager. They include improved customer service, less delays, and less work for you. However, you should have serious concerns about control and the potential for fraud. In particular, there is no control over the possibility of embezzlement by the assistant manager. The assistant manager could steal cash and simply ring up less sales to match the remaining cash. You should reject her suggestion without approval by the manager. Moreover, you should have an ethical concern about the assistant manager's suggestion to ignore store policy.

Guidance Answers to **You Make the Call**

Marketing Manager

You direct your search to the accounting information system. The general journal contains all the revenue information you desire. The difficulty in working with the journal is that you must go through all entries, identify revenues, and compute the total. The ledger also contains the information you desire and is a preferred source as it keeps a running balance of each account and would directly answer your question.

Investor

The debt ratio suggests the stock of Converse is of higher risk than normal and that this risk is rising. Industry ratios reported along with Stride Rite's debt ratios in the chapter further support the conclusion that Converse is of higher risk. In particular, the debt ratio for Converse has been steadily increasing and is now more than double the industry norm of about 0.50. Also, a debt ratio larger than 1.0 indicates negative equity. Excessive losses for Converse led to its negative equity.

Guidance Answers to Flash *backs*

1. External transactions are exchanges between an organization and some other person or organization. Internal transactions are exchanges within an organization, for example, a company using equipment in its operating activities.

2. Examples of source documents are sales tickets, checks, purchase orders, charges to customers, bills from suppliers, employee earnings records, and bank statements.

3. Source documents serve many purposes including recordkeeping and internal control. Source documents, especially if obtained from outside the organization, provide objective evidence about transactions and their amounts for recording. Objective evidence is important because it makes information more reliable and useful.

4.

Assets	Liabilities	Equity
a,c,f	b,e	d

5. An account is a record in an accounting system where increases and decreases in a specific asset, liability, owner's equity, revenue, or expense are recorded and stored. A ledger is a collection of all accounts used by a business.

6. A company's size and diversity affect the number of accounts needed in its accounting system. The types of accounts used by a business depend on information the business needs to both effectively operate and report its activities in financial statements.

7. No. Debit and credit both can mean increase or decrease. The particular meaning in a circumstance depends on the *type of account*. For example, a debit increases the balance of asset and expense accounts but decreases the balance of liability, equity, and revenue accounts.

8. Owner's equity is increased by revenues and by an owner's investments. Owner's equity is decreased by expenses and by an owner's cash withdrawals.

9. The name *double-entry* is used because all transactions affect at least two accounts. There must be at least one debit in one account and at least one credit in another.

10. Answer is *(c)*.

11. The entry is:

Cash	15,000	
Equipment	23,000	
Note Payable		18,000
Sanchez, Capital		20,000

12. A compound journal entry is one that affects three or more accounts.

13. Posting reference numbers are entered in the journal when posting to the ledger as a control over the posting process. They provide a cross-reference that allows the recordkeeper or au-

ditor to trace debits and credits from one record to another. They also create a marker in case the posting process is interrupted.

14. A chart of accounts is a listing of all of a company's accounts and their identifying numbers.

15. Dollar signs are used in financial statements and other reports to identify the kind of currency being used in the reports. At a minimum, they are placed beside the first and last numbers in

each column. Some companies place dollar signs beside any amount that appears after a ruled line to indicate that an addition or subtraction has taken place.

16. The effect of this error is to understate the trial balance's debit column total by $4,000 and overstate the credit column total by $4,000. This results in an $8,000 difference between the two totals.

Demonstration Problem

This demonstration problem is based on the same facts as the demonstration problem at the end of Chapter 2. The following events occurred during the first month of Barbara Schmidt's new haircutting business called The Cutlery:

a. On August 1, Schmidt put $3,000 cash into a checking account in the name of The Cutlery. She also invested $15,000 of equipment that she already owned.

b. On August 2, she paid $600 cash for furniture for the shop.

c. On August 3, she paid $500 cash to rent space in a strip mall for August.

d. On August 4, she furnished the shop by installing the old equipment and some new equipment that she bought on credit for $1,200. This amount is to be repaid in three equal payments at the end of August, September, and October.

e. On August 5, The Cutlery opened for business. Cash receipts from haircutting services provided in the first week and a half of business (ended August 15) were $825.

f. On August 15, Schmidt provided haircutting services on account for $100.

g. On August 17, Schmidt received a $100 check in the mail for services previously rendered on account.

h. On August 17, Schmidt paid $125 to an assistant for working during the grand opening.

i. Cash receipts from haircutting services provided during the second half of August were $930.

j. On August 31, Schmidt paid an installment on the accounts payable from (d).

k. On August 31, she withdrew $900 cash for her personal use.

Required

1. Prepare general journal entries for the preceding transactions.

2. Open the following accounts: Cash (101); Accounts Receivable (102); Furniture (161); Store Equipment (165); Accounts Payable (201); Barbara Schmidt, Capital (301); Barbara Schmidt, Withdrawals (302); Haircutting Services Revenue (403); Wages Expense (623); and Rent Expense (640).

3. Post the journal entries from (1) to the ledger accounts.

4. Prepare a trial balance as of August 31.

Extended Analysis

5. In the coming months, The Cutlery will experience an even greater variety of business transactions. Identify which accounts are debited and credited for the transactions that follow. (Hint: You may have to use some accounts not listed in (2) above.)

a. Purchases supplies with cash.

b. Pays cash for future insurance coverage.

c. Receives cash for services to be provided in the future.

Planning the Solution

■ Analyze each transaction to identify the accounts affected by the transaction and the amount of each effect.

■ Use the debit and credit rules to prepare a journal entry for each transaction.

- Post each debit and each credit in the journal entries to the appropriate ledger accounts and cross-reference each amount in the Posting Reference columns in the journal and account.

- Calculate each account balance and list the accounts with their balances on a trial balance.

- Verify that the total debits in the trial balance equal total credits.

- Analyze future transactions to identify the accounts affected and apply debit and credit rules.

Solution to Demonstration Problem

1. General journal entries:

Date	Account Titles and Explanations	PR	Debit	Credit
Aug. 1	Cash	101	3,000	
	Store Equipment	165	15,000	
	Barbara Schmidt, Capital	301		18,000
	Owner's initial investment.			
2	Furniture	161	600	
	Cash	101		600
	Purchased furniture for cash.			
3	Rent Expense	640	500	
	Cash	101		500
	Paid rent for August.			
4	Store Equipment	165	1,200	
	Accounts Payable	201		1,200
	Purchased additional equipment on credit.			
15	Cash	101	825	
	Haircutting Services Revenue	403		825
	Cash receipts from 10 days of operations.			
15	Accounts Receivable	102	100	
	Haircutting Services Revenue	403		100
	To record revenue for services provided on account.			
17	Cash	101	100	
	Accounts Receivable	102		100
	To record cash received as payment on account.			
17	Wages Expense	623	125	
	Cash	101		125
	Paid wages to assistant.			
31	Cash	101	930	
	Haircutting Services Revenue	403		930
	Cash receipts from second half of August.			
31	Accounts Payable	201	400	
	Cash	101		400
	Paid an installment on accounts payable.			
31	Barbara Schmidt, Withdrawals	302	900	
	Cash	101		900
	Owner withdrew cash from the business.			

2. & 3. Open ledger accounts and post journal entries:

		Cash			Account No. 101	
Date		**Explanation**	**PR**	**Debit**	**Credit**	**Balance**
Aug.	1		G1	3,000		3,000
	2		G1		600	2,400
	3		G1		500	1,900
	15		G1	825		2,725
	17		G1	100		2,825
	17		G1		125	2,700
	31		G1	930		3,630
	31		G1		400	3,230
	31		G1		900	2,330

		Accounts Receivable			Account No. 102	
Date		**Explanation**	**PR**	**Debit**	**Credit**	**Balance**
Aug.	15		G1	100		100
	17		G1		100	0

		Furniture			Account No. 161	
Date		**Explanation**	**PR**	**Debit**	**Credit**	**Balance**
Aug.	2		G1	600		600

		Store Equipment			Account No. 165	
Date		**Explanation**	**PR**	**Debit**	**Credit**	**Balance**
Aug.	1		G1	15,000		15,000
	4		G1	1,200		16,200

		Accounts Payable			Account No. 201	
Date		**Explanation**	**PR**	**Debit**	**Credit**	**Balance**
Aug.	4		G1		1,200	1,200
	31		G1	400		800

		Barbara Schmidt, Capital			Account No. 301	
Date		**Explanation**	**PR**	**Debit**	**Credit**	**Balance**
Aug.	1		G1		18,000	18,000

		Barbara Schmidt, Withdrawals			Account No. 302	
Date		**Explanation**	**PR**	**Debit**	**Credit**	**Balance**
Aug.	31		G1	900		900

Date		Haircutting Services Revenue Explanation	PR	Debit	Account No. 403 Credit	Balance
Aug.	15		G1		825	825
	15		G1		100	925
	31		G1		930	1,855

Date		Wages Expense Explanation	PR	Debit	Account No. 623 Credit	Balance
Aug.	17		G1	125		125

Date		Rent Expense Explanation	PR	Debit	Account No. 640 Credit	Balance
Aug.	3		G1	500		500

4. Prepare trial balance:

THE CUTLERY
Trial Balance
August 31, 2000

	Debit	Credit
Cash	$ 2,330	
Accounts Receivable	0	
Furniture	600	
Store equipment	16,200	
Accounts payable		$ 800
Barbara Schmidt, capital		18,000
Barbara Schmidt, withdrawals	900	
Haircutting services revenue		1,855
Wages expense	125	
Rent expense	500	
Totals	$20,655	$20,655

5a. Supplies debited
    Cash credited
5b. Prepaid Insurance debited
    Cash credited
5c. Cash debited
    Unearned Services Revenue credited

Glossary

Account a place or location within an accounting system in which the increases and decreases in a specific asset, liability, equity, revenue, or expense are recorded and stored. (p. 84).

Account balance the difference between the increases (including the beginning balance) and decreases recorded in an account. (p. 90).

Balance column account an account with debit and credit columns for recording entries and a third column for showing the balance of the account after each entry is posted. (p. 101).

Chart of accounts a list of all accounts used by a company; includes the identification number assigned to each account. (p. 88).

Compound journal entry a journal entry that affects at least three accounts. (p. 100).

Credit an entry that decreases asset and expense accounts or increases liability, equity, and revenue accounts; recorded on the right side of a T-account. (p. 90).

Debit an entry that increases asset and expense accounts or decreases liability, equity, and revenue accounts; recorded on the left side of a T-account. (p. 90).

Debt ratio the ratio of a company's total liabilities to its total assets; used to describe the risk associated with the company's debts. (p. 107).

Double-entry accounting an accounting system where every transaction affects at least two accounts and has at least one debit and one credit; the sum of the debits for each entry must equal the sum of the credits for each entry. (p. 91).

Events happenings that both affect an organization's financial position and can be reliably measured. (p. 83).

External transactions exchanges of economic consideration between an entity and another person or organization. (p. 83).

General journal a record of the debits and credits of transactions; can be used to record any transaction. (p. 100).

Internal transactions exchanges within an organization that can also affect the accounting equation. (p. 83).

Journal a record where transactions are recorded before they are recorded in accounts; amounts are posted from the journal to the ledger; also called the *book of original entry*. (p. 99).

Journalizing the process of recording transactions in a journal. (p. 99).

Ledger a record containing all accounts used by a business. (p. 84).

Note payable an unconditional written promise to pay a definite sum of money on demand or on a defined future date(s); also called a *promissory note*. (p. 85).

Posting the process of transferring journal entry information to the ledger. (p. 99).

Posting reference (PR) column a column in journals where individual account numbers are entered when entries are posted to the ledger. (p. 100).

Promissory note an unconditional written promise to pay a definite sum of money on demand or on a defined future date(s); also called a *note payable* (or *note receivable*). (p. 85).

Source documents another name for *business papers*; these documents are the source of information recorded with accounting entries and can be in either paper or electronic form. (p. 83).

T-account a simple account form used as a helpful tool in showing the effects of transactions and events on specific accounts. (p. 89).

Trial balance a list of accounts and their balances at a point in time; the total debit balances should equal the total credit balances. (p. 104).

Unearned revenues liabilities created when customers pay in advance for products or services; created when cash is received before revenues are earned; satisfied by delivering the products or services in the future. (p. 86).

Questions

1. Discuss the steps in the accounting process.

2. What is the difference between a note receivable and an account receivable?

3. If assets are valuable resources and asset accounts have debit balances, why do expense accounts have debit balances?

4. Why does the recordkeeper prepare a trial balance?

5. Should a transaction be recorded first in a journal or the ledger? Why?

6. Are debits or credits listed first in general journal entries? Are the debits or the credits indented?

7. What kinds of transactions can be recorded in a general journal?

8. If a wrong amount is journalized and posted to the accounts, how should the error be corrected?

9. Review the **NIKE** balance sheet for fiscal year-end 5/31/97 in Appendix A. Identify three accounts on the balance sheet that carry debit balances and three accounts on the balance sheet that carry credit balances.

10. Review the **Reebok** balance sheet for fiscal year-end 12/31/96 in Appendix A. Identify four different liability accounts that include the word *payable* in the account title.

11. Locate **AOL's** income statement in Appendix A. What account titles are used for revenue accounts? Describe these revenue accounts.

12. Reread the chapter's opening scenario describing Maria Sanchez's company, **RecordLink.** Last year RecordLink's revenues exceeded $850,000. Suggest an appropriate account title for RecordLink's revenue account.

Select the items from the following list that are likely to serve as source documents:
a. Income statement   **e.** Owner's withdrawals account
b. Trial balance   **f.** Balance sheet
c. Telephone bill   **g.** Bank statement
d. Invoice from supplier **h.** Sales ticket

Indicate the financial statement on which each of the following accounts appears. Use IS for income statement, SCOE for the statement of changes in owner's equity, and BS for balance sheet:
a. Buildings   **f.** Interest Payable
b. Interest Earned   **g.** Accounts Receivable
c. Owner, Withdrawals   **h.** Salaries Expense
d. Equipment   **i.** Office Supplies
e. Prepaid Insurance   **j.** Repair Services Revenue

Indicate whether a debit or credit is necessary to *decrease* the normal balance of each of the following accounts:
a. Buildings   **f.** Interest Payable
b. Interest Earned   **g.** Accounts Receivable
c. Owner, Withdrawals   **h.** Salaries Expense
d. Owner, Capital   **i.** Office Supplies
e. Prepaid Insurance   **j.** Repair Services Revenue

Identify whether a debit or credit is necessary to result in the indicated change for each of the following accounts:
a. To increase Notes Payable.   **f.** To decrease Cash.
b. To decrease Accounts Receivable. **g.** To increase Utilities Expense.
c. To increase Owner, Capital.   **h.** To increase Fees Earned.
d. To decrease Unearned Fees.   **i.** To increase Store Equipment.
e. To decrease Prepaid Insurance.   **j.** To increase Owner, Withdrawals.

Prepare journal entries for the following transactions:
a. On January 15, Stan Adams opened a landscaping business by investing $60,000 cash and equipment having a $40,000 fair value.
b. On January 20, purchased office supplies on credit for $340.
c. On January 28, received $5,200 in return for providing landscaping services to a customer.

A trial balance has total debits of $21,000 and total credits of $25,500. Which one of the following errors would create this imbalance? Explain.
a. A $4,500 debit to Salaries Expense in a journal entry was incorrectly posted to the ledger as a $4,500 credit, leaving the Salaries Expense account with a $750 debit balance.
b. A $2,250 credit to Consulting Fees Earned in a journal entry was incorrectly posted to the ledger as a $2,250 debit, leaving the Consulting Fees Earned account with a $6,300 credit balance.
c. A $2,250 debit to Rent Expense in a journal entry was incorrectly posted to the ledger as a $2,250 credit, leaving the Rent Expense account with a $3,000 debit balance.

Exercises

Exercise 3-1
Increases, decreases, and normal balances of accounts

C3, C5

Complete the following table by (1) identifying the type of account as an asset, liability, equity, revenue, or expense, (2) entering *debit* or *credit* to identify the kind of entry that would increase or decrease the account balance, and (3) identifying the normal balance of the account.

	Account	Type of Account	Debit or Credit		Normal Balance
			Increase	Decrease	
a.	Land				
b.	H. Cooper, Capital				
c.	Accounts receivable				
d.	H. Cooper, Withdrawals				
e.	Cash				
f.	Equipment				
g.	Unearned revenue				
h.	Accounts payable				
i.	Postage expense				
j.	Prepaid insurance				
k.	Wages expense				
l.	Fees earned				

Exercise 3-2
Analyzing effects of transactions on accounts

A1

Jan Garret recently notified a client that it would have to pay a $48,000 fee for accounting services. Unfortunately, the client did not have enough cash to pay the entire bill. Garret agreed to accept the following items in full payment: (1) $7,500 cash, (2) computer equipment worth $75,000, and (3) assume responsibility for a $34,500 note payable related to the equipment. The entry Garret would make to record this transaction would include which one or more of the following items?

a. $34,500 increase in a liability account.
b. $7,500 increase in the Cash account.
c. $7,500 increase in a revenue account.
d. $48,000 increase in the Jan Garret, Capital, account.
e. $48,000 increase in a revenue account.

Exercise 3-3
Recording effects of transactions in T-accounts

A1

Open the following T-accounts: Cash; Accounts Receivable; Office Supplies; Office Equipment; Accounts Payable; Steve Moore, Capital; Steve Moore, Withdrawals; Fees Earned; and Rent Expense. Record the transactions of Moore Company by recording the debit and credit entries directly in T-accounts. Use the letters beside each transaction to identify entries. Determine the balance of each T-account.

a. Steve Moore invested $12,750 cash in the business.
b. Purchased $375 of office supplies for cash.
c. Purchased $7,050 of office equipment on credit.
d. Received $1,500 cash as fees for services provided to a customer.
e. Paid for the office equipment purchased in transaction *c*.
f. Billed a customer $2,700 as fees for services.
g. Paid the monthly rent with $525 cash.
h. Collected $1,125 of the account receivable created in transaction *f*.
i. Withdrew $1,000 cash from the business.

After recording the transactions of Exercise 3-3 in T-accounts and calculating the balance of each account, prepare a trial balance. Use May 31, 2000, as its date.

Exercise 3-4
Preparing a
trial balance   P2

For each of the listed posting errors, enter in column (1) the amount of the difference the error would create between the two trial balance columns (show a zero if the columns would balance). If there is a difference between the two columns, identify in column (2) the trial balance column that is larger. Identify the account(s) affected in column (3) and the amount by which the account(s) is under- or overstated in column (4). The answer for the first error is shown as an example.

Exercise 3-5
Effects of posting errors
on the trial balance
A1, P2

	Description of Posting Error	(1) Difference between Debit and Credit Columns	(2) Column with the Larger Total	(3) Identify Account(s) Incorrectly Stated	(4) Amount that Account(s) Is Over- or Understated
a.	A $2,400 debit to Rent Expense was posted as a $1,590 debit.	$810	credit	Rent Expense	Rent Expense is understated by $810
b.	A $42,000 debit to Machinery was posted as a debit to Accounts Payable.				
c.	A $4,950 credit to Services Revenue was posted as a $495 credit.				
d.	A $1,440 debit to Store Supplies was not posted at all.				
e.	A $2,250 debit to Prepaid Insurance was posted as a debit to Insurance Expense.				
f.	A $4,050 credit to Cash was posted twice as two credits to the Cash account.				
g.	A $9,900 debit to the owner's withdrawals account was debited to the owner's capital account.				

As the accountant for a company, you are told the column totals in the trial balance are not equal. After going through a careful analysis, you discover only one error. Specifically, the balance of the Office Equipment account has a debit balance of $23,400 on the trial balance. But you discover that a correctly recorded credit purchase of a computer for $5,250 was posted from the journal to the ledger with a $5,250 debit to Office Equipment and another $5,250 debit to Accounts Payable. Answer each of the following questions and show the dollar amount of any misstatement:

a. Is the balance of the Office Equipment account overstated, understated, or correctly stated in the trial balance?

b. Is the balance of the Accounts Payable account overstated, understated, or correctly stated in the trial balance?

c. Is the debit column total of the trial balance overstated, understated, or correctly stated?

d. Is the credit column total of the trial balance overstated, understated, or correctly stated?

e. If the debit column total of the trial balance is $360,000 before correcting the error, what is the total of the credit column?

Exercise 3-6
Analyzing a trial balance
error
A1, P2

Exercise 3-7
Preparing a corrected trial balance

P2

On January 1, Jan Taylor started a new business called The Party Place. Near the end of the year, she hired an accountant without making a careful reference check. As a result, a number of mistakes were made in preparing the following trial balance:

THE PARTY PLACE Trial Balance December 31, 2000		
	Debit	**Credit**
Cash	$ 5,500	
Accounts receivable		$ 7,900
Office supplies	2,650	
Office equipment	20,500	
Accounts payable		9,465
Jan Taylor, capital	16,745	
Services revenue		22,350
Wages expense		6,000
Rent expense		4,800
Advertising expense		1,250
Totals	$45,395	$52,340

Taylor's analysis of the situation reveals:

a. The sum of the debits in the Cash account is $37,175 and the sum of its credits is $30,540.

b. A $275 payment from a credit customer was posted to Cash but was not posted to Accounts Receivable.

c. A credit purchase of office supplies for $400 was completely unrecorded.

d. A transposition error occurred in copying the balance of the Services Revenue account to the trial balance. The correct amount was $23,250.

e. Errors were made in assigning account balances to the debit and credit columns of the trial balance, and in computing totals of the columns.

Use this information to prepare a correct trial balance.

Exercise 3-8
Analyzing account entries and balances

A1

Use the information in each of the following situations to calculate the unknown amount:

1. During October, Ridgeway Company had $97,500 of cash receipts and $101,250 of cash disbursements. The October 31 Cash balance was $16,800. Determine how much cash the company had on hand at the close of business on September 30.

2. On September 30, Ridgeway had a $97,500 balance in Accounts Receivable. During October, the company collected $88,950 from its credit customers. The October 31 balance in Accounts Receivable was $100,500. Determine the amount of sales on account that occurred in October.

3. Ridgeway had $147,000 of accounts payable on September 30 and $136,500 on October 31. Total purchases on account during October were $270,000. Determine how much cash was paid on accounts payable during October.

Exercise 3-9
Describing transactions from T-accounts

A1

Seven transactions were posted to these T-accounts. Provide a short description of each transaction. Include the amounts in your descriptions.

Cash			
(a)	7,000	(b)	3,600
(e)	2,500	(c)	600
		(f)	2,400
		(g)	700

Office Supplies		
(c)	600	
(d)	200	

Prepaid Insurance		
(b)	3,600	

Equipment		
(a)	5,600	
(d)	9,400	

Automobiles		
(a)	11,000	

Accounts Payable		
(f)	2,400	(d)	9,600

Jerry Steiner, Capital		
		(a)	23,600

Delivery Services Revenue		
		(e)	2,500

Gas and Oil Expense		
(g)	700	

Use information from the T-accounts in Exercise 3-9 to prepare general journal entries for the seven transactions (a) through (g).

Exercise 3-10
General journal entries A1

Prepare general journal entries for the following transactions of a new business called PhotoFinish.

Aug. 1	Hannah Young, the owner, invested $7,500 cash and photography equipment valued at $32,500.	
1	Rented a studio, paying $3,000 for the next three months in advance.	
5	Purchased office supplies for $1,400 cash.	
20	Received $2,650 in photography fees earned.	
31	Paid $875 for August utilities.	

Exercise 3-11
Preparing general journal entries
A1

Use the information provided in Exercise 3-11 to prepare an August 31 trial balance for Photo-Finish. Open these T-accounts: Cash; Office Supplies; Prepaid Rent; Photography Equipment; Hannah Young, Capital; Photography Fees Earned; and Utilities Expense. Post the general journal entries to the T-accounts, and prepare a trial balance.

Exercise 3-12
Preparing T-accounts and the trial balance P2

Examine the following transactions and identify those that create revenues for Jarrell Services, a sole proprietorship owned by John Jarrell. Prepare general journal entries to record those transactions and explain why the other transactions did not create revenues.

a. John Jarrell invested $38,250 cash in the business.

b. Provided $1,350 of services on credit.

c. Received $1,575 cash for services provided to a client.

d. Received $9,150 from a client in payment for services to be provided next year.

e. Received $4,500 from a client in partial payment of an account receivable.

f. Borrowed $150,000 from the bank by signing a promissory note.

Exercise 3-13
Analyzing and journalizing revenue transactions
A1

Examine the following transactions and identify those that create expenses for Jarrell Services. Prepare general journal entries to record those transactions and explain why the other transactions did not create expenses.

a. Paid $14,100 cash for office supplies purchased 3 months previously.

b. Paid the $1,125 salary of the receptionist.

c. Paid $45,000 cash for equipment.

d. Paid utility bill with $930 cash.

e. Withdrew $5,000 from the business for personal use.

Exercise 3-14
Analyzing and journalizing expense transactions
A1

1. Calculate the debt ratio for each of the following six seperate cases:

Exercise 3-15
Computing and interpreting the debt ratio
A2

Case	Assets	Liabilities	Owner's Equity
Company 1	$ 88,500	$ 11,000	$ 77,500
Company 2	62,000	46,000	16,000
Company 3	30,500	25,500	5,000
Company 4	145,000	55,000	90,000
Company 5	90,000	30,000	60,000
Company 6	102,500	50,500	52,000

2. Of the six cases, which business relies most heavily on creditor financing?

3. Of the six cases, which business relies most heavily on equity financing?

4. Which two companies indicate the greatest risk?

Problems

Problem 3-1
Recording transactions in T-accounts; preparing a trial balance

A1, P2

Business transactions completed by Kevin Smith during the month of November are as follows:

a. Kevin Smith invests $80,000 cash and office equipment valued at $30,000 in a new sole proprietorship named Apex Consulting.

b. Purchased land and a small office building. The land was worth $30,000, and the building was worth $170,000. The purchase price was paid with $40,000 cash and a long-term note payable for $160,000.

c. Purchased $2,400 of office supplies on credit.

d. Kevin Smith transferred title of his personal automobile to the business. The automobile had a value of $18,000 and was to be used exclusively in the business.

e. Purchased $6,000 of additional office equipment on credit.

f. Paid $1,500 salary to an assistant.

g. Provided services to a client and collected $6,000 cash.

h. Paid $800 for this month's utilities.

i. Paid account payable created in transaction *c*.

j. Purchased $20,000 of new office equipment by paying $18,600 cash and trading in old equipment with a recorded net cost of $1,400.

k. Completed $5,200 of services for a client. This amount is to be paid within 30 days.

l. Paid $1,500 salary to an assistant.

m. Received $3,800 payment on the receivable created in transaction *k*.

n. Withdrew $6,400 cash from the business for personal use.

Required

1. Open the following T-accounts: Cash; Accounts Receivable; Office Supplies; Automobiles; Office Equipment; Building; Land; Accounts Payable; Long-Term Notes Payable; Kevin Smith, Capital; Kevin Smith, Withdrawals; Fees Earned; Salaries Expense; and Utilities Expense.

2. Record the transactions above by entering debits and credits directly in T-accounts. Use the transaction letters to identify each debit and credit entry.

3. Determine the balance of each account and prepare a trial balance as of November 30.

Check Figure
Totals in trial balance, $305,200

Problem 3-2
Recording transactions in T-accounts, preparing a trial balance, and computing a debt ratio

A1, A2, P2

Forest Engineering, a sole proprietorship, completed the following transactions during the month of July:

a. Stephen Forest, the owner, invested $105,000 cash, office equipment with a value of $6,000, and $45,000 of drafting equipment in the business.

b. Purchased land for an office. The land was worth $54,000, and is paid with $5,400 cash and a long-term note payable for $48,600.

c. Purchased a portable building with $75,000 cash and moved it onto the land.

d. Paid $6,000 cash for the premiums on two one-year insurance policies.

e. Completed and delivered a set of plans for a client and collected $5,700 cash.

f. Purchased additional drafting equipment for $22,500. Paid $10,500 cash and signed a long-term note payable for the $12,000 balance.

g. Completed $12,000 of engineering services for a client. This amount is to be paid within 30 days.

h. Purchased $2,250 of additional office equipment on credit.

i. Completed engineering services for $18,000 on credit.

j. Received a bill for rent on equipment that was used on a completed job. The $1,200 rent must be paid within 30 days.

k. Collected $7,200 from the client described in transaction *g*.

l. Paid $1,500 wages to a drafting assistant.

m. Paid the account payable created in transaction *h*.

n. Paid $675 cash for some repairs to an item of drafting equipment.

o. Stephen Forest withdrew $9,360 cash from the business for personal use.

p. Paid $1,500 wages to a drafting assistant.

q. Paid $3,000 cash to advertise in the local newspaper.

Required

1. Open the following T-accounts: Cash; Accounts Receivable; Prepaid Insurance; Office Equipment; Drafting Equipment; Building; Land; Accounts Payable; Long-Term Notes Payable; Stephen Forest, Capital; Stephen Forest, Withdrawals; Engineering Fees Earned; Wages Expense; Equipment Rental Expense; Advertising Expense; and Repairs Expense.

2. Record the transactions by entering debits and credits directly in T-accounts. Use the transaction letters to identify each debit and credit. Prepare a trial balance as of July 31.

3. Calculate the company's debt ratio. Use $236,265 as the ending total assets. Are the assets of the company financed more by debt or equity?

Check Figure
Totals in trial balance,
$253,500

Hector Mendez opened a computer consulting business called Capital Consultants and completed the following transactions during May:

May	1	Mendez invested $100,000 in cash and office equipment valued at $24,000 in the business.
	1	Prepaid $7,200 cash for three months' rent for an office.
	2	Made credit purchases of office equipment for $12,000 and office supplies for $2,400.
	6	Completed services for a client and immediately received $2,000 cash.
	9	Completed an $8,000 project for a client, who will pay within 30 days.
	10	Paid the account payable created on May 2.
	19	Paid $6,000 cash for the annual premium on an insurance policy.
	22	Received $6,400 as partial payment for the work completed on May 9.
	25	Completed work for another client for $2,640 on credit.
	31	Withdrew $6,200 cash from the business for personal use.
	31	Purchased $800 of additional office supplies on credit.
	31	Paid $700 for the month's utility bill.

Problem 3-3
Preparing and posting general journal entries and preparing a trial balance

A1, P1, P2
Ⓖ Ⓢ

Required

1. Prepare general journal entries to record the transactions.

2. Open the following accounts (use the balance column format): Cash (101); Accounts Receivable (106); Office Supplies (124); Prepaid Insurance (128); Prepaid Rent (131); Office Equipment (163); Accounts Payable (201); Hector Mendez, Capital (301); Hector Mendez, Withdrawals (302); Services Revenue (403); and Utilities Expense (690).

3. Post entries to the accounts and enter the balance after each posting.

4. Prepare a trial balance as of the end of this month.

Check Figure
Cash account balance,
$73,900

Art Platt started a business called Able Movers and began operations in July. His accounting skills are weak, and he needs help gathering information at the end of the month. He recorded the following journal entries during July:

Problem 3-4
Interpreting journals, posting, and analyzing trial balance errors

A1, P1, P2

July	1	Cash	60,000	
		Trucks	44,000	
		Art Platt, Capital		104,000
	2	Office Supplies	1,292	
		Cash		1,292
	4	Moving Equipment	12,800	
		Accounts Payable		12,800
	8	Cash	2,000	
		Accounts Receivable	10,000	
		Moving Fees Earned		12,000
	12	Cash	1,600	
		Moving Fees Earned		1,600
	15	Prepaid Insurance	2,700	
		Cash		2,700

21	Cash	10,000	
	Accounts Receivable		10,000
23	Accounts Payable	12,800	
	Cash		12,800
25	Office Equipment	18,800	
	Art Platt, Capital		18,800
29	Office Supplies	2,908	
	Accounts Payable		2,908
31	Art Platt, Withdrawals	4,912	
	Cash		4,912
31	Wages Expense	6,280	
	Cash		6,280

Based on these entries, Platt prepared the following trial balance:

ABLE MOVERS
Trial Balance
For Month Ended July 31, 2000

	Debit	Credit
Cash	$ 45,616	
Accounts receivable	0	
Office supplies	2,400	
Prepaid insurance	2,700	
Trucks	44,000	
Office equipment	18,800	
Moving equipment		$ 12,800
Accounts payable		29,080
Art Platt, capital		122,800
Art Platt, withdrawals	491	
Moving fees earned		13,600
Wages expense	6,280	
Totals	$120,287	$178,280

Preparation Component

1. Platt remembers something about trial balances and realizes the preceding one has at least one error. To help him find the mistakes, set up the following balance column accounts and post entries to them: Cash (101); Accounts Receivable (106); Office Supplies (124); Prepaid Insurance (128); Trucks (153); Office Equipment (163); Moving Equipment (167); Accounts Payable (201); Art Platt, Capital (301); Art Platt, Withdrawals (302); Moving Fees Earned (401); and Wages Expense (623).

Analysis Components

2. Although Platt's journal entries are correct, he forgot to provide explanations. Analyze each entry and present a reasonable explanation of what happened.

3. Prepare a correct trial balance and describe the errors that Platt made.

Check Figure
Totals in trial balance,
$139,308

Problem 3-5
Analyzing account
balances and
reconstructing
transactions

A1, P2

Carlos Young started an engineering firm called Young Engineering. He began operations in March and completed seven transactions, including his initial investment of $17,000 cash. After these transactions, the ledger included the following accounts with their normal balances:

Cash	$26,660
Office supplies	660
Prepaid insurance	3,200
Office equipment	16,500
Accounts payable	16,500
Carlos Young, capital	17,000
Carlos Young, withdrawals	3,740
Engineering fees earned	24,000
Rent expense	6,740

Required

Preparation Component

1. Prepare a trial balance for the business.

Analysis Components

2. Analyze the accounts and their balances and prepare a list that describes each of the seven most likely transactions and their amounts.

3. Present a schedule that shows how the seven transactions in 2 resulted in the $26,660 Cash balance.

Travis McAllister operates a surveying company. For the first few months of the company's life (through April), the accounting records were maintained by an outside accounting service. According to those records, McAllister's owner's equity balance was $75,000 as of April 30. To save on expenses, McAllister decided to keep the records himself. He managed to record May's transactions properly but he had problems properly classifying accounts in financial statements. His first versions of the balance sheet and income statement follow. Using the information contained in these financial statements, prepare revised statements, including a statement of changes in owner's equity, for the month of May.

Problem 3-6
Classifying accounts in financial statements

A1

McALLISTER SURVEYING
Income Statement
For Month Ended May 31, 2000

Revenue:		
Investments by owner		$ 3,000
Unearned surveying fees		6,000
Total revenues		$ 9,000
Operating expenses:		
Rent expense	$3,100	
Telephone expense	600	
Surveying equipment	5,400	
Advertising expense	3,200	
Utilities expense	300	
Insurance expense	900	
Withdrawals by owner	6,000	
Total operating expenses		19,500
Net income (loss)		$(10,500)

McALLISTER SURVEYING
Balance Sheet
For May 31, 2000

Assets		Liabilities	
Cash	$ 3,900	Accounts payable	$ 2,400
Accounts receivable	2,700	Surveying fees earned	18,000
Prepaid insurance	1,800	Short-term notes payable	48,000
Prepaid rent	4,200	Total liabilities	$ 68,400
Office supplies	300		
Buildings	81,000		
Land	36,000	**Owner's Equity**	
Salaries expense	3,000	Travis McAllister, capital	64,500
		Total liabilities and	
Total assets	$132,900	owner's equity	$132,900

Serial Problem
Echo Systems

(This comprehensive problem starts in this chapter and continues in Chapters 4, 5, and 6. Because of its length, this problem is most easily solved if you use the Working Papers that accompany this text.)

On October 1, 2000, Mary Graham organized a computer service company called **Echo Systems.** Echo Systems is organized as a sole proprietorship and will provide consulting services, computer system installations, and custom program development. Graham has adopted the calendar year for reporting and expects to prepare the company's first set of financial statements as of December 31, 2000. The initial chart of accounts for the accounting system includes these items:

Account	No.	Account	No.
Cash	101	Mary Graham, Capital	301
Accounts Receivable	106	Mary Graham, Withdrawals	302
Computer Supplies	126	Computer Services Revenue	403
Prepaid Insurance	128	Wages Expense	623
Prepaid Rent	131	Advertising Expense	655
Office Equipment	163	Mileage Expense	676
Computer Equipment	167	Miscellaneous Expenses	677
Accounts Payable	201	Repairs Expense, Computer	684

Required

1. Prepare journal entries to record each of the following transactions for Echo Systems.

2. Open balance column accounts for the company and post journal entries to them.

Oct.	1	Mary Graham invested $45,000 cash, an $18,000 computer system, and $9,000 of office equipment in the business.
	2	Paid $4,500 for four months' rent.
	3	Purchased computer supplies on credit for $1,320 from Abbott Office Products.
	5	Paid $2,160 cash for one year's premium on a property and liability insurance policy.
	6	Billed Capital Leasing $3,300 for installing a new computer.
	8	Paid for the computer supplies purchased from Abbott Office Products.
	10	Hired Carly Smith as a part-time assistant for $100 per day, as needed.
	12	Billed Capital Leasing another $1,200 for services.
	15	Received $3,300 from Capital Leasing on their account.
	17	Paid $705 to repair computer equipment damaged when moving into the new office.
	20	Paid $1,860 for an advertisement in the local newspaper.
	22	Received $1,200 from Capital Leasing on their account.
	28	Billed Decker Company $3,225 for services.
	31	Paid Carly Smith for seven days' work.
	31	Withdrew $3,600 cash from the business for personal use.
Nov.	1	Reimbursed Mary Graham's business automobile mileage for 1,000 miles at $0.25 per mile.
	2	Received $4,650 cash from Elite Corporation for computer services.
	5	Purchased $960 of computer supplies from Abbott Office Products.
	8	Billed Fostek Co. $4,350 for services.
	13	Received notification from Alamo Engineering Co. that Echo's bid of $3,750 for an upcoming project was accepted.
	18	Received $1,875 from Decker Company against the bill dated October 28.
	22	Donated $750 to the United Way in the company's name.
	24	Completed work for Alamo Engineering Co. and sent them a bill for $3,750.
	25	Sent another bill to Decker Company for the past due amount of $1,350.
	28	Reimbursed Mary Graham's business automobile mileage for 1,200 miles at $0.25 per mile.
	30	Paid Carly Smith for 14 days' work.
	30	Withdrew $1,800 cash from the business for personal use.

BEYOND THE NUMBERS

Refer to the financial statements and related information for **NIKE** in Appendix A.

Reporting in Action

C3, A2

Required

Answer the following questions by analyzing the information in NIKE's statements:

1. How many revenue categories does NIKE report on its consolidated statement of income?
2. What five current assets are reported on NIKE's consolidated balance sheet?
3. What five current liabilities are reported on its balance sheet?
4. What dollar amounts of income taxes are reported on its income statements for the annual reporting periods ending in 1997 and 1996?
5. During the annual reporting period ended May 31, 1997, how much cash did NIKE pay in dividends?
6. What is NIKE's debt ratio at May 31, 1997? (Hint: Use Liabilities = Assets − Stockholders' equity.) How does this compare to its ratio at May, 31 1996?

Swoosh Ahead

7. Obtain access to NIKE's annual report for fiscal years ending after May 31, 1997. You can gain access to NIKE's annual report at its web site [www.nike.com] or through the SEC's EDGAR database [www.sec.gov]. Recompute NIKE's debt ratio with the updated annual report information you have obtained. Compare the May 31, 1997, fiscal year-end debt ratio to any subsequent year's debt ratio that you are able to calculate. Also compare how NIKE's income tax expense has changed since May 31, 1997.

Both **NIKE** and **Reebok** design, produce, market, and sell sports footwear and apparel. Key comparative figures ($ millions) for these two organizations follow:

Comparative Analysis

A2

Key Figures*	NIKE	Reebok
Total liabilities	$2,205	$1,405
Total equity	$3,156	$ 381

* NIKE figures are from its annual report for the fiscal year ended May 31,1997. Reebok figures are from its annual report for the fiscal year ended December 31, 1996.

Required

Use the information in the table above to answer the following questions:

1. What are the total assets for (a) NIKE and (b) Reebok?
2. What is the debt ratio for (a) NIKE and (b) Reebok?
3. Which of the two companies has the higher degree of financial leverage?

Review the **Judgment and Ethics** from the first section of this chapter. Join a class discussion on the nature of the dilemma in this case. The guidance answer suggests that you should not comply with the assistant manager's request.

Ethics Challenge*

C2

Required

Evaluate at least two other courses of action you might consider and why.

Communicating in Practice
A2

The class should be divided into teams. Teams are to select an industry, and each team member is to select a different company in that industry. Each team member is to acquire the annual report of the company selected. Annual reports can be obtained in many ways, including accessing this book's Web page or through the SEC's EDGAR database [**www.sec.gov**].

Required

1. Use the annual report to compute the debt ratio.
2. Communicate with teammates via a meeting, e-mail, or telephone to discuss the meaning of this ratio, how different companies compare to each other, and the industry norm. The team must prepare a single memo reporting the ratios for each company and identify the conclusions or consensus of opinion reached during the team's discussion. The memo is to be duplicated and distributed to the instructor and all classmates.

Taking it to the Net

Visit the **NIKE** annual report Web site at **www.nike.com.** Select the link to visit the financial highlights of NIKE.

Required

1. Of the financial highlights NIKE reports, identify terms you have already discussed in Chapters 1 through 3. Which terms are unfamiliar to you?
2. As a highlight, NIKE reports its stock price at fiscal year-end. Visit the **Yahoo Quote Service** at **quote.yahoo.com.** Use this quote service to locate NIKE's most recent stock price. NIKE's ticker symbol that you will need to use in the quote service is NIKE. How has the price changed since May 31, 1997 when its price was $57.50?

Teamwork in Action
A1

The general ledger shown below reflects the transactions for Musician Makers, a business that provides music lessons for individuals, for the month of November. Your team must validate the accuracy of the information reported. You can divide responsibilities among team members. In rotation, team members must explain to the team how they derived the information required.

MUSICIAN MAKERS
General Ledger

Cash

Beg. Bal.	3900		
(a)	5000	(b)	1000
(c)	400	(g)	500
(d)	50	(h)	120
(j)	120	(i)	200

Accounts Payable

		(e)	125

A. Melody, Capital

		Beg. Bal.	3075
		(a)	5000

Unearned Lesson Revenue

		(j)	120

A. Melody, Withdrawals

(i)	200		

Notes Payable

(b)	1000	Beg. Bal	1000
		(g)	1500

Lesson Revenue

		(c)	400
		(f)	80

Accounts Receivable

Beg. Bal.	75	(d)	50
(f)	80		

Wage Expense	
(h)	120

Supplies	
Beg. Bal.	100
(e)	125

Equipment	
(g)	2000

Required

1. A brief description of each transaction (a) through (j).
2. Compute net income or net loss for November.
3. Compute ending owner's equity.
4. Prove the accounting equation is in balance. Compute the debt ratio.
5. A schedule of cash flows by activities.
6. Prove that the schedule in (5) agrees with the change in the cash account.
7. Explain why cash flow from operating activities doesn't agree with net income.

Obtain a recent copy of the most prominent newspaper distributed in your area. Research the classified section and prepare a report answering the following questions (attach relevant classified clippings to your report). Alternatively, you may want to search the Web for the required job information. One suitable Web site is: **www.ajb.dni.us.** For documentation, you should print copies of Web sites accessed.

1. Identify the number of listings for accounting positions and the various accounting job titles.
2. Identify the number of listings for other job titles, with examples, that require or prefer accounting knowledge/experience but are not specifically accounting positions.
3. Specify the salary range for the accounting and accounting-related positions if provided.
4. Indicate the job that appeals to you, the reason for its appeal, and its requirements.

Hitting the Road

Read the article "Answered Prayers for America Online" in the September 22, 1997, issue of *Business Week*.

Required

1. Identify three setbacks that **AOL** has suffered in the year preceding the time the article was written. Do any of these setbacks deal with accounting practices at AOL? Why would a company consider doing something potentially offensive to its customers?
2. Compare the number of AOL subscribers as of June 30, 1997, to June 30, 1995.
3. A measure of the reliability of the AOL network is the number of simultaneous users it can service. How many users was AOL simultaneously servicing as of August 31, 1997?
4. The article reports that AOL has proposed a deal in which they will exchange part of their company (ANS Communications) for subscribers of the **CompuServe** service. How many subscribers would AOL gain access to if the deal is completed? Would these new subscribers be shown as assets on AOL's balance sheet?

Business Week Activity

C3, A1

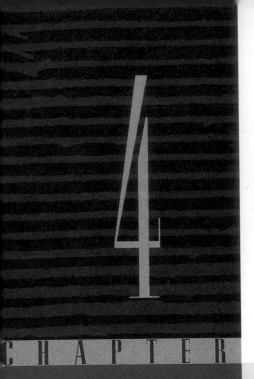

Adjusting Accounts for Financial Statements

▶ A Look Back

Chapter 3 explained the analysis and recording of transactions. We showed how to work with source documents, T-accounts, double-entry accounting, ledgers, postings, and trial balances. These are important parts of the accounting process leading to financial statements.

▶ A Look at This Chapter

This chapter focuses on the timing of reports and the need to adjust accounts. Adjusting accounts is important for recognizing revenues and expenses in the proper period. We describe why adjustments are necessary, how to record them, and their effects on financial statements. We also explain the adjusted trial balance and how we use it to prepare financial statements.

▶ A Look Ahead

Chapter 5 highlights the completion of the accounting cycle. We explain the important final steps in obtaining reliable, relevant, and comparable accounting information. These include closing procedures, post-closing trial balances, and reversing entries.

Chapter Outline

Bad Boys Need Money

NEW YORK—In New York, a mecca for professional and amateur sports teams, there is a new team on the block. It's the **Bronx Bombers,** the "bad boys" of rugby. The Bombers are organized and owned by Rob Burston, a 28-year-old player/coach.

Burston has always been driven. He took just three years to finish college. And he did it while working part-time as a salesperson. So it's no surprise the Bombers, a team Burston organized three years ago, are moving just as fast, topping their division and winning the playoffs. "To take the championship in only our third year is incredible," says Burston proudly. "We wanted it bad, and we believed in each other."

So far, that belief has been a hit on the field and in the stands. Attendance has skyrocketed. This year, between ticket sales, promotional advertising, and other revenues, the Bombers took in over $490,000 in revenues. Just this month, Burston's team signed an exclusive deal with an athletic shoe company to market rugby shoes and apparel. He won't reveal the figure, but the smile on his face is revealing enough.

Burston's next move? He wants to upgrade the facilities and field. "Rugby is a great spectator sport," insists Burston. "And if we do it right, the sky's the limit." Still, it's likely to be a battle. Burston needs money to fund his ideas, and bankers and investors are not accustomed to funding sports teams. A banker, whom Burston has negotiated with, warns of hurdles. "How do you predict income and cash flows in rugby? When do you recognize season ticket sales, promotional revenues, and exclusive contracts? Are facility and field costs expenses or assets? You must overcome these financial hurdles."

Such hurdles don't frighten Burston, who grew up poor with a "can't make it" label. Yet he is a realist who's now working with financial advisors in preparing pro forma statements to see his dream come true. But count on this: Burston and the bad boys of rugby are gunning for the big boys.

CHAPTER PREVIEW

Financial statements reflect revenues when earned and expenses when incurred. This is known as *accrual accounting*. Accrual accounting requires several steps. We described many of these steps in Chapter 3. We showed how companies use accounting systems to collect information about *external* transactions and events. We also explained how journals, ledgers, and other procedures are useful in preparing financial statements.

This chapter emphasizes the accounting process for producing useful information involving *internal* transactions and events. An important part of this process is adjusting the account balances, which are then reported in financial statements. Adjusting of accounts is necessary so that financial statements at the end of a reporting period reflect the effects of all transactions. We also identify and explain an important measure of company performance drawn from these statements (profit margin) and how users put it to work.

Timing and Reporting

Regular, or periodic, reporting is an important part of the accounting process. The point in time or the period of time to which a report refers impacts this process. This section describes the more important impacts of accounting time periods.

The Accounting Period

C1 Explain the importance of periodic reporting and the time period principle.

The value of information is often linked to its timeliness. Useful information must reach decision makers frequently and promptly. To provide timely information, accounting systems prepare reports at regular intervals. This results in an accounting process impacted by the time period (or periodicity) principle. The **time period principle** assumes that an organization's activities can be divided into specific time periods such as a month, a three month quarter, or a year as shown in Exhibit 4.1.

Financial statements are prepared for time periods that are considered important for decision making and regulatory purposes. Time periods covered by statements are called **accounting,** or *reporting*, **periods.** Most organizations use a year as their

"Nike today announced quarterly earnings per share of . . ."

Exhibit 4.1

Accounting Periods

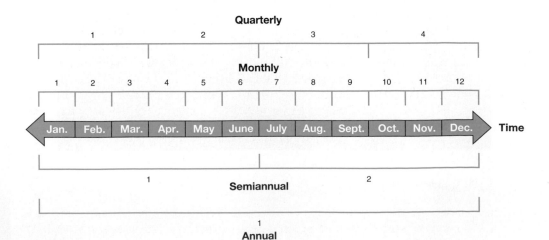

primary accounting period. Reports covering a one-year period are known as **annual financial statements.** Many organizations also prepare **interim financial statements** covering one, three, or six months of activity.

The annual reporting period is not always a calendar year ending on December 31. An organization can adopt a **fiscal year** consisting of any 12 consecutive months. It is also acceptable to adopt an annual reporting period of 52 weeks. For example, **The GAP's** 1997 fiscal year ended on February 1, its 1996 year on February 3, and its 1995 year on January 28.

Companies not experiencing much seasonal variation in sales volume within the year often choose the calendar year as their fiscal year. For example, the financial statements of **Alcoa** reflect a fiscal year that ends on December 31. Companies experiencing seasonal variations in sales often choose a fiscal year corresponding to their natural business year. The **natural business year** ends when sales activities are at their lowest point during the year. The natural business year for retailers ends around January 31, after the holiday season. Examples of these companies include **Wal-Mart, Kmart,** and **Dell.** They start their annual accounting periods on or near February 1.

Purpose of Adjusting

The usual accounting process is to record external transactions and events (with outside parties) during an accounting period. After external transactions are recorded, several accounts in the ledger need adjustments before their balances appear in financial statements. This need arises because internal transactions and events remain unrecorded.

An example is the cost of certain assets that expire as time passes. The Prepaid Insurance account of **FastForward** is one of these. FastForward's trial balance shown in Exhibit 4.2 shows Prepaid Insurance with a balance of $2,400. This amount is the premium for two years of insurance protection beginning on December 1, 1997. By December 31, 1997, one month's coverage is used up, and $2,400 is no longer an accurate amount for the remaining 23 months' prepaid insurance. Because the coverage costs an average of $100 per month ($2,400/24 months), the Prepaid Insurance account balance must be reduced by one month's cost. The income statement must report this $100 cost as insurance expense for December.

Another example is the $3,720 balance in Supplies. This account includes the cost of supplies that were used in December. The cost of the supplies used must be reported as a December expense. The balances of both Prepaid Insurance and Supplies accounts must be adjusted before they are reported on the December 31 balance sheet.

Another adjustment necessary for FastForward relates to one month's usage of equipment. Also, the balances of Unearned Consulting Revenue, Consulting Revenue, and Salaries Expense accounts often need adjusting before appearing on the December statements. We explain in the next section how this adjusting process is carried out.

Recognizing Revenues and Expenses

Decision makers need timely financial information. We use the time period principle in dividing a company's activities into specific time periods. Yet because of the need for regular reporting of information, not all activities are complete at the time financial state-

C2 Describe the purpose of adjusting accounts at the end of a period.

Exhibit 4.2

Trial Balance

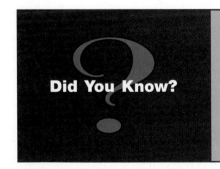

FASTFORWARD Trial Balance December 31, 1997		
	Debit	Credit
Cash	$ 7,950	
Accounts receivable	0	
Prepaid insurance	2,400	
Supplies	3,720	
Equipment	26,000	
Accounts payable		$ 1,100
Unearned consulting revenue		3,000
Note payable		5,100
C.Taylor, capital		30,000
C.Taylor, withdrawals	600	
Consulting revenue		3,800
Rental revenue		300
Rent expense	1,000	
Salaries expense	1,400	
Utilities expense	230	
Total	$43,300	$43,300

ments are prepared. This means we must make some adjustments in reporting to not mislead decision makers.

We rely on two principles in the adjusting process—*revenue recognition* and *matching*. Chapter 2 explains that the revenue recognition principle requires that revenue be reported when earned, not before and not after. Revenue is earned for most companies when services and products are delivered to customers. If FastForward provides consulting to a client in December, the revenue is earned in December. This means it must be reported on the December income statement, even if the client paid for the services in a month other than December. A major goal of the adjusting process is to have revenue recognized (reported) in the time period when it is earned.

Did You Know?

Is It Revenue, or Is It Not?
Centennial Technology, like many companies, recognizes revenue when products are shipped. What is not common is that the CEO of Centennial shipped products to the warehouses of friends and reported it as revenue. **Informix,** a database software maker, also recorded revenue when products were passed to distributors. It admits now that there were "errors in the way revenues had been recorded," and its CEO is in jail. These and other risky revenue recognition practices are often revealed by a large increase in accounts receivable relative to sales ratio.

The **matching principle** aims to report expenses in the same accounting period as the revenues that are earned as a result of these expenses. This matching of costs (expenses) with benefits (revenues) is a major part of the adjusting process. A common example is a business like FastForward that earns monthly revenues while operating out of rented store space. The earning of revenues required rented space. The matching principle tells us that rent must be reported on the income statement for December, even if rent is paid in a month either before or after December. This ensures the rent expense for December is matched with December's revenues.

Matching expenses with revenues often requires us to predict certain events. When we use financial statements we must understand that they involve estimates. This means they include measures that are not precise. **Walt Disney**'s annual report explains that its film and television production costs from movies such as *Flubber* and *Hercules* are matched to revenues based on a ratio of current revenues from the show divided by its predicted total revenues.

Accrual Basis Compared to Cash Basis

Accrual basis accounting uses the adjusting process to recognize revenues when earned and to match expenses with revenues. This means the economic effects of revenues and expenses are recorded when earned or incurred, not when cash is received or paid.

C3 Explain accrual accounting and how it adds to the usefulness of financial statements.

Cash basis accounting means revenues are recognized when cash is received and that expenses are recorded when cash is paid. If a business earns revenue in December but cash is not received from clients until January, then cash basis accounting reports this revenue in January. Because revenues are reported when cash is received and expenses are deducted when cash is paid, the cash basis net income for a period is the difference between revenues received in cash (called *receipts*) and expenses paid in cash (called *expenditures* or *disbursements*).

Cash basis accounting for the income statement, balance sheet, and statement of changes in owner's equity is not consistent with accepted accounting principles. It is commonly held that accrual accounting provides a better indication of business performance than information about current cash receipts and payments.[1] Accrual accounting also increases the *comparability* of financial statements from one period to another. Yet many companies and users of statements still find cash basis accounting useful for several internal reports and decisions.

To see the impact of these different accounting systems, let's consider the Prepaid Insurance of FastForward. FastForward paid $2,400 for two years of insurance coverage beginning on December 1. Accrual accounting means that $100 of insurance expense is reported on December's income statement. Another $1,200 of expense is reported in 1998, and the remaining $1,100 is reported as expense in the first 11 months of 1999. This allocation of insurance cost across these three fiscal years is illustrated in Exhibit 4.3.

A cash basis income statement for December 1997 reports insurance expense of $2,400 as shown in Exhibit 4.4. The income statements for 1998 and 1999 report no insurance expense from this policy.

Exhibit 4.3

Accrual Basis Accounting for Prepaid Insurance

December *Transaction:* Purchase 24 months' insurance beginning December 1997	Insurance Expense 1997				Insurance Expense 1998				Insurance Expense 1999			
	Jan	Feb	Mar	Apr	Jan	Feb	Mar	Apr	Jan	Feb	Mar	Apr
	$0	$0	$0	$0	$100	$100	$100	$100	$100	$100	$100	$100
	May	June	July	Aug	May	June	July	Aug	May	June	July	Aug
	$0	$0	$0	$0	$100	$100	$100	$100	$100	$100	$100	$100
	Sept	Oct	Nov	Dec	Sept	Oct	Nov	Dec	Sept	Oct	Nov	Dec
	$0	$0	$0	$100	$100	$100	$100	$100	$100	$100	$100	$0

---

[1] *Statement of Financial Accounting Concepts No. 1,* "Objectives of Financial Reporting by Business Enterprises" (Norwalk, CT, 1978), par. 44.

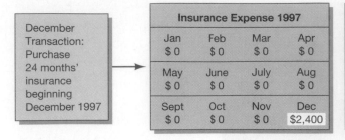

Insurance Expense 1997			
Jan $ 0	Feb $ 0	Mar $ 0	Apr $ 0
May $ 0	June $ 0	July $ 0	Aug $ 0
Sept $ 0	Oct $ 0	Nov $ 0	Dec $2,400

Insurance Expense 1998			
Jan $0	Feb $0	Mar $0	Apr $0
May $0	June $0	July $0	Aug $0
Sept $0	Oct $0	Nov $0	Dec $0

Insurance Expense 1999			
Jan $0	Feb $0	Mar $0	Apr $0
May $0	June $0	July $0	Aug $0
Sept $0	Oct $ 0	Nov $0	Dec $0

December Transaction: Purchase 24 months' insurance beginning December 1997

Exhibit 4.4

Cash Basis Accounting for Prepaid Insurance

The accrual basis balance sheet reports any unexpired premium as a Prepaid Insurance asset. The cash basis never reports this asset. The cash basis information is less useful for most decisions because reported income for 1997–1999 fails to match the cost of insurance with the benefits received for those years.

Accrual basis accounting is generally accepted for external reporting. Yet information about cash flows is also useful and is why companies reporting financial statements according to generally accepted accounting principles must include a statement of cash flows.

Flash back

1. Describe a company's annual reporting period.
2. Why do companies prepare interim financial statements?
3. What accounting principles most directly propel the adjusting process?
4. Is cash basis accounting consistent with the matching principle? Why or why not?
5. If your company pays a $4,800 premium on April 1, 1998, for two years' insurance coverage, how much insurance expense is reported in 1999 using cash basis accounting?

Answers—p. 151

Adjusting Accounts

C4 Identify the types of adjustments and their purpose.

The process of adjusting accounts is similar to our process of analyzing and recording transactions in the prior chapter. We must analyze each account balance and the transactions and events that affect it to determine any needed adjustments. An **adjusting entry** is recorded to bring an asset or liability account balance to its proper amount when an adjustment is needed. This entry also updates the related expense or revenue account. Adjusting entries are posted to accounts like any other entry. This section explains why adjusting entries are needed to provide useful information. We also show the mechanics of adjusting entries and their links to financial statements.

Framework for Adjustments

Adjustments are necessary for transactions and events that extend over more than one period. It is helpful to group adjustments by the timing of cash receipt or payment in relation to the recognition of the related revenues or expenses. Exhibit 4.5 identifies the five main adjustments. These involve both expenses and revenues.

Prepaid expenses, depreciation, and unearned revenues each reflect transactions where cash is paid or received *before* a related expense or revenue is recognized.[2] Accrued expenses and accrued revenues reflect transactions where cash is paid or received *after* a related expense or revenue is recognized. Adjusting entries are necessary for each of

---

[2] Prepaids are also called *deferrals* because the recognition of an expense or revenue is *deferred* until after the related cash is paid or received.

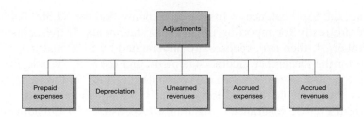

Exhibit 4.5

Framework for Adjustments

these so that revenues, expenses, assets, and liabilities are correctly reported. It is helpful to remember that each adjusting entry affects one or more income statement accounts *and* one or more balance sheet accounts. Also note that an adjusting entry *never* involves the Cash account.

Adjusting Prepaid Expenses

Prepaid expenses refer to items *paid for* in advance of receiving their benefits. Prepaid expenses, also called *deferred expenses,* are assets. As these assets are used, their costs become expenses. Adjusting entries for prepaids involve increasing (debiting) expenses and decreasing (crediting) assets as shown in Exhibit 4.6.

Adjustments are made to reflect transactions and events (including passage of time) that impact the amount of prepaid expenses. This section describes the accounting for three common prepaid expenses: insurance, supplies, and depreciation.

"Here is the first 24 months' insurance in advance."

P1 Prepare and explain adjusting entries for prepaid expenses, depreciation, and unearned revenues.

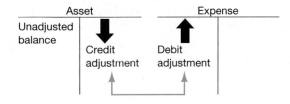

Exhibit 4.6

Adjusting for Prepaid Expenses

Prepaid Insurance

We illustrate prepaid insurance using FastForward's payment of $2,400 for two years of insurance protection beginning on December 1, 1997. The cash payments are illustrated in Exhibit 4.4 for 1997–1999. With the passage of time, the benefit of the insurance protection gradually expires and a portion of the Prepaid Insurance asset becomes expense. For instance, one month's insurance coverage expires by December 31, 1997. This expense is $100, or 1/24 of $2,400. Our adjusting entry to record this expense and reduce the asset is:

Adjustment (a)		
Dec. 31	Insurance Expense	100	
	Prepaid Insurance		100
	To record expired insurance.		

Assets = Liabilities + Equity
−100   −100

Posting this adjusting entry affects the accounts as shown in Exhibit 4.7.

Prepaid Insurance			
Dec. 26	2,400	Dec. 31	100
	−100		
Balance	2,300		

Insurance Expense			
Dec. 31	100		

Exhibit 4.7

Insurance Accounts after Adjusting for Prepaids

After posting, the $100 balance in Insurance Expense and the $2,300 balance in Prepaid Insurance are ready for reporting in financial statements. If the adjustment is *not* made at December 31, then (a) expenses are understated by $100 and net income overstated by $100 for the December income statement, and (b) both Prepaid Insurance and owner's equity (because of net income) are overstated by $100 in the December 31 balance sheet. It is also evident from Exhibit 4.3 that 1998 adjustments must transfer a total of $1,200 from Prepaid Insurance to Insurance Expense, and 1999 adjustments must transfer the remaining $1,100 to Insurance Expense.

Supplies

Supplies are another prepaid expense often requiring adjustment. FastForward purchased $3,720 of supplies in December and used some of them during this month. Consuming these supplies creates expenses equal to their cost. Daily usage of supplies was not recorded in FastForward's accounts because this information was not needed. Also, when we report account balances in financial statements only at the end of a month, record-keeping costs can be reduced by making only one adjusting entry at that time. This entry needs to record the total cost of all supplies used in the month.

Because we prepare an income statement for December, the cost of supplies used during this month must be recognized as an expense. FastForward computes (takes inventory of) the remaining unused supplies. The cost of the remaining supplies is then deducted from the cost of the purchased supplies to compute the amount used. FastForward has $2,670 of supplies remaining out of the $3,720 purchased in December. The $1,050 difference between these two amounts is the cost of the consumed supplies. This amount is December's supplies expense. Our adjusting entry to record this expense and reduce the Supplies asset account is:

Assets = Liabilities + Equity
−1,050   −1,050

	Adjustment (b)		
Dec. 31	Supplies Expense	1,050	
	Supplies		1,050
	To record supplies used.		

Posting this adjusting entry affects the accounts shown in Exhibit 4.8.

The balance of the supplies account is $2,670 after posting and equals the cost of remaining supplies. If the adjustment is *not* made at December 31, then (a) expenses are understated by $1,050 and net income overstated by $1,050 for the December income statement, and (b) both Supplies and owner's equity are overstated by $1,050 in the December 31 balance sheet.

Exhibit 4.8

Supplies Accounts after Adjusting for Prepaids

Supplies					Supplies Expense	
Dec. 2	2,500	Dec. 31	1,050		Dec. 31	1,050	
6	1,100					
26	120					
Total	3,720	Total	1,050			
	−1,050					
Balance	2,670					

Other Prepaid Expenses

There are other prepaid expenses, such as Prepaid Rent, that are accounted for exactly like Insurance and Supplies above. We should also note that some prepaid expenses are both paid for and fully used up within a single accounting period. One example is when a company pays monthly rent on the first day of each month. The payment creates a prepaid expense on the first day of each month that fully expires by the end of the month. In these special cases we can record the cash paid with a debit to the expense account instead of an asset account. This practice is described more completely later in the chapter.

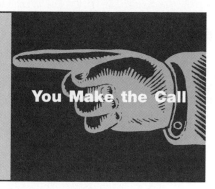

Appraiser

You are hired as an appraiser to estimate the value of a small publishing company. This company recently signed a well-known athlete to write a book. The company agreed to pay the athlete $500,000 to sign plus future royalties on the book. Your analysis of the company's financial statements finds the $500,000 is not reported as an expense. Instead, it is reported as part of Prepaid Expenses. A note to the statement says "prepaid expenses include author signing fees that are matched against future expected sales." Is this accounting for the $500,000 signing bonus acceptable? How does it affect your analysis?

Answer—p. 151

Adjusting for Depreciation

Plant and equipment refers to long-term tangible assets used to produce and sell products and services. These assets are expected to provide benefits for more than one period. Examples of plant and equipment are land, buildings, machines, vehicles, and fixtures. All plant and equipment assets, except for land, eventually wear out or decline in usefulness. The costs of these assets are deferred, but gradually reported as expenses in the income statement over the assets' useful lives (benefit periods). **Depreciation** is the process of computing expense by allocating the cost of these assets over their expected useful lives. Depreciation expense is recorded with an adjusting entry similar to that for prepaid expenses.

FastForward uses equipment in earning revenue. This equipment's cost must be depreciated. Recall that FastForward made two purchases of equipment, one for $20,000 and the other for $6,000, in early December. Chuck Taylor expects this equipment to have a useful life (benefit period) of four years. Taylor expects to sell the equipment for about $8,000 at the end of four years. This means the net cost expected to expire over the useful life is $18,000 ($26,000 − $8,000).[3]

There are several methods we can use to allocate this $18,000 net cost to expense. FastForward uses a method called straight-line depreciation.[4] The **straight-line depreciation method** allocates equal amounts of an asset's cost to depreciation during its useful life. When the $18,000 net cost is divided by the 48 months in the asset's useful life, we get an average monthly cost of $375 ($18,000/48). Our adjusting entry to record monthly depreciation expense is:

	Adjustment (c)		
Dec. 31	Depreciation Expense	375	
	Accumulated Depreciation—Equipment . .		375
	To record monthly depreciation on equipment.		

Assets = Liabilities + Equity
−375   −375

Posting this adjusting entry affects the accounts shown in Exhibit 4.9.

After posting the adjustment, the Equipment account less its Accumulated Depreciation—Equipment account equals the December 31 balance sheet amount for this asset. The balance in the Depreciation Expense—Equipment account is the expense reported

---

[3] For simplicity, we treat this equipment as "one", with a net cost of $18,000. Chapter 11 will explain how we deal with depreciation and its many factors.

[4] We explain the details of depreciation methods in Chapter 11. We briefly describe the straight-line method here to help us understand the adjusting process.

Equipment		
Dec. 3	20,000	
6	6,000	
Bal.	26,000	

Accumulated Depreciation— Equipment		
	Dec. 31	375

Depreciation Expense— Equipment		
Dec. 31	375	

Exhibit 4.9

Accounts after Depreciation Adjustments

in the December income statement. If the adjustment is *not* made at December 31, then (a) expenses are understated by $375 and net income overstated by $375 for the December income statement, and (b) both assets and owner's equity are overstated by $375 in the December 31 balance sheet.

It is common for decreases in an asset account to be recorded with a credit to the account. But this procedure is *not* followed when recording depreciation. Instead, depreciation is recorded in a contra account. A **contra account** is an account linked with another account and having an opposite normal balance. It is reported as a subtraction from the other account's balance. For instance, FastForward's contra account for Accumulated Depreciation—Equipment is subtracted from the equipment account in the balance sheet.

The use of contra accounts allows balance sheet readers to know both the cost of assets and the total amount of depreciation charged to expense. By knowing both these amounts, decision makers can better assess a company's productive capacity and any need to replace assets. FastForward's balance sheet shows both the $26,000 original cost of equipment and the $375 balance in the accumulated depreciation contra account. This information reveals that the equipment is close to new. If FastForward only reports equipment at its net amount of $25,625, users cannot assess the equipment's age or its need for replacement.

The title of this contra account is *Accumulated Depreciation*. It means the account includes total depreciation expense for all prior periods during which the assets were being used. For instance, FastForward's Equipment and Accumulated Depreciation accounts would appear as shown in Exhibit 4.10 on February 28, 1998, after three monthly adjusting entries.

Exhibit 4.10

Accounts after 3 Months of Depreciation Adjustments

Equipment		
Dec. 3	20,000	
6	6,000	
Total	26,000	

Accumulated Depreciation— Equipment		
	Dec. 31	375
	Jan. 31	375
	Feb. 28	375
	Total	1,125

These account balances are reported in the assets section on the February 28 balance sheet as shown in Exhibit 4.11.

Exhibit 4.11

Equipment and Accumulated Depreciation Contra Accounts in the Balance Sheet

Assets		
Cash		$ _____
⋮		
Equipment	$26,000	
Less accumulated depreciation	(1,125)	24,875
Total Assets		$ _____

Small Business Owner

You are preparing to make an offer to purchase a small family-run restaurant. The manager gives you a copy of her depreciation schedule for the restaurant's building and equipment. It shows costs of $75,000 and accumulated depreciation of $55,000. This leaves a net total for building and equipment of $20,000. Is this information valuable in deciding on a purchase offer for the restaurant?

Answer—p. 151

Adjusting Unearned Revenues

Unearned revenues refer to cash *received* in advance of providing products and services. Unearned revenues, also known as *deferred revenues,* are a liability. When cash is accepted, an obligation to provide products and services is accepted. As products and services are provided, the unearned revenues become *earned* revenues. Adjusting entries for unearned revenues involve increasing (crediting) revenues and decreasing (debiting) unearned revenues as shown in Exhibit 4.12.

These adjustments reflect transactions and events (including passage of time) that impact unearned revenues.

An example of unearned revenues is in **America Online**'s annual report in Appendix A. AOL reports Deferred Revenue of $37.95 million among the liabilities on its balance sheet. Another example is **The New York Times,** which reports unexpired (unearned) subscriptions in 1996 of more than $90 million.

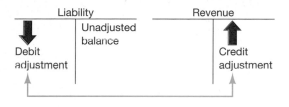

Exhibit 4.12

Adjusting for Unearned Revenues

> Proceeds from subscriptions . . . are deferred at the time of sale and are included in . . . Income on a pro rata basis over the terms of the subscription.

Unearned revenues are over 10% of total current liabilities for both companies.

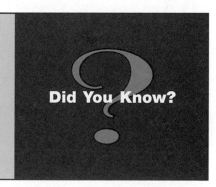

Money Is Celtic Green

Game day for the **Boston Celtics** includes adjusting accounts. When the Celtics receive cash from tickets sales and broadcast fees, it is recorded in an unearned revenue account called "Deferred Game Revenues." The Celtics recognize this unearned revenue on a game-by-game basis. Because the NBA regular season begins in October and ends in April, revenue recognition is mainly limited to this period. For the 1997 season, the Celtics' quarterly (3-month) revenues (in millions) are: $0 for July–Sept.; $21 for Oct.–Dec.; $34 for Jan.–Mar.; and $9 for April–June. [Source: Boston Celtics, Annual & Quarterly Reports.]

Did You Know?

FastForward has unearned revenues. FastForward agreed on December 26 to provide consulting services to a client for a fixed fee of $1,500 per month. On that same day, this client paid the first two months' fees in advance, covering the period December 27 to February 24. The entry to record the cash received in advance is:

$Assets = Liabilities + Equity$
$+3,000 \quad +3,000$

Dec. 26	Cash	3,000	
	Unearned Consulting Revenue		3,000
	Received advance payment for services over the next two months.		

This advance payment increases cash and creates an obligation to do consulting work over the next two months. As time passes, FastForward will earn this payment. There are no external transactions linked with this earnings process. By December 31, Fast-Forward provides five days' service and earns one-sixth of the $1,500 revenue for the first month. This amounts to $250 ($1,500 × 5/30). The *revenue recognition principle* implies that $250 of unearned revenue is reported as revenue on the December income statement. The adjusting entry to reduce the liability account and recognize earned revenue is:

$Assets = Liabilities + Equity$
$\quad\quad\quad -250 \quad\quad +250$

	Adjustment (d)		
Dec. 31	Unearned Consulting Revenue	250	
	Consulting Revenue ($1,500 × 5/30)		250
	To record earned revenue received in advance.		

After posting the adjusting entry the accounts appear as in Exhibit 4.13.

The adjusting entry transfers $250 out of unearned revenue (a liability account) to a revenue account. If the adjustment is *not* made, then (a) revenue and net income are understated by $250 in the December income statement, and (b) Unearned Revenue is overstated and owner's equity understated by $250 on the December 31 balance sheet.

Exhibit 4.13

Revenue Accounts after Adjusting for Prepaids

Unearned Consulting Revenue			
Dec. 31	250	Dec. 26	3,000
			−250
		Balance	2,750

Consulting Revenue			
		Dec. 10	2,200
		12	1,600
		31	250
		Balance	4,050

Adjusting Accrued Expenses

P2 Prepare and describe adjusting entries for accrued expenses and accrued revenues.

Accrued expenses refer to costs that are incurred in a period but are both unpaid and unrecorded. Accrued expenses are incurred expenses that must be reported on the income statement. When costs are incurred in acquiring products and services, there is an obligation to pay for them. The costs of products and services acquired but not yet paid are accrued expenses. Adjusting entries for recording accrued expenses involve increasing (debiting) expenses and increasing (crediting) liabilities as shown in Exhibit 4.14.

Exhibit 4.14

Adjusting for Accrued Expenses

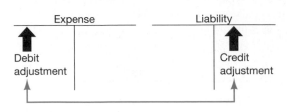

This adjustment recognizes expenses incurred in a period but not yet paid. Common examples of accrued expenses are salaries, interest, rent, and taxes. We use salaries and interest to show how to adjust accounts for accrued expenses.

Accrued Salaries Expense

FastForward's employee earns $70 per day, or $350 for a five-day workweek beginning on Monday and ending on Friday. This employee gets paid every two weeks on Friday.

On December 12 and 26, the wages are paid, recorded in the journal, and posted to the ledger. The *unadjusted* Salaries Expense and Cash paid for salaries appear as shown in Exhibit 4.15:

Salaries Expense		
Dec. 12	700	
26	700	

Cash		
	Dec. 12	700
	26	700

Exhibit 4.15

Salary and Cash Accounts Before Adjusting

The calendar in Exhibit 4.16 shows three working days after the December 26 payday (29, 30, and 31). This means the employee earns three days' salary by the close of business on Wednesday, December 31. While this salary cost has been incurred, it is not yet paid or recorded.

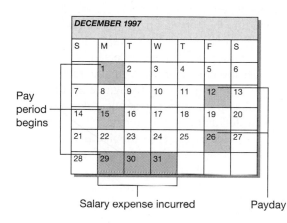

Exhibit 4.16

Salary Accrual and Paydays

The year-end financial statements are incomplete if FastForward fails to report both the added expense and the liability to the employee for unpaid salary. The year-end adjusting entry to account for accrued salaries is:

Adjustment (e)			
Dec. 31	Salaries Expense	210	
	Salaries Payable		210
	To record three days' accrued salary (3 × $70).		

Assets = Liabilities + Equity
+210   −210

After the adjusting entry is posted, the expense and liability accounts appear as shown in Exhibit 4.17:

Salaries Expense		
Dec. 12	700	
26	700	
31	210	
Total	1,610	

Salaries Payable		
	Dec. 31	210

Exhibit 4.17

Salary Accounts After Accrual Adjustments

This means $1,610 of salaries expense is reported on the income statement and that a $210 salaries payable (liability) is reported in the balance sheet. If the adjustment is *not* made, then (a) Salaries Expense is understated and net income overstated by $210 in the December income statement, and (b) Salaries Payable is understated and owner's equity overstated by $210 on the December 31 balance sheet.

Accrued Interest Expense

It is common for companies to have accrued interest expense on notes payable and certain other liabilities at the end of a period. Interest expense is incurred with the passage of time. Unless interest is paid on the last day of an accounting period, we need to adjust accounts for interest expense incurred but not yet paid. This means we must accrue interest cost from the most recent payment date up to the end of the period.[5] We fully describe computation of interest expense later in the book. The adjusting entry is similar to the one for accruing unpaid salary, with a debit to Interest Expense and a credit to Interest Payable (liability).

Adjusting Accrued Revenues

"You can pay me when I finish."

Accrued revenues refer to revenues earned in a period that are both unrecorded and not yet received. Accrued revenues are earned revenues that must be reported on the income statement. An example is a house painter who bills customers when the job is done. If one-third of a house is painted by the end of a period, then one-third of the painter's billing is recorded as revenue in the period even though it is not yet billed or collected. When products and services are delivered, we expect to receive payment for them. Adjusting entries recognize accrued revenues for the value of products and services delivered that are both unrecorded and not yet collected. The adjusting entries increase (debit) assets and increase (credit) revenues as shown in Exhibit 4.18.

This adjustment recognizes revenues earned in a period but not yet received in cash. Common examples of accrued revenues arise from services, products, interest, and rent. We use service fees and interest to show how to adjust accounts for accrued revenues.

Exhibit 4.18

Adjusting for Accrued Revenues

Accrued Services Revenue

Many revenues are recorded when cash is received from a customer or when products and services are sold on credit. Accrued revenues are not recorded until adjusting entries are made at the end of the accounting period. These accrued revenues are earned but unrecorded because either the customer has not yet paid for them or the seller has not yet billed the customer.

FastForward provides us one example. In the second week of December, FastForward agreed to provide consulting services to the athletic department of a college for a fixed fee of $2,700 per month. The terms of the initial agreement call for FastForward to provide services from December 12, 1997 through January 10, 1998, or 30 days of service. The athletic department agrees to pay $2,700 cash to FastForward on January 10, 1998, when the service period is complete.

At December 31, 1997, 20 days of services are already provided to the college. Since the contracted services are not yet entirely provided, the college is not yet billed nor has FastForward recorded the services already provided. FastForward has earned two-thirds of the one-month fee, or $1,800 ($2,700 × 20/30). The *revenue recognition principle* implies we must report the $1,800 on the December income statement because it was earned in December. The balance sheet also must report that this college owes FastForward $1,800. The year-end adjusting entry to account for accrued services revenue is:

---

[5] The formula for computing accrued interest is: Payable amount × Annual interest rate × Fraction of year since last payment date.

Adjustment (f)		
Dec. 31	Accounts Receivable	1,800	
	Consulting Revenue		1,800
	To record 20 days' accrued revenue.		

Assets = Liabilities + Equity
+1,800   +1,800

The debit to accounts receivable reflects the amount owed to FastForward from the college for consulting services already provided. After the adjusting entry is posted, the affected accounts appear as shown in Exhibit 4.19.

Accounts Receivable			
Dec. 12	1,900	Dec. 22	1,900
31	1,800		
Total	3,700	Total	1,900
	−1,900		
Balance	1,800		

Consulting Revenue		
	Dec. 10	2,200
	12	1,600
	31	250
	31	1,800
	Total	5,850

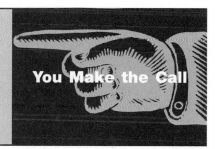

Exhibit 4.19

Receivable and Revenue Accounts after Accrual Adjustments

Accounts receivable are reported on the balance sheet at $1,800, and $5,850 of revenues are reported on the income statement. If the adjustment is *not* made, then (a) both Consulting Revenue and net income are understated by $1,800 in the December income statement, and (b) both Accounts Receivable and owner's equity are understated by $1,800 on the December 31 balance sheet.

Loan Officer

You are a loan officer when an owner of a stereo components store applies for a business loan from your bank. Your analysis of the store's financial statements reveals a record increase in revenues and profits for the current year. Further analysis shows nearly all of this increase is due to a promotional campaign where consumers bought now and pay nothing until January 1 of next year. The store recorded all of these sales as accrued revenue. Do you see any concerns in approving a loan to this store?

You Make the Call

Answer—p. 151

Accrued Interest Revenue

In addition to the accrued interest expense we described earlier, interest can yield an accrued revenue when a company is owed money (or other assets) from a debtor. If a company is holding notes or accounts receivable that produce interest revenue, we must adjust the accounts to record any earned and yet uncollected interest revenue. The adjusting entry is similar to the one for accruing services revenue, with a debit to Interest Receivable (asset) and a credit to Interest Revenue.

Answer—p. 151

Financial Officer

You are the financial officer for a retail outlet company. At year-end when you are reviewing adjusting entries to record accruals, you are called into the president's office. The president asks about accrued expenses and instructs you to not record these expenses until next year because they will not be paid until January or later. The president also asks how much current year's revenues increased by the recent purchase order from a new customer. You state there is no effect on sales until next year because the purchase order says merchandise is to be delivered after January 15 and that is when your company plans to make delivery. The president points out that the order already has been received, that your company is ready to make delivery, and tells you to record this sale in the current year. Your company would report a net income instead of a net loss if you carried out the president's orders for adjusting accruals. What do you do?

Judgment and Ethics

Type	Before Adjusting		Adjusting Entry
	Balance Sheet Account	Income Statement Account	
Prepaid expense	Asset overstated	Expense understated	Dr. Expense Cr. Asset
Depreciation	Asset overstated	Expense understated	Dr. Expense Cr. Contra Asset
Unearned revenues	Liability overstated	Revenue understated	Dr. Liability Cr. Revenue
Accrued Expenses	Liability understated	Expense understated	Dr. Expense Cr. Liability
Accrued Revenues	Asset understated	Revenue understated	Dr. Asset Cr. Revenue

A1 Explain how accounting adjustments link to financial statements.

Adjustments and Financial Statements

The process of adjusting accounts is intended to bring an asset or liability account balance to its correct amount. The adjusting entry also updates a related expense or revenue account. These adjustments are necessary for transactions and events that extend over more than one period. Adjusting entries are posted like any other entry.

Exhibit 4.20 lists the five major types of transactions requiring adjustment. Adjusting entries are necessary for each. Understanding this exhibit is important to understanding the adjusting process and its importance to financial statements. Remember each adjusting entry affects one or more income statement accounts *and* one or more balance sheet accounts. Note that an adjusting entry never affects cash.

Exhibit 4.21 summarizes the adjusting entries of FastForward on December 31. The posting of adjusting entries to individual ledger accounts was shown when we described

Exhibit 4.21

Journalizing Adjusting Entries

GENERAL JOURNAL				Page #
Date	Account Titles and Explanation	PR	Debit	Credit
1997	*Adjusting Entries*			
Dec. 31	Insurance Expense		100	
	Prepaid Insurance			100
	To record expired insurance.			
31	Supplies Expense		1,050	
	Supplies			1,050
	To record supplies used.			
31	Depreciation Expense—Equipment		375	
	Accumulated Depreciation—Equipment			375
	To record monthly depreciation on equipment.			
31	Unearned Consulting Revenue		250	
	Consulting Revenue			250
	To record earned revenue received in advance.			
31	Salaries Expense		210	
	Salaries Payable			210
	To record three days' accrued salary.			
31	Accounts Receivable		1,800	
	Consulting Revenue			1,800
	To record 20 days' accrued revenue.			

each of the transactions and is not repeated here. Adjusting entries are often set apart from other journal entries with the caption <u>Adjusting Entries</u>.

Flash *back*

6. If you omit an adjusting entry for accrued service revenues of $200 at year-end, what is the effect of this error on the income statement and balance sheet?

7. What is a contra account? Explain.

8. What is an accrued expense? Give an example.

9. Describe how an unearned revenue arises. Give an example.

Answers—p. 152

An **unadjusted trial balance** is a listing of accounts and balances prepared *before* adjustments are recorded. An **adjusted trial balance** is a list of accounts and balances prepared *after* adjusting entries are recorded and posted to the ledger. Exhibit 4.22 shows the unadjusted and adjusted trial balances for FastForward at December 31, 1997. Notice several new accounts arising from the adjusting entries. The listing of accounts is also slightly changed to match the order in the chart of account numbers listed near the end of the book.

Adjusted Trial Balance

P3 Explain and prepare an adjusted trial balance.

Exhibit 4.22

Unadjusted and Adjusted Trial Balances

FASTFORWARD
Trial Balances
December 31, 1997

	Unadjusted Trial Balance		Adjusted Trial Balance	
	Dr.	**Cr.**	**Dr.**	**Cr.**
Cash	$ 7,950		$ 7,950	
Accounts receivable			1,800	
Supplies	3,720		2,670	
Prepaid insurance	2,400		2,300	
Equipment	26,000		26,000	
Accumulated depreciation—Equipment				$ 375
Accounts payable		$ 1,100		1,100
Salaries payable				210
Unearned consulting revenue		3,000		2,750
Note payable		5,100		5,100
Chuck Taylor, capital		30,000		30,000
Chuck Taylor, withdrawals	600		600	
Consulting revenue		3,800		5,850
Rental revenue		300		300
Depreciation expense—Equipment			375	
Salaries expense	1,400		1,610	
Insurance expense			100	
Rent expense	1,000		1,000	
Supplies expense			1,050	
Utilities expense	230		230	
Totals	$43,300	$43,300	$45,685	$45,685

Preparing Financial Statements

P4 Prepare financial statements from an adjusted trial balance.

We can prepare financial statements directly from information in the *adjusted* trial balance. An adjusted trial balance includes all balances appearing in financial statements. We know that a trial balance summarizes information in the ledger by listing accounts and their balances. This summary is easier to work from than the entire ledger when preparing financial statements.

Exhibit 4.23 shows how FastForward's revenue and expense balances are transferred from the adjusted trial balance to the (1) income statement and (2) statement of changes in owner's equity. Note how we use the net income and withdrawals account to prepare the statement of changes in owner's equity.

Exhibit 4.24 shows how FastForward's asset and liability balances on the adjusted trial balance are transferred to the balance sheet. The ending owner's equity is determined on the statement of changes in owner's equity and transferred to the balance sheet. There are different formats for the balance sheet. The **account form** lists assets on the left and liabilities and owner's equity on the right side of the balance sheet. Its name comes from its link to the accounting equation, Assets = Liabilities + Equity. The balance sheet in Exhibit 2.17 is in account form. The **report form** balance sheet lists items vertically as shown in Exhibit 4.24. **NIKE** uses a report form. Both forms are widely used and are considered equally helpful to users.

We usually prepare financial statements in the order shown: income statement, statement of changes in owner's equity, and balance sheet.[6] This order makes sense since the balance sheet uses information in the statement of changes in owner's equity, which in turn uses information from the income statement.

Exhibit 4.23

Preparing the Income Statement and Statement of Changes in Owner's Equity from the Adjusted Trial Balance

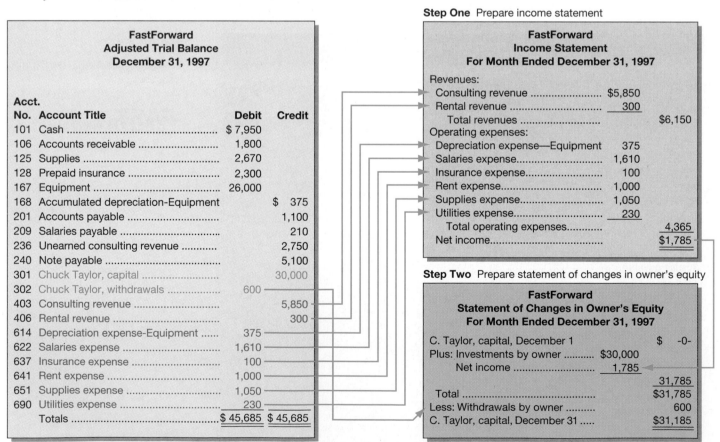

---

[6] The statement of cash flows is often the final statement prepared. The cash ledger account is very helpful for this purpose. Its preparation is illustrated in the next chapter.

Exhibit 4.24

Preparing the Balance Sheet
from the Adjusted Trial Balance

Step Three Prepare balance sheet

FastForward
Adjusted Trial Balance
December 31, 1997

Acct. No.	Account Title	Debit	Credit
101	Cash	$ 7,950	
106	Accounts receivable	1,800	
125	Supplies	2,670	
128	Prepaid insurance	2,300	
167	Equipment	26,000	
168	Accumulated depreciation—Equipment		$ 375
201	Accounts payable		1,100
209	Salaries payable		210
236	Unearned consulting revenue		2,750
240	Note payable		5,100
301	Chuck Taylor, capital		30,000
302	Chuck Taylor, withdrawals	600	
403	Consulting revenue		5,850
406	Rental revenue		300
614	Depreciation expense—Equipment	375	
622	Salaries expense	1,610	
637	Insurance expense	100	
641	Rent expense	1,000	
651	Supplies expense	1,050	
690	Utilities expense	230	
	Totals	$ 45,685	$ 45,685

FastForward
Balance Sheet
December 31, 1997

Assets

Cash		$ 7,950
Accounts receivable		1,800
Supplies		2,670
Prepaid insurance		2,300
Equipment	$ 26,000	
Less accumulated depreciation	(375)	25,625
Total assets		$ 40,345

Liabilities

Accounts payable	$ 1,100	
Salaries payable	210	
Unearned consulting revenue	2,750	
Note payable	5,100	
Total liabilities		$ 9,160

Owner's Equity

C. Taylor, capital, December 31, 1997	$ 31,185
Total liabilities and owner's equity	$ 40,345

From statement of changes
in owner's equity in Exhibit 4.23

Flash back

10. Jordan Air has the following information in its unadjusted and adjusted trial balances:

	Unadjusted		Adjusted	
	Debit	Credit	Debit	Credit
Prepaid insurance	$6,200		$5,900	
Salaries payable				$1,400

What are the adjusting entries that Jordan Air likely recorded?

11. What accounts are taken from the adjusted trial balance to prepare an income statement?

12. In preparing financial statements from an adjusted trial balance, what statement is usually prepared second?

Answers—p. 152

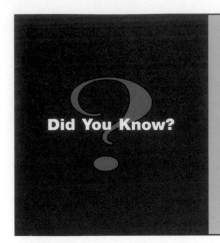

SUN Shines on Accounting

Only three years ago **Sun Microsystems** took almost a month to prepare statements after the end of an accounting period. Today, it takes only 24 hours to deliver preliminary figures to key decision makers at Sun. This gives Sun a big jump on strategic planning for the next period. What is Sun's secret? Transactions are entered in a network of Sun computers so everyone can share and manage data faster. This frees its accounting professionals to take a more active role in managing and strategizing. [Source: *Business Week,* October 28, 1996.]

Accrual Adjustments in Later Periods

P5 Record and describe entries for later periods that result from accruals.

Accrued revenues at the end of one accounting period often result in cash *receipts* from customers in the next period. Also, accrued expenses at the end of one accounting period often result in cash *payments* in the next period. This section explains how we account for these cash receipts or payments in later periods.

Paying Accrued Expenses

FastForward recorded three days of accrued salaries for its employee with this adjusting entry:

Assets = Liabilities + Equity
        +210   −210

Dec. 31	Salaries Expense	210	
	Salaries Payable		210
	To record three days' accrued salary (3 × $70).		

When the first payday of the next period arrives on Friday, January 9, the following entry settles the accrued liability (salaries payable) and records additional salaries expense for work in January:

Assets = Liabilities + Equity
−700   −210   −490

Jan. 9	Salaries Payable (3 days at $70)	210	
	Salaries Expense (7 days at $70)	490	
	Cash		700
	Paid two weeks' salary including three days accrued in December.		

The first debit in the January 9 entry records the payment of the liability for the three days' salary accrued on December 31. The second debit records the salary for January's first seven working days (including the New Year's Day holiday) as an expense of the new accounting period. The credit records the total amount of cash paid to the employee.

Receiving Accrued Revenues

FastForward made the following adjusting entry to record 20 days' accrued revenue earned from its consulting contract with a college:

Assets = Liabilities + Equity
+1,800   +1,800

Dec. 31	Accounts Receivable	1,800	
	Consulting Revenue		1,800
	To record 20 days' accrued revenue.		

When the first month's fee is received on January 10, FastForward makes the following entry to remove the accrued asset (accounts receivable) and recognize the additional revenue earned in January:

Jan. 10	Cash	2,700	
	Accounts Receivable		1,800
	Consulting Revenue		900
	Received cash for accrued asset and earned consulting revenue.		

Assets = Liabilities + Equity
+2,700   +900
−1,800

The debit reflects the cash received. The first credit reflects the removal of the receivable, and the second credit records the earned revenue.

Flash *back*

13. Music-Mart records $1,000 of accrued salaries on December 31. Five days later on January 5 (the next payday), salaries of $7,000 are paid. What is the January 5 entry?

Answer—p. 152

Profit Margin

Preparers of information want financial statements to reflect relevant information about a company's financial performance and condition. A primary goal of this effort is to provide information to help internal and external decision makers evaluate a company's performance during a reporting period. This includes evaluating management's success in producing profits. This type of information can suggest ways to improve operations and helps users in predicting future results.

In using accounting information to evaluate operating results, one helpful measure is the ratio of a company's net income to sales. This ratio is called the **profit margin,** or **return on sales,** and is computed as shown in Exhibit 4.25.

A2 Compute profit margin and describe its use in analyzing company performance.

$$\text{Profit margin} = \frac{\text{Net income}}{\text{Revenues}}$$

Exhibit 4.25

Profit Margin

This ratio can be interpreted as reflecting the portion of profit in each dollar of revenue.

To illustrate how we compute and use the profit margin, we look at the results of **Ben & Jerry's Homemade Ice Cream** in Exhibit 4.26. Profit margin is one measure we can use to evaluate Ben & Jerry's performance during the past few years.

Exhibit 4.26

Ben & Jerry's Profit Margin

	Year Ended					
Accounting measures	**12/28/96**	**12/30/95**	**12/31/94**	**12/30/93**	**12/29/92**	**12/30/91**
Net income (in thousands) .	$ 3,926	$ 5,948	$ (1,869)	$ 7,201	$ 6,675	$ 3,739
Net sales (in thousands) . .	167,155	155,333	148,802	140,328	131,969	96,997
Profit margin	2.3%	3.8%	(1.3%)	5.1%	5.1%	3.9%
Industry profit margin . . .	2.%	2.%	3.%	5.%	4.%	4.%

Ben & Jerry's average profit margin is 3.15% over this period. Year 1994 stands out as the only year with a loss. This is due to a large increase in operating expenses. The profit margin returns to a positive level in both 1995 and 1996. Also note the steady increase in Ben & Jerry's sales, from less than $100 million in 1991 to more than $167 million in 1996.

Our analysis can benefit from a comparison of profit margins with other companies (see last line of Exhibit 4.26). Ben & Jerry's is a relatively small competitor in the super-premium ice cream industry. As a result of selling in this segment of the market, the company's historical profit margins tend to be at or better than those of its competitors. Competition from larger super-premium companies keeps Ben & Jerry's from enjoying a higher margin.

When we evaluate profit margin of a sole proprietorship, we need to modify the above formula by subtracting from net income the value of the owner's efforts. To illustrate this for FastForward, let's assume the efforts of Chuck Taylor, the owner, are worth $1,500 per month. **FastForward's** profit margin for December 1997 is then computed as shown in Exhibit 4.27.

Exhibit 4.27

Modified profit margin

$$\text{Modified profit margin} = \frac{\text{Net income} - \text{Value of owner's efforts}}{\text{Revenues}} = \frac{\$1,785 - \$1,500}{\$6,150} = 4.6\%$$

Flash *back*

14. Define and interpret the profit margin ratio.

15. If Fila's profit margin is 22.5% and its net income is $1,012,500, what are Fila's total revenues for the reporting period?

Answers—p. 152

Summary

C1 Explain the importance of periodic reporting and the time period principle. The value of information is often linked to its timeliness. Useful information must reach decision makers frequently and promptly. To provide timely information, accounting systems prepare periodic reports at regular intervals. The time period principle assumes that an organization's activities can be divided into specific time periods such as a month, a three-month quarter, or a year for periodic reporting.

C2 Describe the purpose of adjusting accounts at the end of a period. After external transactions and events are recorded, several accounts in the ledger often need adjusting for correct balances to appear in financial statements. This need arises because internal transactions and events remain unrecorded. The purpose of adjusting accounts at the end of a period is to recognize revenues earned and expenses incurred during the period that are not yet recorded.

C3 Explain accrual accounting and how it adds to the usefulness of financial statements. Accrual accounting recognizes revenue when earned and expenses when incurred. Accrual accounting reports the effects of transactions and events when they occur, not necessarily when cash inflows and outflows occur. This information is viewed as valuable in assessing a company's financial position and performance. Yet cash flow information is also useful.

C4 Identify the types of adjustments and their purpose. Adjustments can be grouped according to the timing of cash receipts or payments relative to when they're recognized as revenues or expenses. There are five groups: prepaid expenses, de-

preciation, unearned revenues, accrued expenses, and accrued revenues. Adjusting entries are necessary for each of these groups so that revenues, expenses, assets, and liabilities are correctly reported for each period.

A1 Explain how accounting adjustments link to financial statements. Accounting adjustments bring an asset or liability account balance to its correct amount. They also update related expense or revenue accounts. Every adjusting entry affects one or more income statement accounts *and* one or more balance sheet accounts. An adjusting entry never affects cash. Adjustments are necessary for transactions and events that extend over more than one period. Exhibit 4.20 summarizes financial statement links by type of adjustment.

A2 Compute profit margin and describe its use in analyzing company performance. Profit margin is defined as the reporting period's net income divided by revenues for the same period. Profit margin reflects a company's earnings activities by showing how much profit is in each dollar of revenue. Analyzing company performance using this ratio is helped by computing similar ratios for competitors.

P1 Prepare and explain adjusting entries for prepaid expenses, depreciation, and unearned revenues. Prepaid expenses refer to items paid for in advance of receiving their benefits. Prepaid expenses are assets. As a prepaid asset is used, its cost becomes an expense. Adjusting entries for prepaids involve increasing (debiting) expenses and decreasing (crediting) assets. Unearned (or prepaid) revenues refer to cash received in advance of providing products and services. Unearned revenues are a liability. As products and services are provided, the amount of un-earned revenues becomes earned revenues. Adjusting entries for unearned revenues involve increasing (crediting) revenues and de-creasing (debiting) unearned revenues.

P2 **Prepare and describe adjusting entries for accrued ex-penses and accrued revenues.** Accrued expenses refer to costs incurred in a period that are both unpaid and unrecorded. Ac-crued expenses are incurred expenses and are reported on the in-come statement. Adjusting entries for recording accrued expenses involve increasing (debiting) expenses and increasing (crediting) li-abilities. Accrued revenues refer to revenues earned in a period that are both unrecorded and not yet received in cash. Accrued rev-enues are part of revenues and reported on the income statement. Adjusting entries for recording accrued revenues involve increasing (debiting) assets and increasing (crediting) revenues.

P3 **Explain and prepare an adjusted trial balance.** An ad-justed trial balance is a list of accounts and balances pre-pared after adjusting entries are recorded and posted to the ledger.

Financial statements are often prepared from the adjusted trial balance.

P4 **Prepare financial statements from an adjusted trial bal-ance.** We can prepare financial statements directly from the adjusted trial balance. Revenue and expense balances are trans-ferred to the income statement and statement of changes in owner's equity. Asset, liability, and owner's equity balances are transferred to the balance sheet. We usually prepare statements in the following order: income statement, statement of changes in owner's equity, and balance sheet.

P5 **Record and describe entries for later periods that result from accruals.** Accrued revenues at the end of one account-ing period usually result in cash receipts from customers in later periods. Accrued expenses at the end of one accounting period usually result in cash payments in later periods. When cash is re-ceived or paid in these later periods, the entries must account for the accrued assets or liabilities initially recorded.

Guidance Answers to **You Make the Call**

Appraiser

Prepaid expenses are items paid for in advance of receiving their benefits. They also are assets and are expensed as they are used up. The publishing company's treatment of the signing bonus is ac-ceptable provided there are future book sales that we can match against the $500,000 expense. As an appraiser, you are concerned about the likelihood of future book sales and the risks involved. The most conservative appraiser would adjust the records used for analy-sis so that all $500,000 is treated as an expense for the period when the athlete signs. The more risky the likelihood of future book sales is, the more likely your analysis treats the $500,000 as an expense and not a prepaid expense (asset).

Small Business Owner

Depreciation is a process of cost allocation, not asset valuation. Knowing the depreciation schedule of the restaurant is not espe-

cially useful in your estimation of what the restaurant's building and equipment are currently worth. Your assessment of the age, quality, and usefulness of the building and equipment is much more impor-tant. You would also use the current market values of similar assets in estimating the value of this restaurant's building and equipment.

Loan Officer

Your concern in lending to this store arises from analysis of current year sales. While increased revenues and profits are great, your con-cern is with the collectibility of these promotional sales. If the owner sold products to customers with poor records of paying bills, then collectibility of these sales is low. Your analysis must assess this possibility and recognize any expected losses. If the owner sold only to financially secure customers, then you can reliably count on re-ceiving these accrued revenues.

Guidance Answer to **Judgment and Ethics**

Financial Officer

It appears you must make a choice between following the presi-dent's orders or not. The requirements of acceptable practice are clear. Omitting adjustments and early recognition of revenue can mislead users of financial statements (including managers, owners, and lenders). One action is to request a second meeting with the president where you explain that accruing expenses when incurred and recognizing revenue when earned are required practices. You

should also mention the ethical implications of not complying with accepted practice. Point out that the president's orders involve in-tentional falsification of the statements. If the president persists, you might discuss the situation with legal counsel and any auditors in-volved. Your ethical action might cost you this job. But the poten-tial pitfalls of falsification of statements, reputation loss, personal integrity, and other costs are too great.

Guidance Answers to

1. An annual reporting (or accounting) period covers one year and refers to the preparation of annual financial statements. The an-nual reporting period is not always the same as a calendar year that ends on December 31. An organization can adopt a fiscal year consisting of any 12 consecutive months. It is also ac-ceptable to adopt an annual reporting period of 52 weeks.

2. Interim (less than one year) financial statements are prepared to provide decision makers information frequently and promptly.

3. The revenue recognition principle and the matching principle lead most directly to the adjusting process.

4. No. Cash basis accounting is not consistent with the matching principle because it does not always report expenses in the same period as the revenues earned as a result of those expenses.

5. No expense is reported in 1999. Under cash basis accounting the entire $4,800 is reported as expense in 1998 when the pre-mium is paid.

6. If the accrued services revenue adjustment of $200 is not made, then both revenue and net income are understated by $200 on the current year's income statement, and assets and owner's equity are understated by $200 on the balance sheet.

7. A contra account is an account that is subtracted from the balance of a related account. Use of a contra account often provides more complete information than simply reporting a net amount.

8. An accrued expense refers to a cost incurred in a period that is both unpaid and unrecorded prior to adjusting entries. One example is salaries earned by employees but not yet paid at the end of a period.

9. An unearned revenue arises when cash (or other assets) is received from a customer before the services and products are delivered to the customer. Magazine subscription receipts in advance are one example.

10. The probable adjusting entries of Jordan Air are:

Insurance Expense	300	
Prepaid Insurance		300
To record insurance expired.		
Salaries Expense	1,400	
Salaries Payable		1,400
To record accrued salaries.		

11. Revenue accounts and expense accounts.

12. Statement of changes in owner's equity.

13. The January 5 entry to settle the accrued salaries and to pay for the additional salaries from January is:

Jan. 5	Salaries Payable	1,000	
	Salaries Expense	6,000	
	Cash		7,000
	Paid salary including accrual from December.		

14. Profit margin is defined as net income divided by revenues. It can be interpreted as the portion of profit in each dollar of revenue.

15. Fila's profit margin of 22.5% equals $1,012,500 ÷ Revenues. Solving for revenues, we get revenues equal to $4,500,000 (computed as $1,012,500 ÷ 22.5%).

Demonstration Problem

The following information relates to Best Electronics on December 31, 2001. The company uses the calendar year as its annual reporting period. The company initially records prepaid and unearned items in balance sheet accounts.

a. The company's weekly payroll is $8,400, paid every Friday for a five-day workweek. December 31, 2001, falls on a Monday, but the employees will not be paid until Friday, January 4, 2002.

b. Eighteen months earlier, on July 1, 2000, the company purchased equipment that cost $10,000 and had no salvage value. Its useful life is predicted to be five years.

c. On October 1, 2001, the company agreed to work on a new housing development. For installing alarm systems in 24 new homes, the company was paid $144,000 in advance. When the $144,000 cash was received on October 1, that amount was credited to the Unearned Revenue account. Between October 1 and December 31, work on 18 homes was completed.

d. On September 1, 2001, the company purchased a one-year insurance policy for $1,200. The transaction was recorded with a $1,200 debit to Prepaid Insurance.

e. On December 29, 2001, the company renders a $5,000 service which has not been billed as of December 31, 2001.

Required

1. Prepare adjusting entries needed on December 31, 2001, to record the previously unrecorded effects of these transactions and events.

2. Prepare T-accounts for accounts affected by adjusting entries. Post adjusting entries to T-accounts. Determine the adjusted balances for the Unearned Revenue account and the Prepaid Insurance account.

3. Complete the following table describing the effects of your adjusting entries on the 2001 income statement and the December 31, 2001, balance sheet. Use up (down) arrows to indicate an increase (decrease).

Entry	Amount in the Entry	Effect on Net Income	Effect on Total Assets	Effect on Total Liabilities	Effect on Owner's Equity
a					
b					
c					
d					
e					

Planning the Solution

- Analyze information for each situation to determine which accounts need to be updated with an adjustment.
- Calculate the size of each adjustment and prepare the necessary journal entries.
- Show the amount entered by each adjustment in the designated accounts, determine the adjusted balance, and then determine the balance sheet classification that the account falls within.
- Determine each entry's effect on net income for the year and on total assets, total liabilities, and owner's equity at the end of the year.

Solution to Demonstration Problem

1. Adjusting journal entries.

a. Dec. 31	Wages Expense	1,680	
	Wages Payable		1,680
	To accrue wages for the last day of the year ($8,400 × 1/5).		
b. Dec. 31	Depreciation Expense—Equipment	2,000	
	Accumulated Depreciation—Equipment . .		2,000
	To record depreciation expense for the year ($10,000/5 = $2,000).		
c. Dec. 31	Unearned Revenue	108,000	
	Services Revenue		108,000
	To recognize revenues earned ($144,000 × 18/24).		
d. Dec. 31	Insurance Expense	400	
	Prepaid Insurance		400
	To adjust for expired portion of insurance ($1,200 × 4/12).		
e. Dec. 31	Accounts Receivable	5,000	
	Services Revenue		5,000
	To record revenues earned.		

2. T-accounts for adjusting journal entries *a* through *e*.

Wages Expense			
(a)	1,680		

Wages Payable			
		(a)	1,680

Depreciation Expense—Equipment	
(b) 2,000	

Accumulated Depreciation—Equipment	
	(b) 2,000

Unearned Revenue	
Balance	144,000
(c) 108,000	
	Balance 36,000

Services Revenue	
	(c) 108,000
	(e) 5,000
	Balance 113,000

Insurance Expense	
(d) 400	

Prepaid Insurance	
Balance 1,200	(d) 400
Balance 800	

Accounts Receivable	
(e) 5,000	

3. Financial statement effects of adjusting journal entries.

Entry	Amount in the Entry	Effect on Net Income	Effect on Total Assets	Effect on Total Liabilities	Effect on Owner's Equity
a	$1,680	$1,680 ↓	No effect	$1,680 ↑	$1,680 ↓
b	$2,000	$2,000 ↓	$2,000 ↓	No effect	$2,000 ↓
c	$108,000	$108,000 ↑	No effect	$108,000 ↓	$108,000 ↑
d	$400	$400 ↓	$400 ↓	No effect	$400 ↓
e	$5,000	$5,000 ↑	$5,000 ↑	No effect	$5,000 ↑

Alternatives in Accounting for Prepaids

This section explains two alternatives in accounting for prepaid expenses and prepaid (unearned) revenues. We show the accounting for both alternatives.

Recording Prepaid Expenses in Expense Accounts

We explained that prepaid expenses are assets when they are purchased and are recorded with debits to asset accounts. Adjusting entries transfer the costs that expire to expense accounts at the end of an accounting period. We also explained that some prepaid expenses are purchased and fully expire before the end of an accounting period. In these cases, we can avoid adjusting entries by charging the prepaid items to expense accounts when purchased.

There is an alternative practice of recording *all* prepaid expenses with debits to expense accounts. If any prepaids remain unused or unexpired at the end of an accounting period, then adjusting entries must transfer the cost of the unused portions from expense accounts to prepaid expense (asset) accounts. This alternative practice is acceptable. The financial statements are identical under either procedure, but the adjusting entries are different.

To illustrate the accounting differences between these two practices, let's look at Fast-Forward's cash payment of December 26 for 24 months of insurance coverage beginning on December 1. FastForward recorded that payment with a debit to an asset account. But it could have recorded a debit to an expense account. These alternatives are shown in Exhibit 4A.1.

Learning Objectives

Procedural

P6 Identify and explain two alternatives in accounting for prepaids.

P6 Identify and explain two alternatives in accounting for prepaids.

		Payment Recorded as Asset		Payment Recorded as Expense	
Dec. 26	Prepaid Insurance	2,400			
	Cash		2,400		
26	Insurance Expense			2,400	
	Cash				2,400

Exhibit 4A.1

Initial Entry for Prepaid Expenses for Two Alternatives

At the end of the accounting period on December 31, insurance protection for one month is expired. This means $100 ($2,400/24) of the asset expires and becomes an expense for December. The adjusting entry depends on how the original payment is recorded. This is shown in Exhibit 4A.2.

When these entries are posted to the accounts we can see that these two alternatives give identical results. The December 31 adjusted account balances in Exhibit 4A.3 show prepaid insurance of $2,300 and insurance expense of $100 for both methods.

Exhibit 4A.2
Adjusting Entry for Prepaid
Expenses for Two Alternatives

		Payment Recorded as Asset	Payment Recorded as Expense
Dec. 31	Insurance Expense	100	
	Prepaid Insurance	100	
31	Prepaid Insurance		2,300
	Insurance Expense		2,300

Exhibit 4A.3
Account balances under Two
Alternatives for Recording
Prepaid Expenses

Payment Recorded as Asset			Payment Recorded as Expense		
Prepaid Insurance			**Prepaid Insurance**		
Dec. 26	2,400	Dec. 31 100	Dec. 31	2,300	
	−100				
Balance	2,300				

Insurance Expense			Insurance Expense		
Dec. 31	100		Dec. 26	2,400	Dec. 31 2,300
				−2,300	
			Balance	100	

Recording Unearned Revenues in Revenue Accounts

Unearned (prepaid) revenues are liabilities requiring delivery of products and services. We explained how unearned revenues are recorded as credits to liability accounts when cash and other assets are received. Adjusting entries at the end of an accounting period transfer to revenue accounts the earned portion of unearned revenues. Some unearned revenues are received and fully earned before the end of an accounting period. In these cases, we can avoid adjusting entries by recording unearned revenues into revenue accounts when received.

As with prepaid expenses, there is an alternative practice of recording *all* unearned revenues with credits to revenue accounts. If any revenues are unearned at the end of an accounting period, then adjusting entries must transfer the unearned portions from revenue accounts to unearned revenue (liability) accounts. This alternative practice is acceptable. While the adjusting entries are different for these two alternatives, the financial statements are identical.

To illustrate the accounting differences between these two practices, let's look at Fast-Forward's December 26 receipt of $3,000 for consulting services covering the period December 27 to February 24. FastForward recorded this transaction with a credit to a liability account. The alternative is to record it with a credit to a revenue account as shown in Exhibit 4A.4.

By the end of the accounting period (December 31), FastForward earns $250 of this revenue. This means $250 of the liability is satisfied. Depending on how the initial receipt is recorded, the adjusting entry is as shown in Exhibit 4A.5.

Exhibit 4A.4
Initial Entry for Unearned
Revenues for Two Alternatives

		Receipt Recorded as Liability	Receipt Recorded as Revenue
Dec. 26	Cash	3,000	
	Unearned Consulting Revenue	3,000	
26	Cash		3,000
	Consulting Revenue		3,000

	Receipt Recorded as Liability	Receipt Recorded as Revenue
Dec. 31 Unearned Consulting Revenue	250	
Consulting Revenue		250
31 Consulting Revenue		2,750
Unearned Consulting Revenue		2,750

Exhibit 4A.5

Adjusting Entry for Unearned Revenues for Two Alternatives

After adjusting entries are posted, the two alternatives give identical results. The December 31 adjusted account balances in Exhibit 4A.6 show unearned consulting revenue of $2,750 and consulting revenue of $250 for both methods.

Receipt Recorded as Liability

Unearned Consulting Revenue

Dec. 31	250	Dec. 26	3,000
			−250
		Balance	2,750

Consulting Revenue

		Dec. 31	250

Receipt Recorded as Revenue

Unearned Consulting Revenue

		Dec. 31	2,750

Consulting Revenue

Dec. 31	2,750	Dec. 26	3,000
			−2,750
		Balance	250

Exhibit 4A.6

Account Balances under Two Alternatives for Recording Unearned Revenues

Flash back

16. Miller Company records cash receipts of unearned revenues and cash payments of prepaid expenses in balance sheet accounts. Bud Company records these items in income statement accounts. Explain any difference in the financial statements of these two companies from their alternative accounting for prepaids.

Answer—p. 157

Summary of Appendix 4A

P6 Identify and explain two alternatives in accounting for prepaids. It is acceptable to charge all prepaid expenses to expense accounts when they are purchased. When this is done, adjusting entries must transfer any unexpired amounts from expense accounts to asset accounts. It is also acceptable to credit all unearned revenues to revenue accounts when cash is received. In this case the adjusting entries must transfer any unearned amounts from revenue accounts to unearned revenue accounts.

Guidance Answer to Flash backs

16. When adjusting entries are correctly prepared, it does not make any difference whether cash receipts of unearned revenues and cash payments of prepaid expenses are recorded in balance sheet accounts or in income statement accounts. The financial statements of these companies are identical under both methods.

Work Sheet Format for Adjusted Trial Balance

We show in the next chapter how to prepare an adjusted trial balance and financial statements from a work sheet. To focus on the important aspects of the adjusting process in this chapter, we did not introduce the work sheet format. Yet some users prefer this format in introducing the adjusted trial balance, and we present it in Exhibit 4B.1.

Exhibit 4B.1

Work Sheet Format for Preparing the Adjusted Trial Balance

	Unadjusted Trial Balance		Adjustments		Adjusted Trial Balance	
	Dr.	Cr.	Dr.	Cr.	Dr.	Cr.
Cash	$ 7,950				$ 7,950	
Accounts receivable			(f) 1,800		1,800	
Supplies	3,720			(b) 1,050	2,670	
Prepaid insurance	2,400			(a) 100	2,300	
Equipment	26,000				26,000	
Accumulated depreciation— Equipment				(c) 375		$ 375
Accounts payable		$ 1,100				1,100
Salaries payable				(e) 210		210
Unearned consulting revenue		3,000	(d) 250			2,750
Note payable		5,100				5,100
Chuck Taylor, capital		30,000				30,000
Chuck Taylor, withdrawals	600				600	
Consulting revenue		3,800		(d) 250		5,850
				(f) 1,800		
Rental revenue		300				300
Depreciation expense—Equipment			(c) 375		375	
Salaries expense	1,400		(e) 210		1,610	
Insurance expense			(a) 100		100	
Rent expense	1,000				1,000	
Supplies expense			(b) 1,050		1,050	
Utilities expense	230				230	
Totals	$43,300	$43,300	$ 3,785	$ 3,785	$45,685	$45,685

Glossary

Account form balance sheet a balance sheet that lists assets on the left and liabilities and owner's equity on the right side. (p. 146).

Accounting period the length of time covered by financial statements and other reports; also called *reporting period.* (p. 130).

Accrual basis accounting the approach to preparing financial statements that uses the adjusting process to recognize revenues when earned and expenses when incurred; the basis for generally accepted accounting principles. (p. 133).

Accrued expenses costs incurred in a period that are both unpaid and unrecorded; adjusting entries for recording accrued expenses involve increasing (debiting) expenses and increasing (crediting) liabilities. (p. 140).

Accrued revenues revenues earned in a period that are both unrecorded and not yet received in cash (or other assets); adjusting entries for recording accrued revenues involve increasing (debiting) assets and increasing (crediting) revenues. (p. 142).

Adjusted trial balance a listing of accounts and balances prepared after adjustments are recorded and posted to the ledger. (p. 145).

Adjusting entry a journal entry at the end of an accounting period to bring an asset or liability account balance to its proper amount while also updating the related expense or revenue account. (p. 134).

Annual financial statements financial statements covering a one year period; often based on a calendar year, but any twelve consecutive month period is acceptable. (p. 131).

Cash basis accounting revenues are recognized when cash is received and expenses are recorded when cash is paid. (p. 133).

Contra account an account linked with another account and having an opposite normal balance; reported as a subtraction from the other account's balance to provide more complete information than simply the net amount. (p. 138).

Depreciation the expense created by allocating the cost of plant and equipment to the periods in which they are used; represents the expense of using the assets. (p. 137).

Fiscal year the 12 consecutive months (or 52 weeks) chosen as an organization's annual accounting period. (p. 131).

Interim financial statements financial statements covering periods of less than one year; usually based on one- or three- or six-month periods. (p. 131).

Matching principle the principle that requires expenses to be reported in the same period as the revenues that were earned as a result of the expenses. (p. 132).

Natural business year a 12-month period that ends when a company's sales activities are at their lowest point. (p. 131).

Plant and equipment tangible long-lived assets used to produce goods or services. (p. 137).

Prepaid expenses items paid for in advance of receiving their benefits; classified as assets. (p. 135).

Profit margin the ratio of a company's net income to its revenues; measures the portion of profit in each dollar of revenue. (p. 149).

Report form balance sheet a balance sheet that lists items vertically with assets above the liabilities and owner's equity. (p. 146).

Return on sales another name for *profit margin.* (p. 149).

Straight-line depreciation method allocates equal amounts of an asset's net cost to depreciation expense during its useful life. (p. 137).

Time period principle a principle that assumes an organization's activities can be divided into specific time periods such as months, quarters, or years. (p. 130).

Unadjusted trial balance a listing of accounts and balances prepared before adjustments are recorded and posted to the ledger. (p. 145).

Unearned revenues cash received in advance of providing products and services; a liability. (p. 139).

The superscript letter ^A identifies assignment material based on Appendix 4A; the superscript letter ^B identifies material based on Appendix 4B.

Questions

1. What type of business is most likely to select a fiscal year that corresponds to the natural business year instead of the calendar year?
2. What kind of assets requires adjusting entries to record depreciation?
3. What contra account is used when recording and reporting the effects of depreciation? Why is it used?
4. Where is an unearned revenue reported in the financial statements?
5. What is an accrued revenue? Give an example.
6. What is the difference between the cash and accrual bases of accounting?
7. Where is a prepaid expense reported in the financial statements?
8. Why is the accrual basis of accounting preferred over the cash basis?
9^A. If a company initially records prepaid expenses with debits to expense accounts, what type of account is debited in the adjusting entries for prepaid expenses?
10. Why does a sole proprietorship require special procedures in calculating the profit margin?
11. Review the consolidated balance sheet of NIKE in Appendix A. Identify two asset accounts that require adjustment before annual financial state-

ments can be prepared. What would the effect on the income statement be if these two asset accounts were not adjusted?

12. Review the consolidated balance sheet of **Reebok** in Appendix A. As a simplification, assume that the company did not sell or purchase any property, plant, and equipment during 1996. How much depreciation was recorded in the adjusting entry for depreciation at the end of 1996?

13. What current asset account on **America Online's** balance sheet in Appendix A was probably adjusted before the financial statements were prepared as of June 30, 1996? As of June 30, 1995?

14. Review the chapter's opening scenario, *Bad Boys Need Money*. Identify two current sources of revenue for the Bronx Bombers. Identify two additional sources of revenue that the Bronx Bombers might be able to develop. What does it mean when the article states that Burston is currently preparing pro forma financial statements?

Quick Study

QS 4-1
Accrual and cash accounting C3

In its first year of operations, Harris Co. earned $39,000 in revenues and received $33,000 cash from customers. The company incurred expenses of $22,500 but had not paid $2,250 of them at year-end. In addition, Harris prepaid $3,750 for expenses that would be incurred the next year. Calculate the first year's net income under both cash basis and accrual basis accounting.

QS 4-2
Preparing adjusting entries

C4

In recording its transactions during the year, Stark Company records prepayments of expenses in asset accounts and receipts of unearned revenues in liability accounts. At the end of its annual accounting period, the company must make three adjusting entries. They are: (a) accrue salaries expense, (b) adjust the Unearned Services Revenue account to recognize earned revenue, and (c) record the earning of services revenue for which cash will be received the following period. For each of these adjusting entries (a), (b), and (c), use the numbers assigned to the following accounts to indicate the correct account to be debited and the correct account to be credited.

1. Prepaid Salaries Expense
2. Cash
3. Salaries Payable
4. Accounts Receivable
5. Salaries Expense
6. Services Revenue Earned
7. Unearned Services Revenue

QS 4-3
Effects of adjusting entries

C4, A1

In making adjusting entries at the end of its accounting period, Carter Consulting Agency failed to record $1,400 of insurance premiums that had expired. This cost had been initially debited to the Prepaid Insurance account. The company also failed to record accrued salaries payable of $800. As a result of these two oversights, the financial statements for the reporting period will: [choose the best alternative from the following] *(a)* understate assets by $1,400; *(b)* understate expenses by $2,200; *(c)* understate net income by $800; or *(d)* overstate liabilities by $800.

QS 4-4
Intrpreting adjusting entries

C4

The following information is taken from Shank Company's unadjusted and adjusted trial balances:

	Unadjusted		Adjusted	
	Debit	Credit	Debit	Credit
Prepaid insurance	$3,100		$2,950	
Interest payable				$700

Given this information, which of the following items must be included among the adjusting entries?

a. A $150 debit to Insurance Expense and a $700 debit to Interest Expense.

b. A $150 credit to Prepaid Insurance and a $700 debit to Interest Payable.

c. A $150 debit to Insurance Expense and a $700 debit to Interest Payable.

Foster Consulting Company initially records prepaid and unearned items in income statement accounts. Given Foster Consulting Company's practices, which of the following choices applies to the preparation of adjusting entries at the end of the company's first accounting period?

a. Unpaid salaries will be recorded with a debit to Prepaid Salaries and a credit to Salaries Expense.

b. The cost of unused office supplies will be recorded with a debit to Supplies Expense and a credit to Office Supplies.

c. Unearned fees will be recorded with a debit to Consulting Fees Earned and a credit to Unearned Consulting Fees.

d. Earned but unbilled consulting fees will be recorded with a debit to Unearned Consulting Fees and a credit to Consulting Fees Earned.

QS 4-5[A]
Preparing adjusting entries

C4, P6

Revell Company had net income of $37,925 and revenue of $390,000 for the year ended December 31, 2000. Calculate Revell's profit margin. Interpret the profit margin calculation.

QS 4-6
Analyzing profit margin   A2

Classify the following adjusting entries as involving prepaid expenses (P), depreciation (D), unearned revenues (U), accrued expenses (E), or accrued revenues (R).

a. _____ Entry to record annual depreciation expense.

b. _____ Entry to show wages earned but not yet paid.

c. _____ Entry to show revenue earned but not yet billed.

d. _____ Entry to show expiration of prepaid insurance.

e. _____ Entry to show revenue earned that was previously received as cash in advance.

QS 4-7
Identifying accounting adjustments

C4

Adjusting entries affect at least one balance sheet account and at least one income statement account. For the entries listed below, identify the account to be debited and the account to be credited. Indicate which of the two accounts is the income statement account and which is the balance sheet account.

a. Entry to record annual depreciation expense.

b. Entry to record wages earned but not yet paid.

c. Entry to record revenue earned but not yet billed.

d. Entry to record expiration of prepaid insurance.

e. Entry to record revenue earned that was previously received as cash in advance.

QS 4-8
Recording and analyzing adjusting entries

A1

Prepare adjusting journal entries for the financial statements for the year ended December 31, 2000, for each of these independent situations. Assume prepaid expenses are initially recorded in asset accounts. Also, assume fees collected in advance of work are initially recorded as liabilities.

a. Depreciation on the company's equipment for year 2000 is computed to be $16,000.

b. The Prepaid Insurance account had a $7,000 debit balance at December 31, 2000, before adjusting for the costs of any expired coverage. An analysis of the company's insurance policies showed that $1,040 of unexpired insurance remained in effect.

c. The Office Supplies account had a $300 debit balance on January 1, 2000; $2,680 of office supplies were purchased during the year; and the December 31, 2000, physical count showed that $354 of supplies are on hand.

d. One-half of the work for a $10,000 fee received in advance was performed this period.

e. The Prepaid Insurance account had a $5,600 debit balance at December 31, 2000, before adjusting for the costs of any expired coverage. An analysis of the company's insurance policies showed that $4,600 of coverage had expired.

f. Wages of $4,000 have been earned by workers but not paid as of December 31, 2000.

Exercises
Exercise 4-1
Preparing adjusting entries

P1

Exercise 4-2
Adjusting and paying
accrued wages

P2

Resource Management has five part-time employees, each of whom earns $100 per day. They are normally paid on Fridays for work completed on Monday through Friday of the same week. They were all paid in full on Friday, December 28, 2001. The next week, all five of the employees worked only four days because New Year's Day was an unpaid holiday. Show the adjusting entry that would be recorded on Monday, December 31, 2001, and the journal entry that would be made to record paying the employees' wages on Friday, January 4, 2002.

Exercise 4-3
Adjusting entry
classification

C4

In the blank space beside each of these adjusting entries, enter the letter of the explanation that most closely describes the entry:
a. To record this period's depreciation expense.
b. To record accrued salaries expense.
c. To record this period's consumption of a prepaid expense.
d. To record accrued interest income.
e. To record accrued interest expense.
f. To record the earning of previously unearned income.

_____ **1.**	Unearned Professional Fees	18,450	
	Professional Fees Earned		18,450
_____ **2.**	Interest Receivable	2,700	
	Interest Earned		2,700
_____ **3.**	Depreciation Expense	49,500	
	Accumulated Depreciation		49,500
_____ **4.**	Salaries Expense	16,400	
	Salaries Payable		16,400
_____ **5.**	Interest Expense	3,800	
	Interest Payable		3,800
_____ **6.**	Insurance Expense	4,200	
	Prepaid Insurance		4,200

Exercise 4-4
Determining cost flows
through accounts

P1

Determine the missing amounts in each of these four independent situations *a* through *d*:

	a	b	c	d
Supplies on hand—January 1	$ 300	$1,600	$1,360	?
Supplies purchased during the year	2,100	5,400	?	$6,000
Supplies on hand—December 31	750	?	1,840	800
Supplies expense for the year	?	1,300	9,600	6,575

Exercise 4-5
Adjusting and paying
accrued expenses

P2

The following three situations require adjusting journal entries to prepare financial statements as of April 30. For each situation, present the adjusting entry and the entry that would be made to record the payment of the accrued liability during May.

a. The company has a $780,000 note payable that requires 0.8% interest to be paid each month on the 20th of the month. The interest was last paid on April 20 and the next payment is due on May 20.
b. The total weekly salaries expense for all employees is $9,000. This amount is paid at the end of the day on Friday of each week with five working days. April 30 falls on Tuesday of this year, which means that the employees had worked two days since the last payday. The next payday is May 3.
c. On April 1, the company retained an attorney at a flat monthly fee of $2,500. This amount is payable on the 12th of the following month.

On March 1, 1999, a company paid a $16,200 premium on a three-year insurance policy for protection beginning on that date. Fill in the blanks in the following table:

Exercise 4-6
Assets and expenses for accrual and cash accounting

C3

	Balance Sheet Asset under the:			Insurance Expense under the:	
	Accrual Basis	Cash Basis		Accrual Basis	Cash Basis
12/31/1999	$_____	$_____	1999	$_____	$_____
12/31/2000	_____	_____	2000	_____	_____
12/31/2001	_____	_____	2001	_____	_____
12/31/2002	_____	_____	2002	_____	_____
			Total	$_____	$_____

Landmark Properties owns and operates an apartment building and prepares annual financial statements based on a March 31 fiscal year.

a. The tenants of one of the apartments paid five months' rent in advance on November 1, 1999. The rent is $1,500 per month. The journal entry credited the Unearned Rent account when the payment was received. No other entry had been recorded prior to March 31, 2000. Give the adjusting journal entry that should be recorded on March 31, 2000.

b. On January 1, 2000, the tenants of another apartment moved in and paid the first month's rent. The $1,350 payment was recorded with a credit to the Rent Earned account. However, the tenants have not paid the rent for February or March. They have agreed to pay it as soon as possible. Give the adjusting journal entry that should be recorded on March 31, 2000.

c. On April 2, 2000, the tenants described in part *b* paid $4,050 rent for February, March, and April. Give the journal entry to record the cash collection.

Exercise 4-7
Unearned and accrued revenues

P1, P2

Following are two income statements for Pemberton Company for the year ended December 31. The left column was prepared before any adjusting entries were recorded and the right column includes the effects of adjusting entries. The company records cash receipts and disbursements related to unearned and prepaid items in balance sheet accounts. Analyze the statements and prepare the adjusting entries that must have been recorded. Thirty percent of the $6,000 adjustment for Fees Earned was earned but not billed and the other 70% was earned by performing services that the customers had paid for in advance.

Exercise 4-8
Analyzing and preparing adjusting entries

A1, A2, P1, P2

PEMBERTON CO.
Income Statements
For Year Ended December 31

	Before Adjustments	After Adjustments
Revenues:		
Fees earned	$24,000	$30,000
Commissions earned	42,500	42,500
Total revenues	$66,500	$72,500
Operating expenses:		
Depreciation expense, computers		$ 1,500
Depreciation expense, office furniture		1,750
Salaries expense	$12,500	14,950
Insurance expense		1,300
Rent expense	4,500	4,500
Office supplies expense		480
Advertising expense	3,000	3,000
Utilities expense	1,250	1,320
Total operating expenses	$21,250	$28,800
Net income	$45,250	$43,700

Exercise 4-9ᴬ
Adjustments for prepaids recorded in expense and revenue accounts

Classic Customs began operations on December 1. In setting up its accounting procedures, the company decided to debit expense accounts when the company prepays its expenses and to credit revenue accounts when customers pay for services in advance. Prepare journal entries for items *a* through *d* and adjusting entries as of December 31 for items *e* through *g*:

a. Supplies are purchased on December 1 for $3,000.

b. The company prepaid insurance premiums of $1,440 on December 2.

c. On December 15, the company receives an advance payment of $12,000 from a customer for remodeling work.

d. On December 28, the company receives $3,600 from a second customer for remodeling work to be performed in January.

e. By a physical count on December 31, Classic Customs determines that $1,920 of supplies are on hand.

f. An analysis of the insurance policies in effect on December 31 shows that $240 of insurance coverage had expired.

g. As of December 31, only one project is completed. The $6,300 fee for this project had been received in advance.

Exercise 4-10ᴬ
Recording and reporting revenues received in advance

Pavillion Company experienced the following events and transactions during July:

July 1 Received $2,000 in advance of performing work for Andrew Renking.
     6 Received $8,400 in advance of performing work for Matt Swarbuck.
    12 Completed the job for Andrew Renking.
    18 Received $7,500 in advance of performing work for Drew Sayer.
    27 Completed the job for Matt Swarbuck.
    31 The job for Drew Sayer is still unfinished.

a. Give journal entries (including any adjusting entry as of the end of the month) to record these events using the procedure of initially crediting the Unearned Fees account when payment is received from a customer in advance of performing services.

b. Give journal entries (including any adjusting entry as of the end of the month) to record these events using the procedure of initially crediting the Fees Earned account when payment is received from a customer in advance of performing services.

c. Under each method, determine the amount of earned fees reported on the income statement for July and the amount of unearned fees reported on the balance sheet as of July 31.

Exercise 4-11
Computing and interpreting profit margin

A2

Use the following information to calculate the profit margin for each unrelated company *a* through *e*:

	Net Income	Revenues
a.	$ 3,490	$ 31,620
b.	96,744	394,953
c.	110,204	252,786
d.	55,026	1,350,798
e.	79,264	433,914

Which of the five companies is the most profitable according to the profit margin ratio? Interpret the profit margin ratio of the most profitable company.

Garza Company's annual accounting period ends on December 31, 2002. Garza follows the practice of recording prepaid expenses and unearned revenues in balance sheet accounts. The following information concerns the adjusting entries to be recorded as of that date:

a. The Office Supplies account started the year with a $3,000 balance. During 2002, the company purchased supplies at a cost of $12,400, which was added to the Office Supplies account. The inventory of supplies on hand at December 31 had a cost of $2,640.

b. An analysis of the company's insurance policies provided these facts:

Policy	Date of Purchase	Years of Coverage	Total Cost
1	April 1, 2001	2	$15,840
2	April 1, 2002	3	13,068
3	August 1, 2002	1	2,700

The total premium for each policy was paid in full at the purchase date, and the Prepaid Insurance account was debited for the full cost.

c. The company has 15 employees who earn a total of $2,100 in salaries for every working day. They are paid each Monday for their work in the five-day workweek ending on the previous Friday. December 31, 2002, falls on Tuesday, and all 15 employees worked the first two days of the week. Because New Year's Day is a paid holiday, they will be paid salaries for five full days on Monday, January 6, 2003.

d. The company purchased a building on August 1, 2002. The building cost $855,000 and is expected to have a $45,000 salvage value at the end of its predicted 30-year life.

e. Because the company is not large enough to occupy the entire building, it arranged to rent some space to a tenant at $2,400 per month, starting on November 1, 2002. The rent was paid on time on November 1, and the amount received was credited to the Rent Earned account. However, the tenant has not paid the December rent. The company has worked out an agreement with the tenant, who has promised to pay both December's and January's rent in full on January 15. The tenant has agreed not to fall behind again.

f. On November 1, the company rented space to another tenant for $2,175 per month. The tenant paid five months' rent in advance on that date. The payment was recorded with a credit to the Unearned Rent account.

Required

1. Use the information to prepare adjusting entries as of December 31, 2002.

2. Prepare journal entries to record the first subsequent cash transactions for parts *c* and *e*.

Southwest Careers, a school owned by S. Carr, provides training to individuals who pay tuition directly to the school. The school also offers training to groups in off-site locations. The school's unadjusted trial balance as of December 31, 1999 follows. Southwest Careers follows the practice of initially recording prepaid expenses and unearned revenues in balance sheet accounts. Items that require adjusting entries on December 31, 1999, are shown after the trial balance.

Problems

Problem 4-1
Adjusting and subsequent journal entries

A1, P1, P2, P5

Check Figure   Insurance expense, $12,312

Problem 4-2
Adjusting entries, financial statements, and profit margin

P1, P2, P4, A1, A2

S

SOUTHWEST CAREERS
Unadjusted Trial Balance
December 31, 1999

Cash	$ 26,000	
Accounts receivable		
Teaching supplies	10,000	
Prepaid insurance	15,000	
Prepaid rent	2,000	
Professional library	30,000	
Accumulated depreciation—Professional library		$ 9,000
Equipment	70,000	
Accumulated depreciation—Equipment		16,000
Accounts payable		36,000
Salaries payable		
Unearned training fees		11,000
S. Carr, capital		63,600
S. Carr, withdrawals	40,000	
Tuition fees earned		102,000
Training fees earned		38,000
Depreciation expense—Equipment		
Depreciation expense—Professional library		
Salaries expense	48,000	
Insurance expense		
Rent expense	22,000	
Teaching supplies expense		
Advertising expense	7,000	
Utilities expense	5,600	
Totals	$275,600	$275,600

Additional Items

a. An analysis of the company's insurance policies shows that $3,000 of coverage has expired.

b. An inventory shows that teaching supplies costing $2,600 are on hand at the end of the year.

c. Annual depreciation on the equipment is $12,000.

d. Annual depreciation on the professional library is $6,000.

e. On November 1, the company agreed to do a special six-month course for a client. The contract calls for a monthly fee of $2,200, and the client paid the first five months' fees in advance. When the cash was received, the Unearned Training Fees account was credited.

f. On October 15, the school agreed to teach a four-month class for an individual for $3,000 tuition per month payable at the end of the class. The services are being provided as agreed, and no payment has been received.

g. The school's two employees are paid weekly. As of the end of the year, two days' wages have accrued at the rate of $100 per day for each employee.

h. The balance in the Prepaid Rent account represents rent for December.

Required

1. Prepare T-accounts with the balances listed from the unadjusted trial balance.

2. Prepare adjusting journal entries for items *a* through *h* and post them to the T-accounts.

3. Update the balances in T-accounts for the adjusting entries and prepare an adjusted trial balance.

4. Prepare Southwest Careers' income statement and statement of changes in owner's equity for 1999 and prepare its balance sheet as of December 31, 1999.

5. Calculate the company's profit margin for the year.

Check Figure Ending owner's equity, $62,100

A six-column table for RPE Company is shown below. The first two columns contain the unadjusted trial balance for the company as of July 31, 1999. The last two columns contain the adjusted trial balance as of the same date.

Problem 4-3ᴮ
Interpreting unadjusted and adjusted trial balances, preparing financial statements, and calculating profit margin

P1, P2, P4,
A1, A2
S

	Unadjusted Trial Balance		Adjustments		Adjusted Trial Balance	
Cash	$ 27,000				$ 27,000	
Accounts receivable	12,000				22,460	
Office supplies	18,000				3,000	
Prepaid insurance	7,320				4,880	
Office equipment	92,000				92,000	
Accum. depreciation—						
Office equipment		$12,000				$18,000
Accounts payable		9,300				10,200
Interest payable						800
Salaries payable						6,600
Unearned consulting fees . .		16,000				14,300
Long-term notes payable . .		44,000				44,000
R. P. Edds, capital		28,420				28,420
R. P. Edds, withdrawals . . .	10,000				10,000	
Consulting fees earned		156,000				168,160
Depreciation expense—						
Office equipment					6,000	
Salaries expense	71,000				77,600	
Interest expense	1,400				2,200	
Insurance expense					2,440	
Rent expense	13,200				13,200	
Office supplies expense . . .					15,000	
Advertising expense	13,800				14,700	
Totals	$265,720	$265,720			$290,480	$290,480

Required

Preparation Component

1. Prepare this company's income statement and its statement of changes in owner's equity for the year ended July 31, 1999.

2. Prepare the company's balance sheet as of July 31, 1999.

3. Calculate the company's profit margin for the year.

Check Figure Profit margin, 22%

Analysis Component

4. Analyze the differences between the unadjusted and adjusted trial balances to determine the adjustments that must have been made. Show the results of your analysis by inserting amounts from the adjusting journal entries that must have been recorded by the company in the two middle columns. Label each entry with a letter, and provide a short description of the purpose for recording it.

Problem 4-4
Computing accrual
income from cash income

C3

The records for Urban Landscape Co. are kept on the cash basis instead of the accrual basis. But the company is now applying for a loan and the bank wants to know what its net income for year 2000 is under generally accepted accounting principles. Here is the income statement for year 2000 under the cash basis:

URBAN LANDSCAPE CO. Income Statement (Cash Basis) For Year Ended December 31, 2000	
Revenues	$525,000
Expenses	330,000
Net income	$195,000

Additional information was gathered to help convert the income statement to the accrual basis:

	As of 12/31/1999	As of 12/31/2000
Accrued revenues	$12,000	$16,500
Unearned revenues	66,000	21,000
Accrued expenses	14,700	9,000
Prepaid expenses	27,000	20,700

All prepaid expenses from the beginning of the year are consumed or expired, all unearned revenues from the beginning of the year are earned, and all accrued expenses and revenues from the beginning of the year are paid or collected.

Required

Check Figure   Net Income, $243,900

Prepare an accrual basis income statement for this company for year 2000. Provide schedules that explain how you converted from cash revenues and expenses to accrual revenues and expenses.

Problem 4-5
Identifying adjusting and
subsequent entries

C4, P5

For these adjusting and transaction entries, enter the letter of the explanation that most closely describes the adjustment or transaction in the space beside each entry. (You can use letters more than once.)

a. To record receipt of unearned revenue.
b. To record the earning of previously unearned revenue.
c. To record payment of an accrued expense.
d. To record receipt of an accrued revenue.
e. To record an accrued expense.
f. To record an accrued revenue.
g. To record this period's use of a prepaid expense.
h. To record payment of a prepaid expense.
i. To record this period's depreciation expense.

_____	1.	Depreciation Expense	3,000	
		Accumulated Depreciation		3,000
_____	2.	Unearned Professional Fees	2,000	
		Professional Fees Earned		2,000
_____	3.	Rent Expense	1,000	
		Prepaid Rent		1,000
_____	4.	Interest Expense	4,000	
		Interest Payable		4,000

			Debit	Credit
_____	5.	Prepaid Rent	3,500	
		Cash		3,500
_____	6.	Salaries Expense	5,000	
		Salaries Payable		5,000
_____	7.	Insurance Expense	6,000	
		Prepaid Insurance		6,000
_____	8.	Salaries Payable	1,500	
		Cash		1,500
_____	9.	Cash	6,500	
		Unearned Professional Fees		6,500
_____	10.	Cash	9,000	
		Interest Receivable		9,000
_____	11.	Interest Receivable	7,000	
		Interest Earned		7,000
_____	12.	Cash	8,000	
		Accounts Receivable		8,000

The adjusted trial balance below is for Conquest Company as of December 31, 2000:

Problem 4-6
Preparing financial statements from the adjusted trial balance and calculating profit margin

P4, A1, A2

	Debit	Credit
Cash	$ 22,000	
Accounts receivable	44,000	
Interest receivable	10,000	
Notes receivable (due in 90 days)	160,000	
Office supplies	8,000	
Automobiles	160,000	
Accumulated depreciation—Automobiles		$ 42,000
Equipment	130,000	
Accumulated depreciation—Equipment		10,000
Land	70,000	
Accounts payable		88,000
Interest payable		12,000
Salaries payable		11,000
Unearned fees		22,000
Long-term notes payable		130,000
J. Conroe, capital		247,800
J. Conroe, withdrawals	38,000	
Fees earned		420,000
Interest earned		16,000
Depreciation expense—Automobiles	18,000	
Depreciation expense—Equipment	10,000	
Salaries expense	180,000	
Wages expense	32,000	
Interest expense	24,000	
Office supplies expense	26,000	
Advertising expense	50,000	
Repairs expense—Automobiles	16,800	
Total	$998,800	$998,800

Check Figure Total
assets, $552,000

Problem 4-7ᴬ
Recording prepaid
expenses and unearned
revenues

P1, P2, P6

Required

1. Use the information in the trial balance to prepare *(a)* the income statement for the year ended December 31, 2000; *(b)* the statement of changes in owner's equity for the year ended December 31, 2000; and *(c)* the balance sheet as of December 31, 2000.

2. Assume that the value of J. Conroe's services as owner are valued at $30,000 for the year. Calculate the modified profit margin for year 2000.

Trex Company had the following transactions in the last two months of its fiscal year ended December 31:

Nov. 1 Paid $1,500 for future newspaper advertising.

1 Paid $2,160 for insurance through October 31 of the following year.

30 Received $3,300 for future services to be provided to a customer.

Dec. 1 Paid $2,700 for the services of a consultant, to be received over the next three months.

15 Received $7,650 for future services to be provided to a customer.

31 Of the advertising paid for on November 1, $900 worth had not yet been published by the newspaper.

31 Part of the insurance paid for on November 1 had expired.

31 Services worth $1,200 had not yet been provided to the customer who paid on November 30.

31 One-third of the consulting services paid for on December 1 had been received.

31 The company has performed $3,000 of services that the customer paid for on December 15.

Required

Preparation Component

1. Prepare entries for the above transactions under the method that records prepaid expenses as assets and records unearned revenues as liabilities. Also, prepare adjusting entries at the end of the year.

2. Prepare entries for the above transactions under the method that records prepaid expenses as expenses and records unearned revenues as revenues. Also, prepare adjusting entries at the end of the year.

Analysis Component

3. Explain why the alternative sets of entries in requirements 1 and 2 do not result in different financial statement amounts.

Serial Problem

Echo Systems

(This serial problem involving Echo Systems was introduced in Chapter 3 and continues in Chapters 5 and 6. If the Chapter 3 segment has not been completed, the assignment can begin at this point. You need to use the facts presented for the serial problem at the end of Chapter 3. Because of its length, this problem is best solved if you use the Working Papers that accompany this book.)

After the success of its first two months, Mary Graham decides to continue operating Echo Systems. (Transactions that occurred in these first two months are described in Chapter 3.) On December 1, Graham adds these new accounts to the chart of accounts for the ledger:

Account	No.
Accumulated Depreciation—Office Equipment	164
Accumulated Depreciation—Computer Equipment	168
Wages Payable	210
Unearned Computer Services Revenue	236
Depreciation Expense—Office Equipment	612
Depreciation Expense—Computer Equipment	613
Insurance Expense	637
Rent Expense	640
Computer Supplies Expense	652

Required

1. Prepare journal entries to record each of the following transactions for Echo Systems. Post entries to the accounts in the ledger.
2. Prepare adjusting entries to record the transactions and events described on December 31. Post these entries to the accounts in the ledger.
3. Prepare an adjusted trial balance as of December 31, 2000.
4. Prepare an income statement for the three months ended December 31, 2000.
5. Prepare a statement of changes in owner's equity for the three months ended December 31, 2000.
6. Prepare a balance sheet as of December 31, 2000.

Transactions and other information:

Dec. 2   Paid $1,050 to Lakeshore Mall for Echo Systems' share of mall advertising costs.
      3   Paid $600 to repair the company's computer.
      4   Received $3,750 from Alamo Engineering Co. for the receivable from the prior month.
      10 Paid Carly Smith for six days' work at the rate of $100 per day.
      14 Notified by Alamo Engineering Co. that Echo's bid of $6,000 on a proposed project was accepted. Alamo paid an advance of $1,500.
      15 Purchased $1,155 of computer supplies on credit from Abbott Office Products.
      16 Sent a reminder to Fostek Co. to pay the fee for services originally recorded on November 8.
      20 Completed project for Elite Corporation and received $5,625 cash.
   22–26 Took the week off for the holidays.
      28 Received $2,850 from Fostek Co. on their receivable.
      29 Reimbursed Mary Graham's business automobile mileage of 600 miles at $0.25 per mile.
      31 Mary Graham withdrew $1,800 cash from the business.
      31 The following *additional facts* were collected for use in adjusting entries prior to preparing financial statements for the company's first three months:

Additional Facts

a. The December 31 inventory of computer supplies was $720.
b. Three months have passed since the annual insurance premium was paid.
c. As of the end of the year, Carly Smith has not been paid for four days of work at the rate of $100 per day.
d. The computer is expected to have a four-year life with no salvage value.
e. The office equipment is expected to have a three-year life with no salvage value.
f. Prepaid rent for three of the four months has expired.

BEYOND THE NUMBERS

Refer to the financial statements and related information for **NIKE** in Appendix A. Answer the following questions by analyzing the NIKE information:

1. What are the major items making up NIKE's prepaid expenses?
2. What is the total amount recorded as property, plant, and equipment and what is the amount of accumulated depreciation as of May 31, 1997? How do these totals compare to May 31, 1996?
3. What is NIKE's profit margin for 1997 and 1996?

Swoosh Ahead

4. Obtain access to NIKE's annual report for fiscal years ending after May 31, 1997. You can gain access to NIKE's annual report at its web site [www.nike.com] or through the SEC's EDGAR database [www.sec.gov]. Compare the May 31, 1997, fiscal year profit margin to any subsequent year's profit margin that you are able to calculate. Also compare how NIKE's net amount of property, plant, and equipment has changed since May 31, 1997.

Reporting in Action

C4, A1, A2

Comparative Analysis

A2

NIKE Reebok

Both **NIKE** and **Reebok** design, produce, market, and sell sports footwear and apparel. Key comparative figures ($ millions) for these two organizations follow:

Key figures*	NIKE		Reebok	
	1997	1996	1996	1995
Net income	$ 796	$ 553	$ 139	$ 165
Net sales	$9,187	$6,471	$3,479	$3,481

*NIKE figures are from its annual reports for fiscal years ended May 31,1997 and 1996.
 Reebok figures are from its annual reports for fiscal years ended December 31, 1996 and 1995.

Required

1. Compute profit margins for (a) NIKE and (b) Reebok for the two years of data shown above.
2. Which company is more successful on the basis of profit margin?
3. For each company write the following sentence: For every one dollar of sales generated (insert NIKE or Reebok) makes an average profit of _____ cents.
4. Would it be appropriate to calculate the modified profit margin for NIKE or Reebok?

Ethics Challenge

A1

Jackie Houston is a new accountant for Seitzer company. She is learning on the job from Bob Welch, who already has worked several years for Seitzer. Jackie and Bob are preparing adjusting journal entries in anticipation of producing annual financial statements. Jackie has calculated depreciation expense for the fiscal year and records it as:

Depreciation Expense—Equipment $123,546
        Accumulated Depreciation—Equipment   . . $123,546

Bob is rechecking the numbers and says he agrees with her computation. But he says the credit entry should be directly to the equipment account. He argues that while accumulated depreciation is taught in the classroom, "it is a lot less hassle not to use a contra account and just credit the equipment account directly for the annual allocation of depreciation. And, besides, the balance sheet shows the same amount for total assets under both methods."

Required:

1. How should depreciation be recorded? Do you support Jackie or Bob?
2. Evaluate the strengths and weaknesses of Bob's reasons for preferring his method.
3. Indicate whether the situation faced by Jackie is an ethical problem.

Communicating in Practice

C1, C2, A1

Failure to apply accounting principles properly can have significant influence on reported profits as well as on the success or failure of a business. Obtain a copy of the article "KnowledgeWare Accounting Practices Are Questioned," by Timothy O'Brien, *The Wall Street Journal,* September 7, 1994. Read the article and write a summary that includes the following:

1. Identification of the specific accounting principle that this article discusses and an explanation of what this principle requires and prohibits.
2. A description of the accounting practice for **KnowledgeWare** that is questioned in the article.
3. Identification of who has the authority to investigate the challenged practices.
4. Identification of the stakeholders in this case and possible consequences of the questioned accounting practice.
5. An explanation of how this relates to the material in this chapter.

Taking It to the Net

C1, A2

Access the **Cannondale** promotional Web site at http://www.cannondale.com. Visit several hotlinks on the site to get a feel for the company's products.

1. What is the primary product that Cannondale sells?
2. Review the Cannondale 10K—this is the annual financial data required by the SEC. You can access this from the SEC's Edgar system (see this book's Web page). (Hint: Edgar Web site lists numerous recent reports filed with the SEC; click on the one labeled 10K. You will need to scroll down in the 10K report to find the financial statements.)

a. What is the fiscal year-end of Cannondale? Does it appear that Cannondale uses a 12-month or 52-week annual reporting period?

b. What are net sales for Cannondale for the annual accounting period ended June 29, 1996?

c. What is net income for Cannondale for the annual accounting period ended June 29, 1996?

d. Compute profit margin for Cannondale for the annual accounting period ended June 29, 1996.

e. Why do you think Cannondale is employing a fiscal year-end of late June or early July? Does it relate to their natural business year?

Each member of a team will have the responsibility to become a resident expert on a specific type of accounting adjustment. This expertise will be used to facilitate their teammates' understanding of the concepts relevant to the adjustments process and that specific adjustment. Follow the procedures below:

1. Refer to Exhibit 4.20. Each team member is to select their area of expertise by choosing one type of adjustment listed in the exhibit. You have approximately two minutes to make your choices.

2. Learning teams are to disburse and expert teams are to be formed. Expert teams are made up of students who have selected the same area of expertise. The instructor will identify the location where each expert team will meet.

3. Expert teams will collaborate to develop a presentation of items *a–e* listed below. Students must write up the presentations in a format they can show to their learning teams.

a. A specific example (with amounts and dates) of a transaction or event requiring adjustment.

b. The adjusting journal entry for this example with posting as illustrated in T-accounts.

c. Identification and description of the relevant accounting principle bearing on the example.

d. Description of what the post-adjustment account balances reflect, and identification of the statement(s) these balances are reported on.

e. Explanation of how failure to make adjustments affects financial statements.

4. Regroup to original teams. In rotation, experts make the presentations developed in (3) to their own team members. Experts are to encourage and respond to questions.

Teamwork in Action
C4, A1

Pair up with a classmate. Visit the business area of your community or a shopping mall. Identify 10 businesses that operate in the area. Try to construct your list so that it contains a mix of retail and service businesses. Predict whether the companies operate on a 12-month fiscal period that coincides with the calendar year-end or whether they use a natural business fiscal year. Visit each shop in turn, introduce yourself to the employee you are visiting, and try to confirm whether you made a correct determination of the fiscal year-end for the store. In some instances, the personnel available for questioning may not know the answer to your question. If you cannot confirm the answer, thank the employee and note that you could not test your prediction of fiscal year-end. After the visits are complete, compute the percent of fiscal year-ends that you correctly anticipated.

Hitting the Road
C1

Read the short article, "Porsche is back—and then some," in the September 15, 1997, issue of *Business Week*.

Required

1. Contrast the profitability of **Porsche** in 1992 to five years later in 1997.

2. When does Porsche's fiscal year end?

3. What is the amount of sales for Porsche in the 1997 fiscal year?

4. Calculate Porsche's profit margin for the 1997 fiscal year.

5. Despite its recent profitability, what does the article identify as Porsche's weaknesses?

Business Week Activity
A2

CHAPTER 5

Completing the Accounting Cycle

Chapter Outline

Accounting Edge

Washington, DC—Janet Wittes wasn't trying to jump on the latest management bandwagon. But when she founded **Statistics Collaborative** in 1993 to analyze clinical trials of drug companies, her son did her company's accounting. When demand for her services grew—and her son went off to become a journalist—Wittes knew she needed outside accounting help. She lacked work sheets, financial reports, and other tools needed for business decisions. "I realized how little I knew—like not even knowing how to bill clients or pay salaries," said Wittes.

For support, Wittes turned her books over to a local firm called **BusinessMatters.** The firm took care of her basic accounting needs, but it also told her something that shocked her. She was consistently underestimating her expenses—sometimes by as much as 75%. Today, BusinessMatters is not only keeping Wittes' books, it is helping with strategic analyses. Wittes says her profits have doubled since she started using accounting information.

Wittes relies on outsourcing, contracting out accounting services she once did in-house. More business owners are using outsourcing as a strategic tool. Instead of simply looking for cost savings, they seek accounting services at a higher quality than they can do themselves. Providers review every part of the accounting cycle using work sheets and other tools such as what-if and ratio analyses.

A recent survey of executives showed the top two reasons for outsourcing are to improve company focus and reach company potential. Effectively managing data and preparing classified financial reports are important steps in achieving these goals. Coopers & Lybrand found companies that effectively used these services had 22% more revenues than those that didn't and also greater profit margins and cash flows.

Accounting is the gold mine of outsourcers. They look for ways companies can better manage and analyze financial data. The surprise is they tackle tasks with tools readily available to us. The tasks include payroll, recordkeeping, statement preparation, and computing. They now are experimenting with inventory, pensions, and sales—even customer service. There are enormous accounting opportunities for graduates in managing and analyzing data. As one consultant put it, "I have data everywhere but not a drop of information." Work sheets and other analysis tools are one remedy. [Source: *Business Week,* May 13, 1996]

Learning Objectives

Conceptual

C1 Explain why temporary accounts are closed each period.

C2 Identify steps in the accounting cycle.

C3 Explain and prepare a classified balance sheet.

Analytical

A1 Compute the current ratio and describe what it reveals about a company's financial condition.

Procedural

P1 Describe and prepare closing entries.

P2 Explain and prepare a post-closing trial balance.

P3 Prepare a work sheet and explain its usefulness.

CHAPTER PREVIEW

Financial statement preparation is a major purpose of accounting. Many of the important steps leading to financial statements are explained in earlier chapters. We described how transactions and events are analyzed, journalized, and posted. We also described important adjustments that are often necessary to properly reflect revenues when earned and expenses when incurred.

This chapter describes the final steps in the accounting process leading to financial statements. It includes the closing process that prepares revenue, expense, and withdrawal accounts for the next reporting period and updates the owner's capital account. A work sheet is shown as a useful tool in preparing financial statements. We explain how accounts are classified on a balance sheet to give more useful information to decision makers. We also describe the current ratio and explain how it is used by decision makers to assess a company's ability to pay its liabilities in the near future. These tools for managing and analyzing data are the kind Janet Wittes refers to in the opening article. Such tools improve their decision making.

Closing Process

C1 Explain why temporary accounts are closed each period.

The **closing process** is an important step at the end of an accounting period. It prepares accounts for recording the transactions and events of the *next* period. In the closing process we must:

1. Identify accounts for closing.
2. Record and post the closing entries.
3. Prepare a post-closing trial balance.

The purpose of the closing process is twofold. First, it resets revenue, expense, and withdrawal account balances to zero at the end of every period. This is done so that these accounts can measure income and withdrawal amounts for the next period. This is important if we wish to know how a company performs during a period of time. Second, it helps in summarizing a period's revenues and expenses. We use an Income Summary account for this purpose. This section explains the three steps in the closing process.

Temporary and Permanent Accounts

Temporary Accounts

| Revenues |
| Expenses |
| Withdrawals |
| Income Summary |

Permanent Accounts

| Assets |
| Liabilities |
| Owner's Capital |

Temporary, or **nominal, accounts** accumulate data related to one accounting period. They include all income statement accounts, withdrawal accounts, and Income Summary. They are temporary because the accounts are opened at the beginning of a period, used to record events for that period, and then closed at the end of the period. They are nominal because the accounts describe events or changes that have occurred rather than conditions that exist at the end of the period. *The closing process applies only to temporary accounts.*

Permanent, or **real, accounts** report on activities related to one or more future accounting periods. They carry their ending balances into the next period and include all balance sheet accounts. Asset, liability, and owner's equity accounts are not closed as long as a company continues to own the assets, owe the liabilities, and have owner's equity. They are real because they describe existing conditions.

Recording and Posting Closing Entries

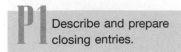

P1 Describe and prepare closing entries.

Recording and posting **closing entries** is to transfer the end-of-period balances in revenue, expense, and withdrawal accounts to the permanent owner's capital account. Closing entries are a necessary step at the end of a period after financial statements are prepared because:

- Revenue, expense, and withdrawal accounts must begin the next period with zero balances.

■ The owner's capital account must reflect (a) increases from revenues and (b) decreases from both expenses and withdrawals.

An income statement aims to report revenues earned and expenses incurred during one accounting period. It is prepared from information recorded in revenue and expense accounts. The statement of changes in owner's equity aims to report changes in the owner's capital account during one period. It uses information on revenues and expenses along with amounts accumulated in the withdrawal account. Because revenue, expense, and withdrawal accounts accumulate information for only one period, they must start each period with zero balances.

To close revenue and expense accounts, we transfer their balances first to an account called Income Summary. **Income Summary** is a temporary account that contains a credit for the sum of all revenues and a debit for the sum of all expenses. Its balance equals net income or net loss and is transferred to the owner's capital account. We then transfer the withdrawal account balance to the owner's capital account. After these closing entries are posted, the revenue, expense, Income Summary, and withdrawal accounts have zero balances. These accounts are then said to be *closed* or *cleared.* This process is illustrated in Exhibit 5.1.

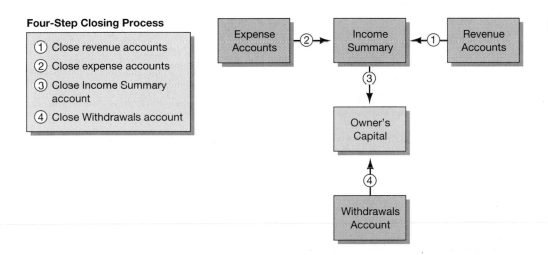

Four-Step Closing Process

1. Close revenue accounts
2. Close expense accounts
3. Close Income Summary account
4. Close Withdrawals account

Exhibit 5.1

Closing Process for a Proprietorship

FastForward's adjusted trial balance on December 31, 1997, is shown in Exhibit 5.2. Exhibit 5.3 uses the adjusted account balances from Exhibit 5.2 to show the four types of entries necessary to close FastForward's revenue, expense, Income Summary, and withdrawal accounts. We explain each of these four types.

Step 1: Close Credit Balances in Revenue Accounts to Income Summary

The first closing entry transfers credit balances in revenue accounts to the Income Summary account. We get accounts with credit balances to zero by debiting them. For FastForward, this journal entry is:

Dec. 31	Consulting Revenue	5,850	
	Rental Revenue	300	
	Income Summary		6,150
	To close revenue accounts.		

This entry closes revenue accounts and leaves them with zero balances. They are now ready to record new revenues for the next period.

The Income Summary account is created and used only for the closing process. The current $6,150 credit balance in Income Summary equals total revenues for the period.

Exhibit 5.2

Adjusted Trial Balance

*FAST*Forward

FASTFORWARD Adjusted Trial Balance December 31, 1997		
Cash	$ 7,950	
Accounts receivable	1,800	
Supplies	2,670	
Prepaid insurance	2,300	
Equipment	26,000	
Accumulated depreciation—Equipment		$ 375
Accounts payable		1,100
Salaries payable		210
Unearned consulting revenue		2,750
Note payable		5,100
Chuck Taylor, capital		30,000
Chuck Taylor, withdrawals	600	
Consulting revenue		5,850
Rental revenue		300
Depreciation expense—Equipment	375	
Salaries expense	1,610	
Insurance expense	100	
Rent expense	1,000	
Supplies expense	1,050	
Utilities expense	230	
Totals	$45,685	$45,685

Exhibit 5.3

Closing entries for FastForward

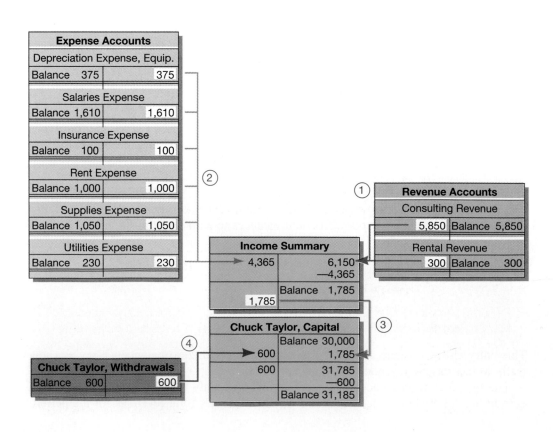

Step 2: Close Debit Balances in Expense Accounts to Income Summary

The second closing entry transfers debit balances in expense accounts to the Income Summary account. This step gathers all the expense account debit balances in the Income Summary account. We get expense accounts' debit balances to zero by crediting them. This allows these accounts to accumulate a record of new expenses in the next period. This second closing entry for FastForward is:

Dec. 31	Income Summary	4,365	
	Depreciation Expense—Equipment		375
	Salaries Expense		1,610
	Insurance Expense		100
	Rent Expense		1,000
	Supplies Expense		1,050
	Utilities Expense		230
	To close expense accounts.		

Exhibit 5.3 shows that posting this entry gives each expense account a zero balance. This prepares each account for expense entries for the next period. The entry makes the balance of Income Summary equal to December's net income of $1,785. All debit and credit balances related to expense and revenue accounts have now been collected in the Income Summary account as shown in Exhibit 5.4.

Income Summary	
4,365	6,150

Exhibit 5.4

Income Summary after Closing Revenue and Expense Accounts

Step 3: Close Income Summary to Owner's Capital

The third closing entry transfers the balance of the Income Summary account to the owner's capital account. This entry closes the Income Summary account and adds the company's net income to the owner's capital account:

Dec. 31	Income Summary	1,785	
	Chuck Taylor, Capital		1,785
	To close the Income Summary account.		

The Income Summary account has a zero balance after posting this entry. It continues to have a zero balance until the closing process occurs at the end of the next period. The owner's capital account has now been increased by the amount of net income. Because the normal balance of owner's capital is a credit, increases to owner's capital from net income are credits.

Step 4: Close Withdrawals Account to Owner's Capital

The fourth closing entry transfers any debit balance in the withdrawals account to the owner's capital account. This entry for FastForward is:

Dec. 31	Chuck Taylor, Capital	600	
	Chuck Taylor, Withdrawals		600
	To close the withdrawals account.		

This entry gives the withdrawals account a zero balance, and the account is ready to accumulate next period's payments to owner. This entry also reduces the capital account balance to the $31,185 amount reported on the balance sheet.

Sources of Closing Entry Information

We can identify the accounts needing to be closed and the amounts in the closing entries by looking to individual revenue, expense, and withdrawal accounts in the ledger.

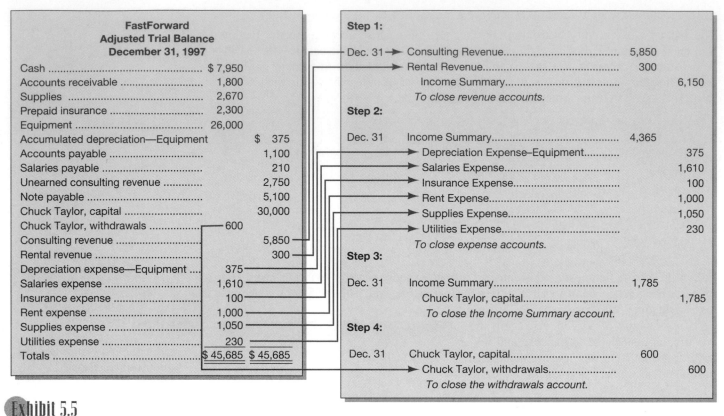

FastForward
Adjusted Trial Balance
December 31, 1997

Cash	$ 7,950	
Accounts receivable	1,800	
Supplies	2,670	
Prepaid insurance	2,300	
Equipment	26,000	
Accumulated depreciation—Equipment		$ 375
Accounts payable		1,100
Salaries payable		210
Unearned consulting revenue		2,750
Note payable		5,100
Chuck Taylor, capital		30,000
Chuck Taylor, withdrawals	600	
Consulting revenue		5,850
Rental revenue		300
Depreciation expense—Equipment	375	
Salaries expense	1,610	
Insurance expense	100	
Rent expense	1,000	
Supplies expense	1,050	
Utilities expense	230	
Totals	$ 45,685	$ 45,685

Step 1:

Dec. 31	Consulting Revenue	5,850	
	Rental Revenue	300	
	Income Summary		6,150
	To close revenue accounts.		

Step 2:

Dec. 31	Income Summary	4,365	
	Depreciation Expense–Equipment		375
	Salaries Expense		1,610
	Insurance Expense		100
	Rent Expense		1,000
	Supplies Expense		1,050
	Utilities Expense		230
	To close expense accounts.		

Step 3:

Dec. 31	Income Summary	1,785	
	Chuck Taylor, capital		1,785
	To close the Income Summary account.		

Step 4:

Dec. 31	Chuck Taylor, capital	600	
	Chuck Taylor, withdrawals		600
	To close the withdrawals account.		

Exhibit 5.5

Preparing Closing Entries from
an Adjusted Trial Balance

If we prepare an adjusted trial balance after the adjusting process, the information for closing entries is easily taken from the trial balance. This is illustrated in Exhibit 5.5 where we show how to prepare closing entries using only the adjusted trial balance.

We are not usually able to make all adjusting and closing entries on the last day of each period. This is because information about certain transactions and events that require adjusting is not always available until several days or even weeks later. This means that some adjusting and closing entries are recorded later but dated as of the last day of the period.

One example is a company that receives a utility bill on January 14 for costs incurred for the month of December. When the bill is received, the company records the expense and the payable as of December 31. Other examples include long-distance phone usage and costs of many Web billings. The income statement for December reflects these additional expenses incurred and the December 31 balance sheet includes these payables even though the amounts are not actually known on December 31.

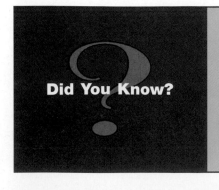

Did You Know?

Virtual Financial Statements
Leading-edge companies venturing into the Information Age are seeing major changes in the accounting process. Quantum leaps in computing technology are increasing the importance of accounting analysis and interpretation. We are moving toward what Clark Johnson, chief financial officer of **Johnson & Johnson,** calls the "virtual financial statement." This means with a click of a mouse we can get up-to-date financials and slash thousands of hours now required in the closing process. Those with knowledge of the accounting process have a competitive edge. [Source: *Business Week,* October 28, 1996.]

Post-Closing Trial Balance

A **post-closing trial balance** is a list of permanent accounts and their balances from the ledger after all closing entries are journalized and posted. It is a list of balances for all accounts not closed. These accounts are a company's assets, liabilities, and owner's equity, and are identical to those in the balance sheet. The aim of a post-closing trial balance is to verify that (1) total debits equal total credits for permanent accounts, and (2) all temporary accounts have zero balances.

FastForward's post-closing trial balance is shown in Exhibit 5.6. The post-closing trial balance is the last step in the accounting process. Like the unadjusted and adjusted trial balances, the post-closing trial balance does not tell us all transactions are recorded or that the ledger is correct.

P2 Explain and prepare a post-closing trial balance.

Exhibit 5.6

Post-Closing Trial Balance

FASTForward

FASTFORWARD Post-Closing Trial Balance December 31, 1997		
Cash	$ 7,950	
Accounts receivable	1,800	
Supplies	2,670	
Prepaid insurance	2,300	
Equipment	26,000	
Accumulated depreciation—Equipment		$ 375
Accounts payable		1,100
Salaries payable		210
Unearned consulting revenue		2,750
Note payable		5,100
Chuck Taylor, capital		31,185
Totals	$40,720	$40,720

Exhibit 5.7 shows the entire ledger of FastForward as of December 31, 1997. We should note that the temporary accounts (revenue, expense, and withdrawal accounts) have balances equal to zero.

Closing Entries for Corporations

Our discussion to this point regarding closing entries relates to activities and accounts of a proprietorship. Closing entries for a partnership are similar to a proprietorship, but some are different for a corporation. The first two closing entries for a corporation are exactly the same. That is, a corporation's revenue and expense accounts are closed to the Income Summary account. The last two closing entries for a corporation are different.

Recall that a corporation's balance sheet shows shareholders' equity as contributed capital and retained earnings. This means the third closing entry for a corporation closes the Income Summary account to the Retained Earnings account. As an example, **Hershey Foods** reported net income of $336 million in 1997. This means the credit balance in the Income Summary account after the revenue and expense accounts are closed is $336 million. **Hershey**'s third closing entry, to update its Retained Earnings account, is (in millions):

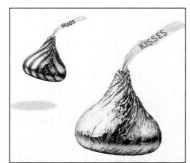

Dec. 31	Income Summary	336	
	Retained Earnings		336
	To close Income Summary to Retained Earnings.		

Exhibit 5.7

Ledger after the Closing
Process for FastForward*

	General Ledger
	Asset Accounts

Cash   Acct. No. 101

Date	Explan.	PR	Debit	Credit	Balance
1997					
Dec. 1		G1	30,000		30,000
2		G1		2,500	27,500
3		G1		20,000	7,500
10		G1	2,200		9,700
12		G1		1,000	8,700
12		G1		700	8,000
22		G1	1,900		9,900
24		G1		900	9,000
24		G1		600	8,400
26		G1	3,000		11,400
26		G1		2,400	9,000
26		G1		120	8,880
26		G1		230	8,650
26		G1		700	**7,950**

Accounts Receivable   Acct. No. 106

Date	Explan.	PR	Debit	Credit	Balance
1997					
Dec. 12		G1	1,900		1,900
22		G1		1,900	0
31	Adj.	G1	1,800		**1,800**

Supplies   Acct. No. 125

Date	Explan.	PR	Debit	Credit	Balance
1997					
Dec. 2		G1	2,500		2,500
6		G1	1,100		3,600
26		G1	120		3,720
31	Adj.	G1		1,050	**2,670**

Prepaid Insurance   Acct. No. 128

Date	Explan.	PR	Debit	Credit	Balance
1997					
Dec. 26		G1	2,400		2,400
31	Adj.	G1		100	**2,300**

Equipment   Acct. No. 167

Date	Explan.	PR	Debit	Credit	Balance
1997					
Dec. 3		G1	20,000		20,000
6		G1	6,000		**26,000**

Accumulated Depreciation— Equipment   Acct. No. 168

Date	Explan.	PR	Debit	Credit	Balance
1997					
Dec. 31	Adj.	G1		375	**375**

	Liability and Equity Accounts

Accounts Payable   Acct. No. 201

Date	Explan.	PR	Debit	Credit	Balance
1997					
Dec. 6		G1		1,100	**1,100**

Salaries Payable   Acct. No. 209

Date	Explan.	PR	Debit	Credit	Balance
1997					
Dec. 31	Adj.	G1		210	**210**

Unearned Consulting Revenue   Acct. No. 236

Date	Explan.	PR	Debit	Credit	Balance
1997					
Dec. 26		G1		3,000	3,000
31	Adj.	G1	250		**2,750**

Note Payable   Acct. No. 240

Date	Explan.	PR	Debit	Credit	Balance
1997					
Dec. 6		G1		6,000	6,000
24		G1	900		**5,100**

Chuck Taylor, capital   Acct. No. 301

Date	Explan.	PR	Debit	Credit	Balance
1997					
Dec. 1		G1		30,000	30,000
31	Closing	G1		1,785	31,785
31	Closing	G1	600		**31,785**

Chuck Taylor, withdrawals   Acct. No. 302

Date	Explan.	PR	Debit	Credit	Balance
1997					
Dec. 24		G1	600		600
31	Closing	G1		600	**0**

*Explanations are omitted for brevity.

Exhibit 5.7 *(continued)*

Revenue and Expense Accounts (including Income Summary)

Consulting Revenue — Acct. No. 403

Date	Explan.	PR	Debit	Credit	Balance
1997 Dec. 10		G1		2,200	2,200
12		G1		1,600	3,800
31	Adj.	G1		250	4,050
31	Adj.	G1		1,800	5,850
31	Closing	G1	5,850		0

Rental Revenue — Acct. No. 406

Date	Explan.	PR	Debit	Credit	Balance
1997 Dec. 12		G1		300	300
31	Closing	G1	300		0

Depreciation Expense, Equipment — Acct. No. 614

Date	Explan.	PR	Debit	Credit	Balance
1997 Dec. 31	Adj.	G1	375		375
31	Closing	G1		375	0

Salaries Expense — Acct. No. 622

Date	Explan.	PR	Debit	Credit	Balance
1997 Dec. 12		G1	700		700
26		G1	700		1,400
31	Adj.	G1	210		1,610
31	Closing	G1		1,610	0

Insurance Expense — Acct. No. 637

Date	Explan.	PR	Debit	Credit	Balance
1997 Dec. 31	Adj.	G1	100		100
31	Closing	G1		100	0

Rent Expense — Acct. No. 641

Date	Explan.	PR	Debit	Credit	Balance
1997 Dec. 12		G1	1,000		1,000
31	Closing	G1		1,000	0

Supplies Expense — Acct. No. 651

Date	Explan.	PR	Debit	Credit	Balance
1997 Dec. 31	Adj.	G1	1,050		1,050
31	Closing	G1		1,050	0

Utilities Expense — Acct. No. 690

Date	Explan.	PR	Debit	Credit	Balance
1997 Dec. 26		G1	230		230
31	Closing	G1		230	0

Income Summary — Acct. No. 901

Date	Explan.	PR	Debit	Credit	Balance
1997 Dec. 31	Closing	G1		6,150	6,150
31	Closing	G1	4,365		1,785
31	Closing	G1	1,785		0

The fourth closing entry for a corporation uses a Dividends Declared account instead of a withdrawal account. **Hershey** declared $122 million in cash dividends. Its fourth closing entry, to update Retained Earnings, is (in millions):

Dec. 31	Retained Earnings	122	
	Dividends Declared		122
	To close Dividends Declared to Retained Earnings.		

Dividends are normally a return of earnings. They are accounted for by reducing the retained earnings of the corporation. We explain and show entries for paying dividends in Chapter 14.

Flash *back*

1. What are the four major closing entries?
2. Why are revenue and expense accounts called temporary? Are there other temporary accounts?
3. What accounts are listed on the post-closing trial balance?

Answers—p. 196

Work Sheet as a Tool

P3 Prepare a work sheet and explain its usefulness.

Accountants use various analyses and internal documents when organizing information for reports to internal and external decision makers. Internal documents are important and are often called **working papers.** One widely used working paper is the **work sheet.** The work sheet is a useful tool for preparers in working with accounting information. It is not usually given to decision makers.

Benefits of a Work Sheet

A work sheet is *not* a required financial report. When a business has only a few accounts and adjustments, preparing a work sheet is unnecessary. Also, computerized accounting systems generate financial statements without the need to generate a work sheet. Yet there are several potential benefits from using a manual or electronic work sheet:

1. It helps preparers avoid errors when working with accounting systems involving many accounts and adjustments.
2. It captures the entire accounting process, linking transactions and events to their effects in financial statements.
3. Auditors of financial statements often use a work sheet for planning and organizing the audit. It can be used to reflect any adjustments necessary as a result of the audit.
4. It is useful in preparing interim (monthly or quarterly) financial statements when journalizing and posting adjusting entries are postponed until the year-end.
5. It is helpful in showing the effects of proposed or "what-if" transactions.

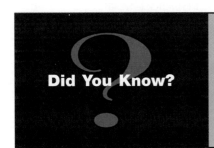

Did You Know?

Silicon Accounting
An electronic work sheet is increasingly common in business. Popular spreadsheet software such as **Excel** is putting electronic work sheets and their benefits within the reach of small business owners. This technology allows us to easily change numbers, assess the impact of alternative strategies, and ease the recordkeeping burden. It can also dramatically decrease the time devoted to the accounting process and other procedures required at the end of a period.

Using a Work Sheet

A work sheet can simplify efforts in preparing financial statements. It is prepared before making adjusting entries at the end of a reporting period. The work sheet stores information about accounts, their needed adjustments, and the financial statements. A complete work sheet contains all information recorded in the journals and shown in the statements. Exhibit 5.8 shows the form of a work sheet and the 5 steps in preparing it.

The multicolumn work sheet provides two columns each for: the unadjusted trial balance, the adjustments, the adjusted trial balance, the income statement, and the balance sheet and statement of changes in owner's equity. A work sheet sometimes has two separate columns for the statement of changes in owner's equity and two separate columns for the balance sheet. Because the statement of changes in owner's equity often includes only a few items, this usually is not done.

We use the information of FastForward to describe and interpret the work sheet. Important steps in preparing the work sheet are explained below. Each step, 1 through 5, is color-coded and explained with reference to Exhibit 5.9.[1]

① *Step 1. Enter Unadjusted Trial Balance*
Refer to Exhibit 5.9, Step 1. The first step in using a work sheet is to list the title of every account with a balance in the company's ledger. The unadjusted debit or credit

---

[1] A traditional acetate overlay presentation is available in *full color* teaching transparencies. A new PowerPoint presentation mimics this overlay option.

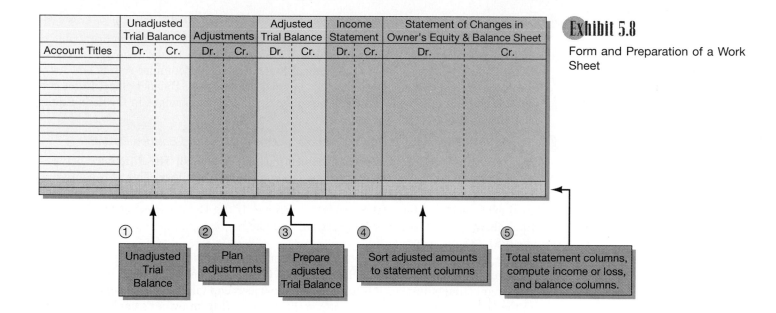

Exhibit 5.8

Form and Preparation of a Work Sheet

balances for accounts in the ledger are then recorded in the two columns of the unadjusted trial balance. The totals of these two columns must be equal. Exhibit 5.9 shows FastForward's work sheet after completing this first step.

The unadjusted trial balance in Exhibit 5.9 reflects the account balances after the December transactions are recorded but *before any adjusting entries are journalized or posted.* Sometimes blank lines are left on the worksheet based on past experience where lines will be needed for adjustments to certain accounts. Exhibit 5.9 shows Accumulated Depreciation as one example. An alternative is to squeeze adjustments on one line or to combine the effects of two or more adjustments in one amount.

② Step 2. Enter Adjustments

Refer to Exhibit 5.9, Step 2. The second step in preparing a work sheet is to enter adjustments in the columns labeled Adjustments, as shown in Exhibit 5.9. The adjustments shown are the same ones we discussed in Chapter 4. An identifying letter relates the debit and credit of each adjustment. This is called *keying* the adjustments. After preparing a work sheet, we still must enter adjusting entries in the journal and post them to the ledger. The identifying letters help match correctly the debit and credit of each adjusting entry. Exhibit 5.9 shows six adjustments for FastForward that we explained in Chapter 4:

a. Expiration of $100 of prepaid insurance.
b. Use of $1,050 of supplies.
c. Depreciation of $375 on equipment.
d. Earning $250 of previously unearned revenue.
e. Accrual of $210 of salaries owed to an employee.
f. Accrual of $1,800 of revenue from a customer.

In entering adjustments, we sometimes identify additional accounts that need to be inserted on the work sheet. The additional accounts can be inserted below the initial list.

③ Step 3. Prepare Adjusted Trial Balance

Refer to Exhibit 5.9, Step 3. The adjusted trial balance is prepared by combining the adjustments with the unadjusted balances for each account. As an example, the Prepaid Insurance account has a $2,400 debit balance in the Unadjusted Trial Balance columns. This $2,400 debit is combined with the $100 credit in the Adjustments columns to give Prepaid Insurance a $2,300 debit in the Adjusted Trial Balance columns. The totals of the Adjusted Trial Balance columns confirm the equality of debits and credits.

(4) *Step 4. Sort Adjusted Trial Balance Amounts to Financial Statements*

Refer to Exhibit 5.9, Step 4. This step involves sorting adjusted trial balance amounts to their proper financial statement columns. Expense items go to the Income Statement Debit column and revenues to the Income Statement Credit column. Assets and withdrawals go to the Statement of Changes in Owner's Equity & Balance Sheet Debit column. Liabilities and owner's capital go to the Statement of Changes in Owner's Equity & Balance Sheet Credit column.

(5) *Step 5. Total Statement Columns, Compute Income or Loss, and Balance Columns*

Refer to Exhibit 5.9, Step 5. Each statement column is totaled. The difference between totals of the Income Statement columns is net income or net loss. This is because revenues are entered in the Credit column and expenses in the Debit column. If the Credit total exceeds the Debit total, there is net income. If the Debit total exceeds the Credit total, there is a net loss. For FastForward, the Credit total exceeds the Debit total, giving a $1,785 net income.

The net income from the Income Statement columns is added to the Statement of Changes in Owner's Equity & Balance Sheet Credit column. Adding net income to the last Credit column implies it is to be added to owner's capital. If a loss occurs, it is added to the Debit column. This implies it is to be subtracted from owner's capital. While the ending balance of owner's capital does not appear in the last two columns as a single amount, it is computed as the owner's capital account balance *plus* net income (or minus net loss) and *minus* the withdrawals account balance.

Exhibit 5.9

Worksheet for FastForward

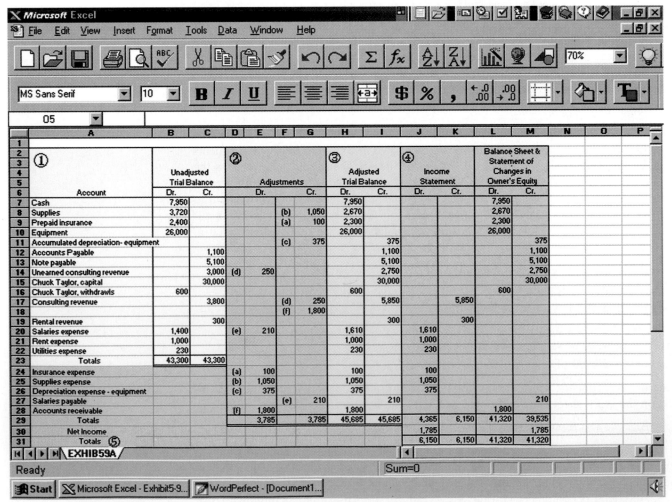

Step 1: ☐ Prepare unadjusted trial balance;   Step 2: ☐ Enter adjustments;   Step 3: ☐ Prepare adjusted trial balance;   Step 4: ☐ Sort adjusted trial balance amounts to financial statement columns;   Step 5: ☐ Total statement columns, compute income or loss, and balance column.

FASTFORWARD
Income Statement
For Month Ended December 31, 1997

Revenues:

Consulting revenue	$ 5,850	
Rental revenue	300	
Total revenues		$ 6,150

Expenses:

Depreciation expense—Equipment	$ 375	
Salaries expense	1,610	
Insurance expense	100	
Rent expense	1,000	
Supplies expense	1,050	
Utilities expense	230	
Total expenses		4,365
Net income		$ 1,785

FASTFORWARD
Statement of Changes in Owner's Equity
For Month Ended December 31, 1997

C. Taylor, capital, December 1, 1997		$ 0
Add: Investment by owner	$30,000	
Net income	1,785	31,785
Total		$31,785
Less: Withdrawal by owner		600
C. Taylor, capital, December 31, 1997		$31,185

FASTFORWARD
Balance Sheet
December 31, 1997

Assets

Cash		$ 7,950
Accounts receivable		1,800
Supplies		2,670
Prepaid Insurance		2,300
Equipment	26,000	
Accumulated depreciation—Equipment	(375)	25,625
Total assets		$40,345

Liabilities

Accounts payable		$ 1,100
Salaries payable		210
Unearned consulting revenue		2,750
Note payable		5,100
Total liabilities		$ 9,160

Owner's Equity

Chuck Taylor, capital		31,185
Total liabilities and owner's equity		$40,345

Exhibit 5.10

Financial Statements from the Work Sheet

When net income or net loss is added to the proper Statement of Changes in Owner's Equity & Balance Sheet column, the totals of the last two columns must balance. If they do not balance, one or more errors were made. The error can be mathematical or can involve error in sorting one or more amounts to columns. A balance in the last two columns is not proof of no errors.

Entering adjustments in the Adjustments columns of a work sheet does not adjust the ledger accounts. Adjusting entries still must be entered in the general journal and posted to ledger accounts. The work sheet helps because its Adjustments columns provide the information for these entries. The adjustments in Exhibit 5.9 are the same as the adjusting entries we described in Chapter 4. In addition, all items in the Income Statement columns must be closed to Income Summary. The net income or net loss shown on the work sheet must be closed to owner's capital. The withdrawals account in the last Debit column must be closed to owner's capital.

Auditor
You are auditing the financial statements of a food service client. This client owns and operates her own restaurant. You ask and receive a printout of her electronic work sheet used to prepare financial statements. There is no depreciation adjustment, yet this client owns a large amount of food service equipment. Does the lack of depreciation adjustment concern you?

Answer—p. 196

Work Sheet Application and Analysis

A work sheet does not substitute for financial statements. The work sheet is a tool we use at the end of an accounting period to help organize and manage data. We use the information in it to prepare financial statements. The financial statements of FastForward are shown in Exhibit 5.10. Its income statement amounts are taken from the Income Statement columns of the work sheet. Similarly, amounts for the statement of changes in owner's equity and the balance sheet are taken from the Statement of Changes in Owner's Equity & Balance Sheet columns of the work sheet. FastForward's statement of cash flows is discussed in the next section and is prepared from the Cash account and supporting documents.

While we can prepare all the statements at this point, we must remember that adjusting entries must be journalized and posted before moving to the closing process. A work sheet is a useful tool, but it is not a substitute for adjusting entries and postings to ledger accounts. These procedures must still be performed as described in Chapter 4.

Work sheets are also useful in analyzing the effects of proposed, or what-if, transactions. This is done by entering their adjusted financial statement amounts in the first two columns, arranging them in the form of financial statements. Proposed transactions are entered in the second two columns. Extended amounts in the last columns show the effects of these proposed transactions on financial statements. These final columns are called **pro forma statements** because they show the statements *as if* the proposed transactions occurred.

Flash *back*

4. Where do we get the amounts to enter in the Unadjusted Trial Balance columns of a work sheet?

5. What are the advantages of using a work sheet in helping us prepare adjusting entries?

Statement of Cash Flows

All of FastForward's cash receipts and cash payments are recorded in its Cash account in the ledger. This Cash account holds information about cash flows from operating, investing, and financing activities. The Cash account for FastForward is shown in Exhibit 5.11.

Cash			
Investment by owner (1)	30,000	Purchase of supplies (2)	2,500
Consulting revenue (5)	2,200	Purchase of equipment (3)	20,000
Collection of account receivable (9) ..	1,900	Payment of rent (6)	1,000
Receipts for future services (12)	3,000	Payment of salary (7)	700
		Payment of note payable (10)	900
		Withdrawal by owner (11)	600
		Payment of insurance (13)	2,400
		Purchase of supplies (14)	120
		Payment of utilities (15)	230
		Payment of salary (16)	700
Total increases	37,100	Total decreases	29,150
Less decreases	−29,150		
Balance	7,950		

Exhibit 5.11

Cash Account of FastForward

The Cash account reports individual cash transactions by types of receipts and payments. These amounts are keyed according to the transactions (1) through (16) from Chapter 3. Adjustments never affect the Cash account; they are not cash-related activities. To prepare the statement of cash flows, we must determine whether a cash inflow or outflow is an operating, investing, or financing activity. We then report amounts in their proper category on the statement of cash flows. FastForward's statement of cash flows is shown in Exhibit 5.12.

FASTFORWARD		
Statement of Cash Flows		
For Month Ended December 31, 1997		
Cash flows from operating activities:		
Cash received from clients	$ 7,100	
Cash paid for supplies	(2,620)	
Cash paid for rent	(1,000)	
Cash paid for insurance	(2,400)	
Cash paid for utilities	(230)	
Cash paid to employee	(1,400)	
Net cash used by operating activities		$ (550)
Cash flows from investing activities:		
Purchase of equipment	$(20,000)	
Net cash used by investing activities		(20,000)
Cash flows from financing activities:		
Investment by owner	$ 30,000	
Partial repayment of note payable	(900)	
Withdrawal by owner	(600)	
Net cash provided by financing activities		28,500
Net increase in cash		$ 7,950
Cash balance, December 1, 1997		0
Cash balance, December 31, 1997		$ 7,950

Exhibit 5.12

Statement of Cash Flows

Our analysis of the Cash account provides us a direct means to prepare the statement of cash flows. But there are two limitations with this method. First, companies often have so many individual cash receipts and disbursements that it is often difficult to review them all. Second, the Cash account often does not contain a description of each cash transaction. Later in this book we show how we can prepare the statement of cash flows when facing these limitations.

Reviewing the Accounting Cycle

C2 Identify steps in the accounting cycle.

The **accounting cycle** refers to the steps in preparing financial statements. It is called a cycle because the steps are repeated each reporting period. Exhibit 5.13 shows the 10 steps in the cycle. They are shown in order, beginning with analyzing transactions and ending with a post-closing trial balance or reversing entries.

Steps 1 through 3 usually occur regularly as a company enters into transactions. Steps 4 through 9 are done at the end of a period. Reversing entries in step 10 are optional and are explained in the appendix to this chapter. Detailed descriptions for all of these steps are in Chapters 3, 4, and 5.

Exhibit 5.13

Steps in the Accounting Cycle*

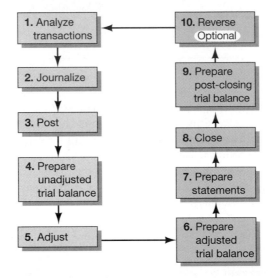

*Steps 4 and 6 can be done on a work sheet. A work sheet is especially useful in planning adjustments and in projecting an adjusted trial balance. But adjustments must always be journalized and posted.

We briefly describe these steps in Exhibit 5.14 to emphasize their importance in providing users relevant and reliable information for decision making.

Exhibit 5.14

Summary of Steps in Accounting Cycle

1. Analyze transaction	Analyze transactions in preparation for journalizing.
2. Journalize	Record debits and credits in a journal.
3. Post	Transfer debits and credits from the journal to the ledger.
4. Prepare unadjusted trial balance	Summarize ledger accounts and amounts.
5. Adjust	Record adjustments to bring account balances up to date; journalize and post adjusting entries.
6. Prepare adjusted trial balance	Summarize adjusted ledger accounts and amounts.
7. Prepare statements	Use adjusted trial balance to prepare statements.
8. Close	Journalize and post entries to close temporary accounts and update the owner's capital account.
9. Prepare post-closing trial balance	Test clerical accuracy of adjusting and closing steps.
10. Reverse (optional)	Reverse certain adjustments in the next period — optional step; see Appendix 5A.

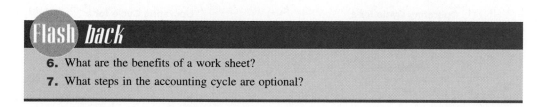

6. What are the benefits of a work sheet?

7. What steps in the accounting cycle are optional?

Answers—p. 196

Our discussion to this point has been limited to *unclassified financial statements*. But companies also prepare classified financial statements. This section focuses on a classified balance sheet. Later in the book we discuss other classified financial statements.

An **unclassified balance sheet** is one where its items are broadly grouped into assets, liabilities and owner's equity. One example is FastForward's balance sheet in Exhibit 5.10. A **classified balance sheet** organizes assets and liabilities into important subgroups. The information in a balance sheet is more useful to decision makers if assets and liabilities are classified into subgroups. One example is information to distinguish liabilities that are due soon from those not due for several years. This information helps us assess a company's ability to meet liabilities when they come due.

Classified Balance Sheet

C3 Explain and prepare a classified balance sheet.

Classification Structure

There is no required layout for a classified balance sheet. Yet a classified balance sheet often contains common groupings as shown in Exhibit 5.15.

Assets	Liabilities and Equity
Current assets	Current liabilities
Long-term investments	Long-term liabilities
Plant and equipment	Owner's equity
Intangible assets	

Exhibit 5.15

Sections of a Classified Balance Sheet

One of the more important classifications is the separation between current and noncurrent items for both assets and liabilities. Current items are those expected to come due (both collected and owed) within the longer of one year or the company's normal operating cycle. An operating cycle is the length of time between (1) purchases of services or products from suppliers to carry out a company's plans and (2) the sale of services or products to customers. The length of a company's operating cycle depends on its activities.

Exhibit 5.16 shows the steps of an operating cycle for both a service company and a merchandising company. For a service company, the **operating cycle** is the average time between (1) paying employees who do the services and (2) receiving cash from customers. For a company selling products, the operating cycle is the average time between (1) paying suppliers for merchandise and (2) receiving cash from customers.

Most operating cycles are less than one year. This means most companies use a one-year period in deciding which assets and liabilities are current. Yet there are companies with an operating cycle longer than one year. For instance, there are companies that routinely allow customers to take more than one year to pay for purchases. Also, producers of certain beverages and products that require aging for several years have operating cycles longer than one year. These companies use their operating cycle in deciding which balance sheet items are current.[2]

---

[2] In these uncommon situations, companies provide supplemental information about their current assets and liabilities to allow users to compare them with other companies.

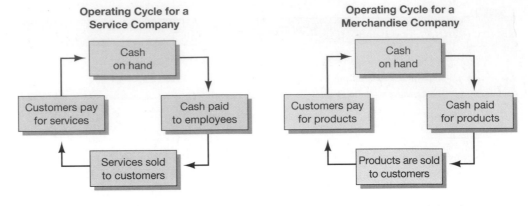

A balance sheet usually lists current assets before long-term assets, and current liabilities before long-term liabilities. This consistency in presentation allows users to quickly identify current assets that are most easily converted to cash, and current liabilities that are shortly coming due. Items in the current group are usually listed in the order of how quickly they will be converted to or paid in cash.

Classification Example

The balance sheet for **Music Components** is shown in Exhibit 5.17. It shows the most commonly used groupings. Its assets are classified as (1) current assets, (2) investments, (3) plant and equipment, and (4) intangible assets. Its liabilities are classified as either current or long term. Not all companies use the same categories of assets and liabilities on their balance sheets. **Compaq**'s balance sheet lists only three asset classes: current assets; property, plant and equipment; and other assets.

Classification Groups

This section describes the most common groups in a classified balance sheet.

Current Assets

Current assets are cash and other resources that are expected to be sold, collected, or used within the longer of one year or the company's operating cycle.[3] Examples are cash, short-term investments in marketable securities, accounts receivable, notes receivable, goods for sale to customers (called *merchandise* or *inventory*), and prepaid expenses. **Wal-Mart**'s 1997 current assets are reported in Exhibit 5.18.

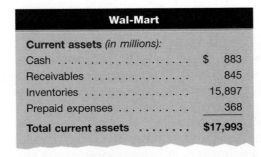

Wal-Mart	
Current assets *(in millions):*	
Cash	$ 883
Receivables	845
Inventories	15,897
Prepaid expenses	368
Total current assets	**$17,993**

A company's prepaid expenses are usually small compared to other assets and are often combined and shown as a single item. It is likely the prepaid expenses in both Exhibit 5.17 and 5.18 include items such as prepaid insurance, prepaid rent, office supplies, and store supplies. Prepaid expenses are usually listed last because they will not be converted to cash.

Long-Term Investments

A second major balance sheet classification often is **long-term investments.** Notes receivable and investments in stocks and bonds are in many cases long-term assets. This

---

[3] FASB, *Accounting Standards—Current Text* (Norwalk, CT, 1995), Sec. B05.105. First published as *Accounting Research Bulletin No. 43*, Chapter 3A, par. 4.

Exhibit 5.17

Classified Balance Sheet

MUSIC COMPONENTS
Balance Sheet
January 31, 2000

Assets

Current assets:

Cash	$ 6,500	
Short-term investments	2,100	
Accounts receivable	4,400	
Notes receivable	1,500	
Merchandise inventory	27,500	
Prepaid expenses	2,400	
Total current assets		$ 44,400

Long-term investments:

Disney common stock	18,000	
Land held for future expansion	48,000	
Total investments		66,000

Plant and equipment:

Store equipment	$ 33,200		
Less accumulated depreciation	8,000	25,200	
Buildings	170,000		
Less accumulated depreciation	45,000	125,000	
Land		73,200	
Total plant and equipment			223,400

Intangible assets:

Trademark		10,000
Total assets		$343,800

Liabilities

Current liabilities:

Accounts payable	$ 15,300	
Wages payable	3,200	
Notes payable	3,000	
Current portion of long-term liabilities	7,500	
Total current liabilities		$ 29,000

Long-term liabilities:

Notes payable (net of current portion)	150,000	
Total liabilities		$179,000

Owner's Equity

D. Bowie, capital		164,800
Total liabilities and owner's equity		$343,800

is because they are held for more than one year or the operating cycle. The *short-term* investments in Exhibit 5.15 are current assets and not shown as long-term investments. We explain the differences between short- and long-term investments later in this book.

Plant and Equipment

Plant and equipment, also called **plant assets,** are tangible long-lived assets used to produce or sell products and services. Examples are equipment, vehicles, buildings, and land. It is important that items in this group are both *long-lived* and *used to produce or sell products and services.* Land held for future expansion is *not* a plant and equipment

asset because it is not used to produce or sell products and services. Plant and equipment assets are also called *property, plant, and equipment* or *land, buildings, and equipment*. The order of listing plant assets within this category varies.

Intangible Assets

Intangible assets are long-term resources used to produce or sell products and services. They lack physical form and their benefits are uncertain. Examples are patents, trademarks, copyrights, franchises, and goodwill. Their value comes from the privileges or rights granted to or held by the owner. **Wang Laboratories** reports intangible assets for 1997 as shown in Exhibit 5.19.

Exhibit 5.19

Intangible Assets Section

Wang Laboratories
Intangible assets, net (in millions) $313

Wang's intangibles include software, licenses, trademarks, and patents.

Current Liabilities

Current liabilities are obligations due to be paid or settled within the longer of one year or the operating cycle. They are usually settled by paying out current assets. Current liabilities include accounts payable, notes payable, wages payable, taxes payable, interest payable, and unearned revenues. Any portion of a long-term liability due to be paid within the longer of one year or the operating cycle is a current liability. Exhibit 5.15 shows how the current portion of long-term liabilities is usually reported. Unearned revenues are current liabilities when they will be settled by delivering products or services within the longer of the year or the operating cycle. While practice varies, current liabilities are often reported in the order of those to be settled first.

Long-Term Liabilities

Long-term liabilities are obligations not due within the longer of one year or the operating cycle. Notes payable, mortgages payable, bonds payable, and lease obligations are common long-term liabilities. If a company has both short- and long-term items in one of these accounts, it is common to separate them in the ledger for later reporting.

Owner's Equity

Owner's equity is the owner's claim on the assets of a company. It is reported in the equity section with an owner's capital account for a proprietorship. For a partnership, the equity section reports a capital account for each partner. For a corporation, the equity section is called Shareholders' Equity and is divided into two main subsections: Capital Stock and Retained Earnings. Chapter 2 described these alternative organization forms in detail.

Flash *back*

8. Identify which of the following assets are classified as (1) current assets or (2) plant and equipment: *(a)* land used in operations; *(b)* office supplies; *(c)* receivables from customers due in 10 months; *(d)* insurance protection for the next nine months; *(e)* trucks used to provide services to customers; *(f)* trademarks used in advertising the company's services.

9. Name two examples of assets classified as investments on the balance sheet.

10. Explain an operating cycle for a service company.

Answers—p. 197

Current Ratio

An important use of financial statements is as an aid in assessing a company's ability to pay its debts in the near future. This type of analysis affects decisions by suppliers in allowing a company to buy on credit. It affects decisions by creditors about lending money to a company. For instance, it can affect creditors' decision about loan terms, including the interest rate, due date, and any requirements for collateral for the loan. An assessment of the ability to pay debts can also affect an internal manager's decisions about using cash to pay existing debts when they come due.

A1 Compute the current ratio and describe what it reveals about a company's financial condition.

The **current ratio** is one important measure used to evaluate a company's ability to pay its short-term obligations. It is computed by dividing current assets by current liabilities:

$$\text{Current ratio} = \frac{\text{Current assets}}{\text{Current liabilities}}$$

Exhibit 5.20

Current Ratio Formula

Using financial information for **Harley-Davidson,** we compute its annual current ratios for the time period 1993–1996. These results are shown in Exhibit 5.21.

Exhibit 5.21

Harley-Davidson's Current Ratio

(in Millions)	Harley-Davidson 1996	1995	1994	1993
Total current assets	$429	$332	$406	$334
Total current liabilities	$264	$233	$216	$191
Current ratio	1.63	1.42	1.88	1.75
Industry current ratio	2.1	1.8	2.2	1.9

Harley's current ratio dipped to 1.42 in 1995 compared to higher ratios for the prior two years, but it rebounded in 1996 to 1.63. The current ratio for all of these years suggests that Harley's short-term obligations can be covered with short-term assets on hand. If the ratio moved closer to 1, Harley would expect to face more problems in covering liabilities. We often look to a company's sales to see if there are sufficient cash inflows to cover liabilities. If the ratio were *less* than 1, it would mean that Harley's current liabilities exceed its current assets, and it would likely face serious problems in covering current liabilities. Harley's current ratio favorably compares with the industry average. Although it appears to be at the lower end of the industry, Harley's ability to pay short-term obligations is good.

Answer—p. 196

Analyst

You are analyzing the financial condition of a sports and fitness club. Your main goal is to assess the club's ability to meet upcoming loan payments in the next period. You compute its current ratio and it is 1.2. You also find a major portion of Accounts Receivable is due from one client who has not made any payments in the past 12 months. Removing this accounts receivable from current assets drops the current ratio to 0.7. What do you conclude?

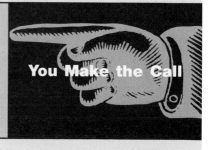

You Make the Call

11. If a company misclassifies a portion of liabilities as long-term when they are short-term, how does this affect its current ratio?

Answer—p. 197

Summary

C1 Explain why temporary accounts are closed each period. Temporary accounts are closed at the end of each accounting period for two main reasons. First, the closing process updates the owner's capital account to include the effects of all transactions and events recorded for the period. Second, it prepares revenue, expense, and withdrawal accounts for the next reporting period by giving them zero balances.

C2 Identify steps in the accounting cycle. The accounting cycle consists of 10 steps: (1) analyze transactions, (2) journalize, (3) post, (4) prepare an unadjusted trial balance, (5) adjust accounts, (6) prepare an adjusted trial balance, (7) prepare statements, (8) close, (9) prepare a post-closing trial balance, and (10) prepare (optional) reversing entries. If a work sheet is prepared, it covers steps 4 and 6.

C3 Explain and prepare a classified balance sheet. Classified balance sheets usually report four groups of assets: current assets, long-term investments, plant and equipment, and intangible assets. They include at least two groups of liabilities: current and long-term. Owner's equity for proprietorships and partners' equity for partnerships both report the capital account balances. A corporation separates shareholders' equity into contributed capital and retained earnings.

A1 Compute the current ratio and describe what it reveals about a company's financial condition. A company's current ratio is defined as current assets divided by current liabilities.

We use it to evaluate a company's ability to pay its current liabilities out of current assets.

P1 Describe and prepare closing entries. Recording and posting closing entries involve transferring the end-of-period balances in revenue, expense, and withdrawal accounts to the owner's capital account. Closing entries involve four steps: (1) close credit balances in revenue accounts to income summary, (2) close debit balances in expense accounts to income summary, (3) close income summary to owner's capital, and (4) close withdrawal account to owner's capital.

P2 Explain and prepare a post-closing trial balance. A post-closing trial balance is a list of permanent accounts and their balances after all closing entries are journalized and posted. Permanent accounts are asset, liability, and owner's equity accounts. The purpose of a post-closing trial balance is to verify that (1) total debits equal total credits for permanent accounts and (2) all temporary accounts have zero balances.

P3 Prepare a work sheet and explain its usefulness. A work sheet can be a useful tool in preparing and analyzing financial statements. It is helpful at the end of a period in preparing adjusting entries, an adjusted trial balance, and financial statements. A work sheet often contains five pairs of columns: unadjusted trial balance, adjustments, adjusted trial balance, income statement, and statement of changes in owner's equity & balance sheet.

Guidance Answers to **You Make the Call**

Auditor

You are concerned about the absence of a depreciation adjustment. Equipment does depreciate, and financial statements recognize this occurrence. Its absence suggests an error or a misrepresentation. You must follow up and require management to adjust the statements for depreciation. Also, if fraud is suggested, you must substantially expand your audit tests, obtain legal advice, and prepare to withdraw from the audit engagement.

Analyst

A current ratio of 1.2 suggests sufficient current assets to cover upcoming current liabilities. But a ratio of 1.2 does not give you much of a buffer in case of error in measuring current assets or current liabilities. Removing tardy receivables further reduces the current ratio to 0.7. This suggests current assets cannot cover current liabilities. Your assessment is that the sports and fitness club will have difficulty meeting upcoming loan payments.

Guidance Answers to

1. The four major closing entries consist of closing: (1) credit balances in revenue accounts to Income Summary, (2) debit balances in expense accounts to Income Summary, (3) Income Summary to owner's capital, and (4) withdrawal account to owner's capital.

2. Revenue and expense accounts are called temporary because they are opened and closed every reporting period. The Income Summary and owner's withdrawal accounts are also temporary accounts.

3. Permanent accounts are listed on the post-closing trial balance. These accounts are the asset, liability, and owner's equity accounts.

4. Amounts in the Unadjusted Trial Balance columns are taken from account balances in the ledger.

5. A work sheet offers the advantage of listing on one page all of the necessary information to make adjusting entries.

6. A worksheet can help in: (a) avoiding errors, (b) linking transactions and events to their effects in financial statements, (c) showing adjustments for audit purposes, (d) preparing interim financial statements, and (e) showing effects from proposed, or what-if, transactions.

7. Reversing entries is an optional step in the accounting cycle. Also, a worksheet is an optional tool in completing steps 4 and 6.

8. Current assets: *b, c, d.* Plant and equipment: *a, e.* Item *f* is an intangible asset.

9. Investment in common stock, investment in bonds, land held for future expansion.

10. The length of a company's operating cycle depends on its activities. For a service company, the operating cycle is the average time between (1) paying employees who do the services and (2) receiving cash from customers from services provided.

11. Since the current ratio is defined as current assets divided by current liabilities, ignoring a portion of current liabilities (1) decreases the reported amount of current liabilities and (2) erroneously increases the current ratio because current assets are now divided by a smaller number.

This partial work sheet shows the December 31, 2000, adjusted trial balance of Westside Appliance Repair Company:

Demonstration Problem

	Adjusted Trial Balance		Income Statement		Statement of Owner's Equity and Balance Sheet	
Cash	$ 83,300					
Notes receivable	60,000					
Prepaid insurance	19,000					
Prepaid rent	5,000					
Equipment	165,000					
Accumulated depreciation—Equipment		$ 52,000				
Accounts payable		37,000				
Long-term notes payable		58,000				
B. Westside, capital		173,500				
B. Westside, withdrawals	25,000					
Repair services revenue		294,000				
Interest earned		6,500				
Depreciation expense—Equipment	26,000					
Wages expense	155,000					
Rent expense	71,000					
Insurance expense	7,000					
Interest expense	4,700					
Totals	$621,000	$621,000				

Required

1. Complete the work sheet by extending the adjusted trial balance totals to the appropriate financial statement columns.

2. Prepare closing entries for Westside Appliance Repair Company.

3. Set up Income Summary and B. Westside, Capital, accounts in the general ledger and post the closing entries to these accounts.

4. Determine the balance of the B. Westside, Capital, account to be reported on the December 31, 2000, balance sheet.

Planning the Solution

• Extend the adjusted trial balance account balances to the appropriate financial statement columns.

• Prepare entries to close the revenue accounts to Income Summary, to close the expense accounts to Income Summary, to close Income Summary to the capital account, and to close the withdrawal account to the capital account.

- Post the first and second closing entries to the Income Summary account. Examine the balance of income summary and verify that it agrees with the net income shown on the work sheet.
- Post the third and fourth closing entries to the capital account.

Solution to Demonstration Problem

1. Completing the work sheet:

	Adjusted Trial Balance		Income Statement		Statement of Changes in Owner's Equity and Balance Sheet	
Cash	$ 83,300				$ 83,300	
Notes receivable	60,000				60,000	
Prepaid insurance	19,000				19,000	
Prepaid rent	5,000				5,000	
Equipment	165,000				165,000	
Accumulated depreciation—Equipment		$ 52,000				$ 52,000
Accounts payable		37,000				37,000
Long-term notes payable		58,000				58,000
B. Westside, capital		173,500				173,500
B. Westside, withdrawals	25,000				25,000	
Repair services revenue		294,000		$294,000		
Interest earned		6,500		6,500		
Depreciation expense—Equipment	26,000		$ 26,000			
Wages expense	155,000		155,000			
Rent expense	71,000		71,000			
Insurance expense	7,000		7,000			
Interest expense	4,700		4,700			
Totals	$621,000	$621,000	$263,700	$300,500	$357,300	$320,500
Net Income			36,800			36,800
Totals			$300,500	$300,500	$357,300	$357,300

2. Closing entries:

Dec. 31	Repair Services Revenue	294,000	
	Interest Earned	6,500	
	Income Summary		300,500
	To close revenue accounts.		
Dec. 31	Income Summary	263,700	
	Depreciation Expense—Equipment		26,000
	Wages Expense		155,000
	Rent Expense		71,000
	Insurance Expense		7,000
	Interest Expense		4,700
	To close expense accounts.		
Dec. 31	Income Summary	36,800	
	B. Westside, capital		36,800
	To close the Income Summary account.		
Dec. 31	B. Westside, capital	25,000	
	B. Westside, withdrawals		25,000
	To close the withdrawals account.		

3. Set up Income Summary and Capital ledger accounts and post the closing entries.

Income Summary   Account No. 999

Date	Explanation	PR	Debit	Credit	Balance
2000 Jan. 1	Beginning balance				0
Dec. 31	Close revenue accounts			300,500	300,500
31	Close expense accounts		263,700		36,800
31	Close income summary		36,800		0

B. Westside, Capital   Account No. 301

Date	Explanation	PR	Debit	Credit	Balance
2000 Jan. 1	Beginning balance				173,500
Dec. 31	Close Income Summary			36,800	210,300
31	Close B. Westside, withdrawals		25,000		185,300

4. The final capital balance of $185,300 (from part 3) will be reported on the December 31, 2000, balance sheet. The final capital balance reflects the increase due to the net income earned during the year and the decrease for the owner's withdrawals during the year.

Reversing Entries and Account Numbering

Learning Objectives

Procedural

P4 Prepare reversing entries and explain their purpose.

This appendix describes both reversing entries and the account numbering system applied in companies.

Reversing Entries

Reversing entries are optional entries. They are linked to any accrued assets and liabilities that were created by adjusting entries at the end of a reporting period. Reversing entries are used to simplify a company's recordkeeping.

Exhibit 5A.1 shows how reversing entries work for **FastForward.** The top of the exhibit shows the adjusting entry FastForward recorded on December 31, 1997, for the employee's earned but unpaid salary. The entry recorded three days' salary to increase December's total salary expense to $1,610. The entry also recognized a liability of $210. The expense is reported on December's income statement. The expense account is then closed. As a result, the ledger on January 1, 1998, reflects a $210 liability and a zero balance in the Salaries Expense account. At this point, the choice is made between using or not using reversing entries.

Accounting without Reversing Entries

The path down the left side of Exhibit 5A.1 is described in detail in Chapter 4. To summarize here, when the next payday occurs on January 9, we record payment with a compound entry that debits both the expense and liability accounts and credits cash. Posting that entry creates a $490 balance in the expense account and reduces the liability account balance to zero because the debt has been settled.

The disadvantage of this approach is the slightly more complex entry required on January 9. Paying the accrued liability means this entry differs from the routine entries made on all other paydays. To construct the proper entry on January 9, we must recall the effect of the adjusting entry. Reversing entries overcome this disadvantage.

Accounting with Reversing Entries

P4 Prepare reversing entries and explain their purpose.

The right side of Exhibit 5A.1 shows how a reversing entry on January 1 overcomes the disadvantage of the January 9 entry from not using reversing entries. A reversing entry is the exact opposite of an adjusting entry. In our example, the Salaries Payable liability

Accrue salaries expense on December 31, 1997

Salaries Expense 210
   Salaries Payable 210

Salaries Expense

Date	Expl.	Debit	Credit	Balance
1997				
Dec. 12	(7)	700		700
26	(16)	700		1,400
31	(e)	210		1,610

Salaries Payable

Date	Expl.	Debit	Credit	Balance
1997				
Dec. 31	(e)		210	210

— OR —

No reversing entry recorded on
January 1, 1998

NO ENTRY

Salaries Expense

Date	Expl.	Debit	Credit	Balance
1998				

Salaries Payable

Date	Expl.	Debit	Credit	Balance
1997				
Dec. 31	(e)		210	210
1998				

Reversing entry recorded on
January 1, 1998

Salaries Payable 210
   Salaries Expense 210

Salaries Expense

Date	Expl.	Debit	Credit	Balance
1998				
Jan. 1			210	(210)

Salaries Payable

Date	Expl.	Debit	Credit	Balance
1997				
Dec. 31	(e)		210	210
1998				
Jan. 1		210		0

Pay the accrued and current salaries on January 9, the first payday in 1998

Salaries Expense 490
Salaries Payable 210
   Cash 700

Salaries Expense

Date	Expl.	Debit	Credit	Balance
1998				
Jan. 9		490		490

Salaries Payable

Date	Expl.	Debit	Credit	Balance
1997				
Dec. 31	(e)		210	210
1998				
Jan. 9		210		0

Salaries Expense 700
   Cash 700

Salaries Expense

Date	Expl.	Debit	Credit	Balance
1998				
Jan. 1			210	(210)
Jan. 9		700		490

Salaries Payable

Date	Expl.	Debit	Credit	Balance
1997				
Dec. 31	(e)		210	210
1998				
Jan. 1		210		0

Under both approaches, the expense and liability accounts have
identical balances after the cash payment on January 9.

Salaries Expense $490
Salaries Payable .... $ 0

is debited for $210, meaning that this account now has a zero balance after the entry is posted. The Salaries Payable account temporarily understates the liability, but this is not a problem since financial statements are not prepared before the liability is settled on January 9. The credit to the Salaries Expense account is unusual because it gives the account an *abnormal credit balance.* We highlight an abnormal balance by circling it.

Because of the reversing entry, the January 9 entry to record payment is straightforward. This entry debits the Salaries Expense account and credits Cash for the full $700 paid. It is the same as all other entries made to record 10 days' salary for the employee.

We should also look at the accounts on the lower right side of Exhibit 5A.1. After the payment entry is posted, Salaries Expense account has a $490 balance that reflects seven days' salary of $70 per day. The zero balance in the Salaries Payable account is now correct.

The lower section of Exhibit 5A.1 shows that the expense and liability accounts have exactly the same balances whether reversing occurs or not. This means either approach produces identical results.

As a general rule, adjusting entries that create new asset or new liability accounts are likely candidates for reversing.

12. How are financial statements affected by a decision to make reversing entries?

Answer—p. 203

Account Numbering System

We described a three-digit account numbering system in Chapter 3. In such a system, the code number assigned to an account both identifies the account and gives information about the account's financial statement category.

In this section we describe a more detailed system, although we see many different systems in practice. The first digit in an account's number identifies its primary balance sheet or income statement category. For example, account numbers beginning with a 1 are assigned to asset accounts and account numbers beginning with a 2 are assigned to liability accounts. Exhibit 5A.2 shows how numbers can be assigned to the accounts of a company that buys and sells merchandise.

Exhibit 5A.2

Account Numbering for a Merchandiser

101–199	Asset accounts
201–299	Liability accounts
301–399	Owner's equity (including withdrawals)
401–499	Sales or revenue accounts
501–599	Cost of goods sold accounts (These are discussed in Chapter 6.)
601–699	Operating expense accounts
701–799	Accounts that reflect unusual and/or infrequent gains
801–899	Accounts that reflect unusual and/or infrequent losses

The second digit of each account number identifies its classification within the primary category. Exhibit 5A.3 shows this identification.

Exhibit 5A.3

Second Digit Account Numbering

101–199	Assets
101–139	Current assets (second digit is 0, 1, 2, or 3)
141–149	Long-term investments (second digit is 4)
151–179	Plant assets (second digit is 5, 6, or 7)
181–189	Natural resources (second digit is 8)
191–199	Intangible assets (second digit is 9)
201–299	**Liabilities**
201–249	Current liabilities (second digit is 0, 1, 2, 3, or 4)
251–299	Long-term liabilities (second digit is 5, 6, 7, 8, or 9)

The third digit completes the unique code for each account. Specific current asset accounts might be assigned the numbers shown in Exhibit 5A.4.

An extensive list of accounts using this code is provided near the end of this book. A three-digit account numbering system is often adequate for smaller businesses. A numbering system for more complex businesses might use four, five, or even more digits.

101–199	Assets
101–139	Current assets
101	Cash
106	Accounts Receivable
110	Rent Receivable
128	Prepaid Insurance

 Exhibit 5A.4

Three-Digit Account Numbering

Summary of Appendix 5A

 P3 **Prepare reversing entries and explain their purpose.** Reversing entries are an optional step. They are applied to accrued assets and liabilities. The purpose of reversing entries is to simplify subsequent journal entries. Financial statements are unaffected by the choice to use or not use reversing entries.

Guidance Answer to Flashbacks

12. Financial statements are unchanged by the choice between using or not using reversing entries.

Glossary

Accounting cycle recurring steps performed each accounting period, starting with analyzing transactions and continuing through the post-closing trial balance. (p. 182).

Classified balance sheet a balance sheet that presents assets and liabilities in relevant subgroups. (p. 188).

Closing entries journal entries recorded at the end of each accounting period that transfer the end-of-period balances in revenue, expense, and withdrawal accounts to the owner's capital account to prepare for the upcoming period and update the owner's capital account. (p. 176).

Closing process steps to prepare accounts for recording the transactions of the next period. (p. 176).

Current assets cash or other assets that are expected to be sold, collected, or used within the longer of one year or the company's operating cycle. (p. 192).

Current liabilities obligations due to be paid or settled within the longer of one year or the operating cycle. (p. 194).

Current ratio a ratio that is used to evaluate a company's ability to pay its short-term obligations, calculated by dividing current assets by current liabilities. (p. 195).

Income Summary a temporary account used only in the closing process to which the balances of revenue and expense accounts are transferred; its balance equals net income or net loss and is transferred to the owner's capital account or the Retained Earnings account for a corporation. (p. 177).

Intangible assets long-term assets (resources) used to produce or sell products or services; these assets lack physical form and their benefits are uncertain. (p. 194).

Long-term investments Assets such as notes receivable or investments in stocks and bonds that are held for more than one year or the operating cycle. (p. 192).

Long-term liabilities obligations that are not due to be paid within the longer of one year or the operating cycle. (p. 194).

Nominal accounts another name for *temporary accounts*. (p. 176).

Operating cycle of a business the average time between paying cash for employee salaries or merchandise and receiving cash from customers. (p. 191).

Owner's equity the owner's claim on the assets of a company. (p. 194).

Permanent accounts accounts that are used to report activities related to one or more future accounting periods; their balances are carried into the next period and include all balance sheet accounts; these balances are not closed as long as the company continues to own the assets, owe the liabilities, and have owner's equity; also called *real accounts*. (p. 176).

Plant and equipment are tangible long-lived assets used to produce or sell products and services; also called *plant assets*. (p. 193).

Post-closing trial balance a list of permanent accounts and their balances from the ledger after all closing entries are journalized and posted; a list of balances for all accounts not closed. (p. 181).

Pro forma statements statements that show the effects of the proposed transactions as if the transactions had already occurred. (p. 187).

Real accounts another name for *permanent accounts*. (p. 176).

Reversing entries optional entries recorded at the beginning of a new year that prepare the accounts for simplified journal entries subsequent to accrual adjusting entries. (p. 200).

Temporary accounts accounts that are used to describe revenues, expenses, and owner's withdrawals for one accounting period; they are closed at the end of the reporting period; also called *nominal accounts*. (p. 176).

Unclassified balance sheet a balance sheet that broadly groups the assets, liabilities, and owner's equity. (p. 188).

Working papers analyses and other informal reports prepared by accountants when organizing the information for formal reports to internal and external decision makers. (p. 184).

Work sheet a 10-column spreadsheet used to draft a company's unadjusted trial balance, adjusting entries, adjusted trial balance, and financial statements; an optional step in the accounting process. (p. 184).

A superscript letter ^A *identifies assignment material based on Appendix 5A.*

Questions

1. What two purposes are accomplished by recording closing entries?
2. What are the four closing entries?
3. What accounts are affected by closing entries? What accounts are not affected?
4. Describe the similarities and differences between adjusting and closing entries.
5. What is the purpose of the Income Summary account?
6. Explain whether an error has occurred if a post-closing trial balance includes the account: Depreciation Expense—Building.
7. How is an unearned revenue classified on the balance sheet?
8. What classes of assets and liabilities are shown on a typical classified balance sheet?
9. What is a company's operating cycle?
10. What are the characteristics of plant and equipment?
11. What tasks are aided by a work sheet?
12. Why are the debit and credit entries in the Adjustments columns of the work sheet identified with letters?
13. How do reversing entries simplify a company's record-keeping efforts?

14.^A If a company accrued unpaid salaries expense of $500 at the end of a fiscal year, what reversing entry could be made? When would it be made?
15. Refer to the May 31, 1997, consolidated balance sheet for **NIKE** in Appendix A. What percent of NIKE's long-term debt is coming due before May 31, 1998?
16. Refer to **Reebok's** Consolidated Statements of Stockholders' Equity in Appendix A. What journal entry was likely recorded as of December 31, 1996, to close the Dividends Declared account?
17. Refer to the financial statements of **America Online** in Appendix A. What journal entry was likely recorded as of June 30, 1996, to close the company's Income Summary account?
18. What are three reasons why a company might wish to outsource services previously performed by a business in-house? Identify five common services that businesses may outsource.

Quick Study

QS 5-1
Effects of closing entries

Jontil Company began the current period with a $14,000 balance in the Peter Jontil, capital, account. At the end of the period, the company's adjusted account balances include the following temporary accounts with normal balances:

Service fees earned	$35,000
Salaries expense	19,000
Depreciation expense	4,000
Interest earned	3,500
Peter Jontil, withdrawals	6,000
Utilities expense	2,300

After closing revenue and expense accounts, what will be the balance of the Income Summary account? After all closing entries are journalized and posted, what will be the balance of the Peter Jontil, capital, account?

QS 5-2
Explaining the accounting cycle

List the following steps of the accounting cycle in their proper order:
a. Preparing the unadjusted trial balance.
b. Preparing the post-closing trial balance.
c. Journalizing and posting adjusting entries.
d. Journalizing and posting closing entries.
e. Preparing the financial statements.
f. Journalizing transactions.
g. Posting the transaction entries.
h. Preparing the adjusted trial balance.
i. Analyze transactions.

The following are common categories on a classified balance sheet:

A. Current assets   **D.** Intangible assets
B. Investments   **E.** Current liabilities
C. Property, plant, and equipment   **F.** Long-term liabilities

For each of the following items, select the letter that identifies the balance sheet category in which the item should appear.

_____ **1.** Store equipment
_____ **2.** Wages payable
_____ **3.** Cash
_____ **4.** Notes payable (due in three years)
_____ **5.** Land not currently used in operations
_____ **6.** Accounts receivable
_____ **7.** Trademarks

QS 5-3
Classifying balance sheet items
C3

Compute Tucker Company's current ratio from the following information about its assets and liabilities:

Accounts receivable	$15,000
Accounts payable	10,000
Buildings	42,000
Cash	6,000
Long-term notes payable	20,000
Office supplies	1,800
Prepaid insurance	2,500
Unearned services revenue	4,000

QS 5-4
Computing current ratio
A1

In preparing a work sheet, indicate the financial statement debit column to which a normal balance of each of the following accounts should be extended. Use IS for the Income Statement Debit column and BS for the Statement of Changes in Owner's Equity or Balance Sheet Debit column.

_____ **1.** Equipment   _____ **4.** Prepaid rent
_____ **2.** Owner, withdrawals   _____ **5.** Accounts receivable
_____ **3.** Insurance expense   _____ **6.** Depreciation expense—Equipment

QS 5-5
Applying a work sheet
P3

The following information is taken from the work sheet for Hascal Company as of December 31, 1999. Using this information, determine the amount for S. Hascal, capital, that should be reported on its December 31, 1999, balance sheet.

	Income Statement		Statement of Changes in Owner's Equity and Balance Sheet	
	Dr.	Cr.	Dr.	Cr.
S. Hascal, capital				65,000
S. Hascal, withdrawals			32,000	
Totals	115,000	174,000		

QS 5-6
Interpreting a work sheet
P3

On December 31, 1999, Yacht Management Co. prepared an adjusting entry for $6,700 of earned but unrecorded management fees. On January 16, 2000, Ace received $15,500 of management fees which included the fees earned in 1999. Assuming the company uses reversing entries, prepare the reversing entry and the January 16, 2000, entry.

QS 5-7ᴬ
Reversing entries
P4

Exercises

Exercise 5-1
Preparing closing entries
CI, PI

The following adjusted trial balance contains the accounts and balances of Painters Company as of December 31, 2000, the end of its fiscal year:

No.	Account Title	Debit	Credit
101	Cash	$18,000	
126	Supplies	12,000	
128	Prepaid insurance	2,000	
167	Equipment	23,000	
168	Accumulated depreciation—Equipment		$ 6,500
301	R. Tanner, capital		46,600
302	R. Tanner, withdrawals	6,000	
404	Services revenue		36,000
612	Depreciation expense—Equipment	2,000	
622	Salaries expense	21,000	
637	Insurance expense	1,500	
640	Rent expense	2,400	
652	Supplies expense	1,200	
	Totals	$89,100	$89,100

Prepare closing entries for Painters Company.

Exercise 5-2
Preparing closing entries and a post-closing trial balance
PI, P2

The adjusted trial balance for West Marketing Co. is shown below. Prepare a table with two columns under each of the following headings: Adjusted Trial Balance, Closing Entries, and Post-Closing Trial Balance. Complete the table by providing four closing entries and the post-closing trial balance.

No.	Account Title	Adjusted Trial Balance	
101	Cash	$ 8,200	
106	Accounts receivable	24,000	
153	Equipment	41,000	
154	Accumulated depreciation—Equip.		$ 16,500
193	Franchise	30,000	
201	Accounts payable		14,000
209	Salaries payable		3,200
233	Unearned fees		2,600
301	F. West, capital		64,500
302	F. West, withdrawals	14,400	
401	Marketing fees earned		79,000
611	Depreciation expense—Equip.	11,000	
622	Salaries expense	31,500	
640	Rent expense	12,000	
677	Miscellaneous expenses	7,700	
901	Income summary		
	Totals	$179,800	$179,800

The following balances of the Retained Earnings and temporary accounts are from High Rider's adjusted trial balance:

Exercise 5-3
Closing entries for a corporation

Account Title	Debit	Credit
Retained earnings		$42,100
Cash dividends declared	$ 7,500	
Services revenue		32,000
Interest earned		5,300
Salaries expense	25,400	
Insurance expense	3,800	
Rental expense	6,400	
Supplies expense	3,100	
Depreciation expense—Trucks	10,600	

Required

a. Prepare the closing entries.

b. Determine the amount of retained earnings to be reported on the company's balance sheet.

Open the following T-accounts with the provided balances. Prepare closing journal entries and post them to the T-accounts.

Exercise 5-4
Preparing and posting closing entries

M. Jones, Capital		
	Dec. 31	41,000

M. Jones, Withdrawals		
Dec. 31	24,000	

Income Summary		

Services Revenue		
	Dec. 31	73,000

Rent Expense		
Dec. 31	8,600	

Salaries Expense		
Dec. 31	20,000	

Insurance Expense		
Dec. 31	3,500	

Depreciation Expense		
Dec. 31	16,000	

Use the following adjusted trial balance of Hanson Trucking Company to prepare a classified balance sheet as of December 31, 2000.

Exercise 5-5
Preparing a classified balance sheet

Account Title	Debit	Credit
Cash	$ 7,000	
Accounts receivable	16,500	
Office supplies	2,000	
Trucks	170,000	
Accumulated depreciation—Trucks		$ 35,000
Land	75,000	
Accounts payable		11,000
Interest payable		3,000
Long-term notes payable		52,000
S. Hanson, capital		161,000
S. Hanson, withdrawals	19,000	
Trucking fees earned		128,000
Depreciation expense—Trucks	22,500	
Salaries expense	60,000	
Office supplies expense	7,000	
Repairs expense—Trucks	11,000	
Total	$390,000	$390,000

Exercise 5-6
Preparing a 10-column worksheet
P3

The following unadjusted trial balance contains the accounts and balances of the Deshaw Delivery Company as of December 31, 2000. Use the following information about the company's adjustments to complete a 10-column worksheet for Deshaw Delivery.

a. Unrecorded depreciation on the trucks at the end of the year is $35,000.
b. The total amount of incurred but unpaid interest at the end of the year is $8,000.
c. The cost of unused office supplies still available at the end of the year is $1,000.

Account Title	Debit	Credit
Cash	$ 14,000	
Accounts receivable	33,000	
Office supplies	4,000	
Trucks	340,000	
Accumulated depreciation—Trucks		$ 70,000
Land	150,000	
Accounts payable		22,000
Interest payable		6,000
Long-term notes payable		104,000
S. Deshaw, capital		322,000
S. Deshaw, withdrawals	38,000	
Delivery fees earned		256,000
Depreciation expense—Trucks	45,000	
Salaries expense	120,000	
Office supplies expense	14,000	
Interest expense	6,000	
Repairs expense, trucks	16,000	
Total	$780,000	$780,000

Exercise 5-7
Computing current ratio A1

Use the information in the adjusted trial balance reported in Exercise 5-5 to compute the current ratio as of the balance sheet date.

Exercise 5-8
Computing current ratio
A1

Calculate the current ratio in each of the following separate cases:

	Current Assets	Current Liabilities
Case 1	$ 78,000	$31,000
Case 2	104,000	75,000
Case 3	44,000	48,000
Case 4	84,500	80,600
Case 5	60,000	99,000

Exercise 5-9
Extending adjusted account balances on a work sheet
P3

These accounts are from the Adjusted Trial Balance columns of a company's 10-column work sheet. In the blank space beside each account, write the letter of the appropriate financial statement column to which a normal account balance is extended.

A. Debit column for the income statement.
B. Credit column for the income statement.
C. Debit column for the statement of changes in owner's equity and balance sheet.
D. Credit column for the statement of changes in owner's equity and balance sheet.

_____ **1.** Service Fees Revenue
_____ **2.** Insurance Expense
_____ **3.** Accumulated Depreciation
_____ **4.** Interest Earned
_____ **5.** Accounts Receivable
_____ **6.** Rent Expense
_____ **7.** Depreciation Expense
_____ **8.** Cash
_____ **9.** Office Supplies
_____ **10.** Accounts Payable
_____ **11.** Owner, capital
_____ **12.** Wages Payable
_____ **13.** Machinery
_____ **14.** Interest Receivable
_____ **15.** Interest Expense
_____ **16.** Owner, withdrawals

Use the following information from the Adjustments columns of a 10-column work sheet to prepare the necessary adjusting journal entries:

Exercise 5-10
Preparing adjusting entries from work sheet

P3

No.	Account Title		Debit		Credit
109	Interest receivable	(d) $	580		
124	Office supplies			(b) $	1,650
128	Prepaid insurance			(a)	900
164	Accumulated depreciation—Office equipment			(c)	3,300
209	Salaries payable			(e)	660
409	Interest earned			(d)	580
612	Depreciation expense—Office equipment	(c)	3,300		
620	Office salaries expense	(e)	660		
636	Insurance expense, office equipment	(a)	432		
637	Insurance expense, store equipment	(a)	468		
650	Office supplies expense	(b)	1,650		
	Totals	$	7,090	$	7,090

Adjustments columns header: **Adjustments** (Debit / Credit)

These partially completed Income Statement columns from a 10-column work sheet are for WinSail Rental Co. Use the information to determine the amount that should be entered on the net income line of the work sheet. In addition, prepare closing entries for WinSail Rental. The owner, Jack Cooper, did not make any withdrawals.

Exercise 5-11
Completing the income statement columns and preparing closing entries

P3

Account Title	Debit	Credit
Rent earned		102,000
Salaries expense	45,300	
Insurance expense	6,400	
Dock rental expense	15,000	
Boat supplies expense	3,200	
Depreciation expense, boats	19,500	
Totals		
Net income		_12600_
Totals		

Exercise 5-12
Extending accounts in a work sheet
P3

The Adjusted Trial Balance columns of a 10-column work sheet for Plummer Company are shown below. Complete the work sheet by extending the account balances into the appropriate financial statement columns and by entering the amount of net income for the reporting period.

No.	Account Title	Adjusted Trial Balance	
101	Cash	$ 6,000	
106	Accounts receivable	26,200	
153	Trucks	41,000	
154	Accumulated depreciation—Trucks		$ 16,500
193	Franchise	30,000	
201	Accounts payable		14,000
209	Salaries payable		3,200
233	Unearned fees		2,600
301	F. Plummer, capital		64,500
302	F. Plummer, withdrawals	14,400	
401	Plumbing fees earned		79,000
611	Depreciation expense—Trucks	5,500	
622	Salaries expense	37,000	
640	Rent expense	12,000	
677	Miscellaneous expenses	7,700	
	Totals	$179,800	$179,800

Exercise 5-13[A]
Reversing entries
P4

Breaker Company records prepaid assets and unearned revenues in balance sheet accounts. The following information was used to prepare adjusting entries for Breaker Corporation as of August 31, the end of the company's fiscal year:

a. The company has earned $5,000 of unrecorded service fees.

b. The expired portion of prepaid insurance is $2,700.

c. Earned $1,900 of the total balance of the Unearned Fees account balance.

d. Depreciation expense for office equipment is $2,300.

e. Employees have earned but have not been paid salaries of $2,400.

Prepare the necessary reversing entries assuming Breaker uses reversing entries in its accounting system.

Exercise 5-14[A]
Reversing entries
P4

The following two events occured for Maxit Co. on October 31, 2000, the end of its fiscal year:

a. Maxit rents a building from its owner for $3,200 per month. By a prearrangement, the company delayed paying October's rent until November 5. On this date, the company paid the rent for both October and November.

b. Maxit rents space in a building it owns to a tenant for $750 per month. By prearrangement, the tenant delayed paying the October rent until November 8. On this date, the tenant paid the rent for both October and November.

Required

1. Prepare adjusting entries that Maxit must record for these events as of October 31.

2. Assuming Maxit does *not* use reversing entries, prepare journal entries to record Maxit's payment of rent on November 5 and the collection of rent on November 8 from Maxit's tenant.

3. Assuming Maxit does use reversing entries, prepare reversing entries and the journal entries to record Maxit's payment of rent on November 5 and collection of rent on November 8 from Maxit's tenant.

Bradshaw Repairs' adjusted trial balance on December 31, 2000, is shown below:

| | BRADSHAW REPAIRS
Adjusted Trial Balance
December 31, 2000 | | |
No.	Account Title	Debit	Credit
101	Cash	$ 13,000	
124	Office supplies	1,200	
128	Prepaid insurance	1,950	
167	Equipment	48,000	
168	Accumulated depreciation—Equipment		$ 4,000
201	Accounts payable		12,000
210	Wages payable		500
301	H. Bradshaw, capital		40,000
302	H. Bradshaw, withdrawals	15,000	
401	Repair fees earned		77,750
612	Depreciation expense—Equipment	4,000	
623	Wages expense	36,500	
637	Insurance expense	700	
640	Rent expense	9,600	
650	Office supplies expense	2,600	
690	Utilities expense	1,700	
	Totals	$134,250	$134,250

Problems

Problem 5-1
Closing entries, financial statements, and current ratio

C3, A1, P1

G S

Check Figure Ending capital balance, $47,650

Required

Preparation Component

1. Prepare an income statement and a statement of changes in owner's equity for the year 2000 and a classified balance sheet at the end of the year. There were no owner investments during the year.

2. Enter the adjusted trial balance in the first two columns of a six-column table that has middle columns for closing entries and the last two columns for a post-closing trial balance. Insert an Income Summary account as the last item in the trial balance.

3. Enter closing entries in the six-column table and prepare journal entries for them.

4. Determine the company's current ratio.

Analysis Component

5. Assume we collect the following two additional information items related to the adjusted trial balance shown above:

a. None of the $700 insurance expense had expired during the year. Instead, it is a prepayment of future insurance protection.

b. There were no earned and unpaid wages at the end of the year.

Describe the changes in financial statements that would result from these two information items.

Problem 5-2
Closing entries, financial
statements, and ratios

C3, A1, P1

The adjusted trial balance for Graw Construction as of December 31, 2000, is shown below:

No.	GRAW CONSTRUCTION Adjusted Trial Balance December 31, 2000 Account Title	Debit	Credit
101	Cash	$ 4,000	
104	Short-term investments	22,000	
126	Supplies	7,100	
128	Prepaid insurance	6,000	
167	Equipment	39,000	
168	Accumulated depreciation—Equipment		$ 20,000
173	Building	130,000	
174	Accumulated depreciation—Building		55,000
183	Land	45,000	
201	Accounts payable		15,500
203	Interest payable		1,500
208	Rent payable		2,500
210	Wages payable		1,500
213	Property taxes payable		800
233	Unearned professional fees		6,500
251	Long-term notes payable		66,000
301	T. Graw, capital		82,700
302	T. Graw, withdrawals	12,000	
401	Professional fees earned		96,000
406	Rent earned		13,000
407	Dividends earned		1,900
409	Interest earned		1,000
606	Depreciation expense—Building	10,000	
612	Depreciation expense—Equipment	5,000	
623	Wages expense	31,000	
633	Interest expense	4,100	
637	Insurance expense	9,000	
640	Rent expense	12,400	
652	Supplies expense	6,400	
682	Postage expense	3,200	
683	Property taxes expense	4,000	
684	Repairs expense	7,900	
688	Telephone expense	2,200	
690	Utilities expense	3,600	
	Totals	$363,900	$363,900

An analysis of other information reveals that Graw Construction is required to make a $6,600 payment on its long-term note payable during 2001. Also, T. Graw invested $50,000 cash at the beginning of year 2000.

Required

1. Prepare the income statement, statement of changes in owner's equity, and classified balance sheet.
2. Prepare the closing entries at the end of the year 2000.
3. Use the information in the financial statements to calculate these ratios:
   a. Return on equity.
   b. Modified return on equity assuming the owner's efforts are valued at $12,000 for the year.
   c. Debt ratio.
   d. Profit margin (use total revenues as the denominator).
   e. Current ratio.

Check Figure Total
assets, $178,100

On June 1, 2000, Jennifer Farrow created a new travel agency called Worldwide Tours. The company records prepaid and unearned items in balance sheet accounts. These transactions occurred during the company's first month:

June 1 Farrow invested $20,000 cash and computer equipment worth $40,000.
2 Rented furnished office space by paying $1,700 rent for the first month.
3 Purchased $1,100 of office supplies for cash.
10 Paid $3,600 for the premium on a one-year insurance policy. Insurance coverage began on June 10.
14 Paid $1,800 for two weeks' salaries to employees.
24 Collected $7,900 of commissions from airlines on tickets obtained for customers.
28 Paid another $1,800 for two weeks' salaries.
29 Paid the month's $650 telephone bill.
30 Paid $250 cash to repair the company's computer.
30 Farrow withdrew $1,500 cash from the business for personal use.

The company's chart of accounts included these accounts:

101	Cash	405	Commissions Earned
106	Accounts Receivable	612	Depreciation Expense—
124	Office Supplies		Computer Equipment
128	Prepaid Insurance	622	Salaries Expense
167	Computer Equipment	637	Insurance Expense
168	Accumulated Depreciation—	640	Rent Expense
	Computer Equipment	650	Office Supplies Expense
209	Salaries Payable	684	Repairs Expense
301	J. Farrow, Capital	688	Telephone Expense
302	J. Farrow, Withdrawals	901	Income Summary

Required

1. Use the balance-column format to create each of the listed accounts.
2. Prepare journal entries to record the transactions for June and post them to the accounts.
3. Prepare an unadjusted trial balance as of June 30.
4. Use the following information to journalize and post adjusting entries for the month:
  a. Two-thirds of one month's insurance coverage was consumed.
  b. There were $700 of office supplies on hand at the end of the month.
  c. Depreciation on the computer equipment was estimated to be $600.
  d. The employees had earned $320 of unpaid and unrecorded salaries.
  e. The company had earned $1,650 of commissions that had not yet been billed.
5. Prepare an income statement, a statement of changes in owner's equity, and a balance sheet.
6. Prepare journal entries to close the temporary accounts and post them to the accounts.
7. Prepare a separate post-closing trial balance.

In the blank space beside each numbered balance sheet item, enter the letter of its balance sheet classification. If the item should not appear on the balance sheet, enter a z in the blank.

a. Current assets
b. Investments
c. Plant and equipment
d. Intangible assets
e. Current liabilities
f. Long-term liabilities
g. Owner's equity
h. Stockholders' equity

_____ **1.** Depreciation expense, trucks
_____ **2.** L. Hale, capital
_____ **3.** Interest receivable
_____ **4.** L. Hale, withdrawals
_____ **5.** Automobiles
_____ **6.** Notes payable—due in three years

Problem 5-3
Applying the accounting cycle

C2, P1, P2

Check Figure Ending capital balance, $60,330

Problem 5-4
Balance sheet classifications

C3

_____ **7.** Accounts payable

_____ **8.** Prepaid insurance

_____ **9.** Common stock

_____ **10.** Unearned services revenue

_____ **11.** Accumulated depreciation—Trucks

_____ **12.** Cash

_____ **13.** Building

_____ **14.** Retained earnings

_____ **15.** Office equipment

_____ **16.** Land (used in operations)

_____ **17.** Repairs expense

_____ **18.** Prepaid property taxes

_____ **19.** Current portion of long-term note payable

_____ **20.** Investment in Chrysler common stock (long-term holding)

Problem 5-5

Work sheet, journal entries, financial statements, and current ratio

C3, A1, P3

This unadjusted trial balance is for Whiten Construction Co. as of the end of its 1999 fiscal year. The beginning balance of the owner's capital was $52,660 and the owner invested another $25,000 cash in the company during the year.

	WHITEN CONSTRUCTION CO. Unadjusted Trial Balance April 30, 1999		
No.	**Account Title**	**Debit**	**Credit**
101	Cash	$ 17,500	
126	Supplies	8,900	
128	Prepaid insurance	6,200	
167	Equipment	131,000	
168	Accumulated depreciation—Equipment		$ 25,250
201	Accounts payable		5,800
203	Interest payable		
208	Rent payable		
210	Wages payable		
213	Property taxes payable		
251	Long-term notes payable		24,000
301	R. Whiten, capital		77,660
302	R. Whiten, withdrawals	30,000	
401	Construction fees earned		134,000
612	Depreciation expense—Equipment		
623	Wages expense	45,860	
633	Interest expense	2,640	
637	Insurance expense		
640	Rent expense	13,200	
652	Supplies expense		
683	Property taxes expense	4,600	
684	Repairs expense	2,810	
690	Utilities expense	4,000	
	Totals	$266,710	$266,710

Required

Preparation Component

1. Prepare a 10-column work sheet for 1999, starting with the unadjusted trial balance and including adjustments based on these additional facts:

a. The supplies on hand at the end of the year had a cost of $3,200.

b. The cost of expired insurance for the year is $3,900.

c. Annual depreciation on equipment is $8,500.

d. The April utilities expense of $550 is not included in the unadjusted trial balance because the bill arrived after it was prepared. The $550 amount owed needs to be recorded.

e. The company's employees have earned $1,600 of accrued wages.

f. The lease for the office requires the company to pay total rent for the year ended April 30 equal to 10% of the company's annual revenues. Rent has been estimated and is being paid to the building owner with monthly payments of $1,100. If the annual rent owed exceeds the total monthly estimated payments, the company must pay the excess before May 31. If the total owed is less than the amount previously paid, the building owner will refund the difference by May 31.

g. Additional property taxes of $900 have been assessed on the equipment but have not been paid or recorded in the accounts.

h. The long-term note payable bears interest at 1% per month, which the company is required to pay by the 10th of the following month. The balance of the Interest Expense account equals the amount paid for the first 11 months of the past fiscal year. The interest for April has not yet been paid or recorded. In addition, the company is required to make a $5,000 payment on the note on June 30, 1999.

2. Use the work sheet to journalize the adjusting and closing entries.

3. Prepare an income statement, a statement of changes in owner's equity, and a classified balance sheet. Calculate the company's current ratio.

Analysis Component

4. Analyze the following errors and describe how each would affect the 10-column work sheet. Explain whether the error is likely to be discovered in completing the work sheet and, if not, the effect of the error on the financial statements.

a. Assume the adjustment for supplies consumption credited Supplies for $3,200 and debited the same amount to Supplies Expense.

b. When completing the adjusted trial balance in the work sheet, the $17,500 cash balance is incorrectly entered in the Credit column.

Check Figure Total assets, $120,250

The unadjusted trial balance for Shooting Ranges as of December 31, 2000, is shown below:

Problem 5-6A
Adjusting, reversing, and subsequent entries

P3, P4

SHOOTING RANGES Unadjusted Trial Balance December 31, 2000		
Cash	$ 13,000	
Accounts receivable		
Supplies	5,500	
Equipment	130,000	
Accumulated depreciation—Equipment		$ 25,000
Interest payable		
Salaries payable		
Unearned membership fees		14,000
Notes payable		50,000
S. Becker, capital		58,250
S. Becker, withdrawals	20,000	
Membership fees earned		53,000
Depreciation expense—Equipment		
Salaries expense	28,000	
Interest expense	3,750	
Supplies expense		
Totals	$200,250	$200,250

Required

1. Prepare a six-column table with two columns under each of the following headings: Unadjusted Trial Balance, Adjustments, and Adjusted Trial Balance. Complete the table by entering adjustments that reflect the following information:

   a. As of December 31, employees have earned $900 of unpaid and unrecorded salaries. The next payday is January 4, and the total amount of salaries to be paid is $1,600.

   b. The cost of supplies on hand at December 31 is $2,700.

   c. The note payable requires an interest payment to be made every three months. The amount of unrecorded accrued interest at December 31 is $1,250, and the next payment is due on January 15. This payment will be $1,500.

   d. An analysis of the unearned membership fees shows $5,600 remains unearned at December 31.

   e. In addition to the membership fees included in the revenue account balance, the company has earned another $9,100 in fees that will be collected on January 21. The company is also expected to collect $8,000 on the same day for new fees earned during January.

   f. Depreciation expense for the year is $12,500.

2. Prepare journal entries for the adjustments entered in the six-column table.

3. Prepare journal entries to reverse the effects of the adjusting entries that involve accruals.

4. Prepare journal entries to record the cash payments and collections that are described for January.

Check Figure Total debits in adjusted trial balance, $224,000

Serial Problem

Echo Systems

(The first two segments of this serial problem were in Chapters 3 and 4, and the final segment is presented in Chapter 6. If the Chapter 3 and 4 segments have not been completed, the assignment can begin at this point. It is recommended you use the Working Papers that accompany this book because they reflect the account balances that resulted from posting the entries required in Chapters 3 and 4.)

The transactions of Echo Systems for October through December 2000 have been recorded in the problem segments in Chapters 3 and 4, as well as the year-end adjusting entries. Prior to closing the revenue and expense accounts for year 2000, the accounting system is modified to include the Income Summary account, which is given the account number 901.

Check Figure Total credits in post-closing trial balance, $78,560.

Required

1. Record and post the necessary closing entries.

2. Prepare a post-closing trial balance.

BEYOND THE NUMBERS

Reporting in Action

Refer to the financial statements and related information for **NIKE** in Appendix A. Find answers to the following questions by analyzing the information in its report:

Required

1. For the fiscal year ended May 31, 1997, what amount will be credited to Income Summary to summarize NIKE's revenues earned for the period?

2. For the fiscal year ended May 31, 1997, what amount will be debited to Income Summary to summarize NIKE's expenses incurred for the period?

3. For the fiscal year ended May 31, 1997, what will be the balance of the Income Summary account before it is closed to Retained Earnings?

4. Consult the Consolidated Statement of Cash Flows for the year ended May 31, 1997. What amount of cash was paid in dividends to common and preferred stockholders?

Swoosh Ahead

5. Obtain access to NIKE's annual report for fiscal years ending after May 31, 1997. You can gain access to NIKE's annual report at its web site [**www.nike.com**] or through the SEC's EDGAR data-

base [www.sec.gov]. How has the amount of net income closed to Income Summary changed in the fiscal years ending after May 31, 1997? How has the amount of cash paid as dividends changed in the fiscal years ending after May 31, 1997?

Both **NIKE** and **Reebok** design, produce, market, and sell sports footwear and apparel. Key comparative figures ($ millions) for these two organizations follow:

Key Figures*	NIKE		Reebok	
	1997	*1996*	*1996*	*1995*
Current assets	$3,831	$2,727	$1,463	$1,333
Current liabilities	$1,867	$1,467	$ 517	$ 432

*NIKE figures are from its annual reports for fiscal years ended May 31, 1997 and 1996. Reebok figures are from its annual reports for fiscal years ended December 31, 1996 and 1995.

Comparative Analysis
A1

Nike
Reebok

Required

1. Compute the current ratios for both years for both companies.
2. Which company has the better ability to pay short-term obligations according to the current ratio?
3. Comment on each company's current ratios for the past two years.
4. How do NIKE's and Reebok's current ratios compare to their industry average ratio of about 1.6?

On January 20, 2000, Jennifer Nelson, the staff accountant for Newby Enterprises, is feeling pressure to complete the preparation of the annual financial statements. The president of the company has said he needs up-to-date financial statements to share with several bankers on January 21 at a dinner meeting that has been called to discuss the possibility of Newby obtaining loan financing for a special building project. Jennifer knows that she won't be able to gather all the needed information in the next 24 hours to prepare the entire set of adjusting entries that must be posted before the financial statements accurately portray the company's performance and financial position for the fiscal period just ended December 31, 1999. Jennifer ultimately decides to estimate several expense accruals at the last minute. When deciding on estimates for the expenses, Jennifer uses low estimates as she doesn't want to make the financial statements look worse than they are. Jennifer finishes the financial statements before the deadline and gives them to the president without mentioning that several accounts use estimated balances as of December 31, 1999.

Ethics Challenge
C2

Required

1. Identify several courses of action that Jennifer could have taken instead of the one she decided on.
2. If you were in Jennifer's situation what would you have done? Briefly justify your response.

Assume one of your classmates said that the *going-concern*, or *continuing-concern, principle* states that the books of a company should be ongoing and therefore not closed until that business is terminated. This classmate does not understand the objective of the closing process or the meaning of the going-concern principle. Write a memo to this classmate that explains the concept of the closing process by drawing analogies between (a) a scoreboard for an athletic event and the revenue and expense accounts of a business or (b) a sports team's record book and the capital account. (Hint: Think about what would happen if the scoreboard was not cleared before the start of a new game.) Your memo should also clarify the meaning of the going-concern principle.

Communicating in Practice
C1

Visit **The Gap's** homepage at **www.gap.com**.

Taking it to the Net
A1

Required

1. Use the hotlink *Company History* to read the story of Gap's creation and evolution. To what does the name "The Gap" refer?

2. Chronicle the new types of stores that The Gap has opened throughout the 1980s and 1990s.

3. Access The Gap's annual financial report by using the hotlink provided. (Hint: If an adobe reader is required and the computer you are using is not so equipped, you may alternatively read the annual report information at www.sec.gov). Compute the current ratio for The Gap for the three years 1995–1997 (the most recent for the year ending January 31, 1998). Comment on the company's trend in liquidity.

Teamwork in Action
P1

The unadjusted trial balance and information for accounting adjustments of Noseworthy Investigators are shown below. Each team member involved in this project is to assume one of the responsibilities listed after the data. After completing each of these responsibilities, the team should work together to prove the accounting equation utilizing information from teammates (1 and 4). If your equation does not balance, you are to work as a team to resolve the error. The team's goal is to complete the task as quickly and accurately as possible.

Unadjusted Trial Balance		
Account Title	Debit	Credit
Cash	$ 15,000	
Supplies	11,000	
Prepaid Insurance	2,000	
Equipment	24,000	
Accumulated Depreciation—Equipment		$ 6,000
Accounts Payable		2,000
D. Noseworthy, capital		31,000
D. Noseworthy, withdrawals	5,000	
Investigation fees earned		32,000
Rent expense	14,000	
Totals	$71,000	$71,000

Additional Year-End Information

a. Expired insurance is $1,200.

b. Equipment depreciation is $3,000.

c. Unused supplies total $4,000.

d. Services in the amount of $500 have been provided and have not been billed or collected.

Responsibilities for individual Team Members

1. Determine the accounts and adjusted balances to be extended to the balance sheet columns of a work sheet. Also, determine total assets and total liabilities.

2. Determine the adjusted revenue account balance and prepare the entry to close this account.

3. Determine the adjusted expense account balances and prepare the entry to close these accounts.

4. Prepare a T-account for D. Noseworthy, Capital, that reflects the unadjusted trial balance amount, and a T-account for Income Summary. Prepare the third closing entry without amounts and the fourth closing entry with amounts. Ask teammates assigned to parts 2 and 3 for the postings for Income Summary. Obtain amounts to complete the third closing entry and post both the third and fourth closing entries. Provide the team with the ending Capital account balance.

5. The entire team should prove the accounting equation.

Hitting the Road
C2

Select a company in your community that you can visit in person or interview on the telephone. Call ahead to the company to arrange a time when you can interview an employee (often an accountant) who helps prepare the annual financial statements for the company. During the interview inquire about the following aspects of the company's accounting cycle:

1. Does the company prepare interim financial statements? What time period is used for the interim statements?
2. Does the company use the cash or accrual basis of accounting?
3. Does the company use a work sheet to aid in the preparation of the financial statements? Why or why not?
4. Does the company use a spreadsheet program to construct the work sheet? If so, which software program is used?
5. How long does it usually take after the end of the 12-month fiscal period to complete annual financial statements?

Read "An Enormous Temptation to Waste" in the February 10, 1997, issue of *Business Week*.

Required

1. What are possible advantages and disadvantages of stockpiling cash?
2. What are some of the reasons for the growth in cash for the companies highlighted in the article?
3. Under what asset subgroup does cash appear on a classified balance sheet?
4. What ratio does the article use to target the companies with the greatest relative amounts of cash?
5. How would the current ratio for the companies be affected by the stockpiling of cash?

Business Week
Activity

C3, A1

6

CHAPTER

Accounting for Merchandising Activities

Fizzling Inventory

BOSTON—By June of last year, 27-year-old Jason Walker was living his dream. He'd just opened **Exotic Fruit Drinks,** a small retail outlet devoted to serving the quirky tastes of young and old alike. But within months, this young entrepreneur's dream had become a nightmare.

Exotic Fruit Drinks started out with a bang. Customers raved about its stock of exotic and unique beverage products. Profit margins on successful drinks far outweighed the costs of unsold products. "We were ready to take on **Nantucket Nectars**," boasted Walker. Within 2 months, however, Walker lost control of inventory, and margins were being squeezed. What happened? Was Exotic Fruit Drinks soon to be another flash in the pan?

Two problems emerged. One was Walker's selection of the periodic inventory system. This system reports inventory levels at periodic intervals such as once a month. This means the inventory system couldn't give Walker up-to-date information on sales and inventory he'd need for stocking and ordering. "Our popular brands were being sold out and nothing was in inventory," says Walker. "We were turning away too many customers." Hardly a ticket for success. The second problem was Walker's lack of negotiating ability regarding purchase contracts. Purchase discounts and returns left too much power and too many decisions with suppliers.

But Walker fought back. With the help of a consultant, he installed a perpetual inventory system and renegotiated purchase contracts. His new inventory system gives up-to-date details on sales and inventory. "We now know what's hot and what's not," says Walker, "And we don't turn away customers." Also, his new contracts allow him to return unsold inventories and to deeply discount others. "This time," claims Walker, "we'll not disappoint!" And the future of Exotic Fruit Drinks looks downright bubbly.

Learning Objectives

Conceptual

C1 Describe merchandising activities and identify business examples.

C2 Identify and explain the components of income for a merchandising company.

C3 Identify and explain the inventory asset of a merchandising company.

C4 Describe both periodic and perpetual inventory systems.

C5 Analyze and interpret cost flows and operating activities of a merchandising company.

Analytical

A1 Analyze and interpret accruals and cash flows for merchandising activities.

A2 Compute the acid-test ratio and explain its use as an indicator of liquidity.

A3 Compute the gross margin ratio and explain its use as an indicator of profitability.

Procedural

P1 Analyze and record transactions for merchandise purchases using a perpetual system.

P2 Analyze and record transactions for sales of merchandise using a perpetual system.

P3 Prepare adjustments and close accounts for a merchandising company.

P4 Define and prepare multiple-step and single-step income statements.

CHAPTER PREVIEW

Merchandising activities are a major part of modern business. Consumers expect a wealth of products, discount prices, inventory on demand, and high quality. This chapter introduces the business and accounting practices used by companies engaged in merchandising activities. These companies buy products and then resell them to customers. We show how financial statements capture these merchandising activities. The new financial statement elements created by merchandising activities are explained. We also analyze and record merchandise purchases and sales transacted by these companies. Adjustments and the closing process for merchandising companies are explained. An understanding of these important topics is what Jason Walker of Exotic Fruit Drinks needed to avoid the problems he encountered.

Merchandising Activities

C1 Describe merchandising activities and identify business examples.

Our emphasis in previous chapters was on the accounting and reporting activities of companies providing services such as **Greyhound Lines, Merrill Lynch, America West Airlines, Avis,** and **Marriott.** In return for services provided to its customers, a service company receives commissions, fares, or fees as revenue. Its net income for a reporting period is the difference between its revenues and the operating expenses incurred in providing services.

A merchandising company's activities are different from those of a service company. A **merchandiser** earns net income by buying and selling merchandise. **Merchandise** consists of products, also called *goods,* that a company acquires for the purpose of reselling them to customers. Merchandisers are often identified as either wholesalers or retailers.

A **wholesaler** is a *middleman* that buys products from manufacturers or other wholesalers and sells them to retailers or other wholesalers. Wholesalers provide promotion, market information, and financial assistance to retailers. They also provide a sales force, reduced inventory costs, less risk, and market information to manufacturers. Wholesalers include companies such as **Fleming, SuperValu, McKesson,** and **Sysco.** A **retailer** is a middleman that buys products from manufacturers or wholesalers and sells them to consumers. Examples of retailers include **The Gap, Oakley, CompUSA, Wal-Mart,** and **Musicland.** Retailers such as **Best Buy** often sell both products and services.

Reporting Financial Performance

Net income to a merchandiser implies that revenue from selling merchandise exceeds both the cost of merchandise sold to customers and the cost of other operating expenses for the period (see Exhibit 6.1). The usual accounting term for revenues from selling merchandise is *sales* and the term used for the cost of buying and preparing the merchandise is *cost of goods sold.*[1] A merchandiser's expenses are often called *operating expenses.*

C2 Identify and explain the components of income for a merchandising company.

Exhibit 6.1

Computing Income for Both a Merchandising Company and a Service Company

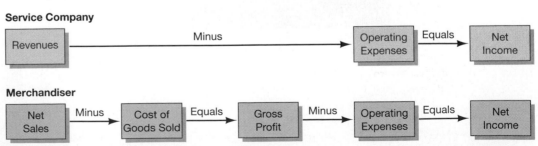

---

[1] Many service companies use the term *sales* in their income statements to describe revenues. **Marriott** is one example. Cost of goods sold is often called *cost of sales* and is described as an operating expense.

The condensed income statement for Z-Mart in Exhibit 6.2 shows how these three elements of net income are related. This statement shows Z-Mart sold products acquired at a cost of $230,400 to customers for $314,700. This yields a $84,300 gross profit. **Gross profit,** also called **gross margin,** equals net sales less cost of goods sold. Gross profit is important to the profitability of merchandisers. Changes in gross profit often greatly impact a merchandiser's operations since gross profit must cover all other expenses plus yield a return for the owner. Z-Mart, for instance, used gross profit to cover $71,400 of other expenses. This left $12,900 in net income for the year 1999.

Z-MART Condensed Income Statement For Year Ended December 31, 1999	
Net sales	$314,700
Cost of goods sold	(230,400)
Gross profit from sales	$84,300
Total other expenses	(71,400)
Net income	$ 12,900

Exhibit 6.2

Condensed Income Statement for a Merchandiser

Reporting Financial Condition

A merchandising company's balance sheet includes an item not on the balance sheet of a service company—a current asset called merchandise inventory. **Merchandise inventory** refers to products a company owns for the purpose of selling to customers. Exhibit 6.3 shows the classified balance sheet for Z-Mart, including merchandise inventory of $21,000. The cost of this asset includes the cost incurred to buy the goods, ship them to the store, and make them ready for sale. Although companies usually hold inventories of other items such as supplies, most companies simply refer to merchandise inventory as *inventory*.

C3 Identify and explain the inventory asset of a merchandising company.

Z-MART Balance Sheet December 31, 1999			
Assets			
Current assets:			
Cash		$ 8,200	
Accounts receivable		11,200	
Merchandise inventory		21,000	
Prepaid expenses		1,100	
Total current assets			$41,500
Plant and equipment:			
Office equipment	$ 4,200		
Less accumulated depreciation	1,400	2,800	
Store equipment	30,000		
Less accumulated depreciation	6,000	24,000	
Total plant and equipment			26,800
Total assets			$68,300
Liabilities			
Current liabilities:			
Accounts payable		$16,000	
Salaries payable		800	
Total liabilities			$16,800
Owner's Equity			
K. Marty, capital			51,500
Total liabilities and owner's equity			$68,300

Exhibit 6.3

Classified Balance Sheet for a Merchandiser

Operating Cycle

A merchandising company's operating cycle begins with the purchase of merchandise and ends with the collection of cash from the sale of merchandise. An example is a merchandiser who buys products at wholesale and distributes and sells them to consumers at retail. The length of an operating cycle differs across the types of businesses. Department stores such as **Sears** and **Dayton Hudson** commonly have operating cycles from three to five months. But operating cycles for grocery merchants such as **Kroger** and **Safeway** usually range from 1 to 2 months.

Exhibit 6.4 illustrates an operating cycle for a merchandiser with (1) cash sales and (2) credit sales. The cash sales cycle moves from (a) merchandise purchases to (b) inventory for sale to (c) cash sales. The credit sales cycle moves from (a) merchandise purchases to (b) inventory for sale to (c) credit sales and (d) accounts receivable to (e) cash. Credit sales delay the receipt of cash until the account receivable is paid by the customer. Companies always try to shorten their operating cycles. Assets tied up in inventory or receivables are not productive assets.

Exhibit 6.4

Operating Cycle of a Merchandiser*

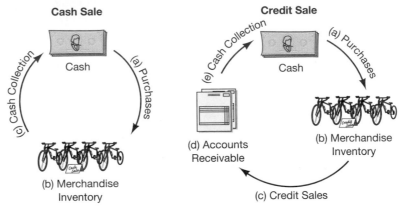

* This exhibit assumes cash purchases. Credit purchases would involve inserting accounts payable before merchandise inventory in the cycle.

Inventory Systems

We explained that a merchandising company's income statement includes an item called *cost of goods sold* and its balance sheet includes a current asset called *inventory*. **Cost of goods sold** is the cost of merchandise sold to customers during a period. It is often the largest single deduction on the income statement of a merchandiser. **Inventory** is products a company owns and expects to sell in its normal operations. These items are part of merchandising activities captured in Exhibit 6.5. This exhibit shows that a company's merchandise available for sale is a combination of what it begins with (beginning inventory) and what it purchases (net cost of purchases). The merchandise available is either sold (cost of goods sold) or kept for future sales (ending inventory).

Exhibit 6.5

Merchandising Cost Flow

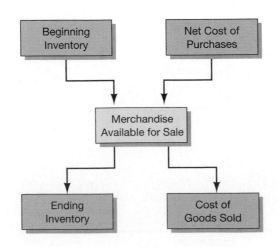

There are two inventory accounting systems used to collect information about cost of goods sold and cost of inventory on hand. The two systems are called *periodic* and *perpetual.*

Periodic Inventory System

A **periodic inventory system** requires updating the inventory account only at the *end of a period* to reflect the quantity and cost of both goods on hand and goods sold. It does not require continual updating of the inventory account. The company records the cost of new merchandise in a temporary *Purchases* account. When merchandise is sold, revenue is recorded but the cost of the merchandise sold is *not* yet recorded as a cost. When financial statements are prepared, the company takes a *physical count of inventory* by counting the quantities of merchandise on hand. Cost of merchandise on hand is determined by relating the quantities on hand to records showing each item's original cost. The cost of merchandise on hand is then used to compute cost of goods sold. The inventory account is adjusted to reflect the amount computed from the physical count of inventory.

Periodic systems were historically used by companies such as hardware, drug, and department stores that sold large quantities of low-value items. Without today's computers and scanners, it was not feasible for accounting systems to track such small items as pencils, toothpaste, paper clips, socks, and toothpicks through inventory and into customers' hands.

Perpetual Inventory System

A **perpetual inventory system** keeps a continual record of the amount of inventory on hand. A perpetual system accumulates the net cost of merchandise purchases in the inventory account and subtracts the cost of each sale from the same inventory account. When an item is sold, its cost is recorded in a *Cost of Goods Sold* account. With a perpetual system we can find out the cost of merchandise on hand at any time by looking at the balance of the inventory account. We can also find out the current balance of cost of goods sold anytime during a period by looking in the Cost of Goods Sold account.

Before advancements in computing technology, a perpetual system was often limited to businesses making a limited number of daily sales such as automobile dealers and major appliance stores. Because there were relatively few transactions, a perpetual system was feasible. In today's information age, with widespread use of computing technology, the use of a perpetual system has dramatically grown. Also, the number of companies using a perpetual system continues to increase.

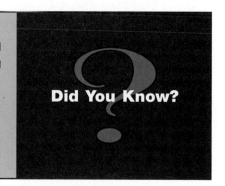

Perpetual Information
Today's information technology is transforming merchandising activities. Computers and perpetual inventory systems are taking the guesswork out of wholesale buying, slashing inventory cycles, keeping popular items in stock, and cutting return rates. These advances have "totally changed the industry from a push industry to a pull industry," says the chairman of **Western Merchandisers,** a supplier of more than 1,000 **Wal-Marts.** Are supermarkets next? A recent study says grocers can cut prices by 11% or more with similar changes in accounting for inventory. [Source: *Business Week,* June 6, 1994.]

Did You Know?

C4 Describe both periodic and perpetual inventory systems.

Because a perpetual inventory system gives users more timely information and is widely used in practice, our discussion in the chapter emphasizes a perpetual system. At **Wal-Mart,** for instance, a majority of suppliers get point-of-sale data. Yet we analyze and record merchandising transactions using *both* periodic and perpetual inventory systems in the appendix to this chapter.

Answers—p. 249

Flash back

1. Describe a merchandiser's cost of goods sold.
2. What is gross profit for a merchandising company?
3. Explain why use of the perpetual inventory system has grown dramatically.

Accounting for Merchandise Purchases

Assets = Liabilities + Equity
+1,200
−1,200

P1 Analyze and record transactions for merchandise purchases using a perpetual system.

We explained that with a perpetual inventory system, the cost of merchandise bought for resale is recorded in the Merchandise Inventory asset account. Z-Mart records a $1,200 cash purchase of merchandise on November 2 with this entry:

Nov. 2	Merchandise Inventory	1,200	
	Cash		1,200
	Purchased merchandise for cash.		

The invoice for this merchandise is shown in Exhibit 6.6. The buyer usually receives the original, while the seller keeps a copy. This source document serves as the purchase invoice of Z-Mart (buyer) and the sales invoice for Trex (seller). The amount recorded for merchandise inventory includes its purchase cost, shipping fees, taxes, and any other costs necessary to make it ready for sale.

To compute the total cost of merchandise purchases, we must adjust the invoice cost for (1) any discounts given to a purchaser by a supplier, (2) any returns and allowances for unsatisfactory items received from a supplier, and (3) any required freight costs paid by a purchaser. This section explains how these items affect our recorded cost of merchandise purchases.

Exhibit 6.6

Invoice

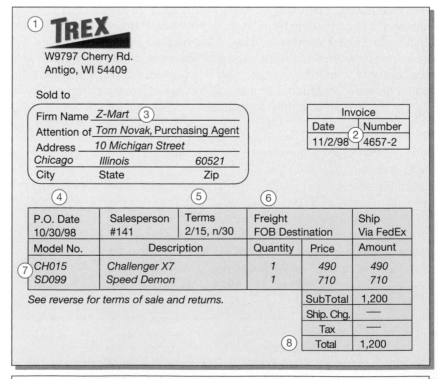

① Seller ② Invoice date ③ Purchaser ④ Order date ⑤ Credit terms
⑥ Freight terms ⑦ Goods ⑧ Total invoice amount

Trade Discounts

When a manufacturer or wholesaler prepares a catalog of items it has for sale, each item is usually given a **list price,** also called a *catalog price.* List price often is not the intended selling price of an item. Instead, the intended selling price equals list price minus a given percent called a **trade discount.**

The amount of trade discount usually depends on whether a buyer is a wholesaler, retailer, or final consumer. A wholesaler buying in large quantities is often granted a larger discount than a retailer buying in smaller quantities. A trade discount reduces a list price and is used to compute the actual selling price of the goods.

Trade discounts are commonly used by manufacturers and wholesalers to change selling prices without republishing their catalogs. When a seller wants to change selling prices, it can notify its customers merely by sending them a new table of trade discounts that they can apply to catalog prices.

Because a list price is not intended to reflect actual selling price of merchandise, a buyer does not enter list prices and trade discounts in its accounts. Instead, a buyer records the net amount of list price minus trade discount. In the November 2 purchase of merchandise by Z-Mart, it received a 40% trade discount for this item that was listed in the seller's catalog at $2,000. Z-Mart's purchase price is $1,200, computed as $2,000 − (40% × $2,000).

Purchase Discounts

The purchase of goods on credit requires a clear statement of expected amounts and dates of future payments to avoid misunderstandings. **Credit terms** for a purchase are a listing of the amounts and timing of payments between a buyer and a seller. Credit terms usually reflect the practices in an industry. In some industries, purchasers expect terms requiring payment within 10 days after the end of a month where purchases occur. These credit terms are entered on sales invoices or tickets as "n/10 EOM." The **EOM** refers to "end of month." In some other industries, invoices are often due and payable 30 calendar days after the invoice date. These credit terms are entered as "n/30." The 30-day period is called the **credit period.** Exhibit 6.7 portrays credit terms.

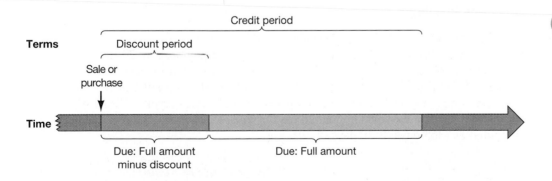

Exhibit 6.7

Credit Terms

Sellers often grant a **cash discount** when the credit period is long and buyers pay within a certain period. A buyer views a cash discount as a **purchase discount.** A seller views a cash discount as a **sales discount.** If cash discounts for early payment exist, they are described in the credit terms on an invoice. As an example, credit terms of "2/10, n/60" mean there is a 60-day credit period before full payment is due. But the seller allows a buyer to deduct 2% of the invoice amount from the payment if it is paid within 10 days of the invoice date. Sellers do this to encourage early payment. A **discount period** is the period where the reduced payment can be made.

To illustrate how a buyer accounts for a purchase discount, we assume Z-Mart's purchase of merchandise for $1,200 was on credit with terms of 2/10, n/30. Z-Mart's entry to record this credit purchase is:[2]

Assets = Liabilities + Equity
+1,200   +1,200

(a) Nov. 2	Merchandise Inventory		1,200	
	Accounts Payable			1,200
	Purchased merchandise on credit, invoice dated November 2, terms 2/10, n/30.			

If Z-Mart takes advantage of the discount and pays the amount due on November 12, the entry to record payment is:

Assets = Liabilities + Equity
−24   −1,200
−1,176

(b) Nov. 12	Accounts Payable		1,200	
	Merchandise Inventory (2% × $1,200) . . .			24
	Cash			1,176
	Paid for the purchase of November 2 less the discount.			

Z-Mart's Merchandise Inventory account now reflects the net cost of merchandise purchased. Its Accounts Payable account shows a zero balance, meaning the debt is satisfied.

Merchandise Inventory					Accounts Payable			
Nov. 2	1,200	Nov. 12	24		Nov. 12	1,200	Nov. 2	1,200
Balance	1,176						Balance	0

Companies' buying practices involving inventory can impact gross profit. **Home Depot,** for instance, reported an increase in gross profit for 1996 over 1995. It explained in its Management Discussion and Analysis section that:

> The improvement resulted primarily from more effective buying practices, which resulted in lowering the cost of merchandise.
>
> **Home Depot**

Managing Discounts

A buyer's failure to pay within a discount period is often quite expensive. If Z-Mart does not pay within the 10-day discount period, it delays the payment by 20 more days. This delay costs Z-Mart an added 2% to the cost of merchandise. Most buyers try to take advantage of purchase discounts. We can approximate Z-Mart's annual rate of interest attached to not paying within the discount period. For Z-Mart's terms of 2/10, n/30, missing the 2% discount for an additional 20 days is equal to an annual interest rate of 36.5%, computed as (365 days ÷ 20 days) × 2%.

Nov. 2. Credit purchase.

Nov. 12. Cash paid in discount period.

[2] Appendix 6A repeats journal entries *(a)* through *(f)* using a periodic inventory system.

Purchasing Agent

You're the purchasing agent for a merchandising company. You purchase a batch of CDs on terms of 3/10, n/90, but your company has limited cash and you must borrow funds at an 11% annual rate if you are to pay within the discount period. Do you take advantage of the purchase discount?

Answer—p. 249

Most companies set up a system to pay invoices with favorable discounts within the discount period. Careful cash management means that no invoice is paid until the last day of a discount period. One technique to achieve this goal is to file each invoice so that it automatically comes up for payment on the last day of its discount period. A simple manual system uses 31 folders, one for each day in a month. After an invoice is recorded, it is placed in the folder matching the last day of its discount period. If the last day of an invoice's discount period is November 12, it is filed in folder number 12. This invoice and other invoices in the same folder are removed and paid on November 12. Computerized systems achieve the same result by using a code identifying the last date in the discount period. When that date occurs, the system automatically identifies accounts to be paid.

Credit Manager

You are the new credit manager for a merchandising company that purchases its merchandise on credit. You are trained for your new job by the outgoing employee. You are to oversee payment of payables to maintain the company's credit standing with suppliers and to take advantage of favorable cash discounts. The outgoing employee explains that the computer system is programmed to prepare checks for amounts net of favorable cash discounts, and checks are dated the last day of the discount period. But you are told checks are not mailed until five days later. "It's simple," this employee explains. "Our company gets free use of cash for an extra five days, and our department looks better. When a supplier complains, we blame the computer system and the mailroom." Your first invoice arrives with a 10-day discount period for a $10,000 purchase. This transaction occurs on April 9 with credit terms of 2/10, n/30. Do you mail the $9,800 check on April 19 or April 24?

Answer—p. 249

Purchase Returns and Allowances

Purchase returns are merchandise received by a purchaser but returned to the supplier. A *purchase allowance* is a reduction in the cost of defective merchandise received by a purchaser from a supplier. Purchasers will often keep defective but still marketable merchandise if the supplier grants an acceptable allowance.

The purchaser usually informs the supplier in writing of any returns and allowances. This is often with a letter or a debit memorandum. A **debit memorandum** is a form issued by the purchaser to inform the supplier of a debit made to the supplier's account, including the reason for a return or allowance. The purchaser sends the debit memorandum to the supplier and also keeps a copy. Exhibit 6.8 shows a debit memorandum prepared by Z-Mart requesting an allowance from Trex for the defective *SpeedDemon* mountain bike. The purchaser's accounting for a debit memorandum requires updating the Merchandise Inventory account to reflect returns and allowances. The November 15 entry by Z-Mart for the purchase allowance requested in the debit memorandum is:

(c) Nov. 15	Accounts Payable	300	
	Merchandise Inventory		300
	Allowance for defective merchandise.		

Assets = Liabilities + Equity
−300   −300

Exhibit 6.8

Debit Memorandum

Case: Z-Mart (buyer) proposes $300 allowance for defective merchandise from Trex (seller)

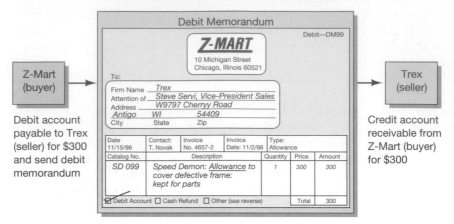

Z-Mart (buyer)

Debit account payable to Trex (seller) for $300 and send debit memorandum

Debit Memorandum

Debit—DM99

Z-MART
10 Michigan Street
Chicago, Illinois 60521

To:
Firm Name ___ *Trex*
Attention of ___ *Steve Servi, Vice-President Sales*
Address ___ *W9797 Cherryy Road*
Antigo   *WI*   *54409*
City   State   Zip

Date 11/15/98	Contact: T. Novak	Invoice No. 4657-2	Invoice Date: 11/2/98	Type: Allowance		
Catalog No.		Description		Quantity	Price	Amount
SD 099		Speed Demon: *Allowance* to cover defective frame: kept for parts		1	300	300
☑ Debit Account ☐ Cash Refund ☐ Other (see reverse)					Total	300

Trex (seller)

Credit account receivable from Z-Mart (buyer) for $300

If this had been a return, then the recorded cost of the defective merchandise would have been entered.[3] Z-Mart's agreement with this supplier says the cost of returned and defective merchandise is offset against Z-Mart's next purchase or its current account payable balance. Some agreements with suppliers involve refunding the cost to a buyer. If there is a refund of cash, then the Cash account is debited for $300 instead of Accounts Payable.

Discounts and Returns

When goods are returned within the discount period, a buyer can take the discount only on the remaining balance of the invoice. As an example, suppose Z-Mart purchases $1,000 of merchandise offered with a 2% cash discount. Two days later, Z-Mart returns $100 of goods before the invoice is paid. When Z-Mart later pays within the discount period, it can take the 2% discount only on the $900 balance. The discount is $18 (2% × $900) and the cash payment is $882 ($900 − $18).

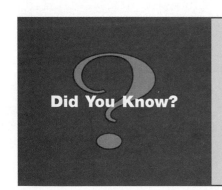

Did You Know?

Clout!

Merchandising companies are unleashing a barrage of demands on suppliers. These include special discounts for new stores, payment of fines for shipping errors, and huge numbers of free samples. One merchandiser warned **Totes** it would impose a fine of $30,000 for errors in bar-coding on products Totes shipped. Merchandisers' goals are to slash inventories, shorten lead times, and eliminate error. [Source: *Business Week*, December 21, 1992.]

Transportation Costs

Depending on terms negotiated with sellers, a merchandiser is sometimes responsible for paying shipping costs on purchases, often called *transportation-in* or *freight-in* costs. Z-Mart's $1,200 purchase on November 2 is on terms of FOB destination. This means Z-Mart is not responsible for paying transportation costs.

A different situation arises when a merchandiser is responsible for paying transportation costs. Such costs are sometimes made to an independent carrier but are also sometimes directly made to the seller. Transportation costs are often included on the invoice when owed to the seller. Transportation costs owed to an independent carrier usually are

---

[3] Recorded cost is the cost reported in an account minus any discounts.

not included on the invoice. The cost principle requires these transportation costs be included as part of the cost of purchased merchandise. This means a separate entry is necessary when they are *not* listed on the invoice. For example, Z-Mart's entry to record a $75 freight charge to an independent carrier for merchandise purchased FOB shipping point is:

(d) Nov. 24	Merchandise Inventory	75	
	Cash		75
	Paid freight charges on purchased merchandise.		

Assets = Liabilities + Equity
+75
−75

Transportation-in costs are different from the costs of shipping goods to customers. Transportation-in costs are included in the cost of merchandise inventory whereas the costs of shipping goods to customers are not. The costs of shipping goods to customers are recorded in a Delivery Expense account when the seller is responsible for these costs. Delivery Expense, also called *freight-out* or *transportation-out*, is reported as a selling expense in the income statement.

Transfer of Ownership

The buyer and seller must reach agreement on who is responsible for paying any freight costs and who bears the risk of loss during transit for merchandising transactions. This is essentially the same as asking at what point does ownership transfer from the seller to the buyer. The point of transfer is called the **FOB** point, where FOB stands for *free on board.* The point when ownership transfers from the seller to the buyer determines who pays transportation costs (and other incidental costs of transit such as insurance).

Exhibit 6.9 identifies two alternative points of transfer. The first is FOB shipping point. *FOB shipping point,* also called *FOB factory,* means the buyer accepts ownership at the seller's place of business. The buyer is then responsible for paying shipping costs and bears the risk of damage or loss when goods are in transit. The goods are part of the buyer's inventory when they are in transit since ownership has transferred to the buyer.

Exhibit 6.9

Identifying Transfer of Ownership

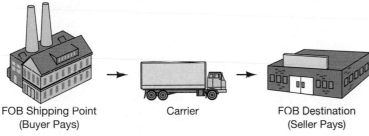

FOB Shipping Point   Carrier   FOB Destination
(Buyer Pays)   (Seller Pays)

	Ownership transfers when goods passed to	Transportation costs paid by
FOB Shipping Point	Carrier	Buyer
FOB Destination	Buyer	Seller

Midway Games is a leader in entertainment software and uses FOB shipping point. Midway has released many outstanding games including Mortal Kombat, Cruis'n USA, Cruis'n World, NBA Jam, Joust, Defender, Pacman, and Space Invaders. Its subsidiary, Atari, has had similar success. Midway is given the right by Nintendo and Sega to self-manufacture cartridges for its platforms. Midway often uses manufacturers in Mexico where the platforms are purchased on an "as is" and "where is" basis. This means they "are delivered to the Company FOB place of manufacture and shipped

at the Company's own expense and risk." Shipping usually takes 3 to 10 days, "depending on the mode of transport and location of manufacturer."[4]

The second point of transfer is FOB destination. *FOB destination* means ownership of the goods transfers to the buyer at the buyer's place of business. The seller is responsible for paying shipping charges and bears the risk of damage or loss in transit. The seller does not record revenue from this sale until the goods arrive at the destination because this transaction is not complete before that point.

Compaq Computer previously shipped its products FOB shipping point. Compaq found delivery companies to be undependable in picking up shipments at scheduled times, which caused backups at the plant, missed deliveries, and unhappy consumers. Compaq then changed its agreements to FOB destination, and its problems were eliminated.

There are situations when the party not responsible for shipping costs pays the carrier. In these cases, the party paying these costs either bills the party responsible or, more commonly, adjusts its account payable or receivable with the other party. For example, a buyer who pays a carrier when terms are FOB destination can decrease its account payable to the seller by the amount of shipping cost. Similarly, a seller who pays a carrier when terms are FOB shipping point can increase its account receivable from the buyer by the amount of shipping cost.

Recording Purchases Information

We explained how purchase discounts, purchase returns and allowances, and transportation-in are included in computing the total cost of merchandise inventory. Purchases are initially recorded as debits to Merchandise Inventory. Any later purchase discounts, returns, and allowances are credited to Merchandise Inventory. Transportation-in is debited to Merchandise Inventory. Z-Mart's 1999 total cost of merchandise purchases is made up of the items listed in Exhibit 6.10.

Exhibit 6.10

Total Cost of Merchandise
Purchases Computation

Z-MART Total Cost of Merchandise Purchases For Year Ended December 31, 1999	
Invoice cost of merchandise purchases	$235,800
Less: Purchase discounts received	(4,200)
Purchase returns and allowances received	(1,500)
Add: Cost of transportation-in	2,300
Total cost of merchandise purchases	$232,400

Combining these costs in the Merchandise Inventory account means this account reflects the net cost of purchased merchandise according to the *cost principle.* Recall that the Merchandise Inventory account is updated after each transaction affecting the cost of goods purchased. We later explain how this account is also updated each time merchandise is sold. These timely updates of the Merchandise Inventory account reflect a perpetual inventory system.

The accounting system described here does not provide separate records for total purchases, total purchase discounts, total purchase returns and allowances, and total transportation-in. Yet managers usually need this information to evaluate and control each of these cost elements. Many companies collect this information in supplementary records. **Supplementary records,** also called *supplemental records,* are a register of information outside the usual accounting records and accounts. We explain in Chapter 8 a process where supplementary records can be maintained.

---

[4] Midway Games Inc., *Form 10-K405* (6-30-97).

4. How long are both the credit and discount periods when credit terms are 2/10, n/60?

5. Identify items subtracted from the *list* amount when computing purchase price: *(a)* freight-in; *(b)* trade discount; *(c)* purchase discount; *(d)* purchase return and/or allowance.

6. Explain the meaning of *FOB*. What does *FOB destination* mean?

Answers—p. 249

We explained how companies buying merchandise for resale need to account for purchases, purchase discounts, and purchase returns and allowances. Merchandising companies also must account for sales, sales discounts, sales returns and allowances, and cost of goods sold. A merchandising company such as Z-Mart reports these items in the gross profit section of an income statement as shown in Exhibit 6.11.

Accounting for Merchandise Sales

Z-MART Computation of Gross Profit For Year Ended December 31, 1999		
Sales		$321,000
Less: Sales discounts	$4,300	
Sales returns and allowances	2,000	6,300
Net sales		$314,700
Cost of goods sold		(230,400)
Gross profit		$ 84,300

Exhibit 6.11

Gross Profit Section of income statement

This section explains how information in this computation is derived from transactions involving sales, sales discounts, and sales returns and allowances.

Sales Transactions

P2 Analyze and record transactions for sales of merchandise using a perpetual system.

Each sales transaction for a seller of merchandise involves two related parts. One part is the revenue received in the form of an asset from a customer. The second part is recognizing the cost of merchandise sold to a customer. Accounting for a sales transaction means capturing information about both parts.

Sales transactions of merchandisers usually include both sales for cash and sales on credit. Whether a sale is for cash or on credit, a sales transaction requires two entries: one for revenue and one for cost. As an example, Z-Mart sold $2,400 of merchandise on credit on November 3. The revenue part of this transaction is recorded as:

(e) Nov. 3	Accounts Receivable	2,400	
	Sales		2,400
	Sold merchandise on credit.		

Assets = Liabilities + Equity
+2,400   +2400

This entry reflects an increase in Z-Mart's assets in the form of an account receivable. It also shows the revenue from the credit sale.[5] If the sale is for cash, the debit is to Cash instead of Accounts Receivable. The cost of the merchandise Z-Mart sold on November 3 is $1,600. We explain in Chapter 7 how the cost of this merchandise is computed. The

---

[5] We describe in Chapter 8 how companies account for sales to customers who use third-party credit cards such as those issued by banks and other organizations.

entry to record the cost part of this sales transaction (under a perpetual inventory system) is:

Assets = Liabilities + Equity
-1,600   -1,600

(e) Nov. 3	Cost of Goods Sold	1,600	
	Merchandise Inventory		1,600
	To record the cost of Nov. 3 sale.		

Since the cost part is recorded each time a sale occurs, the Merchandise Inventory account reflects the cost of the remaining merchandise on hand.

Sales Discounts

Selling goods on credit demands that expected amounts and dates of future payments be made clear to avoid misunderstandings. We explained earlier in this chapter how credit terms often include a discount to encourage early payment. Companies granting cash discounts to customers refer to these as sales discounts. Sales discounts can benefit a seller by decreasing the delay in receiving cash. Prompt payments also reduce future efforts and costs of billing customers.

A seller does not know whether a customer will pay within the discount period and take advantage of a cash discount at the time of a credit sale. This means a sales discount is usually not recorded until a customer pays within the discount period. As an example, Z-Mart completed a credit sale for $1,000 on November 12, subject to terms of 2/10, n/60. The entry to record this sale is:

Assets = Liabilities + Equity
+1,000   +1,000

Nov. 12	Accounts Receivable	1,000	
	Sales		1,000
	Sold merchandise under terms of 2/10, n/60.		

This entry records the receivable and the revenue as if the full amount will be paid by the customer.

But the customer has two options. One option is to wait 60 days until January 11 and pay the full $1,000. In this case, Z-Mart would record the payment as:

Assets = Liabilities + Equity
+1,000
-1,000

Jan. 11	Cash	1,000	
	Accounts Receivable		1,000
	Received payment for November 12 sale.		

The customer's second option is to pay $980 within a 10-day period running through November 22. If the customer pays on or before November 22, Z-Mart would record the payment as:

Assets = Liabilities + Equity
+980   -20
-1,000

Nov. 22	Cash	980	
	Sales Discounts	20	
	Accounts Receivable		1,000
	Received payment for November 12 sale less the discount.		

Sales discounts are recorded in a contra-revenue account called Sales Discounts. This is so management can monitor sales discounts to assess their effectiveness and cost. The Sales Discounts account is deducted from the Sales account when computing a company's net sales (see Exhibit 6.11). While information about sales discounts is useful, it is seldom reported on income statements distributed to external users.

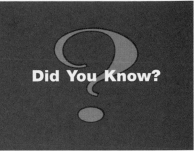
Sales Returns and Allowances

Sales returns refer to merchandise that customers return to the seller after a sale. Many companies allow customers to return merchandise for a full refund. *Sales allowances* refer to reductions in the selling price of merchandise sold to customers. This can occur with damaged merchandise that a customer is willing to purchase with a decrease in selling price. Sales returns and allowances involve dissatisfied customers and the possibility of lost future sales. Managers need information about returns and allowances to monitor these problems. Many accounting systems record returns and allowances in a separate contra-revenue account for this purpose.

Recall Z-Mart's sale of merchandise on November 3. As already recorded, the merchandise is sold for $2,400 and cost $1,600. But what if the customer returns part of the merchandise on November 6, where returned items sell for $800 and cost $600? The revenue part of this transaction must reflect the decrease in sales from the customer's return of merchandise:

(f) Nov. 6	Sales Returns and Allowances	800	
	Accounts Receivable		800
	Customer returned merchandise.		

$$\text{Assets} = \text{Liabilities} + \text{Equity}$$
$$-800 \qquad\qquad\qquad -800$$

Z-Mart can record this return with a debit to the Sales account instead of Sales Returns and Allowances. This method provides the same net sales, but does not provide information managers need in monitoring returns and allowances. By using the Sales Returns and Allowances contra account, this information is available. Published income statements usually omit this detail and show only net sales.

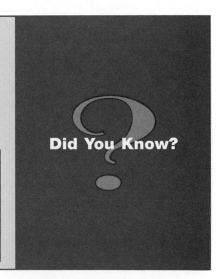

If merchandise returned to Z-Mart is not defective and can be resold to another customer, then Z-Mart returns these goods to its inventory. The entry necessary to restore the cost of these goods to the Merchandise Inventory account is:

Assets = Liabilities + Equity
+600   +600

Nov. 6	Merchandise Inventory	600	
	Cost of Goods Sold		600
	Returned goods to inventory.		

But if the merchandise returned is defective, the seller may discard the returned items. In this case, the cost of returned merchandise is not restored to the Merchandise Inventory account. Instead, most companies leave the cost of defective merchandise in the Cost of Goods Sold account.[6]

Another possibility is that $800 of the merchandise Z-Mart sold on November 3 is defective but the customer decides to keep it because Z-Mart grants the customer a price reduction of $500. The only entry Z-Mart must make in this case is one to reflect the decrease in expected revenue and assets:

Assets = Liabilities + Equity
−500   −500

Nov. 6	Sales Returns and Allowances	500	
	Accounts Receivable		500
	To record sales allowance.		

The seller usually prepares a credit memorandum to confirm a customer's return or allowance. A **credit memorandum** informs a customer of a credit to its Account Receivable account from a sales return or allowance. The information in a credit memorandum is similar to that of a debit memorandum. Z-Mart's credit memorandum issued to the customer for the return of $800 of merchandise on November 6 is shown in Exhibit 6.12.

Exhibit 6.12

Credit Memorandum

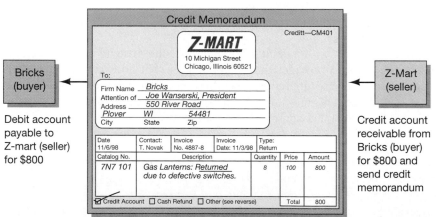

**Case: Z-Mart (seller) accepts $800
of returned merchandise from Bricks (buyer)**

Answers—p. 249

Flash *back*

7. Why are sales discounts and sales returns and allowances recorded in contra-revenue accounts instead of directly in the Sales account?

8. Under what conditions are two entries necessary to record a sales return?

9. When merchandise is sold on credit and the seller notifies the buyer of a price reduction, does the seller send a credit memorandum or a debit memorandum?

---

[6] When managers want to monitor the cost of defective merchandise, a better method is to remove their cost from Cost of Goods Sold and charge it to a Loss from Defective Merchandise account.

This section identifies and explains how merchandising activities affect other accounting processes. We address cost and price adjustments, preparation of adjusting and closing entries, and relations between important accounts.

Cost and Price Adjustments

Buyers and sellers often find they need to adjust the amount owed between them. Such adjustment occurs when purchased merchandise does not meet specifications, unordered goods are received, different quantities are received than were ordered and billed, and errors occur in billing. The original balance can sometimes be adjusted by the buyer without negotiation. For example, when a seller makes an error on an invoice and the buyer discovers it, the buyer can make an adjustment and notify the seller by sending a debit or a credit memorandum. Sometimes adjustments can be made only after negotiations between the buyer and seller. An example is a buyer claims that some merchandise does not meet specifications. In these cases, the amount of allowance given by the seller is usually arrived at only after discussion.

Adjusting Entries

Most adjusting entries are the same for both merchandising companies and service companies. The adjustments for both types of companies involve prepaid expenses, depreciation, accrued expenses, unearned revenues, and accrued revenues.

A merchandising company using a perpetual inventory system is often required to make one additional adjustment. This adjustment updates the Merchandise Inventory account to reflect any losses of merchandise. Merchandising companies can lose merchandise in several ways, including theft and deterioration. **Shrinkage** refers to the loss of inventory for merchandising companies.

While a perpetual inventory system tracks all goods as they move in and out of the company, a perpetual system is unable to directly measure shrinkage. Yet we can compute shrinkage by comparing a physical count of the inventory with recorded quantities. A physical count is usually performed at least once annually to verify the Merchandise Inventory account. Most companies record any necessary adjustment due to shrinkage by charging it to Cost of Goods Sold, assuming shrinkage is not abnormally large.

As an example, Z-Mart's Merchandise Inventory account at the end of 1999 had a balance of $21,250. But a physical count of inventory revealed only $21,000 inventory on hand. The adjusting entry to record this $250 shrinkage is:

Dec. 31	Cost of Goods Sold	250	
	Merchandise Inventory		250
	To adjust for $250 shrinkage revealed by a physical count of inventory.		

Assets = Liabilities + Equity
−250   −250

P3 Prepare adjustments and close accounts for a merchandising company.

Wanted for Shrinkage
Shrinkage can be a sizable cost for many merchandisers. Recent examples of annual losses due to shrinkage are:

| MusicLand | $22 Million |
| Sports Authority | 9 Million |

Companies often invest considerable resources in reducing shrinkage costs.

Did You Know?

Closing Entries

Closing entries are similar for merchandising companies and service companies when using a perpetual system. The one difference is we must close temporary accounts re-

Exhibit 6.13

Adjusted Trial Balance

Z-MART Adjusted Trial Balance December 31, 1999		
Cash	$ 8,200	
Accounts receivable	11,200	
Merchandise inventory	21,000	
Office supplies	550	
Store supplies	250	
Prepaid insurance	300	
Office equipment	4,200	
Accumulated depreciation—Office equipment		$ 1,400
Store equipment	30,000	
Accumulated depreciation—Store equipment		6,000
Accounts payable		16,000
Salaries payable		800
K. Marty, capital		42,600
K. Marty, withdrawals	4,000	
Sales		321,000
Sales discounts	4,300	
Sales returns and allowances	2,000	
Cost of goods sold	230,400	
Depreciation expense—Store equipment	3,000	
Depreciation expense—Office equipment	700	
Office salaries expense	25,300	
Sales salaries expense	18,500	
Insurance expense	600	
Rent expense, office space	900	
Rent expense, selling space	8,100	
Office supplies expense	1,800	
Store supplies expense	1,200	
Advertising expense	11,300	
Totals	$387,800	$387,800

lated to merchandising activities. We show the closing process for Z-Mart using its 1999 adjusted trial balance in Exhibit 6.13.

Z-Mart's trial balance includes several accounts unique to merchandising companies. These include: Merchandise Inventory, Sales, Sales Discounts, Sales Returns and Allowances, and Cost of Goods Sold. Their existence in the ledger means the four closing entries for a merchandiser are slightly different from the ones described in Chapter 5 for a service company. These differences are bolded in the closing entries in Exhibit 6.14.

Merchandising Cost Flows

C5 Analyze and interpret cost flows and operating activities of a merchandising company.

Exhibit 6.15 shows the relations between inventory, purchases, and cost of goods sold across periods. We already explained how the net cost of purchases captures trade discounts, purchase discounts granted, and purchase returns and allowances. These items constituting the cost of purchases are recorded in the Merchandise Inventory account when using a perpetual system. When each sale occurs, the cost of items sold is transferred from Merchandise Inventory to the Cost of Goods Sold account. Cost of goods sold is reported on the income statement. The ending balance in Merchandise Inventory is reported on the balance sheet.

The Merchandise Inventory account balance at the end of period one is the amount of beginning inventory in period two. The sequence of events during period two (and every period) is the same as during period one. The cost of each purchase is added to

Exhibit 6.14

Closing Entries for a
Merchandiser

Step1: Close Credit Balances in Temporary Accounts to Income Summary.

The first entry closes temporary accounts having credit balances. Z-Mart has one temporary
account with a credit balance and it is closed with the entry:

Dec. 31	Sales	321,000	
	Income Summary		321,000
	To close temporary accounts having credit balances.		

Posting this entry to the ledger gives a zero balance to the Sales account and opens the Income
Summary account.

Step 2: Close Debit Balances in Temporary Accounts to Income Summary.

The second entry closes temporary accounts having debit balances. These include Cost of Goods
Sold, Sales Discounts, and Sales Returns and Allowances. This entry also yields the amount of net
income as the balance in the Income Summary account. Z-Mart's second closing entry is:

Dec. 31	Income Summary	308,100	
	Sales Discounts		4,300
	Sales Returns and Allowances		2,000
	Cost of Goods Sold		230,400
	Depreciation Expense—Store Equipment . .		3,000
	Depreciation Expense—Office Equipment .		700
	Office Salaries Expense		25,300
	Sales Salaries Expense		18,500
	Insurance Expense		600
	Rent Expense—Office Space		900
	Rent Expense—Selling Space		8,100
	Office Supplies Expense		1,800
	Store Supplies Expense		1,200
	Advertising Expense		11,300
	To close temporary accounts having debit balances.		

Step 3: Close Income Summary to Owner's Capital.

The third closing entry is the same for a merchandising company and a service company. It closes
the Income Summary account and updates the owner's capital account for income or loss. Z-
Mart's third closing entry is:

Dec. 31	Income Summary	12,900	
	K. Marty, capital		12,900
	To close the Income Summary account.		

The $12,900 amount in the entry is net income reported on the income statement in Exhibit 6.2.

Step 4: Close Withdrawals Account to Owner's Capital.

The fourth closing entry for a merchandising company is the same as the fourth closing entry for a
service company. It closes the withdrawals account and reduces the owner's capital account
balance to the amount shown on the balance sheet. The fourth closing entry for Z-Mart is:

Dec. 31	K. Marty, capital 4,000		
	K. Marty, withdrawals	4,000	
	To close the withdrawals account.		

When this entry is posted, all temporary accounts are cleared and ready to record events for the
year 2000. The Owner's Capital account also is updated and reflects transactions of 1999.

Exhibit 6.15

Merchandising Cost Flow Across Periods*

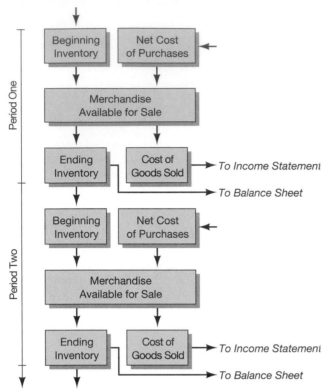

*Cost of goods sold is reported on the Income statement. Ending Inventory is reported on the balance sheet. One period's ending inventory is the next period's beginning inventory.

the Merchandise Inventory account and the cost of each sale is transferred from Merchandise Inventory to Cost of Goods Sold. At the end of the period, the Merchandise Inventory balance is reported on the balance sheet.

Merchandising Cost Accounts

To explain how merchandising transactions affect the Merchandise Inventory and Cost of Goods Sold accounts, we list Z-Mart's merchandising activities during 1999 in Exhibit 6.16 and show the impact of these activities in ledger T-accounts of Exhibit 6.17. The amounts in these exhibits are linked by superscripts a through h.

We explained how the perpetual inventory accounting system does not include separate accounts for purchases, purchase discounts, purchase returns and allowances, and transportation-in. But Z-Mart, like many companies, keeps supplementary records about these items. These supplementary records are used to accumulate the information in Exhibit 6.16. Z-Mart also keeps a separate record for the cost of merchandise returned by customers and restored in inventory.

The Merchandise Inventory and Cost of Goods Sold T-accounts in Exhibit 6.17 reflect the effects of these merchandising activities for Z-Mart. Most amounts in these T-accounts are summary representations of several entries during the year 1999.

The Cost of Goods Sold balance of $230,400 is the amount reported on the income statement in Exhibit 6.2. The Merchandise Inventory balance of $21,000 is the amount reported as a current asset on the balance sheet in Exhibit 6.3. These amounts also appeared on Z-Mart's adjusted trial balance in Exhibit 6.13.

Exhibit 6.16

Summary of Merchandising Activities

Z-Mart's Merchandising Activities for 1999	
Z-Mart's beginning inventory on January 1, 1999	19,000[a]
Invoice cost of merchandise purchases	$235,800[b]
Cost of freight to bring merchandise to Z-Mart's store	2,300[c]
Purchase discounts Z-Mart received from making payments within discount periods	4,200[d]
Refunds and credit granted to Z-Mart from purchase returns and allowances	1,500[e]
Cost of merchandise sold to customers	231,550[f]
Cost of merchandise returned by customers and restored to Z-Mart's inventory	1,400[g]
Cost of inventory shrinkage computed by physical count of inventory at year-end	250[h]

Flash back

10. When a merchandiser uses a perpetual inventory system, why is it often necessary to adjust the Merchandise Inventory balance with an adjusting entry?

11. What temporary accounts do you expect to find in a merchandising business but not in a service business?

12. Describe the closing entries normally made by a merchandising company.

Answers—p. 249

Merchandise Inventory			
Dec. 31, 1998, balance	19,000[a]		
Purchases of merchandise	235,800[b]	Purchase discounts in 1999	4,200[d]
Merchandise returned by customers		Purchase returns and allowances in	
and restored to inventory in 1999	1,400[g]	1999	1,500[e]
Transportation-in costs for 1999	2,300[c]	Cost of sales transactions in 1999	231,550[f]
Total	258,500	Total	237,250
	−237,250		
Dec. 31, 1999 unadjusted balance	21,250		
		Dec. 31 Shrinkage	250[h]
Total	21,250	Total	250
	−250		
Dec. 31, 1999 adjusted balance	21,000		

Cost of Goods Sold			
Cost of sales transactions	231,550[a]	Merchandise returned by customers	
Inventory shrinkage at Dec. 31, 1999,		and restored to inventory in 1999	1,400[g]
adjusting entry	250[h]		
Total	231,800	Total	1,400
	−1,400		
Balance (before closing)	230,400		

Exhibit 6.17

Merchandising Transactions
Reflected in T-Accounts

Income Statement Formats

P4 Define and prepare multiple-step and single-step income statements.

Generally accepted accounting principles do not require companies to use any one format for financial statements. We see many different formats in practice. The first part of this section describes two common income statement formats using Z-Mart's data: multiple-step and single-step. The final part of this section compares accrual and cash flow measures of gross profit for merchandising activities.

Multiple-Step Income Statement

Multiple-step income statements often contain more detail than simply a listing of revenues and expenses. There are two general types of multiple-step income statement. The usual format we see in external reports is what people commonly call the *multiple-step* format. A more detailed format is also available but usually seen only in internal documents. It is called the *classified, multiple-step* format. Both formats can be used in either a perpetual or periodic system.

Classified, Multiple-Step Format

Exhibit 6.18 shows a **classified, multiple-step income statement** for Z-Mart. This format shows detailed computations of net sales and cost of goods sold. Operating expenses are classified separately as selling expenses or general and administrative expenses. This format reports subtotals for various classes of items. This is why it is called a *classified* format.

Z-Mart's sales section is the same as shown earlier in the chapter. The cost of goods sold section draws on supplementary records Z-Mart keeps for merchandise purchases, purchase discounts, purchase returns and allowances, and transportation-in. The difference between net sales and cost of goods sold is Z-Mart's gross profit. Its operating ex-

Exhibit 6.18

Classified, Multiple-Step Income
Statement

Z-MART Income Statement For Year Ended December 31, 1999			
Sales			$321,000
Less: Sales discounts		$ 4,300	
Sales returns and allowances		2,000	6,300
Net sales			$314,700
Cost of goods sold:			
Merchandise inventory, December 31, 1998 ...		$ 19,000	
Total cost of merchandise purchases*		232,400	
Goods available for sale		$251,400	
Merchandise inventory, December 31, 1999 ...		21,000	
Cost of goods sold			230,400
Gross profit from sales			$ 84,300
Operating expenses:			
Selling expenses:			
Depreciation expense, store equipment	$ 3,000		
Sales salaries expense	18,500		
Rent expense, selling space	8,100		
Store supplies expense	1,200		
Advertising expense	11,300		
Total selling expenses		$ 42,100	
General and administrative expenses:			
Depreciation expense, office equipment	$ 700		
Office salaries expense	25,300		
Insurance expense	600		
Rent expense, office space	900		
Office supplies expense	1,800		
Total general and administrative expenses		29,300	
Total operating expenses			71,400
Net income			$ 12,900

* Using *supplementary records,* the total cost of merchandise purchases is composed of: invoice cost of merchandise (235,800) − discounts (4,200) − returns and allowances (1,500) + freight (2,300). See Exhibit 6.10 and related discussion for further explanation.

penses are classified into two categories. **Selling expenses** include the expenses of promoting sales through displaying and advertising merchandise, making sales, and delivering goods to customers. **General and administrative expenses** support the overall operations of a company and include expenses related to accounting, human resource management, and financial management.

Expenses are often divided between categories when they contribute to more than one activity. Exhibit 6.18 shows that Z-Mart allocates the rent expense of $9,000 for its store building between two categories—$8,100 to selling expense and $900 to general and administrative expense.[7]

Multiple-Step Format

Exhibit 6.19 shows a multiple-step income statement format common in external reports. In comparison to Exhibit 6.18, a multiple-step statement leaves out detailed computations of net sales and cost of goods sold. Selling expenses are also combined with general and administrative expenses.

---

[7] These expenses can be recorded in a single ledger account or in two separate accounts. If they are recorded in one account, we allocate its balance between the two expenses when preparing statements.

Z-MART Income Statement For Year Ended December 31, 1999		
Net sales		$314,700
Cost of goods sold		230,400
Gross profit from sales		$ 84,300
Operating expenses:		
Depreciation expense	$ 3,700	
Salaries expense	43,800	
Rent expense	9,000	
Insurance expense	600	
Supplies expense	3,000	
Advertising expense	11,300	
Total operating expenses		71,400
Net income		$ 12,900

Exhibit 6.19

Multiple-Step Income Statement

We frequently see more condensed formats in practice. For example, **Reebok's** income statement in Appendix A shows a single line item titled *Selling, general and administrative expenses.* But its annual report includes management's discussion and analysis of these expenses.

Single-Step Income Statement

A **single-step income statement** is another widely used format. This format is shown in Exhibit 6.20 for Z-Mart. This simple format includes cost of goods sold as an operating expense and shows only one subtotal for total expenses. Operating expenses are highly summarized.

Z-MART Income Statement For Year Ended December 31, 1999		
Net sales		$314,700
Cost of goods sold	$230,400	
Selling expenses	42,100	
General and admin. expenses	29,300	
Total expenses		301,800
Net income		$ 12,900

Exhibit 6.20

Single-Step Income Statement

Many companies use formats that combine features of both the single- and multiple-step statements. As long as income statement items are shown sensibly, management can choose the format it wants.[8] Similar options are available for the statement of changes in owner's equity and statement of cash flows for both merchandising companies and service companies.

Merchandising Cash Flows

Another aspect of effectively reporting on merchandising activities relates to their cash flow impacts. Merchandising sales and costs reported in the income statement usually differ from their cash receipts and payments for the period. This is because an income

A1 Analyze and interpret accruals and cash flows for merchandising activities.

---

[8] We describe some items in later chapters, such as extraordinary gains and losses, that must be shown in certain locations on the income statement.

statement is prepared using accrual accounting, not cash flows. Recognition of sales earned is rarely equal to cash received from customers. Also, recognition of cost of goods sold incurred is rarely equal to cash paid to suppliers.

We use Z-Mart's data in Exhibit 6.21 to illustrate this point. Z-Mart's net sales in the income statement total $314,700. Yet cash receipts from customers are only $309,200 (shown on the right side of Exhibit 6.21). This difference reflects a $5,500 *increase* in Accounts Receivable during 1999 for Z-Mart.

Exhibit 6.21

Analysis of Merchandising Cash Flows

Z-MART For Year Ended December 31, 1999			
Income Statement		**Statement of Cash Flows**	
Net sales	$314,700	Receipts from customers	$309,200
Cost of goods sold ..	230,400	Payments to suppliers	240,900
Gross profit	84,300	Net cash flows from customers and suppliers ..	68,300

An increase in accounts receivable means a delay in Z-Mart's receipt of cash from customers. It also means cash received from customers this period is less than net sales. To see this, recall that net sales and cash received are the same if all net sales are cash sales. But when some or all net sales are credit sales, then net sales and cash are likely different amounts. Since Accounts Receivable increased during the period, we know cash received is less than net sales. But if Accounts Receivable had decreased, then cash received would be greater than net sales. For Z-Mart, this relation is revealed as follows:

Net sales	$314,700
Less increase in accounts receivable ..	5,500
Cash received from customers	$309,200

We apply similar analysis to cost of goods sold. Z-Mart's cost of goods sold reported in its income statement totals $230,400. Yet cash paid to suppliers is $240,900. The difference between cost of goods sold and cash paid to suppliers reflects *two* items: (1) *change in inventory* and (2) *change in accounts payable*. An increase in inventory implies more goods were purchased than sold this period. But a decrease in inventory implies less goods were purchased than sold this period. An increase in accounts payable suggests less cash is paid to suppliers than the cost of this period's purchases. But a decrease in accounts payable suggests more cash is paid to suppliers than the cost of this period's purchases. We know from Exhibit 6.21 that the cash paid to suppliers is $10,500 more than cost of goods sold. This $10,500 difference reflects a $2,000 *increase* in inventory (purchased *more* than sold) and a $8,500 *decrease* in accounts payable (paid for *more* than current purchases) in 1999 for Z-Mart.

Recall that cost of goods sold and cash paid are the same if inventory and account payable levels don't change during the period. But when one or both account balances change, then cost of goods sold and cash paid are likely different amounts. For Z-Mart, this relation for 1999 is shown as follows:

Cost of goods sold	$230,400
Add increase in Inventory	2,000
Add decrease in accounts payable ..	8,500
Cash paid to suppliers	$240,900

Buying and selling merchandise is the most important activity for a merchandiser such as Z-Mart. We need to analyze both accrual and cash flows of this activity for signs of opportunity or problems. The increase in accounts receivable reflects an attempt by Z-Mart to meet competition and increase sales. It is trying to expand its sales by extending credit to more customers. But extending credit to customers who don't pay their bills can backfire. For effective decision making, we must always analyze important differences in accrual and cash flow figures and identify their causes.

Acid-Test and Gross Margin

USING THE INFORMATION

Companies with merchandising activities have at least two major differences from service companies. First, merchandise inventory often makes up a large part of assets, especially current assets. Second, merchandising activities result in cost of goods sold. Cost of goods sold is often the largest cost for these companies. Companies with merchandising activities change the way we use ratio analysis. This is especially the case with the current ratio (see Chapter 5) and the profit margin ratio (see Chapter 4). This section describes adjustments to these ratios to help us analyze merchandising companies.

Acid-Test Ratio

Merchandise inventory is a current asset. For many merchandising companies, inventory makes up a large portion of current assets. This often means a large part of current assets is not readily available for paying liabilities. This is because inventory must be sold and any resulting accounts receivable must be collected before cash is available.

Information about current assets is important since we use it in assessing a company's ability to pay its current liabilities. We explained how the current ratio, defined as current assets divided by current liabilities, is useful in assessing a company's ability to pay current liabilities. Yet since it is sometimes unreasonable to assume inventories are a source of payment for current liabilities, we look to another measure.

One measure used to help us assess a company's ability to pay its current liabilities is the acid-test ratio. The acid-test ratio differs from the current ratio by excluding less liquid current assets such as inventory. *Liquidity* refers to how quickly an item is converted to cash. The less liquid assets or liabilities are those that will take longer to convert to cash. The **acid-test ratio,** also called *quick ratio,* is defined as *quick assets* (cash, short-term investments, and current receivables) divided by current liabilities. This is similar to the current ratio except that the numerator omits inventory and prepaid expenses. Exhibit 6.22 shows both the acid-test and current ratios of **J.C. Penney** for 1993 through 1996.

A2 Compute the acid-test ratio and explain its use as an indicator of liquidity.

(in millions)	1996	1995	1994	1993
J.C. Penney:				
Total quick assets	$ 5,888	$5,380	$5,420	$4,852
Total current assets	$11,712	$9,409	$9,369	$8,565
Total current liabilities	$ 7,966	$4,020	$4,481	$3,883
Acid-test ratio	0.74	1.34	1.21	1.25
Current ratio	1.47	2.34	2.09	2.21
Industry:				
Industry acid-test ratio	1.1	1.3	1.3	1.2
Industry current ratio	3.6	3.9	3.9	3.4

Exhibit 6.22

J.C. Penney's Acid-Test and Current Ratios

The formula for the acid-test ratio is shown in Exhibit 6.23.

Exhibit 6.23
Acid-Test Ratio

$$\text{Acid-test ratio} = \frac{\text{Quick assets}}{\text{Current liabilities}}$$

We compute **Penney's** 1996 acid-test ratio by using information in Exhibit 6.22:

$$\frac{\$5,888}{\$7,966} = 0.74$$

Penney's acid-test and current ratios dropped in 1996 compared with prior years. While the industry ratios also dropped, neither declined to the extent of Penney's ratios. Penney's current ratios for 1993–1996 suggest its short-term obligations can be covered with short-term assets. Yet the acid-test ratio raises a concern in 1996. An acid-test ratio less than 1 means Penney's current liabilities exceed its quick assets. Penney is likely facing some problems in covering current liabilities with liquid assets. This is mainly due to a sharp increase in accounts payable and accrued expenses.

A common rule of thumb is that the acid-test ratio should have a value of at least 1.0 to conclude that a company is unlikely to face liquidity problems in the near future. A value less than 1.0 suggests a liquidity problem unless a company can generate enough cash from sales or if the accounts payable are not due until late in the next period. Similarly, a value greater than 1.0 can hide a liquidity problem if payables are due shortly and receivables won't be collected until late in the next period. Our analysis of Penney's emphasizes that one ratio is seldom enough to reach a conclusion as to strength or weakness. The power of a ratio is often its ability to identify areas we need to analyze in more detail.

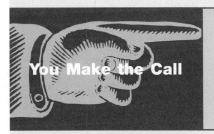
You Make the Call

Supplier
You're a supplier of building materials. A retail store asks you for credit on future purchases of materials. You have no prior experience with this store. You ask and receive the store's financial statements to assess its ability to make payment on purchases. The store's current ratio is 2.1 and its acid-test ratio is 0.5. You find inventory makes up most of current assets. Do you extend credit to this store?

Answer—p. 249

A3 Compute the gross margin ratio and explain its use as an indicator of profitability.

Gross Margin Ratio

A major cost of merchandising companies is its cost of goods sold. For many merchandising companies, cost of goods sold makes up the majority of its costs. This means success for merchandising companies often depends on the relation between sales and cost of goods sold.

We described the importance of the profit margin ratio in Chapter 4. Gross profit, also called *gross margin,* is a major part of the profit margin of merchandising companies. To help us focus on this important item, users often compute a gross margin ratio. Without sufficient gross profit, a merchandising company will likely fail. The gross margin ratio differs from the profit margin ratio by excluding all costs except cost of goods sold. The **gross margin ratio** is defined as gross margin (net sales minus cost of goods sold) divided by net sales. Exhibit 6.24 shows the gross margin ratios of **J.C. Penney** for 1993–1996.

(in millions)	1996	1995	1994	1993
Gross margin	$ 7,606	$ 7,086	$ 7,112	$ 6,581
Net sales	$23,649	$21,419	$21,082	$19,578
Gross margin ratio	32.2%	33.1%	33.7%	33.6%

Exhibit 6.24

J.C. Penney's Gross Margin Ratio

The formula for the gross margin ratio is shown in Exhibit 6.25.

$$\text{Gross margin ratio} = \frac{\text{Gross margin}}{\text{Net sales}}$$

Exhibit 6.25

Gross Margin Ratio

This ratio reflects the gross margin in each dollar of sales. To illustrate how we compute and use the gross margin ratio, we look at the results of J.C. Penney for the past few years as reported in Exhibit 6.24. From the information in this exhibit, we can compute Penney's 1996 gross margin ratio as:

$$\frac{\$7,606}{\$23,649} = 0.32$$

This ratio result means that each $1 of sales for J.C. Penney yields about 32¢ in gross margin to cover all other expenses and still produce a profit for the company.

Results in Exhibit 6.24 show Penney gross margin ratio declined from 1994 to 1996. The 1996 gross margin ratio, for instance, declined to 32.2% from 33.1% in 1995. This nearly 1% decline is an important development. Success for merchandisers such as Penney depends on maintaining an adequate gross margin. Data in this exhibit also reveal that Penney's sales are increasing over this period while its gross margin is decreasing. This shows costs of sales are rising faster than sales.

Chief Financial Officer
You're a chief financial officer of a merchandising company. You're analyzing profitability for your company and compute a 36% gross margin ratio and a 17% net profit margin ratio. Industry averages are 44% for gross margin and 16% for net profit margin. Do these ratios concern you?

You Make the Call

Answer—p. 249

Flash *back*

13. What income statement format shows detailed computations for net sales and cost of goods sold? What format gives no subtotals except total expenses?

14. Which assets are quick assets in computing the acid-test ratio?

15. What ratio is a more strict test of a company's ability to meet its short-term obligations, the acid-test ratio or current ratio?

Answers—p. 249

Summary

C1 Describe merchandising activities and identify business examples. Operations of merchandising companies involve buying products and reselling them. Examples of merchandisers include Wal-Mart, Home Depot, Woolworth, Limited, Circuit City, and Barnes & Noble.

C2 Identify and explain the components of income for a merchandising company. A merchandiser's costs on an income statement include an amount for cost of goods sold. Gross profit, or gross margin, equals sales minus cost of goods sold.

C3 Identify and explain the inventory asset of a merchandising company. The current asset section of a merchandising company's balance sheet includes merchandise inventory. Merchandise inventory refers to the products a merchandiser sells and are on hand at the balance sheet date.

C4 Describe both periodic and perpetual inventory systems. A perpetual inventory system continuously tracks the cost of goods on hand and the cost of goods sold. A periodic system accumulates the cost of goods purchased during the period and does not compute the amount of inventory on hand or the cost of goods sold until the end of a period.

C5 Analyze and interpret cost flows and operating activities of a merchandising company. Net costs of merchandise purchases flow into Merchandise Inventory and from there to Cost of Goods Sold on the income statement. Any remaining Merchandise Inventory balance is reported as a current asset on the balance sheet. This is the beginning inventory for the next period.

A1 Analyze and interpret accruals and cash flows for merchandising activities. Merchandising sales and costs of sales reported in the income statement usually differ from their corresponding cash receipts and payments for the period. Cash received from customers equals net sales less the increase (or plus the decrease) in Accounts Receivable during the period. Cash paid to suppliers equals cost of goods sold less the increase (or plus the decrease) in Accounts Payable and less the decrease (or plus the increase) in Inventory during the period.

A2 Compute the acid-test ratio and explain its use as an indicator of liquidity. The acid-test ratio is computed as quick assets (cash, short-term investments, and current receivables) divided by current liabilities. It is an indicator of a company's ability to pay its current liabilities with its existing quick assets. A ratio equal to or greater than one is often considered adequate.

A3 Compute the gross margin ratio and explain its use as an indicator of profitability. The gross margin (or gross profit) ratio is computed as gross margin (sales minus cost of goods sold) divided by sales. It is an indicator of a company's profitability in merchandising absent operating expenses. A gross margin ratio must be large enough to cover operating expenses and give an adequate net profit margin.

P1 Analyze and record transactions for merchandise purchases using a perpetual system. For a perpetual inventory system, purchases net of trade discounts are added (debited) to the Merchandise Inventory account. Purchase discounts and purchase returns and allowances are subtracted (credited) from Merchandise Inventory, and transportation-in costs are added (debited) to Merchandise Inventory. Many companies keep supplementary records to accumulate information about the total amounts of purchases, purchase discounts, purchase returns and allowances, and transportation-in.

P2 Analyze and record transactions for sales of merchandise using a perpetual system. A merchandiser records sales at list price less any trade discounts. The cost of items sold is transferred from Merchandise Inventory to Cost of Goods Sold. Refunds or credits given to customers for unsatisfactory merchandise are recorded (debited) in Sales Returns and Allowances, a contra account to Sales. If merchandise is returned and restored to inventory, the cost of this merchandise is removed from Cost of Goods Sold and transferred back to Merchandise Inventory. When cash discounts from the sales price are offered and customers pay within the discount period, the seller records (debits) discounts in Sales Discounts, a contra account to Sales. Debit and credit memoranda are documents sent between buyers and sellers to communicate that the sender is either debiting or crediting an account of the recipient.

P3 Prepare adjustments and close accounts for a merchandising company. With a perpetual inventory system, it is often necessary to make an adjustment for inventory shrinkage. This is computed by comparing a physical count of inventory with the Merchandise Inventory account balance. Shrinkage is normally charged to Cost of Goods Sold. Temporary accounts of merchandising companies include Sales, Sales Discounts, Sales Returns and Allowances, and Cost of Goods Sold. Each is closed to Income Summary.

P4 Define and prepare multiple-step and single-step income statements. Multiple-step income statements include greater detail for sales and expenses than do single-step income statements. Classified multiple-step income statements are usually limited to internal use. They show computations of net sales and cost of goods sold. The multiple-step statement reports expenses in categories reflecting different activities. Income statements published for external parties can be either multiple-step or single-step.

Guidance Answers to **You Make the Call**

Purchasing Agent

Delaying payment for 90 days costs your company an additional 3%. You can approximate the annual rate of interest attached to not paying within the discount period. For terms of 3/10, n/90, missing the 3% discount for an additional 80 days is equal to an annual interest rate of 13.69%, computed as (365 days ÷ 80 days) × 3%. Since you can borrow funds at 11% (assuming no other processing costs), it is better to borrow and pay within the discount period. You save 2.69% (13.69% − 11%) in interest costs by not delaying payment.

Supplier

A current ratio of 2.1 suggests there are sufficient current assets to cover current liabilities. But an acid-test ratio of 0.5 is low for most businesses. This says quick assets can only cover about one-half of current liabilities. This implies the store depends on profits from sales of inventory to pay current liabilities. If sales of inventory stall or profit margins decrease, then the likelihood of this store defaulting on its payments increases. Your decision is probably not to extend credit to the store. If you do extend credit, then you are likely to closely monitor the store's financial condition.

Chief Financial Officer

Your company's net profit margin is about equal to the industry average and suggests typical industry performance. However, gross margin reveals a markedly different picture. This ratio indicates your company is paying far more in cost of goods sold or receiving far less in sales than competitors. Your attention must be directed to finding the problem with cost of goods sold, sales, or both. One positive note is that your company's expenses make up 19% of sales (36% − 17%). This favorably compares with competitors' expenses making up 28% of sales (44% − 16%).

Guidance Answer to **Judgment and Ethics**

Credit Manager

Your decision is whether to comply with prior policy or to create a new policy and not abuse discounts offered by suppliers. Your first step should be to meet with your superior to find out if the automatic late payment policy is the actual policy and, if so, its rationale. It is possible the prior employee was reprimanded because of this behavior. If it is the policy to pay late, then you must apply your own sense of right and wrong. One point of view is that the late payment policy is unethical. A deliberate plan to make late payments means the company lies when it pretends to make purchases within the credit terms. There is the potential that your company can lose its ability to get future credit. Another view is that the late payment policy is acceptable. There may exist markets where attempts to take discounts through late payments are accepted as a continued phase of price negotiation. Also, your company's suppliers can respond by billing your company for the discounts not accepted because of late payments. This is a dubious viewpoint, especially given that the old employee proposes you cover up late payments as computer or mail problems, and given that some suppliers have previously complained.

Guidance Answers to **Flashbacks**

1. Cost of goods sold is the cost of merchandise that was purchased from a supplier and is sold to customers during a period.
2. Gross profit (or gross margin) is the difference between net sales and cost of goods sold.
3. Widespread use of computing and related technology in today's information age has dramatically increased use of the perpetual inventory system in practice.
4. Under credit terms of 2/10, n/60, the credit period is 60 days and the discount period is 10 days.
5. *b*
6. FOB means free on board. It is used in identifying the point where ownership transfers from seller to buyer. *FOB destination* means the seller does not transfer ownership of goods to the buyer until they arrive at the buyer's place of business. The seller is responsible for paying shipping charges and bears the risk of damage or loss during shipment.
7. Recording sales discounts and sales returns and allowances separate from sales gives useful information to managers for internal monitoring and decision making.
8. When a customer returns merchandise and the seller restores the merchandise to inventory, two entries are necessary. One entry records the decrease in revenue and credits the customer's account. The second entry debits inventory and reduces cost of goods sold.
9. A credit memorandum.
10. Merchandise Inventory balance may need adjusting to reflect shrinkage.
11. Sales, Sales Discounts, Sales Returns and Allowances, and Cost of Goods Sold.
12. Four closing entries: (1) close credit balances in temporary accounts to Income Summary, (2) close debit balances in temporary accounts to Income Summary, (3) close Income Summary to owner's capital, and (4) close withdrawals account to owner's capital.
13. Classified, multiple-step income statement. Single-step income statement.
14. Cash, short-term investments, and current receivables.
15. Acid-test ratio.

Demonstration Problem

Use the following adjusted trial balance and additional information to complete the requirements:

IOWA ANTIQUES Adjusted Trial Balance December 31, 1999		
Cash	$ 19,000	
Merchandise inventory	50,000	
Store supplies	1,000	
Equipment	44,600	
Accumulated depreciation—Equipment		$ 16,500
Accounts payable		8,000
Salaries payable		1,000
Dee Rizzo, capital		69,000
Dee Rizzo, withdrawals	8,000	
Sales		325,000
Sales discounts	6,000	
Sales returns and allowances	5,000	
Cost of goods sold	148,000	
Depreciation expense—Store equipment	4,000	
Depreciation expense—Office equipment	1,500	
Sales salaries expense	28,000	
Office salaries expense	32,000	
Insurance expense	12,000	
Rent expense (70% is store, 30% is office)	24,000	
Store supplies expense	6,000	
Advertising expense	30,400	
Totals	$419,500	$419,500

Iowa Antiques' *supplementary records* for 1999 reveal the following merchandising activities:

Invoice cost of merchandise purchases	$140,000
Purchase discounts received	3,500
Purchase returns and allowances received	2,600
Cost of transportation-in	4,000

Required

1. Use the supplementary records to compute the cost of merchandise purchases for 1999.
2. Prepare a 1999 classified, multiple-step income statement for internal use. The beginning inventory at January 1, 1999 is $60,100.
3. Prepare a single-step income statement for 1999 similar to the one in Exhibit 6.20.
4. Prepare closing entries for Iowa Antiques at the end of 1999.
5. Compute the acid-test ratio and the gross margin ratio. Explain the meaning of each ratio and interpret them for Iowa Antiques.

Planning the Solution

- Compute the total cost of merchandise purchases for 1999.
- Compute net sales. Then, to compute cost of goods sold, add the net cost of merchandise purchases for the year to beginning inventory and subtract the cost of ending inventory. Subtract cost of goods sold from net sales to get gross profit. Then, classify operating expenses as selling expenses or general administrative expenses.

- To prepare the single-step income statement, begin with net sales. Then, list and subtract the operating expenses.
- The first closing entry debits all temporary accounts with credit balances and opens the Income Summary account. The second closing entry credits all temporary accounts with debit balances. The third entry closes the Income Summary account to the owner's capital account, and the fourth closing entry closes the withdrawals account to the capital account.
- Identify the quick assets on the adjusted trial balance. Compute the acid-test ratio by dividing the quick assets by the amount of current liabilities. Compute the gross margin ratio by dividing the gross profit found in requirement 2 by net sales. Explain and interpret each ratio.

Solution to Demonstration Problem

1.

Invoice cost of merchandise purchases	$140,000
Less: Purchases discounts received	(3,500)
Purchase returns and allowances received	(2,600)
Add: Cost of transportation-in	4,000
Total cost of merchandise purchases	$137,900

2. Classified, multiple-step income statement

IOWA ANTIQUES			
Income Statement			
For Year Ended December 31, 1999			
Sales			$325,000
Less: Sales discounts		$ 6,000	
Sales returns and allowances		5,000	11,000
Net sales			$314,000
Cost of goods sold:			
Merchandise inventory, December 31, 1998		$ 60,100	
Invoice cost of merchandise purchases	$140,000		
Less: Purchase discounts received	(3,500)		
Purchase returns and allowances received .	(2,600)		
Add: Cost of transportation-in	4,000		
Total cost of merchandise purchases		137,900	
Goods available for sale		$198,000	
Merchandise inventory, December 31, 1999		50,000	
Cost of goods sold			148,000
Gross profit from sales			$166,000

(continued)

Operating expenses:

Selling expenses:

Depreciation expense—Store equipment	$ 4,000	
Sales salaries expense	28,000	
Rent expense—Selling space	16,800	
Store supplies expense	6,000	
Advertising expense	30,400	
Total selling expenses		$ 85,200

General and administrative expenses:

Depreciation expense—Office equipment	$ 1,500	
Office salaries expense	32,000	
Insurance expense	12,000	
Rent expense—Office space	7,200	
Total general and administrative expenses		52,700
Total operating expenses		137,900
Net income		$ 28,100

3. Single-step income statement

IOWA ANTIQUES
Income Statement
For Year Ended December 31, 1999

Net sales		$314,000
Operating expenses:		
Cost of goods sold	$148,000	
Selling expenses	85,200	
General and administrative expenses	52,700	285,900
Net income		$ 28,100

4.

Dec. 31	Sales	325,000	
	Income Summary		325,000
	To close temporary accounts with credit balances.		
Dec. 31	Income Summary	296,900	
	Sales Discounts		6,000
	Sales Returns and Allowances		5,000
	Cost of Goods Sold		148,000
	Depreciation Expense—Store Equipment ..		4,000
	Depreciation Expense—Office Equipment ..		1,500
	Sales Salaries Expense		28,000
	Office Salaries Expense		32,000
	Insurance Expense		12,000
	Rent Expense		24,000
	Store Supplies Expense		6,000
	Advertising Expense		30,400
	To close temporary accounts with debit balances.		

Dec. 31	Income Summary	28,100	
	Dee Rizzo, capital		28,100
	To close the Income Summary account.		
Dec. 31	Dee Rizzo, capital	8,000	
	Dee Rizzo, withdrawals		8,000
	To close the withdrawals account.		

5. Acid test ratio = Cash /(Accounts payable + Salaries payable)

$$= \$19{,}000/(\$8{,}000 + \$1{,}000) = \$19{,}000/\$9{,}000 = \underline{\underline{2.11}}$$

Gross margin ratio = Gross profit/Net sales = $166,000/$314,000 = $\underline{\underline{0.53}}$

Iowa Antiques has a healthy acid-test ratio of 2.11. This means it has over $2.00 in liquid assets to satisfy each $1.00 in current liabilities. (Neither supplies nor inventory are considered liquid assets readily convertible into cash for use in satisfying short-term obligations.) The gross margin of .53 shows that Iowa Antiques spends 47 cents of every dollar of net sales on the costs of acquiring the merchandise it sells. This leaves 53 cents of every dollar of net sales to cover other expenses incurred in the business and to provide for a profit.

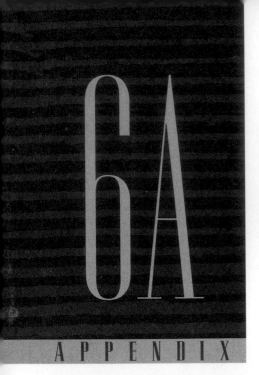

6A

Periodic and Perpetual Inventory Systems: Accounting Comparisons

Learning Objectives

Procedural

P5 Record and compare merchandising transactions using both periodic and perpetual inventory systems.

Recall that under a perpetual system, the Merchandise Inventory account is updated after each purchase and each sale. The Cost of Goods Sold account also is updated after each sale so that during the period the account balance reflects the period's total cost of goods sold to date.

Under a periodic inventory system, the Merchandise Inventory account is updated only once each accounting period. This update occurs at the *end* of the period. During the next period, the Merchandise Inventory balance remains unchanged. It reflects the beginning inventory balance until it is updated again at the end of the period. Similarly, in a periodic inventory system, cost of goods sold is not recorded as each sale occurs. Instead, the total cost of goods sold during the period is computed at the end of the period.

Recording Merchandise Transactions

Under a perpetual system, each purchase, purchase return and allowance, purchase discount, and transportation-in transaction is recorded in the Merchandise Inventory account. Under a periodic system, a separate temporary account is set up for each of these items. At the end of a period, each of these temporary accounts is closed and the Merchandise Inventory account is updated. To illustrate the differences, we use parallel columns to show journal entries for the most common transactions using both periodic and perpetual inventory systems (we drop explanations for simplicity).

Purchases

Z-Mart purchases merchandise for $1,200 on credit with terms of 2/10, n/30. Z-Mart's entry to record this credit purchase is:

(a)

Periodic			Perpetual		
Purchases	1,200		Merchandise Inventory	1,200	
Accounts Payable . .		1,200	Accounts Payable		1,200

The periodic system uses a temporary *Purchases* account that accumulates the cost of all purchase transactions during the period.

Purchase Discounts

When Z-Mart pays the supplier for the previous purchase in (a) within the discount period, the required payment is $1,176 ($1,200 × 98%) and is recorded as:

(b)

Periodic			Perpetual		
Accounts Payable	1,200		Accounts Payable	1,200	
Purchase Discounts .		24	Merchandise Inventory . .		24
Cash		1,176	Cash		1,176

The periodic system uses a temporary *Purchase Discounts* account that accumulates discounts taken on purchase transactions during the period. If payment is delayed until after the discount period expires, the entry under both methods is to debit Accounts Payable and credit Cash for $1,200 each.

Purchase Returns and Allowances

Z-Mart returns merchandise purchased on November 2 because of defects. If the recorded cost of the defective merchandise is $300, Z-Mart records the return with this entry:[9]

(c)

Periodic			Perpetual		
Accounts Payable	300		Accounts Payable	300	
Purchase Returns and Allowances		300	Merchandise Inventory . .		300

This entry is the same if Z-Mart is granted a price reduction (allowance) instead of returning the merchandise. In the periodic system, the temporary Purchase Returns and Allowances account accumulates the cost of all returns and allowances transactions during a period.

Transportation-In

Z-Mart paid a $75 freight charge to haul merchandise to its store. In the periodic system, this cost is charged to a temporary Transportation-In account.

(d)

Periodic			Perpetual		
Transportation-In	75		Merchandise Inventory	75	
Cash		75	Cash		75

Sales

Z-Mart sold $2,400 of merchandise on credit and Z-Mart's cost of this merchandise is $1,600:

(e)

Periodic			Perpetual		
Accounts Receivable . . .	2,400		Accounts Receivable	2,400	
Sales		2,400	Sales		2,400
			Cost of Goods Sold	1,600	
			Merchandise Inventory . .		1,600

Under the periodic system the cost of goods sold is not recorded at the time of sale. We later show how the total cost of goods sold at the end of a period is computed under the periodic system.

---

[9] Recorded cost is the cost recorded in the account after any discounts.

Sales Returns

A customer returns part of the merchandise from the previous transaction in (e), where returned items sell for $800 and cost $600. Z-Mart restores the merchandise to inventory and records the return as:

(f)	Periodic		
Sales Returns and Allowances		800	
Accounts Receivable			800

	Perpetual		
Sales Returns and Allowances		800	
Accounts Receivable . . .			800
Merchandise Inventory		600	
Cost of Goods Sold			600

The periodic system records only the revenue reduction.

Adjusting and Closing Entries

The periodic and perpetual inventory systems show differences in the adjusting and closing entries. Z-Mart's unadjusted trial balances at the end of 1999 under each system are shown in Exhibit 6A.1.

The Merchandise Inventory balance is $19,000 under the periodic system and $21,250 under the perpetual system. Because the periodic system does not revise the Merchandise Inventory balance during the period, the $19,000 amount is the beginning inventory. The $21,250 balance under the perpetual system is the recorded ending inventory before adjusting for any inventory shrinkage.

A physical count of inventory taken at the end of the period disclosed $21,000 of merchandise on hand. We then know inventory shrinkage is: $21,250 - $21,000 = $250. The adjusting entry for shrinkage along with closing entries under the two systems is shown in Exhibit 6A.2.

The periodic system does not require an adjusting entry to record inventory shrinkage. Instead, the periodic system puts the ending inventory of $21,000 in the Merchandise Inventory account in the first closing entry, and removes the $19,000 beginning inventory balance from the account in the second closing entry.

By updating Merchandise Inventory and closing Purchases, Purchase Discounts, Purchase Returns and Allowances, and Transportation-In, the periodic system transfers the cost of goods sold amount to Income Summary. Review the periodic side of Exhibit 6A.2 and notice the color items affect Income Summary as follows:

Credited to Income Summary in the first closing entry:	
Merchandise inventory	$ 21,000
Purchase discounts	4,200
Purchase returns and allowances	1,500
Debited to Income Summary in the second closing entry:	
Merchandise inventory	(19,000)
Purchases	(235,800)
Transportation-in	(2,300)
Net effect on Income Summary	**($230,400)**

Exhibit 6A.1

Comparison of Unadjusted Trial Balances—Periodic and Perpetual

Z-MART Unadjusted Trial Balance December 31, 1999 Periodic	Debit	Credit
Cash	$ 8,200	
Accounts receivable	11,200	
Merchandise inventory	19,000	
Office supplies	550	
Store supplies	250	
Prepaid insurance	300	
Office equipment	4,200	
Accumulated depreciation—Office eq.		$ 1,400
Store equipment	30,000	
Accumulated depreciation—Store eq.		6,000
Accounts payable		16,000
Salaries payable		800
K. Marty, capital		42,600
K. Marty, withdrawals	4,000	
Sales		321,000
Sales discounts	4,300	
Sales returns and allowances	2,000	
Purchases	235,800	
Purchase discounts		4,200
Purchase returns and allowances		1,500
Transportation-in	2,300	
Depreciation expense—Store eq.	3,000	
Depreciation expense—Office eq.	700	
Office salaries expense	25,300	
Sales salaries expense	18,500	
Insurance expense	600	
Rent expense—Office space	900	
Rent expense—Selling space	8,100	
Office supplies expense	1,800	
Store supplies expense	1,200	
Advertising expense	11,300	
	$393,500	$393,500

Z-MART Unadjusted Trial Balance December 31, 1999 Perpetual	Debit	Credit
Cash	$ 8,200	
Accounts receivable	11,200	
Merchandise inventory	21,250	
Office supplies	550	
Store supplies	250	
Prepaid insurance	300	
Office equipment	4,200	
Accum. depreciation—Office eq.		$ 1,400
Store equipment	30,000	
Accum. depreciation—Store eq.		6,000
Accounts payable		16,000
Salaries payable		800
K. Marty, capital		42,600
K. Marty, withdrawals	4,000	
Sales		321,000
Sales discounts	4,300	
Sales returns and allowances	2,000	
Cost of goods sold	230,150	
Depreciation expense—Store eq.	3,000	
Depreciation expense—Office eq.	700	
Office salaries expense	25,300	
Sales salaries expense	18,500	
Insurance expense	600	
Rent expense—Office space	900	
Rent expense—Selling space	8,100	
Office supplies expense	1,800	
Store supplies expense	1,200	
Advertising expense	11,300	
	$387,800	$387,800

Exhibit 6A.2

Comparison of Adjusting and Closing Entries—Periodic and Perpetual

Periodic		
Adjusting entries		
Closing entries		
(1) Sales	321,000	
Merchandise inventory	21,000	
Purchase discounts	4,200	
Purchase returns and allowances	1,500	
Income Summary		347,700
(2) Income Summary	334,800	
Sales discounts		4,300
Sales returns and allowances		2,000
Merchandise inventory		19,000
Purchases		235,800
Transportation-In		2,300
Depreciation Expense—Store eq.		3,000
Depreciation Expense—Office eq.		700
Office Salaries Expense		25,300
Sales Salaries Expense		18,500
Insurance Expense		600
Rent Expense—Office space		900
Rent Expense—Selling space		8,100
Office Supplies Expense		1,800
Store Supplies Expense		1,200
Advertising Expense		11,300
(3) Income Summary	12,900	
K. Marty, capital		12,900
(4) K. Marty, capital	4,000	
K. Marty, withdrawals		4,000

Perpetual		
Adjusting entries		
Cost of Goods Sold	250	
Merchandise Inventory		250
Closing entries		
(1) Sales	321,000	
Income Summary		321,000
(2) Income Summary	308,100	
Sales discounts		4,300
Sales returns and allowances		2,000
Cost of Goods Sold		230,400
Depreciation Expense—Store eq.		3,000
Depreciation Expense—Office eq.		700
Office Salaries Expense		25,300
Sales Salaries Expense		18,500
Insurance Expense		600
Rent Expense—Office space		900
Rent Expense—Selling space		8,100
Office Supplies Expense		1,800
Store Supplies Expense		1,200
Advertising Expense		11,300
(3) Income Summary	12,900	
K. Marty, capital		12,900
(4) K. Marty, capital	4,000	
K. Marty, withdrawals		4,000

This $230,400 effect on Income Summary is the cost of goods sold amount. This figure is confirmed as follows:

Beginning inventory		$ 19,000
Purchases	$235,800	
Less purchase discounts	(4,200)	
Less purchase returns and allowances	(1,500)	
Plus transportation-in	2,300	
Net cost of goods purchased		232,400
Cost of goods available for sale		$251,400
Less ending inventory		(21,000)
Cost of goods sold		**$230,400**

The periodic system transfers cost of goods sold to the Income Summary account but does not use a Cost of Goods Sold account.

The periodic system does not measure shrinkage. Instead it computes cost of goods available for sale, subtracts the cost of ending inventory, and defines the difference as cost of goods sold. This difference, called the *cost of goods,* includes shrinkage.

In our discussion of the periodic system, the change in the Merchandise Inventory account is recorded as part of the closing process. The closing entry method is common in practice. Yet an alternative method, called the *adjusting entry method,* also is commonly used.[10] The *adjusting entry method* records the change in the Merchandise Inventory account with adjusting entries. Under this method, the first two closing entries do not include changes in the Merchandise Inventory account.

Adjusting Entry Method to Record Changes in Merchandise Inventory

Adjusting Entries

Under the adjusting entry method of the periodic system, Z-Mart removes the beginning balance from the Merchandise Inventory account by recording this adjusting entry at the end of 1999:

Dec. 31	Income Summary	19,000	
	Merchandise Inventory		19,000
	To remove the beginning balance from the Merchandise Inventory account.		

A second adjusting entry gives the correct ending balance in the Merchandise Inventory account:

Dec. 31	Merchandise Inventory	21,000	
	Income Summary		21,000
	To insert the correct ending balance in the Merchandise Inventory account.		

After these entries are posted, the Merchandise Inventory account has a $21,000 debit balance:

Merchandise Inventory			
Beg. bal.	19,000		
		19,000	Adj.
Adj.	21,000		
End. bal.	21,000		

These adjustments leave the Income Summary account with a $2,000 credit balance.

Closing Entries

If the adjusting entry method for inventory is used, the closing entries differ only by not including the Merchandise Inventory account. In particular, entries *(1)* and *(2)* in Exhibit 6A.2 are the same except for removing the Merchandise Inventory account and its balance from both entries. Entry *(3)* to close Income Summary is also unchanged. The only difference is that the adjusting entry method took us four entries instead of two to get the net income of $12,900.

---

[10] The adjusting entry method also is used by some computerized accounting systems that do not allow the Merchandise Inventory account (a permanent account) to be changed in the closing process.

Flash *back*

16. What account is used in a perpetual inventory system but not in a periodic system?

17. Which of the following accounts are temporary accounts under a periodic system? (a) Merchandise Inventory; (b) Purchases; (c) Transportation-In.

18. How is cost of goods sold computed under a periodic inventory accounting system?

19. Do reported amounts of ending inventory and net income differ if the adjusting entry method of recording the change in inventory is used instead of the closing entry method?

Answers—p. 260

Summary of Appendix 6A

P5 **Record and compare merchandising transactions using both periodic and perpetual inventory systems.** Transactions involving the sale and purchase of merchandise are recorded and analyzed under both the periodic and perpetual inventory systems. Adjusting and closing entries for both inventory systems are also illustrated and explained.

Guidance Answers to **Flash** *backs*

16. Cost of Goods Sold.

17. (b) Purchases and (c) Transportation-In.

18. Under a periodic inventory system, the cost of goods sold is determined at the end of an accounting period by adding the net cost of goods purchased to the beginning inventory and subtracting the ending inventory.

19. Both methods report the same ending inventory and net income.

Glossary

Acid-test ratio a ratio used to assess the company's ability to settle its current debts with its most liquid assets; it is the ratio between a company's quick assets (cash, short-term investments, and current receivables) and its current liabilities. (p. 245)

Cash discount a reduction in the price of merchandise that is granted by a seller to a purchaser in exchange for the purchaser's making payment within a specified period of time called the *discount period.* (p. 227)

Classified, multiple-step income statement an income statement format that shows intermediate totals between sales and net income and detailed computations of net sales and cost of goods sold. (p. 241)

Cost of goods sold the cost of merchandise sold to customers during a period. (p. 224)

Credit memorandum a notification that the sender has entered a credit in the recipient's account maintained by the sender. (p. 236)

Credit period the time period that can pass before a customer's payment is due. (p. 227)

Credit terms the description of the amounts and timing of payments that a buyer agrees to make in the future. (p. 227)

Debit memorandum a notification that the sender has entered a debit in the recipient's account maintained by the sender. (p. 229)

Discount period the time period in which a cash discount is available and a reduced payment can be made by the buyer. (p. 227)

EOM the abbreviation for *end-of-month*; used to describe credit terms for some transactions. (p. 227)

FOB the abbreviation for *free on board*; the designated point at which ownership of goods passes to the buyer; FOB shipping point (or factory) means that the buyer pays the shipping costs and accepts ownership of the goods at the seller's place of business; FOB destination means that the seller pays the shipping costs and the ownership of the goods transfers to the buyer at the buyer's place of business. (p. 231)

General and administrative expenses expenses that support the overall operations of a business and include the expenses of such activities as providing accounting services, human resource management, and financial management. (p. 242)

Gross margin the difference between net sales and the cost of goods sold; also called *gross profit.* (p. 223)

Gross margin ratio gross margin (sales minus cost of goods sold) divided by sales; also called *gross profit ratio.* (p. 246).

Gross profit the difference between net sales and the cost of goods sold; also called *gross margin.* (p. 223)

Inventory products a company owns and expects to sell in its normal operations. (p. 224)

List price the catalog price of an item before any trade discount is deducted. (p. 227)

Merchandise products, also called *goods,* that a company acquires for the purpose of reselling them to customers. (p. 222)

Merchandiser earns net income by buying and selling merchandise. (p. 222).

Merchandiser inventory products that a company owns for the purpose of selling them to customers. (p. 223).

Periodic inventory system a method of accounting that records the cost of inventory purchased but does not track the quantity on hand or sold to customers; the records are updated at the end of each period to reflect the results of physical counts of the items on hand. (p. 225)

Perpetual inventory system a method of accounting that maintains continuous records of the cost of inventory on hand and the cost of goods sold. (p. 225)

Purchase discount a term used by a purchaser to describe a cash discount granted to the purchaser for paying within the discount period. (p. 227)

Retailer a middleman that buys products from manufacturers or wholesalers and sells them to consumers. (p. 222)

Sales discount a term used by a seller to describe a cash discount granted to customers for paying within the discount period. (p. 227)

Selling expenses the expenses of promoting sales by displaying and advertising the merchandise, making sales, and delivering goods to customers. (p. 242)

Shrinkage inventory losses that occur as a result of shoplifting or deterioration. (p. 237)

Single-step income statement an income statement format that includes cost of goods sold as an operating expense and shows only one subtotal for total expenses. (p. 243)

Supplementary records a register of information outside the usual accounting records and accounts; also called *supplemental records*. (p. 232)

Trade discount a reduction below a list or catalog price that may vary in amount for wholesalers, retailers, and final consumers. (p. 227)

Wholesaler a middleman that buys products from manufacturers or other wholesalers and sells them to retailers or other wholesalers. (p. 222)

The superscript letter ^A^ identifies assignment material based on Appendix 6A.

Questions

1. What items appear in the financial statements of merchandising companies but not in the statements of service companies?

2. Explain how a business can earn a gross profit on its sales and still have a net loss.

3. Why would a company offer a cash discount?

4. What is the difference between a sales discount and a purchase discount?

5. Distinguish between cash discounts and trade discounts. Is the amount of a trade discount on purchased merchandise recorded in the Purchase Discounts account?

6. How does a company that uses a perpetual inventory system determine the amount of inventory shrinkage?

7. Why would a company's manager be concerned about the quantity of its purchase returns if its suppliers allow unlimited returns?

8. Does the sender of a debit memorandum record a debit or a credit in the account of the recipient? Which does the recipient record?

9. What is the difference between single-step and multiple-step income statement formats?

10. In comparing the accounts of a merchandising company with those of a service company, what additional accounts would the merchandising company be likely to use, assuming it employs a perpetual inventory system?

11. Refer to the income statement for **NIKE** in Appendix A. What term is used instead of cost of goods sold? Does the company present a detailed calculation of the cost of goods sold?

12. Refer to the balance sheet for **Reebok** in Appendix A. How does Reebok refer to the inventory account? What is an alternate name that could be used?

13. Refer to the income statement of **America Online** in Appendix A. Does the AOL income statement report a gross profit figure?

14. Jason Walker in the opening article talks about the need to be skillful in negotiating purchase contracts with suppliers. What type of shipping terms should Jason Walker attempt to negotiate to minimize his freight-in costs?

For each description below, identify whether the reference best applies to a periodic or perpetual inventory system.

a. Requires a physical count of inventory to determine the amount of inventory to report on the balance sheet.

b. Records cost of goods sold each time a sales transaction occurs.

c. Provides more timely information to managers.

Quick Study

QS 6-1

Contrast periodic and perpetual systems

d. Traditionally used by drug and department stores that sold large quantities of low-valued items.

e. Requires an adjusting entry to record inventory shrinkage.

QS 6-2
Purchases entries—
perpetual system

P1

Prepare journal entries to record each of the following transactions of a merchandising company. Show any supporting calculations. Assume a perpetual inventory system.

Mar. 5   Purchased 500 units of product with a list price of $5 per unit. The purchaser was granted a trade discount of 20% and the terms of the sale were 2/10, n/60.

Mar. 7   Returned 50 defective units from the March 5 purchase and received full credit.

Mar. 15   Paid the amount due resulting from the March 5 purchase, less the return on March 7.

QS 6-3
Sales entries—perpetual system

P2

Prepare journal entries to record each of the following transactions of a merchandising company. Show any supporting calculations. Assume a perpetual inventory system.

Apr. 1   Sold merchandise for $2,000, granting the customer terms of 2/10, EOM. The cost of the merchandise was $1,400.

Apr. 4   The customer in the April 1 sale returned merchandise and received credit for $500. The merchandise, which had cost $350, was returned to inventory.

Apr. 11   Received payment for the amount due from the April 1 sale less the return on April 4.

QS 6-4
Accounting for
shrinkage—perpetual
system

P3

Beamer Company's ledger on July 31, the end of its fiscal year, includes the following accounts that have normal balances:

Merchandise inventory	$ 34,800
J. Beamer, capital	115,300
J. Beamer, withdrawals	4,000
Sales	157,200
Sales discounts	1,700
Sales returns and allowances	3,500
Cost of goods sold	102,000
Depreciation expense	7,300
Salaries expense	29,500
Miscellaneous expenses	2,000

A physical count of the inventory discloses that the cost of the merchandise on hand is $32,900. Prepare the entry to record this information.

QS 6-5^A
Closing entries

P3

Refer to QS 6-4 and prepare the entries to close the balances in temporary accounts. Do not forget to take into consideration the entry that was made to solve QS 6-4.

QS 6-6
Gross margin analysis

C2, A3

Compute net sales, gross profit, and the gross margin ratio in each of the following situations:

	a	b	c	d
Sales	$130,000	$512,000	$35,700	$245,700
Sales discounts	4,200	16,500	400	3,500
Sales returns and allowances	17,000	5,000	5,000	700
Cost of goods sold	76,600	326,700	21,300	125,900

Interpret the gross margin ratio for situation *a*.

Use the following information to compute the acid-test ratio. Explain what the acid-test ratio of a company measures. Comment on the ratio you compute.

Cash	$1,200
Accounts receivable	2,700
Inventory	5,000
Prepaid expenses	600
Accounts payable	4,750
Other current liabilities	950

QS 6-7
Acid-test ratio and analysis
A2

Explain the similarities and differences between the acid-test ratio and the current ratio. Compare the two ratios.

QS 6-8
Contrasting liquidity ratios
A2

Insert the letter for each term in the blank space beside the definition that it most closely matches:

A. Cash discount   **E.** FOB shipping point   **H.** Purchase discount
B. Credit period   **F.** Gross profit   **I.** Sales discount
C. Discount period   **G.** Merchandise inventory   **J.** Trade discount
D. FOB destination

Exercises
Exercise 6-1
Merchandising terms
C1, C2

_____ **1.** An agreement that ownership of goods is transferred at the buyer's place of business.
_____ **2.** The time period in which a cash discount is available.
_____ **3.** The difference between net sales and the cost of goods sold.
_____ **4.** A reduction in a receivable or payable that is granted if it is paid within the discount period.
_____ **5.** A purchaser's description of a cash discount received from a supplier of goods.
_____ **6.** An agreement that ownership of goods is transferred at the seller's place of business.
_____ **7.** A reduction below list or catalog price that is negotiated in setting the price of goods.
_____ **8.** A seller's description of a cash discount granted to customers in return for early payment.
_____ **9.** The time period that can pass before a customer's payment is due.
_____ **10.** The goods that a company owns and expects to sell to its customers.

Prepare journal entries to record the following transactions for a retail store. Assume a perpetual inventory system.

Mar. 2 Purchased merchandise from Blanton Company under the following terms: $3,600 invoice price, 2/15, n/60, FOB shipping point.
  3 Paid $200 for shipping charges on the purchase of March 2.
  4 Returned to Blanton Company unacceptable merchandise that had an invoice price of $600.
  17 Sent a check to Blanton Company for the March 2 purchase, net of the discount and the returned merchandise.
  18 Purchased merchandise from Fleming Corp. under the following terms: $7,500 invoice price, 2/10, n/30, FOB destination.
  21 After negotiations, received from Fleming Corp. a $2,100 allowance on the purchase of March 18.
  28 Sent a check to Fleming Corp. paying for the March 18 purchase, net of the discount and the allowance.

Exercise 6-2
Recording entries for merchandise purchases

On May 11, Wilson Sales accepted delivery of $30,000 of merchandise it purchased for resale. With the merchandise was an invoice dated May 11, with terms of 3/10, n/90, FOB Hostel Corporation's factory. The cost of the goods to Hostel was $20,000. When the goods were delivered, Wilson paid $335 to Express Shipping Service for delivery charges on the merchandise. On May 12, Wilson returned $1,200 of goods to Hostel, who received them one day later and restored them to inventory. The returned goods had cost Hostel $800. On May 20, Wilson mailed a check to Hostel Corporation for the amount owed on that date. It was received by Hostel the following day.

Exercise 6-3
Analyzing and recording merchandise transactions—both buyer and seller

Required

a. Prepare journal entries that Wilson Sales should record for these transactions. Wilson Sales uses a perpetual inventory system.

b. Prepare journal entries that Hostel Corporation should record for these transactions. Hostel uses a perpetual inventory system.

Exercise 6-4
Analyzing and recording merchandise transactions—both buyer and seller

P1, P2

Sundown Company purchased merchandise for resale from Raintree with an invoice price of $22,000 and credit terms of 3/10, n/60. The merchandise had cost Raintree $15,000. Sundown paid within the discount period. Assume that both the buyer and seller use perpetual inventory systems.

Required

a. Prepare entries that the buyer should record for the purchase and payment.

b. Prepare entries that the seller should record for the sale and collection.

c. Assume that the buyer borrowed enough cash to pay the balance on the last day of the discount period at an annual interest rate of 8% and paid it back on the last day of the credit period. Compute how much the buyer saved by following this strategy. (Use a 365-day year.)

Exercise 6-5
Components of cost of goods sold

C5

Using the data provided from the general ledger and supplementary records, determine each of the missing numbers in the following separate situations:

	a	b	c
Invoice cost of merchandise purchases	$90,000	$40,000	$30,500
Purchase discounts received	4,000	?	650
Purchase returns and allowances received	3,000	1,500	1,100
Cost of transportation-in	?	3,500	4,000
Merchandise inventory (beginning of period)	7,000	?	9,000
Total cost of merchandise purchases	89,400	39,500	?
Merchandise inventory (end of period)	4,400	7,500	?
Cost of goods sold	?	41,600	34,130

Exercise 6-6
Calculating expenses and cost of goods sold

C5

Friar Company's ledger and supplementary records at the end of the period reveal the following:

Sales	$340,000
Sales discounts	5,500
Sales returns	14,000
Merchandise inventory (beginning of period)	30,000
Invoice cost of merchandise purchases	175,000
Purchase discounts received	3,600
Purchase returns and allowances received	6,000
Cost of transportation-in	11,000
Gross profit from sales	145,000
Net income	65,000

Required

Calculate (a) total operating expenses, (b) cost of goods sold, and (c) merchandise inventory (end of period).

Fill in the blanks in the following separate income statements. Identify any losses by putting the amount in parentheses.

	a	b	c	d	e
Sales	$60,000	$42,500	$36,000	$?	$23,600
Cost of goods sold:					
Merchandise inventory (beginning)	$ 6,000	$17,050	$ 7,500	$ 7,000	$ 2,560
Total cost of merchandise purchases	36,000	?	?	32,000	5,600
Merchandise inventory (ending)	?	(2,700)	(9,000)	(6,600)	?
Cost of goods sold	$34,050	$15,900	$?	$?	$ 5,600
Gross profit	$?	$?	$ 3,750	$45,600	$?
Expenses	9,000	10,650	12,150	2,600	6,000
Net income (loss)	$?	$15,950	$ (8,400)	$43,000	$?

Exercise 6-7
Calculating revenues,
expenses, and income

C2, C5

Travis Parts was organized on June 1, 2000, and made its first purchase of merchandise on June 3. The purchase was for 1,000 units at a price of $10 per unit. On June 5, Travis sold 600 of the units for $14 per unit to Decker Co. Terms of the sale were 2/10, n/60. Prepare entries for Travis to record the June 5 sale and each of the following independent alternatives under a perpetual inventory system.

a. On June 7, Decker returned 100 units because they did not fit the customer's needs. Travis restored the units to its inventory.

b. Decker discovered that 100 units were damaged but of some use and, therefore, kept the units. Travis sent Decker a credit memorandum for $600 to compensate for the damage.

c. Decker returned 100 defective units and Travis concluded that these units could not be resold. As a result, Travis discarded the units.

Exercise 6-8
Sales returns and
allowances entries

P2

Refer to Exercise 6-8 and prepare the appropriate journal entries for Decker Co. to record the purchase and each of the three independent alternatives presented. Decker is a retailer that uses a perpetual inventory system and purchased the units for resale.

Exercise 6-9
Purchase returns and
allowances entries

P1

The following amounts from supplementary and accounting records summarize Transeer Company's merchandising activities during year 2000. Set up T-accounts for Merchandise Inventory and Cost of Goods Sold. Then record the summarized activities directly in the T-accounts and calculate the account balances.

Exercise 6-10
Effects of merchandising
activities on accounts

C5

Cost of merchandise sold to customers in sales transactions	$186,000
Merchandise inventory, December 31, 1999	27,000
Invoice cost of merchandise purchases	190,500
Shrinkage determined on December 31, 2000	700
Cost of transportation-in	1,900
Cost of merchandise returned by customers and restored to inventory	2,200
Purchase discounts received	1,600
Purchase returns and allowances received	4,100

The following list includes some permanent accounts and all of the temporary accounts from the December 31, 2000, unadjusted trial balance of Perry Sales, a business owned by Deborah Perry. Use these account balances along with the additional information to journalize adjusting and closing entries. Perry Sales uses a perpetual inventory system.

Exercise 6-11^A
Adjusting and closing
entries for a merchandiser

P3

	Debit	Credit
Merchandise inventory	$ 28,000	
Prepaid selling expenses	5,000	
Deborah Perry, withdrawals	1,800	
Sales		$429,000
Sales returns and allowances	16,500	
Sales discounts	4,000	
Cost of goods sold	211,000	
Sales salaries expense	47,000	
Utilities expense	14,000	
Selling expenses	35,000	
Administrative expenses	95,000	

Additional Information

Accrued sales salaries amount to $1,600. Prepaid selling expenses of $2,000 have expired. A physical count of merchandise inventory discloses $27,450 of goods on hand.

Exercise 6-12
Acid-test and current ratios

A2

Calculate the current and acid-test ratios in each the following separate cases:

	Case X	Case Y	Case Z
Cash	$ 800	$ 910	$1,100
Short-term investments			500
Receivables		990	800
Inventory	2,000	1,000	4,000
Prepaid expenses	1,200	600	900
Total current assets	$4,000	$3,500	$7,300
Current liabilities	$2,200	$1,100	$3,650

Which company case is in the best position to meet short-term obligations? Explain your choice.

Exercise 6-13
Sales returns and allowances information

C2, P2

Briefly explain why a company's manager would want the accounting system to record a customer's return of unsatisfactory goods in the Sales Returns and Allowances account instead of the Sales account. In addition, explain whether the information would be useful for external decision makers.

Exercise 6-14
Physical count error interpreted as shrinkage

P3

A retail company recently completed a physical count of ending merchandise inventory to use in preparing adjusting entries. In determining the cost of the counted inventory, company employees failed to consider that $2,000 of incoming goods had been shipped by a supplier on December 31 under an FOB shipping point agreement. These goods had been recorded in Merchandise Inventory as a purchase, but they were not included in the physical count because they were not on hand. Explain how this overlooked fact affects the company's financial statements and the following ratios: return on equity, debt ratio, current ratio, profit margin, and acid-test ratio.

Exercise 6-15^A
Journal entries to contrast the periodic and perpetual systems

P1, P2, P5

Journalize the following merchandising transactions for Scout Systems assuming (a) a periodic system and (b) perpetual system.

1. On November 1 Scout Systems purchases merchandise for $1,400 on credit with terms of 2/10, n/30.
2. On November 5 Scout Systems pays for the previous purchase.
3. On November 7 Scout Systems discovers and returns $100 of defective merchandise that was purchased on November 1 for a cash refund.
4. On November 10 Scout Systems pays $80 to transport merchandise to its store.

5. On November 13 Scout Systems sells merchandise for $1,500 on account. The cost of the merchandise was $750.

6. On November 16 a customer returns merchandise from the November 13 transaction. The returned item sold for $200 and cost $100.

A company reports the following balances and activities at year-end:

Net sales	$1,005,000
Cost of goods sold	560,000
Increase in accounts receivable for the period	40,000
Cash payments to suppliers	510,000

Exercise 6-16
Profitability and
merchandising cash flows

A1

Required

1. Calculate gross profit.

2. Calculate cash received from customers.

3. Calculate net cash flows from customers and to suppliers.

Prepare journal entries to record the following perpetual system merchandising transactions of Belton Company. (Use a separate account for each receivable and payable; for example, record the purchase on July 1 in Accounts Payable—Jones Company.)

July 1   Purchased merchandise from Jones Company for $6,000 under credit terms of 1/15, n/30, FOB shipping point.

     2   Sold merchandise to Terra Co. for $800 under credit terms of 2/10, n/60, FOB shipping point. The merchandise had cost $500.

     3   Paid $100 for freight charges on the purchase of July 1.

     8   Sold merchandise that cost $1,200 for $1,600 cash.

     9   Purchased merchandise from Keene Co. for $2,300 under credit terms of 2/15, n/60, FOB destination.

   12   Received a $200 credit memorandum acknowledging the return of merchandise purchased on July 9.

   12   Received the balance due from Terra Co. for the credit sale dated July 2, net of the discount.

   16   Paid the balance due to Jones Company within the discount period.

   19   Sold merchandise that cost $900 to Urban Co. for $1,250 under credit terms of 2/15, n/60, FOB shipping point.

   21   Issued a $150 credit memorandum to Urban Co. for an allowance on goods sold on July 19.

   22   Received a debit memorandum from Urban Co. for an error that overstated the total sales invoice by $50.

   24   Paid Keene Co. the balance due after deducting the discount.

   30   Received the balance due from Urban Co. for the credit sale dated July 19, net of the discount.

   31   Sold merchandise that cost $3,200 to Terra Co. for $5,000 under credit terms of 2/10, n/60, FOB shipping point.

Problems

Problem 6-1
Journal entries for
merchandising activities
(perpetual system)

Prepare journal entries to record the following perpetual system merchandising transactions of Hanifin Company. (Use a separate account for each receivable and payable; for example, record the purchase on August 1 in Accounts Payable—Dickson Company.)

Aug. 1   Purchased merchandise from Dickson Company for $6,000 under credit terms of 1/10, n/30, FOB destination.

     4   At Dickson's request, paid $100 for freight charges on the August 1 purchase, reducing the amount owed to Dickson.

     5   Sold merchandise to Griften Corp. for $4,200 under credit terms of 2/10, n/60, FOB destination. The merchandise had cost $3,000.

     8   Purchased merchandise from Kendall Corporation for $5,300 under credit terms of 1/10, n/45, FOB shipping point, plus $240 shipping charges. The invoice showed that at Hanifin's request, Kendall had paid $240 shipping charges and added that amount to the bill.

Problem 6-2
Journal entries for
merchandising activities
(perpetual system)

P1, P2

9 Paid $120 shipping charges related to the August 5 sale to Griften Corp.
10 Griften returned merchandise from the August 5 sale that had cost $500 and been sold for $700. The merchandise was restored to inventory.
12 After negotiations with Kendall Corporation concerning problems with the merchandise purchased on August 8, Hanifin received a credit memorandum from Kendall granting a price reduction of $800.
15 Received balance due from Griften Corp. for the August 5 sale less the return on August 10.
18 Paid the amount due Kendall Corporation for the August 8 purchase less the price reduction granted.
19 Sold merchandise to Farley for $3,600 under credit terms of 1/10, n/30, FOB shipping point. The merchandise had cost $2,500.
22 Farley requested a price reduction on the August 19 sale because the merchandise did not meet specifications. Sent Farley a credit memorandum for $600 to resolve the issue.
29 Received Farley's payment of the amount due from the August 19 purchase.
30 Paid Dickson Company the amount due from the August 1 purchase.

Problem 6-3
Income statement computations and formats

P4, A1

Davison Company's adjusted trial balance as of October 31, 2000, the end of its fiscal year, is shown below:

	Debit	Credit
Merchandise inventory	$ 31,000	
Other assets	128,400	
Liabilities		$ 35,000
B. Davison, capital		117,650
B. Davison, withdrawals	16,000	
Sales		212,000
Sales discounts	3,250	
Sales returns and allowances	14,000	
Cost of goods sold	82,600	
Sales salaries expense	29,000	
Rent expense, selling space	10,000	
Store supplies expense	2,500	
Advertising expense	18,000	
Office salaries expense	26,500	
Rent expense, office space	2,600	
Office supplies expense	800	
Totals	$364,650	$364,650

On October 31, 1999, the company's merchandise inventory amounted to $25,000. Supplementary records of merchandising activities during the 2000 fiscal year disclosed the following:

Invoice cost of merchandise purchases	$91,000
Purchase discounts received	1,900
Purchase returns and allowances received	4,400
Cost of transportation-in	3,900

Required

1. Compute the company's net sales for the year.
2. Compute the company's total cost of merchandise purchased for the year.
3. Prepare a classified, multiple-step income statement (see Exhibit 6.18) that lists the company's net sales, cost of goods sold, and gross profit, as well as the components and amounts of selling expenses and general and administrative expenses.
4. Prepare a condensed single-step income statement that lists these costs: cost of goods sold, selling expenses, and general and administrative expenses.
5. Accounts receivable decreased during the period by $30,000. Compute cash received from customers.

Check Figure Part 4, total expenses, $172,000

Use the data for Davison Company in Problem 6-3 to meet the following requirements:

Required

Preparation Component

1. Prepare closing entries for Davison Company as of October 31, 2000.

Analysis Component

2. All of the company's purchases were made on credit and its suppliers uniformly offer a 3% sales discount. Does it appear that the company's cash management system is accomplishing the goal of taking all available discounts? Explain.

3. In prior years, the company experienced a 4% return and allowance rate on its sales, which means approximately 4% of its gross sales were for items that were eventually returned outright or that caused the company to grant allowances to customers. How does this year's results compare to prior years' results?

The following unadjusted trial balance was prepared at the end of the fiscal year for Tinker Sales Company:

TINKER SALES COMPANY Unadjusted Trial Balance July 31, 2000		
Cash	$ 4,200	
Merchandise inventory	11,500	
Store supplies	4,800	
Prepaid insurance	2,300	
Store equipment	41,900	
Accumulated depreciation—Store equipment		$ 15,000
Accounts payable		9,000
Betsey Tinker, capital		35,200
Betsey Tinker, withdrawals	3,200	
Sales		104,000
Sales discounts	1,000	
Sales returns and allowances	2,000	
Cost of goods sold	37,400	
Depreciation expense—Store equipment		
Salaries expense	31,000	
Insurance expense		
Rent expense	14,000	
Store supplies expense		
Advertising expense	9,900	
Totals	$163,200	$163,200

Rent and salaries expense are equally divided between the selling and the general and administrative functions. Tinker Sales Company uses a perpetual inventory system.

Required

1. Prepare adjusting journal entries for the following:
   a. Store supplies on hand at year-end amount to $1,650.
   b. Expired insurance, an administrative expense, for the year is $1,500.
   c. Depreciation expense, a selling expense, for the year is $1,400.
   d. A physical count of the ending merchandise inventory shows $11,100 of goods on hand.
2. Prepare a multiple-step (not classified) income statement (see Exhibit 6.19).
3. Prepare a single-step income statement (see Exhibit 6.20).
4. Compute the company's current and acid-test ratios as of July 31, 2000.

Problem 6-4
Closing entries and interpreting information about discounts and returns

Check Figure Second closing entry: debit to Income Summary, $189,250

Problem 6-5
Adjusting entries, income statements, and acid-test ratio

A2, P3, P4

Check Figure Part 3, total expenses, $98,750

Serial Problem
Echo Systems

(The first three segments of this comprehensive problem were presented in Chapters 3, 4, and 5. If those segments have not been completed, the assignment can begin at this point. You should use the Working Papers that accompany this text because they reflect the account balances that resulted from posting the entries required in Chapters 3, 4, and 5.)

Earlier segments of this problem have described how Mary Graham created Echo Systems on October 1, 2000. The company has been successful, and its list of customers has grown. To accommodate the growth, the accounting system is ready to be modified to set up separate accounts for each customer. The following list of customers includes the account number used for each account and any balance as of the end of year 2000. Graham decided to add a fourth digit with a decimal point to the 106 account number that had been used for the single Accounts Receivable account. This modification allows the company to continue using the existing chart of accounts. The list also includes the balances that two customers owed as of December 31, 2000:

Customer Account	No.	Dec. 31 Balance
Alamo Engineering Co.	106.1	
Buckman Services	106.2	
Capital Leasing	106.3	
Decker Co.	106.4	$1,350
Elite Corporation	106.5	
Fostek Co.	106.6	$1,500
Grandview Co.	106.7	
Hacienda, Inc.	106.8	
Images, Inc.	106.9	

In response to requests from customers, Graham has decided to begin selling computer software. The company also will extend credit terms of 1/10, n/30 to customers who purchase merchandise. No cash discount will be available on consulting fees. The following additional accounts were added to the General Ledger to allow the system to account for the company's new merchandising activities:

Account	No.
Merchandise Inventory	119
Sales	413
Sales Returns and Allowances	414
Sales Discounts	415
Cost of Goods Sold	502

Because the accounting system does not use reversing entries, all revenue and expense accounts have zero balances as of January 1, 2001.

Required

1. Prepare journal entries to record each of the following transactions for Echo Systems.
2. Post the journal entries to the accounts in the company's General Ledger. (Use asset, liability, and equity accounts that start with balances as of December 31, 2000.)
3. Prepare a partial work sheet consisting of the first six columns similar to the one shown in Appendix 4B that shows the unadjusted trial balance, the March 31 adjustments *(a)* through *(g)*, and the adjusted trial balance. Do not prepare closing entries and do not journalize the adjusting entries or post them to the ledger.
4. Prepare an interim income statement for the three months ended March 31, 2001. Use a single-step format like the one in Exhibit 6.20. List all expenses without differentiating between selling expenses and general and administrative expenses.
5. Prepare an interim statement of changes in owner's equity for the three months ended March 31, 2001.
6. Prepare an interim balance sheet as of March 31, 2001.

Transactions

Jan.	4	Paid Carly Smith for five days' work at the rate of $100 per day. Four of the five days are unpaid days of work from the prior year.
	5	Mary Graham invested an additional $24,000 cash in the business.
	7	Purchased $5,600 of merchandise from Shephard Corp. with terms of 1/10, n/30, FOB shipping point.
	9	Received $1,500 from Fostek Co. as final payment on its account.
	11	Completed a five-day project for Alamo Engineering Co. and billed them $4,500, which is the total price of $6,000 less the advance payment of $1,500.
	13	Sold merchandise with a retail value of $4,200 and a cost of $3,360 to Elite Corporation with terms of 1/10, n/30, FOB shipping point.
	15	Paid $700 for freight charges on the merchandise purchased on January 7.
	16	Received $3,000 cash from Grandview Co. for computer services.
	17	Paid Shephard Corp. for the purchase on January 7, net of the discount.
	20	Elite Corporation returned $400 of defective merchandise from its purchase on January 13. The returned merchandise, which had a cost of $320, was discarded.
	22	Received the balance due from Elite Corporation net of the discount and the credit for the returned merchandise.
	24	Returned defective merchandise to Shephard Corp. and accepted credit against future purchases. Its cost, net of the discount, was $396.
	26	Purchased $8,000 of merchandise from Shephard Corp. with terms of 1/10, n/30, FOB destination.
	26	Sold merchandise with a cost of $4,640 for $5,800 on credit to Hacienda, Inc.
	29	Received a $396 credit memo from Shephard Corp. concerning the merchandise returned on January 24.
	31	Paid Carly Smith for 10 days' work at $100 per day.
Feb.	1	Paid $3,375 to the Lakeshore Mall for another three months' rent in advance.
	3	Paid Shephard Corp. for the balance due, net of the cash discount, less the $396 amount in the credit memo.
	5	Paid $800 to the local newspaper for advertising.
	11	Received the balance due from Alamo Engineering Co. for fees billed on January 11.
	15	May Graham withdrew $4,800 cash.
	23	Sold merchandise with a cost of $2,560 for $3,200 on credit to Grandview Co.
	26	Paid Carly Smith for eight days' work at $100 per day.
	27	Reimbursed Mary Graham's business automobile mileage for 600 miles at $0.25 per mile.
Mar.	8	Purchased $2,400 of computer supplies from Abbott Office Products on credit.
	9	Received the balance due from Grandview Co. for merchandise sold on February 23.
	11	Repaired the company's computer at a cost of $860.
	16	Received $4,260 cash from Images, Inc., for computing services.
	19	Paid the full amount due to Abbott Office Products, including amounts created on December 15 and March 8.
	24	Billed Capital Leasing for $5,900 of computing services.
	25	Sold merchandise with a cost of $1,002 for $1,800 on credit to Buckman Services.
	30	Sold merchandise with a cost of $1,100 for $2,220 on credit to Decker Company.
	31	Reimbursed Mary Graham's business automobile mileage for 400 miles at $0.25 per mile.

Information for the March 31 adjustments and financial statements:

a. The March 31 inventory of computer supplies is $2,115.

b. Three more months have passed since the company purchased the annual insurance policy at a cost of $2,160.

c. Carly Smith has not been paid for seven days of work.

d. Three months have passed since any prepaid rent cost has been transferred to expense. The monthly rent is $1,125.

e. Depreciation on the computer for January through March is $1,125.

f. Depreciation on the office equipment for January through March is $750.

g. The March 31 inventory of merchandise is $980.

BEYOND THE NUMBERS

Reporting in Action

A2, C5

Refer to the financial statements and related information for **NIKE** in Appendix A. Answer the following questions by analyzing that information:

1. Assume the amounts reported for inventories and cost of sales reflect items purchased ready for resale. Compute the net cost of goods purchased during the fiscal year ended May 31, 1997.
2. Calculate the current and acid-test ratios as of the end of the fiscal years ended May 31, 1997, and May 31, 1996. Comment on your ratio results.

Swoosh Ahead

3. Obtain access to NIKE's annual report for fiscal years ending after May 31, 1997. You can gain access to NIKE's annual report at its web site [www.nike.com] or through the SEC's EDGAR database [www.sec.gov]. Recompute the current and acid-test ratios for fiscal years ending after May 31, 1997.

Comparative Analysis

A3

Both **NIKE** and **Reebok** design, produce, market, and sell sports footwear and apparel. Key comparative figures ($ millions) for these two organizations follow:

Key figures	NIKE 1997	NIKE 1996	Reebok 1996	Reebok 1995
Net Sales	$9,187	$6,471	$3,479	$3,481
Cost of Sales	5,503	3,907	2,144	2,114

* NIKE figures are from its annual reports for fiscal years ended May 31, 1997 and 1996.
Reebok figures are from its annual reports for fiscal years ended December 31, 1996 and 1995.

Required

1. Compute the dollar amount of gross margin and the gross margin ratio for the two years shown for both companies.
2. Which company earns more in gross margin for each dollar of net sales?
3. Did the gross margin ratios improve or decline for these companies?

Ethics Challenge

P2

Claire Phelps is a student who attends approximately four dances a year at her school. Each dance requires a new dress and accessories that necessitate a financial outlay of $100-$200 per event. Claire's parents inform her that she is "on her own" with respect to financing the dresses. After incurring a major hit to her savings for the first dance in her freshman year, Claire developed a different approach. She buys the dress on credit the week before the dance, wears it to the dance, and returns the dress the next week to the store for a full refund on her charge card.

Required

1. Comment on the ethics exhibited by Claire and possible consequences of her actions.
2. How does the store account for the dresses that Claire returns?

Communicating in Practice

C4, C5, P3

You are the accountant for **Music, Videos, and More,** a retailer that sells goods for home entertainment needs. The owner of the business, Mr. U. Paah, recently reviewed the annual financial statements and sent you an e-mail stating that he is sure you overstated net income. He explains that he makes this claim because, although he has invested a great deal in security, he is sure shoplifting and other forms of inventory shrinkage have still taken place. He does not see any deduction for such loss on the income statement. The store uses a perpetual inventory system.

Required

Prepare a memorandum that responds to the owner's concerns in paper or e-mail format. If the response is to be made via e-mail, you are to assume your instructor is the owner instead of Mr. U. Paah.

The amount of merchandising activity on the Web has grown dramatically. Use a Web search engine (such as Lycos, Yahoo, or Alta Vista) and search for the word *merchandising*. Explore the Web addresses located by the search engine and make a list of at least 10 products that companies or individuals are trying to market and sell using the Web.

Taking It to the Net

C1

World Brands' ledger and supplementary records at the end of the period disclose the following:

Sales	$430,000
Sales returns	18,000
Merchandise inventory (beginning of period)	49,000
Invoice cost of merchandise purchases	180,000
Purchase discounts received	4,500
Sales discounts	6,600
Purchase returns and allowances received	5,500
Cost of transportation-in	11,000
Operating expenses	20,000
Merchandise inventory (end of period)	42,000

Teamwork in Action

C2, C5, A3

Required

1. *Each* member of the team is to assume responsibility for computing *one* of the amounts listed below. You are not to duplicate your teammates' work. Get necessary amounts from teammate. Each member is to explain his or her computation to the team in preparation for reporting to the class.
   a. Net sales
   b. Total cost of merchandise purchases
   c. Cost of goods sold
   d. Gross profit
   e. Net income
2. Check your net income with the instructor. If correct, proceed to (3).
3. Assume a physical inventory disclosed that the actual ending inventory was $38,000. Discuss how this affects previously computed amounts in (1).

Arrange an interview (in person or by phone) with the manager of a retail shop in a mall or in the downtown area of your community. Explain to the manager that you are an accounting student studying merchandising operations and the accounting for sales returns and sales allowances. Ask the manager what the store policy is regarding returns. Also find out if sales allowances are ever negotiated with customers. Inquire whether management ever perceives that customers are abusing return policies and what actions management takes to counter the abuses. Be prepared to discuss your findings in class.

Hitting the Road

C1

Read the article "An Adrenalin Rush at Adidas," in the September 29, 1997, issue of *Business Week*.

***Business Week* Activity**

P4

Required

1. The article identifies **Adidas** as the number two company in the sporting goods market. What companies are numbers one and three respectively?
2. What new strategy is Adidas using to compete more effectively against its number one rival?
3. After reading the article, do you think the new strategy of Adidas will be effective?
4. Consult the notes of the annual report of **NIKE** in Appendix A. Determine the advertising and promotion expenses incurred by NIKE. Compare the advertising expenses of NIKE to those incurred by Adidas.
5. Identify where the advertising expenses are reported in the financial statements of NIKE.

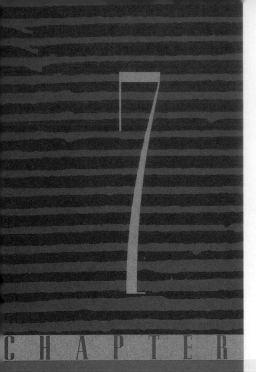

7

CHAPTER

Merchandise Inventories and Cost of Sales

Chapter Outline

Wired in Philly

PHILADELPHIA—Big is not better. Or so says Lenny Russo, the 29-year-old owner of **Wired,** an electronics retailer and service provider. Russo built his business by taking jobs nobody wanted. "Big stores give a hard sell, take your cash, and maybe see you later," says Russo. "Don't get me wrong. They've got a place. It just isn't my place."

What is Russo's place is selling, installing, and servicing home entertainment systems to college students, young families, nightclubs, and other establishments. "I deal with small frys," says Russo. "I give people a great system fitting their needs, and they give me their business." He now has his own store and showroom, and business couldn't be better.

But it wasn't always that way. "The biggest hurdle," bemoans Russo, "was getting the money to get going and to expand." Russo's hurdle was pushing the numbers and getting financial statements together. "The bank wanted to know things like gross margin, turnover, and inventory on hand." Adds Russo, "Til then I thought turnover was something you ate."

The other hurdle Russo faced was measuring inventory. "I started by keeping track of each item sold and recording its cost." But business grew and Russo's system quickly overloaded. He now uses a perpetual system.

Needless to say, Russo has figured a lot of things out in his few years in business. While his tough Philly upbringing shows, he can talk the talk with the best of them. "I can now tell you about turnover, liquidity ratios, and other financial jazz." But, laughs Russo, "don't tell my family!" Somehow, one gets the feeling the Russo family would be proud.

Learning Objectives

Conceptual

C1 Identify the items making up merchandise inventory.

C2 Identify the costs of merchandise inventory.

Analytical

A1 Analyze the effects of inventory methods for both financial and tax reporting.

A2 Analyze the effects of inventory errors on current and future financial statements.

A3 Assess inventory management using both merchandise turnover and days' sales in inventory.

Procedural

P1 Compute inventory in a perpetual system using the methods of specific identification, FIFO, LIFO, and weighted average.

P2 Compute the lower of cost or market amount of inventory.

P3 Apply both the retail inventory and gross profit methods to estimate inventory.

CHAPTER PREVIEW

Activities of merchandising companies involve the purchase and resale of products. We explained accounting for merchandisers in the last chapter and explained how perpetual and periodic inventory systems account for merchandise inventory. In this chapter we extend our study and analysis of inventory by identifying the items making up inventory. We also explain the methods used to assign costs to merchandise inventory *and* cost of goods sold. The assigned costs are not always historical cost.

The principles and methods we describe are used in department stores, grocery stores, and many other merchandising companies that purchase products for resale. These principles and methods affect reported amounts of income, assets, and equity. Understanding these fundamental concepts of inventory accounting increases our ability to analyze and interpret financial statements. As Lenny Russo learned, an understanding of these topics also helps in running one's own business.

Assigning Costs to Inventory

P1 Compute inventory in a perpetual system using the methods of specific identification, FIFO, LIFO, and weighted average.

Accounting for inventory affects both the balance sheet and the income statement. A major goal in accounting for inventory is matching relevant costs against revenues. This is important to properly compute income.[1]

We discussed the *matching principle* in Chapter 4. We use it when accounting for inventory to decide how much of the cost of the goods available for sale is deducted from sales and how much is carried forward as inventory and matched against future sales. Management must make this decision along with several others when accounting for inventory. These decisions include selecting the:

- Costing method (specific identification, FIFO, LIFO, or weighted average)
- Inventory system (perpetual or periodic)
- Items included and their costs
- Use of market or other estimates

Decisions on these factors affect the reported amounts for inventory, cost of goods sold, gross profit, income, current assets, and other accounts. This chapter discusses all of these important issues and their reporting effects.

One of the most important decisions in accounting for inventory is determining the per unit costs assigned to inventory items. When all units are purchased at the same unit cost, this process is simple. But when identical items are purchased at different costs, a question arises as to what amounts are recorded in cost of goods sold when sales occur and what amounts remain in inventory. We must record cost of goods sold and reductions in inventory as sales occur using a perpetual inventory system. A periodic inventory system determines cost of goods sold and inventory amounts at the end of a period (see Appendix 7A). How we assign these costs to inventory and cost of goods sold affects the reported amounts for both systems.

There are four methods commonly used in assigning costs to inventory and cost of goods sold. They are (1) specific identification; (2) first-in, first-out; (3) last-in, first-out; and (4) weighted average. Each method assumes a particular pattern for how costs flow through inventory. Each of the four methods described in this section is acceptable in financial reporting. This is the case whether or not the actual physical flow of goods follows the cost flow assumption.[2] Exhibit 7.1 shows the frequency in use of these methods in practice.

---

[1] FASB, *Accounting Standards—Current Text* (Norwalk, CT, 1995), sec. I78.104. First published as *Accounting Research Bulletin No. 43,* chap. 4, par. 4

[2] Physical flow of goods depends on the type of product and the way it is stored. Perishable goods such as fresh fruit demand that a business attempt to sell them in a first-in, first-out physical flow pattern. Other products such as lanterns or grills can often be sold in a last-in, first-out physical flow pattern. But physical flow and cost flow need not be the same.

We use information from **Trekking,** a sporting goods store, to describe the four methods. Among its many products, Trekking carries one type of mountain bike. Its sales of mountain bikes are directed at biking clubs, and customer purchases are usually in amounts of 10 or more bikes. We use data from Trekking's August 1998 transactions in mountain bikes. Its mountain bike (unit) inventory at the beginning of August and its purchases during August are shown in Exhibit 7.2.

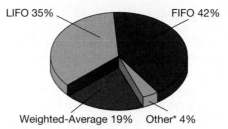

Exhibit 7.1

Frequency in Use of Inventory Methods in Practice

Aug. 1	Beginning inventory	10 units @ $ 91 = $ 910
Aug. 3	Purchases	15 units @ $106 = 1,590
Aug. 17	Purchases	20 units @ $115 = 2,300
Aug. 28	Purchases	10 units @ $119 = 1,190
Total	....	**55 units** $5,990

Exhibit 7.2

Cost of Goods Available for Sale

Trekking ends August with 12 bikes on hand in inventory. This inventory results after Trekking had two large sales of mountain bikes to two different biking clubs in August as shown in Exhibit 7.3:

Aug. 14	Sales	20 units @ $130 = $2,600
Aug. 31	Sales	23 units @ $150 = 3,450
Total	....	**43 units** $6,050

Exhibit 7.3

Retail Sales of Goods

Trekking uses the perpetual inventory system. We explained in the last chapter how use of the perpetual inventory system is increasing due to advances in information and computing technology. Widespread use of electronic scanners and product bar codes supports a perpetual inventory system. For these reasons we discuss Trekking's assigning of costs to inventory in a perpetual system. But in Appendix 7A, we also describe the assigning of costs to inventory using a periodic system. A periodic inventory system computes cost of goods available for sale and allocates it between cost of goods sold and ending inventory at the *end of the period.* By assigning an amount to ending inventory and subtracting it from cost of goods available for sale, we get cost of goods sold.[3]

Trekking's use of a perpetual inventory system means the merchandise inventory account is continually updated to reflect purchases and sales. As described in Chapter 6, the important accounting aspects of a perpetual system are:

- Each purchase of merchandise for resale increases (debit) inventory.
- Each sale of merchandise decreases (credit) inventory and increases (debit) costs of goods sold.
- Necessary costs of merchandise such as transportation-in increase (debit) inventory, and cost reductions such as purchase discounts and purchase returns and allowances decrease (credit) inventory.

Except for any inventory shrinkage, the balance in the merchandise inventory account reflects the amount of merchandise on hand at any time.

---

[3] Similarly, assigning an amount to cost of goods sold also determines the amount of ending inventory.

Specific Identification

When each item in inventory can be directly identified with a specific purchase and its invoice, we can use **specific identification** (also called **specific invoice inventory pricing**) to assign costs. Sales records identify exactly which bikes are sold and when. Trekking's internal documents reveal 6 of the 12 unsold units are from the August 28 purchase and another 6 are from the August 17 purchase. We use this information along with specific identification to assign costs to the goods sold and to ending inventory as shown in Exhibit 7.4.

Exhibit 7.4

Specific Identification Computations

Date	Purchases	Cost of Goods Sold	Inventory Balance
Aug. 1	Beginning balance		10 @ $ 91 = $ 910
Aug. 3	15 @ $106 = $1,590		10 @ $ 91 } = $2,500 15 @ $106
Aug. 14		8 @ $ 91 = $ 728 } = $2,000 12 @ $106 = $1,272	2 @ $ 91 } = $ 500 3 @ $106
Aug. 17	20 @ $115 = $2,300		2 @ $ 91 3 @ $106 } = $2,800 20 @ $115
Aug. 28	10 @ $119 = $1,190		2 @ $ 91 3 @ $106 20 @ $115 } = $3,990 10 @ $119
Aug. 31		2 @ $ 91 = $ 182 3 @ $106 = $ 318 14 @ $115 = $1,610 } = $2,586 4 @ $119 = $ 476	6 @ $115 } = $1,404 6 @ $119

When using specific identification, Trekking's cost of goods sold reported on the income statement is **$4,586,** the sum of $2,000 and $2,586 from the third column of Exhibit 7.4. Trekking's ending inventory reported on the balance sheet is **$1,404,** which is the final inventory balance from the fourth column of Exhibit 7.4. *The assignment of costs to cost of goods sold and inventory using specific identification is the same for both the perpetual and periodic systems.*

First-In, First-Out

The first-in, first-out (FIFO) method of assigning cost to inventory and the goods sold assumes inventory items are sold in the order acquired. When sales occur, costs of the earliest units acquired are charged to cost of goods sold. This leaves the costs from the most recent purchases in inventory. Use of FIFO for Trekking means the costs of mountain bikes are assigned to inventory and goods sold as shown in Exhibit 7.5.

Trekking's cost of goods sold reported on the income statement is **$4,570** ($1,970 + $2,600) and its ending inventory reported on the balance sheet is **$1,420.** *The assignment of costs to cost of goods sold and inventory using FIFO is the same for both the perpetual and periodic systems.*

Last-In, First-Out

The **last-in, first-out (LIFO)** method of assigning cost assumes that the most recent purchases are sold first. Their costs are charged to cost of goods sold, and the costs of the earliest purchases are assigned to inventory. Like the other methods, LIFO is acceptable even when the physical flow of goods does not follow a last-in, first-out pattern.

Date	Purchases	Cost of Goods Sold	Inventory Balance
Aug. 1	Beginning balance		10 @ $ 91 = $ 910
Aug. 3	15 @ $106 = $1,590		10 @ $ 91 15 @ $106 } = $2,500
Aug. 14		10 @ $ 91 = $ 910 10 @ $106 = $1,060 } = $1,970	5 @ $106 = $ 530
Aug. 17	20 @ $115 = $2,300		5 @ $106 20 @ $115 } = $2,830
Aug. 28	10 @ $119 = $1,190		5 @ $106 20 @ $115 10 @ $119 } = $4,020
Aug. 31		5 @ $106 = $ 530 18 @ $115 = $2,070 } = $2,600	2 @ $115 10 @ $119 } = $1,420

Exhibit 7.5

FIFO Computations—Perpetual System

Companies commonly replace the inventory items that they sell. This means the sale of goods causes a company to replace inventory. A good matching of costs with revenues suggests we match the costs of replacements with the sales causing the replacements. While costs for the most recent purchases are not exactly replacement costs, they often are close approximations. One appeal of LIFO is that by assigning costs from the most recent purchases to cost of goods sold, LIFO comes closest to matching replacement costs with revenues (compared to FIFO or weighted average).

Use of LIFO for Trekking means costs of mountain bikes are assigned to inventory and goods sold as shown in Exhibit 7.6.

Date	Purchases	Cost of Goods Sold	Inventory Balance
Aug. 1	Beginning balance		10 @ $ 91 = $ 910
Aug. 3	15 @ $106 = $1,590		10 @ $ 91 15 @ $106 } = $2,500
Aug. 14		15 @ $106 = $1,590 5 @ $ 91 = $ 455 } = $2,045	5 @ $ 91 = $ 455
Aug. 17	20 @ $115 = $2,300		5 @ $ 91 20 @ $115 } = $2,755
Aug. 28	10 @ $119 = $1,190		5 @ $ 91 20 @ $115 10 @ $119 } = $3,945
Aug. 31		10 @ $119 = $1,190 13 @ $115 = $1,495 } = $2,685	5 @ $ 91 7 @ $115 } = $1,260

Exhibit 7.6

LIFO Computations—Perpetual System

Trekking's cost of goods sold reported on the income statement is **$4,730** ($2,045 + $2,685) and its ending inventory reported on the balance sheet is **$1,260.** The assignment of costs to cost of goods sold and inventory using LIFO usually gives different results depending on whether a perpetual or periodic system is used. This is because LIFO under a perpetual system assigns the most recent costs to goods sold at the time of each sale, whereas the periodic system waits to assign costs until the end of a period.

Weighted Average

The **weighted average** (also called **average cost**) method of assigning cost requires computing the average cost per unit of merchandise inventory at the time of each sale. Some systems are set up to compute this average after each purchase. The important point is that we compute weighted average cost at the time of each sale by dividing the cost of goods available for sale by the units on hand. Using weighted average for Trekking means the costs of mountain bikes are assigned to inventory and goods sold as shown in Exhibit 7.7.

Exhibit 7.7

Weighted Average Computations—Perpetual System

Date	Purchases	Cost of Goods Sold	Inventory Balance
Aug. 1	Beginning balance		10 @ $ 91 = $ 910
Aug. 3	15 @ $106 = $1,590		10 @ $ 91 15 @ $106 } = $2,500 (or $100 per unit)[a]
Aug. 14		20 @ $100 = **$2,000**	5 @ $100 = $ 500 (or $100 per unit)[b]
Aug. 17	20 @ $115 = $2,300		5 @ $100 20 @ $115 } = $2,800 (or $112 per unit)[c]
Aug. 28	10 @ $119 = $1,190		5 @ $100 20 @ $115 10 @ $119 } = $3,990 (or $114 per unit)[d]
Aug. 31		23 @ $114 = **$2,622**	12 @ $114 = **$1,368** (or $114 per unit)[e]

[a] $100 per unit = [$2,500 inventory balance ÷ 25 units in inventory].
[b] $100 per unit = [$ 500 inventory balance ÷ 5 units in inventory].
[c] $112 per unit = [$2,800 inventory balance ÷ 25 units in inventory].
[d] $114 per unit = [$3,990 inventory balance ÷ 35 units in inventory].
[e] $114 per unit = [$1,368 inventory balance ÷ 12 units in inventory].

Trekking's cost of goods sold reported on the income statement is **$4,622** ($2,000 + $2,622) and its ending inventory reported on the balance sheet is **$1,368.** The assignment of costs to cost of goods sold and inventory using weighted average usually gives different results depending on whether a perpetual or periodic system is used. This is because weighted average under a perpetual system recomputes the per unit cost at the time of each sale, whereas under the periodic system the per unit cost is only computed at the end of a period.

Inventory Costing and Technology

A perpetual inventory system can be kept in either electronic or manual form. Using a manual form can make a perpetual inventory system too costly for businesses, especially those with many purchases and sales or many units in inventory. But advances in information and computing technology have greatly reduced the cost of a perpetual inventory system. Many companies are now asking whether they can afford *not* to have a perpetual inventory system because timely access to information is being used strategically by companies to gain a competitive advantage. Scanned sales data, for instance, can reveal crucial information on buying patterns. It can also help companies target promotional and advertising activities. These and other applications have greatly increased the use of the perpetual inventory system.

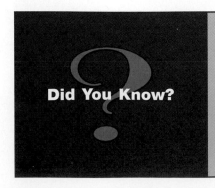

Did You Know?

Whirlwind on the Web
From its roots in a college dorm room in 1984, **Dell** now sells several millions of dollars' worth of computers each week from its Web site. "The Internet," says Michael S. Dell, "is the ultimate direct model." Direct buyers now account for a third of the total PC business. The speed of Web technology has allowed Dell to slash inventories so it can underprice rivals by 10% to 15%. Dell's operating cycle is less than 24 hours and its days' sales in inventory is 13 days. "Speed is everything in this business," adds Mr. Dell. With Dell racing past rivals like Sunday drivers on the Information Highway, there may be a new pace for merchandisers in the Age of the Internet: Dell-ocity. [Source: *Business Week,* April 4, 1997.]

Subsidiary Inventory Records

The Merchandise Inventory account is a controlling account for the subsidiary Merchandise Inventory Ledger. This subsidiary ledger contains a separate record for each product, and it can be in electronic or paper form. A typical ledger is shown in Exhibit 7.8. This record shows both the units and costs for each purchase and sale, along with the balance after each purchase and sale. The record also gives the item, its catalog number, and its location (at the top). The subsidiary Merchandise Inventory Ledger is updated after each purchase and sale transaction. This ledger reveals by its computations that a FIFO cost flow assumption is being used for sports bags.

Exhibit 7.8

Subsidiary Inventory Record

Item	Leather Sports Bags						Location code W18C2		
Catalog No.	LSB-117					Units: Maximum 25	Minimum 5		

	Purchases			Cost of Goods Sold			Inventory Balance		
Date	Units	Cost	Total	Units	Cost	Total	Units	Cost	Total
Aug. 1							10	$100	$1,000
Aug. 12				4	$100	$ 400	6	100	600
Aug. 18	20	$110	$2,200				6	100 }	2,800
							20	110 }	
Aug. 30				6	100	600			
				2	110	220	18	110	1,980
Totals	20		$2,220	12		$ 1,220			

Subsidiary inventory records assist managers in planning and controlling inventory. Exhibit 7.8 reveals a policy of maintaining no more than 25 sports bags to avoid overinvestment in this inventory, and no less than 5 sports bags on hand to avoid out-of-stock occurrences. These records also permit companies to compare a physical count of items on hand to the record. Differences are investigated to identify their cause.

This section identifies the items and costs making up merchandise inventory. This identification is important given the major impact of inventory in financial statements. We also describe the importance and methods of taking a physical count of inventory.

Inventory Items and Costs

C1 Identify the items making up merchandise inventory.

Items in Merchandise Inventory

Merchandise inventory includes all goods owned by a company and held for sale. This rule holds regardless of where goods are located at the time inventory is counted. Most inventory items present no problem when applying this rule. We must simply see that all items are counted and computations are correct. But certain items require special attention. These include goods in transit, goods on consignment, and goods that are damaged or obsolete.

Goods in Transit

Do we include in a purchaser's inventory the goods in transit from a supplier? Our answer depends on whether the rights and risks of ownership have passed from the supplier to the purchaser. If ownership has passed to the purchaser, they are included in the purchaser's inventory. We explained in Chapter 6 how we determine this by looking at the shipping terms—*FOB destination* or FOB *shipping point.* If the purchaser is responsible for paying freight charges, then ownership passes when goods are loaded on the means of transportation. If the supplier is to pay freight charges, ownership passes when goods arrive at their destination.

Goods on Consignment

Goods on consignment are goods shipped by their owner, called the **consignor,** to another party called the **consignee.** A consignee is to sell goods for the owner. Consigned goods are owned by the consignor and are reported in the consignor's inventory. **Score Board,** for instance, pays sports celebrities such as Steve Young and Ken Griffey, Jr., to sign memorabilia. These autographed items (footballs, baseballs, jerseys, photos, etc.) are offered to shopping networks on consignment as well as sold through catalogs and dealers.

Goods Damaged or Obsolete

Damaged goods and obsolete (or deteriorated) goods are not counted in inventory if they are unsalable. If these goods are salable at a reduced price, they are included in inventory at a conservative estimate of their **net realizable value.** Net realizable value is sales price minus the cost of making the sale. The period when damage or obsolescence (or deterioration) occurs is the period when the loss in value is reported.

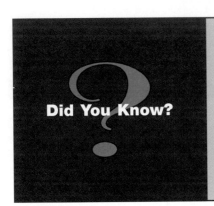

Did You Know?

Inventory Online

Warehouse inventory clerks can now check in hundreds of boxes by quickly scanning bar codes on merchandise. Thanks to **Motorola,** a new wireless portable computer with a two-way radio allows clerks to send and receive data instantly. It gives managers immediate access to up to date information on inventory. Also, the portable computer can withstand dust and harsh weather, and can be dropped on concrete. [Source: *Business Week,* June 6, 1996.]

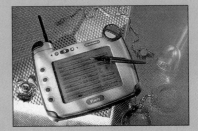

Costs of Merchandise Inventory

C2 Identify the costs of merchandise inventory.

Costs included in merchandise inventory are those expenditures necessary, directly or indirectly, to bring an item to a salable condition and location.[4] This means the cost of an inventory item includes its invoice price minus any discount, plus any added or incidental costs necessary to put it in a place and condition for sale. Added or incidental costs can include import duties, transportation-in, storage, insurance, and costs incurred in an aging process (for example, aging of wine and cheese).

Accounting principles imply that incidental costs are assigned to every unit purchased. This is so all inventory costs are properly matched against revenue in the period when inventory is sold. The *materiality principle* or the *cost-to-benefit constraint* is used by some companies to avoid assigning incidental costs of acquiring merchandise to inventory. These companies argue either that incidental costs are immaterial or that the effort in assigning these costs to inventory outweighs the benefits. Such companies price inventory using invoice prices only. When this is done, the incidental costs are allocated to cost of goods sold in the period when they are incurred.

[4] FASB, *Accounting Standards—Current Text* (Norwalk, CT, 1995), sec. I78.402. First published as *Accounting Research Bulletin No. 43,* ch. 4, par. 5.

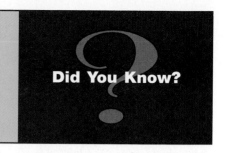

Physical Count of Merchandise Inventory

The Inventory account under a perpetual system is always up to date. Yet events can occur where the Inventory account balance is different from inventory on hand. Such events include theft, loss, damage, and errors. This means nearly all companies take a *physical count of inventory* at least once each year, sometimes called *taking an inventory.* This often occurs at the end of a fiscal year or when inventory amounts are low. This physical count is used to adjust the Inventory account balance to the actual inventory on hand. There is also need for a physical count of inventory under a periodic system (see Appendix 7A).

We determine a dollar amount for the physical count of inventory on hand at the end of a period by: (1) counting the units of each product on hand, (2) multiplying the count for each product by its cost per unit, and (3) adding the costs for all products. When taking a count, items are less likely to be counted more than once or omitted if we use prenumbered inventory tickets. We show a typical inventory ticket in Exhibit 7.9.

> INVENTORY TICKET NO. 1001
>
> Quantity
> counted _____   Purchase date _____
>
> Sales Price $ _____   Cost price $ _____
>
> Counted by _____   Checked by _____

Exhibit 7.9

Inventory Ticket

The process of a physical count is fairly standard. Before beginning a physical count of inventory, we prepare at least one inventory ticket for each product on hand. These tickets are issued to employees doing the count. An employee will count the quantity of a product and obtain information on its purchase date, selling price, and cost. This information is sometimes included with the products but must often be obtained from accounting records or invoices. Once the necessary information is collected, the employee records it on the inventory ticket and signs the form. The inventory ticket is then attached to the counted inventory. Another employee often recounts and rechecks information on the ticket, signs the ticket, and returns it to the manager. To ensure no ticket is lost or missed, internal control procedures verify that all prenumbered tickets are returned. The unit and cost data on inventory tickets are aggregated by multiplying the number of units for each product by its unit cost. This gives us the dollar amount for each product in inventory. The sum total of all products is the dollar amount reported for inventory on the balance sheet.

Flash back

1. What accounting principle most governs allocation of cost of goods available for sale between ending inventory and cost of goods sold?

2. If **NIKE** sells goods to **Target** with terms FOB shipping point, does NIKE or Target report these goods in its inventory while they are in transit?

3. An art gallery purchases a painting for $11,400 on terms FOB shipping point. Additional costs in obtaining and offering the artwork for sale include $130 for transportation-in, $150 for import duties, $100 for insurance during shipment, $180 for advertising, $400 for framing, and $800 for sales salaries. For computing inventory, what cost is assigned to the painting?

Answers—p. 296

Inventory Analysis and Effects

A1 Analyze the effects of inventory methods for both financial and tax reporting.

Exhibit 7.10

Income Statement Effects of Inventory Costing Methods

This section analyzes and compares the effects of using alternative inventory costing methods. We also analyze the tax effects of inventory methods, examine managers' preferences for an inventory method, and look at the effects of inventory errors.

Financial Reporting

When purchase prices don't change, the choice of an inventory costing method is unimportant. All methods assign the same cost amounts when prices don't change. But when purchase prices are rising or falling, the methods are likely to assign different cost amounts. We show these differences in Exhibit 7.10 using Trekking's segment income statement for its mountain bike operations.

TREKKING COMPANY Segment Income Statement—Mountain Bikes Month Ending August 31				
	Specific Identification	FIFO	LIFO	Weighted Average
Sales	$6,050	$6,050	$6,050	$6,050
Cost of goods sold	4,586	4,570	4,730	4,622
Gross profit	$1,464	$1,480	$1,320	$1,428
Operating expenses	450	450	450	450
Income before taxes	$1,014	$1,030	$ 870	$ 978
Income tax expense (30%)	304	309	261	293
Net income	$ 710	$ 721	$ 609	$ 685

The different inventory costing methods show different results for net income. Because Trekking's purchase prices rose in August, FIFO assigned the least amount to cost of goods sold. This led to the highest gross profit and the highest net income. LIFO assigned the highest amount to cost of goods sold. This yields the lowest gross profit and the lowest net income. As expected, amounts from using the weighted average method fell between FIFO and LIFO.[5] The amounts from using specific identification depend on what units are actually sold.

All four inventory costing methods are acceptable in practice. Each method offers certain advantages. One advantage of specific identification is it exactly matches costs and revenues. This is important when each unit has unique features affecting the cost of that unit. An advantage of weighted average is that it tends to smooth out price changes. The advantage of FIFO is it assigns an amount to inventory on the balance sheet that closely approximates current replacement cost. The advantage of LIFO is it assigns the most recent costs incurred to cost of goods sold, and likely better matches current costs with revenues on the income statement.

The choice of an inventory costing method often dramatically impacts amounts on financial statements. **Mobil,** for instance, recently changed its inventory method and reported this change in a news release as follows:

Fairfax, VA—**Mobil Corporation** announced today that it is making a change in its method . . . for crude oil and product inventories. Accordingly, it will reduce . . . year-to-date, net income by a $680 million . . . This inventory accounting change was adopted by Mobil at its board meeting today.

---

[5] The weighted average amount can be outside the FIFO or LIFO amounts if prices do not steadily increase or decrease but exhibit a cyclical pattern.

Companies disclose the inventory method used in their financial statements or notes. This is required by the *full-disclosure principle.*[6]

It is important for us to know and understand inventory costing in our analysis of financial statements. Some companies' financial statements help our analysis by reporting what the difference would be if another costing method were used. **Kmart,** for instance, reports in its 1997 annual report that:

> Inventories valued on LIFO were $457, $440 and $485 lower than amounts that would have been reported using the first-in, first-out (FIFO) method at year end 1997, 1996 and 1995, respectively.

Financial Planner

You are the financial planner for several clients. Your clients periodically request your advice on analysis of financial statements of companies where they have investments. One of these clients asks you if the merchandise inventory account of a company using FIFO needs any "adjustments" in light of recent inflation. What is your advice? Does your advice depend on changes in the costs of these inventories for the company?

Answer—p. 296

Tax Reporting

Trekking's segment income statement in Exhibit 7.10 reflects the company's formation as a corporation. Its income statement includes income tax expense (at a rate of about 30%). Because inventory costs affect net income, they have potential tax effects. Trekking gains a tax advantage by using LIFO. This advantage occurs because LIFO assigns the largest dollar amounts to cost of goods sold when purchase prices are increasing. Trekking's recent purchases are both more costly and assigned to cost of goods sold. This means less income is reported when LIFO is used and purchase prices are rising. This in turn results in the smallest income tax expense.

The Internal Revenue Service (IRS) identifies several methods that are acceptable for inventory costing in reporting taxable income. It is important to know that companies can and often do use different costing methods for financial reporting and tax reporting. *The only exception is when LIFO is used for tax purposes; in this case the IRS requires it be used in financial statements.* Since costs tend to rise, LIFO usually gives a lower taxable income and a tax advantage. Many companies use LIFO for this reason. Yet managers often have incentives to report greater net income for reasons such as bonus plans, job security, and reputation. FIFO is sometimes preferred in these cases due to its tendency to report a higher income when prices are rising.

Flash back

4. Describe one advantage for each inventory costing method: specific identification, FIFO, LIFO, and weighted average.

5. When costs and prices are rising, does LIFO or FIFO report higher net income?

6. When costs and prices are rising, what effect does LIFO have on a balance sheet compared to FIFO?

Answers—p. 296–297

---

[6] FASB, *Accounting Standards—Current Text* (Norwalk, CT, 1995), sec. A10.105, 106. First published as *APB Opinion No. 22,* pars. 12, 13.

Consistency in Reporting

Because inventory costing methods can materially affect amounts on financial statements, some managers might be inclined to choose a method most consistent with their hoped-for results each period. These managers' objective might be to pick the method giving the most favorable financial statement amounts. Managers might also be inclined to pick the method giving them the highest bonus since many management bonus plans are based on net income. If managers were allowed to pick the method each period, it would be more difficult for users of financial statements to compare a company's financial statements from one period to the next. If income increased, for instance, a user would need to decide whether it resulted from successful operations or from the accounting method change. The consistency principle is used to avoid this problem.

The **consistency principle** requires a company to use the same accounting methods period after period so the financial statements are comparable across periods.[7] The consistency principle applies to all accounting methods. Whenever a company must choose between alternative methods, consistency requires that the company continue to use the selected method period after period. Users of financial statements can then assume a company uses the same methods across years and they can make comparisons of a company's statements across periods.

The consistency principle *doesn't* require a company to use one method exclusively. It can use different methods to value different categories of inventory. **Harley-Davidson,** for instance, includes the following note in its 1997 annual report:

> Inventories located in the United States are valued using the last-in, first-out (LIFO) method. Other inventories . . . are valued at the lower of cost or market using the first-in, first-out (FIFO) method.

The consistency principle doesn't mean a company can never change from one accounting method to another. Instead it means a company must argue that the method it is changing to will improve its financial reporting. Under this circumstance, a change is acceptable. Yet when such a change is made, the *full-disclosure principle* requires that the notes to the statements report the type of change, its justification, and its effect on net income.[8]

Judgment and Ethics

Inventory Manager
You are the inventory manager for a merchandiser. Your compensation includes a bonus plan based on the amount of gross profit reported in the financial statements. Your superior comes to you and asks your opinion in changing the inventory costing method from FIFO to LIFO. Since costs have been rising and are expected to continue to rise, your superior predicts the company will save thousands of dollars by switching to LIFO for tax reporting. This is because LIFO matches higher current costs against sales, thereby lowering gross profit and net income. You realize this proposed change will likely reduce your bonus. What do you recommend?

Answer—p. 296

---

[7] FASB, *Statement of Financial Accounting Concepts No. 2,* "Qualitative Characteristics of Accounting Information" (Norwalk, CT, 1980), par. 120.

[8] FASB, *Accounting Standards—Current Text* (Norwalk, CT, 1995), sec. A06.113. First published as *APB Opinion No. 20,* par. 17.

Errors in Reporting Inventory

Companies must take care in both computing and taking a physical count of inventory. If inventory is reported in error, it causes misstatements in cost of goods sold, gross profit, net income, current assets, and equity. It also means misstatements will exist in the next period's statements. This is because ending inventory of one period is the beginning inventory of the next. An error carried forward causes misstatements in the next period's cost of goods sold, gross profit, and net income. Misstatements can reduce the usefulness of financial statements.

A2 Analyze the effects of inventory errors on current and future financial statements.

Income Statement Effects

The income statement effects of an inventory error are evident by looking at the components of cost of goods sold as shown in Exhibit 7.11. The effect of an inventory error on cost of goods sold is determined by computing it with the incorrect component amount and comparing it to cost of goods sold when using the correct component amount.

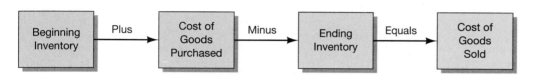

Exhibit 7.11

Cost of Goods Sold Components

We can see, for example, that understating ending inventory will overstate cost of goods sold. An overstatement in cost of goods sold yields an understatement in net income. We can do the same analysis with overstating ending inventory and for an error in beginning inventory. Exhibit 7.12 shows the effects of inventory errors on the current period's income statement amounts.

Inventory Error	Cost of Goods Sold	Net Income
Understate ending inventory	Overstated	Understated
Understate beginning inventory	Understated	Overstated
Overstate ending inventory	Understated	Overstated
Overstate beginning inventory	Overstated	Understated

Exhibit 7.12

Effects of Inventory Errors on This Period's Income Statement

Notice that inventory errors yield opposite effects in cost of goods sold and net income. Inventory errors also carry over to the next period, yielding a reverse effect.

To show these effects, we look at an inventory error for a company with $100,000 in sales for years 1998, 1999, and 2000. If this company maintains a steady $20,000 inventory level during this period and makes $60,000 in purchases in each of these years, then its cost of goods sold is $60,000 and its gross profit is $40,000 each year. But what if this company errs in computing its 1998 ending inventory, and reports $16,000 instead of the correct amount of $20,000? The effects of this error are shown in Exhibit 7.13.

The $4,000 understatement of the 1998 ending inventory causes a $4,000 overstatement in 1998 cost of goods sold and a $4,000 understatement in both 1998 gross profit and 1998 net income. Because 1998 ending inventory becomes the 1999 beginning inventory, this error also causes an understatement in 1999 cost of goods sold and a $4,000 overstatement in both 1999 gross profit and 1999 net income. An inventory error does not affect the third period, year 2000.

If 1998 ending inventory had been overstated, it would have yielded opposite results. In this case the 1998 net income would have been overstated and the 1999 income understated. Because an inventory error causes an offsetting error in the next period, it is

Exhibit 7.13

Effects of Inventory Errors on 3 Periods' Income Statements

| | | Income Statements | |
	1998	1999	2000
Sales	$100,000	$100,000	$100,000
Cost of goods sold:			
Beginning inventory	$20,000	$16,000*	$20,000
Cost of goods purchased .	60,000	60,000	60,000
Goods available for sale . .	$80,000	$76,000	$80,000
Ending inventory	16,000*	20,000	20,000
Cost of goods sold	64,000	56,000	60,000
Gross profit	$ 36,000	$ 44,000	$ 40,000
Operating expenses	10,000	10,000	10,000
Net income	$ 26,000	$ 34,000	$ 30,000

*Correct amount is $20,000.

sometimes said to be *self-correcting*. But don't think this makes inventory errors less serious. Managers, lenders, owners, and other users make important decisions on changes in net income and cost of goods sold. Inventory errors must be avoided.

Balance Sheet Effects

Balance sheet effects of an inventory error are evident by looking at the components of the accounting equation in Exhibit 7.14.

Exhibit 7.14

Accounting Equation

$$\textbf{Assets = Liabilities + Equity}$$

We can see, for example, that understating ending inventory will understate both current and total assets. An understatement in ending inventory also yields an understatement in equity because of the understatement in net income. We can do the same analysis with overstating ending inventory. Exhibit 7.15 shows the effects of inventory errors on the current period's balance sheet amounts.

Exhibit 7.15

Effects of Inventory Errors on This Period's Balance Sheet

Inventory Error	Assets	Equity
Understate ending inventory	Understated	Understated
Overstate ending inventory	Overstated	Overstated

Errors in beginning inventory do not yield misstatements in the balance sheet, but they do affect the income statement.

Flash *back*

7. A company takes a physical count of inventory at the end of 1999 and finds ending inventory is overstated by $10,000. Does this error cause cost of goods sold to be overstated or understated in 1999? In year 2000? By how much?

Answer—p. 297

This section describes other methods to value inventory. Knowledge of these methods is important for understanding and analyzing financial statements.

Other Inventory Valuations

Lower of Cost or Market

We explained how costs are assigned to ending inventory and cost of goods sold using one of four costing methods (FIFO, LIFO, weighted average, or specific identification). Yet the cost of inventory is not necessarily the amount always reported on a balance sheet. *Accounting principles require that inventory be reported at the market value of replacing inventory when market is lower than cost.* Merchandise inventory is then said to be reported on the balance sheet at the **lower of cost or market (LCM).**

P2 Compute the lower of cost or market amount of inventory.

Computing the Lower of Cost or Market

In applying LCM, *market* is defined as the current market value (cost) of replacing inventory. It is the current cost of purchasing the same inventory items in the usual manner.[9] It is also important to know that market is *not* defined as the sales price. A decline in market cost reflects a loss of value in inventory. This is because the recorded cost of inventory is higher than the current market cost. When this occurs, a loss is recognized. This is done by recognizing the decline in merchandise inventory from recorded cost to market cost at the end of the period.

LCM is applied in one of three ways: (1) separately to each individual item, (2) to major categories of items, and (3) to the whole of inventory. The less similar the items are that make up inventory, the more likely it is that companies apply LCM to individual items. Advances in technology further encourage the individual item application.

We show how LCM is applied to the ending inventory of a motorsports retailer. Inventory data for this retailer along with LCM computations are shown in Exhibit 7.16.

Inventory Items	Units on Hand	Per Unit		Total Cost	Total Market	LCM applied to		
		Cost	Market			Items	Categories	Whole
Cycles:								
Roadster	20	$8,000	$7,000	$160,000	$140,000	$140,000		
Sprint	10	5,000	6,000	50,000	60,000	50,000		
Category subtotal				210,000	200,000		200,000	
Off-Road:								
Trax-4	8	5,000	6,500	40,000	52,000	40,000		
Blaz'm	5	9,000	7,000	45,000	35,000	35,000		
Category subtotal				85,000	87,000		85,000	
Total				$295,000	$287,000	$265,000	$285,000	$287,000

Exhibit 7.16

Lower of Cost or Market Computations

When LCM is applied to the *whole* of inventory, the market cost is $287,000. Since this market cost is $8,000 lower than the $295,000 recorded cost, it is the amount reported for inventory on the balance sheet. When LCM is applied to individual *items* of inventory, the market cost is $265,000. Since market is again less than the $295,000 recorded cost, it is the amount reported for inventory. When LCM is applied to the major *categories* of inventory, the market is $285,000. Any one of these three applications of LCM is acceptable. **Best Buy** reports that its:

Merchandise inventories are recorded at the lower of average cost or market.

---

[9] Special exceptions to the definition of market as replacement cost do exist but these are unusual.

The *direct method* is a common way of recording inventory at market. The *direct method* substitutes market value for cost in the inventory account. Using LCM applied on the whole of inventory from Exhibit 7.16 we make the following entry to do this: Cost of Goods Sold Dr. $8,000; Merchandise Inventory Cr. $8,000. The Merchandise Inventory account balance is now $287,000, computed as $295,000 minus $8,000.

Conservatism Principle

We explained how accounting rules require recording inventory down to market when market is less than cost. But inventory usually can't be written up to market when market exceeds cost. If recording inventory down to market is acceptable, why can't we record inventory up to market? One reason is a concern that the gain from a market increase isn't realized until a sales transaction verifies the gain. But this problem also applies to when market is less than cost, and it doesn't stop us from recording it down. The primary reason is the conservatism principle.

The **conservatism principle** says when more than one estimate of amounts to be received or paid in the future are about equally likely, then the less optimistic amount should be used.[10] This principle guides accounting professionals in uncertain situations where amounts must be estimated. LCM is often justified with reference to conservatism. Because the value of inventory is uncertain, recording inventory down when its market value falls is the less optimistic estimate of the amount of inventory.

Flash *back*

8. A company's ending inventory includes the following items:

Product	Units on Hand	Unit Cost	Unit Market Value
A	20	$ 6	$ 5
B	40	9	8
C	10	12	15

Use LCM applied separately to individual items to compute the reported amount for inventory.

Answer—p. 297

P3 Apply both the retail inventory and gross profit methods to estimate inventory.

Retail Inventory Method

Many companies prepare financial statements on a quarterly or monthly basis. Monthly or quarterly statements are called **interim statements** because they are prepared between the traditional annual statements. The cost of goods sold information needed to prepare interim statements is readily available if a perpetual inventory system is used. But a periodic system requires a physical inventory to determine cost of goods sold. To avoid the time-consuming and expensive process of taking a physical inventory each month or quarter, some companies use the **retail inventory method** to estimate cost of goods sold and ending inventory. Some companies even use the retail inventory method to prepare the annual statements. **Home Depot,** for instance, reports in its 1997 annual report that:

> MERCHANDISE INVENTORIES—Inventories are stated at the lower of cost (first-in, first-out) or market, as determined by the retail inventory method.

But all companies should take a physical inventory at least once each year to identify any errors or shortages.

---

[10] FASB, *Statement of Financial Accounting Concepts No. 2* (Norwalk, CT, 1980) par. 95.

Computing the Retail Inventory Estimate

When the retail inventory method is used to estimate inventory, we need to know the amount of inventory a company had at the beginning of the period in both *cost* and *retail* amounts. We already explained the cost of inventory. The retail amount of inventory refers to its dollar amount measured using selling prices of inventory items. We also need the net amount of goods purchased (minus returns, allowances, and discounts) during the period, both at cost and at retail. The amount of net sales at retail is also needed.

A three-step process is used to estimate ending inventory after we compute the amount of goods available for sale during the period both at cost and at retail. This process is shown in Exhibit 7.17.

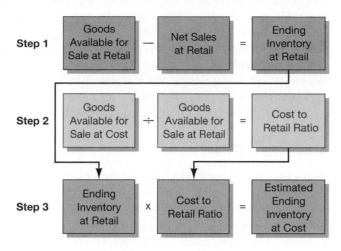

Exhibit 7.17

Inventory Estimation Using Retail Inventory Method

The reasoning behind the retail inventory method is if we can get a good estimate of the cost to retail ratio, then we can apply (multiply) this ratio by ending inventory at retail to estimate ending inventory at cost. We show in Exhibit 7.18 how these steps are applied to estimate ending inventory.

	At Cost	At Retail
Goods available for sale:		
Beginning inventory	$20,500	$ 34,500
Cost of goods purchased	39,500	65,500
Goods available for sale	$60,000	$100,000
Step 1: Deduct net sales at retail		70,000
Ending inventory at retail		$ 30,000
Step 2: Cost to retail ratio: ($60,000 ÷ $100,000) = 60%		
Step 3: Estimated ending inventory at cost ($30,000 × 60%)	$18,000	

Exhibit 7.18

Computing Ending Inventory Using the Retail Inventory Method

Let's recap the steps in Exhibits 7.17 and 7.18 to make certain we understand them. First, there are $100,000 of goods (at retail selling prices) available for sale this period. We see that $70,000 of these goods are sold, leaving $30,000 (retail value) of unsold merchandise in ending inventory. Second, the cost of these goods is 60% of their $100,000 retail value. Third, since cost for this store is 60% of retail, the estimated cost of ending inventory is $18,000.

Estimating Physical Inventory at Cost

Items for sale by retailers usually carry price tags listing selling prices. So when a retailer takes a physical inventory, it commonly totals inventory using selling prices of items on hand. It then reduces the dollar total of this inventory to a cost basis by applying the cost to retail ratio. This is done because selling prices are readily available and by using the cost to retail ratio it eliminates the need to look up invoice prices of items on hand.

To illustrate, assume the company in Exhibit 7.18 estimates its inventory by the retail method and takes a physical inventory using selling prices. If the retail value of this physical inventory is $29,600, then we can compute the cost of this inventory by applying its cost to retail ratio as follows: **$29,600 × 60% = $17,760.** The $17,760 cost figure for ending physical inventory is an acceptable number for annual financial statements. It is also acceptable to the IRS for tax reporting.

Estimating Inventory Shortage at Cost

The inventory estimate in Exhibit 7.18 is an estimate of the amount of goods on hand (at cost). Since it is computed by deducting sales from goods available for sale (at retail), it does not reveal any shrinkage due to breakage, loss, or theft. But we can estimate the amount of shrinkage by comparing the inventory computed in Exhibit 7.18 with the amount from taking a physical inventory. In Exhibit 7.18, for example, we estimated ending inventory at retail as $30,000. But a physical inventory revealed only $29,600 of inventory on hand (at retail). The company has an inventory shortage (at retail) of $400, computed as $30,000 − $29,600. The inventory shortage (at cost) is $240, computed as $400 × 60%.

Gross Profit Method

The **gross profit method** estimates the cost of ending inventory by applying the gross profit ratio to net sales (at retail). A need for this type of estimate can arise when inventory is destroyed, lost, or stolen. These cases need an estimate of inventory so a company can file a claim with its insurer. Users also apply this method to see if inventory amounts from a physical count are reasonable. The gross profit method is useful in these cases. This method uses the historical relation between cost of goods sold and net sales to estimate the proportion of cost of goods sold making up current sales. This cost of goods sold estimate is then subtracted from cost of goods available for sale to give us an estimate of ending inventory at cost. These two steps are shown in Exhibit 7.19.

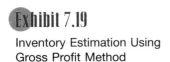

Exhibit 7.19

Inventory Estimation Using
Gross Profit Method

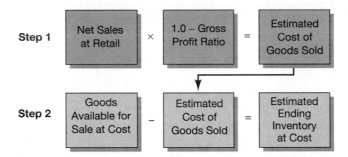

We need certain accounting data to use the gross profit method. This includes the gross profit ratio, beginning inventory (at cost), the net cost of goods purchased, and net sales (at retail). To illustrate, assume a company's inventory is destroyed by fire in March 1999. This company's normal gross profit ratio is 30% of net sales. When the fire occurs, the company's accounts show the following balances:

Sales	$31,500
Sales returns	1,500
Inventory, January 1, 1999	12,000
Net cost of goods purchased	20,500

We can use the gross profit method to estimate this company's inventory loss. We first need to recognize that whatever portion of each dollar of net sales is gross profit, the remaining portion is cost of goods sold. If this company's gross profit ratio is 30%, then 30% of each net sales dollar is gross profit and 70% is cost of goods sold. We show in Exhibit 7.20 how this 70% is used to estimate lost inventory.

Goods available for sale:	
Inventory, January 1, 1999	$12,000
Net cost of goods purchased	20,500
Goods available for sale	32,500
Less estimated cost of goods sold:	
Sales $31,500	
Less sales returns . . . . (1,500)	
Net sales $30,000	
Step 1: Estimated cost of goods sold ($30,000 × 70%)	(21,000)
Step 2: Estimated March inventory loss	$11,500

Exhibit 7.20

Computing Inventory using the Gross Profit Method

To help understand Exhibit 7.20, think of subtracting ending inventory from goods available for sale to get the cost of goods sold. In Exhibit 7.20 we estimate ending inventory by subtracting cost of goods sold from the goods available for sale.

Merchandise Turnover and Days' Sales in Inventory

This section describes how we use information about inventory to assess a company's short-term liquidity (ability to pay) and its management of inventory. Two measures useful for these assessments are presented.

A3 Assess inventory management using both merchandise turnover and days' sales in inventory.

Merchandise Turnover

We described in prior chapters two important ratios useful in evaluating a company's short-term liquidity: current ratio and acid-test ratio. A merchandiser's ability to pay its short-term obligations also depends on how quickly it sells its merchandise inventory. **Merchandise turnover,** also called *inventory turnover*, is one ratio used to evaluate this and is computed as shown in Exhibit 7.21.

$$\text{Merchandise turnover} = \frac{\text{Cost of goods sold}}{\text{Average merchandise inventory}}$$

Exhibit 7.21

Merchandise Turnover

This ratio tells us how many *times* a company turns over its inventory during a period. Average merchandise inventory is usually computed by adding beginning and ending inventory amounts and dividing the total by two. If a company's sales vary within the year, it is often better to take an average of inventory amounts at the end of each quarter or month.

Users apply merchandise turnover to help analyze short-term liquidity. It is also used to assess whether management is doing a good job controlling the amount of inventory on hand. A ratio that is low compared to competitors' ratios suggests inefficient use of assets. The company may be holding more merchandise than is needed to support its sales volume. Similarly, a ratio that is high compared to those of competitors suggests the amount of inventory is too low. This can mean lost sales because customers must back order merchandise. There is no simple rule with merchandise turnover except to say *a high ratio is preferable provided inventory is adequate to meet demand.*

We know how an inventory costing method such as FIFO, LIFO, or weighted average affects reported amounts of inventory and cost of goods sold. The inventory costing method also affects computation of merchandise turnover. To compare merchandise turnover ratios across companies that use different costing methods can be misleading.

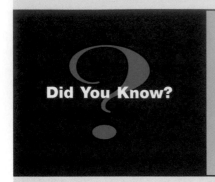

Did You Know?

Pentagon Takes Accounting
The Pentagon is applying accounting skills to shrink inventories and speed deliveries. Inventories in inflation-adjusted dollars dropped from $104 billion in 1990 to $76 billion in 1994 and are predicted to plunge to $55 billion by 2001. Delivery time has been slashed from 25 days to 5 days and the Pentagon now offers a 24-hour emergency service. Delivery from factory to foxhole is speeded up by using bar codes, laser cards, radio tags, and accounting databases to track supplies. "We'll have piles of information instead of piles of stock," says Colonel M.D. Russ. Inventory management is the key. [Source: *Business Week,* December 11, 1995.]

Days' Sales in Inventory

To better interpret merchandise turnover, many users look to measure the adequacy of inventory in meeting sales demand. **Days' sales in inventory,** also called *days' stock on hand,* is a ratio that tells us how much inventory we have on hand in terms of days' sales. It can also be interpreted as the number of days we can sell from inventory if no new items are purchased. This ratio is often viewed as a measure of the buffer against out of stock inventory and is useful in evaluating liquidity of inventory. Days' sales in inventory is computed as shown in Exhibit 7.22.

Exhibit 7.22

Days' Sales in Inventory

$$\text{Days' sales in inventory} = \frac{\text{Ending inventory}}{\text{Cost of goods sold}} \times 365$$

The focus of days' sales in inventory is on ending inventory. Days' sales in inventory estimates how many days it will take to convert inventory on hand at the end of the period into accounts receivable or cash. Notice the different focus of days' sales in inventory and merchandise turnover. Days' sales in inventory focuses on *ending* inventory whereas merchandise turnover focuses on *average* inventory.

Analysis of Inventory Management

Inventory management is a major emphasis of most merchandisers. Merchandisers must both plan and control inventory purchases and sales. **Toys "R" Us** is one of those merchandisers. Its merchandise inventory at February 1, 1997, exceeded $2.2 billion. Toys "R" Us' inventory constituted 70% of it current assets and nearly 30% of its total assets. We apply the analysis tools in this section to Toys "R" Us using its February 1, 1997, financial statements. The relevant data and analysis are shown in Exhibit 7.23.

Exhibit 7.23

Merchandise Turnover and Days' Sales in Inventory for Toys "R" Us

	Year Ended		
	Feb. 1, 1997	**Feb. 3, 1996**	**Jan. 28, 1995**
Cost of goods sold	$6,892.5	$6,592.3	$6,008.0
Ending merchandise inventory	$2,214.6	$1,999.5	$1,999.1
Merchandise turnover	**3.27** times	**3.30** times	**3.18** times
Industry merchandise turnover	3.9 times	3.9 times	3.8 times
Days' sales in inventory	**117.3** days	**110.7** days	**121.4** days
Industry days' sales in inventory . . .	93.9 days	101.4 days	95.6 days

The 1997 merchandise turnover of 3.27 for **Toys "R" Us** is computed as: $6,892.5 ÷ [($2,214.6 + $1,999.5) ÷ 2]. This means Toys "R" Us turns over its inventory about 3.27 times per year, or about once every 112 days (365 days ÷ 3.27). We prefer merchandise turnover to be high provided inventory is not out of stock and the company is not turning away customers. The 1997 days' sales in inventory of 117.3 for Toys "R" Us helps us assess this likelihood and is computed as: ($2,214.6 ÷ $6,892.5) × 365. This tells us Toys "R" Us is carrying more than 117 days of sales in its inventory. This inventory buffer seems more than adequate. Toys "R" Us might benefit from management efforts to increase merchandise turnover. Also, comparisons to 1996 for Toys "R" Us are unfavorable as revealed by a decrease in merchandise turnover and an increase in days' sales in inventory.

Consultant

You are hired as a consultant to analyze inventory management for a retail store. Your preliminary analysis yields a merchandise turnover ratio of 5.0 and a days' sales in inventory measure of 73 days. The industry norm for merchandise turnover is about 4.4 and for days' sales in inventory it is about 74 days. Using this information, where do you direct your attention?

You Make the Call

Answer—p. 296

Flash back

9. The following data pertain to a company's inventory during 1999:

	Cost	Retail
Beginning inventory	$324,000	$530,000
Cost of goods purchased	195,000	335,000
Net sales		320,000

Using the retail method, estimate the cost of ending inventory.

10. Explain how merchandise turnover and days' sales in inventory are both useful in analyzing inventory.

Answers—p. 297

Summary

C1 Identify the items making up merchandise inventory. Merchandise inventory comprises goods owned by a company and held for resale. Three special cases merit our attention. Goods in transit are reported in inventory of the company that holds ownership rights. Goods out on consignment are reported in inventory of the consignor. Goods damaged or obsolete are reported in inventory at a conservative estimate of their net realizable value, computed as sales price minus the cost of making the sale.

C2 Identify the costs of merchandise inventory. Costs of merchandise inventory comprise expenditures necessary, directly or indirectly, in bringing an item to a salable condition and location. This means the cost of an inventory item includes its invoice price minus any discount, plus any added or incidental costs necessary to put it in a place and condition for sale.

A1 Analyze the effects of inventory methods for both financial and tax reporting. When purchase prices don't change, the choice of an inventory method is unimportant. But when purchase prices are rising or falling, the methods are likely to assign different cost amounts to inventory. Specific identification exactly matches costs and revenues. Weighted average smooths out price changes. FIFO assigns an amount to inventory closely approximating current replacement cost. LIFO assigns the most recent costs incurred to cost of goods sold, and likely better matches current costs with revenues. Because inventory methods are also used in tax reporting, they have potential tax effects.

A2 **Analyze the effects of inventory errors on current and future financial statements.** An error in the amount of ending inventory affects assets (inventory), net income (cost of goods sold), and equity for that period. Since ending inventory is next period's beginning inventory, an error in ending inventory affects next period's cost of goods sold and net income. The financial statement effects of errors in one period are offset (reverse) in the next.

A3 **Assess inventory management using both merchandise turnover and days' sales in inventory.** We prefer a high merchandise turnover provided inventory is not out of stock and customers are not being turned away. We use days' sales in inventory to assess the likelihood of inventory being out of stock. We prefer a small number of days' sales in inventory if we can serve customer needs and provide a buffer for uncertainties. Together, each of these ratios helps us assess inventory management and evaluate a company's short-term liquidity.

P1 **Compute inventory in a perpetual system using the methods of specific identification, FIFO, LIFO and weighted average.** Costs are assigned to the cost of goods sold account *each time* a sale occurs in a perpetual system. Specific identification assigns a cost to each item sold by referring to its actual cost (for example, its net invoice cost). Weighted average assigns a cost to items sold by taking the current balance in the

merchandise inventory account and dividing it by the total items available for sale to determine the weighted average cost per unit. We then multiply the number of units sold by this cost per unit to get the cost of each sale. FIFO assigns cost to items sold assuming earliest units purchased are the first units sold. LIFO assigns cost to items sold assuming the most recent units purchased are the first units sold.

P2 **Compute the lower of cost or market amount of inventory.** Inventory is reported at market value when market is *lower* than cost. This is called the lower of cost or market amount of inventory. Market is typically measured as replacement cost. Lower of cost or market can be applied separately to each item, to major categories of items, or to the whole of inventory.

P3 **Apply both the retail inventory and gross profit methods to estimate inventory.** The retail inventory method involves three computations: (1) goods available at retail minus net sales at retail gives ending inventory at retail, (2) goods available at cost divided by goods available at retail gives the cost to retail ratio, and (3) ending inventory at retail multiplied by the cost to retail ratio gives estimated ending inventory at cost. The gross profit method involves two computations: (1) net sales at retail multiplied by one minus the gross profit ratio gives estimated cost of goods sold, and (2) goods available at cost minus estimated cost of goods sold gives estimated ending inventory at cost.

Guidance Answers to **You Make the Call**

Financial Planner

The FIFO method means the oldest costs are the first ones recorded in cost of goods sold. This leaves the most recent costs in ending inventory. You report this to your client and note in most cases the ending inventory of a company using FIFO is reported at or near its market replacement cost. This means your client need not in most cases adjust the reported value of inventory. Your answer changes only if there are major increases in replacement cost compared to the cost of recent purchases reported in inventory. When major increases in costs occur, your client might wish to adjust inventory for the difference between the reported cost of inventory and its market replacement cost. (*Note*: Decreases in costs of purchases are recognized under the lower of cost or market adjustment.)

Consultant

Your client's merchandise turnover is markedly higher than the norm, whereas its days' sales in inventory is approximately at the norm. Since your client's turnover is already 14% better than average, you are probably best served by directing attention at days' sales in inventory. You should see if your client can reduce the level of inventory while maintaining its service to customers. Evidence suggests your client can reduce its level of inventory. This is suggested by recognizing that a company can maintain the same level of days' sales in inventory with a much lower turnover. Given your client's higher turnover, it should be able to hold less inventory.

Guidance Answer to **Judgment and Ethics**

Inventory Manager

Your recommendation is a difficult one. On one hand it seems your company can save (or at least postpone) taxes by switching to LIFO. On the other, switching to LIFO is likely to reduce bonus money that you think you've earned and deserve. Since the U.S. tax code requires companies that use LIFO for tax reporting to also use it for financial reporting, your options are even further constrained. Your

best decision is to tell your superior about the tax savings with LIFO. But you also should discuss your bonus plan and how this is likely to hurt you unfairly. You might propose to compute inventory under the LIFO method for reporting purposes, but use the FIFO method for your bonus calculations. Another solution is to revise the bonus plan to reflect the company's use of the LIFO method.

Guidance Answers to Flash *backs*

1. The matching principle.
2. Target.
3. Total cost is $12,180, computed as: $11,400 + $130 + $150 + $100 + $400.
4. Specific identification exactly matches costs and revenues. Weighted average tends to smooth out price changes. FIFO as-

signs an amount to inventory that closely approximates current replacement cost. LIFO assigns the most recent costs incurred to cost of goods sold, and likely better matches current costs with revenues.

5. FIFO. Specifically, FIFO gives a lower cost of goods sold, a higher gross profit, and a higher net income when prices are rising.

6. LIFO gives a lower inventory figure on the balance sheet as compared to FIFO when prices are rising. FIFO's inventory amount will approximate current replacement costs.

7. Cost of goods sold is understated by $10,000 in 1999 and overstated by $10,000 in year 2000.

8. The reported inventory amount is $540, computed as [(20 × $5) + (40 × $8) + (10 × $12)].

9. The estimated ending inventory (at cost) is $327,000 and is computed as:

   Step 1:   ($530,000 + $335,000) − $320,000 = $545,000

Step 2: $\dfrac{\$324,000 + \$195,000}{\$530,000 + \$335,000} = 60\%$

Step 3: $545,000 \times 60\% = \$327,000$

10. We like merchandise turnover to be high provided inventory is not out of stock and customers are not being turned away. We use days' sales in inventory to assess the likelihood of inventory being out of stock. We want days' sales in inventory to be as low as possible but adequate to serve customer needs and provide a buffer for uncertainties. Together these ratios allow us to assess these effects.

Demonstration Problem

Tale Company uses a perpetual inventory system and had the following beginning inventory and purchases during 1999:

Date		Item X	
		Units	Unit Cost
1/1	Inventory	400	$14
3/10	Purchase	200	15
5/9	Purchase	300	16
9/22	Purchase	250	20
11/28	Purchase	100	21

At December 31, 1999, there were 550 units of X on hand. Sales of units were as follows:

Jan. 15	200 units at $30
April 1	200 units at $30
Nov. 1	300 units at $35

Additional data for use in applying the specific identification method: (1) Jan. 15 sale—200 units @ $14, (2) April 1 sale—200 units @ $15, and (3) Nov. 1 sale—200 units @ $14 and 100 units @ $20.

Required

1. Calculate the cost of goods available for sale.

2. Apply the four different methods of inventory costing (FIFO, LIFO, weighted average, and specific identification) to calculate ending inventory and cost of goods sold under each method.

3. In preparing financial statements for 1999, the accountant was instructed to use FIFO but failed to do so and computed the cost of goods sold according to LIFO. Determine the impact on 1999's income from the accountant's error. Also determine the effect of the error on the year 2000 income. Assume no income taxes.

4. The management of the company would like a report showing how net income would change if the company changes from FIFO to another method. Prepare a schedule showing the cost of goods sold amount under each of the four methods. Calculate the amount by which each cost of goods sold total is different from the FIFO cost of goods sold to inform management how net income would change if another method were used.

Planning the Solution

• Make a schedule showing the calculation of the cost of goods available for sale. Multiply the units of beginning inventory and each purchase by the appropriate unit costs to determine the total cost of goods available for sale.

• Prepare a perpetual FIFO schedule showing the composition of beginning inventory and how the composition of inventory changes after each purchase of inventory and after each sale (see Exhibit 7.5).

- Prepare a perpetual LIFO schedule showing the composition of beginning inventory and how the composition of inventory changes after each purchase of inventory and after each sale (see Exhibit 7.6).
- Make a schedule of purchases and sales recalculating the average cost of inventory after each purchase to arrive at the weighted average cost of ending inventory. Add up the average costs associated with each sale to determine the cost of goods sold using the weighted average method (see Exhibit 7.7).
- Prepare a schedule showing the computation of the cost of goods sold and ending inventory using the specific identification method. Use the information provided to determine which specific units were sold and which specific units remain in inventory (see Exhibit 7.4).
- Compare the ending 1999 inventory amounts under FIFO and LIFO to determine the misstatement of 1999 income that resulted from using LIFO. The 1999 and 2000 errors are equal in amount but have opposite effects.
- Create a schedule showing the cost of goods sold under each method and how net income would differ from FIFO net income if an alternate method were to be adopted.

Solution to Demonstration Problem

1. Cost of goods available for sale:

Item X				
Date		**Units**	**Unit Cost**	**Total Cost**
1/1	Inventory	400	$14	$ 5,600
3/10	Purchase	200	15	3,000
5/9	Purchase	300	16	4,800
9/22	Purchase	250	20	5,000
11/28	Purchase	100	21	2,100
Total cost of goods available for sale				$20,500

2a. FIFO perpetual method:

Date	Purchases	Cost of Goods Sold	Inventory Balance
Jan. 1	Beginning balance		400 @ $14 = $ 5,600
Jan. 15		200 @ $14 = $2,800	200 @ $14 = $ 2,800
Mar. 10	200 @ $15 = $3,000		200 @ $14 200 @ $15 } = $ 5,800
April 1		200 @ $14 = $2,800	200 @ $15 = $ 3,000
May 9	300 @ $16 = $4,800		200 @ $15 300 @ $16 } = $ 7,800
Sept. 22	250 @ $20 = $5,000		200 @ $15 300 @ $16 250 @ $20 } = $12,800
Nov . 1		200 @ $15 = $3,000 100 @ $16 = $1,600	200 @ $16 250 @ $20 } = $ 8,200
Nov. 28	100 @ $21 = $2,100		200 @ $16 250 @ $20 100 @ $21 } = $10,300
Total cost of goods sold		$10,200	

Note to students: **In a classroom situation,** once cost of goods available for sale is known, we can compute the amount for either cost of goods sold or ending inventory—it is a matter of preference. **But in practice,** the costs of items sold are identified as sales are made and immediately transferred from the inventory account to the cost of goods sold account. This transfer then makes it unnecessary to calculate either account balance at the end of a period. The above solution showing the line-by-line approach illustrates actual application, whereas the alternate solution shown below illustrates that, once the concepts are understood, other solution approaches are available.

Alternate FIFO perpetual solution:

[FIFO Alternate No. 1: Computing cost of goods sold first]

Cost of goods available for sale (from 1.)		$20,500
Cost of goods sold:		
1/15 Sold (200 @ $14)	$ 2,800	
4/1 Sold (200 @ $14)	2,800	
11/1 Sold (200 @ $15 and 100 @ $16)	4,600	10,200
Ending inventory		$10,300

[FIFO Alternate No. 2: Computing ending inventory first]

Cost of goods available for sale (from 1.)		$20,500
Ending inventory*:		
11/28 purchase (100 @ $21)	$2,100	
9/22 purchase (250 @ $20)	5,000	
5/9 purchase (200 @ $16)	3,200	
Ending inventory		10,300
Cost of goods sold		$10,200

*Since FIFO assumes earlier costs relate to items sold, we determine ending inventory by assigning the most recent costs first.

2b. LIFO perpetual method:

Date	Purchases	Cost of Goods Sold	Inventory Balance
Jan. 1	Beginning balance		400 @ $14 = $ 5,600
Jan. 15		200 @ $14 = $2,800	200 @ $14 = $ 2,800
Mar. 10	200 @ $15 = $3,000		200 @ $14 200 @ $15 } = $ 5,800
April 1		200 @ $15 = $3,000	200 @ $14 = $ 2,800
May 9	300 @ $16 = $4,800		200 @ $14 300 @ $16 } = $ 7,600
Sept. 22	250 @ $20 = $5,000		200 @ $14 300 @ $16 250 @ $20 } = $12,600
Nov. 1		250 @ $20 = $5,000 50 @ $16 = $ 800	200 @ $14 250 @ $16 } = $ 6,800
Nov. 28	100 @ $21 = $2,100		200 @ $14 250 @ $16 100 @ $21 } = $ 8,900
Total cost of goods sold		$11,600	

Alternate LIFO perpetual solution:

[LIFO Alternate No. 1: Computing cost of goods sold first]

Cost of goods available for sale (from 1.)		$20,500
Cost of goods sold with LIFO perpetual		
1/15 200 units @ $14	$2,800	
4/1 200 units @ $15	$3,000	
11/1 250 units @ $20	$5,000	
50 units @ $16	$ 800	
Cost of goods sold		11,600
Ending inventory		$ 8,900

[LIFO Alternate No. 2: Computing ending inventory first]

Cost of goods available for sale (from 1.)		$20,500
Ending inventory:		
1/1 inventory (200 @ $14)	$2,800	
5/9 purchase (250 @ $16)	4,000	
11/28 purchase (100 @ $21)	2,100	
Ending inventory		8,900
Cost of goods sold		$11,600

2c. Weighted average perpetual method:

Date	Purchases	Cost of Goods Sold	Inventory Balance	
Jan. 1	Beginning balance		400 @ $14	= $5,600
Jan. 15		200 @ $14 = $2,800	200 @ $14	= $2,800
Mar. 10	200 @ $15 = $3,000		200 @ $14 ⎱ 200 @ $15 ⎰ (avg. cost is $14.5)	= $5,800
April 1		200 @ $14.5 = $2,900	200 @ $14.5	= $2,900
May 9	300 @ $16 = $4,800		200 @ $14.5 ⎱ 300 @ $16 ⎰ (avg. cost is $15.4)	= $7,700
Sept. 22	250 @ $20 = $5,000		200 @ $14.5 ⎱ 300 @ $16 ⎰ 250 @ $20 (avg. cost is $16.93)	= $12,700
Nov. 1		300 @ $16.93 = $5,079	450 @ $16.93	= $7618.5
Nov. 28	100 @ $21 = $2,100		450 @ $16.93 ⎱ 100 @ $21 ⎰	= $9718.5
Total cost of goods sold*		$10,779		

*The cost of goods sold ($10,779) plus ending inventory ($9718.5) is slightly less than the cost of goods available for sale ($20,500) due to rounding error.

2d. Specific identification method:

Date	Purchases	Cost of Goods Sold	Inventory Balance
Jan. 1	Beginning balance		400 @ $14 = $ 5,600
Jan. 15		200 @ $14 = $2,800	200 @ $14 = $ 2,800
Mar. 10	200 @ $15 = $3,000		200 @ $14 200 @ $15 } = $ 5,800
April 1		200 @ $15 = $3,000	200 @ $14 = $ 2,800
May 9	300 @ $16 = $4,800		200 @ $14 300 @ $16 } = $ 7,600
Sept. 22	250 @ $20 = $5,000		200 @ $14 300 @ $16 } = $12,600 250 @ $20
Nov. 1		200 @ $14 = $2,800 100 @ $20 = $2,000	300 @ $16 150 @ $20 } = $ 7,800
Nov. 28	100 @ $21 = $2,100		300 @ $16 150 @ $20 } = $ 9,900 100 @ $21
Total cost of goods sold		**$10,600**	

[Specific Identification Alternate No. 1: Computing cost of goods sold first]

Cost of goods available for sale (from 1.)		$20,500
Cost of goods sold:		
1/1 purchase (400 @ $14)	$5,600	
3/10 purchase (200 @ $15)	3,000	
11/28 purchase (100 @ $20)	2,000	
Total cost of goods sold		10,600
Ending inventory		$ 9,900

[Specific Identification Alternate No. 2: Computing ending inventory first]

Cost of goods available for sale (from 1.)		$20,500
Ending inventory:		
5/9 purchase (300 @ $16)	$4,800	
9/22 purchase (150 @ $20)	3,000	
11/28 purchase (100 @ $21)	2,100	
Total ending inventory		9,900
Cost of goods sold		$10,600

3. If LIFO was mistakenly used when FIFO should have been used, cost of goods sold in 1999 would be overstated by $1,400, which is the difference between the FIFO and LIFO amounts of ending inventory. Income would be understated in 1999 by $1,400. In year 2000, income would be overstated by $1,400 because of the understatement of the beginning inventory.

4. Analysis of the effects of alternative inventory methods:

	Cost of Goods Sold	Difference from FIFO Cost of Goods Sold	Effect on Net Income if Adopted Instead of FIFO
FIFO	$10,200	—	—
LIFO	$11,600	+$1,400	$1,400 lower
Weighted average	$10,779	+$ 579	$579 lower
Specific identification	$10,600	+$ 400	$400 lower

Assigning Costs to Inventory—Periodic System

Learning Objectives

Procedural

P4 Compute inventory in a periodic system using the methods of specific identification, FIFO, LIFO, and weighted average.

The basic aim of the periodic system is the same as the perpetual system: to assign costs to the inventory and the goods sold. The same four methods are used in assigning costs under the periodic system—specific identification; first-in, first-out; last-in, first-out; and weighted average. We use information from **Trekking** to describe how we assign costs using these four methods with a periodic system. Data for sales and purchases are reported in the chapter (see Exhibits 7.2 and 7.3) and are not repeated here.

We explained the accounting under a periodic system in Appendix 6A. The important accounting aspects of a periodic system are:

- Each purchase of merchandise for resale increases (debit) the Purchases account.
- Cost of merchandise sold is *not* recorded at the time of each sale. A physical count of inventory at the end of the period is used to compute cost of goods sold and inventory amounts.
- Necessary costs of merchandise such as transportation-in and cost reductions such as purchase discounts and purchase returns and allowances are recorded in separate accounts.

Specific Identification

The amount of costs assigned to inventory and cost of goods sold is the same under the perpetual and periodic systems when using specific identification. This is because specific identification precisely defines which units are in inventory and which are sold.

First-In, First-Out

The first-in, first-out (FIFO) method of assigning cost to inventory and goods sold using the periodic system is shown in Exhibit 7A.1:

Exhibit 7A.1

FIFO Computations—Periodic System

Total cost of 55 units available for sale		$5,990
Less ending inventory priced using FIFO:		
10 units from August 28 purchase at $119 each	$1,190	
2 units from August 17 purchase at $115 each	230	
Ending inventory		1,420
Cost of goods sold		$4,570

Trekking's ending inventory reported on the balance sheet is **$1,420**, and its cost of goods sold reported on the income statement is **$4,570.** These amounts are the same as those computed using the perpetual system. This will always occur because the most recent purchases are in ending inventory under both systems.

Last-In, First-Out

The last-in, first-out (LIFO) method of assigning costs to the 12 remaining units in inventory and to cost of goods sold using the periodic system is shown in Exhibit 7A.2:

Total cost of 55 units available for sale		$5,990
Less ending inventory priced using LIFO:		
10 units in beginning inventory at $ 91 each	$ 910	
2 units from August 3 purchase at $106 each	212	
Ending inventory		1,122
Cost of goods sold		$4,868

Exhibit 7A.2

LIFO Computations—Periodic System

Trekking's ending inventory reported on the balance sheet is **$1,122** and its cost of goods sold reported on the income statement is **$4,868.** When LIFO is used with the periodic system, cost of goods sold is assigned costs from the most recent purchases for the period. With a perpetual system, cost of goods sold is assigned costs from the most recent purchases *prior to each sale.*

Weighted Average

The weighted average method of assigning cost involves three important steps. The first two steps are shown in Exhibit 7A.3. First, multiply the per unit cost for beginning inventory and each particular purchase by their corresponding number of units. Second, add these amounts and divide by the total number of units available for sale to find the weighted average cost per unit.

Step 1:	10 units @ $ 91 = $ 910	
	15 units @ $106 = 1,590	
	20 units @ $115 = 2,300	
	10 units @ $119 = 1,190	
	55	$5,990
Step 2:	$5,990/55 units = $108.91 weighted average cost per unit	

Exhibit 7A.3

Weighted Average Cost per Unit

The third step is to use the weighted average cost per unit to assign costs to inventory and to units sold as shown in Exhibit 7A.4.

Step 3:	Total cost of 55 units available for sale	$5,990
	Less ending inventory priced on a weighted average	
	cost basis: 12 units at $108.91 each	1,307
	Cost of goods sold	$4,683

Exhibit 7A.4

Weighted Average Computations—Periodic

Trekking's ending inventory reported on the balance sheet is **$1,307** and its cost of goods sold reported on the income statement is **$4,683.**

Flash back

11. A company reports the following beginning inventory and purchases, and ends the period with 30 units on hand:

	Units	Cost
Beginning Inventory	100	$10
Purchases #1	40	12
#2	20	14

a. Compute ending inventory using the FIFO periodic system.
b. Compute cost of goods sold using the LIFO periodic system.

Answer—p. 304

Summary of Appendix 7A

P4 **Compute inventory in a periodic system using the methods of specific identification, FIFO, LIFO, and weighted average.** Periodic inventory systems allocate the cost of goods available for sale between cost of goods sold and ending inventory *at the end of a period.* Specific identification and FIFO give identical results whether the periodic or perpetual system is used.

LIFO assigns cost to cost of goods sold assuming the last units purchased for the period are the first units sold. The weighted average cost per unit is computed by taking the total cost of both beginning inventory and net purchases and divided by the total number of units available. Then, multiply cost per unit by the number of units sold to give cost of goods sold.

Guidance Answer to **Flash back**

11. *a.* FIFO periodic ending inventory = (20 × $14) + (10 × $12) = $400.
   b. LIFO periodic cost of goods sold = (20 × $14) + (40 × $12) + (70 × $10) = $1,460.

Glossary

Average cost method another name for weighted average inventory pricing. (p. 279).

Conservatism principle the accounting principle that guides accountants to select the less optimistic estimate when two estimates of amounts to be received or paid are about equally likely. (p. 290)

Consignee one who receives and holds goods owned by another party for the purpose of selling the goods for the owner. (p. 282)

Consignor an owner of goods who ships them to another party who will then sell the goods for the owner. (p. 282)

Consistency principle the accounting requirement that a company use the same accounting methods period after period so that the financial statements of succeeding periods will be comparable. (p. 286)

Days' sales in inventory an estimate of how many days it will take to convert the inventory on hand at the end of the period into accounts receivable or cash; calculated by dividing the ending inventory by cost of goods sold and multiplying the result by 365; also called *days' stock on hand.* (p. 294)

First-in, first-out (FIFO) the method of assigning cost to inventory under the assumption that inventory items are sold in the order acquired; the first items received are the first items sold. (p. 278)

Gross profit method a procedure for estimating an ending inventory in which the past gross profit rate is used to estimate cost of goods sold, which is then subtracted from the cost of goods available for sale to determine the estimated ending inventory. (p. 292)

Interim statements monthly or quarterly financial statements prepared in between the traditional, annual statements. (p. 290)

Last-in, first-out (LIFO) the method of assigning cost to inventory under the assumption that costs for the most recent items purchased are sold first and charged to cost of goods sold. (p. 278)

Lower of cost or market (LCM) the required method of reporting merchandise inventory in the balance sheet where market value is reported when market is lower than cost; market value is usually defined as current replacement cost on the date of the balance sheet. (p. 289)

Merchandise turnover—the number of times a company's average inventory is sold during an accounting period; calculated by dividing cost of goods sold by the average merchandise inventory balance; also called *inventory turnover*. (p. 293)

Net realizable value the expected sale price of an item minus the cost of making the sale. (p. 282)

Retail inventory method a method for estimating an ending inventory based on the ratio of the amount of goods for sale at cost to the amount of goods for sale at marked selling prices. (p. 290)

Specific identification method the pricing of inventory where the purchase invoice of each item in the ending inventory is iden-

tified and used to determine the cost assigned to the inventory. (p. 278)

Specific invoice inventory pricing another name for specific identification method. (p. 278)

Weighted average the method of assigning cost to inventory in which the unit prices of the items making up the current inventory are weighted by the number of units of each in the current inventory. The total of these amounts is then divided by the total number of units available for sale to find the unit cost of the inventory balance and of the units that were sold. (p. 279)

The superscript letter ^A *identifies assignment material based on Appendix 7A.*

Questions

1. What accounts are used in a periodic inventory system but not in a perpetual inventory system?
2. What is meant when it is said that inventory errors correct themselves?
3. If inventory errors correct themselves, why be concerned when such errors are made?
4. Where is merchandise inventory disclosed in the financial statements?
5. Why are incidental costs sometimes ignored in pricing inventory? Under what accounting principle is this permitted?
6. Give the meanings of the following when applied to inventory: *(a)* FIFO; *(b)* LIFO; and *(c)* cost.
7. If prices are falling, will the LIFO or the FIFO method of inventory valuation result in the lower cost of goods sold?
8. Can a company change its inventory method each accounting period?
9. Does the accounting principle of consistency preclude any changes from one accounting method to another?
10. What effect does the full-disclosure principle have if a company changes from one acceptable accounting method to another?

11. What guidance for accountants is provided by the principle of conservatism?
12. What is the usual meaning of the word *market* as it is used in determining the lower of cost or market for merchandise inventory?
13. Refer to **NIKE's** financial statements in Appendix A. On May 31, 1997 what percent of NIKE's current assets was represented by inventory?
14. Refer to **Reebok's** financial statements in Appendix A. Calculate Reebok's cost of goods available for sale as of December 31, 1996.
15. Refer to **AOL's** financial statements in Appendix A. Why does America Online fail to show inventory as a current asset as of June 30, 1996?
16. Refer to the **Wired** article at the beginning of the chapter. What does Russo need to know about Wired to be able to calculate gross margin and inventory turnover?

---

1. At year-end, Carefree Company has shipped $500 of merchandise FOB destination to Stark Company. Which company should include the $500 merchandise that is in transit as part of its inventory at year-end?
2. Carefree Company has shipped $900 of goods to Stark and has an arrangement that Stark will sell the goods for Carefree. Identify the consignor and the consignee. Which company should include any unsold goods as part of inventory?

Quick Study

QS 7-1
Inventory ownership

A car dealer acquires a used car for $3,000, terms FOB shipping point. Additional costs in obtaining and offering the car for sale include $150 for transportation-in, $200 for import duties, $50 for insurance during shipment, $25 for advertising, and $250 for sales staff salaries. For computing inventory, what cost is assigned to the used car acquired?

QS 7-2
Inventory costs

QS 7-3
Calculating cost
of goods available
for sale

A company has beginning inventory of 10 units at $50 each. Every week for four weeks an additional 10 units are purchased at respective costs of $51, $52, $55, and $60. Calculate the cost of goods available for sale and the units available for sale.

QS 7-4
Inventory ownership

Crafts and More, a distributor of handmade gifts, operates out of owner Scott Arlen's home. At the end of the current accounting period, Arlen reports he has 1,500 units of products in his basement, 30 of which were damaged by water and cannot be sold. He also has another 250 units in his van, ready to deliver to fill a customer order, terms FOB destination, and another 70 units out on consignment to a friend who owns a stationery store. How many units should be included in his company's end-of-period inventory?

QS 7-5
Inventory costs

Rigby & Son, antique dealers, purchased the contents of an estate for a price of $37,500. The terms of the purchase were FOB shipping point, and the cost of transporting the goods to Rigby & Son's warehouse was $1,200. Rigby & Son insured the shipment at a cost of $150. Prior to putting the goods up for sale in the store, they cleaned and refurbished merchandise at a cost of $490. Determine the cost of the inventory acquired from the purchase of the estate's contents.

QS 7-6
Inventory costing
methods

A company had the following beginning inventory and purchases during January for a particular item. On January 26, 345 units were sold. What is the cost of the 140 units that remain in the ending inventory, assuming (a) FIFO, (b) LIFO, and (c) weighted average? (Round numbers to the nearest cent.)

	Units	Unit Cost
Beginning inventory on January 1	310	$3.00
Purchase on January 9	75	3.20
Purchase on January 25	100	3.35

QS 7-7
Contrasting inventory
costing methods

Identify the inventory costing method most closely described by each of the following separate statements. Assume a period of rising costs.
a. Matches recent costs against revenue.
b. Provides a tax advantage.
c. Understates the current value of inventory on a balance sheet.
d. Results in a balance sheet inventory closest to replacement costs.
e. Fits best when each unit of product has unique features that affect cost.

QS 7-8^A
Inventory errors

The Weston Company maintains its inventory records on a periodic basis. In taking a physical inventory at the end of year 2000, certain units were counted twice. Explain how this error affects the following: (a) 2000 cost of goods sold, (b) 2000 gross profit, (c) 2000 net income, (d) 2001 net income, (e) the combined two-year income, and (f) income in years after 2001.

QS 7-9
Applying LCM to
inventories

Thrifty Trading Co. has the following products in its ending inventory:

Product	Quantity	Cost	Market
Aprons	9	$6.00	$5.50
Bottles	12	3.50	4.25
Candles	25	8.00	7.00

Compute lower of cost or market (a) for the inventory as a whole and (b) applied separately to each product.

The inventory of Bell Department Store was destroyed by a fire on September 10, 1999. The following 1999 data were available from the accounting records:

QS 7-10
Estimating inventories
P3

Jan. 1 inventory	$180,000
Jan. 1–Sept. 10 purchases (net)	$342,000
Jan. 1–Sept. 10 sales (net)	$675,000
1999 estimated gross profit rate	42%

Estimate the cost of the inventory destroyed in the fire.

Parfour Company made purchases of a particular product in the current year as follows:

Exercises
Exercise 7-1
Inventory costing
methods (perpetual)—
FIFO and LIFO
P1

Jan. 1	Beginning inventory	100 units @ $10 =	$ 1,000
Mar. 14	Purchased	250 units @ $15 =	3,750
July 30	Purchased	400 units @ $20 =	8,000
Oct. 26	Purchased	600 units @ $25 =	15,000
Units available		1,350 units	
Cost of goods available for sale			$27,750

Parfour Company made sales on the following dates at $40 per unit:

Jan. 10	90 units
Mar. 15	140 units
Oct. 5	300 units
Total sales	530 units

Required

Parfour uses a perpetual inventory system. Determine the costs that should be assigned to the ending inventory and to goods sold under each of the following: *(a)* costs are assigned on the basis of FIFO, and *(b)* costs are assigned on the basis of LIFO. Compute gross margin for each method.

Refer to the data in Exercise 7–1. Assume ending inventory is made up of the entire March 14 purchase plus 570 units of the October 26 purchase. Using the specific identification method, calculate the costs of goods sold and the gross margin.

Exercise 7-2
Specific
Identification P1

Trout Company made purchases of a particular product in the current year (1999) as follows:

Exercise 7–3
Inventory costing
methods—perpetual
P1

Jan. 1	Beginning inventory	120 units @ $6.00 =	$ 720
Mar. 7	Purchased	250 units @ $5.60 =	1,400
July 28	Purchased	500 units @ $5.00 =	2,500
Oct. 3	Purchased	450 units @ $4.60 =	2,070
Dec. 19	Purchased	100 units @ $4.10 =	410
	Total	1,420 units	$7,100

Trout Company made sales on the following dates at $15 per unit:

Jan. 10	70 units
Mar. 15	125 units
Oct. 5	600 units
Total	795 units

Required

Trout uses a perpetual inventory system. The ending inventory consists of 625 units, 500 from the July 28 purchase and 125 from the Oct. 3 purchase. Determine the cost assigned to ending inventory and to goods sold under each of the following: *(a)* costs are assigned on the basis of specific identification, *(b)* costs are assigned on a weighted average cost basis, *(c)* costs are assigned on the basis of FIFO, and *(d)* costs are assigned on the basis of LIFO.

Exercise 7-4
Income effects of
inventory methods

A1

Use the data in Exercise 7-3 to construct comparative income statements for Trout Company (year-end 1999) similar to those shown in Exhibit 7.10 for the four inventory methods. Assume operating expenses are $1,250. The applicable income tax rate is 30%.

1. Which method results in the highest net income?

2. Does the weighted average net income fall between the FIFO and LIFO net incomes?

3. If costs were rising instead of falling, which method would result in the highest net income?

Exercise 7-5ᴬ
Alternative cost flow
assumptions—periodic

P4

Paddington Gifts made purchases of a particular product in the current year as follows:

Jan.	1	Beginning inventory	120 units @ $3.00 =	$ 360
Mar.	7	Purchased	250 units @ $2.80 =	700
July	28	Purchased	500 units @ $2.50 =	1,250
Oct.	3	Purchased	450 units @ $2.30 =	1,035
Dec.	19	Purchased	100 units @ $2.05 =	205
		Total	1,420 units	$3,550

Required

The company uses a periodic inventory system, and its ending inventory consists of 150 units, 50 from each of the last three purchases. Determine the cost assigned to ending inventory and to goods sold under each of the following: *(a)* costs are assigned on the basis of specific identification, *(b)* costs are assigned on a weighted average cost basis, *(c)* costs are assigned on the basis of FIFO, and *(d)* costs are assigned on the basis of LIFO. Assuming the company has enough income to require that it pay income taxes, which method provides a current tax advantage?

Exercise 7-6ᴬ
Alternative cost flow
assumptions—periodic

P4

Jasper & Williams Company made purchases of a particular product in the current year as follows:

Jan.	1	Beginning inventory	120 units @ $2.00 =	$ 240
Mar.	7	Purchased	250 units @ $2.30 =	575
July	28	Purchased	500 units @ $2.50 =	1,250
Oct.	3	Purchased	450 units @ $2.80 =	1,260
Dec.	19	Purchased	100 units @ $2.96 =	296
		Total	1,420 units	$3,621

Required

The company uses a periodic inventory system, and its ending inventory consists of 150 units, 50 from each of the last three purchases. Determine the cost assigned to ending inventory and to goods sold under each of the following: *(a)* costs are assigned on the basis of specific identification, *(b)* costs are assigned on a weighted average cost basis, *(c)* costs are assigned on the basis of FIFO, and *(d)* costs are assigned on the basis of LIFO. Assuming the company has enough income to require that it pay income taxes, which method provides a current tax advantage?

Exercise 7-7
Analysis of inventory
errors

A2

The John Henry Company had $900,000 of sales during each of three consecutive years 2000–2002, and it purchased merchandise costing $500,000 during each of the years. It also maintained a $200,000 inventory from the beginning to the end of the three-year period. But in accounting for inventory it made an error at the end of year 2000 that caused its ending year 2000 inventory to appear on its statements as $180,000 rather than the correct $200,000.

Required

1. Determine the actual amount of the company's gross profit in each of the years 2000–2002.

2. Prepare comparative income statements as in Exhibit 7.13 to show the effect of this error on the company's cost of goods sold and gross profit in years 2000–2002.

Showtime Company's ending inventory includes the following items:

Product	Units on Hand	Unit Cost	Replacement Cost per Unit
BB	22	$50	$54
FM	15	78	72
MB	36	95	91
SL	40	36	36

Exercise 7-8
Lower of cost or market

P2

Replacement cost is determined to be the best measure of market. Calculate lower of cost or market for the inventory (a) as a whole and (b) applied separately to each product.

During 1999, Harmony Company sold $130,000 of merchandise at marked retail prices. At the end of 1999, the following information was available from its records:

	At Cost	At Retail
Beginning inventory	$31,900	$64,200
Cost of goods purchased	57,810	98,400

Exercise 7-9
Estimating ending
inventory—retail method

P3

Use the retail inventory method to estimate Harmony's 1999 ending inventory at cost.

In addition to estimating its ending inventory by the retail method, Harmony Company of Exercise 7–9 took a physical inventory at the marked selling prices of the inventory items at the end of 1999. The total of this physical inventory at marked selling prices was $27,300. Determine (a) the estimated amount of this inventory at cost and (b) Harmony's 1999 inventory shrinkage at retail and at cost.

Exercise 7-10
Reducing physical
inventory to
cost—retail method

P3

On January 1, The Parts Store had a $450,000 inventory at cost. During the first quarter of the year, it purchased $1,590,000 of merchandise, returned $23,100, and paid freight charges on purchased merchandise totaling $37,600, terms FOB shipping point. During the past several years, the store's gross profit on sales has averaged 30%. Under the assumption the store had $2,000,000 of net sales during the first quarter of the year, use the gross profit method to estimate its inventory at the end of the first quarter.

Exercise 7-11
Estimating ending
inventory—gross profit
method

P3

From the following information for Russo Merchandising Co., calculate merchandise turnover for 2001 and 2000 and days' sales in inventory at December 31, 2001, and 2000. (Round answers to one decimal place.)

	2001	2000	1999
Cost of goods sold	$643,825	$426,650	$391,300
Inventory (December 31)	96,400	86,750	91,500

Exercise 7-12
Merchandise turnover and
days' sales in inventory

A3

Comment on Russo's efficiency in using its assets to support increasing sales from 2000 to 2001.

Problems

Problem 7-1
Alternative cost flows—
perpetual

Hall Company has the following inventory purchases during the fiscal year ended December 31, 1999:

Beginning	500 units	$45/unit
2/10	250 units	42/unit
3/13	100 units	29/unit
8/21	130 units	50/unit
9/5	245 units	48/unit

Hall Company employs a perpetual inventory system. It had two sales during the period, and the units had a selling price of $75 per unit. The specific units sold are the entire beginning inventory plus 65 units of the 3/13 purchase:

3/15 sales	. . . .	330 units
9/10 sales	. . . .	235 units

Required

Preparation Component

1. Calculate cost of goods available for sale and units available for sale.
2. Calculate units remaining in ending inventory.

3. Calculate the dollar value of ending inventory using *(a)* FIFO, *(b)* LIFO, *(c)* specific identification, and *(d)* weighted average.
4. Calculate the gross profit earned by Hall Company under each of the costing methods in (3).

Analysis Component

5. If the Hall Company's manager earns a bonus based on a percent of gross profit, which method of inventory costing will be preferred?

Problem 7-2^A
Alternative cost flows—
periodic

P4

Mill House Company began 1999 with 20,000 units of Product X in its January 1 inventory that cost $15 each, and it made successive purchases of the product as follows:

Mar. 7	. . . .	28,000 units @ $18 each
May 25	. . . .	30,000 units @ $22 each
Aug. 1	. . . .	20,000 units @ $24 each
Nov. 10	. . . .	33,000 units @ $27 each

The company uses a periodic inventory system. On December 31, 1999, a physical count disclosed that 35,000 units of Product X remained in inventory.

Required

1. Prepare a calculation showing the number and total cost of the units available for sale during 1999.

2. Prepare calculations showing the amounts assigned to the 1999 ending inventory and to cost of goods sold, assuming *(a)* a FIFO basis, *(b)* a LIFO basis, and *(c)* a weighted average basis.

Problem 7-3^A
Income comparisons and
cost flows—periodic

A1, P4

Green Jeans, Inc., sold 5,500 units of its product at $45 per unit during 1999, and incurred operating expenses of $6 per unit in selling the units. It began the year with 600 units and made successive purchases of the product as follows:

January 1 (beginning inventory) . . .	600 units @ $18 per unit
Purchases:	
February 20	1,500 units @ $19 per unit
May 16	700 units @ $20 per unit
October 3	400 units @ $21 per unit
December 11	3,300 units @ $22 per unit
	6,500 units

Chapter 7   Merchandise Inventories and Cost of Sales

311

Required

Preparation Component

1. Prepare a comparative income statement for the company, showing in adjacent columns the net incomes earned from the sale of the product, assuming the company uses a periodic inventory system and prices its ending inventory on the basis of: *(a)* FIFO, *(b)* LIFO, and *(c)* weighted average. Assume an income tax rate of 30%.

Check Figure Net income (LIFO), $69,020

Analysis Component

2. How would the results from the three alternative inventory costing methods change if Green Jeans had been experiencing declining prices in the acquisition of additional inventory?

3. What specific advantages and disadvantages are offered by using LIFO and by using FIFO, assuming the cost trends continue as shown in the purchases data above?

The following amounts were reported in Shockley Company's financial statements:

Problem 7-4
Analysis of inventory errors

	Financial Statements for Year Ended December 31		
	1999	2000	2001
(a) Cost of goods sold	$ 715,000	$ 847,000	$ 770,000
(b) Net income	220,000	275,000	231,000
(c) Total current assets	1,155,000	1,265,000	1,100,000
(d) Owner's equity	1,287,000	1,430,000	1,232,000

In making physical counts of inventory, Shockley made the following errors:
Inventory on December 31, 1999: Understated $66,000
Inventory on December 31, 2000: Overstated $30,000

Required

Preparation Component:

1. For each of the preceding financial statement items—*(a)*, *(b)*, *(c)*, and *(d)*—prepare a schedule similar to the following and show the adjustments necessary to correct the reported amounts.

Check Figure Corrected net income (2000), $179,000

	1999	2000	2001
Cost of goods sold:			
Reported	___	___	___
Adjustments: 12/31/1999 error	___	___	___
12/31/2000 error	___	___	___
Corrected	___	___	___

Analysis Component

2. What is the error in aggregate net income for the three-year period that results from the inventory errors? Explain why this result occurs. Also explain why the understatement of inventory by $66,000 at the end of 1999 resulted in an understatement of equity by the same amount that year.

Problem 7–5
Lower of cost or market

P2

A physical inventory of Electronics Unlimited taken at December 31 reveals the following:

Item	Units on Hand	Per Unit Cost	Per Unit Market
Audio equipment:			
Receivers	335	$ 90	$ 98
CD players	250	111	100
Cassette decks	316	86	95
Turntables	194	52	41
Video equipment:			
Televisions	470	150	125
VCRs	281	93	84
Video cameras	202	310	322
Car audio equipment:			
Cassette radios	175	70	84
CD radios	160	97	105

Check Figure Lower of cost or market: (a) $274,702; (b) $270,332; (c) $263,024

Required

Calculate the lower of cost or market (a) for the inventory as a whole, (b) for the inventory by major category, and (c) for the inventory applied separately to each item.

Problem 7-6
Retail inventory method

P3

The records of Basics Company provide the following information for the year ended December 31:

	At Cost	At Retail
January 1 beginning inventory	$ 471,350	$ 927,150
Cost of goods purchased	3,276,030	6,279,350
Sales		5,495,700
Sales returns		44,600

Required

1. Prepare an estimate of the company's year-end inventory by the retail method.
2. The company took a year-end physical inventory at marked selling prices that totaled $1,675,800. Prepare a schedule showing the store's loss from shrinkage at cost and at retail.

Check Figure Inventory shortage at cost, $41,392

Problem 7-7
Gross profit method

P3

Walker Company wants to prepare interim financial statements for the first quarter of 1999. The company would like to avoid making a physical count of inventory each quarter. During the last five years, the company's gross profit rate has averaged 35%. The following information for the first quarter is available from its records:

January 1 beginning inventory	$ 300,260
Net cost of goods purchased	939,050
Sales	1,191,150
Sales returns	9,450

Check Figure Estimated inventory, $471,205

Required

Use the gross profit method to prepare an estimate of the company's first quarter inventory.

BEYOND THE NUMBERS

Refer to the financial statements and related information for **NIKE** in Appendix A. Answer the following questions by analyzing the information in NIKE's report:

1. What is the total amount of inventories held as current assets by NIKE on May 31, 1997? On May 31, 1996?
2. Inventories represent what percent of total assets on May 31, 1997? On May 31, 1996?
3. Comment on the relative size of inventories NIKE holds compared to other types of assets.
4. What method did NIKE use to determine the inventory amounts reported on its balance sheet?
5. Calculate merchandise turnover for fiscal year ended May 31, 1997 and days' sales in inventory on May 31, 1997. (Note: Cost of sales is cost of goods sold.)

Swoosh Ahead

6. Obtain access to NIKE's annual report for fiscal years ending after May 31, 1997. You can gain access to NIKE's annual report at its web site [**www.nike.com**] or through the SEC's EDGAR database [**www.sec.gov**]. Answer questions 1 through 5 above using the updated NIKE financial information.

Reporting in Action

C2, A3

Both **NIKE** and **Reebok** design, produce, market, and sell sports footwear and apparel. Key comparative figures ($ millions) for these two companies follow:

Key figures	NIKE 1997	NIKE 1996	Reebok 1996	Reebok 1995
Inventory	$1,339	$ 931	$ 545	$ 635
Cost of sales	5,503	3,907	2,144	2,114

*NIKE figures are from its annual reports for fiscal years ended May 31, 1997 and 1996.
Reebok figures are from its annual reports for fiscal years ended December 31, 1996 and 1995.

Required

1. Calculate merchandise turnover for NIKE (1997) and Reebok (1996).
2. Calculate days' sales in inventory for both companies for the two years shown.
3. Comment on your findings in parts *1* and *2*.

Comparative Analysis

A3

Diversion, Inc., is a retail sports store carrying primarily women's golf apparel and equipment. The store is at the end of its second year of operation and, as new businesses often do, is struggling a bit to be profitable. The cost of inventory items has increased in the short time the store has been in business. In the first year of operations the store accounted for inventory costs using the LIFO method. A loan agreement the store has with Dollar Bank, its prime source of financing, requires that the store maintain a certain profit margin and current ratio. The store's owner, Cindy Foor, is currently looking over Diversion's annual financial statements after its year-end inventory has been taken. The numbers are not very favorable and the only way the store can meet the required financial ratios agreed upon with the bank is to change from the LIFO to FIFO method. The store originally decided upon LIFO for inventory costing because of the tax advantages it would afford. Cindy recalculates the ending inventory using FIFO and submits her income statement and balance sheet to the loan officer at the bank for the required bank review of the loan. As Cindy mails the financial statements to the bank, she thankfully reflects on the latitude she has as manager in choosing an inventory costing method.

Ethics Challenge

A1

Required

1. Why does Diversion's use of FIFO improve its profit margin and current ratio?
2. Is the action by Diversion's owner ethical? Explain.

Communicating in Practice
A1

You are a public accountant working for a wholesale produce business that has just completed its first year of operations. Due to catastrophic weather conditions, resulting in the destruction of crops, the cost of acquiring produce to resell has escalated during the later part of this fiscal period. Your client, Mr. Greenhouse, mentioned that because the business sells perishable goods, he has striven to maintain a first-in, first-out flow of goods. Although sales have been good for a first-year business, the high cost of inventory at the end of the year put the business in a tight cash position. Mr. Greenhouse has expressed concern regarding the ability of the business to meet income tax obligations.

Required

Prepare a memorandum or send an e-mail that explains and justifies the inventory valuation method you recommend that your client, Mr. Greenhouse, adopt. If the response is to be made via e-mail, you are to assume your instructor is the owner instead of Mr. Greenhouse.

Taking It to the Net
A3

Visit the **Bausch and Lomb** Web site at **www.bausch.com.** Access the financial statements and financial statement notes and collect the information you need to answer the following questions. If the Bausch and Lomb Web site is not found, consult the Bausch and Lomb financial information at the Edgar database at **www.sec.gov.**

1. What product does Bausch and Lomb sell that is popular with college students?
2. What inventory costing method does Bausch and Lomb use? (Hint: consult the notes to the financial statements to read about Bausch and Lomb's inventory practices.)
3. Calculate Bausch and Lomb's gross margin and gross margin ratio for the most current year's data found at its Web site.
4. Calculate merchandise turnover and days' sales in inventory for the most current year's data found at its Web site.

Teamwork in Action
P1, A1

Each member of the team has the responsibility to become a resident expert on a specific inventory method. This expertise will be used to facilitate teammates' understanding of the concepts relevant to the method he or she has chosen. Follow the procedure outlined below:

1. Each team member is to select their area for expertise by choosing one of the following inventory methods: specific identification, LIFO, FIFO, or weighted average. You have one minute to make your choices.
2. Learning teams are to disburse and expert teams are to be formed. Expert teams will be made up of students who have all selected the same area of expertise. The instructor will identify the location in the room where each expert team will meet.
3. Using data below, expert teams will collaborate to develop a presentation that illustrates each of the relevant procedures and concepts listed below the data. Each student must write up the presentation in a format that can be shown to the learning teams in the next step in the activity.

Data:

Sunmann, Inc., uses a perpetual inventory system. It had the following beginning inventory and current year purchases of a particular product:

Jan.	1	Beginning inventory	50 units @ $10 = $ 500
Jan.	14	Purchased	150 units @ $12 = 1,800
Apr.	30	Purchased	200 units @ $15 = 3,000
Sept.	26	Purchased	300 units @ $20 = 6,000

Sunmann, Inc., made sales on the following dates at $35 a unit:

Jan. 10	30 units	(actual cost $10)
Feb. 15	100 units	(actual cost $12)
Oct. 5	350 units	(actual cost 100 @ $15 and 250 @ $20)

Procedures and concepts to illustrate in expert presentation:

a. Identify and compute the costs to be assigned to the units sold.

b. Identify and compute the costs to be assigned to the units in ending inventory.

c. How likely is it that this inventory costing method will reflect the actual physical flow of goods? How relevant is that factor in determining if this is an acceptable method to use?

d. What is the impact of this method versus others in determining net income and income taxes?

e. How closely does the valuation of the ending inventory reflect replacement costs for these units?

4. Re-form learning teams. In rotation, each expert is to present to their teams that which they developed in (3). Experts are to encourage and respond to questions.

Visit your local mall or downtown retail area with another classmate. Visit five stores. In each store, identify whether the store uses a bar-coding system to help manage its inventory. Try to find at least one store that does not use bar-coding. If a store does not use bar-coding, ask the store's manager or retail clerk whether he or she knows which type of inventory costing method the store employs. Create a table that shows columns for the name of store visited, type of merchandise sold, use or nonuse of bar-coding, and the inventory costing method used if bar-coding is not employed. You might also inquire as to what the store's merchandise turnover is and how often physical inventory is taken.

Hitting the Road
C1, C2

Read the article "Michael Dell: Whirlwind on the Web" in the April 7, 1997, issue of *Business Week*. Answer the following questions:

1. How many days of sales does Dell have in inventory?

2. How does Dell's days of sales in inventory compare with one of its chief competitors?

3. What are three techniques described in the article that Dell uses to improve inventory management?

Business Week Activity
A3

Accounting Information Systems

CHAPTER 8

A Look Back

Chapters 6 and 7 focused on merchandising activities and accounting for inventory. We explained both the perpetual and periodic inventory systems, accounting for inventory transactions, and methods for assigning costs to inventory.

A Look at This Chapter

This chapter emphasizes accounting information systems. We describe fundamental system principles, the system's components, use of special journals and subsidiary ledgers, and technology-based systems. We also discuss segment reporting and how to analyze these data.

A Look Ahead

Chapter 9 focuses on internal controls and accounting for cash and cash equivalents. We explain good internal control procedures and their importance for accounting.

Chapter Outline

Records for Success

MIAMI—It was the worst loss in Maria Lopez's early career as owner of **Outdoors Unlimited.** She'd lobbied hard to carry *REV Sports* products in her sporting goods store. Her rejection letter was harsh, and to the point. "The financial condition and internal controls of Outdoors Unlimited do not support a business relationship at this time . . ." the letter said.

Maria knew she'd pushed the limit in keeping her own records. "I purchased the best accounting software according to small business magazines. But," says Maria, "I didn't have any idea how to use it."

Maria thought she knew how to enter her store's sales and purchases data. Yet it turned out some data were entered in ledgers and not in journals, and vice versa. "The software created lovely reports, but I didn't know if they were correct," admits Maria. "Ledgers, journals, footings, crossfootings—it's all Greek to me!" Most frustrating was that Maria knew her store was doing well, and for unknown reasons, her financials weren't reflecting it.

"I ended up taking an evening course," says Maria. "I learned how to set up an accounting system and to keep special journals. I set up my records as I went through the course."

Maria now regularly creates schedules of accounts payable and accounts receivable. "I use ledgers and aging schedules to identify late-paying customers. I also keep payable records to help me better time payments to suppliers." Maria points out that Outdoors Unlimited now carries *REV*'s products.

And what about that accounting software? "It's great software," says Maria. "But it ought to carry a warning like: *A lack of accounting knowledge can damage your company's health.*"

Learning Objectives

Conceptual

C1 Identify fundamental principles of accounting information systems.

C2 Identify components of accounting information systems.

C3 Explain the goals and uses of special journals.

C4 Describe the use of controlling accounts and subsidiary ledgers.

C5 Explain how technology-based information systems impact accounting.

Analytical

A1 Analyze a company's performance and financial condition by business segments.

Procedural

P1 Journalize and post transactions using special journals.

P2 Prepare and test the accuracy of subsidiary ledgers.

CHAPTER PREVIEW

Accounting for business activities requires collecting and processing information. As the number or complexity of business activities rises, demands placed on accounting information systems increase. Accounting information systems must meet this challenge in an efficient and effective manner. In this chapter, we learn about fundamental principles guiding information systems, and we study components making up these systems. We also explain procedures that use special journals and subsidiary ledgers to make accounting information systems more efficient. Our understanding of the details of accounting reports makes us better decision makers when using financial information, and it improves our ability to analyze and interpret financial statements. Like Maria Lopez in the opening article, knowledge of these topics helps in successfully running a company.

Fundamental System Principles

C1 Identify fundamental principles of accounting information systems.

Accounting information systems collect and process data from transactions and events, organize them in useful forms, and communicate results to decision makers. These systems are crucial to effective decision making for both internal and external users of information. With the increasing complexity of business operations and the growing need for information, accounting information systems are more important than ever before.

All decision makers in practice today need to have a basic knowledge of how accounting information systems work. This knowledge gives decision makers a competitive edge as they gain a better understanding of information constraints, measurement limitations, and potential applications. It allows them to make more informed decisions and to better balance the risks and returns of various strategies. This section explains five fundamental principles of accounting information systems, which are shown in Exhibit 8.1.

Exhibit 8.1
System Principles

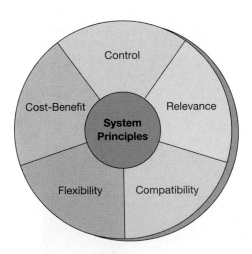

Control Principle

Managers need to control and monitor business activities. To this end, the **control principle** requires an accounting information system to have internal controls. *Internal controls* are methods and procedures allowing managers to control and monitor business activities. They include policies to direct operations toward common goals, procedures to ensure reliable financial reports, safeguards to protect company assets, and methods to achieve compliance with laws and regulations.

Relevance Principle

Decision makers need relevant information to make informed decisions. The **relevance principle** requires that an accounting information system report useful, understandable, timely, and pertinent information for effective decision making. This means an information system is designed to capture data that make a difference in decisions. To ensure this, it is important all decision makers be considered when identifying relevant information for disclosure.

Compatibility Principle

Accounting information systems must be consistent with the aims of a company. The **compatibility principle** requires that an accounting information system conform with a company's activities, personnel, and structure. It also must adapt to the unique characteristics of a company. The system must not be intrusive, but rather work in harmony with and be driven by company goals. **Outdoors Unlimited,** described in the opening article, for example, needs a simple retail information system. **NIKE,** on the other hand, demands both a merchandising and a manufacturing information system able to assemble data from its global operations.

Flexibility Principle

Accounting information systems must be able to adjust to changes. The **flexibility principle** requires that an accounting information system be able to adapt to changes in the company, business environment, and needs of decisions makers. Technological advances, competitive pressures, consumer tastes, regulations, and company activities constantly change. A system must be designed to adapt to these changes.

Cost-Benefit Principle

Accounting information systems must balance costs and benefits. The **cost-benefit principle** requires the benefits from an activity in an accounting information system to out weigh the costs of that activity. The costs and benefits of an activity such as reporting certain information impact the decisions of both external and internal users. They also affect costs of computing, personnel, and other direct and indirect costs. Decisions regarding other systems principles (control, relevance, compatibility, and flexibility) are also affected by the cost-benefit principle.

Accounting information systems consist of people, records, methods, and equipment. The systems are designed to capture information about a company's transactions and to provide output including financial, managerial, and tax reports. Because all accounting information systems have these same goals, they have some basic components. These components apply whether or not a system is heavily computerized. Yet the components of computerized systems usually provide more accuracy, speed, efficiency, and convenience.

There are five basic components of an accounting information system: source documents, input devices, information processors, information storage, and output devices. Exhibit 8.2 shows these components as a series of steps. Yet we know there is a lot of two-way communication between many of these components. We describe each of these key components in this section.

Source Documents

We described source documents in Chapter 3 and explained their importance for both business transactions and information collection. Source documents provide the basic information processed by an accounting system. Most of us are familiar with source documents such as bank statements and checks received from others. Other examples of

Components of Accounting Systems

C2 Identify components of accounting information systems.

Exhibit 8.2

Accounting System Components

| Source Document | Input Devices | Information Processor | Information Storage | Output Devices |

source documents include invoices from suppliers, billings to customers, and employee earnings records.

Source documents are often paper-based. Yet increasingly they are taking other forms such as electronic files and Web communications. Also, a growing number of companies are sending invoices directly from their systems to their customers' systems. The Web is playing a major role in this transformation from paper-based to *paperless* systems.

Accurate source documents are crucial to accounting information systems. Input of faulty or incomplete information seriously impairs the reliability and relevance of the information system. We commonly refer to this as "garbage in, garbage out." Information systems are set up with special attention on control procedures to limit the possibility of entering faulty data in the system.

Input Devices

Input devices capture information from source documents and enable its transfer to the information processing component of the system. These devices often involve converting data on source documents from written or electronic form to a form usable for the system. Journal entries, both electronic and paper-based, are a type of input device. If we record transactions using **GLAS, SPATS,** or **PeachTree** software accompanying this book, our input device is a computer keyboard. Keyboards, scanners, and modems are some of the most common input devices in practice today.

Another increasingly common input device is a *bar-code reader.* Commonly used by merchandisers, bar-code readers are growing in importance as input and control devices for military, law enforcement, and special business applications. Bar-code readers capture code numbers and transfer them to the organization's computer for processing. A *scanner* is another popular input device whose applications are expanding. It can capture writing samples and other input directly from source documents.

Music-In, Rankings-Out

For decades, merchandisers, radio stations, and consumers saw what was hot and what wasn't in *Billboard* magazine's weekly survey. The survey results were compiled from phone interviews with store owners. But a startup company called **SoundScan** began tracking CD sales electronically at checkout counters, producing more accurate results. Its scanners are now in more than 14,000 stores. Among the surprising findings are that country music and small rap labels are far more popular than record executives imagined. Both now get promoted much more heavily. [Source: *Business Week,* June 6, 1994.]

Accounting information systems encourage accuracy by using consistent methods for inputting data. Controls are also used to ensure that only authorized individuals can input data to the system. Controls increase the reliability of the system. They also allow false information to be traced back to its source.

Information Processor

An **information processor** is a system that interprets, transforms, and summarizes information for use in analysis and reporting. An important part of an information processor in accounting systems is professional judgment. Accounting principles are never so structured that they limit the need for professional judgment. Other parts of an information processor include journals, ledgers, working papers, and posting procedures. Each assists in transforming raw data to useful information.

Increasingly, computer technology is assisting manual information processors. This assistance is freeing accounting professionals to take on greater analysis, interpretive, and managerial roles. This assistance to information processors includes both computing hardware and software. Hardware is the computing equipment, and software is the directions for the hardware. Software consists of computer programs that specify operations performed on data. Software often controls much of the accounting system including input, file management, processing, and output. **Microsoft,** the world's largest software producer, is a major part of this evolution. It reported 1996 revenues of more than $8.6 billion, with much of this from software sales.

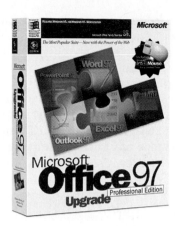

Information Storage

Information storage is the component of an accounting system that keeps data in a form accessible to information processors. After being input and processed, data are usually saved for use in future analysis or reports. This database must be accessible to preparers of periodic financial reports and for other analyses. Information storage is also set up to help in the creation of internal reports. Auditors focus on this database when they audit financial statements. Companies also maintain files of source documents to resolve errors or disputes.

Technology increasingly assists with information storage. While previous systems consisted almost exclusively of paper documents, there is growing use of CDs, hard drives, tapes, and other electronic storage devices. Advances in information storage enable accounting systems to store more detailed data than ever before. This means managers have more data to access and work with in planning and controlling business activities. Information storage can be on-line, meaning data can be accessed whenever it is needed, or it can be off-line, meaning data can't be accessed. Access often requires assistance and authorization. Information storage is increasingly augmented by Web information sources such as SEC databases, FASB standards, and financial and product markets.

Geek Chic

A group of cyberfashion pioneers at **MIT's Media Laboratory** is creating geek chic, a kind of wearable computer. Cyberfashion draws on new technologies. Digital cellular phones mean we can stay connected to the Web wherever we roam. Lithium batteries reduce weight, and miniature monitors are placed at the edge of a pair of glasses. Special conducive thread is woven into clothing to carry low-voltage signals from one part of the system to another and fabric keyboards are sewn into blue jeans. Current offerings include a music synthesizer woven into a dress and a jersey that translates the wearer's words into a foreign language. These creations give new meaning to the term *software*. [Source: *Business Week,* October 20, 1997.]

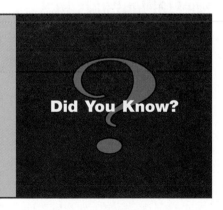

Did You Know?

Output Devices

Output devices are the means to take information out of an accounting system and make it available to users. Output devices provide users with a variety of items including graphics, analysis reports, bills to customers, checks to suppliers, employee paychecks, financial statements, and internal reports. The most common output devices are printers and monitors; others include telephones or direct Web communication with the systems of suppliers or customers. When requests for output occur, an information processor takes the needed data from a database and prepares the necessary report. This report is then sent to an output device.

Information can be output in many forms. For example, a touch-tone telephone can serve as an input/output device when a bank customer calls to learn the balance in his or her account. The customer presses buttons to provide requested authorization and then receives the desired information over the phone line. Another kind of output is an electronic fund transfer (EFT) of payroll from the company's bank account to its employees' bank accounts. One output device to accomplish this is an interface that allows a company's accounting system to send payroll data directly to the accounting system of its bank. Still another EFT output device involves a company recording its payroll data on tape or CD and forwarding it to the bank. This tape or disk is then used by the bank to transfer wages earned to employees' accounts.

Flash *back*

1. Identify the five primary components of an accounting information system.

2. What is the aim of the information processor component of an accounting system?

3. What uses are made of data in the information storage component of an accounting system?

Answers—p. 341

Judgment and Ethics

Certified Public Accountant

You are a CPA consulting with a client. This client's business has grown to the point where its accounting system must be updated to handle both the volume of transactions and management's needs for information. Your client requests your advice in purchasing new software for its accounting system. You have been offered a 10% commission by a software company for each purchase of its system by one of your clients. Do you think your evaluation of software is affected by this commission arrangement? Do you think this commission arrangement is appropriate? Do you tell your client about the commission arrangement before making a recommendation?

Answer—p. 341

Special Journals in Accounting

C3 Explain the goals and uses of special journals.

This section describes the underlying records of accounting information systems. Designed correctly, these records support efficiency in processing transactions and events. They are part of all systems in various forms. They are also increasingly electronically based. But even in technologically advanced systems, a basic understanding of the records we describe in this section aids us in using, interpreting, and applying accounting information. It also improves our understanding of the workings of computer-based systems. We must remember that all accounting systems have common purposes and internal workings whether or not they depend on technology.

This section focuses on special journals and subsidiary ledgers that are an important part of accounting systems. We describe how special journals are used to capture transactions, and we explain how subsidiary ledgers are set up to capture details of certain accounts. This section uses selected transactions of **Outdoors Unlimited** to illustrate these important points.

Outdoors Unlimited uses a *periodic* inventory system, so the special journals are set up using this system. The focus on special journals in a periodic system is appropriate because they are more often used in a periodic system than in a perpetual system. Many perpetual systems are computerized, and thus their "special journals" are usually in electronic form and automate several recordkeeping tasks such as posting and preparing accounts receivable and payable schedules. Appendix 8A describes the slight change in special journals required for a *perpetual* system. We also include a note at the bottom of each of the major journals prepared using the periodic system explaining the minor change required if a company uses a perpetual system.

Basics of Special Journals

A General Journal is an all-purpose journal where we can record any transaction. Yet using a General Journal means that each debit and each credit entered must be individually posted to its respective ledger account. This requires time and effort in posting individual debits and credits, especially for less technologically advanced systems. The costs of posting accounts can be reduced by organizing transactions into common groups and providing a separate special journal. A **special journal** is used in recording and posting transactions of similar type. Most transactions of a merchandiser, for instance, fall into four groups: sales on credit, purchases on credit, cash receipts, and cash disbursements. Exhibit 8.3 shows the special journals for these groups. This section assumes the use of these four special journals along with the General Journal.

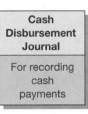

Sales Journal	Cash Receipts Journal	Purchases Journal	Cash Disbursement Journal	General Journal
For recording credit sales	For recording cash receipts	For recording credit purchases	For recording cash payments	For transactions not in special journals

Exhibit 8.3

Using Special Journals with a General Journal

The General Journal continues to be used for transactions not covered by special journals and for adjusting, closing, and correcting entries. We show in the following discussion how special journals are efficient tools in helping journalize and post transactions. This is done, for instance, by accumulating debits and credits of similar transactions, which allows us to post amounts entered in the columns as column *totals* rather than as individual amounts. The advantage of this system increases as the number of transactions increases. Special journals also allow an efficient division of labor. This can be an effective control procedure.

Subsidiary Ledgers

Special journals are helpful for many reasons including collecting information on accounts making up the *General Ledger*. But to understand the details of special journals, it is necessary to know the workings of a subsidiary ledger. A **subsidiary ledger** is a listing of individual accounts with a common characteristic. A subsidiary ledger supports the General Ledger with detailed information on specific accounts, which removes unnecessary details from the General Ledger.

Accounting information systems often include several subsidiary ledgers. Two of the most important are the amounts due from customers, called *accounts receivable,* and amounts owed to creditors, called *accounts payable.* These two common subsidiary ledgers are known as the:

C4 Describe the use of controlling accounts and subsidiary ledgers.

- *Accounts Receivable Ledger* for storing transaction data with individual customers.
- *Accounts Payable Ledger* for storing transaction data with individual creditors.

Individual accounts in subsidiary ledgers are often arranged alphabetically. We describe accounts receivable and accounts payable ledgers in this section. This knowledge will help us in understanding special journals in the next section when we use both of these ledgers.

Accounts Receivable Ledger

When we recorded credit sales in prior transaction analyses, we usually debited Accounts Receivable. Yet when a company has more than one credit customer, the accounts receivable records must show how much *each* customer purchased, paid, and has yet to pay. This information is collected for companies with credit customers by keeping a separate account receivable for each customer.

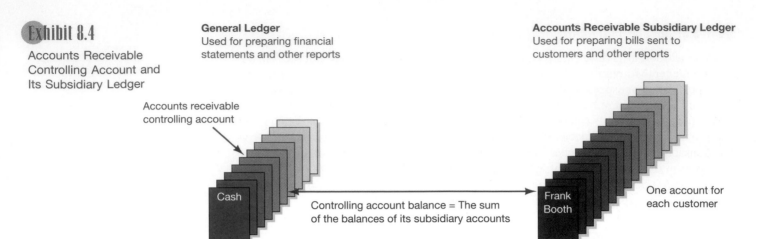

Exhibit 8.4

Accounts Receivable Controlling Account and Its Subsidiary Ledger

A separate account for each customer can be kept in the General Ledger containing the other financial statement accounts. But this is uncommon. Instead, the General Ledger continues to keep a single Accounts Receivable account and a *subsidiary ledger* is set up to keep a separate account for each customer. This subsidiary ledger is called the **Accounts Receivable Ledger** (also called *Accounts Receivable Subsidiary Ledger* or *Customers' Ledger*). Like a General Ledger, a subsidiary ledger can exist in electronic (tape or CD) or paper (book or tray) form. Customer accounts in a subsidiary ledger are kept separate from the Accounts Receivable account in the General Ledger.

Exhibit 8.4 shows the relation between the Accounts Receivable account and its related accounts in the subsidiary ledger. After all items are posted, the balance in the Accounts Receivable account must equal the sum of balances in the customers' accounts. The Accounts Receivable account is said to control the Accounts Receivable Ledger and is called a **controlling account.** Since the Accounts Receivable Ledger is a supplementary record controlled by an account in the General Ledger, it is called a subsidiary ledger.

Accounts Payable Ledger

There are other controlling accounts and subsidiary ledgers. We know, for example, that many companies buy on credit from several suppliers. This means a company must keep a separate account for each creditor. It does this by keeping an Accounts Payable controlling account in the General Ledger and a separate account for each creditor in an **Accounts Payable Ledger** (also called *Accounts Payable Subsidiary Ledger* or *Creditors' Ledger*). The concept of a controlling account and subsidiary ledger as described with accounts receivable also applies to creditor accounts.

Other Subsidiary Ledgers

Subsidiary ledgers are also common for several other accounts. A company with many items of equipment, for example, might keep only one Equipment account in its General Ledger. But this company's Equipment account would control a subsidiary ledger where each item of equipment is recorded in a separate account. Similar treatment is common for investments, inventory, payables, and other large accounts needing separate detailed records.

NIKE reports detailed sales information by geographic area in its 1997 annual report presented in Appendix A. Yet NIKE's accounting system most certainly keeps more detailed sales records than reflected in its annual report. NIKE, for instance, sells hundreds of different products and is able to analyze the sales performance of each one of them. This detail can be captured by many different general ledger sales accounts. But it is likely captured by using supplementary records that function like subsidiary ledgers. The concept of a subsidiary ledger can be applied in many different ways to ensure that the accounting system captures sufficient details to support analyses that decision makers need.

Sales Journal

A **sales journal** is used to record sales of merchandise on credit. Sales of merchandise for cash are not recorded in a sales journal but instead are recorded in a cash receipts journal. Sales of nonmerchandise assets on credit are recorded in the general journal.

Journalizing

Credit sale transactions are recorded with information about each sale entered separately in a Sales Journal. This information is often taken from a copy of the sales ticket or invoice prepared at the time of sale. The top of Exhibit 8.5 shows a Sales Journal from

Journalize and post transactions using special journals.

Exhibit 8.5

Sales Journal with Posting*

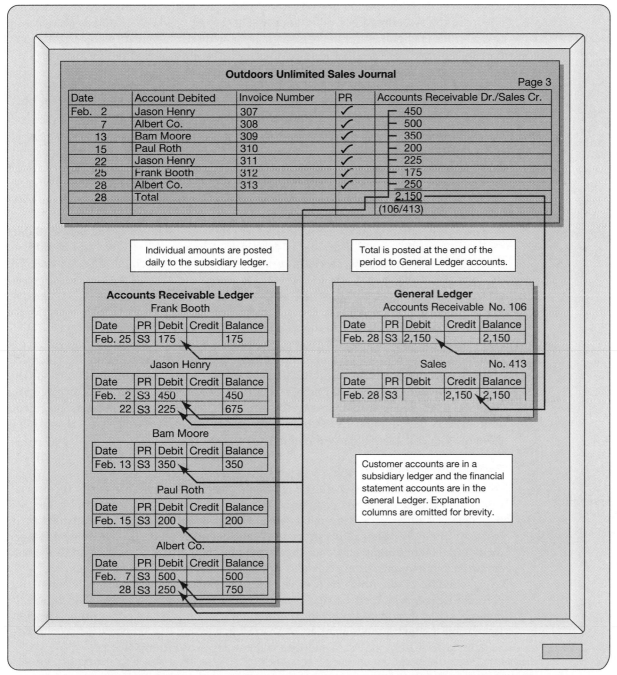

*Sales Journal in a *perpetual* system requires a new column on the far right titled "Cost of Goods Sold Dr., Inventory Cr." (see Exhibit 8.17).

the sporting goods merchandiser, **Outdoors Unlimited.** The Sales Journal in this exhibit is called a columnar journal because it has columns for recording the date, customer's name, invoice number, posting reference, and amount of each credit sale.[1] A **columnar journal** is a journal with more than one column.

Each transaction recorded in the Sales Journal yields a debit to Accounts Receivable and a credit to Sales. We only need one column for these two accounts. An exception is when managers need more information about taxes, returns, items, and other details of transactions. We do not use the posting reference (PR) column when entering transactions; instead this column is used when posting.

Posting

A Sales Journal is posted as shown with the arrow lines in Exhibit 8.5. Individual transactions in the Sales Journal are posted regularly (typically each day) to customer accounts in the Accounts Receivable Ledger. These postings keep customer accounts up to date. This is important for the person granting credit to customers, who needs to know the amount owed by credit-seeking customers. If this information in the customer's account is out of date, an incorrect decision can be made.

When sales recorded in the Sales Journal are individually posted to customer accounts in the Accounts Receivable Ledger, check marks are entered in the Sales Journal's Posting Reference column. Check marks are usually used rather than account numbers because customer accounts are not always numbered. Customer accounts are arranged alphabetically in the Accounts Receivable Ledger for reference. Note that posting debits to Accounts Receivable twice—once to Accounts Receivable and once to the customer's account—does not violate the accounting equation of debits equal credits. The equality of debits and credits is always maintained in the General Ledger. The Accounts Receivable Ledger is a subsidiary record.

The Sales Journal's dollar amount column is totaled at the end of the period (month of February in this case). The total is debited to Accounts Receivable and credited to Sales. The credit records the period's revenue from sales on account. The debit records the increase in accounts receivable. There is a general rule for all postings to a controlling account: The controlling account is debited periodically for an amount or amounts equal to the sum of the debits to the subsidiary ledger, and it is credited periodically for an amount or amounts equal to the sum of the credits to the subsidiary ledger.

When a company uses more than one journal, it identifies in the Posting Reference column of the *ledgers* the journal and page number from which the amount is taken. We identify a journal by using an initial. Items posted from the S̲ales Journal carry the initial *S* before their journal page numbers in a Posting Reference column. Likewise, items from the Cash R̲eceipts Journal carry the initial *R*; items from the Cash D̲isbursements Journal carry the initial *D*; items from the P̲urchases Journal carry the initial *P*; and items from the G̲eneral Journal carry the initial *G*.

Testing the Ledger

P2 Prepare and test the accuracy of subsidiary ledgers.

Account balances in the General Ledger and subsidiary ledgers are tested (or proved) for accuracy after posting is complete. We do this by first preparing a trial balance of the General Ledger to confirm debits equal credits (see Chapter 4 for preparing a trial balance). If debits equal credits in the trial balance, the accounts in the General Ledger, including the controlling accounts, are assumed to be correct. Second, we test the subsidiary ledgers by preparing schedules of individual accounts and amounts.

A **schedule of accounts receivable** is a listing of accounts from the Accounts Receivable Ledger with their balances and the sum of all balances. If this total equals the balance of the Accounts Receivable controlling account, the accounts in the Accounts Receivable Ledger are assumed correct. Exhibit 8.6 shows a schedule of accounts receivable drawn from the Accounts Receivable Ledger of Exhibit 8.5.

---

[1] For brevity, we don't record explanations in any of our special journals.

Additional Issues

This section looks at three additional issues with the Sales Journal: (1) recording sales taxes, (2) recording sales returns and allowances, and (3) using sales invoices as a journal.

Sales Taxes

Many cities and states require retailers to collect sales taxes from customers and to periodically send these taxes to the city or state treasurer. When using a columnar Sales Journal, we can have a record of taxes collected by adding columns to the journal as shown in Exhibit 8.7 for Outdoors Unlimited.

Exhibit 8.6

Schedule of Accounts Receivable

OUTDOORS UNLIMITED Schedule of Accounts Receivable February 28, 2000	
Frank Booth	$ 175
Jason Henry	675
Bam Moore	350
Paul Roth	200
Albert Co.	750
Total accounts receivable	$2,150

Exhibit 8.7

Sales Journal with information on Sales Taxes

Outdoors Unlimited Sales Journal						Page 3
Date	Account Debited	Invoice Number	PR	Accounts Receivable Dr.	Sales Taxes Payable Cr.	Sales Cr.
Dec. 1	Favre Co.	7-1698		103	3	100

We described how column totals of a Sales Journal are commonly posted at the end of each period (month for Outdoors Unlimited). This now includes crediting the Sales Taxes Payable account for the total of the Sales Taxes Payable column. Individual amounts in the Accounts Receivable column are posted daily to customer accounts in the Accounts Receivable Ledger. Individual amounts in the Sales Taxes Payable and Sales columns are not posted. A company that collects sales taxes on its cash sales can also use a special Sales Taxes Payable column in its Cash Receipts Journal.

Sales Returns and Allowances

A company with only a few sales returns and allowances can record them in a General Journal with an entry like:

Mar. 17	Sales Returns and Allowances	414	175	
	Accounts Receivable—Ray Ball	106/✓		175
	Customer returned merchandise.			

Assets = Liabilities + Equity
−175   −175

The debit in this entry is posted to the Sales Returns and Allowances account. The credit is posted to both the Accounts Receivable controlling account and to the customer's account. We also include the account number and the check mark, 106/✓, in the PR column on the credit line. This means both the Accounts Receivable controlling account in the General Ledger and the Ray Ball account in the Accounts Receivable Ledger are credited for $175. Both are credited because the balance of the controlling account in the General Ledger does not equal the sum of the customer account balances in the subsidiary ledger unless both are credited.

A company with a large number of sales returns and allowances can save costs by recording them in a special Sales Returns and Allowances Journal similar to Exhibit 8.8. A company can design and use a special journal for any group of similar transactions if there are enough transactions to warrant a journal. When using a Sales Returns and Allowances Journal to record returns, amounts in the journal are posted daily to customers' accounts. The journal total is posted as a debit to Sales Returns and Allowances and as a credit to Accounts Receivable at the end of the month.

Outdoors Unlimited Sales Returns and Allowances Journal				Page 1
Date	Account Credited	Credit Memo No.	PR	Sales Returns & Allowances Dr. Accounts Receivable Cr.
Mar. 7	Robert Moore	203	✓	10
14	James Warren	204	✓	12
18	T.M. Jones	205	✓	6
23	Sam Smith	206	✓	18
31	Total			46
				(414/106)

Sales Invoices as a Sales Journal

To save costs, some merchandisers avoid using Sales Journals for credit sales. Instead they post each sales invoice total directly to the customer's account in the subsidiary Accounts Receivable Ledger. They then put copies of invoices in numerical order in a file. At the end of the month, they total all invoices for that month and make a general journal entry to debit Accounts Receivable and credit Sales for the total. The bound invoice copies essentially act as a Sales Journal. This procedure is called *direct posting of sales invoices*.

Flash *back*

4. When special journals are used, where are all cash payments by check recorded?

5. How does a columnar journal save posting time and effort?

6. How do debits and credits remain equal when credit sales to customers are posted twice (once to Accounts Receivable and once to the customer's account)?

7. How do we identify the journal from which an amount in a ledger account was posted?

Answers—p. 341

Cash Receipts Journal

A **Cash Receipts Journal** records all receipts of cash. A Cash Receipts Journal is a columnar journal because different accounts are credited when cash is received from different sources.

Journalizing and Posting

Cash receipts usually fall into one of three groups: (1) cash from credit customers in payment of their accounts, (2) cash from cash sales, and (3) cash from other sources. The Cash Receipts Journal in Exhibit 8.9 has a special column for credits when cash is received from one or more of these three sources. We describe how to journalize transactions for each of these three sources in this section. We then describe how to post these transactions.[2]

Cash from Credit Customers

To record cash received in payment of a customer's account, the customer's name is first entered in the Cash Receipts Journal's Account Credited column. Then the amounts debited to Cash and Sales Discount (if any) are entered in their respective journal columns, and the amount credited to the customer's account is entered in the Accounts Receivable Credit column. The February 12 transaction is one example of cash received from credit customers. Note the Accounts Receivable Credit column contains only credits to customer accounts.

---

[2] We include explanations in the Cash Receipts Journal so the reader knows the source of each cash receipt transaction.

Exhibit 8.9

Cash Receipts Journal with
Posting*

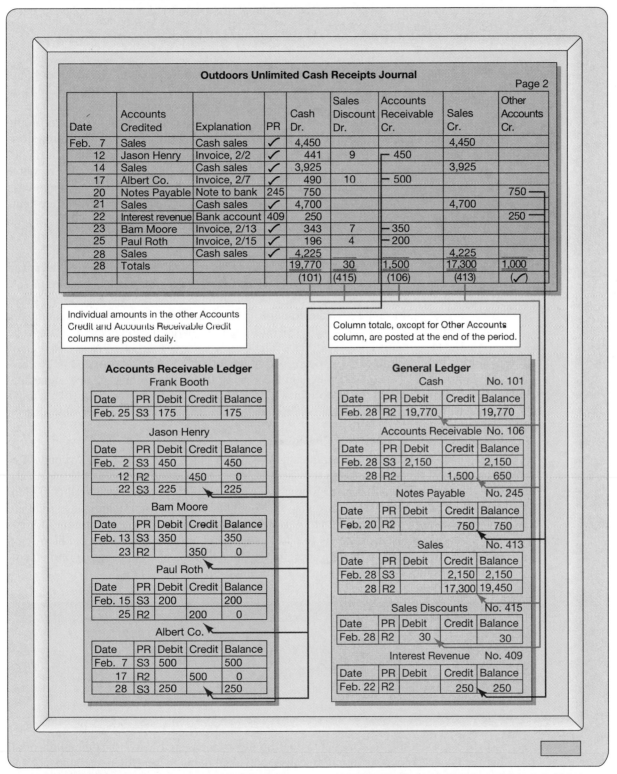

Outdoors Unlimited Cash Receipts Journal

Page 2

Date	Accounts Credited	Explanation	PR	Cash Dr.	Sales Discount Dr.	Accounts Receivable Cr.	Sales Cr.	Other Accounts Cr.
Feb. 7	Sales	Cash sales	✓	4,450			4,450	
12	Jason Henry	Invoice, 2/2	✓	441	9	450		
14	Sales	Cash sales	✓	3,925			3,925	
17	Albert Co.	Invoice, 2/7	✓	490	10	500		
20	Notes Payable	Note to bank	245	750				750
21	Sales	Cash sales	✓	4,700			4,700	
22	Interest revenue	Bank account	409	250				250
23	Bam Moore	Invoice, 2/13	✓	343	7	350		
25	Paul Roth	Invoice, 2/15	✓	196	4	200		
28	Sales	Cash sales	✓	4,225			4,225	
28	Totals			19,770	30	1,500	17,300	1,000
				(101)	(415)	(106)	(413)	(✓)

Individual amounts in the other Accounts Credit and Accounts Receivable Credit columns are posted daily.

Column totals, except for Other Accounts column, are posted at the end of the period.

Accounts Receivable Ledger

Frank Booth

Date	PR	Debit	Credit	Balance
Feb. 25	S3	175		175

Jason Henry

Date	PR	Debit	Credit	Balance
Feb. 2	S3	450		450
12	R2		450	0
22	S3	225		225

Bam Moore

Date	PR	Debit	Credit	Balance
Feb. 13	S3	350		350
23	R2		350	0

Paul Roth

Date	PR	Debit	Credit	Balance
Feb. 15	S3	200		200
25	R2		200	0

Albert Co.

Date	PR	Debit	Credit	Balance
Feb. 7	S3	500		500
17	R2		500	0
28	S3	250		250

General Ledger

Cash No. 101

Date	PR	Debit	Credit	Balance
Feb. 28	R2	19,770		19,770

Accounts Receivable No. 106

Date	PR	Debit	Credit	Balance
Feb. 28	S3	2,150		2,150
28	R2		1,500	650

Notes Payable No. 245

Date	PR	Debit	Credit	Balance
Feb. 20	R2		750	750

Sales No. 413

Date	PR	Debit	Credit	Balance
Feb. 28	S3		2,150	2,150
28	R2		17,300	19,450

Sales Discounts No. 415

Date	PR	Debit	Credit	Balance
Feb. 28	R2	30		30

Interest Revenue No. 409

Date	PR	Debit	Credit	Balance
Feb. 22	R2		250	250

*Cash Receipts Journal in a *perpetual* system requires a new column on the far right titled "Cost of Goods Sold Dr., Inventory Cr." (see Exhibit 8.18).

The posting procedure is twofold. First, individual amounts are posted to subsidiary ledger accounts. Second, column totals are posted to General Ledger accounts. Let's look at the Accounts Receivable Credit column as an example. Individual credits are posted regularly (daily) to customer accounts in the subsidiary Accounts Receivable Ledger. The column total is posted at the end of the period (month) as a credit to the Accounts Receivable controlling account.

Cash Sales

When cash sales are collected, the debits to Cash are entered in the Cash Debit column, and the credits in a special column titled Sales Credit. The February 7 transaction is an example of cash sales. By using a separate Sales Credit column, we can post the total cash sales for a period (month) as a single amount, the column total. When recording daily cash sales in the Cash Receipts Journal, we place a check mark in the Posting Reference (PR) column to indicate that no amount is individually posted from that line of the journal. Sometimes companies also use a double check (✓✓) to identify amounts that are not posted to customer accounts from amounts that are posted. Although cash sales are usually journalized daily (or at point of sale) in practice, cash sales are journalized weekly in Exhibit 8.9 for brevity.

Cash from Other Sources

Most cash receipts are from collections of accounts receivable and from cash sales. But other sources of cash include money borrowed from a bank, interest on account, or sale of unneeded assets. The Other Accounts Credit column is for receipts that do not occur often enough to warrant a separate column. This means items entered in this column are few and are posted to a variety of General Ledger accounts. Postings are less apt to be omitted if these items are posted daily. The Cash Receipts Journal's Posting Reference column is used only for daily postings from the Other Accounts and Accounts Receivable columns. The account numbers in the Posting Reference column refer to items that are posted to General Ledger accounts. Check marks indicate that an item (like a day's cash sales) is either not posted or is posted to the subsidiary Accounts Receivable Ledger.

Footing, Crossfooting, and Posting

At the end of a period (month), the amounts in the Cash, Sales Discount, Accounts Receivable, and Sales columns of the Cash Receipts Journal are posted as column totals. The transactions recorded in all journals must result in equal debits and credits to General Ledger accounts. To be sure that total debits and credits in a columnar journal are equal, we often crossfoot column totals before posting them. To *foot* a column of numbers is to add it. To *crossfoot* is to add the debit column totals, add the credit column totals, and then compare the two sums for equality. Footing and crossfooting of the numbers in Exhibit 8.9 yields the schedule in Exhibit 8.10:

Exhibit 8.10

Footing and Crossfooting Journal Amounts

Debit Columns		Credit Columns	
Sales discounts debit	$ 30	Accounts receivable credit	$ 1,500
Cash debit	19,770	Sales credit	17,300
		Other accounts credit	1,000
Total	$19,800	Total	$19,800

After crossfooting the journal to confirm debits equal credits, we post the totals of all but the Other Accounts column. Because individual items in the Other Accounts column are posted daily, this column total is not posted. We place a check mark below the Other Accounts column to indicate that this column total is not posted. The account numbers of the accounts where the remaining column totals are posted are in parentheses below each column. Posting items daily from the Other Accounts column with a delayed posting of the offsetting items in the Cash column (total) causes the General Ledger to be out of balance during the period. But this doesn't matter because posting the Cash column total causes the offsetting amounts to reach the General Ledger before the trial balance or other financial statements are prepared at the end of the period.

Retailer
You are a retailer in computer equipment and supplies. You want to know how promptly customers are paying their bills. This information can help you in deciding whether to extend credit and in planning your own cash payments. Where might you look for this information?

Answer—p. 341

Purchases Journal

A **Purchases Journal** is used to record all purchases on credit. Purchases for cash are recorded in the Cash Disbursements Journal.

Journalizing

A Purchases Journal usually is more useful if it is a multicolumn journal where all credit purchases, not only merchandise, are recorded. Exhibit 8.11 shows a multicolumn Purchases Journal.

Purchase invoices or other source documents are used in recording transactions in the Purchases Journal. The procedure is similar to that for the Sales Journal. We use the invoice date and terms to compute the date when payment for each purchase is due. Merchandise purchases are recorded in the Purchases Debit column. When a purchase involves an amount recorded in the Other Accounts Debit column, we use the Account column to identify the General Ledger account debited. Outdoors Unlimited also includes a separate column for credit purchases of office supplies. A separate column such as this is useful whenever several transactions involve debits to a specific account. Each company uses its own judgment in deciding on the number of separate columns necessary. The Other Accounts Debit column allows the Purchases Journal to be used for all purchase transactions involving credits to Accounts Payable. The Accounts Payable Credit column is used to record the amounts credited to each creditor's account.

Posting

The amounts in the Accounts Payable Credit column are posted regularly (daily) to individual creditor accounts in a subsidiary Accounts Payable Ledger. Each line of the Account column in Exhibit 8.11 shows the subsidiary ledger account that is posted for these amounts in the Accounts Payable Credit column. Individual amounts in the Other Accounts Debit column usually are posted daily to their General Ledger accounts. At the end of the period (month), all column totals except the Other Accounts Debit column are posted to their General Ledger accounts. The balance in the Accounts Payable controlling account must equal the sum of the account balances in the subsidiary Accounts Payable Ledger after posting.

Testing the Ledger

Account balances in the General Ledger and subsidiary ledgers are tested for accuracy after posting of the Purchases Journal is complete. Similar to the procedures followed for testing the ledger for the Sales Journal, two steps are necessary. First, we prepare a trial balance of the General Ledger to confirm debits equal credits. If debits equal credits in the trial balance, the accounts in the General Ledger, including the controlling accounts, are assumed to be correct. Second, we test the subsidiary ledgers by preparing a schedule of accounts payable. A **schedule of accounts payable** is a listing of accounts from the Accounts Payable Ledger with their balances and the sum of all the balances.

Exhibit 8.11

Purchases
Journal with
Posting*

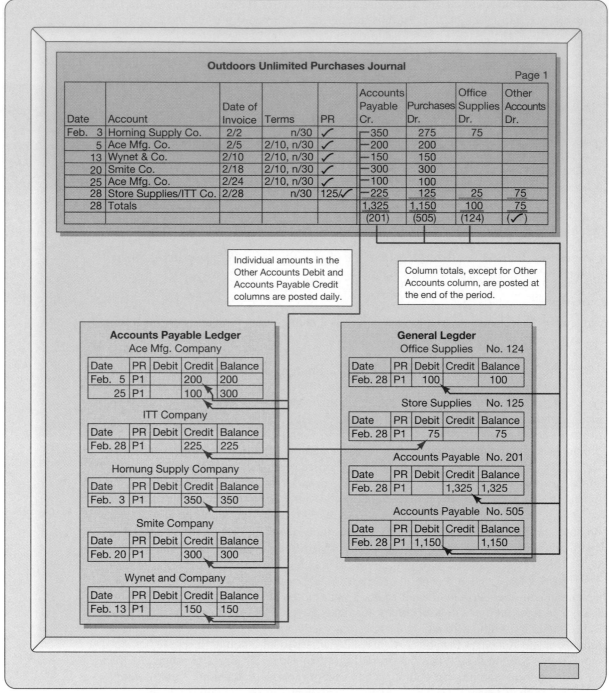

*Purchases Journal in a *perpetual* system replaces "Purchases Dr." with "Inventory Dr." (see Exhibit 8.19).

If this total equals the balance of the Accounts Payable controlling account, the accounts in the Accounts Payable Ledger are assumed correct. Exhibit 8.12 shows a schedule of accounts payable drawn from the Accounts Payable Ledger of Exhibit 8.11.

Cash Disbursements Journal

A **Cash Disbursements Journal,** also called a *Cash Payments Journal,* is used to record all payments of cash. It is a multicolumn journal because cash payments are made for several different purposes.

Journalizing

A Cash Disbursements Journal is like a Cash Receipts Journal except it records repetitive cash payments instead of receipts. Exhibit 8.13 shows the Cash Disbursements Journal for Outdoors Unlimited. We see repetitive credits to the Cash column of this journal. We also commonly see credits to Purchases Discounts and debits to the Accounts Payable account. Many companies purchase merchandise on credit, and therefore, a Purchases column is not often needed. Instead, the occasional cash purchase is recorded in the Other Accounts Debit column and Cash Credit column as illustrated in the February 12 transaction of Exhibit 8.13.

OUTDOORS UNLIMITED Schedule of Accounts Payable February 28, 2000	
Ace Mfg. Company	$ 300
ITT Company	225
Hornung Supply Company	350
Smite Company	300
Wynet & Company	150
Total accounts payable	$1,325

Exhibit 8.12

Schedule of Accounts Payable

The Cash Disbursements Journal has a column titled Ck. No. (check number). For control over cash disbursements, all payments except for very small amounts are made by check.[3] Checks should be prenumbered and entered in the journal in numerical order with each check's number in the column headed Ck. No. This makes it possible to scan the numbers in the column for omitted checks. When a Cash Disbursements Journal has a column for check numbers, it is sometimes called a **Check Register.**

Controller

You are a controller for a merchandising company. You want to analyze your company's cash payments to suppliers, including an analysis of purchases discounts. Where might you look for this information?

You Make the Call

Answer—p. 341

Posting

Individual amounts in the Other Accounts Debit column of a Cash Disbursements Journal are usually posted to their general ledger accounts on a regular (daily) basis. Individual amounts in the Accounts Payable Debit column are also posted regularly (daily) to the specific creditors' accounts in the subsidiary Accounts Payable Ledger. At the end of the period (month), we crossfoot column totals and post the Accounts Payable Debit column total to the Accounts Payable controlling account. Also at the end of the period, the Purchases Discounts Credit column total is posted to the Purchases Discounts account and the Cash Credit column total is posted to the Cash account. The Other Accounts column total is not posted at the end of the period.

Flash *back*

8. What are the normal recording and posting procedures when using special journals and controlling accounts with subsidiary ledgers?

9. What is the rule for posting to a subsidiary ledger and its controlling account?

10. How do we test the accuracy of account balances in the General Ledger and subsidiary ledgers after posting?

Answers—p. 341

General Journal Transactions

When special journals are used we still need a General Journal for adjusting, closing, and correcting entries, and for transactions not recorded in special journals. These special

---

[3] We describe a petty cash system for controlling small cash payments in Chapter 9.

Exhibit 8.13

Cash Disbursements Journal
with Posting*

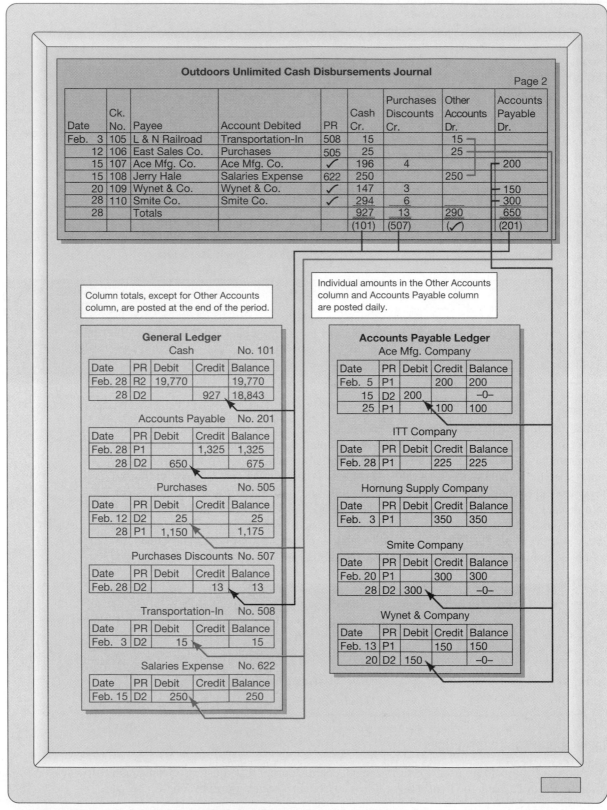

Outdoors Unlimited Cash Disbursements Journal

Page 2

Date	Ck. No.	Payee	Account Debited	PR	Cash Cr.	Purchases Discounts Cr.	Other Accounts Dr.	Accounts Payable Dr.
Feb. 3	105	L & N Railroad	Transportation-In	508	15		15	
12	106	East Sales Co.	Purchases	505	25		25	
15	107	Ace Mfg. Co.	Ace Mfg. Co.	✓	196	4		200
15	108	Jerry Hale	Salaries Expense	622	250		250	
20	109	Wynet & Co.	Wynet & Co.	✓	147	3		150
28	110	Smite Co.	Smite Co.	✓	294	6		300
28		Totals			927	13	290	650
					(101)	(507)	(✓)	(201)

Column totals, except for Other Accounts column, are posted at the end of the period.

Individual amounts in the Other Accounts column and Accounts Payable column are posted daily.

General Ledger

Cash   No. 101

Date	PR	Debit	Credit	Balance
Feb. 28	R2	19,770		19,770
28	D2		927	18,843

Accounts Payable   No. 201

Date	PR	Debit	Credit	Balance
Feb. 28	P1		1,325	1,325
28	D2	650		675

Purchases   No. 505

Date	PR	Debit	Credit	Balance
Feb. 12	D2	25		25
28	P1	1,150		1,175

Purchases Discounts No. 507

Date	PR	Debit	Credit	Balance
Feb. 28	D2		13	13

Transportation-In   No. 508

Date	PR	Debit	Credit	Balance
Feb. 3	D2	15		15

Salaries Expense   No. 622

Date	PR	Debit	Credit	Balance
Feb. 15	D2	250		250

Accounts Payable Ledger

Ace Mfg. Company

Date	PR	Debit	Credit	Balance
Feb. 5	P1		200	200
15	D2	200		–0–
25	P1		100	100

ITT Company

Date	PR	Debit	Credit	Balance
Feb. 28	P1		225	225

Hornung Supply Company

Date	PR	Debit	Credit	Balance
Feb. 3	P1		350	350

Smite Company

Date	PR	Debit	Credit	Balance
Feb. 20	P1		300	300
28	D2	300		–0–

Wynet & Company

Date	PR	Debit	Credit	Balance
Feb. 13	P1		150	150
20	D2	150		–0–

*Cash Disbursements Journal in a *perpetual* system replaces "Purchases Discounts Cr." with "Inventory Cr." (see Exhibit 8.20).

transactions include purchases returns and allowances, purchases of plant assets by issuing a note payable, sales returns if a Sales Returns and Allowances Journal is not used, and receiving a note receivable from a customer. We described how transactions are recorded in a General Journal in Chapter 3.

Flash back

11. How are sales taxes recorded in the context of special journals?

12. What is direct posting of sales invoices?

13. Why does a company need a General Journal when using special journals for sales, purchases, cash receipts, and cash disbursements?

Answers—p. 342

Technology-Based Accounting Information Systems

Accounting information systems are supported with technology, which can range from simple calculators to state-of-the-art advanced electronic systems. Because technology is increasingly important in accounting information systems, we discuss in this section the impact of computer technology, how data processing works with accounting data, and the role of computer networks.

Middleware

The latest buzz in information systems is about "middleware." Middleware is software allowing different computer programs used in a company or across companies to work together. It allows transfer of purchase orders, invoices, and other electronic documents between trading partners' accounting systems. It also helps each partner's bank handle the electronic payments. [Source: *Business Week,* June 16, 1997.]

Did You Know?

Computer Technology in Accounting

Computer technology can be separated into two broad categories—hardware and software. **Computer hardware** is the physical equipment in a computerized accounting information system. The physical equipment includes processing units, hard drives, RAM, modems, CD-ROM drives, speakers, monitors, workstations, servers, notebooks, printers, scanners, and jukeboxes. Computer hardware increasingly assists accounting and accounting-related professionals in their work. Computer hardware often provides accuracy, speed, efficiency, and convenience in performing accounting tasks.

C5 Explain how technology-based information systems impact accounting.

Computer software comprises the programs that direct the operations of computer hardware. A program is a series of commands directing operations such as data access from input or storage, data processing, or data output. A program can be written, for instance, to process customers' merchandise orders. A typical program works as follows. It creates a shipping order identifying products to be sent to customers. If this shipment causes the quantity on hand to fall below some minimum level, the program creates a purchase order to be approved by a manager. If the quantity on hand is less than what a customer ordered, the program creates a partial shipping order and a report to the customer that the remainder is on back order. If replacements are not on order already, the program creates a purchase order. If no units of the ordered product

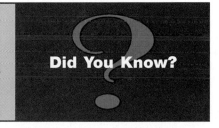

are on hand, the program creates a notification for the customer of a back order and creates a purchase order if necessary. The program continually processes customer orders as they arrive. This program can also be linked with accounting records for sales and accounts receivable, and it can deal with cash and trade discounts that might be offered to customers.

Widespread use of computer technology has increased the type and power of off-the-shelf programs that are ready to use. Off-the-shelf programs include multipurpose software applications for a variety of computer operations. These include familiar word processing programs such as *Word*® and *WordPerfect*®, spreadsheet programs such as *Excel*® and *Lotus 1-2-3*®, and database management programs such as *dBase*®. Other off-the-shelf programs meet the needs of specialized users. These include accounting programs such as *PeachTree*®, *DacEasy*®, and *QuickBooks*®. Off-the-shelf programs are designed to be user-friendly and guide users through all steps.

Off-the-shelf accounting programs can operate more efficiently as *integrated* systems. In an integrated system, actions taken in one part of the system automatically affect related parts. When a credit sale is recorded in an integrated system, for instance, several parts of the system are automatically updated. First, the system stores transaction data (as in a journal) so that we can review the entire entry at a later time. Second, it automatically updates the Cash and Accounts Receivable accounts. Third, it updates the record of amounts owed by a customer. Fourth, it updates the record of products held for sale to show the number of units sold and the number remaining.

Computer hardware and software can dramatically reduce the time and effort devoted to recordkeeping tasks. Less effort directed at recordkeeping tasks means more time for accounting professionals to concentrate on analysis and managerial type decision making. These advances have created an even greater demand for accounting professionals who understand financial reports and can draw insights and information from mountains of processed data. We must remember the primary demand for accounting knowledge is created by the need for information and not by the need for recordkeeping. Accounting professionals are in increasing demand because of expertise in determining relevant and reliable information for decision making. They are also valuable in analyzing the effects of transactions and events on a company and how they are reflected in financial statements and management reports.

Knowledge of the accounting described in this book enables us to understand and use accounting output. It also enables us to understand the transactions and events driving the output. In this way, and in this way only, can we expect to reap the full benefits of accounting reports. All the reports available can't help the external or internal user who fails to understand the accounting principles and methods determining the information.

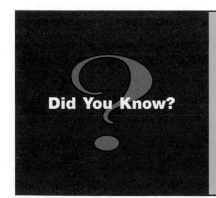

Software CPAs

A new generation of Windows-based accounting software is available. With the touch of a key, users can shift from cash to accrual accounting, and create real-time inventory reports showing all payments, charges, and credit limits at any point in the accounting cycle. Many also include "alert signals" notifying the user when, for example, a large order exceeds a customer's credit limit or purchase orders are needed. This software can also support all four inventory costing methods and do perpetual updating of records as each transaction occurs. **PeachTree Software** is the market leader for small businesses, and most programs cost under $250, with some as low as $50. [Source: *Business Week,* September 1, 1997.]

Data Processing in Accounting

Accounting systems differ in how input is entered and processed. **On-line processing** enters and processes data as soon as source documents are available. This means databases are immediately updated. **Batch processing** accumulates source documents for a period of time and then processes them all at once such as once a day, week, or month.

The advantage of on-line processing is up-to-date databases. This often requires additional costs related to both software and hardware requirements. Common on-line processing in practice includes airline reservations, credit card records, and rapid mail-order processing. The advantage of batch processing is it only requires periodic updating of databases. Records used in sending bills to customers, for instance, might require updating only once a month. The disadvantage of batch processing is the lack of updated databases for management when making business decisions.

Computer Networks in Accounting

Networking, or linking computers with each other, can create technology advantages. **Computer networks** are links among computers giving different users and different computers access to a common database and programs. Many colleges' computer labs, for instance, are networked. A small computer network is called a *local area network (LAN)*. This type of network links machines with *hard-wire* hookups. Large computer networks extending over long distances often rely on *modem* communication.

Demand for information sometimes requires advanced networks such as the system used by **Federal Express** for tracking packages and billing customers, and the system used by **Wal-Mart** for monitoring inventory levels in its stores. These networks include many computers (desktops and mainframes) and satellite communications to gather information and to provide ready access to its database from all locations.

Flash back

14. Identify an advantage of an integrated computer-based accounting system.

15. What advantages do computer systems offer over manual systems?

16. Identify an advantage of computer networks.

Answers—p. 342

Enterprise Application Software[4]

The market for enterprise-application software is soaring. **Enterprise-application software** includes the programs that manage a company's vital operations. They extend from order-taking to manufacturing to accounting. When working properly, these integrated programs can speed decision making, slash costs, and give managers control over global operations with the click of a mouse. Many see enterprise-applications emerging as a company's most strategic asset.

For many managers, enterprise-application software is like a lightbulb illuminating the dark recesses of their company's operations. It allows them to scrutinize a global business, identify where inventories are piling up, and see what plants are most efficient. The software is designed to link every part of a company's operations. This software allowed **Monsanto** to slash production planning from six weeks to three, trim inventories, reduce working capital, and increase its bargaining power with suppliers. **Monsanto** estimates this software saves the company $200 million per year.

There are six major enterprise-applications today. **SAP** dominates the market, with **Oracle** a distant second. SAP software runs the back offices of nearly half of the world's 500 largest companies. It links ordering, inventory, production, purchasing, planning, tracking, and human resources. One transaction or event triggers an immediate chain reaction of events throughout the enterprise. It is making companies more efficient and profitable.

Enterprise-applications are pushing into cyberspace. Now companies can share data with customers and suppliers. Applesauce maker **Mott's** is using SAP so that distribu-

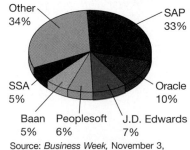

Total Market: $7.2 Billion

Other 34%
SAP 33%
Oracle 10%
J.D. Edwards 7%
Peoplesoft 6%
Baan 5%
SSA 5%

Source: *Business Week,* November 3, 1997.

[4]Source: S. Baker, A. Cortese, and G. Edmondson, "Silicon Valley on the Rhine," *Business Week,* (November 3, 1997).

tors can check the status of orders and place them over the Net, and the **Coca-Cola Company** uses it to ship soda on time. While enterprise-applications may not soon invade small business, it already controls many of our world's largest companies.

USING THE INFORMATION	Business Segments

A1 Analyze a company's performance and financial condition by business segments.

The accounting information system is usually more complex when a company is large and operates in more than one business segment. Special journals and subsidiary ledgers also are usually greater in number and more detailed for these companies.

Information about the business segments of a company is important to both internal and external decision makers. A **business segment** is the part of a company that is separately identified by its products or services or by the geographic market it serves. **NIKE,** for instance, states it operates "in one industry segment," and note 15 of its 1997 annual report shows its four main geographical markets: United States; Europe; Asia/Pacific; and Latin America/Canada. External users of financial statements are especially interested in segment information to better understand a company's business activities.

Information reported about business segments varies in quality and quantity. The full disclosure principle implies we ought to see detailed financial statements for each important segment. But full disclosure by segments is rare because of difficulties in separating segments and management's reluctance to release information that can harm its competitive position.

Companies offering their shares to the public in U.S. stock exchanges must disclose segment information under certain conditions. Accounting standards apply the definition of segments to industries, international activities, export sales, and major customers. A segment is considered important if its sales, operating income, *or* identifiable assets make up 10% or more of their respective totals. Companies are required to report information for these important segments.[5]

Exhibit 8.14 shows the results from a recent survey on the number of companies with business segments. Companies operating in different industries or geographic areas often have different rates of profitability, risk, and growth for these different segments. Evaluating risk and return is a major goal of decision makers, and segment information is useful in this evaluation.

Exhibit 8.14

Types of Segment Reports

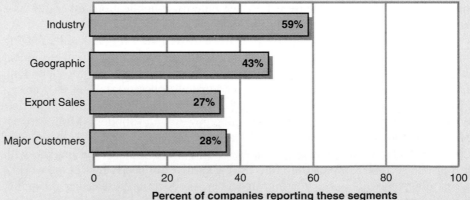

Source: *Accounting Trends & Techniques.* Total exceeds 100% because companies can report one or more segments.

---

[5] For each industry segment, companies must report: (1) net sales, (2) operating income before interest and taxes, (3) identifiable assets, (4) capital expenditures, and (5) depreciation, depletion, and amortization. Guidelines are given for defining a company's international operations, major customers, and export sales and for segmenting operations by geographic areas. Information similar to that reported for industry segments is required. [FASB, *Accounting Standards Current Text* (Norwalk, CT, 1994), sec. §20.101. First published as *FASB Statement No. 15.*]

Analysis of a company's segments is aided by a segment contribution matrix. A **segment contribution matrix** is a table listing of one or more important measures such as sales by segments. This listing usually includes amounts contributed both in dollars and percents, and its growth rate. We prepare a segment contribution matrix for **Woolworth's** sales in Exhibit 8.15.

Woolworth's Segment Contribution Matrix for Sales					
	Sales Contribution (in millions)		Sales Contribution (in %)		1-Year Growth Rate Percent
Segment	1996	1995	1996	1995	
Specialty:					
Athletic Group	$3,615	$3,424	45%	42%	6%
Northern Group	426	367	5%	4%	16%
Specialty Footwear	721	729	9%	9%	−1%
Other Specialty	442	579	5%	7%	−24%
Subtotal	$5,204	$5,099	64%	62%	2%
General Merchandise:					
Germany	$1,624	$1,733	20%	21%	−6%
United States	1,044	1,150	13%	14%	−9%
Other	220	242	3%	3%	−9%
Subtotal	$2,888	$3,125	36%	38%	−8%
Total	$8,092	$8,224	100%	100%	−2%

Exhibit 8.15

Segment Contribution Matrix

The second and third columns in Exhibit 8.15 list 1996 and 1995 sales data by segment. This data is drawn from Note 4 in Woolworth's 1996 annual report. We see that Woolworth's total 1996 sales were $8,092 million, divided into two major segments: (1) specialty and (2) general merchandise. The specialty segment is divided by a product emphasis, whereas the general merchandise segment is divided by geographic area. Standards permit this latitude. While information in these two columns is useful, several questions remain unanswered. What is the contribution of one segment versus another to total sales? Is there evidence of growth or decline by source? What is the highest growth segment? And which is the lowest? A segment contribution matrix provides us a starting point in answering such crucial questions.

Columns four and five of Exhibit 8.15 give us Woolworth's sales contribution in percent by segment. Each number is computed by taking a segment's sales and dividing by total sales. For example, the 1996 sales contribution in percent for the athletic group is computed as: $3,615 ÷ $8,092 = 0.45 or 45%.

The results tell us specialty merchandise makes up more than 60% of total sales, and most of it comes from its athletic group. This suggests Woolworth's sales are highly dependent on one area, the athletic group. A serious analysis of Woolworth demands special attention to this group. This includes assessing future prospects and the risk of competition for the athletic group. If we reviewed Woolworth's Management's Discussion and Analysis report we'd also find its Athletic Group is dominated by its **Foot Locker** stores and less so by its **Champs Sports** and **Going to the Game!** stores.

The far right column of Exhibit 8.15 shows the one-year growth rate in segment sales. A one-year growth rate is computed as: (Current period sales − Prior period sales) ÷ Prior period sales. For example, Woolworth's one-year growth rate in sales for its athletic group is computed as: ($3,615 − $3,424) ÷ $3,424 = 0.06 or 6%. The growth rates reveal several interesting findings. First, the northern group is growing faster than any other segment. Second, other specialty stores such as **After Thoughts** and **The Best of Times** are markedly declining in sales. Third, Woolworth's general merchandise segment reflects declining sales ranging from 6% to 9%. Fourth, while general merchandise has declined 8% in sales, the specialty segment has increased sales by 2%. We can extend our analysis of segment contribution matrixes to other measures such as operating income and assets. We show pie charts of Woolworth's assets breakdown in Exhibit 8.16 as an example of other analyses available to us.

Exhibit 8.16

Segment Asset Analysis
($ in millions)

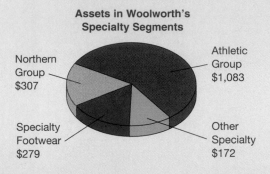

Assets in Woolworth's Specialty Segments

Northern Group $307
Athletic Group $1,083
Specialty Footwear $279
Other Specialty $172

Assets in Woolworth's General Merchandise Segment

Germany $997
United States $364
Other $11

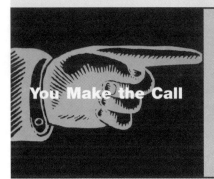

You Make the Call

Banker

You are the banker from whom an owner of a merchandiser in mountain bikes requests a loan to expand operations. The merchandiser's financials reveal a solid net income of $220,000, reflecting a 10% increase over the prior year. You also ask about any segments or geographic focus. The owner tells you that $160,000 of net income was from Cuban operations, reflecting a 60% increase over the prior year. The remaining $60,000 of net income was from U.S. operations, reflecting a 40% decrease. The owner is a Cuban immigrant, and he tells of his relationships with family and friends in Cuba. Does this segment information impact your loan decision?

Answer—p. 341

Flash back

17. What are the advantages of using segment information for analysis of a company?

Answer—p. 342

Summary

C1 Identify fundamental principles of accounting information systems. Accounting information systems are governed by five fundamental principles: control, relevance, compatibility, flexibility, and cost-benefit principles.

C2 Identify components of accounting information systems. There are five basic components of an accounting information system: source documents, input devices, information processors, information storage, and output devices.

C3 Explain the goals and uses of special journals. Special journals are used for recording and posting transactions of similar type, each meant to cover one kind of transaction. Four of the most common special journals are the Sales Journal, Cash Receipts Journal, Purchases Journal, and Cash Disbursements Journal. Special journals are efficient and cost-effective tools in the journalizing and posting processes. Special journals allow an efficient division of labor that is also an effective control procedure.

C4 Describe the use of controlling accounts and subsidiary ledgers. A General Ledger keeps controlling accounts such as Accounts Receivable or Accounts Payable, but details on individual accounts making up the controlling account are kept in a subsidiary ledger (such as an Accounts Receivable Ledger). The balance in a controlling account must equal the sum of its subsidiary account balances after posting is complete.

C5 Explain how technology-based information systems impact accounting. Technology-based information systems aim to increase the accuracy, speed, efficiency, and convenience of accounting procedures. Developments in hardware and software, data processing, and networking all impact accounting in varying degrees.

A1 Analyze a company's performance and financial condition by business segments. A business segment is a part of a company that is separately identified by its products or services or by the geographic market it serves. Analysis of a company's segments is aided by a segment contribution matrix listing of one or more accounting measures such as sales by segments. This listing usually includes amounts contributed both in dollars and percents, and the segment's growth rate.

P1 **Journalize and post transactions using special journals.** Special journals are each devoted to similar kinds of transactions. Transactions are journalized on one line of a special journal, with columns devoted to specific accounts, dates, names, posting references, explanations, and other necessary information. Posting is threefold: (1) individual amounts in the Other Accounts column are posted to their General Ledger accounts on a regular (daily) basis, (2) individual amounts in a column that is posted in total to a controlling account at the end of a period (month) are

posted regularly (daily) to their account in the subsidiary ledger, and (3) total amounts for all columns except the Other Accounts column are posted at the end of a period (month) to their column's account title.

P2 **Prepare and test the accuracy of subsidiary ledgers.** Account balances in the General Ledger and its subsidiary ledgers are tested for accuracy after posting is complete. This procedure is twofold: (1) prepare a trial balance of the General Ledger to confirm debits equal credits, and (2) prepare a schedule of a subsidiary ledger to confirm the controlling account's balance equals the subsidiary ledger's balance. A schedule is a listing of accounts from a subsidiary ledger with their balances and the sum of all balances.

Guidance Answer to **Judgment and Ethics**

Certified Public Accountant

As a CPA you are guided by the AICPA's Code of Professional Conduct described in Chapter 1 and listed near the end of the book. Here the main issue is whether commissions have an actual or perceived impact on the integrity and objectivity of your advice. The Code says you should not accept a commission arrangement if you either perform an audit or a review of the client's financial statements. The

Code also precludes a commission if you compile the client's statements, unless the compilation report discloses a lack of independence. Even in situations where a commission is allowed, the Code requires you tell the client of your commission arrangement. These suggested actions seem appropriate even if you are not bound by the Code. Also, you need to seriously examine the merits of agreeing to a commission arrangement when you are in a position to exploit it.

Guidance Answers to **You Make the Call**

Retailer

The Accounts Receivable Ledger has much of the information you need. It lists detailed information for each customer's account, including the amounts, dates for transactions, and dates of payments. It can be reorganized into an "aging schedule" to show how long customers wait before paying their bills. We describe an aging schedule in Chapter 10.

Banker

This merchandiser's segment information is likely to greatly impact your loan decision. The risks associated with this merchandiser's two sources of net income are quite different. While net income is up by 10%, U.S. operations are performing poorly and Cuban operations are subject to many uncertainties. These uncertainties depend on political events, friends and family relationships, Cuban economic conditions, and a host of other risks. While net income results suggested a low-risk loan opportunity, the segment information reveals a high-risk situation.

Controller

Much of the information you need is in the Accounts Payable Ledger. It contains information for each supplier, the amounts due, and when payments are made. This subsidiary ledger along with information on credit terms should enable you to conduct your analyses.

Guidance Answers to Flashbacks

1. The five primary components are source documents, input devices, information processors, information storage, and output devices.

2. An information processor interprets, transforms, and summarizes the recorded information so that it can be used in analysis and reports.

3. Data saved in information storage are used to prepare periodic financial reports, special-purpose internal reports, and as source documentation for auditors and other users.

4. All cash payments by check are recorded in the Cash Disbursements Journal.

5. Columnar journals allow us to accumulate repetitive debits and credits and post them as column totals rather than as individual amounts.

6. The equality of debits and credits is kept within the General

Ledger. The subsidiary ledger keeps the customer's individual account and is used only for supplementary information.

7. An initial and page number of the journal from which the amount was posted is entered in the Posting Reference column of the ledger account next to the amount.

8. The normal recording and posting procedures are threefold. First, transactions are entered in a special journal column if applicable. Second, individual amounts are posted to the subsidiary ledger accounts. Third, column totals are posted to General Ledger accounts.

9. The controlling account must be debited periodically for an amount or amounts equal to the sum of the debits to the subsidiary ledger, and it must be credited periodically for an amount or amounts equal to the sum of the credits to the subsidiary ledger.

10. Tests for accuracy of account balances in the General Ledger and subsidiary ledgers are twofold. First, we prepare a trial balance of the General Ledger to confirm debits equal credits. Second, we test the subsidiary ledgers by preparing schedules of accounts receivable and accounts payable.

11. A separate column for Sales Taxes Payable can be included in both the Cash Receipts Journal and the Sales Journal.

12. This refers to a procedure of using copies of sales invoices as a Sales Journal. Each invoice total is posted directly to the customer's account, and all invoices are totaled at month-end for posting to the General Ledger accounts.

13. The General Journal is still needed for adjusting, closing, and correcting entries and for special transactions such as sales returns, purchases returns, and plant asset purchases.

14. Integrated systems can save time and minimize errors. This is because actions taken in one part of the system automatically affect and update related parts.

15. Computer systems offer increased accuracy, speed, efficiency, and convenience.

16. Computer networks can create advantages by linking computers, giving different users and different computers access to a common database and programs.

17. Segment information helps us evaluate the risk and return attributes of a company. Companies operating in different business segments often have different rates of profitability, risk, and growth for these segments. This information helps us gain insight into the performance of a segment and its importance for a company's future.

Demonstration Problem

The Pepper Company completed these transactions during March of year 2000:

Mar. 4   Sold merchandise on credit to Jennifer Nelson, Invoice No. 954, $16,800. (Terms of all credit sales are 2/10, n/30.)

6   Purchased office supplies on credit from Mack Company, $1,220. Invoice dated March 3, terms n/30.

6   Sold merchandise on credit to Dennie Hoskins, Invoice No. 955, $10,200.

11   Received merchandise and an invoice dated March 6, terms 2/10, n/30, from Defore Industries, $52,600.

12   Borrowed $26,000 by giving Commerce Bank a long-term promissory note payable.

14   Received payment from Jennifer Nelson for the March 4 sale less the discount.

16   Received a credit memorandum from Defore Industries for unsatisfactory merchandise received on March 11 and returned for credit, $200.

16   Received payment from Dennie Hoskins for the March 6 sale less the discount.

18   Purchased store equipment on credit from Schmidt Supply, invoice dated March 15, terms n/30, $22,850.

20   Sold merchandise on credit to Marjorie Allen, Invoice No. 956, $5,600.

21   Sent Defore Industries Check No. 516 in payment of its March 6 invoice less the returns and the discount.

22   Received merchandise and an invoice dated March 18, terms 2/10, n/30, from the Welch Company, $41,625.

26   Issued a credit memorandum to Marjorie Allen for defective merchandise sold on March 22 and returned for credit $600.

31   Issued Check No. 517, payable to Payroll, in payment of sales salaries for the month, $15,900. Cashed the check and paid the employees.

31   Cash sales for the month were $134,680. (Cash sales are usually recorded daily; however, they are recorded only once in this problem to reduce the repetitive entries.)

31   Post to the customer and creditor accounts. Also, post any amounts that should be posted as individual amounts to General Ledger accounts.

31   Foot and crossfoot the journals and make the month-end postings.

Required

1. Open the following General Ledger accounts: Cash (101), Accounts Receivable (106), Office Supplies (124), Store Equipment (165), Accounts Payable (201), Long-Term Notes Payable (251), Sales (413), Sales Returns and Allowances (414), Sales Discounts (415), Purchases (505), Purchases Returns and Allowances (506), Purchases Discounts (507), and Sales Salaries Expense (621).

2. Open the following Accounts Receivable Ledger accounts: Marjorie Allen, Dennie Hoskins, and Jennifer Nelson.

3. Open the following Accounts Payable Ledger accounts: Defore Industries, Mack Company, Schmidt Supply, and Welch Company.

4. Enter the transactions in a Sales Journal, a Purchases Journal, a Cash Receipts Journal, a Cash Disbursements Journal, and a General Journal similar to the ones illustrated in the chapter. Post at the end of the month. Pepper Co. uses the periodic inventory system.

5. Prepare a trial balance and test the accuracy of subsidiary ledgers by preparing schedules of accounts receivable and accounts payable.

Planning the Solution

- Set up the required general ledger and subsidiary ledger accounts and the five required journals as illustrated in the chapter.
- First read and analyze each transaction and decide in which special journal (or general journal) the transaction is recorded.
- Record each transaction in the proper journal.
- Once you have recorded all transactions, total the journal columns.
- Post from each journal to the appropriate ledger accounts.
- After you have completed posting, prepare a trial balance to prove the equality of the debit and credit balances in your general ledger.
- Prepare schedules of accounts receivable and accounts payable. Compare the total of the schedules to the accounts receivable and accounts payable controlling account balances, making sure that they agree.

Solution to Demonstration Problem

Sales Journal — Page 2

Date		Account Debited	Invoice Number	PR	Accts. Rec. Dr. Sales Cr.
Mar.	4	Jennifer Nelson	954	✓	16,800
	6	Dennie Hoskins	955	✓	10,200
	20	Marjorie Allen	956	✓	5,600
	31	Totals			32,600
					(106/413)

Purchases Journal — Page 3

Date		Account	Date of Invoice	Terms	PR	Accts. Payable Credit	Purchases Debit	Office Supplies Debit	Other Accts. Debit
Mar.	6	Office Supplies/Mack Co	3/3	n/30	✓	1,220		1,220	
	11	Defore Industries	3/6	2/10, n/30	✓	52,600	52,600		
	18	Store Equipment/Schmidt Supp	3/15	n/30	165/✓	22,850			22,850
	22	Welch Company	3/18	2/10, n/30	✓	41,625	41,625		
	31	Totals				118,295	94,225	1,220	22,850
						(201)	(505)	(124)	(✓)

Cash Receipts Journal — Page 3

Date		Account Credited	Explanation	PR	Cash Debit	Sales Discount Debit	Accts. Rec. Credit	Sales Credit	Other Accts. Credit
Mar.	12	L.T. Notes Pay	Note to bank	251	26,000				26,000
	14	Jennifer Nelson	Invoice, 3/4	✓	16,464	336	16,800		
	16	Dennie Hoskins	Invoice, 3/6	✓	9,996	204	10,200		
	31	Sales	Cash sales	✓	134,680			134,680	
	31	Totals			187,140	540	27,000	134,680	26,000
					(101)	(415)	(106)	(413)	(✓)

Cash Disbursements Journal — Page 3

Date		Ck. No.	Payee	Account Debited	PR	Cash Credit	Purch. Disc. Credit	Other Accts. Debit	Accts. Payable Debit
Mar.	21	516	Defore Industries . . .	Defore Industries	✓	51,352	1,048		52,400
	31	517	Payroll	Sales Salaries Expense . . .	621	15,900		15,900	
	31		Totals			67,252	1,048	15,900	52,400
						(101)	(507)	(✓)	(201)

General Journal — Page 2

Mar. 16	Accounts Payable—Defore Industries	201/✓	200	
	Purchases Returns and Allowances	506		200
26	Sales Returns and Allowances	414	600	
	Accounts Receivable—Marjorie Allen	106/✓		600

Accounts Receivable Ledger

Marjorie Allen

Date	Explanation	PR	Debit	Credit	Balance
Mar. 20		S2	5,600		5,600
26		G2		600	5,000

Dennie Hoskins

Date	Explanation	PR	Debit	Credit	Balance
Mar. 6		S2	10,200		10,200
16		R3		10,200	0

Jennifer Nelson

Date	Explanation	PR	Debit	Credit	Balance
Mar. 4		S2	16,800		16,800
14		R3		16,800	0

Accounts Payable Ledger

Defore Industries

Date	Explanation	PR	Debit	Credit	Balance
Mar. 11		P3		52,600	52,600
16		G2	200		52,400
21		D3	52,400		0

Mack Company

Date	Explanation	PR	Debit	Credit	Balance
Mar. 6		P3		1,220	1,220

Schmidt Supply

Date	Explanation	PR	Debit	Credit	Balance
Mar. 18		P3		22,850	22,850

Welch Company

Date	Explanation	PR	Debit	Credit	Balance
Mar. 22		P3		41,625	41,625

General Ledger

Cash   Acct. No. 101

Date	Explanation	PR	Debit	Credit	Balance
Mar. 31		R3	187,140		187,140
31		D4		67,252	119,888

Accounts Receivable   Acct. No. 106

Date	Explanation	PR	Debit	Credit	Balance
Mar. 26		G2		600	(600)
31		S2	32,600		32,000
31		R3		27,000	5,000

Office Supplies   Acct. No. 124

Date	Explanation	PR	Debit	Credit	Balance
Mar. 31		P3	1,220		1,220

Store Equipment   Acct. No. 165

Date	Explanation	PR	Debit	Credit	Balance
Mar. 18		P3	22,850		22,850

Accounts Payable   Acct. No. 201

Date	Explanation	PR	Debit	Credit	Balance
Mar. 6		G2	200		(200)
31		P2		118,295	118,095
31		D3	52,400		65,695

Long-Term Notes Payable   Acct. No. 251

Date	Explanation	PR	Debit	Credit	Balance
Mar. 12				26,000	26,000

Sales   Acct. No. 413

Date	Explanation	PR	Debit	Credit	Balance
Mar. 31		S2		32,600	32,600
31		R3		134,680	167,280

Sales Returns and Allowances   Acct. No. 414

Date	Explanation	PR	Debit	Credit	Balance
Mar. 26		G2	600		600

Sales Discounts   Acct. No. 415

Date	Explanation	PR	Debit	Credit	Balance
Mar. 31		R3	540		540

Purchases   Acct. No. 505

Date	Explanation	PR	Debit	Credit	Balance
Mar. 31		P2	94,225		94,225

Purchases Returns and Allowances   Acct. No. 506

Date	Explanation	PR	Debit	Credit	Balance
Mar. 6		G2		200	200

Purchases Discounts   Acct. No. 507

Date	Explanation	PR	Debit	Credit	Balance
Mar. 31		D4		1,048	1,048

Sales Salaries Expense   Acct. No. 621

Date	Explanation	PR	Debit	Credit	Balance
Mar. 31		D3	15,900		15,900

PEPPER COMPANY
Trial Balance
March 31, 2000

	Debit	Credit
Cash	$119,888	
Accounts receivable	5,000	
Office supplies	1,220	
Store equipment	22,850	
Accounts payable		$ 65,695
Long-term notes payable		26,000
Sales		167,280
Sales returns and allowances	600	
Sales discounts	540	
Purchases	94,225	
Purchases returns and allowances		200
Purchases discounts		1,048
Sales salaries expense	15,900	
Totals	$260,223	$260,223

PEPPER COMPANY
Schedule of Accounts Receivable
March 31, 2000

Marjorie Allen	$5,000
Total accounts receivable	$5,000

PEPPER COMPANY
Schedule of Accounts Payable
March 31, 2000

Mack Company	$ 1,220
Schmidt Supply	22,850
Welch Company	41,625
Total accounts payable	$65,695

Special Journals under a Perpetual System

This appendix shows the special journals under a perpetual inventory system. Each journal is slightly impacted. The Sales Journal and the Cash Receipts Journal each require one new column titled "Cost of Goods Sold Dr., Inventory Cr." The Purchases Journal replaces the "Purchases Dr." column with an "Inventory Dr." column in a perpetual system. The Cash Disbursements Journal replaces the "Purchases Discounts Cr." column with an "Inventory Cr." column in a perpetual system. These changes are illustrated below.

Sales Journal

The Sales Journal for Outdoors Unlimited using the perpetual inventory system is shown in Exhibit 8A.1. The difference in the Sales Journal between the perpetual and periodic system is the addition of a new column to record cost of goods sold and inventory amounts for each sale. The periodic system does not record the increase in cost of goods sold and decrease in inventory at the time of sale. The total of the cost of goods sold and inventory amount column is posted to both of their General Ledger accounts at the end of the period.

Learning Objective

Procedural

P3 Journalize and post transactions using special journals in a perpetual inventory system.

	Outdoors Unlimited Sales Journal				Page 3
Date	Account Debited	Invoice Number	PR	Accounts Receivable Dr. Sales Cr.	Cost of Goods Sold Dr. Inventory Cr.
Feb. 2	Jason Henry	307	✓	450	315
7	Albert Co.	308	✓	500	355
13	Bam Moore	309	✓	350	260
15	Paul Roth	310	✓	200	150
22	Jason Henry	311	✓	225	155
25	Frank Booth	312	✓	175	95
28	Albert Co.	313	✓	250	170
28	Total			2,150	1,500
				(106/413)	(502/119)

Exhibit 8A.1

Sales Journal—Perpetual System

Cash Receipts Journal

The Cash Receipts Journal under the perpetual system is shown in Exhibit 8A.2. Note the addition of a new column on the far right side to record debits to Cost of Goods Sold and credits to Inventory for the cost of merchandise sold. Consistent with the Cash Receipts Journal shown under the periodic system in the chapter, we only show the weekly cash sale entries. But remember that under a perpetual system, these cash sales are recorded at the point of sale. To do that here would make this journal extremely lengthy since Outdoors Unlimited is a retailer with many cash sales every day. Note also that cash received from earlier credit sales does not result in amounts entered in the far right column. This is because the costs for these sales were recorded in the Sales Journal at the point of sale. The total of the cost of goods sold and inventory amount column is posted to both of their General Ledger accounts at the end of the period.

Exhibit 8A.2

Cash Receipts Journal—
Perpetual System

Outdoors Unlimited Cash Receipts Journal									Page 2
Date	Account Credited	Explanation	PR	Cash Dr.	Sales Discount Cr.	Accounts Receivable Cr.	Sales Cr.	Other Accounts Cr.	Cost of Goods Sold Dr. Inventory Cr.
Feb. 7	Sales	Cash sales	✓	4,450			4,450		3,150
12	Jason Henry	Invoice, 2/2	✓	441	9	450			
14	Sales	Cash sales	✓	3,925			3,925		2,950
17	Albert Co.	Invoice, 2/7	✓	490	10	500			
20	Notes Payable	Note to bank	245	750				750	
21	Sales	Cash sales	✓	4,700			4,700		3,400
22	Interest revenue	Bank account	409	250				250	
23	Bam Moore	Invoice, 2/13	✓	343	7	350			
25	Paul Roth	Invoice, 2/15	✓	196	4	200			
28	Sales	Cash sales	✓	4,225			4,225		3,050
28	Totals			19,770	30	1,500	17,300	1,000	12,550
				(101)	(415)	(106)	(413)	(✓)	(502/119)

Purchases Journal

The Purchases Journal under the perpetual system is shown in Exhibit 8A.3. This journal in a perpetual system includes an Inventory column where the periodic system had a Purchases column. All else is identical under the two systems.

Exhibit 8A.3

Purchases Journal—Perpetual
System

Outdoors Unlimited Purchases Journal								Page 1
Date	Account	Date of Invoice	Terms	PR	Accounts Payable Cr.	Inventory Dr.	Office Supplies Dr.	Other Accounts Dr.
Feb. 3	Homung Supply Co.	2/2	n/30	✓	350	275	75	
5	Ace Mfg. Co.	2/5	2/10, n/30	✓	200	200		
13	Wynet and Co.	2/10	2/10, n/30	✓	150	150		
20	Smite Co.	2/18	2/10, n/30	✓	300	300		
25	Ace Mfg. Co.	2/24	2/10, n/30	✓	100	100		
28	Store Supplies/ITT Co.	2/28	n/30	125/✓	225	125	25	75
28	Totals				1,325	1,150	100	75
					(201)	(505)	(124)	(✓)

Cash Disbursements Journal

The Cash Disbursements Journal in a perpetual system is shown in Exhibit 8A.4. This journal includes an Inventory column where the periodic system had the Purchases Discounts column. All else is identical under the two systems. When a company has several cash purchases of inventory, it often adds a new column for Inventory Debit entries.

Exhibit 8A.4

Cash Disbursements Journal—
Perpetual System

Outdoors Unlimited Cash Disbursements Journal								Page 2
Date	Ck. No.	Payee	Account Debited	PR	Cash Cr.	Inventory Cr.	Other Accounts Dr.	Accounts Payable Dr.
Feb. 3	105	L. and N. Railroad	Inventory	508	15		15	
12	106	East Sales Co.	Inventory	505	25		25	
15	107	Ace Mfg. Co.	Ace Mfg. Co.	✓	196	4		200
15	108	Jerry Hale	Salaries Expense	622	250		250	
20	109	Wynet and Co.	Wynet and Co.	✓	147	3		150
28	110	Smite Co.	Smite Co.	✓	294	6		300
28		Totals			927	13	290	650
					(101)	(507)	(✓)	(201)

Summary of Appendix 8A

P3 **Journalize and post transactions using special journals in a perpetual inventory system.** Transactions are journalized and posted using special journals in a perpetual system. The methods are similar to those in a periodic system, with the pri-

mary difference being that the cost of goods sold and inventory need adjusting at the time of each sale. This normally results in the addition of one or more columns devoted to these accounts in each special journal.

Glossary

Accounting information system the people, records, methods, and equipment that collect and process data from transactions and events, organize them in useful forms, and communicate results to decision makers. (p. 318).

Accounts Payable Ledger a subsidiary ledger listing individual creditor accounts. (p. 324).

Accounts Receivable Ledger a subsidiary ledger listing individual credit customer accounts. (p. 324).

Batch processing an approach to inputting data that accumulates source documents for a period of time and then processes them all at once such as once a day, week, or month. (p. 336).

Business segment a part of a company that can be separately identified by the products or services that it provides or a geographic market that it serves. (p. 338).

Cash Disbursements Journal the special journal that is used to record all payments of cash; also called *Cash Payments Journal*. (p. 332).

Cash Receipts Journal the special journal that is used to record all receipts of cash. (p. 328).

Check Register another name for a cash disbursements journal when the journal has a column for check numbers. (p. 383).

Columnar journal a journal with more than one column. (p. 326).

Compatibility principle an information system principle that requires an accounting information system conform with a company's activities, personnel, and structure. (p. 319).

Computer hardware the physical equipment in a computerized accounting information system. (p. 335).

Computer network a link among computers giving different users and different computers access to a common database and programs. (p. 337).

Computer software the programs that direct the operations of computer hardware. (p. 335).

Controlling account a General Ledger account, the balance of which (after posting) equals the sum of the balances of the accounts in a related subsidiary ledger. (p. 324).

Control principle an information system principle that requires an accounting information system to aid managers in controlling and monitoring business activities. (p. 318).

Cost-benefit principle an information system principle that requires the benefits from an activity in an accounting information system to outweigh the costs of that activity. (p. 319).

Enterprise-application software programs that manage a company's vital operations which range from order-taking to manufacturing to accounting. (p. 337).

Flexibility principle an information system principle that requires an accounting information system to be able to adapt to changes in the company, business environment, and needs of decision makers. (p. 319).

Information processor the component of an accounting system that interprets, transforms, and summarizes information for use in analysis and reporting. (p. 320).

Information storage the component of an accounting system that keeps data in a form accessible to information processors. (p. 321).

Input device a means of capturing information from source documents that enables its transfer to the information processing component of an accounting system. (p. 320).

On-line processing an approach to inputting data whereby the data on each source document is inputted as soon as the document is available. (p. 336).

Output devices the means by which information is taken out of the accounting system and made available for use. (p. 321).

Purchases Journal a journal that is used to record all purchases on credit. (p. 331).

Relevance principle an information system principle requiring that an accounting information system report useful, understandable, timely, and pertinent information for effective decision making. (p. 318).

Sales Journal a journal used to record sales of merchandise on credit. (p. 325).

Schedule of accounts payable a list of the balances of all the accounts in the Accounts Payable Ledger that is summed to show the total amount of accounts payable outstanding. (p. 331).

Schedule of accounts receivable a list of the balances of all the accounts in the Accounts Receivable Ledger that is summed to show the total amount of accounts receivable outstanding. (p. 326).

Segment contribution matrix a table listing one or more important measures such as sales by segment; usually includes amounts in dollars and percents along with a growth rate. (p. 339).

Special journal any journal that is used for recording and posting transactions of a similar type. (p. 323).

Subsidiary ledger a listing of individual accounts with a common characteristic; linked to a controlling account in the General Ledger. (p. 323).

Questions

1. When special journals are used, separate journals normally are used to record each of four different types of transactions. What are these four types of transactions?

2. Why should sales to and receipts of cash from credit customers be recorded and posted daily?

3. Both credits to customer accounts and credits to miscellaneous accounts are individually posted from a Cash Receipts Journal similar to the one in Exhibit 8.9. Why not put both kinds of credits in the same column and save journal space?

4. Describe the procedures involving the use of copies of a company's sales invoices as a Sales Journal.

5. When a general journal entry is used to record a returned credit sale, the credit of the entry must be posted twice. Does this cause the trial balance to be out of balance? Why or why not?

6. What notations are entered into the Posting Reference column of a ledger account?

7. What are five basic components of an accounting system?

8. What are source documents? Give some examples.

9. What is the purpose of an input device? Give some examples of input devices for computer systems.

10. What is the difference between data that is stored off-line and data that is stored on-line?

11. What purpose is served by the output devices of an accounting system?

12. What is the difference between batch and on-line processing?

13. Locate the footnote that discusses **NIKE's** industry segment and operations by geographic area in Appendix A. What industry segment does NIKE predominantly operate in? Identify the geographic areas for which NIKE discloses revenues, operating income, and assets.

14. Does the income statement of **Reebok** in Appendix A indicate the Net Income earned by Reebok's business segments? If yes, then list them.

15. Does the balance sheet of **America Online** in Appendix A indicate the identifiable assets owned by America Online's business segments? If yes, then list them.

16. Identify all of the special journals that Maria Lopez is now likely keeping for **Outdoors Limited.** What does Maria mean when she says she now keeps an aging schedule on late-paying customers?

Quick Study

QS 8-1

Special journal identification

C3

Trenton Electronics uses a Sales Journal, a Purchases Journal, a Cash Receipts Journal, a Cash Disbursements Journal, and a General Journal. Trenton recently completed the following transactions. List the transaction letters and next to each letter give the name of the journal in which the transaction should be recorded.

a. Sold merchandise on credit.

b. Purchased shop supplies on credit.

c. Paid an employee's salary.

d. Paid a creditor.

e. Purchased merchandise on credit.

f. Borrowed money from the bank.

g. Sold merchandise for cash.

QS 8-2

Entries in the general journal

C3

The Nostalgic Book Shop uses a Sales Journal, a Purchases Journal, a Cash Receipts Journal, a Cash Disbursements Journal, and a General Journal. The following transactions occurred during the month of November. Journalize the November transactions that should be recorded in the General Journal.

Nov. 2   Purchased merchandise on credit for $2,900 from the Ringdol Co., terms 2/10, n/30.

     12   The owner, G. Werthman, contributed an automobile worth $15,000 to the business.

     16   Sold merchandise on credit to R. Wyder for $1,100, terms n/30.

     19   R. Wyder returned $150 of merchandise originally purchased on November 16.

QS 8-3

Accounting information system components

C2

Identify the most likely role in an accounting system played by each of the lettered items *a* through *j* by assigning a number from the list on the left:

1. Source documents

2. Input devices

3. Information processor

4. Information storage

5. Output devices

_____ a. Bar-code reader

_____ b. Filing cabinet

_____ c. Bank statement

_____ d. Calculator

_____ e. Computer keyboard

_____ f. Floppy diskette

_____ g. Computer monitor

_____ h. Invoice from a supplier

_____ i. Computer software

_____ j. Computer printer

Fill in the blanks to complete the following descriptions:

a. A _____ is an input device that captures writing and other input directly from source documents.

b. _____-_____ _____ are programs that help manage a company's vital operations, from manufacturing to accounting.

c. With _____ processing, source documents are accumulated for a period of time and then processed all at the same time, such as once a day, week, or month.

d. A computer _____ allows different computer users to share access to data and programs.

Trex is a company with publicly traded securities that operates in more than one industry. Which of the following items of information about each industry segment must the company report?

a. Revenues   **e.** Capital expenditures
b. Net sales   **f.** Amortization and depreciation
c. Operating income   **g.** Cash flows
d. Operating expenses **h.** Identifiable assets

Place the letter for each principle in the blank next to its best description below.

A. Control principle   **D.** Flexibility principle
B. Relevance principle   **E.** Cost-Benefit principle
C. Compatibility principle

1. _____ The principle requiring the information system to adapt to the unique characteristics of the company.

2. _____ The principle that affects all other accounting information system principles.

3. _____ The principle requiring the accounting information system to change in response to technological advances and competitive pressures.

4. _____ The principle requiring the accounting information system to help monitor activities.

5. _____ The principle requiring the system to provide timely information for effective decision-making.

Spindle Company uses a Sales Journal, a Purchases Journal, a Cash Receipts Journal, a Cash Disbursements Journal, and a General Journal. The following transactions occurred in the month of February:

Feb. 2 Sold merchandise to S. Mayer for $450 cash, invoice no. 5703.
       5 Purchased merchandise on credit from Camp Corp., $2,300.
       7 Sold merchandise to J. Eason for $1,150, terms 2/10, n/30, invoice no. 5704.
       8 Borrowed $8,000 by giving a note to the bank.
      12 Sold merchandise to P. Lathan for $320, terms n/30, invoice no. 5705.
      16 Received $1,127 from J. Eason to pay for the purchase of February 7.
      19 Sold used store equipment to Whiten, Inc., for $900.
      25 Sold merchandise to S. Summers for $550, terms n/30, invoice no. 5706.

Required

Prepare headings for a Sales Journal like the one in Exhibit 8.5. Journalize the February transactions that should be recorded in the Sales Journal.

SeaMap Company uses a Sales Journal, a Purchases Journal, a Cash Receipts Journal, a Cash Disbursements Journal, and a General Journal. The following transactions occurred in the month of September:

Sept. 3 Purchased merchandise on credit for $3,100 from Pacer Co.
        7 Sold merchandise on credit to J. Namal for $900, subject to a $18 sales discount if paid by the end of the month.
        9 Borrowed $2,750 by giving a note to the bank.
       13 Received a capital contribution of $4,000 from J. Costeau, the owner of the company.
       18 Sold merchandise to B. Baird for $230 cash.
       22 Paid Pacer Co. $3,100 for the merchandise purchased on September 3.
       27 Received $882 from J. Namal in payment of the September 7 purchase.
       30 Paid salaries of $1,600.

Required

Prepare headings for a Cash Receipts Journal like the one in Exhibit 8.9. Journalize the September transactions that should be recorded in the Cash Receipts Journal.

Exercise 8-3
Purchases Journal

Chem Company uses a Sales Journal, a Purchases Journal, a Cash Receipts Journal, a Cash Disbursements Journal, and a General Journal. The following transactions occurred in the month of July:

July 1 Purchased merchandise on credit for $8,100 from Angler, Inc., terms n/30.
8 Sold merchandise on credit to B. Harren for $1,500, subject to a $30 sales discount if paid by the end of the month.
14 Purchased store supplies from Steck Company on credit for $240, terms n/30.
17 Purchased office supplies on credit from Marten Company for $260, terms n/30.
24 Sold merchandise to W. Winger for $630 cash.
28 Purchased store supplies from Hadley's for $90 cash.
29 Paid Angler, Inc., $8,100 for the merchandise purchased on July 1.

Required

Prepare headings for a Purchases Journal like the one in Exhibit 8.11. Journalize the July transactions that should be recorded in the Purchases Journal.

Exercise 8-4
Cash Disbursements Journal

Aeron Supply uses a Sales Journal, a Purchases Journal, a Cash Receipts Journal, a Cash Disbursements Journal, and a General Journal. The following transactions occurred in the month of March:

Mar. 3 Purchased merchandise for $2,750 on credit from Pace, Inc., terms 2/10, n/30.
9 Issued check no. 210 to Narlin Corp. to buy store supplies for $450.
12 Sold merchandise on credit to K. Camp for $670, terms n/30.
17 Issued check no. 211 for $1,500 to repay a note payable to City Bank.
20 Purchased merchandise for $3,500 on credit from LeBaron, terms 2/10, n/30.
29 Issued check no. 212 to LeBaron to pay the amount due for the purchase of March 20, less the discount.
31 Paid salary of $1,700 to E. Brandon by issuing check no. 213.
31 Issued check no. 214 to Pace, Inc., to pay the amount due for the purchase of March 3.

Required

Prepare headings for a Cash Disbursements Journal like the one in Exhibit 8.13. Journalize the March transactions that should be recorded in the Cash Disbursements Journal.

Exercise 8-5
Special journal transactions and error discovery

Simon Pharmacy uses the following journals: Sales Journal, Purchases Journal, Cash Receipts Journal, Cash Disbursements Journal, and General Journal. On June 5, Simon purchased merchandise priced at $12,000, subject to credit terms of 2/10, n/30. On June 14, the pharmacy paid the net amount due. But in journalizing the payment, the accountant debited Accounts Payable for $12,000 and failed to record the cash discount. Cash was credited for the actual amount paid. In what journals would the June 5 and the June 14 transactions have been recorded? What procedure is likely to discover the error in journalizing the June 14 transaction?

Exercise 8-6
Posting to subsidiary ledger accounts

At the end of May, the Sales Journal of Camper Goods appears as follows:

Sales Journal				
Date	Account Debited	Invoice Number	PR	Accounts Receivable Dr. Sales Cr.
May 6	Brad Smithers	190		2,880
10	Dan Holland	191		1,940
17	Sanders Farrell	192		850
25	Dan Holland	193		340
31	Total			6,010

Camper also recorded the return of certain merchandise with the following entry:

May 20	Sales Returns and Allowances	250	
	Accounts Receivable—Sanders Farrell ...		250
	Customer returned merchandise.		

Required

1. Open a subsidiary Accounts Receivable Ledger that has a T-account for each customer listed in the Sales Journal. Post to the customer accounts the entries in the Sales Journal and any portion of the general journal entry that affects a customer's account.

2. Open a General Ledger that has T-accounts for Accounts Receivable, Sales, and Sales Returns and Allowances. Post the Sales Journal and any portion of the general journal entry that affects these accounts.

3. Prepare a schedule of the accounts in the subsidiary Accounts Receivable Ledger and add their balances to show that the total equals the balance in the Accounts Receivable controlling account.

The condensed journals of Tipper Trophies are shown below. The journal column headings are incomplete and they do not indicate whether the columns are debit or credit columns.

Exercise 8-7
Posting from special journals to general and subsidiary ledgers

P1, P2

Sales Journal	
Account	
Jack Hertz	3,700
Trudy Stone	8,400
Dave Waylon	1,000
Total	13,100

Purchases Journal	
Account	
Grass Corp.	5,400
Sulter, Inc.	4,500
McGrew Company	1,700
Total	11,600

Cash Receipts Journal

Account	Cash	Sales Discounts	Accounts Receivable	Sales	Other Accounts
Jack Hertz	3,332	68	3,400		
Sales	2,250			2,250	
Notes Payable	4,500				4,500
Sales	625			625	
Trudy Stone	8,232	168	8,400		
Store Equipment	500				500
Totals	19,439	236	11,800	2,875	5,000

Cash Disbursements Journal

Account	Cash	Purchases Discounts	Other Accounts	Accounts Payable
Prepaid Insurance	850		850	
Sulter, Inc.	4,365	135		4,500
Grass Corp.	4,557	93		4,650
Store Equipment	1,750		1,750	
Totals	11,522	228	2,600	9,150

General Journal

Sales Returns and Allowances	300	
Accounts Receivable—Jack Hertz		300
Accounts Payable—Grass Corp.	750	
Purchases Returns and Allowances		750

Required

1. Prepare T-accounts for the following General Ledger and subsidiary ledger accounts. Separate the accounts of each ledger group as follows:

General Ledger Accounts	Accounts Receivable Ledger Accounts
Cash	Jack Hertz
Accounts Receivable	Trudy Stone
Prepaid Insurance	Dave Waylon
Store Equipment	
Accounts Payable	
Notes Payable	**Accounts Payable Ledger Accounts**
Sales	Grass Corp.
Sales Discounts	McGrew Company
Sales Returns and Allowances	Sulter, Inc.
Purchases	
Purchase Discounts	
Purchase Returns and Allowances	

2. Revise and show complete column headings for the special journals, and post the entries in the journals to their proper T-accounts.

Exercise 8-8
Accounts Receivable Ledger
P1, P2

Skillern Company posts its sales invoices directly and then binds the invoices to make them into a Sales Journal. Skillern had the following sales during January:

Jan.	2	Jay Newton	$ 3,600
	8	Adrian Carr	6,100
	10	Kathy Olivas	13,400
	14	Lisa Mack	20,500
	20	Kathy Olivas	11,200
	29	Jay Newton	7,300
		Total sales	$62,100

Required

1. Open a subsidiary Accounts Receivable Ledger having a T-account for each customer. Post the invoices to the subsidiary ledger.
2. Give the General Journal entry to record the end-of-month total from the Sales Journal.
3. Open an Accounts Receivable controlling T-account and a Sales T-account. Post the General Journal entry from 2.
4. Prepare a schedule of the accounts in the subsidiary Accounts Receivable Ledger and add their balances to show that the total equals the balance in the Accounts Receivable controlling account.

Exercise 8-9
Purchases Journal and error identification
P1

A company that records credit purchases in a Purchases Journal and records purchases returns in a General Journal made the following errors. For each error, indicate when the error should be discovered:
a. Made an addition error in determining the balance of a creditor's account.
b. Made an addition error in totaling the Office Supplies column of the Purchases Journal.
c. Posted a purchases return to the Accounts Payable account and to the creditor's account but did not post to the Purchases Returns and Allowances account.
d. Posted a purchases return to the Purchases Returns and Allowances account and to the Accounts Payable account but did not post to the creditor's account.
e. Correctly recorded a $4,000 purchase in the Purchases Journal but posted it to the creditor's account as a $400 purchase.

Exercise 8-10
Analyzing segment information
A1

Refer to Exhibit 8.15 and complete the segment contribution matrix for Gen X Sports Company. Analyze and interpret the matrix, including identification of segments with the highest and lowest growth rates.

Gen X Sports Company Segment Contribution Matrix for Sales					
	Sales Contribution (in $mil.)		Sales Contribution (in%)		1 Year Growth Rate Percent
Segment	1999	1998	1999	1998	
Segment:					
Skiing Group	$5,235	$3,585			
Skating Group	800	400			
Specialty Footwear	1,200	860			
Other Specialty	975	525			
Subtotal					
General Merchandise:					
South America	$2,725	$1,839			
United States	988	788			
Europe	650	350			
Subtotal					
Total					

Newton Company completed these transactions during April of the current year:

Apr. 2 Purchased merchandise on credit from Baskin Company, invoice dated April 2, terms 2/10, n/60, $13,300.

3 Sold merchandise on credit to Linda Hobart, Invoice No. 760, $3,000. (The terms of all credit sales are 2/10, n/30.)

3 Purchased office supplies on credit from Eau Claire Inc., $1,380. Invoice dated April 2, terms n/10 EOM.

4 Issued Check No. 587 to *U.S. Times* for advertising expense, $999.

5 Sold merchandise on credit to Paul Abrams, Invoice No. 761, $8,000.

6 Received an $85 credit memorandum from Eau Claire Inc. for office supplies received on April 3 and returned for credit.

9 Purchased store equipment on credit from Frank's Supply, invoice dated April 9, terms n/10 EOM, $11,125.

11 Sold merchandise on credit to Kelly Schaefer, Invoice No. 762, $9,500.

12 Issued Check No. 588 to Baskin Company in payment of its April 2 invoice, less the discount.

13 Received payment from Linda Hobart for the April 3 sale, less the discount.

13 Sold merchandise on credit to Linda Hobart, Invoice No. 763, $4,100.

14 Received payment from Paul Abrams for the April 5 sale, less the discount.

16 Issued Check No. 589, payable to Payroll, in payment of sales salaries for the first half of the month, $9,750. Cashed the check and paid employees.

16 Cash sales for the first half of the month were $50,840. (Cash sales are usually recorded daily from the cash register readings. They are recorded only twice in this problem to reduce repetitive transactions.)

17 Purchased merchandise on credit from Spocket Company, invoice dated April 16, terms 2/10, n/30, $12,750.

18 Borrowed $50,000 from First State Bank by giving a long-term note payable.

20 Received payment from Kelly Schaefer for the April 11 sale, less the discount.

20 Purchased store supplies on credit from Frank's Supply, invoice dated April 19, terms n/10 EOM, $730.

23 Received a $400 credit memorandum from Sprocket Company for defective merchandise received on April 17 and returned to sprocket.

23 Received payment from Linda Hobart for the April 13 sale, less the discount.

25 Purchased merchandise on credit from Baskin Company, invoice dated April 24, terms 2/10, n/60, $10,375.

26 Issued Check No. 590 to Sprocket Company in payment of its April 16 invoice, less the return and the discount.

27 Sold merchandise on credit to Paul Abrams, Invoice No. 764, $3,070.

27 Sold merchandise on credit to Kelly Schaefer, Invoice No. 765, $5,700.

Problems

Problem 8-1
Special journals, subsidiary ledgers, and schedule of accounts receivable

30   Issued Check No. 591, payable to Payroll, in payment of the sales salaries for the last half of the month, $9,750.

30   Cash sales for the last half of the month were $70,975.

Required

Preparation Component

1. Prepare a Sales Journal like Exhibit 8.5 and a Cash Receipts Journal like Exhibit 8.9. Number both journal pages as page 3.

2. Review the transactions of Newton Company and enter those transactions that should be journalized in the Sales Journal and those that should be journalized in the Cash Receipts Journal. Ignore any transactions that should be journalized in a Purchases Journal, a Cash Disbursements Journal, or a General Journal.

3. Open the following General Ledger accounts: Cash, Accounts Receivable, Long-Term Notes Payable, Sales, and Sales Discounts. Also open subsidiary Accounts Receivable Ledger accounts for Paul Abrams, Linda Hobart, and Kelly Schaefer.

4. Post items that should be posted as individual amounts from the journals. (Normally, such items are posted daily; but since they are few in number in this problem you are asked to post them only once.)

5. Foot and crossfoot the journals and make the month-end postings.

Check Figure Trial balance totals $205,185

6. Prepare a trial balance of the General Ledger and test the accuracy of the subsidiary ledger by preparing a schedule of accounts receivable.

Analysis Component

7. Assume the sum of the account balances on the schedule of accounts receivable does not equal the balance of the controlling account in the General Ledger. Describe steps you would take to discover the error(s).

Problem 8-2
Special journals, subsidiary ledgers, schedule of accounts payable

The April transactions of Newton Company are listed in Problem 8–1.

Required

1. Prepare a General Journal, a Purchases Journal like Exhibit 8.11, and a Cash Disbursements Journal like Exhibit 8.13. Number all journal pages as page 3.

2. Review the April transactions of Newton Company and enter those transactions that should be journalized in the General Journal, the Purchases Journal, or the Cash Disbursements Journal. Ignore any transactions that should be journalized in a Sales Journal or Cash Receipts Journal.

3. Open the following General Ledger accounts: Cash, Office Supplies, Store Supplies, Store Equipment, Accounts Payable, Long-Term Notes Payable, Purchases, Purchases Returns and Allowances, Purchases Discounts, Sales Salaries Expense, and Advertising Expense. Enter the March 31 balances of Cash ($167,000) and Long-Term Notes Payable ($167,000). Also open subsidiary Accounts Payable Ledger accounts for Frank's Supply, Baskin Company, Sprocket Company, and Eau Claire Inc.

4. Post items that should be posted as individual amounts from the journals. (Normally, such items are posted daily; but since they are few in number in this problem you are asked to post them only once.)

Check Figure Trial balance totals, $191,438

5. Foot and crossfoot the journals and make the month-end postings.

6. Prepare a trial balance of the General Ledger and a schedule of accounts payable.

Problem 8-3
Special journals, subsidiary ledgers, trial balance

(If the Working Papers that accompany this text are not being used, omit this problem.)

It is December 16 and you have just taken over the accounting work of Saskan Enterprises, whose annual accounting period ends December 31. The company's previous accountant journalized its transactions through December 15 and posted all items that required posting as individual amounts (see the journals and ledgers in the working papers). The company completed these transactions beginning on December 16:

Dec. 16   Sold merchandise on credit to Vickie Foresman, Invoice No. 916, $7,700. (Terms of all credit sales are 2/10, n/30.)

17   Received a $1,040 credit memorandum from Shore Company for merchandise received on December 15 and returned for credit.

17   Purchased office supplies on credit from Brown Supply Company, $615. Invoice dated December 16, terms n/10 EOM.

18   Received a $40 credit memorandum from Brown Supply Company for office supplies received on December 17 and returned for credit.

20   Issued a credit memorandum to Amy Ihrig for defective merchandise sold on December 15 and returned for credit, $500.

21   Purchased store equipment on credit from Brown Supply Company, invoice dated December 21, terms n/10 EOM, $6,700.

22   Received payment from Vickie Foresman for the December 12 sale less the discount.

23   Issued Check No. 623 to Sunshine Company in payment of its December 15 invoice less the discount.

24   Sold merchandise on credit to Bill Grigsby, Invoice No. 917, $1,200.

24   Issued Check No. 624 to Shore Company in payment of its December 15 invoice less the return and the discount.

25   Received payment from Amy Ihrig for the December 15 sale less the return and the discount.

26   Received merchandise and an invoice dated December 25, terms 2/10, n/60, from Sunshine Company, $8,100.

29   Sold a neighboring merchant five boxes of file folders (office supplies) for cash at cost, $50.

30   Ken Shaw, the owner of Saskan Enterprises, used Check No. 625 to withdraw $2,500 cash from the business for personal use.

31   Issued Check No. 626 to Jamie Green, the company's only sales employee, in payment of her salary for the last half of December, $2,020.

31   Issued Check No. 627 to Countywide Electric Company in payment of the December electric bill, $710.

31   Cash sales for the last half of the month were $29,600. (Cash sales are usually recorded daily but are recorded only twice in this problem to reduce the repetitive transactions.)

Required

1. Record the transactions listed above in the journals provided in the working papers.

2. Post to the customer and creditor accounts and also post any amounts that should be posted as individual amounts to the General Ledger accounts. (Normally, these amounts are posted daily, but they are posted only once in this problem because they are few in number.)

3. Foot and crossfoot the journals and make the month-end postings.

4. Prepare a December 31 trial balance and test the accuracy of the subsidiary ledgers by preparing schedules of accounts receivable and accounts payable.

Check Figure Trial balance totals, $221,160

Problem 8-4
Special journals, subsidiary ledgers, trial balance

The Bledsoe Company completed these transactions during March of the current year:

Mar. 2   Sold merchandise on credit to Leroy Hackett, Invoice No. 854, $15,800. (Terms of all credit sales are 2/10, n/30.)

3   Purchased office supplies on credit from Arndt Company, $1,120. Invoice dated March 3, terms n/10 EOM.

3   Sold merchandise on credit to Sam Snickers, Invoice No. 855, $9,200.

5   Received merchandise and an invoice dated March 3, terms 2/10, n/30, from Defore Industries, $42,600.

6   Borrowed $72,000 by giving Commerce Bank a long-term promissory note payable.

9   Purchased office equipment on credit from Jett Supply, invoice dated March 9, terms n/10 EOM, $20,850.

10   Sold merchandise on credit to Marjorie Coble, Invoice No. 856, $4,600.

12   Received payment from Leroy Hackett for the March 2 sale less the discount.

13   Sent Defore Industries Check No. 416 in payment of its March 3 invoice less the discount.

13   Received payment from Sam Snickers for the March 3 sale less the discount.

14   Received merchandise and an invoice dated March 13, terms 2/10, n/30, from the Welch Company, $31,625.

15   Issued Check No. 417, payable to Payroll, in payment of sales salaries for the first half of the month, $15,900. Cashed the check and paid the employees.

15   Cash sales for the first half of the month were $164,680. (Normally, cash sales are recorded daily; however, they are recorded only twice in this problem to reduce the repetitive entries.)

15   Post to the customer and creditor accounts and also post any amounts that should be posted as individual amounts to the General Ledger accounts. (Normally, such items are posted daily; but you are asked to post them on only two occasions in this problem because they are few in number.)

16   Purchased store supplies on credit from Arndt Company, $1,670. Invoice dated March 16, terms n/10 EOM.

17   Received a credit memorandum from the Welch Company for unsatisfactory merchandise received on March 14 and returned for credit, $2,425.

19   Received a credit memorandum from Jett Supply for office equipment received on March 9 and returned for credit, $630.

20   Received payment from Marjorie Coble for the sale of March 10 less the discount.

23   Issued Check No. 418 to the Welch Company in payment of its invoice of March 13 less the return and the discount.

27   Sold merchandise on credit to Marjorie Coble, Invoice No. 857, $13,910.

28   Sold merchandise on credit to Sam Snickers, Invoice No. 858, $5,315.

31   Issued Check No. 419, payable to Payroll, in payment of sales salaries for the last half of the month, $15,900. Cashed the check and paid the employees.

31   Cash sales for the last half of the month were $174,590.

31   Post to the customer and creditor accounts and post any amounts that should be posted as individual amounts to the General Ledger accounts.

31   Foot and crossfoot the journals and make the month-end postings.

Required

1. Open the following General Ledger accounts: Cash, Accounts Receivable, Office Supplies, Store Supplies, Office Equipment, Accounts Payable, Long-Term Notes Payable, Sales, Sales Discounts, Purchases, Purchases Returns and Allowances, Purchases Discounts, and Sales Salaries Expense. Open the following Accounts Receivable Ledger accounts: Marjorie Coble, Leroy Hackett, and Sam Snickers. Open the following Accounts Payable Ledger accounts: Arndt Company, Defore Industries, Jett Supply, and the Welch Company.

2. Enter the transactions listed above in a Sales Journal like Exhibit 8.5, a Purchases Journal like Exhibit 8.11, a Cash Receipts Journal like Exhibit 8.9, a Cash Disbursements Journal like Exhibit 8.13, and a General Journal. Post when instructed to do so.

3. Prepare a trial balance of the General Ledger and test the accuracy of the subsidiary ledgers by preparing schedules of accounts receivable and accounts payable.

Check Figure Trial balance totals, $486,966

Comprehensive Problem

Alpine Company

(If the Working Papers that accompany this text are not available, omit this comprehensive problem.)

Assume it is Monday, May 1, the first business day of the month, and you have just been hired as the accountant for Alpine Company, which operates with monthly accounting periods. All of the company's accounting work has been completed through the end of April and its ledgers show April 30 balances. During your first month on the job, you record the following transactions:

May   1   Issued Check No. 3410 to S&M Management Co. in payment of the May rent, $3,710. (Use two lines to record the transaction. Charge 80% of the rent to Rent Expense—Selling Space and the balance to Rent Expense—Office Space.)

2   Sold merchandise on credit to Essex Company, Invoice No. 8785, $6,100. (The terms of all credit sales are 2/10, n/30.)

2   Issued a $175 credit memorandum to Nabors, Inc., for defective merchandise sold on April 28 and returned for credit. The total selling price (gross) was $4,725.

3   Received a $798 credit memorandum from Parkay Products for merchandise received on April 29 and returned for credit.

4   Purchased on credit from Thompson Supply Co.: merchandise, $37,072; store supplies, $574; and office supplies, $83. Invoice dated May 4, terms n/10 EOM.

5   Received payment from Nabors, Inc., for the remaining balance from the sale of April 28 less the May 2 return and the discount.

8   Issued Check No. 3411 to Parkay Products to pay for the $7,098 of merchandise received on April 29 less the May 3 return and a 2% discount.

9   Sold store supplies to the merchant next door at cost for cash, $350.

10   Purchased office equipment on credit from Thompson Supply Co., invoice dated May 10, terms n/10 EOM, $4,074.

11   Received payment from Essex Company for the May 2 sale less the discount.

11   Received merchandise and an invoice dated May 10, terms 2/10, n/30, from Gale, Inc., $8,800.

12   Received an $854 credit memorandum from Thompson Supply Co. for defective office equipment received on May 10 and returned for credit.

15   Issued Check No. 3412, payable to Payroll, in payment of sales salaries, $5,320, and office salaries, $3,150. Cashed the check and paid the employees.

15   Cash sales for the first half of the month, $59,220. (Such sales are normally recorded daily. They are recorded only twice in this problem to reduce the repetitive entries.)

15   Post to the customer and creditor accounts. Also, post individual items that are not included in column totals at the end of the month to the general ledger accounts. (Such items are normally posted daily, but you are asked to post them only twice each month because they are few in number.)

16   Sold merchandise on credit to Essex Company, Invoice No. 8786, $3,990.

17   Received merchandise and an invoice dated May 14, terms 2/10, n/60, from Chandler Corp., $13,650.

19   Issued Check No. 3413 to Gale, Inc., in payment of its May 10 invoice less the discount.

22   Sold merchandise to Oscar Services, Invoice No. 8787, $6,850, terms 2/10, n/60.

23   Issued Check No. 3414 to Chandler Corp. in payment of its May 14 invoice less the discount.

24   Purchased on credit from Thompson Supply Co.: merchandise, $8,120; store supplies, $630; and office supplies, $280. Invoice dated May 24, terms n/10 EOM.

25   Received merchandise and an invoice dated May 23, terms 2/10, n/30, from Parkay Products, $3,080.

26   Sold merchandise on credit to Deaver Corp., Invoice No. 8788, $14,210.

26   Issued Check No. 3415 to Trinity Power in payment of the April electric bill, $1,283.

29   The owner of Alpine Company, Clint Barry, used Check No. 3416 to withdraw $7,000 from the business for personal use.

30   Received payment from Oscar Services for the May 22 sale less the discount.

30   Issued Check No. 3417, payable to Payroll, in payment of sales salaries, $5,320, and office salaries, $3,150. Cashed the check and paid the employees.

31   Cash sales for the last half of the month were $66,052.

31   Post to the customer and creditor accounts. Also, post individual items that are not included in column totals at the end of the month to the General Ledger accounts.

31   Foot and crossfoot the journals and make the month-end postings.

Required

1. Enter the transactions listed above in a Sales Journal, a Purchases Journal, a Cash Receipts Journal, a Cash Disbursements Journal, and a General Journal. Post when instructed to do so. Use a periodic inventory system.

2. Prepare a trial balance in the Trial Balance columns of the provided work sheet form. Complete the work sheet using the following information (Alpine uses the closing entry approach to record the change in the Merchandise Inventory account):

a. Expired insurance, $553.
b. Ending store supplies inventory, $2,632.
c. Ending office supplies inventory, $504.
d. Estimated depreciation of store equipment, $567.
e. Estimated depreciation of office equipment, $329.
f. Ending merchandise inventory, $176,400.

Prepare and post adjusting and closing entries.

3. Prepare a May 2000 classified, multiple-step income statement, a May 2000 statement of changes in owner's equity, and a May 31, 2000 classified balance sheet.

4. Prepare a post-closing trial balance. Also test the accuracy of subsidiary ledgers by preparing schedules of accounts receivable and accounts payable. Prepare a list of the Accounts Receivable Ledger accounts and a list of the Accounts Payable Ledger accounts. Total the balances of each schedule to confirm that their totals equal the balances in the controlling accounts.

BEYOND THE NUMBERS

Refer to the financial statements and related information for **NIKE** in Appendix A. Answer the following questions by analyzing that information.

Reporting in Action

A1

1. Identify the note disclosing NIKE's segment information for total revenue and net income.

2. For fiscal year ended May 31, 1997, compute the percent of both total revenue and operating income that NIKE earns from each segment. Comment on your findings, noting whether the segment with the highest percent of total revenue also generates the highest percent of operating income.

3. Compute the percent change in operating income for each segment and in total from the fiscal year ending in 1996 to 1997. Comment on your findings.

Swoosh Ahead

4. Obtain access to NIKE's annual report for fiscal years ending after May 31, 1997. You can gain access to NIKE's annual report at its web site [www.nike.com] or through the SEC's EDGAR database [www.sec.gov]. Fulfill requirements (2) and (3) using the latest data available to you.

Comparative Analysis
A1

Reebok

Nike

Both **NIKE** and **Reebok** design, produce, market, and sell sports footwear and apparel. Key comparative figures for these two organizations follow ($ thousands):

NIKE Total Revenue by Segment*	Fiscal Year Ended May 31, 1997	Fiscal Year Ended May 31, 1996
United States	$5,529,132	$3,964,662
Europe	1,833,722	1,334,340
Asia/Pacific	1,245,217	735,094
Latin America/Canada and other	578,468	436,529
Total	$9,186,539	$6,470,625

Reebok Net Sales by Segment*	Fiscal Year Ended Dec. 31, 1996	Fiscal Year Ended Dec, 31, 1995
United States	$1,935,724	$2,027,080
United Kingdom	566,196	492,843
Europe	623,209	642,622
Other countries	353,475	318,905
Total	$3,478,604	$3,481,450

*NIKE figures are from its annual reports for fiscal years ended May 31, 1997 and 1996. Reebok figures are from its annual reports for fiscal years ended December 31, 1996 and 1995.

Required

1. Compute the percent change in total revenue (NIKE) and total net sales (Reebok) for the years given. Comment on your findings.
2. Compute the percent change in revenue by each geographic segment for each company. Comment on your findings.
3. Identify the geographic segment experiencing the largest growth in revenue for each company.

Ethics Challenge
C5

John Harris, CPA, is a sole practitioner. He has been practicing as an auditor for 10 years. Recently a long-standing audit client asked John to design and implement an integrated computer accounting information system. The fees associated with this additional engagement with the client are very attractive. However, John wonders if he can remain objective in his evaluation of the client's accounting system and its records on subsequent audits if he puts himself in the position of auditing a system he was responsible for installing. John knows that the professional auditing standards require him to remain independent in fact and appearance from all of his auditing clients.

Required

1. What do you think auditing standards mean when they require independence in fact? In appearance?
2. Why is it important that auditors remain independent of their clients?
3. Do you think John can accept this engagement and remain independent? Justify your response.

Communicating in Practice
C3, C4

Your friend, Ivanna B. Sweeter, has a small retail operation called "Goodies" that sells candies and nuts. Ivanna acquires her goods from a few select vendors. Purchase orders are generally made by phone and on credit. Sales are primarily for cash. Ivanna keeps her own manual accounting system using a general Journal and a General Ledger. At the end of each business day she records one summary entry for cash sales.

Recently, Ivanna began offering goodies packaged in creative gift packages. This has increased sales substantially and she is now receiving orders from corporate clients and others who order quantities and prefer to buy on credit. Increased sales translate to increased purchases. To expand her gift package selection, Ivanna is considering purchasing packaging supplies from other vendors. As a result of increased credit transactions in both purchases and sales, keeping the accounting records has become extremely time-consuming. Ivanna would like to continue to maintain her own manual system. Ivanna calls you for advice. Write a memo to Ivanna advising her as to how she might modify her current manual accounting system to accommodate the expanded business activities described. She is accustomed to checking her ledger by using a trial balance. Your memo should explain the advantages of what you propose and of any other verification techniques you recommend.

This chapter described the reporting of segment information. Companies have criticized current regulatory discussions that seek to expand the information companies must report on their business segments. To learn more about current FASB deliberations on this topic and others, you should visit the FASB's Web site at **www.rutgers.edu/accounting/raw/fasb.**

Required

1. How is the table of contents for the FASB Web site organized? Identify the topical areas one can visit at this Web site.
2. Visit the Quarterly Plan for the FASB Projects area of the Web site. What accounting issues does FASB hope to discuss in the coming year?

Each member of the team is to assume responsibility for one of the six tasks below.
1. Journalizing in the Purchases Journal.
2. Journalizing in the Cash Disbursements Journal
3. Maintaining and verifying the Accounts Payable Ledger
4. Journalizing in the Sales and General Journal
5. Journalizing in the Cash Receipts Journal
6. Maintaining and verifying the Accounts Receivable Ledger
The team should follow the procedures described below in carrying out responsibilities.

Work Procedures

1. After responsibilities 1–6 are assigned, each member of the team is to quickly read through the list of transactions in Problem 8–4, identifying with initials the journal each transaction is to be recorded in. Upon completion, the team leader is to read transaction dates and the appropriate team member is to vocalize responsibility. Any disagreement between teammates must be resolved within the team.
2. Arrange seating to make it easier to access the necessary data for tasks assigned.
3. Journalize and continually update subsidiary ledgers. Journal recorders should alert subsidiary ledger maintainers when they have an entry to be posted to their subsidiary.
4. Team members responsible for tasks 1, 2, 4, and 5 are to summarize and prove journals, while members responsible for tasks 3 and 6 are to prepare schedules.
5. The team leader is to take charge of the General Ledger, rotating team members to obtain amounts to be posted. The person responsible for a journal must complete posting references in the journal. Other team members should verify accuracy of account balance computations. To avoid any abnormal account balances, post in the following order: P, S, G, R, D. *Note: Posting of any necessary individual General Ledger amounts are done at this time as well.*
6. The team leader is to read out General Ledger account balances while another team member fills in the trial balance form. Concurrently, one member should keep a running balance of debit account balance totals and another credit account balance totals. Verify the final total of the trial balance and the schedules. If necessary, the team is to resolve any errors. Turn in the trial balance and schedules to instructor.

Join a classmate and arrange a time when you can conduct a short accounting information systems survey by phone. Select five companies at random from the yellow pages of your community phone book. This survey is probably most easily administered to small service companies in your area. Call each company and ask to speak to a person who is knowledgeable about the accounting system of the company. Explain that you are completing a short phone survey for your accounting class and that it will only take a few minutes to answer your questions. Your survey should ask the following questions:

1. Is the company's accounting system computerized?
2. *If computerized,* what brand of software is used? Is this software a customized program written specifically for the company, or is it a standardized program available to many companies? (Note: Some companies use a combination.)
3. What input device(s) is used to enter transactions into the system?
4. Does the company use on-line or batch processing?
5. Does the company use a network or stand-alone computer workstations?

Read the article "Corporate America Is Fed Up with FASB" in the April 21, 1997, edition of *Business Week.*
1. In the article's table, what key reasons are identified for criticisms of the FASB by companies?
2. Why are companies critical of FASB's proposal on segment reporting?
3. In addition to the reasons cited in the article, are there other reasons you can think of why companies do not wish to expand segment reporting beyond what is currently required?

Internal Control and Cash

CHAPTER 9

Chapter Outline

Losing Control

ANN ARBOR, MI—Jason Barron is a 23-year-old entrepreneur and owner of **Barron Sports.** He's one of the people we see toting a cart full of souvenirs, pennants, and other sports items for fans at football games and other sporting events. "I started doing Michigan football games when I was 15," says Barron. "I now sell at all of Michigan's big sporting events. And I hire people to sell my items at games of other colleges."

But Barron is a victim of employee theft and fraud. "I had no idea of what types of controls I needed when I hired people to sell for me," says Barron. "I was learning on the run, and it nearly cost me everything."

Barron's problems grew from his success. Profit margins on items he sold were enormous, and sales were brisk. He quickly hired additional people to sell for him and began covering more events. But he had no real system of control, either for cash or the salable items.

"I didn't know the first thing about recordkeeping, internal control, or cash accounting," admits Barron. "It really hit home when I sent one load of items to a person working for me in Columbus. It was for the Ohio State vs. Penn State game. The items I sent cost me about $2,500, but they sell for about $9,000." But Barron got back only a little more than $6,800 when everything was supposedly sold. What happened? "The person selling for me had lots of excuses—shoplifting, damage, not delivered—you name it. It was clear to me he had ripped me off to a tune of more than $2,000 in one afternoon! That's when I knew things had to change."

Barron responded with several new control procedures. They included making all employees accountable for salable items and making them pay for items lost or stolen. In return, he substantially increased sales commissions. These changes and others cut into profit margins but nearly eliminated the cost of employee theft and fraud.

"Things are back on track," says Barron. "I want to do the major college Bowl games this year and hopefully be at the Final Four basketball finals." Like a good athlete, Barron has cut distractions and is focused on the sales game.

Learning Objectives

Conceptual

C1 Define internal control and its purpose.

C2 Identify principles of internal control.

C3 Define cash and cash equivalents and how they are reported.

C4 Identify control features of banking activities.

Analytical

A1 Compute days' sales uncollected ratio and use it to analyze liquidity.

Procedural

P1 Apply internal control to cash receipts.

P2 Apply the voucher system to control cash disbursements.

P3 Explain and record petty cash fund transactions.

P4 Apply the net method to control purchase discounts.

P5 Prepare a bank reconciliation.

CHAPTER PREVIEW

We all are aware of reports and experiences involving theft and fraud. These occurrences affect us and produce various actions. Actions include locking doors, chaining bikes, reviewing sales receipts, and acquiring alarm systems. A company also takes actions to safeguard, control, and manage what it owns. Experience tells us small companies are most vulnerable. This is usually due to weak internal controls. It is management's responsibility to set up policies and procedures to safeguard a company's assets, especially cash. To do so, management and employees must understand and apply principles of internal control. This chapter describes these principles and how we apply them. We learn about important internal control policies and procedures. We focus special attention on cash. This is because cash is easily transferable and often at high risk of loss. Several controls for cash are explained including a voucher system, petty cash funds, and reconciling bank accounts. This chapter also describes a method of accounting for purchases that helps us decide whether cash discounts on purchases are being lost and, if so, how much is lost. Our understanding of these controls and procedures makes us more secure in carrying out business activities and in assessing those activities of other companies. Like Jason Barron in the opening article, knowledge of these topics is crucial in successfully running a company.

Internal Control

This section describes internal control and its fundamental principles. We also discuss the impact of computing technology on internal control and the limitations of control procedures.

Purpose of Internal Control

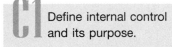

Managers (or owners) of small businesses often control the entire operation. They supervise workers, participate in all activities, and make major decisions. These managers usually buy all the assets and services used in the business. They also hire and manage employees, negotiate all contracts, and sign all checks. These managers know from personal contact and observation whether the business is actually receiving the assets and services paid for. Larger companies find it increasingly difficult to maintain this close personal contact. At some point, managers must delegate responsibilities and rely on formal procedures rather than personal contact in controlling and knowing all operations of the business.

Managers use an internal control system to monitor and control the business's operations. An **internal control system** is all the policies and procedures managers use to:

- Protect assets.
- Ensure reliable accounting.
- Promote efficient operations.
- Urge adherence to company policies.

A properly designed internal control system is a key part of systems design, analysis, and performance. Managers place a high priority on internal control systems because they can prevent avoidable losses, help managers plan operations, and monitor company and human performance. While internal controls don't provide guarantees, they lower the company's risk of loss from not having internal controls.

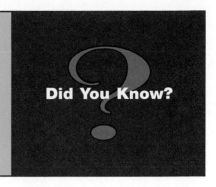
Did You Know?

Principles of Internal Control

Internal control policies and procedures vary from company to company. They depend on factors such as the nature of the business and its size. Yet certain fundamental internal control principles apply to all companies. The **principles of internal control** are:

C2 Identify principles of internal control.

1. Establish responsibilities.
2. Maintain adequate records.
3. Insure assets and bond key employees.
4. Separate recordkeeping from custody of assets.
5. Divide responsibility for related transactions.
6. Apply technological controls.
7. Perform regular and independent reviews.

We explain these seven principles in this section. We also describe how internal control procedures minimize the risk of fraud and theft. These procedures increase the reliability and accuracy of accounting records.

Establish Responsibilities

Proper internal control means that responsibility for each task is clearly established and assigned to one person. When responsibility is not identified, it is difficult to determine who is at fault when a problem occurs. When two salesclerks share access to the same cash register, for instance, it is difficult to identify which clerk is at fault if there is a cash shortage. Neither clerk can prove or disprove the alleged shortage. To prevent this problem, one clerk might be given responsibility for handling all cash sales. Alternately, a company can use a register with separate cash drawers for each clerk. Most of us have experienced waiting in line at a retail counter during a change of shift while employees swap cash drawers.

Maintain Adequate Records

Good recordkeeping is part of an internal control system. It helps protect assets and ensures that employees use prescribed procedures. Reliable records are also a source of information that management uses to monitor company operations. When detailed records of manufacturing equipment and tools are kept, for instance, items are unlikely to be lost or stolen without the discrepancy's being noticed. Similarly, transactions are less likely to be entered in incorrect accounts if a chart of accounts is set up and used carefully. If this chart is not set up or is used incorrectly, managers might never discover excessive expenses or inflated sales.

Many preprinted forms and internal business papers are also designed for use in a good internal control system. When sales slips are properly designed, for instance, sales personnel can record needed information efficiently with less chance of errors or delays to customers. And when sales slips are prenumbered and controlled, each sales slip issued is the responsibility of one salesperson. This means a salesperson is not able to pocket cash by making a sale and destroying the sales slip. Computerized point-of-sale systems achieve the same control results.

Insure Assets and Bond Key Employees

Good internal control means that assets are adequately insured against casualty, and employees handling cash and negotiable assets are bonded. An employee is *bonded* when a company purchases an insurance policy, or a bond, against losses from theft by that employee. Bonding reduces the risk of loss suffered from theft. It also discourages theft because bonded employees know that an independent bonding company is involved when theft is uncovered, and it is unlikely to be sympathetic with an employee involved in theft.

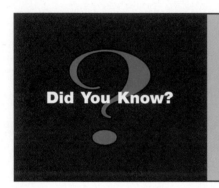

Did You Know?

High-Tech Threads

Theft and counterfeiting are concerns of most companies. **Tracer Detection Technology** has developed a technique for permanently marking paper, currency, and all physical assets. Its new technique involves embedding a one-inch-square tag made of nylon fibers with different light-absorbing properties. Each pattern of fibers creates a unique optical signature. They hope to embed tags in everything from compact disks and credit cards to designer clothes and accessories to help fight theft and counterfeiting. Retailers will be able to verify products by running scanners over the fiber tag. [Source: *Business Week*, October 6, 1997.]

Separate Recordkeeping from Custody of Assets

An important principle of internal control is that a person who controls or has access to an asset must not keep that asset's accounting records. This principle reduces the risk of theft or waste of an asset because the person with control over the asset knows that records of the asset are kept by another person. Also the recordkeeper doesn't have access to the asset and has no reason to falsify records. This means that two people must both agree to commit a fraud, called *collusion*, for the asset to be stolen and the theft is hidden from the records. Because collusion is necessary to commit this type of fraud, it is less likely to occur.

Divide Responsibility for Related Transactions

Good internal control divides responsibility for a transaction or a series of related transactions between two or more individuals or departments. This is to ensure that the work of one acts as a check on the other. But this principle, often called *separation of duties*, is not a call for duplication of work. Each employee or department should perform unduplicated effort.

  Examples of transactions with divided responsibility are placing purchase orders, receiving merchandise, and paying vendors. These tasks shouldn't be given to one individual or department. Assigning responsibility for any of these tasks to one party creates a case where mistakes and perhaps fraud are more likely to occur. Having an independent person, for example, check incoming goods for quality and quantity encourages more care and attention to detail than having the person who placed the order do the checking. Added protection can result from identifying a third person to approve payment of the invoice. Again the risk of both error and fraud is reduced. We can even designate a fourth person with authority to write checks as another measure of protection.

Apply Technological Controls

Cash registers, check protectors, time clocks, mechanical counters, and personal identification scanners are examples of control devices that can improve internal control. Technology often helps them be used effectively. A cash register with a locked-in tape or electronic file makes a record of each cash sale. A check protector perforates the amount of a check into its face and makes it difficult to alter the amount. A time clock registers the exact time an employee both arrives on and departs from the job. Mechanical change and currency counters quickly and accurately count amounts. And personal scanners limit access to only authorized individuals. Each of these and other technological controls are effective parts of many internal control systems.

Face Codes

We're all familiar with bar codes, but how about "face codes"? **Viisage Technology** has licensed a powerful face-recognition program from MIT. It snaps a digital picture of the face and converts key facial features—say, the distance between the eyes—into a series of numerical values. These can be stored on an ID or ATM card as a simple bar code. Searching through tens of thousands of faces is a snap. Welfare agencies in Massachusetts are already using the system to identify fraudulent welfare cases. [Source: *Business Week,* May 5, 1997.]

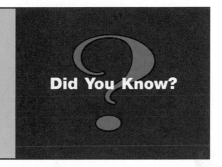

Perform Regular and Independent Reviews

No internal control system is entirely effective. Changes in personnel and technological advances present opportunities for shortcuts and other lapses. So does the stress of time pressures. To counter these changes, regular reviews of internal control systems are needed to ensure that procedures are followed. These reviews are preferably done by internal auditors not directly involved in operations. Their independent perspective encourages an evaluation of the efficiency as well as the effectiveness of the internal control system.

Many companies also pay for audits by independent auditors who are CPAs. These external auditors test the company's financial records and then give an opinion as to whether the company's financial statements are presented fairly in accordance with generally accepted accounting principles. Before external auditors decide on how much testing is needed, they evaluate the effectiveness of the internal control system. In the process of their evaluation, they identify internal controls needing improvement. This information is often helpful to a client.

Political Activist

You are a political activist leading a campaign to improve the health care system. Your funding is limited and you try to hire people who are committed to your cause and who will work for less. A systems analyst recently volunteered her services. One of her recommendations was to require all employees to take at least one week of vacation per year. Why would she recommend a "forced vacation" policy?

Answer—p. 393

Technology and Internal Control

The fundamental principles of internal control are relevant no matter what the technological state of the accounting system, from purely manual to fully automated systems. Yet technology impacts an internal control system in several important ways. Perhaps the most obvious is that technology allows us quicker access to ever-increasing information databases. Used effectively, technology greatly improves managers' ability to monitor and control business operations. This section describes some technological impacts we must be alert to.

Reduced Processing Errors

Technologically advanced systems reduce the number of errors in processing information. Provided the software and data entry are correct, the risk of mechanical and mathematical errors is nearly eliminated. Yet erroneous data entry does occur and one must be alert to that possibility. The decreasing human involvement in later data processing can cause data entry errors to go undiscovered. Similarly, errors in software can produce consistent erroneous processing of transactions. It is important to continually check and monitor all types of systems.

More Extensive Testing of Records

A company's regular review and audit of electronic records can include more extensive testing when information is easily and rapidly accessed. When accounting records are kept manually, auditors and others likely select only small samples of data to test. But when data are accessible with computer technology, then large samples or even complete data files can be quickly reviewed and analyzed.

Limited Evidence of Processing

Because many data processing steps are increasingly done by computer, fewer hard-copy items of documentary evidence are available for review. Yet technologically advanced systems can store some additional evidence. They can, for instance, record information such as who made the entries, the date and time, and the source of their entry. Technology can also be designed to require use of passwords or other identification before access to the system is granted. This means that internal control depends more on the design and operation of the information system and less on analysis of its resulting documents.

Crucial Separation of Duties

Technological advances in accounting information systems are so efficient that they often require fewer employees. This reduction in workforce carries a risk that separation of crucial responsibilities is lost. Companies that use advanced technology also need employees with special skills to operate programs and equipment. The duties of these employees must be controlled and monitored to minimize risk of error and fraud. Better control is maintained if, for instance, the person designing and programming the system does not serve as the operator. Also, the control over programs and files related to cash receipts and disbursements must be separated. To avoid risk of fraud, check-writing activities should not be controlled by a computer operator. Achieving acceptable separation of duties can be especially difficult and costly in small companies with few employees.

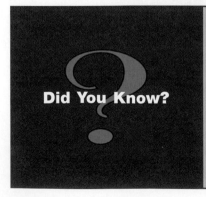

Did You Know?

Calling All Techies

Most internal control systems today rely on information technology. A new study estimates 190,000 jobs in information technology stand vacant. Demand far outstrips supply, producing a bidding war for digital talent. **Bay Networks** recently lost a five-year programmer making $80,000 to a consulting company offering $300,000 per year. And starting salaries for new graduates often exceed $45,000. The most prized programmers are those adept at enterprise programs such as SAP or Oracle. But the demand for techies with Web, intranets, and software expertise is also strong. A recent survey cited the shortage of techies as one of the greatest barriers to company growth. [Source: *Business Week*, March 10, 1997.]

Limitations of Internal Control

All internal control policies and procedures have limitations. Probably the most serious source of these limitations is the human element. Internal control policies and procedures are applied by people and often impact other people. This human element creates several potential limitations that we can categorize as either (1) human error or (2) human fraud.

Human error is a factor whenever internal control policies and procedures are carried out by people. *Human error* can occur from negligence, fatigue, misjudgment, or confusion. *Human fraud* involves intent by people to defeat internal controls for personal gain. Fraudulent behavior can defeat many internal controls. This includes collusion to thwart the separation of duties principle as explained above. This human element highlights the importance of establishing an *internal control environment* to convey management's commitment to internal control policies and procedures.

Another important limitation on internal control is the *cost-benefit principle*. This means the costs of internal controls must not exceed their benefits. Analysis of costs and benefits must consider all factors, including the impact on morale. Most companies, for instance, have a legal right to read employees' e-mail. Yet companies seldom exercise that right unless confronted with evidence of potential harm to the company. The same holds for drug testing, phone tapping, and hidden cameras. The bottom line is that no internal control system is perfect, and that managers must establish internal control policies and procedures with a net benefit to the company.

Flash back

1. Fundamental principles of internal control include:
   a. Responsibility for a series of related transactions (such as placing orders, receiving, and paying for merchandise) should be assigned to one person.
   b. Responsibility for specific tasks should be shared by more than one employee so that one serves as a check on the other.
   c. Employees who handle cash and negotiable assets should be bonded.
2. What are some impacts of computing technology on internal control?

Answers—p. 393

Control of Cash

Cash is a necessary asset of every company. Most companies also include *cash equivalents*, which are similar to cash, as part of cash. We define cash equivalents later in this section. It is important to apply principles of good internal control to cash and cash equivalents. They are the most liquid of all assets and are easily hidden and moved. A good system of internal control for cash provides adequate procedures for protecting both cash receipts and cash disbursements. These procedures should meet three basic guidelines:

1. Handling of cash is separate from recordkeeping for cash.
2. Cash receipts are promptly (daily) deposited in a bank.
3. Cash disbursements are made by check.

The first guideline aims to minimize errors and fraud by division of duties. When duties are separated, two or more people must collude to steal cash and conceal this action in the accounting records. The second guideline aims to use immediate (daily) deposits of all cash receipts to produce a timely independent test of the accuracy of the count of cash received. It also reduces cash theft or loss, and it reduces the risk of an employee personally using the money before depositing it. The third guideline aims to use payments by check to develop a bank record of cash disbursements. This guideline also reduces the risk of cash theft.

One exception to the third guideline is the disbursement of small amounts of currency and coins from a *petty cash fund*. We describe a petty cash fund later in this section. The deposit of cash receipts and the use of checks for cash disbursements also allows a company to use bank records as a separate external record of cash transactions. We explain how to use bank records to confirm the accuracy of a company's own records later in this section.

The exact procedures used to achieve control over cash vary across companies. They depend on such factors as company size, number of employees, volume of cash transactions, and sources of cash. We must therefore view the procedures described in this section as illustrative of those in practice today.

Cash, Cash Equivalents, and Liquidity

C3 Define cash and cash equivalents and how they are reported.

Cash is an important asset for every company and must be managed. Companies also need to carefully control access to cash by employees and others who are sometimes inclined to take it for personal use. Good accounting systems support both goals by managing how much cash is on hand and controlling who has access to it. The importance of accounting for cash is highlighted by the inclusion of a statement of cash flows in a complete set of financial statements. That statement identifies activities affecting cash.[1] The purpose of this section is to define cash and cash equivalents. It also explains liquidity and its relation to cash and cash equivalents.

Cash Defined

Cash includes currency, coins, and amounts on deposit in bank accounts, checking accounts (also called *demand deposits*), and some savings accounts (also called *time deposits*). Cash also includes items that are acceptable for deposit in these accounts such as customers' checks, cashier's checks, certified checks, and money orders.

Cash Equivalents Defined

To increase their return on investment, many companies invest idle cash in assets called *cash equivalents*. **Cash equivalents** are short-term, highly liquid investment assets meeting two criteria:

1. Readily convertible to a known cash amount.
2. Sufficiently close to their maturity date so that market value is not sensitive to interest rate changes.

Only investments purchased within three months of their maturity dates usually satisfy these criteria.[2] Examples of cash equivalents are short-term investments in U.S. treasury bills, commercial paper such as short-term corporate notes payable, and money market funds.

Reporting Cash and Cash Equivalents

Because cash equivalents are similar to cash, most companies combine them with cash as a single item on the balance sheet. **Ford Motor Company,** for instance, reports the following on its December 31, 1997 balance sheet:

Cash and cash equivalents	$ 6,316 (million)

---

[1] We described the statement of cash flows in earlier chapters and discussed cash flow relative to various topics. Chapter 17 explains the statement of cash flows in detail.

[2] FASB, *Accounting Standards—Current Text* (Norwalk, CT, 1995), sec. C25.106. First published in *Statement of Financial Accounting Standards No. 95,* par. 8.

Another example is **Mattel**'s December 31, 1997, balance sheet, which reports a Cash balance of $695 (million). There is no balance or mention of cash equivalents in its balance sheet. But Mattel's Note 1 reports:

> Cash includes cash equivalents, which are highly liquid investments with maturities of three months or less when purchased. Because of the short maturities of these instruments, the carrying amount is a reasonable estimate of fair value.

Liquidity

Cash is the usual means of payment when paying for other assets, services, or liabilities. **Liquidity** is how easily an asset can be converted into another asset or be used in paying for services or obligations. All assets can be judged on their liquidity. Cash and similar assets are called **liquid assets** because they are converted easily into other assets or used to pay for services or liabilities. A company needs more than valuable assets to operate. A company must own some liquid assets, for example, so that bills are paid on time and purchases are made for cash when necessary.

Flash back

3. Why must a company own liquid assets?
4. Why does a company own cash equivalent assets in addition to cash?
5. Identify at least two assets that are classified as cash equivalents.

Answers—p. 393

Control of Cash Receipts

Internal control of cash receipts ensures that all cash received is properly recorded and deposited. Cash receipts arise from many transactions including cash sales, collections of customers' accounts, receipts of interest and rent, bank loans, sale of assets, and owner investments. The principles of internal control apply to all types of cash receipts. This section explains internal control over two important types of cash receipts: over-the-counter and by mail.

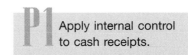

P1 Apply internal control to cash receipts.

Over-the-Counter Cash Receipts

For purposes of internal control, over-the-counter cash sales should be recorded on a cash register at the time of each sale. To help ensure that correct amounts are entered, each register should be located so customers can read the amounts entered. Clerks also should be required to both enter each sale before wrapping merchandise and give the customer a receipt for each sale. The design of each cash register should provide a permanent, locked-in record of each transaction. In many systems, the register is directly linked with computing and accounting services. Many software programs accept cash register transactions and enter them in accounting records. Less technology-dependent registers simply print a record of each transaction on a paper tape or electronic file locked inside the register.

One principle of internal control states that custody over cash should be separate from its recordkeeping. For over-the-counter cash sales, this separation begins with the cash register. The clerk who has access to cash in the register should not have access to its locked-in record. At the end of the clerk's work period, the clerk should count the cash in the register, record the amount, and turn over the cash and a record of its amount to an employee in the cashier's office. The employee in the cashier's office, like the clerk, has access to the cash and should not have access to accounting records (or the register tape or file). A third employee compares the record of total register transactions (or the register tape or file) with the cash receipts reported by the cashier's office. This record (or register tape or file) is the basis for a journal entry recording over-the-counter cash sales. The third employee has access to the records for cash but not to the actual cash. The clerk and the employee from the cashier's office have access to cash but not to the accounting records. This means the accuracy of cash records and amounts are automatically checked. None of them can make a mistake or divert cash without the difference being revealed.

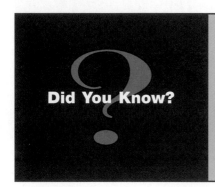

Register Mammoth

Wal-Mart uses an enormous network of information links with its point-of-sale cash registers. With annual sales of more than $100 billion, it uses information systems to coordinate sales, purchases, and distribution. Three Buenos Aires supercenters, for instance, ring up some 15,000 sales on heavy days. **Wal-Mart** is now the dominant discounter in the U.S., Canada, and Mexico. Yet even it makes mistakes, from a glut of ice-fishing huts in tropical Puerto Rico to a dearth of snowshoes in wintertime Ontario. But using cash register information, it is quick to fix mistakes and to capitalize on sales trends. [Source: *Business Week,* June 23, 1997.]

Cash Over and Short

Sometimes errors in making change are discovered when there are differences between the cash in a cash register and the record of the amount of cash sales. Even though a cashier is careful, one or more customers can be given too much or too little change. This means at the end of a work period, the cash in a cash register might not equal the cash sales entered. This difference is reported in the **Cash Over and Short** account. This account is an income statement account recording the income effects of cash overages and cash shortages from errors in making change and missing petty cash receipts. As an example, if a cash register shows cash sales of $550 but the count of cash in the register is $555, the entry to record cash sales and its overage is:

Assets = Liabilities + Equity
+555   +   5
                        +550

Cash	555	
Cash Over and Short		5
Sales		550
To record day's cash sales and overage.		

If a cash register shows cash sales of $625 but the count of cash in the register is $621, the entry to record cash sales and its shortage is:

Assets = Liabilities + Equity
+621   −   4
                        +625

Cash	621	
Cash Over and Short	4	
Sales		625
To record day's cash sales and shortage.		

Because customers are more likely to dispute being shortchanged, the Cash Over and Short account usually has a debit balance at the end of an accounting period. This debit balance reflects an expense. It can be shown on the income statement as an item in general and administrative expenses. But since the amount is usually small, it is often combined with other small expenses and reported as part of *miscellaneous expenses.* If Cash Over and Short has a credit balance at the end of the period, it usually is shown on the income statement as part of *miscellaneous revenues.*

Cash Receipts By Mail

Control of cash receipts that arrive through the mail starts with the person who opens the mail. Preferably, two people are assigned the task of and are present for opening the mail. Because two people are involved, theft of cash receipts by mail usually requires collusion between these two employees. The person opening the mail makes a list (in triplicate) of money received. This list should contain a record of each sender's name, the amount, and an explanation of why the money is sent. The first copy is sent with the money to the cashier. A second copy is sent to the recordkeeper in the accounting area. A third copy is kept by the clerk who opened the mail. The cashier deposits the money in a bank, and the recordkeeper records the amounts received in the accounting records.

This process reflects excellent internal control. First, when the bank balance is reconciled by another person (explained later in the chapter), errors or fraud by the clerk, the cashier, or the recordkeeper are revealed. They are revealed because the bank's record of cash deposited must agree with the records from each of three people. This arrangement virtually eliminates the possibility of errors and fraud. If the clerk does not report all receipts correctly, for instance, customers will question their account balances. If the cashier does not deposit all receipts, for instance, the bank balance does not agree with the recordkeeper's cash balance. The recordkeeper and the person who reconciles the bank balance do not have access to cash and, therefore, have no opportunity to divert cash to themselves. This system makes errors and fraud highly unlikely. The exception is when employees collude.

Control of Cash Disbursements

Control of cash disbursements is especially important for companies. Most large thefts occur from payment of fictitious invoices. One key to controlling cash disbursements is to require that all expenditures be made by check. The only exception is small payments made from petty cash. Another key is to deny access to the accounting records to a person other than the owner who has the authority to sign checks. This separation of duties helps prevent an employee from hiding fraudulent disbursements in the accounting records.

The manager of a small business often signs checks and knows from personal contact that the items being paid for are actually received. This arrangement is impossible in large businesses. Instead, internal control procedures must be substituted for personal contact. These procedures are designed to assure the check signer that the obligations recorded were properly incurred and should be paid. These controls are achieved through a voucher system.

This section describes the voucher system, explains the petty cash system, and describes the management of cash disbursements for purchases.

Paper Chase
Paper documents are still common in business today. Yet companies are increasingly converting to electronic documents. The purposes and features of most documents remain basically the same in either system. But the internal control system must change to reflect different risks and concerns. These include issues of confidentiality and competitive sensitive information that are placed at risk in electronic-based systems.

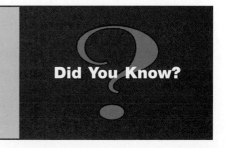

Did You Know?

P2 Apply the voucher system to control cash disbursements.

Voucher System of Control

A **voucher system** is a set of procedures and approvals designed to control cash disbursements and acceptance of obligations. The voucher system of control establishes procedures for:

- Accepting obligations resulting in cash disbursements.
- Verifying, approving, and recording obligations.
- Issuing checks for payment of verified, approved, and recorded obligations.
- Requiring obligations be recorded when incurred.
- Treating each purchase as an independent transaction.

A good voucher system follows these procedures for every transaction. This applies even when many purchases are made from the same company during a period.

A voucher system's control over cash disbursements begins when a company incurs an obligation that will result in payment of cash. A key factor in this system is that only approved departments and individuals are authorized to incur such obligations. The system often limits the kind of obligations that a department or individual can incur. In a large retail store, for instance, only a purchasing department should be authorized to incur obligations from merchandise purchases. Another key factor is that procedures for purchasing, receiving, and paying for merchandise are often divided among several departments. These departments include the one requesting the purchase, the purchasing department, the receiving department, and the accounting department. To coordinate and control responsibilities of these departments, several different business papers are used. Exhibit 9.1 shows how these papers are accumulated in a **voucher.** A voucher is an internal business paper (or folder) that is used to accumulate other papers and information needed to control cash disbursements and to ensure a transaction is properly recorded. We next discuss each document entering a voucher. We show how a company uses this system in controlling cash disbursements for merchandise purchases.

Exhibit 9.1

Document Flow in a Voucher System

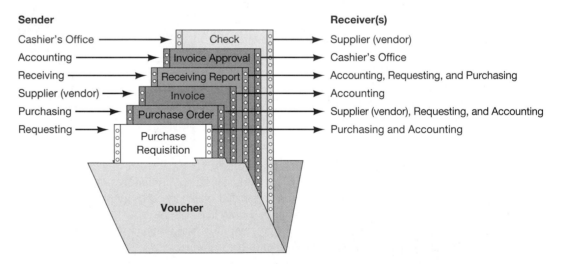

Sender		Receiver(s)
Cashier's Office	Check	Supplier (vendor)
Accounting	Invoice Approval	Cashier's Office
Receiving	Receiving Report	Accounting, Requesting, and Purchasing
Supplier (vendor)	Invoice	Accounting
Purchasing	Purchase Order	Supplier (vendor), Requesting, and Accounting
Requesting	Purchase Requisition	Purchasing and Accounting

Voucher

Purchase Requisition

Department managers in larger stores are usually not allowed to place orders directly with suppliers. If each manager deals directly with suppliers, the merchandise purchased and the resulting liabilities are not well controlled. To gain control over purchases and the resulting liabilities, department managers are often required to place all orders through a purchasing department. When merchandise is needed, a department manager must inform the purchasing department of its needs by preparing and signing a purchase requisition. A **purchase requisition** lists the merchandise needed by a department and requests that it be purchased—see Exhibit 9.2. Two copies of the purchase requisition are sent to the purchasing department. The purchasing department sends one copy to the ac-

```
Purchase Requisition                    No. 917
                          Z-Mart

From ___Sporting Goods Department___      Date _____October 28, 1998____
To _____Purchasing Department_____    Preferred Vendor ___Trex_____

   Request purchase of the following item(s):

   | Model No. | Description  | Quantity |
   | CH 015    | Challenger X7 | 1       |
   | SD 099    | SpeedDemon   | 1        |

   Reason for Request  _____Replenish inventory_____
   Approval for Request_____ J.Z._____


   For Purchasing Department use only: Order Date _10/30/98_   P.O. No. ____P98____
```

Exhibit 9.2

Purchase Requisition

counting department. When the accounting department receives a purchase requisition, it creates and maintains a voucher for this transaction. A third copy of the requisition is kept by the requesting department as backup.

Purchase Order

A **purchase order** is a business paper used by the purchasing department to place an order with a seller, also called a **vendor.** A vendor usually is a manufacturer or wholesaler. A purchase order authorizes a vendor to ship ordered merchandise at the stated price and terms—see Exhibit 9.3. When the purchasing department receives a purchase requisition, it prepares at least four copies of a purchase order. The copies are distributed as follows: *copy 1* is sent to the vendor as a purchase request and as authority to ship merchandise; *copy 2* is sent, along with a copy of the purchase requisition, to the accounting department where it is entered in the voucher and used in approving payment of the invoice; *copy 3* is sent to the requesting department to inform its manager that action is being taken; and *copy 4* is retained on file by the purchasing department.

```
Purchase Order                      No. P98
                          Z-Mart
                     10 Michigan Street
                   Chicago, Illinois 60521

To:  Trex                                 Date _____10/30/98_____
     W9797 Cherry Road                    FOB _____Destination_____
     Antigo, Wisconsin 54409              Ship by _As soon as possible_____
                                          Terms _____2/15, n/30_____

   Request shipment of the following item(s):

   | Model No. | Description   | Quantity | Price | Amount |
   | CH 015    | Challenger X7 | 1        | 490   | 490    |
   | SD 099    | SpeedDemon    | 1        | 710   | 710    |

   All shipments and invoices must        Ordered by
   include purchase order number
                                               J.W.
```

Exhibit 9.3

Purchase Order

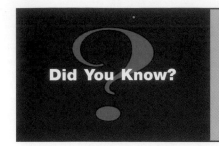

Invoice

An **invoice** is an itemized statement of goods prepared by the vendor (supplier) listing the customer's name, the items sold, the sales prices, and the terms of sale. An invoice is also a bill sent to the buyer from the supplier. From the vendor's point of view, it is a *sales invoice*. The vendor sends the invoice to a buyer, or **vendee**, who treats it as a *purchase invoice*. When receiving a purchase order, the vendor ships the ordered merchandise to the buyer and includes or mails a copy of the invoice covering the shipment to the buyer. The invoice is sent to the buyer's accounting department where it is placed in the voucher. Exhibit 6.6 shows Z-Mart's purchase invoice.

Receiving Report

Many companies maintain a special department to receive all merchandise or other purchased assets. When each shipment arrives, this receiving department counts the goods and checks them for damage and agreement with the purchase order. It then prepares four or more copies of a receiving report. A **receiving report** is used within the company to notify the appropriate persons that ordered goods have been received and to describe the quantities and condition of the goods. One copy is placed in the voucher. Copies are also sent to the requesting department and the purchasing department to notify them that the goods have arrived. The receiving department retains a copy in its files.

Invoice Approval

When a receiving report arrives, the accounting department should have copies of the following papers on file in the voucher: purchase requisition; purchase order; invoice; and receiving report. With the information in these documents, the accounting department can record the purchase and approve its payment before the end of the discount period. In approving an invoice for payment, the department checks and compares information across all documents. To facilitate this checking and to ensure that no step is omitted, the department often uses an **invoice approval,** also called *check authorization.* Exhibit 9.4 shows an invoice approval form. An invoice approval is a checklist of steps necessary for approving an invoice for recording and payment. It is a separate document either filed in the voucher or preprinted on the voucher. It also is sometimes stamped on the invoice. Exhibit 9.4 shows the invoice approval as a separate document.

Exhibit 9.4

Invoice Approval

Invoice Approval			
	No.	By	Date
Purchase requisition	917	72	10/28/98
Purchase order	P98	9w	10/30/98
Receiving report	R85	3K	11/3/98
Invoice:	4657		
Price		9K	11/12/98
Calculations		9K	11/12/98
Terms		9K	11/12/98
Approved for payment		BC	11/12/98

As each step in the checklist is approved, the person initials the invoice approval and records the current date. Final approval implies the following steps have occurred:

1. **Requisition check** Items on invoice are requested, as shown on purchase requisition.
2. **Purchase order check** Items on invoice are ordered, as shown on purchase order.
3. **Receiving report check** Items on invoice are received, as shown on receiving report.
4. **Invoice check:** **Price** Invoice prices are as agreed with the vendor.
   Calculations Invoice has no mathematical errors.
   Terms Terms are as agreed with the vendor.

Voucher

Once an invoice is checked and approved, the voucher is complete. A complete voucher is a record summarizing a transaction. The voucher shows a transaction is certified as correct and it authorizes recording an obligation for the buyer. A voucher also contains approval for paying the obligation on an appropriate date. The physical form of vouchers varies across companies. Many are designed so that the invoice and other related source documents are placed inside the voucher, which is often a folder.

Completion of a voucher usually requires a person to enter certain information required on the inside and outside of the voucher. Typical information required on the inside of a voucher is shown in Exhibit 9.5, and that for the outside is shown in Exhibit 9.6. The information is taken from the invoice and the supporting documents filed in the

Exhibit 9.5

Inside of a Voucher

Z-Mart
Chicago, Illinois

Voucher No. 4657

Date Oct. 28, 1998
Pay to Trex
City Antigo City Wisconsin

For the following: (attach all invoices and supporting papers)

Date of Invoice	Terms	Invoice Number and Other Details	Terms
Nov. 2, 1998	2/15. n/30	Invoice No. 4657	1,200
		Less discount	24
		Net amount payable	1,176

Payment approved
N.O. Neal
Auditor

Exhibit 9.6

Outside of a Voucher

Voucher No. 4657

Accounting Distribution

Account Debited	Amount
Merch. Inventory	1,200
Store Supplies	
Office Supplies	
Sales Salaries	
Other	
Total Vouch. Pay. Cr.	1,200

Due Date November 12, 1998
Pay to Trex
City Antigo
State Wisconsin

Summary of charges:
Total charges 1,200
Discount 24
Net payment 1,176

Record of payment:
Paid
Check No.

voucher. A complete voucher is sent to an authorized individual (often called an *auditor*). This person performs a final review, approves the accounts and amounts for debiting (called the *accounting distribution*), and authorizes recording of the voucher.

When a voucher is approved and recorded, it is filed until its due date, when it is sent to the cashier's office for payment. The person issuing checks relies on the approved voucher and its signed supporting documents as proof that an obligation has been incurred and must be paid. The purchase requisition and purchase order confirm the purchase was authorized. The receiving report shows items have been received, and the invoice approval form verifies that the invoice has been checked for errors. There is little chance for error. There is even less chance for fraud without collusion, unless all the documents and signatures are forged.

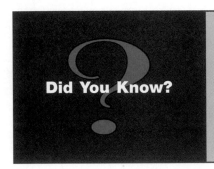

Did You Know?

Anyone Smell a Rat?
Weak internal control contributed to a debacle at **Centennial Technologies,** once a high-tech dynamo. Fictitious sales receipts, altered inventory tags, and recording sales that were never shipped are some of the actions carried out by Centennial's management to deceive auditors, investors, and creditors. CEO Emanuel Pinez was eventually indicted on five counts of fraud. Yet many of these accounting shenanigans could have been avoided with better internal control and oversight. [Source: *Business Week,* March 24, 1997.]

Expenses in a Voucher System

Obligations should be approved for payment and recorded as liabilities as soon as possible after they are incurred. This practice should be applied to all purchases. It should also be applied to all expenses. When a company receives a monthly telephone bill, for instance, the charges (especially long distance and costly calls) should be examined for accuracy. A voucher is prepared and the telephone bill is filed inside the voucher. This voucher is then recorded with a journal entry. If the amount is due at once, a check is issued. If not, the voucher is filed for payment on its due date.

Requiring that vouchers be prepared for expenses when they are incurred helps ensure that every expense payment is valid. Yet invoices or bills for such items as repairs are often not received until weeks after work is done. If no records of repairs exist, it can be difficult to determine whether the invoice amount is correct. Also, if no records exist, it is possible for a dishonest employee to collude with a dishonest seller to get more than one payment for an obligation, or for payment of excessive amounts, or for payment for goods and services not received. An effective voucher system helps prevent each of these frauds.

Flash *back*

6. Good internal control procedures for cash receipts include:
    a. All cash disbursements, other than those for very small amounts, are made by check.
    b. An accounting employee should count cash received from sales and promptly deposit receipts.
    c. Cash receipts by mail should be opened by an accounting employee who is responsible for recording and depositing receipts.
7. Do all companies require a voucher system? At what point in a company's growth do you recommend a voucher system?

Answers—p. 393

Petty Cash System of Control

A basic principle for controlling cash disbursements is that all payments are made by check. An exception to this rule is made for *petty cash disbursements*. Petty cash disbursements are the small payments required in most companies for items such as postage, courier fees, repairs, and supplies. Any amounts other than small payments are excluded. If firms made all small payments by check, it would require numerous checks for small amounts. This system would be both time-consuming and expensive. To avoid writing checks for small amounts, a company usually sets up a petty cash fund and uses the money in this fund to make small payments.

Operating a Petty Cash Fund

Establishing a petty cash fund requires estimating the total amount of small payments likely to be made during a short period such as a week or month. A check is then drawn by the company cashier for an amount slightly in excess of this estimate. This check is recorded with a debit to the Petty Cash account (an asset) and a credit to Cash. The check is cashed, and the currency is given to an employee designated as the *petty cashier*, also called *petty cash custodian*. The petty cashier is responsible for the safekeeping of the cash, for making payments from this fund, and for keeping accurate records.

The petty cashier should keep petty cash in a locked box in a safe place. As each disbursement is made, the person receiving payment signs a *petty cash receipt*, also called *petty cash ticket*—see Exhibit 9.7. The petty cash receipt is then placed in the petty cashbox with the remaining money. Under this system, the sum of all receipts plus the remaining cash equals the total fund amount. A $100 petty cash fund, for instance, contains any combination of cash and cash receipts that total $100 (examples are $100 cash, or $80 cash plus $20 in receipts, or $10 cash plus $90 in receipts). Each disbursement reduces cash and increases the amount of receipts in the petty cashbox. When the cash is nearly gone, the fund should be reimbursed.

Petty Cash Receipt	No. 9
Z-Mart	
For ___Delivery charges___	Date ___11/5/98___
Charge to ___Merchandise Inventory___	Amount ___$6.75___
Approved by ___Jim Gibbs___	Received by ___Dick Fitch___

Exhibit 9.7

Petty Cash Receipt

When it is time to reimburse the petty cash fund, the petty cashier should sort the paid receipts by the type of expense or other accounts to be debited in recording payments from the fund. The accounts are then totaled, and the totals are used in making the entry to record the reimbursement. The petty cashier presents all paid receipts to the company's cashier. The company's cashier stamps all receipts *paid* so they can't be reused, files them for recordkeeping, and gives the petty cashier a check for their sum. When this check is cashed and the money returned to the cashbox, the total money in the box is restored to its original amount. The fund is now ready to begin a new cycle of operations.

Illustration of a Petty Cash Fund

Z-Mart uses a petty cash fund to avoid writing an excessive number of checks for small amounts. Z-Mart initially established a petty cash fund on November 1, 1998. It designated one of its office employees, Jim Gibbs, as petty cashier. A $75 check was drawn,

P3 Explain and record petty cash fund transactions.

cashed, and the proceeds turned over to Gibbs. The entry to record the setup of this petty cash fund is:

Assets = Liabilities + Equity
+75
−75

Nov. 1	Petty Cash	75	
	Cash		75
	To establish a petty cash fund.		

This entry transfers $75 from the regular Cash account to the Petty Cash account. After the petty cash fund is established, the Petty Cash account is not debited or credited again unless the size of the total fund is changed. A fund probably should be increased if it is being used up and reimbursed too frequently. If the fund is too large, some of its money should be redeposited in the cash account.

During November, Jim Gibbs, the petty cashier, made several payments from petty cash. He asked each person who received payment to sign a receipt. On November 27, after making a $26.50 payment for repairs to an office computer, only $3.70 cash remained in the fund. Gibbs then summarized and totaled the petty cash receipts as shown in Exhibit 9.8. He gave this summary and all petty cash receipts to the company's cashier in exchange for a $71.30 check to reimburse the fund. Gibbs cashed the check and put the $71.30 cash in the petty cashbox. The company records the reimbursement check as follows:

Assets = Liabilities + Equity
−71.30   −46.50
                    −15.05
                    − 5.00
                    − 4.75

Nov. 27	Miscellaneous Expenses	46.50	
	Merchandise Inventory	15.05	
	Delivery Expense	5.00	
	Office Expense	4.75	
	Cash		71.30
	To reimburse petty cash.		

Information for this entry is from the petty cashier's summary of payments in Exhibit 9.8. The debits in this entry reflect the petty cash payments.

A petty cash fund is often reimbursed at the end of an accounting period even if the petty cash fund is not low on money. This is done to record expenses in the proper period. If the fund is not reimbursed at the end of a period, the financial statements show both an overstated petty cash asset and understated expenses or assets that were paid out of petty cash. Yet the amounts involved are rarely significant to users of financial statements.

Exhibit 9.8

Petty Cash Payments Report

Z-MART		
Petty Cash Payments Report		
Miscellaneous expenses		
Nov. 2 Washing windows	$10.00	
Nov. 17 Washing windows	10.00	
Nov. 27 Computer repairs	26.50	$46.50
Merchandise inventory (transportation-in)		
Nov. 5 Delivery of merchandise purchased	$ 6.75	
Nov. 20 Delivery of merchandise purchased	8.30	15.05
Delivery expense		
Nov. 18 Customer's package delivered		5.00
Office expense		
Nov. 15 Purchased office supplies		4.75
Total		$71.30

Increasing or Decreasing Petty Cash Fund

A decision to increase or decrease a petty cash fund is often made when reimbursing the fund. To illustrate, let's assume Z-Mart decides to *increase* the petty cash fund of Jim Gibbs to $100 on November 27 when it reimburses the fund. This entry is identical to the one above except for two changes: (1) include a debit to Petty Cash for $25 (this increases the fund from $75 to $100), and (2) credit Cash for $96.30 ($71.30 reimbursement of expenses plus $25 increase in the fund).

Alternatively, if Z-Mart *decreases* the petty cash fund from $75 to $55 on November 27, there are two changes required for the entry on this date: (1) include a credit to Petty Cash for $20 (this decreases the fund from $75 to $55), and (2) credit Cash for $51.30 ($71.30 reimbursement of expense minus $20 decrease in the fund).

Internal Auditor

You are an internal auditor for a company. You are currently making surprise counts of three $200 petty cash funds. You arrive at the office of one of the petty cashiers while she is on the telephone. You explain the purpose of your visit, and the petty cashier asks politely that you come back after lunch so that she can finish the business she's conducting by long distance. You agree and return after lunch. The petty cashier opens the petty cashbox and shows you nine new $20 bills with consecutive serial numbers plus receipts totaling $20. Do you take further action or comment on these events in your report to management?

Answer—p. 393

Cash Over and Short

Sometimes a petty cashier fails to get a receipt for payment. When this occurs and the fund is later reimbursed, the petty cashier often won't recall the purpose of the payment. This mistake causes the fund to be *short*. If the petty cash fund is short, this shortage is recorded as an expense in the reimbursing entry with a debit to the Cash Over and Short account. An overage in the petty cash fund is recorded with a credit to Cash Over and Short in the reimbursing entry.

Flash *back*

8. Why are some cash payments made from a petty cash fund?

9. Why should a petty cash fund be reimbursed at the end of an accounting period?

10. What are two results of reimbursing the petty cash fund?

Answers—p. 393

Control of Purchase Discounts

This section explains how a company can gain more control over purchase discounts. Chapter 6 described entries to record the receipt and payment of an invoice for a purchase of merchandise under the perpetual inventory system. When Z-Mart purchased merchandise with a $1,200 invoice price with terms of 2/10, n/30, it made the entry:

P4 Apply the net method to control purchase discounts.

Nov. 2	Merchandise Inventory	1,200	
	Accounts Payable		1,200
	Purchased merchandise on credit, invoice dated November 2, terms 2/10, n/30.		

Assets = Liabilities + Equity
+1,200   +1,200

When Z-Mart takes advantage of the discount and pays the amount due on November 12, the entry is:

Assets = Liabilities + Equity
−24   −1,200
−1,176

Nov. 12	Accounts Payable	1,200	
	Merchandise Inventory		24
	Cash		1,176
	Paid for the purchase of November 2 less the discount. (2% × $1,200)		

These entries reflect the **gross method** of recording purchases. The gross method records the invoice at its *gross* amount of $1,000 *before* recognizing the cash discount. Many companies record invoices in this way.

Another method of recording purchases is the **net method**. The net method records the invoice at its *net* amount *after* recognizing the cash discount. This method is viewed as providing more useful information to management. If Z-Mart uses the net method of recording purchases, it deducts the potential $24 cash discount from the gross amount and records the initial purchase at the $1,176 net amount:

Assets = Liabilities + Equity
+1,176   +1,176

Nov. 2	Merchandise Inventory	1,176	
	Accounts Payable		1,176
	Purchased merchandise on credit, invoice dated November 2, terms 2/10, n/30.		

If the invoice for this purchase is paid within the discount period, the entry to record the payment debits Accounts Payable and credits Cash for $1,176. But if payment is not made within the discount period and the discount is *lost*, the following entry must be made either on the date the discount is lost or when the invoice is paid:

Assets = Liabilities + Equity
          +24   −24

Dec. 2	Discounts Lost	24	
	Accounts Payable		24
	To record the discount lost.		

A check for the full $1,200 invoice amount is then written, recorded, and sent to the creditor.[3]

The net method gives management an advantage in controlling and monitoring purchase discounts. When invoices are recorded at *gross* amounts, the amount of discounts taken is deducted from the balance of the Merchandise Inventory account. This means the amount of any discounts lost is not reported in any account or on the income statement. Discounts lost recorded in this way are unlikely to come to the attention of management. But when purchases are recorded at *net* amounts, a **discounts lost** expense is brought to management's attention as an operating expense on the income statement. Management can then seek to identify the reason for discounts lost such as oversight, carelessness, or unfavorable terms. This practice gives management better control over persons responsible for paying bills to ensure they take advantage of favorable discounts. In this way, it's less likely that favorable discounts are lost.

Banking Activities as Controls

Banks are used for many different services. One of their most important services is helping companies control cash and cash transactions. Banks safeguard cash, provide detailed and independent records of cash transactions, and are a source of cash financing. This section describes services and documents provided by banking activities that increase managers' control over cash.

---

[3] The discount lost also can be recorded with the payment in a single entry. If financial statements are prepared after a discount is lost, an adjusting entry is required to recognize it if it is not recorded.

Basic Bank Services

This first section explains basic bank services. We include the bank account, the bank deposit, and checking. Each of these services contributes to either or both the control or safeguarding of cash.

Bank Account

A bank account is a record set up by a bank for a customer. It permits this customer to deposit money for safeguarding and check withdrawals. To control access to a bank account, all persons authorized to write checks on the account must sign a **signature card.** Bank employees use signature cards to verify signatures on checks. This lowers the risk of loss from forgery for both banks and customers. Many companies have more than one bank account to serve different needs and handle special transactions such as payroll.

Bank Deposit

Each bank deposit is supported by a deposit ticket. A **deposit ticket** lists the items such as currency, coins, and checks deposited and their corresponding dollar amounts. The bank gives the customer a copy of the deposit ticket or a deposit receipt as proof of the deposit. Exhibit 9.9 shows a deposit ticket.

C4 Identify control features of banking activities.

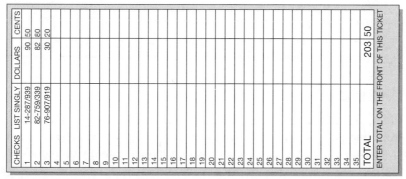

Exhibit 9.9

Deposit Ticket

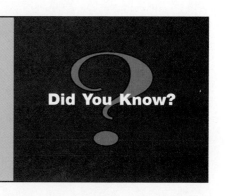

Did You Know?

Bank Check

To withdraw money from an account a customer uses a check. A **check** is a document signed by the depositor instructing the bank to pay a specified amount of money to a designated recipient. A check involves three parties: a *maker* who signs the check, a *payee* who is the recipient, and a *bank* (or *payer*) on which the check is drawn. The bank provides a depositor with checks that are serially numbered and imprinted with the name and address of both the depositor and bank. Both checks and deposit tickets are imprinted with identification codes in magnetic ink for computer processing. Exhibit 9.10 shows a check. This check is accompanied with an optional *remittance advice* giving an explanation for the payment. When a remittance advice is unavailable, the *memo* line is often used for a brief explanation.

Exhibit 9.10

Check with Remittance Advice

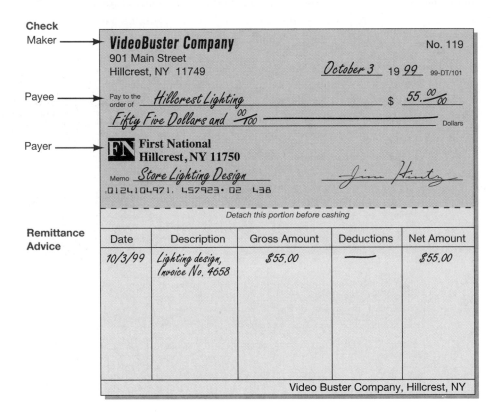

Electronic Funds Transfer

Electronic funds transfer (EFT) is the use of electronic communication to transfer cash from one party to another. No paper documents are necessary. Banks simply transfer cash from one account to another with a journal entry. Companies are increasingly using EFT because of its convenience and low cost. It can cost, for instance, up to a dollar to process a check through the banking system, whereas EFT cost is near zero. We now commonly see items such as payroll, rent, utilities, insurance, and interest payments being handled by EFT. The bank statement lists cash withdrawals by EFT with checks and other deductions. Cash receipts by EFT are listed with deposits and other additions. A bank statement is sometimes a depositor's only notice of an EFT.

Bank Statement

At least once a month, the bank sends each depositor a bank statement showing the activity in that account during the month. Different banks use different formats for their bank statements, yet all of them include the following items of information:

1. Beginning-of-month balance of the depositor's account.

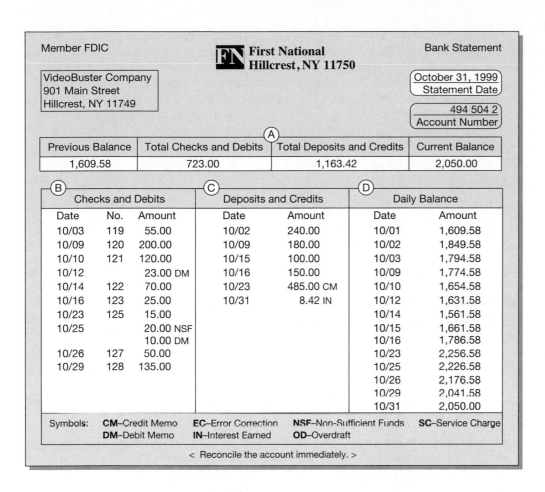

Exhibit 9.11

Bank Statement

2. Checks and other debits decreasing the account during the month.
3. Deposits and other credits increasing the account during the month.
4. End-of-month balance of the depositor's account.

This information reflects the bank's records. Exhibit 9.11 shows a bank statement. Identify each of the four items listed above.

Part A of Exhibit 9.11 summarizes changes in the account. Part B lists paid checks in numerical order along with other debits. Part C lists deposits and credits to the account, and part D shows the daily account balances.

Enclosed with a bank statement are the depositor's canceled checks or images of canceled checks or images of canceled checks along with any debit or credit memoranda affecting the account. **Canceled checks** are checks the bank has paid and deducted from the customer's account during the month. Other deductions also often appear on a bank statement and include: (1) service charges and fees assessed by the bank, (2) customers' checks deposited that are uncollectible, (3) corrections of previous errors, (4) withdrawals through automatic teller machines (ATM), and (5) periodic payments arranged in advance by a depositor.[4] Except for service charges, the bank notifies the depositor of each deduction with a debit memorandum when the bank reduces the balance. A copy of each debit memorandum is usually sent with the monthly statement.[5]

---

[4] Because of a desire to make all disbursements by check, most business checking accounts do not allow ATM withdrawals.

[5] A depositor's account is a liability on the bank's records. This is because the money belongs to the depositor and not the bank. When a depositor increases the account balance, the bank records it with a *credit* to the account. This means that debit memos from the bank produce *credits* on the depositor's books, and credit memos produce *debits* on the depositor's books.

There are also other transactions that increase the depositor's account such as amounts the bank collects on behalf of the depositor and corrections of previous errors. Credit memoranda notify the depositor of all increases when they are recorded. A copy of each credit memorandum is often sent with the bank statement. Another item sometimes added to the bank balance is interest earned by the depositor. Banks that pay interest on checking accounts often compute the amount of interest earned on the average cash balance and credit it to the depositor's account each month. In Exhibit 9.11, the bank credits $8.42 of interest to the account of **VideoBuster.**

Bank Reconciliation

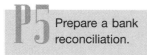

When a company deposits all receipts and when all payments except petty cash payments are by check, the bank statement is a device for proving the accuracy of the depositor's cash records. The company tests the accuracy by preparing a bank reconciliation. A **bank reconciliation** explains the difference between the balance of a checking account according to the depositor's records and the balance reported on the bank statement.

Purpose of Bank Reconciliation

The balance of a checking account reported on the bank statement is rarely equal to the balance in the depositor's accounting records. This is usually due to information that one party has that the other does not. We must therefore prove the accuracy of both the depositor's records and those of the bank. This means we must *reconcile* the two balances and explain or account for any differences in these two balances.

Among the factors causing the bank statement balance to differ from the depositor's book balance are:

1. **Outstanding checks.** These are checks written (or drawn) by the depositor, deducted on the depositor's records, and sent to the payees. Outstanding checks have not yet reached the bank for payment and deduction at the time of the bank statement.

2. **Deposits in transit** (also called **outstanding deposits**). These are deposits made and recorded by the depositor but not recorded on the bank statement. For example, companies often make deposits at the end of a business day, after the bank is closed. A deposit in the bank's night depository on the last day of the month is not recorded by the bank until the next business day and doesn't appear on the bank statement for that month. Also, deposits mailed to the bank near the end of a month may be in transit and unrecorded when the statement is prepared.

3. **Deductions for uncollectible items and for services.** A company sometimes deposits a customer's check that is uncollectible. It usually occurs when the balance in a customer's account is not large enough to cover the check. This check is called a *nonsufficient funds (NSF)* check. The bank initially credits the depositor's account for the amount of the deposited check. When the bank learns the check is uncollectible, it debits (reduces) the depositor's account for the amount of that check. The bank may also charge the depositor a fee for processing an uncollectible check and notify the depositor of the deduction by sending a debit memorandum. While each deduction should be recorded by the depositor when a debit memorandum is received, an entry is sometimes not made until the bank reconciliation is prepared.

    Other possible bank charges to a depositor's account reported on a bank statement include the printing of new checks and a service charge for maintaining the account. Notification of these charges is *not* provided until the statement is mailed.

4. **Additions for collections and for interest.** Banks sometimes act as collection agents for their depositors by collecting notes and other items. Banks can also receive electronic fund transfers to the depositor's account. When a bank collects an item it adds it to the depositor's account, less any service fee. It also sends a credit memorandum to notify the depositor of the transaction. When the memorandum is received, it should be recorded by the depositor. Yet they sometimes remain unrecorded until the time of the bank reconciliation.

Many bank accounts earn interest on the average cash balance in the account during the month. If an account earns interest, the bank statement includes a credit for the amount earned during the past month. Notification of earned interest is provided by the bank statement.

5. **Errors.** Both banks and depositors can make errors. Errors by the bank might not be discovered until the depositor prepares the bank reconciliation. Also, the depositor's errors sometimes are not discovered until the bank balance is reconciled.

Steps in Reconciling a Bank Balance

The employee who prepares the bank reconciliation should not be responsible for cash receipts, processing checks, or maintaining cash records. This employee needs to gather information from the bank statement and from other records. A reconciliation requires this person to:

- Compare deposits on the bank statement with deposits in the accounting records. Identify any discrepancies and determine which is correct. List any errors and unrecorded deposits.

- Inspect all additions (credits) on the bank statement and determine whether each is recorded in the books. Examples are collections by the bank, correction of previous bank statement errors, and interest earned by the depositor. List any unrecorded credits.

- Compare canceled checks on the bank statement with actual checks returned with the statement. For each check, make sure the correct amount is deducted by the bank and the returned check is properly charged to the account. List any discrepancies and errors.

- Compare canceled checks on the bank statement with checks recorded in the books. (The bank statement often lists canceled checks in numerical order to help in this step.) List any outstanding checks. Also, while companies with good internal controls rarely write a check without recording it, we should inspect and list any canceled checks unrecorded in the books.

- Identify any outstanding checks listed on the previous month's bank reconciliation that are not included in the canceled checks on this month's bank statement. List these checks that still remain outstanding at the end of the current month. Send the list to the cashier's office for follow-up with the payees to see if the checks were actually received.

- Inspect all deductions (debits) on the bank statement and determine whether each is recorded in the books. Examples are bank charges for newly printed checks, NSF checks, and monthly service charges. List any unrecorded debits.

When this information is gathered, the employee can complete the reconciliation.

Illustrating a Bank Reconciliation

We use the guidelines listed above and follow nine specific steps in preparing the bank reconciliation. It is helpful to refer to the bank reconciliation for VideoBuster shown in Exhibit 9.12 and the steps ① through ⑨ in preparing it. These nine steps are:

① Identify the bank balance of the cash account (*balance per bank*).

② Identify and list any unrecorded deposits and any bank errors understating the bank balance. Add them to the bank balance.

③ Identify and list any outstanding checks and any bank errors overstating the bank balance. Deduct them from the bank balance.

④ Compute the *adjusted bank balance,* also called *corrected* or *reconciled balance.*

⑤ Identify the company's book balance of the cash account (*balance per book*).

⑥ Identify and list any unrecorded credit memoranda from the bank, interest earned, and errors understating the book balance. Add them to the book balance.

VIDEOBUSTER
Bank Reconciliation
October 31, 1999

①	Bank statement balance		$2,050.00	⑤	Book balance		$1,404.58
②	Add:			⑥	Add:		
	Deposit of 10/31 in transit		145.00		Collect $500 note less $15 fee . . .	$485.00	
					Interest earned	8.42	$ 493.42
			$2,195.00				$1,898.00
③	Deduct:			⑦	Deduct:		
	Outstanding checks:				Check printing charge	$ 23.00	
	No. 124	$150.00			NSF check plus service fee	30.00	$ 53.00
	No. 126	200.00	$ 350.00				
④	**Adjusted bank balance**		**$1,845.00**	⑧	**Adjusted book balance**		**$1,845.00**

⑨ Balances are equal (reconciled)

Exhibit 9.12

Bank Reconciliation

⑦ Identify and list any unrecorded debit memoranda from the bank, service charges, and errors overstating the book balance. Deduct them from the book balance.

⑧ Compute the *adjusted book balance*, also called *corrected* or *reconciled balance.*

⑨ Verify that the two adjusted balances from steps 4 and 8 are equal. If yes, they are reconciled. If not, check for mathematical accuracy and missing data.

In preparing to reconcile the bank account, the VideoBuster employee gathers the following data:

■ Bank balance shown on the bank statement is $2,050.

■ Book balance shown in the accounting records is $1,404.58.

■ A $145 deposit placed in the bank's night depository on October 31 is not recorded on the bank statement.

■ A comparison of canceled checks with the company's books showed two checks outstanding—No. 124 for $150 and No. 126 for $200.

■ Enclosed with the bank statement is a credit memorandum showing the bank collected a note receivable for the company on October 23. The note's proceeds of $500 (minus a $15 collection fee) are credited to the company's account. This credit memorandum is not yet recorded by the company.

■ The bank statement shows a credit of $8.42 for interest earned on the average cash balance in the account. There was no prior notification of this item, and it is not yet recorded on the company's books.

■ Other debits on the bank statement that are not recorded on the books include *(a)* a $23 charge for checks printed by the bank, and *(b)* a NSF check for $20 plus a related $10 processing fee. The NSF check is from a customer, Frank Heflin, on October 16 and was included in that day's deposit.

The bank reconciliation in Exhibit 9.12 reflects these items. The circled numbers in this reconciliation correspond to the nine steps listed earlier.

When the reconciliation is complete, the employee sends a copy to the accounting department so that any needed journal entries are recorded. For instance, entries are needed for any unrecorded debit and credit memoranda and any company mistakes. Another copy goes to the cashier's office. The cashier's copy is especially important if the bank has made an error needing correction.

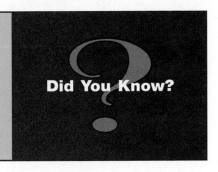

High-Tech Recs

High-tech reconciliations are today available on your PC and via the Web. With little or no fee, one can link into financial information that is updated continuously throughout the day—called real-time reconciliations. These programs do automatic bank reconciliations, and the software highlights such mistakes as transposed numbers or checks not previously recorded. Data can be easily downloaded and used in other applications. But one must still be able to analyze and interpret the reconciliation. [Source: *Business Week,* June 20, 1997.]

Did You Know?

Recording Adjusting Entries from a Bank Reconciliation

A bank reconciliation helps identify errors by both the bank and the depositor. It also identifies unrecorded items that need recording on the company's books. In VideoBuster's reconciliation, the adjusted balance of $1,845 is the correct balance as of October 31. But the company's accounting records show a $1,404.58 balance. We must prepare journal entries to adjust the book balance to the correct balance. It is important to remember that only the items reconciling the book balance require adjustment. A review of Exhibit 9.12 indicates four entries are required for VideoBuster:

Collection of Note

The first entry is to record the net proceeds of VideoBuster's note receivable collected by the bank along with the expense of having the bank perform that service and the reduction in the Notes Receivable account:

Oct. 31	Cash	485	
	Collection Expense	15	
	Notes Receivable		500
	To record collection fee and proceeds of a note collected by the bank.		

Assets = Liabilities + Equity
+485   −15
−500

Interest Earned

The second entry records the interest credited to VideoBuster's account by the bank:

Oct. 31	Cash	8.42	
	Interest Earned		8.42
	To record interest earned on the average cash balance in the checking account.		

Assets = Liabilities + Equity
+8.42   +8.42

Interest earned is a revenue, and the entry recognizes both the revenue and the related increase in Cash.

Check Printing

The third entry debits Miscellaneous Expenses for the check printing charge:

Oct. 31	Miscelianeous Expenses	23	
	Cash		23
	Check printing charge.		

Assets = Liabilities + Equity
−23   −23

NSF Check

The fourth entry records the NSF check that is returned as uncollectible. The $20 check was originally received from Heflin in payment of his account and deposited. The bank charged $10 for handling the NSF check and deducted $30 total from VideoBuster's account. The company must reverse the original entry made when the check was received and also record the $10 fee:

Assets = Liabilities + Equity
+30
−30

Oct. 31	Accounts Receivable—Frank Heflin	30	
	Cash		30
	To charge Heflin's account for NSF check and bank's fee.		

This entry reflects normal business practice by adding the NSF $10 fee to Heflin's account. The company will try to collect the entire $30 from Heflin.

After these four entries are recorded, the balance of cash is increased to the correct amount of $1,845 ($1,404.58 + $485 + $8.42 − $23 − $30).

Flash back

11. What is a bank statement?

12. What is the meaning of the phrase *to reconcile a bank balance?*

13. Why do we reconcile the bank statement balance of cash and the depositor's book balance of cash?

14. List at least two items affecting the bank side of a reconciliation and indicate if the items are added or subtracted.

15. List at least three items affecting the book side of a reconciliation and indicate if the items are added or subtracted.

Answers—p. 393

USING THE INFORMATION   Days' Sales Uncollected

A1 Compute days' sales uncollected ratio and use it to analyze liquidity.

Many companies attract customers by selling to them on credit. This means that cash flows from customers are delayed until accounts receivable are collected. Users of accounting information often want to know how quickly a company can convert its accounts receivable into cash. This is important for evaluating a company's liquidity.

One way users evaluate the liquidity of receivables is by looking at the **days' sales uncollected,** also called *days' sales in receivables.* This measure is computed by taking the current balance of receivables and dividing by net credit sales over the year just completed, and then multiplying by 365 (number of days in a year). But because the amount of net credit sales usually is not reported to external users, the net sales (or revenues) figure is commonly used in the computation. The formula for days' sales uncollected is shown in Exhibit 9.13.

Exhibit 9.13

Days' Sales Uncollected Formula

$$\text{Days' sales uncollected} = \frac{\text{Accounts receivable}}{\text{Net sales}} \times 365$$

Z-Mart, for instance, reports accounts receivable of $11,200 at the end of 1999 (see Exhibit 6.3) and net sales of $314,700 (see Exhibit 6.2) for the year. By dividing $11,200 by $314,700, we find the receivables balance is 3.56% of that year's sales. Because there are 365 days in a year, the $11,200 balance is 3.56% of 365 days of sales, or 13 days of sales.

We use the number of days' sales uncollected to estimate how much time is likely to pass before we receive cash receipts from credit sales equal to the current amount of accounts receivable. For evaluation purposes, we need to compare this estimate to the days' sales uncollected figures for other companies in the same industry. We also make comparisons between current and prior periods.

To illustrate a more thorough analysis of the number of days' sales uncollected, we select data from the annual reports of two toy manufacturers: **Hasbro** and **Mattel.** The days' sales uncollected figures and their component figures for Hasbro and Mattel are shown in Exhibit 9.14.

Company	Figure	($ thousands)		
		1996	1995	1994
Hasbro	Accounts receivable	$ 807	$ 791	$ 718
	Net sales	$3,002	$2,858	$2,670
	Days' sales uncollected	**98 days**	**101 days**	**98 days**
Mattel	Accounts receivable	$ 732	$ 679	$ 762
	Net sales	$3,786	$3,638	$3,205
	Days' sales uncollected	**71 days**	**68 days**	**87 days**

Exhibit 9.14

Analysis Using Days' Sales Uncollected

Days' sales uncollected for Hasbro at the end of 1996 is computed as (in thousands):

$$\frac{\$807}{\$3,002} \times 365 = \textbf{98 days}$$

This means it will take about 98 days to collect cash on ending accounts receivable. This number reflects on one or more of the following factors: a company's ability to collect receivables, the financial health of its customers, customer payment strategies, or sales discount terms.

To better assess this figure for Hasbro, we compare it to the two prior years' numbers and with those of Mattel. We see that Hasbro's days' sales uncollected is steady, varying from 98 to 101 days for the past three years. But in comparison to Mattel, the Hasbro figure is much larger. While Mattel has reduced its days' sales uncollected from 87 days in 1994 to 71 days in 1996, Hasbro has not. This means improved liquidity in receivables for Mattel. Improved liquidity often translates into increased profitability. While we don't show the figures here, the profitability of Mattel exceeds that of Hasbro over 1994–1996. Running a financially successful company requires continuous monitoring of the liquidity of its assets.

Sales Representative
You are a salesperson for a retailer who markets directly to consumers. You and the entire sales staff are told by your accounting division to take action to reduce days' sales uncollected. What can you do to reduce days' sales uncollected?

You Make the Call

Answer—p. 393

Flash back

16. Why is the days' sales uncollected computation usually based on net sales instead of credit sales?

Answer—p. 393

Summary

C1 Define internal control and its purpose. An internal control system consists of the policies and procedures managers use to protect assets, ensure reliable accounting, promote efficient operations, and urge adherence to company policies. It is a key part of systems design, analysis, and performance. It can prevent avoidable losses and help managers both plan operations and monitor company and human performance.

C2 Identify principles of internal control. Principles of good internal control include establishing responsibilities, maintaining adequate records, insuring assets and bonding employees, separating recordkeeping from custody of assets, dividing responsibilities for related transactions, applying technological controls, and performing regular independent reviews.

C3 Define cash and cash equivalents and how they are reported. Cash includes currency and coins and amounts on deposit in a bank checking account and some savings accounts. It also includes items that are acceptable for deposit in these accounts. Cash equivalents are short-term, highly liquid investment assets meeting two criteria: readily convertible to a known cash amount and sufficiently close to their maturity date so that market value is not sensitive to interest rate changes. Examples of cash equivalents are short-term investments in U.S. treasury bills, commercial paper, and money market funds. Because cash equivalents are similar to cash, most companies combine them with cash as a single item on the balance sheet. Cash and cash equivalents are liquid assets because they are converted easily into other assets or used in paying for services or liabilities.

C4 Identify control features of banking activities. Banks offer several basic services that promote the control or safeguarding of cash. These involve the bank account, the bank deposit, and checking. A bank account is a record set up by a bank permitting a customer to deposit money for safeguarding and check withdrawals. A bank deposit is money contributed to the account with a deposit ticket as proof. A check is a document signed by the depositor instructing the bank to pay a specified amount of money to a designated recipient. Electronic funds transfer uses electronic communication to transfer cash from one party to another, and it decreases certain risks while exposing others. Companies increasingly use it because of its convenience and low cost.

P1 Apply internal control to cash receipts. Internal control of cash receipts ensures all cash received is properly recorded and deposited. Cash receipts arise from many transactions including cash sales, collections of customers' accounts, receipts of interest and rent, bank loans, sale of assets, and owner investments. Attention is focused on two important types of cash receipts: over-the-counter and by mail. The principles of internal control are applied in both cases. Good internal control for over-the-counter cash receipts includes use of a cash register, customer review, receipts, a permanent transaction record, and separation of the custody of cash from its recordkeeping. Good internal control for cash receipts by mail includes at least two people assigned to open mail and prepare a list with each sender's name, amount, and explanation.

P2 Apply the voucher system to control cash disbursements. A voucher system is a set of procedures and approvals designed to control cash disbursements and acceptance of obligations. The voucher system of control relies on several important documents, including the voucher and many supporting files. A voucher system's control over cash disbursements begins when a company incurs an obligation that will result in payment of cash. A key factor in this system is that only approved departments and individuals are authorized to incur certain obligations. To coordinate and control responsibilities of these departments, several different business documents are used.

P3 Explain and record petty cash fund transactions. Petty cash disbursements are payments of small amounts for items such as postage, courier fees, repairs, and supplies. To avoid writing checks for small amounts, a company usually sets up one or more petty cash funds and uses the money to make small payments. A petty fund cashier is responsible for safekeeping of the cash, for making payments from this fund, and for keeping receipts and records. A Petty Cash account is debited only when the fund is established or increased in size. The cashier presents all paid receipts to the company's cashier for reimbursement. Whenever the fund is replenished, petty cash disbursements are recorded with debits to expense accounts and a credit to cash.

P4 Apply the net method to control purchase discounts. The net method gives management an advantage in monitoring and controlling purchase discounts. When invoices are recorded at gross amounts, the amount of discounts taken is deducted from the balance of the Merchandise Inventory account. This means the amount of any discounts lost is not reported in any account or on the income statement. Discounts lost are unlikely to come to the attention of management. But when purchases are recorded at net amounts, a discounts lost expense is brought to management's attention as an operating expense on the income statement. Management can then seek to identify the reason for discounts lost, such as oversight, carelessness, or unfavorable terms.

P5 Prepare a bank reconciliation. A bank reconciliation is prepared to prove the accuracy of the depositor's and the bank's records. In completing a reconciliation, the bank statement balance is adjusted for such items as outstanding checks and unrecorded deposits made on or before the bank statement date but not reflected on the statement. The depositor's cash account balance also often requires adjustment. These adjustments include items such as service charges, bank collections for the depositor, and interest earned on the account balance.

A1 Compute days' sales uncollected ratio and use it to analyze liquidity. Many companies attract customers by selling to them on credit. This means cash flows from customers are delayed until accounts receivable are collected. Users of accounting information often want to know how quickly a company can convert its accounts receivable into cash. This is important for evaluating a company's liquidity. The days' sales uncollected ratio is one measure reflecting liquidity. It is computed by dividing the current balance of receivables by net sales over the year just completed, and then multiplying by 365. The number of days' sales uncollected is used to estimate how much time is likely to pass before we receive cash receipts from net sales equal to the current amount of accounts receivable. Our analysis needs to compare this estimate with those for other companies in the same industry and with prior years' estimates.

Guidance Answers to **You Make the Call**

Political Activist

A forced vacation policy is part of a good system of internal controls. When employees are forced to take vacations, their ability to hide any fraudulent behavior decreases. This is because someone must take on the responsibilities of the person on vacation, and the replacement employee potentially can uncover fraudulent behavior or records. A forced vacation policy is especially important for employees in more sensitive positions of handling money or easily transferable assets.

Sales Representative

There are several steps a salesperson can take to reduce days' sales uncollected. These include: (1) decreasing the proportion of sales on account to total sales by encouraging more cash sales; (2) identifying customers most delayed in their payments and encouraging earlier payments or cash sales; and (3) implementing stricter credit policies to eliminate credit sales to customers that never pay.

Guidance Answer to **Judgment and Ethics**

Internal Auditor

Your problem is whether to accept the situation or to dig further to see if the petty cashier is abusing petty cash. Since you were asked to postpone your count and the fund consists of nine new $20 bills, you have legitimate concerns on whether money is being used for personal use. You should conduct further investigation. Perhaps the most recent reimbursement of the fund was for $180 (9 × $20) or more. In that case, this reimbursement can leave the fund with sequentially numbered $20 bills. But if the most recent reimbursement was for less

than $180, the presence of nine sequentially numbered $20 bills suggests that the new bills were obtained from a bank as replacement for bills that had been removed. Neither situation shows the cashier is stealing money. Yet the second case indicates the cashier "borrowed" the cash and later replaced it after the auditor showed up. In writing your report you must not conclude the cashier is unethical unless evidence along with your knowledge of company policies supports it. Your report must present facts according to the evidence.

Guidance Answers to

1. *c*
2. Technology reduces processing errors, allows more extensive testing of records, limits the amount of hard evidence of processing steps, and highlights the importance of maintaining separation of duties.
3. A company owns liquid assets so that it can purchase other assets, buy services, and pay obligations.
4. A company owns cash equivalents because they yield a return greater than what is earned by cash.
5. Examples of cash equivalents are 90-day treasury bills issued by the U.S. government, money market funds, and commercial paper.
6. *a*
7. Not necessarily. A voucher system is used when a manager can no longer control the purchasing procedures through personal supervision and direct participation in business activities.
8. If all cash payments are made by check, numerous checks for small amounts must be written. Because this practice is expensive and time-consuming, a petty cash fund is established for making small cash payments.
9. If the petty cash fund is not reimbursed at the end of an accounting period, the transactions in petty cash are not yet recorded in the accounts and the petty cash asset is overstated. But these amounts are rarely large enough to affect users' decisions based on financial statements.

10. First, when the petty cash fund is reimbursed, the petty cash transactions are recorded in their proper accounts. Second, reimbursement provides money allowing the fund to continue being used. Third, reimbursement identifies any cash shortage or overage in the fund.
11. A bank statement is a report prepared by the bank describing the activities in a depositor's account.
12. To reconcile a bank balance means to explain the difference between the cash balance in the depositor's accounting records and the balance on the bank statement.
13. The purpose of the bank reconciliation is to determine if any errors have been made by the bank or by the depositor and to determine if the bank has completed any transactions affecting the depositor's account that the depositor has not recorded.
14. Outstanding checks—subtracted
    Unrecorded deposits—added
15. Bank service charges—subtracted
    Debit memos—subtracted
    NSF checks—subtracted
    Interest earned—added
    Credit memos—added
16. The calculation is based on net sales because the amount of credit sales normally is not known by statement readers.

Demonstration Problem

Prepare a bank reconciliation for Jamboree Enterprises for the month ended November 30, 2000. The following information is available to reconcile Jamboree Enterprises' book balance of cash with its bank statement balance as of November 30, 2000:

a. After all posting is complete on November 30, the company's book balance of the Cash account had a $16,380 debit balance, but its bank statement showed a $38,520 balance.
b. Checks No. 2024 for $4,810 and No. 2036 for $5,000 are outstanding.

c. In comparing the canceled checks returned by the bank with the entries in the accounting records, we find that Check No. 2025 in payment of rent is correctly drawn for $1,000 but was erroneously entered in the accounting records as $880.

d. The November 30 deposit of $17,150 was placed in the night depository after banking hours on that date, and this amount did not appear on the bank statement.

e. In reviewing the bank statement, a check belonging to Jumbo Enterprises in the amount of $160 was erroneously drawn against Jamboree's account.

f. A credit memorandum enclosed with the bank statement indicated that the bank collected a $30,000 note and $900 of related interest on Jamboree's behalf. This transaction was not recorded by Jamboree before receiving the statement.

g. A debit memorandum for $1,100 listed a $1,100 NSF check. The check had been received from a customer, Marilyn Welch. Jamboree had not recorded the return of this check before receiving the statement.

h. Bank service charges for November totaled $40. These charges were not recorded by Jamboree before receiving the statement.

Planning the Solution

• Set up a bank reconciliation form as shown below with a bank side and a book side for the reconciliation (also see Exhibit 9.12). Leave room on both sides to add several items and to deduct several items. Each column will result in a reconciled and equal balance.

JAMBOREE ENTERPRISES Bank Reconciliation November 30, 2000		
Bank statement balance		Book balance of cash . . . .
Add:		Add:
Deduct:		Deduct:
Adjusted bank balance		Adjusted book balance . . . .

• Examine each item *a* through *h* about Jamboree to determine whether it affects the book balance or the bank balance. For each item decide whether it should be added or deducted from the bank or book balance.

• After all items are analyzed, complete the form and arrive at a reconciled balance between the bank side of the reconciliation and the book side.

• For every reconciling item on the book side prepare an appropriate adjusting entry. Additions to the book side require an adjusting entry that debits cash. Deductions on the book side require an adjusting entry that credits cash.

Solution to Demonstration Problem

JAMBOREE ENTERPRISES Bank Reconciliation November 30, 2000					
Bank statement balance		$38,520	Book balance of cash		$16,380
Add:			Add:		
Deposit of Nov. 30	$17,150		Collection of note . .	$30,000	
Bank error	160	$17,310	Interest earned	900	$30,900
		$55,830			$47,280
Deduct:			Deduct:		
Outstanding checks		9,810	NSF check	$ 1,100	
			Recording error . . .	120	
			Service charge	40	$ 1,260
Adjusted bank balance		**$46,020**	**Adjusted book balance**		**$46,020**

Required Adjusting Entries for Jamboree

Nov. 30	Cash	30,900	
	Notes Receivable		30,000
	Interest Earned		900
	To record collection of note principal and interest.		
Nov. 30	Accounts Receivable—Marilyn Welch	1,100	
	Cash		1,100
	To reinstate account due from an NSF check.		
Nov. 30	Rent Expense	120	
	Cash		120
	To correct recording error on check no. 2025.		
Nov. 30	Bank Service Charges	40	
	Cash		40
	To record bank service charges.		

Glossary

Bank reconciliation an analysis that explains the difference between the balance of a checking account shown in the depositor's records and the balance reported on the bank statement. (p. 386).

Canceled checks checks that the bank has paid and deducted from the customer's account during the month. (p. 385).

Cash includes currency, coins, and amounts on deposit in bank checking or savings accounts. (p. 370).

Cash equivalents short-term, highly liquid investment assets that are readily convertible to a known cash amount and sufficiently close to their maturity date so that market value is not sensitive to interest rate changes. (p. 370).

Cash Over and Short account an income statement account used to record cash overages and cash shortages arising from omitted petty cash receipts and from errors in making change. (p. 372).

Check a document signed by the depositor instructing the bank to pay a specified amount of money to a designated recipient. (p. 384).

Days' sales uncollected a measure of the liquidity of receivables computed by taking the current balance of receivables and dividing by the credit (or net) sales over the year just completed, and then multiplying by 365 (the number of days in a year); also called *days' sales in receivables*. (p. 390).

Deposit ticket lists items such as currency, coins, and checks deposited and their corresponding dollar amounts. (p. 383).

Discounts lost an expense resulting from failing to take advantage of cash discounts on purchases. (p. 382).

Electronic funds transfer (EFT) the use of electronic communication to transfer cash from one party to another. (p. 384).

Gross method a method of recording purchases at the full invoice price without deducting any cash discounts. (p. 382).

Internal control system all the policies and procedures managers use to protect assets, ensure reliable accounting, promote efficient operations, and urge adherence to company policies. (p. 364).

Invoice an itemized statement of goods prepared by the vendor that lists the customer's name, the items sold, the sales prices, and the terms of sale. (p. 376).

Invoice approval a document containing a checklist of steps necessary for approving an invoice for recording and payment; also called *check authorization* (p. 376).

Liquid asset an asset such as cash that is easily converted into other types of assets or used to buy services or pay liabilities. (p. 371).

Liquidity a characteristic of an asset that refers to how easily the asset can be converted into another type of asset or used in paying for services or obligations. (p. 371).

Net method a method of recording purchases at the full invoice price less any cash discounts. (p. 382).

Outstanding checks checks written and recorded by depositor but not yet paid by the bank at the bank statement date (p. 386).

Principles of internal control fundamental principles requiring management to establish responsibility, maintain adequate records, insure assets and bond key employees, separate record-keeping from custody of assets, divide responsibility for related transactions, apply technological controls, and perform regular and independent reviews. (p. 365).

Purchase order a business document used by the purchasing department to place an order with the seller (vendor); authorizes the vendor to ship the ordered merchandise at the stated price and terms. (p. 375).

Purchase requisition a business document listing merchandise needed by a department and requesting it be purchased. (p. 374).

Receiving report a form used within a company to notify the appropriate persons that ordered goods are received and to describe the quantities and condition of the goods. (p. 376).

Signature card includes the signatures of each person authorized to sign checks on the account. (p. 383).

Vendee the buyer or purchaser of goods or services. (p. 376).

Vendor the seller of goods or services, usually a manufacturer or wholesaler. (p. 375).

Voucher an internal business file (or folder) used to accumulate documents and information needed to control cash disbursements and to ensure that a transaction is properly recorded. (p. 374).

Voucher system a set of procedures and approvals designed to control cash disbursements and acceptance of obligations. (p. 374).

Questions

1. Which of the following assets is most liquid and which is least liquid: merchandise inventory, building, accounts receivable, cash?

2. List the seven broad principles of internal control.

3. Why should the person who keeps the record of an asset not be the person responsible for custody of the asset?

4. Internal control procedures are important in every business, but at what stage in the development of a business do they become especially critical?

5. Why should responsibility for a sequence of related transactions be divided among different departments or individuals?

6. Why should all receipts be deposited on the day of receipt?

7. When merchandise is purchased for a large store, why are department managers not permitted to deal directly with suppliers?

8. What is a petty cash receipt? Who signs a petty cash receipt?

9. NIKE's consolidated statement of cash flows in Appendix A describes the changes in cash and cash equivalents that occurred during the year ended May 31, 1997. What amount was provided by (or used in) investing activities? What amount was provided by (or used in) financing activities?

10. Reebok's balance sheet in Appendix A depicts the cash and cash equivalents of Reebok as of December 31, 1996, and December 31, 1995. Contrast the magnitude of cash and cash equivalents with the other current assets as of December 31, 1996. Compare the cash and cash equivalents on hand as of December 31, 1996, with December 31, 1995.

11. Use America Online financial statements in Appendix A to compute the difference in the number of days' sales uncollected on June 30, 1996, and June 30, 1995. (Hint: Use trade accounts receivable only.) Comment on the results.

12. Identify the internal controls that Jason Barron likely implemented to help manage the employee theft he was experiencing. Do you think that increasing the sales commission to employees is a type of internal control? Explain.

Quick Study

QS 9-1
Terminology
C1

What is the difference between the terms *liquidity* and *cash equivalent*?

QS 9-2
Internal control objective
C1, C2

a. What is the main objective of internal control and how is it achieved?
b. Why should recordkeeping for assets be separated from custody over the assets?

QS 9-3
Internal control for cash
P1

A good system of internal control for cash provides adequate procedures for protecting both cash receipts and cash disbursements. Three basic guidelines help achieve this protection. What are these guidelines?

QS 9-4
Petty cash accounting
P3

a. The petty cash fund of the Wee Ones Agency is established at $75. At the end of the month, the fund contained $12.74 and had the following receipts: film rentals, $19.40; refreshments for meetings, $22.81 (both expenditures to be classified as Entertainment Expense); postage, $6.95; and printing, $13.10. Prepare journal entries to record (1) establishment of the fund and (2) reimbursement of the fund at the end of the month.
b. Explain the event(s) causing the Petty Cash account to be credited in a journal entry.

QS 9-5
Bank reconciliation
P5

a. For each of the following items indicate whether its amount (i) affects the bank or book side of the reconciliation and (ii) represents an addition or a subtraction:

(1) Unrecorded deposits   (5) Outstanding checks
(2) Interest on average monthly balance   (6) Debit memos
(3) Credit memos   (7) NSF checks
(4) Bank service charges

b. Which of the items in *a.* require a journal entry?

Which accounting method uses a Discounts Lost account and what is the advantage of this method?

The following account balances are taken from Mountain Snowboards:

	2000	1999
Accounts receivable	$ 75,692	$ 70,484
Net sales	$2,591,933	$2,296,673

What is the difference in the number of days' sales uncollected between years 2000 and 1999? According to this analysis, is the company's collection of receivables improving? Explain your answer.

Lombard Company is a start up business that is growing rapidly. The company's recordkeeper, who was hired two years ago, left town suddenly after the company's manager discovered that a large sum of money had disappeared over the past 18 months. An audit disclosed that the recordkeeper had written and signed several checks made payable to the recordkeeper's fiancé and then recorded the checks as salaries expense. The fiancé, who cashed the checks but never worked for the company, left town with the recordkeeper. As a result, the company incurred an uninsured loss of $84,000.

Evaluate Lombard Company's internal control system and indicate which principles of internal control appear to have been ignored in this situation.

What internal control procedures would you recommend in each of the following situations?

a. A concession company has one employee who sells T-shirts and sunglasses at the beach. Each day, the employee is given enough shirts and sunglasses to last through the day and enough cash to make change. The money is kept in a box at the stand.

b. An antique store has one employee who is given cash and sent to garage sales each weekend. The employee pays cash for merchandise to be resold at the antique store.

Exercise 9-3
Internal control over cash
receipts by mail
P1

Some of Fannin Co.'s cash receipts from customers are sent to the company with the regular mail. Fannin's recordkeeper opens the letters and deposits the cash received each day. What internal control problem exists in this arrangement? What changes do you recommend?

Eanes Co. established a $200 petty cash fund on January 1. One week later, the fund contained $27.50 in cash along with receipts for the following expenditures: postage, $64.00; transportation-in, $19.00; store supplies, $36.50; and miscellaneous expenses, $53.00. Eanes uses the perpetual method to account for merchandise inventory. Prepare journal entries to (a) establish the fund on January 1 and (b) reimburse it on January 8. (c) Prepare the journal entry to reimburse the fund and increase it to $500 on January 8 assuming no entry in part b.

Brady Company established a $400 petty cash fund on September 9. On September 30, the fund had $164.25 in cash along with receipts for the following expenditures: transportation-in, $32.45; office supplies, $113.55; and miscellaneous expenses, $87.60. Brady uses the perpetual method to account for merchandise inventory. The petty cashier could not account for the $2.15 shortage in the fund. Prepare (a) the September 9 entry to establish the fund and (b) the September 30 entry to reimburse the fund and reduce it to $300.

Exercise 9-6
Bank reconciliation

P5

Medline Service Co. deposits all cash receipts on the day when received and makes all cash payments by check. On July 31, 2000, after all posting is complete, its Cash account shows a $11,352 debit balance. Medline's July 31 bank statement shows $10,332 on deposit in the bank on that day. Prepare a bank reconciliation for Medline, using the following information:

a. Outstanding checks total $1,713.

b. The July canceled checks returned by the bank included an $18 debit memorandum for bank services.

c. Check No. 919, returned with the canceled checks, was correctly drawn for $489 in payment of the utility bill and was paid by the bank on July 15. It had been recorded with a debit to Utilities Expense and a credit to Cash in the amount of $498.

d. The July 31 cash receipts of $2,724 were placed in the bank's night depository after banking hours on that date and were unrecorded by the bank when the July bank statement was prepared.

Exercise 9-7
Adjusting entries from bank reconciliation

P5

Give the journal entries that Medline Service Co. must record as a result of having prepared the bank reconciliation in Exercise 9-6.

Exercise 9-8
Bank reconciliation items and adjusting entries

P5

Prepare a table with the following headings for a bank reconciliation as of September 30:

Bank Balance		Book Balance			Not Shown on the Reconciliation
Add	Deduct	Add	Deduct	Adjust	

For each item below, place an *x* in the appropriate columns to indicate whether the item should be added to or deducted from the book or bank balance, or whether it should not appear on the reconciliation. If the book balance is to be adjusted, place a *Dr.* or *Cr.* in the Adjust column to indicate whether the Cash balance should be debited or credited. At the left side of your table, number the entries sequentially to correspond to the numbers in the list.

1. Interest earned on the account.

2. Deposit made on September 30 after the bank was closed.

3. Checks outstanding on August 31 that cleared the bank in September.

4. NSF check from customer returned on September 15 but not recorded by the company.

5. Checks written and mailed to payees on September 30.

6. Deposit made on September 5 that was processed on September 8.

7. Bank service charge.

8. Checks written and mailed to payees on October 5.

9. Checks written by another depositor but charged against the company's account.

10. Principal and interest collected by the bank but not recorded by the company.

11. Special charge for collection of note in No. 10 on company's behalf.

12. Check written against the account and cleared by the bank; erroneously omitted by the company recordkeeper.

Exercise 9-9
Recording invoices at gross or net amounts

P4

Peltier's Imports uses the perpetual method to account for merchandise inventory and had the following transactions during the month of May. Prepare entries to record the transactions assuming Peltier's records invoices (*a*) at gross amounts and (*b*) at net amounts.

May 2 Received merchandise purchased at a $2,016 invoice price, invoice dated April 29, terms 2/10, n/30.

10 Received a $416 credit memorandum (at invoice price) for merchandise received on May 2 and returned for credit.

17   Received merchandise purchased at a $4,480 invoice price, invoice dated May 16, terms 2/10, n/30.

26   Paid for the merchandise received on May 17, less the discount.

28   Paid for the merchandise received on May 2. Payment was delayed because the invoice was mistakenly filed for payment today. This error caused the discount to be lost.

Federated Merchandise Co. reported net sales for 1999 and 2000 of $565,000 and $647,000. The end-of-year balances of accounts receivable were December 31, 1999, $51,000; and December 31, 2000, $83,000. Calculate the days' sales uncollected at the end of each year and describe any changes in the liquidity of the company's receivables.

Exercise 9-10
Liquidity of accounts receivable

A1

Palladium Art Gallery had the following petty cash transactions in February of the current year:

Feb. 2   Drew a $300 check, cashed it, and gave the proceeds and the petty cash box to Nick Reed, the petty cashier.

5   Purchased paper for the copier, $10.13.

9   Paid $22.50 COD charges on merchandise purchased for resale, terms FOB shipping point. Palladium uses the perpetual method to account for merchandise inventory.

12   Paid $9.95 postage to express mail a contract to a client.

14   Reimbursed Gina Barton, the manager of the business, $58 for business mileage on her car.

20   Purchased stationery, $77.76.

23   Paid a courier $18 to deliver merchandise sold to a customer, terms FOB destination.

25   Paid $15.10 COD charges on merchandise purchased for resale, terms FOB shipping point.

28   Paid $64 for stamps.

28   Reed sorted the petty cash receipts by accounts affected and exchanged them for a check to reimburse the fund for expenditures. There was $21.23 cash in the fund, and he could not account for the shortage. The dollar amount of the petty cash fund was increased to $400.

Problems

Problem 9-1
Establishing, reimbursing, and increasing petty cash fund

P3

Required

1. Prepare the journal entry to record establishing the petty cash fund.

2. Prepare a petty cash payments report that has these categories: delivery expense, mileage expense, postage expense, merchandise inventory (transportation-in), and office supplies. Sort the payments into the appropriate categories and total the expenditures in each category.

3. Prepare the journal entry to record the reimbursement and the increase of the fund.

Check Figure   February 28, Cash, $378.77 Cr.

El Gatto Co. has only a General Journal in its accounting system and uses it to record all transactions. The company recently set up a petty cash fund to facilitate payments of small items. The following petty cash transactions were reported by the petty cashier as occurring in April (the last month of the company's fiscal year):

Apr. 1   Received a company check for $250 to establish the petty cash fund.

15   Received a company check to replenish the fund for the following expenditures made since April 1 and to increase the fund to $450.

a.   Paid $78 for janitorial service.

b.   Purchased office supplies for $63.68.

c.   Purchased postage stamps for $43.50.

d.   Paid $57.15 to *The County Crier* for an advertisement in the newspaper.

e.   Counted $11.15 remaining in the petty cash box.

30   The petty cashier reported $293.39 remained in the fund and decided that the April 15 increase in the fund was too large. A company check was drawn to replenish the fund for the following expenditures made since April 15 and to reduce the fund to $400.

f.   Purchased office supplies for $48.36.

g.   Reimbursed office manager for business mileage, $28.50.

h.   Paid $39.75 courier charges to deliver merchandise to a customer, terms FOB destination.

Problem 9-2
Establishing, reimbursing, and adjusting petty cash fund; accounting adjustments

P3

Required

Preparation Component

1. Prepare journal entries to record the establishment of the fund on April 1 and its replenishments on April 15 and on April 30 along with any increases or decreases in the fund balance.

Analysis Component

2. Explain how the company's financial statements are affected if the petty cash fund is not replenished and no entry is made on April 30. (Hint: The amount of office supplies that appears on a balance sheet is determined by a physical count of the supplies on hand.)

Check Figure Cash credits: April 15, $438.85; April 30, $106.61

Problem 9-3
Preparing a bank reconciliation and recording adjustments

The following information is available to reconcile Archdale Company's book balance of cash with its bank statement balance as of October 31, 1999:

a. After all posting is completed on October 31, the company's Cash account has a $26,193 debit balance, but its bank statement shows a $28,020 balance.

b. Checks No. 3031 for $1,380 and No. 3040 for $552 were outstanding on the September 30 bank reconciliation. Check No. 3040 was returned with the October canceled checks, but Check No. 3031 was not. Also, Check No. 3065 for $336 and Check No. 3069 for $2,148, both drawn in October, were not among the canceled checks returned with the statement.

c. In comparing the canceled checks returned by the bank with the entries in the accounting records, it was found that Check No. 3056 for the October rent was correctly drawn for $1,250 but was erroneously entered in the accounting records as $1,230.

d. A credit memorandum enclosed with the bank statement indicates the bank collected a $9,000 noninterest-bearing note for Archdale, deducted a $45 collection fee, and credited the remainder to the account. This event was not recorded by Archdale before receiving the statement.

e. A debit memorandum for $805 lists a $795 NSF check plus a $10 NSF charge. The check had been received from a customer, Jefferson Tyler. Archdale had not recorded the return of this check before receiving the statement.

f. Also enclosed with the statement is a $15 debit memorandum for bank services. It had not been recorded because no previous notification had been received.

g. The October 31 cash receipts of $10,152 were placed in the bank's night depository after banking hours on that date and this amount did not appear on the bank statement.

Required

Preparation Component

Check Figure Reconciled balance, $34,308

1. Prepare a bank reconciliation for the company as of October 31, 1999.

2. Prepare the journal entries necessary to bring the company's book balance of cash into conformity with the reconciled balance.

Analysis Component

3. Assume the October 31, 1999, bank reconciliation for the company is prepared and some items are treated incorrectly. For each of the following errors, explain the effect of the error on: (1) the adjusted bank statement balance and (2) the adjusted cash account book balance.

    a. The company's unadjusted cash account balance of $26,193 is listed on the reconciliation as $26,139.

    b. The bank's collection of a $9,000 note less the $45 collection fee is added to the bank statement balance.

Problem 9-4
Preparing a bank reconciliation and recording adjustments

Walburg Company most recently reconciled its bank and book statement balances of cash on August 31 and showed two checks outstanding at that time, No. 5888 for $1,038.05 and No. 5893 for $484.25. The following information is available for the September 30, 1999, reconciliation:

From the September 30 bank statement:

BALANCE OF PREVIOUS STATEMENT ON 8/31/99	16,800.45
6 DEPOSITS AND OTHER CREDITS TOTALING	11,182.85
9 CHECKS AND OTHER DEBITS TOTALING	9,620.05
CURRENT BALANCE AS OF 9/30/99	18,363.55

=== CHECKING ACCOUNT TRANSACTIONS ===

DATE	AMOUNT	DESCRIPTION	DATE	AMOUNT	DESCRIPTION
09/05	1,103.75	+Deposit	09/25	2,351.70	+Deposit
09/12	2,226.90	+Deposit	09/30	22.50	+Interest
09/17	588.25	−NSF check	09/30	1,385.00	+Credit memo
09/21	4,093.00	+Deposit			

DATE	CHECK NO	AMOUNT	DATE	CHECK NO	AMOUNT
09/03	5888	1,038.05	09/22	5904	2,080.00
09/07	5901*	1,824.25	09/20	5905	937.00
09/04	5902	731.90	09/28	5907*	213.85
09/22	5903	399.10	09/29	5909*	1,807.65

*Indicates a skip in check sequence.

From Walburg Company's accounting records:

Cash Receipts Deposited

Date			Cash Debit
Sept.	5		1,103.75
	12		2,226.90
	21		4,093.00
	25		2,351.70
	30		1,582.75
			11,358.10

Cash Disbursements

Check No.			Cash Credit
5901			1,824.25
5902			731.90
5903			399.10
5904			2,050.00
5905			937.00
5906			859.30
5907			213.85
5908			276.00
5909			1,807.65
			9,099.05

Cash   **Acct. No. 101**

Date		Explanation	PR	Debit	Credit	Balance
Aug.	31	Balance				15,278.45
Sept	30	Total receipts	R12	11,358.10		26,636.55
	30	Total disbursements	D23		9,099.05	17,537.50

Check No. 5904 was correctly drawn for $2,080 to pay for computer equipment; however, the record-keeper misread the amount and entered it in the accounting records with a debit to Computer Equipment and a credit to Cash of $2,050. The NSF check was originally received from a customer, Delia Hahn, in payment of her account. Its return was not recorded when the bank first notified the company. The credit memorandum resulted from the collection of a $1,400 note for Walburg Company by the bank. The bank deducted a $15 collection fee. The collection and fee have not been recorded.

Required

Preparation Component

1. Prepare the September 30 bank reconciliation for this company.

2. Prepare the journal entries to adjust the book balance of cash to the reconciled balance.

Analysis Component

3. The bank statement discloses three places where the canceled checks returned with the bank statement are not numbered sequentially. This means some of the prenumbered checks in the sequence are missing. Several possible situations might explain why canceled checks returned with a bank statement are not numbered sequentially. Describe three of these situations.

Problem 9-5
Analyzing internal control

C2

For the following five scenarios, identify the principle of internal control that is violated. Make a recommendation of what the business should do to ensure adherence to principles of internal control.

1. At Stratford Company, Jill and Joan alternate lunch hours. Normally Jill is the petty cash custodian, but if someone needs petty cash when Jill is at lunch, Joan fills in as custodian.

2. Nadine McDonald does all the posting of patient charges and payments at the Northampton Medical Clinic. Each night Nadine backs up the computerized accounting system to a tape and stores the tape in a locked file at her desk.

3. Jack Mawben prides himself on hiring quality workers who require little supervision. As office manager, Jack gives his employees full discretion over their tasks and has seen no reason to perform independent reviews of their work for years.

4. Bill Clark's manager has told him to reduce overhead. Bill decides to raise the deductible on the plant's property insurance from $5,000 to $10,000. This cuts the property insurance premium in half. In a related move, he decides that bonding of the plant's employees is really a waste of money since the company has not experienced any losses due to employee theft. Bill saves the entire amount of the bonding insurance premium by dropping the bonding insurance.

5. Catherine Young records all incoming customer cash receipts for her employer and also posts the customer payments to their accounts.

BEYOND THE NUMBERS

Reporting in Action

C3, A1

Refer to the financial statements and related information for **NIKE** in Appendix A. Answer the following questions by analyzing information from its statements:

1. For both fiscal year-ends 1997 and 1996, determine the total amount of cash and cash equivalents that NIKE held. Determine the percent this amount represents of total current assets, total current liabilities, total stockholders' equity, and total assets. Comment on any trends.

2. For 1997 use the information in the consolidated statement of cash flows to determine the percent change between the beginning of the year and end of the year amounts of cash and cash equivalents.

3. Compute the days' sales uncollected as of May 31, 1997, and May 31, 1996. Has the collection of receivables improved?

Swoosh Ahead

4. Obtain access to NIKE's annual report for fiscal years ending after May 31, 1997. You can gain access to NIKE's annual report at its web site [**www.nike.com**] or through the SEC's EDGAR database [**www.sec.gov**]. Recompute the days' sales uncollected for any fiscal years ending after May 31, 1997. Compare the days just computed to NIKE's days' sales uncollected in 1997 and 1996.

Comparative Analysis

A1

Both **NIKE** and **Reebok** design, produce, market, and sell sports footwear and apparel. Key comparative figures (in millions) for these two organizations follow:

Key Figures	NIKE* 1997	NIKE* 1996	Reebok* 1996	Reebok* 1995
Accounts receivable	$1,754	$1,346	$ 591	$ 507
Net sales	$9,187	$6,471	$3,479	$3,481

*NIKE figures are from its annual reports for fiscal years ended May 31, 1997 and 1996.
 Reebok figures are from its annual reports for fiscal years ended December 31, 1996 and 1995.

Required

Compute days' sales uncollected for both companies for the two years of data provided. Comment on any trends for both companies. Which company has the larger percent change in days' sales uncollected?

Marge Page, Dot Night, and Colleen Walker work for a family physician, Dr. Thomen, who is in private practice. Dr. Thomen is fairly knowledgeable about office management practices and has segregated the cash receipt duties as follows. Marge opens the mail and prepares a triplicate list of money received. She sends one copy of the list to Dot, the cashier, who deposits the receipts daily in the bank. Colleen, the recordkeeper, also receives a copy of the list and posts payments to patients' accounts. About once a month the office clerks decide to have an expensive lunch compliments of Dr. Thomen. Dot endorses a patient's check in Dr. Thomen's name and cashes it at the bank. Marge destroys the remittance advice accompanying the check. Colleen posts payment to the customer's account as a miscellaneous credit. The clerks justify their actions given their relatively low pay and knowing that Dr. Thomen will likely never miss the payment.

Ethics Challenge

C2

Required

1. Who is the best person in Dr. Thomen's office to reconcile the bank statement?
2. Would a bank reconciliation uncover this office fraud?
3. What are some ways to detect this type of fraud?
4. Suggest additional internal controls that Dr. Thomen may want to implement.

You are a business consultant. The owner of a company sends you an e-mail expressing concern that the company is losing money by not taking advantage of discounts offered by vendors. The company currently uses the gross method of recording purchases. The owner is considering requiring a review of all invoices and payment dates from the previous period. But due to the volume of purchases, the owner recognizes this is time-consuming and costly. The owner seeks your advice as to how the business might monitor purchase discounts in the future. Provide a response.

Communicating in Practice

P4

Visit the internal control Web site at **www.duc.auburn.edu/~auaudit.** Explore this Web site and record answers to the following questions.

1. How does this Web site define internal control?
2. What are some controls this Web site suggests as part of your "personal internal control system"?
3. What purposes do internal controls serve in a university environment?
4. Contrast preventative and detective controls.
5. Who is responsible for implementing and maintaining a system of internal controls?

Taking it to the Net

C1, C2

A team will be called upon to personify the operation of a voucher system. Yet all teams must prepare for the potential to be selected by doing the following:

1. Each team is to identify the documents in a voucher system. The team leader will play the voucher, and each team member is to assume "the role" of one or more documents.
2. To prepare for your individual role you are to:
   a. Find an illustration for the document within the chapter.
   b. Write down your document's function, where you originate, and how you flow through the voucher system.
3. Rehearse the role playing of operating the system. You may use text illustrations as props, and for visual effect you may wear a nametag identifying the part you play.

Teamwork in Action

P2

Browse through a store in your area. Identify between 5 and 10 internal controls this store is implementing.

Hitting the Road

C1

Read the article "The Heavy Burden of Light Fingers" in the December 16, 1996, issue of *Business Week.*

1. What are some schemes employees use to defraud companies?
2. What is the average amount of loss experienced by companies due to employee fraud?
3. According to the article, how are employee frauds uncovered?

***Business Week* Activity**

10

C H A P T E R

Receivables and Short-Term Investments

Chapter Outline

Debt into Gold

TULSA, OK—Today's economy runs on credit sales. Credit sales produce accounts receivable that are often the largest current asset a company owns. But not all accounts receivable are paid. Some end up as "bad debts"—accounts that a company can't collect.

Enter William and Kathryn Bartmann. The Bartmanns first started collecting on other companies' bad debt accounts from their kitchen table in Muskogee, Oklahoma. They used something more powerful than technology and pressure tactics to collect money that debtors owed—they used a philosophy of "respect for people."

The Bartmanns know personally the psychology of debtors, having previously been bankrupt themselves. "You've got to be sympathetic; you've got to listen with your heart as well as your head," says William Bartmann.

The Bartmanns "polite persistence" is paying off. Their entrepreneurial spirit led them to create **CFS,** a Tulsa-based company that is now the nation's largest purchaser of bad credit card debts. Last year, their company earned $137 million. And their net profit margin is a cool 67%!

Through all of its success, CFS has maintained its reputation for ethical dealings in an industry still plagued by abusive and questionable tactics. It also keeps a down-to-earth management style. As one recent example, if revenue targets are met, CFS said it will fly all employees and guests to Las Vegas for a mud-wrestling match—William Bartmann vs. one of his executives. Bartmann has also taken all employees to a baseball game in Kansas City. It's vintage Bartmann—bold and flamboyant.

Interestingly, Bartmann recently turned down a huge cash offer for the company. Why? "It wasn't enough. We're going places," he says. It might be the World Series of profits.

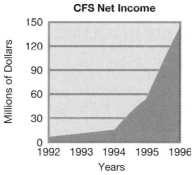

CFS Net Income

Millions of Dollars (0–150), Years 1992–1996

Source: *Business Week,* August 11, 1997

HAPTER PREVIEW

This chapter focuses on accounts receivable, short-term notes receivable, and short-term investments. We describe each of these assets, their use in practice, and how they are accounted for and reported in financial statements. This knowledge helps us use accounting information to make better decisions. It can also help in predicting bad debts as shown in the opening article.

Accounts Receivable

A *receivable* refers to an amount due from another party. Receivables along with cash, cash equivalents, and short-term investments make up the most liquid assets of a company. The two most common receivables are accounts receivable and notes receivable. Other receivables include interest receivable, rent receivable, tax refund receivable, and amounts due from officers and employees.

Accounts receivable refer to amounts due from customers for credit sales. This section begins by describing how accounts receivable arise and their various sources. These sources include sales when customers use credit cards issued by third parties and when a company gives credit directly to customers. When a company extends credit directly to customers it must (1) maintain a separate account receivable for each customer and (2) account for bad debts from credit sales.

Recognizing Accounts Receivable

C1 Describe accounts receivable and how they occur and are recorded.

Accounts receivable arise from credit sales to customers by both retailers and wholesalers. The amount of credit sales has increased in recent years, reflecting several factors including an efficient banking system and a sound economy. Retailers such as **The Limited, Chic by H.I.S, Best Buy,** and **CompUSA** hold millions of dollars in accounts receivable. Similar amounts are held by wholesalers such as **NIKE, Reebok, SUPERVALU, SYSCO,** and **Ace Hardware**. Exhibit 10.1 shows the dollar amount of accounts receivable and its percent of total assets for four companies.

Exhibit 10.1

Accounts Receivable for Selected Companies

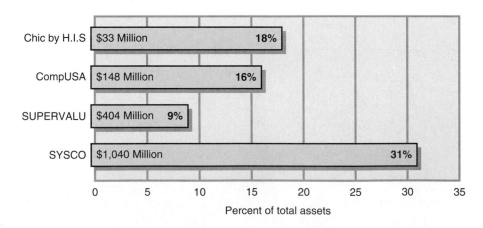

Sales on Credit

We explained in Chapter 8 how credit sales are recorded by debiting an Accounts Receivable account for a specific customer. This is important for showing us how much each customer purchases, how much each customer has paid, and how much each customer still owes. This information provides the basis for sending bills to customers and gives important data for other managerial analyses. To maintain this information, companies that extend credit directly to their customers must maintain a separate account receivable for each of them. The General Ledger continues to report a single Accounts

Receivable amount along with the other financial statement accounts, but a supplementary record is created where a separate account is maintained for each customer. This supplementary record is the *Accounts Receivable Ledger.*.

Exhibit 10.2 shows the relation between the Accounts Receivable account in the General Ledger and the individual customer accounts in the Accounts Receivable Ledger for **TechCom,** a small electronics wholesaler. This exhibit reports the beginning balances of TechCom's accounts receivable for July 15. While TechCom's transactions are mainly in cash, it has two major credit customers: CompStore and RDA Electronics. Exhibit 10.2 shows that the $3,000 total of these two customers' balances in the Accounts Receivable Ledger is equal to the balance of the Accounts Receivable account in the General Ledger.

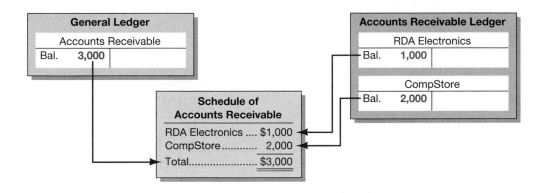

Exhibit 10.2

Accounts Receivable Account and the Accounts Receivable Ledger (before transactions)

To see how accounts receivable from credit sales are recognized in the accounting records, we look at two transactions on July 15 between TechCom and its two major credit customers. The first is a credit sale of $950 to CompStore. A credit sale is posted with both a debit to the Accounts Receivable account in the General Ledger and a debit to the customer account in the Accounts Receivable Ledger. The second transaction is a collection of $720 from RDA Electronics from prior credit sales. Cash receipts from a credit customer are posted with credits to both the Accounts Receivable account in the General Ledger and to the customer account.[1] Both transactions are journalized in Exhibit 10.3.[2]

July 15	Accounts Receivable—CompStore	950	
	Sales		950
	To record credit sales.		
July 15	Cash	720	
	Accounts Receivable—RDA Electronics . .		720
	To record collection of credit sales.		

Exhibit 10.3

Accounts Receivable Transactions

Exhibit 10.4 shows the General Ledger account and the Accounts Receivable Ledger after the two transactions above. The General Ledger account shows the effects of the sale, the collection, and the resulting balance of $3,230. These events are also reflected in the customers' accounts: RDA Electronics has an ending balance of $280 and CompStore now owes $2,950. The $3,230 sum of their accounts equals the debit balance of the General Ledger account.

---

[1] Posting debits or credits to Accounts Receivable twice does not violate the requirement that debits equal credits. The equality of debits and credits is maintained in the General Ledger. The Accounts Receivable Ledger is a supplementary record providing detailed information on each customer.

[2] We omit the cost of sales entries in order to focus on sales and receivables.

Exhibit 10.4

Accounts Receivable Account
and the Accounts Receivable
Ledger (after transactions)

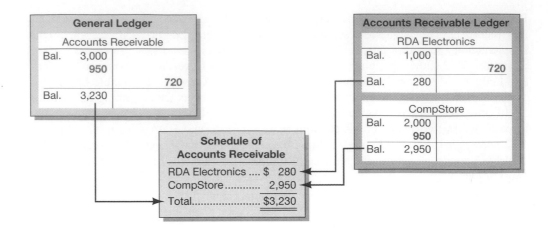

General Ledger		
Accounts Receivable		
Bal. 3,000		
950		
		720
Bal. 3,230		

Schedule of Accounts Receivable	
RDA Electronics	$ 280
CompStore............	2,950
Total......................	$3,230

Accounts Receivable Ledger		
RDA Electronics		
Bal. 1,000		
		720
Bal. 280		
CompStore		
Bal. 2,000		
950		
Bal. 2,950		

Like many companies, TechCom grants credit directly to qualified customers. Many large retailers such as **Sears** and **J.C. Penney** now maintain their own credit cards. This allows them to grant credit to approved customers and to earn interest on any balance not paid within a specified period of time. It also allows them to avoid the fee charged by credit card companies. The entries in this case are the same as those above except for the possibility of added interest revenue. If a customer owes interest on the bill, then we debit Accounts Receivable and credit Interest Revenue for this amount.

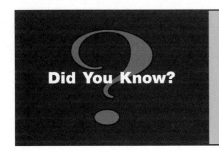

Did You Know?

Cyber Receivables

Cyber receivables are the result of new cyber-merchants. Setting up shop in cyberspace is easier than ever. New programs help merchants build Web storefronts quickly and easily. Merchants simply enter product details such as names and prices, and out comes a respectable-looking site complete with order forms. These storefront programs can be listed as part of a cybermall, and they offer secure credit card orders and track sales and site visits. [Source: *Business Week,* June 9, 1997.]

Credit Card Sales

Many companies allow customers to use credit cards such as **Visa, MasterCard,** or **American Express** to charge purchases. This practice gives customers the ability to make purchases without cash or checks. It also allows them to defer their payments to the credit card company. Once credit is established with the credit card company, the customer does not have to open an account with each store. Customers using credit cards

can make single monthly payments instead of several to different creditors.

There are good reasons why sellers allow customers to use credit cards instead of granting credit directly. First, the seller does not have to evaluate the credit standing of each customer or make decisions about who gets credit and how much. Second, the seller avoids the risk of extending credit to customers who cannot or do not pay. This risk is transferred to the credit card company. Third, the seller typically receives cash from the credit card company sooner than if it granted credit directly to customers. Fourth, a variety of credit options for customers offers a potential increase in sales volume. **Sears,** one of the nation's largest credit providers among retailers, historically offered credit only to customers using a **SearsCharge** card. Sears recently changed its policy to permit customers to charge purchases to third-party companies. It reported this as follows:

SearsCharge increased its share of Sears retail sales even as the company expanded the payment options available to its customers with the acceptance in 1993 of VISA, MasterCard, and American Express in addition to the Discover Card.

In dealing with some credit cards, usually those issued by banks, the seller deposits a copy of each credit card sales receipt in its bank account just like it deposits a customer's check. The seller receives a credit to its checking account without delay. Some credit cards require the seller to send a copy of each receipt to the credit card company. Until payment is received, the seller has an account receivable from the credit card company. In return for the services provided by the credit card company, the seller pays a fee, often ranging from 2% to 5% of credit card sales. This charge is deducted from the credit to the checking account or the cash payment to the seller.

Entrepreneur
You are the owner of a small retail store. You are considering allowing customers to purchase merchandise using credit cards. Until now, your store only accepted cash and checks. What form of analysis do you use to make this decision?

You Make the Call

Answer—p. 433

The procedures used in accounting for credit card sales depend on whether cash is received immediately on deposit or is delayed until paid by the credit card company. For instance, if TechCom has $100 of credit card sales with a 4% fee and cash is received immediately on deposit, then the entry is:

July 15	Cash	96	
	Credit Card Expense	4	
	Sales		100
	To record credit card sales less a 4% credit card expense.		

Assets = Liabilities + Equity
+96   −4
                                +100

If TechCom must send a copy of the credit card sales receipts to a credit card company and wait for payment, then the entry on the date of sale is:

July 15	Accounts Receivable—Credit Card Co.	100	
	Sales		100
	To record credit card sales.		

Assets = Liabilities + Equity
+100   +100

When cash is received from the credit card company, the entry to record the receipt and the deduction of the fee is:

July 30	Cash	96	
	Credit Card Expense	4	
	Accounts Receivable—Credit Card Co.		100
	To record cash receipt less 4% credit card expense.		

Assets = Liabilities + Equity
+96   −4
−100

Note the credit card expense is not recorded until cash is received from the credit card company. This practice is a matter of convenience. By following this practice, the seller avoids computing and recording the credit card expense each time sales are recorded. Instead, the expense related to many sales can be computed once and recorded when cash is received. But the *matching principle* requires reporting credit card expense in the same period as the sale. Therefore, if the sale and cash receipt occur in different periods, we must accrue and report the credit card expense in the period of the sale by using an adjusting entry at the end of the period. If TechCom requires a year-end adjustment of $24 of accrued credit card expense on a $600 receivable that the credit card company has not yet paid, we must make the following entry:

Assets = Liabilities + Equity
−24   −24

Dec. 31	Credit Card Expense	24	
	Accounts Receivable—Credit Card Co. . . .		24
	To accrue credit card expense that is unrecorded at the end of the year.		

The following entry records the cash collection in January:

Assets = Liabilities + Equity
+576
−576

Jan. 5	Cash	576	
	Accounts Receivable—Credit Card Co. . . .		576
	To record collection of amount due from Credit Card Company.		

Some firms report credit card expense in the income statement as a type of discount deducted from sales to get net sales. Other companies classify it as a selling expense or even as an administrative expense. Arguments can be made for all three alternatives.

Flash *back*

1. In recording credit card sales, when do you debit Accounts Receivable and when do you debit Cash?
2. When are credit card expenses recorded in cases where sales receipts must be accumulated before they can be sent to the credit card company? When are these expenses incurred?
3. If payment for a credit card sale is not received by the end of the accounting period, how do you account for the credit card expense from that sale?

Answers—p. 434

Valuing Accounts Receivable

When a company directly grants credit to its customers, there usually are some customers who do not pay what they promised. The accounts of these customers are **uncollectible accounts,** commonly called **bad debts.** The total amount of uncollectible accounts is an expense of selling on credit. Why do companies sell on credit if they expect some accounts to be uncollectible? The answer is that companies believe granting credit will increase revenues and profits to offset bad debts. They are willing to incur bad debts losses if the net effect is to increase sales and profits.

Two methods are used by companies to account for uncollectible accounts: (1) direct write-off method and (2) allowance method. We describe both of these methods.

Credit Woes
The days of easy money are ending for credit card issuers. Costs of financing credit card operations are rising for all issuers, owing to record default rates. Much of this is the fault of issuers who have flooded the market with offers of credit cards with low "teaser" rates. In response, credit card users have greatly increased their debts, and many are unable to pay them. The table here shows the huge increase in bad debts of major credit card issuers. [Source: *Business Week*, March 31, 1997.]

Write-offs for Bad Credit Card Debt		
	12/31/96	12/31/95
Banc One	6.8%	N/A
First Chicago	6.7	3.8%
Discover	6.1	4.5
Citicorp	5.5	3.9
Chase	5.1	4.2
Capital One	5.1	2.6
Advanta	5.1	2.6

Did You Know?

Direct Write-Off Method

The **direct write-off method** of accounting for bad debts records the loss from an uncollectible account receivable at the time it is determined to be uncollectible. No attempt is made to predict uncollectible accounts or bad debts expense. Bad debts expense is recorded when specific accounts are written off as uncollectible. If TechCom determines on January 23 it can't collect $520 owed to it by its customer Jack Kent, the loss is recognized using the direct write-off method as follows:

P1 Apply the direct write-off and allowance methods to account for accounts receivable.

Jan. 23	Bad Debts Expense	520	
	Accounts Receivable—Jack Kent		520
	To write off uncollectible account under the direct write-off method.		

Assets = Liabilities + Equity
−520   −520

The debit in this entry charges the uncollectible amount directly to the current year's Bad Debts Expense account. The credit removes the balance of the account from the subsidiary ledger and from the controlling account.

Sometimes an account written off is later collected. This can be due to factors such as continual collection efforts or the good fortune of a customer. If the account of Jack Kent that was written off directly to Bad Debts Expense is later collected in full, the following two entries record this recovery:

Mar. 11	Accounts Receivable—Jack Kent	520	
	Bad Debts Expense		520
	To reinstate account of Jack Kent previously written off.		
Mar. 11	Cash	520	
	Accounts Receivable—Jack Kent		520
	To record full payment of account.		

Assets = Liabilities + Equity
+520   +520

Assets = Liabilities + Equity
+520
−520

Sometimes an amount previously written off directly to Bad Debts Expense is recovered in the year following the write-off. If there is no balance in the Bad Debts Expense account from previous write-offs and no other write-offs are expected, the credit portion of the entry recording the recovery can be made to a Bad Debts Recoveries revenue account.

Companies must weigh at least two principles when considering use of the direct write-off method: (1) matching principle and (2) materiality principle.

Matching Principle Applied to Bad Debts

The **matching principle** requires expenses to be reported in the same accounting period as the sales they helped produce. This means that if extending credit to customers helped produce sales, the bad debts expense linked to those sales is matched and reported in the same period as the sales. The direct write-off method usually doesn't match revenues and expenses. This mismatch occurs because bad debts expense is not recorded until an account becomes uncollectible, which often does not occur during the same period as the credit sale.

Applying the matching principle to bad debts presents challenges. Managers realize that some portion of credit sales results in bad debts. But knowing what specific credit sale is uncollectible doesn't become apparent until later. If a customer fails to pay within the credit period, most companies send out repeated billings and make other efforts to collect. They don't accept that a customer isn't going to pay until every reasonable means of collection is taken. This decision point may not be reached until one or more accounting periods after the period in which the sale was made. Matching bad debts expense with the revenue it produces therefore requires a company to estimate this unknown amount at the end of each period.

Materiality Principle Applied to Bad Debts

The **materiality principle** states that an amount can be ignored if its effect on the financial statements is unimportant to users. The materiality principle permits use of the direct write-off method in accounting for expenses from bad debts when bad debts expenses are very small in relation to a company's other financial statement items such as sales and net income. This requires that bad debts expense be unimportant for decisions made by users of the company's financial statements.

Allowance Method

The **allowance method** of accounting for bad debts matches the *expected* loss from uncollectible accounts receivable against the sales they helped produce. We must use expected losses since management can't exactly identify the customers who won't pay their bills at the time of sale. This means at the end of each period the allowance method requires us to estimate the total bad debts expected to result from that period's sales. An allowance is then recorded for this expected loss. This method has two advantages over the direct write-off method: (1) bad debts expense is charged to the period when the related sales are recognized, and (2) accounts receivable are reported on the balance sheet at the estimated amount of cash to be collected.

Recording Estimated Bad Debts Expense

The allowance method estimates bad debts expense at the end of each accounting period and records it with an adjusting entry. TechCom, for instance, had credit sales of approximately $300,000 during its first year of operations. At the end of the first year, $20,000 of credit sales remained uncollected. Based on the experience of similar businesses, TechCom estimated that $1,500 of the accounts receivable were uncollectible. This estimated expense is recorded with the following adjusting entry:

Assets = Liabilities + Equity
−1,500   −1,500

Dec. 31	Bad Debts Expense	1,500	
	Allowance for Doubtful Accounts		1,500
	To record estimated bad debts.		

The debit in this entry means the estimated bad debts expense of $1,500 from selling on credit is matched on the income statement with the $300,000 sales it helped produce. The credit in this entry is to a contra asset account called **Allowance for Doubtful Accounts.** A contra account is used because at the time of the adjusting entry, the company does not know which customers will not pay. Because specific bad debts accounts are not identifiable at the time of the adjusting entry, they cannot be removed from the subsidiary Accounts Receivable Ledger. Because the customer accounts are left in the subsidiary ledger, the controlling account for Accounts Receivable cannot be reduced. Instead, the Allowance for Doubtful Accounts *must* be credited.

Bad Debts Related Accounts in Financial Statements

The process of evaluating customers and approving them for credit usually is not assigned to the selling department of a company. Given its goal of increasing sales, the selling department might have different motives in approving customers for credit. Because the selling department is not responsible for granting credit, it should not be held responsible for bad debts expense. This means bad debts expense often appears on the income statement as an administrative expense rather than a selling expense.

Recall TechCom has $20,000 of outstanding accounts receivable at the end of its first year of operations. After the bad debts adjusting entry is posted, TechCom's Accounts Receivable and Allowance for Doubtful Accounts look as shown in Exhibit 10.5.

Accounts Receivable				Allowance for Doubtful Accounts		
Dec. 31	20,000				Dec. 31	1,500

Exhibit 10.5

General Ledger Balances after Bad Debts Adjusting Entry

The Allowance for Doubtful Accounts credit balance of $1,500 has the effect of reducing accounts receivable (net of the allowance) to their estimated realizable value. **Realizable value** is the expected proceeds from converting this asset into cash. Although $20,000 is legally owed to TechCom by its credit customers, only $18,500 is expected to be realized in cash collections from customers.

In the balance sheet, the Allowance for Doubtful Accounts is subtracted from Accounts Receivable to show the amount expected to be realized. This information is often reported as shown in Exhibit 10.6.

Current assets:		
Accounts receivable	$20,000)	
Less allowance for doubtful accounts	(1,500)	$18,500

Exhibit 10.6

Balance Sheet Presentation of Allowance for Doubtful Accounts

Sometimes the contra assets account to Accounts Receivable is not reported separately. This alternative presentation is shown in Exhibit 10.7.

Accounts receivable (net of $1,500 estimated uncollectible accounts)	$18,500

Exhibit 10.7

Alternative Presentation of Allowance for Doubtful Accounts

Writing Off a Bad Debt

When specific accounts are identified as uncollectible, they are written off against the Allowance for Doubtful Accounts. After spending some time trying to collect from Jack Kent, TechCom decides that Kent's $520 account is uncollectible and makes the following entry to write it off:

Jan. 23	Allowance for Doubtful Accounts	520	
	Accounts Receivable—Jack Kent		520
	To write off an uncollectible account.		

Assets = Liabilities + Equity
+520
−520

Posting the credit of this write-off entry to the Accounts Receivable account removes the amount of the bad debt from the controlling account. Posting it to Jack Kent's account removes the amount of the bad debt from the subsidiary ledger. By removing it from the subsidiary ledger, TechCom avoids the cost of additional collection efforts. After this entry is posted, the General Ledger accounts appear as in Exhibit 10.8 (assuming no changes in the balances of related accounts).

Exhibit 10.8

General Ledger Balances after Write-Off

Accounts Receivable			
Dec. 31	20,000		
		Jan. 23	520

Allowance for Doubtful Accounts			
		Dec. 31	1,500
Jan. 23	520		

Note two aspects of this entry and its related accounts. First, while bad debts are an expense of selling on credit, the allowance account is debited in the write-off. The expense account is not debited. The expense account is not debited because bad debts expense is previously estimated and recorded with an adjusting entry at the end of the period in which the sale occurred. Second, while the write-off removes the amount of the account receivable from the ledgers, it doesn't affect the estimated realizable value of TechCom's net accounts receivable, as shown in Exhibit 10.9.

Exhibit 10.9

Realizable Value before and after Write-Off

	Before Write-Off	After Write-Off
Accounts receivable	$20,000	$19,480
Less allowance for doubtful accounts	1,500	980
Estimated realizable accounts receivable	$18,500	$18,500

Neither total assets nor net income are affected by the write-off of a specific account. But both total assets and net income are affected by recognizing the year's bad debts expense in the adjusting entry.

Recovery of a Bad Debt

When a customer fails to pay and the account is written off as uncollectible, his or her credit standing is jeopardized. To help restore credit standing, a customer sometimes later chooses to voluntarily pay all or part of the amount owed. When a recovery of a bad debt occurs, it is recorded in the customer's subsidiary account where this information is retained for use in future credit evaluation.

A company makes two entries when collecting an account previously written off. The first is to reverse the original write-off and reinstate the customer's account. The second entry records the collection of the reinstated account. If on March 11, Jack Kent pays in full his account that TechCom previously wrote off, the entries to record this bad debts recovery are:

Assets = Liabilities + Equity
+520
−520

Assets = Liabilities + Equity
+520
−520

Mar. 11	Accounts Receivable—Jack Kent	520	
	Allowance for Doubtful Accounts		520
	To reinstate the account of Kent previously written off.		
Mar. 11	Cash	520	
	Accounts Receivable—Jack Kent		520
	To record full payment of account.		

Jack Kent paid the entire amount previously written off, but in some cases a customer pays only a portion of the amount owed. A question then arises of whether the entire balance of the account is returned to accounts receivable, or just the amount paid. The answer is a matter of judgment. If we believe this customer will later pay in full, the entire amount owed is returned to accounts receivable. But only the amount paid is returned if we expect no further collection.

Flash *back*

4. Using the matching principle, why must bad debts expenses be estimated?

5. What term describes the balance sheet valuation of accounts receivable less the allowance for doubtful accounts?

6. Why is estimated bad debts expense credited to a contra account rather than to the Accounts Receivable controlling account?

Answers—p. 434

Estimating Bad Debts Expense

Companies with direct credit sales estimate bad debts expense. They do this to help them manage their receivables and to set credit policies. The allowance method of accounting for bad debts also requires an estimate of bad debts expense to prepare the adjusting entry at the end of each accounting period. How does a company estimate bad debts expense? There are two common methods. One is based on the income statement relation between bad debts expense and sales. The second is based on the balance sheet relation between accounts receivable and the allowance for doubtful accounts. Both methods require an analysis of past experience.

P2 Estimate uncollectibles using methods based on sales and accounts receivable.

Percent of Sales Method

The *percent of sales* method uses income statement relations to estimate bad debts. It is based on the idea that a given percent of a company's credit sales for the period are uncollectible.[3] The income statement would then report that percent as the amount of bad debts expense. To illustrate, assume **MusicLand** has credit sales of $400,000 in 1999. Based on past experience and the experience of similar companies, MusicLand estimates 0.6% of credit sales are uncollectible. Using this prediction, MusicLand expects $2,400 of bad debts expense from 1999's sales (computed as $400,000 \times 0.006 = $2,400$). The adjusting entry to record this estimated expense is:

Dec. 31	Bad Debts Expense	2,400	
	Allowance for Doubtful Accounts		2,400
	To record estimated bad debts.		

Assets = Liabilities + Equity
−2,400   −2,400

This entry doesn't mean the December 31, 1999, balance in Allowance for Doubtful Accounts will be $2,400. A $2,400 balance occurs only if the account had a zero balance prior to posting the adjusting entry. For several reasons, the unadjusted balance of Allowance for Doubtful Accounts is not likely to be zero. Unless a company is in its first period of operations, the allowance account will have a zero balance only if the prior amounts written off as uncollectible *exactly* equal the prior estimated bad debts expenses. And that is not likely.

---

[3] Note the focus is on *credit* sales. Cash sales don't produce bad debts, and they are generally not used in this estimation. But if cash sales are relatively small compared to credit sales, there is no major impact from including them.

This means we do not expect the Allowance for Doubtful Accounts to have an unadjusted balance of zero at the end of a period. This also means the adjusted balance reported on the balance sheet normally does not equal the amount of expense reported on the income statement. Expressing bad debts expense as a percent of sales is an estimate based on past experience. As new experience is obtained, we often find the percent used is too high or too low. When this happens, we adjust the rate for future periods.

Accounts Receivable Methods

The *accounts receivable* methods use balance sheet relations to estimate bad debts—primarily the relation between accounts receivable and the allowance amount. It is based on the idea that some portion of the end-of-period accounts receivable balance is not collectible. The objective for this bad debts adjusting entry is to make the Allowance for Doubtful Accounts balance equal to the portion of outstanding accounts receivable estimated as uncollectible. To obtain this required balance for the Allowance for Doubtful Accounts, we compare its balance before the adjustment with our estimated balance. The difference between the two is debited to Bad Debts Expense and credited to Allowance for Doubtful Accounts. Estimating this required balance for the allowance account is done in one of two ways: (1) simple estimate of percent uncollectible from the total outstanding accounts receivable and (2) aging accounts receivable.

Percent of Accounts Receivable Method

The *percent of accounts receivable* approach assumes a given percent of a company's outstanding receivables are uncollectible. This estimated percent is based on past experience and the experience of similar companies. It also is impacted by current conditions such as recent economic trends and difficulties faced by customers. The total dollar amount of all outstanding receivables is multiplied by an estimated percent to get the estimated dollar amount of uncollectible accounts. This amount is reported in the balance sheet as the balance for Allowance for Doubtful Accounts. We prepare an adjusting entry debiting Bad Debts Expense and crediting Allowance for Doubtful Accounts. The amount of the adjustment is the amount necessary to give us the required balance in Allowance for Doubtful Accounts.

Assume **MusicLand** has $50,000 of outstanding accounts receivable on December 31, 1999. Past experience suggests 5% of outstanding receivables are uncollectible. This means that after the adjusting entry is posted, we want the Allowance for Doubtful Accounts to show a $2,500 credit balance (computed as 5% of $50,000). Before the adjustment the account appears as:

Allowance for Doubtful Accounts			
		Dec. 31, 1998, bal.	2,000
Feb. 6	800		
July 10	600		
Nov. 20	400		
		Unadjusted bal.	200

The $2,000 beginning balance is from the December 31, 1998, balance sheet. During 1999, accounts of specific customers are written off on February 6, July 10, and November 20. The account has a $200 credit balance prior to the December 31, 1999, adjustment. The adjusting entry to give the allowance the required $2,500 balance is:

Assets = Liabilities + Equity
−2,300   −2,300

Dec. 31	Bad Debts Expense	2,300	
	Allowance for Doubtful Accounts		2,300
	To record estimated bad debts.		

After this entry is posted, the allowance has a $2,500 credit balance as shown in Exhibit 10.10

Allowance for Doubtful Accounts			
		Dec. 31, 1998, bal.	2,000
Feb. 6	800		
July 10	600		
Nov. 20	400		
		Unadjusted bal.	200
		Dec. 31 adjustment	**2,300**
		Dec. 31, 1999, bal.	2,500

Exhibit 10.10

Allowance for Doubtful Accounts after Bad Debts Adjusting Entry

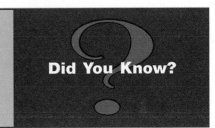

High Tech Estimates

Technology can assist users in estimating bad debts. Both the sales-based and receivables-based methods of estimating bad debts are easily included in computerized information systems. Using current and past data in the system, estimates of bad debts are obtained with adjustments for different assumptions and economic trends. Spreadsheet programs can also be used for estimating bad debts.

Did You Know?

Aging of Accounts Receivable Method

Both the percent of sales (income statement) method and the percent of accounts receivable (balance sheet) method use information from *past* experience to estimate the amount of bad debts expense. Another balance sheet method using receivables information produces a more precise estimate and uses both past experience and current information. The **aging of accounts receivable** method examines *each* account receivable to estimate the amount uncollectible. Receivables are classified by how long they are past their due dates. Then, estimates of uncollectible amounts are made assuming the longer an amount is past due the more likely it is to be uncollectible.

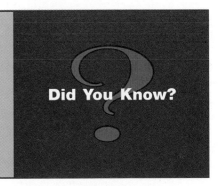

Mining Data and Fool's Gold

Michael Drosnin's best-selling book, *The Bible Code,* claims to find hidden messages in the Bible about dinosaurs, Bill Clinton, and the Land of Magog. The pitfall Drosnin stumbled into reminds us of the dangers of modern technology and "data mining." Done right, data mining can help discover trends, weed out credit card fraud, identify bad credit risks, and estimate uncollectibles. Done wrong, it produces bogus correlations. For instance, historically the single best predictor of the Standard & Poor's 500 stock index was butter production in Bangladesh. The lesson: Use common sense in mining data and beware of fool's gold. [Source: *Business Week,* June 16, 1997.]

Did You Know?

In aging accounts receivable outstanding at the end of a period, we examine each account and classify it by how much time has passed since it was due. Classifications depend on the judgment of a company's management. But classes are often based on 30-day (or one-month) periods. After the outstanding amounts are classified (or aged), past experience is used to estimate the percent of each class that is uncollectible. These percents are applied to the amounts in each class to get the required balance of the Allowance for Doubtful Accounts. This computation is performed by setting up a schedule like Exhibit 10.11 for MusicLand.

Exhibit 10.11

Aging of Accounts Receivable

		MUSICLAND Schedule of Accounts Receivable by Age December 31, 1999					
Customer's Name	Total	Not Yet Due	1 to 30 Days Past Due	31 to 60 Days Past Due	61 to 90 Days Past Due	Over 90 Days Past Due
Charles Abbot	$ 450	$ 450				
Frank Allen	710			$ 710		
George Arden	500	300	$ 200			
Paul Baum	740				$ 100	$ 640
ZZ Services	1,000	810	190			
Totals	$49,900	$37,000	$6,500	$3,500	$1,900	$1,000
Percent uncollectible . . .		× 2%	× 5%	× 10%	× 25%	× 40%
Estimated uncollectible .	$ 2,290	$ 740	$ 325	$ 350	$ 475	$ 400

Exhibit 10.11 lists each customer's account with its total balance. Then, each individual balance is assigned to one of five classes based on its days past due. In computerized systems, this task is often programmed. When all accounts are aged, the amounts in each class are totaled and multiplied by the estimated percent of uncollectible accounts for each class. The reasonableness of the percents used is reviewed regularly to reflect changes in the company and economy. The following excerpt from the 1996 annual report of **Sears** shows such a review:

> Provision for uncollectible accounts increased 58.6% and net charge-offs increased 51.1% from 1995. These increases reflect the 12.6% growth in domestic credit card receivables from 1995 levels and the continuing industry-wide trend of increased delinquencies and bankruptcies. The Company has responded to the aforementioned trend by implementing an aggressive action plan which includes enhanced collection efforts and increased investment in technology designed to improve collection staff productivity.

We see in Exhibit 10.11 that MusicLand has $3,500 in accounts receivable that are 31 to 60 days past due. MusicLand's management estimates 10% of the amounts in this age class are not collectible. The dollar amount of uncollectibles in this class is $350 ($3,500 × 10%).

The final total in the first column tells us the adjusted balance in MusicLand's Allowance for Doubtful Accounts is $2,290 ($740 + $325 + $350 + $475 + $400). Because the allowance account has an unadjusted credit balance of $200, the required adjustment to the Allowance for Doubtful Accounts is $2,090. This computation is shown in Exhibit 10.12.

Exhibit 10.12

Computing Required
Adjustment for Accounts
Receivable Method

Unadjusted balance	$ 200 credit
Required balance	2,290 credit
Required adjustment	**$2,090 credit**

MusicLand records the following end-of-period adjusting entry:

Dec. 31	Bad Debts Expense	2,090	
	Allowance for Doubtful Accounts		2,090
	To record estimated bad debts.		

Assets = Liabilities + Equity
−2,090   −2,090

Alternatively, if MusicLand's allowance had an unadjusted *debit* balance of $500, then its required adjustment is computed as:

Unadjusted balance	$ 500 debit
Required balance	2,290 credit
Required adjustment	**$2,790 credit**

The entry to record this end-of-period adjustment is:

Dec. 31	Bad Debts Expense	2,790	
	Allowance for Doubtful Accounts		2,790
	To record estimated bad debts.		

Assets = Liabilities + Equity
−2,790   −2,790

When the percent of sales (income statement) method is used, MusicLand's bad debts expense for 1999 is estimated at $2,400. When the percent of accounts receivable method is used, the expense is $2,300. And when the aging of accounts receivable method is used, the expense is $2,090. We usually expect these amounts to be different since each method gives only an estimate of future payments. But the aging of accounts receivable method is a more detailed examination of specific accounts and is usually the most reliable.[4] Exhibit 10.13 summarizes the principles guiding all three estimation methods and their focus of analysis.

Income Statement Focus	Balance Sheet Focus	Balance Sheet Focus
Percent of Sales Emphasis on Matching Sales ◄─────► Bad Debts Expense	**Percent of Receivables** Emphasis on Realizable Value Accounts ◄────► Allowance Receivable for Doubtful (total) Accounts	**Aging of Receivables** Emphasis on Realizable Value Accounts ◄────► Allowance Receivable for Doubtful (individual) Accounts

Exhibit 10.13

Methods to Estimate Bad Debts

Flash back

7. SnoBoard Company's end of period 12/31/99 balance in the Allowance for Doubtful Accounts is a credit of $440. By aging accounts receivable, it estimates that $6,142 is uncollectible. Prepare SnoBoard's year-end adjusting entry for bad debts.

8. Record entries for the following transactions assuming the allowance method is used:

January 10, 1999   The $300 account of customer Cool Jam is determined uncollectible.

April 12, 1999   Cool Jam pays in full its account that was deemed uncollectible on January 10, 1999.

Answers—p. 434

---

[4] In many cases, the aging analysis is supplemented with information about specific customers allowing management to decide whether those accounts should be classified as uncollectible. This information often is supplied by the sales and credit department managers.

Installment Accounts Receivable

Many companies allow their credit customers to make periodic payments over several months. When this is done, the selling company's assets may be in the form of installment accounts receivable. *Installment accounts receivable* are amounts owed by customers from credit sales where payment is required in periodic amounts over an extended time period. Source documents for installment accounts receivable include sales slips or invoices describing the sales transactions. When payments are made over several months or if the credit period is long, the customer is usually charged interest. Although installment accounts receivable may have credit periods of more than one year, they should be classified as current assets if the company regularly offers customers such terms.

Companies sometimes allow customers to sign a note receivable for sales. Also, companies sometimes ask for a note to replace an account receivable when a customer requests additional time to pay its past-due account. A note receivable is a written document that promises payment and is signed by the customer. If the credit period is long, the customer is usually charged interest. If the company regularly offers customers this option, these notes receivable are classified as current assets even when their credit period is longer than one year. For legal reasons, sellers generally prefer to receive notes receivable when the credit period is long and the receivable relates to a single sale for a fairly large amount. If a lawsuit is needed to collect from a customer, a note is a written acknowledgment by the buyer of the debt, its amount, and its terms. We explain the details of notes receivable next.

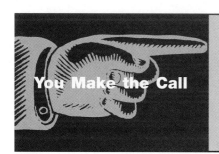

You Make the Call

Labor Union Chief
You are representing your employee union in contract negotiations with management. One week prior to contract discussions, management releases financial statements showing zero growth in earnings. This is far below the 10% growth predicted earlier. In your review of the statements, you find the company increased its "allowance for uncollectible accounts" from 1.5% to 4.5% of accounts receivable. Absent this change, earnings would show a 9% growth. Does this information impact your negotiations?

Answer—p. 434

Notes Receivable

 Describe a note receivable and the computation of its maturity date and interest.

A **promissory note** is a written promise to pay a specified amount of money either on demand or at a definite future date. Promissory notes are used in many transactions, including paying for products and services, in the lending and borrowing of money, and to pay for accounts receivable.

Exhibit 10.14 shows a promissory note dated July 10, 1999. For this note, Julia Browne promises to pay TechCom or to its order (according to TechCom's instructions) a specified amount of money ($1,000), called the **principal** of the note, at a definite future date (October 8, 1999). As the one who signed the note and promised to pay it at ma-

Exhibit 10.14

Promissory Note

turity, Julia Browne is the **maker** of the note. As the person to whom the note is payable, TechCom is the **payee** of the note. To Julia Browne, the note is a liability called a *note payable*. To TechCom, the same note is an asset called a *note receivable*.

The promissory note in Exhibit 10.14 bears interest at 12%, as written on the note. **Interest** is the charge for using (not paying) the money until a later date. To a borrower, interest is an expense. To a lender, it is a revenue.

Computations for Notes

We need knowledge of certain computations for notes to understand them. This section describes these computations. They include determining maturity date, the period covered, and the interest computation.

Maturity Date and Period

The **maturity date** of a note is the day the note (principal and interest) must be repaid. The *period* of a note is the time from the note's date to its maturity date. Many notes mature in less than a full year, and the period covered by them is often expressed in days. When the time of a note is expressed in days, the maturity date is the specified number of days after the note's date. As an example, a five-day note dated June 15 matures and is due on June 20. A 90-day note dated July 10 matures on October 8. This October 8 due date is computed as shown in Exhibit 10.15.

Days in July	31
Minus the date of the note	10
Days remaining in July	21
Add days in August	31
Add days in September	30
Days to equal 90 days, or **Maturity Date, October 8**	8
Period of the note in days	90

Exhibit 10.15

Maturity Date Computation

The period of a note is sometimes expressed in months or years. When months are used, the note matures and is payable in the month of its maturity on the *same day of the month* as its original date. A three-month note dated July 10, for instance, is payable on October 10. The same analysis applies when years are used.

Interest Computation

Interest is the cost of borrowing money for the borrower or the profit from lending money for the lender. Unless otherwise stated, the rate of interest on a note is the rate charged for the use of the principal for one year. The formula for computing interest on a note is shown in Exhibit 10.16.

Principal of the note	×	Annual interest rate	×	Time expressed in years	=	Interest

Exhibit 10.16

Computation of Interest Formula

To illustrate, interest on a $1,000, 12%, six-month note is computed as:

$$\$1,000 \times 12\% \times \frac{6}{12} = \$60$$

To simplify interest computations for notes with periods expressed in days, it is common to treat a year as having 360 days. While this practice is not applied as frequently as it used to be, we **treat a year as having 360 days in our examples and in the as-**

signments to keep computations simple. Using the promissory note above where we have a 90-day, 12%, $1,000 note, the interest is computed as:

$$\$1,000 \times 12\% \times \frac{90}{360} = \$30$$

Receipt of a Note

P3 Record the receipt of a note receivable.

Notes receivable are usually recorded in a single Notes Receivable account to simplify recordkeeping. We need only one account because the original notes are kept on file. This means the maker, rate of interest, due date, and other information can be learned by examining the actual note.[5]

To illustrate the recording for the receipt of a note, we use the $1,000, 90-day, 12% promissory note in Exhibit 10.14. TechCom receives this note at the time of a product sale to Julia Browne. This transaction is recorded as:

Assets = Liabilities + Equity
+1,000   +1,000

July 10	Notes Receivable	1,000	
	Sales		1,000
	Sold merchandise in exchange for a 90-day, 12% note.		

Companies also sometimes accept a note from an overdue customer as a way of granting a time extension on a past-due account receivable. When this occurs, a company may collect part of the past-due balance in cash. This partial payment forces a concession from the customer, reduces the customer's debt (and the seller's risk), and produces a note for a smaller amount. TechCom, for instance, agreed to accept $232 in cash and a $600, 60-day, 15% note from Jo Cook to settle her $832 past-due account. TechCom made the following entry to record receipt of this cash and note:

Assets = Liabilities + Equity
+232
+600
−832

Oct. 5	Cash	232	
	Notes Receivable	600	
	Accounts Receivable—Jo Cook		832
	Received cash and note to settle account.		

Honoring and Dishonoring a Note

The principal and interest of a note are due on its maturity date. The maker of the note usually *honors* the note and pays it in full. But sometimes a maker *dishonors* the note and does not pay it at maturity.

Recording an Honored Note

P4 Record the honoring and dishonoring of a note and adjustments for interest on a note.

We use the TechCom note transaction above to illustrate the honoring of a note. When Jo Cook pays the note on its due date, TechCom records its receipt as:

Assets = Liabilities + Equity
+615   +15
−600

Dec. 4	Cash	615	
	Notes Receivable		600
	Interest Earned		15
	Collected Jo Cook note with interest of $600 × 15% × 60/360.		

Interest Earned, also called Interest Revenue, is reported on the current period's income statement.

---

[5] When a company holds a large number of notes, it sometimes sets up a controlling account and a subsidiary ledger for notes.

Recording a Dishonored Note

When a note's maker is unable or refuses to pay at maturity, the note is dishonored. The act of **dishonoring** a note doesn't relieve the maker of the obligation to pay. The payee should use every legitimate means to collect. But how do companies report this event? The balance of the Notes Receivable account normally includes only those notes that have not matured. When a note is dishonored, we therefore remove the amount of this note from the Notes Receivable account and charge it back to an account receivable from its maker. TechCom, for instance, holds an $800, 12%, 60-day note of Greg Hart. At maturity, Hart dishonored the note. TechCom records this dishonoring of its Notes Receivable as follows:

Oct. 14	Accounts Receivable—Greg Hart	816	
	Interest Earned		16
	Notes Receivable		800
	To charge account of G. Hart for a dishonored note and interest of $800 × 12% × 60/360.		

Assets = Liabilities + Equity
+816   +16
−800

Charging a dishonored note back to the account of its maker serves two purposes. First, it removes the amount of the note from the Notes Receivable account, leaving in the account only notes that have not matured. It also records the dishonored note in the maker's account. Second, and more important, if the maker of the dishonored note applies for credit in the future, his or her account will show all past dealings, including the dishonored note. Restoring the account also reminds the company to continue collection efforts. Note that Hart owes both principal and interest. The above entry records the full amount owed in Hart's account and credits the interest to Interest Earned. This ensures that interest is included in efforts to collect from Hart.

End-of-Period Interest Adjustment

When notes receivable are outstanding at the end of an accounting period, accrued interest is computed and recorded. This recognizes both the interest revenue when it is earned and the added asset (interest) owned by the note's holder. For instance, on December 16, TechCom accepted a $3,000, 60-day, 12% note from a customer in granting an extension on a past-due account. When TechCom's accounting period ends on December 31, $15 of interest has accrued on this note ($3,000 × 12% × 15/360). The following adjusting entry records this revenue:

Dec. 31	Interest Receivable	15	
	Interest Earned		15
	To record accrued interest adjustment.		

Assets = Liabilities + Equity
+15   +15

This adjusting entry means interest earned appears on the income statement for the period when it is earned. It also means interest receivable appears on the balance sheet as a current asset.

Receiving Interest Previously Accrued

When the December 16 note above is collected on February 14, TechCom's entry to record the cash receipt is:

Feb. 14	Cash	3,060	
	Interest Earned		45
	Interest Receivable		15
	Notes Receivable		3,000
	Received payment of a note and its interest.		

Assets = Liabilities + Equity
+3,060   +45
−15
−3,000

Total interest earned on this note is $60. This entry's credit to Interest Receivable records collection of the interest accrued in the December 31 adjusting entry. The interest earned is $45 and reflects TechCom's revenue from holding the note from January 1 to February 14 of the current period.

Flash *back*

9. Wiley purchases $7,000 of merchandise from Stamford Company on December 16, 1999. Stamford accepts Wiley's $7,000, 90-day, 12% note as payment. Stamford's annual accounting period ends on December 31 and it doesn't make reversing entries. Prepare entries for Stamford Company on December 16, 1999, and December 31, 1999.

10. Using the information in Flashback 9., prepare Stamford's March 16, 2000, entry if Wiley dishonors the note.

Answers—p. 434

Converting Receivables to Cash before Maturity

C3 Explain how receivables can be converted to cash before maturity.

Sometimes companies convert receivables to cash before they are due. Reasons for this include the need for cash or a desire to not be involved in collection activities. Converting receivables is usually done either (1) by selling them or (2) by using them as security for a loan. A recent survey showed about 20% of large companies obtain cash from either the sale of receivables or the pledging of receivables as security. In some industries such as textiles and furniture, this is common practice. Recently, this practice has grown to other industries, especially the apparel industry. Also, many small companies use the sale of receivables as an immediate source of cash. This is especially the case for those selling to companies and government agencies that often delay payment.

Selling Accounts Receivable

A company can sell its accounts receivable to a finance company or bank. The buyer, called a *factor*, charges the seller a *factoring fee* and then collects the receivables as they come due. By incurring a factoring fee, the seller receives cash earlier and passes the risk of bad debts to the factor. The seller also avoids costs of billing and accounting for the receivables.

If TechCom, for instance, sells $20,000 of its accounts receivable and is charged a 2% factoring fee, it records this sale as:

Assets = Liabilities + Equity
+19,600   −400
−20,000

Aug. 15	Cash	19,600	
	Factoring Fee Expense	400	
	Accounts Receivable		20,000
	Sold accounts receivable for cash, less a 2% factoring fee.		

Factoring is a major business today. The **CIT Group** is a large factoring firm with volume of about $8 billion in recent years. Interestingly, about 90% of the factoring industry's business comes from textile and apparel businesses.

Pledging Accounts Receivable

A company can also raise cash by borrowing money and then *pledging* its accounts receivable as security for the loan. Pledging receivables doesn't transfer the risk of bad debts to the lender. The borrower retains ownership of the receivables. But if the borrower defaults on the loan, the lender has a right to be paid from cash receipts when the accounts receivable are collected. When TechCom borrowed $35,000 and pledged its receivables as security, it recorded this transaction as:

Aug. 20	Cash	35,000	
	Notes Payable		35,000
	Borrowed money with a note secured by		
	pledging accounts receivable.		

Assets = Liabilities + Equity
+35,000   +35,000

Because pledged receivables are committed as security for a specific loan, the borrower's financial statements should disclose the pledging of accounts receivable. TechCom, for instance, includes the following note with its financial statements regarding its pledged receivables: *Accounts receivable in the amount of $40,000 are pledged as security for a $35,000 note payable to First National Bank.* Another example is from the notes of **Chock Full O'Nuts:**

> Outstanding borrowings . . . are collateralized by, among other things, the trade accounts receivable.

Cash Poor?
Both **Zenith** and **Packard Bell** used receivables to get much needed cash. **Zenith** obtained a 3-year, $60 million credit agreement by pledging accounts receivable as collateral. **Intel** converted accounts receivable to a note receivable for a major customer—widely assumed to be **Packard Bell.** [Source: *Business Week,* December 11, 1995.]

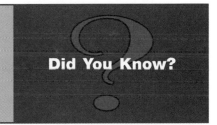

Did You Know?

Discounting Notes Receivable

Notes receivable can be converted to cash before they mature. This can be done by discounting notes receivable at a financial institution or bank. TechCom, for instance, discounted a $3,000, 90-day, 10% note receivable at First National Bank. TechCom held the note for 50 of the 90 days before discounting it. The bank applied a 12% rate in discounting the note, and TechCom received proceeds of $3,034 from the bank.[6] It recorded the discounting of this note as:

Aug. 25	Cash	3,034	
	Interest Revenue		34
	Notes Receivable		3,000
	Discounted a note receivable.		

Assets = Liabilities + Equity
+3,034   +34
−3,000

Notes receivable are discounted without recourse or with recourse. When a note is discounted *without recourse,* the bank assumes the risk of a bad debt loss and the original payee doesn't have a contingent liability. A **contingent liability** is an obligation to make

---

[6] Accounting software and spreadsheet programs are used in practice to compute bank proceeds. TechCom's proceeds from the bank are computed as:

Principal of Note	$3,000
+ Interest from Note ($3,000 × 10% × 90/360)	75
= Maturity Value	3,075
− Bank Discount ($3,075 × 12% × 40/360)	(41)
= Proceeds	$3,034

a future payment if, and only if, an uncertain future event occurs. A note discounted without recourse is like an outright sale of an asset. If a note is discounted *with recourse* and the original maker of the note fails to pay the bank when it matures, the original payee of the note must pay for it. This means a company discounting a note with recourse has a contingent liability until the bank is paid. A company should disclose contingent liabilities in notes to its financial statements. TechCom included the following note: *The Company is contingently liable for a $3,000 note receivable discounted with recourse.* A similar example of a receivables sale with recourse is from the notes of **Tyco:**

> The Company entered into an agreement pursuant to which it sold . . . receivables. The Company has retained substantially the same risk of credit loss as if the receivables had not been sold.

Full Disclosure

The disclosure of contingencies in notes is consistent with the **full disclosure principle.** This principle requires financial statements (including notes) to report all relevant information about the operations and financial position of a company. Relevance is judged by whether its disclosure impacts users' evaluation of a company. Besides contingent liabilities, other items often reported to satisfy the full disclosure principle are long-term commitments under contracts and accounting methods used.

Contingent Liabilities

In addition to discounted notes, a company should disclose any items where it is contingently liable. Examples are potential tax assessments, debts of others guaranteed by the company, and outstanding lawsuits against the company. Information about these helps users predict events that might affect the company. In October 1994, *The Wall Street Journal* reported "**Pennzoil** said it agreed to pay the IRS $454 million in back taxes and interest to resolve a claim stemming from its 1988 settlement with **Texaco.**" Readers of notes to the financial statements of **Pennzoil** were not surprised since Pennzoil included the following note in its annual report the year before:

> Pennzoil received a letter and examination report from the District Director of the IRS that proposes a tax deficiency based on an audit . . . this proposed adjustment is $550.9 million, net of available offsets.

Long-Term Commitments under Contracts

A company should disclose any long-term commitments under contract. The most common example is signing a long-term lease requiring annual payments, even when the obligation doesn't appear in the accounts. Another case is when a company pledges part of its assets as security for loans. These commitments restrict the flexibility of a company.

Accounting Methods Used

When more than one accounting method can be used, a company must describe the one it uses. This is especially important when the choice can materially impact net income.[7] This information helps users in their analysis of a company.

---

[7] FASB, Accounting *Standards—Current Text* (Norwalk, CT, 1995), sec. A10.105. First published as *APB Opinion No. 22*, pars. 12, 13.

Recall from Chapter 9 that cash equivalents are investments that are easily converted to known amounts of cash and they generally mature no more than three months after purchase. Yet many investments mature between 3 and 12 months (or the operating cycle). These investments are **short-term investments,** also called *temporary investments,* or *marketable securities.* Management expects to convert them to cash within one year or the current operating cycle of the business, whichever is longer.[8] Short-term investments are current assets and serve a similar purpose to cash equivalents.

Short-term investments can include both debt and equity securities. *Debt securities* reflect a creditor relationship and include investments in notes, bonds, and certificates of deposit. Debt securities are issued by governments, companies, and individuals. *Equity securities* reflect an ownership relationship and include shares of stock issued by companies. In notes to financial statements, companies usually give a description of their short-term investments.

Accounting for Short-Term Investments

This section explains the basics of accounting for short-term investments in both debt and equity securities.

Debt Securities

Short-term investments in both debt and equity securities are recorded at cost when purchased. TechCom, for instance, purchased short-term notes payable of Intel for $4,000 on January 10. TechCom's entry to record this purchase is:

Jan. 10	Short-Term Investments	4,000	
	Cash		4,000
	Bought $4,000 of Intel notes due May 10.		

Assets = Liabilities + Equity
+4,000
−4,000

These notes mature on May 10 and the cash proceeds are $4,000 plus $120 interest. When the proceeds are received, TechCom records this as:

May 10	Cash	4,120	
	Short-Term Investments		4,000
	Interest Earned		120
	Received cash proceeds from matured notes.		

Assets = Liabilities + Equity
+4,120   +120
−4,000

Equity Securities

The cost of an investment includes all necessary costs to acquire it, including commissions paid. TechCom purchased 100 shares of NIKE common stock as a short-term investment. It paid $50 per share plus $100 in commissions. The entry to record this purchase is

June 2	Short-Term Investments	5,100	
	Cash		5,100
	Bought 100 shares of NIKE stock at 50 plus *$100 commission.*		

Assets = Liabilities + Equity
+5,100
−5,100

The commission is not recorded in a separate account.

[8] FASB, *Accounting Standards—Current Text* (Norwalk, CT, 1995), sec. B05.105. First published as *Accounting Research Bulletin No. 43*, chap. 3A, par. 4.

Short-Term Investments

C4 Describe short-term investments in debt and equity securities.

TechCom received a $0.40 per share cash dividend on its short-term NIKE stock during the current period. This dividend is credited to a revenue account as follows:

Dec. 12	Cash	40	
	Dividends Earned		40
	Received dividend of $0.40 per share on 100 shares of NIKE stock.		

Assets = Liabilities + Equity
+40   +40

Reporting Short-Term Investments

P5 Record the sale of short-term investments.

Companies must report most short-term investments at their fair (market) values.[9] Requirements vary depending on whether short-term investments are classified as (1) held-to-maturity, (2) trading, or (3) available-for-sale securities. This section describes the financial statement presentation for each of these classifications.

Held-to-Maturity Securities

Held-to-maturity securities are *debt securities* that the company has the intent and ability to hold until they mature.[10] **Dairy Queen,** for instance, in notes to its financial statements, stated:

> Management determines the appropriate classification of debt securities at the time of purchase and reevaluates such designation as of each balance sheet date. Debt securities are classified as held-to-maturity because the Company has the positive intent and ability to hold such securities to maturity.

Held-to-maturity securities are reported in current assets if their maturity dates are within one year or the current operating cycle of the company. Held-to-maturity securities are reported at cost.

Trading Securities

Trading securities are either *debt or equity securities* that the company intends to actively trade for profit. These securities are actively managed. This means frequent purchases and sales are made to earn profits on short-term price changes. Trading securities are especially common with financial institutions such as banks and insurance companies.

Valuing and Reporting Trading Securities

Companies report the entire set of trading securities at their fair (or market) values with a "fair value adjustment" to the cost of the set. The resulting unrealized holding gains and losses from changes in the market value for the set of securities from one period to another are reported on the income statement as part of net income or loss. Most users believe accounting reports are more useful for decision making when changes in market values for this set of trading securities are reported in income.

To illustrate, TechCom's set of trading securities had a total cost of $11,500 and a fair market value of $13,000 on December 31, 1998. The difference between the $11,500 cost and the $13,000 fair value reflects a $1,500 gain. Because this gain is not yet confirmed by actual sales of these securities, it is called an **unrealized holding gain.** TechCom records this gain as:

---

[9] FASB, "Accounting for Certain Investments in Debt and Equity Securities," *Statement of Financial Accounting Standards No. 115* (Norwalk, CT, 1995). The requirements of *SFAS 115* also apply to long-term investments in debt and marketable equity securities. We discuss this in Chapter 16.
[10] Ibid., par. 7.

Dec. 31	Trading Securities, Fair Value Adjustment	1,500	
	Unrealized Holding Gain (Loss)		1,500
	To reflect a gain in fair values of trading securities.		

Assets = Liabilities + Equity
+1,500   +1,500

The Unrealized Holding Gain (Loss) is reported in Other Revenues and Gains (Expenses and Losses) on the income statement. After posting this entry, TechCom's investment in trading securities is reported in the current assets section of its balance sheet as:

Current Assets:		
Trading securities (at cost)	$11,500	
Trading securities (fair value adjustment)	1,500	
Trading securities (at fair value)		$13,000

The total cost of the entire set of trading securities is maintained in one account and the fair value adjustment is recorded in a separate account. The fair value adjustment is revised at the end of every period to equal the difference between cost and fair value. Keeping the Trading Securities account at cost helps us compute realized gains or losses when securities are sold, which we describe next.

Selling Trading Securities

When individual trading securities are sold, the difference between the net proceeds from the sale (sale price less brokerage fees) and the cost of the individual trading securities sold is recognized as a gain or a loss. When TechCom sells its $5,100 short-term investment in NIKE stock on December 15 for net proceeds of $5,400, it recognizes a gain of $300. The entry to record this sale is:

Dec. 15	Cash	5,400	
	Gain on Sale of Short-Term Investments ..		300
	Short-Term Investments		5,100
	To record sale of 100 shares of NIKE stock.		

Assets = Liabilities + Equity
+5,400   +300
−5,100

This gain is reported in Other Revenues and Gains on the income statement. If a loss is recorded, it is shown in Other Expenses and Losses. At the end of the period, the fair value adjustment for trading securities excludes the cost and fair values of NIKE stock.

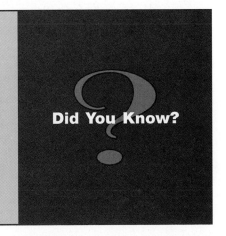

Back to the Future
Before 1938, banks reported fair (market) values for their short-term investments but then switched to historical cost. We now see a return to fair-value reporting for many short-term investments that is driven by S&L and banking problems. Ironically, the Great Depression fueled the 1938 conversion from fair values to historical cost. At that time bank examiners were concerned with protecting bank depositors (Federal Deposit Insurance didn't exist). Examiners had to determine market values for bank assets and liabilities to arrive at bank equity. If a bank's liabilities exceeded or even approximated its assets, its capital was considered impaired. Owners of banks with impaired capital then had to add capital, merge with another bank, or close. This led to bank examiners being blamed for excessive bank closings. Bank appraisal methods were then changed to historical cost.[11]

Did You Know?

---

[11] Source: Dan W. Swenson and Thomas E. Buttross, "Return to the Past: Disclosing Market Values of Financial Instruments." Reprinted with permission of the *Journal of Accountancy,* January 1993, pp. 71–77. Copyright © 1993 by the American Institute of Certified Public Accountants, Inc. Opinions of the authors are their own and do not necessarily reflect policies of the AICPA.

Available-for-Sale Securities

Available-for-sale securities are *debt or equity securities not* classified as trading or held-to-maturity securities. Available-for-sale securities are purchased to earn interest, dividends, or increases in market value. They are not actively managed like trading securities. Many companies own available-for-sale securities.

Valuing and Reporting Available-for-Sale Securities

Similar to trading securities, companies adjust the cost of the entire set of available-for-sale securities to reflect changes in fair value with a fair value adjustment to their total cost. The unrealized holding gains and losses from changes in market value for the set of available-for-sale securities from one period to another are *not* reported on the income statement. Instead, they are reported in the equity section of the balance sheet. Many users believe accounting reports are more useful for decision making when changes in market value of the entire set of available-for-sale securities are not reported in income. Since these securities are not actively traded, they believe including changes in market value would unnecessarily increase the variability of income and decrease its usefulness. We describe the reporting of these securities more fully in Chapter 16.

Selling Available-for-Sale Securities

When individual available-for-sale securities are sold, the difference between the cost of the individual securities sold and the net proceeds from the sale (sale price less brokerage fees) is recognized as a gain or loss. Accounting for the sale of individual available-for-sale securities is identical to that described for the sale of trading securities.

Summary of Accounting for Short-Term Investments

Exhibit 10.17 summarizes accounting for short-term investments in debt and equity securities.

Exhibit 10.17

Accounting for Short-Term Investments in Securities

*Unrealized gains or losses reported on income statement.
**Unrealized gains or losses reported in equity section on balance sheet and in comprehensive income.

The balance sheet presentation of short-term investments usually reports the fair market value for the *total* of all three types of securities instead of each individual type. The cost is also usually reported. A typical presentation of short-term securities is shown in Exhibit 10.18.

Exhibit 10.18

Statement Presentation of Short-Term Investments

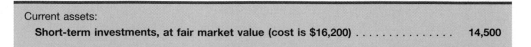

Current assets:
   Short-term investments, at fair market value (cost is $16,200) **14,500**

Even though the contra account to Short-Term Investments is not shown, we can determine its balance is $1,700 by comparing the $16,200 cost with the $14,500 net amount. Companies sometimes report separately the market value and cost for each of the three types of short-term securities.

Flash *back*

11. How are held-to-maturity securities reported on the balance sheet—at cost or fair (market) values?

12. How are trading securities reported on the balance sheet?

13. Unrealized holding gains and losses on available-for-sale securities are reported on what statement?

14. Where are unrealized holding gains and losses on trading securities reported?

Answers—p. 434

Accounts Receivable Turnover

USING THE INFORMATION

In Chapter 7 we discussed *days' sales uncollected* and how it helps us access a company's short-term liquidity or nearness to cash of its receivables. For companies selling on credit, we want to access both the quality and liquidity of its accounts receivable. *Quality* of receivables refers to the likelihood of collection without loss. Experience shows the longer receivables are outstanding beyond their due date, the lower the likelihood of collection. *Liquidity* of receivables refers to the speed of collection.

The **accounts receivable turnover** is a measure of both the quality and liquidity of accounts receivable. It indicates how often, on average, receivables are received and collected during the period. The formula for this ratio is shown in Exhibit 10.19.

A1 Compute accounts receivable turnover and use it to analyze liquidity.

$$\text{Accounts receivable turnover} = \frac{\text{Net sales}}{\text{Average accounts receivable}}$$

Exhibit 10.19

Accounts Receivable Turnover Formula

We prefer net *credit* sales in the numerator because cash sales do not create receivables. But since financial statements rarely report net credit sales, our analysis uses net total sales. The denominator in this turnover formula is the *average* accounts receivable balance during the period. The average is often computed as: (Beginning balance + Ending balance) ÷ 2. This method of estimating the average balance provides a useful result if seasonal changes in the accounts receivable balance during the year are not extreme.

The accounts receivable turnover shows us how often a company converts its average accounts receivable balance into cash during the period. TechCom, for instance, has an accounts receivable turnover of 5.1. This shows its average accounts receivable balance is converted into cash 5.1 times during the year. Exhibit 10.20 shows graphically this turnover activity for TechCom.

Exhibit 10.20

Rate of Accounts Receivable Turnover for TechCom

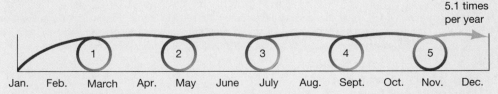

5.1 times per year

Jan. Feb. March Apr. May June July Aug. Sept. Oct. Nov. Dec.

Accounts receivable turnover also helps us evaluate how well management is doing in granting credit to customers in a desire to increase sales revenues. A high turnover in comparison with competitors suggests management should consider using more liberal credit terms to increase sales. A low turnover suggests management should consider stricter credit terms and more aggressive collection efforts to avoid having its resources tied up in accounts receivable.

To illustrate its application, we use data from the annual reports of two competing companies: **Dell Computer** and **Compaq Computer.** Exhibit 10.21 shows results from our computation of accounts receivable turnover for these two companies.

Exhibit 10.21

Analysis Using Accounts Receivable Turnover

Company	Figure ($ millions)	1996	1995	1994
Dell	Net sales	$ 7,759	$ 5,296	$ 3,475
	Average accounts receivable	$ 815	$ 632	$ 475
	Accounts receivable turnover	**9.5**	**8.4**	**7.3**
Compaq	Net sales	$18,109	$14,755	$10,866
	Average accounts receivable	$ 3,155	$ 2,714	$ 1,832
	Accounts receivable turnover	**5.7**	**5.4**	**5.9**

To show how we compute and use accounts receivable turnover, let's look at the numbers for Dell for 1994–1996 as reported in Exhibit 10.21. We compute Dell's 1996 turnover as ($ in millions):

$$\frac{\$7,759}{\$815} = 9.5$$

This means Dell's average accounts receivable balance is converted into cash 9.5 times in 1996. Also, Dell's turnover is continually improving over the period 1994–1996, and it is superior to Compaq. Is Dell's turnover too high? Because sales are growing dramatically over this same period, it doesn't appear Dell's turnover is too high. Instead, Dell's management seems to be doing an excellent job at managing receivables. This is especially apparent when compared to Compaq and most of its other competitors. Turnover for Dell's competitors is generally in the range of 6 to 7 over this same period.[12]

Judgment and Ethics

Family Physician

You are a family physician operating a small practice. Your practice has turned less profitable and you hire a health care analyst to examine your financials and to recommend solutions. The analyst's report highlights several problems including accounts receivable. It states ". . . *accounts receivable turnover is too low. Tighter credit policies are recommended along with discontinuing service to those most delayed in payments.*" How do you interpret these recommendations? What actions do you take?

Answer—p. 434

Flash back

15. A company needs cash and has substantial accounts receivable. What alternatives are available for getting cash from its accounts receivable prior to receiving payments from credit customers? Show the entry made for each alternative.

16. Compute **Mattel's** accounts receivable turnover for 1994 using the following information:

(In thousands)	1994	1993
Accounts receivable	762,024	580,313
Current assets	1,543,523	1,470,750
Net sales	3,205,025	2,704,448
Net income	255,832	117,208

Answers—p. 434

---

[12] As an approximation of *average days' sales uncollected* we can compute an estimate of how many days *(on average)* it takes to collect receivables as follows: 365 days ÷ accounts receivable turnover.

Summary

C1 Describe accounts receivable and how they occur and are recorded. Accounts receivable refer to amounts due from customers for credit sales. The subsidiary ledger lists the amounts owed by individual customers. Credit sales arise from at least two sources: (1) sales on credit and (2) credit card sales. Sales on credit refer to a company's granting credit directly to customers. Credit card sales involve use of a third party's issuing a credit card to customers.

C2 Describe a note receivable and the computation of its maturity date and interest. A note receivable is a written promise to pay a specified amount of money either on demand or at a definite future date. The maturity date of a note is the day the note (principal and interest) must be repaid. Interest rates are typically stated in annual terms. When a note's time to maturity is different than one year, the amount of interest on a note is computed by expressing time as a fraction of one year and multiplying the note's principal by this fraction and the annual interest rate.

C3 Explain how receivables can be converted to cash before maturity. There are three usual means to convert receivables to cash before maturity. First, a company can sell accounts receivable to a factor, who charges a factoring fee. Second, a company can borrow money by signing a note payable that is secured by pledging the accounts receivable. Third, notes receivable can be discounted at a bank, with or without recourse. The full disclosure principle requires companies to disclose the amount of receivables pledged and the contingent liability for notes discounted with recourse.

C4 Describe short-term investments in debt and equity securities. Short-term investments can include both debt and equity securities. *Debt securities* reflect a creditor relationship and include investments in notes, bonds, and certificates of deposit. Debt securities are issued by governments, companies, and individuals. *Equity securities* reflect an ownership relationship and include shares of stock issued by companies.

A1 Compute accounts receivable turnover and use it to analyze liquidity. Accounts receivable turnover is a measure of both the quality and liquidity of accounts receivable. Quality of receivables refers to likelihood of collection without loss. Experience shows the longer receivables are outstanding beyond their due date, the lower the likelihood of collection. Liquidity of receivables refers to speed of collection. The accounts receivable turnover measure indicates how often, on average, receivables are received and collected during the period. Accounts receivable turnover is computed as sales divided by average accounts receivable for the period.

P1 Apply the direct write-off and allowance methods to account for accounts receivable. The direct write-off method charges Bad Debts Expense when accounts are written off as uncollectible. This method is acceptable only when the amount of bad debts expense is immaterial. Under the allowance method, bad debts expense is recorded with an adjustment at the end of each accounting period debiting the Expense account and crediting the Allowance for Doubtful Accounts. The uncollectible accounts are later written off with a debit to the Allowance for Doubtful Accounts.

P2 Estimate uncollectibles using methods based on sales and accounts receivable. Uncollectibles are estimated by focusing on either *(a)* the income statement relation between bad debts expense and credit sales or *(b)* the balance sheet relation between accounts receivable and the Allowance for Doubtful Accounts. The first approach emphasizes the matching principle for the income statement. The second approach can include either a simple percent relation with accounts receivable or the aging of accounts receivable. It emphasizes realizable value of accounts receivable for the balance sheet.

P3 Record the receipt of a note receivable. A note is recorded at its principal amount by debiting the Notes Receivable account. The credit amount is to the asset, product, or service provided in return for the note.

P4 Record the honoring and dishonoring of a note and adjustments for interest on a note. When a note is honored, the payee debits the money received and credits both Notes Receivable and Interest Earned. Dishonored notes are credited to Notes Receivable and debited to Accounts Receivable (to the account of the maker in attempts to collect). The interest earned from holding a note is recorded for the amount of time the note was held in the accounting period.

P5 Record the sale of short-term investments. Short-term investments are recorded at cost, and any dividends or interest from these investments are recorded in their income statement accounts. For presentation in financial statements, short-term investments are classified as held-to-maturity securities, trading securities, or available-for-sale securities. Held-to-maturity securities are reported at cost on the balance sheet. Trading securities and available-for-sale securities are reported at their fair (market) values. Unrealized gains and losses on trading securities are reported in income. Unrealized gains and losses on available-for-sale securities are reported as a separate item in the equity section of the balance sheet. When short-term investments are sold, the difference between the net proceeds from the sale (sales price less brokerage fees) and the cost of the trading securities is recognized as a gain or a loss.

Guidance Answers to **You Make the Call**

Entrepreneur

Your analysis of allowing credit card sales should weigh the benefits against the costs. The primary benefit is the potential to increase sales by attracting customers who prefer the convenience of credit cards. The primary cost is the fee charged by the credit card company for providing this service to your store. Your analysis should therefore estimate the expected increase in sales dollars from allowing credit card sales and then subtract (1) the normal costs and expenses and (2) the credit card fees associated with this expected increase in sales dollars. If your analysis shows an increase in profit from allowing credit card sales, your store should probably allow them.

Labor Union Chief

Yes, this information is likely to impact your negotiations. The obvious question is why the company increased the allowance to such a large extent. This major increase in allowance means a substantial increase in bad debts expense *and* a decrease in earnings. Also, this change coming immediately prior to labor contract discussions raises concerns since it reduces the union's bargaining power for increased compensation. You want to ask management for supporting documentation justifying this increase. Also, you want data for two or three prior years, and similar data from competitors. These data should give you some sense of whether the change in the allowance for uncollectibles is justified.

Guidance Answer to **Judgment and Ethics**

Family Physician

The analyst's recommendations are twofold. First, the analyst is suggesting a more stringent screening of patients according to their credit standing. Second, the analyst suggests dropping those patients who are most overdue or delinquent in their payments. You are likely bothered by these suggestions. While they are probably financially wise recommendations, you are troubled by eliminating services to those less able to pay. One possible alternative is to follow the analyst's recommendations while at the same time implementing a care program directed at those patients less able to pay for services. This allows you to continue services to patients less able to pay, and lets you discontinue services to patients able but unwilling to pay for services.

Guidance Answers to

1. If cash is received as soon as copies of credit card sales receipts are deposited in the bank, the business debits Cash at the time of the sale. If the business does not receive payment until after it submits the receipts to the credit card company, it debits Accounts Receivable at the time of the sale.

2. The credit card expenses are usually *recorded* when the cash is received from the credit card company; however, they are *incurred* at the time of their related sales.

3. An adjusting entry must be made to satisfy the matching principle. The credit card expense must be reported in the same period as their sale.

4. Bad debts expense must be matched with the sales that gave rise to the accounts receivable. This requires that companies estimate bad debts before they learn which accounts are uncollectible.

5. Realizable value (also called net relizable value).

6. The estimated amount of bad debts expense cannot be credited to the Accounts Receivable account because the specific customer accounts that will prove uncollectible cannot be identified and removed from the subsidiary Accounts Receivable Ledger. If the controlling account were credited directly, its balance would not equal the sum of the subsidiary account balances.

7.

1999			
Dec. 31	Bad Debts Expense	5,702	
	Allowance for Doubtful Accounts .		5,702

8.

1999			
Jan. 10	Allowance for Doubtful Accounts	300	
	Accounts Receivable—Cool Jam .		300
Apr. 12	Accounts Receivable—Cool Jam	300	
	Allowance for Doubtful Accounts .		300
Apr. 12	Cash	300	
	Accounts Receivable—Cool Jam .		300

9.

1999			
Dec. 16	Notes Receivable	7,000	
	Sales		7,000
Dec. 31	Interest Receivable	35	
	Interest Earned		35
	($7,000 × 12% × 15/360)		

10.

2000			
Mar. 16	Accounts Receivable—Wiley	7,210	
	Interest Earned		175
	Interest Receivable		35
	Notes Receivable		7,000

11. Securities held-to-maturity are reported at cost.

12. Trading securities are reported at fair (market) value.

13. The equity section of the balance sheet (and in comprehensive income).

14. The income statement.

15. Alternatives are (1) selling their accounts receivable to a factor and (2) pledging accounts receivable as loan security. The entries to record these transactions take the following form:

(1) Cash	#	
Factoring Fee Expense	#	
Accounts Receivable		#
(2) Cash	#	
Notes Payable		#

16. Accounts receivable turnover =

$$\frac{3,205,025}{(762,024 + 580,313)/2} = 4.78 \text{ times}$$

Garden Company completed the following transactions during 1999:

May 8   Purchased 300 shares of Federal Express common stock as a short-term investment in a security available-for-sale. The cost of $40 per share plus $975 in broker's commissions was paid in cash.

July 14   Wrote off a $750 account receivable arising from a sale to Briggs Company several months ago. (Garden Company uses the allowance method.)

30   Garden Company received a $1,000, 3-month, 10% promissory note for a product sale to Sumrell Company.

Aug. 15   Accepted a $2,000 down payment and a $10,000 note receivable from a customer in exchange for an inventory item that normally sells for $12,000. The note is dated August 15, bears 12% interest, and matures in six months.

Sept. 2   Sold 100 shares of Federal Express stock at $47 per share and continued to hold the other 200 shares. The broker's commission on the sale is $225.

15   Received $9,850 in return for discounting without recourse the $10,000 note (dated August 15) at the local bank.

Oct. 2   Purchased 400 shares of McDonald's stock for $60 per share plus $1,600 in commissions. The stock is held as a short-term investment in a security available-for-sale.

Nov. 1   Made a $200 credit card sale with a 4% fee. The cash is received immediately from the credit card company.

5   Made a $500 credit card sale with a 5% fee. The payment from the credit card company is received on Nov. 7.

15   Received the full amount of $750 from Briggs Company that was previously written off on July 14. Record the bad debts recovery.

20   Sumrell Company refused to pay the note that was due to Garden Company on Oct. 30. Make the journal entry to charge the dishonored note plus accrued interest to Sumrell Company's accounts receivable.

Required

1. Prepare journal entries to record these transactions on the books of Garden Company.

2. Prepare an adjusting journal entry as of December 31, 1999, for the following item:

a. Bad debts expense is estimated by an aging of accounts receivable. The unadjusted balance of the Allowance for Doubtful Accounts account is a $1,000 debit, while the required balance is estimated to be a $20,400 credit.

b. Alternatively, assume that bad debts expense is estimated at year-end using a percentage of sales approach. As in (a), assume that the Allowance for Doubtful Accounts account has a $1,000 debit balance before adjustment. The company estimates bad debts to be 1% of credit sales of $2,000,000.

Planning the Solution

- Examine each item to determine which accounts are affected and record the journal entries.
- With respect to the year-end adjustment, record the bad debts expense.

Solution to Demonstration Problem

1.

May 8	Short-Term Investments	12,975	
	Cash		12,975
	Purchased 300 shares of Federal Express. Cost is (300 × $40) + $975.		
July 14	Allowance for Doubtful Accounts	750	
	Accounts Receivable—Briggs Company . .		750
	Wrote off an uncollectible account.		

July 30	Notes Receivable—Sumrell Company	1,000	
	Sales		1,000
	Sold merchandise in exchange for a 3-month, 10% note.		
Aug. 15	Cash	2,000	
	Notes Receivable	10,000	
	Sales		12,000
	Sold merchandise to customer for $2,000 cash and $10,000 note receivable.		
Sept. 2	Cash	4,475	
	Gain on Sale of Investment		150
	Short-Term Investments		4,325
	Sold 100 shares of Federal Express for $47 per share less a $225 commission. The original cost is ($12,975 × 100/300).		
Sept. 15	Cash	9,850	
	Loss on Discounting of Notes	150	
	Notes Receivable		10,000
	Discounted note receivable dated August 15.		
Oct. 2	Short-Term Investments	25,600	
	Cash		25,600
	Purchased 400 shares of McDonald's for $60 per share plus $1,600 in commissions.		
Nov. 1	Cash	192	
	Credit Card Expense	8	
	Sales		200
	To record credit card sale less a 4% credit card expense.		
Nov. 5	Accounts Receivable—Credit Card Company . .	500	
	Sales		500
	To record credit card sale.		
Nov. 7	Cash	475	
	Credit Card Expense	25	
	Accounts Receivable—Credit Card Company		500
	To record cash receipt less a 5% credit card expense.		
Nov. 15	Accounts Receivable—Briggs Company	750	
	Allowance for Doubtful Accounts		750
	To reinstate the account of Briggs Company previously written off.		
Nov. 15	Cash	750	
	Accounts Receivable—Briggs Company . .		750
	In full payment of account.		
Nov. 20	Accounts Receivable—Sumrell Company	1,025	
	Interest Earned		25
	Notes Receivable—Sumrell Company . . .		1,000
	To charge account of Sumrell Company for a dishonored note including interest of $1,000 × 10% × 3/12.		

2a.

Dec. 31	Bad Debts Expense	21,400	
	Allowance for Doubtful Accounts		21,400
	To adjust allowance account from $1,000 debit balance to $20,400 credit balance.		

b.   Alternate approach:

Dec. 31	Bad Debts Expense	20,000	
	Allowance for Doubtful Accounts		20,000
	To provide for bad debts as 1% x $2,000,000		
	in credit sales. (Note: disregard any existing		
	balance in the Allowance account when		
	making the entry using the income statement		
	approach.)		

(*Note to students:* Under the income statement approach which requires estimating bad debts as a percent of sales or net credit sales, the Allowance Account balance is not considered when making the adjusting entry. While this might seem arbitrary, it is not. The income statement approach estimates bad debts expense using the relation between bad debts expense and sales. These are both income statement accounts. The allowance account is a balance sheet account. It is therefore logical that its balance is considered when using the balance sheet approach.)

Glossary

Accounts receivable amounts due from customers for credit sales. (p. 406).

Accounts receivable turnover a measure of both the quality and liquidity of accounts receivable; it indicates how often, on average, receivables are received and collected during the period; computed by dividing credit sales (or net sales) by the average accounts receivable balance. (p. 431).

Aging accounts receivable a process of classifying accounts receivable in terms of how long they are past due for the purpose of estimating the amount of uncollectible accounts. (p. 417).

Allowance for Doubtful Accounts a contra asset account with a balance equal to the estimated amount of accounts receivable that will be uncollectible; also called the Allowance for Uncollectible Accounts. (p. 412).

Allowance method of accounting for bad debts an accounting procedure that (1) estimates and reports bad debts expense from credit sales during the period of the sales and (2) reports accounts receivable at the amount of cash proceeds that is expected from their collection (their estimated realizable value). (p. 412).

Available-for-sale securities investments in debt and equity securities that are not classified as trading securities or held-to-maturity securities. (p. 430).

Bad debts the accounts of customers who do not pay what they have promised to pay; the amount is an expense of selling on credit; also called *uncollectible accounts.* (p. 410).

Contingent liability an obligation to make a future payment if, and only if, an uncertain future event actually occurs. (p. 425).

Direct write-off method of accounting for bad debts a method of accounting for bad debts that records the loss from an uncollectible account receivable at the time it is determined to be uncollectible; no attempt is made to estimate uncollectible accounts or bad debts expense. (p. 411).

Dishonoring a note when a note's maker is unable or refuses to pay at maturity. (p. 423).

Full disclosure principle the accounting principle that requires financial statements (including the notes) to report all relevant information about the operations and financial position of the entity. (p. 426).

Held-to-maturity securities debt securities that the company has the intent and ability to hold until they mature. (p. 428).

Interest the charge for using (not paying) money until a later date. (p. 421).

Maker of a note one who signs a note and promises to pay it at maturity. (p. 421).

Matching principle requires expenses to be reported in the same accounting period as the sales they helped produce. (p. 412).

Materiality principle states that an amount may be ignored if its effect on the financial statements is unimportant to their users. (p. 412).

Maturity date of a note the date on which a note and any interest are due and payable. (p. 421).

Payee of a note the one to whom a promissory note is made payable. (p. 421).

Principal of a note the amount that the signer of a promissory note agrees to pay back when it matures, not including the interest. (p. 420).

Promissory note a written promise to pay a specified amount of money either on demand or at a definite future date. (p. 420).

Realizable value the expected proceeds from converting assets into cash. (p. 413).

Short-term investments current assets that serve a similar purpose to cash equivalents; generally mature between 3 and 12 months (or the operating cycle if longer) at which time management expects to convert them into cash; can be either debt or equity securities (also called *temporary investments*). (p. 427).

Trading securities investments in debt and equity securities that the company intends to actively trade for profit; frequent purchases and sales generally are made with the objective of generating profits on short-term changes in price. (p. 428).

Unrealized holding gain (loss) a gain (loss) not yet realized by an actual transaction or event such as a sale. (p. 428).

Questions

1. Under what conditions should investments be classified as current assets?

2. If a short-term investment in securities held for sale costs $6,780 and is sold for $7,500, how should the difference between the two amounts be recorded?

3. On a balance sheet, what valuation must be reported for short-term investments in trading securities?

4. How do businesses benefit from allowing their customers to use credit cards?

5. Explain why writing off a bad debt against the Allowance account does not reduce the estimated realizable value of a company's accounts receivable.

6. Why does the Bad Debts Expense account usually not have the same adjusted balance as the Allowance for Doubtful Accounts?

7. Why does the direct write-off method of accounting for bad debts usually fail to match revenues and expenses?

8. What is the essence of the accounting principle of materiality?

9. Why might a business prefer a note receivable to an account receivable?

10. What does it mean to sell a receivable without recourse?

11. Review the consolidated balance sheet for NIKE in Appendix A. What percent of accounts receivable as of May 31, 1997, has been set aside as an allowance for doubtful accounts? How does the percent compare to the prior year?

12. Review the consolidated balance sheet for Reebok in Appendix A. Does Reebok use the direct write-off method or allowance method to account for doubtful accounts? What is the realizable value of the accounts receivable as of December 31, 1996? What is another name for the Allowance for Doubtful Accounts?

13. America Online shows cash and cash equivalents of $118,421,000 and short-term investments of $10,712,000 on its consolidated balance sheet as of June 30, 1996 in Appendix A. Since both of these items are current assets, why are they reported separately?

14. Who are likely the major customers of CFS?

Quick Study

QS 10-1
Short-term equity investments

On April 18, Kimmell Industries made a short-term investment in 200 shares of Computer Links common stock. The intent is to actively manage these stocks. The purchase price was $42\frac{1}{2}$ and the broker's fee was $350. On June 30, Kimmell received $2 per share in dividends. Prepare the April 18 and June 30 journal entries.

QS 10-2
Credit card sales

Journalize the following transactions:

a. Sold $10,000 in merchandise on MasterCard credit cards. The sales receipts are immediately deposited in the business's bank account. MasterCard charges a 5% fee.

b. Sold $3,000 on miscellaneous credit cards. Cash will be received within 10 days and a 4% fee will be charged.

QS 10-3
Allowance method for bad debts

Foster Corporation uses the allowance method to account for uncollectibles. On October 31, they wrote off a $1,000 account of a customer, Gwen Rowe. On December 9, they received a $200 payment from Rowe.

a. Make the appropriate entry or entries for October 31.

b. Make the appropriate entry or entries for December 9.

QS 10-4
Percent of accounts receivable method

Duncan Company's year-end trial balance shows accounts receivable of $89,000, allowance for doubtful accounts of $500 (credit), and sales of $270,000. Uncollectibles are estimated to be 1.5% of outstanding accounts receivable.

a. Prepare the December 31 year-end adjustment for uncollectibles.

b. What amount would have been used in the year-end adjustment if the allowance account had a year-end debit balance of $200?

c. Assume the same facts, except that Duncan estimates uncollectibles as 1% of sales. What amount would be used in the adjustment?

On August 2, 2000 SLM Co. received a $5,500, 90-day, 12% note from customer Will Carr as payment on his account. Prepare journal entries for August 2 and the maturity date assuming the note is honored by Carr.

QS 10-5
Note receivable

P3, P4

Seaver Company's December 31 year-end trial balance shows an $8,000 balance in Notes Receivable. This balance is from one note dated December 1, with a period of 45 days and 9% interest. Prepare journal entries for December 31 and the maturity date assuming the note is honored.

QS 10-6
Note receivable

P3, P4

The following facts were extracted from the comparative balance sheets of Ernest Blue, P.C.:

	2000	1999
Accounts receivable	$152,900	$133,700
Net sales	754,200	810,600

Compute the accounts receivable turnover for 2000.

QS 10-7
Accounts receivable turnover

A1

Prepare general journal entries to record the following transactions involving the short-term investments of Morton Co., all of which occurred during 1999:

a. On February 15, paid $150,000 to purchase $150,000 of American General's 90-day short-term debt securities, which are dated February 15 and pay 10% interest.

b. On March 22, bought 700 shares of Royal Industries stock at $25\frac{1}{2}$ plus a $250 brokerage fee.

c. On May 16, received a check from American General in payment of the principal and 90 days' interest on the debt securities purchased in transaction *a*.

d. On July 30, paid $50,000 to purchase $50,000 of OMB Electronics' 8% debt securities, dated July 30, 1999, and due January 30, 2000.

e. On September 1, received a $0.50 per share cash dividend on the Royal Industries stock purchased in transaction *b*.

f. On October 8, sold 350 shares of Royal Industries stock for $32 per share, less a $175 brokerage fee.

g. On October 30, received a check from OMB Electronics for three months' interest on the debt securities purchased in transaction *d*.

Exercises
Exercise 10-1
Short-term investment transactions

C4, P5

Aston Company allows customers to use two credit cards in charging purchases. With the OmniCard, Aston receives an immediate credit when it deposits sales receipts in its checking account. OmniCard assesses a 4% service charge for credit card sales. The second credit card that Aston accepts is Colonial Bank Card. Aston sends its accumulated receipts to Colonial Bank on a weekly basis and is paid by Colonial approximately 10 days later. Colonial Bank charges 2.5% of sales for using its card. Prepare entries in journal form to record the following credit card transactions of Aston Company:

Apr. 6 Sold merchandise for $9,200, accepting the customers' OmniCards. At the end of the day, the OmniCard receipts were deposited in Aston's account at the bank.
     10 Sold merchandise for $310, accepting the customer's Colonial Bank Card.
     17 Mailed $5,480 of credit card receipts to Colonial Bank, requesting payment.
     28 Received Colonial Bank's check for the April 17 billing, less the normal service charge.

Exercise 10-2
Credit card sales

C1

Jenkins Co. recorded the following transactions during November 2000:

Nov. 3	Accounts Receivable—ABC Shop	4,417	
	Sales		4,417
8	Accounts Receivable—Colt Enterprises	1,250	
	Sales		1,250
11	Accounts Receivable—Red McKenzie	733	
	Sales		733

Exercise 10-3
Accounts receivable subsidiary ledger

C1

19	Sales Returns and Allowances	189	
	Accounts Receivable—Red McKenzie . . .		189
28	Accounts Receivable—ABC Shop	2,606	
	Sales		2,606

Required

1. Open a General Ledger having T-accounts for Accounts Receivable, Sales, and Sales Returns and Allowances. Also, open a subsidiary Accounts Receivable Ledger having a T-account for each customer. Post the preceding entries to the General Ledger accounts and the customer accounts.

2. List balances of the accounts in the subsidiary ledger (schedule of accounts receivable), total the balances, and compare the total with the balance of the Accounts Receivable controlling account.

Exercise 10-4
Allowance for doubtful accounts entries
P1, P2

At the end of its annual accounting period, Bali Company estimated its bad debts as one-half of 1% of its $875,000 of credit sales made during the year. On December 31, Bali made an addition to its Allowance for Doubtful Accounts equal to that amount. On the following February 1, management decided the $420 account of Catherine Hicks was uncollectible and wrote it off as a bad debt. Four months later, on June 5, Hicks unexpectedly paid the amount previously written off. Give the journal entries required to record these events.

Exercise 10-5
Percent of accounts receivable method
P1, P2

At the end of each year, Deutch Supply Co. uses the percent of accounts receivable approach to estimate bad debts. On December 31, 2000, it has outstanding accounts receivable of $53,000 and estimates that 4% will be uncollectible. Give the entry to record bad debts expense for year 2000 under the assumption that the Allowance for Doubtful Accounts has a *(a)* $915 credit balance before the adjustment and *(b)* $1,332 debit balance before the adjustment.

Exercise 10-6
Dishonoring a note
P4

Prepare journal entries to record the following transactions of Madison Company:

Mar. 21   Accepted a $3,100, six-month, 10% note dated today from Bradley Brooks in granting a time extension on his past-due account.

Sept. 21   Brooks dishonored his note when it was presented for payment.

Dec. 31   After exhausting all legal means of collection, Madison Company wrote off Brooks' account against the Allowance for Doubtful Accounts.

Exercise 10-7
Honoring a note
P4

Prepare journal entries to record these transactions for Verona Company:

Oct. 31   Accepted a $5,000, six-month, 6% note dated today from Leann Grimes in granting a time extension on her past-due account.

Dec. 31   Adjusted the books for the interest due on the Grimes note.

Apr. 30   Grimes honored her note when presented for payment.

Exercise 10-8
Selling and pledging accounts receivable
C3

On July 31, Konrad International had $125,900 of accounts receivable. Prepare journal entries to record the following August transactions. Also, prepare any footnotes to the August 31 financial statements that should be reported as a result of these transactions.

Aug.   2   Sold merchandise to customers on credit, $6,295.

7   Sold $18,000 of accounts receivable to Fidelity Bank. Fidelity charges a 1.5% fee.

15   Received payments from customers, $3,436.

25   Borrowed $10,000 from Fidelity Bank, pledging $14,000 of accounts receivable as security for the loan.

Exercise 10-9
Accounts receivable turnover
A1

The following information is from the financial statements of Whimsy Company:

	2001	2000	1999
Net sales	$305,000	$236,000	$288,000
Accounts receivable (December 31)	22,900	20,700	17,400

Compute Whimsy's accounts receivable turnover for 2000 and 2001. Compare the two results and give a possible explanation for any significant change.

Prepare journal entries for the following transactions of Barnett Company:

1999

Dec. 16   Accepted a $8,600, 60-day, 7% note dated this day in granting Carmel Karuthers a time extension on her past-due account.

   31   Made an adjusting entry to record the accrued interest on the Karuthers note.

   31   Closed the Interest Earned account.

2000

Feb. 14   Received Karuthers' payment for the principal and interest on the note dated December 16.

Mar. 2   Accepted a $4,000, 8%, 90-day note dated this day in granting a time extension on the past-due account of ATW Company.

   17   Accepted a $1,600, 30-day, 9% note dated this day in granting Leroy Johnson a time extension on his past-due account.

Apr. 16   Johnson dishonored his note when presented for payment.

May 1   Wrote off the Johnson account against Allowance for Doubtful Accounts.

June 10   Received ATW's payment for the principal and interest on the note dated March 2.

Exercise 10-10
Notes receivable
transactions and entries

Checkers Company had no short-term investments prior to 1999 but had the following transactions involving short-term investments in securities available-for-sale during 1999:

Mar. 16   Purchased 3,000 shares of Diamond Shamrock stock at $22\frac{1}{4}$ plus a $1,948 brokerage fee.

Apr. 1   Paid $100,000 to buy 90-day U.S. Treasury bills, $100,000 principal amount, 5%, dated April 1.

June 7   Purchased 1,800 shares of PepsiCo stock at $49\frac{1}{2}$ plus a $1,235 brokerage fee.

   20   Purchased 700 shares of Xerox stock at $15\frac{3}{4}$ plus a $466 brokerage fee.

July 3   Received a check for the principal and accrued interest on the U.S. Treasury bills that matured on June 30.

   15   Received a $0.95 per share cash dividend on the Diamond Shamrock stock.

   28   Sold 1,500 shares of Diamond Shamrock stock at 26 less a $912 brokerage fee.

Sept. 1   Received a $2.10 per share cash dividend on the PepsiCo shares.

Dec. 15   Received a $1.35 per share cash dividend on the remaining Diamond Shamrock stock owned.

   31   Received a $1.60 per share cash dividend on the PepsiCo shares.

Required

Prepare journal entries to record the preceding transactions.

Problems

Problem 10-1
Short-term investment
transactions and entries

Accessories Unlimited allows a few select customers to make purchases on credit. The other customers can use either of two credit cards. Express Bank deducts a 3% service charge for sales on its credit card but credits the checking accounts of its commercial customers immediately when credit card receipts are deposited. Accessories Unlimited deposits the Express Bank credit card receipts at the close of each business day.

   When customers use UniCharge credit cards, Accessories Unlimited accumulates the receipts for several days before submitting them to UniCharge for payment. UniCharge deducts a 2% service charge and usually pays within one week of being billed. Accessories Unlimited completed the following transactions during the month of May:

May 4   Sold merchandise on credit to Anne Bismarck for $565. (The terms of all credit sales are 2/15, n/30, and all sales are recorded at the gross price.)

    5   Sold merchandise for $5,934 to customers who used their Express Bank credit cards. Sold merchandise for $4,876 to customers who used their UniCharge cards.

    8   Sold merchandise for $3,213 to customers who used their UniCharge credit cards.

   10   The UniCharge card receipts accumulated since May 5 were submitted to the credit card company for payment.

   13   Wrote off the account of Mandy Duke against Allowance for Doubtful Accounts. The $329 balance in Duke's account stemmed from a credit sale in October of last year.

   17   Received the amount due from UniCharge.

   18   Received Bismarck's check paying for the purchase of May 4.

Required

Prepare journal entries to record the preceding transactions and events.

Problem 10-2
Sales on credit and credit
card sales

Problem 10-3
Estimating bad debts
P1, P2

On December 31, 2000, SysComm Corporation's records show the following results for the year:

Cash sales	$1,803,750
Credit sales	3,534,000

In addition, the unadjusted trial balance includes the following items:

Accounts receivable	$1,070,100 debit
Allowance for doubtful accounts	15,750 debit

Required

1. Prepare the adjusting entry needed in SysComm's books to recognize bad debts under each of the following independent assumptions:

   a. Bad debts are estimated to be 2% of credit sales.

   b. Bad debts are estimated to be 1% of total sales.

   c. Analysis suggests 5% of outstanding accounts receivable at year-end are uncollectible.

2. Show how Accounts Receivable and the Allowance for Doubtful Accounts appear on the December 31, 2000, balance sheet given the facts in requirement 1a.

3. Show how Accounts Receivable and the Allowance for Doubtful Accounts appear on the December 31, 2000, balance sheet given the facts in requirement 1c.

Check Figure Bad Debts
Expense (1a), $70,680 Dr.

Problem 10-4
Aging accounts receivable
P1, P2

Jewell Company had credit sales of $2.6 million in 1999. On December 31, 1999, the company's Allowance for Doubtful Accounts had a credit balance of $13,400. The accountant for Jewell has prepared a schedule of the December 31, 1999, accounts receivable by age and, on the basis of past experience, has estimated the percent of receivables in each age category that will become uncollectible. This information is summarized as follows:

December 31, 1999 Accounts Receivable	Age of Accounts Receivable	Expected Percent Uncollectible
$730,000	Not due (under 30 days)	1.25%
354,000	1 to 30 days past due	2.00
76,000	31 to 60 days past due	6.50
48,000	61 to 90 days past due	32.75
12,000	Over 90 days past due	68.00

Required

Preparation Component

1. Compute the amount in the December 31, 1999, balance sheet as the Allowance for Doubtful Accounts.

2. Prepare the journal entry to record bad debts expense for 1999.

Check Figure Bad Debts
Expense. $31,625 Dr.

Analysis Component

3. On June 30, 2000, Jewell Company concluded that a customer's $3,750 receivable (created in 1999) is uncollectible and that the account should be written off. What effect will this action have on Jewell's 2000 net income? Explain your answer.

Problem 10-5
Recording accounts
receivable transactions
and bad debts
adjustments
P1, P2

Harrell Industries began operations on January 1, 1999. During the next two years, the company completed a number of transactions involving sales on credit, accounts receivable collections, and bad debts. These transactions are summarized as follows:
1999

a. Sold merchandise on credit for $1,144,500, terms n/30.

b. Wrote off uncollectible accounts receivable in the amount of $17,270.

c. Received cash of $667,100 in payment of outstanding accounts receivable.

d. In adjusting the accounts on December 31, concluded that 1.5% of outstanding accounts receivable would become uncollectible.

2000

e. Sold merchandise on credit for $1,423,800, terms n/30.

f. Wrote off uncollectible accounts receivable in the amount of $26,880.

g. Received cash of $1,103,900 in payment of outstanding accounts receivable.

h. In adjusting the accounts on December 31, concluded that 1.5% of outstanding accounts receivable would become uncollectible.

Check Figure   Year 2000
Bad Debts Expense,
$31,275.30 Dr.

Required

Prepare journal entries to record Harrell's 1999 and 2000 summarized transactions and the adjustments to record bad debts expense at the end of each year.

The following transactions are from The Perry-Finch Company:

1999

Dec. 16   Accepted a $9,600, 60-day, 9% note dated this day in granting Hal Krueger a time extension on his past-due account.

   31   Made an adjusting entry to record the accrued interest on the Krueger note.

   31   Closed the Interest Earned account.

2000

Feb. 14   Received Krueger's payment for principal and interest on the note dated December 16.

Mar. 2   Accepted a $5,120, 10%, 90-day note dated this day in granting a time extension on the past-due account of ARC Company.

   17   Accepted a $1,600, 30-day, 9% note dated this day in granting Penny Bobek a time extension on her past-due account.

Apr. 16   Bobek dishonored her note when presented for payment.

   21   Discounted, with recourse, the ARC Company note at BancFirst at a cost of $50. The transaction was considered to be a loan.

June 2   Received notice from BancFirst that ARC Company defaulted on the note due May 31. Paid the bank the principal plus interest due on the note. (Hint: Create an account receivable for the maturity value of the note.)

July 16   Received payment from ARC Company for the maturity value of its dishonored note plus interest for 45 days beyond maturity at 10%.

Aug. 7   Accepted a $5,440, 90-day, 12% note dated this day in granting a time extension on the past-due account of Mertz & Ivy.

Sept. 3   Accepted a $2,080, 60-day, 10% note dated this day in granting Cecile Duval a time extension on her past-due account.

   18   Discounted, without recourse, the Duval note at BancFirst at a cost of $25.

Nov. 5   Received payment of principal plus interest from Mertz & Ivy for the note of August 7.

Dec. 1   Wrote off the Penny Bobek account against Allowance for Doubtful Accounts.

Problem 10-6
Analysis and journalizing
of notes receivable
transactions

P3, P4

Required

Preparation Component

Prepare journal entries to record Perry-Finch's transactions.

Analysis Component

What reporting is necessary when a business discounts notes receivable with recourse and these notes have not reached maturity by the end of the fiscal period? Explain the reason for this requirement and what accounting principle is being satisfied.

Franklin Security has relatively large idle cash balances and invests them in common stocks that it holds as available-for-sale securities. Following is a series of transactions and events relevant to the short-term investment activity of the company:

1999

Jan. 20   Purchased 900 shares of Johnson & Johnson at $18\frac{3}{4}$ plus a $590 commission.

Feb. 9   Purchased 2,200 shares of Sony Corp. at $46\frac{7}{8}$ plus a $2,578 commission.

Oct. 12   Purchased 500 shares of Mattel, Inc., at $55\frac{1}{2}$ plus an $832 commission.

Problem 10-7
Short-term investment
transactions and entries

C4, P5

2000
Apr. 15 Sold 900 shares of Johnson & Johnson at $21\frac{3}{4}$ less a $685 commission.
July   5 Sold 500 shares of Mattel at $49\frac{1}{8}$ less a $491 commission.
      22 Purchased 1,600 shares of Sara Lee Corp. at $36\frac{1}{4}$ plus a $1,740 commission.
Aug. 19 Purchased 1,800 shares of Eastman Kodak Company at 28 plus a $1,260 commission.

2001
Feb. 27 Purchased 3,400 shares of Microsoft Corp. at $23\frac{5}{8}$ plus a $1,606 commission.
Mar. 3 Sold 1,600 shares of Sara Lee at $31\frac{1}{4}$ less a $1,750 commission.
June 21 Sold 2,200 shares of Sony at 40 less a $2,640 commission.
      30 Purchased 1,200 shares of The Black & Decker Corp. at $47\frac{1}{2}$ plus a $1,995 commission.
Nov. 1 Sold 1,800 shares of Eastman Kodak at $42\frac{3}{4}$ less a $2,309 commission.

Required

Prepare journal entries to record the short-term investment activity for the years shown.

BEYOND THE NUMBERS

Reporting in Action
A1

Refer to the financial statements and related information for **NIKE** in Appendix A. Answer the following questions by analyzing information in its statements:

1. What is NIKE's total amount of cash and cash equivalents on May 31, 1997?
2. NIKE's most liquid assets include "cash and cash equivalents" and "accounts receivable." Express NIKE's most liquid assets as of May 31, 1997, as a percent of current liabilities. Do the same for May 31, 1996. Comment on the company's ability to satisfy current liabilities at the end of the fiscal year 1997 as compared to the end of fiscal year 1996.
3. What criteria did NIKE use to classify items as cash equivalents?
4. Compute NIKE's accounts receivable turnover as of May 31, 1997.

Swoosh Ahead

5. Obtain access to NIKE's annual report for fiscal years ending after May 31, 1997 at its web site **[www.nike.com]** or through the SEC's EDGAR database **[www.sec.gov].** Recompute 2 and 4 above and comment on any changes since May 31, 1997.

Comparative Analysis
A1, P2

Both **NIKE** and **Reebok** design, produce, market, and sell sports footwear and apparel. Key comparative figures (in millions) for these two organizations follow:

Key figures*	NIKE		Reebok	
	1997	1996	1996	1995
Allowance for doubtful accounts	$ 57	$ 43	$ 44	$ 46
Accounts receivable, net	1,754	1,346	591	507
Net sales	9,187	6,471	3,479	3,481

*NIKE figures are from its annual reports for fiscal years ended May 31, 1997 and 1996.
 Reebok figures are from its annual reports for fiscal years ended December 31, 1996 and 1995.

Required

1. Compute the accounts receivable turnover for NIKE as of May 31, 1997, and Reebok as of December 31, 1996.
2. How many days does it take each company, *on average,* to collect its receivables?
3. Which company is more efficient in collecting the accounts receivable?
4. Which company has allowed for a higher percent of uncollectible accounts receivable?

Ethics Challenge
P1, P2

Randy Meyer is the chief executive officer of a medium-size company in Wichita, Kansas. Several years ago Randy persuaded the board of directors of his company to base a percent of his compensation on the net income the company earns each year. Each December Randy estimates year-end financial figures in anticipation of the bonus he will receive. If the bonus is not as high as he would like he offers several accounting recommendations to his controller for year-end adjustments. One of his favorite recommendations is for the controller to reduce the estimate of doubtful accounts. Randy has used this technique with success for several years.

1. What effect does lowering the estimate for doubtful accounts have on the income statement and balance sheet of Randy's company?

2. Do you think Randy's recommendation to adjust the allowance for doubtful accounts is within his right as CEO or do you think this action is an ethics violation? Justify your response.

3. What type of internal control might be useful for this company in overseeing the CEO's recommendations for accounting changes?

As the accountant for Stephenson Distributing, you recently attended a sales managers' meeting devoted to a discussion of the company's credit policies. At the meeting, you reported that bad debts expense for the past year was estimated to be $59,000 and accounts receivable at the end of the year amounted to $1,750,000 less a $43,000 allowance for doubtful accounts. Sylvia Greco, one of the sales managers, expressed confusion over the fact that bad debts expense and the allowance for doubtful accounts were different amounts. You agreed to write a memorandum to her explaining why a difference in bad debts expense and the allowance for doubtful accounts is not unusual. The company estimates bad debts expense to be 2% of sales. Write the memorandum to Greco.

Communicating in Practice
P1, P2

Visit the Web site "How to Collect Debts" at **www.insiderreports.com/BIZRPRTS/B2524.htm.** If you are unable to connect to the Web site listed here, then as an alternate exercise search the Web for five good business tips on effective management of credit customers.

Taking It to the Net
P1

Required

1. Identify four procedures that should routinely be included in dealing with credit customers.
2. What are the author's views in the report ("How to Collect Debts") about phone calls, use of collection agencies, and use of humor in collection letters?
3. Identify the recommended content for a collection letter.

Each member of a team is to participate in estimating uncollectibles based on the aging schedule and estimated percents shown in Problem 10-4A. The division of labor is up to the team. Your goal is to complete this task as soon as possible. After estimating uncollectibles, check your estimate with the instructor. If the team's estimate is correct, the team should proceed using the other information in the problem to prepare the adjusting entry and the presentation of net realizable accounts receivable as it should be shown on the December 31, 1999 Balance Sheet. Your team is to discuss these requirements and ensure all team members concur with and understand the team's solution.

Teamwork in Action
P2

Most of us have seen television commercials that include a comment similar to the following: "Bring your **VISA** because we do not accept **American Express.**" Conduct your own research via interviews, phone calls, or the Internet to determine the reason why companies discriminate in their use of credit cards.

Hitting the Road
C1

Read the article "The Sherlock Holmes of Accounting" in the September 5, 1994 *Business Week* issue.

Business Week Activity
P1

Required

1. Who is the "Sherlock Holmes of Accounting"?
2. How does "Sherlock" decide which companies are investigated?
3. Do companies suffer any consequences if investigated by "Sherlock"?
4. What is a forensic accountant?
5. What criticisms does "Sherlock" make of Seitel with respect to their accounting?

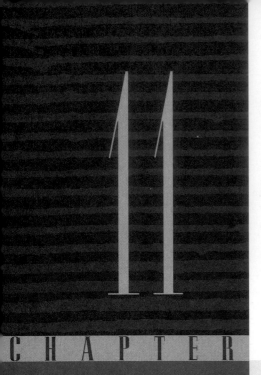

CHAPTER 11

Plant Assets, Natural Resources, and Intangible Assets

Chapter Outline

Bug Killer

ATLANTA, GA—Jenna Lee doesn't fancy herself a consumer crusader. "I'm no Ralph Nader," she says bluntly. But when the 19-year-old Atlanta student stumbled upon a serious glitch in the depreciation calculation in *PCaccount,* an accounting package for PCs, she complained to the program's developer, **Intech.** When the company rudely brushed her off, she got angry enough to take her story to the *Southern Chronicle*—a phone call that helped ignite a national firestorm of controversy.

Shortly after the *Chronicle*'s August 1 exposé, a "deeply distressed" Samuel Carter, Intech's chairman, confessed that his company's line of accounting software contained a "few bugs" in its depreciation and amortization schedules, producing inaccurate calculations. With customers already surly over problems with Intech's customer-service lines, Carter moved quickly. He offered to replace disks on request for Intech's 1 million customers.

The errors are no small problem—particularly to consumers who already used these depreciation programs to prepare their financial or tax reports. Management experts say Intech's aggressive response to the problems helped defuse a potential disaster. "The public loves a confessed sinner," notes Sherry Williams of Consumer Research. Along with the replacement offer, Carter penned an apology in a letter to the product's registered users: "We really let our customers down," he wrote. So far, Carter's willingness to publicly swallow a serving of humble pie appears to be working.

Not everyone is content, though. Even an apologetic telephone call from Intech's president and the offer of a replacement disk haven't managed to mollify Ms. Lee. "It shakes my faith in the whole industry," she says. "Next time, I'm doing my own depreciation calculations!"

Learning Objectives

Conceptual

C1 Describe plant assets and issues in accounting for them.

C2 Explain depreciation and the factors affecting its computation.

C3 Explain depreciation for partial years and changes in estimates.

C4 Identify cash flow impacts of long-term asset transactions.

Analytical

A1 Compare and analyze depreciation for different methods.

A2 Compute total asset turnover and apply it to analyze a company's use of assets.

Procedural

P1 Apply the cost principle to compute the cost of plant assets.

P2 Compute and record depreciation using the straight-line, units-of-production, and declining-balance methods.

P3 Distinguish between revenue and capital expenditures, and account for these expenditures.

P4 Account for asset disposal through discarding, selling, or exchanging an asset.

P5 Account for natural resource assets and their depletion.

P6 Account for intangible assets and their amortization.

CHAPTER PREVIEW

This chapter focuses on long-term assets used in the operation of a company. These assets can be grouped into plant assets, natural resource assets, and intangible assets. Plant assets are a major investment for most companies. They make up a large part of assets on the balance sheet and they yield depreciation, often one of the largest expenses on the income statement. They also affect the statement of cash flows when cash is spent to acquire plant assets or received from their sale. When companies acquire or build a plant asset, it is often referred to as a "capital expenditure." Capital expenditures are important news because they impact both the short- and long-term success of a company. Natural resource assets and intangible assets have similar impacts to plant assets. Because of this and other reasons it is important we understand accounting for each of these long-term assets. This chapter will describe the purchase and use of these assets. We also explain what distinguishes these assets from other types of assets, how to determine their cost, how to allocate their costs to periods benefiting from their use, and how we dispose of long-term assets. This knowledge can help us avoid blind reliance on software that might yield errors as evidenced in the opening article.

SECTION 1—PLANT ASSETS

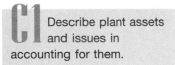

C1 Describe plant assets and issues in accounting for them.

Plant assets are tangible assets that are used in the operations of a company and have a useful life of more than one accounting period. Plant assets are also called *plant and equipment; property, plant, and equipment;* or *fixed assets.* For many companies, plant assets make up the single largest asset they own. Exhibit 11.1 shows plant assets as a percent of total assets for several companies. Not only do they make up a large percent of these companies' assets, but their dollar values are huge. **McDonald's** plant assets, for instance, are reported at more than $14 billion. Also, **Wal-Mart** and **Toys "Я" Us** report plant assets of more than $18 billion and $4 billion, respectively.

Plant assets are set apart from other assets by two important features. First, they are used in operations. This makes them different from, for instance, *inventory* that is held for sale and not used in operations. The distinctive feature here is use and not type of asset. A company that purchases a computer for purposes of reselling it reports it on the balance sheet as inventory. But if the same company purchases the same computer for

Exhibit 11.1

Plant Assets as Percent of Total Assets

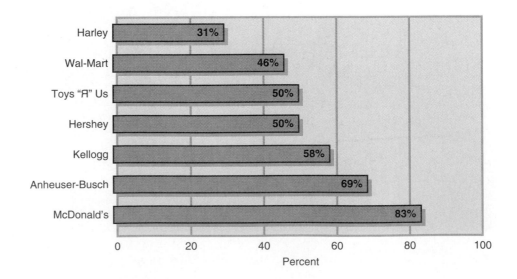

use in operations, it is a plant asset. Another example is *long-term investments* such as land held for future expansion. If this same land holds a factory used in operations, the land is part of plant assets. Still another example is *equipment* held for use in event of a breakdown or for use in peak periods of production. This equipment is reported in plant assets. But if this same equipment is removed from use and held for sale, it is not reported in plant assets.

The second important feature is plant assets have useful lives extending over more than one accounting period. This makes plant assets different from *current assets* such as *supplies* that are usually consumed in a short time after they are placed in use. The cost of current assets is assigned to a single period when they are used. Many *prepaid expenses* are distinguished from plant assets by the length of their useful lives.

The accounting for plant assets reflects these two important features. Since plant assets are used in operations, we try to match their costs against the revenues they generate. Also, since plant assets' useful lives extend over more than one period, our matching of costs and revenues must extend over several periods. We must measure plant assets (balance sheet focus) and allocate their cost to periods benefiting from their use (income statement focus).

Exhibit 11.2 shows the four main accounting issues with plant assets. They are:

1. Computing the costs of plant assets.
2. Allocating the costs of plant assets against revenues for the periods they benefit.
3. Accounting for expenditures such as repairs and improvements to plant assets.
4. Recording the disposal of plant assets.

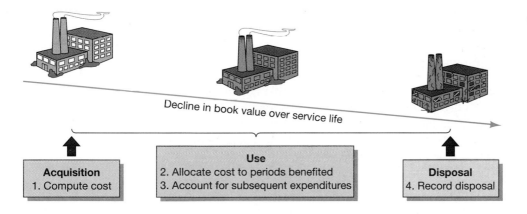

Exhibit 11.2

Issues in Accounting for Plant Assets

This chapter focuses on the decisions and factors surrounding these four important issues, and their accounting.

Cost of Plant Assets

P1 Apply the cost principle to compute the cost of plant assets.

Plant assets are recorded at cost when purchased. This is consistent with the *cost principle.* **Cost** includes all normal and reasonable expenditures necessary to get the asset in place and ready for its intended use. The cost of a factory machine, for instance, includes its invoice price less any cash discount for early payment, plus freight, unpacking, and assembling costs. The cost of a plant asset also includes the necessary costs of installing and testing a machine before placing it in use. Examples are the costs of building a base or foundation for a machine, of providing electrical hook-ups, and of adjusting the machine before using it in operations.

An expenditure must be normal, reasonable, and necessary in preparing an asset for its intended use for it to be charged to and reported as part of the cost of a plant asset. If a machine is damaged during unpacking, the repairs are not added to its cost. Instead, they are charged to an expense account. Also, a traffic fine paid for moving heavy machinery on city streets without a proper permit is not part of the machinery's cost. But payment for a proper permit is included in the cost of machinery. Charges in addition to the purchase price are sometimes incurred to modify or customize a new plant asset. These charges are added to the asset's cost. We explain how to determine the cost of plant assets in the remainder of this section for each of the four major classes of plant assets.

Land

When land is purchased for a building site, its cost includes the total amount paid for the land including any real estate commissions. Its cost also includes fees for insuring the title, legal fees, and any accrued property taxes paid by the purchaser. Payments for surveying, clearing, grading, draining, and landscaping also are included in the cost of land. Other costs of land include assessments by the local government, whether incurred at the time of purchase or later, for items such as roadways, sewers, and sidewalks. These assessments are included because they permanently add to the land's value.

Land purchased as a building site sometimes includes a building that must be removed. In such cases, the total purchase price is charged to the Land account. Also, the cost of removing the building, less any amounts recovered through sale of salvaged materials, is added to the Land account. To illustrate, assume The GAP bought land for a retail store for cash of $167,000. This land contains an old service garage that is removed

Exhibit 11.3

Computing Cost of Land

Net cash price of land	$167,000
Net cost of garage removal	13,000
Closing costs	10,000
Cost of land	**$190,000**

at a net cost of $13,000 ($15,000 in costs less $2,000 proceeds from salvaged materials). Additional closing costs totaled $10,000, consisting of brokerage fees ($8,000), legal fees ($1,500), and title costs ($500). The cost of this land to The GAP is $190,000 and is computed as shown in Exhibit 11.3.

Land Improvements

Because land has an unlimited life and is not consumed when it is used, it is not subject to depreciation. But **land improvements** such as parking lot surfaces, driveways, fences, and lighting systems have limited useful lives. While these costs increase the usefulness of the land, they are charged to a separate Land Improvement account so their costs can be allocated to the periods they benefit.

Buildings

A Building account is charged for the costs of purchasing or constructing a building when it is used in operations. When purchased, the costs of a building usually include its purchase price, brokerage fees, taxes, title fees, and attorney costs. Its costs also include all expenditures to make it ready for its intended use. This includes any necessary repairs or renovations to prepare the building for use such as wiring, lighting, flooring, and wall coverings.

When a building, or any plant asset, is constructed by a company for its own use, its cost includes materials and labor plus a reasonable amount of indirect overhead cost. Overhead includes the costs of heat, lighting, power, and depreciation on machinery used to construct the asset. Cost of construction also includes design fees, building permits, and insurance during construction. But insurance costs for coverage *after* the asset is placed in use are an operating expense. **Wendy's** recently reported constructing plant assets for its own use. They disclosed the following building plans:

> . . . to open or have under construction about 400 new Wendy's restaurants . . . Capital expenditures could total as much as $170 million.

Machinery and Equipment

The cost of machinery and equipment consists of all costs normal and necessary to purchase them and prepare them for their intended use. It includes the purchase price, taxes, transportation charges, insurance while in transit, and the installing, assembling, and testing of machinery and equipment. **Sony,** for instance, disclosed in a recent annual report that:

capital expenditures [much of this machinery and equipment] during the year under review increased 27.9% to . . . $2,817 million . . . Sony intends to further increase its capital expenditures.

Lump-Sum Asset Purchase

Plant assets sometimes are purchased in a group with a single transaction for a lump-sum price. This transaction is called a *lump-sum purchase,* also called *group,* or *basket, purchase.* When this occurs, we allocate the cost of the purchase among the different types of assets acquired based on their *relative market values.* Their market values can be estimated by appraisal or by using the tax-assessed valuations of the assets. To illustrate, Cola Company paid $90,000 cash to acquire land appraised at $30,000, land improvements appraised at $10,000, and a building appraised at $60,000. The $90,000 cost was allocated on the basis of appraised values as shown in Exhibit 11.4.

	Appraised Value	Percent of Total	Apportioned Cost
Land	$ 30,000	30% ($30,000/$100,000)	$27,000 ($90,000 × 30%)
Land improvements	10,000	10 ($10,000/$100,000)	9,000 ($90,000 × 10%)
Building	60,000	60 ($60,000/$100,000)	54,000 ($90,000 × 60%)
Totals	$100,000	100%	$90,000

Exhibit 11.4

Computing Costs in a Lump-Sum Purchase

Flash *back*

1. Identify the asset category for each of the following: *(a)* office supplies, *(b)* office equipment, *(c)* merchandise, *(d)* land held for future expansion, and *(e)* trucks used in operations.

2. Identify the account charged for each of the following expenditures: *(a)* purchase price of a vacant lot to be used in operations and *(b)* cost of paving that vacant lot.

3. What amount is recorded as the cost of a new machine given the following items related to its purchase: gross purchase price, $700,000; sales tax, $49,000; purchase discount taken, $21,000; freight to move machine to plant—terms FOB shipping point, $3,500; assembly costs, $3,000; cost of foundation for machine, $2,500; cost of spare parts used in maintaining the machine, $4,200?

Answers—p. 478

Depreciation

We explained in the prior section how plant assets are tangible assets purchased for use in operations for more than one period. It is helpful to think of a plant asset as an amount of "usefulness" contributing to the operations of a company throughout the asset's useful life. Because the lives of all plant assets other than land are limited, the amount of usefulness expires as an asset is used. This expiration of a plant asset's amount of usefulness is called *depreciation*. **Depreciation** is the process of allocating the cost of a plant asset to expense in the accounting periods benefiting from its use.

When a company buys a delivery truck for use as a plant asset, for instance, it acquires an amount of usefulness in the sense that it obtains a quantity of transportation. The total cost of this transportation is the cost of the truck less the expected proceeds to be received when the truck is sold or traded in at the end of its useful life. This net cost is allocated to the accounting periods that benefit from the truck's use. This allocation of the truck's cost is depreciation.

Note that depreciation doesn't measure the decline in the truck's market value each period. Nor does it measure the physical deterioration of the truck. Depreciation is a process of allocating a plant asset's cost to expense over its useful life, nothing more. Because depreciation reflects the cost of using a plant asset, we do not begin recording depreciation charges until the asset is actually put into use providing services or producing products. This section describes the factors we need to consider in computing depreciation, the depreciation methods used, revisions in depreciation, and depreciation for partial periods.

Factors in Computing Depreciation

Three factors are relevant in determining depreciation: (1) cost, (2) salvage value, and (3) useful life.

Cost

The cost of a plant asset consists of all necessary and reasonable expenditures to acquire it and to prepare the asset for its intended use. We described the computation of cost earlier in this chapter.

Salvage Value

The total amount of depreciation to be charged off over an asset's benefit period equals the asset's cost minus its estimated salvage value. **Salvage value,** also called *residual value* or *scrap value*, is an estimate of the asset's value at the end of its benefit period. This is often viewed as the amount we expect to receive from selling the asset at the end of its benefit period. If we expect an asset to be traded in on a new asset, its salvage value is the expected trade-in value.

Useful (Service) Life

The **useful life** of a plant asset is the length of time it is productively used in a company's operations. Useful life, also called **service life,** may not be as long as the asset's total productive life. As an example, the productive life of a computer is often four to eight years or more. Yet some companies trade in old computers for new ones every two years. In this case, these computers have a two-year useful life. This means the costs of these computers (less their expected trade-in value) are charged to depreciation expense over a two-year period.

Several variables often make the useful life of a plant asset hard to predict. A major variable is the wear and tear from use in operations. But two other variables, inadequacy and obsolescence, also demand consideration. When a company grows more rapidly than expected, its assets sometimes don't meet the company's productive demands. **Inadequacy** refers to the condition where the capacity of a company's plant assets is too small to meet the company's productive demands. Obsolescence, like inadequacy, is hard to predict because the timing of new inventions and improvements normally can't be predicted. **Obsolescence** refers to a condition where, because of new inventions and improvements, a plant asset is no longer useful in producing goods or services with a competitive advantage. A company usually disposes of an obsolete asset before it wears out.

A company is often able to better predict the useful life of a new asset based on its past experience with a similar asset. When it has no experience with a type of asset, a company relies on the experience of others or on engineering studies and judgment. In note 4 of its annual report, **Coca-Cola Bottling** reported the following useful lives:

The principal categories and estimated useful lives of property, plant and equipment were as follows:

Buildings	10–50 years
Machinery and equipment	5–20 years
Transportation equipment	4–10 years
Furniture and fixtures	7–10 years
Vending equipment	6–13 years
Computer equipment and other	3–5 years

Life Expectancy
The life expectancy of plant assets is often in the eye of the beholder. Take **Converse** and **Stride Rite,** for instance. Both compete in the athletic shoe market, yet their buildings' life expectancies are quite different. Converse depreciates buildings over 5 to 10 years, but Stride Rite depreciates their buildings over 12 to 45 years. Such differences can dramatically impact financial statement numbers. [Source: 10K Reports.]

Did You Know?

Depreciation Methods

There are many *depreciation methods* for allocating a plant asset's cost over the accounting periods in its useful life. The most frequently used method of depreciation is the straight-line method. Another common depreciation method is the units-of-production method. We explain both of these methods in this section. This section also describes accelerated depreciation methods, with an emphasis on the declining-balance method.

The computations in this section use information from an athletic shoe manufacturer. In particular, we look at a machine used for inspecting athletic shoes before packaging. This machine is used by manufacturers such as **Converse, Reebok, Adidas,** and **L.A.Gear.** Data for depreciation of this machine are shown in Exhibit 11.5.

Cost	$10,000
Salvage value	1,000
Depreciable cost	$ 9,000
Useful life:	
Accounting periods	5 years
Units inspected	36,000 shoes

P2 Compute and record depreciation using the straight-line, units-of-production, and declining-balance methods.

Exhibit 11.5

Data for Athletic Shoe-Inspecting Machine

Straight-Line Method

Straight-line depreciation charges the same amount to expense for each period of the asset's useful life. A two-step process is used to compute expense. We first compute the *depreciable cost* over the asset's life; this amount is also called the *cost to be depreciated.* It is computed by subtracting the asset's salvage value from its total cost. Second, depreciable cost is divided by the number of accounting periods in the asset's useful life.

The formula and computation for straight-line depreciation of the inspection equipment described above are shown in Exhibit 11.6.

$$\frac{\text{Cost} - \text{Salvage value}}{\text{Useful life in years}} = \frac{\$10,000 - \$1,000}{5 \text{ years}} = \$1,800 \text{ per year}$$

Exhibit 11.6

Straight-Line Depreciation Formula

If this equipment is purchased on December 31, 1998, and used throughout its predicted useful life of five years, the straight-line method allocates an equal amount of depreciation to each of the years 1999 through 2003. We make the following adjusting entry at the end of each of these five years to record straight-line depreciation of this equipment:

Assets = Liabilities + Equity
−1,800   −1,800

Dec. 31	Depreciation Expense	1,800	
	Accumulated Depreciation, Equipment . . .		1,800
	To record annual depreciation over its 5-year useful life.		

The $1,800 Depreciation Expense appears on the income statement among operating expenses. This entry uses the common practice of crediting Accumulated Depreciation, a contra asset account to the Equipment account in the balance sheet.

The graph on the left in Exhibit 11.7 shows that the $1,800 per year expense amount is reported in each of these five years. The graph on the right shows the amounts reported on each of the six December 31 balance sheets while the company owns the asset.

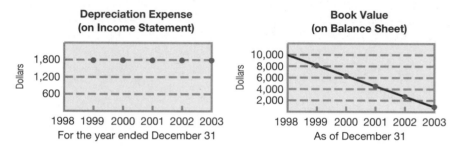

Exhibit 11.7

Financial Statement Effects of Straight-Line Depreciation

The net balance sheet amount is the asset's **book value** for each of those years and is computed as the asset's original cost less its accumulated depreciation. At the end of year two, its book value is $6,400 and is reported in the balance sheet as:

| Equipment . . . . | $10,000 | |
| Less accumulated depreciation . . . . | 3,600 | $6,400 |

The book value declines by $1,800 of depreciation each year. From the graphs we can see why this method is called straight line.

The *straight-line depreciation rate* is computed as 100% divided by the number of periods in the asset's useful life. In the case of our inspection machine, this rate is 20% (100% ÷ 5 years). We use this rate and other information on this machine to compute the machine's *straight-line depreciation schedule* shown in Exhibit 11.8.

Exhibit 11.8

Straight-Line Depreciation Schedule

| | Depreciation for the Period | | | End of Period | |
Period	Depreciable Cost*	Depreciation Rate	Depreciation Expense	Accumulated Depreciation	Book Value**
1998	—	—	—	—	$10,000
1999	$9,000	20%	$1,800	$1,800	8,200
2000	9,000	20	1,800	3,600	6,400
2001	9,000	20	1,800	5,400	4,600
2002	9,000	20	1,800	7,200	2,800
2003	9,000	20	1,800	9,000	1,000

*$10,000 − $1,000.
**Book value is cost minus accumulated depreciation.

Note three items in this schedule. First, depreciation expense is the same each period. Second, accumulated depreciation is the sum of current and prior periods' depreciation expense. Third, book value declines each period until it equals salvage value at the end of its useful life.

Straight line is by far the most frequently applied depreciation method. **Anheuser-Busch,** for instance, discloses its depreciation method in its annual report as follows:

> Depreciation is provided on the straight-line method over the estimated useful lives of the assets.

Units-of-Production Method

While many companies use straight-line depreciation, other methods are common in certain industries. The main purpose of recording depreciation is to provide relevant information about the cost of consuming an asset's usefulness. This means that each accounting period in which an asset is used is charged with a share of its cost. The straight-line method charges an equal share to each period. If plant assets are used about the same amount in each accounting period, this method produces a reasonable matching of expenses with revenues. Yet the use of some plant assets varies greatly from one accounting period to the next. A builder, for instance, may use a piece of construction equipment for a month and then not use it again for several months.

When use of equipment varies from period to period, the units-of-production depreciation method can provide a better matching of expenses with revenues than straight-line depreciation. **Units-of-production depreciation** charges a varying amount to expense for each period of an asset's useful life depending on its usage.

A two-step process is used to compute units-of-production depreciation. We first compute the *depreciation per unit.* It is computed by subtracting the asset's salvage value from its total cost and then dividing by the total number of units expected to be produced during its useful life. Units of production can be expressed in units of product or in any other unit of measure such as hours used or miles driven. This gives us the amount of depreciation per unit of service provided by the asset. The second step is to compute depreciation expense for the period by multiplying the units used in the period by the depreciation per unit.

The formula and computation for units-of-production depreciation for the testing machine described above are shown in Exhibit 11.9 (we expect 7,000 shoes inspected in its first year).

Exhibit 11.9

Units-of-Production
Depreciation Formula

Step 1:

$$\text{Depreciation per unit} = \frac{\text{Cost} - \text{Salvage value}}{\text{Total units of production}} = \frac{\$10,000 - \$1,000}{36,000 \text{ units}} = \$0.25 \text{ per shoe}$$

Step 2:

Depreciation expense = Depreciation per unit × Units used in period

$$\$0.25 \text{ per shoe} \quad \times \quad 7,000 \text{ shoes} \quad = \$1,750$$

Using the production estimates for the machine, we compute the *units-of-production depreciation schedule* shown in Exhibit 11.10. If the machine inspects 7,000 shoes in its first year, depreciation for that first year is $1,750 (7,000 shoes at $0.25 per shoe). If the machine inspects 8,000 shoes in the second year, depreciation for the second year is 8,000 shoes times $0.25 per shoe, or $2,000.

Exhibit 11.10

Units-of-Production
Depreciation Schedule

| | Depreciation for the Period | | | End of Period | |
Period	Number of Units	Depreciation per Unit	Depreciation Expense	Accumulated Depreciation	Book Value
1998	—	—	—	—	$10,000
1999	7,000	$0.25	$1,750	$1,750	8,250
2000	8,000	0.25	2,000	3,750	6,250
2001	9,000	0.25	2,250	6,000	4,000
2002	7,000	0.25	1,750	7,750	2,250
2003	5,000	0.25	1,250	9,000	1,000

Notice that depreciation expense depends on unit output, that accumulated depreciation is the sum of current and prior periods' depreciation expense, and book value declines each period until it equals salvage value at the end of the asset's useful life.

The units-of-production depreciation method is not as frequently applied as straight line. **Boise Cascade,** for instance, is one company using it and states in its annual report:

> Substantially all of the Company's paper and wood products manufacturing facilities determine depreciation by the units-of-production method.

Declining-Balance Method

An **accelerated depreciation method** yields larger depreciation expenses in the early years of an asset's life and smaller charges in later years. While there are several accelerated methods used in financial reporting, the most common is the declining-balance method. The **declining-balance method** of depreciation uses a depreciation rate of up to twice the straight-line rate and applies it to the asset's beginning-of-period book value. Because book value *declines* each period, the amount of depreciation also declines each period.

A common depreciation rate is twice the straight-line rate. This method is called the *double-declining-balance* method. The double-declining-balance method is applied as follows: (1) compute the asset's straight-line depreciation rate; (2) double it; and (3) compute depreciation expense by applying this rate to the asset's beginning-of-period book value. Salvage value is *not* used in these computations.

Let's return to the athletic shoe-testing machine and apply the double-declining-balance method to compute its depreciation expense. Exhibit 11.11 shows this formula and the first year computation for the machine. The three-step process is: (1) divide 100% by five years to determine the straight-line annual depreciation rate of 20% per year, (2) double this 20% rate to get a declining-balance rate of 40% per year, and (3) compute annual depreciation expense as the rate multiplied by the beginning period book value (see Exhibit 11.11).

Exhibit 11.11

Double-Declining-Balance
Depreciation Formula

Step 1:

Straight-line rate = 100% ÷ Useful life = 100% ÷ 5 years = 20%

Step 2:

Double-declining-balance rate = 2 × Straight-line rate = 2 × 20% = 40%

Step 3:

Depreciation expense = Double-declining-balance rate × Beginning period book value

40% × $10,000 = $4,000

The *double-declining-balance depreciation schedule* is shown in Exhibit 11.12. The schedule follows the formula except in year 2003, when depreciation expense is $296. This is not equal to 40% × $1,296, or $518.40. The $296 is computed by subtracting the $1,000 salvage value from the $1,296 book value at the beginning of the fifth year. This is done because an asset is never depreciated below its salvage value. If we had used the $518.40 for depreciation expense in 2003, then ending book value would equal $777.60, which is less than the $1,000 salvage value.

	Depreciation for the Period			End of Period	
Period	Beginning of Period Book Value	Depreciation Rate	Depreciation Expense	Accumulated Depreciation	Book Value
1998	—	—	—	—	$10,000
1999	$10,000*	40%	$4,000	$4,000	6,000
2000	6,000	40	2,400	6,400	3,600
2001	3,600	40	1,440	7,840	2,160
2002	2,160	40	864	8,704	1,296
2003	1,296	40	296*	9,000	**1,000**

Exhibit 11.12

Double-Declining-Balance Depreciation Schedule

*Year 2003 depreciation is $1,296 − $1,000 = $296. This is because book value can't be less than salvage value.

Comparing Depreciation Methods

Exhibit 11.13 shows depreciation expense for the athletic shoe-inspecting machine under each of the three depreciation methods.

A1 Compare and analyze depreciation for different methods.

Period	Straight-Line	Units-of-Production	Double-Declining-Balance
1999	$1,800	$1,750	$4,000
2000	1,800	2,000	2,400
2001	1,800	2,250	1,440
2002	1,800	1,750	864
2003	1,800	1,250	296
	$9,000	$9,000	$9,000

Exhibit 11.13

Depreciation Methods Compared

While the amount of depreciation expense per period is different for different methods, total depreciation expense is the same for the machine's useful life. Each method starts with a total cost of $10,000 and ends with a salvage value of $1,000. The difference is the pattern in depreciation expense over the useful life. The book value of the asset when using straight line is always greater than book value from using double-declining-balance, except at the beginning and end of the asset's useful life. Also, the straight-line method yields a steady pattern of depreciation expense, while the units-of-production does not because it depends on the number of units produced. But both of these methods are acceptable as they allocate cost in a systematic and rational manner.[1]

---

[1] See FASB, *Statement of Financial Accounting Concepts No. 6*, "Elements of Financial Statements of Business Enterprises" (Norwalk, CT, 1985), par. 149.

Trends in Depreciation

A recent survey suggests 80% of companies use straight-line depreciation for their plant assets, 7% use units-of-production, and 4% use declining balance. Another 8% of companies used an unspecified accelerated method, and probably most of these were declining balance. Accelerated depreciation is the preferred method of most companies for income tax reporting. [Source: *Accounting Trends & Techniques*.]

Used with permission from the American Institute of Certified Public Accountants, Inc.

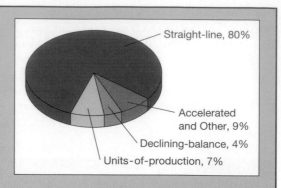

Depreciation for Tax Reporting

The records a company keeps for financial accounting purposes are usually different from the records it keeps for tax accounting purposes. Financial accounting aims to report useful information on financial performance and position, whereas tax accounting reflects government objectives in raising revenues. Differences between these two accounting systems are normal and expected. Depreciation is a common example.

Many companies use accelerated depreciation in computing taxable income. This reduces taxable income with higher depreciation expense in the early years of an asset's life. But taxable income is higher in the later years. A company's goal here is to postpone its tax payments. This means a company can use these resources now to earn additional profit before payment is due.

The United States federal income tax law has rules for depreciating assets. These rules are called the **Modified Accelerated Cost Recovery System (MACRS).** MACRS allows straight-line depreciation for some assets, but it requires accelerated depreciation for most kinds of assets. MACRS separates depreciable assets into different classes and defines the depreciable life and rate for each class. While MACRS is required for tax reporting, MACRS is not acceptable for financial reporting. This mainly is because it allocates costs over an arbitrary period often less than the asset's useful life.

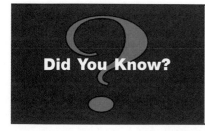

Depreciation Tech

Computer technology greatly simplifies depreciation computations and revisions. There are many inexpensive, off-the-shelf software packages and business calculators that allow a user to choose from a variety of depreciation methods for each asset entered. Detailed depreciation schedules for both financial reporting and income tax reporting are quickly and accurately generated.

Partial Year Depreciation

C3 Explain depreciation for partial years and changes in estimates.

Plant assets are purchased and disposed of at various times during a period. When an asset is purchased (or disposed of) at a time other than the beginning or end of an accounting period, depreciation is recorded for part of a year. This is so the year of purchase or the year of disposal is charged with its share of the asset's depreciation.

To illustrate, let's return to the athletic shoe-inspecting machine. Assume this machine is purchased and placed in service on October 8, 1999, and the annual accounting period ends on December 31. This machine costs $10,000, has a useful life of five years, and a salvage value of $1,000. Because this machine is purchased and used for nearly three months in 1999, the calendar year income statement should report depreciation expense on the machine for part of the year. The amount of depreciation reported usually is based on the assumption that an asset is purchased on the first day of the month nearest the actual date of purchase. In this case, since the purchase occurred on October 8, we assume an October 1 purchase date. This means three months' depreciation is recorded in 1999. If the purchase occurred anytime between October 16 through November 15, depreciation is computed as if the purchase is on November 1. Using straight-line depreciation, we compute three months' depreciation of $450 as follows:

$$\frac{\$10,000 - \$1,000}{5 \text{ years}} \times \frac{3}{12} = \$450$$

A similar computation is necessary when disposal of an asset occurs during a year. For example, let's suppose the machine described above is sold on June 24, 2004. Depreciation is recorded for the period January 1 through June 24 when it is disposed of. This partial year's depreciation, computed to the nearest whole month, is:

$$\frac{\$10,000 - \$1,000}{5 \text{ years}} \times \frac{6}{12} = \$900$$

Revising Depreciation Rates

Because depreciation is based on predictions of salvage value and useful life, depreciation expense is an estimate. During the useful life of an asset, new information may indicate the original predictions are inaccurate. If our estimate of an asset's useful life and/or salvage value changes, what should we do? The answer is to use the new estimate to compute depreciation for current and future periods. This means we revise depreciation expense computation by spreading the cost still to be depreciated over the revised useful life remaining. This approach is used for all depreciation methods.

Let's return to our athletic shoe-inspecting machine using straight-line depreciation. At the beginning of this asset's third year, its book value is $6,400, computed as:

Cost	$10,000
Less two years' accumulated depreciation	3,600
Book value	$ 6,400

At the beginning of its third year, the predicted number of years remaining in its useful life changes from three to four years *and* its estimate of salvage value changes from $1,000 to $400. Depreciation for each of the machine's four remaining years is computed as shown in Exhibit 11.14.

$$\frac{\text{Book value} - \text{Revised salvage value}}{\text{Revised remaining useful life}} = \frac{\$6,400 - \$400}{4 \text{ years}} = \$1,500 \text{ per year}$$

Exhibit 11.14

Computing Revised Depreciation Rates

This means $1,500 of depreciation expense is recorded for the machine at the end of the third through sixth years of its remaining useful life.

Since this asset was depreciated at the rate of $1,800 per year for the first two years, it is tempting to conclude that depreciation expense was overstated in the first two years. But these expenses reflected the best information available at that time. We don't go back and restate past years' financial statements in light of new information. Instead we adjust the current and future periods' statements to reflect this new information.

Revising an estimate of the useful life or salvage value of a plant asset is referred to as a **change in an accounting estimate.** A change in an accounting estimate results "from new information or subsequent developments and accordingly from better insight or improved judgment."[2] A change in an accounting estimate is reflected in future financial statements, and not in prior statements.

Flash back

4. On January 1, 1999, a company pays $77,000 to purchase office furniture with a zero salvage value. The furniture's useful life is somewhere between 7 and 10 years. What is the 1999 straight-line depreciation on the furniture using a (a) 7-year useful life and (b) 10-year useful life?

Answer—p. 478

Reporting Depreciation on Assets

Both the cost and accumulated depreciation of plant assets are reported on the balance sheet. **Motorola,** for instance, reports the following in its balance sheet:

($ in millions)	1996	1995
Property, plant, and equipment:		
Land	$ 261	$ 201
Buildings	5,362	4,754
Machinery	13,975	12,511
	$19,598	$17,466
Less accumulated depreciation	(9,830)	(8,110)
Total	$ 9,768	$ 9,356

Many companies also show plant assets on one line with the net amount of cost less accumulated depreciation. When this is done, the amount of accumulated depreciation is disclosed in a note. **NIKE** reports only the net amount of its property, plant, and equipment in its balance sheet in Appendix A. To satisfy the *full-disclosure principle,* NIKE also describes its depreciation methods in note 1 and the individual amounts comprising plant assets in note 3.[3]

Reporting both the cost and accumulated depreciation of plant assets helps balance sheet readers compare the assets of different companies. For example, a company holding assets costing $50,000 and accumulated depreciation of $40,000 is likely in a situation different from a company with new assets costing $10,000. While the net undepreciated cost is the same in both cases, the first company may have more productive capacity available but likely is facing the need to replace older assets. These insights are not provided if the two balance sheets report only the $10,000 book values.

We emphasize that depreciation is a process of cost allocation. Plant assets are reported on a balance sheet at their remaining undepreciated costs (book value), not at market values. This emphasis on costs rather than market values is based on the *going-concern principle* described in Chapter 2. This principle states that, unless there is evidence to the contrary, we assume a company continues in business. This implies that plant assets are held and used long enough to recover their cost through the sale of products and services. Since plant assets are not sold, their market values are not reported in financial statements. Instead, assets are reported on a balance sheet at cost less accu-

---

[2] FASB, *Accounting Standards—Current Text* (Norwalk, CT, 1995), sec. A35.104 and sec. A06.130. First published as *APB Opinion No. 20*, par. 13 and par. 31.

[3] FASB, *Accounting Standards—Current Text* (Norwalk, CT, 1995), sec. D40.101. First published as *APB Opinion No. 12*, par. 5.

mulated depreciation. This is the remaining portion of the cost that is expected to be recovered in future periods.

Accumulated depreciation on a balance sheet doesn't reflect funds accumulated to buy new assets when the assets currently owned are replaced. Accumulated depreciation is a contra asset account with a credit balance that can't buy us anything. If a company has funds available to buy assets, the funds are shown on the balance sheet in liquid assets such as Cash.

Flash *back*

5. What is the meaning of the term *depreciation* in accounting?

6. A company purchases a new machine for $96,000 on January 1, 1999. Its predicted useful life is five years or 100,000 units of product, and its salvage value is $8,000. During 1999, 10,000 units of product are produced. Compute the book value of this machine on December 31, 1999, assuming (a) straight-line depreciation and (b) units-of-production depreciation.

7. In early January 1999, a company acquires equipment at a cost of $3,800. The company estimates this equipment to have a useful life of three years and a salvage value of $200. Early in 2001, the company changes its estimate to a total four-year useful life and zero salvage value. Using straight-line depreciation, what is depreciation expense on this equipment for the year ended 2001?

Answers—p. 478

Controller

You are the controller for Fascar Company. Fascar has struggled financially for more than two years, and there are no signs of improvement. Fascar's operations require major investments in equipment, and depreciation is a large item in computing income. Fascar's industry normally requires frequent replacements of equipment, and equipment is typically depreciated over three years. Your company's president recently instructed you to revise estimated useful lives of equipment from three to six years and to use a six-year life on all new equipment. You suspect this instruction is motivated by a desire to improve reported income. What actions do you take?

Judgment and Ethics

Answer—p. 478

When a plant asset is acquired and put into service, additional expenditures often are incurred to operate, maintain, repair, and improve it. In recording these added expenditures, we must decide whether they are capitalized or expensed. To capitalize an expenditure is to debit the asset account. A main issue is whether more useful information is provided by reporting these expenditures as current expenses or by adding them to the plant asset's cost and depreciating them over its remaining useful life.

Revenue expenditures are additional costs of plant assets that do not materially increase the asset's life or productive capabilities. They are recorded as expenses and deducted from revenues in the current period's income statement. Examples of revenue expenditures, also called *income statement expenditures,* are supplies, fuel, lubricants, and electric power. **Capital expenditures,** also called *balance sheet expenditures,* are additional costs of plant assets that provide material benefits extending beyond the current period. They are debited to asset accounts and reported on the balance sheet. Capital expenditures increase or improve the type or amount of service an asset provides. Examples are roofing replacement, plant expansion, and major overhauls of machinery and equipment.

Financial statements are affected for several years by the choice between recording costs as revenue expenditures or as capital expenditures. Managers must be careful in classifying them. This classification decision is helped by identifying costs as ordinary repairs, extraordinary repairs, betterments, or low cost asset purchases.

Revenue and Capital Expenditures

P3 Distinguish between revenue and capital expenditures, and account for these expenditures.

Ordinary Repairs

Ordinary repairs are expenditures to keep the asset in normal, good operating condition. They are necessary if an asset is to perform to expectations over its useful life. Or-

dinary repairs don't extend an asset's useful life beyond its original estimate and don't increase its productivity beyond original expectations. Examples are normal costs of cleaning, lubricating, adjusting, and replacing (small) parts of a machine. Ordinary repairs are treated as *revenue expenditures*. This means their costs are reported as expenses on the current income statement. Consistent with this rule, **America West Airlines** reports:

Routine maintenance and repairs are charged to expense as incurred. The cost of major scheduled airframe, engine and certain component overhauls are capitalized . . . over the (future) periods benefited.

Extraordinary Repairs

Extraordinary repairs are expenditures extending the asset's useful life beyond its original estimate. Costs of extraordinary repairs are *capital expenditures* because they benefit future periods. They can be debited to the asset account. But historically they are debited to the asset's accumulated depreciation account to show they restore some effects of past years' depreciation.

Let's return to our inspecting machine purchased for $10,000 and depreciated over five years with a $1,000 salvage value. At the beginning of the machine's fourth year, when the machine's book value is $4,600 (see Exhibit 11.8), it is given a major overhaul at a cost of $2,400. This overhaul extends the machine's useful life by two additional years with no change in salvage value. This means the machine is expected to be used for four more years. The $2,400 cost of the extraordinary repair is recorded as:

Assets = Liabilities + Equity
+2,400
−2,400

Jan. 12	Accumulated Depreciation, Machinery	2,400	
	Cash		2,400
	To record extraordinary repairs.		

This entry increases the book value of the asset from $4,600 to $7,000. For the remaining four years of the asset's life, depreciation is based on this new book value. The effects of the extraordinary repairs are described in Exhibit 11.15.

Exhibit 11.15

Revised Depreciation Schedule from Extraordinary Repairs

	Before	Extraordinary Repair	After
Original cost	$10,000		$10,000
Accumulated depreciation	(5,400)	$2,400	(3,000)
Book value	$ 4,600		$ 7,000
Revised depreciation: ($7,000 − $1,000)/4 years			$ 1,500

Since the $2,400 cost of extraordinary repairs is part of the $7,000 book value computation, it is reflected in the revised depreciation for the asset's remaining life of four years.

Betterments

Betterments, also called *improvements*, are expenditures making a plant asset more efficient or productive. A betterment often involves adding a component to an asset or replacing one of its old components with a better component. A betterment doesn't always increase an asset's useful life. An example is replacing manual controls on a machine with automatic controls to reduce labor costs. This machine will still wear out just as fast as it would with manual controls.[4]

Because a betterment benefits future periods, it is debited to the asset account as a capital expenditure. The new book value (less salvage) is depreciated over the asset's remaining useful life. As an example, suppose a company pays $8,000 for a machine with an eight-year useful life and no salvage value. On January 2, after three years and $3,000 of depreciation, it adds an automated system to the machine at a cost of $1,800. This results in reduced labor cost in operating the machine in future periods. The cost of this betterment is added to the Machinery account with this entry:

Jan. 2	Machinery	1,800	
	Cash		1,800
	To record installation of automated system.		

Assets = Liabilities + Equity
+1,800
−1,800

After the betterment is added, the remaining cost to be depreciated is $6,800, computed as $8,000 − $3,000 + $1,800. Depreciation expense for the remaining five years is $1,360 per year, computed as $6,800/5 years.

Mechanic
You are a mechanic who recently opened your own auto service center. Because of a cash shortage, you are preparing financial statements in the hope of getting a short-term loan from the bank. A friend suggests you treat as many expenses as possible like capital expenditures. What are the impacts on financial statements of treating expenses as capital expenditures? What do you think is the aim of your friend's proposal?

Answers—p. 478

Low Cost Asset Purchases

Maintaining individual plant asset records can be expensive, even in the most advanced system. For that reason, many companies don't keep detailed records for assets costing less than some minimum amount such as $100. Instead, these low cost plant assets are treated as a revenue expenditure. This means their costs are directly charged to an expense account at the time of purchase. This practice is acceptable under the *materiality principle.* Treating immaterial capital expenditures as revenue expenditures is unlikely to mislead users of financial statements. As an example, **Coca-Cola Bottling** discloses that it only capitalizes *major,* or material, betterments in its annual report:

> Additions and major replacements or betterments are added to the assets at cost. Maintenance and repair costs and minor replacements are charged to expense when incurred.

---

[4] One special type of betterment is an *addition.* Examples are a new wing to a factory or a new dock to a warehouse. All additions are capitalized.

Answers—p. 479

Disposals of Plant Assets

P4 Account for asset disposal through discarding, selling, or exchanging an asset.

Exhibit 11.16

Accounting for Disposals of Plant Assets

Plant assets are disposed of for several reasons. Many assets eventually wear out or become obsolete. Other assets are sold because of changing business plans. Sometimes an asset is discarded or sold because it is damaged by fire or accident. Regardless of the cause, disposals of plant assets occur in one of three ways: discarding, sale, or exchange. The accounting for each of these three types of disposals of plant assets is described in Exhibit 11.16.

1. Record depreciation expense up to the date of disposal. This updates the Accumulated Depreciation account.
2. Remove the balances of the disposed asset and related Accumulated Depreciation accounts.
3. Record any cash (and other assets) received or paid in the disposal.
4. Record any gain or loss, computed by comparing the asset's book value with the fair value of assets received.*

*There is one exception to step 4 in the case of asset exchanges that we'll describe later in this section.

Discarding Plant Assets

A plant asset is *discarded* when it is no longer useful to the company and it has no market value. To illustrate, assume a machine costing $9,000 with accumulated depreciation of $9,000 is discarded on June 5. When accumulated depreciation equals the asset's cost it is said to be *fully depreciated* (zero book value). A fully depreciated asset usually doesn't yield a gain or loss on disposal. The entry to record the discarding of this asset is:

Assets = Liabilities + Equity
+9,000
−9,000

June 5	Accumulated Depreciation, Machinery	9,000	
	Machinery		9,000
	To record the discarding of fully depreciated machinery.		

This entry reflects all four steps of Exhibit 11.16. Step 1 is not needed since the machine is fully depreciated. Step 2 is shown in the debit to Accumulated Depreciation and credit to Machinery. Since no cash is involved, step 3 is irrelevant. Also, since book value is zero and no cash is involved, no gain or loss is recorded in step 4.

How do we account for discarding an asset that isn't fully depreciated? Or one whose depreciation is not up to date? To answer this, consider equipment costing $8,000 with accumulated depreciation of $6,000 on December 31 of the prior fiscal year-end. This equipment is being depreciated using straight line over eight years with zero salvage value. On July 1 it is discarded. The first entry is to bring depreciation expense up to date:

Assets = Liabilities + Equity
−500   −500

July 1	Depreciation Expense	500	
	Accumulated Depreciation, Equipment . . .		500
	To record the first six months' depreciation ($1,000 × 6/12).		

The second and final entry reflects steps 2–4 of Exhibit 11.16.

July 1	Accumulated Depreciation, Equipment	6,500	
	Loss on Disposal of Equipment	1,500	
	Equipment		8,000
	To record the discarding of machinery having a $1,500 book value.		

Assets = Liabilities + Equity
+6,500   −1,500
−8,000

The loss is computed by comparing the equipment's $1,500 ($8,000 − $6,000 − $500) book value with the zero net cash proceeds. The loss on disposal is reported in the Other Expenses and Losses section of the income statement. An asset disposal can also sometimes require a cash payment instead of a receipt. Entries like those shown above are made in this case so that the income statement shows any gain or loss from disposal and the balance sheet reflects changes in the asset and accumulated depreciation accounts.

Selling Plant Assets

To illustrate the accounting for selling plant assets, we consider SportsWorld's March 1 sale of its delivery equipment. This equipment had cost $16,000 and had accumulated depreciation of $12,000 on December 31 of the prior calendar year-end. Annual depreciation on this equipment is $4,000 computed using straight-line depreciation. The entry to record depreciation expense and update accumulated depreciation to March 1 is:

March 1	Depreciation Expense	1,000	
	Accumulated Depreciation, Equipment . . .		1,000
	To record the first three months' depreciation ($4,000 × 3/12).		

Assets = Liabilities + Equity
−1,000   −1,000

The second entry to reflect steps 2–4 of Exhibit 11.16 depends on the amount received from the sale. We consider three different possibilities.

Sale at Book Value

If SportsWorld receives $3,000 cash, an amount equal to the equipment's book value, there is no gain or loss on disposal. The entry is:

March 1	Cash	3,000	
	Accumulated Depreciation, Equipment	13,000	
	Equipment		16,000
	To record sale of equipment for no gain or loss.		

Assets = Liabilities + Equity
+3,000
+13,000
−16,000

Sale above Book Value

If SportsWorld receives $7,000 cash, an amount $4,000 above the equipment's book value, there is a gain on disposal. The entry is:

March 1	Cash	7,000	
	Accumulated Depreciation, Equipment	13,000	
	Gain on Disposal of Equipment		4,000
	Equipment		16,000
	To record sale of equipment for a $4,000 gain.		

Assets = Liabilities + Equity
+7000   +4,000
+13,000
−16,000

Sale Below Book Value

If SportsWorld receives $2,500 cash, an amount $500 below the equipment's book value, there is a loss on disposal. The entry is:

Assets = Liabilities + Equity
+2,500   −500
+13,000
−16,000

March 1	Cash	2,500	
	Loss on Disposal of Equipment	500	
	Accumulated Depreciation, Equipment	13,000	
	Equipment		16,000
	To record sale of equipment for a $500 loss.		

Companies at times restructure or downsize operations, which often involves selling plant assets. As part of its restructuring, **Woolworth** sold approximately 120 of its **Woolco** discount stores to **Wal-Mart.** Sale of its Woolco stores yielded a $168 million loss charged against the revenues of Woolworth.

Exchanging Plant Assets

Many plant assets such as machinery, automobiles, and office equipment are disposed of by exchanging them for new assets. In a typical exchange of plant assets, a trade-in allowance is received on the old asset and the balance is paid in cash. Accounting for the exchange of assets is similar to any other disposal unless the old and the new assets are similar in the functions they perform. Trading an old truck for a new truck is an exchange of similar assets, whereas trading a truck for a machine is an exchange of dissimilar assets. The recognition of gains and losses on exchanging plant assets is shown in Exhibit 11.17.

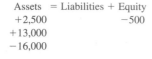

Exhibit 11.17

Gains and Losses on Plant Asset Exchanges

Assets Exchanged	Losses Recognized	Gains Recognized
Dissimilar	Yes	Yes
Similar	Yes	No

Losses on asset exchanges are always recognized. But gains are recognized only for dissimilar asset exchanges. The reason a gain from a similar asset exchange is not recognized is that the exchanged asset's earnings process is not considered complete. The decision to recognize a loss from a similar asset exchange is an application of *accounting conservatism.* This section explains the accounting for these cases.

Exchanging Dissimilar Assets

If a company exchanges a plant asset for another asset that is *dissimilar* in use or purpose, any gain or loss on the exchange is recorded. Any gain or loss is computed by comparing the book value of the asset given up with the fair market value of the asset received (or trade-in allowance).

Receiving More in Exchange: A Gain

Let's assume a company exchanges both an old machine and $16,500 in cash for land. The old machine originally cost $18,000 and has accumulated depreciation of $15,000 at the time of exchange. The land received has a fair market value of $21,000. Using the four steps outlined in Exhibit 11.16, the entry to record this exchange is:

Assets = Liabilities + Equity
+21,000   +1,500
+15,000
−18,000
−16,500

Jan. 2	Land	21,000	
	Accumulated Depreciation, Machinery	15,000	
	Machinery		18,000
	Cash		16,500
	Gain on Exchange of Assets		1,500
	To record exchange of old machine and cash for land.		

We compute the gain on this transaction in the middle columns of Exhibit 11.18. The book value of the assets given totals $19,500. This includes the $16,500 cash and the $3,000 ($18,000 − $15,000) book value of the machine. The total $19,500 book value of assets given is compared to the fair market value of the land received ($21,000). This comparison yields a gain of $1,500 ($21,000 − $19,500).[5]

Dissimilar Plant Asset Exchange	Gain		Loss	
Fair market value of asset(s) received		$21,000		$16,000
Book value of asset(s) given:				
Machine	$ 3,000		$ 3,000	
Cash	16,500	19,500	16,500	19,500
Gain (loss) on exchange		$ 1,500		($ 3,500)

Exhibit 11.18

Computing Gain or Loss on *Dissimilar* Asset Exchanges

Receiving Less in Exchange: A Loss

Let's assume the same facts as in the exchange above *except* the land received has a fair market value of $16,000, not the $21,000 noted previously. The entry to record this exchange is:

Jan. 2	Land	16,000	
	Loss on Exchange of Assets	3,500	
	Accumulated Depreciation, Machinery	15,000	
	Machinery		18,000
	Cash		16,500
	To record exchange of old machine and cash for land.		

Assets − Liabilities + Equity
+16,000   −3,500
+15,000
−18,000
−16,500

We compute the loss on this transaction in the far right columns of Exhibit 11.18. The $19,500 book value of assets given is compared to the fair market value of the land received ($16,000). This yields a loss of $3,500 ($16,000 − $19,500).

Exchanging Similar Assets

Accounting for exchanges of similar assets depends on whether the book value of the asset(s) given up is less or more than the fair market value of the asset(s) received.[6] When the fair market value of the asset(s) received is less than the book value of the asset(s) given, the difference is recognized as a loss. But when the value of the asset(s) received is more than the asset's book value given, the gain is *not* recognized.

Receiving Less in Exchange: A Loss

Let's assume a company exchanges both old equipment and $33,000 in cash for new equipment. The old equipment originally cost $36,000 and has accumulated depreciation of $20,000 at the time of exchange. The new equipment received has a fair market value of $42,000. These details are reflected in the middle columns of Exhibit 11.19.

---

[5] We can also compute a gain or loss by comparing the machine's book value with the trade-in allowance for the machine. Since the fair market value of the land is $21,000 and the cash paid is $16,500, the trade-in allowance for the machine is $4,500. The difference between the machine's $3,000 book value and its $4,500 trade-in allowance gives us the $1,500 gain on exchange.

[6] This rule applies to exchanges of similar assets when the exchange includes a cash payment or when no cash is received or paid. The accounting is slightly different when the exchange involves a cash *receipt*. See FASB, *Accounting Standards—Current Text* (Norwalk, CT, 1995), sec. N35.109. First published as *APB Opinion No. 29*, par. 22.

Exhibit 11.19

Computing Gain or Loss on *Similar* Asset Exchanges

Similar Plant Asset Exchange	Loss		Gain	
Fair market value of asset(s) received		$42,000		$52,000
Book value of asset(s) given:				
Equipment	$16,000		$16,000	
Cash	33,000	49,000	33,000	49,000
Gain (loss) on exchange		($ 7,000)		$ 3,000

The entry to record this similar asset exchange is:

Assets = Liabilities + Equity
+42,000   −7,000
+20,000
−36,000
−33,000

Jan. 3	Equipment (**new**)	42,000	
	Loss on Exchange of Similar Assets	7,000	
	Accumulated Depreciation, Equipment	20,000	
	Equipment (**old**)		36,000
	Cash		33,000
	To record exchange of old equipment and cash for new equipment.		

The book value of the assets given totals $49,000. This includes the $33,000 cash and the $16,000 ($36,000 − $20,000) book value of the old equipment. The total $49,000 book value of assets given is compared to the fair market value of the new equipment received ($42,000). This yields a loss of $7,000 ($42,000 − $49,000).

Receiving More in Exchange: A Gain

Let's assume the same facts as in the similar asset exchange above *except* the new equipment received has a fair market value of $52,000, not the $42,000 noted previously. The entry to record this exchange is:

Assets = Liabilities + Equity
+49,000
+20,000
−36,000
−33,000

Jan. 3	Equipment (**new**)	49,000	
	Accumulated Depreciation, Equipment	20,000	
	Equipment (**old**)		36,000
	Cash		33,000
	To record exchange of old equipment and cash for new equipment.		

We compute a gain on this transaction shown in the far right columns of Exhibit 11.19. But it is *not* recognized in the entry because of the rule prohibiting recognizing a gain on similar asset exchanges.[7] The $49,000 recorded for the new equipment equals its cash price ($52,000) less the unrecognized gain ($3,000) on the exchange. The $49,000 cost recorded is called the *cost basis* of the new machine. This cost basis is the amount we use to compute depreciation and any gain or loss on its eventual disposal. The cost basis of the new asset also can be directly computed by summing book values for the assets given up as shown in Exhibit 11.20.

Exhibit 11.20

Cost Basis of New Asset when Gain Not Recognized

Cost of old equipment	$ 36,000
Less accumulated depreciation	20,000
Book value of old equipment	$ 16,000
Cash paid in the exchange	33,000
Cost recorded for new equipment	**$ 49,000**

---

[7] APB, "Accounting for Nonmonetary Transactions," *APB Opinion No. 29* (New York: AICPA, May 1973), par. 16.

The historical cost principle requires an asset be recorded at the cash or cash equivalent amount given in exchange. The $49,000 cost recorded for the new equipment equals the historical cost book value of the old equipment ($16,000) plus the cash paid in exchange ($33,000). We carry over the old equipment's book value because its earnings process is not considered complete in a similar asset exchange.

Flash back

11. A company acquires equipment on January 10, 1999, at a cost of $42,000. Straight-line depreciation is used, assuming a five-year life and $7,000 salvage value. On June 27, 2000, the company sells this equipment for $32,000. Prepare the entry or entries for June 27, 2000.

12. A company trades an old truck for a new truck. The original cost of the old truck is $30,000, and its accumulated depreciation at the time of the trade is $23,400. The new truck has a cash price of $45,000. Prepare entries to record the trade under two different assumptions: the company receives *(a)* a $3,000 trade-in allowance or *(b)* a $7,000 trade-in allowance.

Answers—p. 479

SECTION 2—NATURAL RESOURCES

Natural Resources

P5 Account for natural resource assets and their depletion.

Natural resources are assets that are physically consumed when used such as standing timber, mineral deposits, and oil and gas fields. Because they are consumed when used, they are often called *wasting assets*. The natural state of these assets represents inventories of raw materials that will be converted into a product by cutting, mining, or pumping. But until that conversion takes place, they are noncurrent assets and reported in a balance sheet using titles such as timberlands, mineral deposits, or oil reserves. These natural resources are reported under either plant assets or a separate category. **Alcoa,** for instance, reports its natural resources under the balance sheet title *Properties, plants and equipment.* In a note to the financial statements, Alcoa reports a separate amount for *Land and land rights, including mines.* **Weyerhaeuser,** on the other hand, reports its huge timber holdings in a separate balance sheet category titled *Timber and timberlands.*

Acquisition Cost and Depletion

Natural resources are initially recorded at cost. Cost includes all expenditures necessary to acquire the resource and prepare it for its intended use. **Depletion** is the process of allocating the cost of natural resources to periods when they are consumed, known as the resource's *useful life.* Natural resources are reported on the balance sheet at cost less *accumulated depletion.* The amount these assets are depleted each year by cutting, mining, or pumping is usually based on units extracted or depleted. This is similar to units-of-production depreciation. **Exxon** uses this approach to amortize the costs of discovering and operating its oil wells.

To illustrate depletion of natural resources, let's consider a mineral deposit with an estimated 500,000 tons of available ore. It is purchased for $500,000 and we expect zero salvage value. The depletion charge per ton of ore mined is $1, computed as $500,000 ÷ 500,000 tons. If 85,000 tons are mined and sold in the first year, the depletion charge for that year is $85,000. These computations are detailed in Exhibit 11.21.

Exhibit 11.21

Depletion Formula and
Computations

Step 1:

$$\text{Depletion per unit} = \frac{\text{Cost} - \text{Salvage value}}{\text{Total units of capacity}} = \frac{\$500,000 - \$0}{500,000 \text{ tons}} = \$1 \text{ per ton}$$

Step 2:

$$\text{Depletion expense} = \text{Depletion per unit} \times \text{Units extracted in period}$$
$$= \$1 \times 85,000 = \$85,000$$

The depletion expense is recorded as:

Dec. 31	Depletion Expense, Mineral Deposit	85,000	
	Accumulated Depletion, Mineral Deposit . .		85,000
	To record depletion of the mineral deposit.		

Assets = Liabilities + Equity
−85,000   −85,000

The balance sheet at the end of this first year reports the deposit as shown in Exhibit 11.22.

Exhibit 11.22

Balance Sheet Presentation of
Natural Resources

| Mineral deposit | $500,000 | |
| **Less accumulated depletion** | 85,000 | $415,000 |

Because the 85,000 tons of mined ore are sold in the year, the entire $85,000 depletion charge is reported on the income statement. But if some of the ore remains unsold at year-end, the depletion cost related to the unsold ore is carried forward on the balance sheet and reported as Unsold Ore Inventory, which is a current asset.

Plant Assets Used in Extracting Resources

The conversion of natural resources by mining, cutting, or pumping usually requires machinery, equipment, and buildings. When the usefulness of these assets is directly related to the depletion of the natural resource, their costs are depreciated over the life of the natural resource in proportion to the depletion charges. This means depreciation is computed using the units-of-production method. For example, if a machine is permanently installed in a mine and one-eighth of the mine's ore is mined and sold in the year, then one-eighth of the machine's cost (less salvage value) is charged to depreciation expense. The same procedure applies if the machine is abandoned once the resources are fully extracted. But if this machine will be moved to another site when extraction is complete, then it is depreciated over its useful life.

SECTION 3—INTANGIBLE ASSETS

Intangible Assets

P6 Account for intangible assets and their amortization.

Intangible assets are rights, privileges, and competitive advantages to the owner of long-term assets that have no physical substance and are used in operations. Examples are patents, copyrights, leaseholds, leasehold improvements, goodwill, and trademarks. Lack of physical substance isn't sufficient for an asset to be an intangible. Notes and accounts receivable, for instance, lack physical substance but aren't used in operations to produce products or services. Assets without physical substance that are not used in operations are reported as either current assets or investments. This section explains accounting for intangible assets and describes the more common types of intangible assets.

Accounting for Intangible Assets

Accounting for intangible assets is similar to that for plant assets. An intangible asset is recorded at cost when purchased. Its cost must be systematically allocated to expense over its estimated useful life through the process of **amortization.** The amortization period for an intangible asset must be 40 years or less.[8] Disposal of an intangible asset involves removing its book value, recording any asset received, and recognizing any gain or loss for the difference.

Amortization of intangible assets is similar to depreciation of plant assets and depletion of natural resources in that it is a process of cost allocation. But only the straight-line method is used for amortizing intangibles *unless* the company can show another method is preferred. Another difference is that the effects of depreciation and depletion are recorded in a contra account (Accumulated Depreciation or Accumulated Depletion), but amortization is usually credited directly to the intangible asset account. This means the original cost of intangible assets is rarely reported on the balance sheet. Instead, only the net amount of unamortized cost is reported.

Some intangibles have limited useful lives due to laws, contracts, or other characteristics of the asset. Examples are patents, copyrights, and leaseholds. Other intangibles such as goodwill, trademarks, and trade names have useful lives that can't be easily determined. The cost of intangible assets is amortized over the periods expected to be benefited by their use. But in no case can this be longer than their legal existence. Also, the amortization period of intangible assets must never be longer than 40 years even when the life of an asset (for example, goodwill) can continue indefinitely into the future.

Intangible assets are often shown in a separate section of the balance sheet immediately after plant assets. **Barnes & Noble,** for instance, follows this approach in reporting $90 million of *intangible assets, net* in its January 31, 1998, balance sheet. Companies also usually disclose the amortization periods they apply to intangibles. **Corning's** annual report, for instance, says it amortizes intangible assets over a maximum of 15 years except for goodwill that is amortized over 40 years. The remainder of our discussion focuses on accounting for specific types of intangible assets.

Patents

The federal government grants patents to encourage the invention of new machines, mechanical devices, and production processes. A **patent** is an exclusive right granted to its owner to manufacture and sell a patented machine or device, or to use a process, for 17 years. When patent rights are purchased, the cost of acquiring the rights is debited to an account called *Patents.* If the owner engages in lawsuits to effectively defend a patent, the cost of lawsuits is debited to the Patents account. The costs of research and development leading to a new patent are expensed when incurred.[9]

Drug War

Mention "drug war" and most people think of fighting cocaine or heroin use. But there's another drug war under way: brand-name drugmakers fight to stop generic copies of their products from hitting the market once their patents expire. Successfully delaying a generic rival means hundreds of millions of dollars in extra sales. [Source: *Business Week,* August 25, 1997.]

Percent of Prescriptions that Specify Generics

(Graph: Percent on vertical axis, from 0 to 60; Years on horizontal axis from 1984 to 1997, showing a rising line from about 20% in 1984 to near 60% in 1997.)

Did You Know?

---

[8] FASB, *Accounting Standards—Current Text* (Norwalk, CT, 1995), sec. I60.110. First published as *APB Opinion No. 17,* par. 29.

[9] FASB, *Accounting Standards—Current Text* (Norwalk, CT, 1995), sec. R50.108. First published as *Statement of Financial Accounting Standards No. 2,* par. 12.

While a patent gives its owner exclusive rights to it for 17 years, the cost of the patent is amortized over its estimated useful life but not to exceed 17 years. If we purchase a patent costing $25,000 with a useful life of 10 years, we make the following adjusting entry at the end of each of the 10 years to amortize one-tenth of its cost:

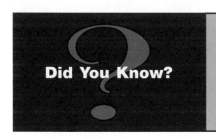

Dec. 31	Amortization Expense, Patents	2,500	
	Patents		2,500
	To write off patent costs over its 10-year useful life.		

Assets = Liabilities + Equity
−2,500   −2,500

The debit of $2,500 to Amortization Expense appears on the income statement as a cost of the product or service provided under the protection of the patent. This entry uses the common practice of crediting the Patents account rather than using a contra account.

Copyrights

A copyright is granted by the federal government or by international agreement. A **copyright** gives its owner the exclusive right to publish and sell a musical, literary, or artistic work during the life of the creator plus 50 years. Yet the useful life of most copyrights is much shorter. The costs of a copyright are amortized over its useful life. The only identifiable cost of many copyrights is the fee paid to the Copyright Office. If this fee is immaterial, it is charged directly to an expense account. But if the identifiable costs of a copyright are material, they are capitalized (recorded in an asset account) and periodically amortized by debiting an account called Amortization Expense, Copyrights.

Did You Know?

Go PHISH

A technology called MP3 allows users to download and upload full-length, CD-quality sound recordings without permission of the copyright holder. Popular groups and individual artists, such as PHISH, Pearl Jam, Van Halen, and Madonna have found their songs freely circulating the Web months before the official release. The industry now uses an automated Web crawler to electronically scan for these online pirates.

Leaseholds

Property is rented under a contract called a **lease.** The property's owner grants the lease and is called the **lessor.** The one who secures the right to possess and use the property is called the **lessee.** A **leasehold** refers to the rights granted to the lessee by the lessor under the terms of the lease. A leasehold is an intangible asset for the lessee.

Certain leases require no advance payment from the lessee but do require monthly rent payments. In this case, we don't need a Leasehold account. Instead, the monthly payments are debited to a Rent Expense account. But if a long-term lease requires the lessee to pay the final period's rent in advance when the lease is signed, the lessee records this advance payment with a debit to a Leasehold account. Because the usefulness of the advance payment is not used until the final period, the Leasehold account balance remains intact until that time. Then, its balance is transferred to Rent Expense.[10]

A long-term lease can increase in value when current rental rates for similar property increase while the required payments under the lease remain constant. This increase in the value of a lease is not reported on the lessee's balance sheet since no extra cost is incurred to acquire it. But if the property is subleased and the new tenant makes a cash payment to the original lessee for the rights under the old lease, the new tenant debits this payment to a Leasehold account. The balance of this Leasehold account is amortized to Rent Expense over the remaining life of the lease.

---

[10] Some long-term leases give the lessee essentially the same rights as a purchaser and result in tangible assets and liabilities reported by the lessee. Chapter 12 describes these leases.

To illustrate how the changing value of a lease can affect business decisions, we consider **La Côte Basque,** a historic restaurant in New York. Late in 1994, La Côte Basque sold the two years remaining on its lease to **Walt Disney Company.** La Côte Basque knew it couldn't renew the lease when it expired because Disney had negotiated a long-term lease of the property with the building owner, **Coca-Cola Company.** La Côte Basque had been operating in this location for 36 years but couldn't compete with the offer by Disney. This led the restaurant to sell the remainder of its lease for a sizable amount and relocate earlier than required.

Leasehold Improvements

Long-term leases sometimes require the lessee to pay for alterations or improvements to the leased property such as partitions, painting, and storefronts. These alterations and improvements are called **leasehold improvements,** and their costs are debited to a *Leasehold Improvements* account. Since leasehold improvements become part of the property and revert to the lessor at the end of the lease, the lessee amortizes these costs over the life of the lease or the life of the improvements, whichever is shorter. The amortization entry debits Rent Expense and credits Leasehold Improvements.

Goodwill

Goodwill has a special meaning in accounting. **Goodwill** is the amount by which the value of a company exceeds the fair market value of this company's net assets if purchased separately. This usually implies the company has certain valuable attributes not measured among its net assets. These can include superior management, skilled workforce, good supplier and customer relations, quality products or services, good location, or other competitive advantages.

Goodwill Illustration

Conceptually, a company has goodwill when its rate of expected future earnings is greater than the rate of normal earnings for its industry. To illustrate this concept, consider the information in Exhibit 11.23 for two competing companies (Winter Gear and Wild Sports). Both are of roughly equal size and compete in the snowboard industry.

	Wild Sports	Winter Gear
Net assets (excluding goodwill)	$190,000	$190,000
Normal rate of return in this industry	10%	10%
Normal return on net assets	$19,000	$19,000
Expected net income	24,000	19,000
Expected net income above-normal	$ 5,000	$ -0-

Exhibit 11.23

Data for Goodwill Illustration

The expected income for Wild Sports is $24,000. This is $5,000 higher than the norm (10%) for this industry. This implies Wild Sports has goodwill that yields above-normal net income. In contrast, Winter Gear's net income of $19,000 is the norm for this industry. This suggests zero goodwill for Winter Gear. What this means is we're willing to pay more for Wild Sports than for Winter Gear because goodwill is a valued asset.

Goodwill is usually recorded only when an entire company or a business segment is purchased. In determining the purchase price of a company, the buyer and seller can estimate the amount of goodwill in more than one way. For instance, how do we value Wild Sports' $5,000 per year above-normal net income? One way is to value goodwill at some *multiple* of above-normal net income. If we choose a multiple of 4, our goodwill estimate for Wild Sports is 4 times $5,000 (or $20,000). Another method is to assume the $5,000 above-normal net income continues indefinitely (often called *capitalizing* the above-normal net income). This is like an *annuity*. If we assume a 16% discount rate, our estimate of goodwill is $5,000/16%, or $31,250. We describe this computation in a later chapter. But whatever method we choose, the value of goodwill is confirmed only by the price the seller is willing to accept and the buyer is willing to pay.

Accounting for Goodwill

To keep financial statement information from being too subjective, goodwill isn't recorded unless it is purchased. Goodwill is measured by subtracting the fair market value of the purchased company's net assets (excluding goodwill) from the purchase price. Goodwill is a major part of many company purchases. For instance, **Procter & Gamble's** purchase of **Revlon's** worldwide Max Factor and Betrix lines of cosmetics for $1,025 million (net of cash acquired) included goodwill and other intangibles of $927 million.

Goodwill is amortized on a straight-line basis over its estimated useful life just like other intangible assets. Since estimating the useful life of goodwill is difficult, there is a wide range of estimates. Exhibit 11.24 shows us results from a recent survey on the goodwill amortization period. The most common amortization period is 40 years. Also, if we assume most of the companies that report "not exceeding 40" actually use 40 years, then we'd have nearly 60% of companies choosing the longest amortization period permitted. This is not surprising because it allows companies to spread goodwill costs over more years.

Exhibit 11.24

Goodwill Amortization Period

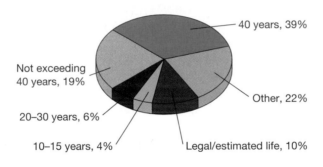

- 40 years, 39%
- Not exceeding 40 years, 19%
- 20–30 years, 6%
- 10–15 years, 4%
- Other, 22%
- Legal/estimated life, 10%

Trademarks and Trade Names

Companies often adopt unique symbols or select unique names and brands in marketing their products. A **trademark** or **trade name** is a symbol, name, phrase, or jingle identified with a company, product, or service. Examples are "I Can," NIKE's swoosh, Marlboro Man, Big Mac, Coca-Cola, and Corvette. Ownership and exclusive right to use a trademark or trade name is often established by showing that one company used it before another. But ownership is best established by registering a trademark or trade name with the government's Patent Office. The cost of developing, maintaining, or enhancing the value of a trademark or trade name by means such as advertising is charged to expense when incurred. But if a trademark or trade name is purchased, its cost is debited to an asset account and amortized.

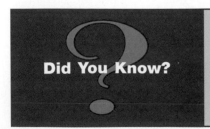

Did You Know?

What's in a Name?
When it comes to brand building, nobody does it better than **NIKE.** Its swoosh is one of the best-known trademarks on the globe. It has helped NIKE pump out sales and earnings growth of nearly 40% for three years straight. Equally impressive is brand identity the **"Intel Inside"** campaign created for a product that consumers never see and few understand. [Source: *Business Week,* March 24, 1997.]

Answers—p. 479

Cash Flow Impacts of Long-Term Assets

Acquisition and disposal transactions involving long-term assets impact the statement of cash flows. Acquisitions of long-term assets are investing activities and are reported in the investing section of the statement of cash flows. Most acquisitions are an immediate *use* of cash and the amount paid at acquisition is deducted in the statement. **NIKE,** for instance, reports the following in its statement of cash flows:

C4 Identify cash flow impacts of long-term asset transactions.

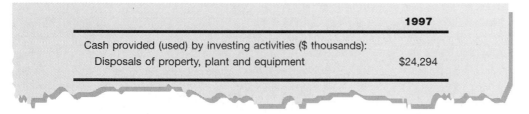

	1997
Cash provided (used) by investing activities ($ thousands):	
Additions to property, plant and equipment	($465,908)

Disposals of long-term assets usually create an immediate receipt of cash. When they do yield cash they are reported as a *source* of cash (an addition) in the investing section of the statement of cash flows. **NIKE** reports its disposals as:

	1997
Cash provided (used) by investing activities ($ thousands):	
Disposals of property, plant and equipment	$24,294

Gain or loss from disposal is the difference between an asset's book value and the value received, and it does not reflect any cash flows from investing activities.[11]

Total Asset Turnover

USING THE INFORMATION

A company's assets are important in determining its ability to generate sales and earn profits. Managers devote a lot of attention to deciding what assets a company acquires, how much is invested in assets, and how assets can be used most efficiently and effectively. Decision makers and other users of financial statements are especially interested in evaluating a company's ability to use its assets in generating sales.

One measure of a company's ability in using its assets is **total asset turnover.** The formula for computing total asset turnover is shown in Exhibit 11.25.

A2 Compute total asset turnover and apply it to analyze a company's use of assets.

---

[11] Also, depreciation and amortization of long-term assets do *not* impact cash (see Chapter 17).

Exhibit 11.25

Total Asset Turnover Formula

$$\text{Total asset turnover} = \frac{\text{Net sales}}{\text{Average total assets}}$$

Total asset turnover can be computed regardless of the type of company being evaluated. It can be applied to manufacturing and merchandising companies, and even to service companies. The numerator, net sales, reflects all operating revenues generated by the company. The denominator, average total assets, is usually measured by averaging total assets at the beginning of the period with total assets at the end of the period.

To illustrate, let's look at a company with total assets of $96,500 at the beginning of the year and $108,500 at the end of the year. Net sales for this company are $440,000 for the year. The company's total asset turnover for the current year is computed as:

$$\text{Total asset turnover} = \frac{\$440,000}{(\$96,500 + \$108,500)/2} = 4.3$$

We describe this company's use of assets in generating net sales by saying "it turned its assets over 4.3 times during the year." This means each $1.00 of assets produced $4.30 of net sales for the year.

Is a total asset turnover of 4.3 good or bad? It is safe to say all companies desire a high total asset turnover. But like many ratio analyses, a company's total asset turnover must be interpreted in comparison with prior years and with similar companies. Interpreting the total asset turnover also requires an understanding of the company's operations. Some operations are capital intensive, meaning a relatively large amount is invested in assets to generate sales. This suggests a relatively lower total asset turnover. Some other companies' operations are labor intensive, meaning sales are generated more by the efforts of people than the use of assets. In this case we expect a higher total asset turnover.[12]

To show how we analyze companies by using total asset turnover, we use data from the annual reports of two competing companies: **Coors** and **Anheuser-Busch.** Exhibit 11.26 shows results from computing total asset turnover for these two companies.

Exhibit 11.26

Analysis Using Total Asset Turnover

Company	Figure (in millions)	1996	1995
Coors	Net sales	$ 1,732	$ 1,680
	Average total assets	$ 1,374	$ 1,378
	Total asset turnover	1.26	1.22
Anheuser-Busch	Net sales	$10,884	$10,341
	Average total assets	$10,527	$10,569
	Total asset turnover	1.03	0.98

To show how we compute and use total asset turnover, let's look at the numbers for Coors in 1995–1996 as reported in Exhibit 11.26. We compute **Coors'** 1996 turnover as:

$$\text{Total asset turnover} = \frac{\$1,732}{\$1,374} = 1.26$$

This means Coors' average total asset balance is converted into sales 1.26 times in 1996. Another way to say this is Coors generated $1.26 of net sales for each $1 of assets. We also see Coors' turnover is steady over the period 1995–1996, and is su-

---

[12] There is a relation between total asset turnover and net profit margin. Companies with low total asset turnover require higher profit margins (examples are hotels and real estate), whereas companies with high total asset turnover can succeed with lower profit margins (examples are food stores and merchandisers).

perior to Anheuser-Busch. Is Coors' turnover high enough? Total asset turnover for Coors' other competitors, available in industry publications such as Dun & Bradstreet, is generally in the range of 1.0 to 1.1 over this same period. It appears Coors is competitive and possibly doing slightly better than its competitors on total asset turnover.

Environmentalist
You are an environmentalist battling a paper manufacturer on environmental concerns. The company claims it can't afford any additional controls. It points to its low total asset turnover of 1.9 and argues it can't compete with other companies where total asset turnover is much higher. Examples mentioned are food stores (5.5), wholesalers (4.0), and builders (3.5). The company suggests it might need to lay off workers to pay for any added costs. How do you respond?

You Make the Call

Answers—p. 478

Summary

C1 Describe plant assets and issues in accounting for them. Plant assets are tangible assets used in the operations of a company and have a useful life of more than one accounting period. Plant assets are set apart from other tangible assets by two important features: use in operations and useful lives longer than one period. There are four main accounting issues with plant assets: (1) computing their costs, (2) allocating their costs to the periods they benefit, (3) accounting for subsequent expenditures, and (4) recording their disposal.

C2 Explain depreciation and the factors affecting its computation. Depreciation is the process of allocating to expense the cost of a plant asset over the accounting periods that benefit from the use of the plant asset. Depreciation doesn't measure the decline in a plant asset's market value, nor does it measure the asset's physical deterioration. Depreciation occurs as an asset is used to produce products or services. Three factors determine depreciation: cost, salvage value, and useful life. Salvage value is an estimate of the asset's value at the end of its benefit period. Useful (service) life is the length of time an asset is productively used in operations.

C3 Explain depreciation for partial years and changes in estimates. Partial years' depreciation is often required because assets are bought and sold throughout the year. Depreciation is revised when changes in estimates such as salvage value and useful life occur. If the useful life of a plant asset changes, for instance, the remaining cost to be depreciated is spread over the remaining (revised) useful life of the asset.

C4 Identify cash flow impacts of long-term asset transactions. Acquisition, depreciation, and disposal of long-term assets impact the statement of cash flows. Both acquisitions and disposals impact the investing section of this statement. Acquisitions are a use of cash, while disposals are a source of cash.

A1 Compare and analyze depreciation for different methods. The amount of depreciation expense per period is usually different for different methods. Yet total depreciation expense is the same for all methods. Each method starts with the same total cost and ends with the same salvage value. The difference is in the pattern of depreciation expense over the asset's useful life. The

book value of an asset when using straight-line is always greater than when using double-declining-balance, except at the beginning and end. The straight-line method yields a steady pattern of depreciation expense, while the units-of-production does not because it depends on the number of units produced. Depreciation methods are acceptable if they allocate cost in a systematic and rational manner.

A2 Compute total asset turnover and apply it to analyze a company's use of assets. Total asset turnover measures a company's ability to use its assets to generate sales. Total asset turnover is defined as net sales divided by average total assets. The turnover measure is interpreted as the dollars of net sales generated for each dollar of assets. While all companies desire a high total asset turnover, it must be interpreted in comparison with prior years and with similar companies.

P1 Apply the cost principle to compute the cost of plant assets. Plant assets are recorded at cost when purchased. Cost includes all normal and reasonable expenditures necessary to get the asset in place and ready for its intended use. The cost of a lump-sum purchase is allocated among its individual assets based on their relative market values.

P2 Compute and record depreciation using the straight-line, units-of-production, and declining-balance methods. The straight-line method of depreciation divides the cost less salvage value by the number of periods in the asset's useful life to determine depreciation expense for each period. The units-of-production method divides the cost less salvage value by the estimated number of units the asset will produce to determine the depreciation per unit. The declining-balance method multiplies the asset's book value by a factor that is usually double the straight-line rate.

P3 Distinguish between revenue and capital expenditures, and account for these expenditures. Revenue expenditures expire in the current period. They are debited to expense accounts and matched with current revenues. Ordinary repairs are an example of revenue expenditures. Capital expenditures benefit future periods and are debited to asset accounts. Examples of capital expenditures include extraordinary repairs and betterments. Immaterial expenditures on plant assets are treated as revenue expenditures.

P4 **Account for asset disposal through discarding, selling, or exchanging an asset.** When a plant asset is discarded, sold, or exchanged, its cost and accumulated depreciation are removed from the accounts. Any cash proceeds from discarding or selling an asset are recorded and compared to the asset's book value to determine gain or loss. When dissimilar assets are exchanged, the new asset is recorded at its fair value, and any gain or loss on disposal is recognized. When similar assets are exchanged, losses are recognized but gains are not. When gains are not recognized, the new asset account is debited for the book value of the old asset plus any cash paid.

P5 **Account for natural resource assets and their depletion.** The cost of a natural resource is recorded in an asset account. Depletion of a natural resource is recorded by allocating its cost to expense using the units-of-production method. Depletion is credited to an Accumulated Depletion account.

P6 **Account for intangible assets and their amortization.** An intangible asset is recorded at the cost incurred to purchase the asset. Allocation of the cost of an intangible asset to expense is done using the straight-line method and is called *amortization*. Amortization is recorded with a credit made directly to the asset account instead of a contra account. Intangible assets include patents, copyrights, leaseholds, goodwill, and trademarks.

Guidance Answers to **You Make the Call**

Mechanic

Treating an expense as a capital expenditure means reported expenses will be lower and income higher in the short run. This is because, unlike an expense, a capital expenditure is not expensed immediately. Instead, the cost of a capital expenditure is spread out over the asset's useful life. Treating an expense as a capital expenditure also means asset and equity totals are reported at a larger amount. This continues until the asset is fully depreciated. Your friend is probably trying to help, but the suggestion hints at unethical behavior. You must remember that only an expenditure benefiting future periods is a capital expenditure. If an item is truly an expense not benefiting future periods, then it must not be treated as a capital expenditure.

Environmentalist

You need to point out that the company's comparison of its total asset turnover with food stores, wholesalers, and builders is misdirected. You must explain these other industries' turnovers are higher because their profit margins are lower (about 2%). Profit margins for the paper industry are usually 3% to 3.5%. You also need to collect data from competitors in the paper industry to show that a 1.9 total asset turnover is about right for this industry. You might even go further and collect data on this company's revenues and expenses, along with compensation data for this company's high-ranking officers and employees.

Guidance Answer to **Judgment and Ethics**

Controller

Before you conclude this instruction is unethical, you might tell the president of your concern that the longer estimate doesn't seem realistic in light of past experience with three-year replacements. You might ask if the change implies a new replacement plan. Depending on the president's response, such a conversation might eliminate your concern. It is possible the president's decision to change estimated useful life reflects an honest and reasonable prediction of the future. Since the company is struggling financially, the president may have concluded the normal pattern of replacing assets every three years can't continue. Perhaps the strategy is to avoid costs of frequent replacements and stretch use of the equipment a few years longer until financial conditions improve. Even if you doubt the company will be able to use the equipment six years, you should consider the possibility the president has a more complete understanding of the situation and honestly believes a six-year life is a good estimate.

On the downside, you may be correct in suspecting the president is acting unethically. If you conclude the president's decision is unethical, you might confront the president with your opinion that it is unethical to change the prediction just to increase income. This is a personally risky course of action and you may want to remind the president of her own ethical responsibility. Another possibility is to wait and see if the auditor will insist on not changing the estimate. You should always insist the statements be based on reasonable estimates.

Guidance Answers to Flash *backs*

1. (*a*) Office supplies—current assets
   (*b*) Office equipment—plant assets
   (*c*) Merchandise—current assets (inventory)
   (*d*) Land held for future expansion—long-term investments
   (*e*) Trucks used in operations—plant assets
2. (*a*) Land
   (*b*) Land Improvements

3. $700,000 + $49,000 − $21,000 + $3,500 + $3,000 + $2,500 = $737,000
4. Straight-line with 7-year life: ($77,000/7) = $11,000
   Straight-line with 10-year life: ($77,000/10) = $7,700
5. Depreciation is a process of allocating and charging the cost of plant assets to the accounting periods that benefit from the assets' use.

6. (a) Book value using straight-line depreciation:
$96,000 − [($96,000 − $8,000)/5] = $78,400
  (b) Book value using units of production:
$96,000 − [($96,000 − $8,000) × (10,000/100,000)]
  = $87,200

7. ($3,800 − $200)/3 = $1,200 (depreciation per year)
$1,200 × 2 = $2,400 (accumulated depreciation)
($3,800 − $2,400)/2 = $700 (revised depreciation)

8.

Accumulated Depreciation, Machinery	12,000	
Cash		12,000

9. A revenue expenditure benefits only the current period and should be charged to expense of the current period. A capital expenditure has a benefit that extends beyond the end of the current period and should be charged to an asset.

10. A betterment involves modifying an existing plant asset to make it more efficient, usually by replacing part of the asset with an improved or superior part. A betterment should be debited to the improved machine's account.

11.

Depreciation Expense	3,500	
Accumulated Depreciation		3,500
Cash	32,000	
Accumulated Depreciation	10,500	
Gain on Sale of Equipment		500
Equipment		42,000

12.

(a)

Truck	45,000	
Loss on Trade-In	3,600	
Accumulated Depreciation	23,400	
Truck		30,000
Cash ($45,000–$3,000)		42,000

(b)

Truck	44,600	
Accumulated Depreciation	23,400	
Truck		30,000
Cash ($45,000–$7,000)		38,000

13. Examples of intangible assets are: patents, copyrights, leaseholds, leasehold improvements, goodwill, trademarks, and exclusive licenses.
Examples of natural resources are: timberlands, mineral deposits, and oil reserves.

14. ($650,000/325,000) × 91,000 = $182,000

15.

Jan. 6	Patents	120,000	
	Cash		120,000
Dec. 31	Amortization Expense	40,000*	
	Patents		40,000

*Amortization computation:
$120,000/3 years = $40,000

On July 14, 1999, Tulsa Company paid $600,000 to acquire a fully equipped factory. The purchase involved the following assets (we include additional facts related to each):

Demonstration Problem

Asset	Appraised Value	Estimated Salvage Value	Estimated Useful Life	Depreciation Method
Land	$160,000			Not depreciated
Land improvements	80,000	$ -0-	10 years	Straight-line
Building	320,000	100,000	10 years	Double-declining-balance
Machinery	240,000	20,000	10,000 units	Units-of-production*
Total	$800,000			

*The machinery is used to produce 700 units in 1999 and 1,800 units in 2000.

Required

1. Allocate the total $600,000 cost among the separate assets.

2. Compute the 1999 (six months) and 2000 depreciation expense for each type of asset and compute total depreciation expense each year for all assets.

3. On the first day of 2001, the machinery and $5,000 cash are exchanged for similar equipment with a fair value of $210,000. Journalize the exchange of similar assets.

4. Assume the exchange in (3) is for dissimilar, not similar, equipment. Journalize the dissimilar asset exchange.

5. On the last day of the fiscal year 2001, the company discards equipment that has been on the books for five years. The original cost of the equipment was $12,000 (estimated life of five years) and the salvage value was $2,000. No depreciation has been recorded for the fifth year before the disposal occurs. Journalize the fifth year of depreciation (straight-line method) and the asset disposal.

6. At the beginning of the year 2001, the company purchases with cash a patent right for $100,000. The company estimates the useful life of the patent to be 10 years. Journalize the patent acquisition and amortization for the year.

7. Late in the year 2001, the company makes its final addition to property and equipment with the acquisition for $600,000 cash of an ore deposit. Access roads and shafts are added for an additional cost of $80,000. Salvage value of the mine is estimated to be $20,000. The company estimates 330,000 tons of available ore. Only 10,000 tons of ore are mined and sold before the end of the year. Journalize the mine's acquisition and first year's depletion.

Planning the Solution

- Complete a three-column schedule showing these amounts for each asset: appraised value, percent of total value, and allocated cost.

- Using the allocated costs, compute the amount of depreciation for 1999 (only one-half year) and 2000 (full year) for each asset. Then summarize those computations in a table showing the total depreciation for each year.

- Remember that gains on exchanges of similar assets are not recognized. Make a journal entry to add the acquired machinery to the books and to remove the machinery, along with its accumulated depreciation, and the cash given in the exchange.

- Remember that gains on exchanges of dissimilar assets are recognized. Make a journal entry to add the acquired machinery to the books and to remove the machinery, along with its accumulated depreciation, and the cash given in the exchange. Also record the gain on the exchange in a separate account titled Gain on Exchange of Dissimilar Assets.

- Remember that all depreciation must be recorded before removing a disposed asset from the books. Calculate and record the depreciation expense for the fifth year using the straight-line method. Since salvage value has not been received at the end of the asset's life, the amount of the salvage value becomes a loss on disposal. Record the loss on the disposal as well as the removal of the asset and its related accumulated depreciation from the books.

- Record the patent as an intangible asset at its purchase price. Use straight-line amortization over the years of useful life to calculate amortization expense. Remember that no accumulated amortization account is used in recording amortization expense. The intangible asset account is credited directly.

- Record the ore deposit as a natural resource asset including all additional costs to ready the mine for use. Calculate depletion per ton using the depletion formula. Multiply the depletion amount per ton by the amount of tons mined since the acquisition to calculate the appropriate depletion expense for the current year.

Solution to Demonstration Problem

1. Allocation of the total cost of $600,000 among the assets:

Asset	Appraised Value	Percent of Total Value	Allocated Cost
Land	$160,000	20%	$120,000 ($600,000 × 20%)
Land improvements	80,000	10	60,000 ($600,000 × 10%)
Building	320,000	40	240,000 ($600,000 × 40%)
Machinery	240,000	30	180,000 ($600,000 × 30%)
Total	$800,000	100%	$600,000

2. Depreciation for each asset:

Land Improvements:

Cost	$ 60,000
Salvage value	-0-
Net cost	$ 60,000
Useful life	10 years
Annual expense ($60,000/10)	$ 6,000
1999 depreciation ($6,000 × 6/12)	$ 3,000
2000 depreciation	$ 6,000

Building:

Straight-line rate = 100%/10 = 10%
Double-declining-balance rate = 10% × 2 = 20%

1999 depreciation ($240,000 × 20% × 6/12)	$ 24,000
2000 depreciation [($240,000 − $24,000) × 20%]	$ 43,200

Machinery:

Cost	$180,000
Salvage value	20,000
Net cost	$160,000
Total expected units	10,000
Expected cost per unit ($160,000/10,000)	$ 16
1999 depreciation ($16 × 700 units)	$ 11,200
2000 depreciation ($16 × 1,800 units)	$ 28,800

Total depreciation expense:

	2000	1999
Land improvements	$ 6,000	$ 3,000
Building	43,200	24,000
Machinery	28,800	11,200
Total	$78,000	$38,200

3. Recording the exchange of similar assets with a gain on the exchange:
The book value on the date of exchange is $240,000 (allocated cost) − $40,000 (accumulated depreciation). The book value of the machinery given in the exchange ($200,000) plus the $5,000 cash is less than the $210,000 value of the machine acquired in the exchange. The entry to record the exchange of similar assets does not recognize this $5,000 gain on exchange:

Machinery (new)	205,000*	
Accumulated Depreciation, Machinery (old)	40,000	
Machinery (old)		240,000
Cash		5,000
To record exchange of similar assets.		

*(Fair market value of acquired asset $210,000 minus $5,000 gain)

4. Recording the exchange of dissimilar assets with a gain on the exchange:

Machinery (new)	210,000	
Accumulated Depreciation, Machinery (old)	40,000	
Machinery (old)		240,000
Cash		5,000
Gain on exchange of dissimilar assets		5,000
To record exchange of dissimilar assets.		

5. Recording the depreciation on the discarded asset:

Depreciation Expense, Equipment	2,000	
Accumulated Depreciation, Equipment		2,000
To record depreciation to date of disposal: ($12,000 − $2,000)/5		

Recording the loss on disposal and the asset removal:

Accumulated Depreciation, Equipment	10,000	
Loss on Disposal of Equipment	2,000	
Equipment		12,000
To record the discarding of machinery with a $2,000 book value.		

6.

Patent	100,000	
Cash		100,000
To record patent acquisition.		

Amortization Expense, Patent	10,000	
Patent		10,000
To record amortization expense: $100,000/10 years = $10,000		

7.

Ore Deposit	680,000	
Cash		680,000
To record ore deposit acquisition and related costs.		

Depletion Expense, Ore Deposit	20,000	
Accumulated Depletion		20,000
To record depletion expense: ($680,000 − $20,000)/330,000 tons available = $2 per ton. $10,000 tons mined and sold × $2 = $20,000 depletion		

Glossary

Accelerated depreciation method depreciation method that produces larger depreciation charges during the early years of an asset's life and smaller charges in the later years. (p. 456).

Amortization a process of systematically allocating the cost of an intangible asset to expense over its estimated useful life. (p. 471).

Betterment an expenditure to make a plant asset more efficient or productive; also called *improvements*. (p. 463).

Book value the original cost of a plant asset less its accumulated depreciation (or depletion, or amortization). (p. 454).

Capital expenditure additional costs of plant assets that provides material benefits extending beyond the current period; also called *balance sheet expenditure*. (p. 461).

Change in an accounting estimate a change in a computed amount used in the financial statements that results from new information or subsequent developments and from better insight or improved judgment. (p. 459).

Copyright a right granted by the federal government or by international agreement giving the owner the exclusive privilege to publish and sell musical, literary, or artistic work during the life of the creator plus 50 years. (p. 472).

Cost includes all normal and reasonable expenditures necessary to get a plant asset in place and ready for its intended use. (p. 449).

Declining-balance depreciation a depreciation method in which a plant asset's depreciation charge for the period is determined by applying a constant depreciation rate (up to twice the straight-line rate) each year to the asset's book value at the beginning of the year. (p. 456).

Depletion the process of allocating the cost of natural resources to periods when they are consumed. (p. 469).

Depreciation the process of allocating the cost of a plant asset to expense in the periods benefiting from its use. (p. 452).

Extraordinary repairs major repairs that extend the useful life of a plant asset beyond original expectations; treated as a capital expenditure. (p. 462).

Goodwill the amount by which the value of a company exceeds the fair market value of the company's net assets if purchased separately. (p. 473).

Inadequacy a condition in which the capacity of the company's plant assets is too small to meet the company's productive demands. (p. 452).

Intangible assets rights, privileges, and competitive advantages to the owner of long-term assets that have no physical substance and are used in operations; examples include patents, copyrights, leaseholds, leasehold improvements, goodwill, and trademarks. (p. 470).

Land improvements assets that increase the usefulness of land but have a limited useful life and are subject to depreciation. (p. 450).

Lease a contract allowing property rental. (p. 472).

Leasehold a name for the rights granted to the lessee by the lessor under the terms of a lease. (p. 472).

Leasehold improvements alterations or improvements to leased property such as partitions, painting, and storefronts. (p. 473).

Lessee the party to a lease who secures the right to possess and use the property. (p. 472).

Lessor the party to a lease who grants the right to possess and use property to another. (p. 472).

Modified Accelerated Cost Recovery System (MACRS) the system of depreciation required by federal income tax law. (p. 450).

Natural resources assets that are physically consumed when used; examples include timber, mineral deposits, and oil and gas fields; also called *wasting assets*. (p. 469).

Obsolescence a condition in which, because of new inventions and improvements, a plant asset can no longer be used to produce goods or services with a competitive advantage. (p. 452).

Ordinary repairs repairs to keep a plant asset in normal, good operating condition; treated as a revenue expenditure. (p. 462).

Patent an exclusive right granted to its owner to manufacture and sell a machine or device, or to use a process, for 17 years. (p. 471).

Plant assets tangible assets that are used in the operations of a company and have a useful life of more than one accounting period. (p. 448).

Revenue expenditure an expenditure that should appear on the current income statement as an expense and be deducted from the period's revenues because it does not provide a material benefit in future periods. (p. 461).

Salvage value management's estimate of the amount that will be recovered at the end of a plant asset's useful life through a sale or as a trade-in allowance on the purchase of a new asset; also called *residual*, or *scrap, value*. (p. 452).

Straight-line depreciation a method that allocates an equal portion of the total depreciation for a plant asset (cost minus salvage) to each accounting period in its useful life. (p. 453).

Total asset turnover a measure of the ability of a company to use its assets to generate sales; computed by dividing net sales by average total assets. (p. 475).

Trademark or **trade name** symbol, name, phrase, or jingle identified with a company or service. (p. 474).

Units-of-production depreciation a method that charges a varying amount to expense for each period of an asset's useful life depending on its usage; expense is computed by taking the cost of the asset less its salvage value and dividing by the total number of units expected to be produced during its useful life. (p. 455).

Useful (or service) life the length of time a plant asset will be productively used in the operations of a business. (p. 452).

Questions

1. What characteristics of a plant asset make it different from other assets?

2. What is the balance sheet classification of land held for future expansion? Why is this type of land not classified as a plant asset?

3. In general, what is included in the cost of a plant asset?

4. What is the difference between land and land improvements?

5. Does the balance of the account, Accumulated Depreciation—Machinery, represent funds accumulated to replace the machinery when it wears out? What does the balance of accumulated depreciation represent?

6. Why is the Modified Accelerated Cost Recovery System not generally accepted for financial accounting purposes?

7. What is the difference between ordinary repairs and extraordinary repairs and how should they be recorded?

8. What accounting principle justifies charging low cost plant asset purchases immediately to an expense account?

9. What are some events that might lead to disposal of a plant asset?

10. Should a gain on an exchange of plant assets be recorded?

11. How does accounting for long-term property and equipment impact the statement of cash flows?

12. How is total asset turnover computed? Why would a financial statement user be interested in total asset turnover?

13. What is the name for the process of allocating the cost of natural resources to expense as natural resources are used?

14. What are the characteristics of an intangible asset?

15. Is the declining-balance method an acceptable means of computing depletion of natural resources?

16. What general procedures are followed in accounting for intangible assets?

17. When does a business have goodwill? Under what conditions can goodwill appear in a company's balance sheet?

18. A company bought an established business and paid for goodwill. If the company plans to incur advertising and promotional costs each year to maintain the value of the goodwill, must the company also amortize the goodwill?

19. Refer to the consolidated balance sheets for NIKE in Appendix A. What title does NIKE use to describe its plant assets? What is NIKE's book value of plant assets as of May 31, 1997, and May 31, 1996?

20. Refer to the consolidated balance sheet of Reebok in Appendix A. How are the property and equipment and intangibles of Reebok presented on its balance sheet?

21. Refer to the consolidated balance sheet of America Online in Appendix A. Identify two different intangible assets owned by American Online.

Quick Study

QS 11-1
Defining plant assets
C1

Explain the difference between (a) plant assets and current assets; (b) plant assets and inventory; and (c) plant assets and long-term investments.

QS 11-2
Cost of plant asset
C1

Starbuck Lanes installed automatic score-keeping equipment. The electrical work required to prepare for the installation was $18,000. The invoice price of the equipment was $180,000. Additional costs were $3,000 for delivery and $12,600 of sales tax. During the installation, a component of the equipment was damaged because it was carelessly left on a lane and hit by the automatic lane cleaning machine during a daily maintenance run. The cost of repairing the component was $2,250. What is the recorded cost of the automatic score-keeping equipment?

QS 11-3
Depreciation methods
P2

On January 2, 1999, Crossfire acquired sound equipment for concert performances at a cost of $55,900. The rock band estimated they would use this equipment for four years, during which time they anticipated performing about 120 concerts. They estimated at that point they could sell the equipment for $1,900. During 1999, the band performed 40 concerts. Compute the 1999 depreciation using (a) the straight-line method and (b) the units-of-production method.

QS 11-4
Computing revised depreciation
C3

Refer to the facts in QS 11–3. Assume that Crossfire chose straight-line depreciation but recognized during the second year that due to concert bookings beyond expectations, this equipment would only last a total of three years. The salvage value would remain unchanged. Compute the revised depreciation for the second year and the third year.

QS 11-5
Double-declining-balance method
P2

A fleet of refrigerated delivery trucks acquired on January 5, 1999, at a cost of $930,000 had an estimated useful life of eight years and an estimated salvage value of $150,000. Compute the depreciation expense for the first three years under the double-declining-balance method.

QS 11-6
Revenue and capital expenditures
P3

a. Classify the following expenditures as revenue or capital expenditures:
   (1) Cost of annual tune-ups for delivery trucks.
   (2) Cost of replacing a compressor for a refrigeration system that extends the estimated life of the system four years, $30,000.
   (3) Cost of $220,000 for an addition of a new wing on an office building.
   (4) Monthly cost of replacement filters on an air conditioning system, $175.
b. Prepare the journal entry to record items (2) and (3) of part a.

Spectrum Flooring owned an automobile with a $15,000 cost and $13,500 accumulated depreciation. In a transaction with a neighboring computer retailer, Spectrum exchanged this auto for a computer with a fair market value of $4,500. Spectrum was required to pay an additional $3,750 cash. Prepare the entry to record this transaction for Spectrum.

QS 11-7
Dissimilar asset
exchanges
P4

Mayes Co. owns an industrial machine that cost $38,400 and has accumulated depreciation of $20,400. Mayes exchanged the machine for a newer model that has a fair market value of $48,000. Record the exchange assuming cash paid of (*a*) $32,000 and then (*b*) $24,000.

QS 11-8
Similar asset
exchange
P4

For each of the following investing activities, identify whether it is a source or use of cash.
Key: **A.** Source of cash from investing activities.
   B. Use of cash for investing activities.

1. _____ Cash purchase of machinery   **3.** _____ Purchase of productive timberland for cash
2. _____ Sale of patents for cash   **4.** _____ Cash sale of factory warehouse

QS 11-9
Cash impacts from
acquisitions and disposals
C4

Eastman Kodak Company reported the following in its annual report: net sales of $13,557 million for 1994 and $12,670 million for 1993; total end-of-year assets of $14,968 million for 1994 and $18,810 million for 1993. Compute its total asset turnover for 1994.

QS 11-10
Computing total
asset turnover
A2

Boise Industries acquired an ore mine at a cost of $1,300,000. It was necessary to incur additional costs of $200,000 to access the mine. The mine is estimated to hold 500,000 tons of ore, and the estimated value of the land after the ore is removed is $150,000.
a. Prepare the entry to record the cost of the ore mine.
b. Prepare the year-end adjusting entry assuming 90,000 tons of ore are mined and sold this year.

QS 11-11
Natural resources and
depletion
P5

Which of the following assets are reported on the balance sheet as intangible assets? Which are reported as natural resources? (*a*) Leasehold, (*b*) Salt mine, (*c*) Building, (*d*) Oil well, (*e*) Trademark.

QS 11-12
Classifying
assets
P6

On January 4 of the current year, Amber's Boutique incurred a $95,000 cost to modernize its store. Improvements included new floors, lighting, and shelving for merchandise. It is estimated these improvements will last for 10 years. Amber's leases its retail space and has 8 years remaining on the lease. Prepare the entry to record the cost of modernization and the amortization entry at the end of the current year.

QS 11-13
Intangible assets
and amortization
P6

Santiago Co. purchased a machine for $11,500, terms 2/10, n/60, FOB shipping point. The seller prepaid the freight charges, $260, adding the amount to the invoice and bringing its total to $11,760. The machine required a special steel mounting and power connections costing $795, and another $375 was paid to assemble the machine and get it into operation. In moving the machine to its steel mounting, it was dropped and damaged. The repairs cost $190. Later, $30 of materials were consumed in adjusting the machine so that it would produce a satisfactory product. The adjustments were normal for this type of machine and were not the result of the damage. Prepare a computation to show the cost of this machine for accounting purposes. (Assume Santiago pays for the purchase within the discount period.)

Exercises
Exercise 11-1
Cost of plant asset

C1

Horizon Company paid $368,250 for real estate plus $19,600 in closing costs. The real estate included land appraised at $166,320; land improvements appraised at $55,440; and a building appraised at $174,240. Prepare a computation showing the allocation of the total cost among the three purchased assets and present the journal entry to record the purchase.

Exercise 11-2
Lump-sum purchase
of plant assets
C1

Planning to build a new plant, Monarch Manufacturing purchased a large lot on which an old building was located. The negotiated purchase price for this real estate was $225,000 for the lot plus $120,000 for the old building. The company paid $34,500 to have the old building torn down and $51,000 for landscaping the lot. It paid a total of $1,440,000 in construction costs, which included the cost of a new building and $85,500 for lighting and paving a parking lot next to the building. Present a single journal entry to record these costs incurred by Monarch, all of which were paid in cash.

Exercise 11-3
Recording costs of real
estate

C1

Exercise 11-4
Alternative
depreciation
methods **C2**

On the first day of the year, Barrow Company installed a computerized machine in its factory at a cost of $42,300. The machine's useful life was estimated at 10 years, or 363,000 units of product, with a $6,000 trade-in value. During its second year, the machine produced 35,000 units of product. Determine the machine's second-year depreciation under the (a) straight-line, (b) units-of-production, and (c) double-declining-balance methods.

Exercise 11-5
Alternative depreciation
methods; partial
year's depreciation **C3**

On April 1, 1999, Rodgers Backhoe Co. purchased a trencher for $250,000. The machine was expected to last five years and have a salvage value of $25,000. Compute depreciation expense for the year 2000, using the (a) straight-line method and (b) double-declining-balance method.

Exercise 11-6
Revising depreciation
rates

C3

BodySmart Fitness Club used straight-line depreciation for a machine that cost $21,750, under the assumption it would have a four-year life and a $2,250 trade-in value. After two years, BodySmart determined that the machine still had three more years of remaining useful life, after which it would have an estimated $1,800 trade-in value. (a) Compute the machine's book value at the end of its second year. (b) Compute the amount of depreciation to be charged during each of the remaining three years in the machine's revised useful life.

Exercise 11-7
Income effects
of alternative
depreciation
methods **A1**

Shamrock Enterprises recently paid $235,200 for equipment that will last five years and have a salvage value of $52,500. By using the machine in its operations for five years, the company expects to earn $85,500 annually, after deducting all expenses except depreciation. Present a schedule showing income before depreciation, depreciation expense, and net income for each year and the total amounts for the five-year period, assuming (a) straight-line depreciation and (b) double-declining-balance depreciation.

Exercise 11-8
Alternate
depreciation
methods **P2**

In January 1999, Labtech purchased computer equipment for $147,000. The equipment will be used in research and development activities for four years and then sold at an estimated salvage value of $30,000. Prepare schedules showing the depreciation and book values for the four years assuming (a) straight-line depreciation and (b) double-declining-balance.

Exercise 11-9
Ordinary repairs,
extraordinary repairs, and
betterments

P3

Archer Company paid $262,500 for equipment that was expected to last four years and have a salvage value of $30,000. Prepare journal entries to record the following costs related to the equipment:

a. During the second year of the equipment's life, $21,000 cash was paid for a new component that was expected to increase the equipment's productivity by 10% each year.

b. During the third year, $5,250 cash was paid for normal repairs necessary to keep the equipment in good working order.

c. During the fourth year, $13,950 was paid for repairs that were expected to increase the useful life of the equipment from four to five years.

Exercise 11-10
Extraordinary repairs;
computations and entries

P3

Flemming Company owns a building that appeared on its prior year's balance sheet at its original $561,000 cost less $420,750 accumulated depreciation. The building has been depreciated on a straight-line basis under the assumption it has a 20-year life and no salvage value. During the first week in January of the current year, major structural repairs were completed on the building at a cost of $67,200. The repairs did not increase the building's capacity, but they did extend its expected life for 7 years beyond the 20 years originally estimated.

a. Determine the building's age as of the end of last year.

b. Give the entry to record the costs of major repairs, which are paid in cash.

c. Determine the book value of the building immediately after the repairs are recorded.

d. Give the entry to record the current year's depreciation.

Exercise 11-11
Partial year's depreciation;
disposal of plant asset

P4

Levy Co. purchased and installed a machine on January 1, 1999, at a total cost of $92,750. Straight-line depreciation was taken each year for four years assuming a seven-year life and no salvage value. The machine was disposed of on July 1, 2003, during its fifth year of service. Prepare entries to record the partial year's depreciation on July 1, 2003, and to record the disposal under the following separate assumptions: (a) the machine is sold for $35,000 cash; and (b) Levy received an insurance settlement of $30,000 resulting from the total destruction of the machine in a fire.

Greenbelt Construction traded in an old tractor for a new tractor, receiving a $28,000 trade-in allowance and paying the remaining $82,000 in cash. The old tractor cost $95,000, and straight-line depreciation of $52,500 had been recorded under the assumption that it would last eight years and have an $11,000 salvage value. Answer the following questions:

a. What was the book value of the old tractor?

b. What is the loss on the exchange?

c. What amount should be debited to the new Tractor account?

Exercise 11-12
Exchanging similar assets

P4

On January 2, 1999, Hammond Service Co. disposed of a machine that cost $42,000 and had been depreciated $22,625. Present the journal entries to record the disposal under each of the following unrelated assumptions:

a. Machine is sold for $16,250 cash.

b. Machine is traded in on a new machine of like purpose having a $58,500 cash price. A $20,000 trade-in allowance is received, and the balance is paid in cash.

c. A $15,000 trade-in allowance is received for the machine on a new machine of like purpose having a $58,500 cash price. The balance is paid in cash.

d. Machine is traded for vacant land next to the shop to be used as a parking lot. The land has a fair value of $37,500, and Hammond paid $12,500 cash in addition to giving up the machine.

Exercise 11-13
Recording plant asset disposals

P4

Refer to the statement of cash flows for **America Online** in Appendix A for the year ended June 30, 1996, to answer the following:

a. What amount of cash is used to purchase property and equipment?

b. What amount of cash is received from sales of property and equipment?

c. How much depreciation and amortization is recorded?

d. What is the total amount of net cash used in investing activities?

e. Are there any gains or losses from sale of property and equipment?

Exercise 11-14
Cash flows related to plant assets

C4

Atherton Co. reports net sales of $4,862,000 for 1999 and $7,542,000 for 2000. End-of-year balances for total assets were: 1998, $1,586,000; 1999, $1,700,000; and 2000, $1,882,000. Compute Atherton's total asset turnover for 1999 and 2000 and comment on the company's efficiency in using its assets.

Exercise 11-15
Evaluating efficient use of assets   A2

On April 2, 1999, Cascade Mining Co. paid $3,633,750 for an ore deposit containing 1,425,000 tons. The company also installed machinery in the mine that cost $171,000, had an estimated seven-year life with no salvage value, and was capable of removing all the ore in six years. The machinery will be abandoned when the ore is completely mined. Cascade began operations on May 1, 1999, and mined and sold 156,200 tons of ore during the remaining eight months of the year. Give the December 31, 1999, entries to record the depletion of the ore deposit and the depreciation of the mining machinery. Depreciation of mining machinery should be in proportion to the mine's depletion.

Exercise 11-16
Depletion of natural resources

P5

The Falstaff Gallery purchased the copyright on an oil painting for $236,700 on January 1, 1999. The copyright legally protects its owner for 19 more years. However, the company plans to market and sell prints of the original for only 12 years. Prepare journal entries to record the purchase of the copyright on January 1, 1999 and the annual amortization of the copyright on December 31, 1999.

Exercise 11-17
Amortization of   P6
intangible assets

Corey Boyd has devoted years to developing a profitable business that earns an attractive return. Boyd is now considering the possibility of selling the business and is attempting to estimate the value of goodwill in the business. The fair value of the net assets of the business (excluding goodwill) is $437,000, and in a typical year net income is about $85,000. Most businesses of this type are expected to earn a return of about 10% on net assets. Estimate the value of the goodwill assuming (a) the value is equal to 10 times the amount that net income is above-normal, and (b) the value is computed by capitalizing the amount that net income is above-normal at a rate of 8%.

Exercise 11-18
Estimating goodwill

Problems

Problem 11-1

Real estate costs; partial year's depreciation

C1, C2, C3

In 1999, Lightscapes paid $2,800,000 for a tract of land and two buildings on it. The plan is to demolish Building One and build a new store in its place. Building Two is to be used as a company office and is appraised at a value of $641,300, with a useful life of 20 years and an $80,000 salvage value. A lighted parking lot near Building One has improvements (Land Improvements One) valued at $408,100 that are expected to last another 14 years and have no salvage value. Without considering the buildings or improvements, the tract of land is valued at $1,865,600. Lightscapes incurred the following additional costs:

Cost to demolish Building One	$ 422,600
Cost of additional landscaping	167,200
Cost to construct new building (Building Three), having a useful life of 25 years and a $390,100 salvage value	2,019,000
Cost of new land improvements near Building Two (Land Improvements Two) which have a 20-year useful life and no salvage value	158,000

Required

1. Prepare a schedule having the following column headings: Land, Building Two, Building Three, Land Improvements One, and Land Improvements Two. Allocate the costs incurred by Lightscapes to the appropriate columns and total each column.
2. Prepare a single journal entry to record all the incurred costs, assuming they are paid in cash on March 31, 1999.
3. Using the straight-line method, prepare December 31 adjusting entries to record depreciation for the nine months of 1999 during which the assets were in use.

Check Figure
Accumulated depreciation, Land Improvements Two, $5,925 Cr.

Problem 11-2

Plant asset costs; partial year's depreciation; alternative methods

C1, C2, C3

G S

Gunner Construction recently negotiated a lump-sum purchase of several assets from a company that was going out of business. The purchase is completed on March 1, 1999, at a total cash price of $787,500 and included a building, land, land improvements, and 12 vehicles. The estimated market values of the assets are: building, $408,000; land, $289,000; land improvements, $42,500; and vehicles, $110,500. The company's fiscal year ends on December 31.

Required

Preparation Component

1. Prepare a schedule to allocate the lump-sum purchase price to the separate assets purchased. Present the journal entry to record the purchase.
2. Compute the 1999 depreciation expense on the building using the straight-line method, assuming a 15-year life and a $25,650 salvage value.
3. Compute the 1999 depreciation expense on the land improvements assuming a five-year life and double-declining-balance depreciation.

Analysis Component

4. Defend or refute this statement: Accelerated depreciation results in less taxes being paid over the life of the asset.

Check Figure 1999 depreciation expense on land improvements, $13,125

Problem 11-3

Alternative depreciation methods; partial year's depreciation; disposal of plant asset

C3, P2 G

Part 1. A machine costing $210,000 with a four-year life and an estimated $20,000 salvage value is installed in Casablanca Company's factory on January 1. The factory manager estimates the machine will produce 475,000 units of product during its life. It actually produces the following units: year 1, 121,400; year 2, 122,400; year 3, 119,600; and year 4, 118,200. The total number of units produced by the end of year 4 exceeds the original estimate. The machine must not be depreciated below the estimated salvage value.

Required

Prepare a form with the following column headings:

Year	Straight-Line	Units-of-Production	Double-Declining-Balance

Check Figure Year 4, units-of-production depreciation expense, $44,640

Then show the depreciation for each year and the total depreciation for the machine under each depreciation method.

Part 2. Casablanca purchased a used machine for $167,000 on January 2. It is repaired the next day at a cost of $3,420 and installed on a new platform costing $1,080. The company predicts the machine will be used for six years and have a $14,600 salvage value. Depreciation is to be charged on a straight-line basis. A full year's depreciation is charged on December 31, the end of the first year of the machine's use. On September 30 of its sixth year in service, it is retired.

Required

a. Prepare journal entries to record the purchase of the machine, the cost of repairing it, and the installation. Cash is paid for all costs incurred.

b. Prepare entries to record depreciation at the machine at December 31 of its first year and on September 30 in the year of its disposal.

c. Prepare entries to record the retirement of the machine under each of the following unrelated assumptions: (i) it is sold for $13,500; (ii) it is sold for $36,000; and (iii) it is destroyed in a fire and the insurance company pays $24,000 in full settlement of the loss claim.

Crenshaw Contractors completed these transactions involving the purchase and operation of equipment:

1999
July 1   Paid $255,440 cash for a new loader plus $15,200 in sales tax and $2,500 for transportation charges. The loader is estimated to have a four-year life and a $34,740 salvage value. Loader costs are recorded in the Equipment account.
Oct. 2   Paid $3,660 to enclose the cab and install air conditioning in the loader. This increased the estimated salvage value of the loader by $1,110.
Dec. 31 Record straight-line depreciation on the loader.

2000
Feb. 17 Paid $920 to repair the loader after the operator backed it into a tree.
June 30 Paid $4,500 to overhaul the loader's engine. As a result, the estimated useful life of the loader is increased by two years.
Dec. 31 Record straight-line depreciation on the loader.

Required

Prepare journal entries to record these transactions.

Problem 11-4
Partial year's depreciation; revising depreciation rates; revenue and capital expenditures

C3, P3

ACT Company completed the following transactions involving delivery trucks:

1999
Mar. 26 Paid $19,415 cash for a new delivery truck plus $1,165 in sales tax. The truck is estimated to have a five-year life and a $3,000 trade-in value. Delivery truck costs are recorded in the Trucks account.
Dec. 31 Record straight-line depreciation on the truck.

2000
Dec. 31 Record straight-line depreciation on the truck. Due to new information obtained earlier in the year, the original estimated useful life of the truck is changed from five years to four years, and the original estimated trade-in value is increased to $3,500.

Check Figure Dec. 31, 2000, Depr. Expense, Equipment, $48,674

Problem 11-5
Partial year's depreciation; revising depreciation rates; exchanging plant assets

C3, P4

2001

July 7   Traded in the old truck and paid $13,565 in cash for a new truck. The new truck is estimated
         to have a six-year life and a $3,125 trade-in value. The invoice for the exchange shows:

Price of the new truck	$22,550
Trade-in allowance granted on the old truck	(9,750)
Balance of purchase price	$12,800
State sales tax	765
Total paid in cash	$13,565

Dec. 31   Record straight-line depreciation on the new truck.

Check Figure   July 7,
2001, Loss on Exchange of
Trucks, $1,527

Required

Prepare journal entries to record these transactions.

Problem 11-6
Partial year's depreciation;
alternative methods;
disposal of plant assets

C3, P2, P4

Wallingford Company completed the following transactions involving machinery:

Machine No. 15-50 is purchased for cash on May 4, 1999, at an installed cost of $158,700. Its use-
ful life is estimated to be six years with a $12,900 trade-in value. Straight-line depreciation is recorded
for the machine at the end of 1999, 2000, and 2001. On April 27, 2002, it is traded for Machine No.
17-95, a similar asset, for an installed cash price of $185,700. A trade-in allowance of $90,330 is received for Machine No. 15-50, and the balance is paid in cash.

Machine No. 17-95's life is predicted to be four years with a $24,600 trade-in value. Double-de-
clining-balance depreciation on this machine is recorded each December 31. On November 5,
2003, it is traded for Machine No. BT-311, a dissimilar asset, for an installed cash price of
$537,000. A trade-in allowance of $81,000 is received for Machine No. 17-95, and the balance is
paid in cash.

It is estimated that Machine No. BT-311 will produce 600,000 units of product during its five-year
useful life, after which it will have a $105,000 trade-in value. Units-of-production depreciation is
recorded for the machine for 2003, a period in which it produces 93,000 units of product. Between
January 1, 2004, and August 24, 2006, the machine produces 324,000 more units. On the latter date,
it is sold for $243,600.

Check Figure   11/5/2003
Gain on Sale of Machinery,
$10,545.

Required

Prepare journal entries to record: *(a)* the purchase of each machine, *(b)* the depreciation expense recorded
on the first December 31 of each machine's life, and *(c)* the disposal of each machine. (Only one entry
is needed to record the exchange of one machine for another.)

Problem 11-7
Intangible assets and
natural resources

P5, P6

Part 1. In 1995, The Pullman Company leased space in a building for 15 years. The lease contract calls
for annual rental payments of $70,000 to be made on each July 1 throughout the life of the lease and
also provides that the lessee must pay for all additions and improvements to the leased property. In 2000,
Pullman decided to sublease the space to Kidman & Associates for the remaining 10 years of the lease.
On June 20, 2000, Kidman paid $185,000 to Pullman for the right to sublease the space and agreed to
assume the obligation to pay the $70,000 annual rent to the building owner beginning July 1, 2000. Af-
ter taking possession of the leased space, Kidman paid for improving the office portion of the leased
space at a cost of $129,840. The improvements were paid for on July 5, 2000, and are estimated to have
a life equal to the 16 years remaining in the life of the building.

Required

Prepare entries for Kidman to record *(a)* its payment to Pullman for the right to sublease the building
space, *(b)* its payment of the 2000 annual rent to the building owner, and *(c)* its payment for the office
improvements. Prepare Kidman's adjusting entries required at the end of 2000 to amortize *(d)* a proper
share of the $185,000 cost of the sublease and *(e)* a proper share of the office improvements.

Part 2. On July 3 of the current year, Jackson Mining Co. paid $4,836,000 for land estimated to contain 7.8 million tons of recoverable ore of a valuable mineral. It installed machinery costing $390,000, which has a 10-year life and no salvage value, and is capable of exhausting the ore deposit in eight years. The machinery is paid for on July 25, nine days before mining operations began. The company removes 400,000 tons of ore during the first five months of operations. Depreciation of the machinery is in proportion to the mine's depletion (it will be abandoned after the ore is fully mined).

Required

Preparation Component

Prepare entries to record *(a)* the purchase of the land, *(b)* the installation of the machinery, *(c)* the first five months' depletion under the assumption the land is valueless after the ore is mined, and *(d)* the first five months' depreciation on the machinery.

Check Figure Depletion Expense, $248,000

Analysis Component

Describe the similarities and differences in amortization, depletion, and depreciation.

American Rental Co., an equipment rental business, has the following balance sheet on December 31, 1999:

Problem 11-8
Goodwill estimation and amortization

Assets	
Cash	$ 93,930
Equipment	678,800
Accumulated depreciation, Equipment	(271,500)
Buildings	340,000
Accumulated depreciation, Buildings	(182,400)
Land	93,000
Total assets	$751,830
Liabilities and Equity	
Accounts payable	$ 18,650
Long-term note payable	337,250
J. Reynolds, capital	395,930
Total liabilities and owner's equity	$751,830

In this industry, net income averages 20% of owner's equity. American Rental regularly expects to earn $100,000 annually. The balance sheet amounts are reasonable estimates of fair market values for all assets except goodwill, which does not appear on the financial statement. In negotiations to sell the business, American Rental proposes that goodwill be measured by capitalizing the amount of above-normal net income at a rate of 15%. The potential buyer thinks that goodwill should be valued at five times the amount that net income is above the average for the industry.

Required

1. Compute the amount of goodwill as proposed by American Rental.
2. Compute the amount of goodwill according to the potential buyer.
3. The buyer purchases the business for the amount of the net assets reported on the December 31, 1999, balance sheet plus the amount proposed by American Rental for the goodwill. If the amount of expected net income (before amortization of goodwill) is obtained the first year, and the goodwill is amortized over the longest permissible time period, what amount of net income will be reported for the first year after the business is purchased?
4. What rate of return on the buyer's investment does the first year's net income represent?

Check Figure Goodwill, (1) $138,760, and (2) $104,070

BEYOND THE NUMBERS

Reporting in Action

A1

Refer to the financial statements and related information for **NIKE** in Appendix A. Answer the following questions by analyzing the information in its annual report:

1. What percent of the original cost of NIKE's property and equipment remains to be depreciated as of May 31, 1997 and 1996? Assume these assets have no salvage value.
2. Over what periods of time is NIKE amortizing intangible assets and goodwill?
3. What is the net change in total property and equipment (before depreciation) for the year ended May 31, 1997? What is the amount of cash generated by (or used for) investment in property and equipment during the year ended May 31, 1997? What is one possible explanation for the difference between these two amounts?
4. Compute NIKE's total asset turnover for the year ended May 31, 1997.

Swoosh Ahead

5. Obtain access to NIKE's annual report for fiscal years ending after May 31, 1997. You can gain access to NIKE's annual report at its web site [**www.nike.com**] or through the SEC's EDGAR database [**www.sec.gov**]. Recompute NIKE's total asset turnover for the additional years' data you collect. Comment on any differences relative to the turnover computed in (4) above.

Comparative Analysis

A2

Both **NIKE** and **Reebok** design, produce, market, and sell sports footwear and apparel. Key comparative figures ($ in millions) for these two companies follow:

	NIKE		Reebok	
Key Figures*	1997	1996	1996	1995
Total Assets	$5,361	$3,952	$1,786	$1,652
Net sales	9,187	6,471	3,479	3,481

*NIKE figures are from its annual reports for fiscal years ended May 31, 1997 and 1996. Reebok figures are from its annual reports for fiscal years ended December 31, 1996 and 1995.

Required

1. Compute NIKE's total asset turnover as of May 31, 1997. Compute Reebok's total asset turnover as of December 31, 1996.

Analysis Component

2. Which company is more efficient in generating net sales given the total assets employed?

Ethics Challenge

C2

Marcia Diamond is a small business owner and handles all the books for her business. Her company just finished a year when a large amount of borrowed funds was invested into a new building addition as well as numerous equipment and fixture additions. Marcia's banker requires that she submit semi-annual financial statements so he can monitor the financial health of her business. He has warned her that if profit margins erode, he might raise the interest rate on the borrowed funds since this means the loan is riskier from the bank's point of view. Marcia knows profit margin is likely to decline in this current year. As she posts year-end adjusting entries, she decides to apply the following depreciation rule: all capital additions are considered put into service the first day of the following month.

Required

1. Identify decisions that managers like Ms. Diamond must make in applying depreciation methods.
2. Is Marcia's decision an ethical violation or is it a legitimate decision managers make in computing depreciation?
3. How will Marcia's depreciation rule affect the profit margin of her business?

The class is divided into teams. Teams are to select an industry, and each team member is to select a different company in that industry. Each team member is to acquire the annual report of the company selected. Annual reports can be obtained in many ways including accessing this book's Web page or through the SEC's EDGAR database [**www.sec.gov**]. Use the annual report to compute total asset turnover. Communicate with teammates via a meeting, e-mail, or telephone to discuss the meaning of this ratio, how different companies compare to each other, and the industry norm. The team must prepare a single memo reporting the ratios for each company and identify the conclusions reached during the team's discussion. The memo is to be duplicated and distributed to the instructor and all classmates.

**Communicating
in Practice**
A2

Visit the Web site of the **U.S. Patent and Trademark Office** at http://patents.uspto.gov. Use the search function to look for any existing patents protecting some of your favorite products. For example, if you search "Coca Cola" you will find numerous patents protecting various aspects of the Coke product from its packaging, to its recipe, to products using it as a theme. Search three different products and note the range of patents protecting the product. (Note: If you have an idea for a new product you might also want to search the database to see if there are any preexisting patents on your idea.)

**Taking It to the
Net**
C1

Each member of the team has the responsibility to become a resident expert on a specific depreciation method. This expertise is used to facilitate their teammates' understanding of the concepts relevant to the method he or she has chosen. Follow the procedure outlined below:

**Teamwork in
Action**
C2, A1, P2

1. Each team member is to select an area for expertise by choosing one of the following depreciation methods: straight line, units of production, and declining balance. You have one minute to make your choices.

2. Learning teams are to disburse and expert teams are to be formed. Expert teams are made up of students who have all selected the same area of expertise. The instructor will identify the location where each expert team meets.

3. Using data below, expert teams are to collaborate and develop a presentation illustrating each of the relevant procedures and concepts required below. Expert team members must write up the presentation in a format they can show to their learning teams in the next step in the activity.

Data: On January 8, 1998, Whitewater Riders purchase a van to transport rafters back to the point of departure at the conclusion of the rafting adventure tours they run. The cost of the van is $44,000. It has an estimated salvage value of $2,000 and is expected to be used for 4 years and driven 60,000 miles. The van is expected to be driven: 12,000 miles in 1998; 18,000 miles in 1999; 21,000 in 2000; and 10,000 in 2001.

Procedures and concepts to illustrate in expert presentation:
   a. Compute annual depreciation expense for each year of the asset's estimated useful life.
   b. Explain when and how annual depreciation is recorded.
   c. Explain the impact of this method versus other methods on net income over the life of the asset.
   d. Identify the book value of the asset over each year of the asset's life and illustrate the reporting of this amount for any one year.

4. Re-form learning teams. In rotation, experts are to present to their teams the results from (3). Experts are to encourage and respond to questions.

Team up with one or more classmates for this activity. You are to brainstorm and do any necessary research to identify companies in your community or your area of the country that have and must account for the following assets: natural resource; patent; lease; leasehold improvement; copyright; trademark; and goodwill. You might need to identify seven different companies given there are seven assets, or you might find a company having more than one type of asset. Once you have matched a company with the asset, identify the accounting this company must use for that asset to allocate its cost to the periods that benefited from its use.

**Hitting the
Road**
C1

Read the article "Guardian of the Famous and the Dead" in the May 8, 1995, issue of *Business Week*.
1. What is the purpose of the **Curtis Management Group** run by CEO Mark A. Roesler?
2. What is the difference between a trademark and rights of publicity?
3. Identify one famous person in each of the following categories represented by the Curtis Management Group: Hollywood, Music, Sports, and Historical.
4. What is the attitude of the U.S. Trade Representatives' office toward the work of the Curtis Management Group?

Business Week
Activity
C1

Current and Long-Term Liabilities

Chapter Outline

Tax Cop

DETROIT, MI—Carmen Benish and her two comrades jump out of their battered Zhiguli and walk briskly to the door of a bicycle sales and services shop in the Moscow suburb of Podolsk. Ducking under bicycle frames hanging from the ceiling, they approach a salesclerk and flash their badges. A few days earlier, an undercover colleague made a purchase that wasn't reported. Benish, Mikail Nikolas, and Val Yaroslav are investigating whether the business is underreporting sales to avoid paying taxes. Two burly policemen in bulletproof vests stand guard as Benish and her fellow investigators confiscate Vladimir Zolov's records. "We pay our taxes on time. We are law-abiding citizens," he protests.

Benish is special. She grew up in a tough inner city environment. But she was determined to stay out of trouble. "I went to college and took accounting and criminal justice," say Benish. "I also joined an international club. I loved the cultural differences." When she graduated with her associate degree this past June, she faced a dilemma. "I like both accounting and criminal justice," says Benish. "I didn't know which way to go."

Fortunately for Benish, her counselor knew the IRS sometimes hires people with exactly the type of background she had. Benish is now an intern in a unique program for international tax investigators at the IRS. "It is a match made in heaven! I get to use my accounting and criminal justice background to help track the underreporting of international income to avoid taxes." Given the huge growth in international sales, this is a high priority at the IRS.

Benish is presently assigned to a one-month internship in Moscow. "Russia is a nightmare for us," says Peter Eastwood, Benish's supervisor at the IRS. "But our job is to ensure that U.S. companies and their affiliates doing business here pay their taxes." These investigators have considerable power. They can levy fines up to three times taxes owed and can seize taxpayers' property and freeze bank accounts during investigations.

But the job is dangerous. Last year in Russia alone, 26 tax officials were killed and 74 wounded, while another 18 tax offices were bombed or sprayed with gunfire. "Sure I'm sometimes scared. But I'm really having fun, and the odds of something bad happening are low," says Benish. "No green eyeshades and cushy desk job for me!"

CHAPTER PREVIEW

Previous chapters introduced us to liabilities for accounts payable, notes payable, wages, and unearned revenues. In this chapter, we learn more about these liabilities and additional ones such as warranties, taxes, payroll, vacation pay, and leases. We also describe contingent liabilities and look at some long-term liabilities. This includes how we define, classify, and measure liabilities for the purpose of reporting useful information about them to decision makers. Understanding tax liabilities is important for Carmen Benish in her IRS work as described in the opening article.

Characteristics of Liabilities

C1 Describe current and long-term liabilities and their characteristics.

This section discusses important characteristics of liabilities, how they are classified, and how they are reported.

Defining Liabilities

A liability is a probable future payment of assets or services that a company is presently obligated to make as a result of past transactions or events.[1] This definition includes three crucial factors:

- Due to a past transaction or event
- Present obligation
- Future payment of assets or services

These three important elements are portrayed visually in Exhibit 12.1.

Exhibit 12.1

Characteristics of a Liability

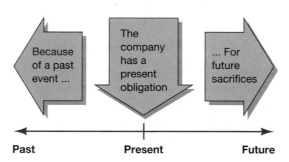

Liabilities do not include all expected future payments. For example, most companies expect to pay wages to its employees in upcoming months and years. But these future payments are not liabilities because there is no past event such as employee work resulting in a present obligation. Future liabilities will arise when employees perform their work and earn the wages.

Classifying Liabilities as Current or Long-Term

Information about liabilities is more useful when the balance sheet identifies them as either current or long-term. Decision makers need to know when obligations are due so they can plan for them and take appropriate action.

Current Liabilities

Current liabilities, also called *short-term liabilities,* are obligations expected to be paid using current assets or by creating other current liabilities.[2] Current liabilities are due within one year or the company's operating cycle, whichever is longer. Examples of current liabilities are accounts payable, short-term notes payable, wages payable, warranty liabilities, lease liabilities, payroll and other taxes payable, and unearned revenues.

---

[1] Financial Accounting Standards Board, *Statement of Financial Accounting Concepts No. 6,* "Elements of Financial Statements" (Norwalk, CT, 1985), par. 35.

[2] FASB, *Accounting Standards—Current Text* (Norwalk, CT, 1995), sec. B05.402. First published as *Accounting Research Bulletin No. 43,* Ch. 3A, par. 7.

Current liabilities are different for different companies. A company's current liabilities depend on its type of operations. **Harley-Davidson,** for instance, recently reported the following items related to its motorcycle operations in its current liabilities section ($ thousands):

Accrued Liabilities

Warranty/recalls . . . . $ 9,384

Dealer incentive programs $29,220

Time Warner, the media and entertainment giant, reports a much different set of current liabilities. For instance, Time Warner reports more than $1 billion in current liabilities made up of items like television programming and royalties.

Long-Term Liabilities

A company's obligations not expected to be paid within one year (or a longer operating cycle) are reported as **long-term liabilities.** Long-term liabilities include long-term notes payable, warranty liabilities, lease liabilities, and bonds payable. They are sometimes reported on the balance sheet in a single long-term liabilities total. **The GAP,** for instance, reports a single total of $762 million long-term liabilities in its recent balance sheet. But many companies show them as two or more items such as *long-term debt* and *other liabilities.* **Dell,** for instance, reports long-term liabilities in its recent balance sheet of (in $ millions): long-term debt, $17; warranties, $225; other, $36. These are reported after current liabilities.

Many liabilities can be either current or long-term depending on their characteristics. A single liability also can be divided between these two sections if a company expects to make payments toward it in both the short and long-term. **Wal-Mart,** for instance, reports in its 1997 balance sheet ($ millions): long-term debt, $7,191; long-term debt due within one year, $1,039. The second item is reported in current liabilities. We also sometimes see liabilities that do not have a fixed due date but are payable on the creditor's demand. These are reported as current liabilities because of the possibility of payment within the year or the company's operating cycle, if longer. Exhibit 12.2 shows amounts of current and long-term liabilities for selected companies.

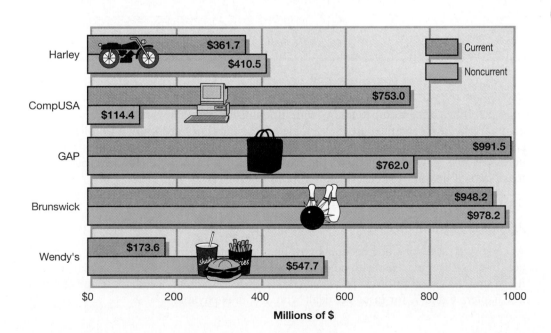

Exhibit 12.2

Current and Long-Term Liabilities

Uncertainty in Liabilities

Accounting for liabilities involves addressing three important questions: Whom to pay? When to pay? How much to pay? Answers to these questions often are decided when a liability is incurred. For example, if a company has an account payable to a specific individual for $100, payable on August 15, 1999, there is no uncertainty about the answers. The company knows whom to pay, when to pay, and how much to pay. But we do see liabilities with uncertainty in one or more of the answers to these three questions.

Uncertainty in Whom to Pay

Some liabilities involve uncertainty in whom to pay. For instance, a company creates a liability with a known amount when issuing a note that is payable to its holder. Although a specific amount is payable to the note's holder at a specified date, the company doesn't know who the holder is until that date. Despite this uncertainty, the corporation reports this liability on its balance sheet.

Uncertainty in When to Pay

A company can have an obligation of a known amount to a known creditor but not know when it must be paid. For example, a legal services firm can accept fees in advance from a client who expects to use its services in the future. This means the legal services firm has a liability that is settled by providing services at an unknown future date. Even though this uncertainty exists, the firm's balance sheet must report this liability. These types of obligations are reported as current liabilities because they are likely to be settled in the short term.

Uncertainty in How Much to Pay

A company can know it has an obligation but not know how much will be required to settle it. For example, a company using electrical power is billed only after the meter is read. This cost is incurred and the liability created before a bill is received. A liability to the power company is reported as an estimated amount if the balance sheet is prepared before a bill arrives.

Flash *back*

1. What is a liability?

2. Is every expected future payment a liability?

3. If a liability is payable in 15 months, is it classified as current or long-term?

Answers—p. 519

Known (Determinable) Liabilities

C2 Identify and describe known current liabilities.

Most liabilities arise from situations with little uncertainty. They are set by agreements, contracts, or laws, and they are measurable. These liabilities are **known liabilities,** also called *definitely determinable liabilities.* Known liabilities include accounts payable, notes payable, payroll, sales taxes, unearned revenues, and leases. How we account for these known liabilities is described in this section.

Accounts Payable

Accounts payable, or trade accounts payable, are amounts owed to suppliers for products or services purchased with credit. Accounting for accounts payable is explained and illustrated in several prior chapters. Much of our discussion of merchandising activities in Chapters 6 and 7, for instance, dealt with accounts payable.

Sales Taxes Payable

Nearly every state and many cities levy taxes on retail sales. Sales taxes are stated as a percent of selling prices. The retailer (seller) collects sales taxes from customers when sales occur and remits (often monthly) these collections to the proper government agency. Since retailers owe these collections to the government, this amount is a current liability for retailers. **Home Depot** reports sales taxes payable of $143 million in 1997. To illustrate, if Home Depot sells materials on August 31 worth $6,000 subject to a 5% sales tax, its entry is:

Aug. 31	Cash	6,300	
	Sales		6,000
	Sales Taxes Payable ($6,000 × 0.05)		300
	To record cash sales and 5% sales tax.		

Assets = Liabilities + Equity
+6,300   +300   +6,000

Sales Taxes Payable is debited and Cash credited when these collections are remitted to the government. Notice Sales Taxes Payable is not tied to any expense. Instead, it arises because laws require retailers to collect this cash from customers for the government.

Unearned Revenues

Unearned revenues (also called *deferred revenues, collections in advance,* and *prepayments*) are amounts received in advance from customers for future products or services. Advance ticket sales for sporting events or music concerts are examples of unearned revenues. The **Boston Celtics,** for instance, reported "deferred game revenues" including advance ticket sales of $6.2 million at March 31, 1998. For example, when the Celtics sell $5 million of season tickets, its entry is:

June 30	Cash	5,000,000	
	Unearned Season Ticket Revenue		5,000,000
	To record sale of of Celtic season tickets.		

Assets   = Liabilities + Equity
+5,000,000   +5,000,000

When each game is played, the Celtics record revenue for the portion earned:

Oct. 31	Unearned Season Ticket Revenue	60,000	
	Season Ticket Revenue		60,000
	To record Celtic season ticket revenues earned.		

Assets = Liabilities + Equity
         −60,000   +60,000

Unearned Season Ticket Revenue is an unearned revenue account and is reported as a current liability. Beyond sporting and music events, unearned revenues arise with airline ticket sales, magazine publishers, construction projects, hotel reservations, and custom orders.

Short-Term Notes Payable

A **short-term note payable** is a written promise to pay a specified amount on a definite future date within one year or the company's operating cycle, whichever is longer. These promissory notes are negotiable (as are checks). This means they can be transferred from party to party by endorsement. The written documentation provided by notes is helpful in resolving disputes and for pursuing legal actions involving these liabilities.

P1 Prepare entries to account for short-term notes payable.

Most notes payable are interest-bearing to compensate for the time until payment is made. Short-term notes payable arise from many transactions. A company purchases merchandise on credit and sometimes extends the credit period by signing a note to replace an account payable. They also arise when money is borrowed from a bank. We describe both of these cases in this section.

Note Given to Extend Credit Period

A company can create a note payable to replace an account payable. Most often, the creditor asks that an interest-bearing note be substituted for an overdue account payable that does not bear interest. A less common situation is where a debtor's weak financial condition encourages the creditor to obtain a note, sometimes for a lesser amount, and then close the account to ensure no additional credit sales are made to this customer.

Illustration of Note to Extend Credit Period

To illustrate, let's assume that on August 23 Wiley asks to extend its past-due $600 account payable to McGraw. After some negotiations, McGraw agrees to accept $100 cash and a 60-day, 12%, $500 note payable to replace the account payable. Wiley records this transaction with this entry:

Aug. 23	Accounts Payable—McGraw Company	600	
	Cash		100
	Notes Payable		500
	Gave $100 cash and a 60-day, 12% note for payment on account.		

Signing the note does not pay off Wiley's debt. Instead, the form of debt is changed from an account payable to a note payable. McGraw prefers the note payable over the account payable because it earns interest and also because it is written documentation of the debt's existence, term, and amount.

When the note comes due, Wiley pays the note and interest by giving McGraw a check for $510. This payment is recorded with this entry:

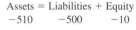

Oct. 22	Notes Payable	500	
	Interest Expense	10	
	Cash		510
	Paid note with interest ($500 × 12% × 60/360).		

The interest expense is computed by multiplying the principal of the note ($500) by the annual interest rate (12%) for the fraction of the year the note is outstanding (60 days/360 days).

Note Given to Borrow from Bank

A bank nearly always requires a borrower to sign a promissory note when making a loan. When the note matures, the borrower repays the note with an amount larger than the amount borrowed. The difference between the amount borrowed and the amount repaid is *interest*. A note often states that the signer of the note promises to pay *principal* (the amount borrowed) plus interest. In this case the *face value* of the note equals principal. Face value is the value shown on the face of the note.

A bank sometimes has a borrower sign a note with a face value that includes both principal and interest. In this case, the signer of the note receives *less* than the note's face value. The difference between the borrowed amount and the note's face value is interest. Since the borrowed amount is less than the note's face value, the difference is sometimes called **discount on note payable.**

To illustrate these two different types of notes, let's assume a company needs $2,000 for a specific project and borrows this money from a bank at 12% annual interest. The loan is made on September 30, 1999, and is due in 60 days.

Face Value Equals Amount Borrowed

The bank in this case requires the company to sign a note with a face value equal to the $2,000 borrowed. The note includes a statement similar to: *"I promise to pay $2,000 plus interest at 12% within 60 days after September 30."* This note is shown in Exhibit 12.3.

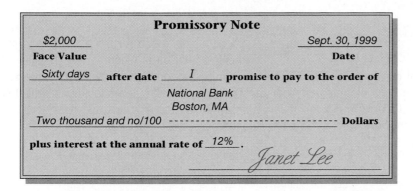

Exhibit 12.3

Note with Face Value Equal to Amount Borrowed

The borrowing company records its receipt of cash and the new liability with this entry:

Sept. 30	Cash	2,000	
	Notes Payable		2,000
	Borrowed $2,000 cash with a 60-day, 12%, $2,000 note.		

Assets = Liabilities + Equity
+2,000   +2,000

When the note and interest are paid 60 days later, the borrowing company records payment with this entry:

Nov. 29	Notes Payable	2,000	
	Interest Expense	40	
	Cash		2,040
	Paid note with interest ($2,000 × 12% × 60/360).		

Assets = Liabilities + Equity
−2,040   −2,000   −40

Face Value Equals Amount Borrowed plus Interest

The bank in this case writes a note with the 12% interest in its face value. This type of note includes a promise similar to: *"I promise to pay $2,040 within 60 days after September 30."* This note is shown in Exhibit 12.4. The note does not refer to the rate used to compute the $40 of interest included in the $2,040 face value. In other respects, this note is identical to the one in Exhibit 12.3. Because this note lacks a stated interest rate, it is sometimes called a **noninterest-bearing note.** This term can be misleading since the note does bear interest, but interest is included in the face value.

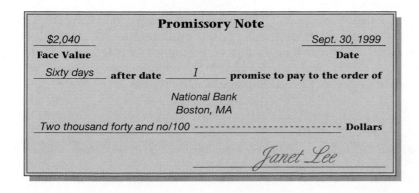

Exhibit 12.4

Note with Face Value Equal to Amount Borrowed plus Interest

When the face value of the note includes principal and interest, the borrowing company usually records this note with an entry to credit Notes Payable for the face value of the note and record the discount in a *contra-liability* account. This entry is:[3]

Sept. 30	Cash	2,000	
	Discount on Notes Payable	40	
	Notes Payable		2,040
	Borrowed $2,000 cash with a 60-day, 12%, $2,040 note.		

Assets = Liabilities + Equity
+2,000   +2,040
                  −40

Discount on Notes Payable is a contra-liability account to the Notes Payable account. If a balance sheet is prepared after this transaction on September 30, the $40 discount is subtracted from the $2,040 balance in the Notes Payable account to reflect the $2,000 net amount borrowed as follows:[4]

| Note payable .... | $2,040 | |
| Less discount on note payable .... | 40 | $2,000 |

When this note matures 60 days later on November 29, the entry to record the company's $2,040 payment to the bank is:

Nov. 29	Notes Payable	2,040	
	Interest Expense	40	
	Cash		2,040
	Discount on Notes Payable		40
	Paid note with interest.		

Assets = Liabilities + Equity
−2,040   −2,040   −40
                  +40

Rock Band

You are a member of a rock band. Your band needs $15,000 to upgrade equipment. You receive loan approvals for $15,000 cash at two banks. One bank's proposed loan contract reads: "Band promises to pay $15,000 plus interest at 14% within 6 months." The competing bank's contract reads: "Band promises to pay $16,000 within 6 months." Which loan do you prefer?

Answer—p. 519

End-of-Period Adjustments to Notes

When the end of an accounting period falls between the signing of a note payable and its maturity date, the *matching principle* requires us to record the accrued but unpaid interest on the note.

To illustrate these end-of-period adjustments, let's return to the short-term note above and assume the company borrowed the $2,000 on December 16, 1999, instead of September 30. This 60-day note then matures on February 14, 2000. Because the company's fiscal year ends on December 31, we need to record interest expense for the 15 days in December. The entries depend on the type of note.

---

[3] The discount is computed as $2,000 × 12% × 60/360.

[4] We approximate the annual interest rate on a short-term loan as: (Interest paid ÷ Amount received) × (360 days ÷ Loan period in days).

Face Value Equals Amount Borrowed

When the note's face value equals the amount borrowed, the accrued interest is charged to expense and credited to an Interest Payable account. To illustrate, we know that 15 days out of the 60-day loan period for the $2,000, 12% note have elapsed by December 31. This means one-fourth (15 days/60 days) of the $40 total interest is an expense of 1999. The borrowing company records this expense with the following adjusting entry at the end of 1999:

1999			
Dec. 31	Interest Expense	10	
	Interest Payable		10
	To record accrued interest on note		
	($2,000 × 12% × 15/360).		

Assets = Liabilities + Equity
       +10   −10

When this note matures on February 14, the company records this entry:

2000			
Feb. 14	Interest Expense ($2,000 × 12% × 45/360)	30	
	Interest Payable	10	
	Notes Payable	2,000	
	Cash		2,040
	Paid note with interest.		

Assets = Liabilities + Equity
−2,040   −10   −30
          −2000

This entry recognizes 45 days of interest expense for year 2000 and removes the balances of the two liability accounts.

Face Value Equals Amount Borrowed plus Interest

We now assume the face value of the note *includes* interest. To illustrate, we assume the borrowing company signs a $2,040 noninterest-bearing note on December 15. When recording this note on December 15, the company credits the $2,040 face value to Notes Payable and debits the $40 discount to a contra-liability account. At year-end, the adjusting entry needed to record the accrual of 15 days of interest for 1999 is:

Dec. 31	Interest Expense	10	
	Discount on Notes Payable		10
	To record accrued interest on note		
	($2,000 × 12% × 15/360).		

Assets = Liabilities + Equity
       +10   −10

Accrued interest is not credited to Interest Payable in this case. Instead, this entry reduces the balance of the contra-liability account from $40 to $30. This increases the net note liability to $2,010 ($2,040 note less $30 discount).

When this note matures, we need an entry both to accrue interest expense for the last 45 days of the note and to record its payment:

2000			
Feb. 14	Interest Expense	30	
	Notes Payable	2,040	
	Discount on Notes Payable		30
	Cash		2,040
	Paid note with interest ($2,000 × 12% × 45/360).		

Assets = Liabilities + Equity
−2,040   −2,040   −30
           +30

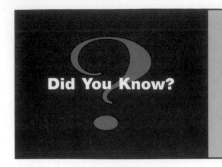

Did You Know?

IHOP Notes
Many franchisors use notes to help entrepreneurs acquire its franchises. **International House of Pancakes** (IHOP) allows about 80% of its franchise fee to be paid with a note payable. Payments on these notes are usually collected weekly.

Flash *back*

4. Why does a creditor want a past-due account replaced by a note?

5. A company borrows money by signing a note payable promising to pay $1,050 in 6 months. In recording the transaction, the company correctly debits $50 to Discount on Notes Payable. How much is borrowed? What annual rate of interest is charged?

Answers—p. 519

Payroll Liabilities

An employer incurs several expenses and liabilities from having employees. These expenses and liabilities are often large and arise from salaries and wages earned, from employee benefits, and from payroll taxes levied on the employer. **Anheuser-Busch,** for instance, reports the following payroll related current liabilities:

Accrued salaries, wages and benefits (in millions) .... $ 214.4

We discuss payroll liabilities and related accounts in this section. The appendix to this chapter describes important details about payroll reports, records, and procedures.

Employee Payroll Deductions

P2 Compute and record *employee* payroll deductions and liabilities.

Gross pay is the total compensation earned by an employee. It includes wages, salaries, commissions, bonuses, and any compensation earned before deductions such as taxes.[5] **Net pay,** also called "take home pay," is gross pay less all deductions.

Payroll deductions, commonly called *withholdings,* are amounts withheld from an employee's gross pay. They are either required or voluntary. Required deductions result from laws and include income taxes and Social Security taxes. Voluntary deductions are at the option of an employee and often include pension and health contributions, union dues, and charitable giving. Exhibit 12.5 shows the typical payroll deductions of an employee. Payroll deductions are withheld from employees' pay by the employer. The employer is obligated to transmit this money to the designated organization. The employer records payroll deductions as current liabilities until these amounts are transmitted. The major payroll deductions are discussed next.

---

[5] Wages usually refer to payments to employees at an hourly rate. Salaries usually refer to payments to employees at a monthly or yearly rate.

Exhibit 12.5

Payroll Deductions

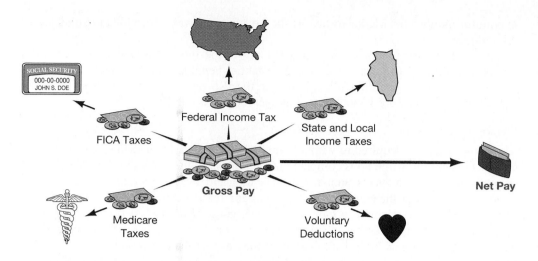

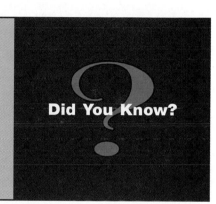

Pay or Else

Delay or failure to pay withholding taxes to government agencies has severe consequences. Fines, for instance, can be imposed at a rate of 5% of taxed owed for each month they're not paid. In severe cases, a 100% penalty can be levied, with interest, on the unpaid balance. The government can even close the company, take its assets, and pursue legal actions against individuals involved.

Did You Know?

Employee FICA Taxes

The federal Social Security system provides qualified workers retirement, disability, survivorship, and medical benefits. Laws *require* employers to withhold **FICA taxes** from employees' pay to cover costs of the system.[6] Employers (and payroll programs) usually separate FICA taxes into two groups: (1) retirement, disability, and survivorship and (2) medical. We follow the same approach in our discussion.

For the first group, the Social Security system provides qualified workers retiring at age 62 or older (until 1999) with monthly cash payments for the rest of their lives. These payments are often called *Social Security benefits.* Starting in 1999, the age for collecting a full benefit begins to rise at a rate of nearly one month per year. The full-benefit retirement age continues increasing until it reaches age 67 in year 2027. The system also provides monthly payments to deceased workers' surviving families and to disabled workers who qualify for assistance.

For the second group, the system provides retirees *Medicare benefits* beginning at age 65. These benefits, like those in the first group, are paid with FICA taxes. Taxes related to the first group are often called *Social Security taxes,* whereas those in the second group (medical) are often called *Medicare taxes.*

Law requires employers to withhold FICA taxes from each employee's salary or wages on each payday. The taxes for Social Security and Medicare are computed separately. For 1998, the amount withheld from each employee's pay for Social Security tax is 6.2% of the first $68,400 earned by the employee in the calendar year, or a maximum of $4,240.80. The Medicare tax is 1.45% of *all* wages earned by the employee. There is no

---

[6] FICA is an abbreviation for the Federal Insurance Contributions Act, the legal source of these taxes.

maximum number for Medicare tax, as the government wants to maintain solvency of this program.

Employers must promptly pay withheld taxes to the Internal Revenue Service (IRS) on specific filing dates during the year. Substantial penalties can be levied against employers who fail to send the withheld taxes to the IRS on time. Until all these taxes are sent to the IRS, they are included in employers' current liabilities.

Employee Income Tax

Most employers are required to withhold federal income tax from each employee's paycheck. The amount withheld is computed using tables published by the IRS. The amount depends on the employee's annual earnings rate and the number of *withholding allowances* claimed by the employee. Allowances are items that reduce the amount of taxes one owes the government. The more allowances you claim, the less tax your employer will withhold. Employees can claim allowances for themselves and their dependents. They also can claim additional allowances if they expect major declines in their taxable income for medical expenses or other deductible items.[7] Most states and many local governments also require employers to withhold income taxes from employees' pay. Income taxes withheld from employees must be paid promptly to the proper government agency. Until they are paid, withholdings are reported as a current liability on the employer's balance sheet.

Employee Voluntary Deductions

Beyond Social Security, Medicare, and income taxes, employers often withhold other amounts from employees' earnings. These withholdings arise from employee requests, contracts, unions, or other agreements. They can include amounts for charitable giving, medical insurance premiums, pension contributions, and union dues. Until they are paid, these withholdings are current liabilities of employers.

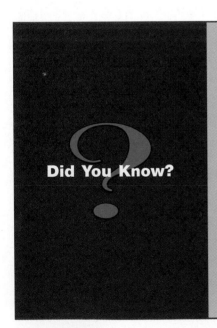

Did You Know?

Pay Stats

Comparing pay is tricky business. **Mexico,** for example, has long been regarded as poor on the hourly base pay scale. But we must recognize that base pay makes up only 30% of a Mexican worker's total compensation as opposed to 70% for a U.S. worker. Mexican workers typically receive full pay 365 days a year—even though they take vacations and holidays, and usually work only 40 to 48 hours a week. They often receive profit-sharing plans, punctuality bonuses, saving plans, and 30 days' extra pay as a Christmas bonus. Even with these benefits, Mexican workers are still estimated to make about $10 less per hour than their U.S. counterparts. [Source: *Business Week,* October 31, 1994.]

---

[7] An employee who claims more allowances than he or she is entitled to is subject to a stiff fine.

Recording Employee Payroll Deductions

Employers must accrue payroll expenses and liabilities at the end of each pay period. To illustrate, let's assume an employee earns a salary of $2,000 per month. At the end of January, the employer's entry to accrue payroll expenses and liabilities for this employee is:

Jan. 31	Salaries Expense	2,000	
	FICA—Social Security Taxes Payable (6.2%)		124
	FICA—Medicare Taxes Payable (1.45%) . .		29
	Employees' Federal Income Taxes Payable* .		213
	Employees' Medical Insurance Payable* . . .		85
	Employees' Union Dues Payable*		25
	Accrued Payroll Payable		1,524
	To record payroll for pay period ended January 31.		

Assets = Liabilities + Equity
+124   −2,000
+29
+213
+85
+25
+1,524

Amounts taken from the employer's accounting records.

Salaries Expense (debit) indicates the employee earned a gross salary of $2,000. The first five payables (credits) record liabilities the employer owes on behalf of this employee to cover FICA taxes, income taxes, medical insurance, and union dues. The Accrued Payroll Payable account (credit) records the $1,524 net pay the employee receives from the $2,000 gross pay earned.

When the employee is paid, another entry (or a series of entries) is required to record the check written and distributed (or funds transferred). The entry to record cash payment to this employee is: Accrued Payroll Payable debited and Cash credited for $1,524.

Check Forgers

More than $600 million annually is estimated to be lost to check schemes. But now companies are fighting back with an internal control technique called **positive pay.** Here's how it works: Using accounting software, a company regularly sends the bank a "positive file" listing all checks written. When a check reaches the bank for payment, the bank compares the check against the positive file. This flags any forged checks, as well as authentic checks whose payee name or payment is altered. Discrepancies are reported to the company, who can stop payment. Many banks such as Texas Commerce Bank offer positive pay plans for free. [Source: *Business Week*, December 8, 1997.]

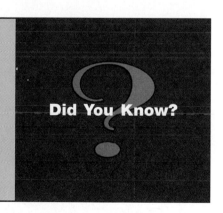

Did You Know?

Employer Payroll Taxes

Employers must pay payroll taxes in addition to those required of employees. These employer taxes include FICA and unemployment taxes.

P3 Compute and record *employer* payroll expenses and liabilities.

Employer FICA Tax

Employers must pay FICA taxes *equal in amount* to the FICA taxes withheld from their employees. An employer's tax is credited to the same FICA Taxes Payable accounts used to record the Social Security and Medicare taxes withheld from employees.[8]

Federal and State Unemployment Taxes

The federal government participates with states in a joint federal-state unemployment insurance program. Under this joint program, each state administers its own program.

---

[8] A self-employed person has to pay both the employee and employer FICA taxes.

These programs provide unemployment benefits to covered workers. The federal government approves state programs and pays a portion of their administrative expenses.

Federal Unemployment Taxes (FUTA). Employers are subject to a federal unemployment tax on wages and salaries paid to their employees. For 1998, the Federal Unemployment Tax Act requires employers to pay a tax of as much as 6.2% of the first $7,000 in salary or wages paid to each employee. But this federal tax can be reduced by a credit of up to 5.4% for taxes paid to a state program. As a result, the net federal unemployment tax is usually only 0.8%.

State Unemployment Taxes (SUTA). All states support their unemployment insurance programs by placing a payroll tax on employers.[9] In most states, the basic rate is 5.4% of the first $7,000 paid each employee. This basic rate is adjusted according to an employer's merit rating. A **merit rating** is assigned by the state and reflects a company's stability or instability in employing workers. A good rating is based on high stability and means an employer can pay less than the basic 5.4% rate. A low rating reflecting high turnover or seasonal hiring and layoffs means an employer pays more. A favorable merit rating translates into cash savings from these taxes. To illustrate, an employer with 100 employees who each earn $7,000 or more per year saves $34,300 annually if it has a merit rating of 0.5% versus 5.4%. This is computed by comparing taxes of $37,800 at the 5.4% rate to only $3,500 at the 0.5% rate.

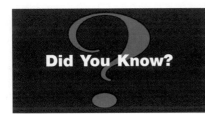
Did You Know?

Tax Aid
Computer technology has reduced errors and increased speed in computing taxes as compared with manual use of tax tables. Tax tables can be stored on computer or downloaded off the Web and then used to accurately compute payroll taxes.

Recording Employer Payroll Taxes

Employer payroll taxes are an added expense beyond the wages and salaries earned by employees. These taxes are often recorded in a journal entry separate from the one recording payroll expenses and deductions (see previous page). To illustrate, assume the $2,000 recorded salaries expense illustrated above is earned by an employee whose earnings have not yet reached $7,000 for the year. Also assume the federal unemployment tax rate is 0.8% and the state unemployment tax rate is 5.4%.

The FICA portion of the employer's tax totals $153, computed by multiplying the 6.2% and 1.45% by the $2,000 gross pay. State unemployment (SUTA) taxes are $108, computed as 5.4% of the $2,000 gross pay. Federal unemployment (FUTA) taxes are $16, computed as 0.8% of $2,000. The entry to record the employer's payroll tax expense and related liabilities is:

Assets = Liabilities + Equity
+124   −277
+29
+108
+16

Jan. 31	Payroll Taxes Expense	277	
	FICA—Social Security Taxes Payable (6.2%)		124
	FICA—Medicare Taxes Payable (1.45%) . . .		29
	State Unemployment Taxes Payable		108
	Federal Unemployment Taxes Payable		16
	To record employer payroll taxes.		

The appendix to this chapter describes payroll reports, records, and procedures applied to a small company. It also illustrates use of accounting software in payroll accounting.

---

[9] A few states require employees to make a contribution. In this book and all its assignments, we assume this tax is only on the employer.

Flash back

6. A company pays its one employee $3,000 per month. This company's net FUTA rate is 0.8% on the first $7,000 earned by the employee, its SUTA rate is 4.0% on the first $7,000, its Social Security tax rate is 6.2% of the first $68,400, and its Medicare tax rate is 1.45% of all amounts earned by the employee. The entry to record this company's March payroll includes what amount for total payroll taxes expense?

7. Identify whether the employer or employee or both pays each of these taxes: *(a)* FICA taxes; *(b)* FUTA taxes; *(c)* SUTA taxes; and *(d)* withheld income taxes.

Answers—p. 519

Lawn Worker

You take a summer job working for a family friend who runs a small lawn mowing service. When the time arrives for your first paycheck, the owner slaps you on the back, gives you full payment in cash, winks, and adds: "No need to pay those high taxes, eh." What are your responsibilities in this case? Do you take any action?

Judgment and Ethics

Answer—p. 519

Estimated Liabilities

An **estimated liability** is a known obligation of an uncertain amount, but one that can be reasonably estimated. Common examples are warranties offered by a seller, income taxes, and employee benefits such as vacation pay, pensions, and health care. We discuss each of these in this section. Other examples of estimated liabilities include property taxes and certain contracts to provide future services.

P4 Account for estimated liabilities, including warranties and income taxes.

Warranty Liabilities

A warranty is an estimated liability of the seller. A **warranty** obligates a seller to pay for replacing or repairing the product (or service) when it fails to perform as expected within a specified period. Most cars, for instance, are sold with a warranty covering parts for a specified period of time. **Ford** reported more than $4 billion in "dealer and customer allowances and claims" in its recent annual report.

To comply with the *full disclosure* and *matching principles,* the seller reports the expected expense of providing the warranty in the period when revenue from the sale of the product is reported. The seller reports this warranty obligation as a liability, even though there is uncertainty about the existence, amount, payee, and date of future sacrifices. The seller's warranty obligation does not require payments unless products fail and are returned for repairs. But future payments are probable and the amount of this liability can be estimated using, for instance, past experience with warranties.

Illustration of Warranty Liabilities

To illustrate, let's consider a dealer who sells a used car for $8,000 on December 1, 1999, with a one-year or 12,000-mile warranty covering parts. This dealer's experience shows warranty expense averages about 4% of a car's selling price. This means expense is expected to be $320 ($8,000 × 4%). The dealer records this estimated expense and liability with this entry:

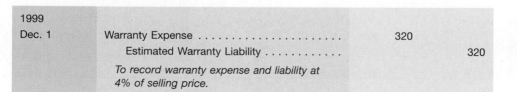

1999			
Dec. 1	Warranty Expense	320	
	Estimated Warranty Liability		320
	To record warranty expense and liability at *4% of selling price.*		

Assets = Liabilities + Equity
      +320   −320

This entry alternatively could be made as part of end-of-period adjustments. Either way, it causes the estimated warranty expense to be reported on the 1999 income statement. It also results in a warranty liability on the balance sheet for December 31, 1999.

To further extend our example, suppose the customer returns the car for warranty repairs on January 9, 2000. The dealer performs this work by replacing parts costing $200. The entry to record partial settlement of the estimated warranty liability is:

Assets = Liabilities + Equity
−200   −200

2000			
Jan. 9	Estimated Warranty Liability	200	
	Auto Parts Inventory		200
	To record costs of warranty repairs.		

This entry does not yield any additional recorded expense in year 2000. Instead, this entry reduces the balance of the estimated warranty liability. Warranty expense was previously recorded in 1999, the year the car was sold with the warranty.

What happens if total warranty costs turn out to be more or less than the estimated 4%, or $320? The answer is that management should monitor actual warranty costs to see whether the 4% rate is accurate. If experience reveals a large difference from estimates, the rate should be changed for future sales. This means while differences are expected, they should be small.

Employee Health and Pension Benefits

Many companies provide **employee benefits** beyond salaries and wages. An employer often pays all or part of medical, dental, life, and disability insurance. Many employers also contribute to pension plans and offer special stock purchase plans to employees. When payroll taxes and charges for employee benefits are added to the employees' basic earnings, employers often find that payroll cost exceeds employees' gross earnings by 25% or more.

To illustrate, we assume an employer agrees to (a) pay an amount for medical insurance equal to $8,000 and (b) to contribute an additional 10% of employees' $120,000 gross salary to a retirement program. The entry to record these benefits is:

Assets = Liabilities + Equity
        +8,000   −20,000
        +12,000

Jan. 31	Employee Benefits Expense	20,000	
	Employees' Medical Insurance Payable . . .		8,000
	Employees' Retirement Program Payable . .		12,000
	To record costs of employee benefits.		

Did You Know?

Post Game
Old timers are taking a swing at baseball. Several ex-players are suing major league baseball over a pension system they say unfairly excludes them and fails to reward their contributions to the game. Gripes include failure to extend pensions to players whose careers ended before 1947, were interrupted by World War II, or were spent in the Negro League. Current major leaguers need only play a quarter of a season to receive a pension. A full pension is about $113,000 a year. [Source: *Business Week*, June 9, 1997.]

Vacation Pay

Many employers offer paid vacation benefits. One example is where employees earn 2 weeks' vacation by working 50 weeks. This benefit increases employer's payroll expenses because employees are paid for 52 weeks but only work for 50 weeks. While total annual salary is the same, the cost per week worked is greater than the amount paid per week. To illustrate, if an employee is paid $20,800 for 52 weeks of employment but works only 50 weeks, then the weekly salary expense to the employer is $416 ($20,800/50 weeks) instead of the $400 paid weekly to the employee ($20,800/52 weeks). The $16 difference between these two amounts is recorded as salary expense and a liability for vacation pay. When the employee takes vacation, the employer reduces the vacation pay liability and does not record any additional expense.

Income Tax Liabilities for Corporations

Financial statements of both proprietorships and partnerships do not include income taxes because these organizations don't pay income taxes. Instead, taxable income for these organizations is carried to the owners' personal tax return and taxed at that level. But corporations are subject to income taxes and must estimate their income tax liability when preparing financial statements. We explain this process in this section. Then, in the next section, we discuss deferred income tax liabilities arising from temporary differences between GAAP and income tax rules.

Income tax expense for a corporation creates a liability until payment is made to the government. Because this tax is created through earning income, a liability is incurred when income is earned. This tax must be paid quarterly under federal regulations.

Illustration of Income Tax Liabilities

To illustrate, let's consider a corporation that prepares monthly financial statements. Based on its income in January 1999, this corporation estimates that it owes income taxes of $12,100. The following adjusting entry records this estimate:

Jan. 31	Income Taxes Expense	12,100	
	Income Taxes Payable		12,100
	To accrue January income tax expense and		
	liability.		

Assets = Liabilities + Equity
        +12,100 −12,100

The tax liability is adjusted each month until the first quarterly payment is made. If estimated taxes for the first three months total $30,000, the entry to record its payment is:

Apr. 10	Income Taxes Payable	30,000	
	Cash		30,000
	Paid quarterly income taxes based on first		
	quarter income.		

Assets = Liabilities + Equity
−30,000   −30,000

This process of accruing and then paying taxes continues through the year. By the time annual financial statements are prepared at year-end, the corporation knows its total earned income and the actual amount of income taxes it must pay. This information allows it to update the expense and liability accounts.

Suppose this corporation has a $22,000 credit balance in the Income Taxes Payable account at December 31, 1999, and year-end information shows the actual liability should be $33,500. The fourth quarter entry to record the final expense and liability adjustment is:

<table>
<tr><td>Dec. 31</td><td>Income Taxes Expense . . . .</td><td>11,500</td><td></td></tr>
<tr><td></td><td>Income Taxes Payable . . . .</td><td></td><td>11,500</td></tr>
<tr><td></td><td colspan="3">*To record additional tax expense and liability.*</td></tr>
</table>

Assets = Liabilities + Equity
+11,500   −11,500

This liability is settled when the corporation makes its final quarterly payment early in year 2000.

Deferred Income Tax Liabilities for Corporations

An income tax liability also can arise when the amount of income before taxes that is reported on a corporation's income statement is not the same as the amount of income reported on its income tax return. This difference occurs because income tax laws and GAAP measure income differently.[10]

Some differences between tax laws and GAAP are temporary. *Temporary differences* arise when the tax return and the income statement report a revenue or expense in different years. As an example, companies are often able to deduct higher amounts of depreciation in the early years of an asset's life and smaller amounts in the later years for tax reporting. But for their income statements, they often report an equal amount of depreciation expense each year. This means in the early years, depreciation expense for tax reporting is more than depreciation expense on the income statement. But in later years, depreciation for tax reporting is less than depreciation on the income statement.

When there are temporary differences between taxable income on the tax return and income before taxes on the income statement, corporations are required to compute income tax expense based on the income reported on the income statement. In the above example involving depreciation, the result is that income taxes expense reported in the early years is more than the amount of income taxes payable. This difference is called a **deferred income tax liability.**

Illustration of Deferred Income Tax Liability

To illustrate, let's assume that in the process of recording its usual quarterly income tax payments, a corporation finds at the end of the year that an additional $25,000 of income tax expense should be recorded. But it also determines only $21,000 is currently due and $4,000 is deferred to future years (a timing difference). The entry to record the required end-of-year adjustment is:

<table>
<tr><td>Dec. 31</td><td>Income Taxes Expense . . . .</td><td>25,000</td><td></td></tr>
<tr><td></td><td>Income Taxes Payable . . . .</td><td></td><td>21,000</td></tr>
<tr><td></td><td>Deferred Income Tax Liability . . . .</td><td></td><td>4,000</td></tr>
<tr><td></td><td colspan="3">*To record tax expense and deferred tax liability.*</td></tr>
</table>

Assets = Liabilities + Equity
+21,000   −25,000
+4,000

The credit to Income Taxes Payable reflects the amount currently due to be paid. The credit to Deferred Income Tax Liability reflects tax payments deferred until future years when the temporary difference reverses.

Many corporations have deferred income tax liabilities. **Coca-Cola Bottling,** for instance, reports deferred income taxes of $108 million in its recent balance sheet.

Temporary differences also can cause a company to pay income taxes before they are reported on the income statement as expense. If so, the company often reports a *deferred income tax asset* on its balance sheet. This is similar to a prepaid expense. **Compaq,** for instance, reports deferred income taxes of $761 million as a current asset in its recent balance sheet.

---

[10] Differences between tax laws and GAAP arise because Congress uses tax laws to generate receipts, stimulate the economy, and influence behavior, whereas GAAP are intended to provide financial information useful for decision making.

Flash *back*

8. Estimated liabilities involve an obligation to pay:

   a. An uncertain but reasonably estimated amount owed on a known obligation.

   b. A known amount to a specific entity on an uncertain due date.

   c. A known amount to an uncertain entity on a known due date.

   d. All of the above.

9. A car is sold for $15,000 on June 1, 1999, with a one-year warranty covering parts. Warranty expense is estimated at 1.5% of selling price. On March 1, 2000, the car is returned for warranty repairs for parts costing $135. The amount recorded as warranty expense at the time of the March 1 repairs is: *(a)* $0; *(b)* $60; *(c)* $75; *(d)* $135; *(e)* $225.

10. Why does a corporation accrue an income tax liability for quarterly reports?

Answers—p. 520

Contingent Liabilities

A **contingent liability** is a potential obligation that depends on a future event arising out of a past transaction or event. A typical example is a lawsuit pending in court. Here a past transaction or event leads to a lawsuit whose result depends on the court's decision. More generally, future payment of a contingent liability depends on whether an uncertain future event occurs.

C3 Explain how to account for contingent liabilities.

Accounting for Contingent Liabilities

Accounting for contingent liabilities depends on the likelihood of a future event's occurring along with our ability to estimate the amount owed in the future if it occurs. Three categories are identified. (1) The first is where the future event is *probable* (likely) and the amount owed can be *reasonably estimated*. We record this amount as a liability.[11] Examples are the estimated liabilities described earlier in the chapter, such as warranties, vacation pay, and income taxes. (2) The second case is where the future event is *remote* (unlikely). We do not record or disclose any information regarding the contingent liability in this case. (3) The third category is where likelihood of the future event is between these two extremes. Here, if the future event is *reasonably possible* (could occur), then we disclose information about the contingent liability in notes to the financial statements.

The next section gives examples of contingent liabilities that often fall in the third category where the future event is reasonably possible. Disclosing information about contingencies in the third category (reasonably possible) is motivated by the *full-disclosure principle*. This principle requires the reporting of information relevant to decision makers.

Reasonably Possible Contingent Liabilities

This section discusses examples of reasonably possible contingent liabilities.

Potential Legal Claims

Many companies are sued or at risk of being sued. The accounting question is: Should the defendant recognize a liability on its balance sheet or disclose a contingent liability in its notes while a lawsuit is outstanding and not yet settled? The answer is that a potential claim is recorded in the accounts only if payment for damages is probable and the amount can be reasonably estimated. If the potential claim can't be reasonably esti-

---

[11] FASB, *Accounting Standards—Current Text* (Norwalk, CT, 1995), sec. C59.105. First published as *FASB Statement No. 5*, par. 8.

mated or it is less than probable but reasonably possible, then it is disclosed. **Ford,** for example, includes the following note in its recent annual report:

> Various legal actions, governmental investigations and proceedings and claims are pending . . . against the company . . . arising out of alleged defects in the company's products.

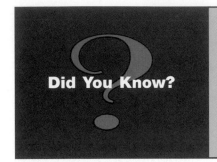

Boiling Mad

Remember the infamous lawsuit against **McDonald's** where an 81-year-old New Mexico woman was awarded $2.9 million—later reduced to $640,000—after spilling hot coffee in her lap? Well, copycat litigation is booming. Fast-food chains are beset by suits over hot-drink and food spills. Companies from **Burger King** to **Starbucks** now print cautions on coffee cups, signs at drive-throughs, and warnings on chili bowls. But restaurateurs continue to have a hard time in court with these claims and remain in hot water over potential legal claims.

Debt Guarantees

Sometimes a company guarantees the payment of debt owed by a supplier, customer, or another company. The guarantor usually discloses the guarantee in its financial statement notes as a contingent liability. But if it is probable the original debtor will default, the guarantor needs to record and report the guarantee in its financial statements as a liability. The **Boston Celtics** have an interesting type of guarantee when it comes to coaches and players as disclosed in its financial report:

> Certain of the contracts provide for guaranteed payments which must be paid even if the employee is injured or terminated.

Other Contingencies

Other examples of contingencies include environmental damages, possible tax assessments, insurance losses, and government investigations. **Sun,** for instance, reports:

> Federal, state, local and foreign laws . . . result in loss contingencies . . . at Sun's refineries, service stations, terminals, pipelines and truck transportation facilities.

Many of these contingencies require disclosure in notes to financial statements since they are reasonably possible. These contingencies sometimes carry characteristics that result in their being recorded as liabilities or omitted altogether.

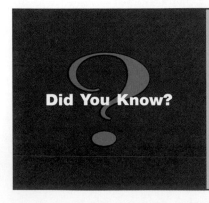

Eco Cops

What's it worth to see from one side of the Grand Canyon to the other? What's the cost when beaches are closed due to pollution? What's the life of a seal worth? These questions are part of measuring environmental liabilities of polluters. One method of measuring these liabilities is called **contingent valuation** by which people are surveyed and asked to answer questions like these.

Their answers are used by regulators to levy fines, assess punitive damages, measure costs of clean-up, and assign penalties for damage to environmental intangibles.

Uncertainties

All organizations face uncertainties from future events such as natural disasters and the development of new competing products or services. If these events occur, they can damage a company's assets or drive it out of business. But these uncertainties are not contingent liabilities because they are future events *not* arising out of past transactions. Financial statements aren't useful if they unduly speculate about the effects of possible future uncertainties such as these.

Flash *back*

11. A future payment is reported as a liability on the balance sheet if payment is contingent on a future event that:
   a. Is not probable but is reasonably possible and the payment cannot be reasonably estimated.
   b. Is probable and the payment can be reasonably estimated.
   c. Is not probable but the payment is known.

12. Under what circumstances is a future payment reported in the notes to the financial statements as a contingent liability?

Answers—p. 520

Long-term liabilities are obligations of a company not requiring payment within one year or its longer operating cycle. Long-term liabilities are often identical to current liabilities except for the greater time interval until the obligation comes due.

Long-term liabilities arise from many different transactions and events. Probably their most common source is money borrowed from a bank or a note issued to buy an asset. They also commonly arise when a company enters into a multiyear lease agreement that is similar to buying the asset. We explain each of these long-term liabilities in the context of discussing known, estimated, and contingent long-term liabilities. A more complete discussion of accounting for long-term liabilities is in Chapter 15.

Long-Term Liabilities

C4 Describe accounting for long-term liabilities.

Known (Determinable) Long-Term Liabilities

Many known or determinable liabilities are long term. These include certain unearned revenues and notes payable. To illustrate, if *Sports Illustrated* sells a five-year magazine subscription, then it records amounts received for this subscription in an Unearned Subscription Revenues account. We know amounts in this account are liabilities, but are they current or long term? The answer is both. The portion of *Sports Illustrated's* Unearned Subscription Revenues account that will be fulfilled in the next year is reported as a current liability. But the remaining portion is reported as a long-term liability.

The same analysis applies to notes payable. The borrower, for instance, reports a two-year note payable as a long-term liability in the first year it is outstanding. But in the second year, the borrower reclassifies this note as a current liability since it is due within one year or the longer operating cycle. Certain other known liabilities are rarely, if ever, reported in long-term liabilities. These include accounts payable, sales taxes, and wages and salaries.

The remainder of this section discusses two additional known liabilities: leases and the current portion of long-term debt.

Lease Liabilities

Leasing is one alternative to purchasing an asset and, in certain situations, is reported like a known liability. A company can lease an asset by agreeing to make a series of rental payments to the property owner, called the *lessor*. Because a lease gives the asset's user (called the *lessee*) exclusive control over the asset's usefulness, the lessee can use it to earn revenues. A lease creates a liability for the lessee if it has essentially the same characteristics as a purchase of an asset on credit.

The lessee must report a leased asset and a lease liability if the lease qualifies as a capital lease. A **capital lease** is a lease agreement transferring the risks and benefits associated with ownership to the lessee. This type of lease spans a number of years and creates a long-term liability that is paid off in a series of payments. **Home Depot,** for instance, reports "certain retail locations are leased under capital leases." The net present value of these long-term capital lease liabilities is about $150 million.

When a capital lease is entered into, the lessee records a leased asset and depreciates it over its useful life. The lessee also records a lease liability and allocates interest expense to the years of the lease. This interest allocation process is the same as that for notes payable.

Leases that are not capital leases are called **operating leases.** The lessee does not record an operating lease as an asset nor as a liability. Instead, the lessee's income statement reports rent expense. It also doesn't report either interest or depreciation expense related to an operating lease. **Home Depot**'s rent expense on its operating leases totaled more than $262 million for the recent year reported.

Current Portion of Long-Term Debt

The **current portion of long-term debt** refers to the part of long-term debt that is due within one year or the longer operating cycle. While long-term debt is reported under long-term liabilities, the current portion due is *reported under current liabilities.* To illustrate, let's assume a $7,500 debt is paid in installments of $1,500 per year for five years. The $1,500 due within the year is reported as a current liability. No journal entry is necessary. Instead, we classify the amounts for debt as either current or long-term when the balance sheet is prepared.

13. Which one of the following requires a lessee to record a liability? *(a)* Operating lease; *(b)* lessor; *(c)* contingent liability; *(d)* capital lease.

Answer—p. 520

Estimated Long-Term Liabilities

Estimated liabilities are both current and long-term. These include employee benefits and deferred income taxes. Pension liabilities to employees are long-term to those workers who will not retire within one year or the longer operating cycle. But for employees who are retired or will retire within the year, a portion of pension liabilities is current in nature. The same analysis applies to employee health benefits, deferred income taxes payable, and warranties. For example, many warranties are for 30 or 60 days in length. Estimated costs under these warranties are properly reported in current liabilities. Yet many automobile warranties are for three years or 36,000 miles. A portion of these warranties is reported as long-term.

Contingent Long-Term Liabilities

Contingent liabilities are both current and long-term in nature. This extends to nearly every contingent liability including litigation, debt guarantees, environmental, government investigation, and tax assessments.

Times Interest Earned

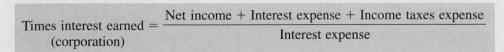

A company incurs interest expense on many of its current and long-term liabilities. Examples extend from its short-term notes and current portion of long-term liabilities to its long-term notes, bonds, and capital leases. Many of these liabilities are likely to remain obligations in one form or another for a substantial period of time even if a company experiences a decline in operations. Because of this, interest expense is often viewed as a *fixed cost.* This means the amount of interest is unlikely to fluctuate much from changes in sales or other operating activities.

While fixed costs can be advantageous when a company is growing, they create risk. This risk stems from the possibility a company might be unable to pay them if sales decline. Let's consider **X-Caliber**'s actual results for 1999 and two possible outcomes for the year 2000 shown in Exhibit 12.6 ($ in thousands). X-Caliber is a manufacturer of water sports equipment and remains a family owned operation.

A1 Compute times interest earned ratio and use it to analyze liabilities.

	Year 1999	Year 2000 If Sales Increase	Year 2000 If Sales Decrease
Sales	$600	$900	$300
Expense (75% of sales)	450	675	225
Income before interest	$150	$225	$ 75
Interest expense (fixed)	60	60	60
Net income	$ 90	$165	$ 15

Exhibit 12.6

X-Caliber's Actual and Projected Results

Exhibit 12.6 shows expenses other than interest are projected to remain at 75% of sales. Expenses changing with sales volume are called *variable expenses.* But interest is expected to remain at $60,000 per year due to its fixed nature.

The middle number column of Exhibit 12.6 shows X-Caliber's income nearly doubles (100%) if sales increase by 50%. But the far right column shows that X-Caliber's profits fall sharply if sales decline by 50%. These numbers show a company's risk is affected by the amount of fixed interest charges it incurs each period.

The risk created by these fixed expenses is captured numerically with the **times interest earned** ratio. We use the formula in Exhibit 12.7 to compute this ratio.

$$\text{Times interest earned} = \frac{\text{Income before interest}}{\text{Interest expense}}$$

Exhibit 12.7

Times Interest Earned Formula

For 1999, X-Caliber's income before interest is $150,000. This means its ratio is computed as $150,000/$60,000, or **2.5 times.** This ratio suggests X-Caliber faces relatively low risk. Its sales must decline sharply before it would be unable to cover its interest expenses. This result is comforting for the company's owners and creditors.

We must use care when computing the times interest earned ratio for a corporation. Since interest is deducted in determining taxable income for a corporation, the numerator for this ratio is adjusted for a **corporation** and expressed as:

$$\text{Times interest earned (corporation)} = \frac{\text{Net income} + \text{Interest expense} + \text{Income taxes expense}}{\text{Interest expense}}$$

Exhibit 12.8

Best Buy's Times Interest Earned Ratio

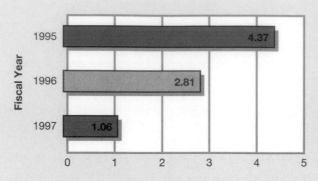

Best Buy's times interest earned ratio for 1995–1997 is shown in Exhibit 12.8. Best Buy's ratio has fallen sharply from 4.37 in 1995 to 1.06 in 1997. This results from a combination of several factors including reduced operating income and increased interest charges. Experience shows when this ratio falls below 1.5 and remains at that level or lower for several periods, the default rate on liabilities increases sharply. This implies increased risk for those decision makers involved with these companies and the creditors.

We must also interpret the times interest earned ratio in light of information about the variability of a company's net income before interest. If this amount is stable from year to year or is growing, the company can afford to take on added risk by borrowing. But if a company's income before interest varies greatly from year to year, fixed interest charges can increase the risk that an owner will not earn a positive return and be unable to pay interest charges.

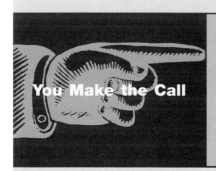

You Make the Call

Entrepreneur

You are an entrepreneur looking to invest in and operate a local franchise of a national chain. You narrow your alternatives to two. Each has an expected annual net income *after* interest of $100,000. Net income for the first franchise includes a regular fixed interest charge of $200,000. But fixed interest charge for the second franchise is $40,000. Which franchise is more risky to you if sales forecasts are not met? Does your decision change if the first franchise likely has more variability in its income before interest?

Answer—p. 519

Flash *back*

14. Times interest earned ratio:
    a. Equals interest expense divided by net income.
    b. Is larger as the amount of fixed interest charges gets larger.
    c. Is best interpreted with information about the variability of income before interest.

Answer—p. 520

Summary

C1   **Describe current and long-term liabilities and their characteristics.** Liabilities are probable future payments of assets or services an entity is presently obligated to make as a result of past transactions or events. Current liabilities are due within one year or the operating cycle, whichever is longer. All other liabilities are long-term liabilities. Distinguishing characteristics among liabilities include uncertainty about the identity of the creditor, due date, and amount to be paid.

C2   **Identify and describe known current liabilities.** Known (or determinable) current liabilities are set by agreements or laws and are measurable with little uncertainty. They include accounts payable, sales taxes payable, unearned revenues, notes payable, payroll liabilities, and the current portion of long-term debt.

C3   **Explain how to account for contingent liabilities.** If an uncertain future payment depends on a probable future event and the amount can be reasonably estimated, the payment is recorded as a liability. But the future payment is reported as a contingent liability if *(a)* the future event is reasonably possible but not probable, or *(b)* the event is probable but the amount of the payment cannot be reasonably estimated.

C4 **Describe accounting for long-term liabilities.** Long-term liabilities are obligations not requiring payment within one year or the longer operating cycle. Long-term liabilities are similar to current liabilities with the exception being the length of time until payment and the likely use of present value concepts. Lease liabilities are one type of long-term liability often used as an alternative to asset purchases. Capital leases are recorded as assets and liabilities. Other leases, called *operating leases,* are recorded as rent expense when the asset is used.

A1 **Compute times interest earned ratio and use it to analyze liabilities.** Times interest earned is computed by dividing a company's net income before interest by the amount of fixed interest charges incurred. If this company is a corporation, the numerator is net income before interest and taxes. This ratio reflects the company's ability to pay interest and earn a profit for its owners against declines in sales.

P1 **Prepare entries to account for short-term notes payable.** Short-term notes payable are current liabilities and most bear interest. When a short-term note is interest-bearing, its face

value equals the amount borrowed. This type of note also identifies a rate of interest to be paid at maturity. When a short-term note is noninterest-bearing, its face value equals the amount to be paid at maturity. This is because its face value includes interest.

P2 **Compute and record *employee* payroll deductions and liabilities.** Employee payroll deductions involve concepts of gross and net pay. Payroll deductions include FICA taxes, income tax, and voluntary deductions such as for pensions and charitable giving.

P3 **Compute and record *employer* payroll expenses and liabilities.** An employer's payroll expenses include gross earnings of the employees, additional employee benefits, and payroll taxes levied against the employer. Payroll liabilities include the net pay of employees, amounts withheld from the employees' wages, employee benefits, and the employer's payroll taxes. Payroll taxes are assessed for Social Security, Medicare, and unemployment programs.

P4 **Account for estimated liabilities, including warranties and income taxes.** Liabilities for warranties and income taxes are recorded with estimated amounts. Both warranties and income taxes are recognized as expenses when incurred. Deferred income tax liabilities are recognized if temporary differences between GAAP and tax rules result in recording more income tax expense than the amount to be currently paid.

Guidance Answers to **You Make the Call**

Rock Band

Both banks have agreed to give the band $15,000 cash, and both loans require repayment in 6 months. Provided terms in these contracts are similar, the only potential difference is in the amount of interest the band must pay. The second bank's contract makes this clear—since $15,000 is borrowed and the band must pay $16,000, the interest charged is $1,000. For the first bank, we must compute interest on the contract. It is $1,050, computed as $15,000 × 14% × 6/12. The band prefers the contract requiring less interest, which is the one reading: "Band promises to pay $16,000 within 6 months."

Entrepreneur

The risk is reflected by the ratio showing the number of times fixed interest charges are covered by net income *before* interest, known as the *times interest earned ratio.* This ratio for the first franchise is 1.5 [($100,000 + $200,000)/$200,000], whereas the ratio for the second franchise is 3.5 [($100,000 + $40,000)/$40,000]. This analysis shows the first franchise is more susceptible to the risk of incurring a loss if its sales decline and, therefore, is more risky. The second question asks about variability of income before interest. If income before interest varies greatly from year to year, this increases the risk an owner will not earn sufficient income to cover interest. Since the first franchise has the greater variability, it makes it an even worse investment.

Guidance Answer to **Judgment and Ethics**

Lawn Worker

You need to be concerned about being an accomplice to unlawful payroll activities. Not paying federal and state taxes on wages earned is illegal and unethical. Such payments also won't provide Social

Security and some Medicare credits. The best course of action is to request payment by check. If this fails to change the owner's payment practices, you must consider quitting this job.

Guidance Answers to **Flash** *backs*

1. Liabilities are probable future payments of assets or services that an entity is presently obligated to make as a result of past transactions or events.

2. No, an expected future payment is not a liability unless an existing obligation was created by a past event or transaction.

3. In most cases, a liability due in 15 months is classified as long-term. But it is classified as a current liability if the company's operating cycle is 15 months or longer.

4. A creditor prefers a note payable instead of an account payable to *(a)* start charging interest and/or *(b)* have positive evidence of the debt and its terms for potential litigation.

5. The amount borrowed is $1,000 ($1,050 − $50). The rate of interest is 5% ($50/$1,000) for six months, which is an annual rate of 10%.

6. $1,000(.008) + $1,000(.04) + $3,000(.062) + $3,000(.0145) = $277.50

7. (a) FICA taxes are paid by both the employee and employer.
(b) FUTA taxes are paid by the employer.
(c) SUTA taxes are paid by the employer.
(d) Withheld income taxes are paid by the employee.

8. *a*

9. *a*

10. A corporation accrues an income tax liability for its quarterly financial statements because income tax expense is incurred when income is earned, not just at the end of the year.

11. *b*

12. A future payment is reported in the notes as a contingent liability if *(a)* the uncertain future event is probable but the amount of payment cannot be reasonably estimated, or *(b)* the uncertain future event is not probable but has a reasonable possibility of occurring.

13. *d*

14. *c*

Demonstration Problem

The following series of transactions and events took place at the Kern Company during its recent calendar reporting year. Describe their effects on financial statements by presenting the journal entries described in each situation.

a. In September 1999, Kern sold $140,000 of merchandise covered by a 180-day warranty. Prior experience shows that costs of fulfilling the warranty equal 5% of sales revenue. Compute September's warranty expense and the increase in the warranty liability and show how it is recorded with a September 30 adjusting entry. Also show the journal entry on October 8 to record an expenditure of $300 cash to provide warranty service on an item sold in September.

b. On October 12, 1999, Kern arranged with a supplier to replace Kern's overdue $10,000 account payable by paying $2,500 cash and signing a note for the remainder. The note matures in 90 days and has a 12% interest rate. Show the entries recorded on October 12, December 31, and January 10, 2000 (when the note matures).

c. In late December, the company learns that it is facing a product liability suit filed by an unhappy customer. The company's lawyer is of the opinion that although the company will probably suffer a loss from the lawsuit it is not possible to estimate the amount of the damages at the present time.

d. Kern Company has made and recorded its quarterly income tax payments. In reviewing its end-of-year tax calculations, the company identifies an additional $50,000 of income tax expense that should be recorded. A portion of this additional expense, $10,000 is deferrable to future years. Record this year-end income tax expense adjusting entry.

e. Kern Company's net income for the year is $1,000,000. Its interest expense and income tax expense for the year are $275,000 and $225,000 respectively. Calculate times interest earned.

f. Sally Kline works for Kern Company. For the pay period ended November 30, her gross earnings were $3,000. Every paycheck Sally has $800 deducted for federal income taxes and $200 for state income taxes. Additionally, a $35 premium is deducted for her health care insurance and $10 as a donation for the United Way. Sally pays FICA Social Security taxes at a rate of 6.2% and FICA Medicare taxes at a rate of 1.45%. Sally has not earned enough this year to be exempt from FICA taxes. Journalize the payment of Sally's wages by Kern Company.

g. On November 1, Kern Company borrows $5,000 from the bank in return for a 60-day, 14% note. Record the issuance of the note on November 1 and repayment of the note with interest on December 31.

h. On December 16, Kern Company issues a noninterest-bearing note promising to pay $2,050 within 60 days. Record the issuance of the note, the interest accrual on December 31, and the repayment of the note on February 14 ($50 of interest is included in the note's face value of $2,050).

Planning the Solution

- For *(a)*, compute the warranty expense for September and record it with an estimated liability. Record the October expenditure as a decrease in the liability.

- For *(b)*, eliminate the liability for the account payable and create the liability for the note payable. Compute interest expense for the 80 days that the note is outstanding in 1999 and record it as an additional liability. Record the payment of the note, being sure to include the interest for the 10 days in 2000.

- For *(c)* decide if the contingent liability for the company needs to be disclosed or accrued (recorded) according to the two necessary criteria—probable loss and reasonably estimable.
- For *(d)* determine how much of the income tax expense is payable in the current year and how much needs to be deferred.
- For *(e)* calculate number of times interest charges are earned according to the formula given in the chapter. Remember that the numerator reflects income before interest and tax expense.
- For *(f)* set up payable accounts for all items in Sally's paycheck that require deductions. After all necessary items are deducted, credit the remaining amount to Accrued Payroll Payable.
- For *(g)* record the issuance of the note. Calculate 60 days' interest due using the 360-day convention in the interest formula.
- For *(h)* record the note as a noninteresting-bearing note. Use the contra account Discount on Notes Payable for the interest portion of the proceeds upon issuance. Make the year-end adjustment for 15 days' interest to Interest Expense and Discount on Notes Payable. Record the repayment of the note, being sure to include the interest for the 45 days in 2000.

Solution to Demonstration Problem

a. Warranty expense = 5% × $140,000 = $7,000

Sept. 30	Warranty Expense	7,000	
	Estimated Warranty Liability		7,000
	To record warranty expense and liability at 5% of sales for the month.		
Oct. 8	Estimated Warranty Liability	300	
	Cash		300
	To record the cost of the warranty service.		

b. Interest expense for 1999 = 12% × $7,500 × 80/360 = $200
Interest expense for 2000 = 12% × $7,500 × 10/360 = $25

Oct. 12	Accounts Payable	10,000	
	Notes Payable		7,500
	Cash		2,500
	Paid $2,500 cash and gave a 90-day, 12% note to extend the due date on the account.		
Dec. 31	Interest Expense	200	
	Interest Payable		200
	To accrue interest on note payable.		
Jan. 10	Interest Expense	25	
	Interest Payable	200	
	Notes Payable	7,500	
	Cash		7,725
	Paid note with interest, including accrued interest payable.		

c. The pending lawsuit should be disclosed in the financial statement notes. Although the loss is probable no liability can be accrued since the loss cannot be reasonably estimated.

d.

Dec. 31	Income Taxes Expense	50,000	
	Income Taxes Payable		40,000
	Deferred Income Tax Liability		10,000
	To record added income tax expense and the deferred tax liability.		

e.

$$\text{Times interest earned} = \frac{\text{Income before interest and taxes}}{\text{Interest expense}}$$

$$\text{Income before interest and taxes} = \text{Net income} + \text{Interest expense} + \text{Income taxes expense}$$

$$\text{Times interest earned} = \frac{\$1,000,000 + \$275,000 + \$225,000}{\$275,000} = \underline{\underline{5.45 \text{ times}}}$$

f.

Nov. 30	Salaries Expense	3,000.00	
	FICA Social Security Taxes Payable (6.2%) .		186.00
	FICA Medicare Taxes Payable (1.45%)		43.50
	Employees' Federal Income Taxes Payable .		800.00
	Employees' State Income Taxes Payable . .		200.00
	Employees' Medical Insurance Payable . . .		35.00
	Employees' United Way Payable		10.00
	Accrued Payroll Payable		1,725.50
	To record Sally Kline's payroll for the pay period ended November 30.		

g.

Nov. 1	Cash	5,000	
	Notes Payable		5,000
	Borrowed cash with a 60-day, 14% note.		

When the note and interest are paid 60 days later, Kern Company records this entry:

Dec. 31	Notes Payable	5,000.00	
	Interest Expense	116.67	
	Cash		5,116.67
	Paid note with interest ($5,000 × 14% × 60/360).		

h.

Dec. 16	Cash	2,000.00	
	Discount on Notes Payable	50.00	
	Notes Payable		2,050.00
	Borrowed cash with a 60-day, noninterest-bearing note.		
Dec. 31	Interest Expense	12.50	
	Discount on Notes Payable		12.50
	To record accrued interest on note payable (15/60 days × $50).		

When the note matures on February 14, 2000, Kern Company records this entry:

2000			
Feb. 14	Interest Expense (45/60 days × $50)	37.50	
	Notes Payable	2,050.00	
	Cash		2,050.00
	Discount on Notes Payable		37.50
	Paid note with interest.		

Payroll Reports, Records, and Procedures

Learning Objectives

Conceptual

C5 Identify and describe payroll reporting.

C6 Identify and describe payroll records.

Procedural

P5 Compute payroll taxes.

P6 Record payment of payroll.

Understanding payroll procedures and keeping adequate payroll reports and records is essential to a company's success. Many companies now use accounting software to maintain their payroll records. This appendix focuses on payroll accounting and its reports, records, and procedures. We also show how accounting software helps with payroll reporting and analysis.

Payroll Reports

Most employees and employers are required to pay local, state, and federal payroll taxes. Payroll expenses involve liabilities to individual employees, to federal and state governments, and to other organizations such as insurance companies. Beyond paying these liabilities, employers are required to prepare and submit reports explaining how these payments are computed.

Reporting FICA Taxes and Income Tax

The Federal Insurance Contributions Act (FICA) requires each employer to file an Internal Revenue Service (IRS) **Form 941,** the **Employer's Quarterly Federal Tax Return.** Form 941 is filed within one month after the end of each calendar quarter. A Form 941 is shown in Exhibit 12A.1 for Phoenix Sales & Service, a landscape maintenance company.

Companies often use accounting software to maintain payroll records. We use an off-the-shelf program, **PeachTree Accounting for Windows,** to generate many of the reports in this section. But several other programs can produce the same reports. Accounting software is helpful in tracking payroll transactions and reporting the accumulated information on Form 941.

Exhibit 12A.1

Form 941

Form **941** (Rev. January 1996) Department of the Treasury Internal Revenue Service (O)	4141	**Employer's Quarterly Federal Tax Return** ▶ See separate instructions for information on completing this return. Please type or print.	

Enter state code for state in which deposits made ▶ [I] (see page 3 of instructions).

Name (as distinguished from trade name): Phoenix Sales and Service

Trade name, if any

Address (number and street): 1214 Mill Road
Phoenix, AZ 85621
USA

Date quarter ended: Dec. 31, 1998

Employer identification number: 86-3214587

City, State, and ZIP code

OMB No. 1545-0029

T
FF
FD
FP
I
T

If address is different from prior return, check here ▶ [ ]

IRS Use: 1 1 1 1 1 1 1 1 1 1   2   3 3 3 3 3   4 4   5 5 5   6   7   8 8 8 8 8   9 9 9   10 10 10 10 10 10 10 10 10 10

If you do not have to file returns in the future, check here ▶ [ ] and enter date final wages paid ▶

If you are a seasonal employer, see Seasonal employers on page 1 of the instructions and check here ▶

1	Number of employees (except household) employed in the pay period that includes March 12th ▶		
2	Total wages and tips, plus other compensation	2	36,599.00
3	Total income tax withheld from wages, tips and sick pay	3	3,056.47
4	Adjustment of withheld income tax for preceding quarters of calendar year	4	
5	Adjusted total of income tax withheld (line 3 as adjusted by line 4—see instructions)	5	3,056.47
6a	Taxable social security wages $ 36,599.00 × 12.4% (.124) =	6a	4,538.28
b	Taxable social security tips $ × 12.4% (.124) =	6a	
7	Taxable Medicare wages and tips $ 36,599.00 × 2.9% (.029) =	7	1,061.36
8	Total social security and Medicare taxes (add lines 6a, 6b, and 7). Check here if wages are not subject to social security and/or Medicare tax ▶ [ ]	8	5,599.64
9	Adjustment of social security and Medicare taxes (see instructions for required explanation) Sick Pay $ _____ ± Fractions of Cents $ _____ ± Other $ _____ =	9	
10	Adjusted total of social security and Medicare taxes (line 8 as adjusted by line 9—see instructions)	10	5,599.64
11	**Total taxes** (add lines 5 and 10)	11	8,656.11
12	Advance earned income credit (EIC) payments made to employees, if any	12	
13	Net taxes (subtract line 12 from line 11). **This should equal line 17, column (d) below** (or line D of Schedule B (Form 941))	13	8,656.11
14	Total deposits for quarter, including overpayment applied from a prior quarter	14	8,656.11
15	**Balance due** (subtract line 14 from line 13). See instructions	15	
16	**Overpayment,** if line 14 is more than line 13, enter excess here ▶ $ _____ 0.00 and check if to be: [ ] Applied to next return **OR** [ ] Refunded.		

- **All filers:** If line 13 is less than $500, you need not complete line 17 or Schedule B.
- **Semiweekly schedule depositors:** Complete Schedule B and check here ▶ [ ]
- **Monthly schedule depositors:** Complete line 17, columns (a) through (d), and check here ▶ [ ]

17	Monthly Summary of Federal Tax Liability.		
(a) First month liability	(b) Second month liability	(c) Third month liability	(d) Total liability for quarter
3,079.11	2,049.76	3,527.24	8,656.11

Sign Here — Under penalties of perjury, I declare that I have examined this return, including accompanying schedules and statements, and to the best of my knowledge and belief, it is true, correct, and complete.

Signature ▶   Print your Name and Title ▶   Date ▶

For Paperwork Reduction Act Notice, see page 1 of separate instructions.   Cat. No. 17001Z   Form **941** (Rev. 1-96)

On line 2 of Form 941 the employer reports the total wages and salaries subject to income tax withholding.[12] The income tax withheld is reported on lines 3 and 5. The combined amount of employees' and employer's FICA (Social Security) taxes for Phoenix Sales & Service is reported on line 6a: taxable Social Security wages, $36,599.00 × 12.4% = $4,538.28. The 12.4% is the sum of the Social Security tax withheld for 1998, computed as 6.2% tax withheld from the employees' wages for the quarter plus the 6.2% tax levied on the employer. The combined amount of employees' Medicare wages is reported on line 7. The 2.9% is the sum of 1.45% withheld from employees' wages for the quarter plus 1.45% tax levied on the employer. Total FICA taxes are reported on lines 8 and 10. They are added to total income taxes withheld of $3,056.47 to yield a total $8,656.11.

---

[12] For brevity, this appendix uses "wages" to refer to both "wages and salaries."

For 1998, income up to $68,400 is subject to Social Security tax. There is no income limit on amounts subject to Medicare tax. Congress sets annual limits on the amount owed for Social Security tax. The total of amounts deposited in a **federal depository bank** is subtracted to determine if a balance remains to be paid. Federal depository banks are authorized to accept deposits of amounts payable to the federal government.

Deposit requirements depend on the amount of tax owed. When the sum of FICA taxes plus the employees' income taxes is less than $500 for a quarter, the taxes can be paid when Form 941 is filed. Companies with large payrolls are often required to pay monthly or semiweekly. Also, if taxes owed are $100,000 or more at the end of any day, they must be paid by the end of the next banking day.

Reporting FUTA Taxes and SUTA Taxes

An employer's federal unemployment taxes (FUTA) are reported on an annual basis by filing an **Annual Federal Unemployment Tax Return,** IRS **Form 940.** It must be mailed on or before January 31 following the end of each tax year. Ten more days are allowed for filing if all required tax deposits are made on a timely basis and the full amount of the tax is paid on or before January 31. Payments of FUTA are made quarterly to a federal depository bank if the total amount due exceeds $100. If $100 or less is due, the taxes are remitted annually with Form 940.

Requirements for paying and reporting of state unemployment taxes (SUTA) vary depending on the laws of each state. But most states require filing quarterly payments and reports.

Reporting Wages and Salaries

Employers are required to give each employee an annual report of the employee's wages subject to FICA and federal income taxes along with the amounts of these taxes withheld. This report is called a **Wage and Tax Statement** or **Form W-2.** It must be given to employees before January 31 following the year covered by the report. Exhibit 12A.2 shows Form W-2 for Phoenix Sales & Service.

Copies of the W-2 Form must be sent to the Social Security Administration. Here they post to each employee's Social Security account the amount of an employee's wages subject to FICA tax and FICA tax withheld. These posted amounts become the basis for determining an employee's retirement and survivors' benefits. The Social Security Ad

Exhibit 12A.2

Form W-2

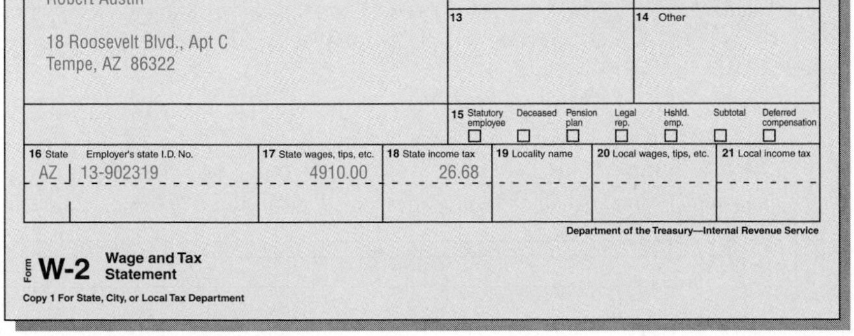

ministration also transmits to the IRS the amount of each employee's wages subject to federal income tax and the amount of taxes withheld.

15. What determines the amount deducted from an employee's wages for federal income taxes?

Answer—p. 530

Payroll Records

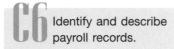

Identify and describe payroll records.

Employers must keep certain payroll records in addition to the reporting and paying of taxes. These records usually include a payroll register. Good records also require an individual earnings report for each employee.

Payroll Register

A **payroll register** shows the pay period dates, hours worked, gross pay, deductions, and net pay of each employee for every pay period. Exhibit 12A.3 shows a payroll register for Phoenix Sales & Service. There is a three-line heading and a one-line explanation of this report. The report is organized into nine columns:

Col. 1 Employee identification (ID); Employee name; Social Security number (SS No); Reference (check number); Date (date check issued)

Col. 2 Pay Type (regular or overtime hours)

Exhibit 12A.3

Payroll Register

Phoenix Sales and Service
Payroll Register
For the Period From Oct. 1, 1998 to Oct. 8, 1998

Employee ID Employee SS No Reference Date	Pay Type	Pay Hrs	Pay Amt	Amount	Gross State SUI_ER	Fed_Income Soc_Sec_ER	Soc_Sec Medicare_ER	Medicare FUTA_ER
AR101 Robert Austin 333-22-9999 9001 10/8/98	Regular	40.00	400.00	338.09	400.00 -2.32 -10.80	-28.99 -24.80	-24.80 -5.80	-5.80 -3.20
CJ102 Judy Cross 299-11-9201 9002 10/8/98	Regular Overtime	40.00 1.00	560.00 21.00	479.35	581.00 -4.24 -15.69	-52.97 -36.02	-36.02 -8.42	-8.42 -4.65
DJ103 John Diaz 444-11-9090 9003 10/8/98	Regular Overtime	40.00 2.00	560.00 42.00	503.75	602.00 -3.87 -16.25	-48.33 -37.32	-37.32 -8.73	-8.73 -4.82
KK104 Kay Keife 909-11-3344 9004 10/8/98	Regular	40.00	560.00	443.10	560.00 -5.49 -15.12	-68.57 -34.72	-34.72 -8.12	-8.12 -4.48
ML105 Lee Miller 444-56-3211 9005 10/8/98	Regular	40.00	560.00	480.18	560.00 -2.74 -15.12	-34.24 -34.72	-34.72 -8.12	-8.12 -4.48
SD106 Dale Sears 909-33-1234 9006 10/8/98	Regular	40.00	560.00	433.10	560.00 -5.49 -15.12	-68.57 -34.72	-34.72 -8.12	-8.12 -4.48
Summary Total 10/1/98 thru 10/31/98	Regular Overtime	240.00 3.00	3,200.00 63.00	2,687.57	3,263.00 -24.15 -88.10	-301.67 -202.30	-202.30 -47.31	47.31 -26.11

Col. 3 Pay Hrs (number of hours worked)[13]

Col. 4 Pay Amt (amount of gross pay)[14]

Col. 5 Amount (Net pay = Gross pay less amounts withheld)

Col. 6 Gross pay; State (state income tax withheld); SUI_ER (state unemployment tax withheld)

Col. 7 Fed_Income (federal income tax withheld); Soc_Sec-ER (Social Security tax withheld, employer)

Col. 8 Soc_Sec (social security tax withheld); Medicare_ER (Medicare tax withheld, employer)

Col. 9 Medicare (Medicare tax withheld); FUTA_ER (FUTA tax withheld, employer)

Exhibit 12A.3 shows separate columns for each type of payroll deduction and for expense accounts where payroll costs are charged. A payroll register includes all data necessary to record payroll in the General Journal. In some accounting software programs such as **PeachTree,** the entries to record payroll are made in a Payroll Journal.

Payroll Check

Payment of payroll is usually done by check or a funds transfer. Exhibit 12A.4 shows a *payroll check* for an employee of Phoenix Sales & Service. This check is accompanied with a detachable *statement of earnings* showing gross pay, deductions, and net pay.

Employee Earnings Report

An **employee earnings report** is a cumulative record of an employee's hours worked, gross earnings, deductions, and net pay. Payroll information on this report is taken from the payroll register. The employee earnings report for Phoenix Sales & Service is shown in Exhibit 12A.5.

Exhibit 12A.4

Check and Statement of Earnings

EMPLOYEE NO.	EMPLOYEE NAME		SOCIAL SECURITY NO.	PAY PERIOD END	CHECK DATE
AR101	Robert Austin		333-22-9999	10/8/98	10/8/98

ITEM	RATE	HOURS	TOTAL	ITEM	THIS CHECK	YEAR TO DATE
Regular	10.00	40.00	400.00	Gross	400.00	400.00
Overtime	15.00			Fed_Income	-28.99	-28.99
				Soc_Sec	-24.80	-24.80
				Medicare	-5.80	-5.80
				State	-2.32	-2.32

HOURS WORKED	GROSS THIS PERIOD	GROSS YEAR TO DATE	NET CHECK	CHECK No.
40.00	400.00	400.00	$338.09	9001

(Detach and retain for your records)

PHOENIX SALES AND SERVICE
1214 Mill Road
Phoenix, AZ 85621
602-555-8900

Phoenix Bank and Trust
Pheonix, AZ 85621
3312-87044

9001

CHECK NO.	DATE	AMOUNT
9001	Oct 8, 1998	**************$338.09*

Three Hundred Thirty–Eight and 9/100 Dollars

PAY TO THE ORDER OF   Robert Austin
18 Roosevelt Blvd., Apt C
Tempe, AZ 86322

Mary Wills
AUTHORIZED SIGNATURE

---

[13] "Pay Hrs" column reports regular hours worked by each employee. If overtime hours apply, the Pay Hrs column shows a second line with overtime hours worked.

[14] The "Pay Amt" column shows regular hours worked on the first line multiplied by the regular pay rate. This equals regular pay. Overtime hours multiplied by the overtime premium rate equals overtime premium pay reported on the second line. If employers are engaged in interstate commerce, the federal law sets a minimum overtime rate of pay to employees. In 1998, this minimum wage is $5.15 per hour. For this company, the minimum overtime premium is 50% of the regular rate for hours worked in excess of 40 per week. This means workers earn at least 150% of their regular rate for hours in excess of 40 per week.

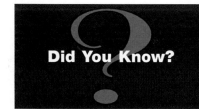

Exhibit 12A.5

Employee Earnings Report

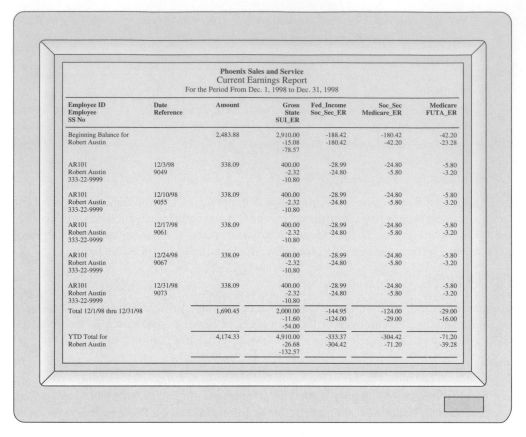

Phoenix Sales and Service
Current Earnings Report
For the Period From Dec. 1, 1998 to Dec. 31, 1998

Employee ID Employee SS No	Date Reference	Amount	Gross State SUI_ER	Fed_Income Soc_Sec_ER	Soc_Sec Medicare_ER	Medicare FUTA_ER
Beginning Balance for Robert Austin		2,483.88	2,910.00 -15.08 -78.57	-188.42 -180.42	-180.42 -42.20	-42.20 -23.28
AR101 Robert Austin 333-22-9999	12/3/98 9049	338.09	400.00 -2.32 -10.80	-28.99 -24.80	-24.80 -5.80	-5.80 -3.20
AR101 Robert Austin 333-22-9999	12/10/98 9055	338.09	400.00 -2.32 -10.80	-28.99 -24.80	-24.80 -5.80	-5.80 -3.20
AR101 Robert Austin 333-22-9999	12/17/98 9061	338.09	400.00 -2.32 -10.80	-28.99 -24.80	-24.80 -5.80	-5.80 -3.20
AR101 Robert Austin 333-22-9999	12/24/98 9067	338.09	400.00 -2.32 -10.80	-28.99 -24.80	-24.80 -5.80	-5.80 -3.20
AR101 Robert Austin 333-22-9999	12/31/98 9073	338.09	400.00 -2.32 -10.80	-28.99 -24.80	-24.80 -5.80	-5.80 -3.20
Total 12/1/98 thru 12/31/98		1,690.45	2,000.00 -11.60 -54.00	-144.95 -124.00	-124.00 -29.00	-29.00 -16.00
YTD Total for Robert Austin		4,174.33	4,910.00 -26.68 -132.57	-333.37 -304.42	-304.42 -71.20	-71.20 -39.28

This report accumulates information showing when an employee's earnings reach the tax-exempt points for FICA, FUTA, and SUTA taxes. It also gives data employers need to prepare Form W-2.

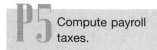

Did You Know?

High-Tech Reports
Computer technology is used to produce many payroll reports including the (a) payroll register, (b) payroll checks, and (c) employee earnings report.

Payroll Procedures

Employers must be able to compute federal income tax in accounting for payroll. This section explains how we compute this tax and shows how to use a payroll bank account.

Computing Federal Income Tax

P5 Compute payroll taxes.

To compute the amount of tax withheld from each employee's wages, we need to determine both the employee's wages earned and the employee's number of *withholding allowances*. Each employee records the number of withholding allowances claimed on a withholding allowance certificate, **Form W-4,** filed with the employer. When the number of withholding allowances increases, the amount of income tax withheld decreases.

Employers often use a **wage bracket withholding table** similar to the one shown in Exhibit 12A.6 to compute the federal income taxes withheld from each employee's gross pay. The table in Exhibit 12A.6 is for a single employee who is paid weekly. Tables are also provided for married employees and for biweekly, semimonthly, and monthly pay periods (most payroll software includes these tables). When using a wage bracket withholding table to compute federal income tax withheld from an employee's gross wages, we need to locate an employee's wage bracket within the first two columns of the table. We then find the amount withheld by looking in the withholding allowance column for that employee.

SINGLE Persons—WEEKLY Payroll Period												
(For Wages Paid in 1998)												
If the wages are —		And the number of withholding allowances claimed is —										
At least	But less than	0	1	2	3	4	5	6	7	8	9	10
		The amount of income tax to be withheld is —										
$600	$610	95	80	68	60	52	44	36	29	21	13	5
610	620	97	83	69	61	53	46	38	30	22	15	7
620	630	100	86	71	63	55	47	39	32	24	16	8
630	640	103	88	74	64	56	49	41	33	25	18	10
640	650	106	91	77	66	58	50	42	35	27	19	11
650	660	109	94	79	67	59	52	44	36	28	21	13
660	670	111	97	82	69	61	53	45	38	30	22	14
670	680	114	100	85	70	62	55	47	39	31	24	16
680	690	117	102	88	73	64	56	48	41	33	25	17
690	700	120	105	91	76	65	58	50	42	34	27	19
700	710	123	108	93	79	67	59	51	44	36	28	20
710	720	125	111	96	82	68	61	53	45	37	30	22
720	730	128	114	99	84	70	62	54	47	39	31	23
730	740	130	116	102	87	73	64	56	48	40	33	25
740	750	134	119	105	90	76	65	57	50	42	34	26

Exhibit 12A.6

Wage Bracket Withholding Table

Flash *back*

16. What amount of income tax is withheld from the salary of a single employee with 3 withholding allowances who earns $675 in a week? (*Hint:* Use the wage bracket withholding table in Exhibit 12A.6.)

Answer—p. 530

Payroll Bank Account

Companies with few employees often pay employees with checks drawn on the company's regular bank account. But a company with many employees often uses a special **payroll bank account** to pay employees. When this account is used, a company either (a) draws one check for total payroll on the regular bank account and deposits it in the payroll bank account or (b) executes an *electronic funds transfer* to the payroll bank account. The entry to record this transaction is:

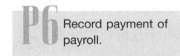

P6 Record payment of payroll.

Oct. 8	Accrued Payroll Payable	2,687.57	
	Cash		2,687.57
	To transfer cash to the payroll bank account.		

Assets = Liabilities + Equity
−2,687.57   −2,687.57

Individual payroll checks are drawn on the company's payroll bank account. Because only one check for the total payroll is drawn on the regular bank account each payday, use of a special payroll bank account helps with internal control. It also helps with reconciling the regular bank account.

When companies use a payroll bank account, they usually include check numbers in the payroll register. Our **PeachTree**-generated payroll register shows check numbers in column 1. For instance, Exhibit 12A.3 reports that check no. 9001 is issued to Robert Austin. With this information, the payroll register serves as a supplementary record of wages earned by and paid to employees.

Flash *back*

17. Which of the following steps are executed when a company draws one check for total payroll and deposits it in a special payroll bank account?
a. Record information on the payroll register with a General Journal entry.
b. Write a check to the payroll bank account for the total payroll and record it with a debit to Accrued Payroll Payable and a credit to Cash.
c. Deposit a check for the total payroll in the payroll bank account.
d. Issue individual payroll checks drawn on the payroll bank account.
e. All of the above.

Answer—p. 530

Summary of Appendix 12A

C5 Identify and describe payroll reporting. Employers report FICA taxes and federal income tax withholdings using Form 941 on a quarterly basis. FUTA taxes are reported annually on Form 940. Annual earnings and deduction information are reported to each employee and to the federal government on Form W-2.

C6 Identify and describe payroll records. An employer's payroll records include a payroll register for each pay period, payroll checks and statements of earnings, and an employee earnings report for each employee. Many companies use accounting software to maintain payroll records. We showed certain reports generated by accounting software including: payroll register, employee earnings report, payroll check, Form 941, and Form W-2.

P5 Compute payroll taxes. Federal income tax deductions depend on the employee's earnings and the number of withholding allowances claimed. Wage bracket withholding tables are available for pay periods of different lengths and for several classes of employees such as single or married.

P6 Record payment of payroll. Employers with a large number of employees often use a separate payroll bank account. When this is done, the payment of employees is recorded with a single credit to Cash. This entry records the transfer of cash from the regular checking account to the payroll checking account.

Guidance Answers to Flash backs

15. An employees' gross earnings and number of withholding allowances determine the amount deducted for federal income taxes.

16. $70

17. e

Glossary

Capital lease a lease that gives the lessee the risks and benefits normally associated with ownership. (p. 516).

Contingent liability a potential liability that depends on a future event arising out of a past transaction. (p. 513).

Current liability obligations due within a year or the company's operating cycle, whichever is longer; paid using current assets or by creating other current liabilities. (p. 496).

Current portion of long-term debt the portion of long-term debt that is due within one year; reported under current liabilities on the balance sheet. (p. 516).

Deferred income tax liability payments of income taxes that are deferred until future years because of temporary differences between GAAP and tax rules. (p. 512).

Discount on note payable the difference between the face value of a note payable and the amount borrowed; represents interest that will be paid on the note over its life. (p. 500).

Employee benefits additional compensation paid to or on behalf of employees, such as premiums for medical, dental, life, and disability insurance; additional benefits include contributions to pension plans, stock purchase plans, and vacations. (p. 510).

Employee earnings report a record of an employee's net pay, gross pay, deductions, and year-to-date information. (p. 527).

Estimated liability obligation of an uncertain amount that can be reasonably estimated. (p. 509).

Federal depository bank a bank authorized to accept deposits of amounts payable to the federal government. (p. 525).

Federal Unemployment Taxes (FUTA) payroll taxes on employers assessed by the federal government to support the federal unemployment insurance program. (p. 508).

FICA taxes taxes assessed on both employers and employees under the Federal Insurance Contributions Act; these taxes fund Social Security and Medicare programs. (p. 505).

Form 940 IRS form used to report an employer's federal unemployment taxes (FUTA) on an annual filing basis. (p. 525).

Form 941 IRS form filed within one month after the end of each calendar quarter to report FICA taxes owed and remitted. (p. 523).

Form W-2 a yearly report given by an employer to each employee showing the employee's wages subject to FICA and federal income taxes along with the annual amounts of these taxes withheld. (p. 525).

Gross pay total compensation earned by an employee. (p. 504).

Known liabilities obligations of a company with little uncertainty; set by agreements, contracts, or laws; also called *definitely determinable liabilities*. (p. 498).

Long-term liability obligations of a company not requiring payment within one year or the company's operating cycle, if longer. (p. 497).

Merit rating a rating assigned to an employer by a state according to the employer's past record for creating or not creating unemployment. (p. 508).

Net pay gross pay less all deductions; also called *take home pay*. (p. 504).

Noninterest-bearing note a note that does not have a stated rate of interest; the interest is included in the face value of the note. (p. 501).

Operating lease a lease that is not a capital lease; costs of operating leases are reported as rent expense. (p. 516).

Payroll bank account a special bank account a company uses solely for paying employees, by depositing in the account each pay period an amount equal to the total employees' net pay and drawing the employees' payroll checks on that account. (p. 504).

Payroll deductions amounts withheld from an employee's gross pay; also called *withholdings.* (p. 504).

Payroll register a record for a pay period that shows the pay period dates and the regular and overtime hours worked, gross pay, net pay for each employee, and deductions. (p. 526).

Short-term note payable current obligation in the form of a written promissory note. (p. 499).

State Unemployment Taxes (SUTA) payroll taxes on employers assessed by states to support unemployment insurance programs. (p. 508).

Times interest earned the ratio of a company's income before interest divided by the amount of interest charges; used to evaluate the risk of being committed to make interest payments when income varies. (p. 517).

Wage bracket withholding table a table that shows the amounts of income tax to be withheld from employees' wages at various levels of earnings. (p. 528).

Warranty an agreement that obligates the seller or manufacturer to repair or replace a product when it breaks or otherwise fails to perform properly within a specified period. (p. 509).

The superscript letter ^{A} identifies assignment material based on Appendix 12A.

Questions

1. What is the difference between a current and a long-term liability?
2. What is an estimated liability?
3. What are the three important questions concerning the certainty of liabilities?
4. Suppose that a company has a facility located in an area where disastrous weather conditions often occur. Should it report a probable loss from a future disaster as a liability on its balance sheet? Why or why not?
5. Why are warranty liabilities usually recognized on the balance sheet as liabilities even when they are uncertain?
6. What is an employer's unemployment merit rating? Why are these ratings assigned to employers?
7. Which payroll taxes are the responsibility of the employee and which taxes are the responsibility of the employer?
8. How can a lease create an asset and a liability for the lessee?
9.^{A} What determines the amount deducted from an employee's wages for federal income taxes?
10.^{A} What is a wage bracket withholding table?
11.^{A} What amount of income tax should be withheld from the salary of a single employee with two withholding allowances who earned $725 per week? What if the employee earned $625 and had no withholding allowances? (Use the wage bracket withholding table in Exhibit 12A.6 to find the answers.)
12.^{A} List two IRS reports that can be generated using PeachTree Accounting for Windows.
13.^{A} What is the 1998 income limit for Social Security tax?
14.^{A} What is the combined amount of the employees' and employer's social security tax?
15. Identify the note on commitments and contingencies in the financial statements of **NIKE** in Appendix A. What are the amounts of minimum annual rental commitments under noncancelable operating leases in future years?
16. Refer to **Reebok**'s balance sheet in Appendix A. What accounts related to income taxes are on the balance sheet? Identify the meaning of each income tax account you identify.
17. Refer to **America Online**'s balance sheet in Appendix A. What account on America Online's balance sheet shows a liability to employees for future benefits?

Quick Study

QS 12-1
Distinguishing between current and long-term liabilities

C1, C2

Which of the following items are normally classified as a current liability for a company that has a 15-month operating cycle?

a. Salaries payable.

b. Note payable due in 18 months.

c. Bonds payable that mature in two years.

d. Note payable due in 11 months.

e. Portion of a long-term note that is due to be paid in 15 months.

QS 12-2
Recording warranty expenses

P4

On September 11, 1999, Valentine's Department Store sells a lawn mower for $400 with a one-year warranty that covers parts. Warranty expense is estimated at 5% of sales. On July 24, 2000, the mower is brought in for repairs covered under the warranty requiring $35 in parts. Prepare the July 24, 2000, entry to record the warranty repairs.

QS 12-3
Recording employer payroll taxes

P3

Yeager Co. has five employees, each of whom earns $2,600 per month. FICA Social Security taxes are 6.2% of gross pay and FICA Medicare taxes are 1.45% of gross pay. FUTA taxes are 0.8% and SUTA taxes are 2.8% of the first $7,000 paid to each employee. Prepare the March 31 journal entry to record March payroll taxes expense.

QS 12-4
Interest-bearing note transactions

P1

On November 7, 2000, the Eggemeyer Company borrowed $150,000 and signed a 90-day, 8% note payable with a face value of $150,000. Compute (a) the accrued interest payable on December 31, 2000, and (b) present the journal entry to record the paying of the note at maturity.

QS 12-5
Noninterest-bearing note transactions

P1

Katie Company signs a noninterest-bearing note promising to pay $4,100 within 60 days after December 16. Record the signing of the note, the interest accrual on December 31, and the repayment of the note on February 14. ($100 of interest is included in the note's face value of $4,100.)

QS 12-6
Recording deferred income tax liability

P4

Longfellow Company has made and recorded its quarterly income tax payments. After a final review of taxes for the year, the company identifies an additional $30,000 of income tax expense that should be recorded. A portion of this additional expense, $8,000, is deferrable to future years. Record the year-end income tax expense adjusting entry for Longfellow Company.

QS 12-7
Accounting for contingent liabilities

C3

The following legal claims exist for the CT Company. Identify the accounting treatment for each legal claim as either (a) a liability that is recorded or (b) an item described in the notes to the financial statements.

1. CT company estimates that this lawsuit could result in damages of $1,000,000; it is reasonably possible that the plaintiff will win the case.

2. CT faces a probable loss on a pending lawsuit; the amount of the judgment cannot be reasonably estimated.

3. CT company estimates damages of this case at $2,500,000 with a high probability of losing the case.

Palm Computing sells $5,000 of merchandise for cash on September 30. The sales tax law requires Palm Computing to collect 4% sales tax on every dollar of merchandise sold. Record the entry for the $5,000 sale and its applicable sales tax. Also record the entry that shows the remittance of the 4% tax on this sale to the state government on October 15.

QS 12-8
Accounting for sales taxes

C2

Ticketmaster receives $4,000,000 in advance cash ticket sales for a four date-tour for the Rolling Stones. Record the advance ticket sales as a lump sum as of October 31. Record the revenue earned for the first concert date played on November 5.

QS 12-9
Unearned revenue

C2

Compute the times interest earned for Trevor Company, which has income after interest expense of $1,575,500 and interest expense of $137,000. Trevor Co. is a proprietorship.

QS 12-10
Times interest earned

A1

Exercises
Exercise 12-1
Classifying liabilities

C1

The following items appear on the balance sheet of a company with a two-month operating cycle. Identify the proper classification of each item as follows: a *C* if it is a current liability, an *L* if it is a long-term liability, or an *N* if it is not a liability.

_____ **a.** Income taxes payable.

_____ **b.** Notes receivable (due in 30 days).

_____ **c.** Mortgage payable (due in 12 months).

_____ **d.** Notes payable (due in 6 to 12 months).

_____ **e.** Bonds payable (mature in 5 years).

_____ **f.** Notes payable (due in 13 to 24 months).

_____ **g.** Wages payable.

_____ **h.** Accounts receivable.

_____ **i.** Notes payable (due in 120 days).

_____ **j.** Mortgage payable (due after 13 months).

Mikado Co. sold a copier with a cost of $3,800 and a two-year parts warranty to a customer on August 16, 1999, for $5,500 cash. Mikado uses the perpetual system to account for inventories. Based on prior experience, Mikado expects to eventually incur warranty costs equal to 4% of this selling price. The liability expense is recorded with an adjusting entry at the end of the year. On November 22, 2000, the copier required on-site repairs that were completed the same day. The cost of the repairs consisted of $199 for the materials taken from the parts inventory. These were the only repairs required in 2000 for this copier.

Exercise 12-2
Warranty expense and liability

P4

a. How much warranty expense does the company report in 1999 for this copier?

b. How much is the warranty liability for this copier as of December 31, 1999?

c. How much warranty expense does the company report in 2000 for this copier?

d. How much is the warranty liability for this copier as of December 31, 2000?

e. Prepare the journal entries that are made to record (1) the sale; (2) the adjustment on December 31, 1999, to record the warranty expense; and (3) the repairs that occurred in November 2000. Mikado uses the perpetual method to account for merchandise inventories.

Constructo Company prepares interim financial statements each month. As part of its accounting process, estimated income taxes are accrued each month for 30% of the current month's net income. The estimated income taxes are paid in the first month of each quarter for the amount accrued in the prior quarter. The following information is available for the last quarter of 1999:

Exercise 12-3
Accounting for income taxes

P4

a. October net income $27,900

November net income   18,200

December net income   32,700

b. After tax computations are completed in early January, the accountant determines that the Income Taxes Payable account balance should be $29,100 on December 31.

Required

1. Determine the amount of the adjustment needed on December 31 to produce the proper ending balance in the Income Taxes Payable account.

2. Prepare journal entries to record the adjustment to the Income Taxes Payable account and to record the January 15 payment of the fourth-quarter taxes.

Exercise 12-4
Computing payroll taxes
P2, P3

Natkin Co. has one employee on its payroll. The employee and the company are subject to the following taxes:

Tax	Rate	Applied to
FICA—Social Security	6.20%	First $68,400
FICA—Medicare	1.45	Gross pay
FUTA	0.80	First $7,000
SUTA	2.90	First $7,000

Compute Natkin's amounts of these four taxes on the employee's gross earnings for September under each of three independent situations *a.* through *c.*:

	Gross Pay through August	Gross Pay for September
a.	$ 6,400	$ 800
b.	18,200	2,100
c.	60,600	7,900

Exercise 12-5
Payroll-related journal entries
P2, P3

Using the data in situation *a* of Exercise 12–4, prepare the employer's September 30 journal entries to record (a) the gross earnings and withholdings for the employee and (b) the employer's payroll taxes. The employee's federal income taxes withheld are $90.

Exercise 12-6
Interest-bearing and noninterest-bearing notes payable
P1

Portable Systems borrowed $94,000 on May 15, 1999, for 60 days at 12% interest by signing a note.

a. On what date will this note mature?

b. How much interest expense results from this note? (Assume a 360-day year.)

c. Suppose the face value of the note equals $94,000, the principal of the loan. Prepare the journal entries to record issuing the note and paying it at maturity.

d. Suppose the face value of the note is $95,880 which includes both the principal of the loan ($94,000) and the interest to be paid at maturity. Prepare the journal entries to record issuing the note and paying it at maturity.

Accura Co. borrowed $150,000 on November 1, 1999, for 90 days at 9% interest by signing a note.

a. On what date will this note mature?

b. How much interest expense results from this note in 1999? (Assume a 360-day year.)

c. How much interest expense results from this note in 2000? (Assume a 360-day year.)

d. Suppose the face value of the note equals $150,000, the principal of the loan. Prepare the journal entries to record issuing the note, to accrue interest at the end of 1999, and to record paying the note at maturity.

e. Suppose the face value of the note is $153,375 which includes both the principal of the loan ($150,000) and the interest to be paid at maturity. Prepare the journal entries to record issuing the note, to accrue interest at the end of 1999, and to record paying the note at maturity.

Exercise 12-7
Interest-bearing and noninterest-bearing short-term notes payable with year-end adjustments

Analysis of Lawrence Co. reveals the following information. Prepare any necessary adjusting entries at December 31, 2000, the company's year-end.

1. During December, Lawrence Company sold 3,000 units of a product that carries a 60-day warranty. December sales for this product total $120,000. The company expects 8% of the units to need repair under warranty, and it estimates that the average repair cost per unit will be $15.

2. The company is being sued by a disgruntled employee. Legal advisors believe it is probable that the company will have to pay damages, the amount of which cannot be reasonably estimated.

3. Employees earn vacation pay at a rate of one day per month. During December, 20 employees qualify for vacation pay. Their average daily wage is $120 per employee.

4. Lawrence Company has guaranteed the $5,000 debt of a supplier. It is not probable that the supplier will default on the debt.

5. The company records an adjusting entry for previously unrecorded cash sales and sales taxes payable at a rate of 5% on $2,000,000.

6. The company recognizes that $50,000 of $100,000 received in advance for products is now earned.

Exercise 12-8
Adjusting entries for liabilities

Rashad Company has the following selected accounts after posting adjusting entries:

Accounts payable	$50,000
Notes payable, 6 month	10,000
Accumulated depreciation, Equipment	20,000
Accrued payroll payable	5,000
Estimated warranty liability	12,000
Discount on notes payable, 6 month	1,000
Payroll taxes expense	2,000
Mortgage payable	100,000

Prepare the current liability section of Rashad Company's balance sheet, assuming $10,000 of the mortgage payable is due within the next year.

Exercise 12-9
Financial statement presentation—current liabilities

Use the following information on proprietorships *a* through *f* to compute times interest earned:

	Net Income (Loss)	Interest Expense
a.	$140,000	$48,000
b.	140,000	15,000
c.	140,000	8,000
d.	265,000	12,000
e.	79,000	12,000
f.	(4,000)	12,000

Exercise 12-10
Computing and interpreting times interest earned

Analysis Component

Which of the cases demonstrates the strongest ability to pay interest charges as they come due?

Exercise 12-11ᴬ
Computing gross and net pay
P5, P6

Norma Bailey, an unmarried employee of a company, worked 48 hours during the week ended January 12. Her pay rate is $12 per hour, and her wages are subject to no deductions other than FICA Social Security, FICA Medicare, and federal income taxes. She claims two withholding allowances. Compute her regular pay, overtime premium pay (overtime premium is 50% of regular rate for hours in excess of 40 per week), gross pay, FICA tax deduction at an assumed rate of 6.2% for the Social Security portion and 1.45% for the Medicare portion, income tax deduction (use the wage bracket withholding table of Exhibit 12A.6), total deductions, and net pay.

Exercise 12-12ᴬ
Payroll entry
P6

Using Exercise 12–11, show the journal entry to record the transfer of cash to the payroll bank account.

Exercise 12-13ᴬ
Computing net pay
P5

The payroll records of Press-A-Software show the following information about Jerry Wood, an employee, for the weekly pay period ending September 30, 1998:

Total earnings current pay period	$ 735
Cumulate earnings previous pay period	$9,700

Jerry Wood is single and claims one deduction. Compute his Social Security tax (6.2%), Medicare tax (1.45%), federal income tax withholding, and state income tax (0.5%). State income tax is 0.5 percent on $9,000 maximum.

Problems

Problem 12-1
Estimating product warranty expenses and liabilities
P4

On October 29, 1999, Sharp Products began to purchase electric razors for resale at $80 each. Sharp uses the perpetual method to account for inventories. The razors are covered under a warranty that requires the company to replace any nonworking razor within 90 days. When a razor is returned, the company simply throws it away and mails a new one from inventory to the customer. The company's cost for a new razor is $18. The manufacturer has advised the company to expect warranty costs to equal 7% of sales. The following transactions and events occurred in 1999 and 2000:

1999
Nov. 11   Sold 75 razors for $6,000 cash.
      30   Recognized warranty expense for November with an adjusting entry.
Dec.   9   Replaced 15 razors that were returned under the warranty.
      16   Sold 210 razors for $16,800 cash.
      29   Replaced 30 razors that were returned under the warranty.
      31   Recognized warranty expense for December with an adjusting entry.

2000
Jan.   5   Sold 130 razors for $10,400 cash.
      17   Replaced 50 razors that were returned under the warranty.
      31   Recognized warranty expense for January with an adjusting entry.

Required

1. How much warranty expense is reported for November and December 1999?
2. How much warranty expense is reported for January 2000?
3. What is the balance of the Estimated Warranty Liability account as of December 31, 1999?
4. What is the balance of the Estimated Warranty Liability account as of January 31, 2000?
5. Prepare journal entries to record these transactions and adjustments.

Check Figure   12/31/1999 estimated liability balance, $786 credit

Langley Company entered into the following transactions involving short-term liabilities in 1999 and 2000:

1999

Apr. 20   Purchased merchandise on credit from Franken, Inc., for $38,500. The terms were 1/10, n/30. Langley uses a perpetual inventory system.

May 19   Replaced the account payable to Franken with a 90-day note bearing 9% annual interest. Langley paid $8,500 cash, with the result that the balance of the note was $30,000.

July   8   Borrowed $60,000 from North Bank by signing a 120-day interest-bearing note for $60,000. The note's annual interest rate is 10%.

?   Paid the note to Franken, Inc., at maturity.

?   Paid the note to North Bank at maturity.

Nov. 28   Signed a noninterest-bearing note with a face value of $21,280 from Crockett Bank that matures in 60 days. The face value includes a principal amount of $21,000.

Dec. 31   Recorded an adjusting entry for the accrual of interest on the note to Crockett Bank.

2000

?   Paid the note to Crockett Bank at maturity.

Required

1. Determine the maturity dates of the three notes described above.

2. Determine the interest due at maturity for the three notes. (Assume a 360-day year.)

3. Determine the interest to be recorded in the adjusting entry at the end of 1999.

4. Determine the interest to be recorded in 2000.

5. Prepare journal entries for all the preceding transactions and events for years 1999–2000.

Legal Consultants pays its employees every week. The employees' gross earnings are subject to these taxes:

Tax	Rate	Applied To
FICA—Social Security	6.20%	First $68,400
FICA—Medicare	1.45	Gross pay
FUTA	0.80	First $7,000
SUTA	2.15	First $7,000

The company is preparing its payroll calculations for the week ended August 25. The payroll records show the following information for the company's four employees:

Name	Gross Pay Through 8/18	This Week	
		Gross Pay	Withholding Tax
Rose	$69,200	$1,800	$252
Chad	29,700	900	99
Mona	6,750	450	54
Jody	1,050	400	36

In addition to the gross pay, the company and each employee pay one-half of the weekly health insurance premium of $32 per employee. The company also contributes 8% of each employee's gross earnings to a pension fund.

Problem 12-2
Short-term notes payable transactions and entries

Check Figure   Total interest for Crockett Bank note, $280

Problem 12-3
Payroll expenses, withholdings, and taxes

Required

Use this information to compute the following for the week ended August 25 (round amounts to the nearest cent):

1. Each employee's FICA withholdings for Social Security.
2. Each employee's FICA withholdings for Medicare.
3. Employer's FICA taxes for Social Security.
4. Employer's FICA taxes for Medicare.
5. Employer's FUTA taxes.
6. Employer's SUTA taxes.
7. Each employee's take-home pay.
8. Employer's total payroll-related expense for each employee.

Check Figure   Part 7: Total take-home pay, $2,885.02

Problem 12-4
Computing and analyzing times interest earned

A1

Here are condensed income statements for two different sole proprietorships:

Foxtrot Co.	
Sales	$500,000
Variable expenses (80%)	400,000
Net income before interest	$100,000
Interest expense (fixed)	30,000
Net income	$ 70,000

Tango Co.	
Sales	$500,000
Variable expenses (60%)	300,000
Net income before interest	$200,000
Interest expense (fixed)	130,000
Net income	$ 70,000

Required

Preparation Component

1. What is the times interest earned for Foxtrot Co.?
2. What is the times interest earned for Tango Co.?
3. What happens to each company's net income if sales increase by 30%?
4. What happens to each company's net income if sales increase by 50%?
5. What happens to each company's net income if sales increase by 80%?
6. What happens to each company's net income if sales decrease by 10%?
7. What happens to each company's net income if sales decrease by 20%?
8. What happens to each company's net income if sales decrease by 40%?

Check Figure   Part 3: Net income for Foxtrot Co., $100,000 (a 43% increase)

Analysis Component

9. Comment on what you observe in relation to the fixed cost strategies of the two companies and the ratio values you computed in parts 1 and 2.

Problem 12–5^A
Entries for payroll transactions

P5, P6

Vaughn Company has 10 employees, each of whom earns $2,600 per month and is paid on the last day of each month. All 10 have been employed continuously at this amount since January 1. Vaughn uses a payroll bank account and special payroll checks to pay its employees. On March 1, the following accounts and balances appeared in its ledger:

a. FICA—Social Security Taxes Payable, $3,224; FICA—Medicare Taxes Payable, $754. (The balances of these accounts represent the liabilities for both the employer's and employees' FICA taxes for the February payroll only.)
b. Employees' Federal Income Taxes Payable, $3,900 (liability for February only).
c. Federal Unemployment Taxes Payable, $416 (liability for January and February together).
d. State Unemployment Taxes Payable, $2,080 (liability for January and February together).

During March and April, the company had the following payroll transactions:

Mar. 15 Issued check payable to Union Bank, a federal depository bank authorized to accept employers' payments of FICA taxes and employee income tax withholdings. The $7,878 check is in payment of the February FICA and employee income taxes.

31 Prepared General Journal entries to record the March Payroll Record, which had the following column totals, and to transfer the funds from the regular bank account to the payroll bank account:

Salaries and Wages				Federal	Federal	
Office Salaries	Shop Wages	Gross Pay	FICA Taxes*	Income Taxes	Total Deductions	Net Pay
$10,400	$15,600	$26,000	$1,612 +$377	$3,900	$5,889	$20,111

*FICA taxes are Social Security and Medicare, respectively.

31 Issued checks payable to each employee in payment of the March payroll.

31 Prepared a General Journal entry to record the employer's payroll taxes resulting from the March payroll. The company has a merit rating that reduces its state unemployment tax rate to 4.0% of the first $7,000 paid each employee. The federal rate is 0.8%.

Apr. 15 Issued check payable to Union Bank in payment of the March FICA and employee income taxes.

15 Issued check to the State Tax Commission for the January, February, and March state unemployment taxes. Mailed the check along with the first quarter tax return to the State Tax Commission.

30 Issued check payable to Union Bank. The check is in payment of the employer's federal unemployment taxes for the first quarter of the year.

30 Mailed Form 941 to the IRS, reporting the FICA taxes and the employees' federal income tax withholdings for the first quarter.

Required

Prepare General Journal entries to record the transactions and events for March and April.

Problem 12-6A
Entries for payroll transactions
P5, P6

On January 8, the end of the first weekly pay period of the year, Prescott Company's Payroll Register showed that its employees had earned $11,380 of office salaries and $32,920 of sales salaries. Withholdings from the employees' salaries include FICA Social Security taxes at the rate of 6.2%, FICA Medicare taxes at the rate of 1.45%, $6,430 of federal income taxes, $670 of medical insurance deductions, and $420 of union dues. No employee earned more than $7,000.

Required

1. Calculate FICA Social Security taxes payable and FICA Medicare taxes payable. Prepare a General Journal entry to record Prescott Company's January 8 payroll.
2. Prepare a General Journal entry to record Prescott's payroll taxes resulting from the January 8 payroll. Prescott has a merit rating that reduces its state unemployment tax rate to 4.0% of the first $7,000 paid each employee. The federal unemployment tax rate is 0.8%.
3. Prescott Company uses a payroll bank account and special payroll checks in paying its employees. Prepare the General Journal entry to transfer funds equal to the payroll from the regular bank account to the payroll bank account.
4. After the entry in part 3 is journalized and posted, are additional journal entries required to record the payroll checks and pay all the employees?

Check Figure Part 3: Accrued Payroll Payable, $33,481.05 Dr.

**Comprehensive
Problem**

**Aardvark
Exterminators**

(Review of Chapters 1–12)

PeachTree

Aardvark Exterminators provides pest control services and sells extermination products manufactured by other companies. The following six-column table contains the company's unadjusted trial balance as of December 31, 2000.

AARDVARK EXTERMINATORS December 31, 2000					
	Unadjusted Trial Balance		Adjustments	Adjusted Trial Balance	
Cash	$ 17,000				
Accounts receivable	4,000				
Allowance for doubtful accounts .		$ 828			
Merchandise inventory	11,700				
Trucks	32,000				
Accum. depreciation, Trucks		0			
Equipment	45,000				
Accum. deprec., Equipment		12,200			
Accounts payable		5,000			
Estimated warranty liability		1,500			
Unearned services revenue		0			
Long-term notes payable		15,000			
Discount on notes payable	3,974				
K. Jones, capital		59,600			
K. Jones, withdrawals	10,000				
Extermination services revenue ..		60,000			
Interest earned		872			
Sales		75,000			
Cost of goods sold	46,300				
Depreciation expense, Trucks ...	0				
Depreciation expense, Equip.	0				
Wages expense	35,000				
Interest expense	0				
Rent expense	9,000				
Bad debts expense	0				
Miscellaneous expenses	1,226				
Repairs expense	8,000				
Utilities expense	6,800				
Warranty expense	0				
Totals	$230,000	$230,000			

The following information applies to the company at the end of the current year:

a. The bank reconciliation as of December 31, 2000, includes these facts:

Balance per bank	$15,100
Balance per books	17,000
Outstanding checks	1,800
Deposit in transit	2,450
Interest earned	52
Service charges (miscellaneous expense)	15

Included with the bank statement was a canceled check that the company had failed to record. (The information in part *b* allows you to determine the amount of the check, which was a payment on account.)

b. An examination of customers' accounts shows that accounts totaling $679 should be written off as uncollectible. It is also determined that the ending balance of the Allowance for Doubtful Accounts should be $700.

c. A truck was purchased and placed in service on July 1, 2000. Its cost is being depreciated with the straight-line method using these facts and estimates:

Original cost	$32,000
Expected salvage value	8,000
Useful life (years)	4

d. Two items of equipment (a sprayer and an injector) were purchased and put into service early in January 1998. Their costs are being depreciated with the straight-line method using these facts and estimates:

	Sprayer	Injector
Original cost	$27,000	$18,000
Expected salvage value	3,000	2,500
Useful life (years)	8	5

e. On August 1, 2000, the company was paid $3,840 in advance to provide monthly service on an apartment complex for one year. The company began providing the services in August. When the cash was received, the full amount was credited to the Extermination Services Revenue account.

f. The company offers a warranty for the services it sells. The expected cost of providing warranty service is 2.5% of sales. No warranty expense has been recorded for 2000. All costs of servicing the warranties in 2000 were properly debited to the liability account.

g. The $15,000 long-term note is a five-year, noninterest-bearing note that was issued to First National Bank on December 31, 1998. The market interest rate on the date of the loan was 8% and interest expense (not yet recorded) is $882 for year 2000.

h. The ending inventory of merchandise was counted and determined to have a cost of $11,700. Aardvark uses a perpetual inventory system.

Required

1. Use the preceding information to determine amounts for the following items:
   a. Correct ending balance of Cash and the amount of the omitted check.
   b. Adjustment needed to obtain the correct ending balance of the Allowance for Doubtful Accounts.
   c. Annual depreciation expense for the truck that was acquired during the year (computed to the nearest month).
   d. Annual depreciation expense for the two items of equipment that were used during the year.
   e. Correct ending balances of the Extermination Services Revenue and Unearned Services Revenue accounts.
   f. Correct ending balances of the accounts for Warranty Expense and Estimated Warranty Liability.
   g. Correct ending balances of the accounts for Interest Expense and Discount on Notes Payable. (Round amounts to nearest whole dollar.)
2. Use the results of part 1 to complete the six-column table by first entering the appropriate adjustments for items *a* through *g* and then completing the adjusted trial balance columns. (Hint: Item *b* requires two entries.)
3. Present journal entries to record the adjustments entered on the six-column table. Assume Aarkvark's adjusted balance for Merchandise Inventory matches the year-end physical count.
4. Prepare a single-step income statement, a statement of changes in owner's equity, and a classified balance sheet.

BEYOND THE NUMBERS

Reporting in Action

C3,A1

Refer to the financial statements and related information for **NIKE** in Appendix A. Answer the following questions by analyzing that information:

1. Compute times interest earned for the years ended May 31, 1997 and 1996. Comment on NIKE's ability to cover its interest expense.

2. Does NIKE's note on commitments provide information allowing one to determine whether the company has entered into any operating or capital leases?

3. What evidence would you look for as an indication that NIKE has any temporary differences between the income reported on the income statement and the income reported on its tax return? Can you find any evidence of these differences for NIKE?

Swoosh Ahead

4. Obtain access to NIKE's annual report for fiscal years ending after May 31, 1997. You can gain access to NIKE's annual report at its Web site [www.nike.com] or through the SEC's EDGAR database [www.sec.gov]. Recompute NIKE's times interest earned for any additional years ending after May 31, 1997, that you have access to.

Comparative Analysis

A1

Both **NIKE** and **Reebok** design, produce, market, and sell sports footwear and apparel. Key comparative figures ($ millions) for these two organizations follow:

	NIKE		Reebok	
Key Figures*	**1997**	**1996**	**1996**	**1995**
Net income	$796	$553	$139	$165
Income tax expense	499	346	84	100
Interest expense	52	39	42	26

*NIKE figures are from its annual reports for fiscal years ended May 31, 1997 and 1996.
Reebok figures are from its annual reports for fiscal years ended December 31, 1996 and 1995.

Required

1. Compute times interest earned using the two years' data shown for each company.

2. Comment on which company appears stronger in its ability to commit to interest payments if income should vary.

Communicating in Practice

C3

Mike Thatcher is a sales manager for an automobile dealership in Chicago. Mike earns a bonus each year based on revenue from the number of autos sold in the year less related warranty expenses. The quality of automobiles sold each year seems to vary since the warranty expenses for autos sold is highly variable. Actual warranty expenses have varied over the past 10 years from a low of 3% of an automobile's selling price to a high of 10%. In the past, Mike has tended toward estimating warranty expenses on the high end just to be conservative. It is the end of the year and once again he must work with the dealership's accountant in arriving at the warranty expense accrual for the cars sold this year.

1. Does the warranty accrual decision present any kind of ethical dilemma for Mike Thatcher?

2. Since warranty expenses are variable, what percent do you think Mike should choose for this year? Justify your response.

Ethics Challenge

P4

Norma Yager is the manager of accounting and finance for a manufacturing company. At the end of the year she must determine whether and how to describe the company's contingencies in financial statements. Her manager, Jonas Perlman, raised an objection to a specific contingency in Yager's proposal. Perlman objects to recognizing an expense and a liability for warranty service on units of a new product that was introduced in the company's fourth quarter. His comment was, "There is no way we can estimate this warranty cost. We don't owe anybody anything until the products break down and are returned for service. Let's report an expense if and when we do the repairs."

Required

Prepare a written response for Yager to send to Perlman addressing his objection in a one-page memorandum dated December 21.

Visit the **Social Security Administration's** Web site at **www.ssa.gov.** Find the link on the homepage to the *Social Security Handbook.* Once you have located the handbook consult the chapter "Wages." In the wages chapter look for information regarding the maximum earnings creditable in any one year. Maximum earnings serve as the threshold amount after which employees and employers do not owe tax during a given year. How does the 1997 level of maximum earnings compare to 1987, 1977, 1967, 1957, and 1947? How are yearly increases in earnings subject to the Social Security tax determined? Is it possible that *all* earnings of a given year will someday be subject to Social Security tax? Why or why not?

Taking It to the Net

P2

Your team is in business and you need to borrow $6,000 for short-term needs. You have been shopping banks for a loan, and you have the following options:

(A) Sign a $6,000, 90-day, 11% interest-bearing note.

(B) Sign a $6,172.5, 90-day, noninterest-bearing note.

Teamwork in Action

P1, C2

Required

1. Discuss these two options and determine the best choice. Ensure that all teammates concur with the decision and understand the rationale. Explain your decision to your instructor.
2. Each member of the team is to prepare *one* of the following entries:
   a. Option A—at date of issuance.
   b. Option B—at date of issuance.
   c. Option A—at maturity date.
   d. Option B—at maturity date.
3. In rotation, each member is to explain the entry prepared in (2) to the team. Ensure that all team members concur with and understand the entries.
4. Assume the funds are borrowed on December 1 and your business has a fiscal year that coincides with a calendar year. Each member of the team is to prepare *one* of the following entries:
   a. Option A—the year-end adjustment.
   b. Option B—the year-end adjustment.
   c. Option A—at maturity date.
   d. Option B—at maturity date.
5. In rotation, each member is to explain the entry prepared in (4) to the team. Ensure that all team members concur with and understand the entries.

Check your local phone book or the **Social Security Administration** Web site (**www.ssa.gov**) to locate the Social Security office nearest to you. Visit the office to request a personal earnings and benefits estimate form. Fill out the form and mail according to the instructions. In several weeks, you will receive a statement from the Social Security Administration regarding your earnings history and future Social Security benefits you can receive. (Note: Formerly the request could be made online. The online request service has been discontinued and is now under review by the Social Security Administration due to security concerns.) It is good to request an earnings and benefit statement every 5 to 10 years to make sure you have received proper credit for all wages earned and for which you and your employer have paid taxes into the system.

Hitting the Road

P2

Read the article "Electronic Stores Get a Cruel Shock," in the January 14, 1991, issue of *Business Week*.

Required

1. Describe the accounting guidelines companies must follow in recognizing revenue from the sale of extended warranties on consumer products.
2. Contrast the rules now in effect with former rules with respect to their effect on the income statements of companies selling extended warranties.
3. What accounting principle likely governed the FASB's decision to change the accounting rules for recognizing warranty revenue?
4. Is the rule on accounting for revenue from warranties consistent with the rules on accounting for expenses related to warranties?

Financial Statement Information

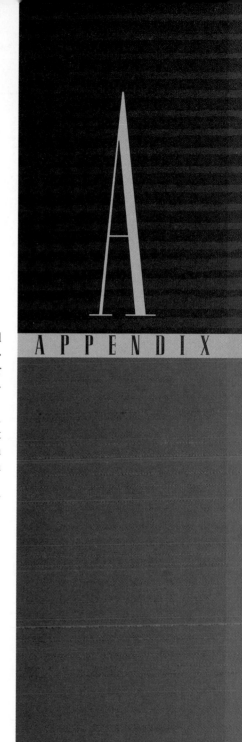

This appendix includes financial statement information for (a) **NIKE** (b) **Reebok** and (c) **America Online.** All of this information is taken from their annual reports. An **annual report** is a summary of the financial results of a company's operations for the year and its future plans. It is directed at external users of financial information, but also affects the actions and decisions of internal users.

An annual report is also used by a company to showcase itself and its products. Many include attractive pictures, diagrams and illustrations related to the company. But the *financial section* is its primary objective. The financial section communicates much information about a company, with most data drawn from the accounting information system.

The layout of the financial section of an annual report is fairly standard and usually includes:

- Letter to Shareholders
- Financial History and Highlights
- Management Discussion and Analysis
- Management's Report
- Report of Independent Accountants (Auditor's Report)
- Financial Statements
- Notes to Financial Statements
- List of Directors and Managers

This appendix provides most of the financial information for NIKE that is contained in its annual report. It also includes the financial statements for Reebok and America Online. The appendix is organized as follows:

- **NIKE   A-2–A-28**
- **Reebok   A-29–A-32**
- **America Online   A-33–A-36**

Many assignments at the end of each chapter refer to information in this appendix. We encourage readers to spend extra time with these assignments as they are especially useful in reinforcing and showing the relevance and diversity of financial accounting and reporting.

FINANCIAL HISTORY

(in thousands, except per share data and financial ratios)

YEAR ENDED MAY 31,	1997	1996	1995	1994
Revenues	$9,186,539	$6,470,625	$4,760,834	$3,789,668
Gross margin	3,683,546	2,563,879	1,895,554	1,488,245
Gross margin %	40.1%	39.6%	39.8%	39.3%
Net income	795,822	553,190	399,664	298,794
Net income per common share	2.68	1.88	1.36	0.99
Average number of common and common equivalent shares	297,000	293,608	294,012	301,824
Cash dividends declared per common share	0.38	0.29	0.24	0.20
Cash flow from operations	323,120	339,672	254,913	576,463
Price range of common stock				
High	76.375	52.063	20.156	18.688
Low	47.875	19.531	14.063	10.781
At May 31:				
Cash and equivalents	$ 445,421	$ 262,117	$ 216,071	$ 518,816
Inventories	1,338,640	931,151	629,742	470,023
Working capital	1,964,002	1,259,881	938,393	1,208,444
Total assets	5,361,207	3,951,628	3,142,745	2,373,815
Long-term debt	296,020	9,584	10,565	12,364
Redeemable Preferred Stock	300	300	300	300
Common shareholders' equity	3,155,838	2,431,400	1,964,689	1,740,949
Year-end stock price	57.500	50 .188	19.719	14.750
Market capitalization	16,633,047	14,416,792	5,635,190	4,318,800
Financial Ratios:				
Return on equity	28.5%	25.2%	21.6%	17.7%
Return on assets	17.1%	15.6%	14.5%	13.1%
Inventory turns	4.8	5.0	5.2	4.3
Current ratio at May 31	2.1	1.9	1.8	3.2
Price/Earnings ratio at May 31	21.5	26.6	14.5	14.9
Geographic Revenues:				
United States	$5,529,132			$2,432,684
Europe	1,833,722			927,269
Asia/Pacific	1,245,217			283,421
Canada, Latin America, and other	578,468			146,294
Total Revenues	$9,186,539	$6,470,625	$4,760,834	$3,789,668

All per common share data has been adjusted to reflect the 2-for-1 stock splits paid October 23, 1996, October 30, 1995 and October 5, 1990. The Company's Class B Common Stock is listed on the New York and Pacific Exchanges and trades under the symbol NKE. At May 31, 1997, there were approximately 300,000 shareholders. Years 1993 and prior have been restated to reflect the implementation of Statement of Financial Accounting Standard No. 109 – Accounting for Income Taxes (see Notes 1 and 6 to the Consolidated Financial Statements).

	1993	1992	1991	1990	1989	1988
	$3,930,984	$3,405,211	$3,003,610	$2,235,244	$1,710,803	$1,203,440
	1,543,991	1,316,122	1,153,080	851,072	635,972	400,060
	39.3%	38.7%	38.4%	38.1%	37.2%	33.2%
	365,016	329,218	287,046	242,958	167,047	101,695
	1.18	1.07	0.94	0.80	0.56	0.34
	308,252	306,408	304,268	302,672	300,576	301,112
	0.19	0.15	0.13	0.10	0.07	0.05
	265,292	435,838	11,122	127,075	169,441	19,019
	22.563	19.344	13.625	10.375	4.969	3.313
	13.750	8.781	6.500	4.750	2.891	1.750
	$ 291,284	$ 260,050	$ 119,804	$ 90,449	$ 85,749	$ 75,357
	592,986	471,202	586,594	309,476	222,924	198,470
	1,165,204	964,291	662,645	561,642	419,599	295,937
	2,186,269	1,871,667	1,707,236	1,093,358	824,216	707,901
	15,033	69,476	29,992	25,941	34,051	30,306
	300	300	300	300	300	300
	1,642,819	1,328,488	1,029,582	781,012	558,597	408,567
	18.125	14.500	9.938	9.813	4.750	3.031
	5,499,273	4,379,574	2,993,020	2,942,679	1,417,381	899,741
	24.5%	27.9%	31.7%	36.3%	34.5%	27.4%
	18.0%	18.4%	20.5%	25.3%	21.8%	16.7%
	4.5	3.9	4.1	5.2	5.1	5.0
	3.6	3.3	2.1	3.1	2.9	2.2
	15.3	13.5	10.5	12.2	8.6	9.0
	$2,528,848	$2,270,880	$2,141,461	$1,755,496	$1,362,148	$ 900,417
	1,085,683	919,763	664,747	334,275	241,380	233,402
	178,196	75,732	56,238	29,332	32,027	21,058
	138,257	138,836	141,164	116,141	75,248	48,563
	$3,930,984	$3,405,211	$3,003,610	$2,235,244	$1,710,803	$1,203,440

FINANCIAL HIGHLIGHTS

(in thousands, except per share data and financial ratios)

YEAR ENDED MAY 31,	1997	1996	% CHG
Revenues	$9,186,539	$6,470,625	42.0%
Gross margin	3,683,546	2,563,879	43.7%
Gross margin %	40.1%	39.6%	
Net income	795,822	553,190	43.9%
Net income per common share	2.68	1.88	42.6%
Return on equity	28.5%	25.2%	13.1%
Stock price at May 31	57.500	50.188	14.6%

SELECTED QUARTERLY FINANCIAL DATA (UNAUDITED)

(in thousands, except per share data)	1st Quarter 1997	1st Quarter 1996*	2nd Quarter 1997	2nd Quarter 1996*	3rd Quarter 1997	3rd Quarter 1996*	4th Quarter 1997	4th Quarter 1996*
Revenues	$2,281,926	$1,700,020	$2,107,034	$1,356,758	$2,423,648	$1,582,039	$2,373,931	$1,852,067
Gross margin	919,807	686,641	829,406	528,629	988,221	628,723	946,112	731,514
Gross margin %	40.3%	40.4%	39.4%	39.0%	40.8%	39.7%	39.9%	39.5%
Net income	226,063	182,098	176,872	97,812	237,133	133,874	155,754	133,727
Net income per common share	0.76	0.62	0.60	0.34	0.80	0.45	0.52	0.45
Average number of common and common equivalent shares	296,368	291,704	297,022	293,988	297,368	294,212	297,252	295,466
Cash dividends declared per common share	0.08	0.06	0.10	0.08	0.10	0.08	0.10	0.07
Price range of common stock								
High	55.625	24.188	64.000	31.313	76.375	35.688	73.125	52.063
Low	47.875	19.531	51.625	22.656	51.500	28.938	51.250	32.688

* For comparable purposes with 1997, quarterly figures for 1996 have been adjusted to reflect the elimination of the one month lag in reporting by certain of the Company's non-U.S. operations. See further discussion in Note 1 to the Consolidated Financial Statements.

MANAGEMENT DISCUSSION AND ANALYSIS

HIGHLIGHTS

Fiscal year 1997 saw record revenues and earnings. Revenues and net income have now increased 13 and 11 consecutive comparable quarters, respectively.

- Revenues grew 42%, an increase of $2.7 billion, compared to the previous year increase of 36%.
- Gross margins established a new record, surpassing 40% of revenues for the first time.
- Selling and administrative costs increased 0.5%, as a percent of revenues, over the previous year.
- Net income was $795.8 million, an increase of 44%.

RESULTS OF OPERATIONS

FISCAL 1997 COMPARED TO FISCAL 1996

Significant growth in worldwide revenues and improved gross margin percentage were the primary factors contributing to record earnings for fiscal 1997 as compared to 1996. In the United States, footwear revenues increased $1 billion, or 36%, demonstrating continued market share gains and industry growth. U.S. apparel exceeded $1 billion in revenues for the first time, increasing $588.5 million, or 70%, over the previous year. Revenues from international (non-U.S.) markets increased 49% over the previous year, and now represent 38% of total revenues. Markets outside the U.S. in which the Company operates, continue to offer tremendous opportunity for growth. The Company continues to invest in infrastructure and local marketing and advertising to capitalize on these opportunities. Through aggressive worldwide marketing efforts and global infrastructure spending, the Company is positioning itself to maintain and to expand markets and gain market share on a worldwide basis.

The Company experienced revenue growth in fiscal 1997 in all breakout categories (see chart). U.S. footwear represents the largest increase in total dollars, improving by almost $1 billion, or 36%, as a result of 28% more pairs sold and a 6% increase in average selling price. The increase in average selling price was due to a change in product mix as well as increased prices in effect during the second half of the fiscal year in certain categories. Men's basketball, men's running, men's cross training, kids, and women's fitness comprise approximately 79% of the total U.S. footwear business, and individually increased 35%, 59%, 26%, 53% and 51%, respectively. Brand Jordan and Golf categories increased significantly over the prior year, improving 133% and 111%, respectively. Two categories experienced revenue reductions, men's court and outdoor, down 22% and 24%, respectively. U.S. apparel experienced growth in all categories, demonstrating the strength of the NIKE brand. Brand revenues outside of the U.S. increased $1.1 billion, or 49%. The U.S. dollar strengthened against nearly all currencies. Had the U.S. dollar remained constant with that of the prior year, non-U.S. revenues would have increased $1.4 billion, or 59%. By region, Asia Pacific increased $511 million, or 70% (84% on a constant dollar basis), Europe increased $497 million, or 38% (48% on a constant dollar basis) and the Americas (which includes Canada and Latin America) increased $137 million, or 44% (46% on a constant dollar basis). The most significant increases were in Japan, Korea, United Kingdom, Italy, and Canada. Other Brands, which includes Bauer Inc., Cole Haan, Sports Specialties, Corp., and Tetra Plastics, Inc., decreased 3% to $504 million. The Company expects revenue growth in fiscal 1998 to be affected by strong demand for the NIKE brand on a global scale, and reduced growth rates in the U.S. given the significance of the existing market share.

The breakdown of revenues follows:

(in thousands)

YEAR ENDED MAY 31,	1997	% CHG	1996	% CHG	1995	% CHG
United States footwear	$3,770,600	36%	$2,772,500	20%	$2,309,400	24%
United States apparel	1,431,000	70	842,500	99	423,900	25
Total United States	5,201,600	44	3,615,000	32	2,733,300	24
Non-U.S. footwear	2,391,000	42	1,682,300	35	1,244,300	25
Non-U.S. apparel	1,089,800	67	651,400	38	472,700	32
Total Non-U.S.	3,480,800	49	2,333,700	36	1,717,000	27
Other brands	504,100	(3)	521,900	68	310,600	38
Total NIKE	$9,186,500	42%	$6,470,600	36%	$4,760,900	26%

Gross margins increased to 40.1% of revenues in fiscal 1997, exceeding 40% for the first time in Company history. The improved percentage was principally driven by price increases in certain U.S. footwear categories in effect the second half of the year. This was offset by slight reductions in gross margin percentages from increased close-out sales as a percentage of total sales, most predominately at Bauer, due to the softening of the in-line skate market and liquidation of non-Bauer brand product to consolidate to a single Bauer brand. Global fiscal 1998 margins could be affected negatively by increasing product costs, added infrastructure to support higher levels of operations, and increased sales of lower priced product including close-outs.

Selling and administrative expenses represented 25.1% of revenues compared with 24.6% in the prior year. NIKE brand expenses increased $353 in the U.S. and $355 million outside the U.S. Increases were largely driven by increased sales and marketing spending, as well as infrastructure-related costs to support growth outside the U.S. The Company intends to continue to invest in growth opportunities and worldwide marketing and advertising in order to ensure the successful sell-through of orders discussed below.

Interest expense increased $12.8 million due to increased short-term and new long-term borrowings needed to fund the increased level of operations, including increased working capital requirements and infrastructure. See further discussion under liquidity and capital resources.

Other income/expense was a net expense of $32.3 million in fiscal 1997, compared with $36.7 million in 1996. The majority of the reduction was attributable to increased interest income, higher gain on disposal of assets and income from a new promotional event staged in Japan, offset by an one-time Bauer restructuring charge of $18 million, which includes, among other things, moving certain products to offshore production and the closing of certain facilities.

Worldwide futures and advance orders for NIKE brand athletic footwear and apparel, scheduled for delivery from June through November, 1997, were approximately $4.9 billion, 18% higher than such orders booked in the comparable period of the prior year. These orders and the percentage growth in these orders are not necessarily indicative of the growth in revenues which the Company will experience for the subsequent periods. This is because the mix of advance/futures and orders at once has shifted significantly toward advance/futures orders as the NIKE brand and futures program become more established in all areas, specifically in the non-U.S. regions. The mix of orders will continue to vary as the non-U.S. operations continue to account for a greater percentage of total revenues and place a greater emphasis on futures programs. Finally, exchange rates can cause differences in comparisons.

Since the Company operates globally, it is exposed to market risks from changes in foreign currency exchange rates. In order to minimize the effect of fluctuations on the Company's foreign currency transactions, the Company uses highly liquid foreign currency spot, forward and purchased options with high credit quality financial institutions. The Company transacts in foreign exchange contracts to hedge underlying economic exposures and does not transact in derivatives for trading or speculative purposes. Where possible, the Company nets its foreign exchange exposures to take advantage of natural offsets that occur in the normal course of business. Firmly committed transactions and the related receivables and payables may be hedged with forward exchange contracts or purchased options. Anticipated, but not yet firmly committed transactions, may be hedged through the use of purchased options. Additional information concerning the Company's hedging activities is presented in Note 14 to the Consolidated Financial Statements.

The Company's non-U.S. operations are subject to the usual risks of doing business abroad, such as the imposition of import quotas or anti-dumping duties. In 1995, the EU Commission, at the request of the European footwear manufacturers, initiated two anti-dumping investigations covering certain footwear imported from the People's Republic of China, Indonesia and Thailand. In January 1997, the Commission imposed significant provisional anti-dumping duties on textile upper shoes imported from China and Indonesia. The Commission has not yet adopted permanent measures nor measures for leather/synthetic shoes, and the Company is unable to determine whether the Commission will do so.

Nevertheless, the investigations and the anti-dumping duties expressly exclude "footwear designed for a sporting activity", and the Company does not currently believe that the Commission will change the exclusion. While the exclusion is subject to inter-pretation and/or amendment by customs authorities, the Company believes that most of its footwear sourced in the target countries for sale in the EU fits within the exclusion and, therefore, the Company will not be materially affected by the results of the anti-dumping investigations. If the Company's footwear were not covered by the exclusion, the Company would consider, in addition to its possible legal remedies, shifting the production of such footwear to other countries in order to maintain competitive pricing. The Company believes that it is prepared to deal effectively with any such anti-dumping measures that may arise and that any adverse impact would be of a short-term nature. The Company continues to closely monitor international trade restrictions and to adopt its multi-country sourcing strategy and contingency plans. The Company believes that its major competitors would be similarly impacted by any such restrictions.

As further explained in Note 1 to the Consolidated Financial Statements, prior to fiscal year 1997, certain of the Company's non-U.S. operations reported their results of operations on a one month lag which allowed more time to compile results. Beginning in the first quarter of fiscal year 1997, the one month lag was eliminated and the May 1996 charge from operations for these entities of $4.1 million was recorded to retained earnings. This change did not have a material effect on the annual results of operations, however, quarterly results changed as certain reporting periods shifted one month. The Selected Quarterly Data section includes adjusted quarterly data for fiscal year 1996 as if the change had been in effect.

FISCAL 1996 COMPARED TO FISCAL 1995

Significant growth in worldwide revenues and improved leverage of selling and administrative costs were the primary factors contributing to record earnings for fiscal year 1996 as compared to 1995.

The Company experienced revenue growth in fiscal 1996 in all breakout categories. The most significant increase in absolute dollars was U.S. footwear, which grew $463.2 million, or 20.1%, as a result of 19% more pairs shipped and a 0.9% increase in average selling price per pair. Men's basketball, women's fitness and men's training comprised approximately half of the U.S. footwear category in terms of total revenues, and individually increased 7%, 29% and 25%, respectively, over the prior year. U.S. apparel increased $418.6 million, or 99%, experiencing growth in all categories and demonstrating the strength of the NIKE brand. Non-U.S. brand revenues also increased significantly, growing $616.7 million, or 35.9%, as a result of increases of $438.0 million (35.2%) and $178.7 million (37.8%) in footwear and apparel, respectively, over the prior year. Non-U.S. revenues were increased 1.2% as a result of the foreign currency translation impact. All NIKE regions outside the U.S. experienced revenue increases greater than 30%. Europe increased 33%, Asia Pacific, 41%, and the Americas, 35%. The most significant increases were in Japan, Italy, United Kingdom, Korea and Canada. Other brands increased $211.3 million, or 68%, over the prior year. Bauer, which was acquired at the end of the Company's third quarter of fiscal 1995, contributed $173.7 million of the increase.

Gross margins were 39.6% in fiscal 1996 compared to 39.8% in 1995. The slight reduction in gross margins compared with 1995 was primarily driven by increased costs of air freight to meet delivery dates on increasing customer orders, and increased footwear product costs not fully recovered through the selling price. These higher expenses were partially offset by improved apparel margins due to significant increases in revenues and a reduction in close-outs as a percentage of total revenues.

Total selling and administrative expenses as a percentage of revenues decreased to 24.6% as compared to 25.4% in 1995. The reduction can be attributed primarily to significant increases in revenues. The increase in absolute dollars was $378.9 million, or 31%. U.S. operations increased $160.5 million and non-U.S. increased $176.3 million, largely a result of increased sales and marketing spending as well as infrastructure to support growth outside the U.S. Bauer accounted for $33 million of the increase.

Interest expense increased $15.3 million due primarily to the higher levels of short term borrowings needed to fund current operations. In 1995, average cash and equivalents were higher, as available cash was used to fund the acquisition of Bauer.

Other income/expense rose $25 million in expense over 1995, primarily as a result of increased goodwill amortization from the acquisition of Bauer, a reduction in interest income due to a net lower cash position compared with the prior year, and increased profit share expense due to increased earnings. These were partially offset by the absence of non-recurring specific obligations which occurred in the prior year related to the shutdown for certain facilities in conjunction with the consolidation of European warehouses.

LIQUIDITY AND CAPITAL RESOURCES

The Company's financial position was very strong at May 31, 1997. Compared to May 31, 1996, total assets grew 36%, or $1.4 billion, to $5.4 billion, and shareholders' equity increased 30%, or $724 million, to $3.2 billion. Working capital increased $704 million, and the Company's current ratio increased to 2.1 at May 31, 1997 from 1.9 at 1996 fiscal year-end.

Cash provided by operations decreased slightly to $323 million for the year ended May 31, 1997, primarily due to improved operating results offset by increased working capital requirements, given the global growth of the Company. Specifically, inventories increased $417 million, representing growth in nearly all areas of the Company. U.S. footwear and apparel inventories increased $71 million (31%) and $52 million (29%), respectively. The largest increases outside of the U.S. were in the European and Asia/Pacific regions with increases of $121 million (54%) and $119 million (134%), respectively, due primarily to the significant increase in operations. Inventory turns on a consolidated basis reduced to approximately 4.8 times, as compared with 5.0 in fiscal 1996. Accounts receivable increased $486 million due, in part, to the higher level of fourth quarter revenues compared with the previous year.

Additions to property, plant and equipment for fiscal 1997 were $466 million, an increase of $250 million over 1996. Additions in the U.S. totaled $266 million for the year due to continued overall expansion of U.S. operations which includes warehouse locations, management information systems, world headquarters expansion and the continued development of NIKETOWN retail locations. Outside the U.S., additions totaled $172 million, compared to $154 million for fiscal 1996, and relates to the continued expansion of infrastructure, investments in information systems and new NIKE retail locations. The remaining additions relate to other brands. Expected capital expenditures for fiscal 1998 approximate $680 million, with the primary components consisting of the continued expansion of the world headquarters, new NIKETOWN retail locations and warehouse expansion in the U.S., Japan and Korea.

Additions to long-term debt of approximately $300 million in fiscal 1997, were used to fund the significant increase in property, plant and equipment, as well as increased working capital requirements. In June 1996, the Company's Japanese subsidiary borrowed 10.5 billion Yen (approximately $100 million) in a private placement, maturing June 26, 2011, to fund construction of a warehouse and distribution center and for other corporate purposes. Additionally, during December 1996 the Company filed a shelf registration statement with the Securities and Exchange Commission for the sale of up to $500 million of debt securities. The filing will enable the Company to issue debt from time to time during the next several years. Under this program, the Company issued $200 million seven-year notes in December 1996, maturing December 1, 2003, and subsequent to May 31, 1997, an additional $100 million medium-term notes were issued, maturing in three to five years. The proceeds were swapped into Dutch Guilders to obtain long-term fixed rate financing to support the growth of the Company's European operations.

Management believes that significant funds generated by operations, together with access to sufficient sources of funds, will adequately meet its anticipated operating, global infrastructure expansion and capital needs. Significant short and long-term lines of credit are maintained with banks which, along with cash on hand, provide adequate operating liquidity. Liquidity is also provided by the Company's commercial paper program under which there was $0 outstanding at both May 31, 1997 and 1996.

Dividends per share of common stock for fiscal 1997 rose $.09 over fiscal 1996 to $.38 per share. Dividend declaration in all four quarters has been consistent since February 1984. Based upon current projected earnings and cash flow requirements, the Company anticipates continuing a dividend and reviewing its amount at the November Board of Directors meeting. The Company's policy continues to target an annual dividend in the range of 15% to 25% of trailing twelve-month earnings.

During fiscal 1994, the Company announced that the Executive Committee of its Board of Directors, acting within limits set by the Board, authorized a plan to repurchase a maximum of $450 million NIKE Class B Common Stock over a period of up to three years. During fiscal 1996, the Board of Directors voted to extend the 1994 stock repurchase program until July 1, 1999. Funding has, and is expected to continue to, come from operating cash flow in combination with occasional short or medium-term borrowings. The timing and the amount of shares purchased will be dictated by working capital needs and stock market conditions. The Company did not repurchase any shares during fiscal 1997 and, as of May 31, 1997, the Company had repurchased 20.6 million shares at a total cost of $301.7 million.

Special Note Regarding Forward-Looking Statements and Analyst Reports

Certain written and oral statements made or incorporated by reference from time to time by NIKE or its representatives this report, other reports, filings with the Securities and Exchange Commission, press releases, conferences, or otherwise, are "forward-looking statements" within the meaning of the Private Securities Litigation Reform Act of 1995 ("the Act"). Forward-looking statements include, without limitation, any statement that may predict, forecast, indicate, or imply future results, performance, or achievements, and may contain the words "believe," "anticipate," "expect," "estimate," "project," "will be," "will continue," "will likely result," or words or phrases of similar meaning. Forward-looking statements involve risks and uncertainties which may cause actual results to differ materially from the forward-looking statements. The risks and uncertainties are detailed from time to time in reports filed by NIKE with the S.E.C., including Forms 8-K, 10-Q, and 10-K, and include, among others, the following: international, national and local general economic and market conditions; the size and growth of the overall athletic footwear, apparel, and equipment markets; intense competition among designers, marketers, distributors and sellers of athletic footwear, apparel, and equipment for consumers and endorsers; demographic changes; changes in consumer preferences; popularity of particular designs, categories of products, and sports; seasonal and geographic demand for NIKE products; the size, timing and mix of purchases of NIKE's products; fluctuations and difficulty in forecasting operating results, including, without limitation, the fact that advance "futures" orders may not be indicative of future revenues due to the changing mix of futures and at-once orders; the ability of NIKE to sustain, manage or forecast its growth; new product development and introduction; the ability to secure and protect trademarks, patents, and other intellectual property; performance and reliability of products; customer service; adverse publicity; the loss of significant customers or suppliers; dependence on distributors; business disruptions; increased costs of freight and transportation to meet delivery deadlines; changes in business strategy or development plans; general risks associated with doing business outside the United States, including, without limitation, import duties, tariffs, quotas and political instability; changes in government regulations; liability and other claims asserted against NIKE; the ability to attract and retain qualified personnel; and other factors referenced or incorporated by reference in this report and other reports. The risks included here are not exhaustive. Other sections of this report may include additional factors which could adversely impact NIKE's business and financial performance. Moreover, NIKE operates in a very competitive and rapidly changing environment. New risk factors emerge from time to time and it is not possible for management to predict all such risk factors, nor can it assess the impact of all such risk factors on NIKE's business or the extent to which any factor, or combination of factors, may cause actual results to differ materially from those contained in any forward-looking statements. Given these risks and uncertainties, investors should not place undue reliance on forward-looking statements as a prediction of actual results.

FINANCIAL REPORTING

Management of NIKE, Inc. is responsible for the information and representations contained in this report. The financial statements have been prepared in conformity with the generally accepted accounting principles we considered appropriate in the circumstances and include some amounts based on our best estimates and judgments. Other financial information in this report is consistent with these financial statements.

The Company's accounting systems include controls designed to reasonably assure that assets are safeguarded from unauthorized use or disposition and which provide for the preparation of financial statements in conformity with generally accepted accounting principles. These systems are supplemented by the selection and training of qualified financial personnel and an organizational structure providing for appropriate segregation of duties.

An Internal Audit department reviews the results of its work with the Audit Committee of the Board of Directors, presently consisting of three outside directors of the Company. The Audit Committee is responsible for recommending to the Board of Directors the appointment of the independent accountants and reviews with the independent accountants, management and the internal audit staff, the scope and the results of the annual examination, the effectiveness of the accounting control system and other matters relating to the financial affairs of the Company as they deem appropriate. The independent accountants and the internal auditors have full access to the Committee, with and without the presence of management, to discuss any appropriate matters.

40

REPORT OF INDEPENDENT ACCOUNTANTS

Portland, Oregon
June 27, 1997
To the Board of Directors and
Shareholders of NIKE, Inc.

In our opinion, the accompanying consolidated balance sheet and the related consolidated statements of income, of cash flows and of shareholders' equity present fairly, in all material respects, the financial position of NIKE, Inc. and its subsidiaries at May 31, 1997 and 1996, and the results of their operations and their cash flows for each of the three years in the period ended May 31, 1997, in conformity with generally accepted accounting principles. These financial statements are the responsibility of the Company's management; our responsibility is to express an opinion on these financial statements based on our audits. We conducted our audits of these statements in accordance with generally accepted auditing standards which require that we plan and perform the audit to obtain reasonable assurance about whether the financial statements are free of material misstatement. An audit includes examining, on a test basis, evidence supporting the amounts and disclosures in the financial statements, assessing the accounting principles used and significant estimates made by management, and evaluating the overall financial statement presentation. We believe that our audits provide a reasonable basis for the opinion expressed above.

Price Waterhouse LLP

41

NIKE, INC. CONSOLIDATED STATEMENT OF INCOME

(in thousands, except per share data)

YEAR ENDED MAY 31,	1997	1996	1995
Revenues	$9,186,539	$6,470,625	$4,760,834
Costs and expenses:			
Costs of sales	5,502,993	3,906,746	2,865,280
Selling and administrative	2,303,704	1,588,612	1,209,760
Interest expense (Notes 4 and 5)	52,343	39,498	24,208
Other income/expense, net (Notes 1, 9 and 10)	32,277	36,679	11,722
	7,891,317	5,571,535	4,110,970
Income before income taxes	1,295,222	899,090	649,864
Income taxes (Note 6)	499,400	345,900	250,200
Net income	$ 795,822	$ 553,190	$ 399,664
Net income per common share (Note 1)	$ 2.68	$ 1.88	$ 1.36
Average number of common and common equivalent shares (Note 1)	297,000	293,608	294,012

The accompanying notes to consolidated financial statements are an integral part of this statement.

NIKE, INC. CONSOLIDATED BALANCE SHEET

(in thousands)

MAY 31,	1997	1996
Assets		
Current Assets:		
Cash and equivalents	$ 445,421	$ 262,117
Accounts receivable, less allowance for		
doubtful accounts of $57,233 and $43,372	1,754,137	1,346,125
Inventories (Note 2)	1,338,640	931,151
Deferred income taxes (Note 6)	135,663	93,120
Prepaid expenses (Note 1)	157,058	94,427
Total current assets	3,830,919	2,726,940
Property, plant and equipment, net (Notes 3 and 5)	922,369	643,459
Identifiable intangible assets and goodwill (Note 1)	464,191	474,812
Deferred income taxes and other assets (Notes 1 and 6)	143,728	106,417
Total assets	$5,361,207	$3,951,628
Liabilities and Shareholders' Equity		
Current Liabilities:		
Current portion of long-term debt (Note 5)	$ 2,216	$ 7,301
Notes payable (Note 4)	553,153	445,064
Accounts payable (Note 4)	687,121	455,034
Accrued liabilities	570,504	480,407
Income taxes payable	53,923	79,253
Total current liabilities	1,866,917	1,467,059
Long-term debt (Notes 5 and 13)	296,020	9,584
Deferred income taxes and other liabilities (Notes 1 and 6)	42,132	43,285
Commitments and contingencies (Notes 11 and 14)	—	—
Redeemable Preferred Stock (Note 7)	300	300
Shareholders' equity (Note 8):		
Common Stock at stated value:		
Class A convertible – 101,711 and 102,240 shares outstanding	152	153
Class B – 187,559 and 185,018 shares outstanding	2,706	2,702
Capital in excess of stated value	210,650	154,833
Foreign currency translation adjustment	(31,333)	(16,501)
Retained earnings	2,973,663	2,290,213
Total shareholders' equity	3,155,838	2,431,400
Total liabilities and shareholders' equity	$5,361,207	$3,951,628

The accompanying notes to consolidated financial statements are an integral part of this statement.

NIKE, INC. CONSOLIDATED STATEMENT OF CASH FLOWS

(in thousands)

YEAR ENDED MAY 31,	1997	1996	1995
Cash provided (used) by operations:			
Net income	$795,822	$553,190	$399,664
Income charges (credits) not affecting cash:			
Depreciation	138,038	97,179	71,113
Deferred income taxes and purchased tax benefits	(47,146)	(73,279)	(24,668)
Amortization and other	30,291	32,685	14,966
Changes in certain working capital components:			
Increase in inventories	(416,706)	(301,409)	(69,676)
Increase in accounts receivable	(485,595)	(292,888)	(301,648)
Increase in other current assets	(56,928)	(20,054)	(10,276)
Increase in accounts payable, accrued liabilities and income taxes payable	365,344	344,248	175,438
Cash provided by operations	323,120	339,672	254,913
Cash provided (used) by investing activities:			
Additions to property, plant and equipment	(465,908)	(216,384)	(154,125)
Disposals of property, plant and equipment	24,294	12,775	9,011
Increase in other assets	(43,829)	(26,376)	(9,499)
(Decrease) increase in other liabilities	(10,833)	(9,651)	3,239
Acquisition of subsidiaries:			
Identifiable intangible assets and goodwill	—	—	(345,901)
Net assets acquired	—	—	(84,119)
Cash used by investing activities	(496,276)	(239,636)	(581,394)
Cash provided (used) by financing activities:			
Additions to long-term debt	300,500	5,044	2,971
Reductions in long-term debt including current portion	(5,190)	(30,352)	(39,804)
Increase in notes payable	92,926	47,964	263,874
Proceeds from exercise of options	26,282	21,150	6,154
Repurchase of stock	—	(18,756)	(142,919)
Dividends – common and preferred	(100,896)	(78,834)	(65,418)
Cash provided (used) by financing activities	313,622	(53,784)	24,858
Effect of exchange rate changes on cash	(166)	(206)	(1,122)
Effect of May 1996 cash flow activity for certain subsidiaries (Note 1)	43,004	—	—
Net increase (decrease) in cash and equivalents	183,304	46,046	(302,745)
Cash and equivalents, beginning of year	262,117	216,071	518,816
Cash and equivalents, end of year	$445,421	$262,117	$216,071
Supplemental disclosure of cash flow information:			
Cash paid during the year for:			
Interest (net of amount capitalized)	$ 44,000	$ 32,800	$ 20,200
Income taxes	543,100	359,300	285,400

The accompanying notes to consolidated financial statements are an integral part of this statement.

NIKE, INC. CONSOLIDATED STATEMENT OF SHAREHOLDERS' EQUITY

(in thousands)	Common Stock				Capital In Excess Of Stated Value	Foreign Currency Translation Adjustment	Retained Earnings	Total
	Class A		Class B					
	Shares	Amount	Shares	Amount				
Balance at May 31, 1994	26,679	$159	46,521	$2,704	$108,284	$(15,123)	$1,644,925	$1,740,949
Stock options exercised			241	2	8,954			8,956
Conversion to Class B Common Stock	(784)	(4)	784	4				—
Repurchase of Class B Common Stock			(2,130)	(13)	(4,801)		(138,106)	(142,920)
Stock issued pursuant to contractual obligations			134	1	9,999			10,000
Translation of statements of non-U.S. operations						16,708		16,708
Net income							399,664	399,664
Dividends on Redeemable Preferred Stock							(30)	(30)
Dividends on Common Stock							(68,638)	(68,638)
Balance at May 31, 1995	25,895	155	45,550	2,698	122,436	1,585	1,837,815	1,964,689
Stock options exercised				3	32,848			32,851
Conversion to Class B Common Stock	(655)	(2)		2				—
Repurchase of Class B Common Stock				(1)	(451)		(18,304)	(18,756)
Two-for-one Stock Split October 30, 1995	25,880							
Translation of statements of non-U.S. operations						(18,086)		(18,086)
Net income							553,190	553,190
Dividends on Redeemable Preferred Stock							(30)	(30)
Dividends on Common Stock							(82,458)	(82,458)
Balance at May 31, 1996	51,120	153	92,509	2,702	154,833	(16,501)	2,290,213	2,431,400
Stock options exercised			1,475	3	55,817			55,820
Conversion to Class B Common Stock	(279)	(1)	279	1				—
Two-for-one Stock Split October 23, 1996	50,870		93,296					
Translation of statements of non-U.S. operations						(14,832)		(14,832)
Net income							795,822	795,822
Dividends on Redeemable Preferred Stock							(30)	(30)
Dividends on Common Stock							(108,249)	(108,249)
Net income for the month ended May 1996, due to the change in fiscal year-end of certain non-U.S. operations (Note 1)							(4,093)	(4,093)
Balance at May 31, 1997	101,711	$152	187,559	$2,706	$210,650	($31,333)	$2,973,663	$3,155,838

The accompanying notes to consolidated financial statements are an integral part of this statement.

NIKE, INC. NOTES TO CONSOLIDATED FINANCIAL STATEMENTS

NOTE 1 – SUMMARY OF SIGNIFICANT ACCOUNTING POLICIES:

Basis of consolidation:

The consolidated financial statements include the accounts of the Company and its subsidiaries. All significant intercompany trans-actions and balances have been eliminated. Prior to fiscal year 1997, certain of the Company's non-U.S. operations reported their results of operations on a one month lag which allowed more time to compile results. Beginning in the first quarter of fiscal year 1997, the one month lag was eliminated. As a result, the May 1996 charge from operations for these entities of $4,093,000 was recorded to retained earnings in the first quarter of the current year.

Recognition of revenues:

Revenues recognized include sales plus fees earned on sales by licensees.

Advertising:

Advertising production costs are expensed the first time the advertisement is run. Media (TV and print) placement costs are expensed in the month the advertising appears. Total advertising and promotion expenses were $978,251,000, $642,498,000 and $495,006,000 for the years ended May 31, 1997, 1996 and 1995, respectively. Included in prepaid expenses and other assets was $111,925,000 and $69,340,000 at May 31, 1997 and 1996, respectively, relating to prepaid advertising and promotion expenses.

Cash and equivalents:

Cash and equivalents represent cash and short-term, highly liquid investments with original maturities three months or less.

Inventory valuation:

Inventories are stated at the lower of cost or market. Cost is determined using the last-in, first-out (LIFO) method for substantially all U.S. inventories. Non-U.S. inventories are valued on a first-in, first-out (FIFO) basis.

Property, plant and equipment and depreciation:

Property, plant and equipment are recorded at cost. Depreciation for financial reporting purposes is determined on a straight-line basis for buildings and leasehold improvements and principally on a declining balance basis for machinery and equipment, based upon estimated useful lives ranging from two to thirty years.

Identifiable intangible assets and goodwill:

At May 31, 1997 and 1996, the Company had patents, trademarks and other identifiable intangible assets with a value of $219,186,000 and $209,586,000, respectively. The Company's excess of purchase cost over the fair value of net assets of businesses acquired (goodwill) was $326,252,000 and $327,555,000 at May 31, 1997 and 1996, respectively.

Identifiable intangible assets and goodwill are being amortized over their estimated useful lives on a straight-line basis over five to forty years. Accumulated amortization was $81,247,000 and $62,329,000 at May 31, 1997 and 1996, respectively. Amortization expense, which is included in other income/expense, was $19,765,000, $21,772,000 and $13,176,000 for the years ended May 31, 1997, 1996 and 1995, respectively. Intangible assets are periodically reviewed by the Company for impairments where the fair value is less than the carrying value.

Other liabilities:

Other liabilities include amounts with settlement dates beyond one year, and are primarily composed of long-term deferred endorse-ment payments of $15,815,000 and $21,674,000 at May 31, 1997 and 1996, respectively. Deferred payments to endorsers relate to amounts due beyond contract termination, which are discounted at various interest rates and accrued over the contract period.

Endorsement contracts:

Accounting for endorsement contracts is based upon specific contract provisions. Generally, endorsement payments are expensed uniformly over the term of the contract after giving recognition to periodic performance compliance provisions of the contracts. Contracts requiring prepayments are included in prepaid expenses or other assets depending on the length of the contract.

Foreign currency translation:

Adjustments resulting from translating foreign functional currency financial statements into U.S. dollars are included in the foreign currency translation adjustment in shareholders' equity.

Derivatives:

The Company enters into foreign currency contracts in order to reduce the impact of certain foreign currency fluctuations. Firmly committed transactions and the related receivables and payables may be hedged with forward exchange contracts or purchased options. Anticipated, but not yet firmly committed, transactions may be hedged through the use of purchased options. Premiums paid on purchased options and any gains are included in prepaid expenses or accrued liabilities and are recognized in earnings when the transaction being hedged is recognized. Gains and losses arising from foreign currency forward and option contracts, and cross-currency swap transactions are recognized in income or expense as offsets of gains and losses resulting from the underlying hedged transactions. Cash flows from risk management activities are classified in the same category as the cash flows from the related investment, borrowing or foreign exchange activity. See Note 14 for further discussion.

Income taxes:

Income taxes are provided currently on financial statement earnings of non-U.S. subsidiaries expected to be repatriated. The Company intends to determine annually the amount of undistributed non-U.S. earnings to invest indefinitely in its non-U.S. operations.

The Company accounts for income taxes using the asset and liability method. This approach requires the recognition of deferred tax liabilities and assets for the expected future tax consequences of temporary differences between the carrying amounts and the tax bases of other assets and liabilities. See Note 6 for further discussion.

Net income per common share:

Net income per common share is computed based on the weighted average number of common and common equivalent (stock option) shares outstanding for the periods reported.

On October 23, 1996 and October 30, 1995, the Company issued additional shares in connection with two-for-one stock splits effected in the form of a 100% stock dividend on outstanding Class A and Class B common stock. The per common share amounts in the Consolidated Financial Statements and accompanying notes have been adjusted to reflect these stock splits.

Management estimates:

The preparation of financial statements in conformity with generally accepted accounting principles requires management to make estimates, including estimates relating to assumptions that affect the reported amounts of assets and liabilities and disclosure of contingent assets and liabilities at the date of financial statements and the reported amounts of revenues and expenses during the reporting period. Actual results could differ from these estimates.

Reclassifications:

Certain prior year amounts have been reclassified to conform to fiscal 1997 presentation. These changes had no impact on previously reported results of operations or shareholders' equity.

NOTE 2 – INVENTORIES:

Inventories by major classification are as follows:

(in thousands)

MAY 31,	1997	1996
Finished goods	$1,248,401	$874,700
Work-in-progress	50,245	28,940
Raw materials	39,994	27,511
	$1,338,640	$931,151

The excess of replacement cost over LIFO cost was $20,716,000 at May 31, 1997, and $16,023,000 at May 31,1996.

NOTE 3 – PROPERTY, PLANT AND EQUIPMENT:

Property, plant and equipment includes the following:

(in thousands)

MAY 31,	1997	1996
Land	$ 90,792	$ 75,369
Buildings	241,062	246,602
Machinery and equipment	735,739	572,396
Leasehold improvements	206,593	83,678
Construction in process	151,561	69,660
	1,425,747	1,047,705
Less accumulated depreciation	503,378	404,246
	$ 922,369	$ 643,459

Capitalized interest expense was $2,765,000, $858,000 and $261,000 for the fiscal years ended May 31, 1997, 1996 and 1995 respectively.

NOTE 4 – SHORT-TERM BORROWINGS AND CREDIT LINES:

Notes payable to banks and interest bearing accounts payable to Nissho Iwai American Corporation (NIAC) are summarized below:

(in thousands)

MAY 31,	1997 Borrowings	1997 Interest Rate	1996 Borrowings	1996 Interest Rate
Banks:				
Non-U.S. Operations	$553,153	4.08%	$445,064	4.38%
	$553,153		$445,064	
NIAC	$414,132	6.14%	$237,413	5.80%

The Company has outstanding loans at interest rates at various spreads above the banks' cost of funds for financing non-U.S. national operations. Certain of these loans can be secured by accounts receivable and inventory.

The Company purchases through Nissho Iwai American Corporation ("NIAC") substantially all of the athletic footwear and apparel it acquires from non-U.S. suppliers. Accounts payable to NIAC are generally due up to 120 days after shipment of goods from the foreign port. Interest on such accounts payable accrues at the ninety day London Interbank Offered Rate (LIBOR) as of the beginning of the month of the invoice date, plus .30%.

At May 31, 1997 and 1996, the Company had no outstanding borrowings under its $500 million unsecured multiple option facility with ten banks, which matures on October 31, 2001. This agreement contains optional borrowing alternatives consisting of a committed revolving loan facility and a competitive bid facility. The interest rate charged on this agreement is determined by the borrowing option and, under the committed revolving loan facility, is either the LIBOR plus .19% or the higher of the Fed Funds rate plus .50% or the Prime Rate. The agreement provides for annual fees of .07% of the total commitment. Under the agreement, the Company must maintain, among other things, certain minimum specified financial ratios with which the Company was in compliance at May 31, 1997.

Ratings for the Company to issue commercial paper, which is required to be supported by committed and uncommitted lines of credit, are A1 by Standard and Poor's Corporation and P1 by Moody's Investor Service. There were no amounts outstanding at May 31, 1997 or May 31, 1996 under these arrangements.

NOTE 5 – LONG-TERM DEBT:

Long-term debt includes the following:

(in thousands)

MAY 31,	1997	1996
6.375% Medium term notes, payable December 1, 2003	$199,211	$ —
4.30% Japanese yen notes, payable June 26, 2011	92,373	—
9.43% capital warehouse lease	—	7,485
Other	6,652	9,400
Total	298,236	16,885
Less current maturities	2,216	7,301
	$296,020	$ 9,584

In December of 1996, the Company filed a $500 million shelf registration with the Securities and Exhange Commission and issued $200 million seven-year notes, maturing December 1, 2003. The proceeds were subsequently exchanged for Dutch Guilders and loaned to a European subsidiary. Interest on the loan is paid semi-annually. The Company entered into swap transactions reducing the effective interest rate to 5.64% as well as to hedge the foreign currency exposure related to the repayment of the intercompany loan. In June of 1997, the Company issued an additional $100 million medium term notes under this program with maturities of June 16, 2000 and June 17, 2002.

In June of 1996, the Company's Japanese subsidiary borrowed 10.5 billion yen in a private placement with a maturity of June 26, 2011. Interest is paid semi-annually. The agreement provides for early retirement after year ten.

The Company's long-term debt ratings are A+ by Standard and Poor's Corporation and A1 by Moody's Investor Service.

Amounts of long-term maturities in each of the five fiscal years 1998 through 2002, respectively, are $2,216,000, $1,891,000, $2,187,000, $188,000 and $47,000.

NOTE 6 – INCOME TAXES:

Income before income taxes and the provision for income taxes are as follows:

(in thousands)

YEAR ENDED MAY 31,	1997	1996	1995
Income before income taxes:			
United States	$1,008,023	$ 644,755	$ 467,548
Foreign	287,199	254,335	182,316
	$1,295,222	$ 899,090	$ 649,864
Provision for income taxes:			
Current:			
United States			
Federal	$ 359,408	$ 247,526	$ 172,127
State	74,716	42,622	34,764
Foreign	112,679	127,345	75,964
	546,803	417,493	282,855
Deferred:			
United States			
Federal	(21,097)	(33,003)	(25,689)
State	(5,062)	(7,657)	(2,430)
Foreign	(21,244)	(30,933)	(4,536)
	(47,403)	(71,593)	(32,655)
	$ 499,400	$ 345,900	$ 250,200

During fiscal 1994 the Company permanently reinvested approximately $56,000,000 of its undistributed non-U.S.earnings in certain subsidiaries.

A benefit has been recognized for foreign loss carry forwards of $138,500,000 and $96,600,000 at May 31, 1997 and 1996, respectively, which have no expiration. As of May 31, 1997, the Company has utilized all foreign tax credits.

51

Deferred tax liabilities (assets) are comprised of the following:

(in thousands)

MAY 31,	1997	1996
Undistributed earnings of foreign subsidiaries	$ 3,026	$ 3,220
Other	13,017	12,040
Gross deferred tax liabilities	16,043	15,260
Allowance for doubtful accounts	(16,092)	(9,050)
Inventory reserves	(30,347)	(20,796)
Deferred compensation	(26,659)	(17,583)
Reserves and accrued liabilities	(50,738)	(42,870)
Tax basis inventory adjustment	(19,263)	(12,363)
Depreciation	(8,379)	(2,594)
Foreign loss carry forwards	(32,100)	(25,162)
Other	(9,582)	(12,978)
Gross deferred tax assets	(193,160)	(143,396)
Net deferred tax assets	$(177,117)	$(128,136)

A reconciliation from the U.S. statutory federal income tax rate to the effective income tax rate follows:

YEAR ENDED MAY 31,	1997	1996	1995
U.S. Federal statutory rate	35.0%	35.0%	35.0%
State income taxes, net of federal benefit	3.5	2.6	3.2
Other, net	.1	.9	.3
Effective income tax rate	38.6%	38.5%	38.5%

NOTE 7 – REDEEMABLE PREFERRED STOCK:

NIAC is the sole owner of the Company's authorized Redeemable Preferred Stock, $1 par value, which is redeemable at the option of NIAC at par value aggregating $300,000. A cumulative dividend of $.10 per share is payable annually on May 31 and no dividends may be declared or paid on the Common Stock of the Company unless dividends on the Redeemable Preferred Stock have been declared and paid in full. There have been no changes in the Redeemable Preferred Stock in the three years ended May 31, 1997. As the holder of the Redeemable Preferred Stock, NIAC does not have general voting rights but does have the right to vote as a separate class on the sale of all or substantially all of the assets of the Company and its subsidiaries, on merger, consolidation, liquidation or dissolution of the Company or on the sale or assignment of the NIKE trademark for athletic footwear sold in the United States.

NOTE 8 – COMMON STOCK:

The authorized number of shares of Class A Common Stock no par value and Class B Common Stock no par value are 110,000,000 and 350,000,000, respectively. The Company announced a two-for-one stock split which was effected in the form of a 100% stock dividend on outstanding Class A and Class B Common Stock, paid October 23, 1996. In the previous year a similar two-for-one stock split was announced, paid October 30, 1995. Each share of Class A Common Stock is convertible into one share of Class B Common Stock. Voting rights of Class B Common Stock are limited in certain circumstances with respect to the election of directors.

The Company's Employee Incentive Compensation Plan (the "1980 Plan") was adopted in 1980 and expired on December 31, 1990. The 1980 Plan provided for the issuance of up to 13,440,000 shares of the Company's Class B Common Stock in connection with the exercise of stock options granted under such plan. No further grants will be made under the 1980 Plan.

In 1990, the Board of Directors adopted, and the shareholders approved, the NIKE, Inc. 1990 Stock Incentive Plan (the "1990 Plan"). The 1990 Plan provides for the issuance of up to 16,000,000 shares of Class B Common Stock in connection with stock options and other awards granted under such plan. The 1990 Plan authorizes the grant of incentive stock options, non-statutory stock options, stock appreciation rights, stock bonuses, and the sale of restricted stock. The exercise price for incentive stock options may not be less than the fair market value of the underlying shares on the date of grant. The exercise price for non-statutory stock options and stock appreciation rights, and the purchase price of restricted stock, may not be less than 75% of the fair market value of the underlying shares on the date of grant. No consideration will be paid for stock bonuses awarded under the 1990 Plan. The 1990 Plan is administered by a committee of the Board of Directors. The committee has the authority to determine the employees to whom awards will be made, the amount of the awards, and the other terms and conditions of the awards. As of May 31, 1997, the committee has granted substantially all non-statutory stock options at 100% of fair market value on the date of grant under the 1990 Plan.

In addition to the option plans discussed above, the Company has several agreements outside of the plans with certain directors, endorsers and employees. As of May 31, 1997, 7,754,000 options with exercise prices ranging from $0.417 per share to $53.625 per share had been granted. The aggregate compensation expenses related to these agreements is $9,530,000 and is being amortized over vesting periods from October 1980 through September 2000. The outstanding agreements expire from December 1998 through September 2006.

During 1995, the Financial Accounting Standards Board issued SFAS 123, "Accounting for Stock Based Compensation," which defines a fair value method of accounting for an employee stock option or similar equity instrument and encouraged, but does not require, all entities to adopt that method of accounting. Entities electing not to adopt the fair value method of accounting must make pro forma disclosures of net income and earnings per share, as if the fair value based method of accounting defined in this statement has been applied.

The Company has elected not to adopt the fair value method; however, as required by SFAS 123, the Company has computed for pro forma disclosure purposes the value of options granted during fiscal years 1997 and 1996 using the Black-Scholes option pricing model. The weighted average assumptions used for stock option grants for 1997 and 1996 were a dividend yield of 1%, expected volatility of the market price of the Company's common stock of 30%, a weighted-average expected life of the options of approximately five years, and interest rates of 6.42 and 6.56 for fiscal 1997 and 5.92 and 5.97 for fiscal 1996. These interest rates are reflective of option grant dates made throughout the year.

Options were assumed to be exercised over the 5 year expected life for purposes of this valuation. Adjustments for forfeitures are made as they occur. For the years ended May 31, 1997 and 1996, the total value of the options granted, for which no previous expense has been recognized, was computed as approximately $29,074,000 and $18,167,000, respectively, which would be amortized on a straight line basis over the vesting period of the options. The weighted average fair value per share of the options granted in 1997 and 1996 are $17.39 and $7.15, respectively.

If the Company had accounted for these stock options issued to employees in accordance with SFAS 123, the Company's net income and pro forma net income and net income per share and pro forma net income per share would have been reported as follows:

YEAR ENDED MAY 31,	1997 Net Income	EPS	1996 Net Income	EPS
As Reported	$795,822	$2.68	$553,190	$1.88
Pro Forma	788,692	2.66	550,426	1.87

The pro forma effects of applying SFAS 123 may not be representative of the effects on reported net income and earnings per share for future years since options vest over several years and additional awards are made each year.

The following summarizes the stock option transactions under plans discussed above (adjusted for all applicable stock splits):

	Shares (in thousands)	Weighted Average Option Price
Options outstanding May 31, 1995	11,916	$10.87
Exercised	(2,281)	7.90
Surrendered	(66)	17.07
Granted	2,690	21.25
Options outstanding May 31, 1996	12,259	13.67
Exercised	(2,012)	11.28
Surrendered	(55)	23.50
Granted	1,692	48.93
Options outstanding May 31, 1997	11,884	19.05
Options exercisable at May 31,		
1996	4,225	8.35
1997	5,219	11.33

The following table sets forth the exercise prices, the number of options outstanding and exercisable, and the remaining contractual lives of the Company's stock options at May 31, 1997:

Exercise Price	Number of Options Outstanding (thousands)	Weighted Average Exercise price	Weighted Average Contractual Life Remaining (years)	Number of Options Exercisable (thousands)	Weighted Average Exercise price
$ 3.125 – $ 9.563	2,841	$ 7.56	2.90	2,841	$ 7.56
11.250 – 14.188	3,027	13.73	5.76	1,108	14.00
14.219 – 21.000	4,132	18.40	7.65	1,263	17.35
22.813 – 71.875	1,884	46.32	8.68	7	32.78

NOTE 9 – BENEFIT PLANS:

The Company has a profit sharing plan available to substantially all employees. The terms of the plan call for annual contributions by the Company as determined by the Board of Directors. Contributions of $18,500,000, $15,500,000 and $11,200,000 to the plan are included in other expense in the consolidated financial statements for the years ended May 31, 1997, 1996 and 1995, respectively.

The Company has a voluntary 401(k) employee savings plan. The Company matches with Common Stock a portion of employee contributions, vesting that portion over 5 years. Company contributions to the savings plan were $6,349,000, $4,660,000 and $3,363,000 for the years ended May 31, 1997, 1996 and 1995, respectively.

NOTE 10 – OTHER INCOME/EXPENSE, NET:

Included in other income/expense for the years ended May 31, 1997, 1996 and 1995, is interest income of $20,089,000, $16,083,000 and $26,094,000, respectively. During the year, the Company's subsidiary, Bauer Inc, recognized a one-time restructuring charge of $18,096,000 for a plan which includes, among other things, moving certain products to offshore production and the closing of certain facilities. The Company recognized $11,412,000 in non-recurring specific obligations associated with the shutdown of certain facilities in conjunction with the consolidation of European warehouses for the year ended May 31, 1995.

NOTE 11 – COMMITMENTS AND CONTINGENCIES:

The Company leases space for its offices, warehouses and retail stores under leases expiring from one to twenty years after May 31, 1997. Rent expense aggregated $84,109,000, $52,483,000 and $43,506,000 for the years ended May 31, 1997, 1996 and 1995, respectively. Amounts of minimum future annual rental commitments under non-cancellable operating leases in each of the five fiscal years 1998 through 2002 are $76,319,000, $65,315,000, $53,776,000, $46,125,000, $42,274,000, respectively, and $326,198,000 in later years.

Lawsuits arise during the normal course of business. In the opinion of management, none of the pending lawsuits will result in a significant impact on the consolidated results of operations or financial position.

NOTE 12 – ACQUISITION OF BAUER INC.:

During the third quarter of fiscal 1995, NIKE acquired all the outstanding shares of Bauer Inc. (formerly Canstar Sports Inc.), the world's largest hockey equipment manufacturer. The acquisition was accounted for using the purchase method of accounting. The cash purchase price, including acqusition costs, was approximately $409 million.

Bauer's assets and liabilities have been recorded in the Company's consolidated balance sheet at their fair values at the acquisition date. Identifiable intangible assets and goodwill relating to the purchase approximated $336 million with estimated useful lives ranging from 5 to 40 years. The amortization period is based on the Company's belief that the combined company has substantial potential for achieving long-term appreciation of the fully integrated global company. Bauer will permit the continued expansion of the current lines of business, as well as the development of new businesses, which can be used to strategically exploit the companies' brand names and products on an accelerated basis. NIKE believes that the combined company will benefit from the acquisition for an indeterminable period of time of at least 40 years and that therefore a 40-year amortization period is appropriate. The proforma effect of the acquisition on the combined results of operations in fiscal 1995 was not significant.

NOTE 13 – FAIR VALUE OF FINANCIAL INSTRUMENTS:

The carrying amounts reflected in the consolidated balance sheet for cash and equivalents and notes payable approximate fair value as reported in the balance sheet because of their short maturities. The fair value of long-term debt is estimated using discounted cash flow analyses, based on the Company's incremental borrowing rates for similar types of borrowing arrangements. The fair value of the Company's long-term debt, including current portion, is approximately $295,863,000, compared to a carrying value of $298,236,000 at May 31, 1997 and $16,840,000, compared to a carrying value of $16,885,000 at May 31, 1996. See Note 14 for fair value of derivatives.

NOTE 14 – FINANCIAL RISK MANAGEMENT AND DERIVATIVES:

The purpose of the Company's foreign currency hedging activities is to protect the Company from the risk that the eventual dollar cash flows resulting from the sale and purchase of products in foreign currencies will be adversely affected by changes in exchange rates. In addition, the Company seeks to manage the impact of foreign currency fluctuations related to the repayment of intercompany borrowings. The Company does not hold or issue financial instruments for trading purposes. It is the Company's policy to utilize derivative financial instruments to reduce foreign exchange risks where internal netting strategies cannot be effectively employed. Fluctuations in the value of hedging instruments are offset by fluctuations in the value of the underlying exposures being hedged.

The Company uses forward exchange contracts and purchased options to hedge certain firm purchases and sales commitments and the related receivables and payables including other third party or intercompany foreign currency transactions. Purchased currency options are used to hedge certain anticipated but not yet firmly committed transactions expected to be recognized within one year. Cross-currency swaps are used to hedge foreign currency denominated payments related to intercompany loan agreements. Hedged transactions are denominated primarily in European currencies, Japanese yen and Canadian dollar. Premiums paid on purchased options and any realized gains are included in prepaid expenses or accrued liabilities and recognized in earnings when the transaction being hedged is recognized. Deferred option premiums paid, net of realized gains, were $14,500,000 and $5,100,000 at May 31, 1997 and 1996, respectively. Gains and losses related to hedges of firmly committed transactions and the related receivables and payables are deferred and are recognized in income or as adjustments of carrying amounts when the offsetting gains and losses are recognized on the hedged transaction. Net realized and unrealized gains on forward contracts deferred at May 31, 1997 and 1996 were $28,000,000 and $20,700,000, respectively.

The estimated fair values of derivatives used to hedge the Company's risks will fluctuate over time. The fair value of the forward exchange contracts is estimated by obtaining quoted market prices. The fair value of option contracts is estimated using option pricing models widely used in the financial markets. These fair value amounts should not be viewed in isolation, but rather in relation to the fair values of the underlying hedged transactions and the overall reduction in the Company's exposure to adverse fluctuations in foreign exchange rates. The notional amounts of derivatives summarized below do not necessarily represent amounts exchanged by the parties and, therefore, are not a direct measure of the exposure to the Company through its use of derivatives. The amounts exchanged are calculated on the basis of the notional amounts and the other terms of the derivatives, which relate to interest rates, exchange rates or other financial indices.

The following table presents the aggregate notional principal amounts, carrying values and fair values of the Company's derivative financial instruments outstanding at May 31, 1997 and 1996.

(in millions)

MAY 31,	1997			1996		
	Notional Principal Amounts	Carrying Values	Fair Values	Notional Principal Amounts	Carrying Values	Fair Values
Currency Swaps	$ 200.0	$19.4	$13.7	$ —	$ —	$ —
Forward Contracts	2,328.5	14.8	47.4	1,422.8	(2.1)	14.5
Purchased Options	413.7	9.7	9.4	280.2	2.6	.5
Total	$2,942.2	$43.9	$70.5	$1,703.0	$ .5	$15.0

At May 31, 1997 and May 31, 1996, the Company had no contracts outstanding with maturities beyond one year except the currency swaps which have maturity dates consistent with the maturity dates of the related debt. All realized gains/losses deferred at May 31, 1997 will be recognized within one year.

The counterparties to derivative transactions are major financial institutions with investment grade or better credit ratings and, additionally, counterparties to derivatives three years or greater are all AAA rated. However, this does not eliminate the Company's exposure to credit risk with these institutions. This credit risk is generally limited to the unrealized gains in such contracts should any of these counterparties fail to perform as contracted and is immaterial to any one institution at May 31, 1997 and 1996. To manage this risk, the Company has established strict counterparty credit guidelines which are continually monitored and reported to Senior Management according to prescribed guidelines. The Company utilizes a portfolio of financial institutions either headquartered or operating in the same countries the Company conducts its business. As a result, the Company considers the risk of counterparty default to be minimal.

NOTE 15 – INDUSTRY SEGMENT AND OPERATIONS BY GEOGRAPHIC AREAS:

The Company operates predominantly in one industry segment, that being the design, production, marketing and selling of sports and fitness footwear, apparel and accessories. During 1997, 1996 and 1995, sales to one major customer amounted to approximately 12%, 12% and 14% of total sales, respectively. The geographic distributions of the Company's identifiable assets, operating income and revenues are summarized in the following table.

(in thousands)

YEAR ENDED MAY 31,	1997	1996	1995
Revenues from unrelated entities:			
United States	$5,529,132	$3,964,662	$2,997,864
Europe	1,833,722	1,334,340	980,444
Asia/Pacific	1,245,217	735,094	515,652
Latin America/Canada and other	578,468	436,529	266,874
	$9,186,539	$6,470,625	$4,760,834
Total revenues:			
United States	$5,531,957	$3,972,815	$3,004,260
Europe	1,833,722	1,341,738	985,882
Asia/Pacific	1,245,217	735,094	515,652
Latin America/Canada and other	730,046	503,591	298,323
Less inter-geographic revenues	(154,403)	(82,613)	(43,283)
	$9,186,539	$6,470,625	$4,760,834
Operating income:			
United States	$ 968,993	$ 697,094	$ 501,685
Europe	170,612	145,722	113,800
Asia/Pacific	174,997	123,585	64,168
Latin America/Canada and other	71,342	55,851	37,721
Less corporate, interest and other income (expense) and eliminations	(90,722)	(123,162)	(67,510)
	$1,295,222	$ 899,090	$ 649,864
Assets:			
United States	$2,994,017	$2,371,991	$1,659,522
Europe	1,272,918	941,522	771,752
Asia/Pacific	665,776	386,485	306,390
Latin America/Canada and other	328,681	188,839	209,389
Total identifiable assets	5,261,392	3,888,837	2,947,053
Corporate cash and eliminations	99,815	62,791	195,692
Total assets	$5,361,207	$3,951,628	$3,142,745

DIRECTORS

William J. Bowerman
Deputy Chairman of the Board of Directors
Eugene, Oregon

Thomas E. Clarke (1)
President and Chief Operating Officer,
NIKE, Inc.
Beaverton, Oregon

Jill K. Conway (4) (5)
Visiting Scholar
Massachusetts Institute of Technology
Boston, Massachusetts

Ralph D. DeNunzio (3) (4)
President, Harbor Point Associates, Inc.,
private investment and consulting firm
New York, New York

Richard K. Donahue
Vice Chairman of the Board
Lowell, Massachusetts

Delbert J. Hayes (2) (3)
Newberg, Oregon

Douglas G. Houser (2)
Assistant Secretary, NIKE, Inc.
Partner – Bullivant, Houser, Bailey,
Pendergrass & Hoffman, Attorneys
Portland, Oregon

John E. Jaqua (4)
Secretary, NIKE, Inc.
Partner – Jaqua & Wheatley,
P.C., Attorneys
Eugene, Oregon

Philip H. Knight (1)
Chairman of the Board
and Chief Executive Officer, NIKE, Inc.
Beaverton, Oregon

Kenichi Ohmae
Former Chairman of the Board
McKinsey & Company
Tokyo, Japan

Charles W. Robinson (3)
President, Robinson & Associates,
venture capital
Santa Fe, New Mexico

A. Michael Spence (2)
Dean, Graduate School of Business
Stanford University
Palo Alto, California

John R. Thompson, Jr. (4)
Head Basketball Coach
Georgetown University
Washington, D.C.

OFFICERS

Philip H. Knight
Chairman of the Board
and Chief Executive Officer

Thomas E. Clarke
President and
Chief Operating Officer

Jeffrey M. Cava
Vice President

Martin P. Coles
Vice President

Gary M. DeStefano
Vice President

Elizabeth G. Dolan
Vice President

Robert S. Falcone
Vice President,
Chief Financial Officer

Stephen D. Gomez
Vice President

Mark G. Parker
Vice President

Lindsay D. Stewart
Vice President, and
Assistant Secretary

David B. Taylor
Vice President

Marcia A. Stilwell
Treasurer

Douglas G. Houser
Assistant Secretary

John E. Jaqua
Secretary

A. Thomas Niebergall
Assistant Secretary

ADVISORY COUNCIL

Michael Jordan
President
The Michael Jordan Foundation
Chicago, Illinois

Gareth C.C. Chang
Senior Vice President – Marketing
GM Hughes Electronics
President and CEO
Hughes International
Los Angeles, California

DIVISION VICE PRESIDENTS

Alexander Bodecker
Beaverton, Oregon

Charlie Denson
Hilversum, The Netherlands

Shelley K. Dewey
Beaverton, Oregon

Dr. Joseph Ha
Beaverton, Oregon

Anders Hanson
Solna, Sweden

Tinker Hatfield
Beaverton, Oregon

Timothy J. Joyce
Beaverton, Oregon

Robert Kreinberg
Beaverton, Oregon

Gary Kurtz
Beaverton, Oregon

Larry Miller
Beaverton, Oregon

Andrew P. Mooney
Beaverton, Oregon

Anthony Peddie
Hong Kong

Kirk T. Stewart
Beaverton, Oregon

Gordon Thompson III
Beaverton, Oregon

Sharon S. Tunstall
Beaverton, Oregon

Matthew F. Wolff
Beaverton, Oregon

Robert C. Wood
Beaverton, Oregon

Craig Zanon
Beaverton, Oregon

(1) Member – Executive Committee
(2) Member – Audit Committee
(3) Member – Finance Committee
(4) Member – Personnel Committee
(5) Member – Compensation Plan Subcommittee

CONSOLIDATED BALANCE SHEETS

Amounts in thousands, except share data

DECEMBER 31,	1996	1995
ASSETS		
Current assets:		
Cash and cash equivalents	$ 232,365	$ 80,393
Accounts receivable, net of allowance for		
doubtful accounts (1996, $43,527; 1995, $46,401)	590,504	506,563
Inventory	544,522	635,012
Deferred income taxes	69,422	65,484
Prepaid expenses and other current assets	26,275	45,418
Total current assets	1,463,088	1,332,870
Property and equipment, net	185,292	192,033
Non-current assets:		
Intangibles, net of amortization	69,700	64,436
Deferred income taxes	7,850	5,455
Other	60,254	56,825
	137,804	126,716
Total Assets	$1,786,184	$1,651,619
LIABILITIES AND STOCKHOLDERS' EQUITY		
Current liabilities:		
Notes payable to banks	$ 32,977	$ 66,682
Current portion of long-term debt	52,684	946
Accounts payable	196,368	166,037
Accrued expenses	169,344	144,585
Income taxes payable	65,588	47,956
Dividends payable		5,742
Total current liabilities	516,961	431,948
Long-term debt, net of current portion	854,099	254,178
Minority interest	33,890	31,081
Commitments and contingencies		
Outstanding redemption value of equity put options		39,123
Stockholders' equity:		
Common stock, par value $.01; authorized 250,000,000 shares;		
issued 92,556,295 shares in 1996, 111,015,133 shares in 1995	926	1,096
Retained earnings	992,563	1,487,006
Less 36,716,227 shares at December 31, 1996 and 36,210,902 at		
December 31, 1995 in treasury at cost	(617,620)	(603,241)
Unearned compensation	(283)	(1,208)
Foreign currency translation adjustment	5,648	11,636
	381,234	895,289
Total Liabilities and Stockholders' Equity	$1,786,184	$1,651,619

The accompanying notes are an integral part of the consolidated financial statements.

Reebok

CONSOLIDATED STATEMENTS OF INCOME

Amounts in thousands, except per share data

YEAR ENDED DECEMBER 31,	1996	1995	1994
Net sales	$3,478,604	$3,481,450	$3,280,418
Other income	4,325	3,126	7,165
	3,482,929	3,484,576	3,287,583
Costs and expenses:			
Cost of sales	2,144,422	2,114,084	1,966,138
Selling, general and administrative expenses	1,065,792	999,731	889,590
Special charges		72,098	
Amortization of intangibles	3,410	4,067	4,345
Interest expense	42,246	25,725	16,515
Interest income	(10,609)	(7,103)	(6,373)
	3,245,261	3,208,602	2,870,215
Income before income taxes and minority interest	237,668	275,974	417,368
Income taxes	84,083	99,753	153,994
Income before minority interest	153,585	176,221	263,374
Minority interest	14,635	11,423	8,896
Net income	$ 138,950	$ 164,798	$ 254,478
Net income per common share	$ 2.00	$ 2.07	$ 3.02
Dividends per common share	$ 0.225	$ 0.300	$ 0.300
Weighted average common and common equivalent shares outstanding	69,618	79,487	84,311

The accompanying notes are an integral part of the consolidated financial statements.

Reebok

CONSOLIDATED STATEMENTS OF STOCKHOLDERS' EQUITY

Dollar amounts in thousands	Common Stock		Additional Paid-in Capital	Retained Earnings	Treasury Stock	Unearned Compensation	Foreign Currency Translation Adjustment
	Shares	Par Value					
BALANCE, DECEMBER 31, 1993	119,902,298	$1,199	$266,890	$1,198,190	$(603,241)	$(3,276)	$(13,145)
Net income				254,478			
Adjustment for foreign currency translation							12,306
Issuance of shares to certain employees	19,293		611			(611)	
Amortization of unearned compensation						827	
Shares repurchased and retired	(3,261,200)	(33)	(112,105)				
Shares retired	(16,000)		(462)			462	
Shares issued under employee stock purchase plans	158,965	2	4,082				
Shares issued upon exercise of stock options	352,255	4	6,172				
Income tax reductions relating to exercise of stock options			2,765				
Dividends declared				(24,610)			
BALANCE, DECEMBER 31, 1994	117,155,611	1,172	167,953	1,428,058	(603,241)	(2,598)	(839)
Net income				164,798			
Adjustment for foreign currency translation							12,475
Issuance of shares to certain employees	43,545		1,558			(1,558)	
Amortization of unearned compensation						1,008	
Shares repurchased and retired	(6,639,600)	(66)	(182,569)	(42,835)			
Shares retired	(67,200)	(1)	(1,385)	(554)		1,940	
Shares issued under employee stock purchase plans	161,377	2	4,253				
Shares issued upon exercise of stock options	361,400	4	6,004				
Put option contracts outstanding			(15)	(39,108)			
Premium received from unexercised equity put options			3,233				
Income tax reductions relating to exercise of stock options			953				
Dividends declared				(23,353)			
BALANCE, DECEMBER 31, 1995	111,015,133	1,096	0	1,487,006	(603,241)	(1,208)	11,636
Net income				138,950			
Adjustment for foreign currency translation							(5,988)
Treasury shares repurchased					(14,379)		
Issuance of shares to certain employees	43,278			1,505		(55)	
Amortization of unearned compensation						292	
Shares repurchased and retired	(18,931,403)	(190)		(672,900)		688	
Shares issued under employee stock purchase plans	157,134	2		4,042			
Shares issued upon exercise of stock options	272,153	3		6,930			
Put option contracts expired		15		39,825			
Income tax reductions relating to exercise of stock options				2,385			
Dividends declared				(15,180)			
BALANCE, DECEMBER 31, 1996	92,556,295	$ 926	$ 0	$ 992,563	$(617,620)	$ (283)	$ 5,648

The accompanying notes are an integral part of the consolidated financial statements.

Reebok

CONSOLIDATED STATEMENTS OF CASH FLOWS

Amounts in thousands

YEAR ENDED DECEMBER 31,	1996	1995	1994
Cash flows from operating activities:			
Net income	$ 138,950	$ 164,798	$ 254,478
Adjustments to reconcile net income to net cash			
provided by operating activities:			
Depreciation and amortization	42,927	39,579	37,400
Minority interest	14,635	11,423	8,896
Deferred income taxes	(6,333)	(1,573)	(13,332)
Special charges		62,743	
Changes in operating assets and liabilities,			
exclusive of those arising from business acquisitions:			
Accounts receivable	(107,082)	16,157	(64,786)
Inventory	77,286	(29,531)	(81,948)
Prepaid expenses	22,650	7,841	(7,752)
Other	11,042	(18,830)	(13,648)
Accounts payable and accrued expenses	67,769	(25,327)	35,211
Income taxes payable	18,419	(55,553)	20,236
Total adjustments	141,313	6,929	(79,723)
Net cash provided by operating activities	280,263	171,727	174,755
Cash flows from investing activities:			
Payments to acquire property and equipment	(29,999)	(63,610)	(61,839)
Proceeds (payments) for business acquisitions and divestitures	6,887		(4,297)
Net cash used for investing activities	(23,112)	(63,610)	(66,136)
Cash flows from financing activities:			
Net borrowings (payments) of notes payable to banks	(36,947)	2,426	37,148
Proceeds from issuance of common stock to employees	13,362	11,216	13,025
Dividends paid	(20,922)	(23,679)	(24,827)
Repayments of long-term debt	(1,290)	(112,445)	(2,585)
Net proceeds from long-term debt	632,108	230,000	
Proceeds from premium on equity put options	717	3,233	
Dividends to minority shareholders	(7,426)	(2,885)	(2,141)
Repurchases of common stock	(686,266)	(225,470)	(112,138)
Net cash used for financing activities	(106,664)	(117,604)	(91,518)
Effect of exchange rate changes on cash	1,485	5,944	(12,512)
Net increase (decrease) in cash and cash equivalents	151,972	(3,543)	4,589
Cash and cash equivalents at beginning of year	80,393	83,936	79,347
Cash and cash equivalents at end of year	$232,365	$ 80,393	$ 83,936
Supplemental disclosures of cash flow information:			
Interest paid	$ 38,738	$ 23,962	$ 19,135
Income taxes paid	101,975	152,690	135,060

The accompanying notes are an integral part of the consolidated financial statements.

America Online, Inc.

Consolidated Statements of Operations

	Year ended June 30,		
(Amounts in thousands, except per share data)	**1996**	1995	1994
Revenues:			
Online service revenues	**$ 991,656**	$ 344,309	$ 98,497
Other revenues	**102,198**	49,981	17,225
Total revenues	**1,093,854**	394,290	115,722
Costs and expenses:			
Cost of revenues	**627,372**	229,724	69,043
Marketing	**212,710**	77,064	23,548
Product development	**53,817**	14,263	5,288
General and administrative	**110,653**	42,700	13,667
Acquired research and development	**16,981**	50,335	–
Amortization of goodwill	**7,078**	1,653	–
Total costs and expenses	**1,028,611**	415,739	111,546
Income (loss) from operations	**65,243**	(21,449)	4,176
Other income (expense), net	**(2,056)**	3,074	1,810
Merger expenses	**(848)**	(2,207)	–
Income (loss) before provision for income taxes	**62,339**	(20,582)	5,986
Provision for income taxes	**(32,523)**	(15,169)	(3,832)
Net income (loss)	**$ 29,816**	$ (35,751)	$ 2,154
Earnings (loss) per share:			
Net income (loss)	**$ 0.28**	$ (0.51)	$ 0.03
Weighted average shares outstanding	**108,097**	69,550	69,035

See accompanying notes.

America Online, Inc.

Consolidated Balance Sheets

(Amounts in thousands, except share data)	June 30, 1996	1995
Assets		
Current assets:		
Cash and cash equivalents	$118,421	$ 45,877
Short-term investments	10,712	18,672
Trade accounts receivable	42,939	32,176
Other receivables	29,674	11,381
Prepaid expenses and other current assets	68,832	25,527
Total current assets	270,578	133,633
Property and equipment at cost, net	101,277	70,919
Other assets:		
Product development costs, net	44,330	18,949
Deferred subscriber acquisition costs, net	314,181	77,229
License rights, net	4,947	5,579
Other assets	35,878	9,121
Deferred income taxes	135,872	35,627
Goodwill, net	51,691	54,356
	$958,754	$405,413
Liabilities and Stockholders' Equity		
Current liabilities:		
Trade accounts payable	$105,904	$ 84,640
Other accrued expenses and liabilities	127,898	23,509
Deferred revenue	37,950	20,021
Accrued personnel costs	15,719	2,863
Current portion of long-term debt	2,435	2,329
Total current liabilities	289,906	133,362
Long-term liabilities:		
Notes payable	19,306	17,369
Deferred income taxes	135,872	35,627
Other liabilities	1,168	2,243
Total liabilities	446,252	188,601
Stockholders' equity:		
Preferred stock, $.01 par value; 5,000,000 shares authorized, 1,000 shares issued and outstanding at June 30, 1996	1	—
Common stock, $.01 par value; 300,000,000 and 100,000,000 shares authorized, 92,626,000 and 76,728,268 shares issued and outstanding at June 30, 1996 and 1995, respectively	926	767
Additional paid-in capital	519,342	252,668
Accumulated deficit	(7,767)	(36,623)
Total stockholders' equity	512,502	216,812
	$958,754	$405,413

See accompanying notes.

America Online, Inc.
Consolidated Statements of Changes in Stockholders' Equity

(Amounts in thousands, except share data)	Preferred Stock Shares	Amount	Common Stock Shares	Amount	Additional Paid-in Capital	Accumulated Deficit	Total
Balances at June 30, 1993	–	–	49,562,136	$495	$ 26,992	$ (3,550)	$ 23,937
Common stock issued:							
Exercise of options and warrants	–	–	2,827,280	28	1,836	–	1,864
Sale of stock, net	–	–	10,713,760	107	66,149	–	66,256
Tax benefit related to stock options	–	–	–	–	4,590	–	4,590
Net income	–	–	–	–	–	2,154	2,154
Balances at June 30, 1994	–	–	63,103,176	630	99,567	(1,396)	98,801
Effect of immaterial poolings	–	–	2,062,756	21	1,032	524	1,577
Balances as Restated	–	–	65,165,932	651	100,599	(872)	100,378
Common stock issued:							
Exercise of options	–	–	2,905,256	29	4,655	–	4,684
Business acquisitions	–	–	4,785,354	48	75,653	–	75,701
Sale of stock, net	–	–	3,871,726	39	56,998	–	57,037
Tax benefit related to stock options	–	–	–	–	14,763	–	14,763
Net loss	–	–	–	–	–	(35,751)	(35,751)
Balances at June 30, 1995	–	–	76,728,268	767	252,668	(36,623)	216,812
Effect of pooling restatement	–	–	–	–	–	(960)	(960)
Balances as Restated	–	–	76,728,268	767	252,668	(37,583)	215,852
Common stock issued:							
Exercise of options and warrants	–	–	10,370,338	104	47,885	–	47,989
Business acquisitions	–	–	465,502	5	16,632	–	16,637
Sale of stock, net	–	–	5,061,892	50	141,320	–	141,370
Sale of preferred stock, net	1,000	$1	–	–	28,314	–	28,315
Tax benefit related to stock options	–	–	–	–	32,523	–	32,523
Net income	–	–	–	–	–	29,816	29,816
Balances at June 30, 1996	**1,000**	**$1**	**92,626,000**	**$926**	**$519,342**	**$(7,767)**	**$512,502**

See accompanying notes.

America Online, Inc.

Consolidated Statements of Cash Flows

(Amounts in thousands)	Year ended June 30,		
	1996	1995	1994
Cash flows from operating activities:			
Net income (loss)	**$ 29,816**	$ (35,751)	$ 2,154
Adjustments to reconcile net income to net cash (used in) provided by operating activities:			
Depreciation and amortization	**33,366**	12,266	2,822
Amortization of subscriber acquisition costs	**126,072**	60,924	17,922
Loss on sale of property and equipment	**44**	37	5
Charge for acquired research and development	**16,981**	50,335	–
Changes in assets and liabilities:			
Trade accounts receivable	**(10,435)**	(14,373)	(4,266)
Other receivables	**(18,293)**	(9,086)	(626)
Prepaid expenses and other current assets	**(43,305)**	(19,635)	(2,873)
Deferred subscriber acquisition costs	**(363,024)**	(111,761)	(37,424)
Other assets	**(26,938)**	(6,051)	(2,542)
Trade accounts payable	**21,150**	60,805	10,224
Accrued personnel costs	**12,856**	1,850	397
Other accrued expenses and liabilities	**104,531**	5,747	9,474
Deferred revenue	**17,929**	7,190	2,322
Deferred income taxes	**32,523**	14,763	3,832
Total adjustments	**(96,543)**	53,011	(733)
Net cash (used in) provided by operating activities	**(66,727)**	17,260	1,421
Cash flows from investing activities:			
Short-term investments	**7,960**	5,380	(18,947)
Purchase of property and equipment	**(50,262)**	(59,255)	(18,010)
Product development costs	**(32,631)**	(13,054)	(5,131)
Sale of property and equipment	**–**	180	95
Purchase costs of acquired businesses	**(4,133)**	(20,523)	–
Net cash used in investing activities	**(79,066)**	(87,272)	(41,993)
Cash flows from financing activities:			
Proceeds from issuance of common stock, net	**189,359**	61,721	68,120
Proceeds from issuance of preferred stock, net	**28,315**	–	–
Principal and accrued interest payments on line of credit and long-term debt	**(935)**	(3,045)	(7,795)
Proceeds from line of credit and issuance of long-term debt	**3,000**	13,488	14,260
Principal payments under capital lease obligations	**(1,402)**	(368)	(83)
Net cash provided by financing activities	**218,337**	71,796	74,502
Net increase in cash and cash equivalents	**72,544**	1,784	33,930
Cash and cash equivalents at beginning of period	**45,877**	44,093	10,163
Cash and cash equivalents at end of period	**$ 118,421**	$ 45,877	$ 44,093
Supplemental cash flow information			
Cash paid during the period for:			
Interest	**$ 1,659**	$ 1,076	$ 577
Income taxes	**–**	–	–

See accompanying notes.

AOL

Accounting Concepts and Alternative Valuations

B

Appendix Outline

Learning Objectives

Conceptual

C1 Explain both descriptive and prescriptive concepts and their development.

C2 Describe the conceptual framework for accounting.

C3 Explain how price changes impact conventional financial statements.

C4 Discuss valuation alternatives to historical cost.

APPENDIX PREVIEW

Accounting concepts are broad ideas developed as a way of *describing* current accounting practices and *prescribing* new and improved practices. In this appendix we explain the accounting concepts the FASB developed in an effort to guide future changes and improvements in accounting. We also discuss alternatives to the historical cost measurements reported in financial statements. Understanding these alternatives helps us with interpreting information in financial statements.

SECTION 1
ACCOUNTING CONCEPTS

Accounting Concepts and Principles

C1 Explain both descriptive and prescriptive concepts and their development.

Accounting concepts are the ideas guiding the selection of transactions and events to be accounted for, the measurement of those transactions and events, and the methods to summarize and report them to users.[1] Accounting concepts serve two main purposes. First, they provide descriptions of existing accounting practices that help us understand and use accounting information. Knowing how concepts are applied enables us to effectively use accounting information in different situations. Also, understanding accounting concepts is more useful than memorizing a list of procedures. Second, accounting concepts are important for the Financial Accounting Standards Board (FASB), which is charged with developing acceptable practices for financial reporting in the United States and with improving the quality of such reporting. They are important because they are used in establishing current and future accounting standards.

We previously defined and illustrated several important accounting *principles* in this book. Several of these major principles are listed in Exhibit B.1. Accounting principles describe in general terms the practices as currently applied. We first explained these principles in Chapter 2, but we referred to them frequently in the book. The term *concepts* includes both these principles and other accounting practices. The FASB also uses the term *concepts* in this way.

Exhibit B.1

Partial List of Accounting Principles

Business Entity
Conservatism
Consistency
Cost
Full Disclosure
Going-Concern
Matching
Materiality
Objectivity
Revenue Recognition
Time Period

As business practices evolved in recent years, accounting concepts were sometimes difficult to apply in dealing with new and different types of transactions. Because they were intended as general descriptions of current accounting practices, these concepts did not necessarily describe what *should* be done. Since these concepts didn't identify weaknesses in accounting practices, they did not lead to major changes or improvements in accounting practices.

The FASB, however, is charged with improving financial reporting. It decided a new set of concepts needed to be developed for this purpose. They also decided this new set of concepts should not merely *describe* what is being done in current practice. Instead, the new concepts should *prescribe* (or guide) what ought to be done to improve things. The project to develop a new set of prescriptive concepts was called the *conceptual framework project.* Before we describe the conceptual framework, we look more closely at the differences between descriptive and prescriptive uses of accounting concepts.

Descriptive and Prescriptive Concepts

Concepts differ in how they are developed and used. Generally, when concepts are intended to describe current practice, they are developed by looking at accepted practices and then making rules to encompass them. This bottom-up, or *descriptive,* approach is shown in Exhibit B.2. It shows arrows going from specific practices to concepts. The outcome of this process is a set of concepts that summarize practice. This process, for instance, leads us to the concept that asset purchases are recorded at cost.

---

[1] FASB, *Scope and Implications of the Conceptual Framework Project* (Stamford, Conn.: FASB, 1976).

Descriptive concepts often fail to show how new problems might be solved. For example, the concept that assets are recorded at cost doesn't provide direct guidance for situations where assets have no cost because they are donated to a company by a local government. The bottom-up approach is based on the presumption that current practices are adequate. They don't lead to development of new and improved accounting methods. The concept that assets are initially recorded at cost doesn't encourage asking the question of whether they should always be carried at that amount.

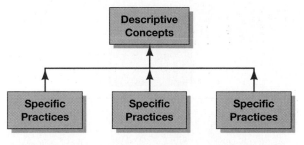

Exhibit B.2

Bottom-Up Development of Descriptive Concepts

When concepts are intended to *prescribe* (or guide) improvements in accounting practice, they are likely to be designed by a top-down approach as shown in Exhibit B.3. The top-down approach starts with broad accounting objectives. The process then generates concepts about the types of information that should be reported. These concepts lead to specific practices that ought to be used. The advantage of this approach is that these concepts are good for solving new problems and evaluating old answers. Its disadvantage is the concepts may not be very descriptive of current practice. The suggested practices may not even be in current use.

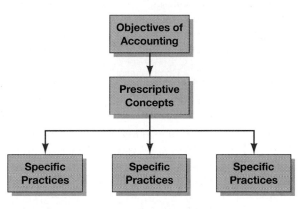

Exhibit B.3

Top-Down Development of Prescriptive Concepts

Since the FASB uses accounting concepts to prescribe accounting practices, the Board used a top-down approach to develop its conceptual framework. The Board's concepts are not necessarily perfect. But the new concepts are intended to provide better guidelines for developing new and improved accounting practices. The FASB declares it will continue to use them as a basis for future actions and already has used them to justify many important changes in financial reporting.

It is crucial in setting accounting standards that the issues be properly identified and described. The conceptual framework helps the FASB do this by providing common objectives and terms. The conceptual framework also helps the Board focus on the important factors in accounting standard-setting and reduces some of the political aspects of policymaking.

Flash back

1. What is the starting point in a top-down approach to developing accounting concepts?

2. What is the starting point in a bottom-up approach to developing accounting concepts?

Answers—p. B-8

The Financial Accounting Standards Board's approach to developing a conceptual framework is diagrammed in Exhibit B.4. The Board has issued six *Statements of Financial Accounting Concepts (SFAC)*. These concepts statements are not the same as the FASB's *Statements of Financial Accounting Standards (SFAS)*. The *SFAS*s are authoritative statements of generally accepted accounting principles, whereas the *SFAC*s are guidelines the Board uses in developing new standards. Accounting professionals are not required to follow the *SFAC*s in practice.

Conceptual Framework

C2 Describe the conceptual framework for accounting.

Exhibit B.4

Conceptual Framework

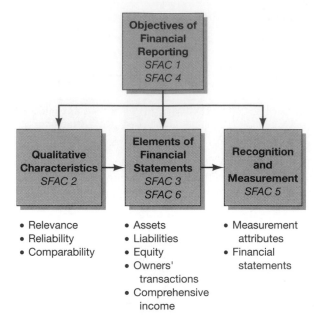

Objectives of Financial Reporting

The first *SFAC* identifies the broad objectives of financial reporting (see Exhibit B.4). The initial and most general objective in *SFAC 1* is to "provide information that is useful to present and potential investors and creditors and other users in making rational investment, credit, and similar decisions."[2] From this starting point, the Board expressed other more specific objectives. These objectives recognize that (1) financial reporting should help users predict future cash flows, and (2) information about a company's resources and obligations is useful in making these predictions.

The concepts making up the conceptual framework are intended to be consistent with these objectives. Current accounting practice already provides information about a company's resources and obligations that are presumably useful for decision makers. While this conceptual framework is intended to be prescriptive of new and improved practices, its concepts are also descriptive of many current practices.

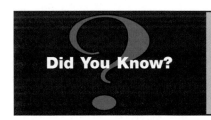

On-line Concepts

The **FASB** has a Web site [www.rutgers.edu/Accounting/raw/fasb] where we can access current FASB documents, planned FASB projects, and summaries and status of all FASB statements. This site also provides access to many current standards and happenings in accounting.

Qualitative Characteristics

Exhibit B.4 shows the next step in the conceptual framework is to identify the qualities (or qualitative characteristics) that financial information should have if it is to be useful in decision making. The Board recognized that information is useful only if it is understandable to users. But the Board assumed users have the training, experience, and motivation to analyze financial reports. With this decision, the Board indicated financial reporting should not try to meet the needs of unsophisticated or casual users.

In *SFAC 2,* the Board stated information is useful if it is (1) relevant, (2) reliable, and (3) comparable. Information is *relevant* if it can make a difference in a decision. Information has this quality when it helps users predict the future or evaluate the past and is received in time to affect their decisions.

Information is *reliable* if users can depend on it to be free from bias and error. Reliable information is verifiable and faithfully represents what is intended to be described. Users can depend on information only if it is neutral. This means the rules used to produce information are not designed to lead users to accept or reject any specific decision.

---

[2] FASB, *Statement of Financial Accounting Concepts No. 1,* "Objective of Financial Reporting by Business Enterprises" (Norwalk, CT, 1978), par. 34.

Information is *comparable* if users can use it to identify differences and similarities between companies. Complete comparability is possible only if companies follow uniform practices. But even if all companies uniformly follow the same practices, comparable reports do not result if the practices are inappropriate. For example, comparable information is not provided if all companies ignored the useful lives of their assets and depreciate them over two years.

Comparability also requires consistency (see Chapter 7). This means a company should not change its accounting practices unless the change is justified as a reporting improvement. Another important concept discussed in *SFAC 2* is materiality (see Chapter 10). An accounting item is material if it affects decisions of users. Items not material are often accounted for in the easiest way possible using cost-benefit criteria.

Elements of Financial Statements

The Board's discussion of financial statement elements, an important part of the conceptual framework, identified and defined categories such as assets, liabilities, equity, revenues, expenses, gains, and losses. In earlier chapters, we drew on many of those definitions. As shown in Exhibit B.4, the Board's original pronouncement on financial statement elements is *SFAC 3*. *SFAC 3* was replaced by *SFAC 6,* which modified the discussion of financial statement elements to include several elements for not-for-profit accounting entities.[3]

Recognition and Measurement

In *SFAC 5,* the Board established concepts for deciding (1) when items should be presented (or recognized) in financial statements and (2) how to assign numbers to (or measure) those items. The Board generally concluded that an item should be recognized in financial statements if it meets the following criteria:

Definable	Meets the definition of an element of financial statements.
Measurable	Has a relevant attribute that's measurable with reliability.
Relevant	Is capable of making a difference in user decisions.
Reliable	Is representationally faithful, verifiable, and neutral.

The question of how an item is measured raises a fundamental question of whether financial statements should be based on cost or on current value. The Board's discussion of this issue is more descriptive of current practice than it is prescriptive of new measurement methods.

In *SFAC 5,* the Board stated that a full set of financial statements should show:

1. Financial position at the end of the period.
2. Earnings for the period. (This is similar to net income reported in current practice.)
3. Comprehensive income for the period. (This concept is broader than earnings and includes all changes in owner's equity other than those that result from transactions with owners. Some changes in asset values are included here but excluded from earnings.)
4. Cash flows during the period.
5. Investments by and distributions to owners during the period.

SFAC 5 is the first pronouncement to call for a statement of cash flows. The statement of cash flows is now required under *SFAS 95,* issued two years after *SFAC 5.*

---

[3] Among the six *Statements of Financial Accounting Concepts* issued by the FASB, one (*SFAC 4*) is directed toward accounting by not-for-profit organizations. Although *SFAC 4* is important, it is beyond the scope of this course.

3. The FASB's conceptual framework is intended to:
   a. Provide a historical analysis of accounting practice.
   b. Describe current accounting practice.
   c. Provide concepts that are prescriptive of what should be done in accounting practice.

4. The notion that accounting practices should be consistent from year to year most directly relates to the FASB's concept that information reported in financial statements should be: *(a)* relevant, *(b)* material, *(c)* reliable, or *(d)* comparable.

5. What characteristics of accounting information make it reliable?

6. What do the *elements of financial statements* refer to?

Answers—p. B-8

ECTION 2 ALTERNATIVE ACCOUNTING VALUATIONS

Historical Cost Accounting and Price Changes

Explain how price changes impact conventional financial statements.

Most agree that conventional (historical cost based) financial statements provide useful information to users. But some also believe conventional financial statements inadequately account for the impact of changing prices. When prices change, users often look for alternative valuations along with the conventional statements when making decisions.

Impact of Price Changes on the Balance Sheet

Conventional financial statements reflect transactions recorded using historical costs. Amounts in these statements are usually not adjusted even though subsequent price changes alter their values.[4] As an example, consider Company X, which purchases 10 acres of land for $25,000. At the end of each accounting period, Company X reports a balance sheet showing "Land . . . $25,000." Several years later, after sharp price increases, Company Y purchases 10 acres of land next to and nearly identical to Company X's land. But Company Y paid $60,000 for its land. Exhibit B.5 shows the conventional balance sheet disclosures of these two companies for the land account.

Exhibit B.5

Conventional Balance Sheet Comparison

	Company X	Company Y
Land	$25,000	$60,000

Without detailed disclosures, a user is likely to conclude that either Company Y has more land than Company X or that Company Y's land is more valuable. In reality, both companies own 10 acres that are identical. The difference is due to price changes.

Impact of Price Changes on the Income Statement

The inability of a conventional balance sheet to reflect price changes also shows up in the income statement. As an example, consider two companies that purchase identical machines but at different times. Company A purchases the machine for $10,000 in 1998,

---

[4] One exception to this is the reporting of certain investments in debt and equity securities at their fair (market) values. We explain this exception in Chapters 10 and 16.

while Company Z purchases the machine in 2000 when its price is $18,000. Both machines are depreciated on a straight-line basis over a 10-year period with no salvage value. Exhibit B.6 shows depreciation expense in the conventional annual income statements for these two companies.

	Company A	Company Z
Depreciation expense, Machinery	$1,000	$1,800

Exhibit B.6

Conventional Income Statement Comparison

Although identical assets are being depreciated, the income statement shows a much higher depreciation expense for Company Z.

This section discusses three alternatives to historical cost valuation in financial statements.

Constant Dollar Accounting

One alternative to conventional financial statements is to adjust the dollar amounts of cost incurred in earlier years for changes in the general price level. This means a specific dollar amount of cost in a previous year is restated in terms of current purchasing power. Restating accounting numbers into dollars of equal purchasing power yields *constant dollar* financial statements. Constant dollar accounting changes the unit of measurement, but it is still based on historical cost.

Current Cost Accounting

All prices do not change at the same rate. When the general price level is rising, some specific prices may be falling. *Current cost* accounting measures financial statement elements at current values. It is not based on historical cost. The result of measuring expenses in current costs is that revenue is matched with current costs of the resources used to earn the revenue (at the time revenue is earned). This means operating profit is not positive unless revenues are large enough to replace all of the resources consumed in the process of producing those revenues. Those who argue for current cost believe that operating profit measured in this fashion provides an improved basis for evaluating the effectiveness of operating activities. On the balance sheet, current cost accounting reports assets at amounts needed to purchase them as of the balance sheet date. Liabilities are reported at amounts needed to satisfy the liabilities as of the balance sheet date.

Mark to Market Accounting

We can also report assets (and liabilities) at current selling prices. On the balance sheet, this means assets are reported at amounts received if the assets were sold. Liabilities are reported at amounts needed to settle the liabilities. This method of valuation is called the *current selling price method* or, more commonly, *mark to market* accounting.

   One argument supporting current selling prices of assets is that the alternative to owning an asset is to sell it. This means the sacrifice a business makes to hold an asset is the amount it would receive if the asset were sold. Also, the benefit derived from holding a liability is the amount the business avoids paying by not settling it. Equity in this case represents the net amount of cash from liquidating the company. This net liquidation value is the amount that can be invested in other projects if the company were liquidated. It is a relevant basis for evaluating whether the income the company earns is enough to justify remaining in business.

Valuation Alternatives to Historical Cost

C4 Discuss valuation alternatives to historical cost.

Some proponents of current selling price believe it should be applied to assets but not liabilities. Others argue it applies equally well to both. Still others believe it should be applied only to assets held for sale. As Chapters 10 and 16 explain, companies use the current selling price approach to value some investments. Investments in trading securities are reported at their fair (market) values, with the related changes in fair values reported on the income statement. Investments in securities available for sale are also reported at their fair values, but the related changes in fair values are not reported on the conventional income statement. Instead, they are reported as part of stockholders' equity.

Summary

C1 Explain both descriptive and prescriptive concepts and their development. Descriptive accounting concepts provide general descriptions of current accounting practices. Prescriptive accounting concepts guide us in the practices that should be followed. These prescriptive concepts are most useful in developing accounting procedures for new types of transactions and making improvements in accounting practice. A bottom-up (descriptive) approach to developing concepts begins by examining the practices currently in use. Then, concepts are developed that provide general descriptions of those practices. A top-down (prescriptive) approach begins by stating the objectives of accounting. From these objectives, concepts are developed that guide us in identifying the types of accounting practices one should follow.

C2 Describe the conceptual framework for accounting. The FASB's conceptual framework begins by stating the broad objectives of financial reporting. Next, it identifies the qualitative characteristics accounting information should possess. The elements contained in financial reports are then defined, followed by recognition and measurement criteria.

C3 Explain how price changes impact conventional financial statements. Conventional financial statements report transactions in terms of historical dollars received or paid. The statements usually are not adjusted to reflect general price level changes or changes in the specific prices of the items reported. Items on financial statements that do not reflect current values can lead to errors in judgment by uninformed users.

C4 Discuss valuation alternatives to historical cost. Constant dollar accounting involves multiplying cost by a factor reflecting the change in the general price level since the cost was incurred. Current cost accounting involves reporting (a) on the balance sheet the dollar amounts needed to purchase the assets or settle the liabilities at the balance sheet date, and (b) on the income statement the amounts needed to acquire operating assets on the date they are used. Mark to market accounting involves reporting current selling prices of assets and liabilities.

Guidance Answers to Flash backs

1. A top-down approach to developing accounting concepts begins by identifying appropriate objectives of accounting reports.
2. A bottom-up approach to developing accounting concepts starts by examining existing accounting practices and determining the general features that characterize those procedures.
3. *c*
4. *d*
5. To have the qualitative characteristic of being reliable, accounting information should be free from bias and error, should be verifiable, should faithfully represent what it is intended to describe, and should be neutral.
6. The elements of financial statements are the objects and events that financial statements should describe; for example, assets, liabilities, revenues, and expenses.

Questions

1. Can a concept be used descriptively and prescriptively?
2. Explain the difference between the FASB's *Statements of Financial Accounting Concepts* and the *Statements of Financial Accounting Standards.*
3. Which three qualitative characteristics of accounting information did the FASB identify as being necessary if the information is to be useful?
4. What is implied by saying that financial information should have the qualitative characteristic of relevance?
5. What are the four criteria an item should satisfy to be recognized in financial statements?
6. Some people argue that conventional financial statements fail to adequately account for inflation. What problem with conventional financial statements generates this argument?
7. What is the fundamental difference in the adjustments made under current cost accounting and under constant dollar accounting?
8. What are three alternatives to historical cost valuation for financial statements?

Identify the following statements as true or false:

1. _____ Accounting concepts are good examples of laws of nature.

2. _____ There are really no viable alternatives to historical cost measurements for financial statement reporting.

3. _____ Specific practices suggested by applying FASB's conceptual framework must be in current use.

4. _____ Accounting professionals are not required to follow the *SFACs* in practice.

5. _____ *SFACs* and *SFASs* are acronyms that both describe authoritative generally accepted accounting principles.

6. _____ Relevance, as an important quality of financial information, is placed above reliability in the conceptual framework hierarchy.

7. _____ When concepts are intended to prescribe improvements in accounting practice, they are likely to be designed by a top-down approach.

Quick Study
QS B-1
Understanding accounting concepts
C1, C2

Match the desired qualities of financial information to their most appropriate characteristics. Use the following codes: **A.** Relevant   **B.** Reliable   **C.** Comparable

1. _____ Timely

2. _____ Neutral

3. _____ Verifiable

4. _____ Requires consistency

5. _____ Makes a difference in decision making

6. _____ Useful in identifying differences between companies

7. _____ Faithful representation

8. _____ Free from bias and error

9. _____ Predictive

QS B-2
Qualities of accounting information
C2

Identify *four* accounts from the following list whose account balances you feel are most likely to mislead users when prices change:

a. Accounts receivable

b. Inventories

c. Land

d. Equipment

e. Accounts payable

f. Cash

g. Long-term stock investments

h. Prepaid expenses

i. Income taxes payable

QS B-3
Impact of price changes on the balance sheet
C3

Match the accounting principle to its best description.

Principle

1. _____ Business entity principle

2. _____ Going-concern principle

3. _____ Objectivity principle

4. _____ Revenue recognition principle

5. _____ Matching principle

6. _____ Time period principle

Description

A. Requires that financial statement information be supported by something other than someone's opinion or imagination.

B. Requires that revenue be recognized at the time it is earned.

C. Assumes the business will continue operating instead of being closed or sold.

D. Requires expenses to be reported in the same period as the revenues earned as the result of the expenses.

E. Requires every business to be accounted for separately and distinctly from its owners.

F. Requires identifying the activities of a business with specific time periods such as quarters or years.

Exercises
Exercise B-1
Reviewing accounting principles
C1

Write a one-page report explaining the difference between descriptive and prescriptive concepts. Indicate why the FASB's conceptual framework is designed to be prescriptive and discuss the issue of whether specific concepts can be both descriptive and prescriptive.

Exercise B-2
Descriptive and prescriptive concepts
C1, C2

Exercise B-3
Mark to market valuation
C4

Exercise B-4
Mark to market valuation
C4

Review **NIKE**'s balance sheet in Appendix A. Identify four account balances that would likely change if its balance sheet were prepared on a mark to market basis rather than using generally accepted accounting principles.

Your employer asks you to prepare the company's balance sheet using mark to market accounting. You realize that some accounts have valuations that don't differ from the historical cost basis, such as cash, accounts receivable, accounts payable, and prepaid expenses. However, there are four accounts that you need to locate market values for. These accounts are inventory, land, equipment, and short-term stock investments. Identify possible sources you may need to consult for these market values.

Present and Future Values

Appendix Outline

- ▶ **Present and Future Value Concepts**
- ▶ **Present Value of a Single Amount**
- ▶ **Future Value of a Single Amount**
- ▶ **Present Value of an Annuity**
- ▶ **Future Value of an Annuity**

Learning Objectives

Conceptual

C1 Describe the earning of interest and the concepts of present and future values.

Procedural

P1 Apply present value concepts to a single amount by using interest tables.

P2 Apply future value concepts to a single amount by using interest tables.

P3 Apply present value concepts to an annuity by using interest tables.

P4 Apply future value concepts to an annuity by using interest tables.

APPENDIX PREVIEW

The concepts of present value are described and applied in Chapter 15. This appendix helps to supplement that discussion with added explanations, illustrations, computations, present value tables, and additional assignments. We also give attention to illustrations, definitions, and computations of future values.

Present and Future Value Concepts

C1 Describe the earning of interest and the concepts of present and future values.

There's an old saying, *time is money.* This saying reflects the notion that as time passes, the assets and liabilities we hold are changing. This change is due to interest. *Interest* is the payment to the owner of an asset for its use by a borrower. The most common example of this type of asset is a savings account. As we keep a balance of cash in our accounts, it earns interest that is paid to us by the financial institution. An example of a liability is a car loan. As we carry the balance of the loan, we accumulate interest costs on this debt. We must ultimately repay this loan with interest.

Present and future value computations are a way for us to estimate the interest component of holding assets or liabilities over time. The present value of an amount applies when we either lend or borrow an asset that must be repaid in full at some future date, and we want to know its worth today. The future value of an amount applies when we either lend or borrow an asset that must be repaid in full at some future date, and we want to know its worth at a future date.

The first section focuses on the present value of a single amount. Later sections focus on the future value of a single amount, and then both present and future values of a series of amounts (or annuity).

Present Value of a Single Amount

We graphically express the present value (p) of a single future amount (f) received or paid at a future date in Exhibit C.1.

Exhibit C.1

Present Value of a Single Amount

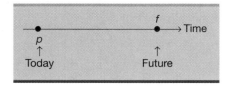

P1 Apply present value concepts to a single amount by using interest tables.

The formula to compute the present value of this single amount is shown in Exhibit C.2 where: p = present value; f = future value; i = rate of interest per period; and n = number of periods.

Exhibit C.2

Present Value of a Single Amount Formula

$$p = \frac{f}{(1 + i)^n}$$

To illustrate the application of this formula, let's assume we need $220 one period from today. We want to know how much must be invested now, for one period, at an interest rate of 10% to provide for this $220.[1] For this illustration the p, or present value, is the unknown amount. In particular, the present and future values, along with the interest rate, are shown graphically as:

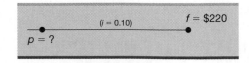

---

[1] Interest is also called a *discount,* and an interest rate is also called a *discount rate.*

Conceptually, we know p must be less than \$220. This is obvious from the answer to the question: Would we rather have \$220 today or \$220 at some future date? If we had \$220 today, we could invest it and see it grow to something more than \$220 in the future. Therefore, if we were promised \$220 in the future, we would take less than \$220 today. But how much less?

To answer that question we can compute an estimate of the present value of the \$220 to be received one period from now using the formula in Exhibit C.2 as:

$$p = \frac{f}{(1 + i)^n} = \frac{\$220}{(1 + .10)^1} = \$200$$

This means we are indifferent between \$200 today or \$220 at the end of one period.

We can also use this formula to compute the present value for *any number of periods*. To illustrate this computation, we consider a payment of \$242 at the end of two periods at 10% interest. The present value of this \$242 to be received two periods from now is computed as:

$$p = \frac{f}{(1 + i)^n} = \frac{\$242}{(1 + .10)^2} = \$200$$

These results tells us we are indifferent between \$200 today, or \$220 one period from today, or \$242 two periods from today.

The number of periods (n) in the present value formula does not have to be expressed in years. Any period of time such as a day, a month, a quarter, or a year can be used. But, whatever period is used, the interest rate (i) must be compounded for the same period. This means if a situation expresses n in months, and i equals 12% per year, then we can assume 1% of an amount invested at the beginning of each month is earned in interest per month and added to the investment. In this case, interest is said to be compounded monthly.

A present value table helps us with present value computations. It gives us present values for a variety of interest rates (i) and a variety of periods (n). Each present value in a present value table assumes the future value (f) is 1. When the future value (f) is different than 1, we can simply multiply present value (p) by that future amount to give us our estimate.

The formula used to construct a table of present values of a single future amount of 1 is shown in Exhibit C.3.

$$p = \frac{1}{(1 + i)^n}$$

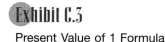

Exhibit C.3

Present Value of 1 Formula

This formula is identical to that in Exhibit C.2 except that f equals 1. Table C.1 at the end of this appendix is a present value table for a single future amount. It is often called a **present value of 1 table.** A present value table involves three factors: p, i, and n.[2] Knowing two of these three factors allows us to compute the third. To illustrate, consider the three possible cases.

Case 1 (solve for p when knowing i and n). Our example above is a case in which we need to solve for p when knowing i and n. To illustrate how we use a present value table, let's again look at how we estimate the present value of \$220 (f) at the end of one period (n) where the interest rate (i) is 10%. To answer this we go to the present value

---

[2] A fourth is f, but as we already explained, we need only multiple the "1" used in the formula by f.

table (Table C.1) and look in the row for 1 period and in the column for 10% interest. Here we find a present value *(p)* of 0.9091 based on a future value of 1. This means, for instance, that $1 to be received 1 period from today at 10% interest is worth $0.9091 today. Since the future value is not $1, but is $220, we multiply the 0.9091 by $220 to get an answer of $200.

Case 2 (solve for *n* when knowing *p* and *i*). This is a case in which we have, say, a $100,000 future value *(f)* valued at $13,000 today *(p)* with an interest rate of 12% *(i)*. In this case we want to know how many periods *(n)* there are between the present value and the future value. A case example is when we want to retire with $100,000, but have only $13,000 earning a 12% return. How long will it be before we can retire? To answer this we go to Table C.1 and look in the 12% interest column. Here we find a column of present values *(p)* based on a future value of 1. To use the present value table for this solution, we must divide $13,000 *(p)* by $100,000 *(f)*, which equals 0.1300. This is necessary because **a present value table defines *f* equal to 1, and *p* as a fraction of 1.** We look for a value nearest to 0.1300 *(p)*, which we find in the row for 18 periods *(n)*. This means the present value of $100,000 at the end of 18 periods at 12% interest is $13,000 or, alternatively stated, we must work 18 more years.

Case 3 (solve for *i* when knowing *p* and *n*). This is a case where we have, say, a $120,000 future value *(f)* valued at $60,000 *(p)* today when there are nine periods *(n)* between the present and future values. Here we want to know what rate of interest is being used. As an example, suppose we want to retire with $120,000, but we only have $60,000 and hope to retire in nine years. What interest rate must we earn to retire with $120,000 in nine years? To answer this we go to the present value table (Table C.1) and look in the row for nine periods. To again use the present value table we must divide $60,000 *(p)* by $120,000 *(f)*, which equals 0.5000. Recall this is necessary because a present value table defines *f* equal to 1, and *p* as a fraction of 1. We look for a value in the row for nine periods that is nearest to 0.5000 *(p)*, which we find in the column for 8% interest *(i)*. This means the present value of $120,000 at the end of nine periods at 8% interest is $60,000 or, in our example, we must earn 8% annual interest to retire in nine years.

Flash back

1. A company is considering an investment expected to yield $70,000 after six years. If this company demands an 8% return, how much is it willing to pay for this investment?

Answer—p. C-8

Future Value of a Single Amount

We use the formula for the present value of a single amount and modify it to obtain the formula for the future value of a single amount. To illustrate, we multiply both sides of the equation in Exhibit C.2 by $(1 + i)^n$. The result is shown in Exhibit C.4.

Exhibit C.4

Future Value of a Single Amount Formula

P2 Apply future value concepts to a single amount by using interest tables.

$$f = p \times (1 + i)^n$$

Future value *(f)* is defined in terms of *p, i,* and *n*. We can use this formula to determine that $200 invested for 1 period at an interest rate of 10% increases to a future value of $220 as follows:

$$
\begin{aligned}
f &= p \times (1 + i)^n \\
&= \$200 \times (1 + .10)^1 \\
&= \$220
\end{aligned}
$$

This formula can also be used to compute the future value of an amount for *any number of periods* into the future. As an example, assume $200 is invested for three periods at 10%. The future value of this $200 is $266.20 and is computed as:

$$f = p \times (1 + i)^n$$
$$= \$200 \times (1 + .10)^3$$
$$= \$266.20$$

It is also possible to use a future value table to compute future values (*f*) for many combinations of interest rates (*i*) and time periods (*n*). Each future value in a future value table assumes the present value (*p*) is 1. As with a present value table, if the future amount is something other than 1, we simply multiply our answer by that amount. The formula used to construct a table of future values of a single amount of 1 is shown in Exhibit C.5.

$$f = (1 + i)^n$$

Exhibit C.5

Future Value of 1 Formula

Table C.2 at the end of this appendix shows a table of future values of a single amount of 1. This type of table is called a **future value of 1 table.**

It is interesting to point out some items in Tables C.1 and C.2. Note in Table C.2 for the row where $n = 0$, that the future value is 1 for every interest rate. This is because no interest is earned when time does not pass. Also notice that Tables C.1 and C.2 report the same information in a different manner. In particular, one table is simply the *inverse* of the other.

To illustrate this inverse relation let's say we invest $100 annually for a period of five years at 12% per year. How much do we expect to have after five years? We can answer this question using Table C.2 by finding the future value (*f*) of 1, for five periods from now, compounded at 12%. From the table we find $f = 1.7623$. If we start with $100, the amount it accumulates to after five years is $176.23 ($100 $\times$ 1.7623).

We can alternatively use Table C.1. Here we find the present value (*p*) of 1, discounted five periods at 12%, is 0.5674. Recall the inverse relation between present value and future value. This means $p = 1/f$ (or equivalently $f = 1/p$).[3] Knowing this we can compute the future value of $100 invested for five periods at 12% as:

$$f = \$100 \times (1 / 0.5674) = \$176.24$$

A future value table involves three factors: *f, i,* and *n.* Knowing two of these three factors allows us to compute the third. To illustrate, consider the three possible cases.

Case 1 (solve for *f* when knowing *i* and *n*). Our example above is a case in which we need to solve for *f* when knowing *i* and *n*. We found that $100 invested for five periods at 12% interest accumulates to $176.24.

Case 2 (solve for *n* when knowing *f* and *i*). This is a case where we have, say, $2,000 (*p*) and we want to know how many periods (*n*) it will take to accumulate to $3,000 (*f*) at 7% (*i*) interest. To answer this, we go to the future value table (Table C.2) and look in the 7% interest column. Here we find a column of future values (*f*) based on a present value of 1. To use a future value table, we must divide $3,000 (*f*) by $2,000 (*p*), which equals 1.500. This is necessary because **a future value table defines *p* equal to 1, and *f* as a multiple of 1.** We look for a value nearest to 1.50 (*f*), which we find in the row for six periods (*n*). This means $2,000 invested for six periods at 7% interest accumulates to $3,000.

---

[3] Proof of this relation is left for advanced courses.

Case 3 (solve for i when knowing f and n). This is a case where we have, say, $2,001 ($p$) and in nine years ($n$) we want to have $4,000 ($f$). What rate of interest must we earn to accomplish this? To answer this, we go to Table C.2 and search in the row for nine periods. To use a future value table, we must divide $4,000 ($f$) by $2,001 ($p$), which equals 1.9990. Recall this is necessary because a future value table defines p equal to 1, and f as a multiple of 1. We look for a value nearest to 1.9990 (f), which we find in the column for 8% interest (i). This means $2,001 invested for nine periods at 8% interest accumulates to $4,000.

Flash *back*

2. Assume you're a winner in a $150,000 cash sweepstakes. You decide to deposit this cash in an account earning 8% annual interest and you plan to quit your job when the account equals $555,000. How many years will it be before you can quit working?

Answer—p. C-8

Present Value of an Annuity

An annuity is a series of equal payments occurring at equal intervals. One example is a series of three annual payments of $100 each. The present value of an *ordinary annuity* is defined as the present value of equal payments at equal intervals as of one period before the first payment. An ordinary annuity of $100 and its present value (p) is illustrated in Exhibit C.6.

Exhibit C.6

Present Value of an Ordinary Annuity

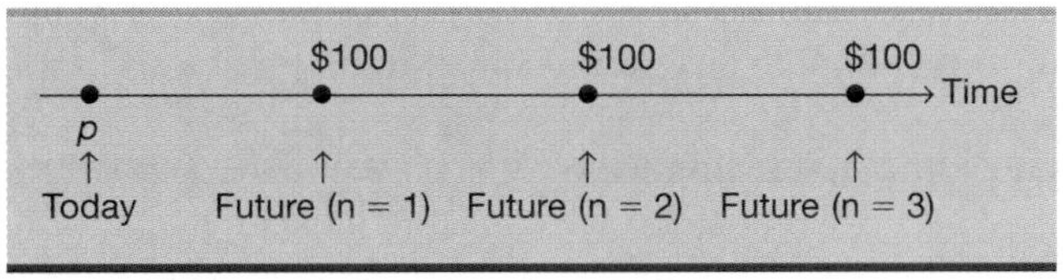

P3 Apply present value concepts to an annuity by using interest tables.

One way for us to compute the present value of an ordinary annuity is to find the present value of each payment using our present value formula from Exhibit C.3. We then would add up each of the three present values. To illustrate, let's look at three, $100 payments at the end of each of the next three periods with an interest rate of 15%. Our present value computations are:

$$p = \frac{\$100}{(1 + .15)^1} + \frac{\$100}{(1 + .15)^2} + \frac{\$100}{(1 + .15)^3} = \$228.32$$

This computation also is identical to computing the present value of each payment (from Table C.1) and taking their sum or, alternatively, adding the values from Table C.1 for each of the three payments and multiplying their sum by the $100 annuity payment.

A more direct way is to use a present value of annuity table. Table C.3 at the end of this appendix is one such table. This table is called a **present value of an annuity of 1 table.** If we look at Table C.3 where $n = 3$ and $i = 15\%$, we see the present value is 2.2832. This means the present value of an annuity of 1 for 3 periods, with a 15% interest rate, is 2.2832.

A present value of annuity formula is used to construct Table C.3. It can also be constructed by adding the amounts in a present value of 1 table.[4] To illustrate, we use Tables C.1 and C.3 to confirm this relation for the prior example:

---

[4] The formula for the present value of an annuity of 1 is: $p = \dfrac{1 - \dfrac{1}{(1 + i)^n}}{i}$

From Table C.1		From Table C.3	
$i = 15\%, n = 1$	0.8696		
$i = 15\%, n = 2$	0.7561		
$i = 15\%, n = 3$	0.6575		
Total	2.2832	$i = 15\%, n = 3$	2.2832

We can also use business calculators or spreadsheet computer programs to find the present value of an annuity.

Flash back

3. A company is considering an investment paying $10,000 every 6 months for 3 years. The first payment would be received in six months. If this company requires an annual return of 8%, what is the maximum amount they are willing to invest?

Answer—p. C-8

Fish'n Pell Lake

Frank and Shirley Capaci went fishing in Pell Lake, Wisconsin, a village of 1,200 people—fishing for money that is. They purchased a ticket in the powerball lottery system and hit the jackpot. The Capaci's had to choose between a $196 million annuity over 25 years or a single amount of $104 million. They chose the latter making it the largest one-time payment in U.S. lottery history. Mr. Capaci, a retired electrician, said they plan to spend the money on their children.

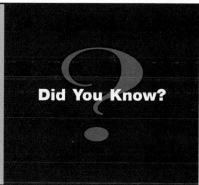

Did You Know?

Future Value of an Annuity

We can also compute the future value of an annuity. The future value of an *ordinary annuity* is the accumulated value of each annuity payment with interest as of the date of the final payment. To illustrate, let's consider the earlier annuity of three annual payments of $100. Exhibit C.7 shows the point in time for the future value (f). The first payment is made two periods prior to the point where future value is determined, and the final payment occurs on the future value date.

$$
\begin{array}{cccc}
 & \$100 & \$100 & \$100 \\
\bullet\!\!-\!\!\!\!-\!\!\!\!-\!\!\!\!-\!\!\bullet\!\!-\!\!\!\!-\!\!\!\!-\!\!\!\!-\!\!\bullet\!\!-\!\!\!\!-\!\!\!\!-\!\!\!\!-\!\!\bullet & & f & \to \text{Time} \\
\uparrow & \uparrow & \uparrow & \uparrow \\
\text{Today} & \text{Future } (n=1) & \text{Future } (n=2) & \text{Future } (n=3)
\end{array}
$$

Exhibit C.7

Future Value of an Ordinary Annuity

One way to compute the future value of an annuity is to use the formula to find the future value of *each* payment and add them together. If we assume an interest rate of 15%, our calculation is:

$$f = \$100 \times (1 + .15)^2 + \$100 \times (1 + .15)^1 + \$100 \times (1 + .15)^0 = \$347.25$$

This is identical to using Table C.2 and finding the sum of the future values of each payment, or adding the future values of the three payments of 1 and multiplying the sum by $100.

P4 Apply future value concepts to an annuity by using interest tables.

A more direct way is to use a table showing future values of annuities. Such a table is called a **future value of an annuity of 1 table.** Table C.4 at the end of this appendix is one such table. We should note in Table C.4 that when $n = 1$, the future values are equal to 1 ($f = 1$) for all rates of interest. That is because the annuity consists of only one payment and the future value is determined on the date of that payment—no time passes between the payment and its future value.

A formula is used to construct Table C.4.[5] We can also construct it by adding the amounts from a future value of 1 table. To illustrate, we use Tables C.2 and C.4 to confirm this relation for the prior example:

From Table C.2		From Table C.4	
$i = 15\%, n = 0$	1.0000		
$i = 15\%, n = 1$	1.1500		
$i = 15\%, n = 2$	1.3225		
Total	3.4725	$i = 15\%, n = 3$	3.4725

Note the future value in Table C.2 is 1.0000 when $n = 0$, but the future value in Table C.4 is 1.0000 when $n = 1$. Is this a contradiction? No. When $n = 0$ in Table C.2, the future value is determined on the date where a single payment occurs. This means no interest is earned, since no time has passed, and the future value equals the payment. Table C.4 describes annuities with equal payments occurring at the end of each period. When $n = 1$, the annuity has one payment, and its future value equals 1 on the date of its final and only payment. Again, no time passes from the payment and its future value date.

Flash back

4. A company invests $45,000 per year for five years at 12% annual interest. Compute the value of this annuity investment at the end of five years.

Answer—p. C-8

Summary

C1 **Describe the earning of interest and the concepts of present and future values.** Interest is payment to the owner of an asset for its use by a borrower. Present and future value computations are a way for us to estimate the interest component of holding assets or liabilities over a period of time.

P1 **Apply present value concepts to a single amount by using interest tables.** The present value of a single amount to be received at a future date is the amount that can be invested now at the specified interest rate to yield that future value.

P2 **Apply future value concepts to a single amount by using interest tables.** The future value of a single amount invested at a specified rate of interest is the amount that would accumulate at a future date.

P3 **Apply present value concepts to an annuity by using interest tables.** The present value of an annuity is the amount that can be invested now at the specified interest rate to yield that series of equal periodic payments.

P4 **Apply future value concepts to an annuity by using interest tables.** The future value of an annuity to be invested at a specific rate of interest is the amount that would accumulate at the date of the final equal periodic payment.

Guidance Answers to Flash backs

1. $70,000 × 0.6302 = $44,114 (using Table C.1, $i = 8\%, n = 6$).
2. $555,000/$150,000 = 3.7000; Table C.2 shows this value is not achieved until after 17 years at 8% interest.
3. $10,000 × 5.2421 = $52,421 (using Table C.3, $i = 4\%, n = 6$).
4. $45,000 × 6.3528 = $285,876 (using Table C.4, $i = 12\%, n = 5$).

---

[5] The formula for the future value of an annuity of 1 is: $f = \dfrac{(1 + i)^n - 1}{i}$

You are asked to make future value estimates using the *future value of 1 table* (Table C.2). Which interest rate column do you use when working with the following rates?

a. 8% compounded quarterly

b. 12% compounded annually

c. 6% compounded semiannually

d. 12% compounded monthly

_____

Flaherty is considering an investment which, if paid for immediately, is expected to return $140,000 five years hence. If Flaherty demands a 9% return, how much is she willing to pay for this investment?

_____

CII, Inc., invested $630,000 in a project expected to earn a 12% annual rate of return. The earnings will be reinvested in the project each year until the entire investment is liquidated 10 years hence. What will the cash proceeds be when the project is liquidated?

QS C-3
Future value of
an amount   P2

_____

Beene Distributing is considering a contract that will return $150,000 annually at the end of each year for six years. If Beene demands an annual return of 7% and pays for the investment immediately, how much should it be willing to pay?

_____

Claire Fitch is planning to begin an individual retirement program in which she will invest $1,500 annually at the end of each year. Fitch plans to retire after making 30 annual investments in a program that earns a return of 10%. What will be the value of the program on the date of the last investment?

_____

Ken Francis has been offered the possibility of investing $2,745 for 15 years, after which he will be paid $10,000. What annual rate of interest will Francis earn? (Use Table C.1.)

QS C-6
Interest rate on
an investment.   P1

_____

Megan Brink has been offered the possibility of investing $6,651. The investment will earn 6% per year and will return Brink $10,000 at the end of the investment. How many years must Brink wait to receive the $10,000? (Use Table C.1.)

QS C-7
Number of periods
of an investment   P1

For each of the following situations identify (1) it as either (a) present or future value and (b) single amount or annuity case, (2) the table you would use in your computations (but don't solve the problem), and (3) the interest rate and time periods you would use.

a. You need to accumulate $10,000 for a trip you wish to take in four years. You are able to earn 8% compounded semiannually on your savings. You only plan on making one deposit and letting the money accumulate for four years. How would you determine the amount of the one-time deposit?

b. Assume the same facts as in (a), except you will make semiannual deposits to your savings account.

c. You hope to retire after working 40 years with savings in excess of $1,000,000. You expect to save $4,000 a year for 40 years and earn an annual rate of interest of 8%. Will you be able to retire with more than $1,000,000 in 40 years?

d. A sweepstakes agency names you a grand prize winner. You can take $225,000 immediately or elect to receive annual installments of $30,000 for 20 years. You can earn 10% annually on investments you make. Which prize do you choose to receive?

_____

Bill Thompson expects to invest $10,000 at 12% and, at the end of the investment, receive $96,463. How many years will elapse before Thompson receives the payment? (Use Table C.2.)

Exercise C-2
Number of periods
of an investment   P2

_____

Ed Summers expects to invest $10,000 for 25 years, after which he will receive $108,347. What rate of interest will Summers earn? (Use Table C.2.)

Exercise C-3
Interest rate on
an investment   P2

Exercise C-4
Interest rate on
an investment   P3

Betsey Jones expects an immediate investment of $57,466 to return $10,000 annually for 8 years, with the first payment to be received in one year. What rate of interest will Jones earn? (Use Table C.3.)

Exercise C-5
Number of periods   P3
of an investment

Keith Riggins expects an investment of $82,014 to return $10,000 annually for several years. If Riggins is to earn a return of 10%, how many annual payments must he receive? (Use Table C.3.)

Exercise C-6
Interest rate on   P4
an investment

Steve Algoe expects to invest $1,000 annually for 40 years and have an accumulated value of $154,762 on the date of the last investment. If this occurs, what rate of interest will Algoe earn? (Use Table C.4.)

Exercise C-7
Number of periods   P4
of an investment

Katherine Beckwith expects to invest $10,000 annually that will earn 8%. How many annual investments must Beckwith make to accumulate $303,243 on the date of the last investment? (Use Table C.4.)

Exercise C-8
Present value   P3
of an annuity

Sam Weber financed a new automobile by paying $6,500 cash and agreeing to make 40 monthly payments of $500 each, the first payment to be made one month after the purchase. The loan bears interest at an annual rate of 12%. What was the cost of the automobile?

Exercise C-9
Future value of   P2
an amount

Mark Welsch deposited $7,200 in a savings account that earns interest at an annual rate of 8%, compounded quarterly. The $7,200 plus earned interest must remain in the account 10 years before it can be withdrawn. How much money will be in the account at the end of the 10 years?

Exercise C-10
Future value of   P4
an annuity

Kelly Malone plans to have $50 withheld from her monthly paycheck and deposited in a savings account that earns 12% annually, compounded monthly. If Malone continues with her plan for 2 1/2 years, how much will be accumulated in the account on the date of the last deposit?

Exercise C-11
Present value   P1, P3
of bonds

Spiller Corp. plans to issue 10%, 15-year, $500,000 par value bonds payable that pay interest semiannually on June 30 and December 31. The bonds are dated December 31, 1999, and are to be issued on that date. If the market rate of interest for the bonds is 8% on the date of issue, what will be the cash proceeds from the bond issue?

Exercise C-12
Future value of an amount
plus an annuity

P2, P4

Starr Company has decided to establish a fund that will be used 10 years hence to replace an aging productive facility. The company will make an initial contribution of $100,000 to the fund and plans to make quarterly contributions of $50,000 beginning in three months. The fund is expected to earn 12%, compounded quarterly. What will be the value of the fund 10 years hence?

Exercise C-13
Present value   P1
of an amount

McAdams Company expects to earn 10% per year on an investment that will pay $606,773 six years hence. Use Table C.1 to compute the present value of the investment.

Exercise C-14
Future value of   P2
an amount

Catten, Inc., invests $163,170 at 7% per year for nine years. Use Table C.2 to compute the future value of the investment nine years hence.

Exercise C-15
Present value of an
amount and   P1, P3
annuity

Compute the amount that can be borrowed under each of the following circumstances:

a. A promise to pay $90,000 in seven years at an interest rate of 6%.

b. An agreement made on February 1, 2000, to make three payments of 20,000 on February 1 of 2001, 2002, and 2003. The annual interest rate is 10%.

On January 1, 2000, a company agrees to pay $20,000 in three years. If the annual interest rate is 10%, determine how much cash the company can borrow with this promise.

Exercise C-16
Present value
of an amount   P1

Find the amount of money that can be borrowed with each of the following promises:

Exercise C-17
Present value of an
amount

P1

Case	Single Future Payment	Number of Years	Interest Rate
a.	$40,000	3	4%
b.	75,000	7	8
c.	52,000	9	10
d.	18,000	2	4
e.	63,000	8	6
f.	89,000	5	2

C&H Ski Club recently borrowed money and agreed to pay it back with a series of six annual payments of $5,000 each. C&H subsequently borrowed more money and agreed to pay it back with a series of four annual payments of $7,500 each. The annual interest rate for both loans is 6%.

a. Use Table C.1 to find the present value of these two annuities. (Round amounts to the nearest dollar.)

b. Use Table C.3 to find the present value of these two annuities.

Exercise C-18
Present values of
annuities

P3

Otto Co. borrowed cash on April 30, 2000, by promising to make four payments of $13,000 each on November 1, 2000, May 1, 2001, November 1, 2001, and May 1, 2002.

a. How much cash is Otto able to borrow if the interest rate is 8%, compounded semiannually?

b. How much cash is Otto able to borrow if the interest rate is 12%, compounded semiannually?

c. How much cash is Otto able to borrow if the interest rate is 16%, compounded semiannually?

Exercise C-19
Present value with
semiannual compounding

C1, P3

Table C.1

Present Value of 1 Due in *n* Periods

Periods	Rate											
	1%	2%	3%	4%	5%	6%	7%	8%	9%	10%	12%	15%
1	0.9901	0.9804	0.9709	0.9615	0.9524	0.9434	0.9346	0.9259	0.9174	0.9091	0.8929	0.8696
2	0.9803	0.9612	0.9426	0.9246	0.9070	0.8900	0.8734	0.8573	0.8417	0.8264	0.7972	0.7561
3	0.9706	0.9423	0.9151	0.8890	0.8638	0.8396	0.8163	0.7938	0.7722	0.7513	0.7118	0.6575
4	0.9610	0.9238	0.8885	0.8548	0.8227	0.7921	0.7629	0.7350	0.7084	0.6830	0.6355	0.5718
5	0.9515	0.9057	0.8626	0.8219	0.7835	0.7473	0.7130	0.6806	0.6499	0.6209	0.5674	0.4972
6	0.9420	0.8880	0.8375	0.7903	0.7462	0.7050	0.6663	0.6302	0.5963	0.5645	0.5066	0.4323
7	0.9327	0.8706	0.8131	0.7599	0.7107	0.6651	0.6227	0.5835	0.5470	0.5132	0.4523	0.3759
8	0.9235	0.8535	0.7894	0.7307	0.6768	0.6274	0.5820	0.5403	0.5019	0.4665	0.4039	0.3269
9	0.9143	0.8368	0.7664	0.7026	0.6446	0.5919	0.5439	0.5002	0.4604	0.4241	0.3606	0.2843
10	0.9053	0.8203	0.7441	0.6756	0.6139	0.5584	0.5083	0.4632	0.4224	0.3855	0.3220	0.2472
11	0.8963	0.8043	0.7224	0.6496	0.5847	0.5268	0.4751	0.4289	0.3875	0.3505	0.2875	0.2149
12	0.8874	0.7885	0.7014	0.6246	0.5568	0.4970	0.4440	0.3971	0.3555	0.3186	0.2567	0.1869
13	0.8787	0.7730	0.6810	0.6006	0.5303	0.4688	0.4150	0.3677	0.3262	0.2897	0.2292	0.1625
14	0.8700	0.7579	0.6611	0.5775	0.5051	0.4423	0.3878	0.3405	0.2992	0.2633	0.2046	0.1413
15	0.8613	0.7430	0.6419	0.5553	0.4810	0.4173	0.3624	0.3152	0.2745	0.2394	0.1827	0.1229
16	0.8528	0.7284	0.6232	0.5339	0.4581	0.3936	0.3387	0.2919	0.2519	0.2176	0.1631	0.1069
17	0.8444	0.7142	0.6050	0.5134	0.4363	0.3714	0.3166	0.2703	0.2311	0.1978	0.1456	0.0929
18	0.8360	0.7002	0.5874	0.4936	0.4155	0.3503	0.2959	0.2502	0.2120	0.1799	0.1300	0.0808
19	0.8277	0.6864	0.5703	0.4746	0.3957	0.3305	0.2765	0.2317	0.1945	0.1635	0.1161	0.0703
20	0.8195	0.6730	0.5537	0.4564	0.3769	0.3118	0.2584	0.2145	0.1784	0.1486	0.1037	0.0611
25	0.7798	0.6095	0.4776	0.3751	0.2953	0.2330	0.1842	0.1460	0.1160	0.0923	0.0588	0.0304
30	0.7419	0.5521	0.4120	0.3083	0.2314	0.1741	0.1314	0.0994	0.0754	0.0573	0.0334	0.0151
35	0.7059	0.5000	0.3554	0.2534	0.1813	0.1301	0.0937	0.0676	0.0490	0.0356	0.0189	0.0075
40	0.6717	0.4529	0.3066	0.2083	0.1420	0.0972	0.0668	0.0460	0.0318	0.0221	0.0107	0.0037

Table C.2

Future Value of 1 Due in *n* Periods

Periods	Rate											
	1%	2%	3%	4%	5%	6%	7%	8%	9%	10%	12%	15%
0	1.0000	1.0000	1.0000	1.0000	1.0000	1.0000	1.0000	1.0000	1.0000	1.0000	1.0000	1.0000
1	1.0100	1.0200	1.0300	1.0400	1.0500	1.0600	1.0700	1.0800	1.0900	1.1000	1.1200	1.1500
2	1.0201	1.0404	1.0609	1.0816	1.1025	1.1236	1.1449	1.1664	1.1811	1.2100	1.2544	1.3225
3	1.0303	1.0612	1.0927	1.1249	1.1576	1.1910	1.2250	1.2597	1.2950	1.3310	1.4049	1.5209
4	1.0406	1.0824	1.1255	1.1699	1.2155	1.2625	1.3108	1.3605	1.4116	1.4641	1.5735	1.7490
5	1.0510	1.1041	1.1593	1.2167	1.2763	1.3382	1.4026	1.4693	1.5386	1.6105	1.7623	2.0114
6	1.0615	1.1262	1.1941	1.2653	1.3401	1.4185	1.5007	1.5869	1.6771	1.7116	1.9738	2.3131
7	1.0721	1.1487	1.2299	1.3159	1.4071	1.5036	1.6058	1.7138	1.8280	1.9487	2.2107	2.6600
8	1.0829	1.1717	1.2668	1.3686	1.4775	1.5938	1.7182	1.8509	1.9926	2.1436	2.4760	3.0590
9	1.0937	1.1951	1.3048	1.4233	1.5513	1.6895	1.8385	1.9990	2.1719	2.3579	2.7731	3.5179
10	1.1046	1.2190	1.3439	1.4802	1.6289	1.7908	1.9672	2.1589	2.3674	2.5937	3.1058	4.0456
11	1.1157	1.2434	1.3842	1.5395	1.7103	1.8983	2.1049	2.3316	2.5804	2.8531	3.4785	4.6524
12	1.1268	1.2682	1.4258	1.6010	1.7959	2.0122	2.2522	2.5182	2.8127	3.1384	3.8960	5.3503
13	1.1381	1.2936	1.4685	1.6651	1.8856	2.1329	2.4098	2.7196	3.0658	3.4523	4.3635	6.1528
14	1.1495	1.3195	1.5126	1.7317	1.9799	2.2609	2.5785	2.9372	3.3417	3.7975	4.8871	7.0757
15	1.1610	1.3459	1.5580	1.8009	2.0789	2.3966	2.7590	3.1722	3.6425	4.1772	5.4736	8.1371
16	1.1726	1.3728	1.6047	1.8730	2.1829	2.5404	2.9522	3.4259	3.9703	4.5950	6.1304	9.3576
17	1.1843	1.4002	1.6528	1.9479	2.2920	2.6928	3.1588	3.7000	4.3276	5.0545	6.8660	10.7613
18	1.1961	1.4282	1.7024	2.0258	2.4066	2.8543	3.3799	3.9960	4.7171	5.5599	7.6900	12.3755
19	1.2081	1.4568	1.7535	2.1068	2.5270	3.0256	3.6165	4.3157	5.1417	6.1159	8.6128	14.2318
20	1.2202	1.4859	1.8061	2.1911	2.6533	3.2071	3.8697	4.6610	5.6044	6.7275	9.6463	16.3665
25	1.2824	1.6406	2.0938	2.6658	3.3864	4.2919	5.4274	6.8485	8.6231	10.8347	17.0001	32.9190
30	1.3478	1.8114	2.4273	3.2434	4.3219	5.7435	7.6123	10.0627	13.2677	17.4494	29.9599	66.2118
35	1.4166	1.9999	2.8139	3.9461	5.5160	7.6861	10.6766	14.7853	20.4140	28.1024	52.7996	133.176
40	1.4889	2.2080	3.2620	4.8010	7.0400	10.2857	14.9745	21.7245	31.4094	45.2593	93.0510	267.864

Table C.3

Present Value of an Annuity of 1 per Period

						Rate						
Periods	1%	2%	3%	4%	5%	6%	7%	8%	9%	10%	12%	15%
1	0.9901	0.9804	0.9709	0.9615	0.9524	0.9434	0.9346	0.9259	0.9174	0.9091	0.8929	0.8696
2	1.9704	1.9416	1.9135	1.8861	1.8594	1.8334	1.8080	1.7833	1.7591	1.7355	1.6901	1.6257
3	2.9410	2.8839	2.8286	2.7751	2.7232	2.6730	2.6243	2.5771	2.5313	2.4869	2.4018	2.2832
4	3.9020	3.8077	3.7171	3.6299	3.5460	3.4651	3.3872	3.3121	3.2397	3.1699	3.0373	2.8550
5	4.8534	4.7135	4.5797	4.4518	4.3295	4.2124	4.1002	3.9927	3.8897	3.7908	3.6048	3.3522
6	5.7955	5.6014	5.4172	5.2421	5.0757	4.9173	4.7665	4.6229	4.4859	4.3553	4.1114	3.7845
7	6.7282	6.4720	6.2303	6.0021	5.7864	5.5824	5.3893	5.2064	5.0330	4.8684	4.5638	4.1604
8	7.6517	7.3255	7.0197	6.7327	6.4632	6.2098	5.9713	5.7466	5.5348	5.3349	4.9676	4.4873
9	8.5660	8.1622	7.7861	7.4353	7.1078	6.8017	6.5152	6.2469	5.9952	5.7950	5.3282	4.7716
10	9.4713	8.9826	8.5302	8.1109	7.7217	7.3601	7.0236	6.7101	6.4177	6.1446	5.6502	5.0188
11	10.3676	9.7868	9.2526	8.7605	8.3064	7.8869	7.4987	7.1390	6.8052	6.4951	5.9377	5.2337
12	11.2551	10.5753	9.9540	9.3851	8.8633	8.3838	7.9427	7.5361	7.1607	6.8137	6.1944	5.4206
13	12.1337	11.3484	10.6350	9.9856	9.3936	8.8527	8.3577	7.9038	7.4869	7.1034	6.4235	5.5831
14	13.0037	12.1062	11.2961	10.5631	9.8986	9.2950	8.7455	8.2442	7.7862	7.3667	6.6282	5.7245
15	13.8651	12.8493	11.9379	11.1184	10.3797	9.7122	9.1079	8.5595	8.0607	7.6061	6.8109	5.8474
16	14.7179	13.5777	12.5611	11.6523	10.8378	10.1059	9.4466	8.8514	8.3126	7.8237	6.9740	5.9542
17	15.5623	14.2919	13.1661	12.1657	11.2741	10.4773	9.7632	9.1216	8.5436	8.0216	7.1196	6.0472
18	16.3983	14.9920	13.7535	12.6593	11.6896	10.8276	10.0591	9.3719	8.7556	8.2014	7.2497	6.1280
19	17.2260	15.6785	14.3238	13.1339	12.0853	11.1581	10.3356	9.6036	8.9501	8.3649	7.3658	6.1982
20	18.0456	16.3514	14.8775	13.5903	12.4622	11.4699	10.5940	9.8181	9.1285	8.5136	7.4694	6.2593
25	22.0232	19.5235	17.4131	15.6221	14.0939	12.7834	11.6536	10.6748	9.8226	9.0770	7.8431	6.4641
30	25.8077	22.3965	19.6004	17.2920	15.3725	13.7648	12.4090	11.2578	10.2737	9.4269	8.0552	6.5660
35	29.4086	24.9986	21.4872	18.6646	16.3742	14.4982	12.9477	11.6546	10.5668	9.6442	8.1755	6.6166
40	32.8347	27.3555	23.1148	19.7928	17.1591	15.0463	13.3317	11.9246	10.7574	9.7791	8.2438	6.6418

Table C.4

Future Value of an Annuity of 1 per Period

						Rate						
Periods	1%	2%	3%	4%	5%	6%	7%	8%	9%	10%	12%	15%
1	1.0000	1.0000	1.0000	1.0000	1.0000	1.0000	1.0000	1.0000	1.0000	1.0000	1.0000	1.0000
2	2.0100	2.0200	2.0300	2.0400	2.0500	2.0600	2.0700	2.0800	2.0900	2.1000	2.1200	2.1500
3	3.0301	3.0604	3.0909	3.1216	3.1525	3.1836	3.2149	3.2464	3.2781	3.3100	3.3744	3.4725
4	4.0604	4.1216	4.1836	4.2465	4.3101	4.3746	4.4399	4.5061	4.5731	4.6410	4.7793	4.9934
5	5.1010	5.2040	5.3091	5.4163	5.5256	5.6371	5.7507	5.8666	5.9847	6.1051	6.3528	6.7424
6	6.1520	6.3081	6.4684	6.6330	6.8019	6.9753	7.1533	7.3359	7.5233	7.7156	8.1152	8.7537
7	7.2135	7.4343	7.6625	7.8983	8.1420	8.3938	8.6540	8.9228	9.2004	9.4872	10.0890	11.0668
8	8.2857	8.5830	8.8923	9.2142	9.5491	9.8975	10.2598	10.6366	11.0285	11.4359	12.2997	13.7268
9	9.3685	9.7546	10.1591	10.5828	11.0266	11.4913	11.9780	12.4876	13.0210	13.5795	14.7757	16.7858
10	10.4622	10.9497	11.4639	12.0061	12.5779	13.1808	13.8164	14.4866	15.1929	15.9374	17.5487	20.3037
11	11.5668	12.1687	12.8078	13.4864	14.2068	14.9716	15.7835	16.6455	17.5603	18.5312	20.6546	24.3493
12	12.6825	13.4121	14.1920	15.0258	15.9171	16.8699	17.8885	18.9771	20.1407	21.3843	24.1331	29.0017
13	13.8093	14.6803	15.6178	16.6268	17.7130	18.8821	20.1406	21.4953	22.9534	24.5227	28.0291	34.3519
14	14.9474	15.9739	17.0863	18.2919	19.5986	21.0151	22.5505	24.2149	26.0192	27.9750	32.3926	40.5047
15	16.0969	17.2934	18.5989	20.0236	21.5786	23.2760	25.1290	27.1521	29.3609	31.7725	37.2797	47.5804
16	17.2579	18.6393	20.1569	21.8245	23.6575	25.6725	27.8881	30.3243	33.0034	35.9497	42.7533	55.7175
17	18.4304	20.012	21.7616	23.6975	25.8404	28.2129	30.8402	33.7502	36.9737	40.5447	48.8837	65.0751
18	19.6147	21.4123	23.4144	25.6454	28.1324	30.9057	33.9990	37.4502	41.3013	45.5992	55.7497	75.8364
19	20.8109	22.8406	25.1169	27.6712	30.5390	33.7600	37.3790	41.4463	46.0185	41.1591	63.4397	88.2118
20	22.0190	24.2974	26.8704	29.7781	33.0660	36.7856	40.9955	45.7620	51.1601	57.2750	72.0524	102.444
25	28.2432	32.0303	36.4593	41.6459	47.7271	54.8645	63.2490	73.1059	84.7009	98.3471	133.334	212.793
30	34.7849	40.5681	47.5754	56.0849	66.4388	79.0582	94.4608	113.283	136.308	164.494	241.333	434.745
35	41.6603	49.9945	60.4621	73.6522	90.3203	111.435	138.237	172.317	215.711	271.024	431.663	881.170
40	48.8864	60.4020	75.4013	95.0255	120.800	154.762	199.635	259.057	337.882	442.593	767.091	1,779.09

Selections from the AICPA Code of Professional Conduct*

Article I—Responsibilities In carrying out their responsibilities as professionals, members should exercise sensitive professional and moral judgments in all their activities.

Article II—The Public Interest Members should accept the obligation to act in a way that will serve the public interest, honor the public trust, and demonstrate commitment to professionalism.

Article III—Integrity To maintain and broaden public confidence, members should perform all professional responsibilities with the highest sense of integrity.

Article IV—Objectivity and Independence A member should maintain objectivity and be free of conflicts of interest in discharging professional responsibilities. A member in public practice should be independent in fact and appearance when providing auditing and other attestation services.

Article V—Due Care A member should observe the professional's technical and ethical standards, strive continually to improve competence and the quality of services, and discharge professional responsibility to the best of the member's ability.

Article VI—Scope and Nature of Services A member in public practice should observe the Principles of the *Code of Professional Conduct* in determining the scope and nature of services to be provided.

The Bylaws of the AICPA require that members adhere to the Rules of the *Code of Professional Conduct*. Departures from the Rules must be justified. The current Rules are:

Rule 101—Independence

Rule 102—Integrity and Objectivity

Rule 201—General Standards

Rule 202—Compliance with Standards

Rule 203—Accounting Principles

Rule 301—Confidential Client Information

Rule 302—Contingent Fees

Rule 501—Acts Discreditable

Rule 502—Advertising and Other Forms of Solicitation

Rule 503—Commissions

Rule 505—Form of Practice and Name

Compliance with the AICPA *Code of Professional Conduct* depends primarily on a member's understanding and voluntary actions. There are provisions for reinforcement by peers and the public through public opinion, and ultimately by disciplinary proceedings. Adherence to the *Code* helps ensure ethical behavior by CPAs.

---

* See, AICPA, *Code of Professional Conduct* (New York: American Institute of Certified Public Accountants, Inc., 1988).

Ethical Standards for Management Accountants

Management accountants have an obligation to the organizations they serve, their profession, the public, and themselves to maintain the highest standards of ethical conduct. In recognition of this obligation, the Institute of Management Accountants has promulgated the following standards of ethical conduct for management accountants. Adherence to these standards is integral to achieving the Objectives of Management Accounting. Management accountants shall not commit acts contrary to these standards, nor shall they condone the commission of such acts by others within their organizations.

Competence

Management accountants have a responsibility to:

- Maintain an appropriate level of professional competence by ongoing development of their knowledge and skills.
- Perform their professional duties in accordance with relevant laws, regulations, and technical standards.
- Prepare complete and clear reports and recommendations after appropriate analyses of relevant and reliable information.

Confidentiality

Management accountants have a responsibility to:

- Refrain from disclosing confidential information acquired in the course of their work except when authorized, unless legally obligated to do so.
- Inform subordinates as appropriate regarding the confidentiality of information acquired in the course of their work and monitor their activities to assure the maintenance of that confidentiality.
- Refrain from using or appearing to use confidential information acquired in the course of their work for unethical or illegal advantage either personally or through third parties.

Integrity

Management accountants have a responsibility to:

- Avoid actual or apparent conflicts of interest and advise all appropriate parties of any potential conflict.

Source: *Statements on Management Accounting,* No. 1C. "Standards of Ethical Conduct for Management Accountants" (New York: Institute of Management Accountants, 1983), pp. 1–2. Reprinted with permission.

- Refrain from engaging in any activity that would prejudice their ability to carry out their duties ethically.
- Refuse any gift, favor, or hospitality that would influence or would appear to influence their actions.
- Refrain from either actively or passively subverting the attainment of the organization's legitimate and ethical objectives.
- Recognize and communicate professional limitations or other constraints that would preclude responsible judgment or successful performance of an activity.
- Communicate unfavorable as well as favorable information and professional judgments or opinions.
- Refrain from engaging in or supporting any activity that would discredit the profession.

Objectivity

Management accountants have a responsibility to:

- Communicate information fairly and objectively.
- Disclose fully all relevant information that could reasonably be expected to influence an intended user's understanding of the reports, comments, and recommendations presented.

Resolution of Ethical Conflict

In applying the standards of ethical conduct, management accountants may encounter problems in identifying unethical behavior or in resolving an ethical conflict. When faced with significant ethical issues, management accountants should follow the established policies of the organization bearing on the resolution of such conflict. If these policies do not resolve the ethical conflict, management accountants should consider the following course of action:

- Discuss such problems with the immediate superior except when it appears that the superior is involved, in which case the problem should be presented initially to the next higher managerial level. If satisfactory resolution cannot be achieved when the problem is initially presented, submit the issues to the next higher managerial level.

  If the immediate superior is the chief executive officer, or equivalent, the acceptable reviewing authority may be a group such as the audit committee, executive committee, board of directors, board of trustees, or owners. Contact with levels about the immediate superior should be initiated only with the superior's knowledge, assuming the superior is not involved.

- Clarify relevant concepts by confidential discussion with an objective advisor to obtain an understanding of possible courses of action.
- If the ethical conflict still exists after exhausting all levels of internal review, the management accountant may have no other recourse on significant matters than to resign from the organization and to submit an informative memorandum to an appropriate representative of the organization.

Except where legally prescribed, communication of such problems to authorities or individuals not employed or engaged by the organization is not considered appropriate.

Chart of Accounts

Assets

Current Assets

101 Cash
102 Petty cash
103 Cash equivalents
104 Short-term investments
105 Short-term investments, fair value
adjustment
106 Accounts receivable
107 Allowance for doubtful accounts
108 Legal fees receivable
109 Interest receivable
110 Rent receivable
111 Notes receivable
115 Subscriptions receivable, common stock
116 Subscriptions receivable, preferred stock
119 Merchandise inventory
120 _____ inventory
121 _____ inventory
124 Office supplies
125 Store supplies
126 _____ supplies
128 Prepaid insurance
129 Prepaid interest
131 Prepaid rent
132 Raw materials inventory
133 Goods in process inventory, _____
134 Goods in process inventory, _____
135 Finished goods inventory

Long-Term Investments

141 Investment in _____ stock
142 Investment in _____ bonds
143 Long-term investments, fair value
adjustment
144 Investment in _____
145 Bond sinking fund

Plant Assets

151 Automobiles
152 Accumulated depreciation, Automobiles
153 Trucks
154 Accumulated depreciation, Trucks
155 Boats
156 Accumulated depreciation, Boats
157 Professional library
158 Accumulated depreciation, Professional
library
159 Law library
160 Accumulated depreciation, Law library
161 Furniture
162 Accumulated depreciation, Furniture
163 Office equipment
164 Accumulated depreciation, Office
equipment
165 Store equipment
166 Accumulated depreciation, Store
equipment
167 _____ equipment
168 Accumulated depreciation, _____
equipment
169 Machinery
170 Accumulated depreciation, Machinery
173 Building _____
174 Accumulated depreciation, Building _____
175 Building _____
176 Accumulated depreciation, Building _____
179 Land improvements _____
180 Accumulated depreciation, Land
improvements _____
181 Land improvements _____
182 Accumulated depreciation, Land
improvements _____
183 Land

Natural Resources

185 Mineral deposit
186 Accumulated depletion, Mineral deposit

Intangible Assets

191 Patents
192 Leasehold
193 Franchise
194 Copyrights
195 Leasehold improvements
196 Organization costs

Liabilities

Current Liabilities

201 Accounts payable
202 Insurance payable
203 Interest payable
204 Legal fees payable
207 Office salaries payable
208 Rent payable
209 Salaries payable
210 Wages payable
211 Accrued payroll payable
214 Estimated warranty liability
215 Income taxes payable
216 Common dividend payable
217 Preferred dividend payable
218 State unemployment taxes payable
219 Employees' federal income taxes payable
221 Employees' medical insurance payable
222 Employees' retirement program payable
223 Employees' union dues payable
224 Federal unemployment taxes payable
225 FICA taxes payable
226 Estimated vacation pay liability

Unearned Revenues

230 Unearned consulting fees
231 Unearned legal fees
232 Unearned property management fees
233 Unearned _____ fees
234 Unearned _____ fees
235 Unearned janitorial revenue
236 Unearned _____ revenue
238 Unearned rent

Notes Payable

240 Short-term notes payable
241 Discount on short-term notes payable
245 Notes payable
251 Long-term notes payable
252 Discount on notes payable

Long-Term Liabilities

253 Long-term lease liability
255 Bonds payable
256 Discount on bonds payable
257 Premium on bonds payable
258 Deferred income tax liability

Equity

Owners' Equity

301 _____, capital
302 _____, withdrawals
303 _____, capital
304 _____, withdrawals
305 _____, capital
306 _____, withdrawals

Contributed Capital

307 Common stock, $ ___ par value
308 Common stock, no par
309 Common stock subscribed
310 Common stock dividend distributable
311 Contributed capital in excess of par value, common stock
312 Contributed capital in excess of stated value, no-par common stock
313 Contributed capital from retirement of common stock
314 Contributed capital, treasury stock transactions
315 Preferred stock
316 Contributed capital in excess of par value, preferred stock
317 Preferred stock subscribed

Retained Earnings

318 Retained earnings
319 Cash dividends declared
320 Stock dividends declared

Other Equity Accounts

321 Treasury stock, common
322 Unrealized holding gain (loss)

Revenues

401 _____ fees earned
402 _____ fees earned
403 _____ services revenue
404 _____ services revenue
405 Commissions earned
406 Rent earned
407 Dividends earned
408 Earnings from investment in _____
409 Interest earned
410 Sinking fund earnings

413 Sales
414 Sales returns and allowances
415 Sales discounts

Cost of Sales

Cost of Goods Sold

502 Cost of goods sold
505 Purchases
506 Purchases returns and allowances
507 Purchases discounts
508 Transportation-in

Manufacturing

520 Raw materials purchases
521 Freight-in on raw materials
530 Factory payroll
531 Direct labor
540 Factory overhead
541 Indirect materials
542 Indirect labor
543 Factory insurance expired
544 Factory supervision
545 Factory supplies used
546 Factory utilities
547 Miscellaneous production costs
548 Property taxes on factory building
549 Property taxes on factory equipment
550 Rent on factory building
551 Repairs, factory equipment
552 Small tools written off
560 Depreciation of factory equipment
561 Depreciation of factory building

Standard Cost Variance

580 Direct material quantity variance
581 Direct material price variance
582 Direct labor quantity variance
583 Direct labor price variance
584 Factory overhead volume variance
585 Factory overhead controllable variance

Expenses

Amortization, Depletion, and Depreciation

601 Amortization expense, _____
602 Amortization expense, _____
603 Depletion expense, _____
604 Depreciation expense, Boats
605 Depreciation expense, Automobiles
606 Depreciation expense, Building _____
607 Depreciation expense, Building _____
608 Depreciation expense, Land improvements _____
609 Depreciation expense, Land improvements _____
610 Depreciation expense, Law library

611 Depreciation expense, Trucks
612 Depreciation expense, _____ equipment
613 Depreciation expense, _____ equipment
614 Depreciation expense, _____
615 Depreciation expense, _____

Employee-Related Expenses

620 Office salaries expense
621 Sales salaries expense
622 Salaries expense
623 _____ wages expense
624 Employees' benefits expense
625 Payroll taxes expense

Financial Expenses

630 Cash over and short
631 Discounts lost
632 Factoring fee expense
633 Interest expense

Insurance Expenses

635 Insurance expense, Delivery equipment
636 Insurance expense, Office equipment
637 Insurance expense, _____

Rental Expenses

640 Rent expense
641 Rent expense, Office space
642 Rent expense, Selling space
643 Press rental expense
644 Truck rental expense
645 _____ rental expense

Supplies Expenses

650 Office supplies expense
651 Store supplies expense
652 _____ supplies expense
653 _____ supplies expense

Miscellaneous Expenses

655 Advertising expense
656 Bad debts expense
657 Blueprinting expense
658 Boat expense
659 Collection expense
661 Concessions expense
662 Credit card expense
663 Delivery expense
664 Dumping expense
667 Equipment expense
668 Food and drinks expense
669 Gas, oil, and repairs expense
671 Gas and oil expense
672 General and administrative expense
673 Janitorial expense
674 Legal fees expense
676 Mileage expense

677 Miscellaneous expenses
678 Mower and tools expense
679 Operating expense
681 Permits expense
682 Postage expense
683 Property taxes expense
684 Repairs expense, _____
685 Repairs expense, _____
687 Selling expense
688 Telephone expense
689 Travel and entertainment expense
690 Utilities expense
691 Warranty expense
695 Income taxes expense

Gains and Losses

701 Gain on retirement of bonds
702 Gain on sale of machinery
703 Gain on sale of short-term investments
704 Gain on sale of trucks
705 Gain on _____
706 Foreign exchange gain or loss
801 Loss on disposal of machinery
802 Loss on exchange of equipment
803 Loss on exchange of _____
804 Loss on sale of notes
805 Loss on retirement of bonds
806 Loss on sale of investments
807 Loss on sale of machinery
808 Loss on sale of _____
809 Loss on _____

Clearing Accounts

901 Income summary
902 Manufacturing summary

Alternate Problems

Klondike Company manufactures, markets, and sells snowmobile equipment. The companies that constitute the recreational vehicle industry earn an average return on investment of 9.5%. The average amount invested, or average total assets, in Klondike Company is $2,000,000. In its most recent year, Klondike earned a profit of $100,000 on sales of $1,200,000.

Required

1. What is Klondike Company's return on investment?
2. Does return on investment seem satisfactory for Klondike given competitors' return on investment?
3. What are the total costs for Klondike Company in its most recent year?
4. What is the average total amount of financing (liabilities and equity) for Klondike Company?

AT&T and GTE produce and market telecommunications products and are direct competitors. Key financial figures (in $ millions) for these businesses over the past year follow:

Key figures	AT&T	GTE
Sales	$79,609	$19,957
Profit	$ 139	$ 2,538
Average invested (assets)	$87,261	$37,019

Required

1. Compute return on investment for (a) AT&T and (b) GTE.
2. Which company is more successful in sales to consumers?
3. Which company is more successful in earning profits from its amount invested?
4. Write a brief memo explaining which company you would invest your money.

All business decisions involve risk and return.

Required

Identify the risk and return in the following activities:
1. Stashing $1,000 under your mattress.
2. Placing a $500 bet on the Kentucky Derby.
3. Investing $10,000 in NIKE stock.
4. Investing $10,000 in U.S. Savings Bonds.

Prepare an outline of an organization's major activities.

A new company will engage in the following activities during their first year of operation. Categorize the activities listed by the following letters:
A. Financing   **B.** Investing   **C.** Operating
_____ **1.** Checking compliance with local laws
_____ **2.** Obtaining a bank loan.
_____ **3.** Purchasing machinery.
_____ **4.** Researching products.
_____ **5.** Supervising workers.
_____ **6.** Contributing personal savings to the business.
_____ **7.** Renting office space.

Problem 2-1A
Analyzing effects of transactions and calculating return on equity

C5, A1, A2

Judith Grimm started a new business called Southwest Consulting and completed the following transactions during its first year of operations:

a. Invested $50,000 cash and office equipment valued at $5,000 in the business.

b. Paid $120,000 for a small building to be used as an office. Paid $10,000 in cash and signed a note payable promising to pay the balance over several years.

c. Purchased $9,000 of office equipment for cash.

d. Purchased $2,000 of office supplies and $3,200 of office equipment on credit.

e. Paid a local newspaper $1,500 for an announcement of the office's opening.

f. Completed a financial plan on credit and billed the client $3,000 for the service.

g. Designed a financial plan for another client and collected a $5,400 cash fee.

h. Withdrew $2,750 cash from the company bank account to pay personal expenses.

i. Received $1,200 from the client described in transaction *f*.

j. Made a $900 payment on the equipment purchased in transaction *d*.

k. Paid $1,900 cash for the office secretary's wages.

Required

Preparation component

1. Create a table like the one presented in Exhibit 2.14, using the following headings for the columns: Cash; Accounts Receivable; Office Supplies; Office Equipment; Building; Accounts Payable; Notes Payable; and Judith Grimm, Capital. Leave space for an explanation column to the right of the Capital column. Identify revenues and expenses by name in the explanation column.

2. Use additions and subtractions to show the effects of the above transactions on the elements of the equation. Show new totals after each transaction. Also, indicate next to each change in the owner's equity whether it was caused by an investment, a revenue, an expense, or a withdrawal.

3. Once you have completed the table, determine the company's net income.

Analysis component

4. Determine the return on Grimm's average owner's equity. Next, assume that Grimm could have earned $3,000 for the period from another job and determine the modified return on equity for the period. State whether you think the business is a good use of Grimm's money if an alternative investment would have returned 10% for the same period.

Problem 2-2A
Preparing a balance sheet, an income statement, and a statement of changes in owner's equity

C1, A1, P1

Andrew Martin began a new business called Universal Maintenance Co. and began operations on June 1. The following transactions were completed during the month:

June	1	Invested $120,000 in the business.
	1	Rented a furnished office of a maintenance company that was going out of business and paid $4,500 cash for the month's rent.
	4	Purchased cleaning supplies for $2,400 cash.
	6	Paid $1,125 cash for advertising the opening of the business.
	8	Completed maintenance services for a customer and immediately collected $750 cash.
	14	Completed maintenance services for First Union Center on credit, $6,300.
	16	Paid $900 cash for an assistant's salary for the first half of the month.
	20	Received payment in full for the services completed for First Union Center on June 14.
	21	Completed maintenance services for Skyway Co. on credit, $3,500.
	22	Purchased additional cleaning supplies on credit, $750.
	24	Completed maintenance services for Comfort Motel on credit, $825.
	29	Received full payment from Skyway Co. for the work completed on June 21.
	29	Made a partial payment of $375 for the cleaning supplies purchased on June 22.
	30	Paid $120 cash for the month's telephone bill.
	30	Paid $525 cash for the month's utilities.
	30	Paid $900 cash for an assistant's salary for the second half of the month.
	30	Purchased insurance protection for the next 12 months (beginning
July	1	by paying a $3,600 premium. Because none of this insurance protection had been used up, it was considered to be an asset called Prepaid Insurance.
	30	Martin withdrew $2,000 from the business for personal use.

Required

1. Arrange the following asset, liability, and owner's equity titles in an equation like Exhibit 2.14: Cash; Accounts Receivable; Cleaning Supplies; Prepaid Insurance; Accounts Payable; Andrew Martin, Capital. Include an explanation column for changes in owner's equity. Identify revenues and expenses by name in the explanation column.

2. Show the effects of the transactions on the elements of the equation by recording increases and decreases in the appropriate columns. Do not determine new totals for the items of the equation after each transaction. Next to each change in owner's equity, state whether it was caused by an investment, a revenue, an expense, or a withdrawal. Determine the final total for each item and verify that the equation is in balance.

3. Prepare a June income statement, a June statement of changes in owner's equity, and a June 30 balance sheet.

The accounting records of Stiller Co. show the following assets and liabilities as of the end of 1999 and 2000:

Problem 2-3A
Calculating and interpreting net income, preparing a balance sheet, and calculating return on equity

C1, A2, P1

	December 31	
	1999	**2000**
Cash	$14,000	$ 10,000
Accounts receivable	25,000	30,000
Office supplies	10,000	12,500
Office equipment	60,000	60,000
Machinery	30,500	30,500
Building		260,000
Land		65,000
Accounts payable	5,000	15,000
Note payable		260,000

Late in December 2000 (just before the amounts in the second column were calculated), Joseph Stiller, the owner, purchased a small office building and moved the business from rented quarters to the new building. The building and the land it occupies cost $325,000. The business paid $65,000 in cash and a note payable was signed for the balance. Stiller had to invest an additional $25,000 to enable it to pay the $65,000. The business earned a satisfactory net income during 2000, which enabled Stiller to withdraw $1,000 per month from the business for personal use.

Required

1. Prepare balance sheets for the business as of the end of 1999 and the end of 2000. (Remember that owner's equity equals the difference between the assets and the liabilities.)

2. By comparing the owner's equity amounts from the balance sheets and using the additional information presented in the problem, prepare a calculation to show how much net income was earned by the business during 2000.

3. Calculate the 2000 return on equity for the business. Also, calculate the modified return on equity, assuming that Stiller's efforts were worth $25,000 for the year.

Cantu Excavating Co., owned by Robert Cantu, began operations in July and completed these transactions during the month:

July 1 Invested $60,000 cash in the business.
1 Rented office space and paid the month's rent of $500.
1 Purchased excavating equipment for $4,000 by paying $800 in cash and agreeing to pay the balance in six months.
6 Purchased office supplies by paying $500 cash.
8 Completed work for a customer and immediately collected $2,200 for doing the work.
10 Purchased $3,800 of office equipment on credit.
15 Completed work for a customer on credit in the amount of $2,400.
17 Purchased $1,920 of office supplies on credit.
23 Paid for the office equipment purchased on July 10.

Problem 2-4A
Analyzing transactions, preparing financial statements, and calculating return on equity

C1, A1, A2, P1

2
CHAPTER

25 Billed a customer $5,000 for completed work; the balance is due in 30 days.
28 Received $2,400 for the work completed on July 15.
31 Paid an assistant's salary of $1,260.
31 Paid the monthly utility bills of $260.
31 Withdrew $1,200 from the business to pay personal expenses.

Required

Preparation Component

1. Arrange the following asset, liability, and stockholders' equity titles in an equation like Exhibit 2.14: Cash; Accounts Receivable; Office Supplies; Office Equipment; Excavating Equipment; Accounts Payable; and Robert Cantu, Capital. Leave space for an explanation column to the right of the Robert Cantu, Capital column. Identify revenues and expenses by name in the explanation column.

2. Use additions and subtractions to show the effects of each transaction on the items in the equation. Show new totals after each transaction. Next to each change in owner's equity, state whether the change was caused by an investment, a revenue, an expense, or a withdrawal.

3. Use the increases and decreases in the last column of the equation to prepare an income statement and a statement of changes in owner's equity for the month. Also, prepare a balance sheet as of the end of the month.

4. Calculate the return on average owner's equity for the month, using the initial investment as the beginning balance of equity.

Analysis Component

5. Assume that Cantu invested $4,000 cash in the business to obtain the excavating equipment on July 1 instead of the purchase conditions described in the transaction. Explain the effect of this change on total assets, total liabilities, owner's equity, and return on equity.

**Computing
Problem 2-5A**
Computing missing
information using
accounting
knowledge

C1, C2

The following financial statement information is known about five unrelated companies:

	Company V	Company W	Company X	Company Y	Company Z
December 31, 1999:					
Assets	$45,000	$70,000	$121,500	$82,500	$124,000
Liabilities	30,000	50,000	58,500	61,500	?
December 31, 2000:					
Assets	49,000	90,000	136,500	?	160,000
Liabilities	26,000	?	55,500	72,000	52,000
During 2000:					
Owner investments	6,000	10,000	?	38,100	40,000
Net income	?	30,000	16,500	24,000	32,000
Withdrawals	4,500	2,000	0	18,000	6,000

Required

1. Answer the following questions about Company V:
  a. What was the owner's equity on December 31, 1999?
  b. What was the owner's equity on December 31, 2000?
  c. What was the net income for 2000?

2. Answer the following questions about Company W:
  a. What was the owner's equity on December 31, 1999?
  b. What was the owner's equity on December 31, 2000?
  c. What was the amount of liabilities owed on December 31, 2000?

3. Calculate the amount of owner investments in Company X made during 2000.

4. Calculate the amount of assets owned by Company Y on December 31, 2000.

5. Calculate the amount of liabilities owed by Company Z on December 31, 1999.

You are to identify how each of the following transactions affects the company's financial statements. For the balance sheet, you are to identify how each transaction affects total assets, total liabilities, and stockholders' equity. For the income statement, you are to identify how each transaction affects net income. For the statement of cash flows, you are to identify how each transaction affects cash flows from operating activities, cash flows from financing activities, and cash flows from investing activities. If there is an increase, place a "+" in the column or columns. If there is a decrease, place a "−" in the column or columns. If there is both an increase and a decrease, place "+/−" in the column or columns. The line for the first transaction is completed as an example.

Problem 2-6A
Identifying effects of transactions on financial statements
C1, C2

	Transaction	Balance Sheet Total Assets	Balance Sheet Total Liab.	Balance Sheet Equity	Income Stmt. Net Income	Statement of Cash Flows Operating	Statement of Cash Flows Financing	Statement of Cash Flows Investing
1	Invests cash	+		+			+	
2	Pays wages with cash							
3	Acquires services on credit							
4	Buys store equipment for cash							
5	Borrows cash with note payable							
6	Sells services for cash							
7	Sells services on credit							
8	Pays rent with cash							
9	Withdraw cash							
10	Collects receivable from (7)							

A new business, Surfnet, has the following cash balance and cash flows for the month of December:

Problem 2A-7
Constructing a statement of cash flows
C1

Cash balance, December 1	$ 0
Withdrawals by owner	1,000
Cash received from customers	7,800
Repayment of debt	1,800
Cash paid for store supplies	5,000
Purchase of equipment	40,000
Cash paid for rent	2,000
Cash paid to employee	1,400
Investment by owner	60,000

Required

Prepare a statement of cash flows for the month of December.

West Consulting completed these transactions during June:

Problem 3-1A
Recording transactions in T-accounts; preparing a trial balance
A1, P2

a. Susan West, the sole proprietor, invested $23,000 cash and office equipment valued at $12,000 in the business.
b. Purchased land and a small office building. The land was worth $8,000 and the building was worth $33,000. The purchase price was paid with $15,000 cash and a long-term note payable for $26,000.
c. Purchased $600 of office supplies on credit.
d. Susan West transferred title of her personal automobile to the business. The automobile had a value of $7,000 and is to be used exclusively in the business.

e. Purchased $1,100 of additional office equipment on credit.

f. Paid $800 salary to an assistant.

g. Provided services to a client and collected $2,700 cash.

h. Paid $430 for this month's utilities.

i. Paid account payable created in transaction *c*.

j. Purchased $4,000 of new office equipment by paying $2,400 cash and trading in old equipment with a recorded net cost of $1,600.

k. Completed $2,400 of services for a client. This amount is to be paid within 30 days.

l. Paid $800 salary to an assistant.

m. Received $1,000 payment on the receivable created in transaction *k*.

n. Susan West withdrew $1,050 cash from the business for personal use.

Required

1. Open the following T-accounts: Cash; Accounts Receivable; Office Supplies; Automobiles; Office Equipment; Building; Land; Accounts Payable; Long-Term Notes Payable; Susan West, Capital; Susan West, Withdrawals; Fees Earned; Salaries Expense; and Utilities Expense.

2. Record the transactions above by entering debits and credits directly in T-accounts. Use the transaction letters to identify each debit and credit entry.

3. Determine the balance of each account and prepare a trial balance as of June 30.

Problem 3-2A
Recording
transactions in T-
accounts; preparing
a trial balance;
computing a debt
ratio

A1, A2, P2

At the beginning of June, Avery Wilson created a custom computer programming company called Softouch. The company had the following transactions during the month:

a. Avery Wilson invested $45,000 cash, office equipment with a value of $4,500, and $28,000 of computer equipment.

b. Purchased land for an office. The land was worth $24,000, and is paid with $4,800 cash and a long-term note payable for $19,200.

c. Purchased a portable building with $21,000 cash and moved it onto the land.

d. Paid $6,600 cash for the premiums on two one-year insurance policies.

e. Provided services to a client and collected $3,200 cash.

f. Purchased additional computer equipment for $3,500. Paid $700 cash and signed a long-term note payable for the $2,800 balance.

g. Completed $3,750 of services for a client. This amount is to be paid within 30 days.

h. Purchased $750 of additional office equipment on credit.

i. Completed client services for $9,200 on credit.

j. Received a bill for rent of a computer testing device that was used on a completed job. The $320 rent must be paid within 30 days.

k. Collected $4,600 from the client described in transaction *i*.

l. Paid $1,600 wages to an assistant.

m. Paid the account payable created in transaction *h*.

n. Paid $425 cash for some repairs to an item of computer equipment.

o. Avery Wilson withdrew $3,875 cash from the business for personal use.

p. Paid $1,600 wages to an assistant.

q. Paid $800 cash to advertise in the local newspaper.

Required

1. Open the following T-accounts: Cash; Accounts Receivable; Prepaid Insurance; Office Equipment; Computer Equipment; Building; Land; Accounts Payable; Long-Term Notes Payable; Avery Wilson, Capital; Avery Wilson, Withdrawals; Fees Earned; Wages Expense; Computer Rental Expense; Advertising Expense; and Repairs Expense.

2. Record the transactions by entering debits and credits directly in T-accounts. Use the transaction letters to identify each debit and credit. Prepare a trial balance as of June 30.

3. Calculate the company's debt ratio. Use $108,000 as the ending total assets. Are the assets of the company financed more by debt or equity?

Leonard Management Services completed these transactions during November:

Nov. 1   Arthur Leonard, the owner, invested $28,000 cash and office equipment valued at $25,000 in the business.

     2   Prepaid $10,500 cash for three months' rent for an office.

     4   Made credit purchases of office equipment for $9,000 and office supplies for $1,200.

     8   Completed work for a client and immediately received $2,600 cash.

   12   Completed a $13,400 project for a client, who will pay within 30 days.

   13   Paid the account payable created on November 4.

   19   Paid $5,200 cash as the annual premium on an insurance policy.

   22   Received $7,800 as partial payment for the work completed on November 12.

   24   Completed work for another client for $1,900 on credit.

   28   Arthur Leonard withdrew $5,300 from the business for personal use.

   29   Purchased $1,700 of additional office supplies on credit.

   30   Paid $460 for the month's utility bill.

Required

1. Prepare general journal entries to record the transactions.

2. Open the following accounts (use the balance column format): Cash (101); Accounts Receivable (106); Office Supplies (124); Prepaid Insurance (128); Prepaid Rent (131); Office Equipment (163); Accounts Payable (201); Arthur Leonard, Capital (301); Arthur Leonard, Withdrawals (302); Service Fees Earned (401); and Utilities Expense (690).

3. Post entries to the accounts and enter the balance after each posting.

4. Prepare a trial balance as of the end of the month.

Problem 3-3A
Preparing and posting general journal entries; preparing a trial balance

A1, P1, P2

Damon Oleson started a business called Knot Board on June 1 and completed several transactions during the month. His accounting skills are weak and he needs some help gathering information at the end of the month. Presented below are the journal entries that he recorded during June:

Problem 3-4A
Interpreting journals; posting; correcting a trial balance

A1, P1, P2

Date		Account	Debit	Credit
June	1	Cash	11,000	
		Store Equipment	9,000	
		Damon Oleson, Capital		20,000
	2	Prepaid Insurance	400	
		Cash		400
	6	Accounts Receivable	1,800	
		Fees Earned		1,800
	9	Office Supplies	700	
		Office Equipment	4,200	
		Accounts Payable		4,900
	11	Cash	2,100	
		Fees Earned		2,100
	14	Accounts Payable	120	
		Office Supplies		120
	20	Cash		1,500
		Accounts Receivable		1,500
	21	Accounts Payable	4,780	
		Cash		4,780
	23	Automobile	8,000	
		Damon Oleson, Capital		8,000
	28	Damon Oleson, Withdrawals	1,000	
		Cash		1,000
	29	Salaries Expense	1,400	
		Cash		1,400
	30	Office Supplies	390	
		Accounts Payable		390

Based on these entries, Oleson prepared the following trial balance:

KNOT BOARD Trial Balance For Month Ended June 30		
	Debit	Credit
Cash	$ 7,200	
Accounts receivable	400	
Office supplies	790	
Prepaid insurance	4,000	
Automobiles	8,000	
Office equipment		$ 4,200
Store equipment		9,000
Accounts payable		930
Damon Oleson, capital		28,000
Damon Oleson, withdrawals		1,000
Fees earned		3,900
Salaries expense	1,500	
Total	$21,890	$47,030

Required

Preparation Component

1. Oleson remembers something about trial balances and realizes the preceding one has at least one error. To help him find the mistakes, set up the following balance column accounts and post entries to them: Cash (101); Accounts Receivable (106); Office Supplies (124); Prepaid Insurance (128); Automobiles (151); Office Equipment (163); Store Equipment (165); Accounts Payable (201); Damon Oleson, Capital (301); Damon Oleson, Withdrawals (302); Fees Earned (401); and Salaries Expense (622).

Analysis Component

2. Although Oleson's journal entries are correct, he forgot to provide explanations. Analyze each entry and present a reasonable explanation of what happened.

3. Prepare a correct trial balance and describe the errors that Oleson made.

Problem 3-5A
Analyzing account balances and reconstructing transactions

A1, P2

Cass Consulting's first seven transactions resulted in the following accounts, which have normal balances:

Cash	$12,485
Office supplies	560
Prepaid rent	1,500
Office equipment	11,450
Accounts payable	11,450
Stephanie Cass, capital	10,000
Stephanie Cass, withdrawals	6,200
Consulting fees earned	16,400
Operating expenses	5,655

Required

Preparation Component

1. Prepare a trial balance for the business.

Analysis Component

2. Analyze the accounts and their balances and prepare a list that describes each of the seven most likely transactions that resulted in the previous account balances.

3. Present a schedule that shows how the seven transactions in 2 resulted in the $12,485 Cash balance.

Rachel Rohr operates a computer programming company specializing in "html" programming and Web site construction. For the first few months of the company's life (through April), the accounting records were maintained by an outside accounting service. According to those records, Rohr's owner's equity balance was $18,500 as of May 1. To save on expenses, Rohr decided to keep the records herself. She managed to record May's transactions properly, but she had problems properly classifying accounts in financial statements. Her first versions of the balance sheet and income statement follow. Using the information contained in these financial statements, prepare revised statements, including a statement of changes in owner's equity, for the month of May.

Problem 3-6A
Classifying accounts in financial statements

A1

3
CHAPTER

R² Consulting
Income Statement
May 31

Revenue:		
Investments by owner		$ 4,000
Unearned programming fees		9,000
Total revenues		$ 13,000
Operating expenses:		
Rent expense	$4,100	
Telephone expense	700	
Office equipment	6,500	
Advertising expense	4,300	
Utilities expense	400	
Insurance expense	800	
Withdrawals by owner	7,000	
Total operating expenses		23,800
Net income (loss)		$(10,800)

R² CONSULTING
Balance Sheet
For Month Ended May 31

Assets		Liabilities	
Cash	$ 4,900	Accounts payable	$ 1,400
Accounts receivable	2,800	Programming fees earned	30,000
Prepaid insurance	1,900	Short-term notes payable	18,000
Prepaid rent	4,100	Total liabilities	$49,400
Office supplies	400		
Computer equipment	40,000	**Owner's Equity**	
Salaries expense	3,000	Rachel Rohr, Capital	7,700
Total assets	$57,100	Total liabilities and owner's equity	$57,100

The Perfecto Company's annual accounting period ends on October 31, 2005. Perfecto follows the practice of recording prepaid expenses and unearned revenues in balance sheet accounts. The following information concerns the adjusting entries that need to be recorded as of that date:

a. The Office Supplies account started the fiscal year with a $500 balance. During the fiscal year, the company purchased supplies at a cost of $3,650, which was added to the Office Supplies account. The inventory of supplies on hand at October 31 had a cost of $700.

b. An analysis of the company's insurance policies provided these facts:

Problem 4-1A
Adjusting and subsequent journal entries **A1,**

P1, P2, P5

4
CHAPTER

Policy	Date of Purchase	Years of Coverage	Total Cost
1	April 1, 2004	2	$3,000
2	April 1, 2005	3	3,600
3	August 1, 2005	1	660

The total premium for each policy was paid in full at the purchase date, and the Prepaid Insurance account was debited for the full cost.

c. The company has 4 employees who earn a total of $800 for every working day. They are paid each Monday for their work in the five-day workweek ending on the previous Friday. October 31, 2005, falls on Monday, and all 4 employees worked the first day of the week. They will be paid salaries for five full days on Monday, November 7, 2005.

d. The company purchased a building on August 1, 2005. The building cost $155,000, and is expected to have a $20,000 salvage value at the end of its predicted 25-year life.

e. Because the company is not large enough to occupy the entire building, it arranged to rent some space to a tenant at $600 per month, starting on September 1, 2005. The rent was paid on time on September 1, and the amount received was credited to the Rent Earned account. However, the tenant has not paid the October rent. The company has worked out an agreement with the tenant, who has promised to pay both October's and November's rent in full on November 15. The tenant has agreed not to fall behind again.

f. On September 1, the company rented space to another tenant for $525 per month. The tenant paid five months' rent in advance on that date. The payment was recorded with a credit to the Unearned Rent account.

Required

1. Use the information to prepare adjusting entries as of October 31, 2005.

2. Prepare journal entries to record the first subsequent cash transactions for parts c and e.

Problem 4-2A
Adjusting entries;
financial statements;
profit margin

P1, P2, P4,
A1, A2

Presented below is the unadjusted trial balance for Design Institute as of December 31, 1999. Design Institute follows the practice of initially recording prepaid expenses and unearned revenues in balance sheet accounts. The institute provides one-on-one training to individuals who pay tuition directly to the business and also offers extension training to groups in off-site locations. Shown after the trial balance are items that will require adjusting entries as of December 31, 1999.

DESIGN INSTITUTE Unadjusted Trial Balance December 31, 1999		
Cash	$ 50,000	
Accounts receivable		
Teaching supplies	60,000	
Prepaid insurance	18,000	
Prepaid rent	2,600	
Professional library	10,000	
Accumulated depreciation—Professional library		$ 1,500
Equipment	30,000	
Accumulated depreciation—Equipment		16,000
Accounts payable		12,200
Salaries payable		
Unearned training fees		27,600
Jay Stevens, capital		68,500
Jay Stevens, withdrawals	20,000	
Tuition fees earned		105,000
Training fees earned		62,000
Depreciation expense—Equipment		
Depreciation expense—Professional library		
Salaries expense	43,200	
Insurance expense		
Rent expense	28,600	
Teaching supplies expense		
Advertising expense	18,000	
Utilities expense	12,400	
Totals	$292,800	$292,800

Additional Items

a. An analysis of the company's insurance policies shows that $6,400 of coverage has expired.

b. An inventory shows that teaching supplies costing $2,500 are on hand at the end of the year.

c. Annual depreciation on the equipment is $4,000.

d. Annual depreciation on the professional library is $2,000.

e. On November 1, the company agreed to do a special four-month course for a client. The contract calls for a $4,600 monthly fee, and the client paid the first two months' fees in advance. When the cash was received, the Unearned Training Fees account was credited.

f. On October 15, the school agreed to teach a four-month class to an individual for $2,200 tuition per month payable at the end of the class. The services are being provided as agreed, and no payment has been received.

g. The school's only employee is paid weekly. As of the end of the year, three days' wages have accrued at the rate of $180 per day.

h. The balance in the Prepaid Rent account represents rent for December.

Required

1. Prepare T-accounts with the balances listed from the unadjusted trial balance.

2. Prepare adjusting journal entries for items *a* through *h* and post them to the T-accounts.

3. Update the balances in T-accounts for the adjusting entries and prepare an adjusted trial balance.

4. Prepare Design Institute's income statement and the statement of changes in owner's equity for 1999, and prepare its balance sheet as of December 31, 1999.

5. Calculate the company's profit margin for the year. The owner was not actively involved in managing the company.

A six-column table for Personal Consulting Company is shown below. The first two columns contain the unadjusted trial balance for the company as of July 31, 2000, and the last two columns contain the adjusted trial balance as of the same date.

Problem 4-3A[B]
Interpreting unadjusted and adjusted trial balances; preparing financial statements; calculating profit margin

P1, P2, P4,
A1, A2

	Unadjusted Trial Balance		Adjustments		Adjusted Trial Balance	
Cash	$ 48,000				$ 48,000	
Accounts receivable	70,000				76,660	
Office supplies	30,000				7,000	
Prepaid insurance	13,200				8,600	
Office equipment	150,000				150,000	
Accumulated depreciation—Office eq. ...		$ 30,000				$ 40,000
Accounts payable		36,000				42,000
Interest payable						1,600
Salaries payable						11,200
Unearned consulting fees		30,000				17,800
Long-term notes payable		80,000				80,000
Dick Persons, capital		70,200				70,200
Dick Persons, withdrawals	10,000				10,000	
Consulting fees earned		264,000				282,860
Depreciation expense—Office eq.					10,000	
Salaries expense	115,600				126,800	
Interest expense	6,400				8,000	
Insurance expense					4,600	
Rent expense	24,000				24,000	
Office supplies expense					23,000	
Advertising expense	43,000				49,000	
Totals	$510,200	$510,200			$545,660	$545,660

Required

Preparation Component

1. Prepare this company's income statement and its statement of changes in owner's equity for the year ended July 31, 2000.
2. Prepare the company's balance sheet as of July 31, 2000.
3. Calculate the company's modified profit margin for the year, assuming the value of the owner's services to the business during the year was $30,000.

Analysis Component

4. Analyze the differences between the unadjusted and adjusted trial balances to determine the adjustments that must have been made. Show the results of your analysis by inserting amounts from the adjusting journal entries that must have been recorded by the company in the two middle columns. Label each entry with a letter and provide a short description of the purpose for recording it.

Problem 4-4A
Computing accrual income from cash income

C3

The records for Craven Products are kept on the cash basis instead of the accrual basis. But the company is now applying for a loan and the bank wants to know what its net income for year 2000 is under generally accepted accounting principles. Here is the income statement for year 2000 under the cash basis:

CRAVEN PRODUCTS Income Statement (Cash Basis) For Year Ended December 31, 2000	
Revenues	$165,000
Expenses	66,000
Net income	$ 99,000

Additional information was gathered to help convert the income statement to the accrual basis:

	As of 12/31/1999	As of 12/31/2000
Accrued revenues	$11,100	$3,600
Unearned revenues	7,050	7,800
Accrued expenses	4,800	11,400
Prepaid expenses	6,300	3,300

All prepaid expenses from the beginning of the year are consumed or expired, all unearned revenues from the beginning of the year are earned, and all accrued expenses and revenues from the beginning of the year are paid or collected.

Required

Prepare an accrual basis income statement for this company for year 2000. Provide schedules that explain how you converted from cash revenues and expenses to accrual revenues and expenses.

Problem 4-5A
Identifying adjusting and subsequent entries

C4, P5

For these adjusting and transaction entries, enter the letter of the explanation that most closely describes the adjustment or transaction in the space beside each entry. (You can use letters more than once.)

a. To record receipt of accrued revenue.
b. To record payment of an accrued expense.
c. To record payment of a prepaid expense.
d. To record this period's depreciation expense.
e. To record the earning of previously unearned revenue.

f. To record this period's use of a prepaid expense.
g. To record an accrued revenue.
h. To record receipt of unearned revenue.
i. To record an accrued expense.

_____	**1.**	Salaries Payable	8,000	
		Cash		8,000
_____	**2.**	Depreciation Expense	6,000	
		Accumulated Depreciation		6,000

			Debit	Credit
____	3.	Unearned Professional Fees	3,500	
		Professional Fees Earned		3,500
____	4.	Interest Receivable	1,500	
		Interest Earned		1,500
____	5.	Cash	5,000	
		Accounts Receivable		5,000
____	6.	Interest Expense	9,000	
		Interest Payable		9,000
____	7.	Cash	4,000	
		Unearned Professional Fees		4,000
____	8.	Insurance Expense	3,000	
		Prepaid Insurance		3,000
____	9.	Rent Expense	6,500	
		Prepaid Rent		6,500
____	10.	Prepaid Rent	7,000	
		Cash		7,000
____	11.	Salaries Expense	1,000	
		Salaries Payable		1,000
____	12.	Cash	2,000	
		Interest Receivable		2,000

The adjusted trial balance below is for Horizon Courier as of December 31, 2000:

Problem 4-6A
Preparing financial statements from the adjusted trial balance; calculating profit margin

P4, A1, A2

	Debit	Credit
Cash	$ 48,000	
Accounts receivable	110,000	
Interest receivable	6,000	
Notes receivable (due in 90 days)	200,000	
Office supplies	12,000	
Trucks	124,000	
Accumulated depreciation—Trucks		$ 48,000
Equipment	260,000	
Accumulated depreciation—Equipment		190,000
Land	90,000	
Accounts payable		124,000
Interest payable		22,000
Salaries payable		30,000
Unearned delivery fees		110,000
Long-term notes payable		190,000
K. Ainesworth, capital		115,000
K. Ainesworth, withdrawals	40,000	
Delivery fees earned		580,000
Interest earned		24,000
Depreciation expense—Trucks	24,000	
Depreciation expense—Equipment	46,000	
Salaries expense	64,000	
Wages expense	290,000	
Interest expense	25,000	
Office supplies expense	33,000	
Advertising expense	26,400	
Repairs expense, trucks	34,600	
Total	$1,433,000	$1,433,000

4
CHAPTER

Required

1. Use the information in the trial balance to prepare (a) the income statement for the year ended December 31, 2000, (b) the statement of changes in owner's equity for the year ended December 31, 2000, and (c) the balance sheet as of December 31, 2000.

2. Assume the services of the owner during year 2000 are valued at $30,000. Calculate the modified profit margin for year 2000.

Problem 4-7A^A
Recording prepaid expenses and unearned revenues

P1, P2, P6

Werthman Company had the following transactions in the last two months of its fiscal year ended July 31:

Apr.	1	Paid $3,450 for future consulting services.
	1	Paid $2,700 for insurance through March 31 of the following year.
	30	Received $7,500 for future services to be provided to a customer.
May	1	Paid $3,450 for future newspaper advertising.
	23	Received $9,450 for future services to be provided to a customer.
	31	Of the consulting services paid for on April 1, $1,500 worth had been received.
	31	Part of the insurance paid for on April 1 had expired.
	31	Services worth $3,600 had not yet been provided to the customer who paid on April 30.
	31	Of the advertising paid for on May 1, $1,050 worth had not been published yet.
	31	The company has performed $4,500 of services that the customer paid for on May 23.

Required

Preparation Component

1. Prepare entries for the above transactions under the method that records prepaid expenses and unearned revenues in balance sheet accounts. Also, prepare adjusting entries at the end of the year.

2. Prepare entries for the above transactions under the method that records prepaid expenses and unearned revenues in income statement accounts. Also, prepare adjusting entries at the end of the year.

Analysis Component

3. Explain why the alternative sets of entries in requirements 1 and 2 do not result in different financial statement amounts.

5
CHAPTER

Problem 5-1A
Closing entries, financial statements, and current ratio

C3, A1, P1

Western Shoe Shops' adjusted trial balance on December 31, 2000, is shown below:

	WESTERN SHOE SHOPS Adjusted Trial Balance December 31, 2000		
	Account Title	**Debit**	**Credit**
101	Cash	$ 13,450	
125	Store supplies	4,140	
128	Prepaid insurance	2,200	
167	Equipment	33,000	
168	Accumulated depreciation—Equipment		$ 9,000
201	Accounts payable		1,000
210	Wages payable		3,200
301	Pearl Jones, capital		31,650
302	Pearl Jones, withdrawals	16,000	
401	Repair fees earned		62,000
612	Depreciation expense—Equipment	3,000	
623	Wages expense	28,400	
637	Insurance expense	1,100	
640	Rent expense	2,400	
651	Store supplies expense	1,300	
690	Utilities expense	1,860	
	Totals	$106,850	$106,850

Required

Preparation Component

1. Prepare an income statement and a statement of changes in owner's equity for the year 2000 and a classified balance sheet at the end of the year. There were no owner investments during the year.

2. Enter the adjusted trial balance in the first two columns of a 6-column table that has middle columns for closing entries and the last two columns for a post-closing trial balance. Insert an Income Summary account as the last item in the trial balance.

3. Enter closing entries in the six-column table and prepare journal entries for them.

4. Determine the company's current ratio.

Analysis Component

5. Assume we collect the following two additional information items related to the adjusted trial balance shown above:

a. None of the $1,100 insurance expense had expired during the year. Instead, it is a prepayment of future insurance protection.

b. There were no earned and unpaid wages at the end of the year.

Describe the changes in financial statements that would result from these two information items.

The adjusted trial balance for Canner Co. as of December 31, 2000 is shown below:

Problem 5-2A
Closing entries, financial statements, and ratios

C3, A1, P1

	CANNER CO. Adjusted Trial Balance December 31, 2000		
No.	**Account Title**	**Debit**	**Credit**
101	Cash	$ 6,400	
104	Short-term investments	10,200	
126	Supplies	3,600	
128	Prepaid insurance	800	
167	Equipment	18,000	
168	Accumulated depreciation—Equipment		$ 3,000
173	Building	90,000	
174	Accumulated depreciation—Building		9,000
183	Land	28,500	
201	Accounts payable		2,500
203	Interest payable		1,400
208	Rent payable		200
210	Wages payable		1,180
213	Property taxes payable		2,330
233	Unearned professional fees		650
251	Long-term notes payable		32,000
301	Joe Canner, capital		91,800
302	Joe Canner, withdrawals	6,000	
401	Professional fees earned		47,000
406	Rent earned		3,600
407	Dividends earned		500
409	Interest earned		1,120
606	Depreciation expense—Building	2,000	
612	Depreciation expense—Equipment	1,000	
623	Wages expense	17,500	
633	Interest expense	1,200	
637	Insurance expense	1,425	
640	Rent expense	1,800	
652	Supplies expense	900	
682	Postage expense	310	
683	Property taxes expense	3,825	
684	Repairs expense	579	
688	Telephone expense	421	
690	Utilities expense	1,820	
	Totals	$196,280	$196,280

An analysis of other information reveals that Canner Company is required to make a $6,400 payment on its long-term note payable during 2001. Also, J. Canner invested $30,000 cash at the beginning of year 2000.

Required

1. Prepare the income statement, statement of changes in owner's equity, and classified balance sheet.
2. Prepare the closing entries at the end of the year 2000.
3. Use the information in the financial statements to calculate these ratios:
   a. Return on equity.
   b. Modified return on equity, assuming the owner's efforts are valued at $15,000 per year.
   c. Debt ratio.
   d. Profit margin (use total revenues as the denominator).
   e. Current ratio.

Problem 5-3A
Applying the accounting cycle

C2, P1, P2

On July 1, 2000, Cindy Tucker created a new self-storage business called Lockit Co. These transactions occurred during the company's first month:

July   1   Tucker invested $20,000 cash and buildings worth $120,000.
       2   Rented equipment by paying $1,800 rent for the first month.
       5   Purchased $2,300 of office supplies for cash.
      10   Paid $5,400 for the premium on a one-year insurance policy.
      14   Paid an employee $900 for two weeks' salary.
      24   Collected $8,800 of storage fees from customers.
      28   Paid another $900 for two weeks' salary.
      29   Paid the month's $300 telephone bill.
      30   Paid $850 cash to repair a leaking roof.
      31   Tucker withdrew $1,600 cash from the business for personal use.

The company's chart of accounts included these accounts:

101	Cash	401	Storage Fees Earned
106	Accounts Receivable	606	Depreciation Expense—Buildings
124	Office Supplies	622	Salaries Expense
128	Prepaid Insurance	637	Insurance Expense
173	Buildings	640	Rent Expense
174	Accumulated Depreciation—Buildings	650	Office Supplies Expense
209	Salaries Payable	684	Repairs Expense
301	Cindy Tucker, Capital	688	Telephone Expense
302	Cindy Tucker, Withdrawals	901	Income Summary

Required

1. Use the balance-column format to create each of the listed accounts.
2. Prepare journal entries to record the transactions for July and post them to the accounts. Record prepaid and unearned items in balance sheet accounts.
3. Prepare an unadjusted trial balance as of July 31.
4. Use the following information to journalize and post adjusting entries for the month:
   a. Two-thirds of one month's insurance coverage was consumed.
   b. There were $1,550 of office supplies on hand at the end of the month.
   c. Depreciation on the buildings was estimated to be $1,200.
   d. The employee had earned $180 of unpaid and unrecorded salary.
   e. The company had earned $950 of storage fees that had not yet been billed.
5. Prepare an income statement, a statement of changes in owner's equity, and a balance sheet.
6. Prepare journal entries to close the temporary accounts and post them to the accounts.
7. Prepare a separate post-closing trial balance.

In the blank space beside each numbered balance sheet item, enter the letter of its balance sheet classification. If the item should not appear on the balance sheet, enter a *z* in the blank.

a. Current assets   **e.** Current liabilities
b. Investments   **f.** Long-term liabilities
c. Plant and equipment   **g.** Owner's equity
d. Intangible assets   **h.** Stockholders' equity

_____ **1.** Office supplies
_____ **2.** Owner, capital
_____ **3.** Common stock
_____ **4.** Notes receivable—due in 120 days
_____ **5.** Accumulated depreciation—Trucks
_____ **6.** Salaries payable
_____ **7.** Commissions earned
_____ **8.** Retained earnings
_____ **9.** Office equipment
_____ **10.** Notes payable—due in three years
_____ **11.** Building
_____ **12.** Prepaid insurance
_____ **13.** Current portion of long-term note payable
_____ **14.** Interest receivable
_____ **15.** Short-term investments
_____ **16.** Land (used in operations)
_____ **17.** Copyrights
_____ **18.** Owner, withdrawals
_____ **19.** Depreciation expense—Trucks
_____ **20.** Investment in Ford common stock (long-term holding)

Shown below is the unadjusted trial balance of Boomer Demolition Company as of the end of its June 30 fiscal year. The beginning balance of the owner's capital balance was $36,900 and the owner invested another $30,000 cash in the company during the year.

Problem 5-5A
Work sheet, journal
entries, financial
statements, and
current ratio

C3, A1, P3

No.	Account Title	Debit	Credit
	BOOMER DEMOLITION COMPANY		
	Unadjusted Trial Balance		
	June 30, 2000		
101	Cash	$ 9,000	
126	Supplies	18,000	
128	Prepaid insurance	14,600	
167	Equipment	140,000	
168	Accumulated depreciation—Equipment		$ 10,000
201	Accounts payable		16,000
203	Interest payable		
208	Rent payable		
210	Wages payable		
213	Property taxes payable		
251	Long-term notes payable		20,000
301	R. Boomer, capital		66,900
302	R. Boomer, withdrawals	24,000	
401	Demolition fees earned		177,000
612	Depreciation expense—Equipment		
623	Wages expense	51,400	
633	Interest expense	2,200	
637	Insurance expense		
640	Rent expense	8,800	
652	Supplies expense		
683	Property taxes expense	8,400	
684	Repairs expense	6,700	
690	Utilities expense	6,800	
	Totals	$289,900	$289,900

Required

Preparation Component

1. Prepare a 10-column work sheet for year 2000, starting with the unadjusted trial balance and including these additional facts:

   a. The supplies on hand at the end of the year had a cost of $8,100.

   b. The cost of expired insurance for the year is $11,500.

   c. Annual depreciation on equipment is $18,000.

   d. The June utilities expense of $700 is not included in the unadjusted trial balance because the bill arrived after it was prepared. The $700 amount owed needs to be recorded.

   e. The company's employees have earned $2,200 of accrued wages.

   f. The lease for the office requires the company to pay total rent for each fiscal year equal to 8% of the company's annual revenues. Rent has been estimated and is being paid to the building owner with monthly payments of $800. If the annual rent owed exceeds the total monthly estimated payments, the company must pay the excess before July 31. If the total owed is less than the amount previously paid, the building owner will refund the difference by July 31.

   g. Additional property taxes of $450 have been assessed on the equipment but have not been paid or recorded in the accounts.

   h. The long-term note payable bears interest at 1% per month, which the company is required to pay by the 10th of the following month. The balance of the Interest Expense account equals the amount paid for the first 11 months of the year. The interest for June has not yet been paid or recorded. In addition, the company is required to make a $4,000 payment on the note on August 30, 2000.

2. Use the work sheet to journalize the adjusting and closing entries.

3. Prepare an income statement, a statement of changes in owner's equity and a classified balance sheet. Calculate the company's current ratio.

Analysis Component

4. Analyze the following separate errors and describe how each would affect the 10-column work sheet. Explain whether the error is likely to be discovered in completing the work sheet and, if not, the effect of the error on the financial statements.

   a. The adjustment for expiration of the insurance coverage credited the Prepaid Insurance account for $3,100 and debited the same amount to the Insurance Expense account.

   b. When completing the adjusted trial balance in the work sheet, the $6,700 Repairs Expense account balance is extended to the Debit column for the balance sheet.

Problem 5-6A^A
Adjusting, reversing, and subsequent entries

P3, P4

This six-column table for Machine Rental Co. includes the unadjusted trial balance as of December 31, 2000:

	MACHINE RENTAL CO. December 31, 2000		
Account Title	**Unadjusted Trial Balance**	**Adjustments**	**Adjusted Trial Balance**
Cash	$ 9,000		
Accounts receivable			
Supplies	6,600		
Machinery	40,100		
Accumulated depreciation—Machinery		$15,800	
Interest payable			
Salaries payable			
Unearned rental fees		5,200	
Notes payable		20,000	
Kara Smith, capital		13,200	
Kara Smith, withdrawals	10,500		
Rental fees earned		37,000	
Depreciation expense—Machinery			
Salaries expense	23,500		
Interest expense	1,500		
Supplies expense			
Totals	$91,200	$91,200	

5
CHAPTER

Required

1. Complete the six-column table by entering adjustments that reflect the following information:

   a. As of December 31, employees have earned $420 of unpaid and unrecorded wages. The next payday is January 4, and the total wages to be paid are $1,250.

   b. The cost of supplies on hand at December 31 is $2,450.

   c. The note payable requires an interest payment to be made every three months. The amount of unrecorded accrued interest at December 31 is $500, and the next payment is due on January 15. This payment will be $600.

   d. An analysis of the unearned rental fees shows that $3,100 remains unearned at December 31.

   e. In addition to the machinery rental fees included in the revenue account balance, the company has earned another $2,350 in fees that will be collected on January 21. The company is also expected to collect $4,400 on the same day for new fees earned during that month.

   f. Depreciation expense for the year is $3,800.

2. Prepare journal entries for the adjustments entered in the six-column table.

3. Prepare journal entries to reverse the effects of the adjusting entries that involve accruals.

4. Prepare journal entries to record the cash payments and collections that are described for January.

Prepare journal entries to record the following perpetual system merchandising transactions of Minchew Company. (Use a separate account for each receivable and payable; for example, record the purchase on May 2 in Accounts Payable—Mobley Co.)

Problem 6-1A
Journal entries for merchandising activities (perpetual system)

P1, P2

6
CHAPTER

May	2	Purchased merchandise from Mobley Co. for $9,000 under credit terms of 1/15, n/30, FOB shipping point.
	4	Sold merchandise to Cornerstone Co. for $1,200 under credit terms of 2/10, n/60, FOB shipping point. The merchandise had cost $750.
	5	Paid $150 for freight charges on the purchase of May 2.
	9	Sold merchandise that cost $1,800 for $2,400 cash.
	10	Purchased merchandise from Richter Co. for $3,450 under credit terms of 2/15, n/60, FOB destination.
	12	Received a $300 credit memorandum acknowledging the return of merchandise purchased on May 10.
	14	Received the balance due from Cornerstone Co. for the credit sale dated May 4, net of the discount.
	17	Paid the balance due to Mobley Co. within the discount period.
	20	Sold merchandise that cost $1,350 to Harrill Co. for $1,875 under credit terms of 2/15, n/60, FOB shipping point.
	22	Issued a $225 credit memorandum to Harrill Co. for an allowance on goods sold on May 20.
	23	Received a debit memorandum from Harrill Co. for an error that overstated the total invoice by $75.
	25	Paid Richter Co. the balance due after deducting the discount.
	31	Received the balance due from Harrill Co. for the credit sale dated May 20, net of the discount.
	31	Sold merchandise that cost $4,800 to Cornerstone Co. for $7,500 under credit terms of 2/10, n/60, FOB shipping point.

Prepare journal entries to record the following perpetual system merchandising transactions of Treadwell Company. (Use a separate account for each receivable and payable; for example, record the purchase on July 3 in Accounts Payable—CMP Corp.)

Problem 6-2A
Journal entries for merchandising activities (perpetual system)

P1, P2

July	3	Purchased merchandise from CMP Corp. for $15,000 under credit terms of 1/10, n/30, FOB destination.
	4	At CMP's request, paid $250 for freight charges on the July 3 purchase, reducing the amount owed to CMS.
	7	Sold merchandise to Harbison Co. for $10,500 under credit terms of 2/10, n/60, FOB destination. The merchandise had cost $7,500.
	10	Purchased merchandise from Cimarron Corporation for $13,250 under credit terms of 1/10, n/45, FOB shipping point, plus $600 shipping charges. The invoice showed that at Treadwell's request, Cimarron had paid the $600 shipping charges and added that amount to the bill.
	11	Paid $300 shipping charges related to the July 7 sale to Harbison Co.
	12	Harbison returned merchandise from the July 7 sale that had cost $1,250 and been sold for $1,750. The merchandise was restored to inventory.
	14	After negotiations with Cimarron Corporation concerning problems with the merchandise purchased on July 10, received a credit memorandum from Cimarron granting a price reduction of $2,000.
	17	Received balance due from Harbison Co. for the July 7 sale less the return on July 12.

20 Paid the amount due Cimarron Corporation for the July 10 purchase less the price reduction granted.
21 Sold merchandise to Hess for $9,000 under credit terms of 1/10, n/30, FOB shipping point. The merchandise had cost $6,250.
24 Hess requested a price reduction on the July 21 sale because the merchandise did not meet specifications. Sent Hess a credit memorandum for $1,500 to resolve the issue.
31 Received Hess's payment of the amount due from the July 21 purchase.
31 Paid CMP Corp. the amount due from the July 3 purchase.

Problem 6-3A
Income statement calculations and formats

P4, A1

Reyna Company's adjusted trial balance as of May 31, 2000, the end of its fiscal year, is shown below:

	Debit	Credit
Merchandise inventory	$ 46,500	
Other assets	192,600	
Liabilities		$ 52,500
Paul Reyna, capital		176,475
Paul Reyna, withdrawals	24,000	
Sales		318,000
Sales discounts	4,875	
Sales returns and allowances	21,000	
Cost of goods sold	123,900	
Sales salaries expense	43,500	
Rent expense—Selling space	15,000	
Store supplies expense	3,750	
Advertising expense	27,000	
Office salaries expense	39,750	
Rent expense—Office space	3,900	
Office supplies expense	1,200	
Totals	$546,975	$546,975

On May 31, 1999, the company's merchandise inventory amounted to $37,500. Supplementary records of merchandising activities during the 2000 fiscal year disclose the following:

Cost of merchandise purchases	$136,500
Purchase discounts received	2,850
Purchase returns and allowances received	6,600
Cost of transportation-in	5,850

Required

1. Calculate the company's net sales for the year.
2. Calculate the company's total cost of merchandise purchased for the year.
3. Present a classified, multiple-step income statement (see Exhibit 6.18) that lists the company's net sales, cost of goods sold, and gross profit, as well the components and amounts of selling expenses and general and administrative expenses.
4. Prepare a condensed single-step income statement that lists these costs: cost of goods sold, selling expenses, and general and administrative expenses.
5. Accounts receivable increased by $50,000 during the period. Calculate cash received from customers.

Problem 6-4A
Closing entries and interpreting information about discounts and returns

P3

Use the data for Reyna Company in Problem 6-3A to meet the following requirements:

Required

Preparation Component

1. Prepare closing entries for Reyna Company as of May 31, 2000.

Analysis Component

2. All of the company's purchases were made on credit and its suppliers uniformly offer a 3% sales discount. Does it appear that the company's cash management system is accomplishing the goal of taking all available discounts? Explain.

3. In prior years, the company experienced a 4% return and allowance rate on its sales, which means approximately 4% of its gross sales were for items that were eventually returned outright or that caused the company to grant allowances to customers. How does this year's results compare to prior years' results?

The following unadjusted trial balance is prepared at the end of the fiscal year for Resource Products Company:

Problem 6-5A
Adjusting entries, income statements, and acid-test ratio

A2, P3, P4

RESOURCE PRODUCTS COMPANY Unadjusted Trial Balance October 31, 2000		
Cash	$ 6,400	
Merchandise inventory	23,000	
Store supplies	9,600	
Prepaid insurance	4,600	
Store equipment	83,800	
Accumulated depreciation—Store equipment		$ 30,000
Accounts payable		16,000
Jan Smithers, capital		70,400
Jan Smithers, withdrawals	6,400	
Sales		208,000
Sales discounts	2,000	
Sales returns and allowances	4,000	
Cost of goods sold	74,800	
Depreciation expense—Store equipment		
Salaries expense	62,000	
Insurance expense		
Rent expense	28,000	
Store supplies expense		
Advertising expense	19,800	
Totals	$324,400	$324,400

Rent and salaries expense are equally divided between the selling and the general and administrative functions. Resource Products Company uses a perpetual inventory system.

Required

1. Prepare adjusting journal entries for the following:
  a. Store supplies on hand at year-end amount to $3,300.
  b. Expired insurance, an administrative expense, for the year is $3,000.
  c. Depreciation expense, a selling expense, is $2,800 for the year.
  d. A physical count of the ending merchandise inventory shows $22,200 of goods on hand.
2. Prepare a multiple-step (not classified) income statement (see Exhibit 6.19).
3. Prepare a single-step income statement (see Exhibit 6.20).
4. Compute the company's current and acid-test ratios as of October 31, 2000.

Clinton Company has the following inventory purchases during the fiscal year ended December 31, 2000:

Problem 7-1A
Alternative cost flows—perpetual

P1

Beg.	600 units	$55/unit
1/10	450 units	56/unit
2/13	200 units	57/unit
7/21	230 units	58/unit
8/5	345 units	59/unit

Clinton Company employs a perpetual inventory system. It had two sales during the period, and the units had a selling price of $90 per unit. The specific units sold are the entire beginning inventory plus 165 units of the 2/13 purchase:

2/15 sales	430 units
8/10 sales	335 units

Required

Preparation Component

1. Calculate cost of goods available for sale and units available for sale.
2. Calculate units remaining in ending inventory.
3. Calculate the dollar value of ending inventory using (a) FIFO, (b) LIFO, (c) specific identification, and (d) weighted average.
4. Calculate the gross profit earned by Hall Company under each of the cost methods in (3).

Analysis Component

5. If the Clinton Company's manager earns a bonus based on a percent of gross profit, which method of inventory costing will be preferred?

Problem 7-2A^A
Alternative cost
flows—periodic

P4

Sea Blue Co. began year 2000 with 6,300 units of Product B in its January 1 inventory that cost $35 each, and it made successive purchases of the product as follows:

January 4	10,500 units @ $33 each
May 18	13,000 units @ $32 each
July 9	12,000 units @ $29 each
November 21	15,500 units @ $26 each

The company uses a periodic inventory system. On December 31, 2000, a physical count disclosed that 16,500 units of Product B remained in inventory.

Required

1. Prepare a calculation showing the number and total cost of the units available for sale during the year.
2. Prepare calculations showing the amounts assigned to the ending inventory and to cost of goods sold assuming *(a)* a FIFO basis, *(b)* a LIFO basis, and *(c)* a weighted average basis.

Problem 7-3A^A
Income
comparisons and
cost flows—periodic

A1, P4

The Denney Company sold 2,500 units of its product at $98 per unit during year 2000, and incurred operating expenses of $14 per unit in selling the units. It began the year with 740 units and made successive purchases of units of the product as follows:

January 1 (beginning inventory) ...	740 units costing $58 per unit
Purchases:	
April 2	700 units @ $59 per unit
June 14	600 units @ $61 per unit
August 29	500 units @ $64 per unit
November 18	800 units @ $65 per unit
	3,340 units

Required

Preparation Component

1. Prepare a comparative income statement for the company, showing in adjacent columns the net incomes earned from the sale of the product, assuming the company uses a periodic inventory system and prices its ending inventory on the basis of: *(a)* FIFO, *(b)* LIFO, and *(c)* weighted average. Assume an income tax rate of 25%.

Analysis Component

2. How would the results from the three alternative inventory costing methods change if Denney had been experiencing decreasing prices in the acquisition of additional inventory?

3. What specific advantages and disadvantages are offered by using LIFO and by using FIFO, assuming a continuing trend of increasing costs?

The following amounts were reported in Matchstick Company's financial statements:

Problem 7-4A
Analysis of
inventory errors

A2

	Financial Statements for Year Ended December 31		
	1999	**2000**	**2001**
(a) Cost of goods sold	$205,200	$212,800	$196,030
(b) Net income	174,800	211,270	183,910
(c) Total current assets	266,000	276,500	262,950
(d) Owner's equity	304,000	316,000	336,000

In making physical counts of inventory, Matchstick made the following errors:

Inventory on December 31, 1999:	Overstated $17,000
Inventory on December 31, 2000:	Understated $25,000

Required

Preparation Component

1. For each of the preceding financial statement items—(a), (b), (c), and (d)—prepare a schedule similar to the following and show the adjustments necessary to correct the reported amounts.

	1999	2000	2001
Cost of goods sold:			
Reported			
Adjustments: 12/31/1999 error			
12/31/2000 error			
Corrected			

Analysis Component

2. What is the error in aggregate net income for the three-year period that results from the inventory errors? Explain why this result occurs.

Problem 7-5A
Lower of cost or
market

P2

A physical inventory of Office Outfitters taken at December 31 reveals the following:

	Units	Per Unit	
Item	on Hand	Cost	Market
Office furniture:			
Desks	436	$261	$305
Credenzas	295	227	256
Chairs	587	49	43
Bookshelves	321	93	82
Filing cabinets:			
Two-drawer	214	81	70
Four-drawer	398	135	122
Lateral	175	104	118
Office equipment:			
Fax machines	430	168	200
Copiers	545	317	288
Typewriters	352	125	117

Required

Calculate the lower of cost or market *(a)* for the inventory as a whole, *(b)* for the inventory by major category, and *(c)* for the inventory applied separately to each item.

Problem 7-6A
Retail inventory
method

P3

The records of The R.E. McFadden Co. provide the following information for the year ended December 31:

	At Cost	At Retail
January 1 beginning inventory	$ 81,670	$114,610
Cost of goods purchased	492,250	751,730
Sales		786,120
Sales returns		4,480

Required

1. Prepare an estimate of the company's year-end inventory by the retail method.
2. The company took a year-end physical inventory at marked selling prices that totaled $78,550. Prepare a schedule showing the store's loss from shrinkage at cost and at retail.

Problem 7-7A
Gross profit method

P3

Four Corners Equipment Co. wants to prepare interim financial statements for the first quarter of year 2000. The company would like to avoid making a physical count of inventory each quarter. During the last five years, the company's gross profit rate has averaged 30%. The following information for the first quarter is available from its records:

January 1 beginning inventory	$ 752,880
Net cost of goods purchased	2,159,630
Sales	3,710,250
Sales returns	74,200

Required

Use the gross profit method to prepare an estimate of the company's March 31, 2000, inventory.

Eldridge Industries completed these transactions during July of the current year:

Problem 8-1A
Special journals,
subsidiary ledgers,
schedule of
accounts receivable

P1, P2

July 1 Purchased merchandise on credit from Beech Company, invoice dated June 30, terms 2/10, n/30, $6,300.

3 Issued Check No. 300 to *The Weekly Journal* for advertising expense, $575.

5 Sold merchandise on credit to Karen Harden, Invoice No. 918, $18,400. (The terms of all credit sales are 2/10, n/30.)

6 Sold merchandise on credit to Paul Kane, Invoice No. 919, $7,500.

7 Purchased store supplies on credit from Blackwater Inc., $1,050. Invoice dated July 7, terms n/10 EOM.

8 Received a $150 credit memorandum from Blackwater Inc. for store supplies received on July 7 and returned for credit.

9 Purchased store equipment on credit from Poppe's Supply, invoice dated July 8, terms n/10 EOM, $37,710.

10 Issued Check No. 301 to Beech Company in payment of its June 30 invoice, less the discount.

13 Sold merchandise on credit to Kelly Grody, Invoice No. 920, $8,350.

14 Sold merchandise on credit to Karen Harden, Invoice No. 921, $4,100.

15 Received payment from Karen Harden for the July 5 sale, less the discount.

15 Issued Check No. 302, payable to Payroll, in payment of sales salaries for the first half of the month, $30,620. Cashed the check and paid employees.

15 Cash sales for the first half of the month were $121,370. (Cash sales are usually recorded daily from the cash register readings. They are recorded only twice in this problem to reduce repetitive transactions.)

16 Received payment from Paul Kane for the July 6 sale, less the discount.

17 Purchased merchandise on credit from Sprague Company, invoice dated July 17, terms 2/10, n/30, $8,200.

20 Purchased office supplies on credit from Poppe's Supply, $750. Invoice dated July 19, terms n/10 EOM.

21 Borrowed $20,000 from College Bank by giving a long-term note payable.

23 Received payment from Kelly Grody for the July 13 sale, less the discount.

24 Received payment from Karen Harden for the July 14 sale, less the discount.

24 Received a $2,400 credit memorandum from Sprague Company for defective merchandise received on July 17 and returned to Sprague.

26 Purchased merchandise on credit from Beech Company, invoice dated July 26, terms 2/10, n/30, $9,770.

27 Issued Check No. 303 to Sprague Company in payment of its July 17 invoice, less the return and the discount.

29 Sold merchandise on credit to Paul Kane, Invoice No. 922, $28,090.

30 Sold merchandise on credit to Kelly Grody, Invoice No. 923, $15,750.

31 Issued Check No. 304, payable to Payroll, in payment of the sales salaries for the last half of the month, $30,620.

31 Cash sales for the last half of the month were $79,020.

Required

Preparation Component

1. Prepare a Sales Journal like Exhibit 8.5 and a Cash Receipts Journal like Exhibit 8.9. Number both journals as page 3.

2. Review the transactions of Eldridge Industries and enter those transactions that should be journalized in the Sales Journal and those that should be journalized in the Cash Receipts Journal. Ignore any transactions that should be journalized in a Purchases Journal, a Cash Disbursements Journal, or a General Journal.

3. Open the following general ledger accounts: Cash, Accounts Receivable, Long-Term Notes Payable, Sales, and Sales Discounts. Also open subsidiary accounts receivable ledger accounts for Karen Harden, Kelly Grody, and Paul Kane.

4. Post the items that should be posted as individual amounts from the journals. (Normally, such items are posted daily; but since they are few in number in this problem you are asked to post them only once.)

5. Foot and crossfoot the journals and make the month-end postings.

6. Prepare a trial balance of the General Ledger and test the accuracy of the subsidiary ledger by preparing a schedule of accounts receivable.

Analysis Component

7. Assume the sum of the account balances on the schedule of accounts receivable does not equal the balance of the controlling account in the General Ledger. Describe steps you would take to discover the error(s).

Problem 8-2A
Special journals;
subsidiary ledgers;
schedule of
accounts payable

P1, P2

The July transactions of Eldridge Industries are listed in Problem 8-1A.

Required

1. Prepare a General Journal, a Purchases Journal like Exhibit 8.11, and a Cash Disbursements Journal like Exhibit 8.13. Number all journal pages as page 3.

2. Review the July transactions of Eldridge Industries and enter those transactions that should be journalized in the General Journal, the Purchases Journal, or the Cash Disbursements Journal. Ignore any transactions that should be journalized in a Sales Journal or Cash Receipts Journal.

3. Open the following General Ledger accounts: Cash, Office Supplies, Store Supplies, Store Equipment, Accounts Payable, Long-Term Notes Payable, Purchases, Purchases Returns and Allowances, Purchases Discounts, Sales Salaries Expense, and Advertising Expense. Enter the June 30 balances of Cash ($165,500) and Long-Term Notes Payable ($165,600). Also open subsidiary Accounts Payable Ledger accounts for Poppe's Supply, Beech Company, Sprague Company, and Blackwater Inc.

4. Post items that should be posted as individual amounts from the journals. (Normally, such items are posted daily; but since they are few in number in this problem you are asked to post them only once.)

5. Foot and crossfoot the journals and make the month-end postings.

6. Prepare a trial balance of the General Ledger and a schedule of accounts payable.

Problem 8-3A
Special journals;
subsidiary ledgers;
trial balance

P1, P2

(If the Working Papers that accompany this text are not being used, omit this problem.)
It is December 16 and you have just taken over the accounting work of Starshine Products, whose annual accounting period ends December 31. The company's previous accountant journalized its transactions through December 15 and posted all items that required posting as individual amounts (see the journals and ledgers in the working papers). The company completed these transactions beginning on December 16:

Dec. 16   Purchased office supplies on credit from Green Supply Company, $765. Invoice dated December 16, terms n/10 EOM.

16   Sold merchandise on credit to Heather Flatt, Invoice No. 916, $4,290. (Terms of all credit sales are 2/10, n/30.)

18   Issued a credit memorandum to Amy Izon for defective merchandise sold on December 15 and returned for credit, $200.

19   Received a $640 credit memorandum from Walters Company for merchandise received on December 15 and returned for credit.

20   Received a $143 credit memorandum from Green Supply Company for office supplies received on December 16 and returned for credit.

20   Purchased store equipment on credit from Green Supply Company, invoice dated December 19, terms n/10 EOM, $7,475.

21   Sold merchandise on credit to Jan Wildman, Invoice No. 917, $5,520.

22   Received payment from Heather Flatt for the December 12 sale less the discount.

25   Received payment from Amy Izon for the December 15 sale less the return and the discount.

25   Issued Check No. 623 to Walters Company in payment of its December 15 invoice less the return and the discount.

25   Issued Check No. 624 to Sunshine Company in payment of its December 15 invoice less a 2% discount.

28   Received merchandise with an invoice dated December 28, terms 2/10, n/60, from Sunshine Company, $6,030.

28   Sold a neighboring merchant a carton of calculator tape (store supplies) for cash at cost, $58.

29   Marlee Levin, the owner of Starshine Products, used Check No. 625 to withdraw $4,000 cash from the business for personal use.

30   Issued Check No. 626 to Midwest Electric Company in payment of the December electric bill, $990.

30   Issued Check No. 627 to Jamie Ford, the company's only sales employee, in payment of her salary for the last half of December, $2,620.

31   Cash sales for the last half of the month were $66,128. (Cash sales are usually recorded daily but are recorded only twice in this problem to reduce the repetitive transactions.)

Required

1. Record the transactions listed above in the journals provided in the working papers.

2. Post to the customer and creditor accounts and also post any amounts that should be posted as individual amounts to the General Ledger accounts. (Normally, these amounts are posted daily, but they are posted only once in this problem because they are few in number.)

3. Foot and crossfoot the journals and make the month-end postings.

4. Prepare a December 31 trial balance and test the accuracy of the subsidiary ledgers by preparing schedules of accounts receivable and accounts payable.

Crystal Company completed these transactions during November of the current year:

Nov. 1   Purchased office equipment on credit from Jett Supply, invoice dated November 1, terms n/10 EOM, $5,062.

2   Borrowed $86,250 by giving Jefferson Bank a long-term promissory note payable.

4   Received merchandise and an invoice dated November 3, terms 2/10, n/30, from Defore Industries, $11,400.

5   Purchased store supplies on credit from Atlas Company, $1,020. Invoice dated November 5, terms n/10 EOM.

8   Sold merchandise on credit to Leroy Holmes, Invoice No. 439, $6,350. (Terms of all credit sales are 2/10, n/30.)

10   Sold merchandise on credit to Sam Spear, Invoice No. 440, $12,500.

11   Received merchandise and an invoice dated November 10, terms 2/10, n/30, from The Welch Company, $2,887.

12   Sent Defore Industries Check No. 633 in payment of its November 3 invoice less the discount.

15   Issued Check No. 634, payable to Payroll, in payment of sales salaries for the first half of the month, $8,435. Cashed the check and paid the employees.

15   Cash sales for the first half of the month were $27,170. (Normally, cash sales are recorded daily; however, they are recorded only twice in this problem to reduce the number of repetitive entries.)

15   Post to the customer and creditor accounts and also post any amounts that should be posted as individual amounts to the General Ledger accounts. (Normally, such items are posted daily; but you are asked to post them on only two occasions in this problem because they are few in number.)

15   Sold merchandise on credit to Marjorie Cook, Invoice No. 441, $4,250.

16   Purchased office supplies on credit from Atlas Company, $559. Invoice dated November 16, terms n/10 EOM.

17   Received a credit memorandum from The Welch Company for unsatisfactory merchandise received on November 10 and returned for credit, $487.

18   Received payment from Leroy Holmes for the November 8 sale less the discount.

19   Received payment from Sam Spear for the November 10 sale less the discount.

19   Issued Check No. 635 to The Welch Company in payment of its invoice of November 10 less the return and the discount.

22   Sold merchandise on credit to Sam Spear, Invoice No. 442, $2,595.

24   Sold merchandise on credit to Marjorie Cook, Invoice No. 443, $3,240.

25   Received payment from Marjorie Cook for the sale of November 15 less the discount.

26   Received a credit memorandum from Jett Supply for office equipment received on November 1 and returned for credit, $922.

30   Issued Check No. 636, payable to Payroll, in payment of sales salaries for the last half of the month, $8,435. Cashed the check and paid the employees.

30   Cash sales for the last half of the month were $35,703.

30   Post to the customer and creditor accounts and post any amounts that should be posted as individual amounts to the General Ledger accounts.

30   Foot and crossfoot the journals and make the month-end postings.

Required

1. Open the following General Ledger accounts: Cash, Accounts Receivable, Office Supplies, Store Supplies, Office Equipment, Accounts Payable, Long-Term Notes Payable, Sales, Sales Discounts, Purchases, Purchases Returns and Allowances, Purchases Discounts, and Sales Salaries Expense. Open the following Accounts Receivable Ledger accounts: Marjorie Cook, Leroy Holmes, and Sam Spear. Open the following Accounts Payable Ledger accounts: Atlas Company, Defore Industries, Jett Supply, and The Welch Company.

Problem 8-4A
Special journals;
subsidiary ledgers;
trial balance

P1, P2

2. Enter the transactions listed above in a Sales Journal like Exhibit 8.5, a Purchases Journal like Exhibit 8.11, a Cash Receipts Journal like Exhibit 8.9, a Cash Disbursements Journal like Exhibit 8.13, and a General Journal. Post when instructed to do so.

3. Prepare a trial balance of the General Ledger and test the accuracy of the subsidiary ledgers by preparing schedules of accounts receivable and accounts payable.

Problem 9-1A
Establishing, reimbursing, and increasing petty cash fund

Dodge & Sons had the following petty cash transactions in July of the current year:

July 5   Drew a $200 check, cashed it, and turned the proceeds and the petty cash box over to Jackie Boone, the petty cashier.

     6   Paid $14.50 COD charges on merchandise purchased for resale, terms FOB shipping point. Dodge & Sons uses the perpetual inventory method to account for merchandise inventory.

   11   Paid $8.75 delivery charges on merchandise sold to a customer, terms FOB destination.

   12   Purchased file folders, $12.13.

   14   Reimbursed Collin Dodge, the manager of the business, $9.65 for office supplies purchased.

   18   Purchased paper for printer, $22.54.

   27   Paid $47.10 COD charges on merchandise purchased for resale, terms FOB shipping point.

   28   Purchased stamps, $16.

   30   Reimbursed Dodge $58.80 for business car mileage.

   31   Boone sorted the petty cash receipts by accounts affected and exchanged them for a check to reimburse the fund for expenditures. There was $11.53 cash in the fund, and she could not account for the overage. The dollar amount of the petty cash fund was increased to $250.

Required

1. Prepare the general journal entry to record establishing the petty cash fund.

2. Prepare a petty cash payments report that has these categories: delivery expense, mileage expense, postage expense, merchandise inventory (transportation-in), and office supplies. Sort the payments into the appropriate categories and total the expenses in each category.

3. Prepare the general journal entry to record the reimbursement and the increase of the fund.

Problem 9-2A
Establishing, reimbursing, and adjusting petty cash fund; accounting adjustments

P3

The accounting system used by The Thrifty Company requires that all entries be journalized in a General Journal. To facilitate payments for small items, Thrifty established a petty cash fund. The following transactions involving the petty cash fund occurred in February (the last month of the company's fiscal year).

Feb. 3   A company check for $150 was drawn and made payable to the petty cashier to establish the petty cash fund.

   14   A company check was drawn to replenish the fund for the following expenditures made since February 3 and to increase the fund to $175.

         a.   Purchased office supplies, $16.29.

         b.   Paid $17.60 COD charges on merchandise purchased for resale, terms FOB shipping point. Thrifty uses the perpetual method to account for merchandise inventory.

         c.   Paid $36.57 to Data Services for minor repairs to a computer.

         d.   Paid $14.82 for items classified as miscellaneous expenses.

         e.   Counted $62.28 remaining in the petty cash box.

   28   The petty cashier noted that $17.35 remained in the fund and decided that the February 14 increase in the fund was not large enough. A company check was drawn to replenish the fund for the following expenditures made since February 14 and to increase it to $250.

         f.   Paid $40 to *The Smart Saver* for an advertisement in a monthly newsletter.

         g.   Paid $28.19 for office supplies.

         h.   Paid $58 to Best Movers for delivery of merchandise to a customer, terms FOB destination.

Required

Preparation Component

1. Prepare journal entries to record the establishment of the fund on February 3 and its replenishment on February 14 and February 28 along with any increases or decreases in the fund balance.

Analysis Component

2. Explain how the company's financial statements are affected if the petty cash fund is not replenished and no entry is made on February 28. (Hint: The amount of Office Supplies that appears on a balance sheet is determined by a physical count of the supplies on hand.)

The following information is available to reconcile Bohannon Co.'s book cash balance with its bank statement balance as of December 31, 2000:

a. After posting is complete, the December 31 cash balance according to the accounting records is $31,743.70, and the bank statement balance for that date is $45,091.80.

b. Check No. 1273 for $1,084.20 and Check No. 1282 for $390, both written and entered in the accounting records in December, were not among the canceled checks returned. Two checks, No. 1231 for $2,289 and No. 1242 for $370.50, were outstanding on November 30 when the bank and book statement balances were last reconciled. Check No. 1231 was returned with the December canceled checks, but Check No. 1242 was not.

c. When the December checks were compared with entries in the accounting records, it was found that Check No. 1267 had been correctly drawn for $2,435 to pay for office supplies but was erroneously entered in the accounting records as $2,453.

d. Two debit memoranda were included with the returned checks and were unrecorded at the time of the reconciliation. One of the debit memoranda was for $749.50 and dealt with an NSF check for $732 that had been received from a customer, Tork Industries, in payment of their account. It also assessed a $17.50 fee for processing. The second debit memorandum covered check printing and was for $79. These transactions were not recorded by Bohannon before receiving the statement.

e. A credit memorandum indicated that the bank had collected a $20,000 note receivable for the company, deducted a $20 collection fee, and credited the balance to the company's account. This transaction was not recorded by Bohannon before receiving the statement.

f. The December 31 cash receipts of $7,666.10 were placed in the bank's night depository after banking hours on that date and did not appear on the bank statement.

Problem 9-3A
Preparing a bank reconciliation and recording adjustments
P5

Required

Preparation Component

1. Prepare a bank reconciliation for the company as of December 31.

2. Prepare the journal entries necessary to bring the company's book balance of cash into conformity with the reconciled balance.

Analysis Component

3. Explain the nature of the communications conveyed by a bank to one of its depositors when the bank sends a debit memo and a credit memo to the depositor.

Safety Systems most recently reconciled its bank balance on April 30 and showed two checks outstanding at that time, No. 1771 for $781 and No. 1780 for $1,325.90. The following information is available for the May 31, 1999, reconciliation:

Problem 9-4A
Preparing a bank reconciliation and recording adjustments

From the May 31 bank statement:

BALANCE OF PREVIOUS STATEMENT ON 04/30/99	18,290.70
5 DEPOSITS AND OTHER CREDITS TOTALING	16,416.80
9 CHECKS AND OTHER DEBITS TOTALING	12,898.90
CURRENT BALANCE AS OF THIS STATEMENT	21,808.60

=== CHECKING ACCOUNT TRANSACTIONS ===

DATE	AMOUNT	DESCRIPTION	DATE	AMOUNT	DESCRIPTION
5/4	2,438.00	+Deposit	5/25	7,200.00	+Credit Memo
5/14	2,898.00	+Deposit	5/26	2,079.00	+Deposit
5/18	431.80	−NSF check	5/31	12.00	−Service charge
5/22	1,801.80	+Deposit			

DATE	CHECK NO	AMOUNT	DATE	CHECK NO	AMOUNT
5/01	1771*	781.00	5/26	1785	157.20
5/04	1782	1,285.50	5/25	1787*	8,032.50
5/02	1783	195.30	5/29	1788	554.00
5/11	1784	1,449.60			

*Indicates a skip in check sequence.

From Safety Systems' accounting records:

Cash Receipts Deposited

Date		Cash Debit
May	4	2,438.00
	14	2,898.00
	22	1,801.80
	26	2,079.00
	31	2,526.30
		11,743.10

Cash Disbursements

Check No.		Cash Credit
1782		1,285.50
1783		195.30
1784		1,449.60
1785		157.20
1786		353.10
1787		8,032.50
1788		544.00
1789		639.50
		12,656.70

Cash   Acct. No. 101

Date		Explanation	PR	Debit	Credit	Balance
Apr.	30	Balance				16,183.80
May	31	Total receipts	R7	11,743.10		27,926.90
	31	Total disbursements	D8		12,656.70	15,270.20

Check No. 1788 was correctly drawn for $554 to pay for May utilities; however, the recordkeeper misread the amount and entered it in the accounting records with a debit to Utilities Expense and a credit to Cash as though it were for $544. The bank paid and deducted the correct amount. The NSF check was originally received from a customer, Goldie Mayer, in payment of her account. Its return was unrecorded. The credit memorandum resulted from a $7,300 note that the bank had collected for the company. The bank deducted a $100 collection fee and deposited the remainder in the company's account. The collection and fee have not been recorded.

Required

Preparation Component

1. Prepare the May 31 bank reconciliation for Safety Systems.

2. Prepare the journal entries to adjust the book balance of cash to the reconciled balance.

Analysis Component

3. The bank statement discloses two places where the canceled checks returned with the bank statement are not numbered sequentially. This means some of the prenumbered checks in the sequence are missing. Several possible situations might explain why canceled checks returned with a bank statement are not numbered sequentially. Describe three of these situations.

For the following five scenarios, identify the principle of internal control that is violated. Make a recommendation of what the business should do to ensure adherence to principles of internal control.

Problem 9-5A
Analyzing internal control

C2

1. Tamerick Company is a fairly small organization but has segregated the duties of cash receipts and cash disbursements. However, the employee responsible for cash disbursements also reconciles the monthly bank account.

2. Stan Spencer is the most computer literate employee in his company. His boss has recently asked him to put password protection on all the office computers. Stan's main job at the company is to process payroll. Stan has put a password in place that only allows his boss access to the file where pay rates are changed and personnel are added/or deleted from the company payroll.

3. Starlight Theater has a computerized order taking system for its tickets. The system is active all week and backed up every Friday night.

4. Trek There Company has two employees handling acquisitions of inventory. One employee places purchase orders and pays vendors. The second employee receives the merchandise.

5. The owner of Holiday Helper uses a check protector to perforate checks, making it difficult for anyone to alter the amount of the check. The check protector sits on the owner's desk in an office that houses company checks and is often unlocked.

McLean Systems had no short-term investments on December 31, 1999, but had the following transactions involving short-term investments in securities available-for-sale during 2000:

Problem 10-1A
Short-term investment transactions and entries

C4, P5

Feb. 6 Purchased 3,400 shares of The Walt Disney Co. stock at $29\frac{1}{2}$ plus a $2,500 brokerage fee.

15 Paid $20,000 to buy six-month U.S. Treasury bills with a principal amount of $20,000, paying 5%, dated February 15.

Apr. 7 Purchased 1,200 shares of The Gillette Co. stock at $13\frac{1}{4}$ plus a $477 brokerage fee.

June 2 Purchased 2,500 shares of Zenith Electronics stock at $32\frac{3}{4}$ plus a $2,865 brokerage fee.

30 Received a $1.75 per share cash dividend on the Disney shares.

Aug. 11 Sold 850 shares of Disney stock at 25 less a $531 brokerage fee.

16 Received a check for the principal and accrued interest on the U.S. Treasury bills purchased February 15.

24 Received a $0.20 per share cash dividend on the Gillette shares.

Nov. 9 Received a $1.00 per share cash dividend on the remaining Disney shares.

Dec. 18 Received a $0.45 per share cash dividend on the Gillette shares.

Required

Prepare General Journal entries to record the preceding transactions.

Ace Office Supply Co. allows a few select customers to make purchases on credit. The other customers can use either of two credit cards. Commerce Bank deducts a 3% service charge for sales on its credit card but immediately credits the checking account of its commercial customers when credit card receipts are deposited. Ace deposits the Commerce Bank credit card receipts at the close of each business day.

Problem 10-2A
Sales on credit and credit card sales

When customers use the Fortune card, Ace accumulates the receipts for several days and then submits them to the Fortune Credit Company for payment. Fortune deducts a 2% service charge and usually pays within one week of being billed. Ace completed the following transactions in July:

July   2   Sold merchandise on credit to J.R. Lacey for $2,780. (Terms of all credit sales are 2/10, n/30; all sales are recorded at the gross price.)

8   Sold merchandise for $3,248 to customers who used their Commerce Bank credit cards. Sold merchandise for $1,114 to customers who used their Fortune cards.

12   Received Lacey's check paying for the purchase of July 2.

13   Sold merchandise for $2,960 to customers who used their Fortune cards.

16   The Fortune card receipts accumulated since July 8 were submitted to the credit card company for payment.

20   Wrote off the account of River City Rentals against Allowance for Doubtful Accounts. The $398 balance in River City's account stemmed from a credit sale in November of last year.

23   Received the amount due from Fortune Credit Company.

Required

Prepare journal entries to record the preceding transactions.

On December 31, 2000, Genie Service Corp's records show the following results for the year:

Cash sales	$1,015,000
Credit sales	1,241,000

In addition, the unadjusted trial balance includes the following items:

Accounts receivable	$475,000 debit
Allowance for doubtful accounts	5,200 credit

Required

1. Prepare the adjusting entry on the books of Genie Service Corp. to estimate bad debts under each of the following independent assumptions:
   a. Bad debts are estimated to be 2.5% of credit sales.
   b. Bad debts are estimated to be 1.5% of total sales.
   c. Analysis suggests 6% of outstanding accounts receivable at year-end are uncollectible.

2. Show how Accounts Receivable and the Allowance for Doubtful Accounts appear on the December 31, 2000, balance sheet given the facts in requirement 1a.

3. Show how Accounts Receivable and the Allowance for Doubtful Accounts appear on the December 31, 2000, balance sheet given the facts in requirement 1c.

Problem 10-4A
Aging accounts receivable

P1, P2

NutraMade Company had credit sales of $3.5 million in 1999. On December 31, 1999, the company's Allowance for Doubtful Accounts had a debit balance of $4,100. The accountant for NutraMade has prepared a schedule of the December 31, 1999, accounts receivable by age and, on the basis of past experience, has estimated the percent of receivables in each age category that will become uncollectible. This information is summarized as follows:

December 31, 1999 Accounts Receivable	Age of Accounts Receivable	Expected Percent Uncollectible
$296,400	Not due (under 30 days)	2.0%
177,800	1 to 30 days past due	4.0
58,000	31 to 60 days past due	8.5
7,600	61 to 90 days past due	39.0
3,700	Over 90 days past due	82.5

Required

Preparation Component

1. Compute the amount in the December 31, 1999, balance sheet as the Allowance for Doubtful Accounts.

2. Prepare the journal entry to record bad debts expense for 1999.

Analysis Component

3. On July 31, 2000, NutraMade concluded that a customer's $2,345 receivable (created in 1999) is uncollectible and that the account should be written off. What effect will this action have on NutraMade's 2000 net income? Explain your answer.

Spring Products Co. began operations on January 1, 1999, and completed a number of transactions during 1999 and 2000 that involved sales on credit, accounts receivable collections, and bad debts. These transactions are summarized as follows:

1999

a. Sold merchandise on credit for $673,490, terms n/30.

b. Received cash of $437,250 in payment of outstanding accounts receivable.

c. Wrote off uncollectible accounts receivable in the amount of $8,330.

d. In adjusting the accounts on December 31, concluded that 1% of outstanding accounts receivable would become uncollectible.

2000

e. Sold merchandise on credit for $930,100, terms n/30.

f. Received cash of $890,220 in payment of outstanding accounts receivable.

g. Wrote off uncollectible accounts receivable in the amount of $10,090.

h. In adjusting the accounts on December 31, concluded that 1% of outstanding accounts receivable would become uncollectible.

Required

Prepare journal entries to record the 1999 and 2000 summarized transactions of Spring Products Co. and the adjustments to record bad debts expense at the end of each year.

Problem 10-5A
Recording accounts receivable transactions and bad debts adjustments

P1, P2

The following transactions are from Metro, Inc.:

1999

Nov. 16   Accepted a $3,700, 90-day, 12% note dated this day in granting Bess Parker a time extension on her past-due account.

Dec. 31   Made an adjusting entry to record the accrued interest on the Parker note.

31   Closed the Interest Earned account.

2000

Feb. 14   Received Parker's payment for principal and interest on the note dated November 16.

28   Accepted a $12,400, 9%, 30-day note dated this day in granting a time extension on the past-due account of The Simms Co.

Mar. 1   Accepted a $5,100, 60-day, 10% note dated this day in granting Bedford Holmes a time extension on his past-due account.

23   Discounted, without recourse, the Holmes note at Security Bank at a cost of $50.

30   The Simms Co. dishonored its note when presented for payment.

June 15   Accepted a $1,900, 60-day, 9% note dated this day in granting a time extension on the past-due account of Sarah Mayfield.

21   Accepted a $9,300, 90-day, 12% note dated this day in granting Vince Soto a time extension on his past-due account.

July 5   Discounted, with recourse, the Soto note at Security Bank at a cost of $200. The transaction was considered to be a loan.

Aug. 14   Received payment of principal plus interest from Mayfield for the note of June 15.

Sept 25   Received notice from Security Bank that the Soto note had been paid.

Nov 30   Wrote off The Simms Co.'s account against Allowance for Doubtful Accounts.

Problem 10-6A
Analyzing and journalizing notes receivable transactions

P3, P4

10
CHAPTER

Required

Preparation Component

Prepare journal entries to record Metro's transactions.

Analysis Component

What reporting is necessary when a business discounts notes receivable with recourse and these notes have not reached maturity by the end of the fiscal period? Explain the reason for this requirement and what accounting principle is being satisfied.

Problem 10-7A
Short-term
investment
transactions and
entries

C4, P5

Dayton Enterprises has idle cash balances and invests them in common stocks that it holds as available-for-sale securities. Following is a series of transactions and events relevant to the short-term investment activity of the company:

1999
Mar. 10   Purchased 2,400 shares of Apple Computer, Inc., at $33\frac{1}{4}$ plus $1,995 commission.
May   7   Purchased 5,000 shares of Ford Motor Co. at $17\frac{1}{2}$ plus $2,625 commission.
Sept.   1   Purchased 1,200 shares of Polaroid Corp. at 49 plus $1,176 commission

2000
Apr. 26   Sold 5,000 shares of Ford at $16\frac{3}{8}$ less $2,237 commission.
       27   Sold 1,200 shares of Polaroid at 52 less $1,672 commission.
June   2   Purchased 3,600 shares of Duracell Int'l., Inc., at $18\frac{7}{8}$ plus $2,312 commission.
       14   Purchased 900 shares of Sears, Roebuck & Co. at $24\frac{1}{2}$ plus $541 commission.

2001
Jan. 28   Purchased 2,000 shares of The Coca-Cola Co. at 41 plus $3,280 commission.
       31   Sold 3,600 shares of Duracell at $16\frac{5}{8}$ less $1,496 commission.
Aug. 22   Sold 2,400 shares of Apple at $29\frac{3}{4}$ less $2,339 commission.
Sept.   3   Purchased 1,500 shares of Motorola, Inc., at 29 plus $870 commission.
Oct.   9   Sold 900 shares of Sears at $27\frac{1}{2}$ less $619 commission.

Required

Prepare journal entries to record the short-term investment activity for the years shown.

11
CHAPTER

Problem 11-1A
Real estate costs;
partial year's
depreciation

C1, C2, C3

In 1999, Spicewood Technologies paid $1,350,000 for a tract of land with two buildings on it. The plan is to demolish Building A and build a new shop in its place. Building B is to be used as a company office and is appraised at a value of $472,770, with a useful life of 15 years and a $90,000 salvage value. A lighted parking lot near Building B has improvements (Land Improvements B) valued at $125,145 that are expected to last another six years and have no salvage value. Without considering the buildings or improvements, the tract of land is valued at $792,585. AutoTech incurred the following additional costs:

Cost to demolish Building A	$ 117,000
Cost of additional landscaping	172,500
Cost to construct new building (Building C), having a useful life of 20 years and a $295,500 salvage value	1,356,000
Cost of new land improvements near Building C (Land Improvements C), which have a 10-year useful life and no salvage value	101,250

Required

1. Prepare a schedule having the following column headings: Land, Building B, Building C, Land Improvements B, and Land Improvements C. Allocate the costs incurred by AutoTech to the appropriate columns and total each column.

2. Prepare a single journal entry to record all the incurred costs, assuming they are paid in cash on October 1, 1999.

3. Using the straight-line method, prepare December 31 adjusting entries to record depreciation for the three months of 1999 during which the assets were in use.

Timberline Company recently negotiated a lump-sum purchase of several assets from a contractor who was planning to change locations. The purchase is completed on September 30, 1999, at a total cash price of $1,610,000 and included a building, land, land improvements, and six trucks. The estimated market values of the assets are: building, $784,800; land, $540,640; land improvements, $226,720; and trucks, $191,840. The company's fiscal year ends on December 31.

Problem 11-2A
Plant asset costs; partial year's depreciation; alternative methods

C1, C2, C3

Required

Preparation Component

1. Prepare a schedule to allocate the lump-sum purchase price to the separate assets purchased. Present the journal entry to record the purchase.

2. Compute the 1999 depreciation expense on the building using the straight-line method, assuming a 12-year life and a $100,500 trade-in value.

3. Compute the 1999 depreciation expense on the land improvements assuming a 10-year life and double-declining-balance depreciation.

Analysis Component

4. Defend or refute this statement: Accelerated depreciation results in more taxes being paid over the life of the asset.

Part 1. On January 2, Brodie Co. purchased and installed a new machine costing $312,000, with a five-year life and an estimated $28,000 salvage value. Management estimates the machine will produce 1,136,000 units of product during its life. Actual production of units is as follows: Year 1, 245,600; Year 2, 230,400; Year 3, 227,000; Year 4, 232,600; and Year 5, 211,200. The total number of units produced by the end of Year 5 exceeds the original estimate. The machine must not be depreciated below the estimated salvage value.

Problem 11-3A
Alternative depreciation methods; partial year's depreciation; disposal of plant assets

C3, P2

Required

Prepare a schedule with the following column headings:

Year	Straight-Line	Units-of-Production	Double-Declining-Balance

Show depreciation for each year and the total depreciation for the machine under each depreciation method.

Part 2. On January 1, Brodie purchased a used machine for $130,000. The next day, it is repaired at a cost of $3,390 and mounted on a new platform costing $4,800. Management estimates the machine will be used for seven years and have a $18,000 salvage value. Depreciation is to be charged on a straight-line basis. A full year's depreciation is charged on December 31 of the first through the fifth years of the machine's use. On April 1 of its sixth year of use, the machine is retired.

Required

a. Prepare journal entries to record the purchase of the machine, the cost of repairing it, and the installation. Cash is paid for all costs incurred.

b. Prepare entries to record depreciation on the machine at December 31 of its first year and on April 1 in the year of its disposal.

c. Prepare entries to record the retirement of the machine under each of the following unrelated assumptions: (i) it is sold for $30,000; (ii) it is sold for $50,000; and (iii) it is destroyed in a fire and the insurance company pays $20,000 in full settlement of the loss claim.

11
CHAPTER

Problem 11-4A
Partial year's
depreciation;
revising depreciation
rates; revenue and
capital expenditures

C3, P3

Rush Delivery Service completed these transactions involving the purchase and operation of delivery equipment:

1999

Mar. 25   Paid cash for a new delivery van, $24,950 plus $1,950 in sales tax. The van is estimated to have a five-year life and a $3,400 salvage value. Van costs are recorded in the Equipment account.

Sept. 30   Paid $1,550 to replace the manual transmission in the van with an automatic transmission. This increased the estimated salvage value of the van by $200.

Dec. 31   Record straight-line depreciation on the van.

2000

May 10   Paid $600 to repair the van after the driver backed it into a loading dock.

Oct. 1   Paid $1,970 to overhaul the van's engine. As a result, the estimated useful life of the van is increased by two years.

Dec. 31   Record straight-line depreciation on the van.

Required

Prepare journal entries to record these transactions.

Problem 11-5A
Partial year's
depreciation;
revising depreciation
rates; exchanging
plant assets

C3, P4

Precision Machine Shop completed the following transactions involving machinery:

1999

June 24   Paid $106,600 cash for a new machine plus $6,400 in sales tax. The machine is estimated to have a six-year life and a $9,800 trade-in value.

Dec. 31   Record straight-line depreciation on the machinery.

2000

Dec. 31   Record straight-line depreciation on the machine. Due to new information obtained earlier in the year, the original estimated useful life of the machinery is changed from six years to four years, and the original estimated trade-in value is increased to $13,050.

2001

Nov. 4   Traded in the old machine and paid $79,500 in cash for a new, similar machine. The new machine is estimated to have an eight-year life and a $10,380 trade-in value. The invoice for the exchange shows:

Price of the new machine	$123,000
Trade-in allowance granted on the old machine	(48,000)
Balance of purchase price	$ 75,000
State sales tax	4,500
Total paid in cash	$ 79,500

Dec. 31   Record straight-line depreciation on the new machine.

Required

Prepare journal entries to record these transactions.

Problem 11-6A
Partial year's
depreciation;
alternative methods;
disposal of plant
assets

C3, P2, P4

Central Printing Co. completed the following transactions involving printing equipment:

Printing press A is purchased for cash on April 3, 1995, at an installed cost of $169,400. Its useful life is estimated to be seven years with a $25,200 trade-in value. Straight-line depreciation is recorded for the press at the end of 1995, 1996, and 1997. On July 2, 1998, it is traded for printing press B, a similar asset, for an installed cash price of $206,400. A trade-in allowance of $112,000 is received for printing press A, and the balance is paid in cash.

Printing press B's life is predicted to be 10 years with a $22,000 trade-in value. Double-declining-balance depreciation is recorded on each December 31 of its life. On March 31, 2000, it is traded for a color laser copier, a dissimilar asset, for an installed cash price of $153,000. A trade-in allowance of $138,000 is received for printing press B, and the balance is paid in cash.

It is estimated that the copier will produce 1,000,000 copies during its four-year useful life, after which it will have a $13,000 trade-in value. Units-of-production depreciation is recorded for the copier for 2000, a period in which it produces 190,000 copies. Between January 1, 2001, and February 10, 2003, the copier produces 640,000 more copies. On the latter date, it is sold for $40,000.

Required

For each item of equipment, prepare journal entries to record: *(a)* its purchase, *(b)* the depreciation expense recorded on the first December 31 of its life, and *(c)* its disposal. (Only one entry is needed to record the exchange of one item of equipment for another.)

Part 1. In 1994, Granite Co. entered into a 12-year lease on a building. The lease contract requires: (1) $26,400 annual rental payments to be made each May 1 throughout the life of the lease and (2) all additions and improvements to the leased property to be paid for by the lessee. In 2000, Granite decided to sublease the space to Magnolia Service Co. for the remaining five years of the lease. On April 25, 2001, Magnolia paid $30,000 to Granite for the right to sublease the space and agreed to assume the obligation to pay the $26,400 annual rent to the building owner beginning May 1, 2001. After taking possession of the leased space, Magnolia paid for improving the office portion of the leased space at a cost of $18,000. The improvements were paid for on May 6, 2001, and are estimated to have a life equal to the 13 years remaining in the life of the building.

Problem 11-7A
Intangible assets and natural resources

P5, P6

Required

Prepare entries for Magnolia to record *(a)* its payment to Granite for the right to sublease the building space, *(b)* its payment of the 2001 annual rent to the building owner, and *(c)* its payment for the office improvements. Prepare Magnolia's adjusting entries required on December 31, 2001, to amortize *(d)* a proper share of the $30,000 cost of the sublease and *(e)* a proper share of the office improvements.

Part 2. On February 19 of the current year, Wayman Industries paid $4,450,000 for land estimated to contain 5 million tons of recoverable ore of a valuable mineral. It installed machinery costing $200,000, which has a 16-year life and no salvage value and is capable of exhausting the ore deposit in 12 years. The machinery is paid for on March 21, 11 days before mining operations began. The company removes 352,000 tons of ore during the first nine months of operations. Depreciation of the machinery is in proportion to the mine's depletion (it will be abandoned after the ore is fully mined).

Required

Preparation Component

Prepare entries to record *(a)* the purchase of the land, *(b)* the installation of the machinery, *(c)* the first nine months' depletion under the assumption the land is valueless after the ore is mined, and *(d)* the first nine months' depreciation on the machinery.

Analysis Component

Describe the similarities and differences in amortization, depletion, and depreciation.

Kudos Casual Wear has the following balance sheet on December 31, 2001:

Problem 11-8A
Goodwill estimation and amortization

Assets	
Cash	$ 138,700
Merchandise inventory	607,950
Buildings	451,500
Accumulated depreciation	(210,800)
Land	192,400
Total assets	$1,179,750
Liabilities and Equity	
Accounts payable	$ 98,325
Long-term note payable	414,050
N. Pursley, capital	667,375
Total liabilities and owner's equity	$1,179,750

In this industry, net income averages 32% of owner's equity. Kudos regularly expects to earn $230,000 annually. The balance sheet amounts are reasonable estimates of fair market values for all assets except goodwill, which does not appear on the financial statements. In negotiations to sell the business, Kudos proposes that goodwill be measured by capitalizing the amount of above-normal net income at a rate of 10%. The potential buyer thinks that goodwill should be valued at eight times the amount that net income is above the average for the industry.

Required

1. Compute the amount of goodwill as proposed by Kudos.

2. Compute the amount of goodwill according to the potential buyer.

3. The buyer purchases the business for the amount of the net assets reported on the December 31, 2001, balance sheet plus the amount proposed by Kudos for the goodwill. If the amount of expected net income (before amortization of goodwill) is obtained the first year, and the goodwill is amortized over the longest permissible time period, what amount of net income will be reported for the first year after the business is purchased?

4. What rate of return on the buyer's investment does the first year's net income represent?

Problem 12-1A
Estimating product warranty expenses and liabilities

P4

On November 10, 1999, Gourmet Co. began to purchase electric coffee grinders for resale at $35 each. Gourmet uses the perpetual method to account for inventories. The grinders are covered under a warranty that requires the company to replace any nonworking coffee grinder within 60 days. When a grinder is returned, the company simply throws it away and mails a new one from inventory to the customer. The company's cost for a new grinder is $14. The manufacturer has advised the company to expect warranty costs to equal 10% of sales. The following transactions and events occurred in 1999 and 2000:

1999
Nov. 16   Sold 50 coffee grinders for $1,750 cash.
     30   Recognized warranty expense for November with an adjusting entry.
Dec. 12   Replaced six grinders that were returned under the warranty.
     18   Sold 150 coffee grinders for $5,250 cash.
     28   Replaced 17 grinders that were returned under the warranty.
     31   Recognized warranty expense for December with an adjusting entry.

2000
Jan.   7   Sold 60 coffee grinders for $2,100 cash.
     21   Replaced 38 grinders that were returned under the warranty.
     31   Recognized warranty expense for January with an adjusting entry.

Required

1. How much warranty expense is reported for November and December 1999?

2. How much warranty expense is reported for January 2000?

3. What is the balance of the Estimated Warranty Liability account as of December 31, 1999?

4. What is the balance of the Estimated Warranty Liability account as of January 31, 2000?

5. Prepare journal entries to record these transactions and adjustments.

Problem 12-2A
Short-term notes payable transactions and entries

P1

Palermo Company entered into the following transactions involving short-term liabilities in 1999 and 2000:

1999
Apr. 22   Purchased merchandise on credit from Omni Products for $4,000. The terms were 1/10, n/30. Palermo uses a perpetual inventory system.
May 23   Replaced the account payable to Omni Products with a 60-day note bearing 15% annual interest. Palermo paid $400 cash, with the result that the balance of the note was $3,600.

July 15   Borrowed $9,000 from the Liberty Bank by signing a 120-day interest-bearing note for $9,000. The note's annual interest rate is 10%.

?   Paid the note to Omni Products at maturity.

?   Paid the note to Liberty Bank at maturity.

Dec. 6   Signed a noninterest-bearing note with a face value of $16,180 from Metro Bank that matures in 45 days. The principal amount on the note is $16,000.

     31   Recorded an adjusting entry for the accrual of interest on the note to the Metro Bank.

2000

?   Paid the note to Metro Bank at maturity.

Required

1. Determine the maturity dates of the three notes described above.
2. Determine the interest due at maturity for the three notes. (Assume a 360-day year.)
3. Determine the interest to be recorded in the adjusting entry at the end of 1999.
4. Determine the interest to be recorded in 2000.
5. Prepare journal entries for all the preceding transactions and events for years 1999–2000.

Jordanaire Company pays its employees every week. The employees' gross earnings are subject to these taxes:

Problem 12-3A
Payroll expenses, withholdings, and taxes

P2, P3

Tax	Rate	Applied To
FICA—Social Security	6.20%	First $68,400
FICA—Medicare	1.45%	Gross pay
FUTA	0.80%	First $7,000
SUTA	1.75%	First $7,000

The company is preparing its payroll calculations for the week ended September 30. The payroll records show the following information for the company's four employees:

Name	Gross Through 9/23	This Week Gross Pay	This Week Withholding Tax
Abel	$69,000	$1,650	$149
Barney	59,085	1,515	182
Crystal	6,650	475	52
Dionne	22,200	600	48

In addition to the gross pay, the company and each employee pay one-half of the weekly health insurance premium of $44 per employee. The company also contributes 5% of each employee's gross earnings to a pension fund.

Required

Use this information to compute the following for the week ended September 30 (round amounts to the nearest cent):

1. Each employee's FICA withholdings for Social Security.
2. Each employee's FICA withholdings for Medicare.
3. Employer's FICA taxes for Social Security.
4. Employer's FICA taxes for Medicare.
5. Employer's FUTA taxes.
6. Employer's SUTA taxes.
7. Each employee's take-home pay.
8. Employer's total payroll-related expense for each employee.

Alternate Problems

Problem 12-4A
Computing and
analyzing times
interest earned

A1

Here are condensed income statements for two different sole proprietorships:

Solstice Co.	
Sales	$120,000
Variable expenses (50%)	60,000
Net income before interest	$ 60,000
Interest expense (fixed)	45,000
Net income	$ 15,000

Equinox Co.	
Sales	$120,000
Variable expenses (75%)	90,000
Net income before interest	$ 30,000
Interest expense (fixed)	15,000
Net income	$ 15,000

Required

Preparation Component

1. What is the times interest earned for Solstice?
2. What is the times interest earned for Equinox?
3. What happens to each company's net income if sales increase by 10%?
4. What happens to each company's net income if sales increase by 40%?
5. What happens to each company's net income if sales increase by 90%?
6. What happens to each company's net income if sales decrease by 20%?
7. What happens to each company's net income if sales decrease by 50%?
8. What happens to each company's net income if sales decrease by 80%?

Analysis Component

9. Comment on what you observe in relation to the fixed cost strategies of the two companies and the ratio values you computed in parts 1 and 2.

Problem 12-5A^A
Entries for payroll
transactions

P5, P6

Capital Company has five employees, each of whom earns $1,200 per month and is paid on the last day of each month. All five have been employed continuously at this amount since January 1. Capital uses a payroll bank account and special payroll checks to pay its employees. On June 1, the following accounts and balances appeared in its ledger:

a. FICA—Social Security Taxes Payable, $744; FICA—Medicare Taxes Payable, $174. (The balances of these accounts represent liabilities for both the employer and employees' FICA taxes for the May payroll only.)

b. Employees' Federal Income Taxes Payable, $900 (liability for May only).

c. Federal Unemployment Taxes Payable, $96 (liability for April and May together).

d. State Unemployment Taxes Payable, $480 (liability for April and May together).

During June and July, the company had the following payroll transactions:

June 15   Issued check payable to First Bank, a federal depository bank authorized to accept employers' payments of FICA taxes and employee income tax withholdings. The $1,818 check is in payment of the May FICA and employee income taxes.

30   Prepared General Journal entries to record the June Payroll Record, which had the following column totals, and to transfer funds from the regular bank account to the payroll bank account:

Salaries and Wages				Federal		
Office Salaries	Shop Wages	Gross Pay	FICA Taxes*	Income Taxes	Total Deductions	Net Pay
$2,000	$4,000	$6,000	$372	$900	$1,359	$4,641
			+$ 87			

*FICA taxes are Social Security and Medicare, respectively.

30 Issued checks payable to each employee in payment of the June payroll.

30 Prepared a General Journal entry to record the employer's payroll taxes resulting from the June payroll. The company has a merit rating that reduces its state unemployment tax rate to 4.0% of the first $7,000 paid each employee. The federal rate is 0.8%.

July 15 Issued check payable to First Bank in payment of the June FICA and employee income taxes.

15 Issued check to the State Tax Commission for the April, May, and June state unemployment taxes. Mailed the check along with the second quarter tax return to the State Tax Commission.

31 Issued check payable to First Bank. The check is in payment of the employer's federal unemployment taxes for the second quarter of the year.

31 Mailed Form 941 to the IRS, reporting the FICA taxes and the employees' federal income tax withholdings for the second quarter.

Required

Prepare the General Journal entries to record the transactions and events for June and July.

Watson Company's first weekly pay period of the year ended on January 8. On that date, the column totals in Watson's Payroll Register indicated its sales employees had earned $69,490, its office employees had earned $42,450, and its delivery employees had earned $2,060. The employees are to have withheld from their wages: FICA Social Security taxes at the rate of 6.2%, FICA Medicare taxes at the rate of 1.45%, $17,250 federal income taxes, $2,320 of medical insurance deductions, and $275 of union dues. No employee earned more than $7,000.

Problem 12-6A[A]
Entries for payroll transactions

P5, P6

Required

1. Calculate FICA Social Security taxes payable and FICA Medicare taxes payable. Prepare a General Journal entry to record Watson Company's January 8 payroll.

2. Prepare a General Journal entry to record Watson's payroll taxes resulting from the January 8 payroll. Watson has a merit rating that reduces its state unemployment tax rate to 3.4% of the first $7,000 paid each employee. The federal unemployment tax rate is 0.8%.

3. Watson Company uses special payroll checks and a payroll bank account in paying its employees. Prepare the General Journal entry to transfer funds equal to the payroll from the regular bank account to the payroll bank account.

4. After the entry in part 3 is journalized and posted, are additional journal entries required to record the payroll checks and pay the employees?

redits

Index